THE UNFINISHED NATION

A Concise History of the American People

Ninth Edition

ALAN BRINKLEY
Columbia University

JOHN GIGGIE
University of Alabama

ANDREW HUEBNER
University of Alabama

Reinforced Binding

What does it mean?

Since high schools frequently adopt for several years, it is important that a textbook can withstand the wear and tear of usage by multiple students. To ensure durability, McGraw-Hill Education has elected to manufacture this textbook with a reinforced binding.

Mc
Graw
Hill
Education

THE UNFINISHED NATION: A CONCISE HISTORY OF THE AMERICAN PEOPLE, NINTH EDITION

Published by McGraw-Hill Education, 2 Penn Plaza, New York, NY 10121. Copyright © 2019 by McGraw-Hill Education. All rights reserved. Printed in the United States of America. Previous editions © 2016, 2014, and 2010. No part of this publication may be reproduced or distributed in any form or by any means, or stored in a database or retrieval system, without the prior written consent of McGraw-Hill Education, including, but not limited to, in any network or other electronic storage or transmission, or broadcast for distance learning.

Some ancillaries, including electronic and print components, may not be available to customers outside the United States.

This book is printed on acid-free paper.

3 4 5 6 7 8 9 LCR 26 25 24 23 22 21 20

ISBN   978-0-076-87659-4 (bound edition)
MHID   0-076-87659-4 (bound edition)

Senior Portfolio Manager: *Jason Seitz*
Lead Product Developer: *Dawn Groundwater*
Product Developer: *Elisa Odoardi*
Marketing Manager: *Will Walter*
Lead Content Project Manager: *Susan Trentacosti*
Content Project Managers: *Emily Windelborn, Sandra Schnee*
Senior Buyer: *Susan K. Culbertson*
Design: *Jessica Cuevas*
Lead Content Licensing Specialist: *Carrie Burger*
Cover Images: *Background: ©Curly Pat/Shutterstock; Map (left): ©Vector Icon Flat/Shutterstock; Map (right): Source: Library of Congress Geography and Map Division [G3301.R2 1767 .P3 Vault.]*
Compositor: *Aptara®, Inc.*

All credits appearing on page or at the end of the book are considered to be an extension of the copyright page.

Library of Congress Cataloging-in-Publication Data
Names: Brinkley, Alan, author. | Giggie, John Michael, 1965- contributor. | Huebner, Andrew, contributor.
Title: The unfinished nation : a concise history of the American people / Alan Brinkley, Columbia University ; with contributions from John Giggie, University of Alabama, Andrew Huebner, University of Alabama.
Description: Ninth edition. | New York, NY : McGraw-Hill Education, [2019]
Identifiers: LCCN 2018025712 | ISBN 978-0-076-87659-4 (alk. paper)
Subjects: LCSH: United States—History.
Classification: LCC E178.1 .B827 2019 | DDC 973—dc23 LC record available at https://lccn.loc.gov/2018025712

The Internet addresses listed in the text were accurate at the time of publication. The inclusion of a website does not indicate an endorsement by the authors or McGraw-Hill Education, and McGraw-Hill Education does not guarantee the accuracy of the information presented at these sites.

mheonline.com/advancedplacement

BRIEF CONTENTS

CONTENTS

©Bettmann/Corbis

JOIN, or DIE.

Source: Library of Congress, Prints and Photographs Division [LC-USZC4-5315]

©MPI/Hulton Archive/Getty Images

Source: National Archives and Records Administration

©Bettmann/Corbis

Source: Yale University Art Gallery

Source: Yale University Art Gallery

©Universal Images Group/Getty Images

©MPI/Archive Photos/Getty Images

©Bettmann/Corbis

Source: Library of Congress, Prints and Photographs Division [LC-USZ62-1138]

Source: Library of Congress, Prints and Photographs Division [LC-USZ61-903]

15 RECONSTRUCTION AND THE NEW SOUTH 352

Source: Library of Congress, Prints and Photographs Division [LC-USZC4-5759]

16 THE CONQUEST OF THE FAR WEST 381

Source: NPS photo by JR Douglas

Source: Library of Congress, Prints and Photographs Division [LC-USZC4-435]

©Corbis

Source: Library of Congress, Prints and Photographs Division [LC-DIG-ppmsca-28490]

Source: Library of Congress, Prints and Photographs Division [LCUSZ62-70382]

21 AMERICA AND THE GREAT WAR 516

For Home and Country

VICTORY LIBERTY LOAN

Source: Library of Congress, Prints and Photographs Division [LC-USZC4-9884]

22 THE NEW ERA 541

©Bettmann/Corbis

23 THE GREAT DEPRESSION 561

Source: Library of Congress,
Prints and Photographs Division
[LC-USF34-009872-E]

©Fotosearch/Archive Photos/GettyImages

SOLDIERS *without guns*

Source: Library of Congress, Prints and Photographs Division [LC-USZC4-1047]

26 THE COLD WAR   642

Source: U.S. Office for Emergency
Management. Office of Civilian Defense.
5/20/1941-6/30/1945/NARA (38174)

27 THE AFFLUENT SOCIETY   668

Source: NASA

28 THE TURBULENT SIXTIES 698

©John Orris/New York Times Co./
Getty Images

29 THE CRISIS OF AUTHORITY 730

©Michael Rougier/The LIFE Images Collection/Getty Images

30 FROM "THE AGE OF LIMITS" TO THE AGE OF REAGAN 761

©Dirck Halstead/The LIFE Images Collection/Getty Images

31 THE AGE OF GLOBALIZATION 784

Source: Official White House Photo by Pete Souza

The title *The Unfinished Nation* is meant to suggest several things. It is a reminder of America's exceptional diversity—of the degree to which, despite all the many efforts to build a single, uniform definition of the meaning of American nationhood, that meaning remains contested. It is a reference to the centrality of change in American history—to the ways in which the nation has continually transformed itself and continues to do so in our own time. And it is also a description of the writing of American history itself—of the ways in which historians are engaged in a continuing, ever unfinished process of asking new questions.

Like any history, *The Unfinished Nation* is a product of its time and reflects the views of the past that historians of recent generations have developed. The writing of our nation's history—like our nation itself—changes constantly. It is not, of course, the past that changes. Rather, historians adjust their perspectives and priorities, ask different kinds of questions, and uncover and incorporate new historical evidence. There are now, as there have always been, critics of changes in historical understanding who argue that history is a collection of facts and should not be subject to "interpretation" or "revision." But historians insist that history is not simply a collection of facts. Names and dates and a record of events are only the beginning of historical understanding. Writers and readers of history interpret the evidence before them, and inevitably bring to the task their own questions, concerns, and experiences.

This edition brings two new authors and therefore a revised and broadened set of ambitions to *The Unfinished Nation.* John Giggie is a historian of race and religion, Andrew Huebner is a historian of war and society, and both more generally study and teach American social and cultural history. Their interests join and complement Alan Brinkley's expansive base of knowledge in the history of American politics, society, and culture. Alan's scholarship inspired John and Andrew as graduate students and they are honored to join him as authors of *The Unfinished Nation.* They endeavor to bring their own scholarly interests and sensitivities to an already vibrant, clear, concise, and balanced survey of American history. The result, we hope, is a text that explores the great range of ideas, institutions, individuals, and events that make up the fabric of society in the United States.

It is a daunting task to attempt to convey the history of the United States in a single book, and the ninth edition of *The Unfinished Nation* has, as have all previous editions, been carefully written and edited to keep the book as concise and readable as possible. It features most notably an enlarged focus on the history of Native Americans, the meaning of the American Revolution, the transformative effects of modern warfare on everyday life, the far-reaching effects of the civil rights movement, and dramatic political and technological change in the twenty-first century. Across these subjects, we recognize that to understand the full complexity of the American past it is necessary to understand both the forces that divide Americans and the forces that draw them together. Thus we've sought to explore the development of foundational ideals like democracy and equality as well as the ways that our nation's fulfillment of those ideals remains, like so much else, unfinished.

ABOUT THE AUTHORS

ALAN BRINKLEY is the Allan Nevins Professor of History at Columbia University. He served as university provost at Columbia from 2003 to 2009. He is the author of *Voices of Protest: Huey Long, Father Coughlin, and the Great Depression*, which won the 1983 National Book Award; *American History: Connecting with the Past; The End of Reform: New Deal Liberalism in Recession and War; Liberalism and Its Discontents; Franklin D. Roosevelt;* and *The Publisher: Henry Luce and His American Century.* He is board chair of the National Humanities Center, board chair of the Century Foundation, and a trustee of Oxford University Press. He is also a member of the Academy of Arts and Sciences. In 1998–1999 he was the Harmsworth Professor of History at Oxford University, and in 2011–2012 the Pitt Professor at the University of Cambridge. He won the Joseph R. Levenson Memorial Teaching Award at Harvard and the Great Teacher Award at Columbia. He was educated at Princeton and Harvard.

JOHN GIGGIE is associate professor of history and African American studies at the University of Alabama where he also serves as director of the Summersell Center for the Study of the South. He is the author of *After Redemption: Jim Crow and the Transformation of African American Religion in the Delta, 1875-1917,* editor of *America Firsthand,* and editor of *Faith in the Market: Religion and the Rise of Commercial Culture.* He is currently preparing a book on civil rights protests in west Alabama. He has been widely honored for his teaching, most recently with a Distinguished Fellow in Teaching Award and Excellence in Community Engagement Award from the University of Alabama. He received his PhD from Princeton University.

ANDREW HUEBNER is associate professor of history at the University of Alabama. He is the author of *Love and Death in the Great War* (2018) and *The Warrior Image: Soldiers in American Culture from the Second World War to the Vietnam Era* (2008). He has written and spoken widely on the subject of war and society in the twentieth-century United States. In 2017, he was named an Organization of American Historians (OAH) Distinguished Lecturer. He received his PhD from Brown University.

AMERICA'S HISTORY IS STILL UNFOLDING

Is American History finished? Not yet! *The Unfinished Nation* shows that as more details are uncovered, dates may not change—but perceptions and reality definitely can. America and her history are in a constant state of change.

Just like America, this edition evolves with two new authors to further Alan Brinkley's established tradition. John Giggie and Andrew Huebner bring expertise and new voices, shedding light on perspectives that will shape an examination of the past. Their aim is to help you, the reader, ask new questions. By doing so, you will find your own answer to the question: is American History finished?

PRIMARY SOURCES HELP STUDENTS THINK CRITICALLY ABOUT HISTORY

Primary sources help students think critically about history and expose them to contrasting perspectives of key events. The Ninth Edition of *The Unfinished Nation* provides features that offer contrasting perspectives or showcase historical artifacts.

Within the print or eBook, the Ninth Edition of *The Unfinished Nation* offers the following features:

CONSIDER THE SOURCE

In every chapter, Consider the Source features guide students through careful analysis of historical documents and prompt them to closely examine the ideas expressed, as well as the historical circumstances. Among the classic sources included are Benjamin Franklin's testimony against the Stamp Act, the Gettysburg Address, a radio address from FDR, and Ronald Reagan on the role of government. Concise introductions provide context, and concluding questions prompt students to understand, analyze, and evaluate each source.

CONSIDER THE SOURCE

BARTOLOMÉ DE LAS CASAS, "OF THE ISLAND OF HISPANIOLA" (1542)

Bartolomé de Las Casas, a Dominican friar from Spain, was an early European settler of the West Indies. He devoted much of his life to describing the culture of native peoples and chronicling the many abuses they suffered at the hands of their colonizers. This excerpt is from a letter he addressed to Spain's Prince Philip.

God has created all these numberless people to be quite the simplest, without malice or duplicity, most obedient, most faithful to their natural Lords, and to the Christians, whom they serve; the most humble, most patient, most peaceful and calm, without strife nor tumults; not wrangling, nor querulous, as free from uproar, hate and desire of revenge as any in the world. . . . Among these gentle sheep, gifted by their Maker with the above qualities, the Spaniards entered as soon as they knew them, like wolves, tigers and lions which had been starving for many days, and since forty years they have done nothing else; nor do they afflict, torment, and destroy them with strange and new, and divers kinds of cruelty, never before seen, nor heard of, nor read of. . . .

The Christians, with their horses and swords and lances, began to slaughter and practice strange cruelty among them. They penetrated into the country and spared neither their children nor the aged, nor pregnant women, nor those in child labour, all of whom they ran through the body and lacerated, as though they were assaulting so many lambs herded in their sheepfold. They made bets as to who would slit a man in two, or cut off his head at one blow or they opened up his bowels. They tore the babes from their mothers' breast by the feet; and dashed their heads

against the rocks. Others they seized by the shoulders and threw into the rivers, laughing and joking, and when they fell into the water they exclaimed: "boil body of so and so!" They spitted the bodies of other babes, together with their mothers and all who were before them, on their swords.

They made a gallows just high enough for the feet to nearly touch the ground, and by thirteens, in honor and reverence of our Redeemer and the twelve Apostles, they put wood underneath and, with fire, they burned the Indians alive.

They wrapped the bodies of others entirely in dry straw, binding them in it and setting fire to it; and so they burned them. They cut off the hands of all they wished to take alive, made them carry them fastened on to them, and said: "Go and carry letters"; that is; take the news to those who have fled to the mountains.

They generally killed the lords and nobles in the following way. They made wooden gridirons of stakes, bound them upon them, and made a slow fire beneath; thus the victims gave up the spirit by degrees, emitting cries of despair in their torture.

UNDERSTAND, ANALYZE, & EVALUATE

1. How did Bartolomé de Las Casas characterize the indigenous people of Hispaniola? How do you think they would have responded to this description?
2. What metaphor did Las Casas use to describe the native peoples and where does this metaphor come from?
3. What role did Las Casas expect the Spaniards to play on Hispaniola? What did they do instead?

Source: MacNutt, Francis Augustus, *Bartholomew de Las Casas: His Life, His Apostolate, and His Writings*, New York: G.P. Putnam's Sons, 1909, 14.

DEBATING THE PAST

Debating the Past essays introduce students to the contested quality of much of the American past, and they provide a sense of the evolving nature of historical scholarship. From examining specific differences in historical understandings of the Constitution, to exploring the causes of the Civil War and the significance of Watergate, these essays familiarize students with the interpretive character of historical understanding.

AMERICA IN THE WORLD

America in the World essays focus on specific parallels between American history and those of other nations and demonstrate the importance of the many global influences on the American story. Topics such as the global Industrial Revolution, the abolition of slavery, and the global depression of the 1920s provide concrete examples of the connections between the history of the United States and the history of other nations.

PATTERNS OF POPULAR CULTURE

Patterns of Popular Culture essays bring fads, crazes, hangouts, hobbies, and entertainment into the story of American history, encouraging students to expand their definition of what constitutes history and gain a new understanding of what popular culture reveals about a society.

McGraw Hill Education

Personalized, Adaptive, and Dynamic
Digital Resources

The Unfinished Nation **is enriched with resources including primary and secondary source activities, and adaptive learning tools that provide students with multiple opportunities to contextualize and apply their understanding.**

Teachers can save time, customize lessons, monitor student progress, and make data-driven decisions in the classroom with the flexible, easy-to-navigate instructional tools.

Intuitive Design

Resources are organized at the chapter level.

The chapter landing page gives students access to

- assigned activities,
- resources and assessments,
- interactive eBook,
- adaptive SmartBook®.

Chapter landing page links students to resources that support success.

Mobile Ready
Access to course content on-the-go is easier and more effective than ever before with the ReadAnywhere mobile app.

Adaptive Study Tools

SMARTBOOK® is the online adaptive study tool. The interactive features engage students and personalize the learning experience with self-guided tools that:

- assess a student's proficiency and knowledge,

- track which topics have been mastered,

- present focused content specific to the student's individual needs.

Highlighted content continuously adapts as students work through exercises.

Practice sets measure depth of understanding and present a personalized learning path.

Teacher Resources

Teachers have access to the interactive eBook, adaptive Smartbook™ plus:

- An online Teacher's Manual with chapter outlines, teaching suggestions, reading strategies, and pacing guides

- Performance reports that allow teachers to identify gaps, and adjust instruction

- Customizable PowerPoint presentations

- Labeled visual aids and additional ideas for lecture enrichment.

Searchable library makes it easy to find and assign resources.

Customizable assignments and quiz banks are automatically graded and populate easy-to-read reports.

Harness technology, unlock success with the digital resources for this text **Visit *my.mheducation.com***

McGraw-Hill Education

CHAPTER-BY-CHAPTER CHANGES

We have extensively revised the narrative and features in this ninth edition to bring in new scholarship, particularly as it relates to the experiences and perspectives of Native Americans, African Americans, and women throughout American history. On the advice of teachers using the book, we have removed the former Chapter 25 on global events from 1921 to 1941 and instead integrated the coverage within chapters on the 1920s, 1930s, and World War II. Another major change in this edition is pedagogical—boldfacing within each chapter all words in the end-of-chapter Key Terms/People/Places/Events list, and creating glossary entries for these boldfaced words. We have also revised every chapter in response to heat map data that pointed to passages where students were struggling. On a chapter-by-chapter basis, major changes include:

Chapter 1, The Collision of Cultures

- Revised timeline with broader representation of cultures involved in the early contact story.
- Updated discussions of Olmecs, Mayas, Mexicas, ancient Pueblo peoples, and the people of Cahokia.
- Revised discussion of women's roles and power in North and South America.
- Revised map of European exploration and conquest to include Native American tribes populating North America.
- Fuller discussion of Oñate's colonizing methods and reactions from native peoples.
- Fuller discussion of Popé's rebellion.
- Revised discussion of the spread of infection among native peoples.
- Updated Debating the Past box on contemporary debates among historians.
- Revised America in the World box, now titled "The International Context of the Early History of the Americas."
- Revised and reorganized discussion of early English exploration and colonization for clarity and flow, including a focus on the Caribbean.

Chapter 2, Transplantations and Borderlands

- Expanded chapter introduction to include the topic of slavery across the colonies.
- Thoroughly revised discussion within "The Early Chesapeake," with an improved narrative sequence, updated scholarship, and greater attention to the agency and contributions of the Powhatans, including a more nuanced discussion of Pocahontas and her life both in North America and in England.
- Fuller treatment of the development of slave codes in the Virginia colony.
- Added recognition of the participation of black men in Bacon's Rebellion and the significance

of the rebellion to the further development of slavery in the colony.
- Greater specificity about the variety of Indian communities in New England.
- Improved discussion of Roger Williams's arguments about tolerance and respect for Narragansett peoples.
- Greater clarity on Anne Hutchinson and the Antinomian heresy.
- Revised discussion of King Philip's War, with a more nuanced discussion of Indian participation and greater attention to the significance of the conflict and its aftermath.
- Revised discussion of the English Civil War and aftermath, with greater attention to its significance for the Caribbean and mainland colonies.
- New information on the role of slaves in the origin and growth of the rice economy of Carolina.
- New discussion of slavery in New York and New York's first free black community.
- Fuller discussion of English colonies in the Caribbean, including slave codes, the social practices developed by slaves, and the economic importance of those colonies.
- Greater specificity on native peoples in "The Southwest Borderlands."
- Updated discussion in "Middle Grounds" about the balance of power between Europeans and Indians.
- Updated Debating the Past box on Native Americans and the Middle Ground.

Chapter 3, Society and Culture in Provincial America

- Expanded chapter introduction, with greater attention to the role of African slaves in colonial life and the interplay of colonists and Indians.
- Fuller discussion clarifies Africans did not journey to the colonies as voluntary immigrants.

- Greater attention to the transition from indentured servant to slave labor in the Chesapeake colonies.
- Expanded coverage of the legal rights of colonial women.
- Better detail on the middle passage, including a description by Olaudah Equiano.
- Updated discussion regarding the evolution of slave codes.
- Revised organization within "The Colonial Economies" to recognize the varieties of slave labor throughout the colonies, North and South.
- Revised map of immigrant groups in colonial America, adding the presence of indigenous peoples.
- Revised map of slavery in colonial America, adding northern colonies.
- Revised description of the realities of plantation life.
- Revised organization of "Patterns of Society" into "Southern Communities" and "Northern Communities."
- Fuller discussion of witchcraft accusations in Salem and beyond.
- Added discussion of the religious heritage of slaves, including the example of Muslim slave Ayuba Suleiman Diallo.
- Revised discussion of the Great Awakening, including its appeal to women and enslaved people.
- Added the role of Cotton Mather's slave Onesimus in fighting smallpox in the colonies.
- Revised chapter conclusion to reflect the many changes within the chapter.

Chapter 4, The Empire in Transition

- Expanded chapter introduction on the changing relationship between the American colonists and their British rulers in the aftermath of the Seven Years' War, and on Native Americans as participants in the war and postwar dynamics.
- Fuller treatment of Native Americans as participants in the French and Indian War, including the following new or expanded topics: role of the Indian leader Tanaghrisson; how Indians viewed alliances with the British and French; the effects of combat and the British victory on Indians; Indian acts of resistance to British power in the Ohio Valley, including Pontiac's rebellion.
- New information on how the Peace of Paris dealt with the enslaved peoples of the Caribbean.
- Clearer discussion of the reasons for colonial resistance to the Sugar Act and the Tea Act.
- Fully rewritten section "The Philosophy of Revolt" for greater clarity and a more nuanced discussion of different revolutionary impulses

and the limits of democracy within colonial assemblies.

Chapter 5, The American Revolution

- Revised discussion in "Defining American War Aims" on the effect of Lord Dunmore's Proclamation and on the purpose of Paine's *Common Sense*.
- Thoroughly updated and clarified the Debating the Past box on how historians have characterized the American Revolution.
- Thoroughly revised section "The War for Independence," with a new organization by region and new material on the combatants, including Native Americans, soldiers of color, and Loyalists.
- In the American in the World box "The Age of Revolutions," expanded discussion of the slave revolt in Saint-Domingue.
- Thoroughly revised "War and Society," with greater detail on how enslaved people, women, and Native Americans participated in and were affected by the Revolution and its outcome.
- Extensively revised discussion in "The Principles of Republicanism" and the limits of democracy.
- Revised discussion of tensions at play in Shays's rebellion.

Chapter 6, The Constitution and the New Republic

- Revised chapter introduction to better establish the context for the Continental Congress and the issues it faced.
- Fuller explanation of the reasons for and functioning of the electoral college.
- New discussion of the limited form of democracy in the early republic, the evolution of citizenship and suffrage rights, and early attempts by free blacks to gain rights.
- Added discussion of the debate over the "necessary and proper" clause.
- Clarified explanation of the quasi war with France.

Chapter 7, The Jeffersonian Era

- Expanded discussion of Native Americans in the lands covered by the Louisiana Purchase.

Chapter 8, Expansion and Division in the Early Republic (previously "Varieties of American Nationalism")

- Expanded chapter introduction to set up chapter themes.
- Improved coverage of New Spain, Mexican independence, and the relationship between American settlers and the Mexican state.

- Added information on the significance of the Mason-Dixon line.
- Added explanation for the demise of the Federalist Party and the emergence of the new two-party system.

Chapter 9, Jacksonian America

- Expanded chapter introduction to frame the goals and attitudes of Jackson and his followers.
- Fuller explanation of the change in the method of choosing electors for the electoral college.
- Added background on Jackson's rise from modest beginnings to plantation owner and a fuller discussion of his ideas about democracy.
- Revised discussion of the Webster-Hayne debate to underscore the issues at stake.
- Improved coverage of the removal of the Indians.
- New Consider the Source box primary source document by Chief John Ross of the Cherokee Nation.
- Revised discussion of the Bank War and the reasons for Jackson's opposition to the Bank of the United States.
- New editorial cartoons illustrating pro and con views of Jackson's economic policies.

Chapter 10, America's Economic Revolution

- Enhanced discussion of the reasons for Irish and German immigration to the United States.
- New coverage of the environmental costs of industrialization.
- Fuller treatment of the Female Labor Reform Association.
- Added explanation of the benefits of new farm tools.

Chapter 11, Cotton, Slavery, and the Old South

- New discussion of northern participation in the international slave trade and indirect support of slavery after the international slave trade was abolished.
- Revised discussion of the priorities and limits of southern transportation systems.
- Revised introduction to "Southern White Society," with a fuller, more nuanced discussion of the sources of southern differences.
- Revised examination of the mythology and sources of power in "The Planter Class."
- Reorganized discussion in "Slave Culture" to include the topic of slave resistance.

Chapter 12, Antebellum Culture and Reform

- New discussion of Margaret Fuller's contribution to transcendentalism and feminist thought.

- Revised explanation of the ideas and appeals of Mormonism.
- Added descriptions of Native Americans.
- Improved connections between sections within the chapter overall.

Chapter 13, The Impending Crisis

- Expanded chapter introduction to preview the issues and stakeholders in the conflict over slavery in the territories.
- New illustrations from the period that show how gold prospects in California were promoted and how the sectional crisis was portrayed.
- Clearer explanation of the free soil and free labor arguments.

Chapter 14, The Civil War

- Clarified discussion of the Union draft.
- Expanded discussion of the economic and social effects of the war for women and enslaved people.
- More nuanced description of the First Battle of Bull Run.

Chapter 15, Reconstruction and the New South

- Revised discussion of Special Field Order No. 15.
- Revised explanation of Lincoln's plans for Reconstruction.
- Fuller description of the rise to power of the Radical Republicans.
- More nuanced view of Grant's presidency and his efforts to protect democracy for black Americans.
- Revised explanation of the rise of Jim Crow.

Chapter 16, The Conquest of the Far West

- Sequence of chapter topics modified for improved connection and flow.
- More clarification regarding nineteenth-century terms.
- Revised description of the military advantages of U.S. forces versus Indians.

Chapter 17, Industrial Supremacy

- Revised section "Making Production More Efficient" (previously titled "The Science of Production") for greater clarity.
- Revised section "Railroad Expansion and the Corporation," with an improved discussion of the importance of government subsidies.

Chapter 18, The Age of the City

- Expanded chapter introduction previewing the problems and attractions of cities in the late nineteenth and early twentieth centuries.

- Revised discussion of the importance of cultural ties to ethnic communities.
- Added to references in America in the World, "Global Migrations" feature.
- More cohesive discussion in "Health and Safety in the Built Environment" (previously headed "Fire and Disease" and "Environmental Degradation").

Chapter 19, From Crisis to Empire

- Improved explanation of the "free silver" debate.
- Thoroughly revised narrative in "The Battle for Cuba."
- Greater attention to the effects of the Philippine War on Filipinos.

Chapter 20, The Progressives

- Fuller explanation for the decline of party influence, including disfranchisement.
- Expanded discussion of McKinley's assassination and the creation of the Secret Service.
- Revised map of national parks, adding ten sites that have been designated since 1992.

Chapter 21, America and the Great War

- Expanded chapter introduction to offer a fuller preview of chapter topics.
- Revised description of Pershing's expedition in Mexico.
- Fuller treatment of African American veterans and the interwar civil rights movement.

Chapter 22, The New Era

- New Consider the Source box titled "American Print Advertisements."
- Thoroughly revised section on the Republican administrations of Harding and Coolidge, now including coverage of the major foreign policy initiatives of the 1920s.

Chapter 23, The Great Depression

- Expanded chapter introduction previewing the effects of the Great Depression and Hoover's response.
- Added discussion of the international context in "The Popular Front and the Left."
- Revised explanation of the limitations of the Reconstruction Finance Corporation.
- "Hoover and the World Crisis" on the rise of fascism added to the discussion of Hoover's presidency.

Chapter 24, The New Deal Era

- Expanded chapter introduction previewing the phases of the New Deal and how it was received.
- New Consider the Source box on Eleanor Roosevelt and civil rights.

- "Isolationism and Internationalism" on Roosevelt's foreign policy and U.S. attitudes toward fascist aggression added to the chapter.

Chapter 25, America in a World at War

- New chapter introduction on the evolution of American foreign policy in the interwar period as a context for World War II.
- New first section "From Neutrality to Intervention" on the events leading up to the American declaration of war.
- Revised narrative of the Allied invasion of Italy.
- New discussion "The Soldier's Experience" under "War on Two Fronts," including the experiences of African American, Native American, and Chinese American soldiers.
- New section "Minority Groups and the War Effort" focusing on the home front.
- Revised discussion of the internment of Japanese Americans.
- Thoroughly revised and updated Debating the Past box on the decision to drop the atomic bomb.

Chapter 26, The Cold War

- Expanded chapter introduction on the context for and main ideas of the Cold War.
- Updated Debating the Past box on how historians have viewed the Cold War.
- Fuller discussion of the implications of the civil war in China.
- Greater context on Soviet expansion and the containment doctrine.
- New Consider the Source box using the "Bert the Turtle (Duck and Cover)."

Chapter 27, The Affluent Society

- Expanded chapter introduction on the forces shaping domestic affairs in the 1950s and early 1960s.
- Fuller explanation of the connection between economic growth and government spending in the postwar period.
- Revised discussion of the reasons for the rise of the modern West.
- Patterns of Popular Culture box "Lucy and Desi" replaces "On the Road."
- Thoroughly revised and expanded section, "The Rise of the Civil Rights Movement," including new material on the Woman's Political Committee and the history of bus boycotts prior to Montgomery.

Chapter 28, The Turbulent Sixties

- Expanded chapter introduction on the social and political issues defining the decade.

- Clearer contrast of JFK's and Nixon's visions of the role of government and of Kennedy's strengths as a candidate.
- Fuller explanation of the New Frontier.
- Revised discussion of how Johnson was able to win support for domestic reform, including the role of Martin Luther King Jr.
- Thoroughly revised section "The Battle for Racial Equality," including vivid accounts of the attack on Freedom Riders in May 1961, the standoff over integration at the University of Alabama, the March on Washington, and the battle for voting rights during Freedom Summer.
- Expanded discussion of the black power movement, the Black Panthers, and Malcolm X. Added discussion regarding Malcolm X's murder.
- Added explanation of the Cold War context for foreign aid initiatives during the Kennedy administration.
- New coverage of the experience of the Vietnam War for the people of South Vietnam.

Chapter 29, The Crisis of Authority

- Expanded chapter introduction previewing the social and cultural revolutions of the 1960s and 1970s.

- Fuller account of the Free Speech Movement and its philosophy.
- Revised section now titled "Women and Social Change," with improved coverage of modern feminism and the abortion issue.
- More accessible explanations of *Furman v. Georgia* and *Roe v. Wade*.
- Revised narrative of the 1972 presidential contest.
- Updated Debating the Past box on Watergate.
- New material on Barbara Jordan's role in calling for Nixon's impeachment.

Chapter 30, From "the Age of Limits" to the Age of Reagan

- Revised description of Ford's pardon of Nixon.
- Added material on Carter's civil rights record.
- Revised discussions of the Sunbelt and religious revivalism in "The Rise of the Conservative Movement."

Chapter 31, The Age of Globalization

- Thoroughly updated chapter on the contemporary period, including the Obama and Trump presidencies and new social, cultural, technological, environmental, and diplomatic trends.
- New coverage of Black Lives Matter and the AIDS epidemic.

ACKNOWLEDGMENTS

We would like to express our deep appreciation to the following individuals who contributed to the development of *The Unfinished Nation, Ninth Edition*:

Academic Reviewers

Kenna Archer, *Angelo State University*
Peter Belser, *Ivy Tech Community College of Indiana*
Kevin W. Caldwell, *Blue Ridge Community College*
Annette Chamberlin, *Virginia Western Community College*
Cara Crowley, *Amarillo College*
Barbara Dunsheath, *East Los Angeles College, Monterey*
Marilyn Howard, *Columbus State Community College*
Katherine Jewell, *Fitchburg State University*
Donald F. Johnson, *North Dakota State University*
Michael Kinney, *Calhoun Community College*
Jordan O'Connell, *Howard College, Big Spring*
Carey Roberts, *Liberty University*
Todd Romero, *University of Houston*
David Snead, *Liberty University*
Dennis Spillman, *North Central Texas College, Gainesville*
Shawna Williams, *Houston Community College, Southeast*

1 | THE COLLISION OF CULTURES

AMERICA BEFORE COLUMBUS
EUROPE LOOKS WESTWARD
THE ARRIVAL OF THE ENGLISH

LOOKING AHEAD

1. How did the societies of native people in the South differ from those in the North in the precontact period (before the arrival of the Europeans)?
2. What effects did the arrival of Europeans have on the native peoples of the Americas?
3. How did patterns of settlement differ within the Americas?

THE DISCOVERY OF THE AMERICAS did not begin with Christopher Columbus. It began many thousands of years earlier, when human beings first crossed into the new continents and began to people them. By the end of the fifteenth century A.D., when the first important contact with Europeans occurred, the Americas were already home to millions of men and women.

These ancient civilizations experienced many changes and many catastrophes during their long history. But it is likely that none of these experiences was as tragically transforming as the arrival of Europeans. In the first violent years of Spanish and Portuguese exploration, the impact of the new arrivals was profound. Europeans brought with them diseases (most notably smallpox) to which native peoples, unlike the invaders, had no experience or immunity. The result was a great demographic catastrophe that killed millions of people, weakened existing societies, and greatly aided the Spanish and Portuguese in their rapid and devastating takeover of the existing American empires.

But the European immigrants were never able to eliminate the influence of the indigenous peoples (whom they came to call "Indians"). In their many interactions, whether beneficial or ruinous, these very different civilizations shaped one another, learned from one another, and changed one another forever.

11,000 YEARS AGO

Migrations into the
Americas begin

300

Mayan writing system
originates

1200

Peak of Cahokian
population in North
America

1325

Tenochtitlán built by
Mexica

1300

Mali Empire
at its peak

1390

Kingdom of Kongo
takes form

1492

Columbus's first
transatlantic voyage

1502

African slaves arrive in
Spanish America

1500

Vast Inca Empire
reaches greatest extent

1518–1530

Smallpox ravages
Indians

1519–1522

Magellan expedition
circumnavigates
globe

1565

St. Augustine, Florida,
founded

1587

Second attempt to
establish Roanoke
colony

1607

Jamestown founded

1608

French establish
Quebec

1609

Spanish found
Santa Fe

1680

Popé leads rebellion
against Spanish

AMERICA BEFORE COLUMBUS

We know relatively little about the first peoples in the Americas, but archaeologists continue to discover ancient artifacts that enlarge our knowledge about the earliest Americans.

THE PEOPLES OF THE PRECONTACT AMERICAS

For many decades, scholars believed that all early migrations into the Americas came from humans crossing an ancient land bridge over the Bering Strait into what is now Alaska, approximately 11,000 years ago. The migrations were probably a result of the development of new stone tools—spears and other hunting implements—used to pursue the large animals that crossed between Asia and North America. All of these land-based migrants are thought to have come from a Mongolian stock related to that of modern-day Siberia. Scholars refer to these migrants as the **"Clovis" people**, so named for a town in New Mexico where archaeologists first discovered evidence of their tools and weapons in the 1930s.

More recent archaeological evidence suggests that not all the early migrants to the Americas came across the Bering Strait. Some migrants from Asia appear to have settled as far south as modern-day Chile and Peru even before people began moving into North America by land. These first South Americans may have come not by land but by sea, using boats.

This new evidence suggests that the early population of the Americas was more diverse and more scattered than scholars used to believe. Recent DNA evidence has identified a possible early population group that does not seem to have Asian characteristics. This suggests that thousands of years before Columbus, there may have been some migration from Europe.

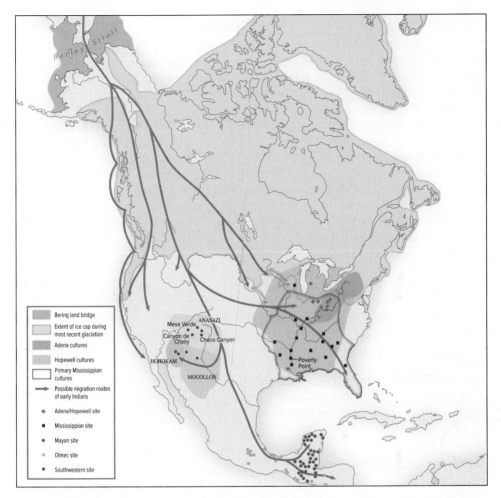

NORTH AMERICAN MIGRATIONS This map tracks some of the very early migrations into, and within, North America in the centuries preceding contact with Europe. It shows the now-vanished land bridge between Siberia and Alaska over which thousands, perhaps millions, of migrating people passed into the Americas. It also shows the locations of some of the earliest settlements in North America. • *What role did the extended glacial field in what is now Canada play in residential patterns in the ancient American world?*

The *Archaic period* is a scholarly term for the early history of humans in America, beginning around 8000 B.C. In the first part of this period, most humans supported themselves through hunting and gathering, using the same stone tools that earlier Americans had brought with them from Asia.

Later in the Archaic period, population groups began to expand their activities and to develop new tools, such as nets and hooks for fishing, traps for smaller animals, and baskets for gathering berries, nuts, seeds, and other plants. Still later, some groups began to farm. Farming, of course, requires people to stay in one place. In agricultural areas, the first sedentary settlements slowly began to form, creating the basis for larger civilizations.

THE GROWTH OF CIVILIZATIONS: THE SOUTH

The most elaborate early civilizations emerged in South and Central America and in Mexico. In Peru, the Incas created the largest empire in the Americas, stretching almost 2,000 miles along western South America. The Incas developed a complex administrative state, an irrigation system, and a large network of paved roads that welded together the populations of many tribes under a single government.

Organized societies emerged around 10,000 B.C. in **Mesoamerica**, a region comprising Mexico and much of Central America. The Olmec people, whose roots trace back to between 1600 and 1500 B.C., were the first complex society in the region. A more sophisticated culture grew up in parts of Central America and in the Yucatán peninsula of Mexico, in an area known as Maya. Mayan civilization, which stretched back to 1800 B.C. and was at its most powerful about A.D. 300, developed a written language, a numerical system similar to the Arabic numeral system, an accurate calendar, an advanced agricultural system, and important trade routes into other areas of the continents.

Gradually, the societies of the Maya region were superseded by other Mesoamerican tribes, who have become known collectively (and somewhat inaccurately) as the Aztecs. They called themselves Mexica. In about A.D. 1325, the Mexicas built the city of Tenochtitlán on a large island in a lake in central Mexico, the site of present-day Mexico City. With a population as high as 100,000 by 1500, Tenochtitlán featured large and impressive public buildings, schools that all male children attended, an organized military, a medical system, and a slave workforce drawn from conquered tribes. It was a city built over water and featuring a sophisticated water navigation system, much like Venice, Italy, but larger. The Mexicas gradually established their dominance over almost all of central Mexico.

The Mesoamerican civilizations were for many centuries the center of civilized life in North and Central America—the hub of culture and trade.

THE CIVILIZATIONS OF THE NORTH

The peoples north of Mexico developed less elaborate but still substantial civilizations. Inhabitants of the northern regions of the continent subsisted on combinations of hunting, gathering, and fishing. They included the Inuit of the Arctic Circle, who fished and hunted seals; big-game hunters of the northern forests, who led nomadic lives based on the pursuit of moose and caribou; tribes of the Pacific Northwest, whose principal occupation was salmon fishing and who created substantial permanent settlements along the coast; and a group of tribes spread through relatively arid regions of the Far West, who developed successful communities based on fishing, hunting small game, and gathering edible plants.

Other societies in North America were agricultural. Among the most developed were those in the Southwest. Between A.D. 900 and 1150, the ancient Pueblo people developed a thriving center of culture and commerce in Chaco Canyon, in modern-day northwestern New Mexico. At its apex, Chaco Canyon boasted a population of 15,000, 12 towns, and 200 villages—one of the largest of which was Pueblo Bonita. Composed of sandstone, timber, and adobe, it soared five stories high and had 600 rooms. There would not be another structure of this size in North America until the 1880s. At roughly the same period, the Hopis lived in small masonry villages, farmed corn, and developed an elaborate irrigation system, ceremonial culture, and trade network stretching across what is now Arizona. And the Zunis, based in the desert areas of present-day Arizona, Utah, and New Mexico, built large stone and adobe villages centered on a plaza, created elaborate pottery, and farmed corn and other grains.

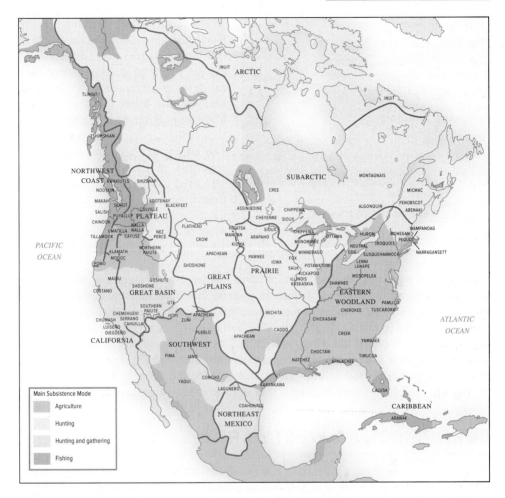

HOW THE EARLY NORTH AMERICANS LIVED This map shows the various ways in which the native tribes of North America supported themselves before the arrival of European civilization. The Native Americans survived largely on the resources available in their immediate surroundings. Note, for example, the reliance on the products of the sea of the tribes along the northern coastlines of the continent, and the way in which tribes in relatively inhospitable climates in the North—where agriculture was difficult—relied on hunting large game. Most Native Americans were farmers. • *What different kinds of farming would have emerged in the very different climates of the agricultural regions shown on this map?*

The eastern third of what is now the United States—much of it covered with forests and inhabited by the Woodland Indians—had the greatest food resources of any area of the continent. Most of the many tribes of the region engaged in farming, hunting, gathering, and fishing simultaneously. In the South there were permanent settlements and large trading networks based on the corn, legumes, and squash grown in the rich lands of the Mississippi River valley. **Cahokia**, a trading center located near present-day St. Louis, had a population of 40,000 at its peak in A.D. 1200. Residents traded not only their crops but also hand tools and pottery they made. Occupying six square miles, Cahokia was the largest and most populous urban center north of Tenochtitlán and would remain so until Philadelphia in 1780.

(©Don Mammoser/Shutterstock)

PUEBLO VILLAGE OF THE SOUTHWEST

The agricultural societies of the Northeast were more mobile. Farming techniques there were designed to exploit the land quickly rather than to develop permanent settlements. Many of the tribes living east of the Mississippi River were linked together loosely by common linguistic roots. The largest of these language groups consisted of the Algonquian tribes, who lived along the Atlantic seaboard from Canada to Virginia; the Iroquois Confederacy, which was centered in what is now upstate New York; and the Muskogean tribes, which consisted of the tribes in the southernmost regions of the eastern seaboard.

Most tribes were matrilineal societies, meaning that family association and clan membership flowed through the mother's heritage. In contrast, in Europe ancestral descent followed paternal lines. All tribes assigned women the majority of work to care for children, prepare meals, and gather certain foods. But the allocation of other tasks varied from one society to another. In the case of the Hopi, women and men shared cultural authority. Women assumed leadership roles in the household, economy, and social system; men tended to predominate in religion and politics. Yet women reserved the power to negate or renegotiate trade or land deals forged by men if they deemed them unjust or imbalanced.

EUROPE LOOKS WESTWARD

Europeans were almost entirely unaware of the existence of the Americas before the fifteenth century. A few early wanderers—Leif Eriksson, an eleventh-century Norse seaman, and others—had glimpsed parts of the eastern Atlantic on their voyages. But even if their discoveries had become common knowledge (and they did not), there would have been little incentive for others to follow. Europe in the Middle Ages (roughly A.D. 500–1500) was too weak, divided, and decentralized to inspire many great ventures. By the end of the fifteenth century, however, conditions in Europe had changed and the incentive for overseas exploration had grown.

COMMERCE AND SEA TRAVEL

Two important social changes encouraged Europeans to look toward new lands. The first was the significant growth in Europe's population in the fifteenth century. The Black Death, a catastrophic epidemic of the bubonic plague that began in Constantinople in 1347, had killed more than a third of the people on the Continent (according to some estimates). But a century and a half later, the population had rebounded. With that growth came a reawakening of commerce. A new merchant class was emerging to meet the rising demand for goods from abroad. As trade increased, and as advances in navigation made long-distance sea travel more feasible, interest in expanding trade grew even more quickly. The second change was the emergence of new governments that were more united and powerful than the feeble political entities of the feudal past. In the western areas of Europe in particular, strong new monarchs were eager to enhance the commercial development of their nations.

Above all, Europeans who craved commercial glory had dreamed of trade with the East. It was not a new dream. In the early fourteenth century, Marco Polo and other adventurers had returned from Asia bearing exotic spices, cloths, and dyes and even more exotic tales. Yet for two centuries, that trade had been limited by the difficulties of the long overland journey to the Asian courts. But in the fourteenth century, talk of finding a faster, safer sea route to East Asia began.

The Portuguese were the preeminent maritime power in the fifteenth century, largely because of Prince Henry the Navigator, who devoted much of his life to the promotion of exploration. In 1486, after Henry's death, the Portuguese explorer Bartholomeu Dias rounded the southern tip of Africa (the Cape of Good Hope). In 1497-1498, Vasco da Gama proceeded all the way around the cape to India. But the Spanish, not the Portuguese, were the first to encounter the *New World,* the term Europeans applied to the ancient lands previously unknown to them.

Christopher Columbus

Christopher Columbus was born and reared in Genoa, Italy. He spent his early seafaring years in the service of the Portuguese, stoking his ambitions of undertaking a great voyage of discovery. By the time he was a young man, he believed he could reach East Asia by sailing west, across the Atlantic, rather than east, around Africa. Columbus thought the world was far smaller than it actually is. He also was convinced that the Asian continent extended farther eastward than it actually does. Most important, he did not realize that anything lay to the west between Europe and the lands of Asia.

Columbus failed to enlist the leaders of Portugal to back his plan, so he turned instead to Spain. The marriage of Spain's two most powerful regional rulers, Ferdinand of Aragon and Isabella of Castile, had produced the strongest and most ambitious monarchy in Europe. Columbus appealed to Queen Isabella for support for his proposed westward voyage, and in 1492, she agreed. Commanding ninety men and three ships—the *Niña,* the *Pinta,* and the *Santa María*—Columbus left Spain in August 1492 and sailed west into the Atlantic. Ten weeks later, he sighted land and assumed he had reached an island off Asia. In fact, he had landed in the Bahamas. When he pushed on and encountered Cuba, he assumed he had reached Japan. He returned to Spain, bringing with him several captured native people as evidence of his achievement. (He called the indigenous people "Indians" because he believed they were from the East Indies in the Pacific.)

But Columbus did not, of course, bring back news of the great khan's court in China or any samples of the fabled wealth of the Indies. And so a year later he tried again, only this time with a much larger expedition. As before, he headed into the Caribbean, discovering several other islands and leaving a small and short-lived **colony** on Hispaniola. On a third voyage, in 1498, he finally reached the mainland and cruised along the northern coast of South America. He then realized, for the first time, that he had encountered not a part of Asia but a separate continent.

Columbus ended his life in obscurity. Ultimately, he was even unable to give his name to the land he had revealed to the Europeans. That distinction went instead to a Florentine merchant, Amerigo Vespucci, who wrote a series of vivid descriptions of the lands he visited on a later expedition to the New World and helped popularize the idea that the Americas were new continents.

Partly as a result of Columbus's initiative, Spain began to devote greater resources and energy to maritime exploration. In 1513, the Spaniard Vasco de Balboa crossed the Isthmus of Panama and became the first known European to gaze westward upon the great ocean

EUROPEAN EXPLORATION AND CONQUEST, 1492–1583 This map shows the many voyages of exploration to and conquest of North America launched by Europeans in the late fifteenth and sixteenth centuries. Note how Columbus and the Spanish explorers who followed him tended to move quickly into the lands of Mexico, the Caribbean, and Central and South America, while the English and French explored the northern territories of North America. In all cases they encountered Indians, whose roots trace back centuries before the arrival of the Europeans. • *What factors might have led these various nations to explore and colonize different areas of the New World?*

that separated America from China. Seeking access to that ocean, Ferdinand Magellan, a Portuguese in Spanish employ, found the strait that now bears his name at the southern end of South America, struggled through the stormy narrows and into the ocean (so calm by contrast that he christened it the *Pacific*), and then proceeded to the Philippines.

There Magellan died in a conflict with local Indians, but his expedition went on to complete the first known circumnavigation of the globe (1519-1522). By 1550, Spaniards had explored the coasts of North America as far north as Oregon in the west and Labrador in the east.

THE SPANISH EMPIRE

In time, Spanish explorers in the New World stopped thinking of America simply as an obstacle to their search for a route to Asia and began instead to consider it a possible source of wealth in itself. The Spanish claimed for themselves the whole of the New World, except for a large part of the east coast of South America (today's Brazil) that was reserved by a papal decree for the Portuguese.

In 1518, Hernando Cortés, who had been an unsuccessful Spanish government official in Cuba for fourteen years, led a small military expedition of about 600 men against the Aztecs in Mexico and their powerful emperor, Montezuma, after hearing stories of their great treasures. Moving his warriors through Mexico, he befriended a native tribe that he labeled the Tlaxcalans, who were rivals of the Aztecs and would become crucial military allies. Approaching Tenochtitlán, Cortés benefited from perfect timing. His arrival seemed to fulfill a popular Aztec prophecy that claimed the god Quetsalcoatl was to return to Earth. The Aztecs mistook Cortés and his fighters—mysterious light skinned men—as divine company and greeted them as honored figures. Cortés, with the support of the Tlaxcalans, quickly took control of the city. Key to his success was the use of body armor that repelled or blunted arrows, steel swords, lances with iron or steel points, and a type of early musket called harquebus—all weapons unknown to the Aztecs. An Aztec counterrebellion, however, soon restored them to power. But not for long.

A smallpox epidemic, begun when a Spanish soldier died from the disease while in Tenochtitlán, spread among the Aztecs and gutted the population. When Cortés re-attacked, again with the backing of the Tlaxcalans, he now fought a depleted people. Even more significantly, he employed a series of new and aggressive military tactics—blocking delivery of food and water to the city, choking off canals, destroying aqueducts—that brought the city to its knees after 75 days. Cortés laid claim to Tenochtitlán, ruthlessly destroying temples and homes and establishing himself as one of the most brutal of the Spanish **conquistadores** (conquerors). Twenty years later, Francisco Pizarro overpowered the Incas in Peru and opened the way for other Spanish advances into South America.

The first Spanish settlers in America were interested largely in exploiting the American stores of gold and silver, and they were fabulously successful. For 300 years, beginning in the sixteenth century, the mines of Spanish America yielded more than ten times as much gold and silver as all the rest of the world's mines combined. Before long, however, most Spanish settlers in America traveled to the New World for other reasons. Many went in hopes of profiting from agriculture. They helped establish elements of European civilization permanently in America. Other Spaniards—priests, friars, and missionaries—went to America to spread Catholicism; through their efforts, the influence of the Catholic Church ultimately extended throughout South and Central America and Mexico. They sometimes evangelized, however, with an iron fist, forcing whole families to forsake their sacred beliefs and practices, be baptized, and adopt the teachings of the Catholic Church or face physical punishment and even death. Yet one of the first friars to work in the colonies, **Bartolomé de Las Casas**, fought for the fair treatment of native peoples by the Spanish as part of his ministry. (See "Consider the Source: Bartolomé de Las Casas, 'Of the Island of Hispaniola.'")

CONSIDER THE SOURCE

BARTOLOMÉ DE LAS CASAS, "OF THE ISLAND OF HISPANIOLA" (1542)

Bartolomé de Las Casas, a Dominican friar from Spain, was an early European settler of the West Indies. He devoted much of his life to describing the culture of native peoples and chronicling the many abuses they suffered at the hands of their colonizers. This excerpt is from a letter he addressed to Spain's Prince Philip.

God has created all these numberless people to be quite the simplest, without malice or duplicity, most obedient, most faithful to their natural Lords, and to the Christians, whom they serve; the most humble, most patient, most peaceful and calm, without strife nor tumults; not wrangling, nor querulous, as free from uproar, hate and desire of revenge as any in the world. . . . Among these gentle sheep, gifted by their Maker with the above qualities, the Spaniards entered as soon as they knew them, like wolves, tigers and lions which had been starving for many days, and since forty years they have done nothing else; nor do they afflict, torment, and destroy them with strange and new, and divers kinds of cruelty, never before seen, nor heard of, nor read of. . . .

The Christians, with their horses and swords and lances, began to slaughter and practice strange cruelty among them. They penetrated into the country and spared neither children nor the aged, nor pregnant women, nor those in child labour, all of whom they ran through the body and lacerated, as though they were assaulting so many lambs herded in their sheepfold. They made bets as to who would slit a man in two, or cut off his head at one blow: or they opened up his bowels. They tore the babes from their mothers' breast by the feet, and dashed their heads against the rocks. Others they seized by the shoulders and threw into the rivers, laughing and joking, and when they fell into the water they exclaimed: "boil body of so and so!" They spitted the bodies of other babes, together with their mothers and all who were before them, on their swords.

They made a gallows just high enough for the feet to nearly touch the ground, and by thirteens, in honor and reverence of our Redeemer and the twelve Apostles, they put wood underneath and, with fire, they burned the Indians alive.

They wrapped the bodies of others entirely in dry straw, binding them in it and setting fire to it; and so they burned them. They cut off the hands of all they wished to take alive, made them carry them fastened on to them, and said: "Go and carry letters": that is; take the news to those who have fled to the mountains.

They generally killed the lords and nobles in the following way. They made wooden gridirons of stakes, bound them upon them, and made a slow fire beneath; thus the victims gave up the spirit by degrees, emitting cries of despair in their torture.

UNDERSTAND, ANALYZE, & EVALUATE

1. How did Bartolomé de Las Casas characterize the indigenous people of Hispaniola? How do you think they would have responded to this description?
2. What metaphor did Las Casas use to describe the native peoples and where does this metaphor come from?
3. What role did Las Casas expect the Spaniards to play on Hispaniola? What did they do instead?

Source: MacNutt, Francis Augustus, *Bartholomew de Las Casas: His Life, His Apostolate, and His Writings.* New York: G.P. Putnam's Sons, 1909, 14.

By the end of the sixteenth century, the Spanish Empire included the Caribbean islands, Mexico, and southern North America. It also spread into South America and included what is now Chile, Argentina, and Peru. In 1580, when the Spanish and Portuguese monarchies temporarily united, Brazil came under Spanish jurisdiction as well.

NORTHERN OUTPOSTS

In 1565, the Spanish established the fort of St. Augustine in Florida, their first permanent settlement in what is now the United States. But it was little more than a small military outpost. A more substantial colonizing venture began in the Southwest in 1598, when Don Juan de Oñate traveled north from Mexico with a party between 600 and 700, claimed for Spain some of the lands of the Pueblo Indians in what is now New Mexico, and began to establish a colony. It was a bloody affair. In October 1898, the Acoma Pueblos refused to turn over food to Oñate's soldiers and, in a small battle killed as many as 13 of them, including Oñate's nephew. In January of the next year, Oñate ordered retribution. His men lay siege to the Acoma village, killing at least 800. They enslaved all survivors older than 12 years for a period of 20 years and cut off the right foot of all men of fighting age.

Oñate granted **encomiendas** (the right to exact tribute and labor from native peoples on large tracts of land) to favored Spaniards. In 1609, Spanish colonists founded Santa Fe. By 1680, there were over 2,000 Spanish colonists living among about 30,000 Pueblos. The economic heart of the colony was cattle and sheep, raised on the *ranchos* that stretched out around the small towns Spanish settlers established.

Part of the Spanish expansion in the North included converting native peoples to Catholicism. As in the South, it met with uneven results. Many native peoples simply rejected the attempt, mixed the precepts and practices of their own faith with Catholicism, or only selectively adopted Catholic rituals and teachings. At other times native peoples and Spanish officials differed over what constituted conversion. Matters came to a head in 1680, when Spanish priests and the colonial government tried to suppress native rituals. In response, **Popé**, an Indian religious leader, led an uprising that killed hundreds of European settlers, captured Santa Fe, and drove the Spanish from the region. Ironically, the rebellion was so widespread and included so many different Indian groups that the native revolutionaries used Spanish as their common language in order to communicate with one other. Twelve years later, however, the Spanish returned and crushed a last revolt in 1696.

Many Spanish colonists now realized that they could not hope to prosper in New Mexico while in constant conflict with a native population that greatly outnumbered them. Although the Spanish intensified their efforts to assimilate the Indians, they also now permitted the Pueblos to own land. They stopped commandeering Indian labor, and they tolerated the survival of tribal religious rituals. There was significant intermarriage between Europeans and Indians. By 1750, the Spanish population had grown to about 4,000. The Pueblo population had declined (through disease, war, and migration) to about 13,000—less than half what it had been in 1680. New Mexico had by then become a reasonably stable but still weak and isolated outpost of the Spanish Empire.

BIOLOGICAL AND CULTURAL EXCHANGES

European and native cultures never entirely merged in the Spanish Empire. Nevertheless, the arrival of whites launched a process of interaction between diverse peoples that left

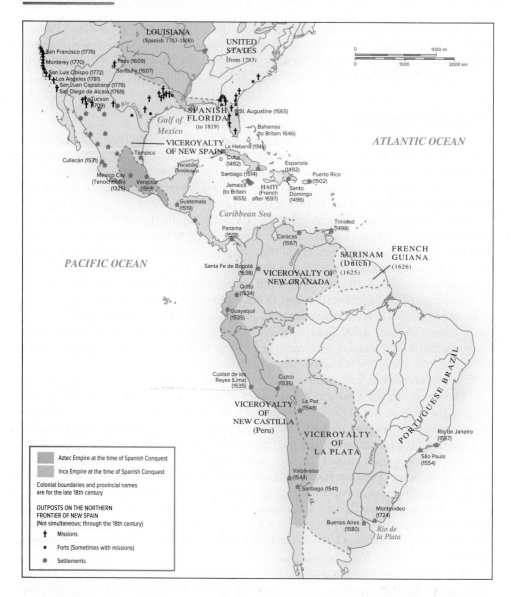

SPANISH AMERICA   From the time of Columbus's initial voyage in 1492 until the mid-nineteenth century, Spain was the dominant colonial power in the New World. From the southern regions of South America to the northern regions of the Pacific Northwest, Spain controlled one of the world's vastest empires. Note how much of the Spanish Empire was simply grafted upon the earlier empires of native peoples—the Incas in what is today Chile and Peru and the Aztecs across much of the rest of South America, Mexico, and the Southwest of what is now the United States. • *What characteristics of Spanish colonization would account for their preference for already settled regions?*

no one unchanged. That Europeans were exploring the Americas at all was a result of early contacts with the native peoples, from whom they had learned of the rich deposits of gold and silver. From then on, the history of the Americas became one of increasing levels of exchanges—some beneficial, others catastrophic—among different peoples and cultures.

(©Dorling Kindersley/Getty Images)

SMALLPOX AMONG THE AZTECS This illustration by a Spanish missionary in the fifteenth century depicts victims of smallpox in various stages of the disease, which was introduced to the Americas by Europeans.

The first and perhaps most profound result of this exchange was the importation of European diseases to the New World. It would be difficult to exaggerate the consequences of the exposure of Native Americans to such illnesses as influenza, measles, typhus, and above all smallpox. Although historians have debated the question of how many people lived in the Americas before the arrival of Europeans, it is estimated that millions died. (See "Debating the Past: Why Do Historians So Often Differ?") Part of the issue was how native cultures traditionally cared for the very ill. They tended to surround the sick with constant companions and visitors as a way to encourage healing—a practice that inadvertently helped spread the highly contagious diseases they were encountering for the first time. Unlike in Europe, where experience with the bubonic plague had taught the benefits of socially isolating the infected, there was no corresponding notion of quarantine among native tribes of the Americas. In some areas, then, native populations were virtually wiped out within a few decades of their first contact with whites. On Hispaniola, where Columbus had landed in the 1490s, the native population quickly declined from approximately one million to about five hundred. In the Maya area of Mexico, as much as 95 percent of the population perished within a few years of the native peoples' first contact with the Spanish. Still, not everyone died, not every community was ravaged, and some rebuilt over time. And many of the tribes north of Mexico were spared the worst of the epidemics. But for other areas of the New World, this was a disaster at least as grave as, and in some places far worse than, the Black Death that had killed over one-third of the population of Europe two centuries before. Some Europeans, watching this biological catastrophe, saw it as evidence of God's will that they should dominate the New World—and its native population.

Why Do Historians So Often Differ?

Early in the twentieth century, when the professional study of history was still relatively new, many historians believed that questions about the past could be answered with the same certainty and precision as questions in more-scientific fields. By sifting through available records, using precise methods of research and analysis, and producing careful, closely argued accounts of the past, they believed they could create definitive histories that would survive without controversy. Scholars who adhered to this view believed that real knowledge can be derived only from direct, scientific observation of clear "fact." They were known as "positivists."

A vigorous debate continues to this day over whether historical research can ever be truly objective. Almost no historian any longer accepts the positivist claim that history could ever be an exact science. Disagreement about the past is, in fact, at the heart of the effort to understand history. Critics of contemporary historical scholarship often denounce the way historians are constantly revising earlier interpretations. Some denounce the act of interpretation itself. History, they claim, is "what happened," and historians should "stick to the facts."

Historians, however, continue to differ with one another both because the facts are seldom as straightforward as their critics claim and because facts by themselves mean almost nothing without an effort to assign meaning to them. Some historical facts, of course, are not in dispute. Everyone agrees, for example, that the Japanese bombed Pearl Harbor on December 7, 1941, and that Abraham Lincoln was elected president in 1860. But many other facts are much harder to determine—among them, for example, the question of how large the American population was before the arrival of Columbus, or how many slaves resisted slavery. This sounds like a reasonably straightforward question, but it is almost impossible to answer with any certainty—because the records of slave resistance are spotty and the definition of "resistance" is a matter of considerable dispute.

Even when a set of facts is clear and straightforward, historians disagree—sometimes quite radically—over what they mean. Those disagreements can be the result of political and ideological disagreements. Some of the most vigorous debates in recent decades have been between scholars who believe that economic interests and class divisions are the key to understanding the past, and those who believe that ideas and culture are at least as important as material interests. Debates can also occur over differences in methodology—between those who believe that quantitative studies can answer important historical questions and those who believe that other methods come closer to the truth.

Most of all, historical interpretation changes in response to the time in which it is written. Historians may strive to be objective in their work, but no one can be entirely free from the assumptions and political concerns of the present. In the 1950s, the omnipresent shadow of the Cold War shaped histories of Communist countries

14 ·

and a view of them as engaged in a war to end democracy. The civil rights movements prompted scholars to reconsider what they knew about the lives and achievements of black Americans, women, Hispanics, and gays and lesbians. The rise of postcolonial societies pushed historians to reexamine assumptions built into the telling of the rise and fall of empires—that they were the products of an elite cadre of men—and rethink the role of workers and the less powerful in influencing the course of events. The "cultural turn" at the end of the twentieth century placed a newfound stress on examining how various forces of culture—gender, sexuality, race, ethnicity, language—deeply affected the ways in which people experienced and understood the world. Its effects are still rippling through the academy, asking historians to ever widen their lens of analysis when seeking to explain people's motivations and actions.

Historians regularly debate over which types of interpretation come closest to capturing the truth of the past with no clear-cut consensus likely to come into focus any time soon. Such debate, though, is a sign of the health of the profession. Scholars need to constantly revisit how they talk about the past and be challenged to defend their decisions in order to make sure they are capturing the full range of human experience when writing their histories. Indeed, understanding the past is a forever continuing—and forever contested—process.

UNDERSTAND, ANALYZE, & EVALUATE

1. What are some of the reasons historians so often disagree? *their own background + opinion*
2. Is there ever a right or wrong in historical interpretation? What value might historical inquiry have other than reaching a right or wrong conclusion?
3. If historians so often disagree, how should a student of history approach historical content? How might disagreement expand our understanding of history?

Europeans entering America ↗

Not all aspects of the exchange were disastrous to the Indians. The Europeans introduced important new crops (among them sugar and bananas), domestic livestock (cattle, pigs, and sheep), and, perhaps most significantly, the horse, which gradually became central to the lives of many native peoples and transformed their societies. Less beneficially, the transfer of European grass seed and the grazing and feeding habits of European animals devastated local flora.

The exchange was at least as important (and more advantageous) to the Europeans. In both North and South America, the arriving white peoples learned from the natives new agricultural techniques appropriate to the demands of the new land. They discovered new crops—above all maize (corn), which Columbus took back to Europe from his first trip to America. Such foods as squash, pumpkins, beans, sweet potatoes, tomatoes, peppers, and potatoes also found their way into European diets.

In South America, Central America, and Mexico, Europeans and native groups lived in intimate, if unequal, contact with one another. Many native people gradually came to speak Spanish or Portuguese, but they created a range of dialects fusing the European languages with elements of their own. European men outnumbered European women by at least ten to one. Intermarriage—often forcible—became frequent between Spanish immigrants and native women. Before long, the population of the colonies came to be dominated (numerically, at least) by people of mixed race, or **mestizos**. A

Virtually all the enterprises of the Spanish and Portuguese colonists depended on Indian workforces. In some places, Indians were sold into slavery. More often, colonists used a

THE INTERNATIONAL CONTEXT OF THE EARLY HISTORY OF THE AMERICAS

Most Americans understand that our nation of late has become intimately bound up with the rest of the world—that we live in what many call the "age of **globalization**." But few extend that idea backward in time and consider how the story of America before Columbus and the effort by European powers to settle it was also part of a global current of ideas and events. Indeed, until recently historians typically studied these early chapters from the nation's past mostly in isolation from larger world events and non-European societies. By contrast today, scholars of early American history now examine what happened in the New World from a broadly international perspective.

That perspective is often called the **"Atlantic World"** and it explores history as the intermingling of peoples from Africa, Europe, and the Americas and the profound effects of those interactions. The phrase has a long intellectual genealogy, stretching back to the foundational work of C. L. R. James, W. E. B. Du Bois, Frantz Fanon, and Eric Williams. They demonstrated that the origins of the New World were deeply enmeshed in the practice and institution of slavery, on the one hand, and that African (and later African American) culture lay at the root of the evolution of culture in the Americas, on the other.

The idea of an Atlantic World rests in part on the obvious connections between western Europe and the Spanish, British, French, and Dutch colonies in North and South America. All the early European civilizations of the Americas were part of a great imperial project launched by the major powers of Europe. The European immigrations to the Americas beginning in the sixteenth century, the advance of slavery and the introduction of it in the New World, the defeat and devastation of native populations, the creation of European agricultural and urban settlements, and the imposition of imperial regulations on trade, commerce, landowning, and political life—all of these forces reveal the influence of Old World **imperialism** on the history of the New World.

But the expansion of empires is only one part of the creation of the Atlantic World. At least equally important—and closely related—is the expansion of commerce from Europe and Africa to the Americas. Although some northern and southern Europeans traveled to the New World in search of religious freedom, or to escape oppression, or to search for adventure, the great majority were in search of economic opportunity. Not surprisingly, therefore, their settlements in the Americas were almost from the start intimately connected to Europe through the growth of commerce between them and to Africa through the capture and import of slaves. This international commercial dynamic between America and Europe was responsible not just for the growth of trade, but also for the increases in migration over time—as the demand for labor in the New World drew more and more settlers from the Old World. Commerce was also a principal reason for the rise of slavery in the Americas, and for the growth of the slave trade between European America and Africa.

Religion was also a powerful force influencing migration to the New World and shaping human interactions there. Depending on the decade, some Europeans—Puritans, Anabaptists—relocated in part to escape persecution for their principles. At other times, Catholics and members of the Church of England built settlements to win converts and extend their religious empires. Significantly, European transplants had to come to terms with the religion of the Indians they encountered, which led to a variety of responses: indifference, evangelism, repression, or the growth of hybrid sacred practices and convictions. Adding to the mix were African slaves, who brought their own indigenous religions. They found themselves the subjects of intense and sometimes brutal proselytizing attempts by Europeans, which met with only uneven success. Some slaves adopted the faith of their owners. But African American religion as a whole generally emerged as a series of spiritual beliefs and rituals that mixed African, European, and sometimes Indian beliefs. It also influenced the religion of Europeans and (to a lesser extent) Indians, particularly in the evolution of their public revivals and preaching traditions in the New World.

The early history of the Americas was also closely bound up with the intellectual life of northern and southern Europe and Latin America. The Enlightenment—the cluster of ideas that emerged in the seventeenth and eighteenth centuries emphasizing the power of human reason—moved quickly to the Americas, producing intellectual ferment throughout the New World. Thinkers from Britain and Spain, for example, stressed the sanctity of individual rights, the proper nature and role of representative government, and the fairness of law that eventually undergirded the history of the American Revolution, the Haitian Revolution, and Latin American revolutions of the eighteenth century. Scientific and technological knowledge—another product of the Enlightenment—traveled constantly across the Atlantic and back. Americans borrowed industrial technology from Britain. Europe acquired much of its early knowledge of electricity from experiments done in America. But the Enlightenment was only one part of the continuing intellectual connections within the Atlantic World, connections that spread artistic, scholarly, and political ideas widely through the lands bordering the ocean.

Instead of thinking of the early history of what became the United States simply as the story of the growth of thirteen small colonies along the Atlantic seaboard of North America, the idea of the Atlantic World encourages us to think of early American history as a vast pattern of exchanges and interactions—trade, migration, religious and intellectual exchange, and many other relationships—among all the societies bordering the Atlantic: northern and southern Europe, western Africa, the Caribbean, and North and South America.

UNDERSTAND, ANALYZE, & EVALUATE

1. What is the Atlantic World?
2. What has led historians to begin studying the idea of an Atlantic World?

coercive (or "indentured") wage system, under which Indians worked in the mines and on the plantations under duress for fixed periods. That was not, in the end, enough to meet the labor needs of the colonists. As early as 1502, European settlers began importing slaves from Africa.

AFRICA AND AMERICA

Over one-half of all the immigrants to the New World between 1500 and 1800 were Africans, sent against their will. Most came from West and Central Africa.

Europeans and white Americans came to portray African society as primitive and uncivilized. But most Africans were, in fact, highly civilized peoples with well-developed economies and political systems. The residents of the Gold Coast had substantial commercial contact with the Mediterranean world—trading ivory, gold, and slaves for finished goods—and, largely as a result, became early converts to Islam. After the collapse of the ancient kingdom of Ghana around A.D. 1100, they created the even larger empire of Mali, whose trading center at Timbuktu became fabled as a learned meeting place of the peoples of many lands. In West Central Africa, the Kingdom of Kongo flourished. It was a regional center for trade, where residents sold goods they manufactured, such as pottery and copper and iron goods. By early 1500, the majority of the ruling class had converted to Catholicism and the Kingdom was sending a formal emissary to the Vatican. And by the end of the sixteenth century its population was nearly 500,000.

As in many Indian societies in America, African families tended to be matrilineal. Women played a major role, often the dominant role, in trade. In many areas, they were also the principal farmers while the men hunted, fished, raised livestock, fought battles; in these areas women choose their own leaders to make decisions and policies for the community as a whole. Everywhere women managed child care and food preparation.

Small elites of priests and nobles stood at the top of many African societies. Most people belonged to a large middle group of farmers, traders, crafts workers, and others. At the bottom of society were slaves—men and women, not all of them African, who were put into bondage after being captured in wars, because of criminal behavior, or as a result of unpaid debts. Slaves in Africa were generally in bondage for a fixed term, and in the meantime they retained certain legal protections (including the right to marry). Children did not inherit their parents' condition of bondage.

The African slave trade long preceded European settlement in the New World. As early as the eighth century, West Africans began selling small numbers of slaves to traders from the Mediterranean and later to the Portuguese. In the sixteenth century, however, the market for slaves increased dramatically as a result of the growing European demand for sugarcane. The small areas of sugar cultivation in the Mediterranean could not meet the demand, and production soon spread to new areas: to the island of Madeira off the African coast, which became a Portuguese colony, and not long thereafter (still in the sixteenth century) to the Caribbean islands and Brazil. Sugar was a labor-intensive crop, and the demand for African workers in these new areas of cultivation was high. At first the slave traders were overwhelmingly Portuguese. By the seventeenth century, though, the Dutch had won control of most of the market. And in the eighteenth century, the English dominated it. By 1700, slavery had spread well beyond its original locations in the Caribbean and South America and into the English colonies to the north. The relationship among European, African, and native peoples—however unequal—reminds us of the global context to the history of America. (See "America in the World: The International Context of the Early History of the Americas.")

THE ARRIVAL OF THE ENGLISH

England's first documented contact with the New World came only five years after Spain's. In 1497, John Cabot (like Columbus, a native of Genoa) sailed to the northeastern coast of North America on an expedition sponsored by King Henry VII, in an unsuccessful search for a northwest passage through the New World to the Orient. But nearly a century passed before the English made any serious efforts to establish colonies in America.

Significantly, England's first experience with colonization came not in the New World but in neighboring Ireland. The English had long laid claim to the island, but only in the late sixteenth century did serious efforts at colonization begin. The long, brutal process by which the English attempted to subdue the Irish created an important assumption about colonization: the belief that settlements in foreign lands must retain a rigid separation from the native populations. Unlike the Spanish in America, the English in Ireland tried to build a separate society of their own, peopled with emigrants from England itself. They would take that concept with them to the New World.

INCENTIVES FOR COLONIZATION

Interest in **colonization** grew in part as a response to social and economic problems in sixteenth-century England. The English people faced frequent and costly European wars as well as almost constant religious strife within their own land. Many suffered, too, from harsh economic changes in their countryside. Because the worldwide demand for wool was growing rapidly, landowners were converting their land from fields for crops to pastures for sheep. The result was a reduction in the amount of land available for growing food. England's food supply declined at the same time that the English population was growing—from 3 million in 1485 to 4 million in 1603. To some of the English, the New World began to seem attractive because it offered something that was growing scarce in England: land.

At the same time, new merchant capitalists were prospering by selling the products of England's growing wool-cloth industry abroad. At first, most exporters did business almost entirely as individuals. In time, however, merchants formed companies, whose **charters** from the king gave them monopolies for trading in particular regions. Investors in these companies often made fantastic profits, and they were eager to expand their trade.

Central to this trading drive was the emergence of a new concept of economic life known as **mercantilism**. Mercantilism rested on the belief that one person or nation could grow rich only at the expense of another, and that a nation's economic health depended, therefore, on selling as much as possible to foreign lands and buying as little as possible from them. The principles of mercantilism spread throughout Europe in the sixteenth and seventeenth centuries. One result was the increased attractiveness of acquiring colonies, which became the source of raw materials and a market for the colonizing power's goods.

In England, the mercantilistic program thrived at first on the basis of the flourishing wool trade with the European continent, and particularly with the great cloth market in Antwerp. In the 1550s, however, that glutted market began to collapse, and English merchants had to look elsewhere for overseas trade. Some English believed colonies would solve their problems.

There were also religious motives for colonization—a result of the **Protestant Reformation**. Protestantism began in Germany in 1517, when Martin Luther challenged some of the basic practices and beliefs of the Roman Catholic Church. Luther quickly won a wide following among ordinary men and women in northern Europe. When the pope excommunicated him in 1520, Luther began leading his followers out of the Catholic Church entirely.

The Swiss theologian John Calvin went even further in rejecting the Catholic belief that human behavior could affect an individual's prospects for salvation. Calvin introduced the doctrine of predestination. God "elected" some people to be saved and condemned others to damnation; each person's destiny was determined before birth, and no one could change that predetermined fate. But those who accepted Calvin's teachings came to believe that the way they led their lives might reveal to them their chances of salvation. A wicked or useless existence would be a sign of damnation; saintliness, diligence, and possibly signs of grace. The new creed spread rapidly throughout northern Europe.

In 1529, King Henry VIII of England, angered by the refusal of the pope to grant him a divorce from his Spanish wife, broke England's ties with the Catholic Church and established himself as the head of the Christian faith in his country. This was known as the English Reformation. After Henry's death, his Catholic daughter, Queen Mary, restored England's allegiance to Rome and persecuted Protestants. But when Mary died in 1558, her half sister, **Elizabeth I**, became England's sovereign and once again severed the nation's connection with the Catholic Church, this time for good.

To many English people, however, the new Church of England was not reformed enough. They clamored for changes that would "purify" the church and quickly became knows as **Puritans**. Most only wanted to simplify worship and reform the leadership of the church. Their frustration mounted steadily as political and ecclesiastical authorities refused to respond to their demands.

Puritan discontent grew rapidly, however, after the death of Elizabeth, the last of the Tudors, and the accession of James I, the first of the Stuarts, in 1603. Convinced that kings ruled by divine right, James quickly antagonized the Puritans by resorting to illegal and arbitrary taxation, favoring English Catholics in the granting of charters and other favors, and supporting "high-church" forms of ceremony, meaning a strong stress on traditional and very formal liturgical practices. By the early seventeenth century, some Puritans were beginning to look for places of refuge outside the kingdom.

The First English Settlements

The first permanent English settlement in the New World was established at Jamestown, in Virginia, in 1607. But for nearly thirty years before that, English merchants and adventurers had been engaged in a series of failed efforts to create colonies in America.

Through much of the sixteenth century, the English had harbored mixed feelings about the New World. They were intrigued by its possibilities, but they were also fearful of Spain, which remained the dominant force in America. In 1588, however, King Philip II of Spain sent one of the largest military fleets in the history of warfare—the Spanish Armada—across the English Channel to attack England itself. The smaller English fleet, taking advantage of its greater maneuverability, defeated the armada and, in a single stroke, ended Spain's domination of the Atlantic. This great shift in naval power caused English interest in colonizing the New World to grow quickly.

The pioneers of English colonization were Sir Humphrey Gilbert and his half brother Sir Walter Raleigh—both veterans of earlier colonial efforts in Ireland. In 1578, Gilbert obtained from Queen Elizabeth a six-year patent granting him the exclusive right "to inhabit and possess any remote and heathen lands not already in the possession of any Christian prince." Five years later, after several setbacks, he led an expedition to Newfoundland, looking for a good place to build a profitable colony. But a storm sank his ship, and he was lost at sea. The next year, Sir Walter Raleigh secured his own six-year grant from the queen and sent a small group of men on an expedition to explore the North American coast. When they returned, Raleigh named the region they had explored Virginia, in honor of Elizabeth, who was known as the "Virgin Queen."

In 1585, Raleigh recruited his cousin, Sir Richard Grenville, to lead a group of men to the island of **Roanoke**, off the coast of what is now North Carolina, to establish a colony. Grenville deposited the settlers on the island, destroyed an Indian village as retaliation for a minor theft, and returned to England. The following spring, with long-overdue supplies and reinforcements from England, Sir Francis Drake unexpectedly arrived in Roanoke. The dispirited colonists boarded his ships and left.

(©The Gallery Collection/Corbis)

ROANOKE A drawing by one of the colonists in the ill-fated Roanoke expedition of 1585 became the basis for this engraving by Theodor de Bry, published in England in 1590. A small European ship approaches the island of Roanoke, in the center. The wreckage of several larger vessels farther out to sea suggests the danger of the journey while the presence of Indian settlements on the mainland and on Roanoke itself reflects the contact between two different cultures to come.

Raleigh tried again in 1587, sending an expedition to Roanoke carrying ninety-one men, seventeen women, and nine children. The settlers attempted to take up where the first group of colonists had left off. John White, the commander of the expedition, returned to England after several weeks, in search of supplies and additional settlers. Because of a war with Spain, he was unable to return to Roanoke for three years. When he did, in 1590, he found the island deserted, with no clue to the fate of the settlers other than the cryptic inscription "Croatoan" carved on a post.

The Roanoke disaster marked the end of Sir Walter Raleigh's involvement in English colonization of the New World. No later colonizers would receive grants of land in America as vast or undefined as those Raleigh and Gilbert had acquired. Yet the colonizing impulse remained very much alive. In the early years of the seventeenth century, a group of London merchants decided to renew the attempt at colonization in Virginia. A rival group of merchants, from the area around Plymouth, was also interested in American ventures and was sponsoring voyages of exploration farther north. In 1606, James I issued a new charter, which divided North America between the two groups. The London group got the exclusive right to colonize the south, and the Plymouth merchants received the same right in the north. Through the efforts of these and other companies, the first enduring English colonies would soon be established in North America.

THE FRENCH AND THE DUTCH IN AMERICA

English settlers in North America encountered not only native groups but also other Europeans who were, like them, driven by mercantilist ideas. There were scattered North American outposts of the Spanish Empire and, more important, there were French and Dutch settlers who were also vying for a stake in the New World.

In the early sixteenth century, eager to discover new trade routes across the Atlantic and locate a new corridor to the Pacific, the French King, Francis I, turned to Giovanni da Verrazzano, an Italian explorer. After rough seas forced him to abort his maiden voyage in 1523, Verrazano set sail the next year and successfully landed at Cape Fear. He charted his way north along the Atlantic Coast, including stops in New York Bay, Long Island, Narraganset Bay, Cape Cod, and finally Newfoundland. Crafting detailed maps and providing accounts of his interactions with Indians, Verrazano laid the pathway for future generations of European explorers.

Nearly 40 years later, in 1562, Frenchman Jean Ribault established a small settlement he called Charlesfort in present-day Parris Island, South Carolina. Poor leadership, inadequate supplies, and a lack of cooperation with local Indians ushered its demise after only a year. But in 1564, Rene Goulaine de Laudonniere, an officer in Ribault's original force, built Fort Caroline, near what is now Jacksonville, Florida. It too nearly collapsed within a year for similar reasons, but a fortuitous stop-over by an English ship allowed residents to trade for much needed supplies. Fort Caroline, however, quickly became entangled in larger territorial conflicts between French and the Spanish, who sacked the fort in 1565, killed most of its residents, and built their own fortification, Fort San Mateo. It lasted until 1569, when a vengeful French force burned it to the ground.

Samuel de Champlain founded the first permanent French settlement in North America at Quebec in 1608, less than a year after the English started their first at Jamestown. Central to its success was Champlain's winning effort to form strong political partnerships with the Montagnais, Algonquins, and Hurons, even going to war with them against the Iroquois. These bonds facilitated the expansion of the French fur trade in the region. Champlain also promoted close interaction between *coureurs de bois*—male French fur traders and trappers—and Indians as a way of knitting together the different cultures. The *coureurs de bois* settled deep in the region, learned Indian languages and customs, and sometimes intermarried. They enlarged the network of fur trading, which helped open the way for French agricultural estates (or *seigneuries*) along the St. Lawrence River and for the development of trade and military centers at Quebec and Montreal.

Jesuit missionaries spread French influence as well. These members of the male-only Catholic Society of Jesus arrived in 1634 and five years later founded the Sainte-Marie-aux-Huron, which as the name suggests was meant to encourage cooperation and conversion among the Hurons. The Jesuits soon expanded the mission, adding a farm, hospital, mill, and church to introduce the Indians to their faith, way of life, and skills like blacksmithing. They learned the local tongue and customs to build new degrees of trust and collaboration and they eventually launched new missions in the region. While their work certainly enhanced relationships with the Indians, the Jesuits faced limits in what they could accomplish. The Hurons, like Indians from other parts of the New World, often challenged attempts to make them into Catholics and farm and live like Frenchmen. They sometimes flat-out resisted or instead sought to mix their traditional religion with Catholicism and create a new faith hybrid, often to the anger of the Jesuits.

The Dutch, too, established a presence in North America. Holland in the early seventeenth century was one of the leading trading nations of the world, and its commerce moved to America in the seventeenth century. In 1609, Henry Hudson, an English explorer in the employ of the Dutch, sailed up the river that was to be named for him in what was then New Netherland. His explorations led to a Dutch claim on the territory. The Dutch built a town on Manhattan Island named New Amsterdam. From it, Dutch trappers moved into the interior toward the Appalachian Mountains and built a profitable trade in furs.

The Dutch, like other the European powers, had a broad global empire of commerce and colonization. In addition to North America, the Dutch settled portions of the Caribbean and South America. They built settlements in Sint Maarten in 1618. St. Croix in 1625, Bonaire and Curacao in 1634, and Sint Eustatius in 1636. For 24 years, from 1630 to 1654, Holland also controlled a giant swath of northeastern Brazil, representing half of all European settlements there at the time. They introduced sugar and the business of sugar trading to Barbados, an English colony, whose networks interestingly were dominated by Jewish merchants who had migrated from Spain to the Netherlands following the Reconquista and the Alhambra Decree of 1492.

CONCLUSION

The lands that Europeans eventually named the Americas were the home of many millions of people before the arrival of Columbus. Having migrated from Asia thousands of years earlier, the pre-Columbian Americans spread throughout the Western Hemisphere and eventually created great civilizations. Among the most notable of them were the Incas in Peru and the Mayas and Aztecs in Mexico. In the regions north of what was later named the Rio Grande, the human population was smaller and the civilizations were less advanced than they were farther south. Even so, North American native peoples created a cluster of civilizations that thrived and expanded. They included the Mississippian peoples, notably the Chickasaws, Cherokees, Choctaws, Muscogees, Creeks, Houmas, Seminoles, and Tunica-Biloxis; as well as the Pueblos of the modern American Southwest and the Algonquians who dwelled mostly in contemporary New England and eastern Canada.

In the century after European contact, these native populations suffered catastrophes that all but destroyed many of the civilizations they had built: brutal invasions by Spanish and Portuguese conquistadores and a series of plagues inadvertently imported by Europeans. By the middle of the sixteenth century, the Spanish and Portuguese—no longer faced with large-scale and effective resistance from the native populations—had established colonial control over all of South America and much of North America.

In the parts of North America that would eventually become the United States, the European presence was for a time much less powerful. The Spanish established an important northern outpost in what is now New Mexico, a society in which Europeans and Indians lived closely together intimately, though on unequal terms. On the whole, however, the North American Indians remained largely undisturbed by Europeans until English, French, and Dutch migrations began in the early seventeenth century.

KEY TERMS/PEOPLE/PLACES/EVENTS

Atlantic World 16
Bartolomé de Las Casas 9
Cahokia 5
charter 19
Christopher Columbus 7
Clovis people 2
colonization 19

colony 7
conquistador 9
Elizabeth I 20
encomienda 11
globalization 16
imperialism 16
mercantilism 19

Mesoamerica 4
mestizo 15
Popé 11
Protestant Reformation 19
Puritans 20
Roanoke 20

RECALL AND REFLECT

1. Why did European countries seek to establish settlements in the New World?
2. How did Indian women occupy different social roles and exercise different social responsibilities than European women?
3. What was the response of Indians to the efforts by Europeans to settle near them?
4. What role did disease play in the settlement of the New World?

2 | TRANSPLANTATIONS AND BORDERLANDS

THE EARLY CHESAPEAKE
THE GROWTH OF NEW ENGLAND
THE RESTORATION COLONIES
BORDERLANDS AND MIDDLE GROUNDS
THE DEVELOPMENT OF EMPIRE

LOOKING AHEAD

1. What were the different English motivations for settling in North America?
2. How did Indians affect the early history of English settlements?
3. How did English colonies differ from another? That is, how did settlements in, say, Virginia differ from the Massachusetts Bay colony?

THE FIRST PERMANENT ENGLISH SETTLEMENTS were small, fragile communities, generally unprepared for the hardships they were to face. Seeking to improve their futures and secure a greater degree of control over their lives, immigrants from the British Isles found a world populated by Native American tribes; by colonists, explorers, and traders from Spain, France, and the Netherlands; and by immigrants from other parts of Europe and, soon, slaves from Africa. American society was from the beginning a fusion of many cultures in which disparate people and cultures coexisted, often quite violently.

All of English North America was, in effect, a borderland during the early years of colonization. Through much of the seventeenth century, English colonies both relied on and did battle with the Indian tribes and struggled with challenges from other Europeans in their midst. Eventually, however, some areas of English settlement—most notably the growing communities along the eastern seaboard—managed to dominate their own regions, marginalizing or expelling Indians and other challengers. In these eastern colonies, the English created significant towns and cities; constructed political, religious, and educational institutions; and built productive agricultural systems. They also instituted slavery here as they did in every colony.

TIME LINE

1607
Jamestown founded

1619
First recorded African slaves in Virginia

Virginia House of Burgesses meets

1620
Pilgrims found Plymouth Colony

1622
Powhatan Indians attack Virginia

1624
Dutch settle Manhattan

1630
Puritans establish Massachusetts Bay colony

1634
Maryland founded

1636
Roger Williams founds Rhode Island

1637
Anne Hutchinson expelled from Massachusetts Bay colony

Pequot War

1663
Carolina chartered

1664
English capture New Netherland

1675
King Philip's War

1676
Bacon's Rebellion

1681
Pennsylvania chartered

1686
Dominion of New England

1688
Glorious Revolution

1732
Georgia chartered

THE EARLY CHESAPEAKE

Once James I had issued his 1606 charters, the London Company moved quickly and decisively to launch a colonizing expedition headed for Virginia—a party of 144 men aboard three ships, the *Godspeed,* the *Discovery,* and the *Susan Constant,* which set sail for America on December 19, 1606.

COLONISTS AND NATIVES

Only 104 men survived the journey. They reached the American coast in late April 1607, sailed into the Chesapeake and up a river they named the James, in honor of their king. They established their colony, **Jamestown**, on a peninsula on the river on May 24. They chose this inland setting because they believed it would provide a measure of comfort and security.

For nearly a decade, Jamestown was a tiny colony constantly verging on collapse. During this time local Indians were more powerful than the English. Coastal Virginia had numerous tribes, many of whom joined forces to form the Powhatan Confederacy, named after its chief, Wahunsonacock, otherwise known as Powhatan. Composed of at least 30 Algonquian-speaking tribes, the Confederacy occupied a broad territory now formed by southern Maryland, Chesapeake Bay, and the Virginia coast. Major tribes included the Arrohateck, the Appamattuck, the Pamunkey, the Chickahominy, and the Mattapony. Chief **Powhatan** initially viewed the English as simply another group among many in his Confederacy, one that posed no immediate threat and could be removed at any time.

The early history of Jamestown certainly gave him little reason to change his mind. Settlers faced ordeals that were to a large degree of their own making. They were vulnerable to local diseases, particularly malaria, which was especially virulent along the marshy rivers they had chosen to settle. They spent more time searching for gold and other exports than growing enough food to be self-sufficient. And they could create no real community without women, who had not been recruited for the expedition. Within a few months after the first colonists arrived in Virginia, only 38 or the 144 men who had sailed to America were alive, the rest killed by diseases and famine.

Jamestown's early survival required the British immigrants to admit their mistakes and learn from Powhatans. This was not easy for the settlers, because they believed that English civilization, with its oceangoing vessels, muskets, and other advanced weaponry, was greatly superior. Yet Indian agricultural techniques were far better adapted to the soil and climate of Virginia than those of English origin. Powhatans were settled farmers whose villages were surrounded by neatly ordered fields. They grew a variety of crops—beans, pumpkins, vegetables, and above all maize (corn). Some of their farmlands stretched over hundreds of acres and supported substantial populations. The colony's leader, the twenty-seven-year-old Captain **John Smith**, convinced the colonists to swallow their pride and learn from the locals what and when to plant and harvest, how to make dugout canoes and navigate local waterways, and where to hunt and fish. They also traded extensively with these Indians for food. Only steady help from Powhatans and Smith's efforts to impose work and order on the community kept Jamestown from completely dying out.

REORGANIZATION AND EXPANSION

As Jamestown struggled to survive, the London Company (now renamed the Virginia Company) was already dreaming of bigger things. In 1609, it obtained a new charter from the king, which increased its power and enlarged its territory. It offered stock in the company to planters who were willing to migrate at their own expense. And it provided free passage to Virginia for poorer people who would agree to serve the company for seven years. In the spring of 1609, two years after the first arrival of the English, a fleet of nine vessels was dispatched to Jamestown with approximately 600 people, including some women and children.

Nevertheless, disaster quickly followed. One of the Virginia-bound ships was lost at sea in a hurricane. Another ran aground in the Bermuda islands and was unable to sail for months. Many of the new settlers succumbed to fevers before winter came. And the winter of 1609–1610 was especially severe, a period that came to be known as "starving time." By then, the natives realized that the colonists were a possible threat to their civilization and they blocked the English from moving inland. Barricaded in the small palisade, unable to hunt or cultivate food, the settlers lived on what they could find: "dogs, cats, rats, snakes, toadstools, horsehides," and even "the corpses of dead men," as one survivor recalled. When the migrants who had run aground in Bermuda finally arrived in Jamestown the following May, they found only about 60 emaciated people still alive. The new arrivals took the survivors onto their ship and sailed for England. But as the refugees proceeded down the James, they met an English ship coming up the river—part of a fleet bringing supplies and the colony's first governor, Lord De La Warr. The departing settlers agreed to return to Jamestown. Relief expeditions soon began to arrive, and the effort to turn a profit in Jamestown resumed.

New settlements began lining the river above and below Jamestown. The immigrants learned about a new crop from the local Indians—tobacco, which was already popular among the Spanish colonies to the south. It was also being imported to Europe and becoming much sought-after by the citizenry, so much so that King James I began to worry about its potential health hazards. John Rolfe, who had arrived in Jamestown in 1610, began experimenting with tobacco in 1612 but needed help to grow it on a large scale. Drawing on local Indian expertise and planting seeds grown in the West Indies, he developed tobacco as Virginia's first profitable crop. His success encouraged other planters to raise tobacco up and down the James River and eventually to move deeper inland, intruding more and more into the native farmlands.

As Jamestown expanded and developed a profitable economy, residents attempted to drive away local Powhatans. During two years of bloody raids, settlers captured Chief Powhatan's young daughter, Pocahontas, in spring 1613. Ironically, only several years earlier she had played a key role in mediating differences between her people and the Europeans. But now, Powhatan refused to ransom her. During her years of captivity living among the English, Pocahontas learned their language, customs, and religion, converting to Christianity and taking (or was given) the name "Rebecca" upon her baptism. In April 1614 she also married John Rolfe and a year later had a son, Thomas, with him. She likely was a key source of education about growing tobacco for Rolfe. While historians generally agree about the course of her life after becoming a prisoner, they are unclear about why Pocahontas pursued this path. Was her conversion genuine or undertaken simply to fulfill the legal requirement for an Indian to marry an Englishman? And was Rolfe's marital intention largely political despite his professed affection for her, as suggested in a letter he penned to Sir Dale describing his motivations as being "for the good of this plantation, for the honour of our country, for the glory of God, for my own salvation, and for the converting

(Source: Photographs in the Carol M. Highsmith Archive, Library of Congress, Prints and Photographs Division [LC-DIG-highsm-13340])

POCAHONTAS In this reproduction of an eighteenth-century painting based itself on a 1616 engraving by Simon van de Passe, Pocahontas is presented to English society as one of its own. She is represented in exclusive European dress—high-neck collar, tailored clothing, and holding Ostrich feathers, symbols of nobility. Her name is inscribed twice, first as Matoaka, a family name given to her as a baby, and then Rebecca, the name she adopted upon converting to Christianity.

to the true knowledge of God and Jesus Christ, an unbelieving creature, namely Pokahuntas [*sic*]. To whom my hearty and best thoughts are, and have a long time been so entangled, and enthralled in so intricate a labyrinth." Regardless, the marriage ushered in a period of uneasy détente between the English and the Powhatan that lasted several years.

This relatively peaceful period accelerated the development of tobacco economy, which in turn created a heavy demand for labor and land. To entice new workers to the colony, the Virginia Company established what it called the **headright system**. Headrights were fifty-acre grants of land. Those who already lived in the colony received two headrights apiece. Each new settler received a single headright for himself or herself. This system encouraged family groups to migrate together, since the more family members who traveled to America, the more land the family would receive. In addition, anyone who paid for the passage of immigrants to Virginia would receive an extra headright for each arrival. As a result, some colonists were quickly able to assemble large plantations, establishing domain over land used by Indians for generations to hunt, fish, and farm.

The Virginia Company also transported ironworkers and other skilled crafts workers to Virginia to diversify the economy. In 1619, it sent 100 English women to become the wives of male colonists. It also promised white male colonists the full rights of "Englishmen," an end to strict and arbitrary rule, and even a share in self-government. On July 30, 1619, delegates from the various communities met as the **House of Burgesses**, the first elected legislature within what was to become the United States.

During these years, Pocahontas and Rolfe had moved to England. Arriving in June 1616, she soon became a subject of popular fascination—the Indian woman who had converted to Christianity and married an English subject. Her unusual status sparked popular debate about the possibility of assimilating Indians and other non-English into English culture. The couple embarked on a return voyage to Virginia in March 1617. But Pocahontas fell gravely ill shortly after embarking, forcing the ship to land near Gravesend on the Thames River, where she died. After burying her, Rolfe continued his travels to Virginia.

A year after Pocahontas's death her father, Chief Powhatan, died. His passing created a vacuum of leadership among the Powhatans, which was eventually filled by his brother, Opechancanough, who sought to stop English encroachment and force them to depart the region. On a March morning in 1622, tribesmen called on the white settlements as if to offer goods for sale; then they suddenly attacked. Not until between 350 and 400 whites of both sexes and all ages lay dead did the Indian warriors finally retreat. Although they killed about one-quarter of the total population of Jamestown, the Powhatans were not seeking to eliminate all settlers; they did not practice what would become known as "total warfare." Instead, they intended to deliver a powerful and graphic message that all newcomers should leave immediately. It did not work, however, and instead set off a series of conflicts that, after more than twenty years, resulted in the defeat of the Powhatans.

SLAVERY AND INDENTURE IN THE VIRGINIA COLONY

In late August of 1619, John Rolfe recorded that "20 and odd Negroes" arrived at Jamestown aboard a Dutch ship. It was actually the British war vessel, the *White Lion,* which had recently raided a Portuguese slave ship for its human cargo. Nevertheless, Rolfe provided the first recorded instance of Africans arriving in North America, though the Spanish had brought some earlier in the South. Historians are uncertain if English colonists in Jamestown initially viewed the Africans as a type of servant, to be held for a term of years and then freed, or as slaves. Likely it was the former, as the majority of laborers at this time were "bonded" to a master or employer for a fixed period of time. Within about ten years, however, English colonists noted that it was "customary practice to hold some Negroes in a form of life service." But they also indicated that some Africans were still able to work for a period of time after which they were freed. This variability in black life would not last long. Virginians began to depend on African laborers to farm tobacco and demanded more of them. The judicial system now begins to codify what blacks could and could not do. In 1639, a law forbade them from owning arms; in 1640, Virginia courts condemned a black runaway servant, John Punch, to "serve his said master . . . for the time of his natural Life"; and most importantly, in 1662, the Virginia General Assembly declared that a "Negro women's children to serve according to the condition of the mother." The 1662 code made it clear that children born to slaves were to be slaves themselves, for life. Even if the father was a free person, black or white, the children's status mirrored that of the mother.

The number of blacks living in Virginia was fairly small during the colony's earliest decades, estimated to be about 23 in 1625 and 300 in 1648. Providing most of the labor to grow the colony at that time were **indentured servants**—who were primarily white English immigrants who inked a contract or an "indenture" that bound them to work for a set period of time for a person or institution in exchange for travel costs to Virginia and all living expenses once there. As tobacco farms increased in size and number and the need for laborers to work them rose accordingly, though, owners slowly turned toward the idea of owning and using black slaves as opposed to indentured servants. They now bought increasing numbers of slaves, and the population in Virginia rose steeply to 3,000 in 1680 and 10,000 by 1704.

During these decades, the Virginia Company in London became defunct. In 1624, James I revoked the company's charter, and the colony came under the control of the crown, where it would remain until 1776. The colony, if not the company, had survived—but at a terrible cost. In Virginia's first seventeen years, more than 8,500 white settlers had arrived in the colony, and nearly 80 percent of them had died. Countless Indians had died as well, and slavery became part of the colony.

Bacon's Rebellion

For more than thirty years, one man—Sir **William Berkeley**, the royal governor of Virginia—dominated the politics of the colony. He took office in 1642 at the age of thirty-six and with but one brief interruption remained in control of the government until 1677. In his first years as governor, he helped open up the interior of Virginia by sending explorers across the Blue Ridge Mountains and crushing a 1644 Indian uprising. The defeated Indians agreed to a treaty ceding to England most of the territory east of the mountains and establishing a boundary, west of which white settlement would be prohibited. But the rapid growth of the Virginia population made this agreement difficult to sustain. Between 1640 and 1660, Virginia's population rose from 8,000 to over 40,000. By 1652, English settlers had established three counties in the territory set aside by the treaty for the Indians.

In the meantime, Berkeley was expanding his own powers. By 1670, the vote for delegates to the House of Burgesses, once open to all white men, was restricted to landowners. Elections were rare, and the same burgesses, representing the established planters of the eastern (or tidewater) region of the colony, remained in office year after year. The more recent settlers on the frontier were underrepresented.

Resentment of the power of the governor and the tidewater aristocrats grew steadily in the newly settled lands of the West (often known as the "backcountry"). In 1676, this resentment helped create a major conflict, which has been named **Bacon's Rebellion** after its leader Nathaniel Bacon, a distant relative of Governor Berkeley. Bacon had a good farm in the West and a seat on the governor's council. But like other members of the new backcountry gentry, he resented the governor's attempts to hold the territorial line. Bacon's hostility toward Berkeley was a result of the governor's refusal to allow white settlers to move farther west. Berkeley forbid further settlement for fear of antagonizing Indians. Adding to the resentment was that Berkeley controlled the lucrative fur trade, which Bacon desperately wanted to profit from.

The turbulence in Virginia reflected not just the tension between Berkeley and Bacon, both of them frontier aristocrats. It was also a result of the consequences of the indentured servant system. By the 1670s, many young men—predominantly white but some black—had finished their term as indentures and had found themselves without a home or any money. Many of them began moving around the colony, sometimes working, sometimes begging, sometimes stealing. This large, landless itinerant group were quickly drawn into what became Bacon's Rebellion.

In 1675, a major conflict erupted in the West between English settlers and natives. As the fighting escalated, Bacon and other concerned landholders demanded that the governor send the militia. When Berkeley refused, Bacon responded by offering to organize a volunteer army of backcountry men who would do their own fighting. Berkeley rejected that offer too. Bacon simply ignored him and launched a series of vicious but unsuccessful pursuits of the Indian challengers.

When Berkeley heard of the unauthorized military effort, he proclaimed Bacon and his men to be rebels. Confused and angry, Bacon now took aim at the governor and all elites, whom he openly criticized for lacking empathy and support for the lower classes. He attracted a range of volunteers and built an alliance of black and white workers as well as African slaves, who asked for an end to their bondage. Bacon led his troops, numbering about 500, east to Jamestown twice. The first time he won a temporary pardon from the governor; the second time, after the governor repudiated the agreement, Bacon burned much of the city and drove the governor into exile. But then Bacon died suddenly of dysentery, and Berkeley regained control. Among the last to surrender were some 400 indentured servants and 80 slaves. In 1677, the Indians reluctantly signed a new treaty that opened new lands to white settlement.

Bacon's Rebellion was part of a continuing struggle to define the Indian and white spheres of influence in Virginia. It also revealed the bitterness of the competition among rival white leaders, and it demonstrated the potential for instability in the colony's large population of free landless men, both black and white, and slaves. Most notably, the uprising forced landed elites in both eastern and western Virginia to recognize a common interest in quelling social unrest from below and shoring up their cultural dominance. As a result, they began to reduce their dependence on indentured laborers and rely more heavily on black slaves. Black slaves, unlike white indentured servants, did not need to be released after a fixed term and hence did not threaten to become an unstable, landless class. Elite whites, perhaps predictably, now sought more slaves and more of them shipped straight from Africa, anticipating that their presumed lack of knowledge about English culture would make them less likely to partner in any rebellion with white workers and servants. To minimize any chance of cooperation between blacks and whites, they also enlisted poor whites to organize slave patrols. Most effectively, they created new laws. In 1705 the Virginia General Assembly passed the Virginia Slave Codes, which formally defined slaves to be property or "real estate" and endowed masters with near limitless power over slaves. The new **slave codes** declared that "All Negro, mulatto and Indian slaves within this dominion . . . shall be held to be real estate. If any slave resist his master . . . correcting such slave, and shall happen to be killed in such correction . . . the master shall be free of all punishment . . . as if such accident never happened." They further specified that slaves needed a written pass to leave their master's home or plantation, that robbery would be met with sixty lashes and time in the stocks, where his or her ears would be loped off, and that associating with whites without official sanction would earn them a whipping, branding, or maiming of some sort. These codes laid the foundation for the practice of slavery for generations to come.

MARYLAND AND THE CALVERTS

The Maryland colony ultimately came to look much like Virginia, but its origins were quite different. **George Calvert**, the first Lord Baltimore, envisioned establishing a colony in America both as a great speculative venture in real estate and as a refuge for English Catholics like himself. Calvert died while he was still negotiating with the king in London for a charter to establish such a colony in the Chesapeake region. But in 1632, his son **Cecilius Calvert**, the second Lord Baltimore, finally received the charter.

religious motives + $$$ motives

THE GROWTH OF THE CHESAPEAKE, 1607–1750 This map shows the political forms of European settlement in the region of Chesapeake Bay in the seventeenth and early eighteenth centuries. Note the several different kinds of colonial enterprises: the royal colony of Virginia, controlled directly by the English crown after the failure of the early commercial enterprises there; and the proprietary regions of Maryland, northern Virginia, and North Carolina, which were under the control of powerful English aristocrats. • *Why were most settlements, regardless of who founded them, found near bodies of water? What does it suggest about the type of economic activities each engaged in?*

Lord Baltimore remained in England, but he named his brother, Leonard Calvert, governor of the colony. In March 1634, two ships—the *Ark* and the *Dove*—bearing Calvert along with 200 or 300 other colonists entered the Potomac River, turned into one of its eastern tributaries, and established the village of St. Mary's on a high, dry bluff. Neighboring Indians, in particular the Susquehannocks, befriended the settlers and provided them with temporary shelter and with stocks of corn.

The Calverts needed to attract thousands of settlers to Maryland if their expensive colonial venture was to pay. As a result, they had to encourage the immigration of Protestants as well as their fellow English Catholics. The Calverts soon realized that Catholics would always be a minority in the colony, and so they adopted a policy of religious toleration: the 1649 "Act Concerning Religion." Dubbed the Maryland Toleration Act, it decreed religious toleration among all resident Christians. Still, politics in Maryland remained plagued for years with chronic tensions, and at times violence, between the Catholic minority and the growing Protestant majority.

At the insistence of the first settlers, the Calverts agreed in 1635 to the calling of a representative assembly—the House of Delegates. But the proprietor retained absolute authority to distribute land as he wished; and since Lord Baltimore granted large estates to his relatives and to other English aristocrats, a distinct upper class soon established itself. By 1640, a severe labor shortage forced a modification of the land-grant procedure; and Maryland, like Virginia, adopted a headright system—a grant of 100 acres to each male settler, another 100 for his wife and each servant, and 50 for each of his children. But the great landlords of the colony's earliest years remained powerful. Like Virginia, Maryland became a center of tobacco cultivation; planters worked their land with the aid, first, of indentured servants imported from Englan and then, beginning late in the seventeenth century, of slaves imported from Africa.

THE GROWTH OF NEW ENGLAND

The northern regions of English North America were slower to attract settlers than those in the South. That was in part because the Plymouth Company was never able to mount a successful colonizing expedition after receiving its charter in 1606. It did, however, sponsor other explorations. Captain John Smith, after departing from Jamestown, made an exploratory journey for the Plymouth merchants, wrote an enthusiastic pamphlet about the lands he had seen, and called them New England.

PLYMOUTH PLANTATION

A discontented congregation of Puritan Separatists in England—those disenchanted with the Church of England and seeking to "separate" from it—established the first enduring European settlement in New England. In 1608, a congregation of Separatists from the English hamlet of Scrooby began emigrating quietly (and illegally), a few at a time, to Leyden, Holland, where they believed they could enjoy freedom of worship. But as foreigners in Holland, they had to work at unskilled and poorly paid jobs. They also watched with alarm as their children began to adapt to Dutch society and drift away from their church. Finally, some of the Separatists decided to move again, this time far across the Atlantic; there, they hoped to create a stable, protected community where they could spread "the gospel of the Kingdom of Christ in those remote parts of the world."

In 1620, leaders of the Scrooby group obtained permission from the Virginia Company to settle in Virginia. The "Pilgrims," as they saw themselves, sailed from Plymouth,

England, in September 1620 on the *Mayflower*, thirty-five "saints" (the Puritan Separatists) and sixty-seven "strangers" (people who were not part of the congregation) were aboard. In November, after a long and difficult voyage, they sighted land—the shore of what is now Cape Cod. That had not been their destination, but it was too late in the year to sail farther south. So the Pilgrims chose a site for their settlement in the area just north of the cape, a place John Smith had labeled "Plymouth" on a map he had drawn during his earlier exploration of New England. Because Plymouth lay outside the London Company's territory, the settlers were not bound by the company's rules. While still aboard ship, the saints in the group drew up an agreement, the **Mayflower Compact**, to establish a government for themselves. Then, on December 21, 1620, they stepped ashore at Plymouth Rock.

The Pilgrims' first winter was a difficult one. Half the colonists perished from malnutrition, disease, and exposure. But the colony survived, in large part because of crucial assistance from the Wampanoags. Significantly, that help was immediately forthcoming from the Wampanoags nor did it betoken their complete trust in the settlers. Earlier English ships had anchored in the area for supplies, captured Indians, and sold them into slavery. An epidemic had broken out before 1615 that killed thousands of Wampanoags and left them vulnerable to attack by their rivals, the Pequot and the Narragansett. Eventually the Wampanoags reached out to the immigrants in part to form an alliance that might help them in any future conflict with their enemies. They now traded with the colonists with furs and showed them how to cultivate corn and how to hunt wild animals for meat. After the first autumn harvest, the settlers invited some Wampanoags to join them in a festival, the original Thanksgiving. But the relationship between the settlers and the local Indians soon was under great strain. Thirteen years after the Pilgrims arrived, a devastating smallpox epidemic wiped out much of the Indian population around Plymouth.

The Pilgrims could not create rich farms on the sandy and marshy soil around Plymouth, but they developed a profitable trade in fish and furs. New colonists arrived steadily from England, and in a decade the population reached 300. The people of **Plymouth Plantation** chose as their governor William Bradford, who ruled successfully for many years. The Pilgrims were always poor. As late as the 1640s, they had only one plow among them. But they were, on the whole, content to be left alone to live their lives in what they considered godly ways.

(©Alexander Sviridov/Shutterstock)

PLYMOUTH PLANTATION (Re-creation)

THE MASSACHUSETTS BAY EXPERIMENT

In 1628, another group of Puritan merchants began organizing a new colonial venture in America. They obtained a grant of land in New England for most of the area now comprising Massachusetts and New Hampshire. They acquired a charter from the king—now Charles I, who had inherited the throne at the death of his father, James I, in 1625—that allowed them to create the **Massachusetts Bay Company** and to establish a colony in the New World. Some members of the Massachusetts Bay Company wanted to create a refuge in New England for Puritans. They bought out the interests of company members who preferred to stay in England, and the new owners elected a governor, **John Winthrop**. They then sailed for New England in 1630. With 17 ships and 1,000 people, it was the largest single migration of its kind in the seventeenth century. Winthrop carried with him the charter of the Massachusetts Bay Company, which meant that the colonists would be responsible to no company officials in England.

The Massachusetts migration quickly produced several settlements. The port of Boston became the capital, but in the course of the next decade colonists established several other towns in eastern Massachusetts: Charlestown, Newtown (later renamed Cambridge), Roxbury, Dorchester, Watertown, Ipswich, Concord, Sudbury, and others.

The Massachusetts Puritans strove to lead useful, conscientious lives of thrift and hard work and they honored material success as evidence of God's favor. Winthrop and the other founders of Massachusetts believed they were building a holy commonwealth, a model—a "city upon a hill"—for the corrupt world to see and emulate. Colonial Massachusetts was a **theocracy**, a society in which the church was almost indistinguishable from the state. Ironically, these Puritans who had sought religious freedom in England now created a society that brooked no tolerance of religious or political dissent. Their strict rules and laws soon produced a new wave of critics who would eventually leave and found new colonies.

Like other new settlements, the Massachusetts Bay colony had early difficulties. During the first winter (1629–1630), nearly 200 people died and many others decided to leave. But the colony soon grew and prospered. The nearby Pilgrims and Wampanoags helped with food and advice. Incoming settlers brought needed tools and other goods. The prevalence of families in the colony helped establish a feeling of commitment to the community and a sense of order among the settlers, and it also ensured that the population would reproduce itself.

THE EXPANSION OF NEW ENGLAND

It did not take long for British settlement to begin moving outward from Massachusetts Bay. Some people migrated in search of soil more productive than the stony land around Boston. Others left because of the oppressiveness of the church-dominated government of Massachusetts.

The Connecticut River valley, about 100 miles west of Boston, began attracting English families as early as the 1630s because of its fertile lands and its isolation from Massachusetts Bay. In 1635, Thomas Hooker, a minister of Newtown (Cambridge), defied the Massachusetts government, led his congregation west, and established the town of Hartford. Four years later, the people of Hartford and of two other newly founded towns nearby adopted a constitution known as the Fundamental Orders of Connecticut, which created an independent colony with a government similar to that of Massachusetts Bay but which gave a larger proportion of the men the right to vote and hold office. Women were barred from voting, as they were virtually everywhere in the colonies.

Another Connecticut colony grew up around New Haven on the Connecticut coast. Unlike Hartford, the Fundamental Articles of New Haven (1639) established a Bible-based government even stricter than that of Massachusetts Bay. New Haven remained independent until 1662, when a royal charter officially gave the Hartford colony jurisdiction over the New Haven settlements.

European settlement in what is now Rhode Island was a result of the vigorous religious and political dissent of **Roger Williams**, a controversial young minister who lived for a time in Salem, Massachusetts. Williams was a confirmed Separatist who argued that the Massachusetts church should abandon all allegiance to the Church of England and permit its citizens to worship as they saw fit. More radically, he proclaimed that the land the colonists were occupying belonged to the local Indians. Not surprisingly the colonial government voted to deport him, but he escaped before they could force him to leave. During the winter of 1635-1636, Williams took refuge with the Narragansetts; the following spring he bought a tract of land from them and, with a few followers, created the town of Providence. He also learned their language and called for the Bible to be translated into Narragansett. In 1644, after obtaining a charter from Parliament, he established a government similar to that of Massachusetts but without any ties to a specific church. That year he famously made the case of a strict separation between church and state, writing "An enforced uniformity of religion throughout a nation or civil state, confounds the civil and religious, denies the principles of Christianity and civility, and that Jesus Christ has come in the flesh." For a time, Rhode Island was the only colony in which all believers, including Jews, Quakers, and Baptists, could worship without interference.

Another challenge to the established religious order in Massachusetts Bay came from **Anne Hutchinson**, a learned and charismatic woman from a substantial Boston family who pushed the limits of religious orthodoxy and the domestic roles of women. She sparked the **Antinomian** heresy, a phrase literally meaning she went against the laws of the ruling society. Specifically, she challenged the clerical doctrine of the covenant of grace, which held that when individuals sincerely confessed belief in Christ, then God promised them salvation. The "elect" then demonstrated their special status by performing good works. Hutchinson differed sharply with this orthodoxy, claiming that one's works and words had no bearing at all on the state of one's salvation. The only matter of significance was whether God selected a person for eternal life or not; what that person did or did not do in the course of daily life mattered none in proving God's favor. Hutchinson's teachings threatened the spiritual authority of established clergy, who spoke on the presumption that they were already saved. As her influence grew and as she began to deliver open attacks on members of the clergy, the Massachusetts hierarchy mobilized to stop her. They would not tolerate any threats to their spiritual authority, especially emanating from a woman occupying a social role—public spokesperson, theological critic—typically reserved for men at this time.

In 1637, Hutchinson was convicted of heresy and sedition and was banished. With her family and some of her followers, she moved to a point on Narragansett Bay not far from Providence. Later she moved south into New York, where in 1643 she and her family died during an Indian uprising.

New Hampshire and Maine were established in 1629 by two English proprietors. But few settlers moved into these northern regions until the religious disruptions in Massachusetts Bay. In 1639, John Wheelwright, a disciple of Anne Hutchinson, led some of his fellow dissenters to Exeter, New Hampshire. Others soon followed. New Hampshire became a separate colony in 1679. Maine remained a part of Massachusetts until 1820.

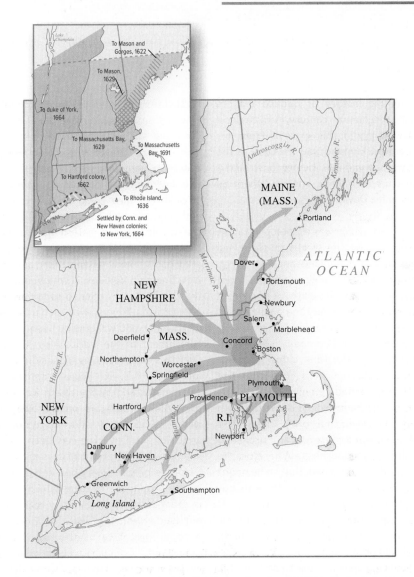

THE GROWTH OF NEW ENGLAND, 1620–1750   The European settlement of New England, as this map reveals, traces its origins primarily to two small settlements on the Atlantic Coast. The first was the Pilgrim settlement at Plymouth, which began in 1620 and spread out through Cape Cod, southern Massachusetts, and the islands of Martha's Vineyard and Nantucket. The second, much larger settlement began in Boston in 1630 and spread rapidly through western Massachusetts, north into New Hampshire and Maine, and south into Connecticut. • *Why would the settlers of Massachusetts Bay have expanded so much more rapidly and expansively than those of Plymouth?*

KING PHILIP'S WAR

In 1637, hostilities broke out between English settlers in the Connecticut Valley and the Pequot Indians of the region. The **Pequot War** resulted in the near elimination of local Indian tribes. But the bloodiest and most prolonged encounter between whites and Indians in the seventeenth century was the fourteen-month conflict that whites called **King Philip's War** and which ultimately killed more than 3,000 Indians and 1,000 colonists.

CONSIDER THE SOURCE

COTTON MATHER ON THE RECENT HISTORY OF NEW ENGLAND (1692)

Reviewing the history of English settlers during the seventeenth century, Puritan cleric Cotton Mather, in this excerpt from his history of New England, saw the Devil as the root of mishap and evil. He demonstrated a real mistrust of Indians and saw them as servants of the Devil.

I believe there never was a poor plantation more pursued by the wrath of the Devil than our poor New England; and that which makes our condition very much the more deplorable is that the wrath of the great God himself at the same time also presses hard upon us. It was a rousing alarm to the Devil when a great company of English Protestants and Puritans came to erect evangelical churches in a corner of the world where he had reigned without any control for many ages; and it is a vexing eyesore to the Devil that our Lord Christ should be known and owned and preached in this howling wilderness. Wherefore he has left no stone unturned, that so he might undermine this plantation and force us out of our country.

First, the Indian Powwows used all their sorceries to molest the first planters here; but God said unto them, "Touch them not!" Then, seducing spirits came to root in this vineyard, but God so rated them off that they have not prevailed much farther than the edges of our land. After this, we have had a continual blast upon some of our principal grain, annually diminishing a vast part of our ordinary food. Herewithal, wasting sicknesses, especially burning and mortal agues, have shot the arrows of death in at our windows. Next, we have had many adversaries of our own language, who have been perpetually assaying to deprive us of those English liberties in the encouragement whereof these territories have been settled. As if this had not been enough, the Tawnies among whom we came have watered our soil with the blood of many hundreds of our inhabitants. Desolating fires also have many times laid the chief treasure of the whole province in ashes. As for losses by sea, they have been multiplied upon us; and particularly in the present French War, the whole English nation have observed that no part of the nation has proportionately had so many vessels taken as our poor New England. Besides all which, now at last the devils are (if I may so speak) in person come down upon us, with such a wrath as is justly much and will quickly be more the astonishment of the world. Alas, I may sigh over this wilderness, as Moses did over his, in Psalm 90.7, 9: "We are consumed by thine anger, and by thy wrath we are troubled: All our days are passed away in thy wrath." And I may add this unto it: the wrath of the Devil too has been troubling and spending of us all our days. . . .

Let us now make a good and a right use of the prodigious descent which the Devil in great wrath is at this day making upon our land. Upon the death of a great man once, an orator called the town together, crying out, "Concurrite cives, dilapsa cunt vestra moenia!" That is, "Come together neighbors, your town walls are fallen down!" But such is the descent of the Devil at this day upon our selves that I may truly tell you, the walls of the whole world are broken down! The usual walls of defense about mankind have such a gap made in them that the very devils are broke in upon us to seduce the souls, torment the bodies, sully the credits, and consume the estates of our neighbors, with impressions both as real and as furious as if the invisible world were becoming incarnate on purpose for the vexing of us. . . .

In as much as the devil is come down in great wrath, we had need labor, with all the care and speed we can, to divert the great wrath of Heaven from coming at the same time upon us. The God of Heaven has with long and loud admonitions been calling us to a reformation of our provoking evils as the only way to avoid that wrath of his which does not only threaten but consume us. It is because we have been deaf to those calls that we are now by a provoked God laid open to the wrath of the Devil himself.

Source: Mather, Cotton, *The Wonders of the Invisible Word.* Boston, 1692, 41–43, 48; cited in Richard Godbeer, *The Salem Witch Hunt: A Brief History with Documents.* Boston: Bedford St. Martin's, 48–49.

UNDERSTAND, ANALYZE, & EVALUATE

1. According to Cotton Mather, what particular hardships did the colonists suffer?
2. What did Mather mean when he wrote that "now at last the devils [have descended] in person"?
3. What deeper explanation did Cotton Mather offer for New England's crisis? What response did he suggest?

In June 1675, the Wampanoags, led by their chief **Metacom** whom the English called "King Philip," joined with Nipmucks, Pocumtucks, and Narragansetts in an attempt to drive out the English settlers and resist any further encroachments upon their land. Stoking Indian resentment as well were efforts by the colonists to force them to recognize English sovereignty. Not all Indians followed Metacom's lead, however, and some actually backed the English, including Nausets, Mohegans, and Pequots. Still, Metacom and his warriors terrorized a string of Massachusetts towns for over a year. In early 1676, however, the tide began to turn when white settlers forged a new alliance with a group of Mohawk allies, who soon ambushed Metacom and beheaded him. Without Metacom, the fragile coalition of the different tribes collapsed and the white settlers were quickly able to crush the uprising. In the aftermath, some survivors fled to Canada. Colonists seized many of those who surrendered and sold them into slavery in the West Indies. The tribes who had originally led the uprising were left greatly weakened as military powers and would never again be able to mount such a major assault against the English settlers.

The conflicts between natives and settlers were crucially affected by earlier exchanges of technology between the English and the tribes. In particular, Indians made effective use of a relatively new European weapon that they had acquired from the English: the flintlock rifle. It replaced the earlier staple of colonial musketry, the matchlock rifle, which proved too heavy, cumbersome, and inaccurate to be effective. The matchlock had to be steadied on a fixed object and ignited with a match before firing. The flintlock could be held up without support and fired without a match.

Despite rules forbidding colonists to instruct natives on how to use and repair the weapons, the natives learned to handle the rifles, and even to repair them very effectively on their own. In King Philip's War, the very high casualties on both sides were partly a result of the use of these more advanced rifles.

The violence of the war and settlers' insatiable appetite for land and uneven respect for Indian culture affected their understanding of recent history. Indeed, leaders increasingly portrayed Indians as "heathens" and barbarians. Religious officials in particular came to consider local tribes as a threat to their hopes of creating a godly community in the New World. (See "Consider the Source: Cotton Mather on the Recent History of New England.")

(Source: Library of Congress, Prints and Photographs Division [LC-USZ62-32055])

A PEQUOT VILLAGE DESTROYED An English artist drew this view of a fortified Pequot village in Connecticut surrounded by English soldiers and their allies from other tribes during the Pequot War in 1637. The invaders massacred more than 600 residents of the settlement.

THE RESTORATION COLONIES

For nearly thirty years after Lord Baltimore received the charter for Maryland in 1632, no new English colonies were established in America. England was dealing with troubles of its own at home.

THE ENGLISH CIVIL WAR

After Charles I dissolved Parliament in 1629 and began ruling as an absolute monarch, he alienated a growing number of his subjects. Finally, desperately in need of money, Charles called Parliament back into session in 1640 and asked it to levy new taxes. But he antagonized the members by dismissing them twice in two years; and in 1642, members of Parliament organized a military force, sparking the English Civil War.

The conflict between the Cavaliers (the supporters of the king) and the Roundheads (the forces of Parliament, who were largely Puritans) lasted seven years. In 1649, the Roundheads defeated the king's forces and shocked all of Europe by beheading the monarch. The stern Roundhead leader Oliver Cromwell assumed the position of "protector." During his reign, Crowell looked westward to expand his influence. He authorized the ambitious Western Design—a vast expedition designed to wrest Jamaica, Puerto Rico, Cuba, and Hispaniola from the Spanish. He earnestly believed that God had called him to engage the Spanish and seize the land for England, but he met with uneven success.

Indeed, his plans failed everywhere except Jamaica. It eventually would become the engine of sugar and slavery in the English colonies in the eighteenth century.

But when Cromwell died in 1658, his son and heir proved unable to maintain his authority. Two years later, Charles II, the son of the executed king, returned from exile and seized the throne, in what became known as the Restoration. Among the results of the Restoration was the resumption of colonization in America. Charles II rewarded faithful courtiers with grants of land in the New World, and in the twenty-five years of his reign he issued charters for four additional colonies: Carolina, New York, New Jersey, and Pennsylvania.

Charles II supported religious toleration—which would allow Catholicism again in England, to the dismay of many Protestants. Parliament refused to agree, however. The prudent Charles was wise enough not to fight for the right of Catholics to worship openly lest it cost him his throne. But he himself made a private agreement with Louis XIV of France that he would become a Catholic—which he did only on his deathbed. His son, James II, faced a hostile Parliament that suspected him of Catholic allegiances.

THE CAROLINAS

In charters issued in 1663 and 1665, Charles II awarded joint title to eight proprietors. They received a vast territory stretching south from Virginia to the Florida peninsula and west to the Pacific Ocean. Like Lord Baltimore, they received almost kingly powers over their grant, which they prudently called Carolina (a name derived from the Latin word for "Charles"). They reserved tremendous estates for themselves and distributed the rest through a headright system similar to those in Virginia and Maryland. Although committed Anglicans themselves, the proprietors guaranteed religious freedom to all Christian faiths. They also created a representative assembly. They hoped to attract settlers from the existing American colonies and to avoid the expense of financing expeditions from England.

But their initial efforts to profit from settlement in Carolina failed dismally. Anthony Ashley Cooper, however, persisted. He convinced the other proprietors to finance expeditions to Carolina from England, the first of which set sail with 300 people in the spring of 1670. The 100 people who survived the difficult voyage established a settlement at Port Royal on the Carolina coast. Ten years later, they founded a city at the junction of the Ashley and Cooper Rivers, which in 1690 became the colonial capital. They called it Charles Town (it was later renamed Charleston).

With the aid of the English philosopher John Locke, Cooper (now the earl of Shaftesbury) drew up the Fundamental Constitution for Carolina in 1669. It divided the colony into counties of equal size and divided each county into equal parcels. It also established a social hierarchy with the proprietors themselves (who were to be known as "seigneurs") at the top, a local aristocracy (consisting of lesser nobles known as "landgraves" or "caciques") below them, and then ordinary settlers ("leet-men"). At the bottom of this stratified society would be poor whites, who would have few political rights, and African slaves. Proprietors, nobles, and other landholders would have a voice in the colonial parliament in proportion to the size of their landholdings.

In reality, Carolina developed along lines quite different from the carefully ordered vision of Shaftesbury and Locke. For one thing, the northern and southern regions of settlement were widely separated and socially and economically distinct from each other. The northern settlers were mainly backwoods farmers. In the South, fertile lands and the good harbor at Charles Town promoted a more prosperous economy and a more stratified, aristocratic society. Settlements grew up rapidly along the Ashley and Cooper Rivers, and colonists established a flourishing trade, particularly (beginning in the 1670s) in rice. Importantly, the development of the rice economy depended heavily on the role of African slaves. It was they who brought the experience and knowledge of how to grow the crop. They grew for themselves and then their masters, who eventually forces their slaves to raise it on a large-scale production.

Southern Carolina very early developed commercial ties to the large (and overpopulated) European colony on the Caribbean island of Barbados. During the first ten years of settlement, in fact, most of the new residents in Carolina were Barbadians, some of whom established themselves as substantial landlords. African slavery had taken root on Barbados earlier than in any of the mainland colonies, and the white Caribbean migrants—tough, uncompromising profit seekers—established a similar slave-based plantation society in Carolina.

Carolina was one of the most divided English colonies in America. There were tensions between the small farmers of the Albemarle region in the North and the wealthy planters in the South. And there were conflicts between the rich Barbadians in southern Carolina and the smaller landowners around them. After Lord Shaftesbury's death, the proprietors proved unable to establish order. In 1719, the colonists seized control of the colony from them. Ten years later, the king divided the region into two royal colonies, North Carolina and South Carolina.

New Netherland, New York, and New Jersey

In 1664, Charles II granted his brother James, the Duke of York, all the territory lying between the Connecticut and Delaware Rivers. This land, however, was also claimed by the Dutch. The growing conflict between the English and the Dutch was part of a larger commercial rivalry between the two nations throughout the world. But the English particularly rejected the Dutch presence in America, because it served as a wedge between the northern and southern English colonies and because it provided bases for Dutch smugglers evading English custom laws. And so months after James received the grant, a English fleet under the command of Richard Nicolls put in at New Amsterdam, the capital of the Dutch colony of New Netherland, and extracted a surrender from the governor, Peter Stuyvesant. Several years later, in 1673, the Dutch reconquered and briefly held their old provincial capital. But they lost it again, this time for good, in 1674.

The Duke of York renamed his territory New York. It contained not only Dutch and English but also Scandinavians, Germans, French, and a large number of Africans (imported as slaves by the Dutch West India Company), as well as members of several different Indian tribes. James wisely made no effort to impose his own Roman Catholicism on the colony. He delegated powers to a governor and a council but made no provision for representative assemblies.

Slavery was different in New York in part because of its Dutch roots. In the 1640s, the Dutch West India Company responded to a petition for freedom from slaves by granting them "half freedom," in which they were technically manumitted but their children were not and they were required to pay a fee to the Company every year. But the Company allowed the slaves to work for wages and also awarded them land, between two and 18 acres, in a watery, hilly region about a mile north from the city, in part to create buffer between Indians and white settlers. The freed slaves eventually inhabited over 130 acres in what was New York's first free black community.

Property holding and political power remained highly divided and highly unequal in New York. In addition to confirming the great Dutch "patroonships" already in existence,

James granted large estates to some of his own political supporters. Power in the colony thus remained widely dispersed among wealthy English landlords, Dutch patroons, wealthy fur traders, and the duke's political appointees. By 1685, when the Duke of York ascended the English throne as James II, New York contained about four times as many people (around 30,000) as it had twenty years before.

Shortly after James received his charter, he gave a large part of the land south of New York to a pair of political allies, both Carolina proprietors, Sir John Berkeley and Sir George Carteret. Carteret named the territory New Jersey. But the venture in New Jersey generated few profits, and in 1674, Berkeley sold his half interest. The colony was divided into two jurisdictions, East Jersey and West Jersey, which squabbled with each other until 1702, when the two halves of the colony were again joined. New Jersey, like New York, was a colony of enormous ethnic and religious diversity, and the weak colonial government made few efforts to impose strict control over the fragmented society. But unlike New York, New Jersey developed no important class of large landowners.

THE QUAKER COLONIES

Pennsylvania was born out of the efforts of a dissenting English Protestant sect, the Society of Friends. They wished to find a home for their own distinctive social order. The Society began in the mid-seventeenth century under the leadership of George Fox, a Nottingham shoemaker, and Margaret Fell. Their followers came to be known as **Quakers** (from Fox's instruction to them to "tremble at the name of the Lord"). Unlike the Puritans, Quakers rejected the concept of predestination (that God foreordained who would go to heaven and to hell) and original sin (that all people were born sinful). Every person, they believed, had divinity within themselves from birth and needed only learn to cultivate it; all could attain salvation.

The Quakers had no formal church government and no paid clergy; in their worship they spoke up one by one as the spirit moved them. Disregarding distinctions of gender and class, they addressed one another with the terms *thee* and *thou,* words commonly used in other parts of British society only in speaking to servants and social inferiors. As confirmed pacifists, they would not take part in wars. Until the mid-eighteenth century, though, Quakers did not oppose slavery and indeed some would own slaves themselves. And in Barbados, many did. Unpopular in England, the Quakers began looking to America for asylum. A few migrated to New England or Carolina, but most Quakers wanted a colony of their own. As members of a despised sect, however, they could not get the necessary royal grant without the aid of someone influential at the court.

Fortunately for the Quaker cause, a number of wealthy and prominent men had converted to the faith. One of them was **William Penn**, an outspoken evangelist who had been in prison several times. Penn worked with George Fox on plans for a Quaker colony in America, and when Penn's father died in 1681, Charles II settled a large debt he had owed to the older Penn by making an enormous grant to the son of territory between New York and Maryland. At the king's insistence, the territory was to be named Pennsylvania, after Penn's late father.

Through his informative and honest advertising, Penn soon made Pennsylvania the best-known and most cosmopolitan of all the British colonies in America. More than any other British colony, Pennsylvania prospered from the outset because of Penn's successful recruiting, his careful planning, and the region's mild climate and fertile soil. Penn sailed to Pennsylvania in 1682 to oversee the laying out of the city he named Philadelphia ("Brotherly Love") between the Delaware and Schuylkill Rivers.

Penn's relatively good relations with Indians were a result in large part of his religious beliefs. Quakerism was a faith that included a refusal to participate in war or any violence and that believed that all people, whatever their background, were capable of becoming Christian. Penn worked to respect the natives and their culture. He recognized Indians' claim to the land in the province, and he was usually scrupulous in reimbursing the natives for their land. In later years, the relationships between the British residents of Pennsylvania and the natives were not always so peaceful.

By the late 1690s, some residents of Pennsylvania were beginning to resist the nearly absolute power of the proprietor. Pressure from these groups grew to the point that in 1701, shortly before he departed for England for the last time, Penn agreed to a Charter of Liberties for the colony. The charter established a representative assembly (consisting, alone among the British colonies, of only one house) that greatly limited the authority of the proprietor. The charter also permitted "the lower counties" of the colony to establish their own representative assembly. The three counties did so in 1703 and as a result became, in effect, a separate colony—Delaware—although until the American Revolution it continued to have the same governor as Pennsylvania.

BORDERLANDS AND MIDDLE GROUNDS

The English colonies clustered along the Atlantic seaboard of North America eventually united, expanded, and became the beginnings of a powerful nation. But in the seventeenth and early eighteenth centuries, their future was not at all clear. In those years, they were small, frail settlements surrounded by other competing ones and Indian societies. The British Empire in North America was, in fact, a much smaller and weaker one than the great Spanish Empire to the south, and in many ways weaker than the enormous French Empire to the north.

The continuing contests for control of North America were most clearly visible in areas around the borders of British settlement—the Caribbean and along the northern, southern, and western borders of the coastal colonies. In the regions of the borderlands emerged societies very different from those in the Briitsh seaboard colonies—areas described as **middle grounds**, in which diverse civilizations encountered one another and, for a time at least, shaped one another. ⮡ CULTURAL BLENDING

THE CARIBBEAN ISLANDS

The Chesapeake was the site of the first permanent English settlements in the North American continent. Throughout the first half of the seventeenth century, however, the most important destinations for British immigrants were the islands of the Caribbean and the northern way station of Bermuda. Far smaller in size than the colonies would eventually become, they still became home to more than half of the English migrants to the New World in the early seventeenth century.

Before the arrival of Europeans, most of the Caribbean islands had substantial Indian populations. But beginning with Christopher Columbus's first visit in 1492, and accelerating after 1496, these populations were severely weakened by European epidemics.

The Spanish Empire claimed title to all the islands in the Caribbean, but Spain created substantial settlements only in the largest of them: Cuba, Hispaniola, and Puerto Rico. English, French, and Dutch traders began settling on some of the smaller islands early in the sixteenth century, despite the Spanish claim to them. After Spain and the Netherlands went to war in 1621 (distracting the Spanish navy and leaving the British in the Caribbean relatively unmolested), the pace of English colonization increased. Its most important settlements were on St. Kitts (1623), Barbados (1627), Antigua (1632), and Jamaica (1655).

In their first years in the Caribbean, English settlers experimented unsuccessfully with tobacco and cotton. But they soon discovered that the most lucrative crop was sugar, for which there was a substantial and growing market in Europe. Sugarcane could also be distilled into rum, for which there was also a booming market abroad. Planters devoted almost all of their land to sugarcane. *need for slaves ↑↑↑*

Because sugar was a labor-intensive crop, British planters quickly found it necessary to import laborers. As in the Chesapeake, they began by bringing indentured servants from England but they soon came to prefer African slaves, over whom they could exert greater control for longer periods. By midcentury, therefore, the English planters in the Caribbean were relying more and more on an enslaved African workforce, which soon substantially outnumbered them. By the early eighteenth century, there were four times as many African slaves as there were white settlers on Barbados and African majorities on all English Leeward Islands. *need for control ↑↑↑*

MASTERS AND SLAVES IN THE CARIBBEAN

Fearful of slave revolts, whites in the Caribbean monitored their labor forces closely and often harshly. Planters paid little attention to the welfare of their workers. Many concluded that it was cheaper to buy new slaves periodically than to protect the well-being of those they already owned, and it was not uncommon for masters literally to work their slaves to death. Few African workers survived more than a decade in the brutal Caribbean working environment—they were either sold to planters in North America or died. Even whites, who worked far less hard than did the slaves, often succumbed to the harsh climate; most died before the age of forty.

Establishing a stable society and culture was extremely difficult for people living in such harsh and even deadly conditions. Still, English Leeward Islands landowners in the Caribbean islands built a range of intuitions that replicated those found in their homeland—government, courts, churches, and juridical codes. Even when many returned home to escape the harsh conditions, the institutions they birthed continued to shape society. The Barbados' slave code of 1661, for example, influenced the practice of slavery in the Caribbean for decades. It empowered masters to treat slaves as they saw fit, including inflicting brutal punishments, with little fear of legal penalty. It stated that for "any Negro or other slave under punishment by his master . . . no person whatsoever shall be liable to any fine therefore." The code also required slaveowners to provide at least one set of clothes to every slave every year, but specified not much else; it said nothing about providing health care, housing, food, or a period of rest. Rewards were promised to slaves who deterred slave uprisings or runaways.

Despite living in subhuman conditions, slaves developed a range of social practices that gave them a measure of comfort and relief, on the one hand, and nurtured an African–Caribbean culture at least partly independent of their masters' control. They sustained African religious and social traditions and blended them with local customs to create new signature expressions of faith. They strove to build families, even though many were destroyed by death or the slave trade. And they challenged their lowly status as slaves by resisting—often quietly and in hidden ways—the circumstances of their lives. They sometimes sabotaged crops, poisoned seeds, set small fires to the harvest, broke hoes and shovels, slowed down their pace of work, or feigned illness to stay out of the fields. Occasionally they revolted, as in 1675 and 1692 in Barbados. While none of these efforts overturned the slave system, they signaled a willingness to buck the system and to build a life of their own making.

The Caribbean settlements were the most important colonies for Britain in the seventeenth and early eighteenth centuries, a vital center in the Atlantic trading world. They were the key source for sugar and rum and a market for goods made in the mainland colonies and in England. More importantly, they were the first principal source of African slaves for the mainland colonies.

The Southwest Borderlands

By the end of the seventeenth century, the Spanish had established a sophisticated and impressive empire. Their capital, Mexico City, was the most dazzling metropolis in the Americas. The Spanish residents, well over a million, enjoyed much greater prosperity than all but a few English settlers in North America.

But the principal Spanish colonies north of Mexico—Florida, Texas, New Mexico, Arizona, and California—were relatively unimportant economically to the empire. They attracted religious minorities, Catholic missionaries, and independent ranchers fleeing the heavy hand of imperial authority. Spanish troops defended the northern flank of the empire, but they remained weak and peripheral parts of the great empire to their south. New Mexico was the most prosperous and populous of these Spanish outposts. By the end of the eighteenth century, New Mexico had a non-Indian population of over 10,000—the largest European settlement west of the Mississippi and north of Mexico—and it was steadily expanding through the region.

The Spanish began to colonize California once they realized that other Europeans—among them English merchants and French and Russian trappers—were beginning to establish a presence in the region. Formal Spanish settlement of California began in the 1760s, when the governor of Baja California was ordered to create outposts of the empire farther north. Soon a string of missions, forts (or *presidios*), and trading communities were springing up along the Pacific Coast, beginning with San Diego and Monterey in 1769 and eventually San Francisco (1776), Los Angeles (1781), and Santa Barbara (1786). They sought to control a local Indian population that had as many as 300 tribes, most notably Tipais, Ipais, Luisenas, Gabrielinos, Chumashs, and Ohlones.

As was historically the case in other European incursions into land occupied by Indians, the arrival of the Spanish in California had a devastating effect on the local population, who died in great numbers from the diseases the colonists imported. As the new settlements spread, the Spanish, here as elsewhere in the Americas, insisted that the remaining Indians convert to Catholicism. And once again they met with mixed results, with some Indians adopting Catholic beliefs and rituals, others rejecting them, and still others creating a hybrid with their traditional convictions. The Spanish colonists were also intent on creating a prosperous agricultural economy. Abetting them was the encomienda program, implemented by the Spanish crown, which authorized colonists to force Indians to go to work for them and pay a yearly tribute or tax. Not all Indians complied, of course, and some ran away or fought back.

The Spanish considered the greatest threat to the northern borders of their empire to be the growing ambitions of the French. In the 1680s, French explorers traveled down the Mississippi Valley to the mouth of the river and claimed those lands for France in 1682. They called the territory Louisiana. Fearful of French incursions farther west, the Spanish began to fortify their claim to Texas by establishing new forts, missions, and settlements there, including San Fernando (later San Antonio) in 1731. Much of the region that is now Arizona was also becoming increasingly tied to the Spanish Empire and was governed from Santa Fe.

THE SOUTHEAST BORDERLANDS

The southeastern areas of what is now the United States posed a direct challenge to English ambitions in North America. After Spain claimed Florida in the 1560s, missionaries and traders began moving northward into Georgia and westward into what is now known as the Florida panhandle. Some ambitious Spaniards began to dream of expanding their empire still farther north, into what became the Carolinas and beyond. The founding of Jamestown in 1607, however, dampened those hopes and replaced them with fears. The English colonies, the Spaniards worried, could threaten their existing settlements in Florida and Georgia. As a result, the Spanish built forts in both regions to defend themselves against the increasing English presence there. Throughout the eighteenth century, the area between the Carolinas and Florida was the site of continuing tension and frequent conflict, between the Spanish and the English—and, to a lesser degree, between the Spanish and the French, who were threatening their northwestern borders with settlements in Louisiana and in what is now Alabama. *European on European conflict*

There was no formal war between England and Spain in these years, but that did not dampen the hostilities in the Southeast. English pirates continually harassed the Spanish settlements and, in 1668, actually sacked St. Augustine. The English encouraged Indians in Florida to rise up against the Spanish missions. The Spanish offered freedom to African slaves owned by English settlers in the Carolinas if they agreed to convert to Catholicism. About 100 Africans accepted the offer, and the Spanish later organized some of them into a military regiment to defend the northern border of New Spain. By the early eighteenth century, the constant fighting in the region had driven almost all the Spanish out of Florida except for settlers in St. Augustine on the Atlantic Coast and Pensacola on the Gulf Coast. *Spanish lose land against English*

Eventually, after more than a century of conflict in the southeastern borderlands, the English prevailed—acquiring Florida in the aftermath of the Seven Years' War (known in America as the French and Indian War) and rapidly populating it with settlers from their colonies to the North. Before that point, however, protecting the southern boundary of the British Empire in North America was a continual concern to the British and contributed in crucial ways to the founding of the colony of Georgia.

THE FOUNDING OF GEORGIA

Georgia—the last English colony to be established in what would become the United States—was founded to create a military barrier against Spanish lands on the southern border of English America. It was also designed to provide a refuge for the impoverished, a place where British men and women without prospects at home could begin anew. Its founders, led by General **James Oglethorpe**, served as unpaid trustees of a society created to serve the needs of the British Empire.

(©Universal History Archive/UIG via Getty Images)

SAVANNAH IN 1734 This view of Savannah by an English artist shows the intensely orderly character of early settlement in the Georgia colony. As the colony grew, its residents gradually abandoned the plan created by Oglethorpe and his fellow trustees.

militaristic motivations
+ settlement motivations

Oglethorpe, himself a veteran of the most recent Spanish wars with Britain, was keenly aware of the military advantages of an English colony south of the Carolinas. Yet his interest in settlement rested even more on his philanthropic commitments. As head of a parliamentary committee investigating English prisons, he had been appalled by the plight of honest debtors rotting in confinement. Such prisoners, and other poor people in danger of succumbing to a similar fate, could, he believed, become the farmer-soldiers of the new colony in America.

In 1732, King George II granted Oglethorpe and his fellow trustees control of the land between the Savannah and Altamaha Rivers. Their colonization policies reflected the vital military purposes of the colony. They limited the size of landholdings to make the settlement compact and easier to defend against Spanish and Indian attacks. They excluded Africans, free or slave; Oglethorpe feared that slave labor would produce internal revolts and that disaffected slaves might turn to the Spanish as allies. The trustees strictly regulated trade with the Indians, again to limit the possibility of wartime insurrection. They also excluded Catholics for fear they might collude with their coreligionists in the Spanish colonies to the south.

Oglethorpe himself led the first colonial expedition to Georgia, which built a fortified town at the mouth of the Savannah River in 1733 and later constructed additional forts south of the Altamaha. In the end, only a few debtors were released from jail and sent to Georgia. Instead, the trustees brought hundreds of impoverished tradesmen and artisans from Britain and Scotland and many religious refugees from Switzerland and Germany. Among the immigrants was a small group of Jews. British settlers made up a lower proportion of the European population of Georgia than of any other English colony.

Oglethorpe (whom some residents of Georgia began calling "our perpetual dictator") created almost constant dissensions and conflict through his heavy-handed regulation of the colony. He also suffered military disappointments, such as a 1740 assault on the Spanish outpost at St. Augustine, Florida, which ended in failure. Gradually, as the threats from Spain receded, he lost his grip on the colony, which over time became more like the rest of British North America, with an elected legislature that loosened the restrictions on settlers. Georgia continued to grow more slowly than the other southern colonies, but in other ways it now developed along lines roughly similar to those of South Carolina.

military purpose ↓, so, control ↓

Middle Grounds

The struggle for the North American continent was not just one among competing European empires. It was also a series of contests among the many different peoples who shared the continent—the Spanish, English, French, Dutch, and other colonists, on one hand, and the many Indian tribes with whom they shared the continent, on the other.

In no part of the Americas did colonial settlers quickly establish their dominance, subjugating and displacing Indians with dispatch. Instead, the balance of power was in constant flux; never was colonial rule inevitable. Along the western borders of English settlement, in particular, Europeans and Indians lived together in regions in which neither side was able to establish clear dominance. In these middle grounds, the two populations—despite frequent conflicts—carved out ways of living together, with each side making concessions to the other. (See "Debating the Past: Native Americans and the Middle Ground.") To be sure, settlers came to power faster in some colonies, like Virginia and parts of New England, but here Indians often continue to live among them. → *Cultural Blending*

It is important to recognize that these western areas tended to fall along the peripheries of European empires, in which the influence of formal colonial governments was at times minimal. European settlers, and the soldiers scattered in forts throughout these regions to protect them, were unable to displace the Indians. So they had to carve out their own relationships with the tribes. In those relationships, the Europeans found themselves obligated to adapt to tribal expectations at least as much as the Indians had to adapt to European ones. *some mutual respect*

In the seventeenth century, before many English settlers had entered the interior, the French were particularly adept at creating successful relationships with the tribes. French missionaries strove to learn local languages and customs and work within relationships between and among Indians. Fur traders practiced similar habits, welcoming the chance to attach themselves to—even to marry within—tribes. They also recognized the importance of treating tribal chiefs with respect and channeling gifts and tributes through them. But by the mid-eighteenth century, French influence in the interior was in decline, and British settlers gradually became the dominant European group. Eventually, the British learned the lessons that the French had long ago absorbed—that simple commands and raw force were ineffective in creating a workable relationship with the tribes; that they too had to learn to deal with Indian leaders through gifts and ceremonies and mediation. In large western regions—especially those around the Great Lakes—they established a precarious peace with the tribes that lasted for several decades.

smaller groups were more collaborative with natives rather than large groups of settlers

NATIVE AMERICANS AND THE MIDDLE GROUND

cultural blending ↰

For many generations, historians chronicling the westward movement of European settlement in North America portrayed Native Americans largely as weak and inconvenient obstacles swept aside by the inevitable progress of "civilization." Indians were presented either as murderous savages or as relatively docile allies of white people, but rarely as important actors of their own. Francis Parkman, the renowned nineteenth-century American historian, described Indians as a civilization "crushed" and "scorned" by the march of European powers in the New World. Many subsequent historians departed little from his assessment.

In the past half century, historians have challenged this traditional view first by examining how white civilization victimized the tribes. Gary Nash's *Red, White, and Black* (1974) was an early important presentation of this approach, as was Ramon Guttierez's *When Jesus Came, the Corn Mothers Went* (1991). They, and other scholars, rejected the optimistic, progressive view of white triumph over adversity and presented, instead, a picture of white brutality and futile Indian resistance, ending in defeat.

History among them selves (

Subsequently, scholars saw Native Americans and Euro-Americans as uneasy partners in the shaping of a new society in which, for a time at least, both were a vital part. Richard White's influential 1991 book, *The Middle Ground*, was among the first significant statements of this view. White examined the culture of the Great Lakes region in the eighteenth century, in which Algonquian Indians created a series of complex trading and political relationships with

French, English, and American settlers and travelers. In this "borderland" between the growing European settlements in the east and the still largely intact Indian civilizations farther west, a new kind of hybrid society emerged in which many cultures intermingled. James Merrell's *Into the American Woods* (1999) contributed further to this new view of collaboration by examining the world of negotiators and go-betweens along the western Pennsylvania frontier in the seventeenth and eighteenth centuries. Like White, he emphasized the complicated blend of European and Native American diplomatic rituals that allowed both groups to conduct business, make treaties, and keep the peace.

Daniel Richter extended the idea of a middle ground further in two important books: *The Ordeal of the Long-house* (1992) and *Facing East from Indian Country* (2001). Richter demonstrates that the Iroquois Confederacy was an active participant in the power relationships in the Hudson River basin; in his later book, he tells the story of European colonization from the Native American perspective, revealing how Western myths of "first contact" such as the story of John Smith and Pocahontas look entirely different when seen through the eyes of Native Americans, who remained in many ways the more powerful of the two societies in the seventeenth century.

Building on Richter but firmly centering the power of Indian societies in the story of European colonization, Kathleen Duval (*The Native Ground: Indians and Colonists in the Heart of the Continent*, 2008) demonstrates how Indian societies often determined the character of relationships with colonial powers. Indeed, she argues that it was Indians who drew Europeans into their practices of diplomacy, warfare, family, agriculture, and gender. Similarly, Pekka Hamalainen, in *The Comanche Empire* (2008), details how the Comanche controlled vast swaths of the American Southwest, besting European colonial powers through their military and economic power throughout the eighteenth and early nineteenth centuries. He portrays the Comanche as building a successful empire that unraveled more because of internal mistakes and divisions than European conquest. And Michael Witgen, in *An Infinity of Nations: How the Native New World Shaped Early North America* (2013), studies how the Anishinaabe and Dakota of the Great Lakes and Northern Plains controlled trade and diplomacy in these regions despite the incursions of Europeans. Even as they interacted with European agents, they were far from conquered or absorbed. Instead, they tended to control the patterns of interaction and cooperation and nurtured an independent culture for generations. •

[handwritten margin note: very different view than others]

UNDERSTAND, ANALYZE, & EVALUATE

1. How have historians' views of Native Americans and their role in the European colonization of North America changed over time?
2. Why do you think scholars changed their portrayal of Indians in early America so radically?

But as the English (and after 1776 American) presence in the region grew, the balance of power between Europeans and natives shifted. Newer settlers had difficulty adapting to the complex rituals that the earlier migrants had developed. The stability of the relationship between the Indians and whites deteriorated. By the early nineteenth century, the middle ground had collapsed, replaced by a European world in which Indians were ruthlessly subjugated and eventually removed. Nevertheless, for a considerable period of early American history the story of the relationship between whites and Indians was not simply a story of conquest and subjugation, but also—in some regions—a story of difficult but stable accommodation and tolerance.

[handwritten note: was not always all bad]

THE DEVELOPMENT OF EMPIRE

The British colonies in America had begun as separate projects, and for the most part they grew up independent of one another and subject to only nominal control from London. But by the mid-seventeenth century, the growing commercial success of the colonial ventures was producing pressure in England for a more uniform structure to the empire.

The English government began trying to regulate colonial trade in the 1650s, when Parliament passed laws to keep Dutch ships out of the British colonies. Later, Parliament passed three important **Navigation Acts**. The first of them, in 1660, closed the colonies to all trade except that carried by English ships. The English also required that tobacco and other items be exported from the colonies only to England or to English possessions. The second act, in 1663, required that all goods sent from Europe to the colonies pass through Britain on the way, where they would be subject to English taxation. The third act, in 1673, imposed duties on the coastal trade among the English colonies, and it provided for the appointment of customs officials to enforce the Navigation Acts. These acts formed the legal basis of England's regulation of the colonies for a century.

colonies were accustomed to independency

THE DOMINION OF NEW ENGLAND

Before the creation of Navigation Acts, all the colonial governments except that of Virginia had operated largely independently of the crown, with governors chosen by the proprietors or by the colonists themselves and with powerful representative assemblies. Officials in London recognized that to increase their control over the colonies, they would have to increase British authority in order to enforce the new laws.

In 1675, the king created a new body, the Lords of Trade, to make recommendations for imperial reform. In 1679, the king moved to increase his control over Massachusetts. He stripped it of its authority over New Hampshire and chartered a separate, royal colony there whose governor he would himself appoint. And in 1684, citing the colonial assembly's defiance of the Navigation Acts, he revoked the Massachusetts charter.

Charles II's brother, James II, who succeeded him to the throne in 1685, went further. He created a single **Dominion of New England**, which combined the government of Massachusetts with the governments of the rest of the New England colonies and later with those of New York and New Jersey as well. He appointed a single governor, Sir Edmund Andros, to supervise the entire region from Boston. Andros's rigid enforcement of the Navigation Acts and his brusque dismissal of the colonists' claims to the "rights of Englishmen" made him highly unpopular.

Struggle for control/power over colonies ↑ tension

THE "GLORIOUS REVOLUTION"

James II, unlike his father, was openly Catholic. In addition, he made powerful enemies when he appointed his fellow Catholics to high offices. The restoration of Catholicism in England led to fears that the Vatican and the pope would soon overtake the country and that the king would support him. At the same time, James II tried to control Parliament and the courts, making himself an absolute monarch. By 1688, the opposition to the king was so great that Parliament voted to force out James II. His daughter, Mary II, and her husband, William of Orange, of the Netherlands—both Protestants—replaced James II to reign jointly. However, James II went to Ireland, raised an army, and fought William but lost. He eventually left the country and spent the rest of his life in France. No Catholic monarch has reigned since. This coup came to be known as the "Glorious Revolution."

When Bostonians heard of the overthrow of James II, they arrested and imprisoned the unpopular Andros. The new sovereigns in England abolished the Dominion of New England and restored separate colonial governments. In 1691, however, they combined Massachusetts with Plymouth and made it a single, royal colony. The new charter restored the colonial assembly, but it gave the crown the right to appoint the governor. It also replaced church membership with property ownership as the basis for voting and office-holding.

Andros had been governing New York through a lieutenant governor, Captain Francis Nicholson, who enjoyed the support of the wealthy merchants and fur traders of the province. Other, less-favored colonists had a long accumulation of grievances against Nicholson and his allies. The leader of the New York dissidents was **Jacob Leisler**, a German merchant. In May 1689, when news of the Glorious Revolution and the fall of Andros reached New York, Leisler raised a militia, captured the city fort, drove Nicholson into exile, and proclaimed himself the new head of government in New York. For two years, he tried in vain to stabilize his power in the colony amid fierce factional rivalry. In 1691, when William and Mary appointed a new governor, Leisler briefly resisted. He was convicted of treason and executed. Fierce rivalry between what became known as the "Leislerians" and the "anti-Leislerians" dominated the politics of the colony for years thereafter. *More power struggles*

In Maryland, many people wrongly assumed that their proprietor, the Catholic Lord Baltimore, who was living in England, had sided with the Catholic James II and opposed William and Mary. So in 1689, an old opponent of the proprietor's government, the Protestant John Coode, led a revolt that drove out Lord Baltimore's officials and led to Maryland's establishment as a royal colony in 1691. The colonial assembly then established the Church of England as the colony's official religion and excluded Catholics from public office. Maryland became a proprietary colony again in 1715, after the fifth Lord Baltimore joined the Anglican Church.

The Glorious Revolution of 1688 in Britian touched off revolutions, mostly bloodless ones, in several colonies. Under the new king and queen, the representative assemblies that had been abolished were revived, and the scheme for colonial unification from above was abandoned. But the Glorious Revolution in America did not stop the reorganization of the empire. The new governments that emerged in America actually increased the crown's potential authority. As the first century of English settlement in America came to its end, the colonists were becoming more a part of the imperial system than ever before.

Theme: Crown's influence + colonial conflict

CONCLUSION

The English colonization of North America was part of a larger effort by several European nations to expand the reach of their increasingly commercial societies. Indeed, for many years, the British Empire in America was among the smallest and weakest of the imperial ventures there, overshadowed by the French to the north and the Spanish to the south.

In the English colonies along the Atlantic seaboard, new agricultural and commercial societies gradually emerged—those in the South centered on the cultivation of tobacco and rice and were reliant on slave labor; those in the northern colonies centered on more traditional food crops and were based mostly on free labor. Substantial trading centers emerged in such cities as Boston, New York, Philadelphia, and Charles Town, and a growing proportion of the population became prosperous and settled in these increasingly complex communities. By the early eighteenth century, English settlement had spread from northern New England (in what is now Maine) south into Georgia.

But this growing English presence coexisted with, and often was in conflict with, other Europeans—most notably the Spanish and the French—in certain areas of North America. In these borderlands, societies did not assume the settled, prosperous form they were taking in the Tidewater and New England. They were raw, sparsely populated settlements in which Europeans, including over time increasing numbers of English, had to learn to accommodate not only one another but also the substantial Indian tribes with whom they shared these interior lands. By the middle of the eighteenth century, there was a significant European presence across a broad swath of North America—from Florida to Maine, and from Texas to Mexico to California. No European power, however, controlled any major part of these large geographic regions. Yet changes were under way within the British Empire that would soon lead to its dominance through a much larger area of North America.

KEY TERMS/PEOPLE/PLACES/EVENTS

Anne Hutchinson 36
Antinomianism 36
Bacon's Rebellion 30
Cecilius Calvert 32
Dominion of New England 52
George Calvert 32
headright system 29
indentured servants 30
Jacob Leisler 52
James Oglethorpe 47

Jamestown 26
John Smith 27
John Winthrop 35
King Philip's War 37
Massachusetts Bay Company 35
Mayflower Compact 34
Metacom 39
middle grounds 44
Navigation Acts 51
Pequot War 37

Plymouth Plantation 34
Powhatan 26
Quakers 43
Roger Williams 36
slave codes 31
theocracy 35
Virginia House of Burgesses 29
William Berkeley 30
William Penn 43

RECALL AND REFLECT

1. Compare patterns of colonization between the Spanish and the English. What similarities do you see? What differences?
2. How did the institution of slavery differ between Virginia and the Caribbean? What accounts for these differences?
3. How did the relationships between European settlers and Indians along the Atlantic seaboard differ from those found in the interior regions near and around what we now call the Great Lakes?
4. How did the Glorious Revolution in England affect England's North American colonies?

3 | SOCIETY AND CULTURE IN PROVINCIAL AMERICA

THE COLONIAL POPULATION
THE COLONIAL ECONOMIES
PATTERNS OF SOCIETY
AWAKENINGS AND ENLIGHTENMENTS

LOOKING AHEAD

1. What accounted for the rapid increase in the colonial population in the seventeenth century?
2. Why did African slavery expand so rapidly in the late seventeenth century?
3. How did religion shape and influence colonial society?

MOST PEOPLE IN ENGLAND and America believed that the English colonies were outposts of the English world. And it is certainly true that as the colonies grew and became more prosperous, they came to closely resemble English society. To be sure, some of the early settlers had come to America to escape what they considered English tyranny. But by the early eighteenth century, many colonists considered themselves British just as much as the men and women in Britain itself did.

However, the colonies were quite different from England and from one other. What distinguished the colonies from England was not simply landscape and climate but also the constant engagement with Indians, experimentation with new systems of local government, attempts to establish religious orthodoxy and the rebellions occasioned with them, and efforts to learn about and raise new crops. African laborers and slaves were stitched into the fabric of colonial life almost from the start. Indeed, the English colonies would eventually become the destination for millions of forcibly transplanted Africans. The area that would become the United States was a magnet for immigrants from many lands other than England: Scotland, Ireland, the European continent, eastern Russia, and the Spanish and French Empires already established in America. Indeed, part of the story of the development of the English colonies is just how distinctive they were becoming from England itself.

1636
America's first college, Harvard, founded

1639
First printing press in colonies begins operation

1685
Huguenots migrate to America

1692
Salem witchcraft trials conclude

1697
Slave importations increase

1720
Cotton Mather starts smallpox inoculation

1734
Great Awakening begins

1739
George Whitefield arrives in America

Great Awakening intensifies

Stono slave rebellion

Zenger trial

1740s
Indigo production begins

THE COLONIAL POPULATION

After uncertain beginnings, the non-Indian population of English North America grew rapidly and substantially, through continued immigration, slave importation, and natural increase. By the late seventeenth century, Europeans and Africans outnumbered the Indians along the Atlantic Coast.

A few of the early settlers were members of the English upper classes, but most were English laborers. Some came independently, such as the religious dissenters in early New England. But in the Chesapeake, at least three-fourths of the immigrants in the seventeenth century arrived as indentured servants.

INDENTURED SERVITUDE

The system of temporary (or "indentured") servitude developed out of practices in England. Most were young men who bound themselves to masters for fixed terms of servitude (usually four to five years) in exchange for passage to America, food, and shelter. Their passage to America was a terrible trial of want and hunger. (See "Consider the Source: Gottlieb Mittelberger, the Passage of Indentured Servants.") Male indentured servants were supposed to receive clothing, tools, and occasionally land upon completion of their service. In reality, however, many left service with nothing. Most women indentures—who constituted roughly one-fourth of the total in the Chesapeake—worked as domestic servants and were expected to marry when their terms of servitude expired.

By the late seventeenth century, the indentured servant population had become one of the largest elements of the colonial population and was creating serious social problems. Some former indentures managed to establish themselves successfully as farmers, tradespeople, or artisans, and some of the women married propertied men. Others found themselves without land, without employment, without families, and without prospects. As a result, there emerged in some areas, particularly in the Chesapeake, a large floating population of young single men who were a source of social unrest that prompted elites to begin to consider African slaves as a better, more dependable and controllable form of laborer.

Shortly after the arrival of African slaves, planters began to view them as critical to their economic successes. Most importantly, they saw great benefit in having a permanent labor population without hope of freedom, consigned to a life of work and servitude and— planters assumed—accepting of their plight. Accelerating their efforts to import more slaves as well were a series of economic and demographic changes. Beginning in the 1670s, a decrease in the birthrate in England and an improvement in economic conditions there reduced the pressures on laboring men and women to emigrate, and the flow of indentured servants into America slowly declined. Those who did travel to America as indentures now generally avoided the southern colonies, where prospects for advancement were slim.

Birth and Death

Immigration remained for a time the greatest source of population growth in the colonies. But the most important long-range factor in the increase of the colonial population was its ability to reproduce itself. Improvement in the reproduction rate began in New England and the mid-Atlantic colonies in the second half of the seventeenth century. After the 1650s, natural increase became the most important source of population growth in those areas. The New England population more than quadrupled through reproduction alone in the second half of the seventeenth century. This rise was a result not only of families having large numbers of children. It was also because life expectancy in New England was unusually high.

Conditions improved much more slowly in the South. The high death rates in the Chesapeake region did not begin to decline to levels found elsewhere until the mid-eighteenth century. Throughout the seventeenth century, the average life expectancy for European men in the region was just over forty years, and for women slightly less. One in four white children died in infancy, and half died before the age of twenty. Children who survived infancy often lost one or both of their parents before reaching maturity. Widows, widowers, and orphans thus formed a substantial proportion of the white Chesapeake population. Only after settlers developed immunity to local diseases (particularly malaria) did life expectancy increase significantly. Population growth was substantial in the region, but it was largely a result of immigration.

The natural increases in the population in the seventeenth century reflected a steady improvement in the balance between men and women in the colonies. In the early years of settlement, more than three-quarters of the white population of the Chesapeake consisted of men. And even in New England, which from the beginning had attracted more families than the southern colonies, 60 percent of the inhabitants were male in 1650. Gradually, however, more women began to arrive in the colonies; and increasing birthrates contributed to shifting the the balance between men and women as well. Throughout the colonial period, the population almost doubled every twenty-five years. By 1775, the non-Indian population of the colonies was over 2 million.

Medicine in the Colonies

There were very high death rates of women who bore children in the colonial era. Physicians had little or no understanding of infection and sterilization. As a result, many women

CONSIDER THE SOURCE

GOTTLIEB MITTELBERGER, THE PASSAGE OF INDENTURED SERVANTS (1750)

Gottlieb Mittelberger, a German laborer, traveled to Philadelphia in 1750 and chronicled his voyage.

Both in Rotterdam and in Amsterdam the people are packed densely, like herrings so to say, in the large sea-vessels. One person receives a place of scarcely 2 feet width and 6 feet length in the bedstead, while many a ship carries four to six hundred souls; not to mention the innumerable implements, tools, provisions, water-barrels and other things which likewise occupy such space.

On account of contrary winds it takes the ships sometimes 2, 3, and 4 weeks to make the trip from Holland to . . . England. But when the wind is good, they get there in 8 days or even sooner. Everything is examined there and the custom-duties paid, whence it comes that the ships ride there 8, 10 or 14 days and even longer at anchor, till they have taken in their full cargoes. During that time every one is compelled to spend his last remaining money and to consume his little stock of provisions which had been reserved for the sea; so that most passengers, finding themselves on the ocean where they would be in greater need of them, must greatly suffer from hunger and want. Many suffer want already on the water between Holland and Old England.

When the ships have for the last time weighed their anchors near the city of Kaupp [Cowes] in Old England, the real misery begins with the long voyage. For from there the ships, unless they have good wind, must often sail 8, 9, 10 to 12 weeks before they reach Philadelphia. But even with the best wind the voyage lasts 7 weeks.

But during the voyage there is on board these ships terrible misery, stench, fumes, horror, vomiting, many kinds of sea-sickness, fever, dysentery, headache, heat, constipation, boils, scurvy, cancer, mouth rot, and the like, all of which come from old and sharply salted food and meat, also from very bad and foul water, so that many die miserably.

Add to this want of provisions, hunger, thirst, frost, heat, dampness, anxiety, want, afflictions and lamentations, together with other trouble, as . . . the lice abound so frightfully, especially on sick people, that they can be scraped off the body. The misery reaches the climax when a gale rages for 2 or 3 nights and days, so that every one believes that the ship will go to the bottom with all human beings on board. In such a visitation the people cry and pray most piteously.

Children from 1 to 7 years rarely survive the voyage. I witnessed . . . misery in no less than 32 children in our ship, all of whom were thrown into the sea. The parents grieve all the more since their children find no resting-place in the earth, but are devoured by the monsters of the sea.

That most of the people get sick is not surprising, because, in addition to all other trials and hardships, warm food is served only three times a week, the rations being very poor and very little. Such meals can hardly be eaten, on account of being so unclean. The water which is served out of the ships is often very black, thick and full of worms, so that one cannot drink it without loathing, even with the greatest thirst. Toward the end we were compelled to eat the ship's biscuit which had been spoiled long ago; though in a whole biscuit there was scarcely a piece the size of a dollar that had not been full of red worms and spiders' nests. . . .

At length, when, after a long and tedious voyage, the ships come in sight of land, so that the promontories can be seen, which the people were so eager and anxious to see, all creep from below on deck to see the land from afar and they weep for joy, and pray and sing, thanking and praising God. The sight of the land makes the people on board the ship, especially the sick and the half dead, alive again, so that their hearts leap within them; they shout and rejoice, and are content to bear their misery in patience, in the hope that they may soon reach the land in safety. But alas!

When the ships have landed at Philadelphia after their long voyage, no one is permitted to leave them except those who pay for their passage or can give good security; the others, who cannot pay, must remain on board the ships till they are purchased, and are released from the ships by their purchasers. The sick always fare the worst, for the healthy are naturally preferred and purchased first; and so the sick and wretched must often remain on board in front of the city for 2 or 3 weeks, and frequently die, whereas many a one, if he could pay his debt and were permitted to leave the ship immediately, might recover and remain alive.

The sale of human beings in the market on board the ship is carried out thus: Every day Englishmen, Dutchmen and High-German people come from the city of Philadelphia and other places, in part from a great distance, say 20, 30, or 40 hours away, and go on board the newly arrived ship that has brought and offers for sale passengers from Europe, and select among the healthy persons such as they deem suitable for their business, and bargain with them how long they will serve for their passage money, which most of them are still in debt for. When they have come to an agreement, it happens that adult persons bind themselves in writing to serve 3, 4, 5 or 6 years for the amount due by them, according to their age and strength. But very young people, from 10 to 15 years, must serve till they are 21 years old.

Many parents must sell and trade away their children like so many head of cattle; for if their children take the debt upon themselves, the parents can leave the ship free and unrestrained; but as the parents often do not know where and to what people their children are going, it often happens that such parents and children, after leaving the ship, do not see each other again for many years, perhaps no more in all their lives. . . . It often happens that whole families, husband, wife and children, are separated by being sold to different purchasers, especially when they have not paid any part of their passage money.

When a husband or wife has died at sea, when the ship has made more than half of her trip, the survivor must pay or serve not only for himself or herself but also for the deceased.

When both parents have died over halfway at sea, their children, especially when they are young and have nothing to pawn or pay, must stand for their own and their parents' passage, and serve till they are 21 years old. When one has served his or her term, he or she is entitled to a new suit of clothes at parting; and if it has been so stipulated, a man gets in addition a horse, a woman, a cow. When a serf has an opportunity to marry in this country, he or she must pay for each year which he or she would have yet to serve, 5 or 6 pounds.

UNDERSTAND, ANALYZE, & EVALUATE

1. What hardships did passengers suffer at sea? What relief could they hope for upon reaching Philadelphia?
2. Explain the different purchase agreements between passengers and masters. How did the death of a family member affect a passenger's indenture contracts?
3. What do the ordeals of indentured servants tell us about prospects in Europe? What do they tell us about the concept of liberty in the colonies?

and babies died from infections contracted during childbirth or surgery. Unaware of bacteria, many communities were plagued with infectious diseases transmitted by garbage or unclean water.

Because of the limited extent of formal medical knowledge, and the lack of regulations for any practitioners at the time, it was relatively easy for people to practice medicine, even without any professional training. The biggest beneficiaries of this were women, who established themselves in considerable numbers as midwives. Midwives assisted women in childbirth, but they also dispensed other medical advice. They were popular because they were usually friends and neighbors of the people they treated, unlike physicians, who were few and therefore not often well known to their patients. But their success also reflected their skill and compassion as health-care providers. Male doctors felt threatened by the midwives and struggled continually to drive them from the field, although they did not make substantial progress in doing so until the nineteenth century.

Midwives and doctors alike practiced medicine on the basis of the prevailing assumptions of their time, most of them derived from the theory of "humoralism" popularized by the famous second-century Roman physician Galen. Galen argued that the human body was governed by four "humors" that were lodged in four bodily fluids: yellow bile (or "choler"), black bile ("melancholy"), blood, and phlegm. In a healthy body, the four humors existed in balance. Illness represented an imbalance and suggested the need for removing from the body the excesses of whatever fluid was causing the imbalance. That was the rationale that lay behind the principal medical techniques of the seventeenth century: purging, expulsion, and bleeding. Bleeding was practiced mostly by male physicians. Midwives favored "pukes" and laxatives. The great majority of early Americans, however, had little contact with physicians, or even midwives, and sought instead to deal with illness on their own. The assumption that treating illness was the exclusive province of trained professionals, so much a part of the twentieth century and beyond, lay far in the distance in the colonial era.

That seventeenth-century medicine rested so much on ideas produced 1,400 years before is evidence of how little support there was for the scientific method in England and America at the time. Bleeding, for example, had been in use for hundreds of years, during which time there had been no evidence at all that it helped people recover from illness; indeed, there was considerable evidence that bleeding could do great harm. But what would seem in later eras to be the simple process of testing scientific assumptions was not yet a common part of Western thought. That was one reason that the birth of the Enlightenment in the late seventeenth century—with its faith in human reason and its belief in the capacity of individuals and societies to create better lives—was important not just to politics but also to science.

WOMEN AND FAMILIES IN THE COLONIES

Because there were many more men than women in seventeenth-century America, few women remained unmarried for long. The average white European woman in America married for the first time at twenty or twenty-one years of age. Because of the large numbers of indentured servants who were forbidden to marry until their terms of service expired, and that female indentured servants frequently had their terms of service extended, premarital sexual relationships were not uncommon. Children born out of wedlock to indentured white women were often taken from their mothers at a young age and were themselves bound as indentured servants.

White women in the Chesapeake could anticipate a life consumed with childbearing. The average wife experienced pregnancies every two years. Those who lived long enough bore an average of eight children apiece (up to five of whom typically died in infancy or early childhood). Since childbirth was one of the most frequent causes of female death, many women did not survive to see their children grow to maturity. Those who did, however, were often widowed, since they were usually much younger than their husbands.

White women lived under the principle of coverture, in which they had their legal rights assumed by their husbands upon marriage. Whereas an adult unmarried woman could own property and enter into contracts on her own, though often under the care of her father, once she married she lost such legal rights. Widows had a considerable amount of power because in most colonies they could inherit and hold property when their husband's died. High death rates meant that some women gained control of property, making them highly desirable for men seeking wives.

In New England, where many more immigrants arrived with family members and where death rates declined more quickly, family structure was much more stable than in the Chesapeake. The sex ratio was more balanced than in the Chesapeake, so most men could expect to marry. As in the Chesapeake, women married young, began producing children early, and continued to do so well into their thirties. In contrast to their southern counterparts, however, northern children were more likely to survive, and their families were more likely to remain intact. Fewer New England women became widows, and those who did generally lost their husbands later in life.

The longer life span in New England meant that parents continued to control their children longer than did parents in the South. Few sons and daughters could choose a spouse entirely independently of their parents' wishes. Men tended to rely on their fathers for land to cultivate. Women needed dowries from their parents if they were to attract desirable husbands.

(©Bettmann/Corbis)

LIFE IN THE AMERICAN COLONIES This colored engraving shows the domestic life of white Americans during the eighteenth century. Depicted are family members at work in their cozy surroundings. The industriousness they show was a virtue of the era.

THE BEGINNINGS OF SLAVERY IN ENGLISH AMERICA

The demand for African servants to supplement the indentured or free labor force existed almost from the first moments of settlement. For a time, however, black workers were hard to find. Not until the mid-seventeenth century, when a substantial commerce in slaves grew up between the Caribbean islands and the southern colonies, did black workers become generally available in North America. Just how slavery actually took root and spread has been a source of endless debate among historians.

The rising demand for slaves in North America beginning in the late seventeenth century helped expand the transatlantic slave trade. Before it ended in the nineteenth century, it was responsible for the forced immigration of as many as 11 million Africans to the Americas and the Caribbean. In the flourishing slave marts on the African coast, native chieftains brought members of rival tribes captured in western and central Africa to the ports. A small number were also captured in raids by European slave traders.

After they were captured and marched to ports along the west African coast, terrified Africans were then tightly packed into the dark, filthy holds of ships for the horrors of the **middle passage**—the long transatlantic journey to the Americas. It took three to four months, during which time up to 600 hundred Africans were chained together in columns deep in the bowels of the ship or stuffed onto shelves running around the hull. So cramped were the quarters that most could not stand up. Men were kept apart from women and children. Food and fresh air were scarce. Many died, their corpses dumped overboard.

Olaadah Equiano, an African from Eboe (present-day Nigeria), was seized by slave traders at the age of 11 in 1745 and sent to the West Indies. He later escaped and penned an autobiography detailing his life, including the middle passage. "I was soon put down under the decks. . . . The closeness of the place, the heat of the climate, added to the number in the ship, which was so crowded that each had scarcely room to turn himself, almost suffocated us. This produced copious perspirations, so that the air soon became unfit for respiration, from a variety of loathsome smells, and brought on a sickness among the slaves, of which many died." Upon arrival in the New World, slaves like Equiano were auctioned off to white landowners and transported, frightened and bewildered, to their new homes.

Most African slaves shipped to the New World landed not in an English colony but the Caribbean islands, Brazil, or territories of the Spanish Empire. From there slaves were sometimes purchased and transported by traders to North America. But not until the 1670s did slave traders start importing blacks directly from Africa to North America. Even then, the flow remained small for a time, mainly because a single group, the Royal African Company of England, monopolized the trade and kept prices high and supplies low. Indeed, only 5 to 7 percent of enslaved Africans were ever sent directly to English North America.

A turning point in the history of the black population in North America was 1697, the year rival traders broke the Royal African Company's monopoly. With the trade now open to competition, prices fell and the number of Africans greatly increased. In 1700, about 25,000 African slaves lived in English North America. Because African Americans were so heavily concentrated in a few southern colonies, they were already beginning to outnumber whites in some areas. By 1760, the number of Africans in the English mainland colonies had increased to approximately a quarter of a million, more of whom lived in the South than the North.

Initially, the legal and social status of the African laborers remained somewhat fluid. In some areas, white and black laborers worked together on terms of relative equality. Some

(Source: Library of Congress, Prints and Photographs
Division [LC-USZ62-44000])

AFRICAN SLAVE TRADE   This image is from a plate from British author Amelia Opie's poem *Black Slaves in the Hold of the Slave Ship: or How to Make Sugar*, published in London in 1826. Opie's poem depicts the life of an African who was captured by slave traders and chronicles his journey to the West Indies on a slave ship and his enforced work on the sugar plantations there. Slaves were fastened and packed like cargo for the long ocean voyage.

blacks were treated much like white hired servants, and some were freed after a fixed term of servitude. But white society eventually determined that slavery promised the most reliable and pliable labor force and beginning in the late seventeenth century began to pass a series of slave codes. In 1662, Virginia declared that slavery followed the condition of the mother, meaning that children of enslaved women were themselves enslaved. Two years later Maryland passed a law stipulating that any free-born woman who married a slave becomes a slave herself. In 1667, Virginia reversed an earlier law and stated that any slave who undergoes the rite of Christian baptism was still a slave. And in 1712 South Carolina announced that "all negro[e]s, mulattoes, mestizo[s] or Indians, which at any time heretofore have been sold, or now are held or taken to be, or hereafter shall be bought and sold for slaves, are hereby declared slaves; and they, and their children, are hereby made and declared slaves."

CHANGING SOURCES OF EUROPEAN IMMIGRATION

The most distinctive and enduring feature of the American population was that it brought together peoples of many different races, ethnic groups, and nationalities. North America was home to a highly diverse population. The British colonies were the home to Native Americans, English immigrants, forcibly imported Africans, and a wide range of other European groups. Among the earliest European immigrants were about French Calvinists (known as Huguenots). The Edict of Nantes of 1598 had assured them freedom of religion in France. But in 1685, the Edict was revoked, driving about 10,000 Huguenots to North America. Germany had similar laws banning Protestantism, driving many Germans to America where they settled in Pennsylvania. They came to be known as the "Pennsylvania Dutch," a corruption of the German term for their nationality, *Deutsch*. Frequent wars in Europe drove many other immigrants to the American colonies.

The most numerous of the newcomers were the so-called **Scotch-Irish**—Scotch Presbyterians who had settled in northern Ireland (in the province of Ulster) in the early seventeenth century. Most of the Scotch-Irish in America pushed out to the western edges of European settlement and occupied land without much regard for who actually claimed to own it.

There were also immigrants from Scotland itself and from southern Ireland. The Irish migrated steadily over a long period. Some abandoned their Roman Catholic religion and much of their ethnic identity after they arrived in America.

POPULATIONS LIVING IN COLONIAL AMERICA, 1760 Even though the entire Atlantic seaboard of what is now the United States had become a series of British colonies by 1760, the nonnative population consisted of people from many places. As this map reveals, English settlers dominated most of the regions of North America. But note the large areas of German settlement in western Chesapeake and Pennsylvania; the swath of Dutch settlement in New York and New Jersey; the Scotch-Irish regions in the western regions of the South; and the large areas in which enslaved Africans were becoming the majority of the population. Note too the presence of multiple Indian nations along the seaboard and interior lands that prefigured the influx of Europeans. They played a vital role in the evolution of the European colonies, sometimes as allies and other times as enemies but always as a key force shaping colonial culture. • *What aspects of the history of these colonies help explain their ethnic composition?*

THE COLONIAL ECONOMIES

Farming, hunting, and fishing dominated almost all areas of European settlement and long-established Indian communities in North America throughout the seventeenth and eighteenth centuries. Even so, no colony was alike. Each developed its own economic focus and character—though all incorporated slavery into the routines of daily life.

SLAVERY AND ECONOMIC LIFE

In every colony, slave labor was essential to economic productivity. Slaves performed different jobs under different conditions depending on their colony of residence, but were an integral and very visible part of every local culture. In Virginia where tobacco was the dominant crop, planters responded to the rising demand from markets in the colonies and Europe by bringing in more slaves to work larger plantations. By the mid-1700s, nearly 150,000 slaves lived in Virginia. South Carolina and Georgia relied on rice production, since the low-lying coastline with its many tidal rivers made it possible to create rice paddies that could be flooded and drained. Rice cultivation was so difficult and unhealthy that many white workers simply refused to perform it, forcing planters in South Carolina and Georgia to grow dependent on slave labor. African workers were highly valued as well because many had lived and worked in rice-producing regions of west Africa and were expert in cultivation techniques and harvesting strategies. In 1765 in South Carolina blacks, nearly all of whom were slaves, outnumbered whites 90,000 to 40,000, and the port of Charleston imported more slaves than any other city in the colonies.

There were fewer slaves in the North, in large part because of the lack of plantation-based economies dominated by a single crop. Slaves in Massachusetts, for example, worked on farms that raised a broad variety of crops, and many served as domestics and tradesmen. The colony was the center of the slave trade for New England and was home to about 4,500 slaves in 1754. The largest slave state in New England, though, was Connecticut. In 1774, nearly 6,500 slaves lived there and about one-half of all ministers, lawyers, judges, and public officials owned slaves.

INDUSTRY AND ITS LIMITS

In northern New England, colder weather and hard, rocky soil made it difficult for colonists to develop the kind of large-scale commercial farming system that southerners were creating. Conditions for agriculture were better in southern New England and the middle colonies, where the soil was fertile and the weather more temperate. New York, Pennsylvania, and the Connecticut River valley were the chief suppliers of wheat to much of New England, parts of the South, and the Caribbean. Even there, however, a substantial commercial economy emerged alongside the agricultural one.

Almost every colonist engaged in a certain amount of industry at home which occasionally provided families with surplus goods they could trade or sell. Beyond these domestic efforts, craftsmen and artisans established themselves in colonial towns as cobblers, blacksmiths, rifle-makers, cabinetmakers, silversmiths, and printers. In some areas, entrepreneurs harnessed water power to run small mills for grinding grain, processing cloth, or milling lumber. And in several coastal areas, large-scale shipbuilding operations began to flourish.

The first effort to establish a significant metals industry in the colonies was an ironworks established in Saugus, Massachusetts, in the 1640s. The Saugus Ironworks used water power

(©MPI/Archive Photos/Getty Images)

TOBACCO PLANT This image clearly links the production of tobacco to the recreational pursuit of smoking. Note that the smoker is white and well-groomed, linking ownership of the tobacco crop to society's elites.

to drive a bellows, which controlled the heat in a charcoal furnace. The carbon from the burning charcoal helped remove the oxygen from the ore and thus reduced its melting temperature. As the ore melted, it trickled down into molds or was taken in the form of simple "sow bars" to a nearby forge to be shaped into iron objects such as pots and anvils. There was also a mill suitable for turning the sow bars into narrow rods that blacksmiths could cut into nails. The Saugus Ironworks was a technological success but a financial failure. It began operations in 1646; in 1668, its financial problems forced it to close its doors.

Metalworks, however, only gradually became an important part of the colonial economy. The largest industrial enterprise anywhere in English North America was the ironworks of the German ironmaster Peter Hasenclever in northern New Jersey. Founded in 1764 with British capital, it employed several hundred laborers. There were other, smaller ironmaking enterprises in every northern colony, and there were ironworks as well in several of the southern colonies. Even so, these and other growing industries did not immediately become the basis for the kind of explosive industrial growth that Great Britain experienced in the late eighteenth century—in part because English parliamentary regulations such as the Iron Act of 1750 restricted metal processing in the colonies. Similar prohibitions limited the manufacture of woolens, hats, and other goods. But the biggest obstacles to industrialization in America were an inadequate labor supply, a small domestic market, and inadequate transportation facilities and energy supplies.

More important than manufacturing were industries that took advantage of the natural resources of the continent. By the mid-seventeenth century, the flourishing fur trade of earlier years was in decline. Taking its place were lumbering, mining, and fishing. These industries provided commodities that could be exported to England in exchange for manufactured goods. And they helped produce the most distinctive feature of the northern economy: a thriving commercial class.

Technological progress, however, did not reach all colonists, even in the North. Up to half of all the farmers did not own a plow, even less a wagon. Substantial numbers of households lacked pots and kettles for cooking and only about half owned guns. Few owned candles because they were unable to afford candle molds or tallow (wax) or because they had no access to commercially produced candles. In the early eighteenth century, very few farmers owned wagons. The low levels of ownership of these and other elementary tools were not because such things were difficult to make but because most Americans remained too poor or too isolated to be able to obtain them.

Indeed, few colonists were self-sufficient in the late seventeenth and early eighteenth centuries. A popular image of early American households is of people who grew their own food, made their own clothes, and bought little from anyone else. In fact, relatively few colonial families owned spinning wheels or looms, which suggests that most people purchased whatever yarn and cloth they needed. Most farmers who grew grain took it to centralized facilities for processing. In general, people who lived in isolated or poor areas owned fewer tools and had less access to advanced technologies than did those in more populous or affluent areas.

The Rise of Colonial Commerce

Perhaps the most remarkable feature of colonial commerce was that it was able to survive at all. American merchants faced bewildering obstacles and lacked so many of the basic institutions of trade that they managed to stay afloat only with great difficulty and through considerable ingenuity. The colonies had almost no gold or silver, and their paper currency was not acceptable as payment for goods from abroad. For many years, colonial merchants had to rely on barter or on money substitutes such as beaver skins, rice, sugar, or tobacco.

A second obstacle was lack of information about the supply and demand of goods and services. Traders had no way of knowing what they would find in foreign ports; American colonial vessels sometimes stayed at sea for years, journeying from one port to another, trading one commodity for another, attempting to find some way to turn a profit. There was also an enormous number of small, fiercely competitive companies, which made the problem of organizing the system of commerce even more acute.

Nevertheless, commerce in the colonies survived and grew. There was elaborate trade among the colonies themselves and with the West Indies. The mainland colonies offered their Caribbean trading partners rum, agricultural products, meat, and fish. The islands offered sugar, molasses, and at times slaves in return. There was also trade with England, continental Europe, and the west coast of Africa. This commerce has often been described, somewhat inaccurately, as the **triangular trade**, suggesting a neat process by which merchants carried rum and other goods from New England to Africa, exchanged their merchandise for slaves, whom they then transported to the West Indies (hence the term *middle passage* for the dreaded journey—it was the second of the three legs of the voyage), and then exchanged the slaves for sugar and molasses, which they shipped back to New England to be distilled into rum. In reality, the so-called triangular trade in rum, slaves, and sugar

THE TRIANGULAR TRADE This map illustrates the complex pattern of trade that fueled the colonial American economy in the seventeenth and eighteenth centuries. A simple explanation of this trade is that the American colonies exported raw materials (agricultural products, furs, and others) to Britain and Europe and imported manufactured goods in return. While that explanation is accurate, it is not complete, largely because the Atlantic trade was not a simple exchange between America and Europe, but a complex network of exchanges involving the Caribbean, Africa, and the Mediterranean. Note the important exchanges between the North American mainland and the Caribbean islands, the important trade between the American colonies and Africa, and the wide range of European and Mediterranean markets in which Americans were active. Not shown on this map, but also very important to colonial commerce, was a large coastal trade among the various regions of British North America. • *Why did the major ports of trade emerge almost entirely in the northern colonies?*

was a complicated maze of highly diverse trade routes. Out of this risky trade emerged a group of adventurous entrepreneurs who by the mid-eighteenth century were beginning to constitute a distinct merchant class. The British Navigation Acts protected them from foreign competition in the colonies. They had ready access to the market in England for such colonial products as furs, timber, and American-built ships. But they also developed markets illegally outside the British Empire—in the French, Spanish, and Dutch West Indies—where they could often get higher prices for their goods than in the British colonies.

THE RISE OF CONSUMERISM

As affluent residents of the colonies grew in number, the growing prosperity and commercialism of British America created both new appetites and new opportunities to satisfy them. The result was an emerging preoccupation with the consumption of material goods.

The growth of eighteenth-century consumerism increased the class divisions in the American colonies. As the difference between the upper and lower classes became more glaring, people of means became more intent on demonstrating their own membership in the upper ranks of society. The ability to purchase and display consumer goods was an important way of doing so, particularly for wealthy people in cities and towns, who did not have large estates to boast their success. But the growth of consumerism was also a product of the early stages of the Industrial Revolution. Although there was relatively little industry in America in the eighteenth century, England and Europe were making rapid advances and producing more and more affordable goods for affluent Americans to buy.

To facilitate the new consumer appetites, merchants and traders began advertising their goods in journals and newspapers. Agents of urban merchants—the ancestors of the traveling salesman—fanned out through the countryside, attempting to interest wealthy landowners and planters in the luxury goods now available to them. George and Martha Washington, for example, spent considerable time and money ordering elegant furnishings for their home at Mount Vernon, goods that were shipped to them mostly from England and Europe.

One feature of a consumer society is that things that once were considered luxuries quickly come to be seen as necessities once they are readily available. In the colonies, items that became commonplace after having once been expensive luxuries included tea, household linens, glassware, manufactured cutlery, crockery, furniture, and many other things. Another result of consumerism is the association of material goods—of the quality of a person's home and possessions and clothing, for example—with virtue and "refinement." The ideal of the cultivated "gentleman" and the gracious "lady" became increasingly powerful throughout the colonies in the eighteenth century. In part that meant striving to become educated and "refined" in speech and behavior. Americans read books on manners and fashion. They bought magazines about London society. And they strove to develop themselves as witty and educated conversationalists. They also commissioned portraits of themselves and their families, devoted large portions of their homes to entertainment, built shelves and cases in which they could display fashionable possessions, constructed formal gardens, and lavished attention on their wardrobes and hairstyles.

PATTERNS OF SOCIETY

Although there were sharp social distinctions in the colonies, the well-defined and deeply entrenched class system of England failed to reproduce itself in America. Aristocracies emerged, to be sure, but they tended to rely less on landownership than control of a substantial workforce, and they were generally less secure and less powerful than their English counterparts. More than in England, white people in America faced opportunities for social mobility—both up and down. There were also new forms of community in America, and they varied greatly from one region to another.

SOUTHERN COMMUNITIES

The plantation system of the American South produced one form of community. The first plantations emerged in the tobacco-growing areas of Virginia and Maryland. Some of the early planters became established aristocrats with vast estates. On the whole, however, seventeenth-century colonial plantations were rough and relatively small. In the early days in Virginia, they were little more than crude clearings where landowners and indentured servants worked side by side in conditions so harsh that death was an everyday occurrence. Most landowners lived in rough cabins or houses, with their servants or slaves nearby. The economy of the plantation was precarious. Planters could not control their markets, so even the largest plantations were constantly at risk. When prices fell, planters faced the prospect of ruin. The plantation economy created many new wealthy landowners, but it also destroyed many.

Enslaved African Americans, of course, lived very differently. On the smaller farms with only a handful of slaves, it was not always possible for a rigid separation to develop between whites and blacks. But by the early eighteenth century, over three-fourths of all slaves lived on plantations of at least ten slaves, and nearly one-half lived in communities of fifty slaves or more. In those settings, they were able to develop a society and culture of their own. Although whites seldom encouraged formal marriages among slaves, many blacks themselves developed strong and elaborate family structures. There were also distinctive forms of slave religion, which variously blended Christianity with African folklore and sacred practices, that became a central element in the emergence of an independent black culture.

Nevertheless, black society was subject to constant intrusions from and interaction with white society. Domestic slaves, for example, were often isolated from their own community. Black women faced sexual assault from owners and overseers; the mixed-race children of these unions were rarely recognized by their white fathers. On some plantations, black workers were treated with a modicum of humanity, but it was not common. More typically they encountered physical brutality and occasionally even sadism, against which they were virtually powerless.

Slaves often resisted their masters, in ways large and small. The most serious example in the colonial period was the **Stono Rebellion** in South Carolina in 1739, during which about 100 slaves banded together, seized weapons, killed several whites, and attempted to escape south to Florida. The uprising was quickly crushed and most participants were executed. A more frequent form of resistance was simply running away, sometimes to nearby Indian tribes in the hope of finding freedom there. Some Indian groups accepted the runaways, but others practiced slavery themselves and also held African slaves or Indian slaves. More often, runaways were caught and returned to their masters before they could reach a protective community. Subtler, often undetected forms of resistance were practiced within the confines of slavery as enslaved people evaded or defied their masters' wishes through lying, cheating, stealing, and foot-dragging.

Most slaves, male and female, worked as field hands. But on the larger plantations that aspired to genuine self-sufficiency, some slaves learned trades and crafts: blacksmithing, carpentry, shoemaking, spinning, weaving, sewing, midwifery, and others. These skilled craftspeople were at times hired out to other planters. Some set up their own establishments in towns or cities and shared their profits with their owners. A few were able to buy their freedom.

NORTHERN COMMUNITIES

It is important to note that slaves in the North experienced much of the same degradation and humiliation as in the South. While fewer in number, they still experienced similar barriers to freedom and white presumptions about their unfitness for citizenship and divine appointment as permanent laborers. No town or city in New England was without black slaves, who worked in the fields, in homes, and in shops and barns.

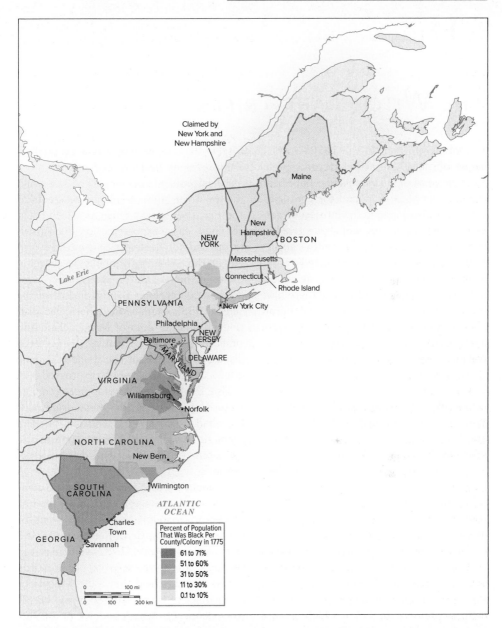

AFRICAN POPULATION AS A PROPORTION OF TOTAL POPULATION, CA. 1775   This map illustrates the parts of the colonies in which slaves made up a large proportion of the population—in some areas, a majority. The slave population was smallest in the western regions of the southern colonies and in the area north of the Chesapeake, although there remained a significant African population in parts of New Jersey and New York (some slave, some free).   •   *What explains the dense concentration of slaves in certain areas?*

The characteristic social unit in New England was not the isolated farm or the large plantation but the town. In the early years of colonization, each new settlement drew up a **covenant** binding all residents tightly together both religiously and socially. Colonists laid out a village, with houses and a meetinghouse arranged around a shared pasture, or "common."

THE WITCHCRAFT TRIALS

The witchcraft trials of the 1690s—which began in Salem, Massachusetts, and spread to other areas of New England—have been the stuff of popular legend for centuries. They have also engaged the interest of generations of historians, who have tried to explain why these seventeenth-century Americans became so committed to the belief that some of their own neighbors were agents of Satan. Although there have been many explanations of the witchcraft phenomenon, some of the most important in recent decades have focused on the central place of women in the story.

Through the first half of the twentieth century, most historians dismissed the witchcraft trials as "hysteria," prompted by the intolerance and rigidity of Puritan society. This interpretation informed the most prominent popular portrayal of witchcraft in the twentieth century: Arthur Miller's play *The Crucible*, first produced in 1953, which was clearly an effort to use the Salem trials as a comment on the great anticommunist frenzy of his own era. But at almost the same time, Perry Miller, the renowned scholar of Puritanism, argued in a series of important studies that belief in witchcraft was not a product of simple public excitement or intolerance but a widely shared part of the religious worldview of the seventeenth century. To the Puritans, witchcraft seemed not only plausible but scientifically rational.

A new wave of interpretation of witchcraft began in the 1970s, with the publication of *Salem Possessed* (1976), by Paul Boyer and Stephen Nissenbaum. Their examination of the town records of Salem in the 1690s led them to conclude that the witchcraft controversy was a product of class tensions between the poorer, more marginal residents of one part of Salem and the wealthier, more privileged residents of another. These social tensions, which could not find easy expression on their own terms, led some poorer Salemites to lash out at their richer neighbors by charging them, or their servants, with witchcraft. A few years later, John Demos, in *Entertaining Satan* (1983), examined witchcraft accusations in a larger area of New England and similarly portrayed them as products of displaced anger about social and economic grievances that could not be expressed otherwise. Demos provided a far more complex picture of the nature of these grievances than had Boyer and Nissenbaum, but like them, he saw witchcraft as a symptom of a persistent set of social and psychological tensions.

At about the same time, however, a number of scholars were beginning to look at witchcraft through the scholarly lens of gender. Famously, Carol Karlsen's *The Devil in the Shape of a Woman* (1987) demonstrated through intensive scrutiny of records across New England that a disproportionate number of those accused of witchcraft were property-owning widows or unmarried women—in other words, women who did not fit comfortably into the normal pattern of male-dominated families. Karlsen concluded that such women were vulnerable to these accusations because they seemed threatening to people (including many women) who were accustomed to women as subordinate members of the community. Mary Beth Norton's *In the Devil's Snare* (2002) placed the witchcraft trials in the context of other events of their time—and in particular the terrifying upheavals and dislocations that the Indian Wars of the late seventeenth century created in Puritan communities. In the face of this crisis, in which refugees from King William's War were fleeing towns destroyed by the Indians and flooding Salem and other eastern towns, fear and social instability grew. Accusations of witchcraft and public trials and executions helped publicize and shore up social norms.

The witchcraft trials helped create a greater-than-normal readiness to connect aberrant behavior—such as the actions of independent or powerful women—to supernatural causes and the result was a wave of deadly witchcraft accusations. •

UNDERSTAND, ANALYZE, & EVALUATE

1. How did the Salem witchcraft trials reflect attitudes toward women and the status of women in colonial New England?
2. Why were colonial New Englanders willing to believe accusations of witchcraft about their fellow colonists?

Thus families generally lived with their neighbors close by. They divided up the outlying fields and woodlands among the residents; the size and location of a family's field depended on the family's numbers, wealth, and social station.

Once a town was established, residents held a yearly "town meeting" to decide important questions and to choose a group of "selectmen," who ran the town's affairs. Participation in the meeting was generally restricted to adult males who were members of the church. Only those who could give evidence of being among the elect assured of salvation (the "visible saints") were admitted to full church membership, although other residents of the town were required to attend church services.

New Englanders did not adopt the English system of primogeniture—the passing of all property to the firstborn son. Instead, a father divided up his land among all his sons. His control of this inheritance gave him great power over the family. Often a son would reach his late twenties before his father would allow him to move into his own household and work his own land. Even then, sons would usually continue to live in close proximity to their fathers.

The early Puritan community was a tightly knit organism. But as the years passed and the communities grew, social strains began to affect this communal structure. This was partly due to the increasing commercialization of New England society. It was also partly due to population growth. In the first generations, fathers generally controlled enough land to satisfy the needs of all their sons. After several generations, however, there was often too little to go around, particularly in communities surrounded by other towns, with no room to expand outward. The result was that in many communities, groups of younger residents broke off and moved elsewhere to form towns of their own.

The tensions building in Puritan communities could produce dramatic events. One example was the widespread excitement in the 1680s and 1690s over accusations of witchcraft—the human exercise of satanic powers—in New England. The most famous outbreak was in Salem, Massachusetts. Fear of the devil's influences spread quickly throughout the town, and hundreds of people, most of them women, were accused of witchcraft. (See "Debating the Past: The Witchcraft Trials.") Twenty residents of Salem were ultimately put to death before the **Salem witchcraft trials** finally ended in 1692. Fourteen were women, all but one of whom was publicly hanged. The other five, including two children, died in prison. Tensions building in Puritan communities could produce dramatic events.

The Salem experience was not unique. Accusations of witchcraft popped up in many New England towns in the early 1690s and centered mostly on women. Research into the background of accused "witches" reveals that most were middle-aged women, often widowed, with few or no children. Some were also of low social position, were often involved in domestic conflicts, had frequently been accused of other crimes, and were considered abrasive by their neighbors. Still others were women who, through inheritance or hard work, had come into possession of substantial property of their own and thus challenged the power of men in the community.

The witchcraft controversies were a reflection of the highly religious character of New England societies. New Englanders believed in the power of Satan. Belief in witchcraft was not a marginal superstition rejected by the mainstream. It was a common feature of Puritan religious conviction.

CITIES

In the 1770s, the two largest colonial ports—Philadelphia and New York—had populations of 28,000 and 25,000, respectively, which made them larger than most English urban centers of their time. Boston (16,000), Charles Town (later Charleston), South Carolina (12,000), and Newport, Rhode Island (11,000), were also substantial communities by the standards of the day.

Colonial cities served as trading centers for the farmers of their regions, as marts for international commerce, and locales where thousands of slaves were bought and sold. Cities were the centers of what industry existed in the colonies. They were the locations of the most advanced schools and sophisticated cultural activities and of shops where imported goods could be bought. In addition, they were communities with urban social problems: crime, vice, pollution, traffic. Unlike smaller towns, cities needed to set up constables' offices and fire departments and develop systems for supporting the urban poor, whose numbers became especially large in times of economic crisis.

Finally, cities were places where new ideas could circulate and be discussed. There were newspapers, books, and other publications from abroad, and hence new intellectual influences. The taverns and coffeehouses of cities provided forums in which people could gather and debate the issues of the day. That is one reason why the Revolutionary crisis, when it began to build in the 1760s and 1770s, originated in the cities.

AWAKENINGS AND ENLIGHTENMENTS

Intellectual life in colonial America revolved around the conflict between the traditional emphasis on a personal God deeply involved in individual lives, and the new spirit of the Enlightenment, which stressed the importance of science and human reason. The old views placed a high value on a stern moral code in which intellect was less important than faith. The Enlightenment suggested that people had substantial control over their own lives and societies.

THE PATTERN OF RELIGIONS

Religious toleration flourished in America to a degree unmatched in any European nation. Settlers in America brought with them so many different religious practices that it proved impossible to impose a single religious code on any large area.

The Church of England was established as the official faith in Virginia, Maryland, New York, the Carolinas, and Georgia. Except in Virginia and Maryland, however, the laws establishing the Church of England as the official colonial religion were largely ignored. Even in New England, where the Puritans had originally believed that they were all part of a single faith, there was a growing tendency in the eighteenth century for different congregations to affiliate with different denominations. In parts of New York and New Jersey, Dutch settlers had established their own Calvinist denomination, Dutch Reformed. American Baptists developed a great variety of sects and shared the belief that rebaptism, usually by total immersion, was necessary when believers reached maturity. But while some Baptists remained Calvinists (believers in predestination), others came to believe in salvation by free will.

Protestants extended toleration to one another more readily than they did to Roman Catholics. New Englanders, in particular, viewed their Catholic neighbors in New France (Canada) not only as commercial and military rivals but also as dangerous agents of Rome. In most of the English colonies, however, Roman Catholics were too few to cause serious conflict. They were most numerous in Maryland, where they numbered 3,000. Perhaps for that reason they suffered the most persecution in that colony. After the overthrow of the original proprietors in 1691, Catholics in Maryland not only lost their political rights but also were forbidden to hold religious services except in private houses.

Jews in provincial America totaled no more than about 2,000 at any time. The largest community lived in New York City. Smaller groups settled in Newport and Charles Town, and there were scattered Jewish families in all the colonies. Nowhere could they vote or hold office. Only in Rhode Island could they practice their religion openly.

African slaves brought their own religious heritage. Though from diverse religious environments in West and western Central Africa, they generally shared a central belief in a Supreme Being or Creator and a pantheon of lesser divinities, whom they appeased and sought favor from through prayer, song, dance, and sacrifice. They aimed to create and sustain a harmonious bond with nature and supernatural beings, including not only gods by also spirits and deceased family ancestors. Many strove to continue traditional practices in their new worlds but faced stern scrutiny and even hostility. Masters regularly compelled their slaves to adopt their own sacred beliefs, which led slaves to build hybrid faiths that blended African religions with Christianity and Judaism or to worship in secret, out of sight and earshot of whites.

Slaves from the Kingdom of Kongo, because of early contact with the Portuguese, tended to be Catholic while those from the Senegambia region often included Muslims. As many as 10 percent of African slaves brought to the colonies were Muslim, but they left only traces of their faith. Like other Africans, they struggled to live their native convictions openly and often took to worshiping clandestinely or integrating their beliefs with their master's principles. Ayuba Suleimon Diallo, born in 1700 into a noble family in Bondu (now Senegal), was captured in 1730, packed on a slave ship, and sold in Annapolis, Maryland, where he worked for two years as a tobacco hand. He ran away, was captured, and placed in jail. There he became known as a devout Muslim of royal lineage whose story of bondage won the sympathy of the Royal African Company, which freed him with the hope he might be of service to them in his native country. He later published an autobiography. African Muslim names appear on muster rolls in the Revolutionary War, such as Yusef ben Ali, Bampett Muhamad, and Joseph Sabo. And in 1777 Thomas Jefferson, arguing for an expansive view of religious tolerance in Virginia and quoting John Locke, wrote that "neither Pagan nor Mahamedan [Muslim] nor Jew ought to be excluded from the civil rights for the Commonwealth because of his religion."

THE GREAT AWAKENING

By the beginning of the eighteenth century, some Americans were growing troubled by the apparent decline in religious piety in their society. The movement of the population westward and the wide scattering of settlements had caused many communities to lose touch with organized religion. The rise of commercial prosperity created a more secular outlook in urban areas. The progress of science and free thought caused at least some colonists to doubt traditional religious beliefs.

Concerns about weakening piety surfaced as early as the 1660s in New England, where the Puritan oligarchy warned of a decline in the power of the church. Ministers preached sermons of despair (known as **jeremiads**), deploring the signs of waning piety. By the standards of other societies or other eras, the Puritan faith remained remarkably strong. But to New Englanders, the "declension" of religious piety seemed a serious problem. By the early eighteenth century, similar concerns about declining piety were emerging in other regions and among members of other faiths. The result was the first great American revival: the **Great Awakening**.

The Great Awakening began in earnest in the 1730s and reached its climax in the 1740s. It was potentially a subversive force in society, challenging traditions of power and deference. The rhetoric of the revival emphasized the potential for every person to break away from the constraints of the past and start anew in his or her relationship with God. Such beliefs reflected in part the desires of many people to break away from their families or communities and start a new life. Not surprisingly, then, the revival had particular appeal to women (the majority of converts) and to younger sons of the third or fourth generation of settlers—those who stood to inherit the least land and who faced the most uncertain futures. Enslaved men and women flocked to hear this message of a new community as well, and even participated, when allowed, in public services.

Powerful **evangelists** from England helped spread the revival. John and Charles Wesley, the founders of Methodism, visited Georgia and other colonies in the 1730s. George Whitefield, a powerful open-air preacher from England, made several evangelizing tours through the colonies and drew massive crowds. He spoke in every colony and multiple times in Massachusetts and Connecticut—so many times, in fact, that it was estimated that every resident heard him preach at least once. But the outstanding preacher of the Great Awakening was the New England Congregationalist **Jonathan Edwards**. From his pulpit in Northampton, Massachusetts, Edwards attacked the new doctrines of easy salvation for all. He preached anew the traditional Puritan ideas of the absolute sovereignty of God, predestination, and salvation by God's grace alone. His vivid descriptions of hell could terrify his listeners.

The Great Awakening led to the division of existing congregations (between "New Light" revivalists and "Old Light" traditionalists) and to the founding of new ones. It also affected areas of society outside the churches. Some of the revivalists denounced book learning as a hindrance to salvation. But other evangelists saw education as a means of furthering religion, and they founded or led schools for the training of New Light ministers.

THE ENLIGHTENMENT

The Great Awakening caused one great cultural upheaval in the colonies. The **Enlightenment** caused another, very different one. The Enlightenment was the product of scientific and intellectual discoveries in Europe in the seventeenth century—discoveries that revealed the "natural laws" that regulated the workings of nature. The new scientific knowledge encouraged many thinkers to begin celebrating the power of human reason and to argue that rational thought, not just religious faith, could create progress and advance knowledge in the world.

In celebrating reason, the Enlightenment encouraged men and women to look to themselves and their own intellect—not just to God—for guidance as to how to live their lives and shape their societies. It helped produce a growing interest in education and a heightened concern with politics and government.

In the early seventeenth century, Enlightenment ideas in America were largely borrowed from Europe—from such thinkers as Francis Bacon and John Locke of England, Baruch Spinoza of Amsterdam, and René Descartes and Jean-Jacques Rousseau of France. Later, however, such Americans as Benjamin Franklin, Thomas Paine, Thomas Jefferson, and James Madison made their own important contributions to Enlightenment thought.

LITERACY AND TECHNOLOGY

White male Americans achieved a high degree of literacy in the eighteenth century. By the time of the Revolution, well over one-half of all white men could read and write. The literacy rate for women lagged behind the rate for men until the nineteenth century. While opportunities for education beyond the primary level were scarce for men, they were almost nonexistent for women.

The large number of colonists who could read created a market for the first widely circulated publications in America other than the Bible: almanacs. By 1700, there were dozens, perhaps hundreds, of almanacs circulating throughout the colonies and even in the sparsely settled lands to the west. Most families had at least one. Almanacs provided medical advice, navigational and agricultural information, practical wisdom, humor, and predictions about the future—most famously, predictions about weather patterns for the coming year, which many farmers used as the basis for decisions about crops, even though the predictions were notoriously unreliable. The most famous almanac in eighteenth-century America was *Poor Richard's Almanac,* published by Benjamin Franklin in Philadelphia.

The wide availability of reading material in colonial America by the eighteenth century was a result of the spread of printing technology. The first printing press began operating in the colonies in 1639, and by 1695 there were more towns in America with printers than there were in England. At first, many of these presses did not get very much use. Over time, however, the rising literacy of the society created a demand for books, pamphlets, and almanacs that the presses rushed to fill.

The first newspaper in the colonies, *Publick Occurrences,* was published in Boston in 1690 using a relatively advanced printing facility. It was the first step toward what would eventually become a large newspaper industry. One reason the Stamp Act of 1765, which imposed a tax on printed materials, created such a furor was that printing technology had by then become central to colonial life.

EDUCATION

Even before Enlightenment ideas penetrated America, colonists placed a high value on formal education. Some families tried to teach their children to read and write at home, although the heavy burden of work in most agricultural households limited the time available for schooling. In Massachusetts, a 1647 law required that every town support a school; and a modest network of public schools emerged as a result. The Quakers and other sects operated church schools, and in some communities widows or unmarried women conducted

> ## Poor Richard, 1743.
>
> A N
>
> # Almanack
>
> For the Year of Chriſt
>
> # 1 7 4 3,
>
> Being the Third after LEAP YEAR.
>
> | *And makes ſince the Creation* | Years |
> |---|---|
> | By the Account of the Eaſtern *Greeks* | 7251 |
> | By the Latin Church, when ☉ ent. ♈ | 6942 |
> | By the Computation of *W. W.* | 5752 |
> | By the *Roman* Chronology | 5692 |
> | By the *Jewiſh* Rabbies | 5504 |
>
> *Wherein is contained,*
>
> The Lunations, Eclipſes, Judgment of the Weather, Spring Tides, Planets Motions & mutual Aſpects, Sun and Moon's Riſing and Setting, Length of Days, Time of High Water, Fairs, Courts, and obſervable Days.
>
> Fitted to the Latitude of Forty Degrees, and a Meridian of Five Hours Weſt from *London,* but may without ſenſible Error, ſerve all the adjacent Places, even from *Newfoundland* to *South-Carolina.*
>
> By *RICHARD SAUNDERS*, Philom.
>
> PHILADELPHIA:
> Printed and ſold by *B. FRANKLIN,* at the New Printing-Office near the Market.

(Source: Library of Congress, Prints and Photographs Division [LC-USZ62-58189])

GUIDE TO THE SEASONS Among their many purposes, almanacs sought to help farmers predict weather and plan for the demands of changing seasons.

"dame schools" in their homes. In cities, some master craftsmen set up evening schools for their apprentices.

African Americans had virtually no access to education. Occasionally a master or mistress would teach slave children to read and write; but as the slave system became more firmly entrenched, strong social (and ultimately legal) sanctions developed to discourage such efforts. Indians, too, remained largely outside the white educational system—to a large degree by choice. Some white missionaries and philanthropists established schools for Native Americans and helped create a small population of Indians literate in spoken and written English.

Harvard, the first American college, was established in 1636 by Puritan theologians who wanted to create a training center for ministers. (The college was named for a Charlestown, Massachusetts, minister, John Harvard, who had left it his library and one-half of his estate.) In 1693, William and Mary College (named for the English king and queen) was established in Williamsburg, Virginia, by Anglicans. And in 1701, conservative Congregationalists, dissatisfied with the growing religious liberalism of Harvard, founded Yale (named for one of its first benefactors, Elihu Yale) in New Haven, Connecticut. Out of the Great Awakening emerged the College of New Jersey, founded in 1746 and known later as Princeton (after the town in which it was located); one of its first presidents was Jonathan Edwards. Despite the religious basis of these colleges, most of them offered curricula that included not only theology but also logic, ethics, physics, geometry, astronomy, rhetoric, Latin, Hebrew, and Greek. King's College, founded in New York City in 1754 and later renamed Columbia, was specifically devoted to the spread of secular knowledge. The Academy and College of Philadelphia, founded in 1755 and later renamed the University of Pennsylvania, was also a secular institution, established by a group of laymen under the inspiration of Benjamin Franklin.

After 1700, most colonial leaders received their entire education in America (rather than attending university in England, as had once been the case). But higher education remained available only to a few relatively affluent white men.

The Spread of Science

The clearest indication of the spreading influence of the Enlightenment in America was an increasing interest in scientific knowledge. Most of the early colleges established chairs in the natural sciences and introduced some of the advanced scientific theories of Europe, including Copernican astronomy and Newtonian physics, to their students. But the most vigorous promotion of science in these years occurred through the private efforts of amateurs and the activities of scientific societies. Leading merchants, planters, and even theologians became corresponding members of the Royal Society of London, the leading English scientific organization. Benjamin Franklin won international fame through his experiments with electricity. Particularly notable was his 1747 theory—and his 1752 demonstration, using a kite—that lightning and electricity were the same. (Previously, most scientists had believed that there were several distinct types of electricity.) His research on the way in which electricity could be "grounded" led to the development of the lightning rod, which greatly reduced fires and other damage to buildings during thunderstorms.

The high value that influential Americans were beginning to place on scientific knowledge was clearly demonstrated by the most controversial scientific experiment of the eighteenth century: inoculation against smallpox. The Puritan theologian **Cotton Mather** credited his onetime slave, whom he had given the name Onesimus after the biblical slave who escaped from Philemon, for teaching him. In a 1716 letter to the Royal Society of London, Mather wrote that Onesimus, after contracting the disease, confided "he had undergone an Operation, which had given him something of ye Small-Pox, & would forever preserve him from it, adding, That it was often used among [Africans] and whoever had ye Courage to use it was forever free from ye Fear of the Contagion." Despite strong opposition, Mather urged inoculation on his fellow Bostonians during an epidemic in the 1720s. The results confirmed the effectiveness of the technique. Other theologians took up the cause, along with many physicians. By the mid-eighteenth century, inoculation had become a common medical procedure in America.

Concepts of Law and Politics

In law and politics, as in other parts of their lives, Americans in the seventeenth and eighteenth centuries believed that they were re-creating in the New World the practices and institutions of the Old World. But as in other areas, they created something very different. Although the American legal system adopted most of the essential elements of the English system, including such ancient rights as trial by jury, significant differences developed in court procedures, punishments, and the definition of crimes. In England, for example, a printed attack on a public official, whether true or false, was considered libelous. At the 1734–1735 trial of the New York publisher **John Peter Zenger**, the courts ruled that criticisms of the government were not libelous if factually true—a verdict that removed some colonial restrictions on the freedom of the press.

More significant for the future relationship between the colonies and England were differences emerging between the American and British political systems. Because the royal government was so far away, Americans created a group of institutions of their own that gave them a large measure of self-government. In most colonies, local communities grew accustomed to running their own affairs with minimal interference from higher authorities. The colonial assemblies came to exercise many of the powers that Parliament exercised in England. Provincial governors (appointed by the king after the 1690s) had broad powers on paper, but their actual influence was limited.

The result of all this was that the provincial governments became accustomed to acting more or less independently of Parliament, and a set of assumptions and expectations about the rights of the colonists took hold in America that was not shared by policymakers in England. These differences caused few problems before the 1760s, because the British did little to exert the authority they believed they possessed. But when, beginning in 1763, the English government began attempting to tighten its control over the American colonies, a great imperial crisis resulted.

(©Fotosearch/Archive Photos/Getty Images)

COLONIAL PUNISHMENT American communities prescribed a wide range of punishments for misconduct and crime. Among the more common punishments were public humiliations—placing offenders in stocks, forcing them to wear badges of shame, or, as in this woodcut, binding them into a "ducking stool" and immersing them in water.

CONCLUSION

Between the 1650s and the 1750s, the English colonies in America grew steadily in population, in the size of their economies, and in the sophistication—and diversity—of their cultures. Although most settlers in the 1750s still believed that they were fully a part of the British Empire, they were in fact living in a very different world.

Diversity and difference characterized individual colonies. They developed their own economies, systems of government, ideas about religious toleration, and rules governing interactions with Indians. What they shared was constant engagement with Indians near the areas of their settlements. Those interactions varied from uneasy peace to outright hostility but always were part of each colony's experience. Also shared was a growing commitment to the enslavement of Africans or African Americans. As increasingly numbers of planters, farmers, landowners, merchants, ministers, and public officials determined that the presence of a slave class benefitted them, colonial governments created slave codes and customs that birthed the colonial culture of human bondage. Many participated in the Great Awakening and embraced evangelical religion, leading to the transcolonial spread of Baptist and Methodist churches. And most colonists shared a belief in certain basic principles of law and politics, which they considered embedded in the English constitution. Their interpretation of that constitution, however, was becoming increasingly different from that of the Parliament in England and was laying the groundwork for future conflict.

KEY TERMS/PEOPLE/PLACES/EVENTS

Cotton Mather 79	jeremiad 76	Scotch-Irish 63
covenant 71	John Peter Zenger 80	Stono Rebellion 70
Enlightenment 76	Jonathan Edwards 76	triangular trade 67
evangelist 76	middle passage 62	
Great Awakening 76	Salem witchcraft trials 73	

RECALL AND REFLECT

1. How did patterns of family life and attitudes toward women differ in the northern and southern colonies?
2. How did the lives of African slaves change over the course of the first century of slavery?
3. Who emigrated to North America in the seventeenth century, and why did they come?
4. What was the intellectual culture of colonial America?
5. How and why did life in the English colonies diverge from life in England?

4 | THE EMPIRE IN TRANSITION

LOOSENING TIES
THE STRUGGLE FOR THE CONTINENT
THE NEW IMPERIALISM
STIRRINGS OF REVOLT
COOPERATION AND WAR

LOOKING AHEAD

1. How did the Seven Years' War change the balance of power in North America and throughout the world?
2. What policies did Parliament implement with regard to the colonies in the 1760s and 1770s, and why did Britain adopt these policies?
3. How did the colonists respond to Parliament's actions?

AS LATE AS THE 1750S, few Americans objected to their membership in the British Empire. The imperial system provided many benefits to the Americans, and for the most part the British government left the colonies alone. Assemblies in those colonies passed laws, levied taxes, and otherwise strove to represent their white constituencies.

By the mid-1770s, the relationship between the American colonies and their British rulers was on the verge of unraveling. A global war between France and Britain had started in North America, and the colonists were thrust into the fight on Britain's side. Most indigenous groups, other than the Iroquois Confederacy, sided with the French. Britain's successes in that conflict left Native Americans divided and weakened, though it did not mark the end of their resistance to colonial encroachment in North America. Yet rather than uniting Britain and the colonists, the peace led to tensions, as London pressured the colonists to help pay for and otherwise contribute to the consolidation of empire. In the spring of 1775, the first shots were fired in a war that would ultimately win America its independence. How had it happened? And why so quickly?

LOOSENING TIES

In one sense, it had not happened quickly at all. Ever since the first days of English settlement, the ideas and institutions of the colonies had been diverging from those in Britain. In another sense, however, the revolutionary crisis emerged in response to relatively sudden changes in the administration of the empire. In 1763, the British government began to enforce a series of colonial policies that brought the differences between the two societies into sharp focus.

A DECENTRALIZED EMPIRE

In the fifty years after the Glorious Revolution, the British Parliament established a growing supremacy over the king. Under Kings George I (1714–1727) and George II (1727–1760), the prime minister and his cabinet became the nation's real executives. Because these kings depended politically on the great merchants and landholders of Britain, they were less inclined than seventeenth-century monarchs to try to tighten control over the empire, which many merchants feared would disrupt profitable commerce with the colonies. As a result, administration of the colonies remained loose, decentralized, and inefficient. What was more, some men appointed to govern the colonies remained in Britain and hired substitutes to take their places in America.

The colonial assemblies, taking advantage of the weak imperial administration, had asserted their own authority to levy taxes, make appropriations, approve appointments, and pass laws. The assemblies came to look upon themselves as little parliaments, each practically as sovereign within its colony as Parliament itself was in Great Britain.

THE COLONIES DIVIDED

Even so, the colonists continued to think of themselves as loyal British subjects. Many

1754 Beginning of French and Indian War

1756 Seven Years' War begins

1760 George III becomes king

1763 Launch of Pontiac's War
Peace of Paris
Proclamation of 1763

1764 Sugar Act

1765 Stamp Act

1766 Stamp Act repealed
Declaratory Act

1767 Townshend Duties

1770 Boston Massacre
Most Townshend Duties repealed

1771 Regulator movement in North Carolina

1772 Committees of correspondence in Boston
Gaspée incident

1773 Tea Act; Boston Tea Party

1774 Coercive Acts
First Continental Congress in Philadelphia

1775 Battles of Lexington and Concord
American Revolution begins

felt stronger ties to Great Britain (as it was called after a 1707 act of unification with Scotland) than they did to the other American colonies. Although the colonies had slowly learned to cooperate with one another on such practical matters as intercolonial trade, road construction, and a colonial postal service, they remained reluctant to cooperate in larger ways, even when, in 1754, they faced a common threat from their old rivals, the French, and France's Indian allies. Delegates from Pennsylvania, Maryland, New York, and New England met in Albany in that year to negotiate a treaty with the Iroquois Confederacy. They tentatively approved a proposal by Benjamin Franklin to set up a "general government" to manage relations with the Indians. War with the French and Indians was already beginning when the **Albany Plan** was presented to the colonial assemblies. None approved it.

THE STRUGGLE FOR THE CONTINENT

The war that raged in North America through the late 1750s and early 1760s, which colonists called the **French and Indian War**, was the final stage in a long struggle among the three principal powers in northeastern North America: the British, the French, and the Iroquois. Two years into the conflict it expanded to Europe and beyond, where it became known as the **Seven Years' War**. The British victory in that struggle confirmed Britain's commercial supremacy and cemented its control over portions of North America.

New France and the Iroquois Nation

By the end of the seventeenth century, the French Empire in America was vast: it constituted the whole length of the Mississippi River and its delta (named Louisiana, after King Louis XIV) and the continental interior as far west as the Rocky Mountains and as far south as the Rio Grande. France claimed, in effect, the entire interior of the continent.

To secure their hold on these enormous claims, they founded a string of communities, fortresses, missions, and trading posts. Would-be feudal lords established large estates *(seigneuries)* along the banks of the St. Lawrence River. On a high bluff above the river stood the fortified city of Quebec. Montreal to the south and Sault Sainte Marie and Detroit to the west marked the northern boundaries of French settlement. On the lower Mississippi there were plantations much like those in the southern colonies of British America, worked by African slaves and owned by **Creoles** (people of European ancestry born in the Americas). New Orleans, founded in 1718 to service the French plantation economy, was soon as big as some of the larger cities of the Atlantic seaboard; Biloxi and Mobile to the east completed the string of French settlement.

Both the French and the British were aware that the battle for control of North America would be determined in part by who could best win the allegiance of native tribes. The British—with their more advanced commercial economy—could usually offer the Indians better and more plentiful goods. But the French offered tolerance. Unlike the British, who were much larger in number, the French settlers in the interior generally adjusted their own behavior to Indian patterns. French fur traders frequently married Indian women and adopted tribal ways. Jesuit missionaries interacted comfortably with the natives and converted them to Catholicism by the thousands without challenging most of their social customs. By the mid-eighteenth century, therefore, the French had better and closer relations with most of the Indians of the interior than did the British.

The most powerful native group, however, had remained aloof from both sides. The **Iroquois Confederacy**—five Indian nations (Mohawk, Seneca, Cayuga, Onondaga, and Oneida) that had formed a defensive alliance in the fifteenth century—had been the most powerful native presence in the Ohio Valley since the 1640s. Although the Iroquois claimed rights to the Valley, they maintained relations with the French and British and cemented their autonomy by trading successfully with both and astutely playing them against each other.

Anglo–French Conflicts

As long as peace and stability in the North American interior lasted, English and French colonists coexisted without serious difficulty. But after the Glorious Revolution in England, a complicated series of Anglo-French wars erupted in Europe and continued intermittently for nearly eighty years, creating important repercussions in America.

King William's War (1689-1697) produced only a few, indecisive clashes between the English and the French in northern New England. Queen Anne's War, which began in 1701 and continued for nearly twelve years, generated more substantial conflicts. The Treaty of Utrecht, which brought the conflict to a close in 1713, transferred substantial territory from the French to the British in North America, including Acadia (Nova Scotia) and Newfoundland. Two decades later, disputes over British trading rights in the Spanish colonies produced a conflict between Great Britain and Spain that soon grew into a much larger European war. The British colonists in America were drawn into the struggle, which they called King George's War (1744-1748). New Englanders captured the French bastion at Louisbourg on Cape Breton Island in Nova Scotia, but the peace treaty that finally ended the conflict forced them to abandon it.

In the aftermath of King George's War, relations among the British, French, and Iroquois in North America quickly deteriorated. The Iroquois granted trading concessions in the interior to British merchants for the first time. The French feared, probably correctly, that the British were using the concessions as a first step toward expansion into French lands. They began in 1749 to construct new fortresses in the Ohio Valley. The British responded by increasing their military forces and building fortresses of their own. The balance of power that the Iroquois had carefully maintained for so long rapidly disintegrated.

For the next five years, tensions between the British and French increased. In the summer of 1754, the governor of Virginia sent a militia force (under the command of an inexperienced young colonel, George Washington) into the Ohio Valley to challenge France's Fort Duquesne, on the site of what is now Pittsburgh. The colonel's men and an allied Indian force under the leader Tanaghrisson were met on the way by a French patrol, and the British–allied force killed a French officer and ten of his men. Washington built a crude stockade (**Fort Necessity**) not far from Fort Duquesne. After the Virginians staged an unsuccessful attack on a French detachment, the French countered with an assault on Fort Necessity, trapping Washington and his soldiers inside. After one-third of them died in the fighting, Washington surrendered. The clash marked the beginning of the French and Indian War.

The Great War for Empire

The French and Indian War lasted nearly nine years, and it moved through three distinct phases. The first phase—from Fort Necessity in 1754 until the expansion of the war to Europe in 1756—was primarily a local, North American conflict, but one that

THE FIRST GLOBAL WAR

The French and Indian War in North America was part of a much larger conflict. Known in Europe as the Seven Years' War, it was one of the longest, most widespread, and most important wars in modern history. The war thrust Great Britain into conflicts across Europe and North America. Winston Churchill once wrote of it as the first "world war."

In North America, the war was a result of tensions along the frontiers of the British Empire. But it arose more broadly from larger conflicts among the great powers in Europe. It began in the 1750s with what historians have called a "diplomatic revolution." Well-established alliances between Britain and the Austro-Hungarian Empire and between France and Prussia collapsed, replaced by a new set of alliances setting Britain and Prussia against France and Austria. The instability that these changing alliances produced helped speed the European nations toward war.

The Austrian–British alliance collapsed because Austria suffered a series of significant defeats at the hands of the Prussians. To the British government, these failures suggested that the Austro-Hungarian Empire was now too weak to help Britain balance French power. As a result, Great Britain launched a search for new partnerships with the rising powers of northern Germany, Austria's enemies. In response, the Austrians sought an alliance with France to help protect them from the power of their former British allies. (One later result of this new alliance was the 1770 marriage of the future French king Louis XVI to the Austrian princess Marie Antoinette.) In the aftermath of these realignments, Austria sought again to defeat the Prussian-Hanover forces in Germany. In the process, Russia became concerned about the Austro-Hungarian Empire's possible dominance in central Europe and allied itself with the British and the Prussians. These complicated realignments eventually led to the Seven Years' War, which soon spread across much of the world. The war engaged not only most of the great powers in Europe, from Britain to Russia, but also the emerging colonial worlds—India, West Africa, the Caribbean, and the Philippines—as the powerful British navy worked to strip France, and eventually Spain, of its valuable colonial holdings.

The Seven Years' War was at heart a struggle for economic power. Colonial possessions, many European nations believed, were critical to their future wealth. The war's outcome affected not only the future of America but also the distribution of power throughout much of the world. It destroyed the French navy and much of the French Empire, and it elevated Great Britain to undisputed preeminence among the colonizing powers—especially when, at the conclusion of the war, India and all of eastern North America fell firmly under British control. The war also reorganized the balance of power in Europe, with Britain now preeminent among the great powers and Prussia (later to become the core of modern Germany) rapidly rising in wealth and military power.

The Seven Years' War was not only one of the first great colonial wars but also one of the last big wars of religion, and it extended the dominance of Protestantism in Europe. In what is now Canada, the war replaced French with British rule and thus replaced Catholic with Protestant dominance. The Vatican, no longer a military power itself, had relied on the great Catholic empires—Spain, France, and Austria-Hungary—as bulwarks of its power and influence. The shift of power toward Protestant governments in Europe and North America weakened the Catholic Church and reduced its geopolitical influence.

The conclusion of the Seven Years' War strengthened Britain and Germany and weakened France. But it did not provide any lasting solution to the rivalries among the great colonial powers. In North America, a dozen years after the end of the conflict, the American Revolution—which in many ways arose from the Seven Years' War—stripped the British Empire of one of its most important and valuable colonial appendages. By the time the American Revolution came to an end, the French Revolution had sparked another lengthy period of conflict, culminating in the Napoleonic Wars of the early nineteenth century, which once again redrew the map of Europe and, for a while, the world. •

UNDERSTAND, ANALYZE, & EVALUATE

1. How did the Seven Years' War change the balance of power among the nations of Europe? Who gained and who lost in the war?
2. Why is the Seven Years' War described as one of the "most important wars in modern history"?

swept up native groups throughout the west. The Iroquois remained largely passive in the conflict. But virtually all the other tribes sided with the French, though a few fought with the British and some with one side then the other. Native Americans tended to view these alliances as means for expelling one power or the other from their lands, not as endorsements of imperial presence in North America. Combat engulfed western white settlements, Indian villages, and frontier forts, featuring clashes between European and colonial armies and native warriors arrayed across the alliances. By late 1755, many British settlers along the frontier had withdrawn east of the Allegheny Mountains to escape the hostilities.

The second phase of the struggle began in 1756, when the Seven Years' War expanded to Europe and beyond. (See "America in the World: The First Global War.") The fighting now spread to the West Indies, India, and Europe itself. But the principal struggle remained the war in North America, where so far Britain had suffered nothing but frustration and defeat. Beginning in 1757, **William Pitt**, the British secretary of state (and future prime minister), brought the war fully under British control. He planned military strategy, appointed commanders, and issued orders to the colonists. British commanders began forcibly enlisting colonists into the army, a practice known as **impressment**. Officers also seized supplies from local farmers and tradesmen and compelled colonists to offer shelter to British troops, all generally without compensation. The Americans resented these new impositions and firmly resisted them. By early 1758, the friction between the British authorities and the colonists was threatening to bring the war effort to a halt.

Beginning in 1758, Pitt initiated the third and final phase of the war by relaxing many of the policies that Americans had found obnoxious. He agreed to reimburse the colonists for all supplies requisitioned by the army. He returned control over recruitment to the colonial assemblies. And he dispatched large numbers of additional British troops to America, where the French had always been outnumbered by the British colonists. These moves turned the tide of battle in Great Britain's favor. After 1756, moreover, the French suffered from a series of poor harvests and were unable to sustain their early military successes.

(Source: Library of Congress, Prints and Photographs Division [LC-DIG-pga-03470])

THE DEATH OF GENERAL WOLFE   This engraving is based on a 1770 painting by Benjamin West of General James Wolfe, lying mortally wounded during the siege of Quebec in 1759. West took much dramatic license in the painting, positioning important and recognizable military figures around Wolfe who in fact were not present. He also depicted a Native American in the manner of a "noble savage," a stock figure in contemporary art and literature simultaneously admired for his uncorrupted virtue but also set apart as irredeemably primitive. This portrayal also romanticized the connections between Indians and the British in the war.

By mid-1758, British regulars and colonial militias were seizing one French stronghold after another. Two British generals, Jeffrey Amherst and James Wolfe, captured the fortress at Louisbourg in July 1758. A few months later Fort Duquesne fell without a fight. The next year, at the end of a siege of Quebec, the army of General Wolfe struggled up a hidden ravine under cover of darkness, surprised the larger forces of the Marquis de Montcalm, and defeated them in a battle in which both commanders were killed. The dramatic fall of Quebec on September 13, 1759, marked the beginning of the end of the American phase of the war. A year later, in September 1760, the French army formally surrendered to Amherst in Montreal. Peace finally came in 1763, with the Peace of Paris, by which the French ceded to Great Britain some of their West Indian islands, most of their colonies in India and Canada, and all other French territory in North America east of the Mississippi. The French then turned over New Orleans and their claims west of the Mississippi to Spain, surrendering all title to the mainland of North America. Yet they kept hold of possessions in the Caribbean central to the economy of empire: Martinique, Guadaloupe, and Saint-Domingue (modern-day Haiti), the most profitable sugar colony in the world and home to hundreds of thousands of enslaved people.

The French and Indian War greatly expanded Britain's territorial claims in the New World. At the same time, the cost of the war greatly enlarged Britain's debt and substantially

(Source: Library of Congress, Prints and Photographs Division
[LC-USZC4-5315])

AN APPEAL FOR COLONIAL UNITY This sketch, one of the first American editorial cartoons, appeared in Benjamin Franklin's Philadelphia newspaper, the *Pennsylvania Gazette*, on May 9, 1754. It was meant to illustrate the need for intercolonial unity against the French and Indians, but later served as a revolutionary rallying cry.

increased British resentment of the Americans. British leaders were contemptuous of the colonists for what they considered American military ineptitude during the war. They were angry that the colonists had made so few financial contributions to a struggle waged, they believed, largely for American benefit. And they were particularly bitter that colonial merchants had been selling food and other goods to the French in the West Indies throughout the conflict. All these factors combined to persuade many British leaders that a major reorganization of the empire would be necessary. London wanted increased authority over the colonies.

The war had an equally profound effect on the American colonists. It was an experience that forced them, for the first time, to act in concert against a common foe. Yet resentments against British impressment and other wartime demands also mobilized common grievances against the government in London. The 1758 return of authority to the colonial assemblies seemed to many Americans to confirm the illegitimacy of British interference in local affairs. Thus Benjamin Franklin's famous woodcut of a divided snake—"Join, or Die"—appeared in 1754 to encourage cooperation with the British against the French and Indians but later served to call for unity against Great Britain itself.

For the Indians of the Ohio Valley, the British victory was disastrous. Many of the territorial spoils came out of Indian land. Disease and starvation plagued indigenous groups, and they held the British responsible. Those tribes that had allied themselves with the French earned the enmity of the British. The Iroquois Confederacy, which had not allied with the French, fared only slightly better. British officials saw the passivity of the Iroquois during the war as evidence of duplicity. In the aftermath of the peace settlement, the fragile Iroquois alliance with the British quickly unraveled. The tribes were increasingly divided and outnumbered, and would seldom again be in a position to deal with their European rivals on terms of military or political equality. But even before the war ended, a coalition under the leadership of a chief named **Pontiac** was planning a united rebellion against British rule. Native groups were to continue contesting the British for control of the Ohio Valley for another fifty years.

THE NEW IMPERIALISM

With the treaty of 1763, Great Britain found itself truly at peace for the first time in more than fifty years. As a result, the British government could now turn its attention to the organization of its empire. Saddled with enormous debts from the many years of war, Britain desperately needed new revenues. Responsible for vast holdings in the New World, the imperial government believed it must increase its administrative capacities in America. The result was a dramatic and, for Britain, disastrous redefinition of the colonial relationship.

BURDENS OF EMPIRE

The experience of the French and Indian War should have suggested that increasing imperial control over the colonies would not be easy. Not only had the resentment of colonists forced Pitt to relax his policies in 1758, but the colonial assemblies continued to defy imperial trade regulations and other British demands. The most immediate problem for London, however, was its staggering war debt. Landlords and merchants in Britain were objecting strenuously to any further tax increases, and the colonial assemblies had repeatedly demonstrated their unwillingness to pay for the war effort. Many officials in Britain believed that only by taxing the Americans directly could the empire effectively meet its financial needs.

At this crucial moment in Anglo–American relations, the government of Great Britain saw the 1760 accession to the throne of **George III**. He was determined to reassert the authority of the monarchy, removing from power the relatively stable coalition of Whigs (opponents of absolute monarchy) that had governed for much of the century and replaced it with a new and very unstable coalition of his own. The weak new ministers that emerged as a result each lasted in office an average of only about two years.

The king had serious intellectual and psychological limitations. He suffered, apparently, from a rare mental disease that produced intermittent bouts of insanity. (Indeed, in the last years of his long reign he was, according to most accounts, unable to perform any official functions.) Yet even when George III was lucid, which was most of the time in the 1760s and 1770s, he was painfully immature and insecure. The king's personality, therefore, contributed both to the instability and to the rigidity of the British government during these critical years.

More directly responsible for the problems that soon emerged with the colonies, however, was **George Grenville**, whom the king made prime minister in 1763. Grenville shared the prevailing opinion within Britain that the colonists should be compelled to pay a part of the cost of defending and administering the empire.

THE BRITISH AND THE TRIBES

With the defeat of the French, frontiersmen from the British colonies began immediately to move over the mountains and into tribal lands in the upper Ohio Valley. An alliance of Ottowas, Potawatomis, and Ojibwes, under the Ottawa chieftain Pontiac, struck back. This "Three Fires Confederacy" maintained a long tradition of native resistance against European powers. Its motivations resembled, as well, the kind of war for independence the colonists would launch against the same British power twelve years later and which other groups (Apaches, Comanches, Utes, Navajos) had waged against the Spanish.

Warriors fighting loosely under Pontiac laid siege to Detroit and captured several British forts, at one point staging a ruse involving a stray lacrosse ball to infiltrate the garrison at

Michilimackinac. Five hundred soldiers and 2,000 white settlers ended up dead in a region spanning from the Great Lakes to the Mississippi River to the Appalachians. The British determined to inflict horrific damage in return. Even as they negotiated, authorities at Fort Pitt gave blankets that had come from a smallpox hospital to a delegation of Delawares. The disease tore through the Indians the following summer.

The British government, fearing a disruption of western trade, issued the **Proclamation of 1763**, which forbade settlers to advance beyond the Appalachian Mountains. Many Indian groups supported the Proclamation as the best bargain available to them. The Cherokees, in particular, worked actively to hasten the drawing of the border, hoping finally to put an end to white encroachment onto their lands. But the much-hoped-for boundary failed to stop white settlers from moving back into lands farther into the Ohio Valley. Meanwhile the **Paxton Boys**, a band of Pennsylvania frontiersmen, massacred Conestoga Indians in 1763–1764. This was the sort of racial terror that animated native certainty that the British intended to "extirpate you from being a people," as one official in 1764 told the Delawares, Shawnees, and Mingoes.

Ultimately, white violence as well as Indian illness, supply shortages, and internal divisions brought the tribal revolt to its end. Native Americans did win membership in trade alliances and promises that the British would enforce the boundary line. But in 1768, new agreements with the western tribes pushed the border outward, and treaties failed to stop the white advance in any event. British settlers who had fought in the Seven Years' War were never going to give up lands they believed they had earned by blood. George Washington dismissed the Proclamation in 1767 as nothing more than "a temporary expedient to quiet the Minds of the Indians." What was more, just as colonists had fumed at being forced to support the war in the West in the 1750s, they now resented being taxed to bankroll the new British commitment to policing the imperial frontier.

BATTLES OVER TRADE AND TAXES

The Grenville ministry tried to increase its authority in the colonies in other ways as well. The **Sugar Act** of 1764 aimed to tighten British control over American trade with French and Spanish colonies through a series of tariffs and rules that would be more strictly enforced than in the past. The duty on French molasses from the Caribbean, for example, was reduced to discourage smugglers who had evaded paying the higher tax. But by lowering the tax and enforcing its payment, the British law aimed to raise revenue from its colony. In addition to regulating imports, the Sugar Act specified that colonists could export timber and iron only to Britain. It also established new vice-admiralty courts in America to try accused smugglers, thus cutting them off from sympathetic local juries. The Currency Act of 1764 required that the colonial assemblies stop issuing paper money.

Regular British troops were stationed permanently in America, and under the Mutiny Act of 1765 the colonists were required to help provision and maintain the army. Ships of the British navy patrolled American waters to search for smugglers. The customs service was reorganized and enlarged. Royal officials were required to take up their colonial posts in person instead of sending substitutes. Colonial manufacturing was restricted so that it would not compete with rapidly expanding industries in Great Britain.

At first, it was difficult for the colonists to resist these unpopular new laws. That was partly because Americans continued to harbor as many grievances against one another as they did against the authorities in London. In 1763, for example, the Paxton Boys descended on Philadelphia to demand tax relief and financial support for their violence against Indians.

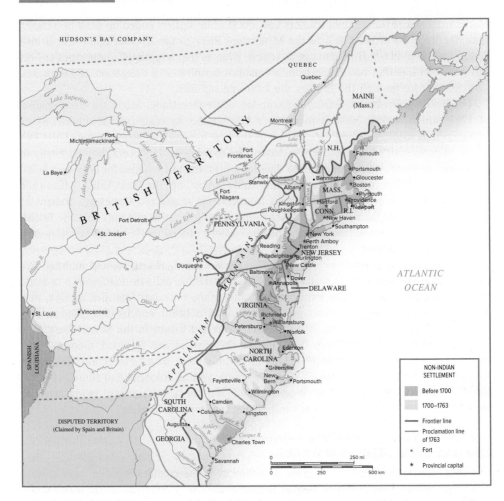

THE THIRTEEN COLONIES IN 1763 This map shows the thirteen colonies at the end of the Seven Years' War. It shows the line of settlement established by the Proclamation of 1763 (the red line), as well as the extent of actual settlement in that year (the blue line). Note that in the middle colonies (North Carolina, Virginia, Maryland, and southern Pennsylvania), settlement had already reached the red line—and in one small area of western Pennsylvania moved beyond it—by the time of the Proclamation of 1763. Note also the string of forts established beyond the Proclamation line. • *How do the forts help explain the efforts of the British to restrict settlement? And how does the extent of actual settlement help explain why it was so difficult for the British to enforce their restrictions?*

Colonial authorities conceded to their demands. In 1771, a small-scale civil war broke out in North Carolina when the "Regulators," farmers of the interior, organized and armed themselves to resist high taxes. The colonial governor appointed sheriffs to enforce the levies. An army of militiamen, most of them from the eastern counties, crushed the Regulator revolt.

The unpopularity of the Grenville program helped the colonists overcome their internal conflicts and led them to regard the policies from London as a threat to all Americans. Northern merchants would suffer from restraints on their commerce. The closing of the West to land speculation and fur trading enraged many colonists. Others were angered by the restriction of opportunities for manufacturing. Southern planters, in debt to British merchants, would be unable to ease their debts by speculating in western land. Small farmers would suffer from the abolition of paper money, which had been the source of most of their loans. Workers in towns faced the prospect of narrowing opportunities, particularly because of the restraints on manufacturing and currency. Everyone stood to suffer from increased taxes.

Most Americans soon found ways to live with the new British laws without terrible economic hardship. But their political grievances remained. Americans were accustomed to wide latitude in self-government. They believed that colonial assemblies had the sole right to control appropriations for the costs of government within the colonies. By attempting to raise extensive revenues directly from the public, the British government was challenging the basis of colonial political power.

STIRRINGS OF REVOLT

By the mid-1760s, a hardening of positions had begun in both Great Britain and America. The result was a progression of events that, more rapidly than imagined, diminished the British Empire in America.

THE STAMP ACT CRISIS

Grenville could not have devised a better method for antagonizing and unifying the colonies than the **Stamp Act** of 1765. Unlike the Sugar Act of a year earlier, which affected only a few New England merchants, the new tax fell on everyone. It levied taxes on every printed document in the colonies: newspapers, almanacs, pamphlets, deeds, wills, licenses. British officials were soon collecting more than ten times as much revenue in America as they had been before 1763. More alarming than these taxes, however, was the precedent they seemed to create. In the past, taxes and duties on colonial trade had always been designed to regulate commerce. The Stamp Act, however, was clearly an attempt by Britain to raise revenue from the colonies without the consent of the colonial assemblies.

Few colonists believed that they could do anything more than grumble until the Virginia House of Burgesses roused Americans to action. The planter and lawyer **Patrick Henry** made a dramatic speech to the House in May 1765, concluding with a vague prediction that if present policies were not revised, George III, like earlier tyrants, might lose his head. Amid shocked cries of "Treason!" Henry introduced a set of resolutions (only some of which the assembly passed) declaring that Americans possessed the same rights as the British, especially the right to be taxed only by their own representatives; that Virginians should pay no taxes except those voted by the Virginia assembly; and that anyone advocating the right of Parliament to tax Virginians should be deemed an enemy of the colony. Henry's resolutions were printed and circulated as the "**Virginia Resolves**."

In Massachusetts at about the same time, James Otis persuaded his fellow members of the colonial assembly to call an intercolonial congress to take action against the new tax. In October 1765, the Stamp Act Congress, as it was called, met in New York with delegates from nine colonies. In a petition to the British government, the congress denied that the colonies could rightfully be taxed except through their own provincial assemblies. Across the ocean, colonial agent **Benjamin Franklin** articulated such grievances before Parliament. (See "Consider the Source: Benjamin Franklin, Testimony against the Stamp Act.")

CONSIDER THE SOURCE

BENJAMIN FRANKLIN, TESTIMONY AGAINST THE STAMP ACT (1766)

In 1765 Parliament passed the first internal tax on the colonists, known as the Stamp Act. Benjamin Franklin was a colonial agent in London at the time, and as colonial opposition to the act grew, he found himself representing these views to the British government. In his testimony from Parliament he describes the role of taxes in Pennsylvania and the economic relationship between the colonies and the mother country.

[handwritten: fear of repeating the past mistakes]

Q. What is your name, and place of abode?

A. Franklin, of Philadelphia.

Q. Do the Americans pay any considerable taxes among themselves?

A. Certainly many, and very heavy taxes.

Q. What are the present taxes in Pennsylvania, laid by the laws of the colony?

A. There are taxes on all estates, real and personal; a poll tax; a tax on all offices, professions, trades, and businesses, according to their profits; an excise on all wine, rum, and other spirit; and a duty of ten pounds per head on all Negroes imported, with some other duties.

[handwritten: occurring at the same time that slavery is present]

Q. For what purposes are those taxes laid?

A. For the support of the civil and military establishments of the country, and to discharge the heavy debt contracted in the last [Seven Years'] war. . . .

Q. Are not all the people very able to pay those taxes?

[handwritten: stamp act sent people over the edge]

A. No. The frontier counties, all along the continent, have been frequently ravaged by the enemy and greatly impoverished, are able to pay very little tax. . . .

Q. Are not the colonies, from their circumstances, very able to pay the stamp duty?

A. In my opinion there is not gold and silver enough in the colonies to pay the stamp duty for one year. *[handwritten: sentiment against the stamp act is very heavy amongst all of Americans]*

Q. Don't you know that the money arising from the stamps was all to be laid out in America?

A. I know it is appropriated by the act to the American service; but it will be spent in the conquered colonies, where the soldiers are, not in the colonies that pay it.

Q. Do you think it right that America should be protected by this country and pay no part of the expense?

A. That is not the case. The colonies raised, clothed, and paid, during the last war, near 25,000 men, and spent many millions.

Q. Were you not reimbursed by Parliament?

A. We were only reimbursed what, in your opinion, we had advanced beyond our proportion, or beyond what might reasonably be expected from us; and it was a very small part of what we spent. Pennsylvania, in particular, disbursed about 500,000 pounds, and the reimbursements, in the whole, did not exceed 60,000 pounds. . . .

Q. Do you think the people of America would submit to pay the stamp duty, if it was moderated?

A. No, never, unless compelled by force of arms. . . .

Q. What was the temper of America towards Great Britain before the year 1763?

A. The best in the world. They submitted willingly to the government of the Crown, and paid, in all their courts, obedience to acts of Parliament. . . .

Q. What is your opinion of a future tax, imposed on the same principle with that of the Stamp Act? How would the Americans receive it?

A. Just as they do this. They would not pay it.

Q. Have not you heard of the resolutions of this House, and of the House of Lords, asserting the right of Parliament relating to America, including a power to tax the people there?

A. Yes, I have heard of such resolutions.

Q. What will be the opinion of the Americans on those resolutions?

A. They will think them unconstitutional and unjust.

Q. Was it an opinion in America before 1763 that the Parliament had no right to lay taxes and duties there?

A. I never heard any objection to the right of laying duties to regulate commerce; but a right to lay internal taxes was never supposed to be in Parliament, as we are not represented there.

Q. Did the Americans ever dispute the controlling power of Parliament to regulate the commerce?

A. No.

Q. Can anything less than a military force carry the Stamp Act into execution?

A. I do not see how a military force can be applied to that purpose.

Q. Why may it not?

A. Suppose a military force sent into America; they will find nobody in arms; what are they then to do? They cannot force a man to take stamps who chooses to do without them. They will not find a rebellion; they may indeed make one.

Q. If the act is not repealed, what do you think will be the consequences?

A. A total loss of the respect and affection the people of America bear to this country, and of all the commerce that depends on that respect and affection.

Q. How can the commerce be affected?

A. You will find that, if the act is not repealed, they will take very little of your manufactures in a short time.

Q. Is it in their power to do without them?

A. I think they may very well do without them.

Q. Is it their interest not to take them?

A. The goods they take from Britain are either necessaries, mere conveniences, or superfluities. The first, as cloth, etc., with a little industry they can make at home; the second they can do without till they are able to provide them among themselves; and the last, which are mere articles of fashion, purchased and consumed because of the fashion in a respected country; but will now be detested and rejected. The people have already struck off, by general agreement, the use of all goods fashionable in mourning.

Q. If the Stamp Act should be repealed, would it induce the assemblies of America to acknowledge the right of Parliament to tax them, and would they erase their resolutions [against the Stamp Act]?

A. No, never.

Q. Is there no means of obliging them to erase those resolutions?

A. None that I know of; they will never do it, unless compelled by force of arms.

Q. Is there a power on earth that can force them to erase them?

A. No power, how great so ever, can force men to change their opinions. . . .

Q. What used to be the pride of the Americans?

A. To indulge in the fashions and manufactures of Great Britain.

Q. What is now their pride?

A. To wear their old clothes over again, till they can make new ones.

UNDERSTAND, ANALYZE, & EVALUATE

1. What kind of taxes did colonists pay according to Franklin? What did the interviewer seem to think of the colonists' tax burden? What disagreements existed between Franklin and his interviewer on the purpose, legality, and feasibility of the stamp tax?

2. How did Franklin characterize the British–colonial relationship prior to 1763?

3. What colonial response to the Stamp Act and other "internal taxes" did Franklin predict? What, if anything, could Parliament do to enforce the colonists' compliance?

Source: *The Parliamentary History of England, London, 1813, vol. XVI*, 138–159; in Charles Morris, *The Great Republic by the Master Historians, vol. II.* R.S. Belcher Co., 1902.

Meanwhile, in the summer of 1765, mobs were rising up in several colonial cities against the Stamp Act. The largest was in Boston, where men belonging to the newly organized **Sons of Liberty** terrorized stamp agents and burned stamps. The mob also attacked such supposedly pro-British aristocrats as the lieutenant governor, Thomas Hutchinson, who had privately opposed passage of the Stamp Act but who felt obliged to support it once it became law. Hutchinson's elegant house was pillaged and virtually destroyed.

The crisis finally subsided largely because Britain backed down. The authorities in London were less affected by the political protests than by economic pressure. Many New Englanders had stopped buying British goods to protest the Sugar Act of 1764, and the Stamp Act caused the boycott to spread. With pressure from British merchants, Parliament—under a new prime minister, the Marquis of Rockingham—repealed the unpopular law on March 18, 1766. To satisfy his strong and vociferous opponents, Rockingham also pushed through the Declaratory Act, which confirmed parliamentary authority over the colonies "in all cases whatsoever." But in their rejoicing over the Stamp Act repeal, most Americans paid little attention to this sweeping declaration of power. *one evil replaces another*

INTERNAL REBELLIONS

The conflicts with Britain were not the only uprisings emerging in the turbulent years of the 1760s. In addition to the Stamp Act crisis and other challenges to London, there were internal rebellions that had their roots in the class system in New York and New England. In the Hudson Valley in New York, great estates had grown up, in which owners had rented out their land to small farmers. The revolutionary fervor of the time led many of these tenants to demand ownership of the land they worked. To emphasize their determination, they stopped paying rents.

The rebellion soon failed, but other challenges continued. In Vermont, which still was governed by New York, insurgent farmers challenged landowners (many of them the same owners whom tenants had challenged on the Hudson) by taking up arms and demanding ownership of the land they worked. Ethan Allen, later a hero of the Revolutionary War and himself a land speculator, took up the cause of the Green Mountain farmers and accused the landowners of trying to "enslave a free people." Allen eventually succeeded in making Vermont into a separate state, which broke up some of the large estates.

THE TOWNSHEND PROGRAM

When the Rockingham government's policy of appeasement met substantial opposition in Britain, the king dismissed the ministry and replaced it with a new government led by the aging but still powerful William Pitt, who was now Lord Chatham. Chatham had in the past been sympathetic toward American interests. Once in office, however, he was at times so incapacitated by mental illness that leadership of his administration fell to the chancellor of the exchequer, Charles Townshend.

With the Stamp Act repealed, the greatest remaining American grievance involved the Mutiny (or Quartering) Act of 1765, which required colonists to shelter and supply British troops. Many colonists objected not so much to the actual burden as to its coercive character. The Massachusetts and New York assemblies went so far as to refuse to grant the mandated supplies to the troops.

Townshend responded in 1767 by disbanding the New York Assembly until the colonists agreed to obey the Mutiny Act. By singling out New York, he believed, he would avoid antagonizing all the colonies at once. He also imposed new taxes, known as the **Townshend Duties**, on various goods imported to the colonies from Great Britain—lead, paint, paper, and tea. Townshend assumed that since these were taxes purely on "external" transactions (imports from overseas), as opposed to the internal transactions the Stamp Act had taxed, the colonists would not object. But all the colonies resented the suspension of the New York Assembly, believing it to be a threat to every colonial government. And all the colonies rejected Townshend's careful distinction between external and internal taxation.

Townshend also established a board of customs commissioners in America. The new commissioners established their headquarters in Boston. They virtually ended smuggling in Boston, although smugglers continued to carry on a busy trade in other colonial seaports. The Boston merchants, angry that the new commission was diverting the lucrative smuggling trade elsewhere, helped organize a boycott of British goods that were subject to the Townshend Duties. Merchants in Philadelphia and New York joined them in a nonimportation agreement in 1768, and later some southern merchants and planters also agreed to cooperate. Throughout the colonies, American homespun and other domestic products became suddenly fashionable. *American Patriotism growing / forming*

Late in 1767, Charles Townshend died. In March 1770, the new prime minister, Lord North, hoping to end the American boycott, repealed all the Townshend Duties except the tea tax.

THE BOSTON MASSACRE

Before news of the repeal reached America, an event in Massachusetts inflamed colonial opinion. The harassment of the new customs commissioners in Boston had grown so intense that the British government had placed four regiments of regular troops in the city. Many of the poorly paid British soldiers looked for jobs in their off-duty hours and thus competed with local workers. Clashes between the two groups were frequent.

On the night of March 5, 1770, a mob of dockworkers, "liberty boys," and others began pelting the sentries at the customs house with rocks and snowballs. Hastily, Captain Thomas Preston of the British regiment lined up several of his men in front of the building to protect it. There was some scuffling, one of the soldiers was knocked down, and in the midst of it all, apparently, several British soldiers fired into the crowd, killing five people.

This murky incident, almost certainly the result of panic and confusion, was quickly transformed by local resistance leaders into the "**Boston Massacre**." It became the subject of such lurid (and inaccurate) accounts as the widely circulated pamphlet *Innocent Blood Crying to God from the Streets of Boston*. A famous engraving by Paul Revere portrayed the massacre as a calculated assault on a peaceful crowd. The British soldiers, tried before a jury of Bostonians and defended by future American president John Adams, were found guilty only of manslaughter and given token punishment. But colonial pamphlets and newspapers convinced many dissidents that the soldiers were guilty of murder.

The leading figure in fomenting public outrage over the Boston Massacre was the colonial official and political philosopher Samuel Adams, second cousin to John. Britain, he

→ American Propaganda used to incite resentment against Brit.

(©Barney Burstein/Corbis Historical/Getty Images)

THE BOSTON MASSACRE (1770), BY PAUL REVERE This sensationalized engraving of the conflict between British troops and Boston laborers is one of many important propaganda documents, by Revere and others, for the revolutionary cause in the 1770s. Among the victims of the massacre listed by Revere was Crispus Attucks, probably the first person of color to die in the struggle for American independence.

argued, had become a morass of sin and corruption; only in America did public virtue survive. In 1772, he proposed the creation of "**committees of correspondence**" in Boston to publicize the grievances against Britain. Other colonies followed Massachusetts's lead, and a loose intercolonial network of political organizations was soon established that kept the spirit of dissent alive through the 1770s.

THE PHILOSOPHY OF REVOLT

Although a superficial calm settled on the colonies after the Boston Massacre, the crises of the 1760s and early 1770s had helped arouse enduring challenges to British authority and had produced powerful instruments for circulating colonial complaints. Yet revolutionary impulses rarely came down to simple arguments for democracy over monarchy, and they rarely pulled in a single direction. Some dissidents rejected or sought to modify British traditions of governance, others lobbied simply for Britain to leave the colonies alone, still others to break away from the monarchy altogether. Gradually these diverse voices would merge to form a political outlook in America that would serve to justify revolt, if not exactly a radical one.

British political philosophy, passed down and amended over time in the unwritten English constitution, called for distributing power among the three elements of society—the monarchy, the aristocracy, and the people—in order to prevent the exercise of unchecked authority. In the late seventeenth and early eighteenth centuries, colonial assemblies in North America resembled the elected and increasingly influential House of Commons in the British Parliament. Neither were particularly democratic, nor did leaders on either side of the Atlantic intend them to be. Though some colonial regions granted voting rights more broadly, most parts of British America and Britain proper endowed the vote rather sparsely to property holders. Through elections for the assemblies, those voters transferred authority over their lives to their representatives, who often went on to govern as they saw fit without much additional consultation from the public. By this political ideology, only independent, landowning men should vote (dependent men could be manipulated by those they depended upon), and only the best minds should hold public office. Two future presidents believed in this model: George Washington in his youth feared the ignorance of the "grazing multitude," John Adams the "common herd of mankind." Some American revolutionaries continued to harbor such suspicions of democracy and the masses up to 1776 and well beyond.

Some colonists opposed the privileges of hereditary aristocracy and the powers of the monarchy. But their galvanizing grievance by the 1770s, as the controversies over duties and quartering demonstrated, concerned matters of representation and **sovereignty**, or the authority to govern. Some colonists objected less to *how* they were governed than to *who* was governing them, or put another way, rejected British *practices* of governance more than their *principles*. This sort of frustration materialized in the slogan, "No taxation without representation." Whatever the nature of a tax, they said, it could not be levied without the consent of the colonists themselves. There were actually some supporters of colonial rights in Britain making such arguments on behalf of the colonists.

But to many other British observers and authorities, this clamor about representation made little sense. According to their constitutional theory, members of Parliament did not represent individuals or particular geographical areas. Instead, each member represented the interests of the whole nation and indeed the whole empire. The many boroughs of Britain that had no representative in Parliament, the whole of Ireland, and the colonies thousands of miles away—all were thus represented in Parliament at London, even though they elected no representatives of their own. This was the theory of **"virtual representation."** Americans, in fact, practiced the very same thing *within* their colonies, whereby assemblies did not reflect universal suffrage yet still claimed to represent their communities.

But for many colonists, the difference was the literal and figurative distance separating themselves from the men supposedly protecting their interests in Parliament. How could officials impose policies and taxes, said a religious leader in Georgia, on those "who never invested them with any such power"? Such thinkers may have believed in virtual representation across miles, but not continents and oceans. Soon enough, the king who shared power with Parliament similarly lost legitimacy. Indeed, this tradition, too, the colonists borrowed from the British, whose outburst of anti-monarchical dissent had separated King Charles I from his head over a century earlier.

TAVERNS IN REVOLUTIONARY MASSACHUSETTS

In colonial Massachusetts, as in many other American colonies in the 1760s and 1770s, taverns (or "public houses," as they were often known) were crucial to the development of popular resistance to British rule. The Puritan culture of New England created some resistance to taverns, and reformers tried to regulate or close them to reduce the problems caused by "public drunkenness," "lewd behavior," and "anarchy." But as the commercial life of the colonies expanded and more people began living in towns and cities, taverns became a central institution in American social life—and eventually in its political life as well.

Taverns were appealing, of course, because they provided alcoholic drinks in a culture where the craving for alcohol and the extent of drunkenness were very high. But taverns had other attractions as well. They were one of the few places where people could meet and talk openly in public; indeed, many colonists considered the life of the tavern as the only vaguely democratic experience available to them. The tavern was a mostly male institution, just as political life was considered a mostly male concern. Male camaraderie and political discourse fused together out of tavern culture.

As the revolutionary crisis deepened, taverns and pubs became central meeting places for cultivating resistance to British policies. Educated and uneducated men alike joined in animated discussions of events. The many who could not read could learn about the contents of revolutionary pamphlets from listening to tavern conversations. They could join in the discussion of

the new republican ideas emerging in America by participating in tavern celebrations of, for example, the anniversaries of resistance to the Stamp Act. Those anniversaries inspired elaborate toasts in public houses throughout the colonies.

In an age before wide distribution of newspapers, taverns and tavernkeepers were important sources of information about the political and social turmoil of the time. Taverns were also the settings for political events. In 1770, for example, a report circulated through the taverns of Danvers, Massachusetts, about a local man who was continuing to sell tea despite the colonial boycott. The Sons of Liberty brought the seller to the Bell Tavern and persuaded him to sign a confession and apology before a crowd of defiant men in the public room.

(Source: Library of Congress, Prints and Photographs Division [LC-USZC2-1367])

TAVERNS AND POLITICS The London Coffee House and other taverns were centers for pre-Revolutionary social and political life in colonial Philadelphia.

Almost all politicians who wanted any real contact with the public found it necessary to visit taverns in colonial Massachusetts. Samuel Adams spent considerable time in the public houses of Boston, where he sought to encourage resistance to British rule while taking care to drink moderately so as not to erode his stature as a leader. His cousin John Adams, although somewhat more skeptical of taverns and more sensitive to the vices they encouraged, also recognized their political value. In taverns, he once said, "bastards and legislatores are frequently begotten." •

UNDERSTAND, ANALYZE, & EVALUATE

1. Why were taverns so important in educating colonists about the relationship with Britain?
2. What gathering places today serve the same purposes as taverns did in colonial America?

SITES OF RESISTANCE

Colonists kept the growing spirit of resistance alive in many ways, but most of all through writing and talking. Dissenting leaflets, pamphlets, and books circulated widely through the colonies. In towns and cities, people gathered in churches, schools, town squares, and, above all, taverns to discuss politics.

Taverns were also places where resistance pamphlets and leaflets could be distributed and where meetings for the planning of protests and demonstrations could be held. Massachusetts had the most elaborately developed tavern culture, which was perhaps one reason why the spirit of resistance grew more quickly there than anywhere else. (See "Patterns of Popular Culture: Taverns in Revolutionary Massachusetts.")

America in the 1760s and early 1770s featured growing resentment about the continued enforcement of the Navigation Acts. Popular anger was visible in occasional acts of rebellion. At one point, colonists seized a British revenue ship on the lower Delaware River. In 1772, angry residents of Rhode Island boarded the British schooner *Gaspée,* set it afire, and sank it.

THE TEA EXCITEMENT

The revolutionary fervor of the 1760s intensified as a result of a new act of Parliament, one that involved the business of selling tea. In 1773, Britain's East India Company (on the verge of bankruptcy) was sitting on large stocks of tea that it could not sell in Britain. In an effort to save the company, the government passed the **Tea Act** of 1773, which gave the company the right to export its merchandise directly to the colonies without paying any of the regular taxes that were imposed on colonial importers. The law provided no new tax on tea, but the original Townshend duty on the commodity survived, and the East India Company was now exempt from paying it. That meant cheaper tea for consumers, which Lord North had assumed would make the law welcome among the colonists.

But resistance leaders in America argued that the law, in effect, imposed an unfair tax on American merchants, who would be undersold by the East India Company and become disadvantaged in the colonial tea trade. The colonists responded by boycotting tea. Unlike earlier protests, most of which had involved relatively small numbers of people, the tea boycott mobilized large segments of the population. It also helped link the colonies together in a common experience of mass popular protest. Particularly important to the movement were the activities of colonial women, who led the boycott. The **Daughters of Liberty**—a recently formed women's organization—proclaimed, "rather than Freedom, we'll part with our Tea."

In the last weeks of 1773, with strong popular support, some colonial leaders made plans to prevent the East India Company from landing its cargoes. In Philadelphia and New York, determined colonists kept the tea from leaving the company's ships, and in Charles Town, South Carolina, they stored it away in a public warehouse. In Boston, local dissenters staged a spectacular drama. On the evening of December 16, 1773, three companies of fifty men each, masquerading as Mohawk Indians, went aboard three ships, broke open the tea chests, and heaved them into the harbor. As the electrifying news of the **Boston Tea Party** spread, colonists in other seaports staged similar acts of resistance.

Parliament retaliated in four acts of 1774: closing the port of Boston, drastically reducing the powers of self-government in Massachusetts, permitting royal officers in America to be tried for crimes in other colonies or in Great Britain, and providing for the quartering of troops by the colonists. These **Coercive Acts** were more widely known in America as the "Intolerable Acts."

The Coercive Acts backfired. Far from isolating Massachusetts, they made the colony a martyr in the eyes of residents of other colonies and sparked new resistance up and down the coast. Colonial legislatures passed a series of resolves supporting Massachusetts. Women's groups mobilized to extend the boycotts of British goods and to create substitutes for the tea, textiles, and other commodities they were shunning. In Edenton, North Carolina, fifty-one women signed an agreement in October 1774 declaring their "sincere adherence" to the anti-British resolutions of their provincial assembly and proclaiming their duty to do "every thing as far as lies in our power" to support the "publick good."

COOPERATION AND WAR

Beginning in 1765, colonial leaders developed a variety of organizations for converting popular discontent into action—organizations that in time formed the basis for an independent government.

NEW SOURCES OF AUTHORITY

The passage of authority from the royal government to the colonists themselves began on the local level. In colony after colony, local institutions responded to the resistance movement by simply seizing authority. At times, entirely new institutions emerged.

The most effective of these new groups were the committees of correspondence. Massachusetts and Virginia and other colonies established these committees to foster continuous cooperation among them. After the royal governor dissolved the assembly in 1774, colonists met in the Raleigh Tavern at Williamsburg, declared that the Intolerable Acts menaced the liberties of every colony, and issued a call for a Continental Congress.

Delegates from all the colonies except Georgia were present when, in September 1774, the **First Continental Congress** convened in Philadelphia. They made five major decisions. First, they rejected a plan for a colonial union under British authority. Second, they endorsed a relatively moderate statement of grievances, which addressed the king as "Most Gracious Sovereign," but which also included a demand for the repeal of all oppressive legislation passed since 1763. Third, they approved a series of resolutions recommending that military preparations be made for defense against possible attack by the British troops in Boston. Fourth, they agreed to a series of boycotts they hoped would stop all trade with Great Britain, and they formed a "Continental Association" to see that these agreements were enforced. Fifth, the delegates agreed to meet again the following spring.

During the winter, the Parliament in London debated proposals for conciliating the colonists, and early in 1775 Lord North finally won approval for a series of measures known as the Conciliatory Propositions. Parliament proposed that the colonies tax themselves at Parliament's demand. With this offer, Lord North hoped to separate the American moderates, whom he believed represented the views of the majority, from the extremist minority. But his offer was too little and too late. It did not reach America until after the first shots of war had been fired. *what would happen if it reached in time*

LEXINGTON AND CONCORD

For months, the farmers and townspeople of Massachusetts had been gathering arms and ammunition and preparing "minutemen" to fight on a moment's notice. The Continental Congress had approved preparations for a defensive war, and the citizen-soldiers waited only for an aggressive move by the British regulars in Boston.

There, General Thomas Gage, commanding the British garrison, considered his army too small to do anything without reinforcements. He resisted the advice of less cautious officers, who assured him that the Americans would back down quickly before any show of British force. When General Gage received orders to arrest the rebel leaders Sam Adams and the wealthy merchant John Hancock, known to be in the vicinity of Lexington, he still hesitated. But when he heard that the minutemen had stored a large supply of gunpowder in Concord (eighteen miles from Boston), he decided to act. On the night of April 18, 1775, he sent a detachment of about 1,000 men out toward Lexington, hoping to surprise the colonials and seize the illegal supplies without bloodshed.

But dissenters in Boston were watching the British movements closely, and during the night two horsemen, William Dawes and Paul Revere, rode out to warn the villages and farms. When the redcoats arrived in Lexington the next day, several dozen minutemen awaited them on the town common. Shots were fired and minutemen fell; eight were killed and ten wounded. Advancing to Concord, the British discovered that the Americans had hastily removed most of the powder supply. All along the road back to Boston, the British were harassed by the gunfire of farmers hiding behind trees, rocks, and stone walls. By the end of the day, the British had lost almost three times as many men as the Americans.

The first shot—the "shot heard 'round the world," as the poet Ralph Waldo Emerson later called it—had been fired. But who had fired it first? According to one of the minutemen at Lexington, the British commander, Major Thomas Pitcairn, had shouted to the colonists on his arrival, "Disperse, ye rebels!" When they ignored him, he ordered his troops to fire. British officers and soldiers claimed that the minutemen had fired first. Whatever the truth, the rebels succeeded in circulating their account well ahead of the British version, adorning it with tales of British atrocities. The effect was to rally thousands of colonists to the rebel cause. *use of bias + propaganda*

It was not immediately clear at the time that the skirmishes at Lexington and Concord were the first battles of a war. But whether people recognized it at the time or not, the American Revolution had begun.

THE BATTLES OF LEXINGTON AND CONCORD, 1775   This map shows the fabled series of events that led to the first battle of the American Revolution. On the night of April 18, 1775, Paul Revere and William Dawes rode out from Boston to warn the outlying towns of the approach of British troops. Revere was captured just west of Lexington, but Dawes escaped and returned to Boston. The next morning, British forces moved out of Boston toward Lexington, where they met armed American minutemen on the Lexington common and exchanged fire. The British dispersed the Americans in Lexington. But they next moved on to Concord, where they encountered more armed minutemen, clashed again, and were driven back toward Boston. All along their line of march, they were harassed by riflemen. • *What impact did the Battles of Lexington and Concord (and the later Battle of Bunker Hill, also shown on this map) have on colonial sentiment toward the British?*

CONCLUSION

When the Seven Years' War ended in 1763, it might have seemed reasonable to expect that relations between the British colonists in America and Great Britain itself would have been cemented more firmly than ever. But in fact, the resolution of that conflict altered the imperial relationship forever, in ways that ultimately drove Americans to rebel against British rule and begin a war for independence. To the British, the lesson of the French and Indian War was that the colonies in America needed firmer control from London. The empire was now much bigger, and it needed better administration. The war had produced great debts, and the Americans—among the principal beneficiaries of the war—should help pay them. And so for more than a decade after the end of the fighting, the British tried one strategy after another to tighten control over and extract money from the colonies.

To the colonists, this effort to tighten imperial rule seemed both a betrayal of the sacrifices they had made in the war and a challenge to their long-developing assumptions about the rights of British people to rule themselves. Gradually, white Americans came to see in the British policies evidence of a conspiracy to establish tyranny in the New World. And so throughout the 1760s and 1770s, the colonists developed an ideology of resistance and defiance. By the time the first shots were fired in the American Revolution in 1775, Britain and America had come to view each other as two very different societies. Their differences, which soon appeared irreconcilable, propelled them into a war that would change the course of history for both sides.

KEY TERMS/PEOPLE/PLACES/EVENTS

Albany Plan 84
Benjamin Franklin 93
Boston Massacre 97
Boston Tea Party 102
Coercive Acts 102
committees of
  correspondence 98
Creole 84
Daughters of Liberty 102
First Continental
  Congress 102

Fort Necessity 85
French and Indian War 84
George Grenville 90
George III 90
impressment 87
Iroquois Confederacy 85
Patrick Henry 93
Paxton Boys 91
Pontiac 89
Proclamation of 1763 91
Seven Years' War 84

Sons of Liberty 96
sovereignty 99
Stamp Act 93
Sugar Act 91
Tea Act 101
Townshend Duties 97
Virginia Resolves 93
virtual representation 99
William Pitt 87

RECALL AND REFLECT

1. What Native Americans fought in the French and Indian War, and how did the war's outcome affect them? What about Native Americans who did not participate in the war?
2. How and why did the colonists' attitude toward Britain change from the time of the Seven Years' War to the beginning of the American Revolution?
3. What were the philosophical underpinnings of the colonists' revolt against Britain?
4. What did the slogan "No taxation without representation" mean, and why was it a rallying cry for the colonists?

5 | THE AMERICAN REVOLUTION

THE STATES UNITED
THE WAR FOR INDEPENDENCE
WAR AND SOCIETY
THE CREATION OF STATE GOVERNMENTS
THE SEARCH FOR A NATIONAL GOVERNMENT

LOOKING AHEAD

1. What were the military strategies (both British and American) of each of the three phases of the American Revolution? How successful were these strategies during each phase?
2. How did the American Revolution become an international conflict, not just a colonial war against the British?
3. How did the new national government of the United States reflect the principles of republicanism?

TWO STRUGGLES OCCURRED SIMULTANEOUSLY during the eight years of war that began in April 1775. The first was the military conflict with Great Britain. The second was a political conflict within America.

The military conflict was, by the standards of later wars, a relatively modest one. By the standards of its own day, however, it was an unusually savage conflict, pitting not only army against army but the civilian population against a powerful external force. The shift of the war from a traditional, conventional struggle to a new kind of conflict—a revolutionary war for liberation—is what made it possible for the United States to defeat the more powerful British.

At the same time, Americans were wrestling with the great political questions that the conflict necessarily produced: first, whether to demand independence from Britain; second, how to structure the new nation they had proclaimed; and third, how to deal with questions that the revolution had raised about slavery, the rights of Indians, the role of women, and the limits of religious tolerance in the new American society.

THE STATES UNITED

Although some Americans had long expected a military conflict with Britain, the actual beginning of hostilities in 1775 found the colonies generally unprepared for war against the world's greatest armed power.

DEFINING AMERICAN WAR AIMS

Three weeks after the Battles of Lexington and Concord, when the **Second Continental Congress** met in Philadelphia, delegates from every colony (except Georgia, which had not yet sent a representative) agreed to support the war. But they disagreed about its purpose. At one extreme was a group led by the Adams cousins (John and Samuel), Richard Henry Lee of Virginia, and others, who already favored independence. At the other extreme was a group led by such moderates as John Dickinson of Pennsylvania, who hoped for a quick reconciliation with Great Britain.

Most Americans believed at first that they were fighting not for independence but for a resolution of grievances against the British Empire. During the first year of fighting, however, many colonists began to change their minds. The costs of the war were so high that the original war aims began to seem too modest to justify them. Many colonists were enraged when the British began trying to recruit Indians, African slaves, and German mercenaries (the hated "Hessians"). Particularly galvanizing for slaveowners in the southern colonies was the royal governor of Virginia's announcement of late 1775 that enslaved people owned by rebels—*not* those enslaved by colonists loyal to the crown—could win freedom if they abandoned their masters and joined the British forces, known as **Lord Dunmore's Proclamation**. When the British government blockaded colonial ports and rejected all efforts at conciliation, many colonists concluded that independence was the only remaining option.

TIME LINE

1775
Second Continental Congress

Washington commands American forces

Lord Dunmores's Proclamation

1776
Paine's *Common Sense*

Declaration of Independence

Battle of Trenton

1777
Articles of Confederation adopted

British defeat at Saratoga

1778
French-American alliance

1781
Articles of Confederation ratified

Cornwallis surrenders at Yorktown

1783
Treaty of Paris

1784
Postwar depression begins

1786
Shays's Rebellion

1787
Northwest Ordinance

THE AMERICAN REVOLUTION

Almost from the moment it ended, historians have debated the character, meaning, and origins of the American Revolution. For the first several generations after 1776, they developed what historians call a "whiggish" view of the rebellion. In this narrative, the colonists proceeded inexorably and with God's approval toward independence from Britain, scoring a preordained victory for Enlightenment ideals and progress, for liberty over tyranny. Later, in the decades before and during the Civil War, the perpetuation of this vision of the Revolution by George Bancroft and others served a contemporary need to emphasize American unity and greatness at a time of roiling division and sectional violence.

In the early twentieth century, historians downplayed the importance of ideology in the Revolution, attributing it, rather, to social and economic forces. Carl Becker, J. Franklin Jameson, Arthur M. Schlesinger, and other "progressive" historians, so named for the period in which they wrote, characterized the Revolution as a burst of radical, populist outrage against not just the monarchy or Parliament but against colonial elites with property, prestige, and power. Thus, said Becker (in 1909), there were really two revolutions, one against Britain, the other against colonial aristocrats, each animated by a different question: "The first was the question of home rule; the second was the question . . . of who should rule at home."

Beginning in the 1950s, with the nation once again searching for unity in the Cold War era, a new generation of scholars began to reemphasize the role of consensus and ideology over class warfare and economic

interests. Edmund S. Morgan (in 1956) argued that most eighteenth-century Americans shared common political principles and that the social and economic conflicts other historians had identified were not severe. Bernard Bailyn, in *The Ideological Origins of the American Revolution* (1967), found Revolutionary rhetoric rooted in deeply and widely held resentments against British imperial oppression. For Bailyn and for Pauline Maier in *From Resistance to Revolution* (1972), the independence movement still tipped radical but in its resentment of monarchical corruption and abuse of power rather than of elite property holders. Scholars of this period argued over what to name the ideologies that drove the rebellion, but they returned to the privileging of ideas over economic motivators.

By the late 1960s, for a new generation of historians, many influenced by the New Left, the pendulum was swinging back to class-based interpretations and to the internal struggles of the Revolutionary generation. Historians like Gary Nash in *The Urban Crucible* (1979) cited economic distress and the actions of mobs in colonial cities, the economic pressures on colonial merchants, and other changes in the character of American culture and society as critical prerequisites for the growth of the Revolutionary movement. Echoing Becker, Nash argued for two revolutions, one by common people against colonial elites and one by colonial elites bent on maintaining their status and power in a post-British environment.

According to many scholars up to the present day, colonial elites succeeded in reclaiming economic and political authority

(©MPI/Hulton Archive/Getty Images)

THE BRITISH SURRENDER This contemporary drawing depicts the formal surrender of British troops at Yorktown on October 19, 1781. Columns of American troops and a large French fleet flank the surrender ceremony, suggesting part of the reason for the British defeat. General Cornwallis, the commander of British forces in Virginia, did not himself attend the surrender. He sent a deputy in his place.

after the British left. These scholars point to the crafting of the Constitution, with its protections for the propertied white male elite and exclusion of everyone else from citizenship rights, as evidence for the victory of an essentially conservative revolution. Along these same lines, groundbreaking work on women during the Revolution by Mary Beth Norton (*Liberty's Daughters*, 1980) and Linda Kerber (*Women of the Republic*, 1980) turned attention to the women who played a major role in the rebellion. They worked in auxiliary functions for the army or as wartime maintainers of home and industry, but in a deeper sense, as cultivators of civic virtue in the home, or "republican mothers." And they lamented that these contributions did not merit citizenship rights in the country's first constitutions.

The pendulum swung again with Gordon Wood, who argued in *The Radicalism of the American Revolution* (1992) for a *socially* radical revolution, whereby the Founders undermined time-worn social patterns of deference, patriarchy, and gender hierarchies. "Americans had become," Wood wrote, "almost overnight, the most liberal, the most democratic, the most commercially minded, and the most modern people in the world." The Revolution did not end slavery or the second-class status of women, he granted, but laid the foundations for those future transformations and should not have its radicalism undercut by those failures.

Others have found the picture Wood painted too rosy. They counter that a new democratic order was short-lived, or came much later, or was driven not by the framers but by societal actors left out of earlier histories of the Revolution. Edward Countryman (*A People in Revolution*, 1989), Woody Holton (*Forced Founders*, 1999; *Unruly Americans*, 2007), and T. H. Breen (*The Marketplace of Revolution*, 2004) argued for a radical Revolution that saw common people, for a time, shape the course of independence. These scholars see in the rebellion rhetorical groundwork for later change or the momentary ignition of possibilities for marginalized groups, but then a retrenchment of elite white rule.

Similarly, scholars of enslaved peoples, women, and Native Americans during the Revolution have tracked the contributions of these groups to the war as well as their appropriation of liberating rhetoric from Revolutionary political culture, but ultimately they have a bleak story to tell. Colin Calloway's *The American Revolution in Indian Country* (1995), Rosemarie Zagarri's *Revolutionary Backlash* (2007), Douglas Egerton's *Death or Liberty* (2009), Carroll Smith-Rosenberg's *This Violent Empire* (2012), and many others have located in the nation's birth foundational commitments to white supremacy, male dominance, and the destruction of indigenous peoples, despite various efforts by these groups to claim the Revolution's transformative potential for themselves. For these and other scholars, America's gradual (and still incomplete) inclusion of marginalized groups came in spite of, rather than because of, the intentions of the country's founders. •

UNDERSTAND, ANALYZE, & EVALUATE

1. In what way was the American Revolution an ideological struggle?
2. In what way was the American Revolution a social and economic conflict?
3. Was the Revolution a fundamentally liberating or constricting event for the nation's people?

Thomas Paine's impassioned pamphlet **Common Sense** crystallized these feelings in January 1776. Paine, who had emigrated from Britain less than two years before, sought to turn the anger of Americans toward parliamentary overreach as well as the British monarchy more broadly. It was simple common sense, Paine wrote, for Americans to break completely with a political system that could inflict such hardships on its own people. Written in plain terms and in English, rather than French or Latin like some treatises, *Common Sense* sold more than 100,000 copies in only a few months and helped build support for the idea of independence in the early months of 1776. (For more on the origins of the rebellion, see "Debating the Past: The American Revolution.")

THE DECLARATION OF INDEPENDENCE

In the meantime, the Continental Congress in Philadelphia was moving toward a complete break with Britain. At the beginning of the summer, it appointed a committee to draft a formal declaration of independence; and on July 2, 1776, it adopted a resolution: "That these United Colonies are, and, of right, ought to be, free and independent states; that they are absolved from all allegiance to the British crown, and that all political connexion between them and the state of Great Britain is, and ought to be, totally dissolved." Two days later, on July 4, Congress approved the **Declaration of Independence** itself, which provided formal justifications for this resolution.

The Declaration launched a period of energetic political innovation, as one colony after another reconstituted itself as a "state." By 1781, most states had produced written constitutions for themselves. At the national level, however, the process was more uncertain. In November 1777, finally, Congress adopted a plan for union, the **Articles of Confederation**. The document confirmed the existing weak, decentralized system.

Thomas Jefferson, a thirty-three-year-old Virginian lawyer and former member of the state House of Burgesses, wrote most of the Declaration. He had help from the Pennsylvania political theorist, inventor, and scientist Benjamin Franklin, and John Adams, a lawyer and Massachusetts delegate to the Second Continental Congress. The Declaration expressed concepts that had been circulating throughout the colonies over the previous few months in the form of at least ninety other, local "declarations of independence"— declarations drafted up and down the coast by town meetings, artisan and militia organizations, county officials, grand juries, Sons of Liberty, and colonial assemblies. Jefferson borrowed heavily from these texts.

The final document had two parts. In the first, the Declaration restated the familiar contract theory of John Locke: that governments were formed to protect what Jefferson called "life, liberty and the pursuit of happiness." Although these lines have become the most famous part of the document, at the time, the second part loomed larger in the minds of the rebels. It listed the alleged crimes of the king, who, with the backing of Parliament, had violated his contract with the colonists and thus had forfeited all claim to their loyalty.

MOBILIZING FOR WAR

Financing the war was difficult. Congress had no authority to levy taxes on its own, and when it requisitioned money from the state governments, none contributed more than a small part of its expected share. Congress had little success borrowing from the public, since few Americans could afford to buy bonds. Instead, Congress issued paper money. Printing presses turned out enormous amounts of "Continental currency," and the states printed currencies of their own. The result, predictably, was soaring inflation, and Congress soon found the Continental currency was virtually worthless. Ultimately, Congress financed the war mostly by borrowing from other nations.

After a surge of revolutionary spirit in 1775, volunteer soldiers became scarce. States had to pay bounties or use a draft to recruit the needed men. At first, the militiamen remained under the control of their respective states. But Congress recognized the need for a centralized military command, and it created a Continental army with a single commander in chief: **George Washington**. An early advocate of independence with considerable military experience, Washington was admired, respected, and trusted by nearly all **American Patriots**, as supporters of independence came to be known. He took command of the new army in June 1775. With the aid of foreign military experts such as the Marquis de Lafayette from France and the Baron von Steuben from Prussia, he built a formidable force.

Though Britain successfully lured many slaves to join its side in exchange for freedom (including some owned by George Washington), several thousand black men fought alongside the colonists, particularly in New England and other parts of the North. Almost all southern states refused to allow slaves to serve, even when Congress offered them money in exchange.

(©Anne S.K. Brown Military Collection, Brown University Library)

REVOLUTIONARY SOLDIERS   Jean Baptist de Verger, a French officer serving in America during the Revolution, kept an illustrated journal of his experiences. Here he portrays four American soldiers carrying different kinds of arms: a black infantryman with a light rifle, a musketman, a rifleman, and an artilleryman.

THE WAR FOR INDEPENDENCE

As the War for Independence began, the British seemed to have overwhelming advantages: the greatest navy and the best-equipped army in the world, the resources of an empire, a coherent structure of command. Yet the United States had advantages, too. Beginning in 1777, Americans received substantial aid from abroad. They were fighting on their own ground. They were more committed to the conflict than the British, who made a series of early miscalculations. The transformation of the war—through three regions—made it a new kind of conflict that the imperial military, for all its strength, was unable to win.

NEW ENGLAND

For the first year of the conflict—from the spring of 1775 to the spring of 1776—many British authorities thought their forces were not fighting a real war, but simply quelling pockets of rebellion in the contentious area around Boston. After the redcoats withdrew from Lexington and Concord in April, American forces besieged them in Boston. In the Battle of Bunker Hill (actually fought on Breed's Hill) on June 17, 1775, the Patriots suffered severe casualties and withdrew. But they inflicted even greater losses on the enemy. The siege continued. Early in 1776, finally, the British decided that Boston was a poor place from which to fight. It was in the center of the most anti-British part of America and tactically difficult to defend because it was easily isolated and surrounded. And so, on March 17, 1776, the redcoats evacuated Boston for Halifax, Nova Scotia, with hundreds of **Loyalist**, or **Tory**, refugees (Americans still loyal to Britain and the king).

In the meantime, the Americans began an invasion of Canada. After General **Benedict Arnold** and Ethan Allen seized Fort Ticonderoga in May 1775, Arnold and General Richard

THE REVOLUTION IN THE NORTH, 1775–1776 After initial battles in and around Boston, the British forces left Massachusetts and (after a brief stay in Halifax, Canada) moved south to New York. In the meantime, American forces moved north in an effort to capture British strongholds in Montreal and Quebec, with little success. • *Why did the British consider New York a better base than Boston?*

Montgomery unsuccessfully threatened Quebec in late 1775 and early 1776 in a battle in which Montgomery was killed and Arnold was wounded.

By the spring of 1776, it had become clear to the British that the conflict was not just a local phenomenon. The American campaigns in Canada, along with new agitation in the mid-Atlantic colonies and the South and growing evidence of colonial unity, all suggested that Great Britain must prepare to fight a much larger conflict.

THE MID-ATLANTIC

During the next phase of the war, which lasted from 1776 until early 1778, the British were in a good position to win. Indeed, only a series of errors and misfortunes prevented them from crushing the rebellion.

The British regrouped quickly after their retreat from Boston. During the summer of 1776, hundreds of British ships and 32,000 British soldiers arrived in New York, under the command of General **William Howe**. He offered Congress a choice: surrender with royal pardon or face a battle against apparently overwhelming odds. To oppose Howe's great force, Washington could muster only about 19,000 soldiers and had no navy at all. Even so, the Americans rejected Howe's offer. The British then pushed the Patriot forces out of Manhattan and off Long Island and drove them in slow retreat over the plains of New Jersey, across the Delaware River, and into Pennsylvania.

The British settled down for the winter in northern and central New Jersey, with an outpost of Hessians at Trenton, on the Delaware River. But Washington did not sit still. On Christmas night 1776, he recrossed the icy Delaware River, surprised and scattered the

Hessians, and occupied Trenton. Then he advanced to Princeton and drove a force of redcoats from their base in the college there. But Washington was unable to hold either Princeton or Trenton and finally took refuge in the hills around Morristown. Still, the campaign of 1776 came to an end with the Americans having triumphed in two minor battles and with their main army still intact.

For the campaigns of 1777, the British devised a strategy to divide the colonies in two. Howe would move from New York up the Hudson to Albany, while another force would come down from Canada to meet him. **John Burgoyne**, commander of the northern force, began a two-pronged attack to the south along both the Mohawk and the upper Hudson approaches to Albany. But having set the plan in motion, Howe strangely abandoned his part of it. Instead of moving north to meet Burgoyne, he went south and captured Philadelphia, hoping that his seizure of the rebel capital would bring the war to a speedy conclusion. Philadelphia fell with little resistance, and the Continental Congress moved into exile in York, Pennsylvania. After launching an unsuccessful attack against the British on October 4 at Germantown (just outside Philadelphia), Washington went into winter quarters at Valley Forge.

Howe's move to Philadelphia left Burgoyne to carry out the campaign in the north alone. He sent Colonel Barry St. Leger up the St. Lawrence River toward Lake Ontario. Burgoyne himself advanced directly down the upper Hudson Valley and easily seized Fort Ticonderoga. But Burgoyne soon experienced two staggering defeats. In one of them—at Oriskany, New York, on August 6—Patriots and Oneidas held off a force of Mohawks, Senecas, Loyalists, and British (all those tribes had once been allied in the Iroquois Confederacy). That allowed Benedict Arnold to close off the Mohawk Valley to St. Leger's advance. In the other battle—at Bennington, Vermont, on August 16—New England militiamen mauled a detachment that Burgoyne had sent to seek supplies. Short of materials, with all help cut off, Burgoyne fought several costly engagements and then withdrew to **Saratoga**, where General Horatio Gates surrounded him. On October 17, 1777, Burgoyne surrendered.

The campaign in upstate New York was not just a British defeat. It signaled the splintering of the Iroquois Confederacy, which had declared its neutrality in 1776 but now saw members ally themselves with both sides. Among those joining the British were a Mohawk brother and sister, **Joseph and Mary Brant**. This ill-fated alliance further divided the already weakened Iroquois Confederacy, because only three of the Iroquois nations (the Mohawks, Senecas, and Cayugas) followed the Brants in support of the British. A year after the defeat at Oriskany, Iroquois forces joined British troops in a series of raids on white settlements in upstate New York.

In late 1779, Patriot forces under the command of General John Sullivan harshly retaliated, burning homes and towns, destroying crops, and leaving the land uninhabitable. The harsh winter that followed saw mass Iroquois starvation and disease. The Patriots wreaked such destruction on Indian settlements that large groups of Iroquois allied with the British fled north into Canada to seek refuge. Many never returned.

Meanwhile the fighting in the North settled into a stalemate. Sir Henry Clinton replaced the unsuccessful William Howe in May 1778 and moved what had been Howe's army from Philadelphia back to New York. The British troops stayed there for more than a year. In the meantime, George Rogers Clark led a Patriot expedition over the Appalachian Mountains and captured settlements in the Illinois country from the British and their Indian allies. On the whole, however, there was relatively little military activity in the North after 1778. There was, however, considerable intrigue. In the fall of 1780, American forces were shocked by the exposure of treason on the part of General Benedict Arnold. Convinced

THE REVOLUTION IN THE MIDDLE COLONIES, 1776-1778 These maps illustrate the major campaigns of the Revolution in the middle colonies—New York, New Jersey, and Pennsylvania—between 1776 and 1778. The large map on the left shows the two prongs of the British strategy: first, a movement of British forces south from Canada into the Hudson Valley and, second, a movement of other British forces, under General William Howe, out from New York. The strategy was designed to trap the American army between the two British movements. • *What movements of Howe helped thwart that plan?* The two smaller maps on the right show a detailed picture of some of the major battles. The upper one reveals the surprising American victory at Saratoga. The lower one shows a series of inconclusive battles between New York and Philadelphia in 1777 and 1778.

that the American cause was hopeless, Arnold conspired with British agents to betray the Patriot stronghold at West Point on the Hudson River. When the scheme was exposed and foiled, Arnold fled to the safety of the British camp, where he spent the rest of the war.

Securing Aid from Abroad

The leaders of the American effort knew that victory would not be likely without aid from abroad. Their most promising allies, they realized, were the French, who stood to gain from seeing Britain lose a crucial part of its empire. At first, France provided the United States with badly needed supplies. But France remained reluctant to formally acknowledge the new nation, despite the efforts of Benjamin Franklin in Paris to lobby for aid and diplomatic recognition. France's foreign minister, the Count de Vergennes, wanted evidence that the Americans had a real chance of winning. The British defeat at Saratoga, he believed, offered that evidence.

When the news from Saratoga arrived in London and Paris in early December 1777, a shaken Lord North made a new peace offer: complete home rule within the empire for Americans if they would quit the war. Vergennes feared the Americans might accept the offer and thus destroy France's opportunity to weaken Britain. Encouraged by Franklin, he agreed on February 6, 1778, to give formal recognition to the United States and to provide it with greatly expanded military assistance.

France's decision made the war an international conflict, which over the years pitted France, Spain, and the Netherlands against Great Britain. That helped reduce the resources available for the British effort in America. But France remained America's most important ally.

THE SOUTH

The American victory at Saratoga and the intervention of the French transformed the war. Instead of mounting a full-scale military struggle against the American army, the British now tried to enlist the support of those elements of the American population who were still loyal to the crown. Since Loyalist sentiment was strongest in the South, and since the British also enticed slaves to rally to their cause, the main focus of their effort shifted there. In the Carolinas in particular, something like a civil war between Loyalists and Patriots had already been brewing.

Late in 1775, colonials fought the British army at Kemp's Landing in Virginia. Three months later, on February 27, 1776, a band of southern Patriots crushed an uprising of Loyalists at Moore's Creek Bridge in North Carolina. The British tried and failed to take Charleston, South Carolina, in June 1776, but were more successful at a different port, Savannah, Georgia, on December 29, 1778. They captured Savannah despite the opposition of a contingent of Patriots, Frenchmen, and black soldiers from Saint-Domingue. British forces then spent three years (from 1778 to 1781) moving through the South, ultimately taking Charleston in May 1780, and then advancing into the interior.

But the British overestimated the extent of Loyalist sentiment, and underestimated the logistical problems they would face. Patriot forces could move at will throughout the region, blending in with the civilian population. Although the southern Continental army had been decimated by the loss of Charleston, the British faced constant harassment from such Patriots as Thomas Sumter, Andrew Pickens, and Francis Marion, the "Swamp Fox." British attempts to destabilize the South by offering refuge to slaves drew tens of thousands of escapees, but also had the effect of galvanizing white southern dedication to the Revolution. With neighbors fighting neighbors in the Carolina backcountry, both regular armies sent commanders to direct the action. **Lord Cornwallis** was named by Clinton to head British forces in the South, Horatio Gates of Saratoga fame to lead the Patriots. Penetrating to Camden, South Carolina, Cornwallis met and crushed a Patriot force under Gates on August 16, 1780. That October, at King's Mountain (near the North Carolina–South Carolina border), a band of Patriot riflemen from the backwoods killed, wounded, or captured every man in a force of 1,100 New York and South Carolina Loyalists upon whom Cornwallis had depended.

Congress recalled Gates, and Washington replaced him with Nathanael Greene, one of the ablest American generals of his time. Once Greene arrived, he confused and exasperated Cornwallis by dividing the American forces into fast-moving contingents while avoiding open, conventional battles. One of the contingents inflicted what Cornwallis admitted was "a very unexpected and severe blow" at Cowpens, near the border between the Carolinas, on January 17, 1781. Finally, after receiving reinforcements, Greene combined all his forces and maneuvered to meet the British at Guilford Court House, North Carolina. After a hard-fought battle there on March 15, 1781, Greene was driven from the field; but Cornwallis had lost so many men that he decided to abandon the Carolina campaign. Instead, he moved north, hoping to conduct raids in the interior of Virginia. But Clinton,

THE REVOLUTION IN THE SOUTH, 1778–1781 The final phase of the American Revolution occurred largely in the South, which the British thought would be a more receptive region for their troops. • *Why did they believe that?* This map reveals the many scattered military efforts of the British and the Americans in those years, none of them conclusive. It also shows the final chapter of the Revolution around Chesapeake Bay and the James River. • *What errors led the British to their surrender at Yorktown?*

fearful that the southern army might be destroyed, ordered him to take up a defensive position at **Yorktown**.

American and French forces quickly descended on Yorktown along with the battle-hardened, all-black First Rhode Island regiment. Washington and the Count de Rochambeau marched a French-American army from New York to join the Marquis de Lafayette in Virginia, while Admiral de Grasse took a French fleet with additional troops up Chesapeake Bay to the York River. These joint operations caught Cornwallis between land and sea. After a few shows of resistance, he surrendered on October 17, 1781, the First Rhode Island having taken part in a key assault on Redoubt 10 a few nights earlier. Two days later, as a military band played "The World Turned Upside Down," he surrendered his whole army of more than 7,000.

WINNING THE PEACE

Cornwallis's defeat provoked outcries in Britain against continuing the war. Lord North resigned as prime minister, Lord Shelburne emerged from the political wreckage to succeed

THE AGE OF REVOLUTIONS

The American Revolution was a result of tensions and conflicts between imperial Britain and its North American colonies. But it was also both a part, and a cause, of what historians have come to call an "age of revolutions," which spread through much of the Western world in the last decades of the eighteenth century and the first decades of the nineteenth.

The modern idea of revolution—the overturning of old systems and regimes and the creation of new ones—was to a large degree a product of the ideas of the Enlightenment. Among those ideas was the notion of popular sovereignty, articulated by, among others, the English philosopher John Locke. Locke argued that political authority did not derive from the divine right of kings or the inherited authority of aristocracies, but from the consent of the governed. A related Enlightenment idea was the concept of individual freedom, which challenged the traditional belief that governments had the right to prescribe the way people act, speak, and even think. Champions of individual freedom in the eighteenth century—among them the French philosopher Voltaire—advocated religious toleration and freedom of thought and expression. The Enlightenment also helped spread the idea of political and legal equality for all people—the end of special privileges for aristocrats and elites and the right of all citizens to participate in the formation of policies and laws. Jean-Jacques Rousseau, a Swiss-French theorist, helped define these new ideas of equality. Together, Enlightenment ideas formed the basis for challenges to existing social orders in many parts of the Western world, and eventually beyond it.

The American Revolution was the first of the Enlightenment-derived uprisings against established orders. It served as an inspiration to people in other lands who opposed unpopular regimes. In 1789, a little over a decade after the beginning of the American Revolution, dissenters rebelled in France—at first through a revolt by the national legislature against the king, and then through a series of increasingly radical challenges to established authority. The monarchy was abolished (and the king and queen publicly executed in 1793), the authority of the Catholic Church was challenged and greatly weakened, and at the peak of revolutionary chaos during the Jacobin period (1793–1794), over 40,000 suspected enemies of the revolution were executed and hundreds of thousands of others imprisoned. The radical phase of the revolution came to an end in 1799, when Napoleon Bonaparte, a young general, seized power and began to build a new French Empire. But France's *ancien regime* of king and aristocracy never wholly recovered.

Together, the French and American Revolutions helped inspire uprisings in many other parts of the Atlantic World, which in many ways sought to expand Enlightenment promises of liberty and equality to *all* people, not just property-holding whites. In 1791, a major slave revolt began in Saint-Domingue, or Haiti, the greatest sugar-producing colony in the world, and soon attracted over 100,000 rebels. The army of enslaved people defeated both the white settlers of the island and the French colonial armies sent to quell their rebellion, then British and Spanish forces attempting to claim the lucrative colony for themselves. Under the leadership of Toussaint-Louverture, they began to agitate for independence, which they obtained on January 1, 1804, a few months after Toussaint's death in a French prison.

The ideas of these revolutions spread next into Spanish and Portuguese colonies in the Americas, particularly among the so-called Creoles, people of European ancestry born in

(©Everett Historical/Shutterstock)

STORMING THE BASTILLE This illustration portrays the storming of the great Parisian fortress and prison, the Bastille, on July 14, 1789. The Bastille was a despised symbol of royal tyranny to many of the French because of the arbitrarily arrested and imprisoned people who were sent there. The July assault was designed to release the prisoners, but in fact the revolutionaries found only seven people in the vast fortress. Even so, the capture of the Bastille—which marked one of the first moments in which ordinary Frenchmen joined the Revolution— became one of the great moments in modern French history. The anniversary of the event, "Bastille Day," remains the French national holiday.

the Americas. In the late eighteenth century, they began to resist the continuing authority of colonial officials from Spain and Portugal and to demand a greater say in governing their own lands. When Napoleon's French armies invaded Spain and Portugal in 1807, they weakened the ability of the European regimes to sustain authority over their American colonies. In the years that followed, revolutions swept through much of Latin America. Mexico became an independent nation in 1821, and provinces of Central America that had once been part of Mexico (Guatemala, El Salvador, Honduras, Nicaragua, and Costa Rica) established their independence three years later. Simón Bolívar, modeling his efforts on those of George Washington, led a movement that helped inspire revolutionary campaigns in Venezuela, Ecuador, and Peru, all of which won their independence in the 1820s. At about the same time, Greek patriots, drawing from the examples of other revolutionary nations, launched a movement to win their independence from the Ottoman Empire, which finally succeeded in 1830.

The age of revolutions left many new, independent nations in its wake. It did not, however, succeed in establishing the ideals of popular sovereignty, individual freedom, and political equality in all the nations it affected. Slavery survived in the United States and in many areas of Latin America. New forms of aristocracy and even monarchy emerged in France, Mexico, Brazil, and elsewhere. Women—many of whom had hoped the revolutionary age would win them new rights—made few legal or political gains in this era. But the ideals that the revolutionary era introduced to the Western world continued to shape the histories of nations throughout the nineteenth century and beyond. •

UNDERSTAND, ANALYZE, & EVALUATE

1. How did the American Revolution influence the French Revolution, and how were other nations affected by it?
2. What was the significance of the revolution in Haiti?

him, and British emissaries appeared in France to talk informally with the American diplomats there: Benjamin Franklin, John Adams, and John Jay.

The Americans were under instructions to cooperate with France in their negotiations with Britain. But Vergennes insisted that France could not agree to any settlement with the British until its ally Spain had achieved its principal war aim: winning back Gibraltar from British control. There was no real prospect of that happening soon, and the Americans began to fear that the alliance with France might keep them at war indefinitely. As a result, the Americans began proceeding on their own, without informing Vergennes, and soon drew up a preliminary treaty with Great Britain, which was signed on November 30, 1782. Benjamin Franklin, in the meantime, skillfully pacified Vergennes and avoided an immediate rift in the French–American alliance.

The final treaty, signed September 3, 1783, was, on the whole, remarkably favorable to the United States. It provided a clear-cut recognition of independence and a large, though ambiguous, cession of territory to the new nation—from the southern boundary of Canada to the northern boundary of Florida and from the Atlantic to the Mississippi. The American people had good reason to celebrate as the last of the British occupation forces left New York. Dissenters around the world, too, found inspiration in news of the Revolution. (See "America in the World: The Age of Revolutions.")

WAR AND SOCIETY

Historians have long debated whether the American Revolution was a social as well as a political revolution, whether it was radical or conservative, whether it arose from economic or ideological agendas. But whatever the intention of those who launched and fought the war, the conflict implicated people from every corner of American society, and accelerated, as wars tend to do, certain kinds of social change, even if temporarily.

LOYALISTS AND RELIGIOUS GROUPS

Estimates differ as to how many Americans remained loyal to Britain during the Revolution, but it is clear that there were many—at least one-fifth (and some historians estimate as much as one-third) of the white population. Some were officeholders in the imperial government. Others were merchants whose trade was closely tied to the imperial system. Still others were people who lived in relative isolation and had simply retained their traditional loyalties. And there were those who, expecting the British to win the war, were currying favor with the anticipated victors. However they came to their positions, Loyalists held what had been the dominant and respected view until rather recently: that colonists should remain faithful to their sovereign.

Many of these Loyalists were hounded by Patriots in their communities and harassed by legislative and judicial actions. Up to 100,000 fled the country. Those who could afford it moved to Britain. Others moved to Canada, establishing the first English-speaking community in the French-speaking province of Quebec. Some returned to America after the war and gradually reentered the life of the nation.

The war weakened other groups as well. The Anglican Church, headed officially by the king and counting many Loyalist members, lost its status as the official religion of Virginia and Maryland. By the time the fighting ended, many Anglican parishes could no longer even afford clergymen. Also weakened were the Quakers, whose pacifism generated widespread derision.

Other Protestant denominations, however, grew stronger. Presbyterian, Congregational, and Baptist churches successfully tied themselves to the Patriot cause. Most American Catholics also supported the Patriots and won increased popularity as a result. Shortly after the peace treaty was signed, the Vatican provided the United States with its own hierarchy and, in 1789, its first bishop.

THE WAR AND SLAVERY

For some African Americans, the war meant freedom because the British enabled escaped slaves to leave the country as a way of disrupting the American war effort. The Dunmore Proclamation was aimed at slaves owned by Patriots, not Loyalists, but many enslaved peoples made no such distinction once they learned of the policy. In South Carolina, for example, nearly one-third of all slaves defected during the war. White southerners in Virginia and Maryland even permitted slaveowners to free—"manumit"—their slaves if they wished, and some southern churches flirted briefly with voicing objections to the system. But these trends, nor the revolutionary ideals of which they were parts, never seriously threatened slavery or white supremacy in the South.

In much of the North, the combination of revolutionary sentiment and evangelical Christian fervor helped spread antislavery ideology widely. But even there, white supremacy flourished, and qualifications to the laws limited the character or speed of emancipation, which tended to be either "absolute" or "gradual." Vermont seceded from New York in 1777 and became the first colony to abolish slavery outright (though it was technically an independent republic until admitted to the union in 1791). Soon New Hampshire and Massachusetts joined on the side of absolute emancipation. In Massachusetts, an enslaved woman named Mum Bett, servant to wealthy revolutionaries, heard talk of freedom and equality and understood her condition to violate such precepts. She successfully sued for her freedom in 1781, taking the name Elizabeth Freeman, and others followed suit, leading to abolition in that state in 1783. (Freeman's great-grandson was civil rights activist W. E. B. Du Bois, born in 1868.) Meanwhile Pennsylvania had become the first state to pass gradual emancipation in 1780, and Rhode Island and Connecticut followed suit in 1784. Gradual emancipation generally meant curtailing the importation of new slaves and granting freedom to those born in bondage after the passage of the laws. Current enslaved people tended to stay enslaved unless states passed full abolition—in the case of Pennsylvania, sixty-seven years later, in 1847.

At war's end, slavery was intact in New York and New Jersey, where the institution played a larger role in the economy than in New England. Both states passed gradual abolition in 1799 and 1804, respectively, but the New York law demonstrated the incomplete and cruel nature of such emancipation. The 1799 measure subjected children born after that date to indentured servitude until young adulthood. Then, the legislature decreed in 1817 that slaves born before 1799 would be freed—but not until 1827. Across the North, a significant though dwindling number of slaves could be found for several decades after the Revolution, and of course they remained in massive numbers in the South. At some point during the war, almost all states in both regions banned the transatlantic slave trade, but in many cases as part of a broader prohibition of commerce with Britain. It resumed after the war, and southern slaveowners succeeded in pushing back a national ban on the importation of slaves until 1808. But the heartbreaking, family-splitting internal traffic in enslaved peoples continued as long as bondage was legal.

Thus the Revolution exposed the continuing contradiction between the nation's commitment to liberty and its simultaneous commitment to slavery, with many colonists even using (without irony) the terminology of "enslavement" to characterize their subjugation by Britain. To people in our time, and even to some people in Revolutionary times like Mum Bett, liberty and slavery were incompatible. But to many white Americans in the eighteenth century, that did not seem obvious. Many white southerners and some northerners believed, in fact, that enslaving Africans—whom they considered inferior and unfit for citizenship— was the best way to ensure liberty for white people. They feared that without slaves, it would be necessary to recruit a servile white workforce in the South, and that the resulting inequalities would jeopardize the survival of liberty. Even men such as Washington and Jefferson, who had moral misgivings about slavery, struggled to envision any alternative to it. Washington, in fact, insisted his slaves be returned to him at war's end by the British, under whom they had served by the terms of Lord Dunmore's Proclamation of 1775, and Jefferson did little to manumit the hundreds of enslaved people in his possession. If slavery was abolished nationwide, these and other white Americans asked, what would happen to black people in America? Few whites, North or South, believed freed men and women could be integrated into American society as equals.

Native Americans and the Revolution

Indians viewed the American Revolution with considerable trepidation, sensing that the battle between white forces was essentially a battle over their own lands. Most tribes chose to stay out of the war, but those who fought did so for their own purposes, purposes in fact shared by the colonists: to secure freedom from encroachment and interference. But because Indians feared the Revolution would replace a somewhat trustworthy ruling group (the British, who had tried to limit the expansion of white settlement) with one they considered hostile to them (the Patriots, who had spearheaded the expansion), most Indians who chose sides joined the British cause. Thus despite their similar agendas, the colonists developed a searing resentment of indigenous groups during the Revolution. In the Declaration of Independence, Thomas Jefferson even counted the inflaming of "merciless Indian Savages" among the British king's crimes.

In the western Carolinas and Virginia, Cherokees led by Chief Dragging Canoe launched a series of attacks on outlying white settlements in the summer of 1776. Patriot militias responded in great force, ravaging Cherokee lands and forcing the chief and many of his followers to flee west across the Tennessee River. Those Cherokees who remained behind agreed to a new treaty by which they gave up still more land. Some Iroquois, despite the setbacks at Oriskany, continued to wage war against Americans in the West and caused widespread destruction in agricultural areas of New York and Pennsylvania. The retaliating American armies inflicted heavy losses on the Indians, but the attacks continued.

In the end, the Revolution generally weakened the position of Native Americans in several ways. The Patriot victory increased white demand for western lands. Many whites resented the assistance such nations as the Mohawk had given the British and insisted on treating them as a conquered people. Others drew from the Revolution a paternalistic view of the tribes. Jefferson, for example, despite his earlier venom, came to view the Indians as "noble savages," uncivilized in their present state but redeemable if they were willing to adapt to the norms of white society.

The triumph of the Patriots in the Revolution contributed to the ultimate defeat of the Indian tribes. To white Americans, independence meant, among other things, their right to move aggressively into the western lands, despite the opposition of the Indians. To the

Indians, American independence was "the greatest blow that could have been dealt us," one tribal leader warned.

Women's Rights and Roles

The long Revolutionary War had a profound effect on white American women. The departure of so many men to fight in the Patriot armies left women in charge of farms and businesses. Often, women handled these tasks with great success. But inflation, the unavailability of male labor, or the threat of enemy troops posed significant challenges. Some women whose husbands or fathers were called away to war did not have even a farm or shop to fall back on. Cities and towns had significant populations of impoverished women, who on occasion led protests against price increases, rioted, or looted food. At other times, women launched attacks on occupying British troops, whom they were required to house and feed at considerable expense.

Not all women stayed behind when the men went off to war. Some joined their male relatives in the camps of the Patriot armies. These female "camp followers" increased army morale and provided a ready source of volunteers to cook, launder, nurse, and do other necessary tasks. In the rough environment of the camps, traditional gender distinctions proved difficult to maintain. Considerable numbers of women became involved, at least intermittently, in combat. A few women even disguised themselves as men to be able to fight. The former indentured servant Deborah Sampson of Massachusetts refashioned herself as Robert Shurtleff and served as a scout and combatant in New York and at the final siege of Yorktown. Her sex was later discovered but the state of Massachusetts granted her an army pension.

The emphasis on liberty and the "rights of man" led some women to begin to question their own position in society. Abigail Adams wrote to her husband, John Adams, in 1776, "In the new code of laws which I suppose it will be necessary for you to make, I desire you would remember the ladies and be more generous and favorable to them than your ancestors." (See "Consider the Source: The Correspondence of Abigail Adams on Women's Rights.") Adams was simply calling for new protections against abusive and tyrannical men. A few women, however, went further. Judith Sargent Murray, one of the leading essayists of the late eighteenth century, wrote in 1779 that women's minds were as good as those of men and that girls as well as boys therefore deserved access to education.

But little changed as a result. Under English common law, an unmarried woman had some legal rights, but a married woman had virtually no rights at all. Everything she owned and everything she earned belonged to her husband. Because she had no property rights, she could not engage in any legal transactions on her own. She could not vote. She had no legal authority over her children. Nor could she initiate a divorce; that, too, was a right reserved almost exclusively for men. After the Revolution, it did become easier for women to obtain divorces in a few states. Otherwise, there were few advances and some setbacks— including the loss of widows' rights to regain their dowries from their husbands' estates. The Revolution, in other words, did not really challenge, but actually confirmed and strengthened, the patriarchal legal system.

Still, the Revolution did encourage people of both sexes to reevaluate the contribution of women to the family and society. As the new republic searched for a cultural identity for itself, it attributed a higher value to the role of women as mothers. The new nation was, many Americans liked to believe, producing a new kind of citizen, steeped in the principles of liberty. Mothers had a particularly important task, therefore, in instructing their children in the virtues that the republican citizenry now was expected to possess.

THE CORRESPONDENCE OF ABIGAIL ADAMS ON WOMEN'S RIGHTS (1776)

Between March and May 1776, Abigail Adams exchanged letters with her husband John on the matter of women's rights in revolutionary America. She was the daughter of a minister and read widely despite lacking a formal education. The couple kept up a regular correspondence on political and social issues of the day.

Abigail Adams to John Adams, March 31, 1776:

I long to hear that you have declared an independency. And, by the way, in the new code of laws which I suppose it will be necessary for you to make, I desire you would remember the ladies and be more generous and favorable to them than your ancestors. Do not put such unlimited power into the hands of the husbands. Remember, all men would be tyrants if they could. If particular care and attention is not paid to the [150] ladies, we are determined to foment a rebellion, and will not hold ourselves bound by any laws in which we have no voice or representation.

That your sex are naturally tyrannical is a truth so thoroughly established as to admit of no dispute; but such of you as wish to be happy willingly give up the harsh title of master for the more tender and endearing one of friend. Why, then, not put it out of the power of the vicious and the lawless to use us with cruelty and indignity with impunity? Men of sense in all ages abhor those customs which treat us only as the vassals of your sex; regard us then as beings placed by Providence under your protection, and in imitation of the Supreme Being make use of that power only for our happiness.

John Adams to Abigail Adams, April 14, 1776:

As to your extraordinary code of laws, I cannot but laugh. We have been told that our struggle has loosened the bonds of government everywhere; that children and apprentices were disobedient; that schools and colleges were grown turbulent; that Indians slighted their guardians, and negroes grew insolent to their masters. But your letter was the first intimation that another tribe, more numerous and powerful than all the rest, were grown discontented. This is rather too coarse a compliment, but you are so saucy, I won't blot it out. Depend upon it, we know better than to repeal our masculine systems. Although they are in full force, you know they are little more than theory. We dare not exert our power in its full latitude. We are obliged to go fair and softly, and, in practice, you know we are the subjects. We have only the name of masters, and rather than give up this, which would completely subject us to the despotism of the petticoat, I hope General Washington and all our brave heroes would fight; I am sure every good politician would plot, as long as he would against despotism, empire, monarchy, aristocracy, oligarchy, or ochlocracy.

Abigail Adams to John Adams, May 7, 1776:

I cannot say that I think you are very generous to the ladies; for, whilst you are proclaiming peace and good-will to men, emancipating all nations, you insist upon retaining an absolute power over wives. But you must remember that arbitrary power is like most other things which are very hard, very liable to be broken; and, notwithstanding all your wise laws and maxims, we have it in our power, not only to free ourselves, but to subdue our masters, and, without violence, throw both your natural and legal authority at our feet;—

"Charm by accepting, by submitting sway, Yet have our humor most when we obey."

1. What was Abigail Adams's opinion of men in power and what did she request of John Adams as they declared independence?
2. To what other social developments did John Adams compare his wife's

request? What did he mean by the "despotism of the petticoat" (a women's undergarment)?
3. What did Abigail Adams predict in her May 7 letter to John Adams? What do you think of her assessment of "arbitrary power"?

Source: Adams, John, Abigail Adams, and Charles Francis Adams, *Familiar Letters of John Adams and His Wife Abigail Adams During the Revolution*. Project Gutenberg, 1776.

THE WAR ECONOMY

The Revolution also produced important changes in the structure of the American economy. After more than a century of dependence on the British imperial system, American commerce suddenly found itself on its own. British ships no longer protected American vessels. In fact, they tried to drive them from the seas. British imperial ports were closed to American trade. But this disruption in traditional economic patterns strengthened the American economy in the long run. Enterprising merchants in New England and elsewhere began to develop new commercial networks in the Caribbean and South America. By the mid-1780s, American merchants were also developing an important trade with Asia.

When British imports to America were cut off, states desperately tried to stimulate domestic manufacturing. No great industrial expansion resulted, but there was a modest increase in production. Trade also increased substantially among the American states.

THE CREATION OF STATE GOVERNMENTS

At the same time as Americans were struggling to win their independence on the battlefield, they were also struggling to create new institutions of government to replace the British system they had repudiated.

THE PRINCIPLES OF REPUBLICANISM

If Americans agreed on nothing else, they agreed that their new governments would be republican. To them, **republicanism** meant a political system in which all power came from the people, rather than from some supreme authority like a king. The success of such a government depended on the character of its citizenry. If the population consisted of sturdy, independent property owners imbued with civic virtue, then the republic could survive. If it consisted of a few powerful aristocrats and a great mass of dependent workers, then it would be in danger. From the beginning, therefore, the ideal of the small freeholder (the independent landowner) was basic to American political ideology. Jefferson, the great champion of the independent **yeoman farmer**, once wrote: "Dependence begets subservience and venality, suffocates the germ of virtue, and prepares fit tools for the designs of ambition."

Another crucial part of republican ideology was the concept of equality. The Declaration of Independence had given voice to the idea in its most ringing phrase: "All men are created equal." This idea would provide a powerful rhetorical framework for claimants to the rights of American citizenship for generations to come.

But for now, those rights went to a limited population of Americans. The United States was not a nation in which all men were independent property holders, and those who were not found their citizenship rights circumscribed. From the beginning, there was a sizable dependent labor force, white and black. White women remained both politically and economically subordinate. Native Americans were systematically exploited and displaced. Nor was there ever full equality of opportunity. American society was more open and fluid than that of most European nations, but the condition of a person's birth was almost always a crucial determinant of success. As we have seen, even in northern states that abolished slavery, emancipation could be a slow process.

Important Revolutionary leaders, including John Adams, continued to defend a very narrow vision of citizenship and suffrage beyond the year 1776 and shuddered at the increasingly egalitarian calls for truly democratic government from the people of the young country. One day, he predicted with fear, "new claims will arise; women will demand a vote; lads from twelve to twenty-one will think their claims not closely attended to; and every man who has not a farthing will demand an equal voice with any other, in all acts of state."

The First State Constitutions

Two states—Connecticut and Rhode Island—already had governments that were republican in all but name. They simply deleted references to England and the king from their charters and adopted them as constitutions. The other eleven states, however, produced new documents.

The first and perhaps most basic decision was that the constitutions were to be written down, unlike Britain's unwritten constitution. The second decision was that the power of the executive, which Americans believed had grown too great in Britain, must be limited. Pennsylvania eliminated the executive altogether. Most other states inserted provisions limiting the power of governors over appointments, reducing or eliminating their right to veto bills, and preventing them from dismissing the legislature. Most important, every state forbade the governor or any other executive officer from holding a seat in the legislature, thus ensuring that, unlike in Britain, the executive and legislative branches of government would remain separate.

Even so, most new constitutions did not embrace direct popular rule. In Georgia and Pennsylvania, the legislature consisted of one popularly elected house. But in every other state, there were upper and lower chambers, and in most cases the upper chamber was designed to represent the "higher orders" of society. There were property requirements for voters—some modest, others substantial—in all states. All of this roughly mimicked the workings of Parliament in Great Britain.

Revising State Governments

By the late 1770s, Americans were growing concerned about the apparent instability of their new state governments. Many believed, once again, the problem was one of too much democracy. As a result, most of the states began to revise their constitutions to limit popular power. Massachusetts, which ratified its first constitution in 1780, became the first state to act on the new concerns.

Two changes in particular differentiated the Massachusetts and later constitutions from the earlier ones. The first was a change in the process of constitution writing itself. Most of the first documents had been written by state legislatures and thus could easily be amended (or violated) by them. Massachusetts created the constitutional convention: a special assembly of the people that would meet only for the purpose of writing the constitution.

The second change was a significant strengthening of the executive. The 1780 Massachusetts constitution made the governor one of the strongest in any state. He was to be elected directly by the people; he was to have a fixed salary (in other words, he would not be dependent on the legislature each year for his wages); he would have significant appointment powers and a veto over legislation. Other states followed. Those with weak or nonexistent upper houses strengthened or created them. Most increased the powers of the governor. Pennsylvania, which had no executive at all at first, now produced a strong one. By the late 1780s, almost every state had either revised its constitution or drawn up an entirely new one in an effort to produce greater stability in government.

Most Americans continued to believe that religion should play some role in government, but they did not wish to give special privileges to any particular denomination. The privileges that churches had once enjoyed were now largely stripped away. In 1786, Virginia enacted the Statute of Religious Liberty, written by Thomas Jefferson, which called for the separation of church and state. But in Massachusetts, state-sponsored religion and religious constitutional clauses survived well into the nineteenth century.

THE SEARCH FOR A NATIONAL GOVERNMENT

Americans were much quicker to agree on state institutions than they were on the structure of their national government. At first, most believed that the central government should remain relatively weak and that each state would be virtually a sovereign nation. It was in response to such ideas that the Articles of Confederation emerged.

THE CONFEDERATION

The Articles of Confederation, which the Continental Congress had adopted in 1777, provided for a national government much like the one already in place before independence. Congress remained the central—indeed the only—institution of national authority. Its powers expanded to give it authority to conduct wars and foreign relations and to appropriate, borrow, and issue money. But it did not have power to regulate trade, draft troops, or levy taxes directly on the people. For troops and taxes, it had to make formal requests of the state legislatures, which could—and often did—refuse them. There was no separate executive; the "president of the United States" was merely the presiding officer at the sessions of Congress. Each state had a single vote in Congress, and at least nine of the states had to approve any important measure. All thirteen state legislatures had to approve any amendment of the Articles.

During the process of ratifying the Articles of Confederation (which required approval by all thirteen states), broad disagreements over the plan became evident. The small states had insisted on equal state representation, but the larger states wanted representation based on population. The smaller states prevailed on that issue. More important, the states claiming western lands wished to keep them, but the rest of the states demanded that all such territory be turned over to the national government. New York and Virginia had to give up their western claims before the Articles were finally approved. They went into effect in 1781.

The Confederation, which existed from 1781 until 1789, was not a complete failure, but it was far from a success. It lacked adequate powers to deal with interstate issues or to enforce its will on the states.

DIPLOMATIC FAILURES

In the peace treaty of 1783, the British had promised to evacuate American territory, but British forces continued to occupy a string of frontier posts along the Great Lakes within the United States. Nor did the British honor their agreement to make restitution to slave-owners whose slaves had made their way to British lines. Disputes also erupted over the northeastern boundary of the new nation and over the border between the United States and Florida. Most American trade remained within the British Empire, and Americans wanted full access to British markets. The government in London, however, placed sharp restrictions on that access.

In 1784, Congress sent John Adams as minister to London to resolve these differences, but Adams made no headway with the British, who were never sure whether he represented a single nation or thirteen different ones. Throughout the 1780s, the British government refused even to send a diplomatic minister to the American capital.

Confederation diplomats agreed to a treaty with Spain in 1786. The Spanish accepted the American interpretation of the Florida boundary. In return, the Americans recognized the Spanish possessions in North America and accepted limits on the right of U.S. vessels to navigate the Mississippi for twenty years. But southern states, incensed at the idea of giving up their access to the Mississippi, blocked ratification.

THE CONFEDERATION AND THE NORTHWEST

The Confederation's most important accomplishment was its resolution of controversies involving the western lands. The Confederation had to find a way to include these areas in the political structure of the new nation.

The Ordinance of 1784, based on a proposal by Thomas Jefferson, divided the western territory into ten self-governing districts, each of which could petition Congress for statehood when its population equaled the number of free inhabitants of the smallest existing state. Then, in the Ordinance of 1785, Congress created a system for surveying and selling the western lands. The territory north of the Ohio River was to be surveyed and marked off into neat rectangular townships, each divided into thirty-six identical sections. In every township, four sections were to be reserved by the federal government for future use or sale (a policy that helped establish the idea of "public land"). The revenue from the sale of one of these federally reserved sections was to support creation of a public school.

The precise rectangular pattern imposed on the Northwest Territory—the grid—became a model for all subsequent land policies of the federal government and for many other planning decisions in states and localities. The grid also became characteristic of the layout of many American cities. It had many advantages. It eliminated the uncertainty about property borders that earlier, more informal land systems had produced. It sped the development of western lands by making land ownership simple and understandable. But it also encouraged a dispersed form of settlement—with each farm family separated from its neighbors—that made the formation of community more difficult. The 1785 Ordinance made a dramatic and indelible mark on the American landscape.

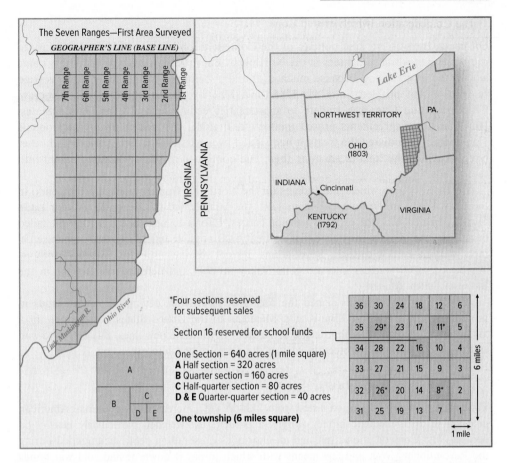

LAND SURVEY: ORDINANCE OF 1785 In the Ordinance of 1785, the Congress established a new system for surveying and selling western lands. These maps illustrate the way in which the lands were divided in an area of Ohio. Note the highly geometrical grid pattern that the ordinance imposed on these lands. Each of the squares in the map on the left was subdivided into 36 sections, as illustrated in the map at the lower right. • *Why was this grid pattern so appealing to the planners of the western lands?*

These ordinances proved highly favorable to land speculators and less so to ordinary settlers, many of whom could not afford the price of the land. Congress compounded the problem by selling much of the best land to the Ohio and Scioto Companies before making it available to anyone else. Criticism of these policies led to the passage in 1787 of another law governing western settlement—legislation that became known as the "**Northwest Ordinance.**" The 1787 Ordinance maintained the grid system, but it abandoned the ten districts established in 1784 and created a single Northwest Territory out of the lands north of the Ohio. The territory could be divided subsequently into three to five territories. It also specified a population of 60,000 as a minimum for statehood, guaranteed freedom of religion and the right to trial by jury to residents of the region, and prohibited slavery throughout the territory.

The western lands south of the Ohio River received less attention from Congress. The region that became Kentucky and Tennessee developed rapidly in the late 1770s as slaveowning territories, and in the 1780s began setting up governments and asking for statehood. The Confederation Congress was never able to resolve the conflicting claims in that region successfully.

INDIANS AND THE WESTERN LANDS

On paper, the western land policies of the Confederation brought order and stability to the process of white settlement in the Northwest. But in reality, order and stability came slowly and at great cost because much of the land belonged to Indians. Congress tried to resolve that problem in 1784, 1785, and 1786 by persuading Iroquois, Choctaw, Chickasaw, and Cherokee leaders to sign treaties ceding lands to the United States. However, those agreements proved ineffective. In 1786, the leadership of the Iroquois Confederacy repudiated the treaty it had signed two years earlier. Other tribes had never really accepted the treaties affecting them and continued to resist white movement into their lands.

Violence between whites and Indians on the Northwest frontier reached a crescendo in the early 1790s. In 1790 and again in 1791, the Miamis, led by the famed warrior Little Turtle, defeated U.S. forces in two major battles. Efforts to negotiate a settlement failed because of the Miamis' insistence that no treaty was possible unless it forbade white settlement west of the Ohio River. Negotiations did not resume until after General Anthony Wayne led 4,000 soldiers into the Ohio Valley in 1794 and defeated the Indians in the **Battle of Fallen Timbers.**

A year later, the Miamis signed the Treaty of Greenville, ceding substantial lands in present-day Ohio, Indiana, Illinois, and Michigan to the United States in exchange for a formal acknowledgment of their claim to territory beyond the new lines. But that hard-won assurance proved a frail protection against the pressure of white expansion.

DEBTS, TAXES, AND DANIEL SHAYS

The postwar depression, which lasted from 1784 to 1787, increased the perennial American problem of an inadequate money supply, a burden that weighed particularly heavily on debtors. The Confederation itself had an enormous outstanding debt, accumulated during the Revolutionary War, and few means with which to pay it down. It had sold war bonds that were now due to be repaid, it owed money to its soldiers, and it carried substantial debts abroad. But with no power to tax, it could request money only from the states, and it received only about one-sixth of the money it asked for. The fragile new nation was faced with the grim prospect of defaulting on its obligations.

This alarming possibility brought to prominence a group of leaders who would play a crucial role in the shaping of the republic for several decades. Robert Morris, the head of the Confederation's treasury, Alexander Hamilton, his young protégé, James Madison of Virginia, and others—all called for a "continental impost," a 5 percent duty on imported goods to be levied by Congress and used to fund the debt. Many Americans, however, feared that the impost plan would concentrate too much financial power in the hands of Morris and his allies in Philadelphia. Congress failed to approve the impost in 1781 and again in 1783.

The states had war debts, too, and they generally relied on increased taxation to pay them. But poor farmers, already burdened by debt, considered such policies unfair. They demanded that the state governments issue paper currency to increase the money supply and make it easier for them to meet their obligations. Resentment was especially high among farmers in New England, who felt that the states were squeezing them to enrich already wealthy bondholders in Boston and other towns. Elite merchants and their allies controlled the state legislatures implementing the taxes in places like Massachusetts, further exacerbating class conflict. Here, in microcosm, were some of the tensions that had concerned the revolutionary generation since 1776. In crafting a decentralized government and favoring the states, the framers of the Confederation made a weak Congress with debts and responsibilities but no way to meet them. When the states exercised their power to tax, it fell on common people to fund the public debt, a burden rather resembling ones of the colonial period. Farmers may have been technically "represented" in the legislatures, but elites still controlled them. Like before 1776, all of this might erupt into mob rule.

True to those fears, throughout the late 1780s, bands of distressed farmers rioted periodically in various parts of New England. Dissidents in the Connecticut Valley and the Berkshire Hills of Massachusetts rallied behind Daniel Shays, a former captain in the Continental army representing farmers already impoverished by the dislocations of the war. Shays issued a set of demands that included paper money, tax relief, a moratorium on debts, and the abolition of imprisonment for debt. During the summer of 1786, the Shaysites prevented the collection of debts, private or public, and used force to keep courts from convening and sheriffs from selling confiscated property. When winter came, the rebels advanced on Springfield, hoping to seize weapons from the arsenal there. In January 1787, an army of state militiamen set out from Boston, met Shays's band, and dispersed his ragged troops.

As a military enterprise, **Shays's Rebellion** was a failure, although it did produce some concessions to the aggrieved farmers. Shays and his lieutenants, at first sentenced to death, were later pardoned, and Massachusetts offered the protesters some tax relief and a postponement of debt payments. But the rebellion had important consequences for the future of the United States, for it added urgency to the movement to produce a new, national constitution.

(©Hi-Story/Alamy)

DANIEL SHAYS AND JOB SHATTUCK   Shays and Shattuck were the principal leaders of the 1786 uprising of poor Massachusetts farmers demanding relief from their indebtedness. Shattuck led an insurrection in the east, which collapsed when he was captured on November 30. Shays organized the rebellion in the west, which continued until it was finally dispersed by state militia in late February 1787. The following year, state authorities pardoned Shays; even before that, the legislature responded to the rebellion by providing some relief to the impoverished farmers. This drawing is part of a hostile account of the rebellion published in 1787 in a Boston almanac.

CONCLUSION

Between a small, inconclusive battle on a village green in New England in 1775 and a momentous surrender at Yorktown in 1781, the American people fought a great and terrible war against the mightiest military nation in the world. Few would have predicted in 1775 that the makeshift armies of the colonies could withstand the forces of the British Empire. But a combination of luck, determination, costly errors by the British, and timely aid from abroad allowed the Patriots, as they began to call themselves, to make full use of the advantages of fighting on their home soil and to frustrate British designs.

This historic military event also propelled the colonies to unite, to organize, and to declare their independence. Having done so, they fought with even greater determination, defending an actual, fledgling nation. By the end of the war, they had created new governments at both the state and national level and had begun experimenting with new political forms.

Yet although the Revolution hinged rhetorically on the notion of freedom from the British monarchy, many of its architects harbored a narrow vision of that concept when it came to the actual practices of governance and power. Many of them openly believed only the best minds and the economically independent should enjoy the rights of citizenship, and in their view, such standards limited those rights to white males and usually just ones with property. But in the republic's first days, the rhetoric of equality was already underwriting murmurings to expand the electorate, frightening some of the founders. And cracks were forming in the edifice of slavery, though it would be many generations before the institution would crumble.

Victory in the American Revolution thus solved many of the problems of the new nation, but it also produced others. What should the United States do about its relations with the Indians and with its neighbors to the north and south? What should it do about the distribution of western lands? What should it do about slavery? How should it balance its commitment to liberty with its need for order? These questions bedeviled the new national government in its first years of existence.

KEY TERMS/PEOPLE/PLACES/EVENTS

Abigail Adams 123
American Patriots 111
Articles of Confederation 111
Battle of Fallen Timbers 130
Benedict Arnold 112
Common Sense 110
Declaration of Independence 111

George Washington 111
Hessians 107
John Burgoyne 114
Joseph and Mary Brant 114
Lord Cornwallis 116
Lord Dunmore's Proclamation 107
Loyalists (Tories) 112
Northwest Ordinance 129
republicanism 125

Saratoga 114
Second Continental Congress 107
Shays's Rebellion 131
Thomas Jefferson 111
William Howe 113
yeoman farmers 125
Yorktown 117

RECALL AND REFLECT

1. What questions did the Second Continental Congress debate, and how did it address them?
2. What was the impact of Thomas Paine's *Common Sense* on Americans' view of the war with Britain?
3. What were the ideals of the new state and national governments, and how did those ideals compare with the realities of American society?
4. What was the purpose of the Articles of Confederation?

6 | THE CONSTITUTION AND THE NEW REPUBLIC

FRAMING A NEW GOVERNMENT
ADOPTION AND ADAPTATION
FEDERALISTS AND REPUBLICANS
ESTABLISHING NATIONAL SOVEREIGNTY
THE DOWNFALL OF THE FEDERALISTS

LOOKING AHEAD

1. What were the most important questions debated at the Constitutional Convention of 1787, and how were they resolved?
2. What were the main tenets of the Federalist and Antifederalist arguments on ratification of the Constitution?
3. What were the origins of America's "first party system"?

BY THE LATE 1780S, many Americans had grown dissatisfied with the Confederation. It was, they believed, ridden with factions, unable to deal effectively with economic problems, and frighteningly powerless in the face of Shays's Rebellion. A decade earlier, Americans had deliberately avoided creating a strong national government, fearing it would encroach on the sovereignty of the individual states. Now they reconsidered.

In the summer of 1787, delegates from every state except Rhode Island gathered in Philadelphia to produce a new governing document for the country. Behind closed doors, disagreements flared over how to represent the states in a new Congress, how to treat the matter of slavery, how to balance individual rights and the common good, and perhaps above all, how to share power between the federal government and the states and mitigate against dangerous aggregations of authority.

By September, the delegates had produced a new constitution that created a much more powerful government with three independent branches. The document then came in for intense debate while the states considered ratification. "Federalists" defended the Constitution and thought it properly checked the power of the masses; "Antifederalists" argued it gave too much power to the federal government and worried about the rights of citizens. In 1788, the last few states to decide voted to ratify, with assurances that amendments would be added to guarantee individual rights. But the adoption of the Constitution did not complete the creation of the republic, for although most people came to agree that the Constitution should guide American governance, they often disagreed on what that document meant.

FRAMING A NEW GOVERNMENT

The Confederation Congress had become so unpopular and ineffectual by the mid-1780s that it began to lead an almost waif-like existence. In 1783, its members timidly withdrew from Philadelphia to escape army veterans demanding their back pay. They took refuge for a while in Princeton, New Jersey, then moved on to Annapolis, Maryland, and in 1785 settled in New York. Delegates were often scarce. Only with great difficulty could Congress produce a quorum to ratify the treaty with Great Britain, ending the Revolutionary War.

ADVOCATES OF REFORM

In the 1780s, some of the wealthiest and most powerful groups in the population began to clamor for a stronger national government. By 1786, such demands had grown so intense that even defenders of the existing system reluctantly agreed that the government needed strengthening at its weakest point—its lack of power to tax.

The most effective advocate of a stronger national government was **Alexander Hamilton**, a successful New York lawyer and illegitimate son of a Scottish merchant in the West Indies. Hamilton now called for a national convention to overhaul the Articles of Confederation. He found an important

TIME LINE

1786
Annapolis Conference

1787
Constitutional Convention; Constitution adopted

1787-1788
States ratify Constitution

1789
Washington becomes first president
Bill of Rights
French Revolution
Judiciary Act

1791
First Bank of U.S. chartered

1792
Washington reelected

1794
Whiskey Rebellion
Jay's Treaty

1795
Pinckney's Treaty

1796
John Adams elected president

1797
XYZ Affair
Alien and Sedition Acts

1798-1799
Quasi war with France
Virginia and Kentucky Resolutions

1800
Jefferson elected president

ally in James Madison of Virginia, who persuaded the Virginia legislature to convene an interstate conference on commercial questions. Only five states sent delegates to the meeting, which took place at Annapolis in 1786, but the conference approved a proposal by Hamilton for a convention of special delegates from all the states to meet in Philadelphia the next year.

At first there seemed little reason to believe the Philadelphia convention would attract any more delegates than had the Annapolis meeting. Then, early in 1787, the news of Shays's Rebellion spread throughout the nation, alarming many previously apathetic leaders, including George Washington, who promptly made plans to travel to Philadelphia for the Constitutional Convention. Washington's support gave the meeting wide credibility.

A DIVIDED CONVENTION

Fifty-five men, representing all the states except Rhode Island, attended one or more sessions of the convention that sat in the Philadelphia State House from May to September 1787. These "Founding Fathers," as they became known much later, averaged forty-four years in age and were well educated by the standards of their time. Most were wealthy property owners, and many feared what one of them called the "turbulence and follies" of democracy. Yet all retained the revolutionary suspicion of concentrated power.

The convention unanimously chose Washington to preside over its sessions and then closed it to the public and press. It then ruled that each state delegation would have a single vote and that major decisions would require not unanimity, as they did in Congress, but a simple majority. Almost all the delegates agreed that the United States needed a stronger central government. But there agreement ended.

Virginia, the most populous state, sent a well-prepared delegation to Philadelphia led by James Madison, who had devised in some detail a plan for a new "national" government. The Virginia Plan shaped the agenda of the convention from the moment Edmund Randolph of Virginia opened the debate by proposing that "a national government ought to be established, consisting of a supreme Legislative, Executive, and Judiciary." Even that brief description outlined a government very different from the Confederation. But the delegates were so committed to fundamental reform that they approved the resolution after only brief debate.

There was less agreement about the details of Madison's **Virginia Plan**. It called for a national legislature of two houses, with states represented in both bodies in proportion to their population. Smaller states, quite predictably, raised immediate objections. William Paterson of New Jersey offered an alternative (the **New Jersey Plan**) that would retain the essence of the Confederation with its one-house legislature in which all states had equal representation. It would, however, give Congress expanded powers to tax and to regulate commerce. The convention rejected Paterson's proposal, but supporters of the Virginia Plan now realized they would have to make concessions to the smaller states. They agreed to permit members of the upper house (what became the Senate) to be elected by state legislatures, not the general voting public.

Many questions remained unresolved. Among the most important was the question of slavery. There was no serious discussion of abolishing slavery during the convention. But other issues were debated heatedly. Would slaves be counted as part of the population in determining representation in Congress? Or would they be considered property, not entitled to representation? Delegates from the states with large slave populations wanted to have it both ways. They argued that slaves should be considered persons in determining representation but as property if the new government levied taxes on the states on the basis of population. Representatives from states where slavery had disappeared or was expected to disappear argued the opposite, that slaves should be included in calculating taxation but not representation.

COMPROMISE

The delegates bickered for weeks. By the end of June, with both temperature and tempers rising, the convention seemed in danger of collapsing. Finally, on July 2, the convention created a "grand committee," comprised of one delegate from each state, which produced a proposal that became the basis of the "Great Compromise." It called for a two-house legislature. In the lower House of Representatives, the states would be represented on the basis of population. Each slave would be counted as three-fifths of a free person in determining the basis for both representation and direct taxation. In the upper Senate the states would be represented equally with two members apiece. On July 16, 1787, the convention voted to accept the compromise.

In the next few weeks, the convention agreed to another important compromise. To placate southern delegates, who feared the new government would interfere with slavery, the convention agreed to bar the new government from stopping the slave trade for twenty years.

Some significant issues remained unaddressed. The **Constitution** provided no definition of citizenship. Nor did it resolve the status of Native American tribes. Most important to many Americans was the absence of a list of individual rights, which would restrain the powers of the national government. Madison opposed the idea, arguing that specifying rights that were reserved to the people would, in effect, limit those rights. Others, however, feared that without such protections the national government might abuse its new authority.

THE CONSTITUTION OF 1787

Many people contributed to the creation of the American Constitution, but the most important person in the process was **James Madison**. Madison had devised the Virginia Plan, and he did most of the drafting of the Constitution itself. Madison's most important achievement, however, was in helping resolve two important philosophical questions: the question of sovereignty and the question of limiting power. (For historians' evolving views on the Constitution's purpose, see "Debating the Past: The Meaning of the Constitution.")

How could a national government exercise sovereignty concurrently with state governments? Where did ultimate sovereignty lie? The answer, Madison and his contemporaries decided, was that all power, at all levels of government, flowed ultimately from the people. Thus neither the federal government nor the state governments were truly sovereign. All of them derived their authority from below. The resolution of the problem of sovereignty made possible one of the distinctive features of the Constitution—its **federalism**, or division of powers between the national and state governments. The Constitution and the government it created were to be the "supreme law" of the land. At the same time, however, the Constitution left important powers in the hands of the states.

In addition to addressing the question of sovereignty, the writers of the Constitution resolved to spread authority over several centers of power. Drawing from the ideas of the French philosopher Baron de Montesquieu, the framers endeavored to prevent any single group, or tyrannical individual, from dominating the government. The Constitution provided for a **separation of powers** within the government, managed by a system of **checks and balances** among the legislative, executive, and judicial branches. The forces within the

THE MEANING OF THE CONSTITUTION

The Constitution of the United States inspired debate from the moment it was drafted. Some argue that the Constitution is a flexible document intended to evolve in response to society's evolution. Others counter that it has a fixed meaning, rooted in the "original intent" of the framers, and that to move beyond that is to deny its value.

Historians, too, disagree about why the Constitution was written and what it meant. To some scholars, the creation of the federal system was an effort to preserve the ideals of the Revolution and to create a strong national government capable of exercising real authority. To others, the Constitution was an effort to protect the economic interests of existing elites, even at the cost of betraying the principles of the Revolution. And to still others, the Constitution was designed to protect individual freedom and to limit the power of the federal government.

The first influential exponent of the heroic view of the Constitution as the culmination of the Revolution was John Fiske, whose book *The Critical Period of American History* (1888) painted a grim picture of political life under the Articles of Confederation. Many problems, including economic difficulties, the weakness and ineptitude of the national government, threats from abroad, interstate jealousies, and widespread lawlessness, beset the new nation. Fiske argued that only the timely adoption of the Constitution saved the young republic from disaster.

In *An Economic Interpretation of the Constitution of the United States* (1913), Charles A. Beard presented a powerful challenge to Fiske's view. According to Beard, the 1780s had been a "critical period" primarily for conservative business interests who feared that the decentralized political structure of

the republic imperiled their financial position. Such men, he claimed, wanted a government able to promote industry and trade, protect private property, and perhaps, most of all, make good the public debt—much of which was owed to them. The Constitution was, Beard claimed, "an economic document drawn with superb skill by men whose property interests were immediately at stake" and who won its ratification over the opposition of a majority of the people.

A series of powerful challenges to Beard's thesis emerged in the 1950s. The Constitution, many scholars now began to argue, was not an effort to preserve property but an enlightened effort to ensure stability and order. Robert E. Brown, for example, argued in 1956 that "absolutely no correlation" could be shown between the wealth of the delegates to the Constitutional Convention and their position on the Constitution. Examining the debate between the Federalists and the Antifederalists, Forrest McDonald, in *We the People* (1958), also concluded that there was no consistent relationship between wealth and property and support for the Constitution. Instead, opinion on the new system was far more likely to reflect local and regional interests. These challenges greatly weakened Beard's argument. Few historians any longer accept his thesis without reservation.

In the 1960s, scholars began again to revive an economic interpretation of the Constitution—one that differed from Beard's but nevertheless emphasized social and economic factors as motives for supporting the federal system. Jackson Turner Main argued in *The Anti-federalists* (1961) that supporters of the Constitution were "cosmopolitan commercialists," eager to advance the economic development of the nation; the

Antifederalists, by contrast, were "agrarian localists," fearful of centralization. Gordon Wood, in *The Creation of the American Republic* (1969), suggested that the debate over the state constitutions in the 1770s and 1780s reflected profound social divisions and that those same divisions helped shape the argument over the federal Constitution. The Federalists, Wood suggested, were largely traditional aristocrats who had become deeply concerned by the instability of life under the Articles of Confederation and were particularly alarmed by the decline in popular deference toward social elites. The creation of the Constitution was part of a larger search to create a legitimate political leadership based on the existing social hierarchy. It reflected the efforts of elites to contain what they considered the excesses of democracy.

More recently, historians have continued to examine the question of "intent." Did the framers intend a strong, centralized political system; or did they intend to create a decentralized system with a heavy emphasis on individual rights? The answer, according to Jack Rakove in *Original Meanings* (1996), and *Revolutionaries* (2010), is both—and many other things as well. The Constitution, he argues, was the result of a long and vigorous debate through which the views of many different groups found their way into the document. James Madison, generally known as the father of the Constitution, was a strong nationalist, as was Alexander Hamilton. They believed that only a powerful central government could preserve stability in a large nation, and they saw the Constitution as a way to protect order and property and defend the nation against the dangers of too much liberty. But if Madison and Hamilton feared too much liberty, they also feared too little. And that made them receptive to the demands of the Antifederalists for protections of individual rights, which culminated in the Bill of Rights. The very "middling sorts" who had exercised more and more power since 1776, scaring many conservative founders, also helped push for such citizen rights, Woody Holton argues in *Unruly Americans and the Origins of the Constitution* (2007).

(Source: National Archives and Records Administration)

The framers differed as well in their views of the proper relationship between the federal government and the state governments. Madison favored unquestioned federal supremacy, while many others, who wanted to preserve the rights of the states, saw in the federal system—and in its division of sovereignty among different levels and branches of government—a guarantee against too much national power. The Constitution is not, Rakove argues, "infinitely malleable." But neither does it have a fixed meaning that can be an inflexible guide to how we interpret it today. •

UNDERSTAND, ANALYZE, & EVALUATE

1. Is the Constitution a conservative, liberal, or radical document?
2. Did the framers consider the Constitution something "finished" (with the exception of constitutional amendments), or did they consider it a document that would evolve in response to changes in society over time?
3. Which parts of the Constitution suggest that the framers' intent was to create a strong, centralized political system? Which parts suggest that the framers' intent was to create a decentralized system with heavy emphasis on individual rights?

government would constantly check one another. Congress would have two chambers, each constraining the other, since both would have to agree before any law could be passed. The president would have the power to veto acts of Congress. The federal courts would be protected from both the executive and the legislature, because judges would serve for life.

The "federal" structure of the government was designed to protect the United States from the kind of despotism that Americans believed had emerged in Britain. Framers of the Constitution wanted a stronger central government, but one not *too* strong. Likewise, they wanted a government representative of and answerable to the popular will, but not *too* much so. Many of them harbored limited trust in the abilities of citizens to put the common good before their individual needs, and pointed to Shays's Rebellion as recent evidence of popular power run amok. Thus in the new government, only the members of the House of Representatives would be elected directly by the people. Senators would be chosen by state legislatures. The president would be chosen by an electoral college, with each state promoting electors to that body however it saw fit but equal to the total number of the state's members of Congress (Senate plus House). No requirement was written into the Constitution that these electors cast their ballots for president and vice president according to the popular will in their states, though that later became the accepted practice when states began recording a popular vote. Federal judges would be appointed by the president and confirmed by the Senate.

On September 17, 1787, thirty-nine delegates signed the Constitution. It was a document that established a democratic republic governed by white people, mostly white men. The framers did not explicitly define **citizenship**—the legal recognition of a person's inclusion in a body politic through the granting of rights and privileges—but common wisdom and jurisprudence held that birth in the United States and whiteness made one a citizen. Congress made this explicit for immigrants with the Naturalization Act of 1790, which helped legalize the stream of newcomers and allowed them to become citizens—provided they were "free white person[s]."

States were left to adjudicate the particulars of citizenship and suffrage rights, but in general they reserved that status for white people and those privileges for white male property owners. New Jersey allowed propertied white women to vote, but brought its suffrage laws into line with those of the other (male suffrage only) states in 1807. A few states would extend citizenship and suffrage rights to free blacks, and free blacks in South Carolina and North Carolina petitioned their state legislature and the U.S. Congress in 1791 and 1797, respectively, for some of the protections afforded white people by the Constitution. Both met rejection, and indeed, black citizenship at the state level was not the norm. They were not, one southern official noted, "constituent members of our society."

Thomas Jefferson worried about excluding "a whole race of men" from the natural rights he had done much to promote. But he could never accept the idea that black men and women could attain the level of knowledge and intelligence of white people, despite an intimate relationship with a black woman, Sally Hemings, who was enslaved on Jefferson's plantation in Virginia. He lived with her after the death of his wife and fathered several of her children, yet he did not change his position on slavery. Unlike George Washington, who freed his slaves after his death, Jefferson (deeply in debt) required his heirs to sell his slaves upon his death, after liberating the Hemings family.

Jefferson did profess to believe Native Americans could be taught the ways of "civilization," taught to live as white Americans did. And indigenous groups had at least the semblance of a legal status within the nation, through treaties that assured them of land possession. But most of these treaties did not survive for long, and native groups found themselves driven farther and farther west without very much of the protection the government had promised. Efforts to teach Anglo farming methods, whereby men did the farming and women cared for the home, clashed with Native American practices and traditions.

Thus indigenous groups, African Americans, and women enjoyed virtually none of the citizenship rights offered to the white population. It was not until 1868 that the Fourteenth Amendment guaranteed people of color born in the United States the status, if not yet the privileges, of citizenship. Indians were not granted birthright citizenship in the United States until the 1920s. And though some states passed woman suffrage laws in the late nineteenth century, it wasn't until 1920 that women secured ratification of the Nineteenth Amendment, giving them the ballot throughout the nation.

ADOPTION AND ADAPTATION

The delegates at Philadelphia had greatly exceeded their instructions from Congress and the states. Instead of making simple revisions in the Articles of Confederation, they had produced a plan for a completely different form of government. They feared that the Constitution would not be ratified under the rules of the Articles of Confederation, which required unanimous approval by the state legislatures. So the convention changed the rules, proposing that the new government would come into being when nine of the thirteen states ratified the Constitution and recommending that state conventions, not state legislatures, be called to ratify it.

FEDERALISTS AND ANTIFEDERALISTS

The Congress in New York accepted the convention's work and submitted it to the states for approval. All the state legislatures except Rhode Island elected delegates to ratifying conventions, most of which began meeting in early 1788. Even before the ratifying conventions convened, however, a great national debate on the new Constitution had begun.

Supporters of the Constitution had a number of advantages. Better organized than their opponents, they seized an appealing label for themselves: **Federalists**—a term that opponents of centralization had once used to describe themselves—thus implying that they were less committed to a "nationalist" government than in fact they were. In addition, the Federalists had the support of not only the two most eminent men in America, Ben Franklin and George Washington, but also the ablest political philosophers of their time: Alexander Hamilton, James Madison, and John Jay. Under the joint pseudonym *Publius*, these three men wrote a series of essays, widely published in newspapers throughout the nation, explaining the meaning and virtues of the Constitution. The essays were later gathered together and published as a book known today as ***The Federalist Papers***. In just one example, the papers defended the controversial "necessary and proper" clause of the Constitution, an important measure that gave Congress sweeping authority to make laws "necessary and proper" to executing the federal government's authority. The *states*, not Congress, had been given that sort of incidental power by the outgoing Articles of Confederation.

The Federalists called their critics "**Antifederalists**," suggesting that their rivals had nothing to offer except opposition. But the Antifederalists, too, led by such distinguished revolutionary leaders as Patrick Henry and Samuel Adams, had serious arguments. They were, they believed, the defenders of the true principles of the Revolution. They believed that the Constitution would increase taxes, weaken the states, wield dictatorial powers, favor the "well-born" over the common people, and abolish individual liberty. Antifederalists found the necessary and proper clause a particularly frightening transfer of powers not expressly "delegated" by the Constitution from the states to the federal government. But their biggest complaint was that the Constitution lacked a bill of rights. Only by enumerating the natural rights of the people, they argued, could there be any certainty that those rights would be protected.

Despite the efforts of the Antifederalists, ratification proceeded quickly during the winter of 1787–1788. The Delaware convention, the first to act, ratified the Constitution unanimously, as did the New Jersey and Georgia conventions. And in June 1788, New Hampshire, the critical ninth state, ratified the document. It was now theoretically possible for the Constitution to go into effect. But a new government could not hope to succeed without Virginia and New York, the largest states, whose conventions remained closely divided. By the end of June, first Virginia and then New York consented to the Constitution by narrow margins, and on the assumption that a bill of rights would be added in the form of amendments to the Constitution. North Carolina's convention adjourned without taking action, waiting to see what happened with the amendments. Rhode Island, controlled by staunch opponents of centralized government, did not even consider ratification.

COMPLETING THE STRUCTURE

The first elections under the Constitution were held in the early months of 1789. There was never any doubt about who would be the first president. George Washington had presided at the Constitutional Convention, and many who had favored ratification did so only because they expected him to preside over the new government as well. Washington received the votes of all the presidential electors. (**John Adams**, a leading Federalist, became vice

(Source: National Gallery of Art, Washington)

GEORGE WASHINGTON AT MOUNT VERNON Washington was in his first term as president in 1790 when an anonymous folk artist painted this view of his home at Mount Vernon, Virginia. Washington appears in uniform, along with members of his family, on the lawn. After he retired from office in 1797, Washington returned happily to his plantation and spent the two years before his death in 1799 "amusing myself in agricultural and rural pursuits." He also played host to an endless stream of visitors from throughout the country and Europe.

president.) After a journey from his estate at Mount Vernon, Virginia, marked by elaborate celebrations along the way, Washington was inaugurated in New York on April 30, 1789.

The first Congress served in many ways as a continuation of the Constitutional Convention. Its most important task was drafting a bill of rights. By early 1789, even Madison had come to agree that some sort of bill of rights would be essential to legitimize the new government. On September 25, 1789, Congress approved twelve amendments, ten of which were ratified by the states by the end of 1791. These first ten amendments to the Constitution comprise what we know as the **Bill of Rights**. Nine of them placed limitations on the new government by forbidding it to infringe on certain fundamental rights: freedom of religion, speech, and the press, immunity from arbitrary arrest, trial by jury, and others.

The Bill of Rights had very specific terms. Provisions for the judiciary branch were more vague. The Constitution said only: "The judicial power of the United States shall be vested in one Supreme Court, and in such inferior courts as the Congress may from time to time ordain and establish." It was left to Congress to determine the number of Supreme Court judges to be appointed and the kinds of lower courts to be organized. In the Judiciary Act of 1789, Congress provided for a Supreme Court of six members and a system of lower district courts and courts of appeal. It also gave the Supreme Court the power to make the final decision in cases involving the constitutionality of state laws.

The Constitution also said little about the organization of the executive branch. It referred indirectly to executive departments but did not specify which ones or how many there should be. The first Congress created three such departments—state, treasury, and war—and also established the offices of the attorney general and postmaster general. To the office of secretary of the treasury, Washington appointed Alexander Hamilton of New York. For secretary of war, he chose a Massachusetts Federalist, General Henry Knox. He named Edmund Randolph of Virginia as attorney general and chose another Virginian, Thomas Jefferson, for secretary of state.

FEDERALISTS AND REPUBLICANS

The framers of the Constitution had dealt with many controversies by papering them over with a series of vague compromises. As a result, the disagreements survived to plague the new government.

At the heart of the controversies of the 1790s was the same basic difference in philosophy that had fueled the debate over the Constitution. On one side stood a powerful group who envisioned America as a genuine nation-state, with centralized authority and a complex commercial economy. On the other side stood thinkers who envisioned a more modest national government. Rather than aspire to be a highly commercial or urban nation, it should remain predominantly rural and agrarian. The centralizers became known as the Federalists and gravitated to the leadership of Alexander Hamilton. Their opponents acquired the name **Republicans** and admired the views of Thomas Jefferson as well as James Madison, who grew skeptical of Federalist rule.

Hamilton and the Federalists

For twelve years, the Federalists retained firm control over the new government. That was in part because George Washington had always envisioned a strong national government. But the president, Washington believed, should stand above political controversies, and so he avoided personal involvement in the deliberations of Congress. As a result, the dominant figure in his administration became Alexander Hamilton. Of all the national leaders of his time, Hamilton was one of the most aristocratic in his political philosophy. He believed a stable and effective government required an elite ruling class. Thus the new government needed the support of the wealthy and powerful, and to get that, it needed to give elites a stake in its success.

Hamilton proposed, therefore, that the existing public debt be "funded." This meant that the various certificates of indebtedness that the old Congress had issued during and after the Revolution—many of them now in the possession of wealthy speculators—be called in and exchanged for interest-bearing bonds. He also recommended that the states' revolutionary debts be "assumed" (taken over) to cause state bondholders also to look to the central government for eventual payment. Hamilton wanted to create a permanent national debt, with new bonds being issued as old ones were paid off. He hoped to motivate the wealthy classes, who were the most likely to lend money to the government, to support perpetually the survival of that centralized state.

Hamilton also wanted to create a national bank. It would provide loans and currency to businesses, give the government a safe place for the deposit of federal funds, facilitate the collection of taxes and the disbursement of the government's expenditures, and provide a stable center to the nation's small and feeble banking system. The bank would be chartered by the federal government, but much of its capital would come from private investors.

The funding and assumption of debts would require new sources of revenue. Hamilton recommended two kinds of taxes to complement the receipts anticipated from the sales of public land. One was an excise tax on alcoholic beverages, a tax that would be most burdensome to the whiskey distillers of the backcountry, small farmers who converted part of their corn and rye crops into whiskey. The other was a tariff on imports, which Hamilton saw not only as a way to raise money but also as a way to protect domestic industries from foreign competition. In his famous "Report on Manufactures" of 1791, he outlined a plan for stimulating the growth of industry and spoke glowingly of the advantages to society of a healthy manufacturing sector.

The Federalists, in short, offered more than a vision of a stable new government. They offered a vision of the sort of nation America should become—a nation with a wealthy, enlightened ruling class, a vigorous, independent commercial economy, and a thriving manufacturing sector.

Enacting the Federalist Program

Few members of Congress objected to Hamilton's plan for funding the national debt, but many did oppose his proposal to exchange new bonds for old certificates of indebtedness on a dollar-for-dollar basis. Many of the original holders had been forced to sell during the hard times of the 1780s to speculators, who had bought them at a fraction of their face value. James Madison, now a House representative from Virginia, argued for a plan by which the new bonds would be divided between the original purchasers and the speculators. But Hamilton's allies insisted that the honor of the government required a literal fulfillment of its earlier promises to pay whoever held the bonds. Congress finally passed the funding bill Hamilton wanted.

Hamilton's proposal that the federal government assume the state debts encountered greater difficulty. Its opponents argued that if the federal government took over the state debts, the states with small debts would have to pay taxes to service the states with large ones. Massachusetts, for example, owed much more money than did Virginia. Only by striking a bargain with the Virginians were Hamilton and his supporters able to win passage of the assumption bill.

The deal involved the location of the national capital, which the Virginians wanted near them in the South. Hamilton and Jefferson met and agreed to exchange northern support for placing the capital in the South for Virginia's votes for the assumption bill. The bargain called for the construction of a new capital city on the banks of the Potomac River, which divided Maryland and Virginia, on land to be selected by George Washington.

Hamilton's bank bill produced the most heated debates. Madison, Jefferson, Randolph, and others argued that because the Constitution made no provision for a national bank, Congress had no authority to create one. But Congress agreed to Hamilton's bill despite these objections, and Washington signed it. The Bank of the United States began operations in 1791.

Hamilton also had his way with the excise tax, although protests from farmers later forced revisions to reduce the burden on smaller distillers. He failed to win passage of a tariff as highly protective as he had hoped for, but the tariff law of 1792 did raise the rates somewhat.

Once enacted, Hamilton's program won the support of manufacturers, creditors, and other influential segments of the population. But others found it less appealing. Small farmers complained they were being taxed excessively. They and others began to argue that the Federalist program served the interests of a small number of wealthy elites rather than the people at large. From these sentiments, an organized political opposition arose.

THE REPUBLICAN OPPOSITION

The Constitution made no reference to political parties. Most of the framers believed that organized parties were dangerous "factions" to be avoided. Disagreement was inevitable on particular issues, but they believed that such disagreements need not and should not lead to the formation of permanent factions.

Yet not many years had passed after the ratification of the Constitution before Madison and others became convinced that Hamilton and his followers had become dangerous and self-interested. The Federalists had used the powers of their offices to reward their supporters and win additional allies. They were doing many of the same things, their opponents believed, that the corrupt British governments of the early eighteenth century had done.

Because the Federalists appeared to their critics so menacing and tyrannical, there was no alternative but to organize a vigorous opposition. The result was the emergence of an alternative political organization, whose members ultimately called themselves "Democratic-Republicans" or just Republicans. (These first Republicans are not institutionally related to the modern Republican Party, which was created in the 1850s.) By the late 1790s, Republicans were going to even greater lengths than Federalists to create vehicles of partisan influence. In every state they formed committees, societies, and caucuses. Republican groups banded together to influence state and local elections. Neither side was willing to admit that it was acting as a party, nor would either concede the right of the other to exist. This institutionalized factionalism is known to historians as the "first party system."

From the beginning, the preeminent figures among the Republicans were Thomas Jefferson and James Madison. The most prominent spokesman for the cause, Jefferson promoted a vision of an agrarian republic in which most citizens would farm their own land. Jefferson did not scorn commercial or industrial activity. But he believed that the nation should be wary of too much urbanization and industrialization.

Although both parties had supporters across the country and among all classes, there were regional and economic differences. Federalists were most numerous in the commercial

(Source: National Gallery of Art, Washington)

THE JEFFERSONIAN IDYLL American artists in the early nineteenth century were drawn to tranquil rural scenes, symbolic of the Jeffersonian vision of a nation of small, independent farmers. By 1822, when Francis Alexander painted *Ralph Wheelock's Farm*, the simple agrarian republic was already being transformed by rapid economic growth.

centers of the Northeast and in such southern seaports as Charleston. Republicans were stronger in rural areas of the South and West. The difference in their philosophies was visible in, among other things, their reactions to the progress of the French Revolution. As that revolution grew increasingly radical in the 1790s, the Federalists expressed horror. But the Republicans applauded the democratic, anti-aristocratic spirit they believed the French Revolution embodied.

When the time came for the nation's second presidential election, in 1792, both Jefferson and Hamilton urged Washington to run for a second term. The president reluctantly agreed. But while Washington had the respect of both factions, he was, in reality, more in sympathy with the Federalists than with the Republicans.

ESTABLISHING NATIONAL SOVEREIGNTY

The Federalists consolidated their position by acting effectively in managing the western territories and diplomacy.

Securing the West

Despite the Northwest Ordinance, the old Congress had largely failed to tie the outlying western areas of the country firmly to the national government. Farmers in western Massachusetts had rebelled. Settlers in Vermont, Kentucky, and Tennessee had flirted with seceding from the Union. At first, the new government under the Constitution faced similar problems.

In 1794, farmers in western Pennsylvania raised a major challenge to federal authority when they refused to pay the new whiskey excise tax and began terrorizing tax collectors in the region. But the federal government did not leave settlement of the so-called **Whiskey Rebellion** to the authorities of Pennsylvania. At Hamilton's urging, Washington called out the militias of three states and assembled an army of nearly 15,000, and he personally led the troops into Pennsylvania. At the approach of the militiamen, the rebellion quickly collapsed.

The federal government won the allegiance of the whiskey rebels through intimidation. It secured the loyalties of other western people by accepting new states as members of the Union. The last two of the original thirteen colonies joined the Union once the Bill of Rights had been appended to the Constitution—North Carolina in 1789 and Rhode Island in 1790. Vermont became the fourteenth state in 1791, after New York and New Hampshire agreed to give up their rights to it. Next came Kentucky, in 1792, when Virginia relinquished its claim to that region. After North Carolina ceded its western lands to the Union, Tennessee became a state in 1796.

The new government faced a greater challenge in more distant areas of the Northwest and the Southwest. The ordinances of 1784–1787, establishing the terms of white settlement in the West, had produced a series of border conflicts with indigenous peoples. The new government inherited these tensions, which continued with few interruptions for nearly a decade.

Such clashes revealed another issue the Constitution had done little to resolve: the place of Native Americans within the new federal structure. The Constitution gave Congress power to "regulate Commerce . . . with the Indian tribes." And it bound the new government to respect treaty agreements negotiated by the Confederation, most of which had been struck with tribal representatives. But none of this did very much to clarify the precise legal standing of Indians within the United States. The tribes received no direct representation in the new government. Above all, the Constitution did not address the major issue of land. Native Americans lived within the boundaries of the United States, yet they claimed (and the white government at times agreed) that they had some measure of sovereignty over their own land. But neither the Constitution nor common law offered any clear guide to the rights of a "nation within a nation" or to the precise nature of indigenous sovereignty.

Maintaining Neutrality

A crisis in Anglo-American relations emerged in 1793, when the revolutionary French government went to war with Great Britain. Both the president and Congress took steps to establish American neutrality in the conflict, but that neutrality was severely tested.

Early in 1794, the Royal Navy began seizing hundreds of American ships engaged in trade in the French West Indies. Hamilton was deeply concerned. War would mean an end to imports from Britain, and most of the revenue for maintaining his financial system came from duties on those imports. Hamilton and the Federalists did not trust the State Department, now in the hands of the ardently pro-French Edmund Randolph, to find a solution to the crisis. So they persuaded Washington to name a special commissioner—the chief justice of the Supreme Court, John Jay—to go to England and negotiate a solution. Jay was instructed to secure compensation for the recent British assaults on American shipping, to demand withdrawal of British forces from their posts on the frontier of the United States, and to negotiate a commercial treaty with Britain.

The long and complex treaty Jay negotiated in 1794 failed to achieve all these goals. But it settled the conflict with Britain, avoiding a likely war. It provided for undisputed American sovereignty over the entire Northwest and produced a reasonably satisfactory

CONSIDER THE SOURCE

WASHINGTON'S FAREWELL ADDRESS, *AMERICAN DAILY ADVERTISER*, SEPTEMBER 19, 1796

In this open letter to the American people, drafted by James Madison in 1792 and later revised with the aid of Alexander Hamilton, President Washington defended the young Constitution and warned against disunity among the nation's various states and political factions. Here he cautions citizens about another threat to the republic—entangling engagements abroad.

Observe good faith and justice toward all nations. Cultivate peace and harmony with all. Religion and morality enjoin this conduct. And can it be that good policy does not equally enjoin it? It will be worthy of a free, enlightened, and, at no distant period, a great nation to give to mankind the magnanimous and too novel example of a people always guided by an exalted justice and benevolence. . . .

In the execution of such a plan nothing is more essential than that permanent, inveterate antipathies against particular nations and passionate attachments for others should be excluded, and that, in place of them just and amicable feelings toward all should be cultivated. The nation which indulges toward another an habitual hatred or an habitual fondness is in some degree a slave. It is a slave to its animosity or to its affection either of which is sufficient to lead it astray from its duty and its interest. The nation prompted by ill will and resentment sometimes impels to war the government, contrary to the best calculations of policy. The government sometimes participates in the national propensity, and adopts through passion what reason would reject. . . .

So, likewise, a passionate attachment of one nation for another produces a variety of evils. Sympathy for the favorite nation, facilitating the illusion of an imaginary common interest in cases where no real common interest exists, and infusing into one the enmities of the other, betrays the former into a participation in the quarrels and wars of the latter without adequate inducement or justification. . . .

As avenues to foreign influence in innumerable ways, such attachments are particularly alarming to the truly enlightened and independent patriot. How many opportunities do they afford to tamper with domestic factions to practice the arts of seduction, to mislead public opinion, to influence or awe the public councils! Such an attachment of a small or weak toward a great and powerful nation dooms the former to be the satellite of the latter.

Against the insidious wiles of foreign influence (I conjure you to believe me, fellow citizens) the jealousy of a free people ought to be constantly awake, since history and experience prove that foreign influence is one of the most baneful foes of republican government. . . .

The great rule of conduct for us in regard to foreign nations is, in extending our commercial relation to have with them as little political connection as possible. So far as we have already formed engagements, let them be fulfilled with perfect good faith. Here let us stop.

Europe has a set of primary interests which to us have no, or a very remote, relation. Hence she must be engaged in frequent controversies, the causes of which are essentially foreign to our concerns. Hence, therefore, it must be unwise in us to implicate ourselves by artificial ties in the ordinary vicissitudes of her politics, or the ordinary combinations and collisions of her friendships or enmities.

Our detached and distant situation invites and enables us to pursue a different course. If we remain one people, under an efficient government, the period is not far off when we may defy material injury from external annoyance; when we may take such an attitude as will cause the neutrality we may at any time resolve upon to be scrupulously respected; when belligerent nations, under the impossibility of making acquisitions upon us, will not lightly hazard giving us provocation; when we may choose peace or war, as our interest, guided by justice, shall counsel.

Why forego the advantages of so peculiar a situation? Why quit our own to stand upon foreign ground? Why, by interweaving our destiny with that of any part of Europe, entangle our peace and prosperity in the toils of European ambition, rivalship, interest, humor, or caprice?

It is our true policy to steer clear of permanent alliances with any portion of the foreign world, so far, I mean, as we are now at liberty to do it. For let me not be understood as capable of patronizing infidelity to existing engagements. I hold the maxim of less applicable to public than to private affairs that honesty is always the best policy. I repeat therefore, let those engagements be observed in their genuine sense. But in my opinion it is unnecessary and would be unwise to extend them.

Taking care always to keep ourselves by suitable establishments on a respectable defensive posture, we may safely trust to temporary alliances for extraordinary emergencies.

Harmony, liberal intercourse with all nations, are recommended by policy, humanity, and interest. But even our commercial policy should hold an equal and impartial hand, neither seeking nor granting exclusive favors or preferences; . . . constantly keeping in view that it is folly in one nation to look for disinterested favors from another; that it must pay with a portion of its independence for whatever it may accept under that character; that by such acceptance it may place itself in the condition of having given equivalents for nominal favors, and yet of being reproached with ingratitude for not giving more. There can be no greater error than to expect or calculate upon real favors from nation to nation. It is an illusion which experience must cure, which a just pride ought to discard.

UNDERSTAND, ANALYZE, & EVALUATE

1. What advice did George Washington offer on foreign policy?
2. Did Washington advocate the complete isolation of the United States from Europe? Explain.
3. How did Washington characterize Europe? What circumstances of the 1790s may have inspired this assessment?

Source: www.senate.gov/artandhistory/history/minute/Washingtons_Farewell_Address.htm.

commercial relationship. Nevertheless, when the terms became known in America, criticism was intense. Opponents of the treaty—Jeffersonian Republicans fearful that economic ties to Britain would fund and strengthen the Federalist agenda—went to great lengths to defeat it. But in the end the Senate ratified what was by then known as **Jay's Treaty**.

Jay's Treaty paved the way for a settlement of important American disputes with Spain. Under **Pinckney's Treaty** (negotiated by Thomas Pinckney and signed in 1795), Spain recognized the right of Americans to navigate the Mississippi to its mouth and to deposit goods at New Orleans for reloading on oceangoing ships; agreed to fix the northern boundary of Florida along the 31st parallel; and commanded its authorities to prevent Native Americans in Florida from launching raids north across that border. (For President Washington's views on such matters of foreign policy, see "Consider the Source: Washington's Farewell Address.")

THE DOWNFALL OF THE FEDERALISTS

Since almost everyone in the 1790s agreed there was no place in a stable republic for organized parties, the emergence of the Republicans as a powerful and apparently permanent opposition seemed to Federalists a grave threat to national stability. And so when international perils confronted the government in the 1790s, Hamilton and his followers moved forcefully against what they considered illegitimate dissent.

THE ELECTION OF 1796

George Washington refused to run for a third term as president in 1796. Jefferson was the obvious presidential candidate of the Republicans that year, but the Federalists faced a more difficult choice. Hamilton had created too many enemies to be a credible candidate. Vice President John Adams, who was not directly associated with any of the controversial Federalist achievements, received the party's nomination for president at a caucus of Federalists in Congress.

The Federalists were still clearly the dominant party. But without Washington to mediate, they fell victim to fierce factional rivalries. Adams defeated Jefferson by only three electoral votes and assumed the presidency as head of a divided party facing a powerful opposition. Jefferson became vice president by finishing second. (Not until the adoption of the Twelfth Amendment in 1804 did electors vote separately for president and vice president.)

THE QUASI WAR WITH FRANCE

American relations with Great Britain and Spain improved as a result of Jay's and Pinckney's treaties. But the nation's relations with revolutionary France quickly deteriorated. French vessels captured American ships on the high seas. The French government refused to receive Charles Cotesworth Pinckney when he arrived in Paris as the new American minister. In an effort to stabilize relations, Adams appointed a bipartisan commission to negotiate with France. When the Americans arrived in Paris in 1797, three agents of the French foreign minister, Prince Talleyrand, demanded a loan for France and a bribe for French officials before any negotiations could begin. Pinckney, a member of the commission, responded, "No! No! Not a sixpence!"

Even when Adams heard of the failure of diplomacy, he remained reluctant to go to war. Under pressure from Congress, including Federalists eager to fight the French, he sent that body the commissioners' report, though not before deleting the names of the three French agents and designated them only as Messrs. X, Y, and Z. When the report was published, the "**XYZ Affair**," as it quickly became known, provoked widespread popular outrage at France's actions and strong popular support for the Federalists' response. For nearly two years, 1798 and 1799, the United States found itself engaged in a **quasi war** with France.

Adams never asked for a declaration of war, but Congress passed measures cutting off all trade with France, nullifying the Treaty of Alliance of 1778, authorizing American vessels to capture French armed ships, and creating the Department of the Navy. The new maritime force soon won a number of battles and captured a total of eighty-five French ships. The United States also began cooperating closely with the British. At last, the French began trying to conciliate the United States. Adams sent another commission to Paris in 1800, and the new French government (headed now by "First Consul" Napoleon Bonaparte) agreed to a treaty with the United States that canceled the old agreements of 1778 and established new commercial arrangements. As a result, the "war" came to a reasonably peaceful end.

REPRESSION AND PROTEST

The conflict with France helped the Federalists increase their majorities in Congress in 1798. They now began to consider ways to silence the Republican opposition. The result was some of the most controversial legislation in American history: the **Alien and Sedition Acts**.

The Alien Act placed new obstacles in the way of foreigners who wished to become American citizens. The Sedition Act allowed the government to prosecute those who engaged in "sedition" against the government. In theory, only libelous or treasonous activities were subject to prosecution, but since such activities had no clear definition, the law, in effect, gave the government authority to stifle virtually any opposition. The Republicans interpreted the new laws as part of a Federalist campaign to destroy them.

President Adams signed the new laws but was cautious in implementing them. He did not deport any aliens, and he prevented the government from launching a broad crusade against the Republicans. But the Alien Act discouraged immigration and encouraged some foreigners already in the country to leave. And the administration used the Sedition Act to arrest and convict ten men, most of them Republican newspaper editors whose only crime had been criticism of Federalists in government.

Republican leaders contemplated ways to reverse the Alien and Sedition Acts. Some looked to the state legislatures for help. They developed a theory to justify action by the

(Source: Library of Congress, Prints and Photographs Division [LC-DIG-ppmsca-31832])

CONGRESSIONAL BRAWLERS, 1798 This cartoon was inspired by the celebrated fight on the floor of the House of Representatives between Matthew Lyon, a Republican representative from Vermont, and Roger Griswold, a Federalist from Connecticut. Griswold (at right) attacks Lyon with his cane, and Lyon retaliates with fire tongs. Other members of Congress are portrayed enjoying the battle.

states against the federal government in two sets of resolutions of 1798–1799, one written (anonymously) by Jefferson and adopted by the Kentucky legislature, and the other drafted by Madison and approved by the Virginia legislature. The **Virginia and Kentucky Resolutions**, as they were known, relied on the ideas of John Locke and the Tenth Amendment to the Constitution, which gave to the states powers not explicitly granted to the federal government. They argued that the federal government had been formed by a "compact," or contract, among the states and possessed only certain delegated powers. Whenever a state decided that the central government had exceeded those powers, it had the right to "nullify" the appropriate laws.

The Republicans did not win wide support for the nullification idea. They did, however, succeed in elevating their dispute with the Federalists to the level of a national crisis. By the late 1790s, the entire nation was deeply and bitterly politicized. State legislatures at times resembled battlegrounds. Even the U.S. Congress was plagued with violent disagreements. In one celebrated incident in the chamber of the House of Representatives, Matthew Lyon, a Republican from Vermont, responded to an insult from Roger Griswold, a Federalist from Connecticut, by spitting in Griswold's eye. Griswold attacked Lyon with his cane, Lyon fought back with a pair of fire tongs, and soon the two men were wrestling on the floor.

The "Revolution" of 1800

These bitter controversies shaped the presidential election of 1800. The presidential candidates were the same as four years earlier: Adams for the Federalists, Jefferson for the Republicans. But the campaign of 1800 was very different from the one preceding it. Adams and Jefferson themselves displayed reasonable dignity, but their supporters showed no such restraint. The Federalists accused Jefferson of being a dangerous radical whose followers were wild men who, if they should come to power, would bring on a reign of terror comparable to that of the French Revolution. The Republicans portrayed Adams as a tyrant conspiring to become king, and they accused the Federalists of plotting to impose slavery on the people. The election was close, and the crucial contest was in New York. There, Aaron Burr mobilized an organization of Revolutionary War veterans, the Tammany Society, to serve as a Republican political machine. Through Tammany's efforts, the party carried the city by a large majority, and with it the state. Jefferson, it seemed, had won.

But an unexpected complication soon jeopardized the Republican victory. The Constitution called for each elector to "vote by ballot for two persons." The expectation was that an elector would cast one vote for his party's presidential candidate and the other for his party's vice presidential candidate. To avoid a tie, the Republicans had intended that one elector would refrain from voting for the party's vice presidential candidate, Aaron Burr. But when the votes were counted, Jefferson and Burr each had 73. No candidate had a majority, and the House of Representatives had to choose between the two top candidates, Jefferson and Burr. Each state delegation would cast a single vote.

The new Congress, elected in 1800 with a Republican majority, was not to convene until after the inauguration of the president, so it was the Federalist Congress that had to decide the question. After a long deadlock, several leading Federalists concluded, following Hamilton's advice, that Burr was too unreliable to trust with the presidency. On the thirty-sixth ballot, Jefferson was elected.

After the election of 1800, the only branch of the federal government left in Federalist hands was the judiciary. The Adams administration spent its last months in office taking steps to make the party's hold on the courts secure. With the Judiciary Act of 1801, the Federalists reduced the number of Supreme Court justiceships by one but greatly increased the number of federal judgeships as a whole. Adams quickly appointed Federalists to the newly created positions. He also appointed a leading Federalist, John Marshall, to be chief justice of the Supreme Court, a position Marshall held for thirty-four years. Indeed, there were charges that he stayed up until midnight on his last day in office to finish signing the new judges' commissions. These officeholders became known as the "midnight appointments."

Even so, the Republicans viewed their victory as almost complete. The nation had, they believed, been saved from tyranny. The exuberance with which the victors viewed the future—and the importance they ascribed to the defeat of the Federalists—was evident in the phrase Jefferson himself later used to describe his election. He called it the "**Revolution of 1800.**"

CONCLUSION

The Constitution of 1787 created a federal system of dispersed authority, divided among national and state governments and among an executive, a legislature, and a judiciary. The young nation thus sought to balance its need for an effective central government against its fear of concentrated and despotic power. The ability of the delegates to the Constitutional Convention to compromise revealed their yearning for a stable political system. The same willingness to compromise allowed the greatest challenge to the ideals of the new democracy—slavery—to survive intact.

The writing and ratifying of the Constitution settled some questions about the shape of the new nation. The first twelve years under the government created by the Constitution solved others. And yet by the year 1800, a basic disagreement about the future of the nation remained unresolved and was creating bitter divisions and conflicts on the political scene. The election of Thomas Jefferson to the presidency that year opened a new chapter in the nation's public history. It also brought to a close, at least temporarily, savage political conflicts that had seemed to threaten the nation's future.

KEY TERMS/PEOPLE/PLACES/EVENTS

Alexander Hamilton 135
Alien and Sedition Acts 151
Antifederalists 141
Bill of Rights 143
checks and balances 137
citizenship 140
Constitution 137
federalism 137

Federalists 141
James Madison 137
Jay's Treaty 149
John Adams 142
New Jersey Plan 136
Pinckney's Treaty 149
quasi war 150
Republicans 143

Revolution of 1800 153
separation of powers 137
The Federalist Papers 141
Virginia and Kentucky
  Resolutions 152
Virginia Plan 136
Whiskey Rebellion 147
XYZ Affair 150

RECALL AND REFLECT

1. How did the Constitution of 1787 attempt to resolve the weaknesses of the Articles of Confederation?
2. What role did *The Federalist Papers* play in the battle over ratification of the Constitution?
3. What were the main tenets of Alexander Hamilton's financial program?
4. What diplomatic crises did the United States face in the first decade of its existence, and how did the new government respond to these crises?
5. What was the "Revolution of 1800" and in what way was it a revolution?

7 | THE JEFFERSONIAN ERA

THE RISE OF CULTURAL NATIONALISM

STIRRINGS OF INDUSTRIALISM

JEFFERSON THE PRESIDENT

DOUBLING THE NATIONAL DOMAIN

EXPANSION AND WAR

THE WAR OF 1812

LOOKING AHEAD

1. How successful was Jefferson's effort to create a "republican" society dominated by sturdy, independent farmers?
2. How did the Napoleonic Wars affect the United States?
3. What events and issues led to the War of 1812?

THOMAS JEFFERSON AND HIS FOLLOWERS assumed control of the national government in 1801 as the champions of a distinctive vision of America. They favored a society of sturdy, independent farmers, happily free from the workshops, industrial towns, and urban mobs of Europe. They celebrated localism and simplicity. Above all, they proposed a federal government of sharply limited power.

Almost nothing worked out as they had planned, for during the Republican years in power the young republic was developing in ways that made much of their vision obsolete. The American economy became steadily more diversified and complex, making the ideal of a simple, agrarian society impossible to maintain. American cultural life was dominated by a vigorous and ambitious nationalism. Jefferson himself contributed to the changes by exercising strong national authority at times and by arranging the greatest single increase in the size of the United States in its history.

THE RISE OF CULTURAL NATIONALISM

In many respects, American cultural life in the early nineteenth century reflected the Republican vision of the nation's future. Opportunities for education increased, the nation's literary and artistic life began to free itself from European influences, and American religion began to adjust to the spread of Enlightenment rationalism. In other ways, however, the new culture was posing a serious challenge to Republican ideals.

EDUCATIONAL AND LITERARY NATIONALISM

Central to the Republican vision of America was the concept of a virtuous and enlightened citizenry. Republicans believed, therefore, in the creation of a nationwide system of public schools in which all male citizens would receive free education. Such hopes were not fulfilled, as it would be many decades before some states, particularly in the South, established viable public education systems. Schooling remained primarily the responsibility of private institutions, most of which were open only to those who could afford to pay for them. In southern and mid-Atlantic states, most schools were run by religious groups. In New England, private academies were often more secular, many of them modeled on those founded by the Phillips family at Andover, Massachusetts, in 1778, and at Exeter, New Hampshire, three years later. Many were frankly aristocratic in outlook. Some educational institutions were open to the poor, but not nearly enough to accommodate everyone, and the education they offered was usually clearly inferior to that provided for more prosperous students.

Private secondary schools such as those in New England as well as many public schools generally excluded females from the classroom. Yet the late eighteenth and early nineteenth centuries did see some important advances in education for women. As Americans began to place a higher value on the importance of the "republican mother" who would help train the new generation for citizenship, people began to ask how mothers could raise their children to be enlightened if the mothers themselves were uneducated. Such concerns helped speed the creation of female academies throughout the nation, usually for the daughters of affluent families. In 1789, Massachusetts required that its public schools serve females as well as males. Other states, although not all, soon followed.

Some women aspired to more. In 1784, **Judith Sargent Murray** published an essay defending the right of women to education. Women and men were equal in intellect and potential, Murray argued, so their educational opportunities should be equivalent. And they should have opportunities to earn their own livings and establish roles in society apart from their husbands and families. Murray's ideas attracted relatively little support.

Because Jefferson and his followers liked to think of Native Americans as "noble savages" (uncivilized but not necessarily uncivilizable), they hoped that schooling the Indians in white culture would "uplift" the tribes. Missionaries and mission schools proliferated among the tribes. But there were no comparable efforts to educate enslaved African Americans.

Higher education similarly diverged from Republican ideals. The number of colleges and universities in America grew substantially, from nine at the time of the Revolution to twenty-two in 1800. None of the new schools, however, were truly public. Even universities established by state legislatures relied on private contributions and tuition fees to survive. Scarcely more than one white man in a thousand (and virtually no women, blacks, or indigenous people) had access to any college education, and those few who did attend universities were, almost without exception, members of prosperous, propertied families.

MEDICINE AND SCIENCE

Medicine and science were not always closely connected to each other in the early nineteenth century, but many physicians were working hard to strengthen the link. The University of Pennsylvania created the first American medical school in 1765. Most doctors, however, studied medicine by working with an established practitioner. Some American physicians believed in applying new scientific methods to medicine, but they had to struggle against age-old prejudices and superstitions. Efforts to teach anatomy, for example, encountered strong public hostility because of the dissection of cadavers that the study required. Municipal authorities had virtually no understanding of medical science and almost no idea of what to do in the face of the severe epidemics that often swept their populations; only slowly did they respond to warnings that the lack of adequate sanitation programs was to blame for much disease.

Individual patients often had more to fear from their doctors than from their illnesses. Even the leading advocates of scientific medicine often embraced ineffective or dangerous treatments. George Washington's death in 1799 was probably less a result of the minor throat infection that had afflicted him than of his physicians' efforts to cure him by bleeding and purging.

The medical profession also used its newfound commitment to the scientific method to justify expanding its control over kinds of care that had traditionally been outside its domain. Most childbirths, for example, had been attended by female midwives in the eighteenth century. In the early nineteenth century, physicians began to handle deliveries themselves. Among the results of that change were a narrowing of opportunities for women and a restriction of access to childbirth care for poor mothers, who could afford midwives but not physicians.

CULTURAL ASPIRATIONS OF THE NEW NATION

Many Americans dreamed of an American literary and artistic life that would rival the greatest achievements of Europe. The 1772 "Poem on the Rising Glory of America" predicted that America was destined to become the "seat of empire" and the "final stage" of civilization. **Noah Webster**, the Connecticut schoolmaster, lawyer, and author of widely used American spellers and dictionaries, echoed such sentiments, arguing that the American schoolboy should be educated as a nationalist. "As soon as he opens his lips," Webster wrote, "he should rehearse the history of his own country; he should lisp the praise of liberty, and of those illustrious heroes and statesmen who have wrought a revolution in her favor."

A growing number of writers began working to create a strong American literature. Among the most popular was **Washington Irving** of New York, who won popular acclaim for his satirical histories of early American life and his powerful fables of society in the New World. His folktales, recounting the adventures of American fictional literary heroes such as Ichabod Crane and Rip Van Winkle, made him the widely acknowledged leader of American literary life in the early eighteenth century.

RELIGION AND REVIVALISM

By elevating ideas of individual liberty and reason, the American Revolution had weakened traditional forms of religious practice and challenged many ecclesiastical traditions. By the 1790s, only a small proportion of white Americans were members of formal churches, and ministers were complaining about the "decay of vital piety."

Religious traditionalists were particularly alarmed about the emergence of new, "rational" religious doctrines—theologies that reflected modern, scientific attitudes. **Deism**, which had originated among Enlightenment philosophers in France, attracted such educated Americans as Jefferson and Benjamin Franklin and by 1800 was reaching a moderately broad popular audience. Deists accepted the existence of God, but they considered God a remote "watchmaker" who, after having created the universe, had withdrawn from direct involvement with the human race and its sins. Religious skepticism also produced the philosophies of "universalism" and "unitarianism." Disciples of these new ideas rejected the traditional Calvinist belief in predestination and the idea of the Trinity. Jesus was only a great religious teacher, they claimed, not the son of God.

But religious skepticism attracted relatively few people. Most Americans who remained religious clung to more traditional faiths. And beginning in 1801, those traditions staged a dramatic comeback in a wave of revivalism known as the **Second Great Awakening**. The origins of the Awakening lay in the efforts of conservative theologians to fight the spread of religious rationalism. Presbyterians expanded their efforts on the western fringes of white settlement. Itinerant Methodist preachers traveled throughout the nation to win recruits for their new church, which soon became the fastest-growing denomination in America. Almost as successful were the Baptists, who found an especially fervent following in the South.

By the early nineteenth century, the revivalist energies of all these Protestant denominations were combining to create the greatest surge of evangelical fervor since the first Great Awakening sixty years before. In only a few years, membership in churches embracing revivalism was mushrooming. At **Cane Ridge**, Kentucky, in the summer of 1801, a group of evangelical ministers presided over the nation's first "camp meeting"—an extraordinary revival that lasted several days and impressed all who saw it with its fervor and its size (some estimated that 25,000 people attended). Such events became common in subsequent years.

(Source: Library of Congress, Prints and Photographs Division [LC-USZC4-772])

METHODIST CAMP MEETING, c. 1819 Camp (or revival) meetings were popular among some evangelical Christians in America as early as 1800. By the 1820s, there were approximately 1,000 meetings a year, most of them in the South and the West. After one such meeting in 1806, a participant wrote: "Will I ever see anything more like the day of Judgement on the side of eternity—to see the people running, yes, running from every direction to the stand, weeping, shouting, and shouting for joy. . . . O! Glorious day they went home singing shouting." This image from the 1810s suggests the degree to which women participated in many revivals.

The basic message of the Second Great Awakening was that individuals must readmit God and Christ into their daily lives. They must embrace a fervent, active piety, and they must reject the skeptical rationalism that threatened traditional beliefs. Yet the wave of revivalism did not restore the religion of the past whole cloth. Few denominations any longer accepted the idea of predestination, and the belief that people could affect their own destinies added intensity to the individual's search for salvation. The Awakening, in short, combined a more active piety with a belief in a God whose grace could be attained through faith and good works.

One of the striking features of the Awakening was the preponderance of women within it. Female converts far outnumbered males. That may have been due in part to the movement of industrial work out of the home and into the factory. That process robbed women of one of their roles as part of a household-based economy and left many feeling isolated. Religious enthusiasm provided, among other things, access to a new range of activities— charitable societies ministering to orphans and the poor, missionary organizations, and others—in which women came to play important parts.

In some areas of the country, revival meetings were open to people of all races. From these revivals emerged a group of black preachers who became important figures within the enslaved community. Some of them translated the apparently egalitarian religious message of the Awakening—that salvation was available to all—into a similarly liberating message for blacks in the present world. Out of black revival meetings in Virginia, for example, arose an elaborate plan in 1800 (devised by Gabriel Prosser, the brother of a black preacher) for a slave rebellion and an attack on Richmond. The plan was discovered and foiled in advance by whites, but revivalism continued in subsequent years to create occasional racial unrest in the South.

The spirit of revivalism was particularly strong among Native Americans. Presbyterian and Baptist missionaries were active among the southern tribes and sparked a wave of conversions. But the most important revivalist was **Handsome Lake**, a Seneca whose seemingly miraculous "rebirth" after years of alcoholism helped give him a special stature within his tribe. Handsome Lake blended traditionalism and change, calling for a revival of Indian ways and a repudiation of the individualism of white society, but also encouraging Christian missionaries to become active within the tribes and Iroquois men to abandon their roles as hunters and become sedentary farmers. As in much of white society, Iroquois women, who had traditionally done the farming, were to move into more domestic roles. His mixture of messages spread through the scattered Iroquois communities that had survived the military and political setbacks of previous decades and inspired many Indians to give up whiskey, gambling, and other destructive customs derived from white society.

STIRRINGS OF INDUSTRIALISM

While Americans had been engaged in a revolution to win their independence, a momentous economic transformation had been in progress in Great Britain: the **Industrial Revolution**. Power-driven machines were permitting manufacturing to become more rapid and extensive, with profound social and economic consequences. (See "America in the World: The Global Industrial Revolution.")

TECHNOLOGY IN AMERICA

Nothing comparable to the European Industrial Revolution occurred in America in the first two decades of the nineteenth century. Yet even while Jeffersonians warned of the dangers of rapid economic change, they witnessed a series of technological advances that would ultimately transform the United States. Some of these innovations were British imports. Despite efforts by the London government to prevent the export of textile machinery or the emigration of skilled mechanics, a number of immigrants with advanced technological knowledge arrived in the United States, eager to introduce the new machines to America. Samuel Slater, for example, used knowledge he had acquired before leaving England to build a spinning mill in Pawtucket, Rhode Island, for the Quaker merchant Moses Brown in 1790.

America also produced notable inventors of its own. In 1793, **Eli Whitney** developed a machine that performed the arduous task of removing the seeds from short-staple cotton quickly and efficiently. It was dubbed the cotton "gin," a derivative of "engine." With the device, a single operator could clean as much cotton in a few hours as it once took a group of workers to do in a day. The results were profound. Previously cotton cultivation had been restricted largely to the coast and the Sea Islands, the only places where long-staple cotton—easily cleaned by hand—could be grown. With the invention of an efficient mechanical means for cleaning short-staple cotton, it too became a profitable crop, and one that could be grown throughout the South. Cotton cultivation spread, and within a decade, the total crop increased eightfold. African American slavery, which with the decline of tobacco

(©Bettmann/Corbis)

PAWTUCKET BRIDGE AND FALLS One reason for the growth of the textile industry in New England in the early nineteenth century was that there were many sources of water power in the region to run the machinery in the factories. That was certainly the case with Slater's Mill, one of the first American textile factories. It was located in Pawtucket, Rhode Island, alongside a powerful waterfall, demonstrating the critical importance of water power to early American industry.

production had seemed to be a dwindling institution, expanded and firmly fixed itself upon the South. The large supply of domestically produced fiber also encouraged entrepreneurs in New England and elsewhere to develop a native textile industry.

Whitney was an important figure in the history of American technology for another reason as well. He helped introduce the concept of interchangeable parts to the United States. As machines such as the cotton gin became widely used, it was increasingly important for owners of such machines to have access to spare parts, and for the parts to be made so that they fit the machines properly. Whitney designed not only the cotton gin, but also machine tools that could manufacture its component parts to exact specifications. The U.S. government later commissioned Whitney to manufacture 1,000 muskets for the army. Each part of the gun had to be interchangeable with the equivalent part in every other gun.

Interchangeability was of great importance in the United States because of the great distances many people had to travel to reach towns or cities and the relatively limited transportation systems available to them. Interchangeable parts meant a farmer could repair a machine himself. But interchangeability was not easy to achieve. In theory, many parts were designed to be interchangeable. In reality, the actual manufacturing of such parts was for many years not nearly precise enough. Farmers and others often had to do considerable fitting before the parts would work in their equipment. Not until later in the century would machine tools be developed to the point that they could make truly interchangeable parts.

THE GLOBAL INDUSTRIAL REVOLUTION

While Americans were engaged in a revolution to win their independence, they were also taking the first steps toward another great revolution—one that was already in progress in England and Europe. It was the emergence of modern industrialism. Historians differ over precisely when the Industrial Revolution began, but it is clear that by the end of the eighteenth century it was well under way in many parts of the world. A hundred years later, the global process of industrialization had transformed the societies of Britain, most of continental Europe, Japan, and the United States. Its social and economic consequences were complex and profound and continue to shape the nature of global society.

For Americans, the Industrial Revolution largely resulted from rapid changes in Great Britain, the nation with which they had the closest relations. Britain was the first nation to develop significant industrial capacity. The factory system took root in Britain in the late eighteenth century, revolutionizing the manufacture of cotton thread and cloth. One invention followed another in quick succession. Improvements in weaving drove improvements in spinning, and these changes created a demand for new devices for carding (combing and straightening the fibers for the spinner). Water, wind, and animal power continued to be important in the textile industry. But more important was the emergence of steam power, which began to proliferate after the appearance of James Watt's advanced steam engine (patented in 1769). Cumbersome and inefficient by modern standards, Watt's engine was nevertheless a major improvement over earlier "atmospheric" engines. Britain's textile industry quickly became the most

profitable in the world, and it helped encourage comparable advances in other fields of manufacturing as well.

Despite the efforts of the British government to prevent the export of industrial technology, knowledge of the new machines reached other nations quickly, usually through the emigration of people who had learned the technology in British factories. America benefited the most because it received more immigrants from Great Britain than from any other country, but technology spread quickly to the nations of continental Europe as well. Belgium was the first, developing a significant coal, iron, and armaments industry in the early nineteenth century. France, profiting from the immigration of approximately fifteen thousand British workers with advanced technological skills, had created a substantial industrial capacity in textiles and metals by the end of the 1820s, which in turn contributed to a great boom in railroad construction later in the century. German industrialization progressed rapidly after 1840, beginning with coal and iron production and then, in the 1850s, moving into large-scale railroad construction. By the late nineteenth century, Germany had created some of the world's largest industrial corporations. In Japan, the sudden intrusion of American and European traders helped spur the so-called Meiji reforms of the 1880s and 1890s, which launched a period of rapid industrialization there as well.

Industrialization changed not just the world's economies but also its societies. First in England and then in Europe, America, and Japan, social systems underwent wrenching changes. Hundreds of thousands of men and women moved from rural areas into cities to work in factories, where they experienced both the benefits and the costs of industrialization. The standard of living of the new working class, when objectively quantified, was usually significantly higher than that of the rural poor, and factory laborers experienced some improvement in nutrition and other material circumstances. But the psychological costs of being suddenly uprooted from one way of life and thrust into a fundamentally different one could outweigh the economic gains. There was little in most workers' prior experience to prepare them for the nature of industrial labor. It was disciplined, routinized work with a fixed and rigid schedule, a sharp contrast to the varying, seasonal work pattern of the rural economy. Nor were many factory workers prepared for life in the new industrial towns and expanding cities.

Industrial workers experienced, too, a fundamental change in their relationship with their employers. Unlike rural landlords and local aristocrats, factory owners and managers were usually remote and inaccessible figures. The new class of industrial **capitalists**, many of them accumulating unprecedented wealth, dealt with their workers impersonally, and the result was a growing schism between the two classes, each lacking access to or understanding of the other. Working men and women throughout the globe began thinking of themselves as a distinct class, with common goals and interests. And their efforts simultaneously to adjust to their new way of life and to resist its most damaging aspects sometimes created great social turbulence. Battles between workers and employers became a characteristic feature of industrial life throughout the world.

Life in industrial nations changed at every level. Populations grew rapidly, and people began to live longer. At the same time, pollution, crime, and infectious disease (until modern sanitation systems emerged) increased greatly in industrialized cities. Around the industrial world, middle classes expanded and came, in varying degrees, to dominate the economy, although not always the culture or the politics, of their nations.

Not since the agrarian revolution thousands of years earlier, when many humans had turned from hunting to farming for sustenance, had there been an economic change comparable to the Industrial Revolution. Centuries of traditions, social patterns, and cultural and religious assumptions were challenged and often shattered. The tentative stirrings of industrialism in the United States in the early nineteenth century, therefore, were part of a vast movement that over the course of the next century transformed much of the globe. •

UNDERSTAND, ANALYZE, & EVALUATE

1. Why did the British government attempt to prevent the export of Britain's industrial technology?
2. What did the Industrial Revolution mean for ordinary people around the world?

TRANSPORTATION INNOVATIONS

One of the prerequisites for industrialization is a transportation system that allows the efficient movement of raw materials to factories and of finished goods to markets. The United States had no such system in the early years of the republic, and thus it had no domestic market extensive enough to justify large-scale production. But projects were under way that would ultimately expand the transportation network.

One such project was the development of the steamboat. Britain had pioneered steam power, and even steam navigation, in the eighteenth century, and there had been experiments in America in the 1780s and 1790s in various forms of steam-powered transportation.

HORSE RACING

Informal horse racing began in North America almost as soon as Europeans settled the English colonies. Formal racing followed quickly. The first racetrack in North America—New Market (named for a popular racecourse in England)—was established in 1665 on Long Island, near present-day Garden City, New York. Tracks quickly developed wide appeal, and soon horse racing had spread up and down the Atlantic Coast. By the time of the American Revolution, it was popular in almost every colony and was moving as well into the newly settled areas of the Southwest. Andrew Jackson was a founder of the first racetrack in Nashville, Tennessee, in the early nineteenth century. Kentucky—whose native bluegrass was early recognized as ideal for grazing horses—had eight tracks by 1800.

Like almost everything else in the life of early America, the world of horse racing was bounded by lines of class and race. For many years, it was considered the exclusive preserve of "gentlemen," so much so that in 1674, a Virginia court fined James Bullocke, a tailor, for proposing a race, "it being contrary to Law for a Labourer to make a race, being a sport only for Gentlemen." But while white aristocrats retained control of racing, they were not the only people who participated in it. Southern planters often trained young male slaves as jockeys for their horses, just as northern horse owners employed the services of free blacks as riders. In the North and the South, African Americans eventually emerged as some of the most talented and experienced trainers of racing horses. And despite social and legal pressures, free blacks and poor whites often staged their own informal races.

Racing also began early to reflect the growing sectional rivalry between North and South. In 1824, the Union Race Course on Long Island established an astounding $24,000 purse for a race between two famous thoroughbreds: American Eclipse (from the North) and Sir Henry (from the South). American Eclipse won two of the three heats. A southern racehorse prevailed in another such celebrated contest in 1836. These intersectional races, which drew enormous crowds and created tremendous publicity, continued into the 1850s, until the North–South rivalry began to take a more deadly form.

Horse racing remained popular after the Civil War, but two developments changed its character considerably. One was the successful effort to drive African Americans out of the sport. At least until the 1890s, black jockeys and trainers remained central to racing. At the first Kentucky Derby, in 1875, fourteen of the fifteen horses had African American riders. One black man, Isaac Murphy, won a remarkable 44 percent of all races in which he rode, including three Kentucky Derbys. Gradually, however, the same social dynamics that enforced racial segregation in so many other areas of American life penetrated racing as well. By the beginning of the twentieth century, white jockeys and organized jockey clubs had driven almost all black riders and many black trainers out of the sport.

The second change was the introduction of formalized betting. In the late nineteenth century, racetracks created betting systems to lure customers to the races. At the same time that the breeding of racehorses was moving into the hands of enormously

(Source: Bequest of Adele S. Colgate, 1962/The Metropolitan Museum of Art)

"TROTTING CRACKS" ON THE SNOW, 1858   This lithograph by Louis Maurer portrays trotting racehorses hitched to sleighs. The publishing duo Currier and Ives circulated this and many other images of trotters, reflecting and contributing to the popularity of the sport in the nineteenth century.

wealthy families, the audience for racing was becoming increasingly working class and lower middle class. The people who now came to racetracks were mostly white men, and some white women, who were lured not by a love of horses but by the usually futile hope of quick and easy riches through gambling.   •

UNDERSTAND, ANALYZE, & EVALUATE

1. Why do you think horse racing was such a popular spectator sport in early America? Why has it continued to be popular?

2. How did changes in the sport of horse racing reflect similar changes in American society at large?

A major advance emerged out of the efforts of the inventor **Robert Fulton** and the promoter Robert R. Livingston, who made possible the launching of a steamboat large enough to carry passengers. Their *Clermont,* equipped with paddle wheels and a British-built engine, sailed up the Hudson River in the summer of 1807.

Meanwhile, what was to become known as the "turnpike era" had begun. In 1794, a corporation built a toll road running the sixty miles from Philadelphia to Lancaster, Pennsylvania, with a hard-packed surface of crushed stone that provided a good year-round surface with effective drainage, but was very expensive to construct. The Pennsylvania venture proved so successful that similar turnpikes, so named from the kind of tollgate frequently used, were laid out from other cities to neighboring towns. Like they do today, travelers on these roads paid to use them.

The process of building the turnpikes was a difficult one. Companies had to survey their routes with many things in mind, particularly elevation. Horse-drawn vehicles had great difficulty traveling along roads with more than a five-degree incline, which required many roads to take very circuitous routes to avoid steep hills. Building roads over mountains was an almost insurmountable task, and no company was successful in doing so until governments began to participate in the financing of the projects.

COUNTRY AND CITY

Despite all these changes, America remained an overwhelmingly rural and agrarian nation. Only 3 percent of the population lived in towns of more than 8,000 in 1800. Even the nation's largest cities could not begin to compare with such European capitals as London and Paris, though Philadelphia, with 70,000 residents, New York, with 60,000, and others were becoming centers of commerce, learning, and urban culture comparable to many of the secondary cities of Europe.

People in cities and towns lived differently from the vast majority of Americans who continued to work as farmers. Among other things, urban life often required affluence, and affluent people sought increasing elegance and refinement in their homes, their grounds, and their dress. They also looked for diversions—music, theater, dancing, and, for many people, horse racing. Informal horse racing had begun as early as the 1620s, and the first formal race course in North America opened near New York City in 1665. By the early nineteenth century, it was a popular activity in most areas of the country. The crowds that gathered at horse races were an early sign of the vast appetite for popular, public entertainments that would be an enduring part of American culture. (See "Patterns of Popular Culture: Horse Racing.")

It was still possible for some to believe that this small nation might not become a complex modern society. But the forces pushing such a transformation were already at work. And Thomas Jefferson, for all his commitment to the agrarian ideal, found himself as president obliged to confront and accommodate them.

JEFFERSON THE PRESIDENT

Privately, Thomas Jefferson may well have considered his victory over John Adams in 1800 to be what he later termed it: a revolution "as real . . . as that of 1776." Publicly, however, he was restrained and conciliatory, attempting to minimize the differences between the two parties and calm the passions that the bitter campaign had aroused. There was no public repudiation of Federalist policies, no true "revolution." Indeed, at times Jefferson seemed to outdo the Federalists at their own work.

THE FEDERAL CITY AND THE "PEOPLE'S PRESIDENT"

The modest character of the federal government during the Jeffersonian era was symbolized by the newly founded national capital, the city of **Washington, D.C.** There were many who envisioned that the uncompleted town, designed by the French architect Pierre L'Enfant, would soon emerge as the Paris of the United States.

In reality, throughout most of the nineteenth century Washington remained little more than a straggling, provincial village. Although the population increased steadily from the 3,200 counted in the 1800 census, it never rivaled that of New York, Philadelphia, or the other major cities of the nation and remained a raw, inhospitable community. Members of Congress viewed Washington not as a home but as a place to visit briefly during sessions of the legislature. Most lived in a cluster of simple boardinghouses in the vicinity of the Capitol. It was not unusual for a member of Congress to resign his seat in the midst of a session to return home if he had an opportunity to accept the more prestigious post of member of his state legislature.

Jefferson was a wealthy planter by background, but as president he conveyed to the public an image of plain, almost crude disdain for pretension. Like an ordinary citizen, he walked to and from his inauguration at the Capitol. In the presidential mansion, which had not yet acquired the name "White House," he disregarded the courtly etiquette of his predecessors. He did not always bother to dress up, prompting the British ambassador to complain of being received by the president in clothes that were "indicative of utter slovenliness and indifference to appearances."

Yet Jefferson managed to impress most of those who knew him. He probably had a wider range of interests and accomplishments than any other major political figure in American history, with the possible exception of Benjamin Franklin. In addition to politics and diplomacy, he was an active architect, educator, inventor, farmer, and philosopher-scientist.

Jefferson was a shrewd and practical politician. He worked hard to exert influence as the leader of his party, giving direction to Republicans in Congress by quiet and sometimes even devious means. Although the Republicans had objected strenuously to the efforts of their Federalist predecessors to build a network of influence through patronage, Jefferson

(©Bettmann/Getty Images)

THOMAS JEFFERSON This 1805 portrait by the noted American painter Rembrandt Peale shows Jefferson at the beginning of his second term as president. It also conveys (through the simplicity of dress and the slightly unkempt hair) the image of democratic simplicity that Jefferson liked to project as the champion of the "common man."

used his powers of appointment as an effective political weapon. Like Washington before him, he believed that federal offices should be filled with men loyal to the principles and policies of the administration. By the end of his second term, practically all federal jobs were held by loyal Republicans. Jefferson was a popular president and had little difficulty winning reelection against Federalist Charles C. Pinckney in 1804. Jefferson won by the overwhelming electoral college majority of 162 to 14, and Republican membership of both houses of Congress increased.

Dollars and Ships

Under Washington and Adams, the Republicans believed, the government had been needlessly extravagant. Yearly federal expenditures had almost tripled between 1793 and 1800, as Hamilton had hoped. The public debt had also risen, and an extensive system of internal taxation had been erected.

The Jefferson administration moved deliberately to reverse these trends. In 1802, the president persuaded Congress to abolish all internal taxes, leaving customs duties and the sale of western lands as the only sources of revenue for the government. Meanwhile, Secretary of the Treasury Albert Gallatin drastically reduced government spending. Although Jefferson was unable entirely to retire the national debt as he had hoped, he did cut it almost in half (from $83 million to $45 million).

Jefferson also scaled down the armed forces. He reduced the already tiny army of 4,000 men to 2,500 and pared down the navy from twenty-five ships in commission to seven. Anything but the smallest of standing armies, he argued, might menace civil liberties and civilian control of government. Yet Jefferson was not a pacifist. At the same time that he was reducing the size of the army and navy, he helped establish the U.S. Military Academy at West Point, founded in 1802. And when trouble started brewing overseas, he began again to build up the fleet. Such trouble appeared first in the Mediterranean, off the coast of northern Africa.

For years the Barbary states of North Africa—Morocco, Algiers, Tunis, and Tripoli—had been demanding protection money from all nations whose ships sailed the Mediterranean. Even Great Britain regularly paid off the Barbary pirates to ensure safe passage. During the 1780s and 1790s the United States, too, had agreed to treaties providing for annual tribute to the Barbary states to protect American vessels trading in the region. But Jefferson showed reluctance to continue this policy of appeasement. "Tribute or war is the usual alternative of these Barbary pirates," he said. "Why not build a navy and decide on war?"

He got it. In 1801, the pasha (leader) of Tripoli forced Jefferson's hand. Unhappy with American responses to his demands for tribute, he ordered the flagpole of the American consulate chopped down and declared war. Jefferson built up American naval forces in the area and the Marines defeated a contingent of the pasha's forces. Finally, in 1805, Jefferson agreed to terms by which the United States ended the payment of tribute to Tripoli but paid a substantial ransom for the release of American prisoners seized by Barbary pirates.

Conflict with the Courts

Having won control of the executive and legislative branches of government, the Republicans looked with suspicion on the judiciary, which remained largely in the hands of Federalist judges. Soon after Jefferson's first inauguration, his followers in Congress launched an attack on this last preserve of the opposition. Their first step was the repeal of the Judiciary Act of 1801, thus eliminating the judgeships to which Adams had made his "midnight appointments."

The debate over the courts led to one of the most important judicial decisions in the history of the nation. Federalists had long maintained that the Supreme Court had the authority to nullify acts of Congress, and the Court itself had actually exercised the power of judicial review in 1796 when it upheld the validity of a law passed by Congress. But the Court's authority in this area would not be secure, it was clear, until it actually declared a congressional act unconstitutional. In 1803, in the case of *Marbury v. Madison*, it did so. William Marbury, one of Adams's midnight appointments, had been named a justice of the peace in the District of Columbia. But his commission, although signed and sealed, had not been delivered to him before Adams left office. When Jefferson took office, his secretary of state, James Madison, refused to hand over the commission. Marbury asked the Supreme Court to direct Madison to perform his official duty. But the Court ruled that while Marbury had a right to his commission, the Court had no authority to order Madison to deliver it. On the surface, therefore, the decision was a victory for the administration. But of much greater importance than the relatively insignificant matter of Marbury's commission was the Court's reasoning in the decision.

The original Judiciary Act of 1789 had given the Court the power to compel executive officials to act in such matters as the delivery of commissions, and it was on that basis that Marbury had filed his suit. But the Court ruled that Congress had exceeded its authority, that the Constitution defined the powers of the judiciary, and that the legislature had no right to expand them. The relevant section of the 1789 act was, therefore, unconstitutional and void. In seeming to deny its own authority, the Court was in fact radically enlarging it. The justices had repudiated a relatively minor power (the power to force the delivery of a commission) by asserting a vastly greater one (the power to nullify an act of Congress).

The chief justice of the United States at the time of the ruling (and until 1835) was **John Marshall**. A leading Federalist and prominent Virginia lawyer, he had served John Adams as secretary of state. Ironically, it was Marshall who had failed to deliver Marbury's commission. In 1801, just before leaving office, Adams had appointed him chief justice, and almost immediately Marshall established himself as the dominant figure of the Court, shaping virtually all its most important rulings, including *Marbury v. Madison*. Through a succession of Republican presidents, he battled to give the federal government unity and strength. And in so doing, he established the judiciary as a coequal branch of government with the executive and the legislature.

DOUBLING THE NATIONAL DOMAIN

In the same year Jefferson was elected president of the United States, Napoleon Bonaparte made himself ruler of France with the title of first consul. In the year Jefferson was reelected, Napoleon named himself emperor. The two men had little in common, yet for a time they were of great assistance to each other in international politics.

JEFFERSON AND NAPOLEON

Having failed in a grandiose plan to seize India from the British Empire, Napoleon began to dream of restoring French power in the New World. The territory east of the Mississippi, which France had ceded to Great Britain in 1763, was now part of the United States, but Napoleon hoped to regain the lands west of the Mississippi, which had belonged to Spain since the end of the Seven Years' War. In 1800, under the secret Treaty of San Ildefonso,

France regained title to Louisiana, which included almost the whole of the Mississippi Valley to the west of the river. The Louisiana Territory would, Napoleon hoped, become the heart of a great French empire in America.

Jefferson was unaware at first of Napoleon's imperial ambitions in America. For a time he pursued a foreign policy that reflected his well-known admiration for France. But he began to reassess American relations with the French when he heard rumors of the secret transfer of Louisiana. Particularly troubling to Jefferson was French control of New Orleans, the outlet through which the produce of the fast-growing western regions of the United States was shipped to the markets of the world.

Jefferson was even more alarmed when, in the fall of 1802, he learned that the Spanish intendant at New Orleans (the French had not yet taken formal possession) had announced a disturbing new regulation. American ships sailing the Mississippi River had for many years been accustomed to depositing their cargoes in New Orleans for transfer to oceangoing vessels. The intendant now forbade the practice, even though Spain had guaranteed Americans that right in the Pinckney Treaty of 1795.

Westerners demanded that the federal government do something to reopen the river, and the president faced a dilemma. If he yielded to the frontier clamor and tried to change the policy by force, he would run the risk of a major war with France. If he ignored the westerners' demands, he would lose political support. But Jefferson envisioned another solution. He instructed Robert Livingston, the American ambassador in Paris, to negotiate for the purchase of New Orleans. Livingston, on his own authority, proposed that the French sell the United States the rest of Louisiana as well.

(Source: Library of Congress, Prints and Photographs Division [LC-DIG-pga-00809])

THE LEVEE IN NEW ORLEANS Because of its location near the mouth of the Mississippi River, New Orleans was the principal port of western North America in the early nineteenth century. Through it, western farmers shipped their produce to markets in the East and Europe. This 1884 lithograph shows a busy traffic in goods through the port.

In the meantime, Jefferson persuaded Congress to appropriate funds for an expansion of the army and the construction of a river fleet, and he hinted that American forces might descend on New Orleans and that the United States might form an alliance with Great Britain if the problems with France were not resolved. Perhaps in response, Napoleon suddenly decided to offer the United States the entire Louisiana Territory.

Napoleon had good reasons for the decision. His plans for an empire in America had already gone seriously awry, partly because a yellow fever epidemic had wiped out much of the French army sent to quell the rebellion in Saint-Domingue (present-day Haiti) and partly because the expeditionary force he wished to send to reinforce the troops had been icebound in a Dutch harbor through the winter of 1802–1803. By the time the harbor thawed in the spring of 1803, Napoleon was preparing for a renewed war in Europe. He would not, he realized, have the resources to secure an empire in America.

THE LOUISIANA PURCHASE

Faced with Napoleon's sudden proposal, Livingston and James Monroe, whom Jefferson had sent to Paris to assist in the negotiations, had to decide whether they should accept it even if they had no authorization to do so. But fearful that Napoleon might withdraw the offer, they decided to proceed. After some haggling over the price, Livingston and Monroe signed an agreement with Napoleon on April 30, 1803.

By the terms of the treaty, the United States was to pay a total of $15 million to the French government, a bargain at under three cents an acre. The Americans would also grant certain exclusive commercial privileges to France in the port of New Orleans and incorporate the white residents of Louisiana into the Union with the same rights and privileges as other citizens. The boundaries of the purchase were not clearly defined. What was clear, however, was that the lands were far from uninhabited. The Osages, Kiowas, Mandans, Pawnees, Arapahos, Cheyennes, Shoshones, Omahas, Arikaras, Sioux, Otos, Crows, and other tribes lived within the Louisiana Purchase. But terrible smallpox epidemics had ravaged the West during the Revolution and then again in 1801. The decimation, though not destruction, of the native population allowed white people in the east to tell themselves stories of an empty West awaiting divinely ordained American expansion.

In Washington, the president was both pleased and embarrassed when he received the treaty. He was pleased with the terms of the bargain, but he was uncertain about his authority to accept it, since the Constitution said nothing about the acquisition of new territory. But Jefferson's advisers persuaded him that his treaty-making power under the Constitution would justify the purchase, and Congress promptly approved it. Finally, late in 1803, General James Wilkinson, a commissioner of the United States, took formal control of the territory. Before long, the Louisiana Territory was organized on the general pattern of the Northwest Territory, with the assumption that it would be divided eventually into states. The first of these was admitted to the Union as the state of Louisiana in 1812.

EXPLORING THE WEST

Meanwhile, a series of explorations revealed the geography of the far-flung new territory to white Americans. In 1803, Jefferson helped plan an expedition that was to cross the continent to the Pacific Ocean, gather geographical information, and investigate prospects for trade with indigenous peoples. (See "Consider the Source: Thomas Jefferson to Meriwether Lewis.") The expedition began in May 1804. He named as its leader the twenty-nine-year-old

CONSIDER THE SOURCE

THOMAS JEFFERSON TO MERIWETHER LEWIS (1803)

In the summer of 1803, between the purchase and the incorporation of the Louisiana Territory, President Jefferson sent the following instructions to the explorer Meriwether Lewis. Here Jefferson reveals not only his own expansive curiosity, but also his administration's plans for the newly acquired lands.

To Meriwether Lewis, esquire, Captain of the 1st regiment of infantry of the United States of America: Your situation as Secretary of the President of the United States has made you acquainted with the objects of my confidential message of Jan. 18, 1803, to the legislature . . . you are appointed to carry them into execution.

Instruments for ascertaining by celestial observations the geography of the country thro' which you will pass, have already been provided. Light articles for barter, & presents among the Indians, arms for your attendants, say for from 10 to 12 men, boats, tents, & other travelling apparatus, with ammunition, medicine, surgical instruments & provisions you will have prepared with such aids as the Secretary at War can yield in his department; & from him also you will receive authority to engage among our troops, by voluntary agreement, the number of attendants above mentioned, over whom you, as their commanding officer are invested with all the powers the laws give in such a case. . . .

Your mission has been communicated to the Ministers here from France, Spain & Great Britain, and through them to their governments: and such assurances given them as to it's objects as we trust will satisfy them. The country of Louisiana having been ceded by Spain to France, the passport you have from the Minister of France, the representative of the present sovereign of the country, will be a protection with all its subjects: And that from the Minister of England will entitle you to the friendly aid of any traders of that allegiance with whom you may happen to meet.

The object of your mission is to explore the Missouri river, & such principal stream of it, as, by it's course & communication with the waters of the Pacific Ocean, may offer the most direct & practicable water communication across this continent, for the purposes of commerce.

Beginning at the mouth of the Missouri, you will take observations of latitude & longitude, at all remarkable points on the river, & especially at the mouths of rivers, at rapids, at islands & other places & objects distinguished by such natural marks & characters of a durable kind, as that they may with certainty be recognized hereafter. . . . The interesting points of the portage between the heads of the Missouri & the water offering the best communication with the Pacific Ocean should also be fixed by observation, & the course of that water to the ocean, in the same manner as that of the Missouri.

Your observations are to be taken with great pains & accuracy, to be entered distinctly, & intelligibly for others as well as yourself, to comprehend all the elements necessary, with the aid of the usual tables, to fix the latitude and longitude of the places at which they were taken, & are to be rendered to the war office, for the purpose of having the calculations made concurrently by proper persons within the U.S. Several copies of these, as well as your other notes, should be made at leisure times & put into the care of the most trustworthy of your attendants, to guard by multiplying them, against the accidental losses to which they will be exposed. A further guard would be that one of these copies be written on the paper of the birch, as less liable to injury from damp than common paper.

The commerce which may be carried on with the people inhabiting the line you will pursue, renders a knowledge of these people important. You will therefore endeavor to make yourself acquainted, as far as a diligent pursuit of your journey shall admit, with the names of the nations & their numbers; the extent & limits of their possessions; their relations with other tribes or nations; their language, traditions, monuments; their ordinary occupations in agriculture, fishing, hunting, war, arts, & the implements for these; their food, clothing, & domestic accomodations; the diseases prevalent among them, & the remedies they use; moral & physical circumstances which distinguish them from the tribes we know; peculiarities in their laws, customs & dispositions; and articles of commerce they may need or furnish, & to what extent.

And considering the interest which every nation has in extending & strengthening the authority of reason & justice among the people around them, it will be useful to acquire what knowledge you can of the state of morality, religion & information among them, as it may better enable those who endeavor to civilize & instruct them, to adapt their measures to the existing notions & practises of those on whom they are to operate.

Other objects worthy of notice will be the soil & face of the country, it's growth & vegetable productions; especially those not of the U.S.; the animals of the country generally, & especially those not known in the U.S., the remains and accounts of any which may be deemed rare or extinct; the mineral productions of every kind; but more particularly metals, limestone, pit coal & saltpetre; salines & mineral waters, noting the temperature of the last, & such circumstances as may indicate their character. Volcanic appearances. Climate as characterized by the thermometer, by the proportion of rainy, cloudy & clear days, by lightening, hail, snow, ice, by the access & recess of frost, by the winds prevailing at different seasons, the dates at which particular plants put forth or lose their flowers, or leaf, times of appearance of particular birds, reptiles or insects.
[. . .]

In all your intercourse with the natives treat them in the most friendly & conciliatory manner which their own conduct will admit; allay all jealousies as to the object of your journey, satisfy them of it's innocence, make them acquainted with the position, extent, character, peaceable & commercial dispositions of the U.S., of our wish to be neighborly, friendly & useful to them, & of our dispositions to a commercial intercourse with them; confer with them on the points most convenient as mutual emporiums, & the articles of most desireable interchange for them & us. If a few of their influential chiefs, within practicable distance, wish to visit us, arrange such a visit with them, and furnish them with authority to call on our officers, on their entering the U.S. to have them conveyed to this place at public expence. If any of them should wish to have some of their young people brought up with us, & taught such arts as may be useful to them, we will receive, instruct & take care of them, such a mission.

UNDERSTAND, ANALYZE, & EVALUATE

1. At the time that Jefferson wrote this letter, who held official possession of Louisiana? What European nations were present in the Louisiana Territory?
2. What do the details of this letter reveal about Jefferson's own interest in nature and science?
3. What guidance did Jefferson offer Lewis in regard to natives? What policy toward Native Americans did Jefferson seem to have in mind for the future?

Source: Barth, Gunther (ed.), *The Lewis and Clark Expedition: Selections from the Journals, Arranged by Topic.* New York: Bedford St. Martin's, 1998, 18–22. Original manuscript in *Bureau of Rolls, Jefferson Papers*, ser. 1, vol. 9, doc. 269, reprinted in Thwaites, *Original Journals of the Lewis and Clark Expedition*, 7:247–252.

Meriwether Lewis, a veteran of wars against Native Americans who was skilled in the ways of the wilderness. Lewis chose as a colleague the thirty-four-year-old William Clark, an experienced frontiersman and soldier. **Lewis and Clark**, with a company of four dozen men, started up the Missouri River from St. Louis. With the Shoshone woman Sacajawea as their interpreter, they eventually crossed the Rocky Mountains, descended along the Snake and Columbia Rivers, and in the late autumn of 1805 camped on the Pacific Coast. In September 1806, they were back in St. Louis with elaborate records of the geography and the native civilizations they had observed along the way.

While Lewis and Clark explored, Jefferson dispatched groups to other parts of the Louisiana Territory. Lieutenant Zebulon Montgomery Pike, twenty-six years old, led an expedition in the fall of 1805 from St. Louis into the upper Mississippi Valley. In the summer of 1806, he set out again, proceeding up the valley of the Arkansas River and into what later became Colorado. His account of his western travels helped create an enduring (and inaccurate) impression among most Americans that the land between the Missouri River and the Rockies was an uncultivable desert.

EXPLORING THE LOUISIANA PURCHASE, 1804–1807 When Jefferson purchased the Louisiana Territory from France in 1803, he doubled the size of the nation. But few Americans knew what they had bought. The Lewis and Clark expedition set out in 1804 to investigate the new territory, and this map shows their route, along with that of another explorer, Zebulon Pike. Note the vast distances the two parties covered (including, in both cases, a great deal of land outside the Louisiana Purchase), as well as the fact these lands were already inhabited by indigenous groups. Note, too, how much of this enormous territory lay outside the orbit of even these ambitious explorations. • *What might explain why the explorers took such winding routes through the territories?*

THE BURR CONSPIRACY

Jefferson's triumphant reelection in 1804 suggested that most of the nation approved of the new territorial acquisition. But some New England Federalists raged against it. They realized that the more new states joined the Union, the less power their region and party would retain. In Massachusetts, a group of the most extreme Federalists, known as the Essex Junto, concluded that the only recourse for New England was to secede from the Union and form a separate "northern confederacy." If such a breakaway state were to have any hope for survival, the Federalists believed, it would have to include New York and New Jersey as well as New England. But the leading Federalist in New York, Alexander Hamilton, refused to support the secessionist scheme.

Federalists in New York then turned to Hamilton's greatest political rival, Vice President Aaron Burr. Burr accepted a Federalist proposal that he become their candidate for governor of New York in 1804, and there were rumors he had also agreed to support the Federalist plans for **secession**. Hamilton accused Burr of plotting treason and made numerous private remarks, widely reported in the press, about Burr's "despicable" character. When Burr lost the election, he blamed his defeat on Hamilton's malevolence and challenged him to a duel. Hamilton feared that refusing Burr's challenge would brand him a coward. And so, on a July morning in 1804, the two men met at Weehawken, New Jersey. Hamilton was wounded and died the next day.

Burr now had to flee New York to avoid an indictment for murder. He found new outlets for his ambitions in the West. Even before the duel, he had begun corresponding with General James Wilkinson, now governor of the Louisiana Territory. Burr and Wilkinson, it seems clear, hoped to lead an expedition that would capture Mexico from the Spanish. But there were also rumors they wanted to separate the Southwest from the Union and create a western empire that Burr would rule. (There is little evidence that these rumors were true.)

Whether true or not, many of Burr's opponents chose to believe the rumors, including, ultimately, Jefferson himself. When Burr led a group of armed followers down the Ohio River by boat in 1806, disturbing reports flowed into Washington (the most alarming from Wilkinson, who had suddenly turned against Burr) that an attack on New Orleans was imminent. Jefferson ordered the arrest of Burr and his men as traitors. Burr was brought to Richmond for trial. But to Jefferson's chagrin, Chief Justice Marshall limited the evidence the government could present and defined the charge in such a way the jury had little choice but to acquit. Burr soon faded from the public eye. But when he learned of the Texas revolution against Mexico years later, he said, "What was treason in me thirty years ago is patriotic now."

The Burr conspiracy was in part the story of a single man's soaring ambitions and flamboyant personality. But it also exposed the larger perils still facing the new nation. With a central government that remained deliberately weak, with ambitious political leaders willing, if necessary, to circumvent normal channels in their search for power, the legitimacy of the federal government—and indeed the existence of the United States as a stable and united nation—remained tenuous.

EXPANSION AND WAR

Two very different conflicts were taking shape in the last years of Jefferson's presidency. One was the continuing tension in Europe, which in 1803 escalated once again into a full-scale conflict (the Napoleonic Wars). As fighting between the British and the French increased, each side took steps to prevent the United States from trading with the other. The other conflict occurred in North America itself, a result of the ceaseless westward expansion of white settlement, which was colliding with a native population committed to protecting its lands from intruders. In both the North and the South, the threatened tribes mobilized to resist white encroachments. They began as well to forge connections with British forces in Canada and Spanish forces in Florida. The Indian conflict on land, therefore, became intertwined with the European conflict on the seas, and ultimately helped cause the War of 1812.

CONFLICT ON THE SEAS

In 1805, at the Battle of Trafalgar, a British fleet virtually destroyed what was left of the French navy. Because France could no longer challenge the British at sea, Napoleon now chose to pressure Britain in other ways. The result was what he called the Continental System, designed to close the European continent to British trade. Napoleon issued a series of decrees barring British and neutral ships touching at British ports from landing their cargoes at any European port controlled by France or its allies. The British government replied to Napoleon's decrees by establishing a blockade of the European coast. The blockade required that any goods being shipped to Napoleon's Europe be carried either in British vessels or in neutral vessels stopping at British ports—precisely what Napoleon's policies forbade.

In the early nineteenth century, the United States had developed one of the most important merchant marines in the world, one that soon controlled a large proportion of the trade between Europe and the West Indies. But the events in Europe now challenged that control, because American ships were caught between Napoleon's decrees and Britain's blockade. If they sailed directly for the European continent, they risked being captured by the British navy. If they sailed by way of a British port, they ran the risk of seizure by the French. Both of the warring powers were violating America's rights as a neutral nation. But most Americans considered the British, with their greater sea power, the worse offender—especially since British vessels frequently stopped American ships on the high seas and seized sailors off the decks, making them victims of **impressment**.

IMPRESSMENT

Many British sailors called their navy—with its floggings, low pay, and terrible shipboard conditions—a "floating hell." Few volunteered. Most had had to be "impressed" (forced) into service, and at every opportunity they deserted. By 1807, many of these deserters had emigrated to the United States and joined the American merchant marine or navy. To check this loss of manpower, the British claimed the right to stop and search American merchantmen and reimpress deserters. They did not claim the right to take native-born Americans, but they did insist on the right to seize naturalized Americans born on British soil. In practice, the British navy often made no careful distinctions, impressing British deserters and native-born Americans alike.

In the summer of 1807, the British went to more provocative extremes. Sailing from Norfolk, with several alleged deserters from the British navy among the crew, the American naval frigate *Chesapeake* was hailed by the British ship *Leopard*. When the American commander, James Barron, refused to allow the British to search the *Chesapeake*, the *Leopard* opened fire. Barron had no choice but to surrender, and a boarding party from the *Leopard* dragged four men off the American frigate.

When news of the *Chesapeake-Leopard* incident reached the United States, there was a great popular clamor for revenge. Jefferson and his secretary of state James Madison tried to maintain the peace. Jefferson expelled all British warships from American waters to lessen the likelihood of future incidents. Then he sent instructions to his minister in London, James Monroe, to demand from the British government an end to impressment. Britain disavowed the actions of the *Leopard*'s commanding officer and recalled him, offered compensation for those killed and wounded in the incident, and promised to return three of the captured sailors (the fourth had been hanged). But the British cabinet refused to renounce impressment and instead reasserted its right to recover deserting seamen.

"PEACEABLE COERCION"

To prevent future incidents that might bring the nation again to the brink of war, Jefferson persuaded Congress to pass a drastic measure late in 1807. Known as the Embargo Act, it prohibited all foreign trade. The **embargo** was widely evaded, but it was effective enough to create a serious depression throughout most of the nation. Hardest hit were the merchants and shipowners of the Northeast, most of them Federalists.

The presidential election of 1808 came in the midst of this embargo-induced depression. James Madison was elected president, but the Federalist candidate, Charles Pinckney again, ran much more strongly than he had in 1804. The Embargo Act was clearly a growing political liability, and Jefferson decided to back down. A few days before leaving office, he approved a bill ending his experiment with what he called "peaceable coercion."

(©North Wind Picture Archives/Alamy)

STRUGGLING WITH THE EMBARGO This cartoon shows a merchant being injured by the terms of the U.S. embargo, which is personified by the snapping turtle. The word *Ograbme* is "embargo" spelled backward. The embargo not only enraged American merchants but also failed to resolve the maritime tensions with the British that ultimately helped lead to war in 1812.

To replace the embargo, Congress passed the Non-Intercourse Act just before Madison took office. It reopened trade with all nations but Great Britain and France. A year later, in 1810, the Non-Intercourse Act expired and was replaced by Macon's Bill No. 2, which reopened free commercial relations with those two powers but authorized the president to prohibit commerce with either belligerent if it should continue violating neutral shipping after the other had stopped. Napoleon, in an effort to induce the United States to reimpose the embargo against Britain, announced that France would no longer interfere with American shipping. Madison announced that an embargo against Great Britain alone would automatically go into effect early in 1811 unless Britain renounced its restrictions on American shipping.

In time, this new, limited embargo persuaded London to repeal its blockade of Europe. But the repeal came too late to prevent war. In any case, naval policies were only part of growing tensions between Britain and the United States.

THE "INDIAN PROBLEM" AND THE BRITISH

Given the ruthlessness with which white settlers in North America had continued to dislodge native tribes, it was hardly surprising that indigenous peoples continued to look to England for protection. The British in Canada, for their part, had relied on Native Americans as partners in the lucrative fur trade. There had been relative peace in the Northwest for over a decade after Jay's Treaty and Anthony Wayne's victory over the tribes at Fallen Timbers in 1794. But the 1807 war crisis following the *Chesapeake-Leopard* incident revived the conflict between Indians and white settlers.

The Virginia-born **William Henry Harrison**, already a veteran of combat against Native Americans at age twenty-six, went to Washington as the congressional delegate from the Northwest Territory in 1799. An advocate of development in the western lands, he was largely responsible for the passage in 1800 of the so-called Harrison Land Law, which enabled white settlers to acquire farms from the public domain on much easier terms than before.

In 1801, Jefferson appointed Harrison governor of the Indiana Territory to administer the president's proposed solution to the "Indian problem." Jefferson offered native groups a choice: they could convert themselves into settled farmers and become part of white society, or they could migrate west of the Mississippi. In either case, they would have to agree by treaty to give up claims to their tribal lands in the Northwest.

Jefferson considered the assimilation policy a benign alternative to continuing conflict between Indians and white settlers. But to the tribes, the new policy seemed terribly harsh, especially given the cruel efficiency with which Harrison set out to implement it. He used threats, bribes, trickery, and whatever other tactics he felt would help him conclude treaties. In the first decade of the nineteenth century, the number of white Americans who had settled west of the Appalachians had grown to more than 500,000—a population far larger than that of the Native Americans. The tribes would face ever-growing pressure to move out of the way of the rapidly growing white settlements. By 1807 the United States had extracted treaty rights to eastern Michigan, southern Indiana, and most of Illinois from reluctant tribal leaders.

Meanwhile, in the Southwest, white Americans were taking millions of acres from other tribes in Georgia, Tennessee, and Mississippi. The Indians wanted desperately to resist, but the separate tribes were helpless by themselves against the power of the United States. Yet two new factors emboldened them. One was the policy of British authorities in Canada. After the *Chesapeake* incident, they began to expect an American invasion of Canada and therefore renewed efforts to forge alliances with the Indians. A second and more important factor was the rise of two remarkable native leaders, Tenskwatawa and **Tecumseh**.

Tecumseh and the Prophet

Tenskwatawa was a charismatic religious leader and orator known as "**the Prophet**." Like Handsome Lake, he had experienced a mystical awakening in the process of recovering from alcoholism. Having freed himself from what he considered the evil effects of white culture, he began to speak to his people of the superior virtues of Indian civilization and the sinfulness and corruption of the white world. In the process, he inspired a religious revival that spread through numerous tribes and helped unite them. The Prophet's headquarters at the meeting of Tippecanoe Creek and the Wabash River (known as Prophetstown) became a sacred place for people of many tribes. Out of their common religious experiences, they began to consider joint military efforts as well. Tenskwatawa advocated an Indian society entirely separate from that of white Americans and a culture rooted in tribal tradition. The effort to trade with the Anglos and to borrow from their culture would, he argued, lead to the death of native ways.

Tecumseh—the chief of the Shawnees, called by his tribe "the Shooting Star"—was in many ways more militant than his brother Tenskwatawa. "Where today are the Pequot," he thundered. "Where are . . . the other powerful tribes of our people? They have vanished before the avarice and oppression of the white man." He warned of his tribe's extermination if they did not take action against the white Americans moving into their lands.

Tecumseh understood that only through united action could the tribes hope to resist the steady advance of white civilization. Beginning in 1809, he set out to unite all the tribes of the Mississippi Valley into what became known as the Tecumseh Confederacy. Together, he promised, they would halt white expansion, recover the whole Northwest, and make the Ohio River the boundary between the United States and Indian country. He maintained that Harrison and others, by negotiating treaties with individual tribes, had obtained no real title to land. The land belonged to all the tribes; none of them could rightfully cede any of it without the consent of the others. In 1811, Tecumseh left Prophetstown and traveled down the Mississippi to visit the tribes of the South and persuade them to join the alliance.

During Tecumseh's absence, Governor Harrison saw a chance to destroy the growing influence of the two Indian leaders. With 1,000 soldiers, he camped near Prophetstown, and on November 7, 1811, he provoked an armed conflict. Although the white forces suffered losses as heavy as those of the Native Americans, Harrison drove off the Indians and burned the town. The Battle of Tippecanoe, named for the creek, disillusioned many of the Prophet's followers, and Tecumseh returned to find the confederacy in disarray. But there were still warriors eager for combat, and by the spring of 1812 they were raiding white settlements along the frontier.

The mobilization of the tribes resulted largely from indigenous initiative, but Britain's agents in Canada had encouraged and helped supply the uprising. To Harrison and most white residents of the regions, there seemed only one way to make the West safe for Americans: drive the British out of Canada and annex that province to the United States.

Florida and War Fever

While white frontiersmen in the North demanded the conquest of Canada, those in the South looked to the acquisition of Spanish Florida. The territory was a continuing threat to whites in the southern United States. Enslaved people escaped across the Florida border, and Indians there launched frequent raids north. But white southerners also coveted Florida's network of rivers that could provide residents of the Southwest with access to valuable ports on the Gulf of Mexico.

In 1810, American settlers in West Florida (presently part of Mississippi, Alabama, and Louisiana) seized the Spanish fort at Baton Rouge and asked the federal government to annex the territory to the United States. President Madison happily agreed and then began planning to get the rest of Florida, too. The desire for Florida became yet another motivation for war with Britain. Spain was Britain's ally, and a war might provide an excuse for taking Spanish as well as British territory.

By 1812, therefore, war fever was raging on both the northern and southern borders of the United States. The demands of the residents of these areas found substantial support in Washington among a group of determined young congressmen who earned the name **War Hawks**.

In the congressional elections of 1810, voters elected a large number of representatives of both parties eager for war with Britain. The most influential of them came from the new states in the West or from the backcountry of the old states in the South. Two of their leaders, both recently elected to the House of Representatives, were Henry Clay of Kentucky and John C. Calhoun of South Carolina, men of great intellect, magnetism, and ambition. Both were supporters of war with Great Britain.

Clay was elected Speaker of the House in 1811, and he appointed Calhoun to the crucial Committee on Foreign Affairs. Both men began agitating for the conquest of Canada. Madison still preferred peace but was losing control of Congress. On June 18, 1812, he approved a declaration of war against Britain.

THE WAR OF 1812

The British were not eager for conflict with the United States. Even after the Americans declared war, Britain largely ignored them for a time, occupied as they were with fighting the French in the Napoleonic Wars. But in the fall of 1812, Napoleon launched a catastrophic campaign against Russia that left his army in disarray. By late 1813, with the French Empire on its way to final defeat, Britain was able to turn its military attention to America.

BATTLES WITH THE TRIBES

In the summer of 1812, American forces invaded Canada through Detroit. They soon had to retreat back to Detroit and in August surrendered the fort there. Other invasion efforts also failed. In the meantime, Fort Dearborn (later Chicago) fell before an Indian attack.

Things went only slightly better for the United States on the seas. At first, American frigates won some spectacular victories over British warships. But by 1813, the British navy was counterattacking effectively, driving the American frigates to cover and imposing a blockade on the United States.

The United States did, however, achieve significant early military successes on the Great Lakes. First, the Americans took command of Lake Ontario, permitting them to raid and burn York (now Toronto), the capital of Canada. American forces then seized control of Lake Erie, mainly through the work of the young Oliver Hazard Perry, who engaged and dispersed a British fleet at Put-in-Bay on September 10, 1813. This made possible, at last, a more successful invasion of Canada by way of Detroit. William Henry Harrison pushed up the Thames River into upper Canada and on October 5, 1813, won a victory notable for the death of Tecumseh, who was serving as a brigadier general in the British army. The Battle of the Thames resulted in no lasting occupation of Canada, but it weakened and disheartened the Native Americans of the Northwest.

In the meantime, another white military leader was striking an even harder blow at Indians in the Southwest. The Creek, supplied by the Spaniards in Florida, had been attacking white settlers near the Florida border. Andrew Jackson, a wealthy Tennessee planter and a general in the state militia, set off in pursuit of the Creek. On March 27, 1814, in the Battle of Horseshoe Bend, Jackson's men took terrible revenge on the Indians, slaughtering women and children along with warriors. The tribe agreed to cede most of its lands to the United States and would eventually retreat westward. The vicious battle also won Jackson a commission as major general in the U.S. Army, and in that capacity he led his men south into Florida. On November 7, 1814, he seized the Spanish fort at Pensacola.

BATTLES WITH THE BRITISH

But the victories over the tribes did not end the war. After the surrender of Napoleon in 1814, Britain decided to invade the United States. A British armada sailed up the Patuxent River

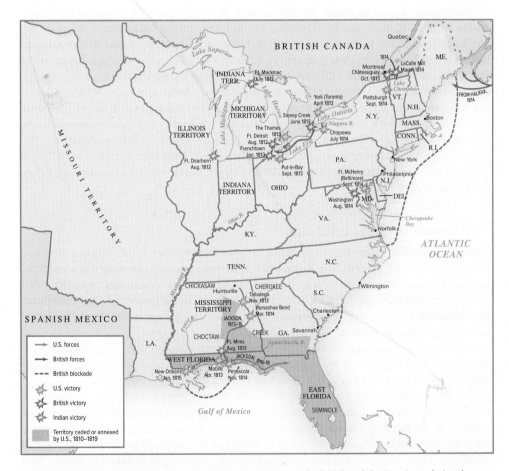

THE WAR OF 1812 This map illustrates the military maneuvers of the British and the Americans during the War of 1812. It shows all the theaters of the war, from New Orleans to southern Canada, the extended land and water battle along the Canadian border and in the Great Lakes, and the fighting around Washington and Baltimore. Note how in all these theaters there are about the same number of British and American victories. • *What finally brought this inconclusive war to an end?*

from Chesapeake Bay and landed an army that marched to nearby Bladensburg, on the outskirts of Washington, where it dispersed a poorly trained force of American militiamen. On August 24, 1814, British troops entered Washington and put the government to flight. Then they set fire to several public buildings, including the White House, in retaliation for the earlier American burning of the Canadian capital at York.

Leaving Washington in partial ruins, the invading army proceeded up the bay toward Baltimore. But that city, guarded by Fort McHenry, was prepared. To block the approaching fleet, the American garrison had sunk several ships in the Patapsco River (the entry to Baltimore's harbor), thus forcing the British to bombard the fort from a distance. Through the night of September 13, Francis Scott Key, a Washington lawyer on board one of the British ships to negotiate the return of prisoners, watched the bombardment. The next morning, "by the dawn's early light," he could see the flag on the fort still flying. He recorded his pride in the moment by writing a poem, "The Star-Spangled Banner." The British withdrew from Baltimore, and Key's words were soon set to the tune of an old English drinking song. (In 1931 "The Star-Spangled Banner" became the official national anthem.)

Meanwhile, American forces repelled another British invasion in northern New York. At the Battle of Plattsburgh, on September 11, 1814, they turned back a much larger British naval and land force. In the South, a formidable array of battle-hardened British veterans landed below New Orleans and prepared to advance north up the Mississippi. Awaiting the British was Andrew Jackson with a contingent of Tennesseans, Kentuckians, Creoles, blacks, pirates, and regular army troops drawn up behind earthen breastworks. On January 8, 1815, the redcoats advanced on the American fortifications, but the exposed British forces were no match for Jackson's well-protected men. After the Americans had repulsed several waves of attackers, the British finally retreated, leaving behind 700 dead, 1,400 wounded, and 500 prisoners. Jackson's losses were 8 killed and 13 wounded. Only later did news reach North America that the United States and Britain had signed a peace treaty several weeks before the Battle of New Orleans.

THE REVOLT OF NEW ENGLAND

With a few notable exceptions, the military efforts of the United States between 1812 and 1815 had failed. As a result, the Republican government became increasingly unpopular. In New England, opposition both to the war and to the Republicans was so extreme that some Federalists celebrated British victories. In Congress, in the meantime, the Republicans had continual trouble with the Federalist opposition, led by the young New Hampshire congressman Daniel Webster.

By now the Federalists were in the minority in the country, but they were still the majority party in New England. Some of them began to dream once again of creating a separate nation. Talk of secession reached a climax in the winter of 1814–1815.

On December 15, 1814, delegates from the New England states met in Hartford, Connecticut, to discuss their grievances against the Madison administration. The would-be seceders at the **Hartford Convention** were outnumbered by a comparatively moderate majority. But while the convention's report only hinted at secession, it reasserted the right of nullification and proposed seven amendments to the Constitution designed to protect New England from the growing influence of the South and the West.

Because the war was going so badly, the New Englanders assumed that the Republicans would have to agree to their demands. Soon after the convention adjourned, however, the news of Jackson's victory at New Orleans reached the cities of the Northeast. A day or two later, reports of a peace treaty arrived from abroad. In the changed atmosphere, the aims of the Hartford Convention and the Federalist Party came to seem futile, irrelevant, even treasonable. The party would never recover from those associations with disloyalty.

THE PEACE SETTLEMENT

Negotiations between the United States and Britain began in August 1814, when American and British diplomats met in Ghent, Belgium. John Quincy Adams, Henry Clay, and Albert Gallatin led the American delegation. Although both sides began with extravagant demands, the final treaty did little except end the fighting itself. The Americans gave up their demand for a British renunciation of impressment and for the cession of Canada to the United States. The British abandoned their call for the creation of an Indian buffer state in the Northwest and made other, minor territorial concessions. The treaty was signed on Christmas Eve 1814.

Both sides had reason to accept this skimpy agreement. The British, exhausted and in debt from their prolonged conflict with Napoleon, were eager to settle the lesser dispute in North America. The Americans realized that with the defeat of Napoleon in Europe, the British would no longer have much incentive to interfere with American commerce.

Other settlements followed the Treaty of Ghent. A commercial treaty in 1815 gave Americans the right to trade freely with England and much of the British Empire. The Rush-Bagot agreement of 1817 provided for mutual disarmament on the Great Lakes. Eventually, though not until 1872, the Canadian–American boundary became the longest "unguarded frontier" in the world.

For Native Americans east of the Mississippi, the conflict dealt another disastrous blow to their ability to resist white expansion. Tecumseh was dead. The British were gone from the Northwest. And the intertribal alliance of Tecumseh and the Prophet had collapsed. As the end of the war spurred a new white movement westward, indigenous peoples were less able than ever to defend their land.

CONCLUSION

Thomas Jefferson called his election to the presidency the "Revolution of 1800," and his supporters believed that his victory would bring a dramatic change in the character of the nation—a retreat from Hamilton's dreams of a powerful, developing nation and a return to an ideal of a simple agrarian republic.

But American society was changing rapidly, making it virtually impossible for the Jeffersonian dream to prevail. The nation's population was expanding and diversifying. Its cities were growing, and its commercial life was becoming ever more important. In 1803, the Jefferson administration made one of the most important contributions to the growth of the United States: the Louisiana Purchase, which dramatically expanded the physical boundaries of the nation and extended white settlement deeper into the continent. In the process, it greatly widened the battles between Europeans and Native Americans.

The growing national pride and commercial ambitions of the United States gradually created another serious conflict with Great Britain: the War of 1812, a war that was settled finally in 1814 on terms at least mildly favorable to the United States. By then, the bitter party rivalries that had characterized the first years of the republic had to some degree subsided, and the nation was poised to enter what became known, quite inaccurately, as the "era of good feelings."

KEY TERMS/PEOPLE/PLACES/EVENTS

Cane Ridge 158
capitalists 163
deism 158
Eli Whitney 160
embargo 177
Handsome Lake 160
Hartford Convention 182
impressment 176
Industrial Revolution 160

John Marshall 169
Judith Sargent Murray 157
Lewis and Clark 174
Marbury v. Madison 169
Noah Webster 158
Robert Fulton 165
secession 175
Second Great
    Awakening 158

Tecumseh 178
the Prophet
    (Tenskwatawa) 179
War Hawks 180
Washington Irving 158
Washington, D.C. 166
William Henry
    Harrison 178

RECALL AND REFLECT

1. What was the impact of the Second Great Awakening on women, African Americans, and Native Americans?
2. What was the long-term significance of the *Marbury v. Madison* ruling?
3. How did Americans respond to the Louisiana Purchase?
4. What foreign entanglements and questions of foreign policy did Jefferson have to deal with during his presidency? How did these affect his political philosophy?
5. What were the consequences of the War of 1812?

8 | EXPANSION AND DIVISION IN THE EARLY REPUBLIC

STABILIZING ECONOMIC GROWTH
EXPANDING WESTWARD
THE "ERA OF GOOD FEELINGS"
SECTIONALISM AND NATIONALISM
THE REVIVAL OF OPPOSITION

LOOKING AHEAD

1. How did the economic developments and territorial expansion of this era affect American nationalism?
2. What was the "era of good feelings," and why was it given that name?
3. How did the Marshall Court seek to establish a strong national government?

LIKE A "FIRE BELL IN THE NIGHT," as Thomas Jefferson said, the issue of slavery arose after the War of 1812 to threaten the unity of the nation. The debate began when the territory of Missouri applied for admission to the Union, raising the question of whether it would be a free or a slaveholding state. But the larger issue, one that would rise again and again to plague the republic, was whether the vast new western regions of the United States would ultimately align politically with the North or the South.

The Missouri crisis, settled in 1820, was significant because it was a sign of sectional crises to come. But at the time, it was also significant because it stood in such sharp contrast to the rising American nationalism of the years following the war. Whatever forces might have been working to pull the nation apart, stronger ones were acting, at least for a time, to draw it together. A set of widely shared sentiments and ideals worked to unite white Americans of what historians call the early republic: the memory of the Revolution, the veneration of the Constitution, the belief that America had a special mission in the world.

In their twilight years, Thomas Jefferson and John Adams, members of opposing parties, one a northerner, one a southerner, kept up a correspondence in which they fretted over looming sectional conflict. Then, on July 4, 1826, the fiftieth anniversary of the adoption of the Declaration of Independence, the two founders died within hours of each other. Bedside witnesses reported Jefferson asking at the end, "Is it the Fourth?" Adams, meanwhile, comforted those around him moments before his death by saying, "Thomas Jefferson still survives." In fact the Virginian had died a few hours earlier.

1815
U.S. treaties take western lands from Indians

1816
Second Bank of U.S.

Monroe elected president

1818
Seminole War ends

1819
Panic and depression

Dartmouth College v. Woodward; McCulloch v. Maryland

1820
Missouri Compromise

Monroe reelected

1823
Monroe Doctrine

1824
John Quincy Adams elected president

1828
Tariff of abominations

Jackson elected president

STABILIZING ECONOMIC GROWTH

After the War of 1812, the United States continued its economic growth and territorial expansion. Yet a vigorous postwar boom led to a disastrous bust in 1819. This collapse was evidence the United States continued to lack some of the basic institutions necessary to sustain long-term growth.

THE GOVERNMENT AND ECONOMIC GROWTH

The War of 1812 produced chaos in shipping and banking, and it exposed dramatically the inadequacy of the nation's existing transportation and financial systems. The aftermath of the war, therefore, led to new efforts to strengthen national economic development.

The wartime experience underlined the need for another national bank. After the expiration of the first bank's charter, a large number of state banks had issued vast quantities of banknotes, creating a confusing variety of currency of widely differing value. It was difficult to tell what any banknote was really worth, and counterfeiting was easy. In response to these problems, Congress chartered a second Bank of the United States in 1816, much like its predecessor of 1791 but with more capital. The national bank could not forbid state banks from issuing notes, but its size and power enabled it to compel the state banks to issue only sound notes or risk being forced out of business.

Congress also acted to promote manufacturing, which the war (by cutting off imports) had already greatly stimulated. The American textile industry, in particular, had grown dramatically. Between 1807 and 1815, the total number of cotton spindles in the country increased more than fifteenfold, from 8,000 to 130,000. Before the war, the textile factories clustered in New England produced only yarn and thread, while families operating hand looms at home did the actual weaving of cloth. Then the Boston merchant **Francis Cabot Lowell**, after examining British textile machinery, developed a power loom that improved upon it. In 1813, in Waltham, Massachusetts, Lowell founded the first mill in America to carry on the processes of spinning and weaving under a single roof.

The end of the war suddenly dimmed the prospects for American industry. British ships swarmed into American ports and unloaded cargoes of manufactured goods, many priced below cost. In response, in 1816, protectionists in Congress passed a tariff law that effectively limited competition from abroad on a wide range of items, including cotton cloth, despite objections from agricultural interests, who stood to pay higher prices for manufactured goods.

TRANSPORTATION

A pressing economic need of the early republican period was a better transportation system to link the vast territories of the growing United States. But should the federal government help finance roads and other "internal improvements"? The idea of using government funds to finance road building was not a new one. When Ohio entered the Union in 1803, the federal government agreed that part of the proceeds from the sale of public lands there should finance road construction. And in 1807, Congress enacted a law proposed by the Jefferson administration that permitted using revenues from Ohio land sales to finance a National Road from the Potomac River to the Ohio. By 1818, the highway ran as far as Wheeling, Virginia, on the Ohio River; and the Lancaster Pike, financed in part by the state of Pennsylvania, extended westward to Pittsburgh.

At the same time, steam-powered shipping was expanding rapidly. By 1816, river steamers were sailing up the Mississippi to the Ohio River and up the Ohio as far as Pittsburgh. Steamboats were soon carrying more cargo on the Mississippi than all the earlier forms of river transport combined—flatboats, barges, and others. They stimulated the agricultural economy of the West and the South by providing cheaper access to markets, and they enabled eastern manufacturers to send their finished goods west much more readily.

(Source: National Gallery of Art, Washington)

STEAMBOATS ON THE HUDSON Inventor Robert Fulton developed an engine that could propel a boat from Manhattan to Albany, a distance of about 150 miles, in 32 hours. His steam-powered vessels were the first to be large and reliable enough for commercial use. This painting from 1854 by James Bard depicts the towboat "John Birkbeck."

Nevertheless, serious gaps in the nation's transportation network remained, as the War of 1812 had shown. Once the British blockade had cut off Atlantic shipping, the coastal roads had become choked by the unaccustomed volume of north–south traffic. Congress passed a bill introduced by Representative John C. Calhoun that would use government funds to finance internal improvements. But President James Madison, on his last day in office, vetoed it. He believed that Congress lacked authority to fund the improvements without a constitutional amendment. For a time, state governments and private enterprise were left on their own to build the transportation network necessary for the growing American economy.

EXPANDING WESTWARD

Another reason for the rising interest in internal improvements was the dramatic westward surge of white Americans. By 1820, white settlers had pushed well beyond the Mississippi River, and the western population of citizens was increasing more rapidly than the rest of the nation.

THE GREAT MIGRATION

The westward movement of Euro-Americans was one of the most important developments of the early republican period and the nineteenth century more broadly. It occurred for several reasons.

One was population growth, which drove many white Americans out of the crowded East. Between 1800 and 1820, the American population nearly doubled—from 5.3 million to 9.6 million. Most Americans were still farmers, and the agricultural lands of the East were by now largely occupied or exhausted. In the South, the spread of the plantation system limited opportunities for new settlers. Another reason for westward migration was that the West itself was increasingly attractive to white settlers. Land there was much more plentiful than in the East. And in the aftermath of the War of 1812, the federal government continued its policy of pushing Native Americans westward, signing treaties in 1815 that took more land from the tribes. Migrants from throughout the East flocked in increasing numbers to what was then known as the Old Northwest (part of the present-day Midwest). Most settlers floated downstream on flatboats on the Ohio River, then left the river, often at Cincinnati, and traveled overland with wagons, handcarts, packhorses, cattle, and hogs.

WHITE SETTLERS IN THE OLD NORTHWEST

Having arrived at their new lands, most settlers built lean-tos or cabins, hewed clearings out of the forest, and planted crops of corn to supplement wild game and domestic animals. It was a rough and lonely existence. Men, women, and children worked side by side in the fields, and at times had virtually no outside contact for weeks or months.

Life in the western territories was not, however, entirely solitary or individualistic. Migrants often journeyed westward in groups and built communities with schools, churches, and stores. The labor shortage in the interior led neighbors to develop systems of mutual aid. They gathered periodically to raise a barn, clear land, or harvest crops.

Another common feature of life in the Old Northwest was mobility. Individuals and families were constantly on the move, settling for a few years in one place and then selling their land (often at a significant profit) and resettling somewhere else. When new areas for settlement opened farther to the west, it was often the people already on the western edges of white settlement—rather than those coming from the East—who flocked to them first.

THE PLANTATION SYSTEM IN THE OLD SOUTHWEST

In the Old Southwest (later known as the Deep South), the new agricultural economy emerged along different lines. The market for cotton continued to grow, and the Old Southwest contained a broad zone where cotton could thrive. That zone became known as the Black Belt, a region of dark, productive soil in Alabama and Mississippi.

The first whites to arrive in the Old Southwest were usually small farmers who made rough clearings in the forest. But wealthier planters soon followed. They bought up the cleared land, as the original settlers moved farther west. Success in the wilderness was by no means assured, even for the wealthiest settlers. Many planters managed to do little more than subsist in their new environment, and others experienced utter ruin. But some planters soon expanded small clearings into vast cotton fields. They replaced the cabins of the early pioneers with more sumptuous log dwellings and ultimately with imposing mansions. They also built up large enslaved workforces.

The rapid seizure and settlement of the Old Northwest and Southwest resulted in the admission of four new states to the Union: Indiana in 1816, Mississippi in 1817, Illinois in 1818, and Alabama in 1819.

TRADE AND TRAPPING IN THE FAR WEST

In the early decades of the nineteenth century, few Anglo-Americans ventured into the far western areas of the continent. The lands comprising what is now Texas, California, and much of the rest of the far Southwest belonged to the Spanish colony of New Spain. But the revolutionary fervor of the age stimulated an independence movement, and in 1821 insurgents declared victory, replacing New Spain with the independent Mexican Empire. Several years later the Mexican Empire became a republic.

After independence, Mexico almost immediately opened its northern territories to trade with and settlement by Americans. The new government hoped that settlers, who were to become Mexican citizens, would help secure their northern border, and that traders would strengthen their connection to the continental economy. Instead, American traders quickly displaced Indian and Mexican traders. In New Mexico, for example, the Missouri merchant William Becknell began in 1821 to offer American manufactured goods for sale, priced considerably below the Mexican goods that had dominated the market in the past. Mexico effectively lost its markets in its own territory as a steady traffic of commercial wagon trains began moving back and forth along the Santa Fe Trail between Missouri and New Mexico. Over in Texas, American land speculators like Moses Austin and his son Stephen sold off parcels of their huge land grants from Mexico to small farmers. Rather than assimilating into the Mexican state, the Texas settlers maintained a separate identity and practiced slavery that was banned elsewhere in the republic.

Fur traders created a wholly new kind of commerce. After the War of 1812, John Jacob Astor's American Fur Company and other firms extended their operations from the Great Lakes area westward to the Rockies. At first, fur traders did most of their business by purchasing pelts from indigenous peoples. But increasingly, white trappers entered the region and joined the Iroquois and other Indians in pursuit of beaver and other furs.

(Source: Yale University Art Gallery)

THE TRAPPERS' CAMP-FIRE This illustration by British artist F. F. Palmer imagines a moment of camaraderie among trappers, with the Rocky Mountains in the background.

The trappers, or "mountain men," who began trading in the Far West were small in number, and mostly young, single men. But they developed important commercial relationships with the Indian and Mexican residents of the West. Some entered into intimate relationships with native and Mexican women. They also recruited women as helpers in the difficult work of preparing furs and skins for trading. In some cases, though, white trappers clashed violently with the Mojave and other tribes.

In 1822, Andrew and William Ashley founded the Rocky Mountain Fur Company and recruited white trappers to move permanently into the Rockies. The Ashleys dispatched supplies annually to their trappers in exchange for furs and skins. The arrival of the supply train became the occasion for a gathering of scores of mountain men, some of whom lived much of the year in considerable isolation. But however isolated their daily lives, these mountain men were closely bound up with the expanding market economy, an economy in which the bulk of the profits from the trade flowed to the merchants, not the trappers.

Eastern Images of the West

Americans in the East were only dimly aware of the world of the trappers. They were more aware of the explorers, many of them dispatched by the U.S. government. In 1819 and 1820, the War Department ordered **Stephen H. Long** to journey up the Platte and South Platte Rivers through what is now Nebraska and eastern Colorado (where he discovered the peak that would be named for him). He then returned eastward along the Arkansas River through what is now Kansas. Long wrote an influential report on his trip, which echoed the dismissive conclusions of Zebulon Pike fifteen years before. The region "between the Missouri River and the Rocky Mountains," Long wrote, "is almost wholly unfit for cultivation, and of course uninhabitable by a people depending upon agriculture for their subsistence." On the published map of his expedition, he labeled the Great Plains the "Great American Desert."

THE "ERA OF GOOD FEELINGS"

The expansion of the economy, the growth of white settlement and trade in the West, the creation of new states—all reflected the rising spirit of nationalism that was spreading through the United States in the years following the War of 1812. That spirit found reflection for a time as well in the character of early republican national politics.

THE END OF THE FIRST PARTY SYSTEM

Ever since 1800, the presidency seemed to have been the possession of Virginians. After two terms in office, Jefferson secured the presidential nomination for his secretary of state, James Madison, and after two more terms, Madison did the same for *his* secretary of state, James Monroe, in 1816. Many in the North resented the so-called Virginia Dynasty, but the Republicans had no difficulty electing their candidate that year. Monroe received 183 ballots in the electoral college. His Federalist opponent, Rufus King of New York, received only 34.

Monroe entered office under what seemed to be favorable circumstances. With the decline of the Federalists amid their disloyal talk during the War of 1812, his party faced no serious opposition. And with the conclusion of that conflict, the nation faced no important international threats. Some American politicians had dreamed since the first days of the republic of a time in which partisan divisions and factional disputes might come to an end. In the prosperous postwar years, Monroe attempted to use his office to realize that dream.

He made that clear, above all, in the selection of his cabinet. For secretary of state, he chose former Federalist **John Quincy Adams** of Massachusetts, son of the second president. Jefferson, Madison, and Monroe had all served as secretary of state before becoming president. Adams thus became the heir apparent, suggesting the Virginia Dynasty would soon come to an end. Speaker of the House Henry Clay declined an offer to be secretary of war, so Monroe named John C. Calhoun instead.

Soon after his inauguration, Monroe made a goodwill tour through the country. In New England, so recently the scene of rabid Federalist discontent, he was greeted everywhere with enthusiastic demonstrations. The *Columbian Centinel,* a Federalist newspaper in Boston, observed that an "era of good feelings" had arrived. And on the surface, at least, that seemed to be the case. In 1820, Monroe was reelected without opposition. For all practical purposes, the Federalist Party had ceased to exist.

JOHN QUINCY ADAMS AND FLORIDA

John Quincy Adams had spent much of his life in diplomatic service before becoming secretary of state. He was a committed nationalist, and he considered his most important task to be the promotion of American expansion.

His first challenge was Florida. The United States had already annexed West Florida, but that claim was in dispute. Most Americans, moreover, still believed the nation should gain possession of the entire peninsula. In 1817, Adams began negotiations with the Spanish minister, Luis de Onís, over the territory.

In the meantime, however, events in Florida were taking their own course. Andrew Jackson, now in command of American troops along the Florida frontier, had orders from Secretary of War Calhoun to "adopt the necessary measures" to stop continuing raids on

(©North Wind Picture Archives/Alamy)

CELEBRATING THE NATION Celebrations of Independence Day, like this one in New York City, became major festive events throughout the United States in the early nineteenth century, a sign of rising American nationalism.

American territory by Seminole Indians south of the border. Jackson used those orders as an excuse to invade Florida and seize the Spanish forts at St. Marks and Pensacola. This became the first of several operations known as the **Seminole Wars**.

Instead of condemning Jackson's raid, Adams urged the government to assume responsibility for it. The United States, he said, had the right under international law to defend itself against threats from across its borders. Jackson's raid demonstrated to the Spanish that the United States could easily take Florida by force. Adams implied that the nation might consider doing so.

Onís realized, therefore, that he had little choice but to negotiate a settlement. Under the provisions of the **Adams-Onís Treaty** of 1819, Spain ceded all of Florida to the United States and gave up its claim to territory north of the 42nd parallel in the Pacific Northwest. In return, the American government gave up its claims to Texas—for a time.

The Panic of 1819

The Monroe administration had little time to revel in its diplomatic successes, for the nation was facing a serious economic crisis: the **Panic of 1819**. It followed a period of high foreign demand for American farm goods and thus of exceptionally high prices for American farmers. But the rising prices for farm goods stimulated a land boom in the western United States. Fueled by speculative investments, land prices soared.

The availability of easy credit to settlers and speculators—from the government (under the land acts of 1800 and 1804), from state banks and wildcat banks, even for a time from the rechartered Bank of the United States—fueled the land boom. Beginning in 1819, however, new management at the national bank began tightening credit, calling in loans, and foreclosing mortgages. This precipitated a series of failures by state banks. The result was a financial panic. Six years of depression followed.

Some Americans saw the Panic of 1819 and the widespread distress that followed as a warning that rapid economic growth and territorial expansion would destabilize the nation. But by 1820, most Americans were irrevocably committed to the idea of growth and expansion.

SECTIONALISM AND NATIONALISM

For a brief but alarming moment in 1819–1820, the increasing differences between the North and the South threatened the unity of the United States—until the Missouri Compromise averted a sectional crisis.

THE MISSOURI COMPROMISE

When Missouri applied for admission to the Union as a state in 1819, slavery was already well established there. Even so, Representative James Tallmadge Jr. of New York proposed an amendment to the Missouri statehood bill that would prohibit the further introduction of slaves into Missouri and provide for the gradual emancipation of those already there. The **Tallmadge Amendment** provoked a controversy that raged for the next two years.

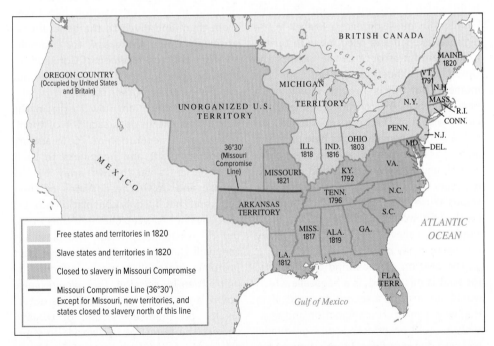

THE MISSOURI COMPROMISE, 1820   This map illustrates the way in which the Missouri Compromise proposed to settle the controversy over slavery in the new western territories of the United States. The compromise rested on the virtually simultaneous admission of Missouri and Maine to the Union, one a slave state and the other a free one. Note the red line extending beyond the southern border of Missouri, which in theory established a permanent boundary between areas in which slavery could be established and areas where it could not be. • *What precipitated the Missouri Compromise?*

THOMAS JEFFERSON REACTS TO THE MISSOURI COMPROMISE (1820)

In this letter to Massachusetts congressman John Holmes, the former president writes of the sectional divisions supposedly resolved by the recent Missouri Compromise. Jefferson wonders how the Union will hold together amid sharp disagreements over slavery and westward expansion.

Monticello, April 22, 1820 I thank you, Dear Sir, for the copy you have been so kind as to send me of the letter to your constituents on the Missouri question. It is a perfect justification to them. I had for a long time ceased to read newspapers, or pay any attention to public affairs, confident they were in good hands, and content to be a passenger in our bark to the shore from which I am not distant. But this momentous question, like a firebell in the night, awakened and filled me with terror. I considered it at once as the knell of the Union. It is hushed, indeed, for the moment. But this is a reprieve only, not a final sentence. A geographical line, coinciding with a marked principle, moral and political, once conceived and held up to the angry passions of men, will never be obliterated; and every new irritation will mark it deeper and deeper. I can say, with conscious truth, that there is not a man on earth who would sacrifice more than I would to relieve us from this heavy reproach, in any *practicable* way.

The cession of that kind of property, for so it is misnamed, is a bagatelle which would not cost me a second thought, if, in that way, a general emancipation and *expatriation* could be effected; and gradually, and with due sacrifices, I think it might be. But as it is, we have the wolf by the ears, and we can neither hold him, nor safely let him go. Justice is in one scale, and self-preservation in the other. Of one thing I am certain, that as the passage of slaves from one state to another would not make a slave of a single human being who would not be so without it, so their diffusion over a greater surface would make them individually happier, and proportionally facilitate the accomplishment of their emancipation, by dividing the burden on a greater number of coadjutors. An abstinence too, from this act of power, would remove the jealousy excited by the undertaking of Congress to regulate the condition of the different descriptions of men composing a state. This certainly is the exclusive right of every state, which nothing in the Constitution has taken from them and given to the general government. Could Congress, for example, say that the non-freemen of Connecticut shall be freemen, or that they shall not emigrate into any other state?

I regret that I am now to die in the belief, that the useless sacrifice of themselves by the generation of '76, to acquire self-government and happiness to their country, is to be thrown away by the unwise and unworthy passions of their sons, and that my only consolation is to be, that I live not to weep over it. If they would but dispassionately weigh the blessings they will throw away against an abstract principle more likely to be effected by union than by scission, they would pause before they would perpetrate this act of suicide on themselves, and of treason against the hopes of the world. To yourself, as the faithful advocate of the Union, I tender the offering of my high esteem and respect.

UNDERSTAND, ANALYZE, & EVALUATE

1. What does Jefferson's metaphor of "a firebell in the night" suggest about his own feelings about the Missouri Compromise and its geographical line?

2. What was Jefferson referring to when he wrote that Americans had "the wolf by the ears"? How appropriate is this metaphor in your assessment?

3. What seemed to be Jefferson's position on the powers of states and the federal government with respect to slavery?

Source: Library of Congress, *Thomas Jefferson Papers, Series 1. General Correspondence. 1651–1827, Thomas Jefferson to John Holmes, April 22, 1820,* http://memory.loc.gov; reproduced in Wayne Franklin (ed.), *The Selected Writings of Thomas Jefferson, A Norton Critical Edition.* New York: W.W. Norton & Company, 2010, 361–362.

Since the beginning of the republic, new states had come into the Union mostly in pairs, one from the North, another from the South. In 1819, there were eleven free states and eleven slave states. The admission of Missouri would upset that balance, hence the controversy over slavery and freedom in Missouri.

Complicating the Missouri question was the admission of Maine as a new (and free) state. Speaker of the House **Henry Clay** informed northern members that if they blocked Missouri from entering the Union as a slave state, southerners would block the admission of Maine. But ultimately the Senate agreed to combine the Maine and Missouri proposals into a single bill. Maine would be admitted as a free state, Missouri as a slave state. Then Senator Jesse B. Thomas of Illinois proposed an amendment prohibiting slavery in the rest of the Louisiana Purchase territory north of the southern boundary of Missouri (the 36°30′ parallel). The Senate adopted the Thomas Amendment, and Speaker Clay, with great difficulty, guided the amended Maine-Missouri bill through the House.

Nationalists in both the North and South hailed this settlement—which became known as the **Missouri Compromise**—as the happy resolution of a danger to the Union. Former president Thomas Jefferson was less convinced that sectional harmony would last. (See "Consider the Source: Thomas Jefferson Reacts to the Missouri Compromise.") Indeed, during the debate, members of Congress referred to the Mason-Dixon line, surveyed by two Englishmen before the Revolution and separating Pennsylvania and Maryland. That line, now, along with the new parallel and the Ohio River in between, would separate the worlds of slavery and freedom (other than the state of Missouri itself), and in popular parlance, the sociocultural distinctions between North and South.

MARSHALL AND THE COURT

John Marshall served as chief justice of the U.S. Supreme Court from 1801 to 1835. More than anyone but the framers themselves, he molded the development of the Constitution: strengthening the Supreme Court, increasing the power of the federal government, and advancing the interests of the propertied and commercial classes.

Committed to promoting commerce, the Marshall Court staunchly defended the inviolability of contracts. In *Fletcher v. Peck* (1810), which arose out of a series of notorious land frauds in Georgia, the Court had to decide whether the Georgia legislature of 1796 could repeal the act of the previous legislature granting lands under shady circumstances to the Yazoo Land Companies. In a unanimous decision, Marshall held that a land grant was a valid contract and could not be repealed even if corruption was involved.

(©Stock Montage/Archive Photos/Getty Images)

JOHN MARSHALL   A former secretary of state, Marshall served as chief justice from 1801 until his death in 1835 at the age of eighty. Such was the power of his intellect and personality that he dominated his fellow justices throughout that period, regardless of their previous party affiliations or legal ideologies. Marshall established the independence of the Court, gave it a reputation for nonpartisan integrity, and established its powers, which were only vaguely described by the Constitution.

Dartmouth College v. Woodward (1819) further expanded the meaning of the contract clause of the Constitution. Having gained control of the New Hampshire state government, Republicans tried to revise Dartmouth College's charter to convert the private college into a state university. Daniel Webster argued the college's case. The Dartmouth charter, he insisted, was a contract, protected by the same doctrine that the Court had already upheld in *Fletcher v. Peck*. The Court ruled for Dartmouth, proclaiming that corporation charters such as the one the colonial legislature had granted the college were contracts and thus inviolable. The decision placed important restrictions on the ability of state governments to control corporations.

In overturning the act of the legislature and the decisions of the New Hampshire courts, the justices also implicitly claimed for themselves the right to override the decisions of state courts. But advocates of states' rights, especially in the South, continued to challenge this right. In *Cohens v. Virginia* (1821), Marshall explicitly affirmed the constitutionality of federal review of state court decisions. The states had given up part of their sovereignty in ratifying the Constitution, he explained, and their courts must submit to federal jurisdiction.

Meanwhile, in *McCulloch v. Maryland* (1819), Marshall confirmed the "implied powers" of Congress by upholding the constitutionality of the Bank of the United States. The Bank had become so unpopular in the South and the West that several states tried to drive branches out of business. This case presented two constitutional questions to the Supreme Court: Could Congress charter a bank? And if so, could individual states ban it or tax it? Daniel Webster, one of the Bank's attorneys, argued that establishing such an institution came within the "necessary and proper" clause of the Constitution and that the power to tax involved a "power to destroy." If the states could tax the Bank at all, they could tax it to death. Marshall adopted Webster's words in deciding for the Bank.

In the case of ***Gibbons v. Ogden*** (1824), the Court strengthened Congress's power to regulate interstate commerce. The state of New York had granted the steamboat company of Robert Fulton and Robert Livingston the exclusive right to carry passengers on the Hudson River to New York City. Fulton and Livingston then gave Aaron Ogden the business of carrying passengers across the river between New York and New Jersey. But Thomas Gibbons, who had a license granted by Congress, began competing with Ogden for the ferry traffic. Ogden brought suit against him and won in the New York courts. Gibbons appealed to the Supreme Court. The most important question facing the justices was whether Congress's power to give Gibbons a license superseded the state of New York's power to grant Ogden a monopoly. Marshall claimed that the power of Congress to regulate interstate commerce (which, he said, included navigation) was "complete in itself" and might be "exercised to its utmost extent." Ogden's state-granted monopoly, therefore, was void.

The highly nationalist decisions of the Marshall Court established the primacy of the federal government over the states in regulating the economy and opened the way for an increased federal role in promoting economic growth. They protected corporations and other private economic institutions from local government interference.

THE COURT AND THE TRIBES

The nationalist inclinations of the Marshall Court were visible as well in a series of decisions concerning the legal status of indigenous tribes. But these decisions did not simply affirm the supremacy of the United States. They also carved out a distinctive position for Native Americans within the constitutional structure.

The first of the crucial Indian decisions was *Johnson v. McIntosh* (1823). Leaders of the Illinois and Pinakeshaw tribes had sold parcels of their land to a group of white settlers (including Johnson) but had later signed a treaty with the federal government ceding territory that included those same parcels to the United States. The government proceeded to grant homestead rights to new white settlers (among them McIntosh) on the land claimed by Johnson. The Court was asked to decide which claim had precedence. Marshall's ruling, not surprisingly, favored the United States. But in explaining it, he offered a preliminary definition of the place of Indians within the nation. Native Americans had a basic right to their tribal lands, he said, that preceded all other American law. Individual American citizens could not buy or take land from the tribes. Only the federal government—the supreme authority—could do that.

Even more important was the Court's 1832 decision in *Worcester v. Georgia*, in which the Court invalidated a Georgia law that attempted to regulate access by U.S. citizens to Cherokee country. Only the federal government could do so, Marshall claimed. The tribes, he explained, were sovereign entities in much the same way Georgia was a sovereign entity— "distinct political communities, having territorial boundaries within which their authority is exclusive." In defending the power of the federal government, he was also affirming, indeed expanding, the rights of the tribes to remain free from the authority of *state* governments.

The Marshall decisions, therefore, did what the Constitution itself had not: define a place for Indian tribes within the American political system. The tribes had basic property rights.

(©Culture Club/Hulton Archive/Getty Images)

CHEROKEE LEADER SEQUOYAH Sequoyah (who also used the name George Guess) was a mixed-blood Cherokee who translated his tribe's language into writing through an elaborate syllabary (equivalent to an alphabet) of his own invention, pictured here. He opposed Indian assimilation into white society and saw the preservation of the Cherokee language as a way to protect the culture of his tribe. He moved to Arkansas in the 1820s and became a chief of the western Cherokee tribes.

They were sovereign entities not subject to the authority of state governments. But the federal government, like a "guardian" governing its "ward," had ultimate authority over tribal affairs.

THE LATIN AMERICAN REVOLUTION AND THE MONROE DOCTRINE

Just as the Supreme Court was asserting American nationalism in shaping the country's economic life, so the Monroe administration was asserting nationalism in formulating foreign policy. American diplomacy had been principally concerned with Europe. But in the 1820s, dealing with Europe forced the United States to develop a policy toward Latin America.

Americans looking southward in the years following the War of 1812 beheld a gigantic spectacle: the Spanish Empire in its death throes and a whole continent in revolt. Already the United States had developed a profitable trade with Latin America. Many believed the success of the anti-Spanish revolutions would further strengthen America's position in the region.

In 1815, the United States proclaimed neutrality in the wars between Spain and its rebellious colonies. But the United States sold ships and supplies to the revolutionaries, a clear indication that it was trying to help the revolutions. Finally, in 1822, President Monroe established diplomatic relations with five new nations—La Plata (later Argentina), Chile, Peru, Colombia, and Mexico—making the United States the first country to recognize them.

In 1823, Monroe went further and announced a policy that would ultimately be known (beginning some thirty years later) as the **Monroe Doctrine**, even though it was primarily the work of John Quincy Adams. "The American continents," Monroe declared, "are henceforth not to be considered as subjects for future colonization by any European powers." The United States would consider any foreign challenge to the sovereignty of existing American nations as an unfriendly act. At the same time, he proclaimed, "Our policy in regard to Europe . . . is not to interfere in the internal concerns of any of its powers."

But Monroe also vowed not to interfere with *current* European powers operating in the Americas, and indeed, without a viable seafaring force, the United States relied on the British Royal Navy to make the implicit threats in the statement credible. The intended targets here were the French, Spain's allies, who Americans feared might help Spain retake its lost empire, and the Russians, encroaching on the northern Pacific coastline.

The Monroe Doctrine had few immediate effects, but it was important as an expression of the growing spirit of nationalism in the United States in the 1820s. And it established the idea of the United States as the dominant power in the Western Hemisphere.

THE REVIVAL OF OPPOSITION

After 1816, the Federalist Party ceased to exist, discredited by its seemingly treasonous behavior during the War of 1812 and outmatched in several consecutive presidential races by the party of Jefferson. The Republican Party became the only national political organization in America for a short time. In many ways, it now resembled the defunct Federalist Party in its commitment to economic growth and centralized government.

But divisions were growing, just as they had in the late eighteenth century. By the 1820s, a two-party system was emerging once again. The full name of the mighty Republican Party had always been the Democratic-Republican Party. It now split along the lines its name suggested, with the divisions visible in 1824 but explicit in 1828. By the latter election, there would be a Democratic Party, which leaned toward the old Jeffersonian vision of a decentralized nation. The Democrats opposed the federal government's growing role in the economy. The other party was the National Republican Party (later the Whigs and unrelated to the modern Republican Party), which leaned toward the old Federalist belief in a powerful central government. The Whigs believed in a strong national bank and a centralized economy. Both parties believed in economic growth and expansion. But they disagreed on whether the national government should oversee the economy or release it from federal interference.

THE "CORRUPT BARGAIN"

Until 1820, presidential candidates were nominated by party caucuses in Congress. But in 1824, "King Caucus" was overthrown. The Republican caucus nominated William H. Crawford of Georgia, the favorite of the extreme states' rights faction of the party. But other candidates received nominations from state legislatures and won endorsements from irregular mass meetings throughout the country.

One of them was Secretary of State John Quincy Adams. But he was a man of cold and forbidding manners, with little popular appeal. Another contender was Henry Clay, the Speaker of the House. He had a devoted personal following and a definite and coherent program: the **American System**, which proposed creating a great home market for factory and farm producers by raising the protective tariff, strengthening the national bank, and financing internal improvements. Andrew Jackson, the fourth major candidate, had no significant political record, even though he was a new member of the U.S. Senate. But he was a military hero and had the help of shrewd political allies from his home state of Tennessee. All four of these candidates technically ran as Democratic-Republicans, but the splintering of the party was obvious.

Jackson received more popular and electoral votes than any other candidate, but not a majority. The Twelfth Amendment to the Constitution (passed in the aftermath of the contested 1800 election) required the House of Representatives, with one vote per state delegation regardless of population, to choose among the three candidates with the largest numbers of electoral votes. Crawford was seriously ill. Clay was out of the running, but he was in a strong position to influence the result. Jackson was Clay's most dangerous political rival in the West, so Clay supported Adams, in part because Adams was an ardent nationalist and a likely supporter of the American System. With Clay's endorsement, Adams won election in the House.

The Jacksonians believed that their large popular and electoral pluralities entitled their candidate to the presidency, and they were enraged when he lost. But they grew angrier still when Adams named Clay his secretary of state. The State Department was the well-established route to the presidency, and Adams thus appeared to be naming Clay as his own successor. The outrage the Jacksonians expressed at what they called a "corrupt bargain" haunted Adams throughout his presidency.

THE SECOND PRESIDENT ADAMS

Adams proposed an ambitiously nationalist program reminiscent of Clay's American System, but Jacksonians in Congress blocked most of it. Adams also experienced diplomatic frustrations. He appointed delegates to an international conference that the Venezuelan liberator Simón Bolívar had called in Panama in 1826. But Haiti was one of the participating nations, and southerners in Congress opposed the idea of white Americans mingling with the black delegates. Congress delayed approving the Panama mission so long that the American delegation did not arrive until after the conference was over.

Even more damaging to the administration was its support for a new tariff on imported goods in 1828. This measure originated with the demands of New England woolen manufacturers. But to win support from middle and western states, the administration had to accept duties on other items. In the process, it antagonized the original supporters of the bill; the benefits of protecting their manufactured goods from foreign competition now had to be weighed against the prospects of having to pay more for raw materials. Adams signed the bill, earning the animosity of southerners, who cursed it as the "tariff of abominations."

JACKSON TRIUMPHANT

By the time of the 1828 presidential election, the new two-party system was now in place. On one side stood the supporters of John Quincy Adams and the National Republicans. Opposing them were the followers of Andrew Jackson, the Democrats. Adams attracted the support of most remaining Federalists. Jackson appealed to a broad coalition that opposed the "economic aristocracy."

But issues seemed to count for little in the end, as the campaign degenerated into a war of personal invective. The Jacksonians charged that Adams had been guilty of gross waste and extravagance. Adams's supporters hurled even worse accusations at Jackson. They called him a murderer and distributed a "coffin handbill," which listed, within coffin-shaped outlines, the names of militiamen whom Jackson was said to have shot in cold blood during the War of 1812. (The men had been deserters who were legally executed after sentence by a court-martial.) And they called his wife a bigamist. Jackson had married his beloved Rachel at a time when the pair incorrectly believed her first husband had divorced her. (When Jackson's wife read of the accusations against her, she collapsed and, a few weeks later, died.)

Jackson's victory was decisive, but sectional. Adams swept virtually all of New England and showed significant strength in the mid-Atlantic region. Nevertheless, the Jacksonians considered their victory as complete and as important as Jefferson's in 1800. Once again, the forces of privilege had been driven from Washington. Once again, a champion of democracy would occupy the White House. America had entered, some Jacksonians claimed, a new era of democracy, the "era of the common man."

CONCLUSION

In the aftermath of the War of 1812, a vigorous nationalism increasingly came to characterize the political and popular culture of the United States. In all regions of the country, white men and women celebrated the achievements of the early leaders of the republic, the genius of the Constitution, and the success of the nation in withstanding serious challenges from both without and within. Party divisions faded.

But the broad nationalism of the "era of good feelings" disguised some deep divisions. Indeed, philosophies of governance differed substantially from one region, and one group, to another. Battles continued between those who favored a strong central government committed to advancing the economic development of the nation and those who wanted a decentralization of power to open opportunity to more people. Battles continued as well over the role of slavery in American life—and in particular over the place of slavery in the new western territories. The Missouri Compromise of 1820 postponed the day of reckoning on that issue, but only for a time.

KEY TERMS/PEOPLE/PLACES/EVENTS

Adams-Onís Treaty 192
American System 199
Francis Cabot Lowell 187
Gibbons v. Ogden 197
Henry Clay 195

John Quincy Adams 191
McCulloch v. Maryland 196
Missouri Compromise 195
Monroe Doctrine 198
Panic of 1819 192

Seminole Wars 192
Stephen H. Long 190
Tallmadge Amendment 193
Worcester v. Georgia 197

RECALL AND REFLECT

1. How did the War of 1812 stimulate the national economy?
2. What were the reasons for the rise of sectional differences in this era? What attempts were made to resolve these differences? How successful were those attempts?
3. Why was the Monroe Doctrine proclaimed?
4. What was the significance of Andrew Jackson's victory in the election of 1828?

9 | JACKSONIAN AMERICA

THE RISE OF MASS POLITICS
"OUR FEDERAL UNION"
THE REMOVAL OF THE INDIANS
JACKSON AND THE BANK WAR
THE CHANGING FACE OF AMERICAN POLITICS
POLITICS AFTER JACKSON

LOOKING AHEAD

1. How did the electorate expand during the Jacksonian era, and what were the limits of that expansion?
2. What events fed the growing tension between nationalism and states' rights, and what were the arguments on both sides of that issue?
3. What was the second party system, and how did its emergence change national politics?

MANY AMERICANS IN THE 1830s were growing apprehensive about the future of their expanding republic. Some feared that rapid economic and territorial growth would produce social chaos or overextension. They insisted that the country's first priority was to establish order and a clear system of authority. Others argued that the greatest danger facing the nation was the growth of inequality and privilege. They wanted to eliminate the favored status of powerful elites and make opportunity more widely available. Advocates of this latter vision seized control of the federal government in 1829 with the inauguration of Andrew Jackson.

The democratization of government over which Jackson presided came wrapped in the rhetoric of equality and aroused the excitement of working people. But Jackson and his followers were not egalitarians. They accepted economic inequality and social gradation. Jackson himself was a frontier aristocrat who surrounded himself with advisers of wealth and prestige. However, many in Jackson's circle had risen to prominence, in their own accounting, by talent and energy rather than accidents of birth. These national leaders considered it their mission to ensure others would have the opportunity to do the same.

But Jackson and his followers did not imagine women, indigenous peoples, or African Americans, whether slave or free, as part of these democratic visions. Neither would poor farmers nor workers be their primary concern. Rather, the Jacksonians sought to challenge the power of eastern elites on behalf of the rising entrepreneurs of the South and West.

THE RISE OF MASS POLITICS

On March 4, 1829, thousands of Americans from all regions of the country crowded before the U.S. Capitol to watch the inauguration of **Andrew Jackson**. After the ceremonies, the crowd poured into a public reception at the White House, where, in their eagerness to shake the new president's hand, they filled the state rooms to overflowing, trampled one another, soiled the carpets, and damaged the upholstery. "It was a proud day for the people," wrote Amos Kendall, one of Jackson's closest political associates. Supreme Court Justice Joseph Story, a friend and colleague of John Marshall, remarked with disgust: "The reign of King 'Mob' seems triumphant."

In fact, the "age of Jackson" was much less a triumph of the common people than Kendall hoped and Story feared. But it did mark a transformation of American politics. Once restricted to a relatively small elite of property owners, politics now became open to virtually all the nation's white male citizens. In a political sense at least, the period had some claim to the title the Jacksonians gave it: the "era of the common man."

EXPANDING DEMOCRACY

What some have called the "age of Jackson" did not really bring economic equality. The distribution of wealth and property in America was little different at the end of the Jacksonian era than it had been at the start. But the extension of suffrage to new groups stimulated a transformation of American politics.

Until the 1820s, relatively few Americans had been permitted to vote. Most states restricted the franchise to white male property owners or taxpayers or both. But even before Jackson's election, the franchise began to expand. Change came first in Ohio and other new states of the West, which, on joining the Union, adopted constitutions that guaranteed

TIME LINE

1830
Webster and Hayne debate

1830–1838
Indians expelled from Southeast

1831
Anti-Mason Party holds first convention

1832–1833
Nullification crisis

1832
Jackson vetoes recharter of Bank of U.S.

Jackson reelected

1833
Jackson removes deposits from Bank of U.S.

1835
Taney named chief justice of Supreme Court

1835–1842
Seminole Wars

1836
Specie circular

Van Buren elected president

1837–1844
Panic and depression

1840
William Henry Harrison elected president

Independent Treasury Act

1841
Harrison dies; Tyler becomes president

all adult white males—not just property owners or taxpayers—the right to vote and permitted all voters the right to hold public office. Older states, concerned about the loss of their population to the West, began to drop or reduce their own property ownership or taxpaying requirements.

The wave of state reforms was generally peaceful, but in Rhode Island, democratization efforts created considerable instability. The Rhode Island constitution barred more than half the adult males in the state from voting in the 1830s. In 1840, the lawyer and activist Thomas L. Dorr and a group of his followers formed a "People's party," held a convention, drafted a new constitution, and submitted it to a popular vote. It was overwhelmingly approved, and the Dorrites began to set up a new government, with Dorr as governor. The existing legislature, however, rejected the legitimacy of Dorr's constitution. And so, in 1842, two governments were claiming power in Rhode Island. The old state government declared Dorr and his followers rebels and began to imprison them. The Dorrites, meanwhile, made an ineffectual effort to capture the state arsenal. The **Dorr Rebellion** quickly failed, but the episode helped spur the old guard to draft a new constitution with expanded suffrage.

The democratization process was far from complete. In the South, of course, no slaves could vote. In addition, southern election laws continued to favor the planters and politicians of the older counties. Free blacks could not vote anywhere in the South and hardly anywhere in the North. In no state could women vote. Nowhere was the ballot secret, and often it was cast as a spoken vote, which meant that voters could be easily bribed or intimidated. Despite the persisting limitations, however, the number of voters increased much more rapidly than did the population as a whole.

One of the most striking political trends of the early nineteenth century was the change in the method of choosing presidential electors for the electoral college. In 1800, the

(Source: Yale University Art Gallery)

CANVASSING FOR A VOTE (1853). This lithograph of a painting by George Caleb Bingham depicts a politician (in top hat) speaking with potential voters outside a hotel in Arrow Rock, Missouri. The men represent different social classes and ages. Women and blacks were barred from voting, but political rights expanded substantially in the 1830s and 1840s among white males.

legislatures had chosen the presidential electors (and thus determined those electors' votes for president) in ten states; the electors were chosen by the people in only six states. By 1828, electors were chosen by popular vote in every state but South Carolina, which meant that state electors in the college would cast their votes for president and vice president in accordance with the popular vote (as is common practice today). In short, these changes gave common voters a greater say in who won elections. In the presidential election of 1824, fewer than 27 percent of adult white males had voted. Only four years later, the figure was 58 percent; and in 1840, 80 percent.

TOCQUEVILLE AND *DEMOCRACY IN AMERICA*

The rapid growth of the electorate—and the emergence of political parties—was among the most striking events of the early nineteenth century. As the right to vote spread widely in these years, it came to be the mark of freedom and democracy. One of the most important commentaries on this extraordinary moment in American life was a book by the French aristocrat **Alexis de Tocqueville**. He spent two years in the United States in the 1830s watching the dramatic political changes in the age of Andrew Jackson. The French government had requested that he make a study of American prisons, which were thought to be more humane and effective institutions than those in Europe. But Tocqueville quickly went far beyond the study of imprisonment and wrote a classic study of American life, titled *Democracy in America*. Tocqueville examined not just the politics of the United States, but also the daily lives of many groups of Americans and their cultures, their associations, and their visions of democracy. In France in the early decades of the nineteenth century, the fruits of democracy were largely restricted to landowners and aristocrats. But Tocqueville recognized that traditional aristocracies were rapidly fading in America and that new elites could rise and fall no matter what their backgrounds.

Tocqueville also realized that the rising democracy of America had many limits. Democracy was a powerful, visible force in the lives of most white men. Few women could vote, although some shared the democratic ethos through their families. For many other Americans, democracy was a distant hope. Tocqueville wrote of the limits of equality and democracy:

> he first who attracts the eye, the first in enlightenment, in power and in happiness, is the white man, the European, man par excellence; below him appear the Negro and the Indian. These two unfortunate races have neither birth, nor face, nor language, nor mores in common; only their misfortunes look alike. Both occupy an equally inferior position in the country that they inhabit; both experience the effects of tyranny; and if their miseries are different, they can accuse the same author for them.

Tocqueville's book helped define the character of American democracy for readers in France and other European nations. Only later did it become widely read and studied in the United States as a remarkable portrait of the emerging democracy of the United States.

THE LEGITIMIZATION OF PARTY

The high level of voter participation was only partly the result of an expanded electorate. It resulted as well from growing interest in politics, a strengthening of party organization, and increasing party loyalty. Although party competition had been part of American politics almost from the beginning, acceptance of the idea of party had not. For more than thirty years, most Americans who had opinions about the nature of government considered parties evils to be avoided and thought the nation should seek a broad consensus without permanent factional lines. But in the 1820s and 1830s, those assumptions gave way to a new view that permanent, institutionalized parties were a desirable part of the political process, that they were indeed essential to democracy.

JACKSONIAN DEMOCRACY

To many Americans in the 1820s and 1830s, Andrew Jackson was a champion of democracy, a symbol of the spirit of antielitism and egalitarianism that was sweeping American life. Historians, however, have disagreed sharply not only in their assessments of Jackson himself but in their portrayal of American society in his era.

The "progressive" historians of the early twentieth century tended to see Jacksonian politics as a forebear of their own battles against economic privilege and political corruption. Frederick Jackson Turner encouraged scholars to see Jacksonianism as a protest by the frontier against the conservative aristocracy of the East. Jackson represented those who wanted to make government responsive to the will of the people rather than to the power of special interests. The culmination of this progressive interpretation of Jacksonianism was Arthur M. Schlesinger's *The Age of Jackson* (1945). Less interested in the regional basis of Jacksonianism than the disciples of Turner had been, Schlesinger argued that Jacksonian democracy was an effort "to control the power of the capitalist groups, mainly Eastern, for the benefit of non-capitalist groups, farmers and laboring men, East, West, and South." He portrayed Jacksonianism as an early version of modern reform efforts to "restrain the power of the business community."

Richard Hofstadter, in an influential 1948 essay, sharply disagreed. Jackson, he argued, was the spokesman of rising entrepreneurs—aspiring businessmen who saw the road to opportunity blocked by the monopolistic power of eastern aristocrats. The Jacksonian leaders were less sympathetic to the

aspirations of those below them than they were to the destruction of obstacles to their own success. Bray Hammond, writing in 1957, argued similarly that the Jacksonian cause was "one of enterpriser against capitalist." Other historians saw Jacksonianism less as a democratic reform movement than as a nostalgic effort to restore a lost past. Marvin Meyers's *The Jacksonian Persuasion* (1957) argued that Jackson and his followers looked with misgivings on the new industrial society emerging around them and yearned instead for a restoration of the agrarian, republican virtues of an earlier time.

In the 1960s, historians began taking less interest in Jackson and his supporters and more in the social and cultural bases of American politics in the time of Jackson. Lee Benson's *The Concept of Jacksonian Democracy* (1961) used quantitative techniques to demonstrate the role of religion and ethnicity in shaping party divisions. Edward Pessen's *Jacksonian America* (1969) portrayed America in the Jacksonian era as an increasingly stratified society. This inclination to look more closely at society than at formal "Jacksonianism" continued into the late twentieth and early twenty-first centuries. Sean Wilentz, in *Chants Democratic* (1984) and in *The Rise of American Democracy* (2005), examined the rise of powerful movements among ordinary citizens who were attracted less to Jackson himself than to the notion of popular democracy.

Gradually, this attention to the nature of society has led to reassessments of Jackson himself and the nature of his regime. In *Fathers and Children* (1975), Michael Rogin portrays Jackson as a leader determined to secure the supremacy of white men in the

United States. Alexander Saxton, in *The Rise and Fall of the White Republic* (1990), makes the related argument that "Jacksonian Democracy" was explicitly a white man's democracy that rested on the subjugation of slaves, women, and Native Americans. But the portrayal of Jackson as a champion of the common people has not vanished from scholarship entirely. The most renowned postwar biographer of Jackson, Robert V. Remini, argued that despite the flaws in his democratic vision, he was a genuine "man of the people." The journalist Jon Meacham reaches a similar conclusion in his Pulitzer Prize–winning *American Lion* (2009).

UNDERSTAND, ANALYZE, & EVALUATE

1. What was Jacksonian democracy? Was it a reform movement against conservative special interests? Was it a regional movement designed to shift power to the West? Or was it a class-based movement to elevate workers and farmers?

2. Jackson was known as a "man of the people." Which people were attracted to him?

The elevation of party occurred first at the state level, most prominently in New York. There, after the War of 1812, Martin Van Buren led a dissident political faction (known as the "Bucktails") that challenged the established political elite led by the aristocratic governor, DeWitt Clinton. The Bucktails argued that Clinton's closed circle made genuine democracy impossible. They advocated institutionalized political parties in its place, based on the support of a broad public constituency. A party would need a permanent opposition, they insisted, because competition would force it to remain sensitive to the will of the people. Parties would check and balance one another in much the same way as the different branches of government did.

By the late 1820s, this new idea of party had spread beyond New York. The election of Jackson in 1828, the result of a popular movement that stood apart from the usual political elites, seemed further to legitimize it. In the 1830s, finally, a fully formed two-party system began to operate at the national level. The anti-Jackson forces began to call themselves **Whigs**. Jackson's followers, once again, called themselves Democrats, thus giving a permanent name to what is now the nation's oldest political party.

PRESIDENT OF THE COMMON PEOPLE

Andrew Jackson had been born to recent Irish immigrants in 1767. From modest beginnings he went on to study law, then served as a representative, senator, and judge. By the early nineteenth century, he was prospering as a planter and merchant in Tennessee, serving in the militia, and earning notoriety for his armed campaigns against Native Americans in the Southeast and the British in New Orleans. Soon more than a hundred slaves labored at his plantation and home, the Hermitage.

Unlike Thomas Jefferson, Jackson was no democratic philosopher. The Democratic Party, much less than the old Jeffersonian Republicans, embraced no clear or uniform ideological position. But Jackson himself did embrace a distinct and simple theory of democracy. Government, he said, should offer "equal protection and equal benefits" to all its white male citizens and favor no one region or class over another, with a major exception—people of color could expect no protection from the administration. Jackson would ultimately expel Native Americans from the Southeast and try (unsuccessfully) to ban antislavery literature from the mails. Rather, Jackson's brand of popular politics meant launching an assault on what he considered the citadels of the eastern aristocracy and extending opportunities to the rising classes of the West and the South. (For historians' changing assessments of Jackson, see "Debating the Past: Jacksonian Democracy.")

Jackson's first target was the entrenched officeholders in the federal government, whom he bitterly denounced. Offices, he said, belonged to the people, not to a self-serving bureaucracy. Equally important, a large turnover in the bureaucracy would allow him to reward his own supporters with offices. One of Jackson's allies, William L. Marcy of New York, once explained, "To the victors belong the spoils." Patronage, the process of giving out jobs as political rewards, became known as the **spoils system**. Although Jackson removed no more than one-fifth of existing federal officeholders, his embrace of the spoils system helped cement its place in party politics.

Jackson's supporters also worked to transform the process by which presidential candidates were selected. In 1832, the president's followers staged a national convention to renominate him. Through the convention, its founders believed, power in the party would arise directly from the people rather than from such elite political institutions as the congressional caucus.

"OUR FEDERAL UNION"

Jackson's commitment to extending power beyond entrenched elites led him to want to reduce the functions of the federal government. A concentration of power in Washington would, he believed, restrict opportunity to people with political connections. But Jackson was also strongly committed to the preservation of the Union. Thus, at the same time as he was promoting an economic program to reduce the power of the national government, he was asserting the supremacy of the Union in the face of a potent challenge. For no sooner had he entered office than his own vice president—**John C. Calhoun**—began to champion a controversial constitutional theory: nullification.

CALHOUN AND NULLIFICATION

Once an outspoken protectionist, Calhoun had strongly supported the tariff of 1816. But by the late 1820s, he had come to believe that the tariff was responsible for the stagnation of South Carolina's economy, though the exhaustion of the state's farmland was the real reason for the decline. Some exasperated Carolinians were ready to consider a drastic remedy: secession.

With his future political hopes resting on how he met this challenge in his home state, Calhoun developed the theory of **nullification**. Drawing from the ideas of Madison and Jefferson and citing the Tenth Amendment to the Constitution, Calhoun argued that since the federal government was a creation of the states, the states—not the courts or Congress—were the final arbiters of the constitutionality of federal laws. If a state concluded that Congress had passed an unconstitutional law, then it could hold a special convention and declare the federal law null and void within the state. The nullification doctrine—and the idea of using it to nullify the 1828 tariff—quickly attracted broad support in South Carolina. But it did nothing to help Calhoun's standing within the new Jackson administration, in part because he had a powerful rival in **Martin Van Buren**.

THE RISE OF VAN BUREN

Van Buren had served briefly as governor of New York before becoming Jackson's secretary of state in 1829. He soon established himself as a member both of the official cabinet and of the president's unofficial circle of political allies, known as the "Kitchen Cabinet." And

Van Buren's influence with the president grew stronger still as a result of a quarrel over etiquette that drove a wedge between Jackson and Calhoun.

Peggy O'Neale was the daughter of a Washington tavernkeeper with whom both Andrew Jackson and his friend John H. Eaton had taken lodgings while serving as senators from Tennessee. O'Neale was married, but rumors circulated in Washington in the mid-1820s that she and Senator Eaton were having an affair. O'Neale's husband died in 1828, and she and Eaton were soon married. A few weeks later, Jackson named Eaton secretary of war and thus made the new Mrs. Eaton a cabinet wife. The rest of the administration wives, led by Mrs. Calhoun, refused to receive her. Jackson, who blamed slanderous gossip for the death of his own wife, was furious, and demanded that the members of the cabinet accept her into their social world. Calhoun, under pressure from his wife, refused. Van Buren, a widower, befriended the Eatons and thus ingratiated himself with Jackson. By 1831, Jackson had tapped Van Buren as his preferred successor in the White House, apparently ending Calhoun's dreams of the presidency.

THE WEBSTER–HAYNE DEBATE

In January 1830, in the midst of a routine debate over federal policy toward western lands, a senator from Connecticut suggested that all land sales and surveys be temporarily discontinued. Robert Y. Hayne, a young senator from South Carolina, charged that slowing down the growth of the West was simply a way for the East to retain its political and economic power. Hayne and other southerners believed the South and West might join an alliance to check the strength of the East; that slavery would only thrive with new western lands opened up to the institution; and most crucially, that states, not the federal government, should control local matters like the sale of land and thereby nullify federal laws attempting such control.

Daniel Webster, now a senator from Massachusetts, attacked Hayne (and through him Calhoun) for what he considered an attack on the integrity of the Union and the power of the federal government. Southern states, Webster charged, were putting crass economic and political advantages ahead of the survival of a strong nation unified by common respect for federal law. Hayne responded with a defense of nullification. Webster then spent two full afternoons delivering what became known as his "Second Reply to Hayne." He concluded with the ringing appeal: "Liberty and Union, now and for ever, one and inseparable!" The exchange over federal versus state power became known as the **Webster-Hayne debate**.

Both sides waited to hear what President Jackson thought of the argument. That became clear at the annual Democratic Party banquet in honor of Thomas Jefferson. After dinner, guests delivered a series of toasts. The president arrived with a written text in which he had underscored certain words: "Our Federal Union—It must be preserved." While he spoke, he looked directly at Calhoun. The diminutive Van Buren, who stood on his chair to see better, thought he saw Calhoun's hand shake and a trickle of wine run down his glass as he responded to the president's toast with his own: "The Union, next to our liberty most dear."

THE NULLIFICATION CRISIS

In 1832, the controversy over nullification finally produced a crisis when South Carolinians responded angrily to a congressional tariff bill that offered them no relief from the 1828 tariff of abominations. Almost immediately, the legislature summoned a state convention, which voted to nullify the tariffs of 1828 and 1832 and to forbid the collection of duties within the state. At the same time, South Carolina elected Hayne to serve as governor and Calhoun to replace Hayne as senator.

Jackson insisted that nullification was treason. He strengthened the federal forts in South Carolina and ordered a warship to Charleston. When Congress convened early in 1833, Jackson proposed a force bill authorizing the president to use the military to see that acts of Congress were obeyed. Violence seemed a real possibility.

Calhoun faced a predicament as he took his place in the Senate. Not a single state had come to South Carolina's defense. But the timely intervention of Henry Clay, also newly elected to the Senate, averted a crisis. Clay devised a compromise by which the tariff would be lowered gradually so that by 1842 it would reach approximately the same level as in 1816. The compromise and the force bill were passed on the same day, March 1, 1833. Jackson signed them both. In South Carolina, the convention reassembled and repealed its nullification of the tariffs. But unwilling to allow Congress to have the last word, the convention nullified the force act—a purely symbolic act, since the tariff had already been amended. Calhoun and his followers claimed a victory for nullification, which had, they insisted, forced the revision of the tariff. But the episode taught Calhoun and his allies that no state could defy the federal government alone.

THE REMOVAL OF THE INDIANS

There had never been any doubt about Andrew Jackson's attitude toward the Indian tribes whose lands were now encircled by the eastern states and territories of the United States. He wanted them to move west. Since his early military expeditions in Florida, Jackson had harbored a deep hostility toward the Indians. In this he was little different from most white Americans.

White Attitudes toward the Tribes

In the eighteenth century, many whites had shared Thomas Jefferson's view of the Indians as "noble savages," with an inherent dignity that made civilization possible among them if they would only mimic white social, cultural, political, and economic practices. Yet by the first decades of the nineteenth century, many whites were coming to view Native Americans simply as "savages" who should be removed from all the lands east of the Mississippi. White westerners also favored removal to put an end to violence and competition in the western areas of white settlement. Most of all, they wanted valuable land that the tribes still possessed.

Events in the Northwest added urgency to the issue of removal. In Illinois, an alliance of Sauk (or Sac) and Fox Indians under Black Hawk fought white settlers in 1831–1832 in an effort to overturn what Black Hawk considered an illegal cession of tribal lands to the United States. The **Black Hawk War** was notable for its viciousness. White forces attacked the Indians even when they attempted to surrender, pursued them as they retreated, and slaughtered many of them. The brutal war only reinforced the determination of whites to remove all the tribes to the West.

The "Five Civilized Tribes"

Even more troubling to the government in the 1830s were the remaining Indian tribes of the South, who possessed lands southerners coveted for their growing cotton empire. In western Georgia, Alabama, Mississippi, and Florida lived what were known as the

(Source: National Gallery of Art, Washington)

BLACK HAWK AND FIVE OTHER SAUK PRISONERS After his defeat by white settlers in Illinois in 1832, Black Hawk and other Sauk warriors were captured and sent on a tour by Andrew Jackson, displayed to the public as trophies of war. This painting, by George Catlin, shows six Sauk prisoners the year of their capture at Jefferson Barracks near St. Louis. Black Hawk is third from left, holding the feather. The Sauks insisted on being portrayed with the cannon balls chained to their legs.

"Five Civilized Tribes"—the Cherokees, Creeks, Seminoles, Chickasaws, and Choctaws. These groups had adopted various Euro-American institutions and practices, including literacy, organized government, laws, agricultural economies, and even slavery. In 1830, both the federal government and several southern states were accelerating efforts to remove the tribes to the West. That year Congress passed the **Indian Removal Act**, which authorized the financing of federal negotiations to relocate the southern tribes to the West. Some Indians believed removal the least disagreeable option—better, perhaps, than the prospect of destitution, white encroachment, and violence. Others fought back.

The Cherokees tried to stop Georgia, which had passed its own laws of forcible removal, from taking their lands. The Supreme Court actually supported the tribe's contention in *Worcester v. Georgia* that the state had no authority to negotiate with tribal representatives, a sovereign "nation" of sorts. But Jackson repudiated the decisions, reportedly responding to news of the rulings with the contemptuous statement: "John Marshall has made his decision. Now let him enforce it."

Then, in 1835, the U.S. government extracted a treaty from a minority faction of the Cherokees that ceded to Georgia the tribe's land in that state in return for $5 million and a reservation west of the Mississippi. With removal inevitable, this Cherokee "Treaty Party" reasoned, a deal for cash and land to the west was the best alternative available. But the great majority of the 17,000 Cherokees, including their leader John Ross, did not recognize the treaty as legitimate. (See "Consider the Source: Letter from Chief John Ross.") Jackson sent an army of 7,000 under General Winfield Scott to round them up and drive them westward.

LETTER FROM CHIEF JOHN ROSS TO THE SENATE AND HOUSE OF REPRESENTATIVES (1836)

Chief John Ross, leader of the Cherokee Nation, wrote the U.S. Congress to object to the Treaty of New Ochota. Signed by a minority faction within the tribe, the treaty's terms pledged the removal of Cherokees from all lands east of the Mississippi in return for money and land in present-day Oklahoma. Despite Ross's protests, the army forced the Cherokees westward on the "Trail of Tears." Thousands died on the route.

Red Clay Council Ground, Cherokee Nation, September 28, 1836

It is well known that for a number of years past we have been harassed by a series of vexations, which it is deemed unnecessary to recite in detail, but the evidence of which our delegation will be prepared to furnish. With a view to bringing our troubles to a close, a delegation was appointed on the 23rd of October, 1835, by the General Council of the nation, clothed with full powers to enter into arrangements with the Government of the United States, for the final adjustment of all our existing difficulties. The delegation failing to effect an arrangement with the United States commissioner, then in the nation, proceeded, agreeably to their instructions in that case, to Washington City, for the purpose of negotiating a treaty with the authorities of the United States.

After the departure of the Delegation, a contract was made by the Rev. John F. Schermerhorn, and certain individual Cherokees, purporting to be a "treaty, concluded at New Echota, in the State of Georgia, on the 29th day of December, 1835, by General William Carroll and John F. Schermerhorn, commissioners on the part of the United States, and the chiefs, headmen, and people of the Cherokee tribes of Indians." A spurious Delegation, in violation of a special injunction of the general council of the nation, proceeded to Washington City with this pretended treaty, and by false and fraudulent representations supplanted in the favor of the Government the legal and accredited Delegation of the Cherokee people, and obtained for this instrument, after making important alterations in its provisions, the recognition of the United States Government. And now it is presented to us as a treaty, ratified by the Senate, and approved by the President [Andrew Jackson], and our acquiescence in its requirements demanded, under the sanction of the displeasure of the United States, and the threat of summary compulsion, in case of refusal. It comes to us, not through our legitimate authorities, the known and usual medium of communication between the Government of the United States and our nation, but through the agency of a complication of powers, civil and military.

By the stipulations of this instrument, we are despoiled of our private possessions, the indefeasible property of individuals. We are stripped of every attribute of freedom and eligibility for legal self-defence. Our property may be plundered before our eyes; violence may be committed on our persons; even our lives may be taken away, and there is none to regard our complaints. We are denationalized; we are disfranchised. We are deprived of membership in the human family! We have neither land nor home, nor resting place that can be called our own. And this is effected by the provisions of a compact which assumes the venerated, the sacred appellation of treaty.

We are overwhelmed! Our hearts are sickened, our utterance is paralized, when we reflect on the condition in which we are placed, by the audacious practices of unprincipled men, who have managed their stratagems with so much dexterity as to impose on the Government of the United States, in the face of our earnest, solemn, and reiterated protestations.

The instrument in question is not the act of our Nation; we are not parties to its covenants; it has not received the sanction of our people. The makers of it sustain no office nor appointment in our Nation, under the designation of Chiefs, Head men, or any other title, by which they hold, or could acquire, authority to assume the reins of Government, and to make bargain and sale of our rights, our possessions, and our common country. And we are constrained solemnly to declare, that we cannot but contemplate the enforcement of the stipulations of this instrument on us, against our consent, as an act of injustice and oppression, which, we are well persuaded, can never knowingly be countenanced by the Government and people of the United States; nor can we believe it to be the design of these honorable and highminded individuals, who stand at the head of the Govt., to bind a whole Nation, by the acts of a few unauthorized individuals. And, therefore, we, the parties to be affected by the result, appeal with confidence to the justice, the magnanimity, the compassion, of your honorable bodies, against the enforcement, on us, of the provisions of a compact, in the formation of which we have had no agency.

UNDERSTAND, ANALYZE, & EVALUATE

1. On what grounds did Chief Ross object to the removal treaty?
2. What did the Cherokees stand to lose by the terms of removal, according to Chief Ross?
3. What options were available to native groups in their attempts to negotiate with the United States?

Source: Moulton, Gary E., ed. *The Papers of Chief John Ross, vol. 1, 1807–1839*. Norman, OK: University of Oklahoma Press, 1985.

TRAIL OF TEARS

About 1,000 Cherokees fled to North Carolina, where eventually the federal government provided them with a small reservation in the Smoky Mountains that survives today. But most of the rest made a long, forced trek to "**Indian Territory**," what later became Oklahoma, beginning in the winter of 1838. Thousands, perhaps a quarter or more of the émigrés, perished before reaching their unwanted destination. In the harsh new reservations, the survivors remembered the terrible journey as "The Trail Where They Cried," the **Trail of Tears**.

Between 1830 and 1838, virtually all the Five Civilized Tribes were forced to travel to Indian Territory. The Choctaws of Mississippi and western Alabama were the first to make the trek, beginning in 1830. The army moved out the Creeks of eastern Alabama and western Georgia in 1836. A year later, the Chickasaws in northern Mississippi began their long march westward and the Cherokees, finally, a year after that.

The Seminoles in Florida were able to resist removal, but even their success was limited. Like other tribes, the Seminoles had agreed under pressure to a settlement by which they ceded their lands to the United States and agreed to move to Indian Territory within three years. Most did move west, but a substantial minority, under the leadership of the chieftain Osceola, balked and staged an uprising beginning in 1835 to defend their lands, the second of the Seminole Wars. Joining the Indians in their struggle was a group of runaway African American slaves, who had been living with the tribe. Jackson sent troops to Florida, but the Seminoles and their black allies were masters of guerrilla warfare in the junglelike Everglades. Finally, in 1842, the government abandoned the war. By then, many of the Seminoles had been either killed or forced westward.

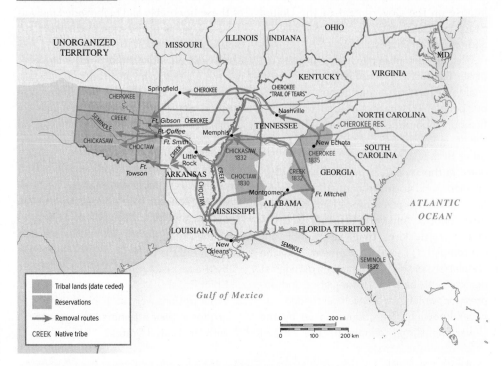

THE EXPULSION OF THE TRIBES, 1830-1835 Well before he became president, Andrew Jackson was famous for his military exploits against the tribes. Once in the White House, he ensured that few Indians would remain in the southern states of the nation, now that white settlement was increasing there. The result was a series of dramatic "removals" of Indian tribes out of their traditional lands and into new territories west of the Mississippi—mostly in Oklahoma. Note the very long distance many of these tribes had to travel. • *Why was the route of the Cherokee, shown in the upper portion of the map, known as the Trail of Tears?*

THE MEANING OF REMOVAL

By the end of the 1830s, most of the Indian societies east of the Mississippi had been removed to the West. The tribes had ceded over 100 million acres to the federal government and had received in return about $68 million and 32 million acres in the far less hospitable lands west of the Mississippi, territory that already had established native populations. There they lived, divided by tribe into a series of separate reservations, in a territory surrounded by a string of U.S. forts and whose climate and topography bore little relation to anything they had known before.

What, if any, were the alternatives to the removal of the Indians? There was probably never any realistic possibility that the government could stop white expansion westward. But there were alternatives to the brutal removal policy. The West was filled with examples of white settlers and native tribes living side by side. In the pueblos of New Mexico, in the fur trading posts of the Pacific Northwest, and in parts of Texas and California, Indians and the newcomers from Mexico, Canada, and the United States had created societies in which the various groups mingled intimately. Sometimes close contact between whites and Indians was beneficial to both sides; often it was cruel and exploitative. But the early multiracial societies of the West did not separate whites and Indians. They demonstrated ways in which the two cultures could interact, each shaping the other.

By the mid-nineteenth century, however, white Americans had adopted a different model. Much as the early British settlers along the Atlantic Coast had established "plantations," from which natives were, in theory, to be excluded, so the western whites of later years believed that Indians could not be partners in the creation of new societies in the West. They were obstacles to be removed and, as far as possible, isolated.

JACKSON AND THE BANK WAR

Jackson was quite willing to manipulate the Indian tribes. But in other contexts, he was very reluctant to use federal authority, as shown by his 1830 veto of a congressional measure providing a subsidy to the proposed Maysville Road in Kentucky. The bill was unconstitutional, Jackson argued, because the road in question lay entirely within Kentucky and was not, therefore, a part of "interstate commerce." Jackson also thought the bill unwise because it committed the government to what he considered extravagant expenditures. A similar resistance to federal power lay behind Jackson's war against the Bank of the United States.

BIDDLE'S INSTITUTION

The Bank of the United States held a monopoly on federal deposits, provided credit to growing enterprises, issued banknotes that served as a dependable medium of exchange, and exercised a restraining effect on the less well-managed state banks. **Nicholas Biddle**, who ran the Bank from 1823 on, had done much to put the institution on a sound and prosperous basis. Nevertheless, many Americans—among them Andrew Jackson—were determined to destroy it.

Opposition to the Bank came from two very different groups: the "soft-money" and "hard-money" factions. Advocates of soft money consisted largely of state bankers and their allies. They objected to the Bank because it restrained state banks from issuing notes freely. The hard-money faction, which included Andrew Jackson, believed that gold or silver coin (specie) was the only safe currency, and they condemned *all* banks that issued banknotes, state or federal. Jackson inherently distrusted paper bills, which were essentially promissory in character and would become worthless if the specie that backed them dried up.

But his critiques of Biddle's bank went deeper than that. The Bank of the United States was the largest corporation in the country, partially public and partially private: it owed its existence to Congress but could float loans to state banks, businesses, and individuals as it saw fit. Jackson attacked it as both an overly centralized and domineering federal institution and also as a greedy private enterprise currying favor with the rich and powerful. Thus like many political issues then and now, the battle over the Bank became a focal point for broader antagonisms of privilege, governance, and power. Jackson made clear that he would not favor renewing the charter of the Bank of the United States, which was due to expire in 1836.

A Philadelphia aristocrat unaccustomed to politics, Biddle began granting banking favors to influential men. In particular, he relied on Daniel Webster, whom he named the Bank's legal counsel and director of the Boston branch. Webster helped Biddle enlist the support of Henry Clay as well. Clay, Webster, and other advisers persuaded Biddle to apply to Congress for a recharter bill in 1832, four years ahead of the expiration date. Congress passed the recharter bill, Jackson vetoed it, and the Bank's supporters in Congress failed to override the veto. The Bank question then emerged as the paramount issue of the 1832 election, just as Clay had hoped.

In 1832, Clay ran for president as the unanimous choice of the Whigs. But the "**Bank War**" failed to provide Clay with the winning issue he had hoped for. Jackson, with Van Buren as his running mate, won an overwhelming victory with 55 percent of the popular vote and 219 electoral votes.

THE "MONSTER" DESTROYED

Jackson was now more determined than ever to destroy the "monster." He could not legally abolish the Bank before the expiration of its charter. But he could weaken it by removing the government's deposits from it. When his secretary of the treasury, believing that such an action would destabilize the financial system, refused to give the order, Jackson fired him and appointed a replacement. When the new secretary similarly procrastinated, Jackson fired him, too, and named a third: **Roger B. Taney**, the attorney general, a close friend and loyal ally of the president.

Taney soon began taking the government's deposits out of the Bank of the United States and putting them in a number of state banks. In response, Biddle called in loans and raised interest rates, explaining that without the government deposits the Bank's resources, previously quite strong, were now stretched thin. His actions shrunk or destroyed corporations, led to worker layoffs, and precipitated a short recession, all done deliberately to reveal and protest the impact of Jackson's withdrawal.

Indeed, as financial conditions worsened in the winter of 1833–1834, supporters of the Bank sent petitions to Washington urging its rechartering. But the Jacksonians blamed the recession on Biddle. He had the money, they said, not the government. In the court of public opinion, claims of Biddle's overly broad power over the economy appeared to have been borne out. When the banker finally carried his contraction of credit too far and had to reverse himself to appease the business community, his hopes of winning a recharter of the Bank died in the process. Jackson had won a considerable political victory. But when the Bank of the United States expired in 1836, the country was left with a fragmented and chronically unstable banking system that would plague the economy for many years.

In the aftermath of the Bank War, Jackson moved against the most powerful remaining institution of economic nationalism: the Supreme Court. In 1835, when John Marshall died, the president appointed as the new chief justice his trusted ally Roger B. Taney. Taney did not bring a sharp break in constitutional interpretation, but he did help modify Marshall's vigorous nationalism. Perhaps the clearest indication of the new judicial climate was the celebrated case of *Charles River Bridge v. Warren Bridge* of 1837. The case involved a dispute between two Massachusetts companies over the right to build a bridge across the Charles River between Boston and Cambridge. Reversing the spirit of many Marshall decisions, Taney argued that a state could amend or nullify a contract if such action was necessary to advance the well-being of the community. The decision reflected one of the cornerstones of the Jacksonian idea: that the key to democracy was an expansion of economic opportunity, which would not occur if older corporations could maintain monopolies.

THE CHANGING FACE OF AMERICAN POLITICS

Jackson's forceful—some people claimed tyrannical—tactics in crushing first the nullification movement and then the Bank of the United States helped galvanize a growing opposition coalition. It began as a gathering of national political leaders opposed to Jackson's

(Source: Library of Congress, Prints and Photographs Division [LC-USZ62-1562])

KING ANDREW THE FIRST This parody appeared sometime in 1833 in response to Andrew Jackson's withdrawal of federal funds from the Bank of the United States and his veto of its recharter the previous year. Jackson, trampling on a torn Constitution and the coat of arms of Pennsylvania, where the Bank was located, holds a veto in his left hand and a scepter in his right.

use of power. Denouncing the president as "King Andrew I," they began to refer to themselves as Whigs, after the party in England that traditionally worked to limit the power of the king. With the emergence of the Whigs, the nation once again had two competing political parties. What scholars now call the "second party system" had begun its relatively brief life.

Democrats and Whigs

The philosophy of the Democratic Party in the 1830s bore the stamp of Andrew Jackson. The federal government, the Democrats believed, should be limited in power, except to the degree that it worked to eliminate social and economic arrangements that entrenched privilege and stifled opportunity. The rights of states should be protected except to the extent that state governments interfered with social and economic mobility. Jacksonian Democrats celebrated "honest workers," "simple farmers," and "forthright businessmen" and contrasted them to the corrupt, monopolistic, aristocratic forces of established wealth. Democrats were more likely than Whigs to support territorial expansion, which would, they believed, widen opportunities for aspiring Americans. Radical members of the party—the so-called Loco Focos, mainly workingmen, small businessmen, and professionals in the Northeast—called for a vigorous assault on privileged elites and what they saw as the government's economic manipulations on their behalf. A Loco Foco protest against inflation turned into a riot of hungry New York workers in February 1837, but the group's philosophies later found official expression in an 1840 act of Congress separating banking from the federal government.

In contrast, the political philosophy that became known as Whiggery favored the expansion of federal power and industrial and commercial development. Whigs were cautious about westward expansion, fearful that rapid territorial growth would produce instability. And although Whigs insisted that their vision would result in increasing opportunities for all Americans, they tended to attribute particular value to the entrepreneurs and institutions that most effectively promoted economic growth.

The Whigs were strongest among the more substantial merchants and manufacturers of the Northeast, the wealthier planters of the South, and the ambitious farmers and rising commercial class of the West. The Democrats drew more support from smaller merchants and the workingmen of the Northeast, as well as southern and western planters who favored a predominantly agrarian economy. Whigs tended to be wealthier, to have more aristocratic backgrounds, and to be more commercially ambitious than the Democrats. But Whigs and Democrats alike were more interested in winning elections than in maintaining philosophical purity. And both parties made adjustments from region to region to attract the largest possible number of voters.

In New York, for example, the Whigs developed a popular following through a movement known as Anti-Masonry. The Anti-Mason Party had emerged in the 1820s in response to widespread resentment against the secret and exclusive, hence supposedly undemocratic, Society of Freemasons. Such resentment increased in 1826 when a former Mason, William Morgan, mysteriously disappeared from his home in Batavia, New York, shortly before he was scheduled to publish a book that would allegedly expose the secrets of Freemasonry. With help from a widespread assumption that Morgan had been abducted and murdered by vengeful Masons, Whigs seized on the Anti-Mason frenzy to launch spirited attacks on Jackson and Van Buren (both Freemasons), implying that the Democrats were connected with the antidemocratic conspiracy.

Religious and ethnic divisions also played an important role in determining the constituencies of the two parties. Irish and German Catholics tended to support the Democrats, who appeared to share their own vague aversion to commercial development and who seemed to respect their cultural values. Evangelical Protestants gravitated toward the Whigs because they associated the party with constant development and improvement. They envisioned a society progressing steadily toward unity and order, and they looked on the new immigrant communities as groups that needed to be disciplined and taught "American" ways.

The Whig Party was more successful at defining its positions and attracting a constituency than it was at uniting behind a national leader. No one person was ever able to command the loyalties of the party in the way Jackson commanded those of the Democrats. Instead, Whigs tended to divide their allegiance among the "Great Triumvirate" of Henry Clay, Daniel Webster, and John C. Calhoun.

Clay won support from many who favored internal improvements and economic development with what he called the American System. But Clay's image as a devious political operator and his identification with the West were a liability. He ran for president three times and never won. Daniel Webster won broad support among the Whigs with his passionate speeches in defense of the Constitution and the Union; but his close connection with the Bank of the United States and the protective tariff, his reliance on rich men for financial support, and his excessive fondness for brandy prevented him from developing enough of a national constituency to win him his desired office. John C. Calhoun never considered himself a true Whig, and his identification with the nullification controversy in effect disqualified him from national leadership in any case. Yet he sided with Clay and Webster on the issue of the national bank, and he shared with them a strong animosity toward Andrew Jackson.

The Whigs competed relatively evenly with the Democrats in congressional, state, and local races, but they managed to win only two presidential elections in the more than twenty years of their history. Their problems became particularly clear in 1836. While the Democrats united behind Andrew Jackson's personal choice for president, Martin Van Buren, the Whigs could not agree on a single candidate. Instead, they ran several candidates in different regions, hoping they might separately draw enough votes from Van Buren to throw the election to the House of Representatives, where the Whigs might be better able to elect one of their candidates. In the end, however, Van Buren won easily, with 170 electoral votes to 124 for all his opponents combined.

POLITICS AFTER JACKSON

Andrew Jackson retired from public life in 1837, the most beloved political figure of his age. Martin Van Buren was less fortunate. He could not match Jackson's personal magnetism, and his administration suffered from economic difficulties that hurt both him and his party.

VAN BUREN AND THE PANIC OF 1837

Van Buren's success in the 1836 election was a result in part of a nationwide economic boom. Canal and railroad builders operated at a peak of activity. Prices were rising, credit was plentiful, and the land business, in particular, was booming. Between 1835 and 1837, the government sold nearly 40 million acres of public land, nearly three-fourths of it to speculators. These land sales, along with revenues the government received from the tariff of 1833, created a series of substantial federal budget surpluses and made possible a steady reduction of the national debt. From 1835 to 1837, the government for the first and only time in its history was out of debt, with a substantial surplus in the Treasury.

Congress and the administration now faced the question of what to do with the Treasury surplus. Support soon grew for returning the federal surplus to the states. An 1836 "distribution" act required the federal government to pay its surplus funds to the states each year in four quarterly installments as interest-free, unsecured loans. No one expected the "loans" to be repaid. The states spent the money quickly, mainly to promote the construction of highways, railroads, and canals. The distribution of the surplus thus gave further stimulus to the economic boom. At the same time, the withdrawal of federal funds strained the state banks in which they had been deposited by the government; the banks had to call in their own loans to make the transfer of funds to the state governments.

Congress did nothing to check the speculative fever. But Jackson feared that the government was selling land for state banknotes of questionable value. In 1836, he issued an executive order, the "**specie circular**." It provided that in payment for public lands, the government would accept only gold or silver coins or currency backed by gold or silver. The specie circular produced a financial crisis that began in the first

(Source: Library of Congress, Prints and Photographs Division [LC-USZ62-89594])

HUMBUG GLORY BANK This image mocked opponents of the specie circular, and more broadly, ridiculed the issuance of currency not backed by gold or silver. It reflected Andrew Jackson's charge that banks, here led by "Honest Amos," would circulate worthless paper rather than gold or silver coin (specie) or currency backed by those precious metals.

months of Van Buren's presidency, the **Panic of 1837**. Banks and businesses failed; unemployment grew; bread riots shook some of the larger cities; and prices fell, especially the price of land. Many railroad and canal projects failed; several of the debt-burdened state governments ceased to pay interest on their bonds, and a few repudiated their debts, at least temporarily. The worst depression in American history to that point, it lasted for five years, and it was a political catastrophe for Van Buren and the Democrats.

The Van Buren administration did little to fight the depression. In fact, some of the steps it took—borrowing money to pay government debts and accepting only specie for payment of taxes—may have made things worse. Other efforts failed in Congress: a "preemption" bill that would have given settlers the right to buy government land near them before it was opened for public sale, and another bill that would have lowered the price of land. Van Buren did succeed in establishing a ten-hour workday on all federal projects via a presidential order, but he had few legislative achievements.

The most important and controversial measure in the president's program was a proposal for a new financial system. Under Van Buren's plan, known as the "independent treasury" or "subtreasury" system, government funds would be placed in an independent treasury in Washington and in subtreasuries in other cities. No private banks would have the government's money or name to use as a basis for speculation. Van Buren called a special session of Congress in 1837 to consider the proposal, but it failed in the House. In 1840, however, the administration finally succeeded in driving the measure through both houses of Congress.

THE LOG CABIN CAMPAIGN

As the campaign of 1840 approached, the Whigs realized that they would have to settle on one candidate for president. In December 1839, they held their first nominating convention. Passing over Henry Clay, they chose **William Henry Harrison**, a renowned soldier and a popular national figure. The Democrats again nominated Van Buren.

The 1840 campaign was the first in which the new and popular "penny press" carried news of the candidates to large audiences. (See "Patterns of Popular Culture: The Penny Press.") Such newspapers were deliberately livelier and more sensationalist than the newspapers of the past, which had been almost entirely directed at the upper classes. The *Sun,* the first of the new breed, began publishing in 1833 and was from the beginning self-consciously egalitarian. It soon had the largest circulation in New York. Other, similar papers soon began appearing in other cities—reinforcing the increasingly democratic character of political culture and encouraging the inclination of both parties to try to appeal to ordinary voters as they planned their campaigns.

The campaign of 1840 also illustrated how fully the spirit of party competition had established itself in America. The Whigs—who had emerged as a party largely because of their opposition to Andrew Jackson's common-people democracy—presented themselves in 1840 as the party of the common people. So, of course, did the Democrats. The Whig campaign was particularly effective in portraying William Henry Harrison, a wealthy member of the frontier elite with a considerable estate, as a simple man of the people who loved log cabins and hard cider. The Democrats, already weakened by the depression, had no effective defense against such tactics. Harrison won the election with 234 electoral votes to 60 for Van Buren and with a popular majority of 53 percent.

(Source: Library of Congress, Prints and Photographs Division [LC-USZ62-40740])

HARRISON AND REFORM   This poster announced a meeting of supporters of William Henry Harrison. It conveys Harrison's presumably humble beginnings in a log cabin. In reality, Harrison was a wealthy, aristocratic man, but the unpopularity of the aristocratic airs of his opponent, President Martin Van Buren, persuaded the Whig Party that it would be good political strategy to portray Harrison as a humble "man of the people."

THE PENNY PRESS

On September 3, 1833, a small newspaper appeared in New York City for the first time: the *Sun*, published by a young former apprentice from Massachusetts named Benjamin Day. Four pages long, it contained mostly trivial local news, with particular emphasis on sex, crime, and violence. It sold for a penny, launching a new age in the history of American journalism, the age of the "penny press."

Before the advent of the penny press, newspapers in America were far too expensive for most ordinary citizens to buy. But several important changes in both the business of journalism and the character of American society paved the way for Benjamin Day and others to challenge the established press. New technologies—the steam-powered cylinder printing press, new machines for making paper, railroads and canals for distributing issues to a larger market—made it possible to publish newspapers inexpensively and to sell them widely. A rising popular literacy rate, a result, in part, of the spread of public education, created a bigger reading public.

The penny press was also a response to the changing culture of the 1820s and 1830s. The spread of an urban market economy contributed to the growth of the penny press by drawing a large population of workers, artisans, and clerks into large cities, where they became an important market for the new papers. The spirit of democracy—symbolized by the popularity of Andrew Jackson and the rising numbers of white male voters across the country—helped create an appetite for journalism that spoke to and for "the people." The *Sun* and other papers like it were committed to feeding the appetites of the people of modest means, who constituted most of their readership. "Human interest stories" helped solidify their hold on the working public.

Within six months of its first issue, the *Sun* had the largest circulation in New York—8,000 readers, more than twice the number of its nearest competitors. James Gordon Bennett's *New York Herald*, which began publication in 1835, soon surpassed the *Sun* in popularity, with its lively combination of sensationalism and local gossip and its aggressive pursuit of national and international stories. The *Herald* pioneered a "letters to the editor" column, was the first paper to have regular reviews of books and the arts, and launched the first daily sports section. By 1860, its circulation of more than 77,000 was the largest of any daily newspaper in the world.

Not all the new penny papers were as sensationalistic as the *Sun* and the *Herald*. The *New-York Tribune*, founded in 1841 by Horace Greeley, prided itself on serious reporting and commentary. As serious as the *Tribune*, but more sober and self-consciously "objective" in its reportage, was the *New York Times*, which Henry Raymond founded in 1851. "We do not mean to write as if we were in a passion—unless that shall really be the case," the *Times* huffily proclaimed in its first issue, in an obvious reference to Greeley and his impassioned reportage, "and we shall make it a point to get into a passion as rarely as possible."

The newspapers of the penny press initiated the process of turning journalism into a profession. They were the first papers to pay their reporters, and they were also the first to rely heavily on advertisements, often devoting up to half their space to paid advertising. They tended to be sensationalistic and opinionated, but they were also usually aggressive in uncovering serious and important news—in police stations, courts, jails, streets, and private homes as well as in city halls, state capitals, Washington, and the world.

(Source: Library of Congress, Chronicling America: Historic American Newspapers [sn83030311-18360101])

THE *HERALD* This 1836 front page of the *Herald,* which had begun publication the prior year, contains advertisements for medicines and insurance, markets the services of a doctor, a school, and a furniture maker, and announces the enlargement of the newspaper.

UNDERSTAND, ANALYZE, & EVALUATE

1. How were the penny press newspapers a product of the Jacksonian era?
2. Before the advent of the penny press, newspapers in America were aimed at a much narrower audience. Some published mainly business news, and others worked to advance the aims of a political party. What nationally circulated newspapers and other media today continue this tradition?

THE FRUSTRATION OF THE WHIGS

Despite their decisive victory, the Whigs found the four years after their resounding victory frustrating and divisive. The trouble began when their appealing new president died of pneumonia just one month after taking office. Vice President **John Tyler** of Virginia succeeded him.

Tyler was a former Democrat who had left the party in reaction to what he considered Jackson's excessively egalitarian program; Tyler's approach to public policy still showed signs of his Democratic past. The president did agree to bills abolishing Van Buren's independent-treasury system and raising tariff rates. But he refused to support Clay's attempt to recharter the Bank of the United States, and he vetoed several internal improvement bills sponsored by Clay and other congressional Whigs. Finally, a conference of congressional Whigs voted Tyler out of the party. Every cabinet member but Webster, who was serving as secretary of state, resigned. Five former Democrats took their places. When Webster, too, left the cabinet, Tyler appointed Calhoun, who had rejoined the Democratic Party, to replace him.

A new political alignment was taking shape. Tyler and a small band of conservative southern Whigs were preparing to rejoin the Democrats. Into the common people's party of Jackson and Van Buren was arriving a faction with decidedly aristocratic political ideas, men who thought that government had an obligation to protect and even expand the institution of slavery and who believed in states' rights with almost fanatical devotion.

WHIG DIPLOMACY

In the midst of these domestic controversies, anti-British factions in Canada launched an unsuccessful rebellion against the colonial government there in 1837. When the insurrection failed, some of the rebels took refuge near the United States border and chartered an American steamship, the *Caroline,* to ship them supplies across the Niagara River from New York. British authorities in Canada seized the *Caroline* and burned it, killing one American in the process. Resentment over the *Caroline* affair in the United States grew rapidly. At the same time, tensions flared over the boundary between Canada and Maine, which had been in dispute since the treaty of 1783. In 1838, rival groups of Americans and Canadians, mostly lumberjacks, began moving into the Aroostook River region in the disputed area, precipitating a violent brawl that became known as the "Aroostook War."

Several years later, in 1841, an American ship, the *Creole,* sailed from Virginia for New Orleans with more than 100 slaves aboard. En route the slaves mutinied, seized possession of the ship, and took it to the Bahamas. British officials there declared the slaves free, and the London government refused to overrule them. Many Americans, especially southerners, were furious.

At this critical juncture, a new government eager to reduce tensions with the United States came to power in Great Britain. It sent Lord Ashburton, an admirer of America, to negotiate an agreement on the Maine boundary and other matters. The result was the **Webster-Ashburton Treaty** of 1842, under which the United States received slightly more than half the disputed area and agreed to a northern boundary as far west as the Rocky Mountains. Ashburton also eased the memory of the *Caroline* and *Creole* affairs by expressing regret and promising no future "officious interference" with American ships. Anglo-American relations improved significantly.

During the Tyler administration, the United States established its first diplomatic relations with China. In the 1844 Treaty of Wang Hya, American diplomats secured the same trading privileges as the British. In the next ten years, American trade with China steadily increased.

In their diplomatic efforts, at least, the Whigs were able to secure some important successes. But by the end of the Tyler administration, the party could look back on few other victories. And in the election of 1844, the Whigs lost the White House to James K. Polk, a Democrat with an explicit agenda of westward expansion.

CONCLUSION

The election of Andrew Jackson in 1828 reflected the emergence of a new political world. Throughout the nation, the laws governing political participation were loosening, and the number of people permitted to vote was increasing to include most white males but almost no one else. Along with this expansion of the electorate was emerging a new spirit of party politics.

Jackson set out as president to entrench his party, the Democrats, in power. A fierce defender of the West and a sharp critic of what he considered the stranglehold of the aristocratic East on the nation's economic life, he sought to limit the role of the federal government in economic affairs and worked to destroy the Bank of the United States, which he considered a corrupt vehicle of aristocratic influence. And he confronted the greatest challenge yet to American unity—the nullification crisis of 1832-33—with a strong assertion of the power and importance of the Union. These positions won him broad popularity and ensured his reelection in 1832 and the election of his designated successor, Martin Van Buren, in 1836.

But a new coalition of anti-Jacksonians, who called themselves the Whigs, launched a powerful new party that used much of the same anti-elitist rhetoric to win support for their own, much more nationalistic program. Their emergence culminated in the campaign of 1840 with the election of William Henry Harrison, the first Whig president. When his death led to the accidental presidency of John Tyler, however, further realignments were set in motion.

KEY TERMS/PEOPLE/PLACES/EVENTS

Alexis de Tocqueville 205
Andrew Jackson 203
Bank War 216
Black Hawk War 210
Daniel Webster 209
Dorr Rebellion 204
Five Civilized Tribes 211
Indian Removal Act 211

Indian Territory 213
John C. Calhoun 208
John Tyler 224
Martin Van Buren 208
Nicholas Biddle 215
nullification 208
Panic of 1837 220
Roger B. Taney 216

specie circular 219
spoils system 208
Trail of Tears 213
Webster-Ashburton Treaty 224
Webster-Hayne debate 209
Whigs 207
William Henry Harrison 220

RECALL AND REFLECT

1. What was Andrew Jackson's political philosophy, and how was it reflected in the policies and actions of his administration?
2. Who benefited under Jacksonian democracy? Who suffered?
3. How did Andrew Jackson change the office of the presidency?
4. Who supported and who opposed the Bank of the United States, and why? Who was right?
5. How and why did white attitudes toward Native Americans change, and how did these changes lead to the Indian Removal Act and the Trail of Tears?
6. How did Native Americans in the Southeast respond to white efforts to seize their land and remove them to the West?

10 | AMERICA'S ECONOMIC REVOLUTION

THE CHANGING AMERICAN POPULATION
TRANSPORTATION AND COMMUNICATIONS
REVOLUTIONS
COMMERCE AND INDUSTRY
MEN AND WOMEN AT WORK
PATTERNS OF SOCIETY
THE AGRICULTURAL NORTH

LOOKING AHEAD

1. What were the factors sparking the U.S. economic revolution of the mid-nineteenth century?
2. How did the U.S. population change between 1820 and 1840, and how did the population change affect the nation's economy, society, and politics?
3. Why did America's Industrial Revolution affect the northern economy and society differently than it did the southern economy and society?

WHEN THE UNITED STATES ENTERED the War of 1812, it was still an essentially agrarian nation. There were, to be sure, some substantial cities in America and also modest but growing manufacturing centers, mainly in the Northeast. But the overwhelming majority of Americans were farmers and tradespeople.

By the time the Civil War began in 1861, however, the United States had transformed itself. Most Americans were still rural people. But even most farmers were now part of a national, and even international, market economy. Equally important, the United States was starting to challenge the industrial nations of Europe for supremacy in manufacturing. The nation had experienced the beginning of its own Industrial Revolution.

1817–1825

Erie Canal constructed

1830s

Immigration from Ireland and Germany begins

1837

Native American Association fights immigration

1845

Native American Party formed

1847

John Deere manufactures steel plows

1830

Baltimore and Ohio Railroad begins operation

1834

Lowell Mills women strike

McCormick patents mechanical reaper

1844

Morse sends first telegraph message

1846

Rotary press invented

1852

American Party (Know-Nothings) formed

THE CHANGING AMERICAN POPULATION

The American Industrial Revolution was a result of many factors: advances in transportation and communications, the growth of manufacturing technology, the development of new systems of business organization, and perhaps above all, surging population growth.

POPULATION TRENDS

Three trends characterized the American population during the **antebellum** period: rapid increase, movement westward, and the growth of towns and cities where demand for work was expanding.

The American population, 4 million in 1790, had reached 10 million by 1820 and 17 million by 1840. Improvements in public health played a role in this growth. Epidemics declined in both frequency and intensity, and the death rate as a whole dipped. But the population increase was also a result of a high birthrate. In 1840, white women bore an average of 6.14 children each.

The African American population increased more slowly than the white population. After 1808, when the importation of slaves became illegal, the proportion of blacks to whites in the nation as a whole steadily declined. The slower increase of the black population was also a result of its comparatively high death rate. Slave mothers had large families, but life was shorter for both slaves and free blacks than for whites—a result of the enforced poverty and harsh working conditions in which virtually all African Americans lived.

Immigration, choked off by wars in Europe and economic crises in America, contributed little to the American population in the first three decades of the nineteenth century. Of the total 1830 population of nearly 13 million, the foreign-born numbered fewer than 500,000. Soon, however, immigration began to grow once again. Famine and political unrest in European countries fueled people's desire to emigrate, while the transatlantic voyage became quicker and more affordable as steamships replaced older ships powered by wind alone.

Much of this new European immigration flowed into the rapidly growing cities of the Northeast. But urban growth was a result of substantial internal migration as well. As agriculture in New England and other areas grew less profitable, more and more people picked up stakes and moved—some to promising agricultural regions in the West, but many to eastern cities.

IMMIGRATION AND URBAN GROWTH, 1840–1860

The growth of cities accelerated dramatically between 1840 and 1860. The population of New York, for example, rose from 312,000 to 805,000, making it the nation's largest and most commercially important city. Philadelphia's population grew over the same twenty-year period from 220,000 to 565,000; Boston's, from 93,000 to 177,000. By 1860, 26 percent of the population of the free states was living in towns (places of 2,500 people or more) or cities, up from 14 percent in 1840. The urban population of the South, by contrast, increased from 6 percent in 1840 to only 10 percent in 1860.

The booming agricultural economy of the West produced significant urban growth as well. Between 1820 and 1840, communities that had once been small villages or trading posts became major cities: St. Louis, Pittsburgh, Cincinnati, Louisville. All became centers of the growing carrying trade that connected the farmers of the Midwest with New Orleans and, through it, the cities of the Northeast. After 1830, however, an increasing proportion of this trade moved from the Mississippi River to the Great Lakes, creating such important new port cities as Buffalo, Detroit, Milwaukee, and Chicago, which gradually overtook the river ports.

Immigration from Europe swelled. Between 1840 and 1850, more than 1.5 million Europeans moved to America. In the 1850s, the number rose to 2.5 million. Almost half the residents of New York City in the 1850s were recent immigrants. In St. Louis, Chicago, and Milwaukee, the foreign-born outnumbered those of native birth. Comparatively few immigrants settled in the South.

The newcomers came from many different countries, but the overwhelming majority were from Ireland and Germany. By 1860, there were more than 1.5 million Irish-born and approximately 1 million German-born people in the United States. Many of the Irish were rural farmers escaping brutal poverty, British rule, and especially the Potato Famine that, from 1845 to 1852, rotted crops, caused widespread starvation, and helped spread disease. It killed nearly one million Irish. Most Irish immigrants abandoned their agricultural roots and stayed in the very eastern cities where they landed, becoming part of the unskilled labor force. The largest group of Irish immigrants comprised young, single women, who typically worked in factories or as domestics. Like the Irish, many German-speaking immigrants hungered for improved agricultural conditions, especially when wheat prices plummeted. But others came for explicitly political reasons. Many fled Europe in search of democracy after the failed revolutions of 1848. And those who were Jewish hoped to leave behind increasing anti-Semitism. Germans tended to arrive in America with more money and often came in family groups. They generally moved on to the Northwest, where they established farms or opened businesses.

The Rise of Nativism

Many politicians, particularly Democrats, eagerly courted the support of the new arrivals. Other citizens, however, viewed the growing foreign population with alarm. Some people argued that the immigrants were racially inferior or that they corrupted politics by selling their votes. Others complained that they were stealing jobs from the native workforce. Protestants worried that the growing Irish population would increase the power of the Catholic Church in America. Older-stock Americans feared that immigrants would become a radical force in politics. Out of these fears and prejudices emerged a number of secret societies to combat the "alien menace."

The first was the Native American Association, founded in 1837, which in 1845 became the Native American Party. In 1850, it joined with other groups supporting **nativism** to form the Supreme Order of the Star-Spangled Banner, whose demands included banning Catholics or aliens from holding public office, enacting more restrictive naturalization laws, and establishing literacy tests for voting. The order adopted a strict code of secrecy, which included a secret password: "I know nothing." Ultimately, members of the movement came to be known as the "**Know-Nothings.**"

After the 1852 elections, the Know-Nothings created a new political organization that they called the American Party. It scored an immediate and astonishing success in the elections of 1854. The Know-Nothings did well in Pennsylvania and New York and actually won control of the state government in Massachusetts. Outside the Northeast, however, their progress was more modest. After 1854, the strength of the Know-Nothings declined, and the party soon disappeared.

(Source: Library of Congress, Prints and Photographs Division [LC-USZC4-5004])

KNOW-NOTHING SOAP   This illustrated advertising label for soap manufactured in Boston alludes to the Know-Nothing or nativist movement. The Indian depicted in the foreground and teepees and camp in the background symbolize the movement's prejudice against new arrivals.

TRANSPORTATION AND COMMUNICATIONS REVOLUTIONS

Just as the Industrial Revolution required an expanding population, it also required an efficient system of transportation and communications. The first half of the nineteenth century saw dramatic changes in both.

THE CANAL AGE

From 1790 until the 1820s, the so-called turnpike era, the United States had relied largely on roads for internal transportation. But roads alone were not adequate for the nation's expanding needs. And so, in the 1820s and 1830s, Americans began to turn to other means of transportation as well.

Larger rivers like the Mississippi became increasingly important as steamboats replaced the slow barges that had previously dominated water traffic. The new riverboats carried the corn and wheat of northwestern farmers and the cotton and tobacco of southwestern planters to New Orleans, where oceangoing ships took the cargoes on to eastern ports or abroad.

But this roundabout river–sea route satisfied neither western farmers nor eastern merchants, who wanted a new way to ship goods cheaper and more directly to the urban markets and ports of the Atlantic Coast. New highways across the mountains provided a partial solution to the problem. But the costs of hauling goods overland, although lower than before, were still too

CANALS IN THE NORTH, 1823–1860 Note how the East and West are being connected through a growing transportation network. The great success of the Erie Canal, which opened in 1825, inspired decades of energetic canal building in many areas of the United States, as this map illustrates. But none of the new canals had anything like the impact of the original Erie Canal, and thus none of New York's competitors—among them Baltimore, Philadelphia, and Boston—were able to displace it as the nation's leading commercial center. • *How did the emergence of canals change the distribution of goods in America?*

high for anything except the most compact and valuable merchandise. And so interest grew in building canals—human-made waterways that connected bodies of water and were wide and deep enough for commercial vessels.

The job of financing canals fell largely to the states. New York was the first to act. It had the natural advantage of a good land route between the Hudson River and Lake Erie through the only break in the Appalachian chain. But the engineering tasks were still imposing. The more than 350-mile-long route was interrupted by high ridges and thick woods. After a long public debate, canal advocates prevailed, and digging began on July 4, 1817.

The **Erie Canal** was the greatest construction project Americans had ever undertaken. The canal itself was basically a simple ditch forty feet wide and four feet deep, with towpaths along the banks for the horses or mules that were to draw the canal boats. But its construction involved hundreds of difficult cuts and fills to enable the canal to pass through hills and over valleys, stone aqueducts to carry it across streams, and eighty-eight locks of heavy masonry with great wooden gates to permit ascents and descents. Still, the Erie Canal opened in October 1825 amid elaborate ceremonies and celebrations, and traffic was soon so heavy that within about seven years, tolls had repaid the entire cost of construction. By providing a route to the Great Lakes, the canal gave New York access to Chicago and the growing markets of the West. The Erie Canal also contributed to the decline of agriculture in New England. Now that it was so much cheaper for western farmers to ship their crops east, people farming marginal land in the Northeast found themselves unable to compete.

The system of water transportation extended farther when Ohio and Indiana, inspired by the success of the Erie Canal, provided water connections between Lake Erie and the Ohio River. These canals made it possible to ship goods by inland waterways all the way from New York to New Orleans.

One of the immediate results of these new transportation routes was increased white settlement in the Northwest, because it was now easier for migrants to make the westward journey and to ship their goods back to eastern markets. Much of the western produce continued to go downriver to New Orleans, but an increasing proportion went east to New York. And manufactured goods from throughout the East now moved in growing volume through New York and then to the West via the new water routes.

Rival cities along the Atlantic seaboard took alarm at New York's access to (and control over) so vast a market, largely at their expense. But they had limited success in catching up. Boston, its way to the Hudson River blocked by the Berkshire Mountains, did not even try to connect itself to the West by canal. Philadelphia, Baltimore, Richmond, and Charleston all aspired to build water routes to the Ohio Valley but never completed them. Some cities, however, saw opportunities in a different and newer means of transportation. Even before the canal age had reached its height, the era of the railroad was beginning.

THE EARLY RAILROADS

Railroads played a relatively small role in the nation's transportation system in the 1820s and 1830s, but railroad pioneers laid the groundwork in those years for the great surge of railroad building in the midcentury. Eventually, railroads became the primary transportation system for the United States, as well as critical sites of development for innovations in technology and corporate organization.

Railroads emerged from a combination of technological and entrepreneurial innovations: the invention of tracks, the creation of steam-powered locomotives, and the development of trains as public carriers of passengers and freight. By 1804, both English and American inventors had experimented with steam engines for propelling land vehicles. In 1820, John Stevens

(©Universal Images Group/Getty Images)

RACING ON THE RAILROAD Peter Cooper designed and built the first steam-powered locomotives in America in 1830 for the Baltimore and Ohio Railroad. On August 28 of that year, he raced his locomotive (the "Tom Thumb") against a horse-drawn railroad car. This sketch depicts the moment when Cooper's engine overtook the horse-drawn railroad car.

ran a locomotive and cars around a circular track on his New Jersey estate. And in 1825, the Stockton and Darlington Railroad in England became the first line to carry general traffic.

American entrepreneurs quickly grew interested in the English experiment. The first company to begin actual operations was the **Baltimore and Ohio Railroad**, which opened a thirteen-mile stretch of track in 1830. In New York, the Mohawk and Hudson began running trains along the sixteen miles between Schenectady and Albany in 1831. By 1836, more than a thousand miles of track had been laid in eleven states.

THE TRIUMPH OF THE RAILS

Railroads gradually supplanted canals and all other forms of transport. In 1840, the total railroad trackage of the country was under 3,000 miles. By 1860, it was over 27,000 miles, mostly in the Northeast. Railroads even crossed the Mississippi at several points by great iron bridges. Chicago eventually became the rail center of the West, securing its place as the dominant city of that region.

The emergence of the great train lines diverted traffic from the main water routes—the Erie Canal and the Mississippi River. By lessening the dependence of the West on the Mississippi, the railroads also helped weaken further the connection between the Northwest and the South.

Railroad construction required massive amounts of capital. Some came from private sources, but much of it came from government funding. State and local governments invested in railroads, but even greater assistance came from the federal government in the form of public land grants. By 1860, Congress had allotted over 30 million acres to eleven states to assist railroad construction.

It would be difficult to exaggerate the impact of the rails on the American economy, on American society, even on American culture. Where railroads went, towns, ranches, and farms grew up rapidly along their routes. Areas once cut off from markets during winter found that the railroad could transport goods to and from them year-round. Most of all, the railroads cut the time of shipment and travel. In the 1830s, traveling from New York to Chicago by lake and canal took roughly three weeks. By railroad in the 1850s, the same trip took less than two days.

The railroads were much more than a fast and economically attractive form of transportation. They were also a breeding ground for technological advances, a key to the nation's economic growth, and the birthplace of the modern corporate form of organization. They became a symbol of the nation's technological prowess. To many people, railroads were the most visible sign of American advancement and greatness.

RAILROAD GROWTH, 1850–1860 These two maps illustrate the dramatic growth of American railroads in the 1850s. Note the particularly extensive increase in mileage in the upper Midwest (known at the time as the Old Northwest). Note, too, the relatively smaller increase in railroad mileage in the South. Railroads forged a close economic relationship between the upper Midwest and the Northeast and weakened the Midwest's relationship with the South. • *How did this contribute to the South's growing sense of insecurity within the Union?*

THE TELEGRAPH

What the railroad was to transportation, the telegraph was to communication—a dramatic advance over traditional methods and a symbol of national progress and technological expertise.

Before the telegraph, communication over great distances could be achieved only by direct, physical contact. That meant that virtually all long-distance communication relied on the mail, which traveled first on horseback and coach and later by railroad. There were obvious disadvantages to this system, not the least of which was the difficulty in coordinating the railroad schedules. By the 1830s, experiments with many methods of improving long-distance communication had been conducted, among them a procedure for using the sun and reflective devices to send light signals as far as 187 miles.

In 1832, Samuel F. B. Morse—a professor of art with an interest in science—began experimenting with a different system. Fascinated with the possibilities of electricity, Morse set out to find a way to send signals along an electric cable. Technology did not yet permit the use of electric wiring to send reproductions of the human voice or any complex information. But Morse realized that electricity itself could serve as a communication device—that pulses of electricity could themselves become a kind of language. He experimented at first with a numerical code, in which each number would represent a word on a list available to recipients. Gradually, however, he became convinced of the need to find a more universal telegraphic "language," and he developed what became the **Morse code**, in which alternating long and short bursts of electric current would represent individual letters.

In 1843, Congress appropriated $30,000 for the construction of an experimental telegraph line between Baltimore and Washington; in May 1844 it was complete, and Morse succeeded in transmitting the news of James K. Polk's nomination for the presidency over the wires. By 1860, more than 50,000 miles of wire connected most parts of the country; a year later, the Pacific Telegraph, with 3,595 miles of wire, opened between New York and San Francisco. By then, nearly all the independent lines had joined in one organization, the **Western Union Telegraph Company**. The telegraph spread rapidly across Europe as well, and in 1866, the first transatlantic cable was laid, allowing telegraphic communication between America and Europe.

(©villorejo/Alamy)

THE TELEGRAPH The telegraph provided rapid communication across the country—and eventually across oceans—for the first time. Samuel F. B. Morse was one of a number of inventors who helped create the telegraph, but he was the most commercially successful of the rivals.

One of the first beneficiaries of the telegraph was the growing system of rails. Wires often ran alongside railroad tracks, and telegraph offices were often located in railroad stations. The telegraph allowed railroad operators to communicate directly with stations in cities, small towns, and even rural hamlets—to alert them to schedule changes and warn them about delays and breakdowns. Among other things, this new form of communication helped prevent accidents by alerting stations to problems that engineers in the past had to discover for themselves.

New Technology and Journalism

Another beneficiary of the telegraph was American journalism. The wires delivered news in a matter of hours—not days, weeks, or months, as in the past—across the country and the world. Where once the exchange of national and international news relied on the cumbersome exchange of newspapers by mail, now it was possible for papers to share their reporting. In 1846, newspaper publishers from around the nation formed the Associated Press to promote cooperative news gathering by wire.

Other technological advances spurred the development of the American press. In 1846, Richard Hoe invented the steam-powered cylinder rotary press, making it possible to print newspapers much more rapidly and cheaply than had been possible in the past. Among other things, the rotary press spurred the dramatic growth of mass-circulation newspapers. The *New York Sun,* the most widely circulated paper in the nation, had 8,000 readers in 1834. By 1860, its successful rival the *New York Herald*—benefiting from the speed and economies of production the rotary press made possible—had a circulation of 77,000.

COMMERCE AND INDUSTRY

By the mid-nineteenth century, the United States had developed the beginnings of a modern capitalist economy and an advanced industrial capacity. But the economy had developed along highly unequal lines—benefiting some classes and some regions far more than others.

The Expansion of Business, 1820–1840

American business grew rapidly in the 1820s and 1830s in part because of important innovations in management. Individuals or limited partnerships continued to operate most businesses, and the dominant figures were still the great merchant capitalists, who generally had sole ownership of their enterprises. In some larger businesses, however, the individual merchant capitalist was giving way to the corporation. Corporations, which had the advantage of combining the resources of a large number of shareholders, began to develop particularly rapidly in the 1830s, when some legal obstacles to their formation were removed. Previously, a corporation could obtain a charter only by a special act of a state legislature; by the 1830s, states began passing general incorporation laws, under which a group could secure a charter merely by paying a fee. The laws also permitted a system of limited liability, in which individual stockholders risked losing only the value of their own investment—and not the corporation's larger losses as in the past—if the enterprise failed. These changes made possible much larger manufacturing and business enterprises.

THE EMERGENCE OF THE FACTORY

The most profound economic development in mid-nineteenth-century America was the rise of the factory. Before the War of 1812, most manufacturing took place within households or in small workshops. Later in the nineteenth century, however, New England textile manufacturers began using new water-powered machines that allowed them to bring their operations together under a single roof. This **factory system**, as it came to be known, soon penetrated the shoe industry and other industries as well.

Between 1840 and 1860, American industry experienced particularly dramatic growth. For the first time, the value of manufactured goods was roughly equal to that of agricultural products. More than half of the approximately 140,000 manufacturing establishments in the country in 1860, including most of the larger enterprises, were located in the Northeast. The Northeast thus produced more than two-thirds of the manufactured goods and employed nearly three-quarters of the men and women working in manufacturing.

ADVANCES IN TECHNOLOGY

Even the most highly developed industries were still relatively immature. American cotton manufacturers, for example, produced goods of coarse grade; fine items continued to come from England. But by the 1840s, significant advances were occurring.

Among the most important was in the manufacturing of machine tools—the tools used to make machinery parts. The government supported much of the research and development of machine tools, often in connection with supplying the military. For example, a government armory in Springfield, Massachusetts, developed two important tools—the turret lathe (used for cutting screws and other metal parts) and the universal milling machine (which replaced the hand chiseling of complicated parts and dies)—early in the nineteenth century. The precision grinder (which became critical to, among other things, the construction of sewing machines) was designed in the 1850s to help the army produce standardized rifle parts. By the 1840s, the machine tools used in the factories of the Northeast were already better than those in most European factories.

One important result of better machine tools was that the principle of interchangeable parts spread into many industries. Eventually, interchangeability would revolutionize watch and clock making, the manufacturing of locomotives, the creation of steam engines, and the making of many farm tools and guns. It would also help make possible bicycles, sewing machines, typewriters, cash registers, and eventually the automobile.

Industrialization was also profiting from new sources of energy. The production of coal, most of it mined around Pittsburgh in western Pennsylvania, leaped from 50,000 tons in 1820 to 14 million tons in 1860. The new power source, which replaced wood and water power, made it possible to locate mills away from running streams and thus permitted the wider expansion of the industry.

The great industrial advances owed much to American inventors. In 1830, the number of inventions patented was 544; in 1860, it stood at 4,778. Several industries provide particularly vivid examples of how a technological innovation could produce major economic change. In 1839, Charles Goodyear, a New England hardware merchant, discovered a method of vulcanizing rubber (treating it to give it greater strength and elasticity); by 1860, his process had found over 500 uses and had helped create a major American rubber industry. In 1846, Elias Howe of Massachusetts constructed a sewing machine; Isaac Singer made improvements on it, and the Howe-Singer machine was soon being used in the manufacture of ready-to-wear clothing.

(Source: Library of Congress, Prints and Photographs Division [LC-USZ62-69112])

THE ENVIRONMENTAL COSTS OF INDUSTRIALIZATION Nineteenth-century factories like this print works in Manchester contributed to unprecedented levels of air pollution.

Industrialization was not without environmental costs, however. It brought unprecedented levels of water and air pollution that eventually triggered early efforts at reform and contributed to growing public awareness about the need to protect the environment and citizens. To stop toxic runoff from cattle processing plants, for example, Wisconsin passed the Slaughterhouse Offal Act of 1862 that prohibited dumping slaughter wastes in surface water. By 1861 Chicago and Cincinnati had both implemented smoke laws aimed at decreasing the soot, ash, and heavy smog produced by coal and iron factories, railroads, and ships.

RISE OF THE INDUSTRIAL RULING CLASS

The merchant capitalists remained figures of importance in the 1840s. In such cities as New York, Philadelphia, and Boston, influential mercantile groups operated shipping lines to southern ports or dispatched fleets of trading vessels to Europe and Asia. But merchant capitalism was declining by the middle of the century. This was partly because British competitors were stealing much of America's export trade, but mostly because there were greater opportunities for profit in manufacturing than in trade. That was one reason why industries developed first in the Northeast: an affluent merchant class with the money and the will to finance them already existed there. They supported the emerging industrial capitalists and soon became the new aristocrats of the Northeast, with far-reaching economic and political influence.

MEN AND WOMEN AT WORK

In the 1820s and 1830s, factory labor came primarily from the native-born population. After 1840, the growing immigrant population became the most important new source of workers.

RECRUITING A NATIVE WORKFORCE

Recruiting a labor force was not an easy task in the early years of the factory system. Ninety percent of the American people in the 1820s still lived and worked on farms. Many urban residents were skilled artisans who owned and managed their own shops, and the available unskilled workers were not numerous enough to meet industry's needs. But dramatic improvements in agricultural production, particularly in the Midwest, meant that each region no longer had to feed itself; it could import the food it needed. As a result, rural people from relatively unprofitable farming areas of the East began leaving the land to work in the factories.

Two systems of recruitment emerged to bring this new labor supply to the expanding textile mills. One, common in the mid-Atlantic states, brought whole families from the farm to work together in the mill. The second system, common in Massachusetts and New England in general, enlisted young women, mostly farmers' daughters in their late teens and early twenties. It was known as the **Lowell or Waltham system**, after the towns in which it first emerged. Many of these women worked for several years, saved their wages, and then returned home to marry and raise children. Others married men they met in the factories or in town. Most eventually stopped working in the mills and took up domestic roles instead.

Labor conditions in these early years of the factory system, hard as they often were, remained significantly better than they would later become. The Lowell workers, for example, were generally well fed, carefully supervised, and housed in clean boardinghouses and dormitories, which the factory owners maintained. (See "Consider the Source: *Handbook to Lowell*.") Wages for the Lowell workers were relatively generous by the standards of the time. The women even published a monthly magazine, the *Lowell Offering*.

Yet even these relatively well-treated workers found the transition from farm life to factory work difficult. Forced to live among strangers in a regimented environment, many women had trouble adjusting to the nature of factory work. However uncomfortable women may have found factory work, they had few other options. Work in the mills was in many cases virtually the only alternative to returning to farms that could no longer support them.

The factory system of Lowell did not, in any case, survive for long. In the competitive textile market of the 1830s and 1840s, manufacturers found it difficult to maintain the high living standards and reasonably attractive working conditions of before. Wages declined; the hours of work lengthened; the conditions of the boardinghouses deteriorated. In 1834, mill workers in Lowell organized a union—the **Factory Girls Association**—which staged a strike to protest a 25 percent wage cut. Two years later, the association struck again—against a rent increase in the boardinghouses. Both strikes failed, and a recession in 1837 virtually destroyed the organization. Eight years later, the Lowell women, led by the militant **Sarah Bagley**, created the Female Labor Reform Association, which grew to around 500 members in five months. It was one of the first American labor organizations created by women. Members published the *Voice of Industry* to air their grievances and political goals, which included a ten-hour day and improvements in conditions in the mills. The new association also asked state governments for legislative investigation of conditions in the mills. Although mill owners reduced the workday by 30 minutes, larger labor reforms would have to wait. The association dissolved in 1848 because the character of the factory workforce was changing again, lessening the urgency of their demands. Many mill girls were gradually moving into other occupations: teaching, domestic service, or homemaking. And textile manufacturers were turning to a less demanding labor supply: immigrants.

THE IMMIGRANT WORKFORCE

The increasing supply of immigrant workers after 1840 was a boon to manufacturers and other entrepreneurs. These new workers, because of their growing numbers and their unfamiliarity with their new country, had even less leverage than the women they displaced,

HANDBOOK TO LOWELL (1848)

Strict rules governed the working life of the young women who worked in the textile mills in Lowell, Massachusetts, in the first half of the nineteenth century. Equally strict rules regulated their time away from work (what little leisure time they enjoyed) in the company-supervised boardinghouses in which they lived. The excerpts from the *Handbook to Lowell* from 1848 that follow suggest the tight supervision under which the Lowell mill girls worked and lived.

FACTORY RULES

REGULATIONS TO BE OBSERVED by all persons employed in the factories of the Hamilton Manufacturing Company. The overseers are to be always in their rooms at the starting of the mill, and not absent unnecessarily during working hours. They are to see that all those employed in their rooms are in their places in due season, and keep a correct account of their time and work. They may grant leave of absence to those employed under them, when they have spare hands to supply their places and not otherwise, except in cases of absolute necessity.

All persons in the employ of the Hamilton Manufacturing Company are to observe the regulations of the room where they are employed. They are not to be absent from their work without the consent of the overseer, except in cases of sickness, and then they are to send him word of the cause of their absence. They are to board in one of the houses of the company and give information at the counting room, where they board, when they begin, or, whenever they change their boarding place; and are to observe the regulations of their boarding-house.

Those intending to leave the employment of the company are to give at least two weeks' notice thereof to their overseer.

All persons entering into the employment of the company are considered as engaged for twelve months, and those who leave sooner, or do not comply with all these regulations, will not be entitled to a regular discharge.

The company will not employ anyone who is habitually absent from public worship on the Sabbath, or known to be guilty of immorality.

A physician will attend once in every month at the counting-room, to vaccinate all who may need it, free of expense.

Anyone who shall take from the mills or the yard, any yarn, cloth or other article belonging to the company will be considered guilty of stealing and be liable to prosecution.

Payment will be made monthly, including board and wages. The accounts will be made up to the last Saturday but one in every month, and paid in the course of the following week.

These regulations are considered part of the contract, with which all persons entering into the employment of the Hamilton Manufacturing Company, engage to comply.

BOARDING-HOUSE RULES

REGULATIONS FOR THE BOARDING-HOUSES of the Hamilton Manufacturing Company. The tenants of the boarding-houses are not to board, or permit any part of their houses to be occupied by any person, except those in the employ of the company, without special permission.

They will be considered answerable for any improper conduct in their houses, and are not to permit their boarders to have company at unseasonable hours.

The doors must be closed at ten o'clock in the evening, and no person admitted after that time, without some reasonable excuse.

The keepers of the boarding-houses must give an account of the number, names and employment of their boarders, when required, and report the names of such as are guilty of any improper conduct, or are not in the regular habit of attending public worship.

The buildings, and yards about them, must be kept clean and in good order; and if they are injured, otherwise than from ordinary use, all necessary repairs will be made, and charged to the occupant.

The sidewalks, also, in front of the houses, must be kept clean, and free from snow, which must be removed from them immediately after it has ceased falling; if neglected, it will be removed by the company at the expense of the tenant.

It is desirable that the families of those who live in the houses, as well as the boarders, who have not had the kine pox, should be vaccinated, which will be done at the expense of the company, for such as wish it.

Some suitable chamber in the house must be reserved, and appropriated for the use of the sick, so that others may not be under the necessity of sleeping in the same room.

JOHN AVERY, Agent.

UNDERSTAND, ANALYZE, & EVALUATE

1. What do these rules suggest about the everyday lives of the mill workers?
2. What do the rules suggest about the company's attitude toward the workers? Do the rules offer any protections to the employees, or are they all geared toward benefiting the employer?
3. Why would the company enforce such strict rules? Why would the mill workers accept them?

Source: *Handbook to Lowell,* 1848.

and thus they often experienced far worse working conditions. Poorly paid construction gangs, made up increasingly of Irish immigrants, performed the heavy, unskilled work on turnpikes, canals, and railroads. Many of them lived in flimsy shanties, in grim conditions that endangered the health of their families (and reinforced native prejudices toward the "shanty Irish"). Irish workers began to predominate in the New England textile mills as well in the 1840s. Employers began paying piece rates rather than a daily wage and used other devices to speed up production and exploit the labor force more efficiently. The factories themselves were becoming large, noisy, unsanitary, and often dangerous places to work; the average workday was extending to twelve, often fourteen hours; and wages were declining. Women and children, whatever their skills, earned less than most men.

THE FACTORY SYSTEM AND THE ARTISAN TRADITION

Factories were also displacing the trades of skilled artisans. Artisans were as much a part of the older, republican vision of America as sturdy yeoman farmers. Independent craftspeople clung to a vision of economic life that was very different from that promoted by the new capitalist class. The **artisans** embraced not just the idea of individual, acquisitive success but also a sense of a "moral community." Skilled artisans valued their independence, their stability, and their relative equality within their economic world.

Some artisans made successful transitions into small-scale industry. But others found themselves unable to compete with the new factory-made goods. In the face of this competition, skilled workers in cities such as Philadelphia, Baltimore, Boston, and New York formed societies for mutual aid. During the 1820s and 1830s, these craft societies began to combine on a citywide basis and set up central organizations known as trade unions. In 1834, delegates from six cities founded the National Trades' Union, and in 1836, printers and cordwainers (makers of high-quality shoes and boots) set up their own national craft unions.

Hostile laws and hostile courts handicapped the unions, as did the Panic of 1837 and the depression that followed. But some artisans managed to retain control over their productive lives.

Fighting for Control

Industrial workers made continuous efforts to improve their lots. They tried, with little success, to persuade state legislatures to pass laws setting a maximum workday and regulating child labor. Their greatest legal victory came in Massachusetts in 1842, when the state supreme court, in *Commonwealth v. Hunt*, declared that unions were lawful organizations and that the strike was a lawful weapon. Other state courts gradually accepted the principles of the Massachusetts decision, but employers continued to resist.

Virtually all the early craft unions excluded women. As a result, women began establishing their own, new protective unions in the 1850s. Like the male craft unions, the female unions had little power in dealing with employers. They did, however, serve an important role as mutual aid societies for women workers.

Many factors combined to inhibit the growth of better working standards. Among the most important obstacles was the flood into the country of immigrant laborers, who were usually willing to work for lower wages than native workers. Because they were so numerous, manufacturers had little difficulty replacing disgruntled or striking workers with eager immigrants. Ethnic divisions often led workers to channel their resentments into internal bickering among one another rather than into their shared grievances. Another obstacle was the sheer strength of the industrial capitalists, who possessed not only economic but also political and social power.

PATTERNS OF SOCIETY

The Industrial Revolution was making the United States both dramatically wealthier and increasingly unequal. It was transforming social relationships at almost every level.

The Rich and the Poor

The commercial and industrial growth of the United States greatly elevated the average income of the American people. But this increasing wealth was being distributed highly unequally. Substantial groups of the population—slaves, Indians, landless farmers, and many of the unskilled workers on the fringes of the manufacturing system—shared hardly at all in the economic growth. But even among the rest of the population, disparities of income were growing. Merchants and industrialists were accumulating enormous fortunes; and in the cities, a distinctive culture of wealth began to emerge.

In large cities, people of great wealth gathered together in neighborhoods of astonishing opulence. They founded clubs and developed elaborate social rituals. They looked increasingly for ways to display their wealth—in great mansions, showy carriages, lavish household goods, and the elegant social establishments they patronized. New York developed a

(©Everett Historical/Shutterstock)

CENTRAL PARK   Daily carriage rides allowed the wealthy to take in fresh air while showing off their finery to their neighbors.

particularly elaborate high society. The construction of Central Park, which began in the 1850s, was in part a result of pressure from the members of high society, who wanted an elegant setting for their daily carriage rides.

A significant population of genuinely destitute people also emerged in the growing urban centers. These people were almost entirely without resources, often homeless, and dependent on charity or crime, or both, for survival. Substantial numbers of people actually starved to death or died of exposure. Some of these "paupers," as contemporaries called them, were recent immigrants. Some were widows and orphans, stripped of the family structures that allowed most working-class Americans to survive. Some were people suffering from alcoholism or mental illness, unable to work. Others were victims of native prejudice—barred from all but the most menial employment because of race or ethnicity. The Irish were particular victims of such prejudice.

The worst victims in the North were free blacks. Most major urban areas had significant black populations. Some of these African Americans were descendants of families who had lived in the North for generations. Others were former slaves who had escaped or been released by their masters. In material terms, at least, life was not always much better for them in the North than it had been in slavery. Most had access to very menial jobs at best. In most parts of the North, blacks could not vote, attend public schools, or use any of the public services available to white residents. Even so, most African Americans preferred life in the North, however arduous, to life in the South.

SOCIAL AND GEOGRAPHICAL MOBILITY

Despite the contrasts between conspicuous wealth and poverty in antebellum America, there was relatively little overt class conflict at this time. For one thing, life, in material terms at least, was better for most factory workers than it had been on the farms or in Europe. Laborers also found that it was possible to move up the economic ladder, especially when compared to opportunities in much of Europe. A significant amount of mobility within the working class also helped limit discontent. A few workers—a very small number, but enough to support the dreams of others—managed to move from poverty to riches by dint of work, ingenuity, and luck. And a much larger number of workers managed to move at least one notch up the ladder—for example, becoming in the course of a lifetime a skilled, rather than an unskilled, laborer.

More important than social mobility was geographical mobility. Some workers saved money, bought land, and moved west to farm it. But few urban workers, and even fewer poor ones, could afford to make such a move. Much more common was the movement of laborers from one industrial town to another. These migrants, often the victims of layoffs, looked for better opportunities elsewhere. Their search seldom led to marked improvement in their circumstances. The rootlessness of this large and distressed segment of the work-force made effective organization and protest difficult.

MIDDLE-CLASS LIFE

Despite the visibility of the very rich and the very poor in antebellum society, the fastest-growing group in America was the middle class. Economic development opened many more opportunities for people to own or work in shops or businesses, to engage in trade, to enter professions, and to administer organizations. In earlier times, when landownership had been the only real basis of wealth, society had been divided between those with little or no land (people Europeans generally called peasants) and a landed gentry (which in Europe usually became an inherited aristocracy). Once commerce and industry became a source of wealth, these rigid distinctions broke down; many people could become prosperous without owning land, but by providing valuable services.

Middle-class life in the antebellum years rapidly established itself as the most influential cultural form of urban America. Solid, substantial middle-class houses lined city streets, larger in size and more elaborate in design than the cramped, functional rowhouses in working-class neighborhoods—but also far less lavish than the great houses of the very rich. Middle-class people tended to own their homes, often for the first time. Workers and arti-sans remained mostly renters.

Middle-class women usually remained in the household, although increasingly they were also able to hire servants—usually young, unmarried immigrant women. In an age when doing the family's laundry could take an entire day, one of the aspirations of middle-class women was to escape from some of the drudgery of housework.

New household inventions altered, and greatly improved, the character of life in middle-class homes. Perhaps the most important was the invention of the cast-iron stove, which began to replace fireplaces as the principal vehicle for cooking in the 1840s. These wood- or coal-burning devices were hot, clumsy, and dirty by later standards, but compared to the inconvenience and danger of cooking on an open hearth, they seemed a great luxury. Stoves gave cooks greater control over food preparation and allowed them to cook several things at once.

Middle-class diets were changing rapidly, and not just because of the wider range of cooking that the stove made possible. The expansion and diversification of American agri-culture and the ability of distant farmers to ship goods to urban markets by rail greatly increased the variety of food available in cities. Fruits and vegetables were difficult to ship over long distances in an age with little refrigeration, but families had access to a greater variety of meats, grains, and dairy products than in the past. A few wealthy households acquired iceboxes, which allowed them to keep meat and dairy products fresh for several days. Most families, however, did not yet have any refrigeration. For them, preserving food meant curing meat with salt and preserving fruits in sugar. Diets were generally much heavier and starchier than they are today, and middle-class people tended to be considerably stouter than would be considered healthy or fashionable now.

Middle-class homes came to differentiate themselves from those of workers and artisans in other ways as well. The spare, simple styles of eighteenth-century homes gave way to the much more elaborate, even baroque household styles of the Victorian era—styles increasingly characterized by crowded, even cluttered rooms, dark colors, lush fabrics, and heavy furniture and draperies. Middle-class homes also became larger. It became less common for children to share beds and for all members of a family to sleep in the same room. Parlors and dining rooms separate from the kitchen—once a luxury—became the norm among the middle class. Some urban middle-class homes had indoor plumbing and indoor toilets by the 1850s—a significant advance over outdoor wells and privies.

THE CHANGING FAMILY

The new industrializing society produced profound changes in the nature of the family. Among them was the movement of families from farms to urban areas. Sons and daughters in urban households were much more likely to leave the family in search of work than they had been in the rural world. This was largely because of the shift of income-earning work out of the home. In the early decades of the nineteenth century, the family itself had been the principal unit of economic activity. Now most income earners left home each day to work in a shop, mill, or factory. A sharp distinction began to emerge between the public

(©Fotosearch/Archive Photos/Getty Images)

FAMILY TIME, 1842 This illustration for *Godey's Lady's Book*, a magazine whose audience was better-off white women, offers an idealized image of family life. The father reads to his family from a devotional text; two servants off to the side listen attentively as well. What does this image communicate about the roles of the household members?

world of the workplace and the private world of the family. The world of the family was now dominated not by production but by housekeeping, child rearing, and other primarily domestic concerns.

There was a significant decline in the birthrate, particularly in urban areas and in middle-class families. In 1800, the average American woman could be expected to give birth to approximately seven children. By 1860, the average woman bore five children.

The "Cult of Domesticity"

The growing separation between the workplace and the home sharpened distinctions between the social roles of men and women. Those distinctions affected not only factory workers and farmers but also members of the growing middle class.

With fewer legal and political rights than men, most women remained under the virtually absolute authority of their husbands. They were seldom encouraged to pursue education above the primary level. Women students were not accepted in any college or university until 1837. For a considerable time after that, only Oberlin in Ohio offered education to both men and women, and Mount Holyoke in Massachusetts was founded by Mary Lyon as an academy for women.

However unequal the positions of men and women in the preindustrial era, those positions had generally been defined within the context of a household in which all members played important economic roles. In the middle-class family of the new industrial society, by contrast, the husband was assumed to be the principal, usually the only, income producer. The image of women changed from one of contributors to the family economy to one of guardians of the "domestic virtues." Middle-class women learned to place a higher value on keeping a clean, comfortable, and well-appointed home; on entertaining; and on dressing elegantly and stylishly.

Within their own separate sphere, middle-class women began to develop a distinctive female culture. A "lady's" literature began to emerge. Romantic novels written for female readers focused on the private sphere that middle-class women now inhabited, as did women's magazines that focused on fashions, shopping, homemaking, and other purely domestic concerns.

This **cult of domesticity**, as some scholars have called it, provided many women greater material comfort than they had enjoyed in the past and placed a higher value on their "female virtues." At the same time, it left women increasingly detached from the public world, with fewer outlets for their interests and energies. Except for teaching and nursing, work by women outside the household gradually came to be seen as a lower-class preserve.

Working-class women continued to work in factories and mills, but under conditions far worse than those that the original, more "respectable" women workers of Lowell and Waltham had experienced. Domestic service became another frequent source of female employment.

Leisure Activities

Leisure time was scarce for all but the wealthiest Americans. Most people worked long hours every day without any vacation. For the lucky, Sunday was a day off, set aside for rest and religion. Not surprising, then, holidays took on a special importance, as suggested by the strikingly elaborate celebrations of the Fourth of July in the nineteenth century. The celebrations were not just expressions of patriotism, but a way of enjoying one of the few nonreligious holidays from work available to most Americans.

For urban people, leisure was something to be seized in what few free moments they had. Men gravitated to taverns for drinking, talking, and game-playing after work. Women gathered in one another's homes for conversation and card games. For educated people, reading became one of the principal leisure activities. Newspapers and magazines proliferated rapidly, and books became staples of affluent homes. In contrast, rural Americans, because of the seasonal nature of farm work, enjoyed more free time in the late fall and winter. They pursued similar past times as urbanites, but within the home.

A public culture of leisure emerged too, especially in larger cities. Theaters became popular and attracted audiences that crossed class lines. Much of the popular theater of the time consisted of melodrama based on novels or American myths. Also popular were Shakespeare's plays, reworked to appeal to American audiences. Tragedies were given happy endings; comedies were interlaced with regional humor; lines were rewritten with American dialect; and scenes were abbreviated or cut so that the play could be one of several in an evening's program. So familiar were many Shakespearean plots that audiences took delight in seeing them parodied in productions such as *Julius Sneezer* and *Hamlet and Egglet*.

(©Bettmann/Corbis)

P. T. BARNUM AND TOM THUMB P. T. Barnum stands next to his star Charles Stratton, whose stage name was General Tom Thumb after the fairy-tale character. Stratton joined Barnum's touring company as a child, singing, dancing, and playing roles such as Cupid and Napoleon Bonaparte. The adult Stratton and Barnum became business partners.

Minstrel shows—in which white actors wearing blackface mimicked (and ridiculed) African American culture—became staples among white audiences. Public sporting events—boxing, horse racing, cockfighting (already becoming controversial), and others—often attracted considerable audiences. Baseball, not yet organized into professional leagues, was beginning to attract large crowds when played in city parks or fields. A particularly exciting event in many communities was the arrival of the circus.

Popular tastes in public spectacle tended toward the bizarre and the fantastic. Relatively few people traveled; and in the absence of film, radio, television, or even much photography, Americans hungered for visions of unusual phenomena. People going to the theater or the circus or the museum wanted to see things that amazed and even frightened them. The most celebrated provider of such experiences was the famous and unscrupulous showman P. T. Barnum, who opened the American Museum in New York in 1842—not a showcase for art or nature, but as an exhibit of "human curiosities" that included people with dwarfism, Siamese twins, magicians, and ventriloquists. Barnum was a genius in publicizing his ventures with garish posters and elaborate newspaper announcements. Later, in the 1870s, he launched the famous circus for which he is still best remembered.

Lectures were one of the most popular forms of entertainment in nineteenth-century America. Men and women flocked in enormous numbers to lyceums, churches, schools, and auditoriums to hear lecturers explain the latest advances in science, describe their visits to exotic places, provide vivid historical narratives, or rail against the evils of alcohol or slavery. Messages of social uplift and reform attracted rapt audiences, particularly among women.

THE AGRICULTURAL NORTH

Even in the rapidly urbanizing and industrializing Northeast, and more so in what nineteenth-century Americans called the Northwest, most people remained tied to the agricultural world. But agriculture, like industry and commerce, was becoming increasingly a part of the new capitalist economy.

NORTHEASTERN AGRICULTURE

The story of agriculture in the Northeast after 1840 is one of decline and transformation. Farmers of this section of the country could no longer compete with the new and richer soil of the Northwest. In 1840, the leading wheat-growing states were New York, Pennsylvania, Ohio, and Virginia. In 1860, they were Illinois, Indiana, Wisconsin, Ohio, and Michigan. Illinois, Ohio, and Missouri also supplanted New York, Pennsylvania, and Virginia as growers of corn. In 1840, the most important cattle-raising areas in the country were New York, Pennsylvania, and New England. By the 1850s, the leading cattle states were Illinois, Indiana, Ohio, and Iowa in the Northwest and Texas in the Southwest.

Some eastern farmers responded to these changes by moving west themselves and establishing new farms. Still others moved to mill towns and became laborers. Some farmers, however, remained on the land and turned to what was known as "truck farming"—supplying food to the growing cities. They raised vegetables or fruit and sold their produce in nearby towns. Supplying milk, butter, and cheese to local urban markets also attracted many farmers in central New York, southeastern Pennsylvania, and various parts of New England.

THE OLD NORTHWEST

Life was different in the states of the Old Northwest (now known as the Midwest). In the two decades before the Civil War, this section of the country experienced steady industrial growth, particularly in and around Cleveland (on Lake Erie) and Cincinnati, the center of meatpacking in the Ohio Valley. Farther west, Chicago was emerging as the national center of the agricultural machinery and meatpacking industries. Most of the major industrial activities of the Old Northwest either served agriculture (as in the case of farm machinery) or relied on agricultural products (as in flour milling, meatpacking, whiskey distilling, and the making of leather goods).

Some areas of the Old Northwest were not yet dominated by whites. Indians remained the most numerous inhabitants of large portions of the upper third of the Great Lakes states until after the Civil War. In those areas, hunting and fishing, along with some sedentary agriculture, remained the principal economic activities.

For the settlers who populated the lands farther south, the Old Northwest was primarily an agricultural region. Its rich lands made farming highly lucrative. Thus the typical citizen of the Old Northwest was not the industrial worker or poor, marginal farmer, but the owner of a reasonably prosperous family farm.

Industrialization, in both the United States and Europe, provided the greatest boost to agriculture. With the growth of factories and cities in the Northeast, the domestic market for farm goods increased dramatically. The growing national and worldwide demand for farm products resulted in steadily rising farm prices. For most farmers, the 1840s and early 1850s were years of increasing prosperity.

The expansion of agricultural markets also had profound effects on sectional alignments in the United States. The Old Northwest sold most of its products to the Northeast and became an important market for the products of eastern industry. A strong economic relationship was emerging between the two sections that was profitable to both—and that was increasing the isolation of the South within the Union.

By 1850, the growing western white population was moving into the prairie regions on both sides of the Mississippi. These farmers cleared forest lands or made use of fields the Indians had cleared many years earlier. And they developed a timber industry to make use of the remaining forests. Although wheat was the staple crop of the region, other crops—corn, potatoes, and oats—and livestock were also important.

The Old Northwest also increased production by adopting new agricultural techniques. Farmers began to cultivate new varieties of seed, notably Mediterranean wheat, which was hardier than the native type; and they imported better breeds of animals, such as hogs and sheep from England and Spain. Most important were improved tools and farm machines. The cast-iron plow, invented in 1814, had the advantage of being more durable than older wooden plows, more capable of breaking up hard and stony fields, and eventually having replaceable parts. But it was still ineffective at churning up the thick sod and clay soils found throughout the Midwest. It was replaced in 1847 by the steel plow, manufactured by the John Deere company in Moline, Illinois, and the steel plow quickly became a farming staple.

Two new machines heralded a coming revolution in grain production. The automatic reaper, the invention of Cyrus H. McCormick of Virginia, took the place of sickle, cradle, and hand labor. Pulled by a team of horses, it had a row of horizontal knives on one side for cutting wheat; the wheels drove a paddle that bent the stalks over the knives, which then fell onto a moving belt and into the back of the vehicle. The reaper enabled a crew of six or seven men to harvest in a day as much wheat as fifteen men could harvest using the older methods. McCormick, who had patented his device in 1834, established a factory

(©Oxford Science Archive/Print Collector/Getty Images)

CYRUS MCCORMICK'S AUTOMATIC REAPER

at Chicago in 1847. By 1860, more than 100,000 reapers were in use. Almost as important to the grain grower was the thresher—a machine that separated the grain from the wheat stalks—which appeared in large numbers after 1840. (Before that, farmers generally flailed grain by hand or used farm animals to tread it.) The Jerome I. Case factory in Racine, Wisconsin, manufactured most of the threshers. (Modern "harvesters" later combined the functions of the reaper and the thresher.)

The Old Northwest was the most self-consciously democratic section of the country. But its democracy was of a relatively conservative type—capitalistic, property-conscious, middle-class. Abraham Lincoln, an Illinois Whig, voiced the optimistic economic opinions of many of the people of his section. "I take it that it is best for all to leave each man free to acquire property as fast as he can," said Lincoln. "When one starts poor, as most do in the race of life, free society is such that he knows he can better his condition; he knows that there is no fixed condition of labor for his whole life."

RURAL LIFE

Life for farming people varied greatly from one region to another. In the more densely populated areas east of the Appalachians and in the easternmost areas of the Old Northwest, farmers made extensive use of the institutions of communities—churches, schools, stores, and taverns. As white settlement moved farther west, farmers became more isolated and had to struggle to find any occasions for contact with people outside their own families.

Religion drew farm communities together more than any other force in remote communities. Town or village churches were popular meeting places, both for services and for social events—most of them dominated by women. Even in areas with no organized churches, farm families—and women in particular—gathered in one another's homes for prayer meetings, Bible readings, and other religious activities. Weddings, baptisms, and funerals also united communities.

But religion was only one of many reasons for interaction. Farm people joined together frequently to share tasks such as barn raising. Large numbers of families gathered at harvesttime to help bring in crops, husk corn, or thresh wheat. Women came together to share domestic tasks, holding "bees" in which groups of women made quilts, baked goods, preserves, and other products.

Despite the many social gatherings farm families managed to create, they had much less contact with popular culture and public life than people who lived in towns and cities. Most rural people treasured their links to the outside world—letters from relatives and friends in distant places, newspapers and magazines from cities they had never seen, catalogs advertising merchandise that their local stores never had. Yet many also valued the relative autonomy that a farm life gave them. One reason many rural Americans looked back nostalgically on country life once they moved to the city was that they sensed that in the urban world they had lost some control over the patterns of their daily lives.

CONCLUSION

Between the 1820s and the 1850s, the American economy experienced the beginnings of an industrial revolution—a change that transformed almost every area of life in fundamental ways.

The American Industrial Revolution was a result of many things: population growth, advances in transportation and communication, new technologies that spurred the development of factories and mass production, the recruiting of a large industrial labor force, and the creation of corporate bodies capable of managing large enterprises. The new economy expanded the ranks of the wealthy, helped create a large new middle class, and introduced high levels of inequality.

Culture in the industrializing areas of the North changed, too, as did the structure and behavior of the family, the role of women, and the way people used their leisure time and encountered popular culture. The changes helped widen the gap in experience and understanding between the generation of the Revolution and the generation of the mid-nineteenth century. They also helped widen the gap between North and South.

KEY TERMS/PEOPLE/PLACES/EVENTS

antebellum 228
artisan 241
Baltimore and Ohio
Railroad 233
Commonwealth v. Hunt 242
cult of domesticity 246
Erie Canal 232

Factory Girls
Association 239
factory system 237
industrialization 237
Know-Nothings 230
Lowell or Waltham
system 239

Morse code 235
nativism 230
Sarah Bagley 239
Western Union Telegraph
Company 235

RECALL AND REFLECT

1. What were the political responses to immigration in mid-nineteenth-century America? Do you see any parallels to responses to immigration today?
2. Why did the rail system supplant the canal system as the nation's major transportation network?
3. How did the industrial workforce change between the 1820s and the 1840s? What were the effects on American society of changes in the workforce?
4. How did America's Industrial Revolution and the factory system change family life and women's social and economic roles?
5. How did agriculture in the North change as a result of growing industrialization and urbanization?

11 | COTTON, SLAVERY, AND THE OLD SOUTH

THE COTTON ECONOMY
SOUTHERN WHITE SOCIETY
SLAVERY: THE "PECULIAR INSTITUTION"
THE CULTURE OF SLAVERY

LOOKING AHEAD

1. How did slavery shape the southern economy and society, and how did it make the South different from the North?
2. What was the myth and what was the reality of white society in the South? Why was the myth so pervasive and widely believed?
3. How did slaves resist their enslavement? How successful were their efforts? What was the response of whites?

THE SOUTH, LIKE THE NORTH, experienced significant growth in the middle years of the nineteenth century. The southern agricultural economy grew increasingly productive and prosperous. Trade in such staples as sugar, rice, tobacco, and above all cotton made the South a major force in international commerce. It also tied the South securely to the emerging capitalist world of the United States and its European trading partners.

Yet despite all these changes, the South experienced a much less fundamental transformation in these years than did the North. It had begun the nineteenth century as a primarily agricultural region; it remained overwhelmingly so in 1860. It had begun the century with few important cities and little industry; and so it remained sixty years later. In 1800, a plantation system dependent on slave labor had dominated the southern economy; by 1860, that system had only strengthened its grip on the region. And by the outbreak of the Civil War, few southern white leaders could imagine the health and prosperity of their homeland without slavery.

Gabriel Prosser's
unsuccessful slave
revolt

1808

Slave importation
banned

1820s

Depression in tobacco
prices begins

High cotton production
in Southwest

1822

Denmark Vesey's
conspiracy

1831

Nat Turner
slave rebellion

1833

John Randolph
frees 400 slaves

1837

Cotton prices plummet

1846

*De Bow's Commercial
Review* founded

1849

Cotton production
boom

THE COTTON ECONOMY

The most important economic development in the mid-nineteenth-century South was the shift of economic power from the "upper South," the original southern states along the Atlantic Coast, to the "lower South," the expanding agricultural regions in the new states of the Southwest. That shift reflected above all the growing dominance of cotton in the southern economy.

THE RISE OF KING COTTON

Much of the upper South continued to rely on the cultivation of tobacco. But the market for that crop was notoriously unstable, and tobacco rapidly exhausted the land on which it grew. By the 1830s, therefore, many farmers in the old tobacco-growing regions of Virginia, Maryland, and North Carolina were shifting to other crops, while the center of tobacco cultivation was moving westward, into the Piedmont area.

The southern regions of the coastal South—South Carolina, Georgia, and parts of Florida—continued to rely on the cultivation of rice, a more stable and lucrative crop. But rice demanded substantial irrigation and needed an exceptionally long growing season (nine months), so its cultivation remained restricted to a relatively small area. Sugar growers along the Gulf Coast similarly enjoyed a reasonably profitable market for their crop. But sugar cultivation required intensive (and debilitating) labor and a long growing time; only relatively wealthy planters could afford to grow it. In addition, producers faced major competition from the great sugar plantations of the Caribbean. Sugar cultivation, therefore, did not spread much beyond a small area in southern Louisiana and eastern Texas. Long-staple (Sea Island) cotton was another lucrative crop, but like rice and sugar, it could grow only in a limited area—the coastal regions of the Southeast.

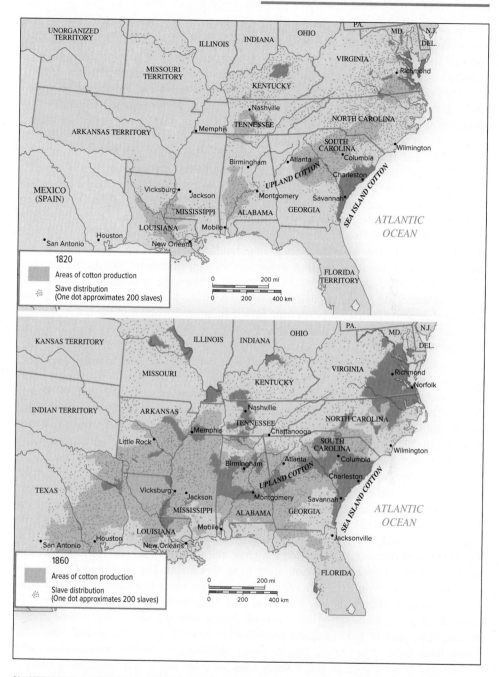

SLAVERY AND COTTON IN THE SOUTH, 1820 AND 1860 These two maps show the remarkable spread of cotton cultivation in the South in the decades before the Civil War. Both maps show the areas of cotton cultivation (the green-colored areas) as well as areas with large slave populations (the brown-dotted areas). Note how in the top map, which represents 1820, cotton production is concentrated largely in the East, with a few areas scattered among Alabama, Mississippi, Louisiana, and Tennessee. Slavery is concentrated along the Georgia and South Carolina coast, areas in which long-staple cotton was grown, with only a few other areas of highly dense slave populations. By 1860, the South had changed dramatically. Cotton production had spread throughout the lower South, from Texas to northern Florida, and slavery had moved with it. Slavery was much denser in the tobacco-growing regions of Virginia and North Carolina, which had also grown. • *How did this economic shift affect the white South's commitment to slavery?*

The decline of the tobacco economy and the limits of the sugar, rice, and long-staple cotton economies might have forced the region to shift its attention to other, nonagricultural pursuits had it not been for the growing importance of a new product that soon overshadowed all else: short-staple cotton. It was a hardier and coarser strain of cotton that could grow successfully in a variety of climates and soils. It was harder to process than the long-staple cotton because its seeds were difficult to remove from the fiber. But the invention of the cotton gin in 1793 had largely solved that problem.

Demand for cotton increased rapidly in Britain in the 1820s and 1830s and in New England in the 1840s and 1850s. From the western areas of South Carolina and Georgia, production moved into Alabama and Mississippi and then into northern Louisiana, Texas, and Arkansas. By the 1850s, cotton had become the linchpin of the southern economy. By the time of the Civil War, cotton constituted nearly two-thirds of the total export trade of the United States.

Cotton production boomed in the lower South (later known as the "Deep South"). Some began to call it the "**cotton kingdom.**" The prospect of tremendous profits drew settlers to the lower South by the thousands. Some were wealthy planters from the older states, but most were small slaveholders or slaveless farmers who hoped to move into the planter class.

A similar shift, if an involuntary one, occurred in the slave population. Between 1840 and 1860, hundreds of thousands of slaves moved from the upper South to the cotton states—either accompanying masters who were themselves migrating to the lower South or (more often) sold to planters already there.

This "**second middle passage,**" as the historian Ira Berlin has called it (using a term usually associated with the transatlantic slave trade), was a traumatic experience for perhaps a million dislocated African Americans. Slave families were broken up and scattered across the expanding cotton kingdom. Marched over hundreds of rugged miles, tied together in "coffles" (as on the earlier slave ships coming from Africa), they arrived in unfamiliar and usually forbidding territory, where they were made to construct new plantations and work in cotton fields. The sale of slaves to the lower South became an important economic activity for whites in the upper South, where agricultural production was declining.

Even as slavery slowly became the lifeblood of the southern economy and society, it was never strictly a southern phenomenon. In the North during the Colonial era, the enslaved populations numbered about 40,000, mostly concentrated in seabound cities and inland farms. In New York City in 1740, for example, about 20 percent of the entire population was enslaved. Northern sea merchants profited handsomely by trafficking in slaves, be it from African or Caribbean or eastern port cities or between those cities themselves. After the American Revolution, however, slavery in the North began to slowly die out. The Northwest Ordinance of 1787 outlawed slavery in the Northwest Territory and the states that developed in this area— Ohio, Indiana, Michigan, Illinois, Wisconsin, and Minnesota—were always "free" states. By 1804, all other northern states had outlawed slavery, although some implemented gradual emancipation. And in 1807 Congress enacted a law banning the importation of slaves from foreign lands to the United States. Despite these prohibitions, the North continued to indirectly support slavery. Its commerce and industry relied on crops and cotton produced by slaves in the South, and thus it largely tolerated southern slavery, at least until the late antebellum era.

SOUTHERN TRADE AND INDUSTRY

While slave-based agriculture boomed, other forms of economic activity were slow to develop in the South. Flour milling and textile and iron manufacturing grew, particularly in the upper South, but industry remained a relatively insignificant force in comparison with the agricultural economy. The total value of southern textile manufactures in 1860 was $4.5 million—a threefold increase over the value of those goods twenty years before. But the value of cotton exports alone was approximately $200 million.

The limited nonfarm commercial sector that did develop in the South was largely intended to serve the needs of the plantation economy. Particularly important were the brokers, or "factors," who, in the absence of banks, marketed the planters' crops and provided planters with credit. Other obstacles to economic development included the South's inadequate transportation system: what little there was tended to serve the interests of planters first. Canals were almost nonexistent; most roads were crude and unsuitable for heavy transport; railroads, although they expanded substantially in the 1840s and 1850s, failed to tie the region together effectively. In fact, a key aim of many southern railroads was to link larger plantations to cities and their markets. Not surprisingly then, the principle means of large-scale transportation was by steamboats and other larger watercraft along major rivers or the sea to Charleston, New Orleans, Savannah, Houston, Mobile, and other port cities. While this system benefited planters, who typically located near major waterways, it made it difficult for industry to grow in landlocked areas far from cities.

The South, therefore, was becoming more and more dependent on the industrial manufacturers, merchants, and professionals of the North. Concerned by this trend, some southerners began to advocate economic independence for the region, among them James D. B. De Bow of New Orleans, whose magazine, *De Bow's Commercial Review,* called for southern commercial expansion and economic independence from the North. Yet even *De Bow's Commercial Review* was filled with advertisements from northern manufacturing firms; and its circulation was far smaller in the South than such northern magazines as *Harper's Weekly.*

SOUTHERN WHITE SOCIETY

An important question about antebellum southern history concerns why the region did so little to develop a larger industrial and commercial economy of its own. Why did it remain so different from the North?

Part of the reason was the great profitability of the region's agricultural system. In the Northeast, many people had turned to manufacturing as the agricultural economy of the region declined. In the South, the agricultural economy was booming, and ambitious capitalists had little incentive to look elsewhere. Another reason was that wealthy southerners had so much capital invested in land and slaves that they had little left for other investments. Some historians have also suggested that the southern climate—with its long, hot, steamy summers—was less suitable for industrial development than the climate of the North.

The South's resistance to transforming its economy was also tied to a culture that blindly celebrated the wealth and profit planters wrung from the labor of slaves and that viewed slavery itself as a benevolent institution in which slaves were well cared for, even loved. Not only was slavery an oppressive institution, but much of this culture failed to reflect the reality of southern society.

Significantly, only a very small minority of southern whites owned slaves. Indeed, most white southerners were **yeoman farmers**, meaning they farmed their own small plots of land usually without the assistance of slaves. In 1860, when the white population was just above 8 million, the number of slaveholders was only 383,637. Even with all members of slaveowning families included in the figures, those living in slaveowning households still amounted to perhaps no more than one-quarter of the white population. And only a small proportion of this relatively

CONSIDER THE SOURCE

SENATOR JAMES HENRY HAMMOND DECLARES, "COTTON IS KING" (1858)

James Henry Hammond, a U.S. senator from South Carolina, was a leading advocate for the overwhelming significance of cotton to the economy of the South and the nation. He famously made his point in 1858 in his "Cotton Is King" speech.

If we never acquire another foot of territory for the South, look at her. Eight hundred and fifty thousand square miles. As large as Great Britain, France, Austria, Prussia, and Spain. Is not that territory enough to make an empire that shall rule the world? . . . With the finest soil, the most delightful climate, whose staple productions none of those great countries can grow, we have three thousand miles of continental shore line, so indented with bays and crowded with islands, that, when their shore lines are added, we have twelve thousand miles. Through the heart of our country runs the great Mississippi, the father of waters, into whose bosom are poured thirty-six thousand miles of tributary streams; and beyond we have the desert prairie wastes, to protect us in our rear. Can you hem in such a territory as that? . . .

[. . .] Upon our muster-rolls we have a million of militia. In a defensive war, upon an emergency, every one of them would be available. At any time, the South can raise, equip, and maintain in the field, a larger army than any Power of the earth can send against her, and an army of soldiers—men brought up on horseback, with guns in their hands.

[. . .] It appears, by going to the reports of the Secretary of the Treasury, which are authentic, that last year the United States exported in round numbers $279,000,000 worth of domestic produce, excluding gold and foreign merchandise re-exported. Of this amount $158,000,000 worth is the clear produce of the South; . . .

[. . .] [W]e have nothing to do but to take off restrictions on foreign merchandise and open our ports, and the whole world will come to us to trade. They will be too glad to bring and carry for us, and we never shall dream of a war. Why the South has never yet had a just cause of war. Every time she has drawn her sword it has been on the point of honor, and that point of honor has been mainly loyalty to her sister colonies and sister States, who have ever since plundered and calumniated her.

But if there were no other reason why we should never have war, would any sane nation make war on cotton? Without firing a gun, without drawing a sword, should they make war on us we can bring the whole world to our feet. The South is perfectly competent to go on, one, two, or three years without planting a seed of cotton. I believe that if she was to plant but half her cotton for three years to come, it would be an immense advantage to her. I am not so sure but that after three total years' abstinence she would come out stronger than ever she was before and better prepared to enter afresh upon her great career of enterprise. . . . England would topple headlong and carry the whole civilized world with her, save the South. No, you dare not make war on cotton. No power on earth dares to make war upon it. Cotton *is* king.

In all social systems there must be a class to do the menial duties, to perform the drudgery of life. That is, a class requiring but a low order of intellect and but little skill. Its requisites are vigor, docility, fidelity. . . . Fortunately for the South, she found a race adapted to that purpose to her hand—a race inferior to her own, but eminently qualified in temper, in vigor, in docility, in capacity to stand the climate, to answer all her purposes. We use them for our purpose, and call them slaves. We found them slaves by the "common consent of mankind," which, according to Cicero, *"lex naturae est"*; the highest proof of what is Nature's law. We are old-fashioned at the South yet; it is a word discarded now by "ears polite." I will not characterize that class at the North by that term; but you have it; it is there; it is everywhere; it is eternal.

Source: Hammond, James Henry, Speech on the Kansas-Lecompton Constitution, U.S. Senate, March 4, 1858, in *Congressional Globe*, 35th Cong., 1st Sess., Appendix, 70–71, in Regina Lee Blaszczyk and Philip B. Scranton (eds.), *Major Problems in American Business History*, Boston: Houghton Mifflin Company, 2006, 149–154.

UNDERSTAND, ANALYZE, & EVALUATE

1. How did Hammond describe the South in comparison to the North? Compare this assessment with the experience of the South in the Civil War. How did Hammond view the South in a global context? What do you think of this assessment?

2. What justifications did Hammond offer for slavery? Describe the comparison Hammond drew between northern wage labor and southern slavery.

small number of slaveowners owned slaves in substantial numbers. Yet as the cotton economy surged in the late 1850s, white supporters such as Senator **James Henry Hammond** championed its value to southern society and argued for a ruling planter class and working slave class. (See "Consider the Source: Senator James Henry Hammond Declares, 'Cotton Is King.'")

THE PLANTER CLASS

How, then, did the South come to be seen as a society dominated by fabulously wealthy slaveowning planters when, in fact, there were very few of them? In large part, it was because the **planter class** exercised power and influence far in excess of its numbers and because yeoman farmers, even when they resented the superiority of planters, supported and identified with the institution of slavery. Indeed, most aspired to be slaveholders themselves.

Nor was the world of the planter nearly as leisured and genteel as the aristocratic myth would suggest. Growing staple crops was a tough business. Planters focused on the hard, stubborn basics of running their business: buying and selling slaves, anticipating fluctuations in markets, arranging for the transportation of the harvest, controlling costs, and winning a profit at year's end. Sometimes they managed poorly and lost everything. Planters were just as much competitive capitalists as the industrialists of the North. Even many affluent planters lived rather modestly, their wealth so heavily invested in land and slaves that there was often little left for personal comfort. And white planters, including some substantial ones, tended to move frequently as new and presumably more productive areas opened up to cultivation.

Wealthy southern whites sustained their image as aristocrats in many ways. They adopted an elaborate code of "chivalry," which obligated white men to defend their "honor," often through dueling. They tended to avoid such "coarse" occupations as trade and commerce; those who did not become planters often gravitated toward the military. The aristocratic ideal also found reflection in the definition of a special role for southern white women.

THE "SOUTHERN LADY"

In some respects, affluent white women in the South occupied roles very similar to those of middle-class white women in the North. Their lives generally centered in the home, where (according to the South's social ideal) they served as companions to and hostesses for their husbands and as nurturing mothers for their children. "Genteel" southern white women seldom engaged in public activities or found income-producing employment.

But the life of the "southern lady" was also very different from that of her northern counterpart. For one thing, the **cult of honor** dictated that southern white men give particular importance to the defense of women. In practice, this generally meant that white men were even more dominant and white women even more subordinate in southern culture than they were in the North. Social theorist George Fitzhugh wrote in the 1850s: "Women, like children, have but one right, and that is the right to protection. The right to protection involves the obligation to obey."

More important in determining the role of southern white women, however, was that the vast majority of them lived on farms, with little access to the "public world" and thus few opportunities to look beyond their roles as wives and mothers. For many white women, living on farms of modest size meant a fuller engagement in the economic life of the family than was typical for middle-class women in the North. These women engaged in spinning, weaving, and other production; they participated in agricultural tasks; they helped supervise the slave workforce. On the larger plantations, however, even these limited roles were often considered unsuitable for white women, and the "plantation mistress" became, in some cases, more an ornament for her husband than an active part of the economy or the society. Southern white women also had less access to education than their northern counterparts. The few female "academies" in the South trained women primarily to be suitable wives.

Southern white women had other special burdens as well. The southern white birthrate remained nearly 20 percent higher than that of the nation as a whole, but infant mortality in the region remained higher than elsewhere. The slave labor system also had a mixed impact on white women. It helped spare many of them from certain kinds of arduous labor, but it also damaged their relationships with their husbands. Male slaveowners had frequent forced sexual relationships with the female slaves on their plantations; the children of those unions served as a constant reminder to white women of their husbands' infidelities and violence. Black women (and men) were obviously the most important victims of such practices, but white women suffered, too.

THE LOWER CLASSES

Below planters on the economic scale were yeoman farmers, and below them were the landless poor. Some yeoman devoted themselves largely to subsistence farming; others grew cotton or other crops for the market but usually could not produce enough to allow them to expand their operations or even get out of debt.

One reason for the class divide was the southern educational system. For the sons of wealthy planters, the region provided ample opportunities to gain an education. In 1860, there were 260 southern colleges and universities, public and private, with 25,000 students enrolled in them. But as in the rest of the United States, universities were only within the reach of the upper class. The elementary and secondary schools of the South were not only fewer than but also inferior to those of the Northeast. The South had more than 500,000 illiterate whites, over half the nation's total. The subordination of the lower classes to the planter class raises an important question: Why did lower-class whites not oppose the aristocratic social system from which they benefited so little?

Some did oppose the planter elite, but for the most part in limited ways and in isolated areas. These were mainly the "hill people," who lived in the Appalachian ranges east of the Mississippi, in the Ozarks to the west of the river, and in other "hill country" or "back-country" areas. They practiced a simple form of subsistence agriculture, owned practically no slaves, and were, in most respects, unconnected to the cotton economy. Such whites frequently expressed animosity toward the planter aristocracy. Unsurprisingly, the mountain regions were the only parts of the South to resist the movement toward secession in the early 1860s. Even during the Civil War itself, many refused to support the Confederacy.

Far greater in number, however, were the nonslaveowning whites who lived in the midst of the plantation system. Many, perhaps most of them, accepted that system because they were tied to it in important ways. Small farmers depended on the local plantation aristocracy for access to cotton gins, markets for their modest crops and their livestock, and credit or other financial assistance in time of need. In many areas, moreover, the poorest resident of a county might easily be a cousin of the richest aristocrat. In the 1850s, the cotton boom allowed many small farmers to improve their economic fortunes. Some bought more land, became slaveowners, and moved into at least the fringes of plantation society. Others simply felt more secure in their positions as independent yeomen and hence were more likely to embrace the fierce regional loyalty that was spreading throughout the white South in these years.

There were other white southerners, however, who were known at the time variously as "crackers," "sand hillers," or "poor white trash." Occupying the infertile lands of the pine barrens, the red hills, and the swamps, they lived in genuine squalor. Many owned no land and supported themselves by foraging or hunting. Others worked at times as common laborers for their neighbors. Their degradation resulted partly from dietary deficiencies and disease. Forced to resort at times to eating clay (hence the tendency of more-affluent whites to refer to them disparagingly as "clay eaters"), they suffered from pellagra, hookworm, and malaria. Planters and small farmers alike held them in contempt.

Even among these southerners—the true outcasts of white society—there was no real opposition to the plantation system or slavery. In part, this was because they were so benumbed by poverty that they had little strength to protest. But the single greatest unifying factor among the southern white population was their perception of race. However poor and miserable white southerners might be, they could still look down on the black population of the region and feel a bond with their fellow whites and a sense of racial supremacy.

SLAVERY: THE "PECULIAR INSTITUTION"

White southerners often referred to slavery as the "**peculiar institution**," meaning that it was distinctive, special. And indeed it was. The South in the mid-nineteenth century was the only area in the Western world—except for Brazil, Cuba, and Puerto Rico—where slavery still existed. Slavery, more than any other single factor, isolated the South from the rest of American society and much of the world.

Within the South itself, slavery produced paradoxical results. On one hand, it isolated blacks from whites. As a result, African Americans under slavery began to develop a society and culture of their own. On the other hand, slavery created a unique bond between blacks and whites—slaves and masters—in the South. The two groups may have maintained separate spheres, but each sphere was deeply influenced by the other. In both cases, slavery profoundly affected all aspects of southern and even American society. (See "Debating the Past: Analyzing Slavery.")

ANALYZING SLAVERY

No issue in American history has produced a more spirited debate than the nature of plantation slavery. The debate began well before the Civil War, when **abolitionists** strove to expose slavery to the world as a brutal, dehumanizing institution, while southern defenders of slavery tried to depict it as a benevolent and paternalistic system. But by the late nineteenth century, with white Americans eager for sectional conciliation, most northern and southern chroniclers of slavery began to accept a romanticized and unthreatening picture of the Old South and its peculiar institution.

The first major scholarly examination of slavery was Ulrich B. Phillips's *American Negro Slavery* (1918), which portrayed slavery as an essentially benign institution in which kindly masters looked after submissive and generally contented African Americans. Phillips's apologia for slavery remained the authoritative work on the subject for nearly thirty years.

In the 1940s, challenges to Phillips began to emerge. Melville J. Herskovits disputed Phillips's contention that black Americans retained little of their African cultural inheritance. Herbert Aptheker published a chronicle of slave revolts as a way of refuting Phillips's claim that blacks were submissive and content.

A somewhat different challenge to Phillips emerged in the 1950s from historians who emphasized the brutality of the institution. Kenneth Stampp's *The Peculiar Institution* (1956) and Stanley Elkins's *Slavery* (1959) described a labor system that did serious physical and psychological damage to its victims. They portrayed slavery as something like a prison, in which men and women had virtually no space to develop their own social and cultural lives. Elkins compared the system to Nazi concentration camps and likened the childlike "Sambo" personality of slavery to tragic distortions of character produced by the Holocaust.

In the early 1970s, an explosion of new scholarship on slavery shifted the emphasis away from the damage the system inflicted on African Americans and toward the striking success of the slaves themselves in building a culture of their own. John Blassingame in 1973 argued that "the most remarkable aspect of the whole process of enslavement is the extent to which the American-born slaves were able to retain their ancestors' culture." Herbert Gutman, in *The Black Family in Slavery and Freedom* (1976), challenged the prevailing belief that slavery had weakened and even destroyed the African American family. On the contrary, Gutman argued, the black family survived slavery with impressive strength, although with some significant differences from the prevailing form of the white family. Eugene Genovese's *Roll, Jordan, Roll* (1974) revealed how African Americans manipulated white paternalist assumptions to build a large cultural space of their own where they could develop their own family life, social traditions, and religious patterns. That same year, Robert Fogel and Stanley Engerman published the controversial *Time on the Cross,* a highly quantitative study that supported some of the claims of Gutman and Genovese about black achievement but that went much further in portraying slavery as a successful and reasonably humane (if ultimately immoral) system. Slave workers, they argued, were better treated and lived in greater comfort than most northern industrial workers of the same era. Their conclusions produced a storm of criticism.

(Source: Library of Congress, Prints and Photographs Division [LC-USZC4-5251])

NURSING THE MASTER'S CHILD   This 1855 photograph of a slave woman and master's child is documentary evidence of the complex relationships that historians of slavery have studied.

Other important scholarship includes African American slave women. Elizabeth Fox-Genovese's *Within the Plantation Household* (1988) examined the lives of both white and black women on the plantation. She portrayed slave women as defined by their dual roles as members of the plantation workforce and anchors of the black family. Slave women, she argued, professed loyalty to their mistresses when forced to serve them as domestics; but their real loyalty remained to their own communities and families.

More recent studies by Walter Johnson and Ira Berlin mark an at least partial return to the "damage" approach to slavery of the 1970s. Johnson's *Soul by Soul* (2000) examines the South's largest slave market, New Orleans. For whites, he argues, purchasing slaves was a way of fulfilling the middle-class male fantasy of success and independence. For the slaves themselves, the trade was dehumanizing and destructive to black families and communities. Berlin's *Many Thousands Gone* (2000) and *Generation of Captivity* (2003)—among the most important studies of slavery in a generation—similarly emphasize the dehumanizing character of the slave market and show that, whatever white slaveowners might say, slavery was less a social system than a commodification of human beings.   •

UNDERSTAND, ANALYZE, & EVALUATE

1. Why might the conclusions drawn by Robert Fogel and Stanley Engerman in *Time on the Cross* have provoked vehement criticism?
2. What might be some reasons for the resurrection of focus on the "damage" thesis of slavery, as in the works by Walter Johnson and Ira Berlin?

VARIETIES OF SLAVERY

Southern **slave codes** forbade slaves to hold property, to leave their masters' premises without permission, to be out after dark, to congregate with other slaves except at church, to carry firearms, to testify in court against white people, or to strike a white person even in self-defense. The codes prohibited whites from teaching slaves to read or write. The laws contained no provisions to legalize slave marriages or divorces. If an owner killed a slave while punishing him, the act was generally not considered a crime. Slaves, however, faced the death penalty for killing or even resisting a white person and for inciting revolt. The codes also contained extraordinarily rigid provisions for defining a person's race. Anyone with a trace (or, often, even a rumor) of African ancestry was defined as black.

Enforcement of the codes, however, was spotty and uneven. Some slaves did acquire property, did become literate, and did assemble with other slaves. White owners themselves handled most transgressions by their slaves and inflicted widely varying punishments. In other words, despite the rigid provisions of law, there was in reality considerable difference within the slave system. Some slaves lived in almost prisonlike conditions, rigidly and harshly controlled by their masters. Many (probably most) others experienced considerable flexibility and autonomy.

The nature of the relationship between masters and slaves depended in part on the size of the plantation. White farmers with few slaves generally supervised their workers directly and often worked closely alongside them. The paternal relationship between such masters

(Source: Library of Congress, Prints and Photographs Division [LC-USZC4-2524])

THE LASH This illustration, by H. L. Stephens, is a harsh reminder of the ever present risk of physical violence and suffering that permeated southern slavery. Published in 1863 in Philadelphia, it was part of a set of cards distributed by abolitionists to dramatize and protest the inhumanity of slavery.

and their slaves could be warm and benevolent, or tyrannical and cruel. In general, African Americans themselves preferred to live on larger plantations, where they had a chance for a social world of their own.

Although the majority of slaveowners were small farmers, the majority of slaves lived on plantations of medium or large size, with substantial slave workforces. Thus the relationship between master and slave was much less intimate for the typical slave than for the typical slaveowner. Substantial planters often hired overseers and even assistant overseers to represent them. "Head drivers," trusted and responsible slaves often assisted by several subdrivers, acted under the overseer as foremen.

Life under Slavery

Most, but not all, slaves received an adequate if rude diet, consisting mainly of cornmeal, salt pork, molasses, and, on rare occasions, fresh meat or poultry. Many slaves cultivated gardens for their own use. Their masters provided them with cheap clothing and shoes. They lived in rough cabins, called slave quarters. The plantation mistress or a doctor retained by the owner provided some medical care, but slave women themselves—as "healers," midwives, or simply as mothers—often were the more important source of medical attention.

Slaves worked hard, beginning with light tasks as children. They toiled from sun-up to sun-down, and even longer during harvesttime. Slave women worked particularly hard. They generally labored in the fields with the men, and they also handled cooking, cleaning, and child rearing. Many slave families were divided. Husbands and fathers often lived on neighboring plantations; at times, one spouse (usually the male) would be sold to a plantation owner far away. As a result, black women often found themselves acting in effect as single parents.

Slaves were, as a group, much less healthy than southern whites. After 1808, when the importation of slaves became illegal, the proportion of blacks to whites in the nation as a whole steadily declined as a result of the comparatively high black death rate. Slave mothers had large families, but the enforced poverty in which virtually all African Americans lived ensured that fewer of their children would survive to adulthood than the children of white parents. Even those who did survive typically died at a younger age than the average white person.

Household servants had a somewhat easier life—physically at least—than did field hands. On a small plantation, the same slaves might do both field work and housework. But on a large estate, there would generally be a separate domestic staff: nursemaids, housemaids, cooks, butlers, coachmen. These people lived close to the master and his family, eating the leftovers from the family table. Between the blacks and whites of such households, affectionate, almost familial relationships might develop. More often, however, house servants resented their isolation from their fellow slaves and the lack of privacy and increased discipline that came with living in such close proximity to the master's family. When emancipation came after the Civil War, it was often the house servants who were the first to leave the plantations of their former owners.

Female household servants were especially vulnerable to sexual abuse by their masters and white overseers. In addition to being subjected to unwanted sexual attention from white men, female slaves often received vindictive treatment from white women. Plantation mistresses naturally resented the sexual liaisons between their husbands and female slaves. Punishing their husbands was not usually possible, so they often punished the slaves instead—with arbitrary beatings, increased workloads, and various forms of psychological torment. Indeed, slave punishments tended to be violent and brutal. Runaways, thieves, and

(Source: *The Life and Adventures of Jonathan Jefferson Whitlaw, or, Scenes on the Mississippi, Vol. II*, by Frances Trollope, 1836)

CLEAR STARCHING IN LOUISIANA This 1837 etching by French artist Auguste Hervieu depicts a plantation mistress verbally abusing a slave woman and child. Hervieu traveled to America with British writer and abolitionist Frances Trollope. This illustration is from Trollope's 1836 novel *The Life and Adventures of Jonathan Jefferson Whitlaw: Or, Scenes on the Mississippi*, a work that exposed the degrading effects of slavery on both slaves and slaveowners.

laggards faced the lash, but in reality, any action by a slave deemed inappropriate or wary by the master could bring swift and severe physical retribution. This ever-present threat of arbitrary and brutal discipline, oddly enough, rarely undercut white popular ideals of southern aristocracy as gracious and refined.

SLAVERY IN THE CITIES

The conditions of urban slavery differed significantly from those in the countryside. On the relatively isolated plantations, slaves had little contact with free blacks and lower-class whites, and masters maintained a fairly direct and effective control. In the city, however, a master often could not supervise his slaves closely and at the same time use them profitably. Even if they slept at night in carefully watched backyard barracks, they moved about during the day alone, performing errands of various kinds.

There was a considerable market in the South for common laborers, particularly since, unlike in the North, there were few European immigrants to perform menial chores. As a result, masters often hired out slaves for such tasks. Slaves on contract worked in mining and lumbering (often far from cities), but others worked on the docks and on construction sites, drove wagons, and performed other unskilled jobs in cities and towns. Slave women and children worked in the region's few textile mills. Particularly skilled workers such as blacksmiths or carpenters were also often hired out. After regular working hours, many of them fended for themselves; thus urban slaves gained numerous opportunities to mingle with free blacks and with whites. In the cities, the line between slavery and freedom was less distinct than on the plantation.

Free African Americans

Over 250,000 free African Americans lived in the slaveholding states by the start of the Civil War, more than half of them in Virginia and Maryland. In some cases, they were slaves who had somehow earned money to buy their own and their families' freedom. It was most often urban blacks, with their greater freedom of movement and activity, who could take that route. One example was **Elizabeth Keckley**, a slave woman who bought freedom for herself and her son with proceeds from sewing. She later became a seamstress, personal servant, and companion to Mary Todd Lincoln in the White House. But few masters had any incentive, or inclination, to give up their slaves, so this route was open to relatively few people.

Some slaves were set free by a master who had moral qualms about slavery, or by a master's will after his death—for example, the more than 400 slaves belonging to John Randolph of Roanoke, freed in 1833. From the 1830s on, however, state laws governing slavery became stricter, in part in response to the fears Nat Turner's revolt created among white southerners. The new laws made **manumission**, or the ability of a slaveowner to free his slaves, much more difficult and in some cases practically impossible.

A few free blacks attained wealth and prominence. Some even owned slaves themselves, usually relatives whom they had bought to ensure their ultimate emancipation. In a few cities—New Orleans, Natchez, and Charleston—free black communities managed to flourish with relatively little interference from whites and with some economic stability. Most southern free blacks, however, lived in abject poverty. Yet, great as were the hardships of freedom, blacks much preferred it to slavery.

The Slave Trade

The domestic slave trade—transfer of slaves from one part of the South to another—was one of the most important and terrible consequences of slavery. Sometimes slaves moved to the new cotton lands in the company of their original owners, who were migrating themselves. More often, however, the transfer occurred through the efforts of professional slave traders. The traders took slaves to such central markets as Natchez, New Orleans, Mobile, and Charleston, where purchasers bid for them. A sound young field hand could fetch a price that might vary in the 1840s and 1850s from $500 to $1,700, depending on fluctuations in the market (and the health and age of the slaves).

The domestic slave trade dehumanized all who were involved in it. It separated children from parents, and parents from each other. Even families kept together by scrupulous owners might be broken up in the division of the estate after the master's death. Planters might deplore the trade, but they eased their consciences by holding the traders in contempt.

While the domestic slave trade operated legally within the South, the importation of slaves from Africa and other foreign countries had been banned since 1808. However, some enslaved people continued to be smuggled into the United States as late as the 1850s. At the annual southern commercial conventions, planters began to discuss the legal reopening of the foreign slave trade. "If it is right to buy slaves in Virginia and carry them to New Orleans," William L. Yancey asked his fellow delegates in 1858, "why is it not right to buy them in Cuba, Brazil, or Africa." The convention that year voted to repeal all the laws against slave imports, but the federal government never acted on their proposal.

The continued smuggling of slaves was not without resistance. In 1839, a group of 53 Africans who had been abducted by Portuguese slave hunters and shipped to Cuba took charge of a ship, the *Amistad*, that was transporting them to a Caribbean plantation. Their

(Source: Library of Congress, Prints and Photographs Division [LC-USZ62-27657])

THE BUSINESS OF SLAVERY The offices of slave dealers were familiar sights on the streets of pre–Civil War southern cities and towns. They provide testimony to the way in which slavery was not just a social system but a business, deeply woven into the fabric of southern economic life.

goal was to sail back to their homelands in Africa. The slaves had no experience with sailing, and they tried to compel the crew to steer them across the Atlantic. Instead, the ship sailed up the Atlantic Coast until it was captured by a ship of the U.S. Revenue Service. Many Americans, including President Van Buren, thought the slaves should be returned to Cuba. But at the request of a group of abolitionists, former president John Quincy Adams went before the Supreme Court to argue that they should be freed. Adams claimed that the foreign slave trade was illegal and thus the *Amistad* rebels could not be returned to slavery. The Court accepted his argument in 1841, and those who survived were returned to Africa, with funding from American abolitionists.

Two years later, another group of slaves revolted onboard a ship and took control of it–this time an American vessel bound from Norfolk, Virginia, to New Orleans, Louisiana– and steered it (and its 135 slaves) to the British Bahamas, where slavery was illegal and the slaves were given sanctuary. Such shipboard revolts were rare, but they were symbols of the continued effort by Africans to overcome slavery.

THE CULTURE OF SLAVERY

Fleeing America by commandeering a ship was a very small if very dramatic part of how slaves responded to their plight. Much more common was an elaborate process of cultural adaptation. One of the ways blacks adapted was by developing their own, separate culture, one that enabled them to sustain a sense of racial pride and unity.

Slave Religion

Almost all African Americans were Christians by the early nineteenth century. Some had converted voluntarily and others in response to coercion from their masters and Protestant missionaries who evangelized among them. Masters expected their slaves to join their denominations and worship under the supervision of white ministers. A separate slave religion was not supposed to exist. Indeed, autonomous black churches were banned by law.

Nevertheless, blacks throughout the South developed their own version of Christianity, at times incorporating into it such practices as voodoo or other polytheistic religious traditions of Africa. Or they simply bent religion to the special circumstances of bondage.

African American religion was often more emotional than its white counterpart and reflected the influence of African customs and practices. Slave prayer meetings routinely involved fervent chanting, spontaneous exclamations from the congregation, and ecstatic conversion experiences. Black religion was also generally more joyful and affirming than that of many white denominations. And above all, African American religion emphasized the dream of freedom and deliverance. In their prayers and songs and sermons, black Christians talked and sang of the day when the Lord would "call us home," "deliver us to freedom," or "take us to the Promised Land." While whites generally chose to interpret such language merely as the expression of hopes for life after death, many blacks used the images of Christian salvation to express their own dreams of freedom in the present world.

Language and Music

In many areas, slaves retained a language of their own. Having arrived in America speaking many different African languages, the first generations of slaves had as much difficulty communicating with one another as they did with white people. To overcome these barriers, they learned a simple, common language (known to linguists as "pidgin"). It retained some African words, but it drew primarily, if selectively, from English. And while slave language grew more sophisticated as blacks spent more time in America, some features of this early pidgin survived in black speech for many generations.

Music was especially important in slave society. Again, the African heritage was an important influence. African music relied heavily on rhythm, and so did black music in America. Slaves often created instruments for themselves out of whatever materials were at hand. The banjo became important to slave music. But more important were voices and song.

Field workers often used songs to pass the time; since they sang them in the presence of the whites, they usually attached relatively innocuous words to them. But African Americans also created more politically challenging music in the relative privacy of their own religious services. It was there that the tradition of the spiritual emerged. Through the spiritual, Africans in America not only expressed their religious faith, but also lamented their bondage and expressed continuing hope for freedom.

Slave songs were rarely written down and often seemed entirely spontaneous; but much slave music was really derived from African and Caribbean traditions passed on through generations. Performers also improvised variations on songs they had heard. When the setting permitted it, African Americans danced to their music—dances very different from and much more spontaneous than the formal steps that nineteenth-century whites generally learned. They also used music to accompany another of their important cultural traditions: storytelling.

THE SLAVE FAMILY

The slave family was the other crucial institution of black culture in the South. Like religion, it suffered from legal restrictions. Nevertheless, what we now call the "nuclear family" consistently emerged as the dominant kinship model among African Americans.

Black women generally began bearing children at younger ages than most whites, often as early as fourteen or fifteen (sometimes as a result of unwanted sexual relations with their masters). Slave communities did not condemn premarital pregnancy in the way white society did, and black couples would often begin living together before marrying. It was customary, however, for couples to marry—in a ceremony involving formal vows—soon after conceiving a child. Husbands and wives on neighboring plantations sometimes visited each other with the permission of their masters, but often such visits had to be in secret, at night. Family ties among slaves were generally no less strong than those of whites.

When marriages did not survive, it was often because of circumstances over which blacks had no control. Up to a third of all black families were broken apart by the slave trade. Extended kinship networks were strong and important and often helped compensate for the breakup of nuclear families. A slave forced suddenly to move to a new area, far from his or her family, might create fictional kinship ties and become "adopted" by a family in the new community. Even so, the impulse to maintain contact with a spouse and children remained strong long after the breakup of a family. One of the most frequent causes of flight from the plantation was a slave's desire to find a husband, wife, or child who had been sent elsewhere. After the Civil War, white and black newspapers were filled with notices from former slaves seeking to reconnect with family members separated during bondage.

However much blacks resented their lack of freedom, they often found it difficult to maintain an entirely hostile attitude toward their owners. They depended on whites for the material means of existence—food, clothing, and shelter—and they relied on them as well for security and protection. There was, in short, a paternal relationship between slave and master—frequently harsh, at other times kindly, but always important. That paternalism, in fact, became a vital instrument of white control. By creating a sense of mutual dependence, whites helped minimize though never came close to eliminating resistance to an institution that served only the interests of the ruling race.

SLAVE RESISTANCE

Slaveowners liked to argue that the slaves were generally content and "happy with their lot." But it is clear that the vast majority of southern blacks yearned for freedom and detested the peculiar institution. Evidence for that can be found, if nowhere else, in the reaction of slaves when emancipation finally came. Virtually all reacted to freedom with great joy; few chose to remain in the service of the whites who had owned them before the Civil War.

Rather than contented acceptance, the dominant response of African Americans to slavery was a complex one: a combination of adaptation and resistance. At the extremes, slavery could produce two very different reactions, each of which served as the basis for a powerful stereotype in white society. One extreme was what became known as the "Sambo"— the shuffling, grinning, head-scratching, deferential slave who acted out what he recognized as the role the white world expected of him. But the Sambo pattern of behavior was a charade put on by blacks, a façade assumed in the presence of whites. The other extreme was the slave rebel—the African American who resisted either acceptance or accommodation but remained forever rebellious.

Actual slave revolts were extremely rare, but the knowledge that they were possible struck terror into the hearts of white southerners. In 1800, **Gabriel Prosser** gathered 1,000 rebellious slaves outside Richmond; but two African Americans gave away the plot, and the Virginia militia stymied the uprising before it could begin. Prosser and thirty-five others were executed. In 1822, the Charleston free black **Denmark Vesey** and his followers—rumored to total 9,000—made preparations for revolt; but again word leaked out and suppression and retribution followed. On a summer night in 1831, **Nat Turner**, a slave preacher, led a band of African Americans armed with guns and axes from house to house in Southampton County, Virginia. They killed sixty white men, women, and children before being overpowered by state and federal troops. More than a hundred blacks were executed in the aftermath.

For the most part, however, resistance to slavery took other, less violent forms. Some blacks attempted to resist by running away. A small number managed to escape to the North or to Canada, especially after sympathetic whites and free blacks began organizing secret escape routes, known as the "underground railroad," to assist them in flight. But the odds against a successful escape were very high. The hazards of distance and the slaves' ignorance of geography were serious obstacles, as were the white "slave patrols," which stopped wandering blacks on sight and demanded to see travel permits. Despite all the obstacles to success, however, blacks continued to run away from their masters in large numbers.

Perhaps the most important method of resistance was simply a pattern of everyday behavior by which blacks defied their masters. That whites so often considered blacks to be lazy and shiftless suggests one means of resistance: refusal to work hard. Some slaves stole from their masters or from neighboring whites. Others performed isolated acts of

(©MPI/Archive Photos/Getty Images)

HARRIET TUBMAN WITH ESCAPED SLAVES Harriet Tubman (ca. 1820–1913) was born into slavery in Maryland. In 1849, when her master died, she escaped to Philadelphia to avoid being sold out of state. Over the next ten years, she assisted first members of her own family and then up to 300 other slaves escape from Maryland to freedom. She is shown here, on the far left, with some of the slaves she had helped free.

sabotage: losing or breaking tools or performing tasks improperly. In extreme cases, blacks might make themselves useless by cutting off their fingers or even committing suicide. A few turned on their masters and killed them. The extremes, however, were rare. For the most part, blacks resisted by building subtle methods of rebellion into their normal patterns of behavior.

CONCLUSION

While the North was creating a complex and rapidly developing commercial-industrial economy, the South was expanding its agrarian economy without making many fundamental changes in the region's character. Great migrations took many southern whites, and even more African American slaves, into new agricultural areas in the Deep South, where they created a booming "cotton kingdom." The cotton economy created many great fortunes and some modest ones. It also entrenched the planter class as the dominant force within southern society—both as owners of vast numbers of slaves and as patrons, creditors, politicians, landlords, and marketers for the large number of poor whites who lived on the edge of the planter world.

The differences between the North and the South were a result of differences in natural resources, social structure, climate, and culture. Above all, they were the result of the existence within the South of an unfree labor system that prevented the kind of social fluidity that an industrializing society usually requires. Within that system, however, slaves created a vital, independent culture and religion in the face of white subjugation.

KEY TERMS/PEOPLE/PLACES/EVENTS

abolitionist 262
Amistad 267
cotton kingdom 256
cult of honor 260
Denmark Vesey 271

Elizabeth Keckley 267
Gabriel Prosser 271
James Henry Hammond 259
manumission 267
Nat Turner 271

peculiar institution 261
planter class 259
second middle passage 256
slave codes 264
yeoman farmer 257

RECALL AND REFLECT

1. Why did cotton become the leading crop of the South?
2. Why did industry fail to develop in the South to the extent that it did in the North?
3. How did slavery function economically and socially?
4. What was the effect of slavery on white slaveowners? On slaves? On nonslaveowning whites? On free blacks?
5. Through what means did slaves maintain a distinct African American culture?

12 | ANTEBELLUM CULTURE AND REFORM

THE ROMANTIC IMPULSE
REMAKING SOCIETY
THE CRUSADE AGAINST SLAVERY

LOOKING AHEAD

1. How did an American national culture of art, literature, philosophy, and communal living develop in the nineteenth century?
2. What were the issues on which social and moral reformers tried to "remake the nation"? How successful were their efforts?
3. Why did the crusade against slavery become the preeminent issue of the reform movement?

THE UNITED STATES IN THE MID-NINETEENTH CENTURY was growing rapidly in size, population, and economic complexity. Most Americans were excited by the new possibilities these changes produced. But many people were also painfully aware of the problems that accompanied them.

One result of these conflicting attitudes was the emergence of movements to "reform" the nation—to refine and improve it. Some reforms rested on an optimistic faith in human nature, a belief that within every individual resided a spirit that was basically good and that society should attempt to unleash. A second impulse was a desire for order and control. With their traditional values and institutions being challenged and eroded, many Americans yearned for above all stability and discipline. By the end of the 1840s, however, one issue—slavery—had come to overshadow all others. And one group of reformers—the abolitionists—had become the most influential of all.

1821
New York constructs
first penitentiary

1826
Cooper's *The Last of
the Mohicans*

1830
Joseph Smith publishes
the Book of Mormon

1831
The *Liberator* begins
publication

1833
American Antislavery
Society founded

1837
Horace Mann
appointed secretary
of Massachusetts
Board of Education

1840
Liberty Party formed

1841
Brook Farm founded

1845
Frederick Douglass's
autobiography

1848
Women's rights
convention at Seneca
Falls, N.Y.

Oneida Community
founded

1850
Hawthorne's
The Scarlet Letter

1851
Melville's *Moby Dick*

1852
Stowe's
Uncle Tom's Cabin

1854
Thoreau's *Walden*

1855
Whitman's
Leaves of Grass

THE ROMANTIC IMPULSE

"In the four quarters of the globe," wrote the English wit Sydney Smith in 1820, "who reads an American book? or goes to an American play? or looks at an American picture or statue?" The answer, he assumed, was obvious: no one.

American intellectuals were painfully aware of the low regard in which Europeans held their culture, and they tried to create an artistic life that would express their own nation's special virtues. At the same time, many of the nation's cultural leaders were striving for another kind of liberation, which was—ironically—largely an import from Europe: the spirit of romanticism. In literature, in philosophy, in art, even in politics and economics, American intellectuals were committing themselves to the liberation of the human spirit.

NATIONALISM AND ROMANTICISM IN AMERICAN PAINTING

Despite Sydney Smith's contemptuous question, a great many people in the United States were, in fact, looking at American paintings—and they were doing so because they believed Americans were creating important new artistic traditions of their own.

American painters sought to capture the power of nature by portraying some of the nation's grandest landscapes. The first great school of American painters—known as the **Hudson River school**—emerged in New York. Frederic Church, Thomas Cole, Thomas Doughty, Asher Durand, and others painted the spectacular vistas of the largely untamed Hudson Valley. Like Ralph Waldo Emerson and Henry David Thoreau, whom many of the painters read and admired, they considered nature—far more than civilization—the best source of wisdom and fulfillment. In portraying the Hudson Valley, they seemed to announce that in America, unlike in

Europe, "wild nature" still existed; and that America, therefore, was a nation of greater promise than the overdeveloped lands of the Old World.

In later years, some of the Hudson River painters traveled farther west. Their enormous canvases of great natural wonders–the Yosemite Valley, Yellowstone, the Rocky Mountains–touched a passionate chord among the public. Some of the most famous of their paintings–particularly the works of Albert Bierstadt and Thomas Moran–traveled around the country attracting enormous crowds.

AN AMERICAN LITERATURE

The effort to create a distinctively American literature made considerable progress in the 1820s through the work of the first great American novelist: James Fenimore Cooper. What most distinguished his work was its evocation of the American West. Cooper had a lifelong fascination with the human relationship to nature and with the challenges (and dangers) of America's expansion westward. His most important novels–among them *The Last of the Mohicans* (1826) and *The Deerslayer* (1841)–examined the experience of rugged white frontiersmen with Indians, pioneers, violence, and the law. Cooper evoked the ideal of the independent individual with a natural inner goodness–an ideal that many Americans feared was in jeopardy.

Another, later group of American writers displayed more clearly the influence of romanticism. **Walt Whitman's** book of poems *Leaves of Grass* (1855) celebrated democracy, the liberation of the individual spirit, and the pleasures of the flesh. In helping free verse from traditional, restrictive conventions, he also expressed a yearning for emotional and physical release and personal fulfillment–a yearning perhaps rooted in part in his own experience as a homosexual living in a society profoundly intolerant of unconventional sexuality.

Less exuberant was **Herman Melville**, perhaps the greatest American writer of his era. *Moby Dick,* published in 1851, is Melville's most important–although not, in his lifetime, his most popular–novel. It tells the story of Ahab, the powerful, driven captain of a whaling vessel, and his obsessive search for Moby Dick, the great white whale that had once maimed him. It is a story of courage and the strength of human will. But it is also a tragedy of pride and revenge. In some ways it is an uncomfortable metaphor for the harsh, individualistic, achievement-driven culture of nineteenth-century America.

LITERATURE IN THE ANTEBELLUM SOUTH

The South experienced a literary flowering of its own in the mid-nineteenth century, and it produced writers and artists who were, like their northern counterparts, concerned with defining the nature of America. But white southerners tended to produce very different images of what society was and should be.

The southern writer Edgar Allan Poe penned stories and poems that were primarily sad and macabre. His first book, *Tamerlane and Other Poems* (1827), received little recognition. But later works, including his most famous poem, "The Raven" (1845), established him as a major, if controversial, literary figure. Poe evoked images of individuals rising above the narrow confines of intellect and exploring the deeper–and often painful and horrifying–world of the spirit and emotions.

Other southern novelists of the 1830s (among them Nathaniel Beverley Tucker, William Alexander Caruthers, and John Pendleton Kennedy) produced historical romances and eulogies for the plantation system of the upper South. The most distinguished of the region's authors was William Gilmore Simms. For a time, his work expressed a broad nationalism that transcended his regional background; but by the 1840s, he too became a strong defender of southern institutions—especially slavery—against the encroachments of the North. There was, he believed, a unique quality to southern life that fell to intellectuals to defend.

One group of southern writers, however, produced works that were more broadly American. These writers from the fringes of plantation society—Augustus B. Longstreet, Joseph G. Baldwin, Johnson J. Hooper, and others—depicted the world of the backwoods South and focused on ordinary people and poor whites. Instead of romanticizing their subjects, they were deliberately and sometimes painfully realistic, seasoning their sketches with a robust, vulgar humor that was new to American literature. These southern realists established a tradition of American regional humor that was ultimately to find its most powerful voice in Mark Twain.

THE TRANSCENDENTALISTS

One of the outstanding expressions of the romantic impulse in America came from a group of New England writers and philosophers known as the **transcendentalists**. Borrowing heavily from German and English writers and philosophers, the transcendentalists promoted a theory of the individual that rested on a distinction between what they called "reason" and "understanding." Reason, as they defined it, had little to do with rationality. It was, rather, the individual's innate capacity to grasp beauty and truth by giving full expression to the instincts and emotions. Understanding, by contrast, was the use of intellect in the narrow, artificial ways imposed by society; it involved the repression of instinct and the victory of externally imposed learning. Every person's goal, therefore, should be the cultivation of "reason"—and, thus, liberation from "understanding." Each individual should strive to "transcend" the limits of the intellect and allow the emotions, the "soul," to create an "original relation to the Universe."

Transcendentalist philosophy emerged first in America among a small group of intellectuals centered in Concord, Massachusetts, and led by **Ralph Waldo Emerson**. A Unitarian minister in his youth, Emerson left the clergy in 1832 to devote himself to writing, teaching, and lecturing. In "Nature" (1836), Emerson wrote that in the quest for self-fulfillment, individuals should work for a communion with the natural world: "in the woods, we return to reason and faith. . . . Standing on the bare ground,—my head bathed by the blithe air, and uplifted into infinite space,—all mean egotism vanishes. . . . I am part and particle of God." In other essays, he was even more explicit in advocating a commitment to individuality and the full exploration of inner capacities.

Emerson's stress on individuality and the search for inner meaning apart from society inspired Margaret Fuller. In 1840 she became the first editor of the transcendentalist journal *The Dial,* where she argued for the important relationship between the discovery of the "self" and the questioning of the prevailing gender roles of her era. In *Women in the Nineteenth Century*, published in 1845 and considered an important work in the early history of feminism, Fuller wrote, "Many women are considering within themselves what they need and what they have not." She urged readers, especially women, to set aside conventional thinking about the place of women in society.

Henry David Thoreau went even further than Emerson and Fuller in repudiating the repressive forces of society, which produced, he said, "lives of quiet desperation." Each individual should work for self-realization by resisting pressures to conform to society's

(Source: Library of Congress, Prints and Photographs Division [LC-USZ62-47039])

MARGARET FULLER   Margaret Fuller was in the forefront of efforts to probe how contemporary gender roles limited the free expression of women's souls and abilities.

expectations and responding instead to his or her own instincts. Thoreau's own effort to free himself—immortalized in *Walden* (1854)—led him to build a small cabin in the Concord woods on the edge of Walden Pond, where he lived alone for two years as simply as he could, attempting to liberate himself from what he considered society's excessive interest in material comforts. In his 1849 essay "Resistance to Civil Government," he extended his critique of artificial constraints in society to government, arguing that when government required an individual to violate his or her own morality, it had no legitimate authority. The proper response was "civil disobedience," or "passive resistance"—a public refusal to obey unjust laws. It was a belief that would undergird some antislavery reforms and, much later in the mid-twentieth century, attacks on racial segregation.

THE DEFENSE OF NATURE

As Emerson's and Thoreau's tributes to nature suggest, a small but influential group of Americans in the nineteenth century feared the impact of capitalism on the integrity of the natural world. "The mountains and cataracts, which were to have made poets and painters," wrote the essayist Oliver Wendell Holmes, "have been mined for anthracite and dammed for water power."

To the transcendentalists and others, nature was not just a setting for economic activity, as many farmers, miners, and others believed. It was the source of deep, personal human inspiration—the vehicle through which individuals could best realize the truth within their own souls. Genuine spirituality, they argued, did not come from formal religion but through communion with the natural world.

In making such claims, the transcendentalists were among the first Americans to anticipate the conservation movement of the late nineteenth century and the environmental movement of the twentieth century. They had no scientific basis for their defense of the wilderness and little sense of the twentieth-century notion of the interconnectedness of species. But they did believe in, and articulate, an essential unity between humanity and nature—a spiritual unity, they believed, without which civilization would be impoverished. They looked at nature, they said, "with new eyes," and with those eyes they saw that "behind nature, throughout nature, spirit is present."

Visions of Utopia

Although transcendentalism was at its heart an individualistic philosophy, it helped spawn one of the most famous nineteenth-century experiments in communal living: Brook Farm. The dream of the Boston transcendentalist George Ripley, Brook Farm was established in 1841 as an experimental community in West Roxbury, Massachusetts. There, according to Ripley, individuals would gather to create a new society that would permit every member to have full opportunity for self-realization. All residents would share equally in the labor of the community so that all could share as well in the leisure, which was essential for cultivation of the self. The tension between the ideal of individual freedom and the demands of a communal society, however, eventually took its toll on Brook Farm. Many residents became disenchanted and left. When a fire destroyed the central building of the community in 1847, the experiment dissolved.

Among the original residents of Brook Farm was the writer **Nathaniel Hawthorne**, who expressed his disillusionment with the experiment and, to some extent, with transcendentalism in a series of novels. In *The Blithedale Romance* (1852), he wrote scathingly of Brook Farm itself. In other novels—most notably *The Scarlet Letter* (1850) and *The House of the Seven Gables* (1851)—he wrote equally passionately about the price individuals pay for cutting themselves off from society. Egotism, he claimed (in an indirect challenge to the transcendentalist faith in the self), was the "serpent" that lay at the heart of human misery.

Brook Farm was only one of many experimental communities in the years before the Civil War. The Scottish industrialist and philanthropist Robert Owen founded an experimental community in Indiana in 1825, which he named New Harmony. It was to be a "Village of Cooperation," in which every resident worked and lived in total equality. The community was an economic failure, but the vision that had inspired it continued to enchant some Americans. Dozens of other "Owenite" experiments were established in other locations in the ensuing years.

Redefining Gender Roles

Inspired by the transcendentalist emphasis on liberating the individual from the constraints of social convention, many of the new utopian communities revised the traditional relationship between men and women. Some even experimented with radical redefinitions of gender roles.

One of the more radical of the utopian colonies of the nineteenth century was the Oneida Community, established in 1848 in upstate New York by John Humphrey Noyes. The **Oneida "Perfectionists,"** as residents of the community called themselves, rejected traditional notions of family and marriage. All residents, Noyes declared, were "married" to all other residents; there were to be no permanent conjugal ties. But Oneida was not, as horrified critics often claimed, an experiment in unrestrained "free love." It was a place where the community carefully monitored sexual behavior, where women were protected from unwanted childbearing, and where children were raised communally, often seeing little of their own parents. The Oneidans took pride in what they considered their liberation of women from the demands of male "lust" and from the traditional restraints of family. Their numbers were never large—only once did they count more than 300 members—and the community itself lasted only 30 years.

The **Shakers**, too, redefined traditional gender roles. Founded by "Mother" Ann Lee in the 1770s, the society of the Shakers survived through the twentieth century. (A tiny remnant is left today.) But the Shakers attracted a particularly large following in the mid-nineteenth century and established more than twenty communities throughout the Northeast and Northwest in the 1840s. They derived their name from a unique religious ritual—in which members of a congregation would "shake" themselves free of sin while performing a loud chant and an ecstatic dance.

The most distinctive feature of Shakerism, however, was its commitment to complete celibacy—which meant, of course, that no one could be born into the faith. All Shakers had to choose it voluntarily. Shakerism attracted about 6,000 members in the 1840s, more women than men. They lived in communities where contacts between men and women were strictly limited, and they endorsed the idea of sexual equality, although women exercised the greater power.

The Shakers were not, however, motivated only by a desire to escape the burdens of traditional gender roles. They were also trying to create a society set apart from the chaos and disorder they believed had come to characterize American life. In that, they were much like other dissenting religious sects and utopian communities of their time.

THE MORMONS

Among the most important religious efforts to create a new and more ordered society was that of the Church of Jesus Christ of Latter-day Saints—the Mormons. The original Mormons were white men and women, many of whom felt that social changes had left them economically marginalized and in doubt about the fundamental tenets of traditional Christianity. They discovered in Mormonism a new history of the world, a new establishment of the Christian church, a new book of scripture and set of prophets to join those of the Bible, a new call to prepare for the Second Coming, and a new promise that—just as God had once been a man—all believers could become like God himself.

Mormonism began in upstate New York through the efforts of **Joseph Smith**. In 1830, when he was just twenty-four, he organized the church and published a remarkable document—the Book of Mormon, named for the ancient prophet who he claimed had been its chief editor. It was, he said, a translation of a set of golden tablets he had found in the hills of New York, revealed to him by Moroni, an angel of God and the book's last prophet. The Book of Mormon told the story of two ancient civilizations in America, whose people had anticipated the coming of Christ and were rewarded when Jesus actually came to America after his resurrection. Ultimately, both civilizations collapsed because of their rejection of Christian principles. But Smith believed their history as righteous societies could serve as a model for building a new holy community in the United States.

In 1831, gathering a small group of believers around him, Smith began searching for a sanctuary for his new community of "saints," an effort that would continue unhappily for more than fifteen years. Time and again, the Latter-day Saints, as they called themselves, attempted to establish peaceful communities. Time and again, they met with persecution

(©Everett Historical/Shutterstock)

MORMONS HEADING WEST This lithograph by William Henry Jackson imagines the physical challenges that Mormon pioneers faced in their journey to Utah in 1850. Many of the men are shown pulling their families and possessions on handcarts.

from their neighbors, who were suspicious of their radical religious doctrines—their claims of new prophets, new scripture, and divine authority. Opponents were also concerned by their rapid growth and their increasing political strength. Near the end of his life, Joseph Smith introduced the practice of polygamy (giving a man the right to take several wives), which became public knowledge after Smith's death. From then on, polygamy became a central target of anti-Mormon opposition.

Driven from their original settlements in Independence, Missouri, and Kirtland, Ohio, the Mormons founded a new town in Illinois that they named Nauvoo. In the early 1840s, it became an imposing and economically successful community. In 1844, however, bitter enemies of Joseph Smith published an inflammatory attack on him. Smith ordered his followers to destroy the offending press, and he was subsequently arrested and imprisoned in nearby Carthage. There, an angry mob attacked the jail and fatally shot him. The Mormons soon abandoned Nauvoo and, under the leadership of Smith's successor, Brigham Young, traveled—12,000 strong, in one of the largest single group migrations in American history—across the Great Plains and the Rocky Mountains. They established several communities in Utah, including the present Salt Lake City, where, finally, the Mormons were able to create a lasting settlement.

REMAKING SOCIETY

Central to romanticism and transcendentalism was a reform impulse—the drive to improve the life and health of men and women. Seeking to uncover the divinity of the individual inspired larger quests to perfect the world itself. The reform impulse helped create new movements to remake mainstream society—movements in which, to a striking degree, women formed both the rank and file and the leadership. By the 1830s, such movements had become organized reform societies.

REVIVALISM, MORALITY, AND ORDER

Along with romanticism and transcendentalism, Protestant revivalism was another powerful source of the popular effort to rewrite society. It was the movement that had begun with the Second Great Awakening early in the century and had, by the 1820s, evolved into a powerful force for social reform.

The New Light evangelicals embraced the optimistic belief that every individual was capable of salvation through his or her own efforts. Partly as a result, revivalism soon became not only a means of personal salvation but also an effort to reform the larger society. In particular, revivalism produced a crusade against personal immorality.

Evangelical Protestantism greatly strengthened the crusade against drunkenness. No social vice, **temperance** advocates argued, was more responsible for crime, disorder, and poverty than the excessive use of alcohol. Women complained that men spent money their families needed on alcohol and that drunken husbands often beat and abused their wives. Temperance also appealed to those who were alarmed by immigration; drunkenness, many nativists believed, was responsible for violence and disorder in immigrant communities. By 1840, temperance had become a major national movement, with powerful organizations and more than a million followers who had signed a formal pledge to forgo hard liquor.

(Source: Library of Congress, Prints and Photographs Division [LC-USZC4-1629])

THE DRUNKARD'S PROGRESS This 1846 lithograph by Nathaniel Currier shows what temperance advocates argued was the inevitable consequence of alcohol consumption. Beginning with an apparently innocent "glass with a friend," the young man rises step by step to the summit of drunken revelry, then declines to desperation and suicide while his abandoned wife and child grieve.

Health, Science, and Phrenology

For some Americans, the search for individual and social perfection led to an interest in new theories of health and knowledge. In the nineteenth century, more than half of those who contracted cholera—a severe bacterial infection of the intestines, usually contracted from contaminated food or water—died. Nearly a quarter of the population of New Orleans in 1833 perished from the disease. Many cities established health boards to try to find ways to prevent epidemics. But the medical profession of the time, not yet aware of the nature of bacterial infections, had no answers.

Instead, many Americans turned to nonscientific theories for improving health. Affluent men and especially women flocked to health spas for the celebrated "water cure" (known to modern scientists as hydrotherapy), which purported to improve health through immersing people in hot or cold baths or wrapping them in wet sheets. Other people adopted new dietary theories. Sylvester Graham, a Connecticut-born Presbyterian minister and committed reformer, won many followers with his prescriptions for eating fruits, vegetables, and bread made from coarsely ground flour—a prescription not unlike some dietary theories today—and for avoiding meat. (The graham cracker is made from a kind of flour named for him.)

Perhaps strangest of all to modern sensibilities was the widespread belief in the new "science" of phrenology, which appeared first in Germany and became popular in the United States beginning in the 1830s through the efforts of Orson and Lorenzo Fowler, publishers of the *Phrenology Almanac*. Phrenologists argued that the shape of an individual's skull was an important indicator of his or her character and intelligence. They made elaborate measurements of bumps and indentations to calculate the size (and, they claimed, the strength) of different areas of the brain. Phrenology seemed to provide a way of measuring an individual's fitness for various positions in life and to promise an end to the arbitrary process by which people matched their talents to occupations and responsibilities. The theory is now universally believed to have no scientific value at all.

Medical Science

In an age of rapid technological and scientific advances, medicine sometimes seemed to lag behind. In part, that was because of the character of the medical profession, which—in the absence of any significant regulation or prescribed pathway of schooling—attracted many poorly educated people and not a few quacks. Efforts to regulate the profession were beaten back in the 1830s and 1840s by those who considered the licensing of physicians to be a form of undemocratic monopoly. The prestige of the profession, therefore, remained uneven.

The biggest problem facing American medicine, however, was the absence of basic knowledge about disease. The great medical achievement of the eighteenth century—the development of a vaccination against smallpox by Edward Jenner—came from no broad theory of infection but from a brilliant adaptation of folk practices among country people. The development of anesthetics in the nineteenth century came not from medical doctors at first, but from a New England dentist, William Morton, who was looking for ways to help his patients endure the extraction of teeth. Beginning in 1844, Morton began experimenting with sulfuric ether. John Warren, a Boston surgeon, soon began using ether to sedate surgical patients. Even these advances met with stiff resistance from some traditional physicians, who mistrusted innovation and experimentation.

In the absence of any broad acceptance of scientific methods and experimental practice in medicine, it was very difficult for even the most talented doctors to make progress in treating disease. Even so, halting progress toward the discovery of the germ theory did occur in antebellum America. In 1843, the Boston essayist, poet, and physician Oliver Wendell Holmes published a study of large numbers of cases of "puerperal fever" (septicemia in children) and concluded that the disease could be transmitted from one person to another. This discovery of contagion met with a storm of criticism but was later vindicated by the clinical success of the Hungarian physician Ignaz Semmelweis, who noticed that infection seemed to be spread by medical students who had been working with diseased corpses. Once he began requiring students to wash their hands and disinfect their instruments, the infections virtually disappeared.

EDUCATION

One of the most important reform movements of the mid-nineteenth century was the effort to produce a system of universal public education. As of 1830, no state had such a system. Soon after that, however, interest in public education began growing rapidly.

The greatest of the educational reformers was **Horace Mann**, the first secretary of the Massachusetts Board of Education, which was established in 1837. To Mann and his followers, education was the only way to preserve democracy, for an educated electorate was essential to the workings of a free political system. Mann reorganized the Massachusetts school system, lengthened the academic year (to six months), doubled teachers' salaries, broadened the curriculum, and introduced new methods of professional training for teachers. Other states followed by building new schools, creating teachers' colleges, and offering many children access to education for the first time. By the 1850s, the principle (although not yet the reality) of tax-supported elementary schools was established in every state.

The quality of public education continued to vary widely. In some places—Massachusetts, for example—educators were generally capable men and women, often highly trained. In other areas, however, barely literate teachers and severely limited funding hindered education. Among the highly dispersed population of the West, many children had no access to schools at all. In the South, all African Americans were barred from education, and only about a third of all white children of school age were actually enrolled in schools in 1860. In the North, 72 percent were enrolled, but even there, many students attended classes only briefly and casually.

Among the goals of educational reformers was to teach children the social values of thrift, order, discipline, punctuality, and respect for authority. Horace Mann, for example, spoke of the role of public schools in extending democracy and expanding individual opportunity. But he spoke, too, of their role in creating social order: "Train up a child in the way he should go, and when he is old he will not depart from it."

The interest in education contributed to the growing movement to educate American Indians. Some reformers believed that Indians could be "civilized" if only they could be taught the ways of the white world. Efforts by missionaries and others to educate Indians and encourage them to assimilate were particularly prominent in such areas of the Far West as Oregon, where conflicts with the natives had not yet become acute. Nevertheless, the great majority of Native Americans remained outside the reach of white educational reform.

Despite limitations and inequities, the achievements of the school reformers were impressive. By the beginning of the Civil War, the United States had one of the highest literacy rates of any nation in the world: 94 percent of the population of the North, and 83 percent of the white population of the South.

REHABILITATION

The belief in the potential of the individual also sparked the creation of new institutions to help individuals with disabilities—institutions that formed part of a great network of charitable activities known as the Benevolent Empire. Among them was the Perkins School for the Blind in Boston. Nothing better exemplified the romantic reform spirit of the era than the conviction of those who founded Perkins. They believed that even society's supposedly most disadvantaged members could be helped to discover their own inner strength and wisdom.

Similar impulses produced another powerful movement of reform: the creation of "asylums" for criminals and those who were mentally ill. In advocating prison and hospital reform, Americans were reacting against one of society's most glaring ills: antiquated jails and mental institutions whose inmates lived in almost inhuman conditions. Beginning in the 1820s, many states built new penitentiaries and mental asylums. New York built the first penitentiary at Auburn in 1821. In Massachusetts, the reformer Dorothea Dix began a national movement for new methods of treating individuals with mental illness.

New forms of prison discipline were designed to reform and rehabilitate criminals. Solitary confinement and the imposition of silence on work crews (both instituted in Pennsylvania and New York in the 1820s) were meant to give prisoners opportunities to meditate on their wrongdoings and develop "penitence" (hence the name "penitentiary").

Some of the same impulses that produced asylums underlay the emergence of a new "reform" approach to the challenge of working with Native Americans. For several decades, the dominant thrust of the United States' policy toward the Indians had been relocation—getting the tribes out of the way of white civilization. But among some whites, there had also been another intent: to move the Indians to a place where they would be allowed to develop to a point at which assimilation might be possible.

It was a small step from the idea of relocation to the idea of the reservation. Just as prisons, asylums, and orphanages would provide society with an opportunity to train and uplift misfits and unfortunates within white society, so the reservations might provide a way to undertake what one official called "the great work of regenerating the Indian race." These optimistic goals failed to meet the expectations of the reformers.

THE RISE OF FEMINISM

Many women who became involved in reform movements in the 1820s and 1830s came to resent the social and legal restrictions that limited their participation. Out of their concerns emerged the first American feminist movement. Sarah and Angelina Grimké, sisters who became active and outspoken abolitionists, ignored claims by men that their activism was inappropriate to their gender. "Men and women were created equal," they argued. "They are both moral and accountable beings, and whatever is right for man to do, is right for women to do." Other reformers—Catharine Beecher, **Harriet Beecher Stowe** (her sister), **Lucretia Mott, Elizabeth Cady Stanton, Susan B. Anthony**, and **Dorothea Dix**—similarly pressed at the boundaries of "acceptable" female behavior.

In 1840, American female delegates arrived at a world antislavery convention in London, only to be turned away by the men who controlled the proceedings. Angered at the rejection, several of the delegates became convinced that their first duty as reformers should now be to elevate the status of women. Over the next several years, Mott, Stanton, and others began drawing pointed parallels between the plight of women and the plight of slaves; and in 1848, in **Seneca Falls**, New York, they organized a convention to discuss the question of women's rights. Out of the meeting came the Declaration of Sentiments and Resolutions, which stated that "all men and women are created equal," and that women no less than men are endowed with certain inalienable rights. (See "Consider the Source: Declaration of Sentiments and Resolutions, Seneca Falls, New York.") In demanding the right to vote, they launched a movement for woman suffrage that would survive until the battle was finally won in 1920.

Many of the women involved in these feminist efforts were Quakers. Quakerism had long embraced the ideal of sexual equality and had tolerated, indeed encouraged, the emergence of women as preachers and community leaders. Of the women who drafted the Declaration of Sentiments, all but Elizabeth Cady Stanton were Quakers.

Feminists benefited greatly from their association with other reform movements, most notably abolitionism, but they also suffered as a result. The demands of women were usually assigned a secondary position to what many considered the far greater issue of the rights of slaves.

STRUGGLES OF BLACK WOMEN

Among the leading voices for women's rights was **Sojourner Truth**, a black woman born into slavery in Ulster County in New York in 1799 but who escaped to freedom at age 29. Born Isabella Baumfree, she changed her name after becoming a Methodist in 1843 and believed that God had called her to testify to the truth of freedom from sin and slavery. A staunch abolitionist, she attended the Ohio Women's Rights Convention in Akron, Ohio, in 1851, and delivered an impassioned and well-publicized call for equal rights for women and blacks. Afterward Truth became a leading spokesperson for both causes.

While black women like Sojourner Truth campaigned publicly for women's and blacks' civil rights, others attempted to reform society from within their religious traditions. Like white clerics, black preachers in African American churches widely banned female congregants from becoming ordained and obtaining a license to preach and often required them to seek special permission to serve as class and prayer leaders. Indeed, no black denomination formally recognized a woman as a cleric until the African Methodist Episcopal Church ordained Julia Foote in 1895. Still, black women sought to preach throughout the colonial and antebellum eras. Among the first was **Jarena Lee**, born free in 1783 in Cape May, New Jersey. As a twenty-one-year-old woman then living in Philadelphia, she preached in public with such verve and passion that she earned an invitation from Rev. Richard Allen to speak at his church. Yet few other ministers welcomed her, which Lee struggled to understand theologically. As she argued in 1833, "If the man may preach, because the Savior died for him, why not the women, seeing he died for her also? Is he not a whole Savior, instead of a half one, as those who hold it wrong for a woman to preach, would seem to make it appear? Did not Mary *first* preach the risen Savior? Then did not Mary, a woman, preach the gospel?"

A more radical contemporary of Lee's was **Rebecca Cox Jackson**. Growing up a free woman in Philadelphia during the early 1800s, she lived much of her life with her brother, Joseph Cox, an African Methodist Episcopal minister. Following instructions given to her by a heavenly spirit in 1830, Jackson began to host prayer meetings that quickly surged in popularity. She stirred controversy by tossing aside convention and inviting men and women to worship side by side. She earned a temporary reprieve, however, after a visit by Rev. Morris Brown, who succeeded Rev. Richard Allen as bishop of the African Methodist Episcopal Church. Brown came to one of Jackson's meetings with the idea of silencing her, but left thoroughly impressed by her preaching and ordered that she be left alone. In 1833 Jackson embarked on a preaching tour outside Philadelphia but met with new and greater resistance. Her insistence on her right to preach, open refusal to join a church, and radical views on sexuality that included celibacy within marriage angered area clerics and, Jackson claimed, motivated some to assault her. Eventually she broke ranks with the free black church movement and joined a Shaker group in Watervliet, New York. In 1851 she returned to Philadelphia and founded a Shaker community composed mainly of black women.

DECLARATION OF SENTIMENTS AND RESOLUTIONS, SENECA FALLS, NEW YORK (1848)

On July 19 and 20, 1848, leaders of the women's rights movement gathered in Seneca Falls, New York, to host a national conversation about "the social, civil, and religious conditions and rights of women." They outlined their grievances and goals in the Declaration of Sentiments and Resolutions, which helped shape a national reform movement.

When, in the course of human events, it becomes necessary for one portion of the family of man to assume among the people of the earth a position different from that which they have hitherto occupied, but one to which the laws of nature and of nature's God entitle them, a decent respect to the opinions of mankind requires that they should declare the causes that impel them to such a course.

We hold these truths to be self-evident: that all men and women are created equal; that they are endowed by their Creator with certain inalienable rights; that among these are life, liberty, and the pursuit of happiness; that to secure these rights governments are instituted, deriving their just powers from the consent of the governed. Whenever any form of government becomes destructive of these ends, it is the right of those who suffer from it to refuse allegiance to it, and to insist upon the institution of a new government, laying its foundation on such principles, and organizing its powers in such form, as to them shall seem most likely to effect their safety and happiness. Prudence, indeed, will dictate that governments long established should not be changed for light and transient causes; and accordingly all experience hath shown that mankind are more disposed to suffer, while evils are sufferable, than to right themselves by abolishing the forms to which they are accustomed. But when a long train of abuses and usurpations, pursuing invariably the same object, evinces a design to reduce them under absolute despotism, it is their duty to throw off such government, and to provide new guards for their future security. Such has been the patient sufferance of the women under this government, and such is now the necessity which constrains them to demand the equal station to which they are entitled. The history of mankind is a history of repeated injuries and usurpations on the part of man toward woman, having in direct object the establishment of an absolute tyranny over her. To prove this, let facts be submitted to a candid world.

He has never permitted her to exercise her inalienable right to the elective franchise. He has compelled her to submit to laws, in the formation of which she had no voice. He has withheld from her rights which are given to the most ignorant and degraded men—both natives and foreigners.

Having deprived her of this first right of a citizen, the elective franchise, thereby leaving her without representation in the halls of legislation, he has oppressed her on all sides. He has made her, if married, in the eye of the law, civilly dead.

He has taken from her all right in property, even to the wages she earns.

He has made her, morally, an irresponsible being, as she can commit many crimes with impunity, provided they be done in the presence of her husband. In the covenant of marriage, she is compelled to promise obedience to her husband, he becoming, to all intents and purposes, her master—the law giving him power to deprive her of her liberty, and to administer chastisement.

He has so framed the laws of divorce, as to what shall be the proper causes, and in case of separation, to whom the guardianship of the children shall be given, as to be wholly regardless of the happiness of women—the law, in all cases, going upon a false supposition of the supremacy of man, and giving all power into his hands.

After depriving her of all rights as a married woman, if single, and the owner of property, he has taxed her to support a government which recognizes her only when her property can be made profitable to it.

He has monopolized nearly all the profitable employments, and from those she is permitted to follow, she receives but a scanty remuneration. He closes against her all the avenues to wealth and distinction which he considers most honorable to himself. As a teacher of theology, medicine, or law, she is not known.

He has denied her the facilities for obtaining a thorough education, all colleges being closed against her.

He allows her in church, as well as state, but a subordinate position, claiming apostolic authority for her exclusion from the ministry, and, with some exceptions, from any public participation in the affairs of the church.

He has created a false public sentiment by giving to the world a different code of morals for men and women, by which moral delinquencies which exclude women from society, are not only tolerated, but deemed of little account in man.

He has usurped the prerogative of Jehovah himself, claiming it as his right to assign for her a sphere of action, when that belongs to her conscience and to her God.

He has endeavored, in every way that he could, to destroy her confidence in her own powers, to lessen her self-respect, and to make her willing to lead a dependent and abject life.

Now, in view of this entire disfranchisement of one-half the people of this country, their social and religious degradation—in view of the unjust laws above mentioned, and because women do feel themselves aggrieved, oppressed, and fraudulently deprived of their most sacred rights, we insist that they have immediate admission to all the rights and privileges which belong to them as citizens of the United States.

UNDERSTAND, ANALYZE, & EVALUATE

1. What central claim about the relationship of men and women lies at the heart of this declaration? What evidence did the authors produce to support their claim?
2. With what demand did the authors conclude their resolution? How would you have reacted to this text?

Source: Stanton, Elizabeth Cady, *A History of Woman Suffrage, vol. 1.* Rochester, NY: Fowler and Wells, 1889, 70–71.

Lee and Jackson rejected the limitations placed on their preaching because of their gender. Like other black women, they found confirmation for their efforts not in any church rule or clerical pronouncement but rather through their personal interpretation of the Bible and, more important, an unflagging conviction that God had called them to preach. Though denied official recognition as preachers, they still touched the lives of many and represented a vital dimension to the religious lives of northern blacks.

THE CRUSADE AGAINST SLAVERY

The antislavery movement was not new to the mid-nineteenth century. Nor was it primarily a domestic crusade. Indeed, the struggle to end slavery took root in countries around the world. (See "America in the World: The Abolition of Slavery.") But not until 1830 in America did the antislavery movement begin to gather the force that would ultimately enable it to overshadow virtually all other efforts at social reform.

THE ABOLITION OF SLAVERY

The United States formally abolished slavery through the Thirteenth Amendment of the Constitution in 1865, in the aftermath of the Civil War. But the effort to abolish slavery did not begin or end in North America. Emancipation in the United States was part of a worldwide antislavery movement that began in the late eighteenth century and continued through the end of the nineteenth.

The end of slavery, like the end of monarchies and established aristocracies, was one of the ideals of the Enlightenment, which inspired new concepts of individual freedom and political equality. As Enlightenment ideas spread throughout the Western world in the seventeenth and eighteenth centuries, people on both sides of the Atlantic began to examine slavery anew. Some Enlightenment thinkers, including some of the founders of the American republic, believed that freedom was appropriate for white people but not for people of color. But others came to believe that all human beings had an equal claim to liberty, and their views became the basis for an escalating series of antislavery movements.

Opponents of slavery first targeted the slave trade—the vast commerce in human beings that had grown up in the seventeenth and eighteenth centuries and had come to involve large parts of Europe, Africa, the

(Source: Library of Congress, Prints and Photographs Division [LC-USZC4-5321])

ANTISLAVERY MESSAGE The image of an enslaved man praying to God was popular in both British and American antislavery circles. It began as the seal of the Committee for the Abolition of the Slave Trade, a British abolitionist group formed in 1787, accompanied by the quote, "Am I not a man and a brother?" This example from 1837 was used to illustrate John Greenleaf Whittier's antislavery poem "Our Countrymen in Chains."

Caribbean, and North and South America. In the aftermath of the revolutions in America, France, and Haiti, the attack on the slave trade quickly gained momentum. Its central figure was the English reformer William Wilberforce, who spent years attacking Britain's connection with the slave trade on moral and religious grounds. After the Haitian Revolution, Wilberforce and other antislavery activists denounced slavery on the grounds that its continuation would create more slave revolts. In 1807, he persuaded Parliament to pass a law ending the slave trade within the entire British Empire. The British example foreshadowed many other nations to make the slave trade illegal as well: the United States in 1808, France in 1814, Holland in 1817, Spain in 1845. Trading in slaves persisted within countries and colonies where slavery remained legal (including the United States), and some illegal slave trading continued throughout the Atlantic World. But the international sale of slaves steadily declined after 1807. The last known shipment of slaves across the Atlantic—from Africa to Cuba—occurred in 1867.

Ending the slave trade was a great deal easier than ending slavery itself, in which many people had major investments and on which much agriculture, commerce, and industry depended. But pressure to abolish slavery grew steadily throughout the nineteenth century, with Wilberforce once more helping to lead the international outcry against the institution. In Haiti, the slave revolts that began in 1791 eventually abolished not only slavery but also French rule. In some parts of South America, slavery came to an end with the overthrow of Spanish rule in the 1820s. Simón Bolívar, the great leader of Latin American independence, considered abolishing slavery an important part of his mission, freeing those who joined his armies and insisting on constitutional prohibitions of slavery in several of the constitutions he helped frame. In 1833, the British parliament passed a law abolishing slavery throughout the British Empire and compensated slaveowners for freeing their slaves. France abolished slavery in its empire, after years of agitation from abolitionists, in 1848. In the Caribbean, Spain followed Britain in slowly eliminating slavery from its colonies. Puerto Rico abolished slavery in 1873; and Cuba became the last colony in the Caribbean to end slavery, in 1886, in the face of increasing slave resistance and the declining profitability of slave-based plantations. Brazil was the last nation in the Americas to abolish slavery, ending the system in 1888. The Brazilian military began to turn against slavery after the valiant participation of slaves in Brazil's war with Paraguay in the late 1860s; eventually, educated Brazilians began to oppose the system too, arguing that it obstructed economic and social progress.

In the United States, the power of world opinion—and the example of Wilberforce's movement in England—became an important influence on the abolitionist movement as it gained strength in the 1820s and 1830s. American abolitionism, in turn, helped reinforce the movements abroad. Frederick Douglass, the former American slave turned abolitionist, became a major figure in the international antislavery movement and was a much-admired and much-sought-after speaker in England and Europe in the 1840s and 1850s. No other nation paid such a terrible price for abolishing slavery as did the United States during its Civil War, but American emancipation was nevertheless part of a worldwide movement toward emancipation. •

UNDERSTAND, ANALYZE, & EVALUATE

1. Why did opponents of slavery focus first on ending the slave trade, rather than abolishing slavery itself? Why was ending the slave trade easier than ending slavery?

2. How do William Wilberforce's arguments against slavery compare with those of the abolitionists in the United States?

EARLY OPPOSITION TO SLAVERY

In the early years of the nineteenth century, those who opposed slavery were, for the most part, a calm and genteel lot, expressing moral disapproval but doing little else. To the extent that there was an organized antislavery movement, it centered on the effort to resettle American blacks in Africa or the Caribbean. In 1817, a group of prominent white Virginians organized the American Colonization Society (ACS), which proposed a gradual freeing of slaves, with masters receiving compensation. The liberated black men and women would then be transported out of the country and helped establish a new society of their own. The ACS received some private funding, some funding from Congress, and some funding from the legislatures of Virginia and Maryland. And it successfully arranged to have several groups of blacks transported out of the United States to the west coast of Africa, where in 1830 they established the nation of **Liberia**. (In 1846, Liberia became an independent black republic, with its capital, Monrovia, named for the American president who had presided over the initial settlement.)

But the ACS was in the end a negligible force. There were far too many blacks in America in the nineteenth century to be transported to Africa by any conceivable program. The ACS met resistance, in any case, from blacks themselves, many of whom were now three or more generations removed from Africa and, despite their loathing of slavery, had no wish to emigrate. They viewed themselves as entitled to fair treatment as Americans.

GARRISON AND ABOLITIONISM

In 1830, with slavery spreading ideology rapidly in the South and the antislavery movement seemingly on the verge of collapse, a new figure emerged: **William Lloyd Garrison**. Born in Massachusetts in 1805, Garrison was in the 1820s an assistant to the New Jersey Quaker Benjamin Lundy, who published the leading antislavery newspaper of the time. Garrison grew impatient with his employer's moderate tone, so in 1831 he returned to Boston to found his own newspaper, *The Liberator*.

Garrison's philosophy was so simple that it was genuinely revolutionary. Opponents of slavery, he said, should not talk about the evil influence of slavery on white society but rather the damage the system did to slaves. And they should, therefore, reject "gradualism" and demand the immediate abolition of slavery and the extension of all the rights of American citizenship to both slaves and free African Americans. Garrison wrote in a relentless, uncompromising tone. "I am aware," he wrote in the very first issue of *The Liberator*, "that many object to the severity of my language; but is there not cause for severity? I will be as harsh as truth, and as uncompromising as justice. . . . I am in earnest—I will not equivocate—I will not excuse—I will not retreat a single inch—and I will be heard."

Garrison soon attracted a large group of followers throughout the North, enough to enable him to found the New England Antislavery Society in 1832 and, a year later, after a convention in Philadelphia, the American Antislavery Society.

BLACK ABOLITIONISTS

Abolitionism obviously had a particular appeal to the free black population of the North. These free blacks typically lived in conditions of poverty and oppression and faced a barrage of local customs and state laws that frequently reminded them of their lowly social positions. For all their problems, however, northern blacks were fiercely proud of their freedom and sensitive to the plight of those members of their race who remained in bondage. Many in the 1830s came to support Garrison. But they also rallied to leaders of their own.

Among the earliest black abolitionists was **David Walker**, who preceded even Garrison in publicly calling for an uncompromising opposition to slavery on moral grounds. In 1829, Walker, a free black man who had moved from North Carolina to Boston, published a harsh pamphlet—*An Appeal to the Coloured Citizens of the World*—that described slavery as a sin that would draw divine punishment if not abolished. "America is more our country than it is the whites'—we have enriched it with our blood and tears." He urged slaves to "kill [their masters] or be killed."

Most black critics of slavery were somewhat less violent in their rhetoric but equally uncompromising in their commitment to abolition. The greatest African American abolitionist of all—and one of the most electrifying orators of his time, black or white—was **Frederick Douglass**. Born a slave in Maryland, Douglass escaped to Massachusetts in 1838, became an outspoken leader of antislavery sentiment, and spent two years lecturing

(Source: Digital image courtesy of the Getty's Open Content Program)

FUGITIVE SLAVE LAW CONVENTION Abolitionists gathered in Cazenovia, New York, in August 1850 to consider how to respond to the law recently passed by Congress requiring northern states to return fugitive slaves to their owners. Frederick Douglass is seated just to the left of the table in this photograph of some of the participants. The gathering was unusual among abolitionist gatherings in including substantial numbers of African Americans.

in England. On his return to the United States in 1847, Douglass purchased his freedom from his Maryland owner and founded an antislavery newspaper, *The North Star,* in Rochester, New York. He achieved wide renown as well for his autobiography, *Narrative of the Life of Frederick Douglass* (1845), in which he presented a damning picture of slavery. Douglass demanded not only freedom but also full social and economic equality for blacks.

"What, to the American slave, is your 4th of July?," Douglass harshly asked in an Independence Day speech in Rochester, New York, in 1854. "I answer: a day that reveals to him, more than all other days in the year, the gross injustice and cruelty to which he is the constant victim. . . . There is not a nation on earth guilty of practices, more shocking and bloody, than are the people of these United States at this very hour."

Black abolitionists had been active for years before Douglass emerged as a leader of their cause. They held their first national convention in 1830. But with Douglass's leadership, they became a more influential force than any other African American. They began, too, to forge an alliance with white antislavery leaders such as Garrison.

ANTI-ABOLITIONISM

The rise of abolitionism provoked a powerful opposition. Almost all white southerners, of course, were bitterly hostile to the movement. But even in the North, abolitionists were a small, dissenting minority. Some whites feared that abolitionism would produce a destructive civil war. Others feared that it would lead to a great influx of free blacks into the North and displace white workers.

The result of such fears was an escalating wave of violence. A mob in Philadelphia attacked the abolitionist headquarters there in 1834, burned it to the ground, and began a bloody race riot. Another mob seized Garrison on the streets of Boston in 1835 and threatened to hang him. He was saved from death only by being locked in jail. Elijah Lovejoy, the editor of an abolitionist newspaper in Alton, Illinois, was victimized repeatedly and finally killed when he tried to defend his printing press from attack.

That so many men and women continued to embrace abolitionism in the face of such vicious opposition suggests that abolitionists were not people who took their political commitments lightly. They were strong-willed, passionate crusaders who displayed not only enormous courage and moral strength but, at times, a fervency that many of their contemporaries found deeply disturbing. The mobs were only the most violent expression of a hostility to abolitionism that many, perhaps most, other white Americans shared.

ABOLITIONISM DIVIDED

By the mid-1830s, the unity of the abolitionist crusade began to crack. One reason was the violence of the anti-abolitionists, which persuaded some members of the abolition movement that a more moderate approach was necessary. Another reason was the growing radicalism of William Lloyd Garrison, who shocked even many of his own allies (including Frederick Douglass) by attacking not only slavery but the government itself. The Constitution, he said, was "a covenant with death and an agreement with hell." In 1840, Garrison precipitated a formal division within the American Antislavery Society by insisting that women be permitted to participate in the movement on terms of full equality. He continued after 1840 to arouse controversy with new and even more radical stands: an extreme pacifism that rejected even defensive wars; opposition to all forms of coercion—not just slavery, but prisons and asylums; and finally, in 1843, a call for northern disunion from the South.

From 1840 on, therefore, abolitionism moved in many channels and spoke with many different voices. The radical and uncompromising Garrisonians remained influential. But so were others who operated in more moderate ways, arguing that abolition could be accomplished only as the result of a long, patient, peaceful struggle. They appealed to the conscience of the slaveholders; and when that produced no results, they turned to political action, seeking to induce the northern states and the federal government to aid the cause. They joined the Garrisonians in helping runaway slaves find refuge in the North or in Canada through the underground railroad.

The abolitionists also helped fund the legal battle over the Spanish slave vessel, *Amistad*. After the Supreme Court (in *Prigg v. Pennsylvania,* 1842) ruled that states need not aid in enforcing the 1793 law requiring the return of fugitive slaves to their owners, abolitionists won passage in several northern states of "personal liberty laws," which forbade state officials to assist in the capture and return of runaways. The antislavery societies also petitioned Congress to abolish slavery in places where the federal government had jurisdiction—in the territories and in the District of Columbia—and to prohibit the interstate slave trade.

Antislavery sentiment underlay the formation in 1840 of the Liberty Party, which ran Kentucky antislavery leader James G. Birney for president. But this party and its successors never campaigned for outright abolition. They stood instead for "Free Soil," for keeping slavery out of the territories. Some Free-Soilers were concerned about the welfare of blacks; others were people who cared nothing about slavery but simply wanted to keep the West a country for whites. But the Free-Soil position would ultimately do what abolitionism never could: attract the support of large numbers of the white population of the North.

The slow progress of abolitionism drove some critics of slavery to embrace more drastic measures. A few began to advocate violence. A group of prominent abolitionists in New England, for example, funneled money and arms to John Brown for his bloody uprisings in Kansas and Virginia. Others attempted to arouse public anger through propaganda.

The most powerful of all abolitionist propaganda was Harriet Beecher Stowe's novel *Uncle Tom's Cabin,* published as a book in 1852. It sold more than 300,000 copies within a year of publication and was reissued again and again. It succeeded in bringing the message of abolitionism to an enormous new audience—not only those who read the book but also those who watched countless theater companies reenact it across the nation. When Abraham Lincoln was introduced to Stowe once in the White House, he reportedly said to her: "So you are the little lady that has brought this great war." Reviled throughout the South, Stowe became a hero to many in the North. And in both regions, her novel helped inflame sectional tensions to a new level of passion.

Stowe's novel emerged not just out of abolitionist politics but also a popular tradition of sentimental novels written by, and largely for, women. (See "Patterns of Popular Culture: Sentimental Novels.") Stowe artfully integrated the emotional conventions of the sentimental novel with the political ideas of the abolitionist movement, and to sensational effect. Her novel, by embedding the antislavery message within a familiar literary form in which women were the key protagonists serving to improve society, brought that message to an enormous new audience.

SENTIMENTAL NOVELS

"America is now wholly given over to a damned mob of scribbling women," Nathaniel Hawthorne complained in 1855, "and I should have no chance of success while the public taste is occupied with their trash." Hawthorne, one of the leading novelists of his time, was complaining about the most popular form of fiction in mid-nineteenth-century America—not his own dark and brooding works, but the "sentimental novel," a genre of literature written and read mostly by middle-class women.

In an age when affluent women occupied primarily domestic roles, and in which finding a favorable marriage was the most important thing many women could do to secure or improve their lots in life, the sentimental novel gave voice to both female hopes and female anxieties. The plots of sentimental novels were usually filled with character-improving problems and domestic trials, but most of them ended with the heroine securely and happily married. They were phenomenally successful, many of them selling more than 100,000 copies each—far more than almost any other books of the time.

Sentimental heroines were almost always beautiful and endowed with specifically female qualities—"all the virtues," one novelist wrote, "that are founded in the sensibility of the heart: Pity, the attribute of angels, and friendship, the balm of life, delight to dwell in the female breast." Women were highly sensitive creatures, the sentimental writers believed, incapable of disguising their feelings, and subject to fainting, mysterious illnesses, trances, and, of course, tears—things rarely expected of men. But they were also capable of a kind of nurturing love and natural sincerity that was hard to find in the predominantly male public world. In Susan Warner's *The Wide, Wide World* (1850), for example, the heroine, a young girl named Ellen Montgomery, finds herself suddenly thrust into the "wide, wide world" of male competition after her father loses his fortune. She is unable to adapt to this world, but she is saved in the end when she is taken in by wealthy relatives, who will undoubtedly prepare her for a successful marriage. They restore to her the security and comfort to which she had been born and without which she seemed unable to thrive.

Sentimental novels accepted uncritically the popular assumptions about women's special needs and desires, and they offered stirring tales of how women satisfied them. But sentimental novels were not limited to romanticized images of female fulfillment through protection and marriage. They hinted as well at the increasing role of women in reform movements. Many such books portrayed women dealing with social and moral problems—and using their highly developed female sensibilities to help other women escape from their troubles. Women were particularly suitable for such reform work, the writers implied, because they were specially gifted at helping and nurturing others.

The most famous sentimental novelist of the nineteenth century was Harriet Beecher Stowe. Most of her books—*The Minister's Wooing, My Wife and I, We and Our Neighbors,* and others—portrayed the travails and ultimate triumphs of women as they became wives, mothers, and hostesses. But Stowe

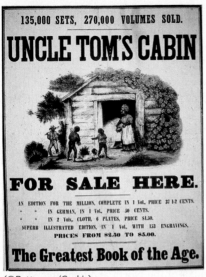

135,000 SETS, 270,000 VOLUMES SOLD.

UNCLE TOM'S CABIN

FOR SALE HERE.

AN EDITION FOR THE MILLION, COMPLETE IN 1 Vol, PRICE 37 1-2 CENTS.
" " IN GERMAN, IN 1 Vol. PRICE 50 CENTS.
" " IN 2 Vols, CLOTH, 6 PLATES, PRICE $1.50.
SUPERB ILLUSTRATED EDITION, IN 1 Vol, WITH 153 ENGRAVINGS,
PRICES FROM $2.50 TO $5.00.

The Greatest Book of the Age.

(©Bettmann/Corbis)

UNCLE TOM'S CABIN *Uncle Tom's Cabin* did much to inflame public opinion in both the North and the South in the last years before the Civil War. At the time, however, Stowe was equally well known as one of the most successful American writers of sentimental novels.

sentimental novels encounter in their struggles to find security and tranquillity in their lives.

Another way in which women were emerging from their domestic sphere was in becoming consumers of the expanding products of America's industrializing economy. The female characters in sentimental novels searched not just for love, security, and social justice; they also searched for luxury and for the pleasure of buying some favored item. Susan Warner illustrated this aspect of the culture of the sentimental novel—and the desires of the women who read them—in *The Wide, Wide World*, in her description of the young Ellen Montgomery in an elegant bookstore, buying a Bible: "Such beautiful Bibles she had never seen; she pored in ecstasy over their varieties of type and binding, and was very evidently in love with them all." •

was and remains best known for her 1852 antislavery novel, *Uncle Tom's Cabin,* one of the most influential books ever published in America. As a story about slavery, and about an aging black man—Uncle Tom— who is unfailingly submissive to his white masters, it is in many ways very different from her other novels. But *Uncle Tom's Cabin* is a sentimental novel, too. Stowe's critique of slavery is based partly on her belief in the importance of domestic values and family security. Slavery's violation of those values, and its denial of that security, is what made it so abhorrent to her. The simple, decent Uncle Tom faces many of the same dilemmas that the female heroines of other

UNDERSTAND, ANALYZE, & EVALUATE

1. How did the lives of the heroines of the sentimental novels compare with the lives of real women of the nineteenth century? What made them so popular?

2. How did the sentimental novels encourage women's participation in public life? Did the novels reinforce prevailing attitudes toward women or broaden the perception of women's "proper role"?

3. *Uncle Tom's Cabin* is probably one of the best-known works of American fiction. Why was this novel so much more powerful than other sentimental novels? Why has it endured?

Even divided, abolitionism remained a powerful influence on the life of the nation. Only a relatively small number of people before the Civil War ever accepted the abolitionist position that slavery must be entirely eliminated in a single stroke. But the crusade that Garrison had launched, and that thousands of committed men and women kept alive for three decades, was a constant, visible reminder of how deeply the institution of slavery was dividing America.

CONCLUSION

The rapidly changing society of antebellum America encouraged interest in a wide range of reforms. Writers, artists, intellectuals, and others drew heavily from new European notions of personal liberation and fulfillment—a set of ideas often known as romanticism. But they also strove to create a truly American culture. The literary and artistic life of the nation expressed the rising interest in personal liberation—in giving individuals the freedom to explore their own souls and to find in nature a full expression of their divinity. It also called attention to some of the nation's glaring social problems.

Reformers, too, made use of the romantic belief in the divinity of the individual. They flocked to religious revivals, worked on behalf of such "moral" reforms as temperance, supported education, and articulated some of the first statements of modern feminism. And in the North, they rallied against slavery. Out of this growing antislavery movement emerged a new and powerful phenomenon: abolitionism, which insisted on immediate emancipation of slaves. The abolitionist movement galvanized much of the North and contributed greatly to the growing schism between North and South.

KEY TERMS/PEOPLE/PLACES/EVENTS

David Walker 291
Dorothea Dix 284
Elizabeth Cady Stanton 284
Frederick Douglass 291
Harriet Beecher
 Stowe 284
Henry David Thoreau 276
Herman Melville 275
Horace Mann 283

Hudson River school 274
Jarena Lee 285
Joseph Smith 279
Liberia 290
Lucretia Mott 284
Nathaniel Hawthorne 278
Oneida "Perfectionists" 278
Ralph Waldo Emerson 276
Rebecca Cox Jackson 285

Seneca Falls
 Convention 284
Shakers 279
Sojourner Truth 285
Susan B. Anthony 284
temperance 281
transcendentalism 276
Walt Whitman 275
William Lloyd Garrison 290

RECALL AND REFLECT

1. What is "romanticism" and how was it expressed in American literature and art?
2. How did religion affect reform movements, and what was the effect of these movements on religion?
3. What were the aims of the women's movement of the nineteenth century? How successful were women in achieving these goals?
4. What arguments and strategies did the abolitionists use in their struggle to end slavery? Who opposed them and why?

13 | THE IMPENDING CRISIS

LOOKING WESTWARD
EXPANSION AND WAR
THE SECTIONAL DEBATE
THE CRISES OF THE 1850s

LOOKING AHEAD

1. How did the annexation of western territories intensify the conflict over slavery and lead to deeper divisions between the North and the South?
2. What compromises attempted to resolve the conflicts over the expansion of slavery into new territories? To what degree were these compromises successful? Why did they eventually fail to resolve the differences between the North and the South?
3. What were the major arguments for and against slavery and its expansion into new territories?

UNTIL THE 1840s, POLITICAL TENSIONS between the North and the South remained relatively contained and, other than African American writers and clerics, few predicted that sectional tensions could ever lead the country into a civil war.

But midcentury brought a rash of explosive issues that politicians struggled—and ultimately failed—to resolve peacefully. In the North the abolitionist movement picked up steam and inspired legions of supporters, the most aggressive of whom sought to fight slavery with the sword as well as the pen. The South birthed a generation of militant pro-slavery spokesmen who brooked no compromise over a state's right to embrace slavery and the society based on it. From the West emerged raging controversies over the political fate of the territories and whether they would enter the Union as either slave or free states. Partisans recruited sympathizers from across the nation and even took up arms to win their point.

TIME LINE

1836
Texas declares independence from Mexico

1844
Polk elected president

1846
Oregon boundary dispute settled

U.S. declares war on Mexico

Wilmot Proviso

1848
Treaty of Guadalupe Hidalgo

Taylor elected president

California gold rush begins

1850
Compromise of 1850

Taylor dies; Fillmore becomes president

1852
Pierce elected president

1853
Gadsden Purchase

1854
Kansas-Nebraska Act

Republican Party formed

1855–1856
"Bleeding Kansas"

1856
Buchanan elected president

1857
Dred Scott decision

1858
Lecompton constitution defeated

1859
John Brown raids Harpers Ferry

1860
Lincoln elected president

LOOKING WESTWARD

More than a million square miles of new territory came under the control of the United States during the 1840s. By the end of the decade, the nation possessed all the territory of the present-day United States except Alaska, Hawaii, and a few relatively small areas acquired later through border adjustments. Many factors accounted for this great new wave of expansion, but one of the most important was an ideology known as **Manifest Destiny**.

MANIFEST DESTINY

Manifest Destiny reflected both the growing pride that characterized American nationalism in the mid-nineteenth century and the idealistic vision of social perfection that fueled so much of the reform energy of the time. It rested on the idea that America was destined—by God and by history—to expand its boundaries over a vast area.

By the 1840s, publicized by the rise of inexpensive newspapers dubbed "penny press," the idea of Manifest Destiny had spread throughout the nation. Some advocates of Manifest Destiny envisioned a vast new "empire of liberty" that would include Canada, Mexico, Caribbean and Pacific islands, and ultimately (for the most ardent believers) much of the rest of the world. Countering such bombast were politicians such as Henry Clay and others, who warned that territorial expansion would reopen the painful controversy over slavery. Their voices, however, could not compete with the enthusiasm over expansion in the 1840s, which began with the issues of Texas and Oregon.

AMERICANS IN TEXAS

Twice in the 1820s, the United States had offered to purchase Texas from the Republic of Mexico, and twice Mexico refused. But Mexican officials were desperate to populate this frontier region because they believed it to be threatened by nomadic indigenous groups like the Comanche Indians and possibly Spain. As a result, they enacted what would be viewed in hindsight as a curious policy—namely, a colonization law that offered cheap land and a four-year exemption from taxes to any American willing to move into Texas. Thousands of Americans flocked into the region, the great majority of them white southerners and their slaves, intent on establishing cotton plantations. By 1830, there were about 7,000 Americans living in Texas, more than twice the number of Mexicans there.

Most of the settlers came to Texas through the efforts of American intermediaries, who received sizable land grants from Mexico in return for bringing new residents into the region. The most successful was **Stephen F. Austin**, a young immigrant from Missouri who established the first legal American settlement in Texas in 1822. Austin and others created centers of power in the region that competed with the Mexican government. Not surprisingly, in 1830 the Mexican government barred any further American immigration into the region. But Americans kept flowing into Texas anyway.

Friction between the American settlers and the Mexican government was already growing in the mid-1830s when instability in Mexico itself drove General **Antonio López de Santa Anna** to seize power as a dictator. He increased the powers of the Mexican government at the expense of the state governments, a measure that Texans from the United States assumed was aimed specifically at them. Sporadic fighting between Americans and Mexicans in Texas erupted in 1835. The next year, the American settlers defiantly proclaimed their independence from Mexico.

Santa Anna led a large army into Texas, where the American settlers were divided into several squabbling factions. Mexican forces annihilated an American garrison at the **Alamo** mission in San Antonio after a famous, if futile, defense by a group of Texas "patriots" that included, among others, the renowned frontiersman and former Tennessee congressman Davy Crockett. Another garrison at Goliad suffered substantially the same fate. By the end of 1836, the rebellion appeared to have collapsed.

But General **Sam Houston** managed to keep a small force together. And on April 21, 1836, at the Battle of San Jacinto, he defeated the Mexican army and took Santa Anna prisoner. Santa Anna, under pressure from his captors, signed a treaty giving Texas independence.

(©Kathie Rees/EyeEm/Getty Images)

THE LONE STAR FLAG Texas was an independent republic for nine years. The tattered banner pictured here was one of the republic's original flags.

A number of Mexican residents of Texas (*Tejanos*) had fought with the Americans in the revolution. But soon after Texas won its independence, their positions grew difficult. The Americans did not trust them, feared that they were agents of the Mexican government, and in effect drove many of them out of the new republic. Most of those who stayed had to settle for a politically and economically subordinate status.

One of the first acts of the new president of Texas, Sam Houston, was to send a delegation to Washington with an offer to join the Union. But President Jackson, fearing that adding a large new slave state to the Union would increase sectional tensions, blocked annexation and even delayed recognizing the new republic until 1837.

Spurned by the United States, Texas cast out on its own. England and France, concerned about the surging power of the United States, saw Texas as a possible check on its growth and began forging ties with the new republic. At that point, President Tyler persuaded Texas to apply for statehood again in 1844. But northern senators, fearing the admission of a new slave state, defeated it. Statehood would have to wait until after the election of President Polk.

OREGON

Control of what was known as "Oregon country," in the Pacific Northwest, was also a major political issue in the 1840s. Both Britain and the United States claimed sovereignty in the region. Unable to resolve their conflicting claims diplomatically, they agreed in an 1818 treaty to allow citizens of each country equal access to the territory. This "joint occupation" continued for twenty years.

At the time of the treaty neither Britain nor the United States had established much of a presence in Oregon country. White settlement in the region consisted largely of scattered American and Canadian fur trading posts. But American interest in Oregon grew substantially in the 1820s and 1830s.

By the mid-1840s, white Americans substantially outnumbered the British in Oregon. They had also devastated much of the Indian population, in part through a measles epidemic that spread through the Cayuse Indians. American settlements were sprouting up along the Pacific Coast, and the new settlers were urging the U.S. government to take possession of the disputed Oregon country.

THE WESTWARD MIGRATION

The migrations into Texas and Oregon were part of a larger movement that took hundreds of thousands of white and black Americans into the far western regions of the continent between 1840 and 1860. The largest number of migrants were from the Old Northwest. Most were relatively young people who had traveled in family groups. Few were wealthy, but many were relatively prosperous. Poor people who could not afford the trip on their own usually had to join other families or groups as laborers—men as farm or ranch hands; women as domestic servants, teachers, or, in some cases, prostitutes. Groups heading for areas where mining or lumbering was the principal economic activity consisted mostly of men. Those heading for farming regions traveled mainly as families.

Migrants generally gathered in one of several major depots in Iowa and Missouri (Independence, St. Joseph, or Council Bluffs), joined a wagon train led by hired guides, and set off with their belongings piled in covered wagons, livestock trailing behind. The major route west was the 2,000-mile **Oregon Trail**, which stretched from Independence across the Great Plains and through the South Pass of the Rocky Mountains. From there, migrants moved

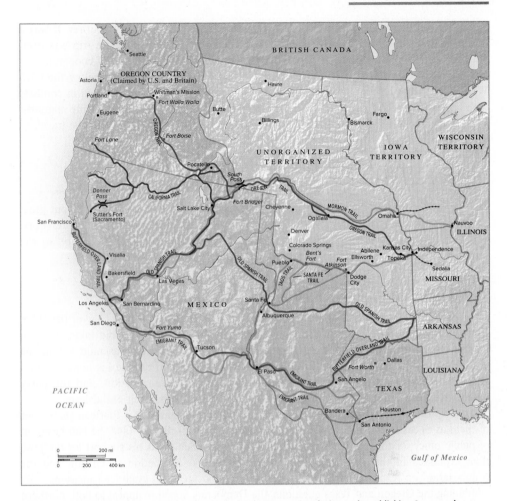

WESTERN TRAILS IN 1860 As settlers began the long process of exploring and establishing farms and businesses in the West, major trails began to develop to facilitate travel and trade between the region and the more thickly settled areas to the east. Note how many of the trails led to California and how few of them led into any of the far northern regions of U.S. territory. Note, too, the important towns and cities that grew up along these trails. • *What forms of transportation later performed the functions that these trails performed prior to the Civil War?*

north into Oregon or south (along the California Trail) to the northern California coast. Other migrations moved along the Santa Fe Trail, southwest from Independence into New Mexico.

However they traveled, overland migrants faced an arduous journey. Most lasted five or six months (from May to November), and travelers always felt the pressure to get through the Rockies before the snows began, often not an easy task given the very slow pace of most wagon trains. To save their horses for pulling the wagons, they walked most of the way. Diseases, including cholera, decimated and slowed many groups traveling west. The women, who did the cooking and washing at the end of the day, generally worked harder than the men, who usually rested when the caravan halted.

Despite the traditional image of westward migrants as rugged individualists, most travelers found the journey to be a communal experience. That was partly because many expeditions consisted of groups of friends, neighbors, or relatives who had decided to pull up stakes and move west together. And it was also because of the intensity of the journey. It was a rare expedition in which there were not some internal conflicts before the trip was over; but those who made the journey successfully generally learned the value of cooperation.

Only a few expeditions experienced Indian attacks. In the twenty years before the Civil War, fewer than 400 migrants (slightly more than one-tenth of 1 percent) died in conflicts with tribes. In fact, Indians were usually more helpful than dangerous to the white migrants. They often served as guides and traded horses, clothing, and fresh food with the travelers.

EXPANSION AND WAR

The growing number of white Americans in the lands west of the Mississippi put great pressure on the government in Washington to annex Texas, Oregon, and other territory. And in the 1840s, these expansionist pressures helped push the slavery question to the forefront of political debate and move the United States ever closer to war.

THE DEMOCRATS AND EXPANSION

In preparing for the election of 1844, the two leading candidates—Henry Clay of the Whig Party and Martin Van Buren of the Democratic Party—both tried to avoid taking a stand on the controversial annexation of Texas. Sentiment for expansion was mild within the Whig Party, and Clay had no difficulty securing the nomination despite his noncommittal position. But many southern Democrats strongly supported annexation, and the party passed over Van Buren to nominate **James K. Polk**, who shared their enthusiasm.

Polk had represented Tennessee in the House of Representatives for fourteen years, four of them as Speaker, and had subsequently served as governor. But by 1844, he had been out of public office for three years. What made his victory possible was his support for the position, expressed in the Democratic platform, "that the re-occupation of Oregon and the re-annexation of Texas at the earliest practicable period are great American measures." By combining the Oregon and Texas questions, the Democrats hoped to appeal to both northern and southern expansionists—and they did. Polk carried the election, 170 electoral votes to 105.

Polk entered office with a clear set of goals and with plans for attaining them. John Tyler accomplished the first of Polk's ambitions for him in the last days of his own presidency. Interpreting the election returns as a mandate for the annexation of Texas, the outgoing president won congressional approval for it in February 1845. That December, Texas became a state.

Polk himself resolved the Oregon question. The British minister in Washington brusquely rejected a compromise that would establish the U.S.–Canadian border at the 49th parallel. Incensed, Polk again asserted the American claim to all of Oregon. There was loose talk of war on both sides of the Atlantic—talk that in the United States often took the form of the bellicose slogan "Fifty-four forty or fight!" (a reference to where the Americans hoped to draw the northern boundary of their part of Oregon). But neither country really wanted war. Finally, the British government accepted Polk's original proposal to divide the territory at the 49th parallel. On June 15, 1846, the Senate approved a treaty that fixed the boundary there.

THE SOUTHWEST AND CALIFORNIA

One of the reasons the Senate and the president had agreed so readily to the British offer to settle the Oregon question was that their attention was turning to new tensions emerging

THE OREGON BOUNDARY, 1846 One of the last major boundary disputes between the United States and Great Britain involved the territory known as Oregon—the large region on the Pacific Coast north of California (which in 1846 was still part of Mexico). For years, America and Britain had overlapping claims on the territory. The British claimed land as far south as the present state of Oregon, while the Americans claimed land extending well into what is now Canada. Tensions over the Oregon border at times rose to the point that many Americans were demanding war, some using the slogan "Fifty-four forty or fight!" referring to the latitude of the northernmost point of the American claim. • *How did President James K. Polk defuse the crisis?*

in the Southwest. As soon as the United States admitted Texas to statehood in 1845, the Mexican government broke off diplomatic relations with Washington. Mexican–American relations grew still worse when a dispute developed over the boundary between Texas and Mexico. Texans claimed the Rio Grande as their western and southern border. Mexico, although still not conceding the loss of Texas, argued nevertheless that the border had always been the Nueces River, to the north of the Rio Grande. Polk accepted the Texas claim, and in the summer of 1845 he sent a small army under General Zachary Taylor to Texas to protect the new state against a possible Mexican invasion.

Part of the area in dispute was New Mexico, whose Spanish and Indian residents lived in a multiracial society that by the 1840s had endured for nearly a century and a half. In the 1820s, the Mexican government had invited American traders into the region, hoping to speed development of the province. But New Mexico, like Texas, soon became more

American than Mexican, particularly after a flourishing commerce developed between Santa Fe and Independence, Missouri.

Americans were also increasing their interest in California. In this vast region lived members of several western Indian tribes and perhaps 7,000 Mexicans. Gradually, however, white Americans began to arrive: first maritime traders and captains of Pacific whaling ships, who stopped to barter goods or buy supplies; then merchants, who established stores, imported goods, and developed a profitable trade with the Mexicans and Indians; and finally pioneering farmers, who entered California from the east and settled in the Sacramento Valley. Some of these new settlers began to dream of bringing California into the United States.

President Polk soon came to share their dream and committed himself to acquiring both New Mexico and California for the United States. At the same time that he dispatched the troops under Taylor to Texas, he sent secret instructions to the commander of the Pacific naval squadron to seize the California ports if Mexico declared war. Representatives of the president quietly informed Americans in California that the United States would respond sympathetically to a revolt against Mexican authority there.

THE MEXICAN WAR

Having appeared to prepare for war, Polk turned to diplomacy by dispatching a special minister to try to buy off the Mexicans. But Mexican leaders rejected the American offer to purchase the disputed territories. On January 13, 1846, as soon as he heard the news, Polk ordered Taylor's army in Texas to move across the Nueces River, where it had been stationed, to the Rio Grande. For months, the Mexicans refused to fight. But finally, according to disputed American accounts, some Mexican troops crossed the Rio Grande and attacked a unit of American soldiers. On May 13, 1846, Congress declared war by votes of 40 to 2 in the Senate and 174 to 14 in the House.

Whig critics charged that Polk had deliberately maneuvered the country into the conflict and had staged the border incident that had precipitated the declaration. Many opponents also claimed that Polk had settled for less than he should have because he was preoccupied with Mexico. Opposition intensified as the war continued and as the public became aware of the rising casualties and expense.

Victory did not come as quickly as Polk had hoped. The president ordered Taylor to cross the Rio Grande, seize parts of northeastern Mexico, beginning with the city of Monterrey, and then march on to Mexico City itself. Taylor captured Monterrey in September 1846, but he let the Mexican garrison evacuate without pursuit. Polk now began to fear that Taylor lacked the tactical skill for the planned advance against Mexico City. He also feared that, if successful, Taylor would become a powerful political rival (as, in fact, he did).

In the meantime, Polk ordered other offensives against New Mexico and California. In the summer of 1846, a small army under Colonel Stephen W. Kearny captured Santa Fe with no opposition. He then proceeded to California, where he joined a conflict already in progress that was being staged jointly by American settlers, a well-armed exploring party led by John C. Frémont, and the American navy: the so-called Bear Flag Revolt. Kearny brought the disparate American forces together under his command, and by the autumn of 1846 he had completed the conquest of California.

But Mexico still refused to concede defeat. At this point, Polk and General Winfield Scott, the commanding general of the army and its finest soldier, launched a bold new campaign. Scott assembled an army at Tampico, which the navy transported down the Mexican coast to Veracruz. With an army that never numbered more than 14,000, Scott

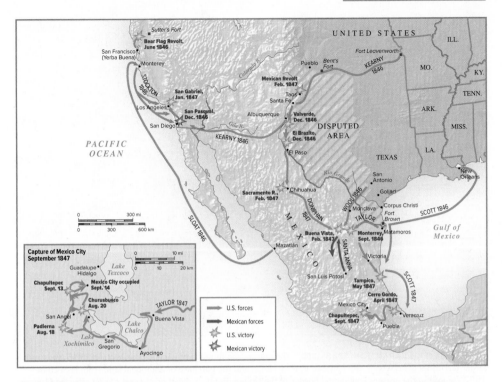

THE MEXICAN WAR, 1846-1848 Shortly after the settlement of the Oregon border dispute with Britain, the United States entered a war with Mexico over another contested border. This map shows the movement of Mexican and American troops during the fighting, which extended from the area around Santa Fe south to Mexico City and west to the coast of California. Note the American use of its naval forces to facilitate a successful assault on Mexico City, and others on the coast of California. Note, too, how unsuccessful the Mexican forces were in their battles with the United States. Mexico won only one battle—a relatively minor one at San Pasqual near San Diego—in the war. • *How did President Polk deal with the popular clamor for the United States to annex much of present-day Mexico?*

advanced 260 miles along the Mexican National Highway toward Mexico City, kept American casualties low, and never lost a battle before finally seizing the Mexican capital. A new Mexican government took power and announced its willingness to negotiate a peace treaty.

President Polk continued to encourage those who demanded that the United States annex much of Mexico itself. At the same time, he was growing anxious to get the war finished quickly. Polk sent a special presidential envoy, Nicholas Trist, to negotiate a settlement. On February 2, 1848, he reached agreement with the new Mexican government on the **Treaty of Guadalupe Hidalgo**, by which Mexico agreed to cede California and New Mexico to the United States and acknowledge the Rio Grande as the boundary of Texas. In return, the United States promised to assume any financial claims its new citizens had against Mexico and to pay the Mexicans $15 million. Trist had obtained most of Polk's original demands, but he had not satisfied the new, more expansive dreams of acquiring additional territory in Mexico itself. Polk angrily claimed that Trist had violated his instructions, but he soon realized that he had no choice but to accept the treaty to silence a bitter battle growing between ardent expansionists demanding the annexation of "All Mexico!" and antislavery leaders charging that the expansionists were conspiring to extend slavery to new realms. The president submitted the Trist treaty to the Senate, which approved it by a vote of 38 to 14.

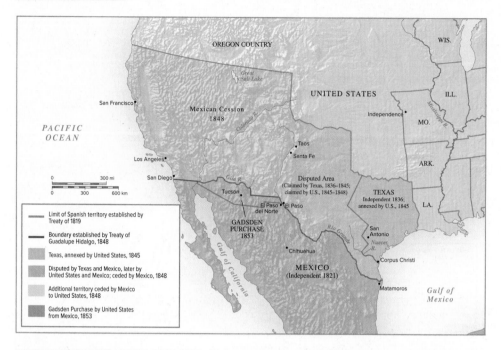

SOUTHWESTERN EXPANSION, 1845–1853 The annexation of much of what is now Texas in 1845, the much larger territorial gains won in the Mexican War in 1848, and the purchase of additional land from Mexico in 1853 completed the present continental border of the United States. • *What great event shortly after the Mexican War contributed to a rapid settlement of California by migrants from the eastern United States?*

THE SECTIONAL DEBATE

James Polk tried to be a president whose policies transcended sectional divisions. But conciliating the sections was becoming an ever more difficult task, and Polk gradually earned the enmity of northerners and westerners alike, who believed his policies favored the South at their expense.

SLAVERY AND THE TERRITORIES

In August 1846, while the Mexican War had been still in progress, Polk had asked Congress to appropriate $2 million for purchasing peace with Mexico. Immediately arising was the question of whether slavery would be allowed in any newly acquired territory. Representative David Wilmot of Pennsylvania, an antislavery Democrat, introduced an amendment to the appropriation bill prohibiting slavery in any territory acquired from Mexico. The so-called **Wilmot Proviso** passed the House but failed in the Senate. (See "Consider the Source: Wilmot Proviso.") Southern militants contended that all Americans had equal rights in the new territories, including the right to move their slaves (which they considered property) into them.

As the sectional debate intensified, President Polk supported a proposal to extend the Missouri Compromise line through the new territories to the Pacific Coast, banning slavery north of the line and permitting it south of the line. Others supported a plan, originally known as "squatter sovereignty" and later by the more dignified phrase "**popular sovereignty**," that would allow the people of each territory to decide the status of slavery there. The debate over these various proposals dragged on for many months.

The presidential campaign of 1848 dampened the controversy for a time as both Democrats and Whigs tried to avoid the slavery question. When Polk, in poor health, declined to run again, the Democrats nominated Lewis Cass of Michigan, a dull, aging party regular. The Whigs nominated General **Zachary Taylor** of Louisiana, hero of the Mexican War but a man with no political experience. Opponents of slavery found the choice of candidates unsatisfying, and out of their discontent emerged the new **Free-Soil Party**, whose candidate was former president Martin Van Buren.

Taylor won a narrow victory. But while Van Buren failed to carry a single state, he polled an impressive 291,000 votes (10 percent of the total), and the Free-Soilers elected ten members to Congress. The emergence of the Free-Soil Party as an important political force signaled the inability of the existing parties to contain the political passions slavery was creating. It was also an early sign of the coming collapse of the second party system in the 1850s.

THE CALIFORNIA GOLD RUSH

By the time Taylor took office, the pressure to resolve the question of slavery in the far western territories had become more urgent as a result of dramatic events in California. In January 1848, a foreman working in a sawmill owned by John Sutter (one of California's leading ranchers) found traces of gold in the foothills of the Sierra Nevada. Within months, news of the discovery had spread throughout the nation and much of the world. Almost immediately, hundreds of thousands of people began flocking to California in a frantic search for gold.

The atmosphere in California at the peak of the gold rush was one of almost crazed excitement and greed. Most migrants to the Far West prepared carefully before making the journey. But the California migrants (known as "**Forty-niners**") threw caution to the winds, abandoning farms, jobs, homes, and families, piling onto ships and flooding the overland trails. The overwhelming majority of the Forty-niners (perhaps 95 percent) were white men, and the society they created in California was unusually fluid and volatile because of the almost total absence of white women, children, or families.

The gold rush also attracted some of the first Chinese migrants to the western United States. News of the discoveries created great excitement in China, particularly in impoverished areas. It was, of course, extremely difficult for a poor Chinese peasant to get to America; but many young, adventurous people (mostly men) decided to go anyway—in the belief that they could quickly become rich and then return to China. Emigration brokers loaned many migrants money for passage to California, which the migrants were to pay off out of their earnings there.

The gold rush produced a serious labor shortage in California, as many male workers left their jobs and flocked to the gold fields. That created opportunities for many people who needed work (including Chinese immigrants). It also led to a frenzied exploitation of Indians that resembled slavery in all but name. A new state law permitted the arrest of "loitering" or orphaned Indians and their assignment to a term of "indentured" labor.

The gold rush was of critical importance to the growth of California, but not for the reasons most of the migrants hoped. There was substantial gold in the hills of the Sierra Nevada, and many people got rich from it. But only a tiny fraction of the Forty-niners ever found gold. Some disappointed migrants returned home after a while; however, many stayed in California and swelled both the agricultural and urban populations of the territory. By 1856, for example, San Francisco—whose population had been 1,000 before the gold rush—was the home of over 50,000 people. By the early 1850s, California, which had always had

WILMOT PROVISO (1846)

To counter rising tensions over the question of whether territory acquired from Mexico would be slave or free, Representative David Wilmot of Pennsylvania spearheaded an effort to ban slavery from that territory forever. His amendment passed the House twice but failed in the Senate, because of heated opposition from northern pro-slavery politicians.

Provided, that, as an express and fundamental condition to the acquisition of any territory from the Republic of Mexico by the United States, by virtue of any treaty which may be negotiated between them, and to the use by the Executive of the moneys herein appropriated, neither slavery nor involuntary servitude shall ever exist in any part of said territory, except for crime, whereof the party shall first be duly convicted.

UNDERSTAND, ANALYZE, & EVALUATE

1. What condition did the proviso impose on future territory?
2. Why did this simple provision prove so controversial? What were its consequences?
3. Do you recognize the last two lines of the provision? Where do they later reappear?

(Source: Library of Congress, Prints and Photographs Division [LC-DIG-ppmsca-32195])

LOOKING FOR GOLD In this 1850s lithograph, the unnamed artist presents the West as a world of abundance and great wealth available to all with just a little bit of pluck and luck. Gold is there for the taking, and happiness befalls all who pan for riches. Absent is any sense of failure, hard work, and suffering.

a diverse population, had become even more heterogeneous. The gold rush had attracted not just white Americans but also Europeans, Chinese, South Americans, Mexicans, free blacks, and slaves who accompanied southern migrants. Conflicts over gold intersected with racial and ethnic tensions to make the territory an unusually turbulent place.

Rising Sectional Tensions

Zachary Taylor believed statehood could become the solution to the issue of slavery in the territories. As long as the new lands remained territories, the federal government was responsible for deciding the fate of slavery within them. But once they became states, he thought, their own governments would be able to settle the slavery question. At Taylor's urging, California quickly adopted a constitution that prohibited slavery, and in December 1849 Taylor asked Congress to admit California as a free state.

Congress balked, in part because of several other controversies concerning slavery that were complicating the debate. One was the effort of antislavery forces to abolish slavery in the District of Columbia. Another was the emergence of personal liberty laws in northern states, which barred courts and police officers from returning runaway slaves to their owners in defiance of the Constitution's Fugitive Slave Clause. But the biggest obstacle to the president's program was the white South's fear that new free states would be added to the northern majority. The number of free and slave states was equal in 1849—fifteen each. The admission of California would upset the balance; and New Mexico, Oregon, and Utah—all candidates for statehood—might upset it further.

(Source: Library of Congress, Prints and Photographs Division [LC-USZ62-11138])

STIRRING THE POT OF SECTIONAL TENSIONS   James Baillie's 1850 lithograph, *The Hurly-Burly Pot*, warns of sharpening antagonisms between the North and the South and the rising threat of disunion. He targets the most vocal partisans: from the North, abolitionist William Lloyd Garrison, Free-Soil promoter David Wilmot, and journalist Horace Greeley; and from the South, states' rights promoter Senator John C. Calhoun. Like the witches in Shakespeare's *Macbeth*, the first three dance around a bubbling cauldron, adding to it sacks branded "Free Soil," "Abolition," and "Fourierism" (tossed in by Greeley, a supporter of utopian socialist Charles Fourier). Behind them looms John Calhoun, who crows about this act of treason: "For success to the whole mixture, we invoke our great patron Saint Benedict Arnold."

Even many otherwise moderate southern leaders now began to talk about secession from the Union. In the North, every state legislature but one adopted a resolution demanding the prohibition of slavery in the territories.

THE COMPROMISE OF 1850

Faced with this mounting crisis, moderates and unionists spent the winter of 1849–1850 trying to frame a great compromise. The aging Henry Clay, who was spearheading the effort, believed that no compromise could last unless it settled all the issues in dispute. As a result, he took several measures that had been proposed separately, combined them into a single piece of legislation, and presented it to the Senate on January 29, 1850. Among the bill's provisions were the admission of California as a free state; the formation of territorial governments in the rest of the lands acquired from Mexico, without restrictions on slavery; the abolition of the slave trade, but not slavery itself, in the District of Columbia; and a new and more effective fugitive slave law. These resolutions launched a debate that raged for seven months.

Finally in midyear, the climate for compromise improved. President Taylor suddenly died, and Vice President Millard Fillmore of New York took his place. Fillmore, who understood the important of flexibility, supported the compromise and persuaded northern Whigs to do so as well. Where the Old Guard's omnibus bill had failed, **Stephen A. Douglas**, a Democratic senator from Illinois, proposed breaking up the bill. Thus representatives of different sections could support those elements of the compromise they liked and oppose those they did not. Douglas also gained support with complicated backroom deals linking

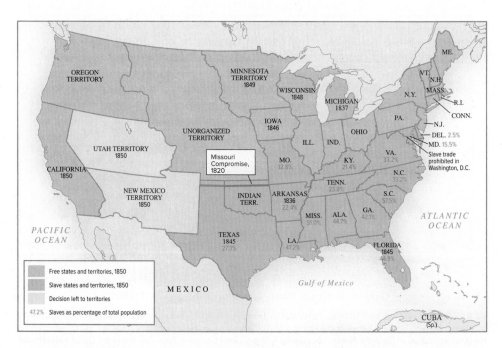

SLAVE AND FREE TERRITORIES UNDER THE COMPROMISE OF 1850   The acquisition of vast new western lands raised the question of the status of slavery in new territories organized for statehood by the United States. Tension between the North and the South on this question led in 1850 to a great compromise, forged in Congress, to settle this dispute. The compromise allowed California to join the Union as a free state and introduced the concept of "popular sovereignty" for other new territories. • *How well did the Compromise of 1850 work?*

the compromise to such nonideological matters as the sale of government bonds and the construction of railroads. As a result of his efforts, by mid-September Congress had enacted all the components of the compromise.

The **Compromise of 1850** was a victory of individual self-interest. Still, members of Congress hailed the measure as a triumph of statesmanship; and Millard Fillmore, signing it, called it a just settlement of the sectional problem, "in its character final and irrevocable."

THE CRISES OF THE 1850s

For a few years after its passage, the Compromise of 1850 seemed to work. Sectional conflict appeared to fade amid booming prosperity and growth. But the tensions between the North and the South never really disappeared.

THE UNEASY TRUCE

With the run-up to the presidential election of 1852, both major parties endorsed the Compromise of 1850 and nominated candidates unidentified with sectional passions. The Democrats chose the obscure New Hampshire politician Franklin Pierce, and the Whigs chose the military hero General Winfield Scott. But the sectional question quickly became a divisive influence in the election and the Whigs were the principal victims. They suffered massive defections from antislavery members who were angered by the party's evasiveness on the issue. Many of them flocked to the Free-Soil Party, whose antislavery presidential candidate, John P. Hale, repudiated the Compromise of 1850. The divisions among the Whigs helped produce a victory for the Democrats in 1852.

Franklin Pierce attempted to maintain harmony by avoiding divisive issues, particularly slavery. But it was an impossible task. Northern opposition to the Fugitive Slave Act intensified quickly after 1850. Mobs formed in some northern cities to prevent enforcement of the fugitive slave law, and several northern states also passed their own laws barring the deportation of fugitive slaves. White southerners watched with growing anger and alarm as the one element of the Compromise of 1850 that they had considered a victory seemed to become meaningless in the face of northern defiance.

"YOUNG AMERICA"

One of the ways Franklin Pierce hoped to dampen sectional controversy was through his support of a movement in the Democratic Party known as **"Young America."** Its adherents saw the expansion of American democracy throughout the world as a way to divert attention from the controversies over slavery. The great liberal and nationalist revolutions of 1848 in Europe stirred them to dream of a republican Europe with governments based on the model of the United States. They dreamed as well of acquiring new territories in the Western Hemisphere.

But efforts to extend the nation's domain could not avoid becoming entangled with the sectional crisis. Pierce had been pursuing diplomatic attempts to buy Cuba from Spain (efforts begun in 1848 by Polk). In 1854, however, a group of Pierce's envoys sent him a private document from Ostend, Belgium, making a case for seizing Cuba by force. When the Ostend Manifesto, as it became known, was leaked to the public, antislavery northerners charged the administration with conspiring to bring a new slave state into the Union.

The South, for its part, opposed all efforts to acquire new territory that would not support a slave system. The kingdom of Hawaii agreed to join the United States in 1854, but the treaty died in the Senate because it contained a clause prohibiting slavery in the islands. A powerful movement to annex Canada to the United States similarly foundered, at least in part because of slavery.

Slavery, Railroads, and the West

What fully revived the sectional crisis, however, was the same issue that had produced it in the first place: slavery in the territories. By the 1850s, the line of substantial white settlement had moved beyond the boundaries of Missouri, Iowa, and what is now Minnesota into a great expanse of plains, which many white Americans had once believed was unfit for cultivation. Now it was becoming apparent that large sections of this region were, in fact, suitable for farming. In the states of the Old Northwest, prospective settlers urged the government to open the area to them, provide territorial governments, and dislodge local Indians to make room for white settlers. There was relatively little opposition from any segment of white society to this proposed violation of Indian rights. But the interest in further settlement raised two issues that did prove highly controversial and that gradually became entwined with each other: railroads and slavery.

As the nation expanded westward, broad support began to emerge for building a transcontinental railroad. The problem was where to place it—and in particular, where to locate the railroad's eastern terminus, where the line could connect with the existing rail network east of the Mississippi. Northerners favored Chicago, while southerners supported St. Louis, Memphis, or New Orleans. The transcontinental railroad had also become part of the struggle between the North and the South.

Pierce's secretary of war, Jefferson Davis of Mississippi, removed one obstacle to a southern route. Surveys indicated that a railroad with a southern terminus would have to pass through an area in Mexican territory. But in 1853, Davis sent James Gadsden, a southern railroad builder, to Mexico, where he persuaded the Mexican government to accept $10 million in exchange for a strip of land that today comprises parts of Arizona and New Mexico. The so-called **Gadsden Purchase** only accentuated the sectional rivalry as it added more slave territory.

The Kansas–Nebraska Controversy

The momentum for an intercontinental railroad continued to build, but the first great barrier was the debate over where to put it. The acknowledged leader of northwestern Democrats and senator from Illinois, Stephen A. Douglas, wanted the transcontinental railroad to run north through his state, but he also recognized, as many did, that a northern route through the territories would run mostly through Indian populations. As a result, he introduced a bill in January 1854 to organize (and thus open to white settlement and railroads) a huge new territory, known as Nebraska, west of Iowa and Missouri from the still unorganized territory of the Louisiana Purchase.

Douglas knew the South would oppose his bill because organized territories over time become states, and the proposed territory was north of the Missouri Compromise line (36°3′) and hence closed to slavery since 1820. Initially, Douglas attempted to appease southerners by including a provision that territorial legislatures would decide the status of slavery. In theory, the region could choose to open itself to slavery, effectively repealing the Missouri Compromise. When southern Democrats demanded more, Douglas also agreed to divide the area into two territories—Nebraska and Kansas—instead of one. The new, second territory (Kansas) was thought more likely to become a slave state. In its final form, the measure was known as the **Kansas-Nebraska Act**. President Pierce supported the bill, and after a strenuous debate, it became law in May 1854 with the unanimous support of the South and the partial support of northern Democrats.

No piece of legislation in American history produced so many immediate, sweeping, and ominous political consequences. It split and destroyed the Whig Party. It divided the northern Democrats (many of whom were appalled at the repeal of the Missouri Compromise) and drove many of them from the party. Most important, it spurred the creation of a new party that was frankly sectional in composition and creed. People in both major parties who opposed Douglas's bill began to call themselves Anti-Nebraska Democrats and Anti-Nebraska Whigs. In 1854, they formed a new organization and named it the Republican Party, and it instantly became a major force in American politics. In the elections of that year, the Republicans won enough seats in Congress to permit them, in combination with allies among the Know-Nothings, to organize the House of Representatives.

"Bleeding Kansas"

White settlers began moving into Kansas almost immediately after the passage of the Kansas-Nebraska Act. In the spring of 1855, elections were held for a territorial legislature. There were only about 1,500 legal voters in Kansas by then, but thousands of Missourians, some traveling in armed bands into Kansas, swelled the vote to over 6,000. As a result, pro-slavery forces elected a majority to the legislature, which immediately legalized slavery. Outraged free-staters elected their own delegates to an independent constitutional convention, which met at Topeka and adopted a constitution excluding slavery. They then chose their own governor and legislature and petitioned Congress for statehood. But President Pierce denounced them as traitors and threw the full support of the federal government behind the pro-slavery territorial legislature. A few months later, a pro-slavery federal marshal assembled a large posse, consisting mostly of Missourians, to arrest the free-state leaders, who had set up their headquarters in Lawrence. The posse sacked the town, burned the "governor's" house, and destroyed several printing presses. Retribution came quickly.

Among the most fervent abolitionists in Kansas was **John Brown**, a grim, fiercely committed zealot who had moved to Kansas to fight to make it a free state. After the events in Lawrence, he gathered six followers (including four of his sons) and in one night murdered five pro-slavery settlers. This terrible episode, known as the Pottawatomie Massacre, led to more civil strife in Kansas including more armed bands engaged in guerrilla warfare with some more interested in land claims or loot than slavery. Northerners and southerners alike came to believe that the events in Kansas illustrated (and were caused by) the aggressive designs of the rival section. "Bleeding Kansas" became a powerful symbol of the sectional controversy.

Another symbol soon appeared, in the U.S. Senate. In May 1856, **Charles Sumner** of Massachusetts, a strong antislavery leader, rose to give a speech titled "The Crime Against Kansas." In it he gave particular attention to Senator Andrew P. Butler of South Carolina, an outspoken defender of slavery. The South Carolinian was, Sumner claimed, the "Don Quixote" of slavery, having "chosen a mistress . . . who, though ugly to others, is always lovely to him, though polluted in the sight of the world, is chaste in his sight . . . the harlot slavery."

The pointedly sexual references and the general viciousness of the speech enraged Butler's nephew, Preston Brooks, a member of the House of Representatives from South Carolina.

(Source: Library of Congress, Prints and Photographs
Division [LC-USZ62-2472])

JOHN BROWN   Even in this formal photographic portrait (taken in 1859, the last year of his life), John Brown
conveys the fierce sense of righteousness that fueled his extraordinary activities in the fight against slavery.

Several days after the speech, Brooks approached Sumner at his desk in the Senate chamber
during a recess, raised a heavy cane, and began beating him repeatedly on the head and
shoulders. Sumner, trapped in his chair, rose in agony with such strength that he tore the
desk from the bolts holding it to the floor. Then he collapsed, bleeding and unconscious.
So severe were his injuries that he was unable to return to the Senate for four years.
Throughout the North, he became a hero—a martyr to the barbarism of the South. In the
South, Preston Brooks became a hero, too. Censured by the House, he resigned his seat,
returned to South Carolina, and stood successfully for reelection.

The Free-Soil Ideology

What had happened to produce such deep hostility between the two sections? In part, the
tensions were reflections of the two sections' differing economic and territorial interests.
But they were also reflections of a hardening of ideas in both the North and the South.

In the North, assumptions about the proper structure of society came to center on the
belief in "free soil" and "free labor." Most white northerners came to believe that the existence of slavery was dangerous not only because of what it did to blacks but because of
what it threatened to do to whites. At the heart of American democracy, they argued, was
the right of all citizens to own property, to control their own labor, and to have access to
opportunities for advancement. Slavery, as a system of coerced labor, make a mockery of
this belief. At the same time, many, but not all, northern whites shared a conviction that
slavery was morally wrong. Northern blacks also embraced free labor ideology but fused
to it a staunch antislavery conviction.

According to this vision, the South was the antithesis of democracy—a closed, static
society, in which slavery preserved an entrenched aristocracy. While the North was growing

and prospering, the South was stagnating, rejecting the values of individualism and progress. The South, northern free-laborites further maintained, was engaged in a conspiracy to extend slavery throughout the nation and thus to destroy the openness of northern capitalism and replace it with the closed, aristocratic system of the South. The only solution to this "slave power conspiracy" was to fight the spread of slavery and extend the nation's democratic (i.e., free-labor) ideals to all sections of the country.

This ideology, which lay at the heart of the new Republican Party, also strengthened the commitment of Republicans to the Union. Since the idea of continued growth and progress was central to the free-labor vision, the prospect of dismemberment of the nation was to the Republicans unthinkable.

THE PRO-SLAVERY ARGUMENT

In the meantime, in the South a very different ideology was emerging. It was a result of many things: the Nat Turner uprising in 1831, which terrified southern whites; the expansion of the cotton economy into the Deep South, which made slavery unprecedentedly lucrative; and the growth of the Garrisonian abolitionist movement, with its strident attacks on southern society. The popularity of Harriet Beecher Stowe's *Uncle Tom's Cabin* was perhaps the most glaring evidence of the power of those attacks, but other abolitionist writings had been antagonizing white southerners for years.

In response to these pressures, a number of white southerners produced a new intellectual defense of slavery. Professor Thomas R. Dew of the College of William and Mary helped begin that effort in 1832. Twenty years later, apologists for slavery summarized their views in an anthology that gave their ideology its name: *The Pro-Slavery Argument*. John C. Calhoun stated the essence of the case in 1837: Slavery was "a good—a positive good." It was good for the slaves because they enjoyed better conditions than industrial workers in the North, good for southern society because it was the only way the two races could live together in peace, and good for the entire country because the southern economy, based on slavery, was the key to the prosperity of the nation.

Above all, southern apologists argued, slavery was good because it served as the basis for the southern way of life—a way of life superior to any other in the United States, perhaps in the world. White southerners looking at the North saw a spirit of greed, debauchery, and destructiveness. "The masses of the North are venal, corrupt, covetous, mean and selfish," wrote one southerner. Others wrote with horror of the factory system and the crowded, pestilential cities filled with unruly immigrants. But the South, they believed, was a stable, orderly society, free from the feuds between capital and labor plaguing the North. It protected the welfare of its workers. And it allowed the aristocracy to enjoy a refined and accomplished cultural life. It was, in short, an ideal social order in which all elements of the population were secure and content.

The defense of slavery rested, too, on increasingly elaborate arguments about the biological inferiority of African Americans, who were, white southerners claimed, inherently unfit to take care of themselves, let alone exercise the rights of citizenship.

BUCHANAN AND DEPRESSION

In this unpromising climate, the presidential campaign of 1856 began. Democratic Party leaders wanted a candidate who, unlike President Pierce, was not closely associated with the explosive question of "Bleeding Kansas." They chose James Buchanan of Pennsylvania, who as minister to England had been safely out of the country during the recent controversies. The Republicans, participating in their first presidential contest, endorsed a Whiggish program of internal improvements, thus combining the idealism of antislavery with the economic aspirations of the North. The Republicans nominated John C. Frémont, who had made a national reputation as an explorer of the Far West and who had no political record. The Native American, or Know-Nothing, Party was beginning to break apart, but it nominated former president Millard Fillmore, who also received the endorsement of a small remnant of the Whig Party.

After a heated, even frenzied campaign, Buchanan won a narrow victory over Frémont and Fillmore. Whether because of age and physical infirmities or because of a more fundamental weakness of character, he became a painfully timid and indecisive president at a critical moment in history. In the year Buchanan took office, a financial panic struck the country, followed by a depression that lasted several years. In the North, the depression strengthened the Republican Party because distressed manufacturers, workers, and farmers came to believe that the hard times were the result of the unsound policies of southern-controlled, pro-slavery Democratic administrations. They expressed their frustrations by moving into an alliance with antislavery elements and thus into the Republican Party.

THE *DRED SCOTT* DECISION

On March 6, 1857, the U.S. Supreme Court projected itself into the sectional controversy with one of the most controversial and notorious decisions in its history—*Dred Scott v. Sandford*. Dred Scott was a Missouri slave, once owned by an army surgeon who had taken Scott with him into Illinois and Wisconsin, where slavery was forbidden. In 1846, after the surgeon died, Scott sued his master's widow for freedom on the grounds that his residence in free territory had liberated him from slavery. The claim was well grounded in Missouri law, and in 1850 the circuit court in which Scott filed the suit declared him free. By now, John Sanford, the brother of the surgeon's widow, was claiming ownership of Scott, and he appealed the circuit court ruling to the state supreme court, which reversed the earlier decision. When Scott appealed to the federal courts, Sanford's attorneys claimed that Scott had no standing to sue because he was not a citizen.

The Supreme Court (which misspelled Sanford's name in its decision) was so divided that it was unable to issue a single ruling on the case. The thrust of the various rulings, however, was a stunning defeat for the antislavery movement. Chief Justice Roger Taney, who wrote one of the majority opinions, declared that Scott could not bring a suit in the federal courts because he was not a citizen. Blacks had no claim to citizenship, Taney argued. Slaves were property, and the Fifth Amendment prohibited Congress from taking property without "due process of law." Consequently, Taney concluded, Congress possessed no authority to pass a law depriving persons of their slave property in the territories. The Missouri Compromise, therefore, had always been unconstitutional.

The ***Dred Scott* decision** decision did nothing to challenge the right of an individual state to prohibit slavery within its borders, but the statement that the federal government was powerless to act on the issue was a drastic and startling one. Southern whites were elated: the highest tribunal in the land had sanctioned parts of the most extreme southern argument. In the North, the ruling produced widespread dismay. The decision, the *New York Tribune* wrote, "is entitled to just so much moral weight as would be the judgment of a majority of those congregated in any Washington bar-room." Republicans threatened that when they won control of the national government, they would reverse the decision—by "packing" the Court with new members.

DEADLOCK OVER KANSAS

President Buchanan timidly endorsed the *Dred Scott* decision. At the same time, he tried to resolve the controversy over Kansas by supporting its admission to the Union as a slave state. In response, the pro-slavery territorial legislature called an election for delegates to a constitutional convention. The free-state residents refused to participate, claiming that the legislature had discriminated against them in drawing district lines. As a result, the pro-slavery forces won control of the convention, which met in 1857 at Lecompton, framed a constitution legalizing slavery, and refused to give voters a chance to reject it. When an election for a new territorial legislature was called, the antislavery groups turned out in force and won a majority. The new antislavery legislature promptly submitted the Lecompton constitution to the voters, who rejected it by more than 10,000 votes.

Both sides had resorted to fraud and violence, but it was clear nevertheless that a majority of the people of Kansas opposed slavery. Buchanan, however, pressured Congress to admit Kansas under the pro-slavery Lecompton constitution. Stephen A. Douglas and other northern and western Democrats refused to support the president's proposal, which died in the House of Representatives. Finally, in April 1858, Congress approved a compromise: The Lecompton constitution would be submitted to the voters of Kansas again. If it was approved, Kansas would be admitted to the Union; if it was rejected, statehood would be postponed. Again, Kansas voters decisively rejected the Lecompton constitution. Not until the closing months of Buchanan's administration in 1861 did Kansas enter the Union—as a free state.

THE EMERGENCE OF LINCOLN

Given the gravity of the sectional crisis, the congressional elections of 1858 took on a special importance. Of particular note was the U.S. Senate contest in Illinois, which pitted Stephen A. Douglas, the most prominent northern Democrat, against **Abraham Lincoln**, who was largely unknown outside Illinois.

Lincoln was a successful lawyer who had long been involved in state politics. He had served several terms in the Illinois legislature and one undistinguished term in Congress. But he was not a national figure like Douglas, and so he tried to increase his visibility by engaging Douglas in a series of debates. The Lincoln–Douglas debates attracted enormous crowds and received wide attention.

At the heart of the debates was a basic difference on the issue of slavery. Douglas appeared to have no moral position on the issue, Lincoln claimed. He stated that Douglas did not care whether slavery was "voted up, or voted down." Lincoln's opposition to slavery was more fundamental. If the nation could accept that blacks were not entitled to basic human rights, he argued, then it could accept that other groups—immigrant laborers, for example—could be deprived of rights, too. And if slavery were to extend into the western territories, he argued, opportunities for poor white laborers to better their lots there would be lost. The nation's future, Lincoln argued (reflecting the central idea of the Republican Party), rested on the spread of free labor.

Lincoln believed slavery was morally wrong, but he was not an abolitionist. That was in part because he could not envision an easy alternative to slavery in the areas where it already existed. He shared the prevailing view among northern whites that the black race was not prepared to live on equal terms with whites. But even while Lincoln accepted the inferiority of black people, he continued to believe that they were entitled to basic rights. "I have no purpose to introduce political and social equality between the white and the black races. . . . But I hold that . . . there is no reason in the world why the negro is not entitled to all the natural rights enumerated in the Declaration of Independence, the right to life, liberty, and the pursuit of happiness. I hold that he is as much entitled to these as the white man." Lincoln and his party would "arrest the further spread" of slavery. They would not directly challenge it where it already existed but would trust that the institution would gradually die out there of its own accord.

Douglas's popular sovereignty position satisfied his followers sufficiently to produce a Democratic majority in the state legislature, which returned him to the Senate but aroused little enthusiasm. Lincoln, by contrast, lost the election but emerged with a growing following both in and beyond the state. And outside Illinois, the elections went heavily against the Democrats. The party retained control of the Senate but lost its majority in the House, with the result that the congressional sessions of 1858 and 1859 were bitterly deadlocked.

John Brown's Raid

The battles in Congress, however, were almost entirely overshadowed by an event that enraged and horrified the South. In the fall of 1859, John Brown, the antislavery radical whose bloody actions in Kansas had inflamed the crisis there, staged an even more dramatic episode, this time in the South itself. With private encouragement and financial aid from some prominent abolitionists, he made elaborate plans to seize a mountain fortress in Virginia from which, he believed, he could foment a slave insurrection in the South. On October 16, he and a group of eighteen followers attacked and seized control of a U.S. arsenal in **Harpers Ferry**, Virginia. But the slave uprising Brown hoped to inspire did not occur, and he quickly found himself besieged in the arsenal by citizens, local militia companies, and, before long, U.S. troops under the command of Robert E. Lee. After ten of his men were killed, Brown surrendered. He was promptly tried in a Virginia court for treason and sentenced to death. He and six of his followers were hanged.

No other single event did more than the Harpers Ferry raid to convince white southerners that they could not live safely in the Union. Many southerners believed (incorrectly) that John Brown's raid had the support of the Republican Party, and it suggested to them that the North was now committed to producing a slave insurrection.

The Election of Lincoln

As the presidential election of 1860 approached, the Democratic Party was torn apart by a battle between southerners, who demanded a strong endorsement of slavery, and westerners, who supported the idea of popular sovereignty. When the party convention met in April in Charleston, South Carolina, and endorsed popular sovereignty, delegates from eight states in the lower South walked out. The remaining delegates could not agree on a presidential candidate and finally adjourned after agreeing to meet again in Baltimore. The decimated convention at Baltimore nominated Stephen Douglas for president. In the meantime, disenchanted southern Democrats met in Richmond and nominated John C. Breckinridge of Kentucky.

The Republican leaders, in the meantime, were trying to broaden their appeal in the North. The platform endorsed such traditional Whig measures as a high tariff, internal improvements, a homestead bill, and a Pacific railroad to be built with federal financial assistance. It supported the right of each state to decide the status of slavery within its borders. But it also insisted that neither Congress nor territorial legislatures could legalize slavery in the territories. The Republican convention chose Abraham Lincoln as the party's presidential nominee. Lincoln was appealing because of his growing reputation for eloquence, because of his firm but moderate

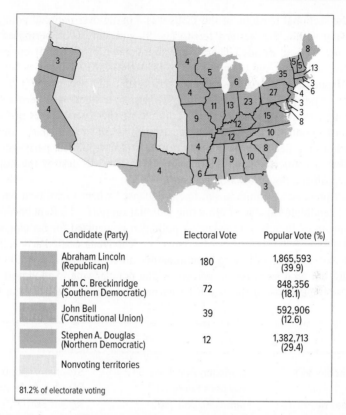

Candidate (Party)	Electoral Vote	Popular Vote (%)
Abraham Lincoln (Republican)	180	1,865,593 (39.9)
John C. Breckinridge (Southern Democratic)	72	848,356 (18.1)
John Bell (Constitutional Union)	39	592,906 (12.6)
Stephen A. Douglas (Northern Democratic)	12	1,382,713 (29.4)
Nonvoting territories		

81.2% of electorate voting

THE ELECTION OF 1860 The stark sectional divisions that helped produce the Civil War were clearly visible in the results of the 1860 presidential election. Abraham Lincoln, the antislavery Republican candidate, won virtually all the free states. Stephen Douglas, a northern Democrat with no strong position on the issue of slavery, won two of the border states, and John Bell, a supporter of both slavery and union, won others. John Breckinridge, a strong pro-slavery southern Democrat, carried the entire Deep South. Lincoln won under 40 percent of the popular vote but, because of the four-way division in the race, managed to win a clear majority of the electoral vote. • *What impact did the election of Lincoln have on the sectional crisis?*

position on slavery, and because his relative obscurity ensured that he would have none of the drawbacks of other, more prominent (and therefore more controversial) Republicans.

In the November election, Lincoln won the presidency with a majority of the electoral votes but only about two-fifths of the fragmented popular vote. Therefore, his victory was far from decisive. And his party, moreover, failed to win a majority in Congress. Even so, many white southerners interpreted the election of Lincoln as the death knell to their power and influence in the Union. And within a few weeks of Lincoln's victory, the process of disunion began—a process that would quickly lead to a prolonged and bloody war.

CONCLUSION

In the decades following the War of 1812, a vigorous nationalism pervaded much of American life, helping smooth over the growing differences among the very distinct societies emerging in the United States. During the 1850s, however, the forces that had worked to hold the nation together in the past fell victim to new and much more divisive pressures.

Driving the sectional tensions of the 1850s was a battle over national policy toward the place of slavery within the western territories. Should slavery be permitted in the new states? And who should decide? There were strenuous efforts to craft compromises and solutions to this dilemma: the Compromise of 1850, the Kansas-Nebraska Act of 1854, and others. But despite these efforts, positions on slavery continued to harden in both the North and the South. Bitter battles in the territory of Kansas over whether to permit slavery there; growing agitation by abolitionists in the North and pro-slavery advocates in the South; the Supreme Court's controversial *Dred Scott* decision in 1857; the popularity of *Uncle Tom's Cabin* throughout the decade; and the emergence of a new political party—the Republican Party—openly and centrally opposed to slavery: all worked to destroy the hopes for compromise and push the South toward secession.

In 1860, all pretense of common sentiment collapsed when no political party presented a presidential candidate capable of attracting national support. The Republicans nominated Abraham Lincoln of Illinois, a little-known politician recognized for his eloquent condemnations of slavery in a Senate race two years earlier. The Democratic Party split apart, with its northern and southern wings each nominating different candidates. Lincoln won the election easily, but with less than 40 percent of the popular vote. And almost immediately after his victory, the states of the South began preparing to secede from the Union.

KEY TERMS/PEOPLE/PLACES/EVENTS

Abraham Lincoln 317
Alamo 299
Antonio López de
  Santa Anna 299
Charles Sumner 313
Compromise of 1850 311
Dred Scott decision 316
Forty-niners 307
Free-Soil Party 307

Gadsden Purchase 312
Harpers Ferry 318
James K. Polk 302
John Brown 313
Kansas-Nebraska Act 313
Manifest Destiny 298
Oregon Trail 300
popular sovereignty 306
Sam Houston 299

Stephen A. Douglas 310
Stephen F. Austin 299
Tejanos 300
Treaty of Guadalupe
  Hidalgo 305
Wilmot Proviso 306
Young America 311
Zachary Taylor 307

RECALL AND REFLECT

1. How were the boundary disputes over Oregon and Texas resolved? Why were the resolutions in the two cases so different?
2. How did Polk's decisions and actions as president intensify the sectional conflict?
3. What was the issue at stake in "Bleeding Kansas," and how did events in Kansas reflect the growing sectional division between the North and the South?
4. What was the *Dred Scott* decision? What was the decision's impact on the sectional crisis?
5. How did the growing sectional crisis affect the nation's major political parties?

14 | THE CIVIL WAR

THE SECESSION CRISIS
THE MOBILIZATION OF THE NORTH
THE MOBILIZATION OF THE SOUTH
STRATEGY AND DIPLOMACY
CAMPAIGNS AND BATTLES

LOOKING AHEAD

1. How did the North's mobilization for war differ from mobilization in the South? What accounts for these differences?
2. How did the war affect the North and the South differently?
3. What were the military strategies employed by the North and the South from the opening clashes in 1861 through the Union victory in 1865, and how did these strategies differ?

AMERICA FACED A TIME OF RECKONING by the end of 1860. As had been long predicted by black critics of American society like David Walker and Frederick Douglass, the country was being brought to knees by the institution of slavery. The shared political beliefs and institutions that had bound the Union for generations now lay tattered. The second party system had collapsed, no longer able to contain sectional differences and find compromises over the meaning and expansion of the peculiar institution. Politicians leapt at one another's throats, each eager to protect his state's particular economy, society, and views on the morality and legality of slavery. The federal government itself was no longer a remote, unthreatening presence to most citizens. Forced to resolve the status of territories and settle the question of whether they would be open to slavery or not, Washington now became a more direct presence in the lives of Americans. The presidential election of 1860 brought these political tensions to a head and forced Americans to confront the possibility that the nation would no longer exist. It precipitated the bloodiest war in nation's history whose outcome—which was always in doubt until the very end—ultimately remade the meaning of American democracy.

1861

Confederate States of
America formed

Davis president of
Confederacy

Conflict at Fort Sumter

First Battle of Bull Run

1862

Battles of Shiloh,
Antietam,
Second Bull Run

Confederacy enacts
military draft

1863

Emancipation
Proclamation

Battle of Gettysburg

Vicksburg surrenders

Union enacts military
draft

New York City
antidraft riots

1864

Battle of the Wilderness

Sherman's
March to the Sea

Lincoln reelected

1865

Lee surrenders to Grant

13th Amendment

THE SECESSION CRISIS

Almost as soon as news of Abraham Lincoln's election reached the South, militant leaders began to demand an end to the Union.

THE WITHDRAWAL OF THE SOUTH

South Carolina, long the hotbed of Southern separatism, seceded first, on December 20, 1860. By the time Lincoln took office, six other Southern states—Mississippi (January 9, 1861), Florida (January 10), Alabama (January 11), Georgia (January 19), Louisiana (January 26), and Texas (February 1)—had withdrawn from the Union. In February 1861, representatives of the seven seceded states met at Montgomery, Alabama, and formed a new nation—the **Confederate States of America**. Two months earlier, President James Buchanan told Congress that no state had the right to secede from the Union but that the federal government had no authority to stop a state if it did.

The seceding states immediately confiscated the federal property within their boundaries. But they did not at first have sufficient military power to seize two fortified offshore military installations: **Fort Sumter**, in the harbor of Charleston, South Carolina, garrisoned by a small force under Major Robert Anderson; and Fort Pickens, in Pensacola, Florida. Buchanan refused to yield Fort Sumter when South Carolina demanded it. Instead, in January 1861, he ordered an unarmed merchant ship to proceed to Fort Sumter with additional troops and supplies. Confederate guns turned it back. Still, neither section was yet ready to concede that war had begun. And in Washington, efforts began once more to forge a compromise.

THE FAILURE OF COMPROMISE

Gradually, the compromise efforts came together around a proposal from John J. Crittenden of Kentucky. Known as the

Crittenden Compromise, it proposed reestablishing the Missouri Compromise line and extending it westward to the Pacific. Slavery would be prohibited north of the line and permitted south of it. Southerners in the Senate seemed willing to accept the plan. But the compromise would have required the Republicans to abandon their most fundamental position—that slavery not be allowed to expand—and they rejected it. Whether the failure to compromise and find common ground between Northern and Southern politicians triggered the Civil War has been a topic of debate among historians for generations. (See "Debating the Past: The Causes of the Civil War.")

When Abraham Lincoln arrived in Washington, talk of secession and possible war filled the air. In his inaugural address, Lincoln insisted that acts of force or violence to support secession were insurrectionary and that the government would "hold, occupy, and possess" federal property in the seceded states—a clear reference to Fort Sumter.

But Fort Sumter was running short of supplies. So Lincoln sent a relief expedition to the fort and informed the South Carolina authorities that he would send no troops or munitions unless the supply ships met with resistance. The new Confederate government ordered General P. G. T. Beauregard, commander of Confederate forces at Charleston, to take the fort. When Anderson refused to give up, the Confederates bombarded it for two days. On April 14, 1861, Anderson surrendered. The Civil War had begun.

Almost immediately, four more slave states seceded from the Union and joined the Confederacy: Virginia (April 17), Arkansas (May 6), Tennessee (May 7), and North Carolina (May 20). The four remaining slave states, Maryland, Delaware, Kentucky, and Missouri—under heavy political pressure from Washington—remained in the Union.

THE OPPOSING SIDES

All the important material advantages for waging war lay with the North, most notably an advanced industrial system able by 1862 to manufacture almost all the North's own war materials. The South had almost no industry at all.

In addition, the North had a superior transportation system, with more and better railroads than did the South. During the war, the Confederate railroad system steadily deteriorated and by early 1864 had almost collapsed.

But the South also had advantages. The Southern armies were, for the most part, fighting a defensive war on familiar land with local support. The Northern armies, on the other hand, were fighting mostly within the South amid hostile local populations; they had to maintain long lines of communication. The commitment of the white population of the South to the war was, with limited exceptions, clear and firm throughout much of the early years of fighting. In the North, opinion was more divided, and support remained shaky until very near the end. A major Southern victory at any one of several crucial moments might have proved decisive in breaking the North's will to continue the struggle. Finally, the dependence of the English and French textile industries on Southern cotton inclined many leaders in those countries to favor the Confederacy; and Southerners hoped, with some reason, that one or both might intervene on their behalf.

BILLY YANK AND JOHNNY REB

The vast majority of Civil War soldiers were volunteers. Recruiters for the Union often pulled in groups of men from the same town or ethnic group. There were entire companies and even regiments of Irish Americans, German Americans, Italian Americans, or,

THE CAUSES OF THE CIVIL WAR

Abraham Lincoln, in his 1865 inaugural address, looked back at the terrible war that was now nearing its end and said, "All knew [that slavery] was somehow the cause of the war." Few historians dispute that. But disagreement has been sharp over whether slavery was the only, or even the principal, cause of the war.

The debate began even before the war itself. In 1858, Senator William H. Seward of New York took note of the two competing explanations of the sectional tensions that were then inflaming the nation. On one side, he said, stood those who believed the conflicts to be "accidental, unnecessary, the work of interested or fanatical agitators." Opposing them stood those (among them Seward himself) who believed there to be "an irrepressible conflict between opposing and enduring forces."

The "irrepressible conflict" argument dominated historical discussion of the war from the 1860s to the 1920s. War was inevitable, some historians claimed, because there was no room for compromise on the central issue of slavery. Others deemphasized slavery and pointed to the economic differences between the agrarian South and the industrializing North. Charles and Mary Beard, for example, wrote in 1927 of the "inherent antagonisms" between the interests of planters and those of industrialists. Still others cited social and cultural differences as the source of an irrepressible conflict. Slavery, the historian Allan Nevins argued, was only one factor that was making residents of the North and South "separate peoples." Fundamental differences in "assumptions, tastes, and cultural aim" made it virtually impossible for the two societies to live together in peace.

More recent proponents of irrepressible-conflict arguments similarly emphasize culture and ideology but define the concerns of the North and the South in different terms. Eric Foner, writing in 1970, argued that the moral concerns of abolitionists and the economic concerns of industrialists were less important in explaining Northern hostility to the South than was the broad-based "free-labor" ideology of the region. Northerners opposed slavery because they feared it might spread into their own region or into the West and threaten the position of free white laborers.

Other historians have argued that the war was not inevitable, beginning with a group of scholars in the 1920s known as the "revisionists." James G. Randall and Avery Craven were the two leading proponents of the view that the differences between the North and the South were not so great as to require a war, that only a "blundering generation" of leaders caused the conflict. Michael Holt revived the revisionist argument in a 1978 book, in which he, too, emphasized the partisan ambitions of politicians. Holt was, along with Paul Kleppner, Joel Silbey, and William Gienapp, one of the creators of an "ethnocultural" interpretation of the war that emphasized the collapse of the party system and the role of temperance and nativism, which was central to the coming of the conflict. •

1. Some arguments regarding the Civil War as inevitable focus on economic differences between the North and the South. What were these differences and how might they have led—inevitably—to war?

2. Some revisionist scholars attribute the Civil War to a "blundering generation" of political leaders. Who were these leaders and what blunders did they make? Could better decisions have avoided war?

later, African Americans. Initially, these soldiers and their officers were haphazardly trained and unprepared for battle. Many officers jokingly referred to their troops as armed mobs.

Because individual states outfitted their soldiers at the outset of the war, Union uniforms were at first far from uniform, ranging from the dark blue jackets and light blue pants of the regular army to dark blue and red "Zouave" uniforms based on the French colonial regiments in Algeria. "Federals" did not consistently wear blue uniforms until 1862, when the federal government provided them along with shoes, weapons, cartridge boxes, knapsacks, blankets, canteens, and other basic supplies.

Northerners generally saw themselves fighting to restore the Union and preserve the American democratic experiment. They questioned how the nation might endure if parts of it could secede at every undesirable election result. Most white Northerners understood that divisions over slavery had caused the Civil War, but they did not fight, at first, to abolish it. Later, when it became clear that abolishing slavery would help end the rebellion, emancipation joined reunion as a war aim. (In contrast, black Northerners immediately understood the war to be a struggle for emancipation.) Otherwise, beyond the timeless motivations of comradeship, honor, and adventure shared by soldiers in many wars, Union troops generally fought to sustain "the best government on earth."[1]

Like his Union counterpart, the average Confederate soldier rarely had proper military training and tended to serve with comrades from the same area. When on the march, fully provisioned Southern soldiers carried an ammunition cartridge box on their belts, a rolled-up blanket, a haversack, a tin cup, frying pan, and cloth-covered canteen. Many Confederate soldiers supplied their own shotguns, hunting rifles, or ancient flintlock muskets, and cavalrymen often provided their own horses. Regiments wore different uniforms, and even after the Confederacy adopted gray, the government was never able to clothe every soldier. Meals were meager, with soldiers on both sides subsisting on dried vegetables, salt pork and beef, coffee, and tough crackers known as hardtack.

Southerners saw themselves as the protectors of sacred American values. They defended the right of states to secede if they found the federal government oppressive, just as the colonies had claimed the right to declare independence from an oppressive Britain in the Revolutionary War. And they interpreted their defense of slavery as a defense of individual property rights in general. Indeed, slavery was at the heart of the rights Confederates sought to protect and of the life and economy they fought to preserve. Confederate vice president Alexander Stephens called slavery the "cornerstone" of the Confederacy. Outraged at the thought of living under an antislavery president, secessionists relished independence.

1 James McPherson, *Battle Cry of Freedom: The Civil War Era* (New York: Oxford University Press, 1988), p. 309.

(Source: The Metropolitan Museum of Art, New York, Gift of Mrs. Frank B. Porter, 1922)

THE COST OF BATTLE Seeking to capture the moment when Union Brigadier General Francis Channing Barlow captures three Confederate officers on June 21, 1864, at Petersburg, Virginia, Winslow Homer offers a sharp portrait of defeat and victory. Beyond providing a picture of the soldiers' different uniforms, he looks ahead to the state of America after the war. In the unapologetic glare of the Confederate most closely facing Barlow, Homer questions how quickly or coherently the nation can knit itself back together.

"Thank God!" wrote one Mississippian the summer after secession. "We have a country at last . . . to live for, to pray for, to fight for, and if necessary, to die for."[2]

Beyond these abstract motivations, however, many rebels fought to protect their homes and families from the invading Yankees.

THE MOBILIZATION OF THE NORTH

In the North, the war produced considerable discord, frustration, and suffering. But it also produced prosperity and economic growth. With the South now gone from Congress, the Republican Party enjoyed almost unchallenged supremacy. During the war, it enacted an aggressively nationalistic program to promote economic development.

ECONOMIC NATIONALISM

Two 1862 acts assisted the rapid development of the West. The **Homestead Act** permitted any citizen or prospective citizen to purchase 160 acres of public land for a small fee after living on it for five years. The Morrill Act transferred substantial public acreage to the state governments, which could now sell the land and use the proceeds to finance public education. This act led to the creation of many new state colleges and universities, the so-called land-grant institutions. Congress also passed a series of tariff bills that by the end of the

2 James McPherson, *Battle Cry of Freedom: The Civil War Era* (New York: Oxford University Press, 1988), p. 310.

war had raised duties to the highest level in the nation's history—a great boon to domestic industries eager for protection from foreign competition, but a hardship for many farmers and other consumers. Without the seceding states to block their legislation, Congress bent to the political will of the Northern and western factions.

Congress also moved to spur completion of a transcontinental railroad. It created two new federally chartered corporations: the Union Pacific Railroad Company, which was to build westward from Omaha, and the Central Pacific, which was to build eastward from California. The two projects were to meet in the middle and complete the link, which they did in 1869 at Promontory Point, Utah.

The National Bank Acts of 1863–1864 created a new national banking system. Existing or newly formed banks could join the system if they had enough capital and were willing to invest one-third of it in government securities. In return, they could issue U.S. Treasury notes as currency. This eliminated much (although not all) of the chaos and uncertainty surrounding the nation's currency.

More difficult was financing the war itself. The government tried to do so in three ways: levying taxes, issuing paper currency, and borrowing. Congress levied new taxes on almost all goods and services and in 1861 levied an income tax for the first time. But taxation raised only a small proportion needed to fight the war, and strong popular resistance prevented the government from raising the rates.

At least equally controversial was the printing of paper currency, or "**greenbacks.**" The new currency was backed not by gold or silver but (as today) simply by the good faith and credit of the government. The value of the greenbacks fluctuated according to the fortunes of the Northern armies. Early in 1864, with the war effort bogged down, a greenback dollar was worth only 39 percent of a gold dollar. But at the close of the war, with confidence high, it was worth 67 percent of a gold dollar.

By far the largest source of financing for the war was loans. The Treasury persuaded ordinary citizens to buy over $400 million worth of bonds. Yet public bond purchases constituted only a small part of the government's borrowing, which in the end totaled $2.6 billion, most of it from banks and large financial interests.

Raising the Union Armies

At the beginning of 1861, the regular army of the United States consisted of only 16,000 troops, many of them stationed in the West. So the Union, like the Confederacy, had to raise its army mostly from scratch. After the surrender of Fort Sumter, on April 15, 1863, Lincoln directed individual state militias to help him create a new federal force of 75,000 soldiers by providing men for an initial term of three months. But it would be far from enough. When Congress convened in July 1861, it authorized enlisting 500,000 volunteers for three-year terms.

This voluntary system of recruitment produced adequate forces only briefly, during the first flush of enthusiasm for the war. By March 1863, Congress was forced to pass a national draft law. Virtually all young adult males were eligible to be drafted, although a man could escape service by hiring someone to go in his place or by paying the government a fee of $300.

To many who were accustomed to a remote and inactive national government, **conscription** was strange and threatening. Opposition to the draft law was widespread, particularly among laborers, immigrants, and Democrats opposed to the war (known as "Peace Democrats" or "Copperheads" by their opponents). Occasionally opposition to the draft erupted into violence such as when demonstrators rioted in New York City for four days in July 1863, after the first names were selected for conscription. More than 100 people died. Irish workers were at the center of violence. They were angry because black strikebreakers had been used against them in a recent longshoremen's strike. They blamed African Americans generally for the war, which they thought was being fought for the benefit of slaves. The rioters lynched several African Americans and burned down black homes, businesses, and even an orphanage, leaving more than 100 dead. Only the arrival of federal troops direct from the Battle of Gettysburg halted the violence.

WARTIME POLITICS

When Abraham Lincoln arrived in Washington, many Republicans considered him a minor prairie politician who would be easily controlled by the real leaders of his party. But Lincoln was not cowed by the distinguished figures around him. The new president understood his own (and his party's) weaknesses, and he assembled a cabinet representing every faction of the Republican Party and every segment of Northern opinion. He moved boldly to use the war powers of the presidency, blithely ignoring inconvenient parts of the Constitution because, he said, it would be foolish to lose the whole by being afraid to disregard a part. And so he sent troops into battle without asking Congress for a declaration of war, arguing that the conflict was a domestic insurrection, and he unilaterally proclaimed a naval blockade of the South.

Lincoln's greatest political problem was the widespread popular opposition to the war in the North. Lincoln ordered military arrests of civilian dissenters and suspended the right of habeas corpus (the right of an arrested person to receive a speedy trial). At first, Lincoln used these methods only in sensitive areas such as the border states; but by 1862, he proclaimed that all persons who discouraged enlistments or engaged in disloyal practices were subject to martial law.

Repression was not the only tool the North used to strengthen support for the war. In addition to arresting "disloyal" Northerners, Lincoln's administration used new tools of persuasion to build popular opinion in favor of the war. In addition to pro-war pamphlets, posters, speeches, and songs, the war mobilized a significant corps of photographers—organized by the renowned Mathew Brady, one of the first important photographers in American history—to take pictures of the war. The photographs that resulted from this effort—new to warfare—were among the grimmest ever made to that point, many of them displaying the vast numbers of dead on the Civil War battlefields. For some Northerners, the images of death contributed to a revulsion for the war. But for most they gave evidence of the level of sacrifice that had been made for the preservation of the Union and thus spurred the nation on to victory. (Southerners used similar propaganda in the Confederacy, although less effectively.)

By the time of the 1864 election, the North was in political turmoil. The Republicans had suffered heavy losses in the midterm elections of 1862, and in response party leaders tried to create a broad coalition of all the groups that supported the war. They called the new organization the Union Party, but it was, in reality, little more than the Republican Party and a small faction of War Democrats. They nominated Lincoln for a second term and Andrew Johnson of Tennessee, a War Democrat who had opposed his state's decision to secede, for the vice presidency.

The Democrats nominated **George B. McClellan**, a celebrated former Union general. The party adopted a platform denouncing the war and calling for a truce. McClellan repudiated that demand, but the Democrats were clearly the peace party in the campaign, trying to profit from growing war weariness. For a time, Lincoln's prospects for reelection seemed doubtful.

At this crucial moment, however, several Northern military victories, particularly the capture of Atlanta, Georgia, early in September 1864, rejuvenated Northern morale and boosted Republican prospects. With the overwhelming support of Union troops, Lincoln won reelection comfortably, with 212 electoral votes to McClellan's 21.

THE POLITICS OF EMANCIPATION

Despite their surface unity in supporting the war and their general agreement on most economic matters, the Republicans disagreed sharply with one another on the issue of slavery. "Radical Republicans"—led in Congress by such men as Representative Thaddeus Stevens of Pennsylvania and Senators Charles Sumner of Massachusetts and Benjamin Wade of Ohio—wanted to use the war to abolish slavery immediately and completely. "Conservative Republicans" favored a more cautious policy—in part to placate the slave states that remained, precariously, within the Union.

Nevertheless, momentum began to gather behind emancipation early in the war. In 1861, Congress passed the **Confiscation Acts**, which declared that all slaves used for "insurrectionary" purposes (that is, in support of the Confederate military effort) would be considered freed. Subsequent laws in the spring of 1862 abolished slavery in the District of Columbia and the western territories and provided for the compensation of owners. In July 1862, Radicals pushed through Congress the second Confiscation Act, which declared free the slaves of persons supporting the insurrection and authorized the president to employ African Americans as soldiers.

As the war progressed, many in the North slowly accepted emancipation as a central war aim; nothing less, they believed, would justify the enormous sacrifices the struggle had required. As a result, the Radicals gained increasing influence within the Republican Party—a development that did not go unnoticed by the president, who decided to seize the leadership of the rising antislavery sentiment himself.

On September 22, 1862, after the Union victory at the Battle of Antietam, the president announced his intention to use his war powers to issue an executive order freeing all slaves in the Confederacy. And on January 1, 1863, he formally signed the **Emancipation Proclamation**, which declared forever free the slaves inside the Confederacy. The proclamation did not apply to the Union slave states; nor did it affect those parts of the Confederacy already under Union control (Tennessee, western Virginia, and southern Louisiana). It applied, in short, only to slaves over whom the Union had no control. Still, the document was of great importance. It clearly and irrevocably established that the war was being fought not only to preserve the Union but also to eliminate slavery. Eventually, as federal armies occupied much of the South, the proclamation became a practical reality and led directly to the freeing of thousands of slaves.

Even in areas not directly affected by the proclamation, the antislavery impulse gained strength. The U.S. government's tentative measures against slavery were not, at first, a major factor in the liberation of slaves. Instead, the war helped African Americans liberate themselves, and they did so in increasing numbers as the war progressed. Many slaves were taken from their plantations and put to work as workers building defenses and other chores. Once transported to the front, many of them found ways to escape across Northern lines, where they were treated as "contraband"—goods seized from people who had no right to them. They could not be returned to their masters. By 1862, the Union army often penetrated deep into the Confederacy. Almost everywhere they went, escaped slaves flocked to join them by the thousands, often whole families. Some of them joined the Union army, others simply stayed with the troops until they could find their way to free states. When the Union captured New Orleans and much of southern Louisiana, slaves refused to work for their former masters, even though the Union occupiers had not made any provisions for liberating African Americans.

By the end of the war, two Union slave states (Maryland and Missouri) and three Confederate states occupied by Union forces (Tennessee, Arkansas, and Louisiana) had abolished slavery. In 1865, Congress finally approved and the states ratified the **Thirteenth Amendment**, which abolished slavery in all parts of the United States. After more than two centuries, legalized slavery finally ceased to exist in the United States.

AFRICAN AMERICANS AND THE UNION CAUSE

About 186,000 emancipated blacks served as soldiers, sailors, and laborers for the Union forces. Yet in the first months of the war, African Americans were largely excluded from the military. A few black regiments eventually took shape in some of the Union-occupied areas of the Confederacy. But once Lincoln issued the Emancipation Proclamation, black enlistment increased rapidly and the Union military began actively to recruit African American soldiers and sailors in both the North and, where possible, the South.

Some of these men were organized into fighting units, of which the best known was probably the Fifty-fourth Massachusetts Infantry, which (like most black regiments) had a white commander: Robert Gould Shaw, a member of an aristocratic Boston family.

Most black soldiers, however, were assigned menial tasks behind the lines, such as digging trenches and transporting water. Even though many fewer blacks than whites died in combat, the African American mortality rate was actually higher than the rate for white soldiers because so many black soldiers died of diseases contracted while working long,

(Source: Library of Congress, Prints and Photographs Division [LC-B8184-841])

AFRICAN AMERICAN TROOPS Although most of the black soldiers who enlisted in the Union army performed noncombat jobs behind the lines, some black combat regiments—members of one of which are pictured here—fought with great success and valor in critical battles.

arduous hours in unsanitary conditions. Conditions for blacks and whites were unequal in other ways as well. Until 1869, black soldiers were paid a third less than were white soldiers. But however dangerous, onerous, or menial the tasks that black soldiers were given, most of them felt enormous pride in their service—pride they retained throughout their lives, and often through the lives of their descendants. Many moved from the army into politics and other forms of leadership (in both the North and, after the war, the Reconstruction South). Black fighting men captured by the Confederates were sent back to their masters (if they were escaped slaves) or executed. In 1864, Confederate soldiers killed over 260 black Union soldiers after capturing them in Tennessee.

WOMEN, NURSING, AND THE WAR

Thrust into new and often unfamiliar roles by the war, women took over positions vacated by men as teachers, salesclerks, office workers, mill and factory hands, and above all nursing. The **United States Sanitary Commission**, an organization of civilian volunteers, mobilized large numbers of female nurses to serve in field hospitals. By the end of the war, women were the dominant force in nursing.

Female nurses encountered considerable resistance from male doctors, many of whom thought it inappropriate for women to take care of male strangers. The Sanitary Commission countered such arguments by presenting nursing in domestic terms: as a profession that made use of the same maternal, nurturing roles women played as wives and mothers.

Some women came to see the war as an opportunity to win support for their own goals. Elizabeth Cady Stanton and Susan B. Anthony together founded the Women's National Loyal League in 1863 and worked simultaneously for the abolition of slavery and the awarding of suffrage to women.

THE MOBILIZATION OF THE SOUTH

Early in February 1861, representatives of the seven seceding states met at Montgomery, Alabama, to create a new Southern nation. When Virginia seceded several months later, the leaders of the Confederacy moved to Richmond.

There were, of course, important differences between the new Confederate nation and the nation it had left. But there were also significant similarities.

THE CONFEDERATE GOVERNMENT

The Confederate constitution was almost identical to the Constitution of the United States, with several significant exceptions. It explicitly acknowledged the sovereignty of the individual states (although not the right of secession). And it specifically sanctioned slavery and made its abolition (even by one of the states) practically impossible.

The constitutional convention at Montgomery named a provisional president and vice president: **Jefferson Davis** of Mississippi and **Alexander H. Stephens** of Georgia, who were later elected by the general public, without opposition, for six-year terms. Davis had been a moderate secessionist before the war. Stephens had argued against secession. The Confederate government, like the Union government, was dominated throughout the war by men of the political center.

Davis was a reasonably able administrator and encountered little interference from the generally tame members of his unstable cabinet. But he rarely provided genuinely national leadership, spending too much time on routine items. Unlike Lincoln, he displayed a strict—even obsessive—regard for legal and constitutional requirements.

Although there were no formal political parties in the Confederacy, its politics were fiercely divided nevertheless. Some white Southerners opposed secession and war altogether. Most white Southerners supported the war, but as in the North, many were openly critical of the government and the military, particularly as the tide of battle turned against the South.

States' rights had become such a cult among many white Southerners that they resisted virtually all efforts to exert national authority, even those necessary to win the war. States' rights enthusiasts obstructed conscription and restricted Davis's ability to impose martial law and suspend habeas corpus. Governors such as Joseph Brown of Georgia and Zebulon M. Vance of North Carolina tried at times to keep their own troops apart from the Confederate forces.

But the national government was not impotent. It experimented, successfully for a time, with a "food draft," which permitted soldiers to feed themselves by seizing crops from farms in their path. The Confederacy also seized control of the railroads and shipping; it impressed slaves to work as laborers on military projects and imposed regulations on industry; it limited corporate profits. States' rights sentiment was a significant handicap, but the South nevertheless took important steps in the direction of centralization.

MONEY AND MANPOWER

Financing the Confederate war effort was a monumental task. The Confederate congress tried at first to requisition funds from the individual states; but the states were as reluctant to tax their citizens as the congress was. In 1863, therefore, the congress enacted an income tax. But taxation produced only about 1 percent of the government's total income. Borrowing was not much more successful. The Confederate government issued bonds in such vast amounts that the public lost faith in them, and efforts to borrow money in Europe, using cotton as collateral, fared no better.

As a result, the Confederacy had to pay for the war through the least stable, most destructive form of financing: paper currency, which it began issuing in 1861. By 1864, the Confederacy had issued the staggering total of $1.5 billion in paper money. The result was a disastrous inflation—a 9,000 percent increase in prices in the course of the war (in contrast to 80 percent in the North).

Like the United States, the Confederacy first raised armies by calling for volunteers. And as in the North, by the end of 1861 voluntary enlistments were declining. In April 1862, therefore, the congress enacted the Conscription Act, which subjected all white males between the ages of eighteen and thirty-five to military service for three years. As in the North, a draftee could avoid service if he furnished a substitute. But since the price of substitutes was high, the provision aroused such opposition from poorer whites that it was repealed in 1863.

Even so, conscription worked for a time, in part because enthusiasm for the war was intense and widespread among white men in most of the South. At the end of 1862, about 500,000 soldiers were in the Confederate army, not including the many slave men and women recruited by the military to perform such services as cooking, laundry, and manual labor. Small numbers of slaves and free blacks enlisted in the Confederate army, and a few participated in combat.

After 1862, however, conscription began producing fewer men, and by 1864 the Confederate government faced a critical manpower shortage. The South was suffering from intense war weariness, and many Southerners had concluded that defeat was inevitable. Nothing could attract or retain an adequate army any longer. In a frantic final attempt to raise men, the congress authorized the conscription of 300,000 slaves, but the war ended before the government could attempt this incongruous experiment.

ECONOMIC AND SOCIAL EFFECTS OF THE WAR

The war cut off Southern planters and producers from Northern markets, and a Union blockade of Confederate ports eventually reduced the sale of cotton outside of the region and overseas by nearly 95 percent. As a result, the South redoubled effort to diversify and expand its crops, bolster its textile industry, and make armaments and wartime provisions. Nothing came close to replacing cotton, however. Indeed, in the South, production of all goods during the war declined by more than a third; in the North, production grew. Above all, the fighting itself wreaked havoc on the Southern landscape, destroying farmland, towns, cities, and railroads. As the war continued, the shortages, the inflation, and the carnage slowly destabilized Southern society. Resistance to conscription, food impressment, and taxation rose throughout the Confederacy, as did hoarding and black-market commerce. Even before emancipation, the war had far-reaching effects on the lives of slaves. Confederate leaders enforced slave codes with particular severity, but many slaves—especially those near the front—still escaped their masters and crossed Union lines.

Some recreational pursuits found new popularity. Baseball emerged as a favorite pastime for Confederate and Union troops alike, who set up makeshift games within their ranks to relieve the pressures of the war. At the same time, civilians in Northern cities flocked to cheer on local teams in the newly founded National Association of Base Ball Players. (See "Patterns of Popular Culture: Baseball and the Civil War.")

The war turned the meaning of work upside down for women. Because their fathers, brothers, and husbands had all gone to war, and some would never return, many white women assumed greater responsibility for raising crops, caring for animals, hunting, and fishing; others turned to mills and manufacturing jobs to earn money for food. To support the Confederate cause more directly, they joined relief associations and wrote letters, sent food, sewed uniforms and blankets, and worked in hospitals. Slave women also saw their labors expand. They too were forced to take on duties vacated by masters gone to fight and by male slaves who accompanied their masters, were impressed, or ran away. Now they cooked, cleared land, and farmed even more and took up new livery and hunting duties.

STRATEGY AND DIPLOMACY

The military initiative in the Civil War lay mainly with the North, since it needed to destroy the Confederacy as quickly as possible. Southerners needed only to survive; however, survival required diplomatic recognition from other nations, especially Great Britain, and the financial and military aid that would accompany it. Lincoln and his diplomatic corps worked tirelessly to keep foreign powers and their resources out of the Confederacy while the Union navy blockaded Southern ports.

BASEBALL AND THE CIVIL WAR

Long before the great urban stadiums, the lights, the cameras, and the multimillion-dollar salaries, baseball was the most popular game in America. During the Civil War, it was a treasured pastime for soldiers and for thousands of men (and some women) behind the lines, in both the North and the South.

The legend that baseball was invented by Abner Doubleday—who probably never even saw the game—was created by Albert G. Spalding, a patriotic sporting-goods manufacturer eager to prove that the game had purely American origins. In fact, baseball was derived from a variety of earlier games, especially the English pastimes of cricket and rounders. American baseball took its own distinctive form beginning in the 1840s, when Alexander Cartwright, a shipping clerk, formed the New York Knickerbockers, laid out a diamond-shaped field with four bases, and declared that batters with three strikes were out and that teams with three outs were retired.

Cartwright moved West in search of gold in 1849, settling finally in Hawaii, where he introduced the game to Americans in the Pacific. But the game did not languish in his absence. Henry Chadwick, an English-born journalist, spent much of the 1850s popularizing the game and regularizing its rules. By 1860, baseball was being played by college students and Irish workers, by urban elites and provincial farmers, by people of all classes and ethnic groups from New England to Louisiana. Students at Vassar College formed "ladies" teams in the 1860s, and in Philadelphia, free black men formed the Pythians, the first of what was to become a great network of African American

baseball teams. From the beginning, they were barred from playing against most white teams.

When young men marched off to war in 1861, some took their bats and balls with them. Almost from the start of the fighting, soldiers in both armies took advantage of idle moments to lay out baseball diamonds and organize games. Games on battlefields were sometimes interrupted by gunfire and cannon fire. "It is astonishing how indifferent a person can become to danger," a soldier wrote home to Ohio in 1862. "The report of musketry is heard but a very little distance from us, . . . yet over there on the other side of the road is most of our company, playing Bat Ball." After a skirmish in Texas, another Union soldier lamented that, in addition to casualties, his company had lost "the only baseball in Alexandria, Texas." Far from discouraging baseball, military commanders—and the United States Sanitary Commission, the Union army's medical arm—actively encouraged the game during the war. It would, they believed, help keep up the soldiers' morale.

Away from the battlefield, baseball continued to flourish. In New York City, games between local teams drew crowds of ten thousand to twenty thousand. The National Association of Base Ball Players, founded in 1859, had recruited ninety-one clubs in ten Northern states by 1865; a North Western Association of Baseball Players, organized in Chicago in 1865, indicated that the game was becoming well established in the West as well. In Brooklyn, William Cammeyer drained a skating pond on his property, built a board fence around it, and created the first enclosed baseball field in America—the Union Grounds. He charged ten cents for admission. The professionalization of the game had begun.

Despite all the commercialization and spectacle that came to be associated with baseball in the years after the Civil War, the game remained for many Americans what it was to millions of young men fighting in the most savage war in the nation's history—an American passion that at times, even if briefly, erased the barriers dividing groups from one another. "Officers and men forget, for a time, the differences in rank," a Massachusetts private wrote in 1863, "and indulge in the invigorating sport with a schoolboy's ardor." •

UNDERSTAND, ANALYZE, & EVALUATE

1. How could a competitive game of baseball erase "the barriers dividing groups from one another"?
2. Baseball during the Civil War crossed the lines of cultural differences between the North and the South. Does baseball today—professional or amateur—continue to cross lines of cultural differences?

THE COMMANDERS

The most important Union military leader was Abraham Lincoln. He ultimately succeeded as commander in chief because he recognized the North's material advantages, and he realized that the proper objective of his armies was to destroy the Confederate armies' ability to fight. Despite his missteps and inexperience, the North was fortunate to have Lincoln, but the president struggled to find a general as well suited for his task as Lincoln was for his.

From 1861 to 1864, Lincoln tried repeatedly to find a chief of staff capable of orchestrating the Union war effort. He turned first to General Winfield Scott, the ailing seventy-four-year-old hero of the Mexican War who had already contributed strategic advice to the president, but Scott was no longer physically capable of leading an army. Lincoln then appointed the young George B. McClellan, the commander of the Union forces in the East, the Army of the Potomac. Unfortunately, the proud and overly cautious McClellan seemed too slow to act for Lincoln's tastes. Lincoln returned McClellan to his previous command in March 1862. For most of the rest of the year, Lincoln had no chief of staff at all. When he eventually appointed General Henry W. Halleck to the post, he found him ineffectual as well. Not until March 1864 did Lincoln finally find a general he trusted to command the war effort: **Ulysses S. Grant**, who shared Lincoln's belief in unremitting combat and in making enemy armies and resources the target of military efforts.

Lincoln's handling of the war effort faced constant scrutiny from the Committee on the Conduct of the War, a joint investigative committee of the two houses of Congress. Established in December 1861 and chaired by Senator Benjamin E. Wade of Ohio, the committee complained constantly of the inadequate ruthlessness of Northern generals, which Radicals on the committee attributed (largely inaccurately) to a secret sympathy among the officers for slavery. The committee's efforts often seriously interfered with the conduct of the war.

Southern military leadership centered on President Davis, a trained soldier who nonetheless failed to create an effective central command system. Early in 1862, Davis named General **Robert E. Lee** as his principal military adviser. But in fact, Davis had no intention of sharing control of strategy with anyone. After a few months, Lee left Richmond to command forces in the field, and for the next two years, Davis planned strategy alone. In February 1864, he named General Braxton Bragg as a military adviser, but Bragg never provided much more than technical advice.

(Source: Library of Congress, Prints and Photographs Division [LC-USZ61-903]; Library of Congress, Prints and Photographs Division [LC-DIG-cwpb-04406])

GRANT (LEFT) AND LEE Of the Union general, an observer said: "He habitually wears an expression as if he had determined to drive his head through a brick wall, and was about to do it." It was an apt metaphor for Grant's military philosophy, which relied on constant, unrelenting assault. The Confederate general, in contrast, was known for his dignified and disciplined demeanor. He became a symbol to white Southerners of the "Lost Cause."

At lower levels of command, men of markedly similar backgrounds controlled the war in both the North and the South. Many of the professional officers on both sides were graduates of the U.S. Military Academy at West Point and the U.S. Naval Academy at Annapolis. Amateur officers played an important role in both armies as commanders of volunteer regiments. In both the North and the South, such men were usually economic or social leaders in their communities who rounded up troops to lead. Sometimes this system produced officers of real ability; more often it did not.

THE ROLE OF SEA POWER

The Union had an overwhelming advantage in naval power. It played two important roles in the war: enforcing a blockade of the Southern coast and assisting the Union armies in field operations.

The blockade, which began in the first weeks of the war, kept most oceangoing ships out of Confederate ports, but for a time small blockade runners continued to slip through. Gradually, however, federal forces tightened the blockade by seizing the Confederate ports themselves. The last important port in Confederate hands—Wilmington, North Carolina— fell to the Union early in 1865.

The Confederates made a bold attempt to break the blockade with an ironclad warship, constructed by plating with iron a former U.S. frigate, the *Merrimac.* On March 8, 1862, the refitted *Merrimac,* renamed the *Virginia,* left Norfolk to attack a blockading squadron of wooden ships at nearby Hampton Roads. It destroyed two of the ships and scattered the rest. But the Union government had already built ironclads of its own, including the *Monitor,* which arrived only a few hours after the *Virginia*'s dramatic foray. The next day, it met the *Virginia* in battle. Neither vessel was able to sink the other, but the *Monitor* put an end to the *Virginia*'s raids and preserved the blockade.

The Union navy was particularly important in the western theater of the war, where the major rivers were navigable by large vessels. The navy transported supplies and troops and joined in attacking Confederate strong points. The South had no significant navy of its own and could defend against the Union gunboats only with ineffective fixed land fortifications.

EUROPE AND THE DISUNITED STATES

Judah P. Benjamin, the Confederate secretary of state for most of the war, was an intelligent but undynamic man who attended mostly to routine administrative tasks. William Seward, his counterpart in Washington, gradually became one of the outstanding American secretaries of state. He had invaluable assistance from Charles Francis Adams, the American minister to London. This gap between the diplomatic skills of the Union and the Confederacy was a decisive factor in the war.

At the beginning of the conflict, the sympathies of the ruling classes of England and France lay largely with the Confederacy, partly because the two nations imported much Southern cotton; but it was also because they were eager to weaken the United States, an increasingly powerful rival to them in world commerce. France was unwilling to take sides in the conflict unless England did so first. And in England, the government was reluctant to act because there was powerful popular support for the Union—particularly from the large and influential English antislavery movement. After Lincoln issued the Emancipation Proclamation, antislavery groups worked particularly avidly for the Union. Southern leaders hoped to counter the strength of the British antislavery forces by arguing that access to Southern cotton was vital to the English and French textile industries. But English manufacturers had a surplus of both raw cotton and finished goods on hand in 1861 and could withstand a temporary loss of access to American cotton. Later, as the supply began to diminish, both England and France managed to keep at least some of their mills open by importing cotton from Egypt, India, and elsewhere. Equally important, even the 500,000 English textile workers thrown out of jobs as a result of mill closings continued to support the North. In the end, therefore, no European nation offered diplomatic recognition, financial support, or military aid to the Confederacy. No nation wanted to antagonize the United States unless the Confederacy seemed likely to win, and the South never came close enough to victory to convince its potential allies to support it. In the end, the Confederacy was on its own.

Even so, tension, and on occasion near hostilities, continued between the United States and Britain. The Union government was angry when Great Britain, France, and other nations declared themselves neutral early in the war, thus implying that the two sides to the conflict had equal stature. Leaders in Washington insisted that the conflict was simply a domestic insurrection, not a war between two legitimate governments.

A more serious crisis, the so-called *Trent* affair, began in late 1861. Two Confederate diplomats, James M. Mason and John Slidell, had slipped through the then-ineffective Union blockade to Havana, Cuba, where they boarded an English steamer, the *Trent,* for England. Waiting in Cuban waters was the American frigate *San Jacinto,* commanded by the impetuous Charles Wilkes. Acting without authorization, Wilkes stopped the British vessel, arrested the diplomats, and carried them in triumph to Boston. The British government demanded the release of the prisoners, reparations, and an apology. Lincoln and Seward were aware that Wilkes had violated maritime law. They were unwilling to risk war with England, and they eventually released the diplomats with an indirect apology.

CAMPAIGNS AND BATTLES

In the absence of direct intervention by the European powers, the two contestants in North America were left to resolve the conflict between themselves. They did so in four long years of bloody combat. More than 618,000 Americans died in the course of the Civil War, far more than the 112,000 who perished in World War I or the 405,000 who died in World War II. There were nearly 2,000 deaths for every 100,000 of population during the Civil War. In World War I, the comparable figure was only 109, and in World War II the comparable figure was 241. In some respects, the Civil War was the bloodiest war in modern times.

THE TECHNOLOGY OF WAR

Much of what happened on the battlefield in the Civil War was a result of new technologies that transformed the nature of combat.

The most obvious change was the nature of the armaments. Among the most important was the introduction of repeating weapons. Samuel Colt had patented a repeating pistol (the revolver) in 1835, but more important for military purposes was the repeating rifle, introduced in 1860 by Oliver Winchester. Also significant were greatly improved cannons and artillery, a result of earlier advances in iron and steel technology.

These new armaments made it impossibly deadly to fight battles as they had been fought for centuries, with lines of infantry soldiers standing erect in the field firing volleys at their opponents until one side withdrew. Soldiers quickly learned that the proper position for combat was staying low to the ground and behind cover. For the first time in the history of organized warfare, therefore, infantry did not fight in formation, and the battlefields became more chaotic places. Gradually, the deadliness of the new weapons encouraged armies on both sides to spend a great deal of time building elaborate fortifications and trenches to protect themselves from enemy fire. The sieges of Vicksburg and Petersburg, the defense of Richmond, and many other military events all produced the construction of vast fortifications around both cities and attacking armies. (They were the predecessors to the vast network of trenches of World War I.)

Other weapons technologies were less central to the fighting of the war, but important nevertheless. The relatively new technology of hot-air balloons was employed intermittently to provide a view of enemy formations in the field. The ironclad ships—and even torpedoes and submarine technology, which made fleeting appearances in the 1860s—suggested the dramatic changes that would soon overtake naval warfare.

Critical to the conduct of the war, however, were two other relatively new technologies: the railroad and the telegraph. The railroad was particularly important in mobilizing millions of soldiers and transferring them to the front. Transporting such enormous numbers of soldiers, and the supplies necessary to sustain them, by foot or by horse and wagon would have been almost impossible. But, ironically, railroads also limited the mobility of the armies. Commanders were forced to organize their campaigns at least in part around the location of the railroads rather than on the basis of the best topography or most direct land route to a destination. The dependence on the rails—and the resulting necessity of concentrating huge numbers of men in a few places—also encouraged commanders to prefer great battles with large armies rather than smaller engagements with fewer troops.

The impact of the telegraph on the war was limited both by the scarcity of qualified telegraph operators and by the difficulty of bringing telegraph wires into the fields where battles were being fought. Things improved somewhat after the new U.S. Military Telegraph Corps, headed by Thomas Scott and Andrew Carnegie, trained and employed over 1,200 operators. Gradually, too, both the Union and Confederate armies learned to string telegraph wires along the routes of their troops, so that field commanders were able to stay in close touch with one another during battles.

The Opening Clashes, 1861

The Union and the Confederacy fought their first major battle of the war in northern Virginia. A Union army of over 30,000 men under General Irvin McDowell was stationed just outside Washington. About thirty miles away, at Manassas, sat a slightly smaller Confederate army commanded by General P. G. T. Beauregard. If the Northern army could destroy the Southern one, Union leaders believed, the war might end at once. In mid-July, McDowell marched his inexperienced troops toward Manassas. Beauregard moved his troops behind Bull Run, a small stream north of Manassas, and called for reinforcements, which reached him the day before the battle.

On July 21, in the **First Battle of Bull Run**, or First Battle of Manassas, McDowell almost succeeded in dispersing the Confederate forces. But the Southerners managed to fight off a last strong Union assault and then counterattacked savagely. Surprised, the Union troops panicked, broke ranks, and ran helter skelter. Caught off guard himself, and unable to readily identify his soldiers because of mismatched and irregular uniforms (some regiments actually gray uniforms), McDowell failed to reorganize the troops. Instead he ordered a retreat to Washington—which quickly became a wild, chaotic withdrawal complicated by the presence along the route of many civilians, who had ridden down from the capital, picnic baskets in hand, to watch the battle from nearby hills. The Confederates, disorganized by the turn of events, did not pursue. But they hailed the outcome of the battle as a smashing success and a sure sign of future victories. By contrast, the battle was a severe blow to Union morale and to the president's confidence in his officers.

Elsewhere, Union forces achieved some small but significant victories in 1861. A Union force under General George B. McClellan moved east from Ohio into western Virginia. By the end of 1861, it had "liberated" the antisecession mountain people of the region, who created their own state government loyal to the Union; the state was admitted to the Union as West Virginia in 1863.

THE WESTERN THEATER

After the battle at Bull Run, military operations in the East settled into a long and frustrating stalemate. The first decisive operations occurred in the western theater in 1862. Here Union forces were trying to seize control of the southern part of the Mississippi River from both the north and south, moving down the river from Kentucky and up from the Gulf of Mexico toward New Orleans.

In April, a Union squadron commanded by Flag Officer David G. Farragut smashed past weak Confederate forts near the mouth of the Mississippi and from there sailed up to New Orleans. The city was virtually defenseless because the Confederate high command had expected the attack to come from the north. The surrender of New Orleans on April 25, 1862, was an important turning point in the war. From then on, the mouth of the Mississippi was closed to Confederate trade, and the South's largest city and most important banking center was in Union hands.

Farther north in the western theater, Confederate troops under General Albert Sidney Johnston were stretched out in a long defensive line around two forts in Tennessee, Fort Henry and Fort Donelson. Early in 1862, Ulysses S. Grant attacked Fort Henry, whose defenders, awed by the ironclad riverboats accompanying the Union army, surrendered with almost no resistance. Grant then moved both his naval and ground forces to Fort Donelson, where the Confederates put up a stronger fight but finally, on February 16, had to surrender. Grant thus gained control of river communications and forced Confederate troops out of Kentucky and half of Tennessee.

With about 40,000 men, Grant now advanced south along the Tennessee River. At Shiloh, Tennessee, he met a force almost equal to his own, commanded by Albert Sidney Johnston and P. G. T. Beauregard. The result was the Battle of **Shiloh**, April 6–7, 1862. In the first day's fighting (during which Johnston was killed), the Southerners drove Grant back to the river. But the next day, reinforced by 25,000 fresh troops, Grant recovered the lost ground and forced Beauregard to withdraw. After the narrow Union victory at Shiloh, Northern forces occupied Corinth, Mississippi, and took control of the Mississippi River as far south as Memphis.

General Braxton Bragg, now in command of the Confederate army in the West, gathered his forces at Chattanooga, in eastern Tennessee, where he faced a Union army trying to capture the city. The two armies maneuvered for advantage inconclusively in northern Tennessee and southern Kentucky for several months until December 31–January 2, when they finally clashed in the Battle of Murfreesboro, or Stone's River. Bragg was forced to withdraw to the South in defeat.

By the end of 1862, Union forces had made considerable progress in the West. But the heart of the war remained in the East.

THE VIRGINIA FRONT, 1862

During the winter of 1861–1862, George B. McClellan, commander of the Army of the Potomac, concentrated on training his army of 150,000 men near Washington. Finally, he designed a spring campaign to capture the Confederate capital at Richmond. But instead of heading overland directly, McClellan chose a complicated route that he thought would circumvent the Confederate defenses. The navy would carry his troops down the Potomac to a peninsula east of Richmond, between the York and James Rivers; the army would approach the city from there in what became known as the Peninsular campaign.

THE WAR IN THE WEST, 1861–1863 While the Union armies in Virginia were meeting with repeated frustrations, the Union armies in the West were scoring notable successes in the first two years of the war. This map shows a series of Union drives in the western Confederacy. Flag Officer David Farragut's ironclads led to the capture of New Orleans—a critical Confederate port—in April 1862, while forces farther north under the command of Ulysses S. Grant drove the Confederate army out of Kentucky and western Tennessee. These battles culminated in the Union victory at Shiloh, which led to Union control of the upper Mississippi River. • *Why was control of the Mississippi so important to both sides?*

McClellan set off with 100,000 men, reluctantly leaving 30,000 members of his army behind, under General Irvin McDowell, to protect Washington. McClellan eventually persuaded Lincoln to send him the additional men. But before the president could do so, a Confederate army under General **Thomas J. ("Stonewall") Jackson** staged a rapid march north through the Shenandoah Valley, as if preparing to cross the Potomac and attack Washington. Lincoln postponed sending reinforcements to McClellan, retaining McDowell's corps to head off Jackson. In the Valley campaign of May 4–June 9, 1862, Jackson defeated two separate Union forces and slipped away before McDowell could catch him.

Meanwhile, McClellan was fighting Confederate troops under General Joseph E. Johnston outside Richmond in the two-day Battle of Fair Oaks, or Seven Pines (May 31–June 1), and holding his ground. Johnston, badly wounded, was replaced by Robert E. Lee, who then recalled Stonewall Jackson from the Shenandoah Valley. With a combined force of 85,000 to face McClellan's 100,000, Lee launched a new offensive, known as the Battle of the Seven Days (June 25–July 1), in an effort to cut McClellan off from his base on the York River. But McClellan fought his way across the peninsula and set up a new base on the James.

McClellan was now only twenty-five miles from Richmond and in a good position to renew the campaign. But despite continuing pressure from Lincoln, he did not advance. Hoping to force a new offensive against Richmond along the direct overland route he had always preferred, Lincoln finally ordered the army to move back to northern Virginia and join up with a smaller force under General John Pope. As the Army of the Potomac left the peninsula by water, Lee moved north with the Army of northern Virginia to strike Pope before McClellan could join him. Pope was as rash as McClellan was cautious, and he attacked the approaching Confederates without waiting for the arrival of all of McClellan's troops. In the Second Battle of Bull Run, or Manassas (August 29–30), Lee threw back the assault and routed Pope's army, which fled to Washington. With hopes for an overland campaign against Richmond now in disarray, Lincoln removed Pope from command and put McClellan back in charge of all the federal forces in the region.

Lee soon went on the offensive again, heading north through western Maryland, and McClellan moved out to meet him. McClellan had the good luck to get a copy of Lee's orders, which revealed that a part of the Confederate army, under Stonewall Jackson, had separated from the rest to attack Harpers Ferry. But instead of attacking quickly before the Confederates could recombine, McClellan stalled, again giving Lee time to pull most of his forces back together behind **Antietam** Creek, near the town of Sharpsburg. There, on September 17, McClellan's 87,000-man army repeatedly attacked Lee's force of 50,000, with staggering casualties on both sides. Late in the day, just as the Confederate line seemed ready to break, the last of Jackson's troops arrived from Harpers Ferry to reinforce it. McClellan might have broken through with one more assault. Instead, he allowed Lee to retreat into Virginia. Technically, Antietam was a Union victory; but in reality, McClellan had squandered an opportunity to destroy much of the Confederate army. In November, Lincoln finally removed McClellan from command for good.

McClellan's replacement, General Ambrose E. Burnside, was a short-lived mediocrity. He tried to move toward Richmond by crossing the Rappahannock River at Fredericksburg. There, on December 13, he launched a series of attacks against Lee, all of them bloody, all of them hopeless. After losing a large part of his army, he withdrew to the north bank of the Rappahannock. He was relieved at his own request. The year 1862 ended, therefore, with a series of frustrations for the Union.

THE PROGRESS OF THE WAR

Why did the Union—with its much greater population, its much larger population, and its much better transportation and technology than the Confederacy—make so little decisive progress in the first two years of the war? Had there been a crushing victory by the North early in the war—for example, a routing at the First Battle of Bull Run—the conflict might have ended quickly by destroying the Confederacy's morale. But none occurred.

Many Northerners blamed the military stalemate on timid or incompetent Union generals, and there was some truth to that view. But the more important reason for the drawn-out conflict was that it was not a war of traditional tactics and military strategy. It was, even if the leaders of both sides were not yet fully aware of it, a war of attrition, and the Confederacy could survive only if the Union quit fighting. Winning or losing battles here and there would not determine the outcome of the war. What would bring the war

July 1861–July 1862

August–December 1862

1863

Confederate forces
Union forces
Confederate victories
Union victories
Inconclusive

THE VIRGINIA THEATER, 1861–1863   Much of the fighting during the first two years of the Civil War took place in what became known as the Virginia theater—although the campaigns in this region eventually extended north into Maryland and Pennsylvania. The Union hoped for a quick victory over the newly created Confederate army. But as these maps show, the Southern forces consistently thwarted such hopes. The map at top left shows the battles of 1861 and the first half of 1862, almost all of them won by the Confederates. The map at lower left shows the last months of 1862, during which the Southerners again defeated the Union in most of their engagements—although Northern forces drove the Confederates back from Maryland in September. The map on the right shows the troop movements that led to the climactic battle of Gettysburg in 1863. • *Why were the Union forces unable to profit more from material advantages during these first years of the war?*

to a conclusion was the steady destruction of the resources that were necessary for victory. More than two bloody years of fighting were still to come. But those last years were a testimony to the slow, steady deterioration of the Confederacy's ability to maintain the war, and the consistent growth of the resources that allowed the Union armies to grow steadily stronger.

1863: YEAR OF DECISION

At the beginning of 1863, General Joseph Hooker was commanding the still-formidable Army of the Potomac, which remained north of the Rappahannock, opposite Fredericksburg. Taking part of his army, Hooker crossed the river above Fredericksburg and moved toward the

THE SIEGE OF VICKSBURG, MAY–JULY 1863   In the spring of 1863, Grant began a campaign to win control of the final piece of the Mississippi River still controlled by the Confederacy. To do that required capturing the Southern stronghold at Vicksburg—a well-defended city sitting above the river. Vicksburg's main defenses were to the north, so Grant boldly moved men and supplies around the city and attacked it from the south. Eventually, he cut off the city's access to the outside world, and after a six-week siege, its residents finally surrendered. • *What impact did the combined victories at Vicksburg and Gettysburg have on Northern commitment to the war?*

town and Lee's army. But at the last minute, he drew back to a defensive position in a desolate area of brush and scrub trees known as the Wilderness. Lee divided his forces for a dual assault on the Union army. In the Battle of Chancellorsville, May 1-5, Stonewall Jackson attacked the Union right and Lee himself charged the front. Hooker barely managed to escape with his army. Lee had frustrated Union objectives, but he had not destroyed the Union army. And his ablest officer, Jackson, was fatally wounded in the course of the battle.

While the Union forces were suffering repeated frustrations in the East, they were winning some important victories in the West. In the spring of 1863, Ulysses S. Grant was driving at Vicksburg on the Mississippi River. Vicksburg was well protected on land and had good artillery coverage of the river itself. But in May, Grant boldly moved men and supplies—over land and by water—to an area south of the city, where the terrain was reasonably good. He then attacked Vicksburg from the rear. Six weeks later, on July 4, Vicksburg—whose residents were by then starving as a result of the prolonged siege—surrendered. At almost the same time, the other Confederate strongpoint on the river, Port Hudson, Louisiana, also surrendered to a Union force that had moved north from New Orleans. With the achievement of one of the Union's basic military aims—control of the whole length of the Mississippi—the Confederacy was split in two, with Louisiana, Arkansas, and Texas cut off from the other seceded states. The victories on the Mississippi were one of the great turning points of the war.

During the siege of Vicksburg, Lee proposed an invasion of Pennsylvania, which would, he argued, divert Union troops north. Further, he argued, if he could win a major victory on Northern soil, England and France might come to the Confederacy's aid. The war-weary North might even quit the war before Vicksburg fell.

In June 1863, Lee moved up the Shenandoah Valley into Maryland and then entered Pennsylvania. The Union Army of the Potomac, commanded first by Hooker and then (after June 28) by General George C. Meade, moved north, too. The two armies finally encountered each other at the small town of **Gettysburg**, Pennsylvania. There, on July 1-3, 1863, they fought the most celebrated battle of the war.

Meade's army established a strong, well-protected position on the hills south of the town. Lee attacked, but his first assault on the Union forces on Cemetery Ridge failed. A day later, he ordered a second, larger effort. In what is remembered as Pickett's Charge, a force of 15,000 Confederate soldiers advanced for almost a mile across open country while being swept by Union fire. Only about 5,000 made it up the ridge, and this remnant finally had to surrender or retreat. By now, Lee had lost nearly a third of his army. On July 4, the same day as the surrender of Vicksburg, Lee withdrew from Gettysburg. The retreat was another major turning point in the war. Never again were the weakened Confederate forces able seriously to threaten Northern territory. Months later Lincoln visited the battlefield site and delivered one of the most famous speeches in American history. (See "Consider the Source: The Gettysburg Address.")

Before the end of the year, there was one more important turning point, this time in Tennessee. After occupying Chattanooga on September 9, Union forces under General William Rosecrans began an unwise pursuit of Bragg's retreating Confederate forces. The two armies engaged in western Georgia, in the Battle of Chickamauga (September 19-20). Union forces could not break the Confederate lines and retreated back to Chattanooga.

Bragg now began a siege of Chattanooga itself, seizing the heights nearby and cutting off fresh supplies to the Union forces. Grant came to the rescue. In the Battle of Chattanooga (November 23-25), the reinforced Union army drove the Confederates back into Georgia. Union forces had now achieved a second important objective: control of the Tennessee River.

CONSIDER THE SOURCE

THE GETTYSBURG ADDRESS (1863)

Lincoln gave this speech on November 19, 1863, on the occasion of the dedication of the Soldiers' National Cemetery in Gettysburg, Pennsylvania, four months after the famous battle.

Four score and seven years ago our fathers brought forth on this continent, a new nation, conceived in Liberty, and dedicated to the proposition that all men are created equal.

Now we are engaged in a great civil war, testing whether that nation, or any nation so conceived and so dedicated, can long endure. We are met on a great battlefield of that war. We have come to dedicate a portion of that field, as a final resting place for those who here gave their lives that that nation might live. It is altogether fitting and proper that we should do this.

But, in a larger sense, we can not dedicate—we can not consecrate—we can not hallow—this ground. The brave men, living and dead, who struggled here, have consecrated it, far above our poor power to add or detract. The world will little note, nor long remember what we say here, but it can never forget what they did here. It is for us the living, rather, to be dedicated here to the unfinished work which they who fought here have thus far so nobly advanced. It is rather for us to be here dedicated to the great task remaining before us—that from these honored dead we take increased devotion to that cause for which they gave the last full measure of devotion—that we here highly resolve that these dead shall not have died in vain—that this nation, under God, shall have a new birth of freedom—and that government of the people, by the people, for the people, shall not perish from the earth.

UNDERSTAND, ANALYZE, & EVALUATE

1. What purpose did Lincoln ascribe to the Civil War in the first two sentences of his speech?
2. Why did Lincoln state that he and his audience could not dedicate the battlefield?
3. What significance did Lincoln ascribe to the Battle of Gettysburg in the last sentence of this speech?
4. Why do you think this address endeared President Lincoln to many of his contemporaries and so many Americans since?

Source: Johnson, Michael P. (ed.), *Abraham Lincoln, Slavery, and the Civil War: Selected Writings and Speeches*, Boston, MA: Bedford St. Martin's, 2010, 263.

THE LAST STAGE, 1864–1865

By the beginning of 1864, President Lincoln had appointed General Ulysses S. Grant as chief of all the Union armies. Grant, like Lincoln, believed in using the North's great advantage in troops and material resources to overwhelm the South. He planned two great offensives for 1864. In Virginia, the Army of the Potomac would advance toward Richmond and force Lee into a decisive battle. In Georgia, the western army, under General **William T. Sherman**, would advance east toward Atlanta and destroy the remaining Confederate force, now under the command of Joseph E. Johnston.

GETTYSBURG, JULY 1–3, 1863 Gettysburg was the most important single battle of the Civil War. Had Confederate forces prevailed at Gettysburg, the future course of the war might well have been very different. The map on the left shows the distribution of Union and Confederate forces at the beginning of the battle, July 1, after Lee had driven the Northern forces south of town. The map on the right reveals the pattern of the attacks on July 2 and 3. Note, in particular, Pickett's bold and costly charge, whose failure on July 3 was the turning point in the battle and, some chroniclers have argued, the war. • *Why did Robert E. Lee believe that an invasion of Pennsylvania would advance the Confederate cause?*

The Northern campaign began when the Army of the Potomac, 115,000 strong, plunged into the rough, wooded Wilderness area of northwestern Virginia in pursuit of Lee's 75,000-man army. After avoiding an engagement for several weeks, Lee turned Grant back in the Battle of the Wilderness (May 5–7). Without stopping to rest or reorganize, Grant resumed his march toward Richmond and met Lee again in the bloody Battle of Spotsylvania Court House (May 8–21) in which 12,000 Union troops and a large, but unknown, number of Confederates fell. Grant kept moving, but victory continued to elude him. Lee kept his army between Grant and the Confederate capital and on June 1–3 repulsed the Union forces again, just northeast of Richmond, at Cold Harbor.

Grant now moved his army east of Richmond and headed south toward the railroad center at Petersburg. If he could seize Petersburg, he could cut off the capital's communications with the rest of the Confederacy. But Petersburg had strong defenses; and once Lee came to the city's relief, the assault became a prolonged siege.

In Georgia, meanwhile, Sherman was facing less ferocious resistance. With 90,000 men, he confronted Confederate forces of 60,000 under Johnston. As Sherman advanced, Johnston tried to delay him by maneuvering. The two armies fought only one real battle— Kennesaw Mountain, northwest of Atlanta, on June 27—where Johnston scored an impressive victory. Even so, he was unable to stop the Union advance toward Atlanta, prompting Davis to replace him with General John B. Hood. Sherman took the city on September 2 and burned it.

VIRGINIA CAMPAIGNS, 1864–1865   From the Confederate defeat at (and retreat from) Gettysburg until the end of the war, most of the eastern fighting took place in Virginia. By now, Ulysses S. Grant was commander of all Union forces and had taken over the Army of the Potomac. Although Confederate forces won a number of important battles during the Virginia campaign, the Union army grew steadily stronger and the Southern forces steadily weaker. Grant believed that the Union strategy should reflect the North's greatest advantage: its superiority in men and equipment. • *What effect did this decision have on the level of casualties?*

Hood now tried unsuccessfully to draw Sherman out of Atlanta by moving back up through Tennessee and threatening an invasion of the North. Sherman sent Union troops to reinforce Nashville. In the Battle of Nashville on December 15–16, 1864, Northern forces practically destroyed what was left of Hood's army.

Meanwhile, Sherman had left Atlanta to begin his soon-to-be-famous "March to the Sea." Living off the land, destroying supplies it could not use, his army cut a sixty-mile-wide swath of desolation across Georgia. Sherman sought not only to deprive the Confederate army of war materials and railroad communications. He was also determined to break the will of the Southern people by burning towns and plantations along his route. By December 20, he had reached Savannah, which surrendered two days later. Early in 1865, Sherman continued his destructive march, moving northward through South Carolina. He was virtually unopposed until he was well inside North Carolina, where a small force under Johnston could do no more than cause a brief delay.

In April 1865, Grant's Army of the Potomac—still engaged in the prolonged siege at Petersburg—finally captured a vital railroad junction southwest of the town. Without rail access to the South, and plagued by heavy casualties and massive desertions, Lee informed the Confederate government that he could no longer defend Richmond. Within hours, Jefferson Davis, his cabinet, and as much of the white population as could find transportation fled. That night, mobs roamed the city, setting devastating fires. And the next morning, Northern forces entered the Confederate capital. With them was Abraham Lincoln, who walked through the streets of the burned-out city surrounded by black men and women cheering him as the "Messiah" and "Father Abraham." In one particularly stirring moment, the president turned to a former slave kneeling on the street before him and said: "Don't kneel to me. . . . You must kneel to God only, and thank Him for the liberty you will enjoy hereafter."

With the remnant of his army, now about 25,000 men, Lee began moving west in the forlorn hope of finding a way around the Union forces so that he could move south and link up with Johnston in North Carolina. But the Union army pursued him and blocked his escape route. Lee finally recognized that further bloodshed was futile. He arranged to meet Grant at a private home in the small town of **Appomattox Court House**, Virginia, where on April 9 he surrendered what was left of his forces. Nine days later, near Durham, North Carolina, Johnston surrendered to Sherman. The long war was now effectively over. Jefferson Davis was finally captured in Georgia. A few Southern diehards continued to fight, but even their resistance collapsed before long. General George Meade's shout, "It's all over," described in simple terms one of the most momentous events in the nation's history.

The war ensured the permanence of the Union, but many other issues remained far from settled. What would happen to the freedmen (the term used for slaves who were now liberated)? Could the South and the North reconcile? Would the massive industrial growth in

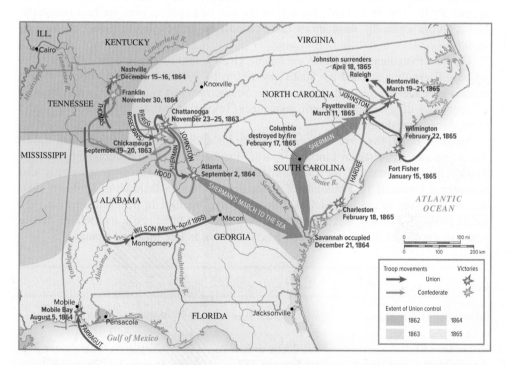

SHERMAN'S MARCH TO THE SEA, 1864-1865 While Grant was wearing down Lee in Virginia, General William Tecumseh Sherman was moving east across Georgia. After a series of battles in Tennessee and northwest Georgia, Sherman captured Atlanta and then marched unimpeded to Savannah, on the Georgia coast—deliberately devastating the towns and plantations through which his troops marched. Note that after capturing Savannah by Christmas 1864, Sherman began moving north through the Carolinas. A few days after Lee surrendered to Grant at Appomattox, Confederate forces farther south surrendered to Sherman. • *What did Sherman believe his devastating March to the Sea would accomplish?*

the North during the Civil War spread to the South, or would the South remain an agrarian region with much less wealth than in the North? The end of the war was the beginning of more than a generation of struggle to determine the legacy of the Civil War.

CONCLUSION

The American Civil War began with high hopes and high ideals on both sides. In the North and the South alike, thousands of men enthusiastically enlisted in local regiments and went off to war. Four years later, over 600,000 of them were dead and many more maimed and traumatized for life. A fight for "principles" and "ideals"—a fight few people had thought would last more than a few months—had become one of the longest wars, and by far the bloodiest war, in American history, before or since.

During the first two years of fighting, the Confederate forces seemed to have all the advantages. They were fighting on their own soil. Their troops seemed more committed to the cause than those of the North. Their commanders were exceptionally talented, while Union forces were, for a time, erratically led. Gradually, however, the Union's advantages began to assert themselves. The North had a stabler political system led by one of the greatest leaders in the nation's history. It had a much larger population, a far more developed industrial economy, superior financial institutions, and a better railroad system. By the middle of 1863, the tide of the war had shifted; over the next two years, Union forces gradually wore down the Confederate armies before finally triumphing in 1865.

The war strengthened the North's economy, giving a spur to industry and railroad development. It greatly weakened the South's by destroying millions of dollars of property and depleting the region's young male population. Southerners had gone to war in part because of their fears of growing Northern dominance. Ironically, the war itself confirmed and strengthened that dominance.

But most of all, the Civil War was a victory for millions of African American slaves. The war produced Abraham Lincoln's epochal Emancipation Proclamation and, later, the Thirteenth Amendment to the Constitution, which abolished slavery altogether. It also encouraged hundreds of thousands of slaves literally to free themselves, to desert their masters and seek refuge behind Union lines—at times to fight in the Union armies. The future of the freed slaves was not to be an easy one, but three and a half million people who had once lived in bondage emerged from the war as free men and women.

KEY TERMS/PEOPLE/PLACES/EVENTS

Alexander H. Stephens 331

Antietam 342

Appomattox Court House 349

Confederate States of America 322

Confiscation Acts 329

conscription 327

Emancipation Proclamation 329

First Battle of Bull Run 339

Fort Sumter 322

George B. McClellan 328

Gettysburg 345

greenbacks 327

Homestead Act 326

Jefferson Davis 331

Robert E. Lee 335

Shiloh 340

Thirteenth Amendment 330

Thomas J. ("Stonewall") Jackson 341

Ulysses S. Grant 335

United States Sanitary Commission 331

William T. Sherman 346

RECALL AND REFLECT

1. Assess the advantages of the North and those of the South at the beginning of the Civil War. How did the advantages of each side change over the course of the war?
2. How did the Confederate government differ from the federal government of the United States?
3. How did the war affect the lives of women in the North and in the South?
4. Compare Lincoln and Davis as heads of government and commanders in chief.
5. Why did Lincoln issue the Emancipation Proclamation, and what were its effects?

15 | RECONSTRUCTION AND THE NEW SOUTH

THE PROBLEMS OF PEACEMAKING
RADICAL RECONSTRUCTION
THE SOUTH IN RECONSTRUCTION
THE GRANT ADMINISTRATION
THE ABANDONMENT OF RECONSTRUCTION
THE NEW SOUTH

LOOKING AHEAD

1. What were the various plans for Reconstruction proposed by Lincoln, Johnson, and Congress? Which plan was enacted and why?
2. What were the effects of Reconstruction for blacks and whites in the South?
3. What were the political achievements and failures of the Grant administration?

FEW PERIODS IN THE HISTORY of the United States have produced as much bitterness or created such enduring controversy as the era of Reconstruction—the years following the Civil War during which Americans attempted to reunite their shattered nation. To many white Southerners, Reconstruction was a vicious and destructive experience—a period when vindictive Northerners inflicted humiliation and revenge on the defeated South. Northern defenders of Reconstruction, in contrast, argued that their policies were the only way to prevent unrepentant Confederates from restoring Southern society to what it had been before the war.

To most African Americans at the time, and to many people of all races since, Reconstruction was notable for other reasons. Neither a vicious tyranny, as white Southerners charged, nor a thoroughgoing reform, as many Northerners hoped, it was instead an important first step in the effort to secure civil rights and economic power for the former slaves. Reconstruction did not provide African Americans with either the enduring legal protections or the material resources to ensure anything like real equality. Most black men and women still had little formal power to overturn their oppression for many decades.

And yet for all its shortcomings, Reconstruction did help African Americans create new institutions and some important legal precedents that helped them survive and that ultimately, well into the twentieth century, became the basis of later efforts to win greater freedom and equality.

THE PROBLEMS OF PEACEMAKING

Although it was clear in 1865 that the war was almost over, the path to actual peace was not yet clear. Abraham Lincoln could not negotiate a treaty with the defeated government; he continued to insist that the Confederacy had no legal right to exist. Yet neither could he simply readmit the Southern states into the Union.

THE AFTERMATH OF WAR AND EMANCIPATION

The South after the Civil War was a desolate place. Towns had been gutted, plantations burned, fields neglected, bridges and railroads destroyed. Many white Southerners—stripped of their slaves through emancipation and of capital invested in now worthless Confederate bonds and currency—had almost no personal property. More than 258,000 Confederate soldiers had died in the war, and thousands more returned home wounded or sick. Some white Southerners faced starvation and homelessness.

If the physical conditions were bad for Southern whites, they were far worse for Southern blacks—the 3.5 million men and women now emerging from bondage. As soon as the war ended, hundreds of thousands of them left their plantations in search of a new life in freedom. But most had nowhere to go, and few had any possessions except the clothes they wore.

COMPETING NOTIONS OF FREEDOM

For blacks and whites alike, Reconstruction became a struggle to define the meaning of the war and, above all, the meaning of freedom. But the former slaves and the defeated whites had very different conceptions of what freedom meant.

For most white Southerners, freedom meant the ability to control their own

TIME LINE

1863
Lincoln announces Reconstruction plan

1864
Lincoln vetoes Wade-Davis Bill

1865
Confederacy surrenders

Lincoln assassinated; Johnson is president

Freedmen's Bureau

Joint Committee on Reconstruction

1866
Republicans gain in congressional elections

1867
Congressional Reconstruction begins

1868
Johnson impeached and acquitted

14th Amendment ratified

Grant elected president

1869
Congress passes 15th Amendment

1872
Grant reelected

1873
Panic and depression

1877
Hayes wins disputed election

Compromise of 1877 ends Reconstruction

1883
Supreme Court upholds segregation

1890s
Jim Crow laws in South

1895
Atlanta Compromise

1896
Plessy v. Ferguson

(Source: Library of Congress, Prints and Photographs Division [LC-USZC4-4593])

RICHMOND, 1865 By the time Union forces captured Richmond in early 1865, the Confederate capital had been under siege for months and much of the city lay in ruins, as this photograph reveals. On April 4, President Lincoln, accompanied by his son Tad, visited Richmond. As he walked through the streets of the shattered city, hundreds of former slaves emerged from the rubble to watch him pass. "No triumphal march of a conqueror could have equalled in moral sublimity the humble manner in which he entered Richmond," a black soldier serving with the Union army wrote. "It was a great deliverer among the delivered. No wonder tears came to his eyes."

destinies without interference from the North or the federal government. And in the immediate aftermath of the war, this meant trying to restore their society to its antebellum form. When these white Southerners fought for what they considered freedom, they were fighting above all to preserve local and regional autonomy and white supremacy.

For African Americans, freedom meant independence from white control. In the wake of advancing Union armies, millions of black Southerners sought to secure that freedom with economic opportunity, which for many meant landownership. An African American man in Charleston told a Northern reporter, "Gib us our own land and we take care ourselves."[1] For a short while during the war, Union generals and federal officials cooperated, awarding confiscated land to the former slaves who had worked it.

In November 1862, when Union forces occupied the Sea Islands of South Carolina and their main harbor, Port Royal, the islands' white property owners fled to the mainland. Ten thousand former slaves seized control of the vacated land, marking the beginning of the "Port Royal Experiment" in which formerly enslaved blacks were permitted to farm and raise crops for sale. Some saved enough money to purchase the land they worked from the federal government, totaling about 33,000 acres. Union officials and Northern missionaries recruited teachers, nurses, and doctors to build schools and hospitals for the newly freed people of the Sea Islands. Later in the war saw a broader redistribution of land. At the urging of black leaders, General William Sherman issued Special Field Order No. 15 on January 16, 1865; the order granted former Confederate land in coastal Georgia and South Carolina (including the Sea Islands) to the region's ex-slaves. Within five months, nearly 400,000 acres had been distributed to newly freed people, most of it in 40-acre plots.

In the war's immediate aftermath, the federal government attempted to help ex-slaves forge independent lives by establishing the Bureau of Refugees, Freedmen, and Abandoned Lands, which Congress authorized in March 1865. The **Freedmen's Bureau**, as it became known, helped feed, clothe, educate, and provide medical care for ex-slaves. It also settled land disputes and set labor contracts between freedmen and white property owners. Headed by General Oliver O. Howard, the Freedman's Bureau operated on a shoestring budget with fewer than 1,000 agents, some of whom were corrupt, yet it still emerged as a key federal institution shaping black and white life in the South after the war.

The Freedmen's Bureau, for a while at least, also supported the redistribution of land, overseeing the allocation of 850,000 acres of confiscated land to former slaves. General Howard instructed his agents in his famous "Circular 13" to lease the land in 40-acre plots to former slaves with the intention of eventually selling it to them. A small number of freedmen purchased land outright under the Southern Homestead Act of 1866 that Howard had championed; the act made 46 million acres of public land for sale in 160-acre plots in Alabama, Arkansas, Florida, Louisiana, and Mississippi. (The law was repealed before many ex-slaves were able to take advantage of it.) Some of Howard's officials and other army personnel secured mules for freed people as well, fulfilling the common wisdom that 40 acres and a mule were the building block of any stable household. The bureau also settled land disputes and set labor contracts between freedmen and white property owners.

PLANS FOR RECONSTRUCTION

Political control of **Reconstruction** rested in the hands of the Republicans, who were deeply divided in their approach to the issue. There were three major groups of Republicans. Conservatives insisted that the South accept abolition, but they proposed few other conditions for the readmission of the seceded states. The **Radicals**, led by Representative **Thaddeus Stevens** of Pennsylvania and Senator **Charles Sumner** of Massachusetts, urged a much harsher course, including disenfranchising large numbers of Southern whites, protecting black civil rights, confiscating the property of wealthy whites who had aided the Confederacy, and distributing the land among the freedmen. Finally the Moderates rejected the most stringent demands of the Radicals but supported extracting at least some concessions from the South on black rights.

Ultimately two major plans for Reconstruction in the South emerged under President Lincoln. Lincoln himself favored a lenient policy, believing that Southern Unionists (mostly former Whigs) could become the nucleus of new, loyal state governments. He announced his vision in December 1863, more than a year before the war ended. It came to be known as the "Ten Percent Plan" because it declared that any Southern state could be readmitted to the Union once 10 percent of eligible voters—defined as those present on the voter roles of the 1860 election—pledged an oath of loyalty to the government and accepted the abolition of slavery. These loyal voters could then elect representatives to fashion new state constitutions and governments. At the same time, Lincoln offered full amnesty to all Southerners except high-ranking military officers and government leaders of the Confederacy. He also proposed extending suffrage to African Americans who were educated, owned property, or had served in the Union army. Three Southern states—Louisiana, Arkansas, and Tennessee, all under Union occupation—reestablished loyal governments under the Lincoln formula in 1864.

Outraged at the mildness of Lincoln's program, the Radical Republicans refused to admit representatives from the three "reconstructed" states to Congress. In July 1864, they pushed

RECONSTRUCTION

Debate over the nature of Reconstruction has been unusually intense. Indeed, few issues in American history have raised such deep and enduring passions.

Beginning in the late nineteenth century and continuing well into the twentieth, a relatively uniform and highly critical view of Reconstruction prevailed among historians. William A. Dunning's *Reconstruction, Political and Economic* (1907) was the principal scholarly expression of this view. Dunning portrayed Reconstruction as a corrupt and oppressive outrage imposed on a prostrate South by a vindictive group of Northern Republican Radicals. Unscrupulous carpetbaggers flooded the South and plundered the region. Ignorant and unfit African Americans were thrust into political offices. Reconstruction governments were awash in corruption and compiled enormous levels of debt. The Dunning interpretation dominated several generations of historical

scholarship and helped shape such popular images of Reconstruction as those in the novel and film *Gone with the Wind*.

W. E. B. Du Bois, the great African American scholar, offered one of the first alternative views in *Black Reconstruction* (1935). To Du Bois, Reconstruction was an effort by freed blacks (and their white allies) to create a more democratic society in the South, and it was responsible for many valuable social innovations. In the early 1960s, John Hope Franklin and Kenneth Stampp, building on a generation of work by other scholars, published new histories of Reconstruction that also radically revised the Dunning interpretation. Reconstruction, they argued, was a genuine, if inadequate, effort to solve the problem of race in the South. Congressional Radicals were not saints, but they were genuinely concerned with protecting the rights of former slaves. Reconstruction had brought important, if temporary, progress to the

(©Corbis)

A FREEDMEN'S BUREAU SCHOOL African American students and teachers stand outside a school for former slaves, one of many run by the Freedmen's Bureau throughout the defeated Confederacy in the first years after the war.

South and had created no more corruption there than was evident in the North at the same time. What was tragic about Reconstruction, the revisionists claimed, was not what it did to Southern whites but what it failed to do for Southern blacks. It was, in the end, too weak and too short-lived to guarantee African Americans genuine equality.

In more recent years, some historians have begun to question the assessment of the first revisionists that, in the end, Reconstruction accomplished relatively little. Leon Litwack argued in *Been in the Storm So Long* (1979) that former slaves used the protections Reconstruction offered them to carve out a certain level of independence for themselves within Southern society: strengthening churches, reuniting families, and resisting the efforts of white planters to revive the gang labor system.

Eric Foner's *Reconstruction: America's Unfinished Revolution* (1988) and *Forever Free* (2005) also emphasized how far African Americans moved toward freedom and independence in a short time and how important they were in shaping the execution of Reconstruction policies. Reconstruction, he argues, "can only be judged a failure" as an effort to secure "blacks' rights as citizens and free laborers." But it "closed off even more oppressive alternatives. . . . The post-Reconstruction labor system embodied neither a return to the closely supervised gang labor of antebellum days, nor the complete dispossession and immobilization of the black labor force and coercive apprenticeship systems envisioned by white Southerners in 1865 and 1866. . . . The doors of economic opportunity that had opened could never be completely closed." •

UNDERSTAND, ANALYZE, & EVALUATE

1. What are the popular interpretations of Reconstruction today? Do romanticized ideals of a benighted Old South, as seen in *Gone with the Wind*, still persist?

2. A new view of Reconstruction began to emerge in the 1960s, the end of the civil rights movement. Why do you think the civil rights movement might have encouraged historians and others to reexamine Reconstruction?

their own plan through Congress: the **Wade-Davis Bill**. Named for Senator Benjamin Wade of Ohio and Representative Henry Davis of Maryland, it called for the president to appoint a provisional governor for each conquered state. In contrast to Lincoln's Ten Percent Plan, the Wade-Davis Bill specified that only when 50 percent of eligible voters in a state declared loyalty to the Union could the process of readmission begin. At that point the provisional governor could summon a state constitutional convention, whose delegates were to be elected by voters who had never borne arms against the United States. The new state constitutions would be required to abolish slavery, disenfranchise Confederate civil and military leaders, and repudiate debts accumulated by the state governments during the war. Only then would Congress formally readmit the states to the Union. Like the president's proposal, the Wade-Davis Bill left the question of political rights for blacks up to the states.

Congress passed the bill a few days before it adjourned in 1864, but Lincoln disposed of it with a pocket veto, meaning that he killed the bill by refusing to sign it—keeping it "in his pocket" until it was too late for Congress to act on it during the legislative session. Predictively, Lincoln's pocket veto enraged Radical leaders and set up a showdown with the president over the future of Reconstruction policy. The debate between Congress and Lincoln over the proper course of Reconstruction and its purpose and objectives was one that scholars would soon pick up. Indeed, beginning in the latter stages of Reconstruction, historians struggled to make sense of its meaning to America. They continue to do so today. (See "Debating the Past: Reconstruction.")

THE DEATH OF LINCOLN

What plan the president might have produced no one can say. On the night of April 14, 1865, Lincoln and his wife attended a play at Ford's Theater in Washington. John Wilkes Booth, an actor fervently committed to the Southern cause, entered the presidential box from the rear and shot Lincoln in the head. Early the next morning, the president died.

The circumstances of Lincoln's death earned him immediate martyrdom. They also produced something close to hysteria throughout the North, especially because it quickly became clear that Booth had been the leader of a conspiracy. One of his associates shot and wounded Secretary of State **William H. Seward** on the night of the assassination, and another abandoned at the last moment a plan to murder Vice President Andrew Johnson. Booth himself escaped on horseback into the Maryland countryside, where, on April 26, he was cornered by Union troops and shot to death in a blazing barn. Eight other people were convicted by a military tribunal of participating in the conspiracy. Four were hanged.

To many Northerners, however, the murder of the president seemed evidence of an even darker conspiracy—one masterminded and directed by the unrepentant leaders of the defeated South to challenge the very authority of the nation's elected officials. Militant Republicans exploited such suspicions relentlessly in the ensuing months.

(Source: Library of Congress, Prints and Photographs Division [LC-USZ62-12380])

ABRAHAM LINCOLN   This haunting photograph of Abraham Lincoln, showing clearly the weariness and aging that four years as a war president had created, was taken in Washington only four days before his assassination in 1865.

JOHNSON AND "RESTORATION"

Leadership of the Moderates and Conservatives fell immediately to Lincoln's successor, **Andrew Johnson** of Tennessee. A Democrat until he had joined the Union ticket in 1864, he became president at a time of growing partisan passions.

Johnson revealed his plan for Reconstruction—or "Restoration," as he preferred to call it—soon after he took office and implemented it during the summer of 1865 when Congress was in recess. Like Lincoln, he offered some form of amnesty to Southerners who would take an oath of allegiance. In most other respects, however, his plan resembled the Wade-Davis Bill. The new president appointed a provisional governor in each state and charged him with inviting qualified voters to elect delegates to a constitutional convention. To win readmission to Congress, a state had to revoke its ordinance of secession, abolish slavery and ratify the Thirteenth Amendment, and repudiate Confederate and state war debts.

By the end of 1865, all the seceded states had formed new governments—some under Lincoln's plan, others under Johnson's—and awaited congressional approval of them. But Radicals in Congress vowed not to recognize the Johnson governments, for, by now, Northern opinion had become more hostile toward the South. Delegates to the Southern conventions had angered much of the North by their apparent reluctance to abolish slavery and by their refusal to grant suffrage to any blacks. Southern states had also seemed to defy the North by electing prominent Confederate leaders to represent them in Congress, such as Alexander Stephens of Georgia, the former vice president of the Confederacy.

RADICAL RECONSTRUCTION

Reconstruction under Johnson's plan—often known as "presidential Reconstruction"—continued only until Congress reconvened in December 1865. At that point, Congress refused to seat the representatives of the "restored" states and created a new Joint Committee on Reconstruction to frame a policy of its own. The period of "congressional," or "Radical," Reconstruction had begun.

THE BLACK CODES

Meanwhile, events in the South were driving Northern opinion in still more radical directions. Throughout the South in 1865 and early 1866, state legislatures enacted sets of laws known as the **Black Codes**, which authorized local officials to apprehend unemployed blacks, fine them for vagrancy, and hire them out to private employers to satisfy the fines. Some codes forbade blacks to own or lease farms or to take any jobs other than as plantation workers or domestic servants, jobs formerly held by slaves. Former slaves raised an alarm immediately and called for swift intervention by the federal troops and for new legislation to protect them. (See "Consider the Source: Southern Blacks Ask for Help.")

Congress first responded to the Black Codes by passing an act extending the life and expanding the powers of the Freedmen's Bureau so that it could nullify work agreements forced on freedmen under the Black Codes. Then, in April 1866, Congress passed the first Civil Rights Act, which declared blacks to be fully fledged citizens of the United States and gave the federal government power to intervene in state affairs to protect the rights of citizens. Johnson vetoed both bills, but Congress overrode him on each of them.

SOUTHERN BLACKS ASK FOR HELP (1865)

Even before the war ended, groups of former slaves gathered in conventions to petition the federal government for steady support for black civil rights, including the use of the U.S. Army to subdue unrepentant ex-Confederates. In this example, African Americans from Virginia publicly air their hopes and fears only three months after Appomattox.

We, the undersigned members of a Convention of colored citizens of the State of Virginia, would respectfully represent that, although we have been held as slaves, and denied all recognition as a constituent of your nationality for almost the entire period of the duration of your Government, and that by your *permission* we have been denied either home or country, and deprived of the dearest rights of human nature; yet when you and our immediate oppressors met in deadly conflict upon the field of battle—the one to destroy and the other to save your Government and nationality, we, with scarce an exception, in our inmost souls espoused your cause, and watched, and prayed, and waited, and labored for your success. . . .

When the contest waxed long, and the result hung doubtfully, you appealed to us for help, and how well we answered is written in the rosters of the two hundred thousand colored troops now enrolled in your Service; and as to our undying devotion to your cause, let the uniform acclamation of escaped prisoners, "whenever we saw a black face we felt sure of a friend," answer.

Well, the war is over, the rebellion is "put down," and we are *declared* free! Four fifths of our enemies are paroled or amnestied, and the other fifth are being pardoned, and the President has, in his efforts at the reconstruction of the civil government of the States, late in rebellion, left us entirely at the mercy of these subjugated but unconverted rebels, in *everything* save the privilege of bringing us, our wives and little ones, to the auction block. *We know* these men—know them well—and we assure you that, with the majority of them, loyalty is only "lip deep," and that their professions of loyalty are used as a cover to the cherished design of getting restored to their former relations with the Federal Government, and then, by all sorts of "unfriendly legislation," to render the freedom you have given us more Intolerable than the slavery they intended for us.

We warn you in time that our only safety is in keeping them under Governors of the *military persuasion* until you have so amended the Federal Constitution that it will prohibit the States from making any distinction between citizens on account of race or color. In one word, the only salvation for us besides the power of the Government, is in the *possession of the ballot*. Give us this, and we will protect ourselves. . . . But, 'tis said we are ignorant. Admit it. Yet who denies we *know* a traitor from a loyal man, a gentleman from a rowdy, a friend from an enemy? . . . All we ask is an *equal chance* with the white *traitors* varnished and japanned with the oath of amnesty. Can you deny us this and still keep faith with us? . . .

We are "sheep in the midst of wolves," and nothing but the military arm of the Government prevents us and all the *truly* loyal white men from being driven from the land of our birth. Do not then, we beseech you, give to one of these "wayward sisters" the rights they abandoned and forfeited when they rebelled until you have secured our rights by the aforementioned amendment to the Constitution.

1. What did the authors of this petition emphasize in the first two paragraphs, and why did they feel this was important?
2. Why did the authors emphasize that they had been "declared" free? What dangers to their prospect of freedom did they observe?
3. What federal legal responses did they propose? Can you recognize these suggestions in the constitutional changes that came with Reconstruction?

Source: "Proceedings of the Convention of the Colored People of Virginia, Held in the City of Alexandria, August 2, 3, 4, 5, 1865," Alexandria, Va., 1865, in W. L. Fleming (ed.), *Documentary History of Reconstruction*. Cleveland, Ohio, 1906, vol. 1, 195–196; located in "Southern Blacks Ask for Help (1865)," in Thomas A. Bailey and David M. Kennedy (eds.), *The American Spirit*, vol. 1, 7th ed., Lexington, Mass., 1991, 466–467.

THE FOURTEENTH AMENDMENT

In April 1866, the Joint Committee on Reconstruction proposed the **Fourteenth Amendment** to the Constitution. Without the support of Johnson, Congress approved it in early summer and sent it to the states for ratification. It offered the first constitutional definition of American citizenship. Everyone born in the United States, and everyone naturalized, was automatically a citizen and entitled to all the "privileges and immunities" guaranteed by the Constitution, including equal protection of the laws by both the state and national governments. There could be no other requirements for citizenship. For the first time in the nation's history, race or a prior condition of servitude was discarded as a barrier to full citizenship. The amendment also prohibited former members of Congress or other former federal officials who had aided the Confederacy from holding any state or federal office unless two-thirds of Congress voted to pardon them.

Congressional Radicals offered to readmit to the Union any state whose legislature ratified the Fourteenth Amendment. Only Tennessee did so. All the other former Confederate states, along with Delaware and Kentucky, refused, leaving the amendment temporarily without the necessary approval of three-fourths of the states.

Radicals, however, were undeterred and even began to grow in confidence and determination as they anticipated gaining new levels of support in the upcoming congressional election in the fall. And they were right. Bloody race riots in New Orleans and other Southern cities swiftly drew attention to the need for more vigorous legal and physical protection for African Americans and to the failure of Johnson's policies to restore peace and order. Johnson himself undercut his own popularity and that of his party by delivering intemperate and mean-spirited speeches in which he openly disparaged the Radicals, blamed the recent violence on them, and accused them of treating blacks like pawns. He nearly fell off the stage delivering several speeches, which gave rise to rampant speculation that he was drinking too much. In the 1866 congressional elections, the voters returned an overwhelming majority of Republicans, most of them Radicals, to Congress. In the Senate, there were now 42 Republicans to 11 Democrats; in the House, 143 Republicans to 49 Democrats. Congressional Republicans were now strong enough to enact a plan of their own even over the president's objections.

THE CONGRESSIONAL PLAN

The Radicals passed three Reconstruction bills early in 1867 and overrode Johnson's vetoes of all of them. Nearly two years after the end of the war, these bills finally established a coherent plan for Reconstruction.

Under the congressional plan, Tennessee, which had ratified the Fourteenth Amendment granting the franchise to all male citizens over twenty-one, was promptly readmitted. But Congress rejected the Lincoln–Johnson governments of the other ten Confederate states and, instead, combined those states into five military districts. A military commander governed each district and had orders to register qualified voters (defined as all adult black males and those white males who had not participated in the war). Once registered, voters would elect conventions to prepare new state constitutions, which had to include provisions for black suffrage. And once voters ratified the new constitutions, they could elect state governments. Congress had to approve a state's constitution, and the state legislature itself had to ratify the Fourteenth Amendment. Once enough states ratified the amendment to make it part of the Constitution, the former Confederate states could be restored to the Union.

By 1868, seven of the ten remaining former Confederate states had fulfilled these conditions and were readmitted to the Union. Conservative whites held up the return of Virginia and Texas until 1869 and Mississippi until 1870. By then, Congress had added an additional requirement for readmission—ratification of the **Fifteenth Amendment**, which forbade the states and the federal government to deny suffrage on account of "race, color, or previous condition of servitude." This opened the ballot box of all male citizens regardless of color, but kept it shut to all women. Ratification by the states was completed in 1870.

To stop Johnson from interfering with their plans, the congressional Radicals passed two remarkable laws of dubious constitutionality in 1867. One, the Tenure of Office Act, forbade the president to remove civil officials, including members of his own cabinet, without the consent of the Senate. The principal purpose of the law was to protect the job of Secretary of War Edwin M. Stanton, who was cooperating with the Radicals. The other

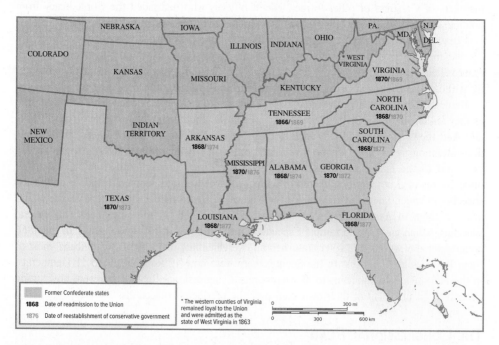

RECONSTRUCTION, 1866–1877 This map provides the date when each former Confederate state was read-mitted by presidential order to the Union, as well as the date when a traditional white conservative elite took office as a majority in each state—an event white Southerners liked to call "redemption." • *What had to happen for a state to be readmitted to the Union? What had to happen before a state could experience "redemption"?*

law, the Command of the Army Act, prohibited the president from issuing military orders except through the commanding general of the army (General Grant), who could not be relieved or assigned elsewhere without the consent of the Senate.

The congressional Radicals also took action to stop the Supreme Court from interfering with their plans. In 1866, the Court had declared in the case of *Ex parte Milligan* that military tribunals were unconstitutional in places where civil courts were functioning. Radicals in Congress immediately proposed several bills that would require two-thirds of the justices to support any decision overruling a law of Congress, would deny the Court jurisdiction in Reconstruction cases, would reduce its membership to three, and would even abolish it. The justices apparently took notice. Over the next two years, the Court refused to accept jurisdiction in any cases involving Reconstruction.

THE IMPEACHMENT OF ANDREW JOHNSON

President Johnson had long since ceased to be a serious obstacle to the passage of Radical legislation, but he was still the official charged with administering the Reconstruction programs. As such, the Radicals believed, he remained a major impediment to their plans. Early in 1867, they began looking for reasons to begin formal efforts that would result in his **impeachment**. Republicans found it, they believed, when Johnson dismissed Secretary of War Stanton despite Congress's refusal to agree. Elated Radicals in the House quickly impeached the president for violating the recently passed Tenure of Office Act and sent the case to the Senate for trial.

The trial lasted throughout April and May 1868 but things eventually broke Johnson's way. The Radicals put heavy pressure on all the Republican senators, but the Moderates vacillated. On the first three charges to come to a vote, seven Republicans joined the Democrats and independents to support acquittal. The Senate vote was 35 to 19, one vote short of the constitutionally required two-thirds majority needed to remove Johnson from office. After that, the Radicals dropped the impeachment effort.

THE SOUTH IN RECONSTRUCTION

Reconstruction may not have immediately accomplished what its framers intended, but it did have profound effects on the South.

THE RECONSTRUCTION GOVERNMENTS

Critics branded Southern white Republicans with the derogatory terms **scalawags** and **carpetbaggers**. Scalawags, the slang term for "scoundrels," were former Whigs who had never felt comfortable in the Democratic Party or farmers who lived in remote areas where there had been little or no slavery. Carpetbaggers were white men originally from the North, most of them veterans of the Union army, who looked on the South as a more promising frontier than the West and had traveled there at war's end as hopeful planters, businessmen, or professionals. The term refers to their use of a cheap travel bag made from carpeting material.

The most numerous Republicans in the South were the black freedmen, few of whom had any previous experience in politics. They tried to build institutions through which they could learn to exercise their power. In several states, African American voters held their own conventions to chart their future course. Their newfound religious independence from white churches also helped give them unity and self-confidence.

THE "STRONG" GOVERNMENT 1869—1877.

(Source: Library of Congress, Prints and Photographs Division [LC-DIG-ppmsca-15783])

CRITICS' VIEW OF RECONSTRUCTION   This Reconstruction-era cartoon expresses the view held by Southern white Democrats that they were being oppressed by Northern Republicans. President Grant (whose hat bears Abraham Lincoln's initials) rides in comfort in a giant carpetbag, guarded by bayonet-wielding soldiers, as the South staggers under the burden in chains. Evidence of military occupation is in the scarred background.

African Americans played significant roles in the politics of the Reconstruction South. They served as delegates to the constitutional conventions and held public offices of practically every kind. Between 1869 and 1901, twenty blacks served in the U.S. House of Representatives, two in the Senate. Blacks served, too, in state legislatures and in various other state offices. Southern whites complained loudly about "Negro rule," but in the South as a whole, the percentage of black officeholders was small—and always far lower than the percentage of blacks in the population.

The record of the Reconstruction governments is mixed. Critics at the time and later denounced them for corruption and financial extravagance, and there is some truth to both charges. But the corruption in the South, real as it was, was hardly unique to the Reconstruction governments. Corruption had been rife in some antebellum and Confederate governments, and it was at least as rampant in the Northern states. And the large state expenditures of the Reconstruction years were huge only in comparison with the meager budgets of the antebellum era. They represented an effort to provide the South with desperately needed services that antebellum governments had never provided.

EDUCATION

Perhaps the most important accomplishment of the Reconstruction governments was a dramatic improvement in Southern education. Much of the impetus for educational reform in the South came from outside groups—the Freedmen's Bureau, Northern private philanthropic organizations, the many Northern white women who traveled to the South to teach in freedmen's schools—and from African Americans themselves. Over the opposition of many Southern whites, who feared that education would give blacks "false notions of equality," these reformers established a large network of schools for former slaves—4,000 schools by 1870, staffed by 9,000 teachers (half of them black), teaching 200,000 students. In the 1870s, Reconstruction governments began to build a comprehensive public school system. By 1876, more than half of all white children and about 40 percent of all black children were attending schools in the South (although almost all such schools were racially segregated). Several black "academies," offering more advanced education, also began operating. Gradually, these academies grew into an important network of black colleges and universities.

LANDOWNERSHIP AND TENANCY

The most ambitious goal of the Freedmen's Bureau, and of some Republican Radicals in Congress, was to reform landownership in the South. The effort failed. By June 1865, the bureau had settled nearly 10,000 black families on their own land—most of it drawn from abandoned plantations in areas occupied by the Union armies. By the end of that year, however, Southern plantation owners were returning and demanding the restoration of their property. President Johnson supported their demands, and the government eventually returned most of the confiscated lands to their original white owners.

Even so, the distribution of landownership in the South changed considerably in the postwar years. Among whites, there was a striking decline in landownership, from 80 percent before the war to 67 percent by the end of Reconstruction. Some whites lost their land because of unpaid debt or increased taxes; others left the marginal lands they had owned to move to more fertile areas, where they rented. Among blacks, during the same period, the proportion of landowners rose from virtually none to more than 20 percent.

Still, most blacks, and a growing minority of whites, did not own their own land during Reconstruction and, instead, worked for others in one form or another. Many black agricultural laborers—perhaps 25 percent of the total—simply worked for wages. Most, however, became tenants of white landowners—that is, they worked their own plots of land and paid their landlords either a fixed rent or a share of their crops (hence the term **sharecropping**). As tenants and sharecroppers, blacks enjoyed at least a physical independence from their landlords and had the sense of working their own land, even if in most cases they could never hope to buy it. But tenantry also benefited landlords in some ways, relieving them of the cost of purchasing slaves and of responsibility for the physical well-being of their workers.

INCOMES AND CREDIT

In some respects, the postwar years were a period of remarkable economic progress for African Americans in the South. The per capita income of blacks (when the material benefits of slavery are counted as income) rose 46 percent between 1857 and 1879, while the per capita income of whites declined 35 percent. African Americans were also able to work less than they had under slavery. Women and children were less likely to labor in the fields, and adult men tended to work shorter days. In all, the black labor force worked about one-third fewer hours during Reconstruction than it had been compelled to work under slavery—a reduction that brought the working schedule of blacks roughly into accord with that of white farm laborers.

But other developments limited these gains. While the black share of profits was increasing, the total profits of Southern agriculture were declining. Nor did the income redistribution of the postwar years lift many blacks out of poverty. Black per capita income rose from about one-quarter of white per capita income (which was itself low) to about one-half in the first few years after the war. After this initial increase, however, it rose hardly at all.

Blacks and poor whites alike found themselves virtually imprisoned by the **crop-lien system.** Few of the traditional institutions of credit in the South—the "factors" and banks—returned after the war. In their stead emerged a new credit system, centered in large part on local country stores—some of them owned by planters, others owned by independent merchants. Blacks and whites, landowners and tenants—all depended on these stores. And since most who made their livelihood from the land did not have the same steady cash flow as other workers, they usually had to rely on credit from these merchants to purchase what they needed. Most local stores had no competition and thus could set interest rates as high as 50 or 60 percent. Poor farmers had to give the merchants a lien (or claim) on their crops as collateral for the loans (thus the term *crop-lien*). Those who suffered a few bad years in a row, as many did, could become trapped in a cycle of debt from which they could never escape.

As a result of this burdensome credit system, some blacks who had acquired land during the early years of Reconstruction, and many poor whites who had owned land for years, gradually lost it as they fell into debt. Southern farmers also became almost wholly dependent on cash crops—and most of all on cotton—because only such marketable commodities seemed to offer any possibility of escape from debt. The relentless planting of cotton ultimately contributed to soil exhaustion, which undermined the Southern agricultural economy over time.

THE AFRICAN AMERICAN FAMILY IN FREEDOM

A major reason for the rapid departure of so many blacks from plantations was the desire to find lost relatives and reunite families. Thousands of African Americans wandered through the South looking for husbands, wives, children, or other relatives from whom they had been separated. Former slaves rushed to have their marriages, previously without legal standing, sanctified by church and law.

Within the black family, the definition of male and female roles quickly came to resemble that within white families. Many women and children at first ceased working in the fields. Such work, they believed, was a badge of slavery. Instead, many women restricted themselves largely to domestic tasks. Still, economic necessity often compelled black women to engage in income-producing activities: working as domestic servants, taking in laundry, even helping their husbands in the fields. By the end of Reconstruction, half of all black women over the age of sixteen were working for wages.

(Source: Library of Congress, Prints and Photographs Division [LC-USZC4-5759])

LABORING OVER LAUNDRY   One of the most common occupations of women recently emancipated from slavery was taking in laundry from white families who no longer had enslaved servants. This photograph illustrates how arduous a task laundry was.

THE GRANT ADMINISTRATION

American voters in 1868 yearned for a strong, stable figure to guide them through the troubled years of Reconstruction. They turned trustingly to General **Ulysses S. Grant**.

THE SOLDIER PRESIDENT

Grant could have had the nomination of either party in 1868. But believing that Republican Reconstruction policies were more popular in the North, he accepted the Republican nomination. The Democrats nominated former governor Horatio Seymour of New York. The campaign was a bitter one, and Grant's triumph was surprisingly narrow. Indeed, without the 500,000 new black Republican voters in the South, he would have had a minority of the popular vote.

Grant entered the White House with no formal political experience, relying instead on his slow but steady rise through the ranks of the army and his recent years as a general. The new president did not pick the best advisers, surrounding himself with wealthy friends intent on protecting their interests and appointing ineffective cabinet members, with the exception of secretary of state Hamilton Fish. Grant also relied heavily on established party leaders—the group most ardently devoted to patronage, and his administration used the spoils system even more blatantly than most of its predecessors. It was a choice of counsel that would eventually come back to haunt him.

Although his selection of colleagues was suspect, Grant steadily supported the citizenship of former slaves and the policies of Radical Reconstruction even as such a position increasingly posed political risk. Refusing to compromise much on matters of racial politics, he alienated the many Northerners who were growing disillusioned with the prolonged federal presence in the South and effort to protect and extend democracy to black Americans.

By the end of Grant's first term, therefore, members of a substantial faction of the party—who referred to themselves as Liberal Republicans—had come to oppose what they derisively called "Grantism." Some Republicans suspected, correctly as it turned out, that there was corruption in the Grant administration itself. In 1872, hoping to prevent Grant's reelection, they bolted the party and nominated their own presidential candidate: Horace Greeley, veteran editor and publisher of the *New York Tribune*. The Democrats, somewhat reluctantly, named Greeley their candidate as well, hoping that the alliance with the Liberals would enable them to defeat Grant. But the effort was in vain. Grant won a substantial victory, polling 286 electoral votes to Greeley's 66.

THE GRANT SCANDALS

During the 1872 campaign, the first of a series of political scandals came to light that would plague Grant and the Republicans for the next four years. It involved the French-owned Crédit Mobilier construction company, which had helped build the Union Pacific Railroad. The heads of Crédit Mobilier had used their positions as Union Pacific stockholders to steer large fraudulent contracts to their construction company, thus bilking the Union Pacific of millions. To prevent investigations, the directors had given Crédit Mobilier stock to key members of Congress. But in 1872, Congress conducted an investigation that revealed that some highly placed Republicans—including Schuyler Colfax, now Grant's vice president—had accepted stock.

One dreary episode of malfeasance followed another in Grant's second term. Benjamin H. Bristow, Grant's third Treasury secretary, discovered that some of his officials and a group of distillers operating as a "whiskey ring" were cheating the government out of taxes by filing false reports. Then a House investigation revealed that William W. Belknap, secretary of war, had accepted bribes to retain an Indian-post trader in office (the so-called Indian ring). Other, lesser scandals also added to the growing impression that "Grantism" had brought rampant corruption to government.

THE GREENBACK QUESTION

Compounding Grant's problems was a financial crisis, known as the Panic of 1873. It began with the failure of a leading investment banking firm, Jay Cooke and Company, which had invested too heavily in postwar railroad building. There had been panics before—in 1819, 1837, and 1857—but this was the worst one yet.

Debtors now pressured the government to redeem federal war bonds with greenbacks, which would increase the amount of money in circulation. But Grant and most Republicans wanted a "sound" currency—based solidly on gold reserves—that would favor the interests of banks and other creditors. There was approximately $356 million in paper currency issued during the Civil War that was still in circulation. In 1873, the Treasury issued more in response to the panic. But in 1875, Republican leaders in Congress passed the Specie Resumption Act, which provided that after January 1, 1879, greenback dollars would be redeemed by the government and replaced with new certificates, firmly pegged to the price of gold. The law satisfied creditors, who had worried that debts would be repaid in paper currency of uncertain value. But "resumption" made things more difficult for debtors because the gold-based money supply could not easily expand.

In 1875, the "Greenbackers" formed their own political organization: the National Greenback Party. It failed to gain widespread support, but the money issue was to remain one of the most controversial and enduring issues in late-nineteenth-century American politics.

REPUBLICAN DIPLOMACY

The Johnson and Grant administrations achieved their greatest successes in foreign affairs as a result of the work not of the presidents themselves but of two outstanding secretaries of state: William H. Seward and Hamilton Fish.

An ardent expansionist, Seward acted with as much daring as the demands of Reconstruction politics and the Republican hatred of President Johnson would permit. He accepted a Russian offer to buy Alaska for $7.2 million, despite criticism from many who derided the purchase as "Seward's Folly." In 1867, Seward also engineered the American annexation of the tiny Midway Islands, west of Hawaii.

Hamilton Fish's first major challenge was resolving the long-standing controversy over the American claims that Britain had violated neutrality laws during the Civil War by permitting English shipyards to build ships (among them the *Alabama*) for the Confederacy. American demands that England pay for the damage these vessels had caused became known as the "*Alabama* claims." In 1871, after a number of failed efforts, Fish forged an agreement, the Treaty of Washington, that provided for international arbitration.

THE ABANDONMENT OF RECONSTRUCTION

As the North grew increasingly preoccupied with its own political and economic problems, interest in Reconstruction began to wane. By the time Grant left office, Democrats had taken back seven of the governments of the former Confederate states. For three other states—South Carolina, Louisiana, and Florida—the end of Reconstruction had to wait for the withdrawal of the last federal troops in 1877.

THE SOUTHERN STATES "REDEEMED"

In the states where whites constituted a majority—the states of the upper South—overthrowing Republican control was relatively simple. By 1872, all but a handful of Southern whites had regained suffrage. Now a clear majority, they needed only to organize and elect their candidates.

In other states, where blacks were a majority or where the populations of the two races were almost equal, whites used outright intimidation and violence to undermine the Reconstruction regimes. Secret societies—the **Ku Klux Klan**, the Knights of the White Camellia, and others—used terrorism to frighten or physically bar blacks from voting. Paramilitary organizations—the Red Shirts and White Leagues—armed themselves to "police" elections and worked to force all white males to join the Democratic Party. Strongest of all, however, was the weapon of economic pressure. Some planters simply refused to rent land to Republican blacks; storekeepers refused to extend them credit; and employers refused to give them work or, when they did, pay them fairly.

The Republican Congress responded to this wave of repression with the **Enforcement Acts** of 1870 and 1871 (better known as the Ku Klux Klan Acts), which prohibited states from discriminating against voters on the basis of race and gave the national government the authority to prosecute crimes by individuals under federal law. The laws also authorized the president to use federal troops to protect civil rights—a provision President Grant used in 1871 in nine counties of South Carolina. The Enforcement Acts, although seldom enforced, discouraged Klan violence, which declined by 1872.

Waning Northern Commitment

But this Northern commitment to civil rights did not last long. After the adoption of the Fifteenth Amendment in 1870, some reformers convinced themselves that their long campaign on behalf of black people was now over, that with the vote blacks ought to be able to take care of themselves. Former Radical leaders such as Charles Sumner and Horace Greeley now began calling themselves Liberals, cooperating with the Democrats, and even denouncing what they viewed as black-and-carpetbag misgovernment. Within the South itself, many white Republicans now moved into the Democratic Party as voters threw out Republican politicians whom they blamed for the financial crisis.

The Panic of 1873 further undermined support for Reconstruction. In the congressional elections of 1874, the Democrats won control of the House of Representatives for the first time since 1861. To appeal to Southern white voters, Grant even reduced the use of military force to prop up the Republican regimes in the South.

The Compromise of 1877

Grant had hoped to run for another term in 1876, but most Republican leaders—shaken by recent Democratic successes and scandals by the White House—resisted. Instead, they settled on Rutherford B. Hayes, three-time governor of Ohio and a champion of civil service reform. The Democrats united behind Samuel J. Tilden, the reform governor of New York, who had been instrumental in overthrowing the corrupt Tweed Ring of New York City's Tammany Hall.

Although the campaign was a bitter one, few differences of principle distinguished the candidates from one another. The election produced an apparent Democratic victory. Tilden carried the South and several large Northern states, and his popular margin over Hayes was nearly 300,000 votes. But disputed returns from Louisiana, South Carolina, Florida, and Oregon, whose electoral votes totaled 20, threw the election in doubt. Hayes could still win if he managed to receive all 20 disputed votes.

The Constitution had established no method to determine the validity of disputed returns. The decision clearly lay with Congress, but it was not obvious with which house or through what method. (The Senate was Republican, and the House was Democratic.) Members of each party naturally supported a solution that would yield them the victory. Finally, late in January 1877, Congress tried to break the deadlock by creating a special electoral commission composed of five senators, five representatives, and five justices of the Supreme Court. The congressional delegation consisted of five Republicans and five Democrats. The Court delegation would include two Republicans, two Democrats, and the only independent, Justice David Davis. But when the Illinois legislature elected Davis to the U.S. Senate, the justice resigned from the commission. His seat went instead to a Republican justice. The commission voted along straight party lines, 8 to 7, awarding every disputed vote to Hayes.

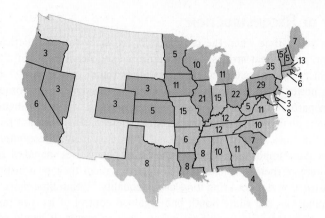

	Candidate (Party)	Electoral Vote	Popular Vote (%)
	Rutherford B. Hayes (Republican)	185	4,036,298 (48)
	Samuel J. Tilden (Democratic)	184	4,300,590 (51)

81.8% of electorate voting

THE ELECTION OF 1876 The election of 1876 was one of the most controversial in American history. As in the elections of 1824, 1888, 2000, and 2016, the winner of the popular vote—Samuel J. Tilden—was not the winner of the electoral vote, which he lost by one vote. The final decision as to who would be president was not made until the day before the official inauguration in March. • *How did the Republicans turn this apparent defeat into a victory?*

Behind this seemingly partisan victory, however, lay a series of elaborate and sneaky compromises among leaders of both parties. When a Democratic filibuster threatened to derail the electoral commission's report, Republican Senate leaders met secretly with Southern Democratic leaders. As the price of their cooperation, the Southern Democrats exacted several pledges from the Republicans, which became known as the **Compromise of 1877**: the appointment of at least one Southerner to the Hayes cabinet, control of federal patronage in their areas, generous internal improvements, federal aid for the Texas and Pacific Railroad, and most important, withdrawal of the remaining federal troops from the South.

In his inaugural address, Hayes announced that the South's most pressing need was the restoration of "wise, honest, and peaceful local self-government," and he soon withdrew the troops and let white Democrats take over the remaining Southern state governments. That produced charges that he was paying off the South for acquiescing in his election—charges that were not wholly untrue. The outcome of the election created such bitterness that not even Hayes's promise to serve only one term could mollify his critics.

The president and his party hoped to build up a "new Republican" organization in the South committed to modest support for black rights. Although many white Southern leaders sympathized with Republican economic policies, resentment of Reconstruction was so deep that supporting the party became politically impossible. The "solid" Democratic South, which would survive until the mid-twentieth century, was taking shape.

THE LEGACY OF RECONSTRUCTION

Reconstruction was a time when the promise of democracy for all Americans, regardless of race or color, made great strides. Never before had the civil rights of citizens become so clearly enumerated and extended to those other than landholding white men; never before had the power of the federal government been marshaled so vigorously to protect these rights. In particular, African Americans achieved a new level of dignity and power in America unimaginable only a few years earlier. There was a significant redistribution of income among the races and a more limited but still noteworthy redistribution of landownership. Perhaps most important, African Americans themselves managed to carve out a society and culture of their own and to create or strengthen their own institutions.

Still, Reconstruction did not bring long-lasting equality. Within little more than a decade after a devastating war, the white South had regained control of its own institutions and, to a great extent, restored its traditional ruling class to power. It would soon dismantle many of the legal freedoms won by African Americans and support an ideology of white supremacy. The federal government itself imposed no drastic economic reforms on the region, and few political changes of any kind other than the abolition of slavery would stay in effect after the 1870s.

Reconstruction was notable, finally, for its limitations. For in those years, the United States failed in its first serious effort to resolve its oldest and deepest social problem—the problem of racial injustice.

Given the odds confronting them, however, African Americans had reason for considerable pride in the gains they were able to make during Reconstruction. And future generations would be grateful for the two great charters of freedom—the Fourteenth and Fifteenth Amendments to the Constitution—which, although widely ignored at the time, would one day serve as the basis for a "Second Reconstruction" that would renew the fight to bring freedom to all Americans.

THE NEW SOUTH

The Compromise of 1877 was supposed to be the first step toward developing a stable, permanent Republican Party in the South. In that respect, at least, it failed. In the years following the end of Reconstruction, white southerners established the Democratic Party as the only viable political organization for the region's whites. Even so, the South did change in some of the ways that the framers of the Compromise had hoped.

THE "REDEEMERS"

Many white southerners rejoiced at the restoration of what they liked to call "home rule." But in reality, political power in the region was soon more restricted than at any time since the Civil War. Once again, most of the South fell under the control of a powerful, conservative ruling class, whose members were known variously as the "**Redeemers**" or the "Bourbons."

In some places, this post-Reconstruction ruling class was much the same as it was in the antebellum period. In Alabama, for example, the old planter elite retained much of its former power. In other areas, however, the Redeemers constituted a genuinely new ruling class of merchants, industrialists, railroad developers, and financiers. Some of them were former planters, some of them northern immigrants, some of them ambitious, upwardly mobile white southerners from the region's lower social tiers. They combined a defense of "home rule" and social conservatism with a commitment to economic development.

The various Bourbon governments of the New South behaved in many respects quite similarly. Virtually all the new Democratic regimes lowered taxes, reduced public spending, and drastically diminished state services. One state after another eliminated or cut its support for public school systems.

INDUSTRIALIZATION AND THE NEW SOUTH

Many white southern leaders in the post-Reconstruction era hoped to see their region develop a vigorous industrial economy, a "**New South**." Henry Grady, editor of the *Atlanta Constitution,* and other New South advocates seldom challenged white supremacy, but they did promote the virtues of thrift, industry, and progress—qualities that prewar southerners had often denounced in northern society.

Southern industry did expand dramatically in the years after Reconstruction, most visibly in textile manufacturing. In the past, southern planters had usually shipped their cotton to manufacturers in the North or in Europe. Now textile factories appeared in the South itself—many of them drawn to the region from New England by the abundance of water power, the ready supply of cheap labor, the low taxes, and the accommodating conservative governments. The tobacco processing industry similarly established an important foothold in the region. In the lower South, and particularly in Birmingham, Alabama, the iron (and, later, steel) industry grew rapidly.

Railroad development also increased substantially in the post-Reconstruction years. Between 1880 and 1890, trackage in the South more than doubled. And in 1886, the South changed the gauge (width) of its trackage to correspond with the standards of the North. No longer would it be necessary for cargoes heading into the South to be transferred from one train to another at the borders of the region.

Yet southern industry developed within strict limits, and its effects on the region were never even remotely comparable to the effects of industrialization on the North. The southern share of national manufacturing doubled in the last twenty years of the century, but it was still only 10 percent of the total. Similarly, the region's per capita income increased 21 percent in the same period, but average income in the South was still only 40 percent of that in the North; in 1860 it had been more than 60 percent. And even in those industries where development had been most rapid—textiles, iron, railroads—much of the capital had come from, and many of the profits thus flowed to, the North.

The growth of southern industry required the region to recruit a substantial industrial workforce for the first time. From the beginning, a high percentage of the factory workers were women. Heavy male casualties in the Civil War had helped create a large population of unmarried women who desperately needed employment. Hours were long (often as much as twelve hours a day), and wages were far below the northern equivalent; indeed, one of the greatest attractions of the South to industrialists was that employers were able to pay workers there as little as one-half of what northern workers received. Life in most mill towns was rigidly controlled by the owners and managers of the factories, who rigorously suppressed attempts at protest or union organization. Company stores sold goods to workers at inflated prices and issued credit at exorbitant rates (much as country stores did in agrarian areas), and mill owners ensured that no competing merchants were able to establish themselves in the community.

Some industries, such as textiles, offered few opportunities to African American workers. But many did, like tobacco, iron, and lumber. In towns hosting these industries black and white cultures came into close contact, which fueled the determination of local white leaders to take additional measures to protect white supremacy.

TENANTS AND SHARECROPPERS

The most important economic problem in the post-Reconstruction South was the impoverished state of agriculture. The 1870s and 1880s saw an acceleration of the process that had begun in the immediate postwar years: the imposition of systems of tenantry and debt peonage on much of the region; the reliance on a few cash crops rather than on a diversified agricultural system; and increasing absentee ownership of valuable farmlands. During Reconstruction, perhaps a third or more of the farmers in the South were tenants; by 1900, the figure had increased to 70 percent.

AFRICAN AMERICANS AND THE NEW SOUTH

The "New South creed" was not the property of whites alone. Many African Americans were attracted to the vision of progress and self-improvement as well. Some former slaves (and, as the decades passed, their offspring) succeeded in elevating themselves into the

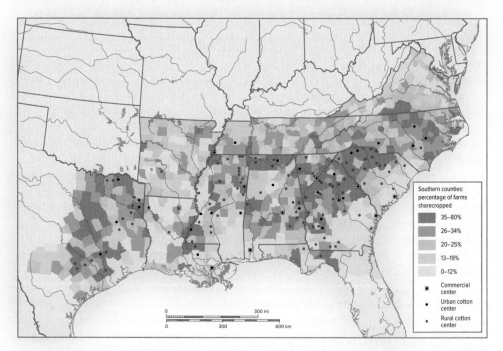

THE CROP-LIEN SYSTEM IN 1880 In the years after the Civil War, more and more southern farmers—white and black—became tenants or sharecroppers on land owned by others. This map shows the percentage of farms that were within the so-called crop-lien system, the system by which people worked their lands for someone else, who had a claim (or "lien") on part of the farmers' crops. Note the high density of sharecropping and tenant farming in the most fertile areas of the Deep South, the same areas where slaveholding had been most dominant before the Civil War. • *How did the crop-lien system contribute to the shift in southern agriculture toward one-crop farming?*

middle class, acquired property, established small businesses, or entered professions. Believing strongly that education was vital to the future of their people, they expanded the network of black colleges and institutes that had taken root during Reconstruction into an important educational system.

The chief spokesman for this commitment to education was **Booker T. Washington**, founder and president of the Tuskegee Institute in Alabama. Born into slavery, Washington had worked his way out of poverty after acquiring an education (at Virginia's Hampton Institute). He urged other blacks to follow the same road to self-improvement.

Washington's message was both cautious and hopeful. African Americans should attend school, learn skills, and establish a solid footing in agriculture and the trades. Industrial, not classical, education should be their goal. Blacks should, moreover, refine their speech, improve their dress, and adopt habits of thrift and personal cleanliness; they should, in short, adopt the standards of the white middle class. Only thus, Washington claimed, could they win the respect of the white population.

In a famous speech in Georgia in 1895, Washington outlined a controversial philosophy of race relations that became widely known as the **Atlanta Compromise**. Blacks, he said, should forgo agitation for political rights and concentrate on self-improvement and preparation for equality. Washington offered a powerful challenge to those whites who wanted to discourage African Americans from acquiring an education or winning any economic gains. But his message was also intended to assure whites that blacks would not challenge the emerging system of segregation.

THE BIRTH OF JIM CROW

Few white southerners had ever accepted the idea of racial equality. That the former slaves acquired any legal and political rights at all after emancipation was in large part the result of their own efforts and crucial federal support. That outside support all but vanished after 1877, when the last federal troops withdrew and the Supreme Court stripped the Fourteenth and Fifteenth Amendments of much of their significance. In the so-called civil rights cases of 1883, the Court ruled that the Fourteenth Amendment prohibited state governments from discriminating against people because of race but did not restrict private organizations or individuals from doing so. Popular culture reflected these frightening political developments. The rise of **minstrel shows**—slapstick dramatic representations of black culture—typically embodied racist ideas. "Corked-up" whites (a reference to the black makeup made by burning cork) grossly caricatured African American culture as silly, unintelligent, sensual, and immoral. Late in the 1800s, however, blacks founded their own minstrel shows in part to modify these stereotypes, though with only modest success. (See "Patterns of Popular Culture: The Minstrel Show.")

Eventually, the Court also validated state legislation that institutionalized the separation of the races. In *Plessy v. Ferguson* (1896), a case involving a Louisiana law that required segregated seating on railroads, the Court held that separate accommodations did not deprive blacks of equal rights if the accommodations were equal. In *Cumming v. County Board of Education* (1899), the Court ruled that communities could establish schools for whites only, even if there were no comparable schools for blacks.

Even before these dubious decisions, white southerners were working to separate the races to the greatest extent possible, and were particularly determined to strip African Americans of the right to vote. In some states, disenfranchisement had begun almost as soon as Reconstruction ended. But in other areas, black voting continued for some time

THE MINSTREL SHOW

The minstrel show was one of the most popular forms of entertainment in America in the second half of the nineteenth century. It was also a testament to the high awareness of race (and the high level of racism) in American society both before and after the Civil War. Minstrel performers were mostly white, usually disguised as black. But African American performers also formed their own minstrel shows and transformed them into vehicles for training black entertainers and developing new forms of music and dance.

Before and during the Civil War, when minstrel shows consisted almost entirely of white performers, performers blackened their faces with cork and presented grotesque stereotypes of the slave culture of the American South. Among the most popular of the stumbling, ridiculously ignorant characters invented for these shows were such figures as "Zip Coon" and "Jim Crow" (whose name later resurfaced as a label for late-nineteenth-century segregation laws). A typical minstrel show presented a group of seventeen or more

(Source: Library of Congress, Prints and Photographs Division [LC-USZ62-2659])

MINSTRELSY AT HIGH TIDE   The Primrose & West minstrel troupe—a lavish and expensive entertainment that drew large crowds in the 1800s—was one of many companies to offer this brand of entertainment to eager audiences all over the country. Although minstrelsy began with white musicians performing in blackface, the popularity of real African American minstrels encouraged the impresarios of the troupe to include groups of white and black performers alike.

men seated in a semicircle facing the audience. The man in the center ran the show, played the straight man for the jokes of others, and led the music—lively dances and sentimental ballads played on banjos, castanets, and other instruments and sung by soloists or the entire group.

After the Civil War, white minstrels began to expand their repertoire. Drawing from the famous and successful freak shows of P. T. Barnum and other entertainment entrepreneurs, some began to include Siamese twins, bearded ladies, and even a supposedly eight-foot two-inch "Chinese giant" in their shows. They also incorporated sex, both by including women in some shows and, even more popularly, by recruiting female impersonators. One of the most successful minstrel performers of the 1870s was Francis Leon, who delighted crowds with his female portrayal of a flamboyant "prima donna."

One reason white minstrels began to move in these new directions was that they were now facing competition from black performers, who could provide more-authentic versions of black music, dance, and humor. They usually brought more talent to the task than white performers. The Georgia Minstrels, organized in 1865, was one of the first all-black minstrel troupes, and it had great success in attracting white audiences in the Northeast for several years. By the 1870s, touring African American minstrel groups were numerous. The black minstrels used many of the conventions of the white shows. There were dances, music, comic routines, and sentimental recitations. Some black performers even chalked their faces to make themselves look as dark as the white blackface performers with whom they were competing. Black minstrels sometimes denounced slavery (at least indirectly) and did not often speak demeaningly of the capacities of their race. But they could not entirely escape caricaturing African American life as they struggled to meet the expectations of their white audiences.

The black minstrel shows had few openly political aims. They did help develop some important forms of African American entertainment and transform them into a part of the national culture. Black minstrels introduced new forms of dance, derived from the informal traditions of slavery and black community life. They showed the "buck and wing," the "stop time," and the "Virginia essence," which established the foundations for the tap and jazz dancing of the early twentieth century. They also improvised musically and began experimenting with forms that over time contributed to the growth of ragtime, jazz, and rhythm and blues.

Eventually, black minstrelsy—like its white counterpart—evolved into other forms of theater, including the beginnings of serious black drama. At Ambrose Park in Brooklyn in the 1890s, for example, the celebrated black comedian Sam Lucas (a veteran of the minstrel circuit) starred in the play *Darkest America,* which one black newspaper later described as a "delineation of Negro life, carrying the race through all their historical phases from the plantation, into reconstruction days and finally painting our people as they are today, cultured and accomplished in the social graces, [holding] the mirror faithfully up to nature."

But interest in the minstrel show did not die altogether. In 1927, Hollywood released *The Jazz Singer,* the first feature film with sound. It was about the career of a white minstrel performer, and its star was one of the most popular singers of the twentieth century: Al Jolson, whose career had begun on the blackface minstrel circuit years before. •

UNDERSTAND, ANALYZE, & EVALUATE

1. How did minstrel shows performed by white minstrels reinforce prevailing attitudes toward African Americans?
2. Minstrel shows performed by black minstrels often conformed to existing stereotypes of African Americans. Why?
3. Can you think of any popular entertainments today that carry remnants of the minstrel shows of the nineteenth century?

after Reconstruction—largely because conservative whites believed they could control the black electorate and use it to beat back the attempts of poor white farmers to take control of the Democratic Party.

In the 1890s, however, franchise restrictions became much more rigid. During those years, some small white farmers began to demand complete black disenfranchisement—because they objected to the black vote being used against them by the Bourbons. At the same time, many members of the conservative elite began to doubt their ability to influence black voters and fear that poor whites might unite politically with poor blacks to challenge them.

In devising laws to disenfranchise black males, the southern states had to find ways to evade the Fifteenth Amendment, which prohibited states from denying anyone the right to vote because of race. Two devices emerged before 1900 to accomplish this goal: the poll tax, or some form of property qualification (few blacks were prosperous enough to meet such requirements); and the "literacy" or "understanding" test, which required voters to demonstrate an ability to read and to interpret the Constitution. Even those African Americans who could read had a hard time passing the difficult test white officials gave them, which often required them to interpret an arcane part of the Constitution to the satisfaction of a white elected official. (The laws affected poor white voters as well as blacks.) By the late 1890s, the black vote had decreased by 62 percent, the white vote by 26 percent.

Laws restricting the franchise and segregating schools were only part of a network of state and local statutes—collectively known as the **Jim Crow laws**—that by the first years of the twentieth century had institutionalized an elaborate system of racial hierarchy reaching into almost every area of southern life. Blacks and whites could not ride together in the same railroad cars, sit in the same waiting rooms, use the same washrooms, eat in the same restaurants, or sit in the same theaters. Blacks had no access to many public parks, beaches, or picnic areas; they could not be patients in many hospitals. Much of the new legal structure did no more than confirm what had already been widespread social practice in the South. But the Jim Crow laws also stripped blacks of many of the modest social, economic, and political gains they had made in the late nineteenth century.

More than legal efforts were involved in this process. The 1890s witnessed a dramatic increase in white violence against blacks, which, along with the Jim Crow laws, served to inhibit black agitation for equal rights. The worst such violence—lynching of blacks by white mobs—reached appalling levels. In the nation as a whole in the 1890s, there was an average of 187 lynchings each year, more than 80 percent of them in the South. The vast majority of victims were black men accused of crimes they did not commit and who rarely enjoyed due process or a fair trial. Those who participated in lynchings often saw their actions as a legitimate form of law enforcement, but also as a way to deliver a powerful message about the power of white supremacy—namely, that they could use intimidation as means of controlling the black population.

The rise of lynchings shocked the conscience of many white Americans in a way that other forms of racial injustice did not. In 1892, **Ida B. Wells**, a committed black journalist, published a series of impassioned articles after the lynching of three of her hometown friends in Memphis, Tennessee; her articles launched what became an international antilynching movement. The movement gradually attracted substantial support from whites in the North and even the South, particularly from women. Its goal was a federal antilynching law, which would allow the national government to do what state and local governments in the South were generally unwilling to do: punish those responsible for lynchings. Although such a law was introduced to Congress in 1918 and reintroduced in the 1920s, 1930s, and 1940s, it never made it past southern senators.

(Source: Library of Congress, Prints and Photographs Division [LC-USZ62-29285])

LYNCHING OF HENRY SMITH, PARIS, TEXAS, 1893 A large, almost festive crowd numbering about 10,000 gathers to watch the lynching of a Henry Smith. Accused of murdering a four-year-old white girl who was the daughter of a law enforcement officer, Smith was mutilated and burned on this scaffold. Over 4000 lynchings occurred between the end of slavery and the late 1930s, mostly in the South. They reached their peak in the 1890s and the first years of the twentieth century. Lynchings such as this one—publicized well in advance and attracting whole families who traveled great distances to see them—were relatively infrequent. Most lynchings were the work of smaller groups, operating with less visibility.

Opposition to lynching, however, paled in contrast to the overwhelming support among most southern whites for actions that kept African Americans subordinate to them and without the power to effect change. As in the antebellum period, poor whites generally aligned themselves politically with wealthy whites out of a shared feeling of racial superiority, despite having economic concerns in common with African Americans.

CONCLUSION

Reconstruction was a profoundly important moment in American history. Despite the bitter political battles in Washington and throughout the South, culminating in the unsuccessful effort to remove President Andrew Johnson from office, the most important result of the effort to reunite the nation after its long and bloody war was a reshaping of the lives of ordinary people in all regions.

In the North, Reconstruction solidified the power of the Republican Party. The rapid expansion of the northern economy accelerated, drawing more and more of its residents into a burgeoning commercial world.

In the South, Reconstruction fundamentally rearranged the relationship between white and black citizens. African Americans initially participated actively and effectively in southern politics. After a few years of widespread black voting and significant black officeholding, however, the forces of white supremacy shoved most African Americans to the margins of the southern political world, where they would mostly remain until the 1960s.

In other ways, however, the lives of southern blacks changed dramatically and permanently. Overwhelmingly, they left the plantations. Some sought work in towns and cities. Others left the region altogether. But the great majority began farming on small farms of their own—not as landowners, except in rare cases, but as tenants and sharecroppers on land owned by whites. The result was a form of economic bondage, driven by debt, only scarcely less oppressive than the legal bondage of slavery. Within this system, however, African Americans managed to carve out a much larger sphere of social and cultural activity than they had ever been able to create under slavery. Black churches proliferated in great numbers. African American schools and printing presses emerged in some communities, and black colleges began to operate in the region. Some former slaves owned businesses and flourished.

Strenuous efforts by "New South" advocates to advance industry and commerce in the region produced impressive results in a few areas. But the South on the whole remained what it had always been: a largely rural society with a sharply defined class structure. It also maintained a deep commitment among its white citizens to the subordination of African Americans—a commitment solidified in the 1890s and the early twentieth century when white southerners erected an elaborate legal system of segregation (the Jim Crow laws). Tragically, the promise of the great Reconstruction amendments to the Constitution—the Fourteenth and Fifteenth—remained largely unfulfilled in the South as the century drew to its close.

KEY TERMS/PEOPLE/PLACES/EVENTS

Andrew Johnson 359
Atlanta Compromise 375
Black Codes 359
Booker T. Washington 375
carpetbagger 363
Charles Sumner 355
Compromise of 1877 371
crop-lien system 366
Enforcement Acts 370
Fifteenth Amendment 362

Fourteenth
  Amendment 361
Freedmen's Bureau 355
Ida B. Wells 378
impeachment 363
Jim Crow laws 378
Ku Klux Klan 369
minstrel show 375
New South 373
Plessy v. Ferguson 375

Radical Republicans 355
Reconstruction 355
Redeemers 372
scalawag 363
sharecropping 365
Thaddeus
  Stevens 355
Ulysses S. Grant 367
Wade-Davis Bill 357
William H. Seward 358

RECALL AND REFLECT

1. What were the principal questions facing the nation at the end of the Civil War?
2. What were the achievements of Reconstruction? Where did it fail and why?
3. What new problems arose in the South as the North's interest in Reconstruction waned?
4. What was the Compromise of 1877, and how did it affect Reconstruction?
5. How did the "New" South differ from the South before the Civil War?

16 | THE CONQUEST OF THE FAR WEST

THE SOCIETIES OF THE FAR WEST

THE ROMANCE OF THE WEST

THE CHANGING WESTERN ECONOMY

THE DISPERSAL OF THE TRIBES

THE RISE AND DECLINE OF THE WESTERN FARMER

LOOKING AHEAD

1. What various ethnic and racial groups populated the American West, and how did they interact?

2. How did the arrival and settlement of substantial numbers of Anglo-Americans transform the society and economy of the West?

3. What role did the federal government play in shaping the development of the West?

BY THE MID-1840S, WHITE AMERICAN MIGRANTS, along with many others, from the eastern regions of the nation had settled in the West in substantial numbers. Farmers, ranchers, and miners all found opportunity in the western lands. By the end of the Civil War, the West had become legendary in the eastern states. No longer the Great American Desert, it was now widely viewed as the "frontier": an empty land awaiting settlement and civilization; a place of wealth, adventure, opportunity, and untrammeled individualism.

In fact, the real West of the mid-nineteenth century bore little resemblance to its popular image. It was a diverse land, with many different regions, climates, and stores of natural resources. And it was extensively populated. The English-speaking migrants of the late nineteenth century did not find an empty, desolate land. They found Indians, Mexicans, African Americans, French and British Canadians, Asians, and others, some of whose families had been living in the West for generations.

1862
Homestead Act

1865-1867
Sioux Wars

1869
Transcontinental railroad completed

1873
Barbed wire invented

1874
Black Hills gold rush

1876
Battle of the Little Bighorn

1877
Desert Land Act

1882
Chinese Exclusion Act

1885
Twain's *Huckleberry Finn*

1887
Dawes Act

1889
Oklahoma opened to white settlement

1890
Battle of Wounded Knee

1893
Turner thesis

THE SOCIETIES OF THE FAR WEST

The Far West was in fact a composite of many lands. It contained both the most arid regions and some of the wettest and lushest areas of the United States. It contained the flattest plains and the highest mountains. It also contained many peoples.

THE WESTERN TRIBES

The Indian tribes made up the largest and most important western population group before the great white migration. Some were members of eastern tribes who had been forcibly resettled west of the Mississippi. But most were members of indigenous tribes whose roots stretched back generations.

More than 300,000 Indians (among them the Serrano, Chumash, Pomo, Maidu, Yurok, and Chinook) had lived on the Pacific Coast before the arrival of Spanish settlers. They supported themselves through a combination of fishing, foraging, and simple agriculture. The Pueblos of the Southwest had long lived largely as farmers and had established permanent settlements there.

The most widespread Indian groups in the West were the Plains Indians. They were, in fact, made up of many different tribal and language groups. Some lived more or less sedentary lives as farmers, but many subsisted largely through hunting buffalo. Riding small but powerful horses, the tribes moved through the grasslands following the herds, constructing tepees as temporary dwellings. The buffalo, or bison, provided the economic basis for the Plains Indians' way of life. The flesh of the large animal was their principal source of food, and its skin supplied materials for clothing, shoes, tepees, blankets, robes, and utensils. "Buffalo chips"—dried manure—provided fuel; buffalo bones became knives and arrow tips; buffalo tendons formed the strings of bows.

The Plains warriors proved to be the most formidable foes that white settlers would encounter. But the tribes were usually unable to unite against white aggression. At times, tribal warriors even faced white forces who were being assisted by guides and even fighters from rival tribes. Some tribes, however, were able to overcome their divisions and cooperate effectively. By the mid-nineteenth century, for example, the Sioux, Arapaho, and Cheyenne had forged a powerful alliance that dominated the northern plains. That proved no protection, however, against the greatest danger to the tribes: ecological and economic decline. Indians were highly vulnerable to eastern infectious diseases, such as the smallpox epidemics that decimated the Pawnee in Nebraska in the 1840s. And the tribes were, of course, at a considerable disadvantage in any long-term battle against an enemy with a deadlier and more plentiful weaponry, especially repeating rifles guns and cannons.

Hispanic New Mexico

For centuries, much of the Far West had been part of the Spanish Empire and, later, the Mexican Republic. When the United States acquired its new lands there in the 1840s, it also acquired many Mexican residents.

In New Mexico, the centers of Spanish-speaking society were farming and trading communities established in the seventeenth century. Descendants of the original Spanish settlers (and more recent migrants from Mexico) engaged primarily in cattle and sheep ranching. When the United States acquired title to New Mexico in the aftermath of the Mexican War, General Stephen Kearny—who had commanded the American troops in the region—tried to establish a territorial government out of the approximately 1,000 Anglo-Americans in the region, ignoring the more than 50,000 Hispanics. There were widespread fears among Hispanics and Indians that the new American rulers would confiscate their lands. In 1847, before the new government had established itself, Taos Indians rebelled, killing the new governor and other Anglo-American officials before being subdued by U.S Army forces. New Mexico remained under military rule for three years, until the United States finally organized a territorial government there in 1850. The U.S. Army finally broke the power of the Navajo, Apache, and other tribes in the region.

The Anglo-American presence in the Southwest grew rapidly once the railroads heavily penetrated the region in the 1880s and early 1890s. With the railroads came extensive new ranching, farming, and mining. This expansion of economic activity attracted a new wave of Mexican immigrants, who moved across the border in search of work. The English-speaking proprietors of the new enterprises, however, commonly restricted most Mexicans to the lowest-paying and least stable jobs.

Hispanic California and Texas

In California, Spanish settlement began in the eighteenth century with a string of Catholic missions along the Pacific Coast. The missionaries and the soldiers who accompanied them gathered most of the coastal Indians into their communities, some forcibly and others by persuasion. In the 1830s, after the new Mexican government began reducing the power of the church, the mission society largely collapsed. In its place emerged a secular Mexican aristocracy, which controlled a chain of large estates in the fertile lands west of the Sierra mountains. For them, the acquisition of California by the United States was disastrous. So vast were the numbers of English-speaking immigrants that the *Californios* (as the Hispanic residents of the region were known) had struggled to resist the onslaught. English-speaking prospectors organized to exclude them, sometimes violently, from the mines during the gold rush. Many *Californios* also lost their lands—either through corrupt business deals or through outright seizure.

Increasingly, Mexicans and Mexican Americans became part of the lower end of the state's working class, clustered in *barrios* in Los Angeles or elsewhere or laboring as migrant farmworkers. Even small Hispanic landowners who managed to hang on to their farms found themselves unable to raise livestock, as once-communal grazing lands fell under the control of powerful Anglo ranchers.

A similar pattern occurred in Texas after it joined the United States. Many Mexican landowners lost their land—some as a result of fraud and coercion, others because even the most substantial Mexican ranchers could not compete with the emerging Anglo-American ranching kingdoms. In 1859, angry Mexicans, led by the rancher Juan Cortina, raided the jail in Brownsville and freed all the Mexican prisoners inside. But such resistance had little long-term effect. As in California, Mexicans in southern Texas became an increasingly impoverished working class, relegated largely to unskilled farm or industrial labor.

THE CHINESE MIGRATION

At the same time that ambitious or impoverished Europeans were crossing the Atlantic in search of opportunities in the New World, many Chinese were crossing the Pacific in hopes of better lives. Not all came to the United States. Many Chinese—some as "**coolies**" (a nineteenth-century term meaning indentured servants whose conditions were close to slavery)—moved to Hawaii, Australia, Latin America, South Africa, and even the Caribbean.

A few Chinese traveled to the American West even before the gold rush, but after 1848 the flow increased dramatically. By 1880, more than 200,000 Chinese had settled in the United States. Almost all came as free laborers. For a time, white Americans welcomed the Chinese as a conscientious, hardworking people. Very quickly, however, white opinion turned hostile—in part because the Chinese were so industrious and successful that some white Americans began considering them rivals.

In the early 1850s, large numbers of Chinese immigrants joined the hunt for gold. Many of them were well-organized, hardworking prospectors, and for a time some enjoyed considerable success. But opportunities for the Chinese to prosper in the mines were fleeting. In 1852, the California legislature began trying to exclude the Chinese from gold mining by enacting a "foreign miners" tax. Gradually, the effect of the discriminatory laws, the hostility of white miners, and the declining profitability of the surface mines drove most Chinese out of prospecting.

As mining declined as a source of wealth and jobs for the Chinese, railroad employment grew. Beginning in 1865, over 12,000 Chinese found work building the transcontinental railroad, forming 90 percent of the labor force of the Central Pacific. The company preferred them to white laborers because they worked hard, made few demands, and accepted relatively low wages.

Work on the Central Pacific was arduous and often dangerous. In the winter, many Chinese tunneled into snowbanks at night to create warm sleeping areas for themselves, even though such tunnels frequently collapsed, suffocating those inside. In the spring of 1866, 5,000 Chinese railroad workers rebelled against the terrible conditions and went on strike to demand higher wages and a shorter workday. The company isolated them, surrounded them with strikebreakers, and starved them into submission.

In 1869, the transcontinental railroad was completed, and thousands of Chinese lost their jobs. Some moved into agricultural work usually in menial positions. Increasingly, however, the Chinese flocked to cities. By far the largest single Chinese community was in San Francisco. Much of community life there, and in other "Chinatowns" throughout the West, revolved around organizations, somewhat like benevolent societies, that filled many of the roles that

(Source: National Archives and Records Administration)

A CHINESE FAMILY IN SAN FRANCISCO This portrait of Chun Duck Chin and his seven-year-old son Chun Jan Yut was taken in a studio in San Francisco in the 1870s. Both father and son appear to have dressed up for the occasion, in traditional Chinese garb, and the studio—which likely took many such portraits of Chinese families—provided a formal Chinese backdrop. The son is holding what appears to be a chicken, perhaps to impress relatives in China with his family's prosperity.

political machines often served in immigrant communities in eastern cities. Often led by prominent merchants (in San Francisco, they were known as the "Six Companies"), these organizations became, in effect, employment brokers, unions, arbitrators of disputes, defenders against outside persecution, and dispensers of social services. They also organized elaborate festivals and celebrations that were a conspicuous and important part of life in Chinatowns.

Other Chinese organizations were secret societies known as "tongs." Some of the tongs were violent criminal organizations, involved in the opium trade and prostitution. Few people outside the Chinese communities were aware of their existence, except when rival tongs engaged in violent conflict (or "tong wars").

In San Francisco and other western cities, the Chinese usually occupied the lower rungs of the employment ladder. Many worked as common laborers, servants, and unskilled factory hands. Some established their own small businesses, especially laundries. There were few commercial laundries in China, but they could be started in America with very little capital and required only limited command of English. By the 1890s, Chinese constituted over two-thirds of all the laundry workers in California.

During the earliest Chinese migrations to California, virtually all the relatively small number of women who made the journey did so because they had been sold into prostitution. As late as 1880, nearly half the Chinese women in California were prostitutes. Gradually, however, the overall number of Chinese women increased, and Chinese men in America became more likely to seek companionship in families.

ANTI-CHINESE SENTIMENTS

As Chinese communities grew larger, more visible, and more powerful, anti-Chinese sentiment among white residents intensified. Anti-Chinese activities, some of them bloody, reflected the resentment of many white workers toward Chinese laborers for accepting lower wages. As the political value of attacking the Chinese grew in California, the Democratic Party took up the call. So did the Workingmen's Party of California—founded in 1878 by Denis Kearney, an Irish immigrant—which gained significant power in the state largely because of its hostility to the Chinese. By the mid-1880s, anti-Chinese agitation and violence had spread up and down the Pacific Coast and into other areas of the West.

In 1882, Congress responded to the political pressure and the growing racial violence by passing the **Chinese Exclusion Act**, which banned Chinese immigration into the United States for ten years and barred Chinese already in the country from becoming naturalized citizens. Congress renewed the law for another ten years in 1892 and made it permanent in 1902. It had a dramatic effect on the Chinese population, which declined by more than 40 percent in the forty years after the act's passage.

MIGRATION FROM THE EAST

The scale of post–Civil War white migration to the American West dwarfed everything that had preceded it. In previous decades, the settlers had come in thousands. Now they came in millions. Most of the new settlers were from the established Anglo-American societies of the eastern United States, but substantial numbers—over 2 million between 1870 and 1900—were foreign-born immigrants from Europe: Scandinavians, Germans, Irish, Russians, Czechs, and others.

They came to the West for many reasons. Settlers were attracted by gold and silver deposits, by the short-grass pasture for cattle and sheep, and ultimately by the rich sod of the plains and the meadowlands of the mountains. The completion of the great transcontinental railroad line in 1869, and the construction of the many subsidiary lines that spidered out from it, encouraged rapid settlement. So did the land policies of the federal government. The **Homestead Act** of 1862 permitted settlers to buy plots of 160 acres for a small fee if they occupied the land they purchased for five years and improved it.

Supporters of the Homestead Act believed it would create new markets and new outposts of commercial agriculture for the nation's growing economy. But a unit of 160 acres, while ample in much of the East, was too small for the grazing and grain farming of the Great Plains. Eventually, the federal government provided some relief. The Timber Culture Act (1873) permitted homesteaders to receive grants of 160 additional acres if they planted 40 acres of trees on them. The Desert Land Act (1877) allowed claimants to buy 640 acres at $1.25 an acre, provided they irrigated part of their holdings within three years. These and other laws ultimately made it possible for individuals to acquire as much as 1,280 acres of land at little cost.

Political organization followed on the hard heels of settlement. By the mid-1860s, territorial governments were in operation in the new provinces of Nevada, Colorado, Dakota, Arizona, Idaho, Montana, and Wyoming. Statehood rapidly followed. Nevada became a state in 1864, Nebraska in 1867, and Colorado in 1876. In 1889, North and South Dakota,

Montana, and Washington won admission; Wyoming and Idaho entered the next year. Congress denied Utah statehood until its Mormon leaders convinced the government in 1896 that polygamy (the practice of men taking several wives) had been abandoned. At the turn of the century, only Arizona, New Mexico, and Oklahoma remained outside the Union.

THE ROMANCE OF THE WEST

The rapidly developing West occupied a special place in the Anglo-American imagination. Many white Americans continued to consider it a romantic place, a wilderness where individuals could experience true freedom. But such thinking was more fiction than fact.

THE WESTERN LANDSCAPE AND THE COWBOY

Part of the attraction of the West was its spectacular natural landscape. Painters of the new "**Rocky Mountain school**"—of whom the best known were Albert Bierstadt and Thomas Moran—celebrated the new West in grandiose canvases, some of which toured the eastern and midwestern states and attracted enormous crowds eager for a vision of the Great West.

Gradually, paintings and photographs inspired a growing wave of tourism among people eager to see the natural wonders of the region. In the 1880s and 1890s, resort hotels began to spring up near some of the region's most spectacular landscapes.

Even more appealing was the rugged, free-spirited lifestyle that many Americans associated with the West. Many nineteenth-century Americans came especially to idealize the figure of the cowboy. Western novels such as Owen Wister's *The Virginian* (1902) romanticized the cowboy's supposed freedom from traditional social constraints, his affinity with nature, even his supposed propensity for violence. Wister's character—one of the most enduring in popular American literature—was a semi-educated man whose natural decency, courage, and compassion made him a powerful symbol of the supposed virtues of the "frontier." But *The Virginian* was only the most famous example of a type of literature that soon swept throughout the United States. Novels and stories glorified the West and the lives of cowboys in particular, in boys' magazines, pulp novels, theater, and serious literature.

Among the reasons for the widespread admiration of the cowboy were the remarkably popular Wild West shows that traveled throughout the United States and Europe. Most successful were the shows of Buffalo Bill Cody, a former Pony Express rider, Indian fighter, and hero of popular dime novels for children. Cody's Wild West show, which spawned dozens of imitators, exploited his own fame and romanticized the life of the cowboy through reenactments of Indian battles and displays of horsemanship and riflery (many of them by the famous sharpshooter Annie Oakley). Buffalo Bill and his imitators confirmed the popular image of the West as a place of romance and glamour and helped keep that image alive for later generations.

THE IDEA OF THE FRONTIER

It was not simply the particular character of the new West that resonated in the nation's imagination. It was also that many Americans considered it the last natural frontier. Since the earliest moments of European settlement in America, the image of uncharted territory to the west had always comforted and inspired those who dreamed of starting life anew.

THE FRONTIER AND THE WEST

The emergence of the history of the American West as an important field of scholarship can be traced to a paper Frederick Jackson Turner delivered to the American Historical Association in 1893: "The Significance of the Frontier in American History." Turner stated his thesis simply. The settlement of the West by white Americans—"the existence of an area of free land, its continuous recession, and the advance of American settlement westward"—was the central story of the nation's history. The process of westward expansion had transformed a desolate and savage land into modern civilization and had continually renewed American ideas of democracy and individualism.

In the first half of the twentieth century, virtually everyone who wrote about the West echoed at least part of Turner's argument. Ray Allen Billington's *Westward Expansion* (1949) was almost wholly consistent with the Turnerian model. In *The Great Plains* (1931) and *The Great Frontier* (1952), Walter Prescott Webb similarly emphasized the bravery and ingenuity of white settlers in the Southwest.

Serious efforts to displace the Turner thesis as the explanation of western American history began after World War II. In *Virgin Land* (1950), Henry Nash Smith examined many of the same heroic images of the West that Turner and his disciples had presented; but he treated those images less as descriptions of reality than as myths. Earl Pomeroy challenged Turner's notion of the West as a place of individualism, innovation, and democratic renewal. "Conservatism, inheritance, and continuity bulked at least as large," he claimed. Howard Lamar, in *Dakota Territory, 1861–1889* (1956) and *The Far Southwest* (1966), emphasized the highly diverse character of the West.

The western historians who emerged since the late 1970s launched an even more emphatic attack on the Turner thesis and the idea of the "frontier." "New western historians" such as Richard White, Patricia Nelson Limerick, William Cronon, Donald Worster, Peggy Pascoe, and many others challenged the Turnerians on a number of points.

Turner saw the nineteenth-century West as "free land" awaiting the expansion of Anglo-American settlement and American democracy. The more recent western historians reject the concept of an empty "frontier," emphasizing instead the elaborate and highly developed civilizations that already existed in the region. White, English-speaking Americans, they have argued, did not so much "settle" the West as conquer it. And they continued to share the region not only with the Indians and Hispanics who preceded them there, but also with African Americans, Asians, Latin Americans, and others who flowed into the West at the same time they did.

The Turnerian West was a place of heroism, triumph, and above all progress, dominated by the feats of brave white men. The West that the new western historians describe was a less triumphant (and less masculine) place in which bravery and success coexisted with oppression, greed, and failure; in which decaying ghost towns, bleak Indian reservations, impoverished barrios, and ecologically devastated landscapes have been as characteristic of western development as great ranches, rich farms, and prosperous cities.

To Turner and his disciples, the nineteenth-century West was a place where rugged individualism flourished and replenished American democracy. The newer scholars point out that the region was inextricably tied

to a national and international capitalist economy. Westerners depended on government-
subsidized railroads for access to markets,
federal troops for protection from Indians,
and (later) government-funded dams and
canals for irrigating their fields and sustaining their towns.

And while Turner defined the West as a
process—a process of settlement that
came to an end with the "closing of the
frontier" in the late nineteenth century—
the newer historians see the West as a

region. Its distinctive history did not end in
1890 but continues into our own time. •

UNDERSTAND, ANALYZE, & EVALUATE

1. How and why did the portrayal of the
West by the newer western historians differ from the West that Turner described?
2. Why did the newer western historians
challenge Turner's views, and why has
their depiction of the West, in turn,
provoked such controversy?

same year as Hayes election

Mark Twain gave voice to this romantic vision of the frontier in a series of novels and
memoirs. In *The Adventures of Tom Sawyer* (1876) and *The Adventures of Huckleberry Finn*
(1885), he produced characters who repudiated the constraints of organized society and
attempted to escape into a more natural world. (For Huck Finn, the vehicle of escape was
a small raft on the Mississippi.) This yearning for freedom reflected a larger vision of the
West as the last refuge from the constraints of civilization.

One of the most beloved and successful artists of the nineteenth century was Frederic
Remington, a painter and sculptor whose works came to represent the romance of the

(Source: Library of Congress, Prints and Photographs Division [LC-DIG-ppmsca-09855])

AMERICAN PROGRESS, 1872   The Brooklyn artist John Gast painted this image of hardy settlers marching
toward the frontier for western travel guides. The goddess of progress, holding a schoolbook and telegraph line,
leads the way. Native Americans, buffalo, and a bear are pushed off to the margins by the pioneers' approach.

West. He portrayed the cowboy as a natural aristocrat, much like Wister's *The Virginian,* living in a natural world in which all the normal supporting structures of "civilization" were missing.

Theodore Roosevelt also contributed to the romanticizing of the West. He traveled to the Dakota badlands in the mid-1880s to recover from the sudden death of his young wife. In the 1890s, he published a four-volume history, *The Winning of the West,* with a heroic account of the spread of white civilization into the frontier.

Perhaps the most influential statement of the romantic vision of the frontier came from the young historian Frederick Jackson Turner, in a memorable paper he delivered as a thirty-two-year-old in Chicago in 1893 titled "The Significance of the Frontier in American History." In it he boldly claimed that the experience of western expansion had stimulated individualism, nationalism, and democracy; kept opportunities for advancement alive; and made Americans the distinctive people that they were. "Now," Turner concluded portentously, "the frontier has gone and with its going has closed the first period of American history." The **Turner thesis** was widely accepted by his contemporaries, but later historians have challenged it. (See "Debating the Past: The Frontier and the West.")

In accepting the idea of the "passing of the frontier," many Americans were acknowledging the end of one of their most cherished myths. As long as it had been possible for them to see the West as an empty, open land, it was possible to believe that there were constantly revitalizing opportunities in American life. But by the end of the nineteenth century, there was a vague and ominous sense of opportunities foreclosed.

THE CHANGING WESTERN ECONOMY

Turner accurately captured the popular view of the West as a place of unrivaled opportunity for growth and wealth that was a key motivation for the millions who migrated in the decades after the Civil War. This great wave of Anglo-American and European settlement transformed the economy of the Far West and tied the region firmly to the growing industrial economy of the East.

LABOR IN THE WEST

As commercial activity increased, many farmers, ranchers, and miners found it necessary to recruit a paid labor force—not an easy task given the small labor pool compared to that found in established cities. This labor shortage led to higher wages for some workers than were typical in the East. But working conditions were often treacherous, and job security was almost nonexistent. Once a railroad was built, a crop harvested, a herd sent to market or a mine played out, hundreds and even thousands of workers could find themselves suddenly unemployed.

The western working class was highly multiracial. English-speaking whites worked alongside African Americans and immigrants from southern and eastern Europe, as they did in the East. Even more, they worked with Chinese, Filipinos, Mexicans, and Indians. But the workforce was highly stratified along racial lines. In almost every area of the western economy, white workers (whatever their ethnicity) occupied the upper tiers of employment: management and skilled labor. The lower tiers—unskilled work in the mines, on the railroads, or in agriculture—were filled overwhelmingly by nonwhites.

The western economy was, however, no more a single entity than the economy of the East. In the late nineteenth century, the region produced three major industries, each with distinctive history and characteristics: mining, ranching, and commercial farming.

THE ARRIVAL OF THE MINERS

The first economic boom in the Far West was the result of mining. The mining boom began around 1860 and flourished until the 1890s. Then it abruptly declined.

At first it was news of a gold or silver strike that would start a stampede. The California gold rush of 1849 was the first and most famous gold rush. But it was followed by others. Individual prospectors would pan for gold, extracting the first shallow deposits of ore largely by hand, a method known as placer mining. After these surface deposits dwindled, corporations moved in to engage in lode or quartz mining, which dug deeper beneath the surface. Then, as those deposits dwindled, commercial mining declined, and ultimately ranchers and farmers moved in and established a longer-lasting agricultural economy.

The first great mineral strikes (other than the California gold rush) occurred just before the Civil War. In 1858, gold was discovered in the Pike's Peak district of what would soon be the territory of Colorado; the following year, 50,000 prospectors stormed in. Denver and other mining camps blossomed into "cities" overnight. Almost as rapidly as they had developed, the booms ended. Later, the discovery of silver near Leadville supplied a new source of mineral wealth.

While the Colorado rush of 1859 was still in progress, news of another strike drew miners to Nevada. Gold had been found in the Washoe district. Even more plentiful and more valuable was the silver found in the great Comstock Lode (first discovered in 1858 by Henry Comstock) and other Washoe veins. The first prospectors to reach the Washoe fields came from California, and from the beginning, Californians dominated the settlement and development of Nevada. A remote desert without railroad transportation, the territory produced no supplies of its own, and everything had to be shipped from California to Virginia City, Carson City, and other roaring camp towns. When the first placer (or surface) deposits ran out, Californian and eastern capitalists bought the claims of the pioneer prospectors and began to use the more difficult process of quartz mining, which enabled them to retrieve silver from deeper veins. For a few years, these outside owners reaped tremendous profits: from 1860 to 1880, the Nevada lodes yielded bullion worth $306 million. After that, the mines quickly played out.

The next important mineral discoveries came in 1874, when gold was found in the Black Hills of southwestern Dakota Territory. Prospectors swarmed into the remote area. Like the others, the boom flared for a time, until surface resources faded and corporations took over—above all, the enormous Homestake Mining Company—and came to dominate the fields. The Dakotas, like other boom areas of the mineral empire, ultimately developed a largely agricultural economy.

The gold and silver discoveries generated the most popular excitement. But less glamorous natural resources proved more important to western development. The great Anaconda copper mine, launched by William Clark in 1881, marked the beginning of an industry that would remain important to Montana for many decades. In other areas, mining operations had significant success with lead, tin, quartz, and zinc.

Men greatly outnumbered women in the mining towns, and younger men in particular had difficulty finding female companions of comparable age. Those women who did gravitate to the new communities often came with their husbands. Single women, or women whose husbands were earning no money, did work for wages at times, as cooks, laundresses, and tavernkeepers. And in the sexually imbalanced mining communities, there was always a ready market for prostitutes.

The thousands of people who flocked to the mining towns in search of quick wealth and failed to find it often remained as wage laborers in corporate mines after the boom period, working in almost uniformly terrible conditions. In the 1870s, one worker in every thirty was disabled in the mines, and one in every eighty was killed. That rate fell later in the nineteenth century, but mining remained one of the most dangerous and arduous working environments in the United States.

THE CATTLE KINGDOM

A second important element of the changing economy of the Far West was cattle ranching. The open range—the vast grasslands of the public domain—provided a huge area on the Great Plains where cattle raisers could graze their herds.

The western cattle industry was born slowly and through the pioneering work of Mexicans, Texans, white settlers, and free and enslaved blacks. Long before citizens of the United States entered the Southwest, Mexican ranchers had developed the techniques and equipment that the cattlemen and cowboys of the Great Plains later employed: branding, roundups, roping, and the gear of the herders—their lariats, saddles, leather chaps, and spurs. Americans in Texas, with the largest herds of cattle in the country, adopted these methods and carried them to the northernmost ranges of the cattle kingdom. From Texas, too, came the small, muscular horses (broncos and mustangs) that enabled cowboys to control the herds.

At the end of the Civil War, an estimated 5 million cattle roamed the Texas ranges. Eastern markets offered good prices for steers. The challenge facing the cattle industry lay in getting the animals from the range to towns on major rail lines. Early in 1866, some Texas cattle ranchers began driving their combined herds, up to 260,000 steers, north to Sedalia, Missouri, on the Missouri Pacific Railroad. The caravan suffered heavy losses but established a new and important feature of their business: namely, that cattle could be driven to distant markets and pastured along the trail. This earliest of the **long drives** established the first, tentative link between the isolated cattle breeders of west Texas and the booming urban markets of the East.

Market facilities soon grew up at Abilene, Kansas, on the Kansas Pacific Railroad, and for years the town reigned as the railhead of the cattle kingdom. But by the mid-1870s, agricultural development in western Kansas had eaten away at the open-range land. Cattlemen had to develop other trails and other market outlets. As the railroads reached farther west, other locations began to rival Abilene as major centers of stock herding: Dodge City and Wichita in Kansas, Ogallala and Sidney in Nebraska, Cheyenne and Laramie in Wyoming, and Miles City and Glendive in Montana.

There had always been an element of risk and speculation in the open-range cattle business. Rustlers and Indians frequently seized large numbers of animals. But as the settlement of the plains increased, new forms of competition arose. Sheep breeders from California and Oregon brought their flocks onto the range to compete for grass. Farmers ("nesters") from the East threw fences around their claims, blocking trails and breaking up the open range. A series of "**range wars**"—between sheepmen and cattlemen, ranchers, and farmers—erupted out of the tensions among these competing groups.

Accounts of the lofty profits to be made in the cattle business tempted eastern, English, and Scottish capital to the plains. Increasingly, the structure of the cattle economy became

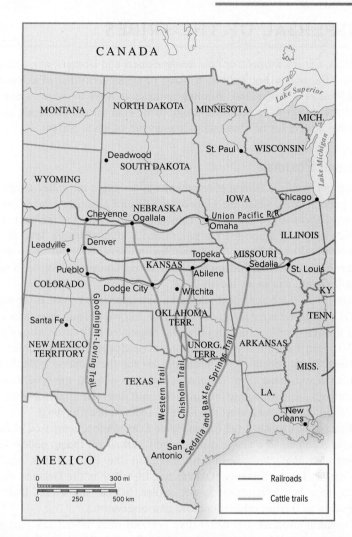

THE CATTLE KINGDOM, CA. 1866-1887 Cattle ranching and cattle drives are among the most romanticized features of the nineteenth-century West. But they were also hardheaded businesses, made possible by the growing eastern market for beef and the availability of reasonably inexpensive transportation—thanks to the dense network of trails and railroads—to take cattle to the urban markets. • *Why was the open range necessary for the great cattle drives, and what eventually ended the cattle trails?*

corporate; in one year, twenty corporations with a combined capital of $12 million were chartered in Wyoming. The result of this frenzied, speculative expansion was that the ranges, already shrunk by the railroads and the farmers, became overstocked. There was not enough grass to support the crowding herds or sustain the long drives. Two severe winters, in 1885-1886 and 1886-1887, and a searing summer between them scorched the plains. Streams and grass dried up. Hundreds of thousands of cattle died. Princely ranches and costly investments disappeared in a season.

The open-range industry never recovered, and the long drive finally disappeared for good. Railroads displaced the trail as the route to market for livestock. But some established cattle ranches survived, grew, and prospered, eventually producing more beef than ever.

THE DISPERSAL OF THE TRIBES

Be they ranchers, miners, farmers, or railroad developers and laborers, migrants to the West tended to view the region not only as a place of opportunity but of conquest. Having imagined the West as a "virgin land" awaiting civilization by white people, many Americans tried to force the region to match their image of it. That meant, above all, ensuring that the Indian tribes would not be obstacles to the spread of white society.

WHITE TRIBAL POLICIES

The traditional policy of the federal government was to regard the tribes simultaneously as independent nations (with which the United States could negotiate treaties) and as wards of the president (who would exercise paternalistic authority over the Indians). The concept of Indian sovereignty had supported the government's attempt before 1860 to erect a permanent frontier between whites and Indians. But the belief in tribal sovereignty and the treaties or agreements with the Indians were not strong enough to withstand the desire of white settlers for more and more Indian lands.

By the early 1850s, the government adopted a new approach known as the **concentration policy**. In 1851, the government assigned each tribe its own defined reservation, confirmed by individual treaties—treaties often illegitimately negotiated with unauthorized Indian "representatives" chosen by whites, people known sarcastically as "treaty chiefs." The new arrangement had many benefits for whites and few for the Indians. It divided the tribes from one another and made them easier to control. It allowed the government to force tribes into scattered locations and to take over the most desirable lands for white settlement. But concentration did not survive as the basis of Indian policy for long.

In 1867, Congress established the Indian Peace Commission, composed of both soldiers and civilians, to recommend a new and presumably permanent Indian policy. The commission recommended that the government move all the Plains tribes into two large reservations—one in Indian Territory (Oklahoma), the other in the Dakotas. At a series of meetings with the tribes, government agents cajoled, bribed, and tricked their representatives into agreeing to treaties establishing the new reservations.

But this "solution" worked little better than previous ones for Indians. Part of the problem were the corrupt or incompetent agents of the Bureau of Indian Affairs who administered the reservations. The problem was also exacerbated by the relentless slaughter of buffalo herds by whites that destroyed the tribes' way of life. After the Civil War, professional and amateur hunters—even casual visitors shooting from passing trains—swarmed over the plains, slaughtering the huge animals. Some Indian tribes (notably the Blackfeet) also began killing large numbers of buffalo to sell in the booming new market for their hides and meat. In 1865, there had been at least 15 million buffalo; two decades later, fewer than 1,000 of the great beasts survived. By destroying the buffalo herds, whites were destroying the Indians' source of food and supplies and their ability to resist white advance.

THE INDIAN WARS

Whites and Indians fought incessantly from the 1850s to the 1880s, as Indians struggled against the growing threats to their civilizations. Indian warriors attacked wagon trains, stagecoaches, and isolated ranches, often in retaliation for earlier attacks on them by whites. As the U.S. Army became more deeply involved in the fighting, the tribes began to focus more of their attacks on white soldiers.

(Source: NPS photo by JR Douglas)

BUFFALO HIDE MANIA A boom in the popularity of Buffalo hides after the Civil War led to the widespread and indiscriminate slaughter of Buffalo, rendering the species nearly extinct by the late 1800s.

At times, this small-scale fighting escalated. During the Civil War, the eastern Sioux in Minnesota, cramped on a small reservation and exploited by corrupt white agents, suddenly rebelled. Led by Little Crow, they killed more than 700 whites before being subdued. Thirty-eight of the Indians were hanged, and the tribe was exiled to the Dakotas.

At the same time, fighting flared up in eastern Colorado, where the Arapaho and Cheyenne were coming into conflict with white miners settling in the region. Bands of Indians attacked stagecoach lines and settlements in an effort to regain territory they had lost. In response to these incidents, whites called up a large territorial militia. The governor urged all friendly Indians to congregate at army posts for protection before the army began its campaign. One Arapaho and Cheyenne band under Black Kettle, apparently in response to the invitation, camped near Fort Lyon on Sand Creek in November 1864. Some members of the party were warriors, but Black Kettle believed he was under official protection and exhibited no hostile intention. Nevertheless, Colonel J. M. Chivington led a volunteer militia force—largely consisting of unemployed miners, many of whom were apparently drunk—to the unsuspecting camp and massacred 133 people, 105 of them women and children. Black Kettle himself escaped the Sand Creek massacre. But four years later, in 1868, he and Cheyenne soldiers went to war with the whites. The Indians were caught on the Washita River, near the Texas border, by Colonel George A. Custer. White troops killed the chief and his people.

At the end of the Civil War, white troops stepped up their wars against the western Indians on several fronts. The most serious and sustained conflict was in Montana, where the army was attempting to build a road, the Bozeman Trail, to connect Fort Laramie, Wyoming, to the new mining centers. The western Sioux resented this intrusion into the heart of their buffalo range. Led by one of their great chiefs, Red Cloud, they so harried the soldiers and the construction party that the road could not be used.

But it was not only the U.S. military that harassed the tribes. White vigilantes engaged in what became known as "Indian hunting" or unofficial campaigns of violence. Sometimes the killing was in response to Indian raids on white communities. But considerable numbers of whites were committed to the goal of literal "elimination" of the tribes whatever their behavior, a goal that rested on the belief in the essential inhumanity of Indians and the impossibility of white coexistence with them. In California, civilians killed close to 5,000 Indians between 1850 and 1880—one of many factors (disease and poverty being the more important) that steadily reduced the Indian population of the state from 150,000 before the Civil War to 30,000 in 1870.

The treaties negotiated in 1867 brought a temporary lull to many of the conflicts. But new forces soon shattered the peace again. In the early 1870s, more waves of white settlers, mostly miners, began to penetrate the lands in Dakota Territory supposedly guaranteed to the tribes in 1867. Indian resistance flared anew. In the northern plains, the Sioux rose up in 1875 and left their reservation. When white officials ordered them to return, bands of warriors gathered in Montana and united under two great leaders: Crazy Horse and Sitting Bull. Three U.S. Army columns set out to round them up and force them back onto the reservation. With the expedition, as colonel of the famous Seventh Cavalry, was the colorful and controversial George A. Custer. At the Battle of the **Little Bighorn** in southern Montana in 1876, an unprecedentedly large army, perhaps 2,500 tribal warriors, surprised Custer and part of his regiment, surrounded them, and killed every soldier.

But the Indians did not have the political organization or the supplies to keep their troops united. Soon the warriors drifted off in bands to elude pursuit or search for food, and the army ran them down and returned them to Dakota. The power of the Sioux quickly collapsed. They accepted defeat and life on reservations.

One of the most dramatic episodes in Indian history occurred in Idaho in 1877. The Nez Percé were a small and relatively peaceful tribe, some of whose members had managed to live unmolested in Oregon into the 1870s without ever signing a treaty with the United States. But under pressure from white settlers, the U.S. government forced them to move onto a reservation. With no realistic prospect of resisting, the Indians began the journey to the reservation; but on the way, several younger Indians, drunk and angry, killed four white settlers.

The leader of the band, **Chief Joseph**, persuaded his followers to flee from the inevitable retribution. American troops pursued and attacked them, only to be driven off in a battle at White Bird Canyon. After that, the Nez Percé scattered in several directions and became part of a remarkable chase. Joseph moved with 200 warriors and 350 women, children, and old people in an effort to reach Canada. Pursued by four columns of American soldiers, the Indians covered 1,321 miles in seventy-five days, repelling or evading the army time and again. They were finally caught just short of the Canadian boundary. Some escaped and slipped across the border; but Joseph and most of his followers, weary and discouraged, finally gave up. "Hear me, my chiefs," Joseph said after meeting with the American general Nelson Miles, "I am tired. My heart is sick and sad. From where the sun now stands, I will fight no more forever."

The last Indians to maintain organized resistance against the whites were the Chiricahua Apache. The two ablest chiefs of this tribe were Mangas Colorados and Cochise. Mangas was murdered during the Civil War by white soldiers who tricked him into surrendering. In 1872 Cochise agreed to peace in exchange for a reservation that included some of the tribe's traditional land. But Cochise died in 1874, and his successor, **Geronimo**, fought on for more than a decade longer, establishing bases in the mountains of Arizona and Mexico and leading warriors in intermittent raids against white outposts. With each raid, however, the number of warring Apache dwindled, as some warriors died and others drifted away to the reservation. By 1886, Geronimo's band consisted of only about 30 people, including women and children, while his white pursuers numbered perhaps 10,000. Geronimo recognized the odds and surrendered.

The Apache Wars, the most violent of all the Indian conflicts, produced brutality on both sides. But it was the whites who committed the most flagrant atrocities. That did not end with the conclusion of the Apache Wars. Another tragic encounter occurred in 1890 as a result of a religious revival among the Sioux—a revival that itself symbolized the catastrophic effects of the white assaults on Indian civilization. As other tribes had done in trying times in the past, many of these Indians turned to a prophet who led them in a religious revival.

This time the prophet was Wovoka, a Paiute who inspired a fervent spiritual awakening that began in Nevada and spread quickly to the plains. Wovoka predicted the imminent coming of a messiah. The new revival's most conspicuous feature was a mass, emotional "Ghost Dance," which inspired ecstatic, mystical visions—including images of the retreat of white people from the plains and a restoration of the great buffalo herds. White agents on the Sioux reservation, bewildered and fearful, warned the army that dances might be the prelude to hostilities.

On December 29, 1890, the Seventh Cavalry tried to round up a group of about 350 cold and starving Sioux at **Wounded Knee**, South Dakota. Fighting broke out in which about 40 white soldiers and up to 200 Indians died. An Indian may have fired the first shot, but the battle soon turned into a one-sided massacre, as the white soldiers turned their new machine guns on the Indians and mowed them down in the snow.

THE DAWES ACT

Even before the Ghost Dance and the Wounded Knee tragedies, the federal government had moved to destroy forever the tribal structure that was the cornerstone of Indian culture. Reversing its policy of nearly fifty years, Congress abolished the practice by which tribes owned reservation lands communally. The new policy required Indians to become landowners and farmers, to abandon their collective society and culture and become part of white civilization. Some supporters of the new policy believed they were acting for the good of the Indians, whom they considered a "vanishing race" in need of rescue by and assimilation into white society.

The **Dawes Severalty Act** of 1887 provided for the gradual elimination of most tribal ownership of land and the allotment of tracts to individual owners: 160 acres to the head of a family, 80 acres to a single adult or orphan, 40 acres to each dependent child. Adult owners were given U.S. citizenship, but unlike other citizens, they could not gain full title to their property for twenty-five years (supposedly to prevent them from selling the land to speculators).

In applying the Dawes Act, the Bureau of Indian Affairs relentlessly promoted the idea of assimilation that lay behind it. Not only did agents of the bureau try to move Indian families onto their own plots of land, they also took many Indian children away from their families and sent them to boarding schools run by whites. They moved as well to stop Indian religious rituals and encouraged the spread of Christianity and the creation of Christian churches on the reservations.

CARLISLE INDIAN SCHOOL. This 1904 photo captures young Native American men at work in a metal shop at The Carlisle School in Carlisle, Pennsylvania. The Carlisle School was a federally-funded boarding school dedicated to "remaking" Indian children and adolescents into hard-working citizens capable of participating in white society. Students were expected to leave behind their tribal culture and clothing and adopt the behavior, values, and fashion of white America. Thousands of Indians from dozens of tribes attended Carlisle during its existence from 1879 to 1918. It was one of twenty-six such schools operated by the Bureau of Indian Affairs at the turn of the twentieth century.

Few Indians were prepared for this wrenching change. In any case, white administration of the Dawes Act was so corrupt and inept that ultimately the government simply abandoned most efforts to enforce it. Much of the reservation land, therefore, was never distributed to individual owners.

THE RISE AND DECLINE OF THE WESTERN FARMER

The arrival of the miners, the empire building of the cattle ranchers, the dispersal of the Indian tribes—all served as a prelude to the decisive phase of white settlement of the Far West. Even before the Civil War, farmers had begun moving into the plains region, challenging the dominance of the ranchers and the Indians. By the 1870s, what was once a trickle had become a deluge. Western journalists and visitors alike told tall tales of money to be had for the taking: the region's healthy climate, pure water, fertile soil, and nutrient-rich grasses, they crowed, made industries like cattle ranching into can't-miss investment opportunities. (See "Consider the Source: Walter Baron Von Richthofen, *Cattle Raising on the Plains in North America*.") And they came. Farmers poured into the plains and beyond, enclosed land that had once been hunting territory for Indians and open range for cattle, and established a new agricultural region.

For a time in the late 1870s and early 1880s, the new western farmers flourished, enjoying the fruits of an agricultural economic boom. Beginning in the mid-1880s, however, the boom turned to bust, and the western agricultural economy began a long, steady decline.

FARMING ON THE PLAINS

Many factors combined to produce the surge of post–Civil War western agricultural settlement, but the most important was the railroads. Before the war, the Great Plains had been accessible only through a difficult journey by wagon. But beginning in the 1860s, a great new network of railroad lines made huge areas of settlement accessible for the first time.

(Source: Library of Congress, American Memory Collection [rbpe.13401300])

RAILROAD LAND ADVERTISEMENT. Like many railroad companies in the late 1800s, the Burlington & Missouri sponsored migration to the West by offering favorable terms of credit for land purchase to interested parties.

CONSIDER THE SOURCE

WALTER BARON VON RICHTHOFEN, *CATTLE RAISING ON THE PLAINS IN NORTH AMERICA* (1885)

Boosters of the West's lucrative economy were plentiful. Walter Baron Von Richthofen, an immigrant and scion of an aristocratic German Austrian family, lauded cattle ranching as a western industry that begged for investors eager to make easy money.

The immense profits which have been universally realized in the Western cattle business for the past, and which will be increased in the future, owing to the more economical methods pursued, so long as ranges can be purchased at present prices, may seem incredible to many of my readers, who, no doubt, have considered the stories of the fortunes realized as myths. Yet it is true that many men who started only a few years ago with comparatively few cattle, are now wealthy, and, in some cases, millionaires. They certainly did not find the gold upon the prairies, nor did they have any source of revenue beyond the increase of their cattle. The agencies producing this immense wealth are very natural and apparent.

The climate of the West is the healthiest on the earth; the pure, high mountain air and dry atmosphere are the natural remedies, or rather preventives, against sickness among cattle in general, and against all epidemic diseases in particular; for "nowhere in the Western states do we find any traces of pleuro-pneumonia, foot or mouth, and such like contagious diseases."

The pure, clear water of the mountain rivers affords to cattle another health preserver, and the fine nutritious and bountiful grasses, and in winter the naturally cured hay, furnish to them the healthiest natural food.

Formerly these pastures cost nothing, and at present only a trifle . . . so that the interest on the investment in purchasing land is of little importance in the estimate of the cost of keeping a herd. In fact, ownership of land is now indispensable for a herd-owner. This land in less than ten years will be a considerable factor in the profits of the cattle business, as the value of pastures will constantly-increase.

The principal cost of raising cattle is only the herding and watching the cattle by herders, without any cost for sheltering or feeding. In time even these expenses will be reduced, as now already herds are kept in large fenced ranges, and many of the herders are dispensed with.

The losses of cattle, as shown by statistics, are larger among Eastern and European herds, which are sheltered in stables and fed the whole year round, than among the shelterless herds of the West. The losses in the West . . . are practically reduced by long experience to a certain percentage, which enables the stockmen to calculate infallibly the profits and losses of their business.

This annual loss is found to average 2 to 3 per cent. We may safely put the loss in the extreme Northern states at about 3 per cent, and in the more Southern and temperate districts at 2 or less per cent. The annual cost of herding the cattle . . . is about $.70 per head; adding the other expenses, such as taxes, loss of interest on the purchase-money of land, etc., we find that the entire annual expense is less than $1.50 per head.

Now let me illustrate the profits realized from one Texas cow, worth $30.00. In ten years she will have eight calves, which, if they are all steers, will have produced at the end of fourteen years $320, or a profit of $272.00. The cow herself still remains, and is worth about her original cost for the butcher. These figures are made without reference to any increase in the value of cattle or beef, and without reference to any improvement of the stock by crossing it with better blood. . . .

Ten years ago an Irish servant-girl wanted money due her, amounting to $150, from a cattle-raiser who lived in Montana. Cattle had been dull, and he could not dispose of any of his herd, but agreed to her to brand fifteen cows in her name, give her the increase, and carry them with his herd, free of cost, until she was ready to sell, he to have the first privilege of purchase. She accepted, held on to her purchase, and last May sold out her master for $25,000.

Source: Von Richthofen, Walter Baron, *Cattle Raising on the Plains of North America*, 1885; repr., Norman, OK: University of Oklahoma Press, 1964, 70–73, 80; located in Marilynn S. Johnson (ed.), *Violence in the West: The Johnson County Range War and the Ludlow Massacre: A Brief History with Documents*, Boston, MA: Bedford St. Martin's, 2009, 37–39.

UNDERSTAND, ANALYZE, & EVALUATE

1. How did Von Richthofen describe the land and natural resources for cattle ranching in the North American plains? Why did Von Richthofen stress the importance of landownership?
2. Does Von Richthofen strike you as a cautious businessman? What might explain the confidence he showed in his projections?
3. Why do you think the author concluded with the example of the Irish servant girl?

The building of the transcontinental train line—completed in 1869 when the two lines met at Promontory Point, Utah—was a dramatic and monumental achievement. But the construction of subsidiary lines in the following years proved of greater importance to the West. State governments, imitating Washington, subsidized railroad development by offering direct financial aid, favorable loans, and more than 50 million acres of land (on top of the 130 million acres the federal government had already provided). Although built and operated by private corporations, the railroads were in many respects public projects.

The railroad companies actively promoted settlement to create new markets. New communities would consume and generate the goods their lines would transport, and the railroads could profit by selling the land they had gained for free, or for very little money, from local and federal government.

Contributing further to the great surge of white agricultural expansion was a pronounced but temporary change in the climate of the Great Plains. For several years in succession, beginning in the 1870s, rainfall in the plains states was well above average. White Americans now rejected the old idea that the region was the "Great American Desert."

But even under the most favorable conditions, farming on the plains presented special problems. First was the problem of fencing. Farmers had to enclose their land, but materials for traditional wood or stone fences were unavailable. In the mid-1870s, however, two Illinois farmers, Joseph H. Glidden and I. L. Ellwood, solved this problem by developing and marketing barbed wire, which became standard equipment on the plains and revolutionized fencing practices all over the world.

The second problem was water. Water was scarce even when rainfall was above average. After 1887, a series of dry seasons began, and lands that had been fertile now returned to semidesert. Some farmers dealt with the problem by using deep wells pumped by steel windmills, by turning to "dryland farming" (a system of tillage designed to conserve moisture in the soil by covering it with a dust blanket), or by planting drought-resistant crops. In many areas of the plains, however, only large-scale irrigation could save the endangered farms. But irrigation projects of the necessary magnitude required government assistance, and neither the federal nor the state governments were prepared to fund the projects.

Most of the people who moved into the region had previously been farmers in the Midwest, the East, or Europe. In the booming years of the early 1880s, with land values rising, the new farmers had no problem obtaining extensive and easy credit. But the arid years of the late 1880s—during which crop prices fell while production became more expensive—changed the farmers' prospects. Tens of thousands of farmers could not pay their debts and were forced to abandon their farms. There was, in effect, a reverse migration: white settlers moving back east, sometimes turning once-flourishing western communities into desolate ghost towns. Those who remained continued to suffer from falling prices (for example, wheat, which had sold for $1.60 a bushel at the end of the Civil War, dropped to 49 cents in the 1890s) and persistent indebtedness.

COMMERCIAL AGRICULTURE

By the late nineteenth century, the sturdy, independent farmer of popular myth was being replaced by the commercial farmer—attempting to do in the agricultural economy what industrialists were doing in the manufacturing economy. Commercial farmers specialized in cash crops that were sold in national or world markets. They did not often make their own household supplies or grow their own food but bought them from merchants. This kind of farming, when it was successful, raised farmers' living standards. But it also made them dependent on bankers and interest rates, railroads and freight rates, national and European markets, world supply and demand. And unlike the capitalists of the industrial order, they could not regulate their production or influence the prices of what they sold.

Between 1865 and 1900, farm output increased dramatically, not only in the United States but in Brazil, Argentina, Canada, Australia, New Zealand, Russia, and elsewhere. Beginning in the 1880s, worldwide overproduction led to a drop in prices for most agricultural goods and hence to great economic distress for many of the more than 6 million American farm families. By the 1890s, 27 percent of the farms in the country were mortgaged; by 1910, 33 percent. In 1880, 25 percent of all farms had been operated by tenants; by 1910, the proportion had grown to 37 percent. Commercial farming made some people fabulously wealthy. But the farm economy as a whole was suffering a significant decline relative to the rest of the nation.

THE FARMERS' GRIEVANCES

American farmers were painfully aware that something was wrong. But few people yet understood the implications of national and world overproduction. Instead, they concentrated their attention and anger on more immediate, more comprehensible—and no less real—problems: inequitable freight rates, high interest charges, and an inadequate currency.

The farmers' first and most burning grievance was against the railroads. In many cases, the railroads charged higher rates for farm goods than for other goods, and for transport in the South and West than in the Northeast. Railroads also controlled elevator and warehouse facilities in buying centers and charged arbitrary storage rates.

Farmers also resented the institutions controlling credit—banks, loan companies, insurance corporations. Since sources of credit in the West and South were few, farmers had to take loans on whatever terms they could get, often at very high interest rates ranging from 10 to 25 percent. Many farmers had to pay back these loans in years when crop prices were dropping and, after 1873, when the supply of money in circulation contracted because the federal government eliminated the minting of silver coins. During times when the money supply tightened, banks and creditors assessed borrowers like farmers much higher fees and interest rates. As a result, expansion of the currency became an increasingly important issue to farmers.

A third grievance concerned prices. A farmer could plant a large crop at a moment when its price was high and find that by the time of the harvest the price had declined. Farmers' fortunes rose and fell in response to unpredictable forces. But many farmers became convinced (often with some reason) that "intermediaries"—speculators, bankers, regional and local agents—were conspiring with one another to fix prices so as to benefit themselves at the growers' expense. Many farmers also came to believe (again, not entirely without reason) that manufacturers in the East were colluding to keep the prices of farm goods low and the prices of industrial goods high. Although farmers sold their crops in a competitive world market, they bought manufactured goods in a domestic market protected by tariffs and dominated by trusts and corporations.

The Agrarian Malaise

These economic difficulties helped produce social and cultural resentments. Among them was the isolation of farm life. Farm families in some parts of the country were virtually cut off from the outside world. During the winter months, the loneliness and boredom could become nearly unbearable. Many farmers lacked access to adequate education for their children. They had few or no proper medical facilities. There were few organized recreational or cultural activities. Older farmers felt the sting of watching their children leave the farm for the city. They felt the humiliation of being ridiculed as "hayseeds" by the new urban culture that was coming to dominate American life.

This sense of isolation and obsolescence led to a growing malaise among many farmers, a discontent that helped create a great national political movement in the 1890s. It found reflection, too, in some of the literature that emerged from rural America. Writers in the late nineteenth century might romanticize the rugged life of the cowboy and the western miner. For the farmers, however, the image of the agricultural world was different. Hamlin Garland, for example, reflected the growing disillusionment in a series of novels and short stories. In the introduction to his novel *Jason Edwards* (1891), he wrote that in the past, the agrarian frontier had seemed to be "the Golden West, the land of wealth and freedom and happiness." Now, however, the bright promise had faded. The trials of rural life were crushing the human spirit. "So this is the reality of the dream!" a character in *Jason Edwards* exclaims, "A shanty on a barren plain, hot and lone as a desert. My God!" Once, sturdy yeoman farmers had viewed themselves as the backbone of American life. Now they were becoming painfully aware that their position was declining in relation to the rising urban-industrial society to the east.

CONCLUSION

To many Americans in the late nineteenth century, the West seemed an untamed "frontier" in which hardy pioneers were creating a new society. The reality of the West in these years, however, was very different from this enduring image. White Americans moved into the vast regions west of the Mississippi at a remarkable rate in the years after the Civil War, and many of them indeed settled in lands far from any civilization they had ever known. But the West was not an empty place. It contained a large population of Indians, with whom the white settlers sometimes lived uneasily and with whom they sometimes battled; but almost always in the end, the Indians were pushed aside and (with help from the federal government) relocated onto lands whites did not want. There were significant numbers of Mexicans in some areas, small populations of Asians in others, and African Americans moving in from the South in search of land and freedom. The West was no barren frontier but a place of many cultures.

The West was also closely and increasingly tied to the emerging capitalist-industrial economy of the East. The miners who flooded into California, Colorado, Nevada, the Dakotas, and elsewhere were responding to the demand in the East for gold and silver, but even more for iron ore, copper, lead, zinc, and quartz. Cattle and sheep ranchers produced meat, wool, and leather for eastern consumers and manufacturers. Farmers grew crops for sale in national and international commodities markets. The West certainly looked different from the East. But the growth of the West was very much a part of the growth of the rest of the nation. And the culture of the West, despite the romantic images of pioneering individuals embraced by easterners and westerners alike, was at its heart as much a culture of economic growth and capitalist ambition as was that of the rest of the nation.

KEY TERMS/PEOPLE/PLACES/EVENTS

Californios 383
Chief Joseph 396
Chinese Exclusion Act 386
concentration policy 394
coolies 384

Dawes Severalty Act 397
Geronimo 396
Homestead Act 386
Little Bighorn 396
long drive 392

Mark Twain 389
range wars 392
Rocky Mountain school 387
Turner thesis 390
Wounded Knee 397

RECALL AND REFLECT

1. How did ethnic, racial, and cultural prejudice affect western society?
2. What were the three major industries involved in the development of the West, and how did these industries transform the western economy?
3. What was the romantic image of the West, and how was this image expressed in art, literature, and popular culture?
4. How did actions and policies of the federal government affect the fate of Indians in the West?

17 | INDUSTRIAL SUPREMACY

SOURCES OF INDUSTRIAL GROWTH
CAPITALISM AND ITS CRITICS
THE ORDEAL OF THE WORKER

LOOKING AHEAD

1. What factors drove America's industrial expansion in the late nineteenth and early twentieth centuries?
2. Who were the critics of America's new industrial economy, what were their criticisms, and what solutions did they propose?
3. How did the conditions and characteristics of the workforce change during this period of rapid industrialization?

"TWENTY-FIVE YEARS AFTER THE DEATH of Lincoln, America had become, in the quantity and value of her products, the leading manufacturing nation of the world. What England had accomplished in a hundred years, the United States had achieved in half the time." So boasted the historians Charles and Mary Beard in the 1920s, expressing the amazement many Americans felt when they considered the remarkable expansion of their industrial economy in the late nineteenth century.

In fact, America's rise to industrial supremacy was not as sudden as such observers suggested. The nation had been building a manufacturing economy since early in the nineteenth century. But Americans were clearly correct in observing that the accomplishments of the last three decades of the nineteenth century overshadowed all the earlier progress.

The remarkable growth did much to increase the wealth and improve the lives of many Americans. But such benefits were unequally shared. While industrial titans and a growing middle class were enjoying a prosperity without precedent in the nation's history, workers, farmers, and others were experiencing an often painful ordeal that slowly edged the United States toward a great economic and political crisis.

1859
First oil well drilled

1866
National Labor Union
founded

First transatlantic cable

1870
Rockefeller founds
Standard Oil

1873
Carnegie Steel founded

Economic panic

1876
Bell invents telephone

1877
Nationwide railroad
strike

1879
Edison invents electric
lightbulb

1881
American Federation of
Labor founded

1886
Haymarket bombing

1888
Bellamy's *Looking
Backward*

1892
Homestead steel strike

1893
Depression begins

1894
Pullman strike

1901
Carnegie publishes
The Gospel of Wealth

1903
Wright brothers'
airplane flight

1914
Ford introduces factory
assembly lines

SOURCES OF INDUSTRIAL GROWTH

Many factors contributed to the growth of American industry: abundant raw materials, a large and growing labor supply, a surge in technological innovation, the emergence of a talented and often ruthless group of entrepreneurs, a federal government eager to assist the growth of business, and an expanding domestic market for the products of manufacturing.

INDUSTRIAL TECHNOLOGIES

The rapid emergence of new technologies, together with the discovery of new materials and productive processes, were among the principal sources of late-nineteenth-century industrial growth. Some of the most important innovations were in communications. In 1866, Cyrus W. Field laid a transatlantic telegraph cable to Europe. During the next decade, Alexander Graham Bell developed the first telephone with commercial capacity. By 1900, there were 1.35 million telephones, and by 1920, 13.3 million. And the Italian inventor Guglielmo Marconi was taking the first steps toward the development of radio in the 1890s; the technology he pioneered quickly found its way to the United States. Other inventions that speeded the pace of business organization were the typewriter (by Christopher L. Sholes in 1868), the cash register (by James Ritty in 1879), and the calculating, or adding, machine (by William S. Burroughs in 1891).

Among the most revolutionary innovations was the introduction in the 1870s of electricity as a source of light and power. The pioneers of electric lighting included Charles F. Brush, who devised the arc lamp for street illumination, and Thomas A. Edison, who invented the incandescent lamp (or lightbulb). Edison and others designed improved generators and built large power plants to furnish electricity to whole cities. By the turn of the century, electric power was becoming commonplace in street railway systems, in the elevators of urban skyscrapers, in factories, and increasingly in offices and homes.

Particularly important to trade and industry was the development of new high-efficiency steam engines capable of powering larger ships at faster speeds than ever before. The new high-speed freighters, for example, made it cheaper for Britain to buy wheat grown in Canada and the United States than to grow it at home. The introduction of refrigerated ships in the 1870s made it possible to transport meat from North America, and even Australia and Asia, to Europe.

The Technology of Iron and Steel Production

Iron production had developed slowly in the United States through most of the nineteenth century, mostly driven by the demand for iron rails; steel production had developed hardly at all by the end of the Civil War. In the 1870s and 1880s, however, iron production soared as railroads added 40,000 new miles of track, and steel production made great strides toward its eventual dominance in the metals industry.

An Englishman, Henry Bessemer, and an American, William Kelly, developed, almost simultaneously, a process for converting iron into the much more durable and versatile steel. (The process, which took Bessemer's name, consisted of blowing air through molten iron to burn out the impurities and create a much stronger metal.) The Bessemer process also relied on the discovery by the British metallurgist Robert Mushet that ingredients could be added during the conversion process to give steel additional strength. In 1868, the New Jersey ironmaster Abram S. Hewitt introduced from Europe another method of making steel—the open-hearth process. These techniques made possible the production of steel in great quantities and large dimensions, for use in the manufacture of locomotives, rails, and girders for the construction of tall buildings.

The steel industry emerged first in western Pennsylvania and eastern Ohio, partly because iron ore could be found there in abundance. It was also because the new forms of steel production created a demand for new kinds of fuel—and particularly for the anthracite (or hard) coal that was plentiful in Pennsylvania. Later, new techniques made it possible to use bituminous (or soft) coal, also easily mined in western Pennsylvania. As a result, Pittsburgh quickly became the center of the steel world. New sources of ore soon emerged. The upper peninsula of Michigan, the Mesabi Range in Minnesota, and central Alabama became important ore-producing locales and new centers of steel production grew up near them: Cleveland, Detroit, Chicago, and Birmingham, among others.

Until the Civil War, iron and steel furnaces were mostly made of stone and usually built against the side of a hill to reduce construction demands. By the 1870s, however, furnaces were redesigned as cylindrical iron shells lined with brick. These massive new furnaces were 75 feet tall and higher and could produce over 500 tons a week.

As the steel industry spread, new transportation systems emerged to serve it. Steel production in the Great Lakes region produced steam freighters that could carry ore on the lakes. Shippers used new steam engines to speed the unloading of ore. The demand for vessels capable of transporting oil and the development of new and more powerful steam engines led to the design of larger and heavier freighters.

There was an even closer relationship between the emerging steel companies and the railroads. Steel manufacturers provided rails and parts for cars; railroads were both markets for and transporters of manufactured steel. But the relationship soon became more intimate than that. The Pennsylvania Railroad, for example, actually created the Pennsylvania Steel Company.

(Source: Library of Congress, Prints and Photographs Division [LC-USZ62-63520])

PIONEER OIL RUN, 1865 The American oil industry emerged first in western Pennsylvania, where speculators built makeshift facilities almost overnight. An oil field on the other side of the hill depicted here had been producing 600 barrels a day, and the wells quickly spilled over the hill and down the slope shown in the photograph.

The steel industry's need for lubrication for its machines helped create another important new industry in the late nineteenth century—oil. (Not until later did oil become important primarily for its potential as a fuel.) The existence of petroleum reserves in western Pennsylvania had been common knowledge for some time. The Pennsylvania businessman George Bissell showed that the substance could be burned in lamps and that it could also yield such products as paraffin, naphtha, and lubricating oil. Bissell raised money to begin drilling; and in 1859, Edwin L. Drake, one of Bissell's employees, established the first oil well near Titusville, Pennsylvania, which soon produced 500 barrels of oil a month. Demand for petroleum grew quickly, and promoters soon developed other oil fields in Pennsylvania, Ohio, and West Virginia.

THE AUTOMOBILE AND THE AIRPLANE

Among the most important technological innovations was the invention of the automobile. Two technologies led to its development: gasoline and the self-contained engine. Gasoline (or petrol) was the product of an extraction process developed in the late nineteenth century in the United States by which lubricating oil and fuel oil were removed separately from crude oil. As early as the 1870s, designers in France, Germany, and Austria had begun to develop an "internal combustion engine," which used the expanding power of burning gas to drive pistons. A German, Nicolaus August Otto, created a gas-powered "four-stroke" engine in the mid-1860s, which was a precursor to automobile engines. But he did not develop a way to untether it from gas lines to be used portably in machines. One of Otto's former employees, Gottfried Daimler, later perfected an engine that could be used in automobiles. Today's automotive giant Daimler-Benz, maker of Mercedes-Benz vehicles, bears his name.

The American automobile industry developed rapidly in the aftermath of these European breakthroughs. Charles and Frank Duryea built the first gasoline-driven motor vehicle in America in 1893. Three years later, **Henry Ford** produced the first of the famous cars that would bear his name. In 1895, there were only four automobiles on the American highways. By 1917, there were nearly 5 million.

The search for a means of human flight, as old as civilization, had been almost entirely futile until the late nineteenth century, when engineers, scientists, and tinkerers in both the United States and Europe began to experiment with a wide range of aeronautic devices. Balloonists began to consider ways to make dirigibles useful vehicles of transportation. Others experimented with kites and gliders.

Two brothers in Ohio, **Wilbur and Orville Wright**, began to construct a glider in 1899 that could be propelled through the air by an internal combustion engine. Four years later, Orville made a celebrated test flight near Kitty Hawk, North Carolina, in which an airplane took off by itself and traveled 120 feet in twelve seconds under its own power before settling back to earth. By the fall of 1904, the Wright brothers had improved the plane to the point where they were able to fly over twenty-three miles, and in the following year they began to take a few passengers on their flights with them.

Although the first working airplane was built in the United States, aviation technology was slow to gain a foothold in America. Most of the early progress in airplane design occurred in France, where there was substantial government funding for research and development. The U.S. government created the National Advisory Committee on Aeronautics in 1915, twelve years after the Wright brothers' flight, and American airplanes became a significant presence in Europe during World War I. But the prospects for commercial flight seemed dim until the 1920s, when Charles Lindbergh's famous solo flight from New York to Paris electrified the nation and the world.

Research and Development

New industrial technologies persuaded many businesses to build their own research operations. The corporate research-and-development (R&D) laboratories coincided with a decline in government support for research, helping corporations attract skilled researchers. It also decentralized the sources of research funding and ensured that inquiry would move in many directions, and not just along paths determined by the government.

A rift began to emerge between scientists and engineers. Engineers—both inside and outside of universities—became increasingly tied up with the R&D agendas of corporations. Many scientists continued to scorn this "commercialization" of knowledge and preferred to stick to basic research that had no immediate practical applications. But many American scientists were more closely connected to practical challenges than were their European counterparts, and some joined engineers in corporate R&D laboratories, which over time began to sponsor both practical and basic research.

Making Production More Efficient

Central to the growth of the automobile and other industries were changes in the techniques of production. By the turn of the century, many industrialists embraced the new principles of "scientific management," dubbed "**Taylorism**" after its leading theoretician, Frederick Winslow Taylor. Taylor aimed to make human labor compatible with the demands of the machine age. He urged employers to reorganize the production process by subdividing tasks into small simple steps that did not require enormous skill or training to complete. The goal

(©Everett Collection Historical/Alamy)

WOMEN ON THE ASSEMBLY LINE This photograph, from 1902, shows women at work on the lock and drill department assembly line at the National Cash Register Company in Dayton, Ohio.

was to minimize worker errors, speed up the production process, and make workers more interchangeable and therefore easier to replace. Scientific management, Taylor claimed, would create a more efficient and less costly workplace.

The most important change in industrial technology was the emergence of mass production and, along with it, the moving assembly line, which Henry Ford introduced in his automobile plants in 1914. The assembly line was a particular place—a factory through which automobiles moved as they were assembled by workers who specialized in particular tasks. It was also a concept. The concept stressed the complete interchangeability of parts. General Motors adopted the same philosophy. Automobile production relied on other technologies, too, in particular the intensive use of electricity—to drive the assembly line, to light the factories, and to run the critical ventilating systems that kept dust from interfering with the machines. The revolutionary assembly-line technique enabled Ford to raise wages and reduce hours while cutting the base price of his Model T from $950 in 1914 to $290 in 1929. It became a standard for many other industries.

RAILROAD EXPANSION AND THE CORPORATION

The principal agent of industrial development in the late nineteenth century was still the expansion of the railroads. Railroads gave industrialists access to distant markets and remote sources of raw materials. Their expansion across the country created thousands of jobs and fueled the growth of hundreds of new and established communities. Their steady demand for track and train boosted the fortunes of steel plants and coal mines, while their sale of excess land stimulated westward migration.

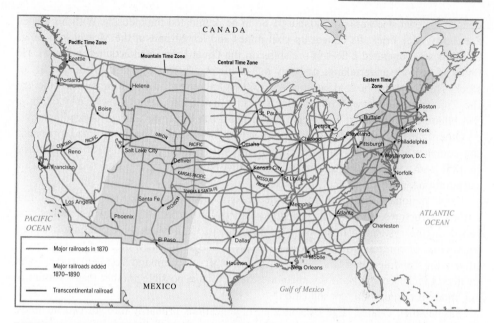

RAILROADS, 1870–1890 This map illustrates the rapid expansion of railroads in the late nineteenth century. In 1870, there was already a dense network of rail lines in the Northeast and Midwest, illustrated here by the green lines. The red lines show the further expansion of rail coverage between 1870 and 1890, much of it in the South and the areas west of the Mississippi River. • *Why were railroads so essential to the nation's economic growth in these years?*

Total railroad trackage increased from 30,000 miles in 1860 to 193,000 in 1900. Vital to this progress was the help of local, state, and federal governments, who provided loans and subsidies. Equally important was the emergence of great railroad "combinations" or mergers that facilitated the development of the industry by concentrating power and resources in the hands of a few powerful men. The achievements and excesses of these tycoons—Cornelius Vanderbilt, James J. Hill, Collis P. Huntington, and others—became symbols to much of the nation of concentrated economic power. But railroad development was less significant for the individual barons it created than for its contribution to the growth of a new institution: the modern corporation.

There had been various forms of corporations in America since colonial times, but the modern corporation emerged as a major force only after the Civil War. By then, railroad magnates and other industrialists realized that their great ventures could not be financed by any single person.

Under the laws of incorporation passed in many states in the 1830s and 1840s, business organizations could raise money by selling stock to members of the public; after the Civil War, one industry after another began doing so. What made these stocks appealing was that investors now had only "limited liability"—they risked only the amount of their investments and were not liable for any debts the corporation might accumulate beyond that point. The ability to sell stock to a broad public made it possible for entrepreneurs to gather vast sums of capital and undertake great projects with manageable financial risk.

The Pennsylvania and other railroads were among the first to adopt the new corporate form of organization. But incorporation quickly spread beyond the railroad industry. **Andrew Carnegie**, a Scottish immigrant, worked his way up from modest beginnings and, in 1873, opened his own steelworks in Pittsburgh. Soon he dominated the industry. With his associate Henry Clay Frick, he bought up coal mines and leased part of the Mesabi iron range in Minnesota, operated a fleet of ore ships on the Great Lakes, and acquired railroads. He financed his vast undertakings not only out of his own profits but also out of the sale of stock. Then, in 1901, he sold out for $450 million to the banker **J. P. Morgan**, who merged the Carnegie interests with others to create the giant United States Steel Corporation—a $14 billion enterprise that controlled almost two-thirds of the nation's steel production.

Other industries developed similarly. Gustavus Swift forged a relatively small meatpacking company into a great national corporation. Isaac Singer patented a sewing machine in 1851 and created I. M. Singer and Company—one of the first modern manufacturing corporations.

Large, national business enterprises needed methodical and highly standardized administrative structures. As a result, corporate leaders introduced managerial techniques that relied on the systematic division of responsibilities. Companies built carefully designed hierarchies of control, strict cost-accounting procedures, and a new breed of business executives: the "middle managers," who formed a layer of command between workers and owners. Efficient administrative capabilities helped make possible another major feature of the modern corporation: consolidation.

Businessmen created large consolidated organizations primarily through two methods. **Horizontal integration** combined a number of firms engaged in the same enterprise into a single corporation such as the consolidation of many different railroad lines into one company. Through **vertical integration**, a company took over all the different businesses on which it relied for its primary function, for example, Carnegie Steel, which came to control not only steel mills but also mines, railroads, and other enterprises. In both cases of integration, the result was similar: a new form of business organization that largely eliminated or severely minimized competition from rivals.

The most celebrated corporate empire of the late nineteenth century was Standard Oil, owned by **John D. Rockefeller**. Shortly after the Civil War, Rockefeller launched a refining company in Cleveland and immediately began trying to eliminate his competition. Allying himself with other wealthy capitalists, he formed the Standard Oil Company of Ohio in 1870, which in a few years had acquired twenty of the twenty-five refineries in Cleveland, as well as plants in Pittsburgh, Philadelphia, New York, and Baltimore.

So far, Rockefeller had expanded only horizontally—buying many refineries. But soon he began expanding vertically as well. He built his own barrel factories, terminal warehouses, and pipelines. Standard Oil owned its own freight cars and developed its own marketing organization. By the 1880s, Rockefeller had established such dominance within the petroleum industry that to much of the nation he served as a leading symbol of monopoly.

Rockefeller and other industrialists saw consolidation as a way to cope with what they believed was the greatest curse of the modern economy: "cutthroat competition." Most businessmen claimed to believe in free enterprise and a competitive marketplace, but in fact they feared that substantial competition could spell instability and ruin for all.

As the movement toward consolidation accelerated, new vehicles emerged to facilitate it. The railroads began with so-called pool arrangements—informal agreements among various companies to stabilize rates and divide markets (arrangements that would, in later years, be known as cartels). But the pool arrangements were too weak and could not ensure cost stability.

The failure of the pools led to new techniques of consolidation. The next effort to stabilize prices was the creation of the "trust"—pioneered by Standard Oil in the early 1880s and the banker J. P. Morgan. Under a trust agreement, stockholders in individual corporations transferred their stocks to a small group of trustees in exchange for shares in the trust itself. Owners of trust certificates often had no direct control over the decisions of the trustees; they simply received a share of the profits of the combination. The trustees themselves, on the other hand, might literally own only a few companies but could exercise effective control over many.

In 1889, the state of New Jersey helped produce a third form of consolidation by changing its laws of incorporation to permit companies to buy up rivals. Other states soon followed. Once actual corporate mergers were permitted, the original trusts became unnecessary. Rockefeller, for example, quickly relocated Standard Oil to New Jersey and created what became known as a "holding company"—a central corporate body that would buy up the stock of various members of the Standard Oil trust and establish direct, formal ownership of them.

By the end of the nineteenth century, 1 percent of the corporations in America were able to control more than 33 percent of the manufacturing. A system of economic organization was emerging that lodged enormous power in the hands of very few men—the great bankers of New York such as Morgan, industrial titans such as Rockefeller (who himself gained control of a major bank), and others.

The industrial giants of the era clearly contributed to substantial economic growth. They were also creating the basis for one of the greatest public controversies of their era: a raging debate over concentrated economic and political power that continued well into the twentieth century.

CAPITALISM AND ITS CRITICS

The inequality of the roaring capitalism of the late nineteenth century was not without its critics. Farmers, workers, middle-class businessmen, and many others considered the new capitalism to be a threat to their own destinies. But the industrial titans built a powerful defense for the new corporate economy.

SURVIVAL OF THE FITTEST

The new rationale for capitalism was based on the belief of individualism—an ideology that would remain at the heart of American conservatism for many decades. Wealthy capitalists defended their wealth by saying that they had earned their wealth and power through their own hard work and their acquisitiveness and thrift. Those who failed had only themselves to blame—a result of ignorance, stupidity, or laziness.

Conservative social theories helped support the belief that through "survival of the fittest" wealthy capitalists deserved their success. Among them was the theory of **Social Darwinism.** Darwin's theories argued that the fittest forms of life survived over thousands of years because of their biological fitness. Social Darwinism argued that individuals rose or fell in society because of their innate "fitness." (Darwin himself, along with most scientists, debunked Social Darwinism, but many Americans embraced it nevertheless.) The English philosopher and biologist Herbert Spencer introduced the theory of Social Darwinism in his book *Principles of Biology* (1864). Society, he argued, benefited from the elimination of the unfit and the survival of the strong and talented. William Graham Sumner, a sociologist at Yale, borrowed from Spencer's theory and created a theory of his own in his famous 1906 book *Folkways*. Those who failed, he argued in a 1913 essay, were unfit for success: "Before the tribunal of nature a man has no more right to life than a rattlesnake; he has no more right to liberty than any wild beast; his right to pursuit of happiness is nothing but a license to maintain the struggle for existence." Wealthy corporate leaders were attracted to the ideas of Spencer and Sumner. Their success confirmed their own virtues and "fitness."

Capitalists argued that they earned their wealth through the honest, all-American virtues of competition and the free market. But critics of the industrial and financial titans claimed that they earned their wealth not because of the innate fitness of those who succeeded, but because they replaced the natural workings of the marketplace by building great monopolies that would protect them from competition.

THE GOSPEL OF WEALTH

Some businessmen attempted to temper the harsh philosophy of Social Darwinism with a gentler, if in some ways equally self-serving, idea: the "**gospel of wealth**." People of great wealth, they argued, had not only great power but also a great responsibility to use their riches to advance social progress. Elaborating on this creed in his 1889 article "The Gospel of Wealth," and elaborated on in the 1901 book of the same title, Andrew Carnegie wrote that people of wealth should consider all revenues in excess of their own needs to be "trust funds" used for the good of the community. (See "Consider the Source: Andrew Carnegie Explains 'The Gospel of Wealth.'") Carnegie was only one of many industrialists who devoted large parts of their fortunes to philanthropic works.

The idea of private wealth as a public blessing existed alongside another popular concept: the notion of great wealth as something available to all. Russell H. Conwell, a Baptist minister, became one of the most prominent spokesmen for the idea by delivering one lecture, "Acres of Diamonds," more than 6,000 times between 1880 and 1900. Conwell told a series of stories, which he claimed were true, of individuals who had found opportunities for extraordinary wealth in their own backyards. (One such story involved a modest farmer who discovered a vast diamond mine in his own fields.) Most of the millionaires in the country, Conwell claimed (inaccurately), had begun on the lowest rung of the economic ladder and had worked their way to success.

But the most famous promoter of the success story was **Horatio Alger**. He was originally a minister in a small town in Massachusetts but was driven from his pulpit as a result of sexual scandals. He moved to New York, where he wrote over a hundred celebrated novels—all of them tributes to social mobility and the ability of Americans to rise from "rags to riches." (See "Patterns of Popular Culture: The Novels of Horatio Alger.")

If Alger's rags-to-riches tales captured the aspiration of many men, **Louisa May Alcott**'s enormously popular novels helped give voice to the often unstated ambitions of many women. Alcott was the daughter of a noted New England reformer, but her family nevertheless experienced considerable hardship. After serving as a nurse in the Civil War and writing a series of popular adventure novels (under a pen name, A. M. Barnard, that disguised her gender), she became a major literary figure with the publication of *Little Women* in 1869 and two sequels over the next twenty years. The main character in these novels, Jo March, struggles to build a life for herself that is not defined by conventional women's roles and ambitions. She spurns a traditional marriage and eventually weds a professor who appears to support her literary ambitions. "Girls write to ask who the little women marry, as if that was the only end and aim of a woman's life," Alcott wrote a friend. "I won't marry Jo to Laurie [the attractive, wealthy neighbor who proposes to her] to please any one." Alcott's female characters, in some ways like Alger's male ones, are remarkable for their independence and drive. Jo March is willful, rebellious, stubborn, ambitious, and often selfish—far from the posed, romantic, submissive women in most popular sentimental novels of Alcott's time aimed at female audiences.

ALTERNATIVE VISIONS

Alongside the celebrations of competition and the justifications for great wealth stood a group of alternative philosophies, challenging the corporate ethos and, at times, capitalism itself.

One such philosophy came from the sociologist Lester Frank Ward. In *Dynamic Sociology* (1883) and other books, he argued that civilization was not governed by natural selection but by human intelligence, which could shape society as it wished. In contrast to Sumner, who believed that state intervention to remodel the environment was futile, Ward thought that an active government engaged in positive planning was society's best hope.

Other Americans adopted more-radical approaches to reform. Some dissenters found a home in the Socialist Labor Party, founded in the 1870s and led for many years by Daniel De Leon, an immigrant from the West Indies. Although De Leon attracted a following in the industrial cities, the party never became a major political force and never polled more than 82,000 votes. A dissident faction of De Leon's party, eager to forge stronger ties with organized labor, broke away and in 1901 formed the more enduring **American Socialist Party**.

Other radicals gained a wider following. Among them was the California writer and activist **Henry George**. His angrily eloquent *Progress and Poverty,* published in 1879, became one of the best-selling nonfiction works in American publishing history. George blamed social problems on the ability of a few monopolists to grow wealthy as a result of rising land values. An increase in the value of land, he claimed, was not a result of any effort by the owner, but an "unearned increment," produced by the growth of society around the land. Such profits were rightfully the property of the community. And so George proposed a "single tax" on land, to replace all other taxes, which would return the increment to the people. The tax, he argued, would destroy monopolies, distribute wealth more equally, and eliminate poverty.

Rivaling George in popularity was **Edward Bellamy**, whose utopian novel *Looking Backward,* published in 1888, sold more than 1 million copies. It described the experiences of a young Bostonian who went into a hypnotic sleep in 1887 and awoke in the year 2000 to find a new social order in which want, politics, and vice were unknown. The new society had emerged through a peaceful, evolutionary process: the large trusts of the late nineteenth century had continued to grow in size and to combine with one another until ultimately they formed a single, great trust, controlled by the government, which distributed the abundance of the industrial economy equally among all the people. "Fraternal cooperation" had replaced competition. Class divisions had disappeared. Bellamy labeled the philosophy behind this vision "nationalism."

THE PROBLEMS OF MONOPOLY

Relatively few Americans shared the views of those who questioned capitalism itself. But as time went on, a growing number of people were becoming deeply concerned about the growth of **monopoly.**

By the end of the century, a wide range of groups had begun to assail monopoly and economic concentration. In the absence of competition, they argued, monopolistic industries

CONSIDER THE SOURCE

ANDREW CARNEGIE EXPLAINS "THE GOSPEL OF WEALTH" (1889)

Writing for a general audience in the literary and culture magazine the _North American Review_, billionaire Andrew Carnegie made one of the industrial age's most famous arguments about the inherent justness of the unequal distribution of economic power and wealth.

The problem of our age is the proper administration of wealth, that the ties of brotherhood may still bind together the rich and poor in harmonious relationship. The conditions of human life have not only been changed, but revolutionized, within the past few hundred years. In former days there was little difference between the dwelling, dress, food, and environment of the chief and those of his retainers. The Indians are today where civilized man then was. . . . The contrast between the palace of the millionaire and the cottage of the laborer with us to-day measures the change which has come with civilization. This change, however, is not to be deplored, but welcomed as highly beneficial. It is well, nay, essential, for the progress of the race that the houses of some should be homes for all that is highest and best in literature and the arts,—and for all the refinements of civilization, rather than that none should be so. Much better this great irregularity than universal squalor. . . . The "good old times" were not good old times. Neither master nor servant was as well situated then as to-day. A relapse to old conditions would be disastrous to both—not the least so to him who serves—and would sweep away civilization with it. But whether the change be for good or ill, it is upon us, beyond our power to alter, and, therefore, to be accepted and made the best of. It is a waste of time to criticize the inevitable.

It is easy to see how the change has come. . . . In the manufacture of products we have the whole story. . . . To-day the world obtains commodities of excellent quality at prices which even the preceding generation would have deemed incredible. The poor enjoy what the rich could not before afford. What were the luxuries have become the necessaries of life. The laborer has now more comforts than the farmer had a few generations ago. The farmer has more luxuries than the landlord had, and is more richly clad and better housed. The landlord has books and pictures rarer and appointments more artistic than the king could then obtain.

The price we pay for this salutary change is, no doubt, great. . . . Under the law of competition, the employer of thousands is forced into the strictest economies, among which the rates paid to labor figure prominently, and often there is friction between the employer and the employed, between capital and labor, between rich and poor. Human society loses homogeneity.

The price which society pays for the law of competition, like the price it pays for cheap comforts and luxuries, is also great; but the advantages of this law are also greater still than its cost—for it is to this law that we owe our wonderful material development, which brings improved conditions in its train. But, whether the law be benign or not, we must say of it, as we say of the change in the conditions of men to which we have referred: It is here; we cannot evade it; no substitutes for it have been found; and while the law may be sometimes hard for the individual, it is best for the race, because it insures the survival of the fittest in every department. Social Darwinism?

What is the proper mode of administering wealth after the laws upon which civilization is founded have thrown it into the hands of the few? . . .

There remains . . . only one mode of using great fortunes; in this we have the true antidote for the temporary unequal distribution of wealth, the reconciliation of the rich and the poor—a reign of harmony. . . . It is founded upon the present most intense Individualism, and the race is prepared to put it in practice by degrees whenever it pleases. Under its sway we shall have an ideal State, in which the surplus wealth of the few will become, in the best sense, the property of the many, because administered for the common good; and this wealth, passing through the hands of the few, can be made a much more potent force for the elevation of our race than if distributed in small sums to the people themselves. Even the poorest can be made to see this, and to agree that great sums gathered by some of their fellow-citizens and spent for public purposes, from which the masses reap the principal benefit, are more valuable to them than if scattered among themselves in trifling amounts through the course of many years. . . .

Poor and restricted are our opportunities in this life, narrow our horizon, our best work most imperfect; but rich men should be thankful for one inestimable boon. They have it in their power during their lives to busy themselves in organizing benefactions from which the masses of their fellows will derive lasting advantage, and thus dignify their own lives. The highest life is probably to be reached, not by such imitation of the life of Christ as Count Tolstoi gives us, but, while animated by Christ's spirit, by recognizing the changed conditions of this age, and adopting modes of expressing this spirit suitable to the changed conditions under which we live, still laboring for the good of our fellows, which was the essence of his life and teaching, but laboring in a different manner.

This, then, is held to be the duty of the man of wealth: To set an example of modest, unostentatious living, shunning display or extravagance; to provide moderately for the legitimate wants of those dependent upon him; and, after doing so, to consider all surplus revenues which come to him simply as trust funds, which he is called upon to administer, and strictly bound as a matter of duty to administer in the manner which, in his judgment, is best calculated to produce the most beneficial results for the community—the man of wealth thus becoming the mere trustee and agent for his poorer brethren, bringing to their service his superior wisdom, experience, and ability to administer, doing for them better than they would or could do for themselves. . . .

[T]he best means of benefiting the community is to place within its reach the ladders upon which the aspiring can rise—free libraries, parks, and means of recreation, by which men are helped in body and mind; works of art, certain to give pleasure and improve the public taste; and public institutions of various kinds, which will improve the general condition of the people; in this manner returning their surplus wealth to the mass of their fellows in the forms best calculated to do them lasting good.

Thus is the problem of rich and poor to be solved. The laws of accumulation will be left free, the laws of distribution free. Individualism will continue, but the millionaire will be but a trustee for the poor, intrusted for a season with a great part of the increased wealth of the community, but administering it for the community far better than it could or would have done for itself. . . .

Such, in my opinion, is the true gospel concerning wealth, obedience to which is destined some day to solve the problem of the rich and the poor, and to bring "Peace on earth, among men good will."

UNDERSTAND, ANALYZE, & EVALUATE

1. What did Carnegie think of the inequality of wealth in industrial America? What were the wealthy supposed to do in this inequality of wealth, and what role did Andrew Carnegie envision for the poor?

2. What was the price of this new inequality?

Source: Carnegie, Andrew, "Wealth," *North American Review*, 1889, located in: Michael P. Johnson, *Reading the American Past: Selected Historical Documents*, vol. 2: From 1865, 5th ed., Boston, MA: Bedford St. Martin's, 2012, 52–55.

THE NOVELS OF HORATIO ALGER

A young boy, perhaps an orphan, makes his way through life on the rough streets of the city by selling newspapers or peddling matches. One day, his energy and determination catch the eye of a wealthy man, who gives him a chance to improve himself. Through honesty, charm, hard work, and aggressiveness, the boy rises in the world to become a successful man.

That, in a nutshell, is the story that Horatio Alger presented to his vast public in novel after novel—over a hundred of them in all—for over forty years. During his lifetime, Americans bought millions of copies of his novels. After his death in 1899, his books (and others written in his name) continued to sell at an astonishing rate. Even today, when the books themselves are largely forgotten, the name Horatio Alger has come to represent the idea of individual advancement through (in a phrase Alger coined) "pluck and luck."

Alger was born in 1832 into a middle-class New England family, attended Harvard, and spent a short time as a Unitarian minister. In the mid-1850s, he turned to writing stories and books, and he continued to do so for the rest of his life. His most famous novel, *Ragged Dick*, was published in 1868. Almost all of his books were fables of a young man's rise "from rags to riches." The purpose of his writing, he claimed, was twofold. He wanted to "exert a salutary influence upon the class of whom [he] was writing, by setting before them inspiring examples of what energy, ambition, and an honest purpose may achieve." He also wanted to show his largely middle-class readers "the life and experiences of the friendless and vagrant children to be found in all our cities."

Most Americans of the late nineteenth and early twentieth centuries were attracted to Alger's stories because the stories helped them believe in one of the most cherished national myths: that with willpower and hard work, individuals could rise in the world. That belief was all the more important in the late nineteenth century when large-scale corporate industrialization was making it increasingly difficult for individuals to control their own fates.

THE WESTERN BOY
OR,
THE ROAD TO SUCCESS.
By Horatio Alger, Jr.

(Source: Library of Congress, Prints and Photographs Division [LC-USZ62-61588])

A NEWSBOY'S STORY Alger's novels were even more popular after his death in 1899 than they had been in his lifetime. This reprint of one of his many rags-to-riches stories—about a New York newsboy's rise to wealth and success—was typical of his work.

Alger placed great emphasis on the moral qualities of his heroes; their success was a reward for their virtue. But many of his readers ignored the moral message and clung simply to the image of sudden and dramatic success. After the author's death, his publishers abridged many of Alger's works, eliminating the parts of his stories where the heroes do good deeds and focusing solely on the success of Alger's heroes in rising in the world.

Alger himself had very mixed feelings about the new industrial order he described. His books were meant to reveal not just the opportunities for advancement it sometimes created, but also its cruelty. That was one reason that in almost all his books, his heroes triumphed not just because of their own virtues or efforts, but because of some amazing stroke of luck. To Alger, at least, the modern age did not guarantee success through hard work alone; there had to be some providential assistance as well. Over time, however, Alger's admirers ignored his own misgivings about industrialism and portrayed his books purely as celebrations of (and justifications for) laissez-faire capitalism and the accumulation of wealth.

An example of the transformation of Alger into a symbol of individual achievement is the Horatio Alger Award, established in 1947 by the American Schools and Colleges Association to honor "living individuals who by their own efforts [have] pulled themselves up by their bootstraps in the American tradition." Among its recipients have been Presidents Dwight D. Eisenhower and Ronald Reagan, evangelist Billy Graham, and Supreme Court Justice Clarence Thomas. •

UNDERSTAND, ANALYZE, & EVALUATE

1. How do Alger's novels both defend industrial capitalism and criticize it?
2. According to the essay, Alger placed great emphasis on the moral qualities of his heroes, but his publishers later eliminated that aspect of the novels. Why?

could charge whatever prices they wished. Railroads, in particular, charged very high rates along some routes because they knew their customers had no choice but to pay them. Beginning in 1873, the economy fluctuated erratically, producing severe recessions every five or six years, each worse than the last.

(Source: Library of Congress, Prints and Photographs Division [LC-USZC4-435])

A MONSTROUS VISION OF VERTICAL INTEGRATION This 1905 image from *Puck* magazine captures the growing popular fear that businesses like Standard Oil had too much power. See that the Standard Oil octopus controls all in its reach—its tentacles encoil copper, oil, and steel industries as well as a State House and the U.S. Capitol.

THE ORDEAL OF THE WORKER

Most workers in the late nineteenth century experienced a real rise in their standard of living. But they did so at the cost of arduous and often dangerous working conditions, diminishing control over their own work, and a growing sense of powerlessness.

THE IMMIGRANT WORKFORCE

The industrial workforce expanded dramatically in the late nineteenth century as a result of massive migration into industrial cities. Rural Americans continued to flow into factory towns and cities—people disillusioned with or bankrupted by life on the farm. There was also a great wave of immigration from abroad in the decades following the Civil War, primarily from Europe, but also from China, Canada, and Mexico. The 25 million immigrants who arrived in the United States between 1865 and 1915 were more than four times the number who had arrived in the previous fifty years.

In the 1870s and 1880s, most of the immigrants came from England, Ireland, and northern Europe. By the end of the century, however, the major sources of immigrants had shifted, with large numbers of southern and eastern Europeans (Italians, Poles, Russians, Greeks, Slavs, and others) moving into the country and into the industrial workforce.

The new immigrants came to America in part to escape poverty and oppression in their homelands. But they were also attracted by expectations of new opportunities. Railroads lured immigrants into their western landholdings by distributing misleading advertisements overseas. Industrial employers actively recruited immigrant workers under the Labor Contract Law, which—until its repeal in 1885—permitted them to pay for the passage of workers in advance and deduct the amount later from their wages. Even after the repeal of the law, employers continued to encourage the immigration of unskilled laborers, often with the assistance of foreign-born labor brokers, such as the Greek and Italian *padrones,* who recruited work gangs of their fellow nationals.

The arrival of these new groups heightened ethnic tensions within the working class. Low-paid Poles, Greeks, and French Canadians began to displace higher-paid British and Irish workers in the textile factories of New England. Italians, Slavs, and Poles emerged as a major source of labor for the mining industry. Chinese and Mexicans competed with Anglo-Americans and African Americans in mining, farmwork, and factory labor in California, Colorado, and Texas.

WAGES AND WORKING CONDITIONS

At the turn of the century, the average income of the American worker was $400 to $500 a year—below the $600 figure that many believed was required to maintain a reasonable level of comfort. Nor did workers have much job security. All were vulnerable to the boom-and-bust cycle of the industrial economy and the instability caused by technological advances. Even those who kept their jobs could find their wages suddenly and substantially cut in hard times. Few workers, in other words, were ever very far from poverty.

Many first-generation workers, accustomed to the patterns of agrarian life, had trouble adjusting to the nature of modern industrial labor: routine, repetitive tasks on a strict and monotonous schedule. Skilled artisans, whose once-valued tasks were now performed by machines, found the new system impersonal and demeaning. Most factory laborers worked ten hours a day, six days a week; in the steel industry they worked twelve hours a day. Industrial accidents were frequent.

(Source: Library of Congress, Prints and Photographs Division [LC-DIG-nclc-01581])

SPINDLE BOYS Young boys, some of them barefoot, clamber among the great textile machines in a Georgia cotton mill, mending broken threads and replacing empty bobbins. Many of them were the children or siblings of women who worked in the plant. The photograph is by Lewis Hine, who traveled around the country documenting abuses for the National Child Labor Committee.

The decreasing need for skilled work in factories induced many employers to increase the use of women and children, whom they could hire for lower wages than adult males. By 1900, 20 percent of all manufacturing workers were women. Women labored in all areas of industry, even in some of the most arduous jobs. Most women, however, worked in a few industries where unskilled and semiskilled machine labor (as opposed to heavy manual labor) prevailed. The textile industry remained the largest single industrial employer of women. Domestic service, though, remained the most common female occupation overall. Women worked for wages well below the minimum necessary for survival and well below the wages paid to men working the same jobs.

At least 1.7 million children under sixteen years of age were employed in factories and fields; 10 percent of all girls aged ten to fifteen, and 20 percent of all boys, held jobs. Under public pressure, thirty-eight states passed child labor laws in the late nineteenth century. But 60 percent of child workers were employed in agriculture, which was typically exempt from the laws. For children employed in factories, the laws merely set a minimum age of twelve years and a maximum workday of ten hours, standards that employers often ignored in any case.

Emerging Unionization

Laborers attempted to fight back against such conditions by creating national unions. By the end of the century, however, their efforts had met with little success.

There had been craft unions in America, representing small groups of skilled workers, since well before the Civil War. But most unions could not hope to exert significant power in the economy. And during the turbulent recession years of the 1870s, unions faced the additional problem of widespread public hostility. When labor disputes with employers turned bitter and violent, as they occasionally did, much of the public instinctively blamed the workers for the trouble, rarely the employers. Particularly alarming to middle-class Americans was the emergence of the "**Molly Maguires**," an Irish secret society, in the anthracite coal region of western Pennsylvania. This militant labor organization sometimes used violence and even murder in its battle with coal operators.

Excitement over the Molly Maguires paled beside the near hysteria that gripped the country during the railroad strike of 1877, which began when the eastern railroads announced a 10 percent wage cut and soon expanded into something approaching a class war. Strikers disrupted rail service from Baltimore to St. Louis, destroyed equipment, and rioted in the streets of Pittsburgh and other cities. State militias were called out, and in July President Hayes ordered federal troops to suppress the disorders. In Baltimore, eleven demonstrators died and forty were wounded in a conflict between workers and militiamen. In Philadelphia, the state militia killed twenty people when the troops opened fire on thousands of workers and their families who were attempting to block the railroad crossings. In all, over one hundred people died before the strike finally collapsed several weeks after it had begun. The Great Railroad Strike was America's first major national labor conflict.

THE KNIGHTS OF LABOR

In the first major effort to create a genuinely national labor organization, the Noble Order of the **Knights of Labor** was founded in 1869 under the leadership of Uriah S. Stephens. Membership was open to all who "toiled" a definition that included all workers, most business and professional people, and virtually all women—whether they worked in factories, as domestic servants, or in their own homes. Only lawyers, bankers, liquor dealers, and professional gamblers were excluded. The Knights of Labor championed an eight-hour workday and the abolition of child labor, but they were more interested in long-range reform of the economy. The Knights hoped to replace the "wage system" with a new "cooperative system," in which workers would themselves control their workplaces.

For several years, the Knights remained a secret fraternal organization. But in the late 1870s under the leadership of Terence V. Powderly, the order moved into the open and entered a period of spectacular expansion. By 1886, it claimed a total membership of over 700,000. Local unions or assemblies associated with the Knights launched a series of railroad and other strikes in the 1880s in defiance of Powderly's wishes. Their failures to win any meaningful concessions helped discredit the organization. By 1890, membership of the Knights had shrunk to 100,000. A few years later, the organization disappeared altogether.

THE AMERICAN FEDERATION OF LABOR

Even before the Knights began to decline, a rival association appeared. In 1881, representatives of a number of craft unions formed the Federation of Organized Trade and Labor Unions of the United States and Canada. Five years later, this body took the name it has borne ever since, the **American Federation of Labor (AFL)**.

Rejecting the Knights' idea of one big union for everybody, the federation was an association of essentially autonomous craft unions that represented mainly skilled workers. **Samuel Gompers**, the powerful leader of the AFL, concentrated on labor's immediate objectives: wages, hours, and working conditions. As one of its first objectives, the AFL demanded a national eight-hour workday and called for a general strike if the goal was not achieved by May 1, 1886. On that day, strikes and demonstrations for a shorter workday took place all over the country.

In Chicago, a center of labor and radical strength, a strike was already in progress at the McCormick Harvester Company. City police had been harassing the strikers, and labor and radical leaders called a protest meeting at Haymarket Square on May 1. When the police ordered the crowd to disperse, someone threw a bomb that killed seven policemen and injured sixty-seven others. The police, who had killed four strikers the day before, fired into the crowd and killed four more people. Conservative, property-conscious Americans—frightened and outraged—blamed the protesters and demanded retribution. Chicago officials finally rounded up eight anarchists and charged them with murder, on the grounds that their statements had incited whoever had hurled the bomb. All eight scapegoats were found guilty after a remarkably injudicious trial. Seven were sentenced to death. One of them committed suicide, four were executed, and two had their sentences commuted to life imprisonment.

To most middle-class Americans, the **Haymarket bombing** was an alarming symbol of social chaos and radicalism. "Anarchism" now became in the public mind a code word for terrorism and violence, even though most anarchists were relatively peaceful. For the next thirty years, the specter of anarchism remained one of the most frightening concepts in the American imagination. Business owners exploited it to smear labor leaders and disrupt their activities. It became a constant obstacle to the goals of the AFL and other labor organizations, and it did particular damage to the Knights of Labor. However much they tried to distance themselves from radicals, labor leaders were always vulnerable to accusations of anarchism, as the violent strikes of the 1890s occasionally illustrated.

THE HOMESTEAD STRIKE

The Amalgamated Association of Iron and Steel Workers was the most powerful trade union in the country in the late 1800s. Its members were skilled workers, in great demand by employers, and they had long been able to exercise significant power in the workplace. In the mid-1880s, however, demand for skilled workers declined as new production methods changed the steelmaking process. In the streamlined Carnegie system, which was coming to dominate the steel industry, the union was able to maintain a foothold in only one of the corporation's three major factories—the Homestead plant near Pittsburgh.

By 1890, Carnegie and his chief lieutenant, Henry Clay Frick, had decided that the Amalgamated "had to go." Over the next two years, they repeatedly cut wages at Homestead. At first, the union begrudgingly acquiesced, aware that it was not strong enough to wage a successful strike. But in 1892, when the company stopped even discussing its financial decisions with the union and gave it two days to accept another wage cut, the Amalgamated called for a strike.

Frick abruptly shut down the plant and called in 300 guards from the Pinkerton Detective Agency, well known as strikebreakers, to enable the company to hire nonunion workers. They approached the plant by river, on barges, on July 6, 1892. The strikers poured gasoline on the water, set it on fire, and then met the Pinkertons at the docks with guns and dynamite. After several hours of fighting, which killed 3 guards and ten strikers and injured many others, the Pinkertons surrendered and were escorted roughly out of town.

But the workers' victory in the **Homestead strike** was temporary. The governor of Pennsylvania, at the company's request, sent the state's entire National Guard contingent, some 8,000 men, to Homestead. Production resumed, with strikebreakers now protected by troops. And public opinion turned against the strikers when a radical made an attempt to assassinate Frick. Slowly, workers drifted back to their jobs, and finally—four months after the strike began—the Amalgamated surrendered. By 1900, every major steel plant in the Northeast had broken with the Amalgamated. Its membership shrank from a high of 24,000 in 1891 (two-thirds of all eligible steelworkers) to fewer than 7,000 a decade later.

THE PULLMAN STRIKE

A dispute of greater magnitude, if less violence, was the **Pullman strike** in 1894. The Pullman Palace Car Company manufactured railroad sleeping and parlor cars at a plant near Chicago. There the company constructed a 600-acre town, Pullman, and rented its trim, orderly houses to the employees. George M. Pullman, owner of the company, saw the town as a model—a solution to the problems of industrial workers. But many residents chafed at the regimentation (and the high rents). In the winter of 1893–1894, the Pullman Company slashed wages by about 25 percent, citing its own declining revenues in the depression, without reducing the rent it charged its employees. Workers went on strike and persuaded the militant American Railway Union, led by **Eugene V. Debs**, to support them by refusing to handle Pullman cars and equipment. Within a few days, thousands of railroad workers in twenty-seven states and territories were on strike, and transportation from Chicago to the Pacific Coast shut down.

Unlike most elected politicians, the governor of Illinois, John Peter Altgeld, was a man with demonstrated sympathies for workers and their grievances. He refused to call out the militia to protect employers. Infuriated, railroad operators bypassed Altgeld and asked the federal government to send regular army troops to Illinois, using the pretext that the strike was preventing the movement of mail on the trains. In July 1894, President Grover Cleveland ordered 2,000 troops to the Chicago area. A federal court issued an injunction forbidding the union to continue the strike. When Debs and his associates defied it, they were arrested and imprisoned. With federal troops protecting the hiring of new workers and with the union leaders in a federal jail, the strike quickly collapsed.

SOURCES OF LABOR WEAKNESS

In the last decades of the nineteenth century, labor made few real gains despite militant organizing efforts. Industrial wages rose hardly at all. To be sure, labor leaders won a few legislative victories—the abolition of the Contract Labor Law, the establishment of an eight-hour day for government employees, compensation for some workers injured on the job, and others. But many such laws were not enforced, and most business leaders laughed at them. Widespread strikes and protests, and many other working-class forms of resistance, large and small, led to scant enduring gains. The end of the century found most workers with less political power and less control of the workplace than they had had forty years before.

Workers failed to make greater gains for many reasons. The principal labor organizations represented only a small percentage of the industrial workforce; the AFL, the most important, blatantly excluded unskilled workers and most women, blacks, and recent immigrants. Divisions within the workforce, such as tensions among different ethnic and racial groups, contributed further to union weakness.

Another source of labor weakness was the shifting nature of the workforce. Many immigrant workers came to America intending to earn some money and then return home. The assumption that they had no long-range future in the country tamed their enthusiasm to organize. Other workers were in constant motion, moving from one job to another, one town to another, seldom in a single place long enough to establish any institutional ties or exert any real power.

Above all, perhaps, workers made few gains in the late nineteenth century because they faced corporate organizations of vast wealth and power, which were generally determined to crush any efforts by workers to challenge their prerogatives. And as the Homestead and Pullman strikes suggest, the corporations usually had the support of local, state, and federal authorities, who were willing to send in troops to "preserve order" and crush labor uprisings on demand.

Despite the creation of new labor unions and a wave of strikes and protests, workers in the late nineteenth century failed on the whole to create successful organizations or to protect their interests. In the battle for power within the emerging industrial economy, almost all the advantages seemed to lie with capital.

CONCLUSION

In the four decades after the Civil War, the United States propelled itself into the forefront of the industrializing nations of the world. Large areas of the nation remained overwhelmingly rural, to be sure. But even so, America's economy, and along with it the nation's society and culture, was being profoundly transformed.

New technologies, new forms of corporate management, and new supplies of labor helped make possible the rapid growth of the nation's industries and the construction of its railroads. The factory system contributed to the growth of the nation's cities. Immigration provided a steady supply of new workers for the growing industrial economy. The result was a steady increase in national wealth, rising living standards for much of the population, and the creation of great new fortunes.

But industrialization did not spread its fruits evenly. Large areas of the country, most notably the South, and large groups in the population, most notably minorities, women, and recent immigrants, profited relatively little from economic growth. Industrial workers experienced arduous conditions of labor. Small merchants and manufacturers found themselves overmatched by great new combinations.

Industrialists strove to create a rationale for their power and to persuade the public that everyone had something to gain from it. But many Americans remained skeptical of modern capitalism, and some—workers struggling to form unions, reformers denouncing trusts, socialists envisioning a new world, and many others—created broad and powerful critiques of the new economic order. Industrialization brought both progress and pain to late-nineteenth-century America. Controversies over its effects defined the era and would continue to define the first decades of the twentieth century.

KEY TERMS/PEOPLE/PLACES/EVENTS

American Federation of
  Labor (AFL) 422
American Socialist
  Party 415
Andrew Carnegie 411
Edward Bellamy 415
Eugene V. Debs 424
gospel of wealth 414
Haymarket bombing 423

Henry Ford 409
Henry George 415
Homestead strike 423
Horatio Alger 414
horizontal integration 412
John D. Rockefeller 412
J. P. Morgan 412
Knights of Labor 422
Louisa May Alcott 414

Molly Maguires 422
monopoly 415
Pullman strike 424
Samuel Gompers 422
Social Darwinism 413
Taylorism 409
vertical integration 412
Wilbur and Orville
  Wright 409

RECALL AND REFLECT

1. Who were some of the business and industrial titans of the late nineteenth century, and what did they contribute to America's industrial growth?
2. What changes took place in corporate organization in the late nineteenth century, and how did these changes affect the nation's economy?
3. What was the gospel of wealth?
4. How did Social Darwinism attempt to justify the social consequences of industrial capitalism?
5. How did workers respond to the expansion of industrialization and the new industrial economy?

18 | THE AGE OF THE CITY

THE NEW URBAN GROWTH
THE URBAN LANDSCAPE
STRAINS OF URBAN LIFE
THE RISE OF MASS CONSUMPTION
LEISURE IN THE CONSUMER SOCIETY
HIGH CULTURE IN THE URBAN AGE

LOOKING AHEAD

1. What were some of the problems that resulted from rapid urbanization, and how did urban governments respond to these problems?
2. How did the sources of immigration to America shift in the late nineteenth century, and what was the native response to the change?
3. How did the rise of mass consumption affect leisure and entertainment?

THE INDUSTRIALIZATION AND COMMERCIALIZATION of America changed the face of society in countless ways. Nowhere were those changes more profound than in the growth of cities and the creation of an urban society and culture. From its roots as a primarily agrarian republic, the United States in the late nineteenth century was becoming an urban nation.

Cities grew so rapidly that their facilities and institutions could not keep pace. Housing, transportation, sewer systems, social services, governments—all lagged far behind the enormous demands urban populations placed on them. And to observers at the time, crime, poverty, and conflict between groups living in densely packed environments were portents of looming urban chaos.

But despite their problems, people flocked to cities to take advantage of economic, educational, and cultural opportunities. As centers of wealth, cities in the United States and around the world became the sites of great civic projects that came to define the urban experience. These included public parks, museums, theaters, opera houses, railroad stations, libraries, and commercial boulevards. The city of the late nineteenth and early twentieth centuries thus showcased the achievements of modern society as well as the tensions that urbanization generated.

THE NEW URBAN GROWTH

The urban population in America increased sevenfold in the half century after the Civil War. In 1920, the census revealed that for the first time, a majority of the American people lived in "urban" areas—defined as communities of 2,500 people or more. Natural increase accounted for only a small part of urban growth. Families in cities experienced a high rate of infant mortality, a declining fertility rate, and a high death rate from disease. It was immigration, rather, that expanded the urban population so dramatically.

THE MIGRATIONS

In the late nineteenth century, Americans left the declining agricultural regions of the East at a dramatic rate. Some moved to the newly developing farmlands of the West. But almost as many moved to the growing cities of the East and the Midwest.

Among those leaving rural America for industrial cities in the 1880s were black men and women trying to escape the poverty, debt, violence, and oppression they faced in the rural South. They were also seeking new opportunities in cities. Factory jobs for African Americans were rare and professional opportunities almost nonexistent. Urban black people tended to work in service occupations as cooks, janitors, domestic servants, and so on. Because many such jobs were considered women's work, black women often outnumbered black men in the cities.

The most important source of urban population growth, however, was the great number of new immigrants from abroad, part of a larger pattern of mobility around the world. (See "America in the World: Global Migrations.") Some came from Canada, Latin America, and—particularly on the West Coast—China and Japan. But

TOTAL IMMIGRATION, 1861–1900 Over 10 million immigrants from abroad entered the United States in the last forty years of the nineteenth century, with particularly high numbers arriving in the 1880s and 1890s. This chart shows the pattern of immigration in five-year intervals. • *What external events might help explain some of the rises and falls in the rates of immigration in these years?*

the greatest number came from Europe. After 1880, the flow of new arrivals began to include large numbers of people from southern and eastern Europe. By the 1890s, more than half of all immigrants came from these regions.

In earlier years, most new immigrants from Europe (particularly Germans and Scandinavians) had arrived with at least some money and education. Most of them arrived at one of the major port cities on the Atlantic Coast, the greatest number landing at New York's immigrant depot at Castle Garden, and then headed west. But the new immigrants of the late nineteenth century, many coming through Ellis Island after 1892, generally lacked the capital to buy farmland and lacked the education to establish themselves in professions. So, like similarly poor Irish immigrants before the Civil War, they settled overwhelmingly in industrial cities, where they worked largely in unskilled jobs.

The Ethnic City

By 1890, most of the population of the major cities consisted of immigrants: 87 percent of the population in Chicago, 80 percent in New York, 84 percent in Milwaukee and

GLOBAL MIGRATIONS

The great waves of immigration that transformed American society in the nineteenth and early twentieth centuries were not unique to the United States. They were part of a great, global movement of peoples—unprecedented in history—that affected every continent in the world and that has continued to this day. These great migrations were the product of two related forces: population growth and industrialization.

The population of Europe grew faster in the second half of the nineteenth century than ever before and ever since—almost doubling between 1850 and the beginning of World War I. The population growth was a result of growing economies able to support more people and of more efficient and productive agriculture that helped end debilitating famines. But the rapid growth nevertheless strained the resources of many parts of Europe and affected, in particular, rural people, who were now too numerous to live off the available land. Many decided to move to other parts of the world where land was more plentiful.

At the same time, industrialization drew millions of people out of the countryside and into cities—sometimes into cities in their own countries but often to industrial cities in other nations. Historians of migration speak of "push" factors (pressures on people to leave their homes) and "pull" factors (the lure of new lands) in explaining population movements. The "push" for many nineteenth-century migrants was poverty and inadequate land at home; for others it was political and religious oppression. The "pull" was the availability of land or industrial jobs in other regions—and, for some, the prospect of greater freedom abroad. Faster, cheaper, and easier transportation—railroads, steamships, and much later, airplanes—also aided large-scale immigration.

From 1800 to the start of World War I, 50 million Europeans migrated overseas. They left almost all areas of Europe, but in the later years of the century, when migration reached its peak, most came from poor rural areas in southern and eastern Europe. Italy, Russia, and Poland were among the biggest sources of late-nineteenth-century migrants. Almost two-thirds of these immigrants came to the United States. But nearly 20 million Europeans migrated to other lands. Migrants from England and Ireland (among others) moved in large numbers to those areas of the British Empire with vast, seemingly open territory: Canada, Australia, New Zealand, and South Africa. Large numbers of Italians moved to Argentina and other parts of South America. Many migrants moved to open land in these countries and established themselves as farmers, using the new mechanical farming devices made possible by industrialization. In many places—Australia, New Zealand, Argentina, South Africa, and the United States—immigrants evicted native residents and created societies

(Source: Library of Congress, Prints and Photographs Division [LC-DIG-ggbain-01561])

of their own. Many others settled in the industrial cities that were growing up in all these regions and formed distinctive ethnic and national communities within them.

But it was not only Europeans who were transplanting themselves in these years. Tremendous numbers of poor people left Asia, Africa, and the Pacific Islands in search of better lives. Most of them could not afford the journey abroad on their own. They moved instead as indentured servants, in much the same way many European migrants moved to America in the seventeenth century, agreeing to a term of servitude in their new land in exchange for food, shelter, and transportation. Recruiters of indentured servants fanned out across China, Japan, areas of Africa and the Pacific Islands, and above all, India. French and British recruiters brought hundreds of thousands of Indian migrants to work in plantations in their own Asian and African colonies. Chinese laborers were recruited to work on plantations in Cuba and Hawaii; mines in British Malaya, Peru, South Africa, and Australia; and railroad projects in Canada, Peru, and the United States. African indentured servants moved in large numbers to the Caribbean, and Pacific Islanders tended to move to other islands or to Australia.

The immigration of European peoples was largely voluntary and brought most migrants to the United States, where indentured servitude was illegal, although sometimes imposed on workers through labor contracts. But the migration of non-European peoples often involved an important element of coercion and brought relatively small numbers of people to the United States. This non-European migration was a function of the growth of European empires, and it was made possible by the imperial system—by its labor recruiters, by its naval resources, by its law, and by its economic needs. Together, these various forms of migration produced one of the greatest population movements in the history of the world and transformed not just the United States but much of the globe.   •

UNDERSTAND, ANALYZE, & EVALUATE

1. What were some of the "push" and "pull" factors that motivated the migration of both Europeans and non-Europeans?
2. Why did more Europeans than non-Europeans migrate to the United States?

Detroit. Equally striking was the diversity of new immigrant populations. In other countries experiencing heavy immigration in this period, most of the new arrivals were coming from one or two sources. But in the United States, no single national group dominated.

Most of the new arrivals were rural people, and for many of them the adjustment to city life was painful. To help ease the transition, some immigrant groups formed close-knit ethnic communities within the cities, in neighborhoods often called immigrant "ghettoes." Ethnic neighborhoods offered newcomers much that was familiar, including newspapers and theater in their native languages, stores selling their native foods, and church and fraternal organizations that provided links to their national pasts. Many immigrants also maintained close ties with their native countries. They stayed in touch with relatives who had remained behind, and perhaps as many as a third in the early years returned to their homelands after a relatively short time. Others helped bring the rest of their families to America. The cultural cohesiveness of ethnic communities clearly eased the pain of separation from the immigrants' native lands.

But immigrants who aroused strong racial prejudice among native-born whites found it very difficult to advance, whatever their talents. Those white immigrants who arrived with a valuable skill or with some capital did better than those who did not. And over time,

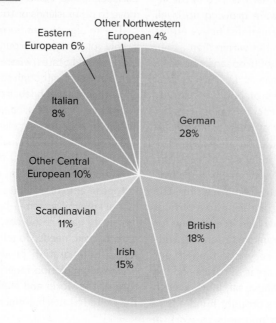

SOURCES OF IMMIGRATION FROM EUROPE, 1860–1900 This pie chart shows the sources of European immigration in the late nineteenth century. The largest number of immigrants continued to come from Britain, Ireland, Germany, and Scandinavia, but the beginnings of what in the early twentieth century would become a major influx of immigrants from new sources—southern and eastern Europe in particular—are already visible here. There was also some immigration from other sources—Mexico, South and Central America, and Asia. • *Why would these newer sources of European and other kinds of immigration create controversy among older-stock Americans?*

those who lived in cities where people of their own nationality came to predominate—for example, the Irish in New York and Boston or the Germans in Milwaukee—gained an advantage as they learned to exert their political power.

ASSIMILATION AND EXCLUSION

Despite the many differences among the various immigrant communities, virtually all groups had certain things in common. Most immigrants shared the experience of settling in cities. Most were young; the majority of newcomers were between fifteen and forty-five years old. And in most communities of the foreign-born, ethnic ties had to compete against the desire for assimilation.

Many of the new arrivals had come with romantic visions of the New World. However disillusioning they might have found their first contact with the United States, they usually retained the dream of becoming true "Americans." Second-generation immigrants were especially likely to attempt to break with old ways. Young women, in particular, sometimes rebelled against parents who tried to arrange or prevent marriages or who opposed women entering the workplace.

Old-stock Americans encouraged or demanded assimilation in countless ways. Public schools taught children in English, and employers often insisted that workers speak English on the job. Most non-ethnic stores sold mainly American products, forcing immigrants to adapt their diets, clothing, and lifestyles to American norms. Church leaders were often native-born Americans or more assimilated immigrants who encouraged their parishioners to adopt American ways. Some even embraced reforms to make their religion more compatible with the norms of the new country. Reform Judaism, imported from Germany in the late nineteenth century, was an effort by American Jewish leaders (as it had been by German ones) to make their faith less "foreign" to the dominant culture.

The vast numbers of new immigrants and their distinctive communities provoked fear and resentment among some native-born Americans just as earlier arrivals had done. In 1887, Henry Bowers, a self-educated lawyer, founded the American Protective Association, a group committed to stopping immigration. By 1894, membership in the organization reportedly reached 500,000, with chapters throughout the Northeast and Midwest. That same year, five Harvard alumni in Boston founded the Immigration Restriction League, which proposed screening immigrants through literacy tests and other standards to separate the "desirable" from the "undesirable."

The government responded to popular concern about immigration even earlier. In 1882, Congress excluded the Chinese, denied entry to "undesirables"—convicts, paupers, those with mental illness—and placed a tax of 50 cents on each person admitted. Later legislation of the 1890s enlarged the list of those barred from immigrating.

But these laws kept out only a small number of aliens, and more ambitious restriction proposals made little progress in Congress, for immigration provided a cheap and plentiful labor supply to the rapidly growing economy. Many argued that America's industrial as well as agricultural development would be impossible without it.

THE URBAN LANDSCAPE

The city was a place of remarkable contrasts. It had homes of almost unimaginable size and grandeur and hovels of indescribable squalor. It had conveniences unknown to earlier generations and problems that seemed beyond the capacity of society to solve.

THE CREATION OF PUBLIC SPACE

There were a few early American cities that were planned from the beginning, Philadelphia and Washington most prominently. By the mid-nineteenth century, reformers, planners, architects, and others began to call for more ordered visions of many other cities.

Among the most important urban innovations of the mid-nineteenth century were great city parks, which reflected the desire of urban leaders to provide an antidote to the congestion of the city landscape. Parks, they argued, would allow city residents a healthy, restorative escape from the strains of urban life by reacquainting them with the natural world. This notion of the park as refuge was most effectively promoted by the landscape designers Frederick Law Olmsted and Calvert Vaux, who together in the late 1850s designed New York's Central Park. They deliberately created a public space that would look as little like the city as possible. Instead of the ordered, formal spaces common in some European cities, they created a space that seemed entirely natural. Central Park was from the start one of the most popular and admired public spaces in the world.

At the same time that cities were creating great parks, they were also creating great public buildings: libraries, art galleries, natural history museums, theaters, and concert and opera halls. New York's Metropolitan Museum of Art was the largest and best known of many great museums taking shape in the late nineteenth century, but giant museums grew up quickly in Boston, Philadelphia, Chicago, and other places. In one city after another, new and lavish public libraries appeared, as if to confirm the city's role as a center of learning and knowledge.

Wealthy residents were the principal force behind the creation of the great art museums, concert halls, opera houses, and, at times, even parks. As their own material and social aspirations grew, they wanted the public life of the city to provide them with amenities to match their expectations. Becoming an important patron of a major cultural institution was an especially effective route to social distinction.

As both the size and aspirations of great cities increased, urban leaders launched monumental projects to remake them. Some cities began to clear away older neighborhoods and streets and create grand, monumental avenues lined with new and more impressive buildings. A particularly important event in inspiring such efforts was the 1893 Columbian Exposition in Chicago, a world's fair constructed to honor the 400th anniversary of Columbus's first voyage to America. At the center of the wildly popular exposition was a cluster of neoclassical buildings—the "Great White City"—arranged symmetrically around a formal lagoon. It became the inspiration for the **city beautiful movement**, led by the architect of the Great White City, Daniel Burnham. The movement strove to impose a similar order and symmetry on the disordered life of cities around the country. Only rarely, however, were planners able to overcome the obstacles of private landowners and complicated urban politics to realize more than a small portion of their dreams.

The effort to remake the city did not focus only on redesigning existing landscapes. It occasionally led to the creation of entirely new ones. In one of the largest public works projects ever undertaken in America to that point, the city of Boston gradually filled in a large area of marshy tidal land in the late 1880s to create the neighborhood known as "Back Bay." Chicago claimed large areas from Lake Michigan and at one point raised the street level for the entire city to help avoid the problems the marshy land created. In New York and other cities, the response to limited space was not so much to create new land as to annex adjacent territory. A great wave of annexations expanded the boundaries of many American cities in the 1890s and beyond, most notably New York City's 1898 annexation of Brooklyn, which had itself been a large and important city.

THE SEARCH FOR HOUSING

One of the greatest urban problems was to provide housing for the thousands of new residents pouring into the cities every day. For the prosperous, housing was seldom a worry. The availability of cheap labor reduced the cost of building and permitted anyone with even a moderate income to afford a house. Some of the richest urban residents lived in palatial mansions located in exclusive neighborhoods in the heart of the city—Fifth Avenue in New York, Back Bay and Beacon Hill in Boston, Society Hill in Philadelphia, Lake Shore Drive in Chicago, Nob Hill in San Francisco, and many others.

Many of the moderately well-to-do city dwellers took advantage of less expensive land on the edges of cities and settled in new suburbs, linked to the downtowns by trains or streetcars. Chicago in the 1870s, for example, connected nearly a hundred residential suburbs to the downtown by railroad. Real estate developers worked to create suburban communities that would appeal to many city dwellers' nostalgia for the countryside, promoting them with lawns, trees, and houses designed to look manorial.

Most urban residents, however, could not afford either to own a house in the city or to move to the suburbs. Instead, they stayed in the city centers and rented. Landlords tried to

(©Bettmann/Corbis)

A TENEMENT LAUNDRY This woman, shown here with some of her children, was typical of many working-class mothers who found income-producing activities they could pursue in the home (in this case, laundry).

squeeze as many rent-paying residents as possible into the smallest available space. In Manhattan, for example, the average population density in 1894 was 143 people per acre, a rate far higher than that of any other American or European city then or since. In the cities of the South—Charleston, New Orleans, Richmond—poor African Americans lived in crumbling former slave quarters. In Boston, immigrants moved into cheap three-story wooden houses ("triple-deckers"). In Baltimore and Philadelphia, the new arrivals crowded into narrow brick row houses. And in New York and many other cities, they lived in **tenements**.

The word *tenement* had originally referred simply to a multiple-family rental building, but by the late nineteenth century it had become a term for slum dwellings only. The first tenements, built in 1850, had been hailed as a great improvement in housing for the poor. But most were, in fact, miserable places, with many windowless rooms and little or no plumbing or heating. **Jacob Riis**, a Danish immigrant and New York newspaper photographer, shocked many middle-class Americans with his sensational descriptions and pictures of tenement life in his 1890 book *How the Other Half Lives.* But the solution reformers often adopted was simply to raze slum dwellings without building any new housing to replace them.

Urban Technologies: Transportation and Construction

Urban growth posed monumental transportation challenges. Sheer numbers of people mandated the development of mass transportation. Streetcars drawn on tracks by horses had been introduced into some cities even before the Civil War. But the horsecars were not fast enough, so many communities developed new forms of mass transit. In 1870, New York opened its first elevated railway, whose noisy, steam-powered trains moved rapidly above the city streets on massive iron structures. New York, Chicago, San Francisco, Boston, and other cities also experimented with cable cars, towed by continuously moving underground cables. Richmond, Virginia, introduced the first electric trolley line in 1888, and in 1897, Boston opened the first American subway. At the same time, cities were developing new techniques of road and bridge building. One of the great technological marvels of the 1880s was the completion of the Brooklyn Bridge in New York—a dramatic steel-cable suspension span designed by John A. Roebling.

Cities grew upward as well as outward. In Chicago, the 1884 construction of the first modern "skyscraper"—a ten-story building—launched a new era in urban architecture. Critical to the creation of the skyscraper was a new technology of construction, which emerged as a result of several related developments. New kinds of steel girders could support much greater tension than the metals of the past. The invention and development of the passenger elevator made much taller buildings possible. And the search for ways to protect cities from the ravages of great fires, which caused such terrible destruction in wood-frame cities of the late nineteenth century, led to steel-frame construction that, among other things, made cities more fireproof. Once the technology existed to permit the construction of tall buildings, there were few obstacles to building taller and taller structures. The early Chicago skyscrapers paved the way for some of the great construction achievements later in the twentieth century: the Chrysler Building and the Empire State Building in New York, the LaSalle Building in Chicago, and ultimately the vast numbers of steel and glass skyscrapers of post-1945 cities around the world.

STRAINS OF URBAN LIFE

Increasing urban congestion and the absence of adequate public services produced serious hazards. Crime, fire, disease, and indigence all placed strains on the capacities of metropolitan institutions, and both governments and private agencies were for a time poorly equipped to respond.

HEALTH AND SAFETY IN THE BUILT ENVIRONMENT

Chicago and Boston suffered great fires in 1871, and other cities experienced similar disasters. The terrible experience of the fires encouraged the construction of fireproof buildings and the development of professional fire departments. They also forced cities to rebuild at a time when new technological and architectural innovations were available. Some of the high-rise downtowns of American cities arose out of the rubble of great fires.

An even greater hazard than fire was disease, especially in poor neighborhoods with inadequate sanitation facilities. An epidemic that began in a poor neighborhood could and often did spread easily into other neighborhoods as well. Few municipal officials recognized the relationship of improper sewage disposal and water contamination to such epidemic diseases as typhoid fever and cholera. Many cities lacked adequate systems for disposing of human waste until well into the twentieth century. Flush toilets and sewer systems began to appear in the 1870s, but they could not solve the problem as long as sewage continued to flow into open ditches or streams, polluting cities' water supplies. Contributing to the same problem was the urban presence of domestic animals, including horses, cows, and pigs.

Air quality in many cities was poor as well. Few Americans had the severe problems that London experienced in the late nineteenth century with its seemingly perpetual "fogs" created by the burning of soft coal. But air pollution from factories and from stoves and furnaces in offices, homes, and other buildings was constant and at times severe. The incidence of respiratory infection and related diseases was much higher in cities than it was in rural areas, and it accelerated rapidly in the late nineteenth century.

Modern notions of environmental science were unknown to most Americans in these years. But the environmental degradation of many American cities was a visible and disturbing fact of life. The frequency of great fires, the dangers of disease, the crowding of working-class neighborhoods—all exemplified the environmental costs of industrialization and rapid urbanization.

Yet by the early twentieth century, reformers crusading to improve the environmental conditions of cities were beginning to achieve some notable successes. By 1910, most large American cities had constructed sewage disposal systems, often at great cost, to protect the drinking water of their inhabitants and prevent the great bacterial plagues that impure water had helped create in the past, such as the yellow fever epidemic in Memphis that killed 5,000 people.

In 1912, the federal government created the **Public Health Service**, which was charged with preventing such occupational diseases as tuberculosis, anemia, and carbon dioxide poisoning, which were common in the garment industry and other trades. It attempted to create common health standards for all factories; but since the agency had few powers of enforcement, it had limited impact. The creation of the Occupational Safety and Health Administration in 1970, which gave government the authority to require employers to create safe and healthy workplaces, was a legacy of the Public Health Service's early work.

Urban Poverty, Crime, and Violence

Urban expansion spawned widespread and often desperate poverty. Public agencies and private philanthropic organizations offered some relief, but they were generally poorly funded and also dominated by middle-class people who believed that too much assistance would breed dependency. Most tried to restrict aid to the "deserving" poor, those who truly could not help themselves. Charitable organizations conducted elaborate investigations to separate the "deserving" from the "undeserving." Other charitable societies—for example, the Salvation Army, which began operating in America in 1879—concentrated more on religious revivalism than on relief of the homeless and hungry. Middle-class people grew particularly alarmed over the rising number of poor children in the cities, some of them orphans or runaways. They attracted greater attention from reformers than any other group, although that attention produced no lasting solutions to their problems.

Poverty and crowding bred crime and violence. The American murder rate rose rapidly in the late nineteenth century, from twenty-five murders for every million people in 1880 to over a hundred by the end of the century. That reflected in part a very high level of violence in some nonurban areas: the American South, where lynching and homicide were particularly high, and the West, where the rootlessness and instability of new communities (cow towns, mining camps, and the like) created much violence. But the big cities contributed their share to the increase as well. Native-born Americans liked to believe that crime was a result of the violent proclivities of immigrant groups, and they cited the rise of gangs and criminal organizations in various ethnic communities. But native-born Americans in the cities were as likely to commit crimes as immigrants. The rising crime rates encouraged many cities to develop larger and more professional police forces. But police forces themselves could spawn corruption and brutality.

Some members of the middle class, fearful of urban insurrections, felt the need for even more substantial forms of protection. Urban National Guard groups built imposing armories on the outskirts of affluent neighborhoods and stored large supplies of weapons and ammunition in preparation for uprisings that, in fact, virtually never occurred.

The city was a place of strong allure and great excitement. Yet it was also a place of alienating impersonality and, to some, of degradation and exploitation. The novel *Sister Carrie* (1900), written by **Theodore Dreiser**, exposed one troubling aspect of urban life: the plight of single women like Dreiser's heroine, Carrie, who found themselves without any means of support. Carrie first took an exhausting and ill-paying job in a Chicago shoe factory, then drifted into a life of "sin," exploited by predatory men.

(Source: Library of Congress, Prints and Photographs Division [LC-USZC4-7884])

PUCK MAGAZINE   *Puck* (1871–1918) was the first successful humor magazine published in the United States. It offered political cartoons, caricatures, and satire on the issues of the day. This cover shows a beer and wine seller shuttering his store by order of the government. The Tammany man indicates that the merchant will be able to operate without penalty in exchange for his support.

THE MACHINE AND THE BOSS

For newly arrived immigrants and other inner-city residents struggling to adjust to urban life, the principal source of assistance was the political "machine." The urban machine owed its existence to the power vacuum that the chaotic growth of cities had created and to the potential voting power of large immigrant communities. Out of that combination emerged urban "bosses." The principal function of the political boss was simple: to win votes for his organization. That meant winning the loyalty of his constituents. To do so, a boss might provide them with occasional relief—a basket of groceries or a bag of coal. He might step in to save those arrested for petty crimes from jail. When he could, he found work for the unemployed. Above all, he rewarded many of his followers with patronage: with jobs in city government or in the police, which the machine's elected officials often controlled; with jobs building or operating the new transit systems; and with opportunities to rise in the political organization itself.

Machines were also vehicles for making money. Politicians enriched themselves and their allies through various forms of graft and corruption. A politician might discover in advance where a new road or streetcar line was to be built, buy land near it, and sell it at a profit when property values rose as a result of the construction. There was also covert graft. Officials received kickbacks from contractors in exchange for contracts to build public projects, and they sold franchises for the operation of public utilities. The most famously corrupt city boss was **William M. Tweed**, head of New York City's **Tammany Hall** in the 1860s and 1870s, whose extravagant use of public funds and kickbacks landed him in jail in 1872.

The urban machine was not without competition. Reform groups frequently mobilized public outrage at the corruption of the bosses and often succeeded in driving machine politicians from office. But the reform organizations typically lacked the permanence of the machine.

THE RISE OF MASS CONSUMPTION

In the last decades of the nineteenth century, developments in urban America began shaping a broader ethos of mass consumption. Much of this phenomenon was driven by middle-class tastes, but more and more Americans participated in the new consumer culture and thereby connected themselves to national trends, styles, and products.

PATTERNS OF INCOME AND CONSUMPTION

Incomes rose for almost everyone in the industrial era, although highly unevenly. One result of the new economy was the creation of vast fortunes, but perhaps the most important result for society as a whole was the growth and increasing prosperity of the middle class. Clerks, accountants, middle managers, and other "white-collar" workers saw their salaries rise by an average of a third between 1890 and 1910. Doctors, lawyers, and other professionals experienced a particularly dramatic increase in both the prestige and the profitability of their professions. Working-class incomes rose in those years as well, although from a much lower base and more slowly. The iron and steel industries saw workers' hourly wages increase by a third between 1890 and 1910; but industries with large female workforces—shoes, textiles, and paper—saw more modest increases, as did almost all industries in the South. Wages for African Americans, Mexicans, and Asians also rose more slowly than those for white workers.

CONSIDER THE SOURCE

JOHN WANAMAKER, THE FOUR CARDINAL POINTS OF THE DEPARTMENT STORE (1874)

The Philadelphia merchant John Wanamaker was one of the most successful and innovative businessmen of his day. A pioneer of the department store, Wanamaker ran this advertisement explaining the policies and benefits for consumers of his new commercial venue.

FOUR CARDINAL POINTS

By which we will hereafter steer our craft

FULL GUARANTEE   CASH PAYMENT

ONE PRICE   CASH RETURNED

Explanation and Elaboration of the New Plan

FIRST POINT—"CASH"—Houses doing a credit business must provide for losses on bad debts, interest on long-standing accounts, capital locked up, etc. To bear such losses themselves would drive them out of business. Therefore a per cent is added to the price of each article sold to cover this leakage, and cash buyers, whether they know it or not, really pay the bad debts and the interest on the long credits of the other customers. Under the cash payment system one pays only for what he gets, and contributes nothing to a "Sinking Fund."

By this radical change we shall lose some of our customers, no doubt, but we will gain ten where we lose one, the advantages being so great to all who can avail themselves of them. So we say CASH THROUGHOUT. Bring money for Clothing and we will supply it at prices possible under no other plan.

SECOND POINT—"ONE PRICE"—The fairness of this feature of our plan all will praise. It is simply treating all alike—exacting nothing from indisposition to bargain or ignorance, and, at the same time, conceding all that shrewdness on the shrewdest customer's part could possibly extort, because the "One Price" which we mark on our goods shall invariably be Not the "First" Price, but the Last and Lowest Price.

Not the "Top" Price, but the Very Bottom Price.

THIRD POINT—"FULL GUARANTEE"— A printed guarantee, bearing the signature of our firm will accompany each garment as a warrantee. This binds us in every sense, and will be honored as quickly as a good draft of the Government of the United States. This is a sample of the full guarantee, and tells its own story—Guarantee.

WE HEREBY GUARANTEE

First—That the prices of our goods shall be as low as the same quality of material and manufacture are sold anywhere in the United States.

Second—That prices are precisely the same to everybody for same quality, on same day of purchase.

Third—That the quality of goods is as represented on printed labels.

Fourth—That the full amount of cash paid will be refunded, if customers find the articles unsatisfactory, and return them unworn and uninjured within ten days of date of purchase.

FOURTH POINT—"CASH RETURNED"— This is simply a concession on our part to our customers, to secure them full confidence in dealing for goods they know very little about, and we thus prevent any occasion for dissatisfaction from any and every cause whatsoever. If the garment is not exactly what you thought, if your taste changes, if the "home folks" prefer another color or another shape, if you find you can buy the same material and style elsewhere for less money, if you conclude you don't need it after you get home, if the season changes suddenly and you wish you had not bought it, bring it back unworn and uninjured, and the full amount of money you paid will be returned on the spot. What more can we do for our customers than this, when we make our clothing so that they can draw the money value with it equally as well as with a check on the banks?

The ADVANTAGES incident to a system having for its cardinal points these which we have now explained, are simply innumerable. Saving of time and temper, perfect security, absence of all huckstering, etc., etc.

But above all this . . .

All of these "By-ways" lead direct to CHEAPNESS; and this without lowering the quality or style of our celebrated make of MEN'S AND BOY'S CLOTHING.

UNDERSTAND, ANALYZE, & EVALUATE

1. What were the benefits of Wanamaker's four cardinal points for consumers? What were the benefits for Wanamaker? Judging by Wanamaker's new way of doing business, what must business practices and customer service have looked like before?

2. Why might these assurances have been particularly important for a large department store? Why might they have been essential for the urban consumer market?

Source: *Golden Book of the Wanamaker Stores, Jubilee Year, 1861–1911,* Philadelphia, PA: John Wanamaker, 1911, 152–154. This advertisement was originally published in 1874. Located in Regina Lee Blaszczyk and Philip B. Scranton (eds.), *Major Problems in American Business History,* Boston, MA: Houghton Mifflin Company, 2006, 298–299.

Rising incomes created new markets for consumer goods, which were now available to a mass market for the first time, as a result of technological innovations and new merchandising techniques. An example of such changes was the emergence of ready-made clothing. In the early nineteenth century, most Americans had made their own clothing. The invention of the sewing machine and the Civil War demand for uniforms spurred the manufacture of clothing and helped create an enormous industry devoted to producing ready-made garments. By the end of the century, almost all Americans bought their clothing from stores. Partly as a result, much larger numbers of people became concerned with personal style. Interest in women's fashion, for example, had once been a luxury reserved for the relatively affluent. Now middle-class and even working-class women could strive to emulate distinctive styles of dress.

Buying and preparing food also became a critical part of the new **consumerism**. The development and mass production of tin cans in the 1880s created a large new industry devoted to packaging and selling canned food and condensed milk. Refrigerated railroad cars made it possible for perishable foods to be transported over long distances without spoiling. Artificially frozen ice enabled many households to afford iceboxes. The changes brought improved diets and better health. Life expectancy rose six years in the first two decades of the twentieth century.

CHAIN STORES, MAIL-ORDER HOUSES, AND DEPARTMENT STORES

Changes in marketing also altered the way Americans bought goods. New "chain stores" could usually offer a wider array of goods at lower prices than the small local stores with which they competed. The Atlantic and Pacific Tea Company (A&P) began a national network of grocery stores in the 1870s. F. W. Woolworth built a chain of dry goods stores. Sears and Roebuck established a large market for its mail-order merchandise by distributing an enormous catalog each year.

In larger cities, the emergence of great department stores helped make shopping more alluring and glamorous. Marshall Field in Chicago created one of the first American

(©Corbis)

DEPARTMENT STORES Department stores often created "events" to help promote sales of their many wares. Here, Strawbridge and Clothier department store creates a stir on Market Street in Philadelphia in 1907.

department stores, a place deliberately designed to produce a sense of wonder and excitement. Similar stores emerged in New York, Brooklyn, Boston, Philadelphia, and other cities. (For the philosophy of one of the leading department store innovators, see "Consider the Source: John Wanamaker, the Four Cardinal Points of the Department Store.")

WOMEN AS CONSUMERS

The rise of mass consumption had particularly dramatic effects on American women. Women's clothing styles changed much more rapidly than men's, which encouraged more frequent purchases. Women generally bought and prepared food for their families, so the availability of new food products changed not only how people ate but also how women shopped and cooked.

The consumer economy produced new employment opportunities for women as salesclerks and waitresses. And it spawned the creation of a new movement in which women played a vital role: the consumer protection movement. The **National Consumers League (NCL)**, formed in the 1890s under the leadership of Florence Kelley, attempted to mobilize the power of women as consumers to force retailers and manufacturers to improve wages and working conditions. The NCL encouraged women to buy only products with the League's "white label," which indicated that the product was made under fair working conditions.

LEISURE IN THE CONSUMER SOCIETY

Closely related to the rise of consumption was a growing interest in leisure time. Members of the urban middle and professional classes had large blocks of time during which they were not at work—evenings, weekends, even paid vacations. Working hours in many factories declined, from an average of nearly seventy hours a week in 1860 to under sixty in 1900. Even farmers found that the mechanization of agriculture gave them more free time. As many people's lives became more compartmentalized, with clear distinctions between work and leisure, many Americans began to search for new forms of recreation and entertainment.

Redefining Leisure

In earlier eras, relatively few Americans had considered leisure a valuable thing. Many equated it with laziness. In the late nineteenth century, however, the beginnings of a redefinition of leisure appeared. The economist Simon Patten articulated this new view of leisure in *The Theory of Prosperity* (1902), *The New Basis of Civilization* (1910), and other works. He challenged the centuries-old assumption that the normal condition of civilization was a scarcity of goods. In earlier times, Patten argued, fear of scarcity had caused people to place a high value on thrift, self-denial, and restraint. But in modern industrial societies, new economies could create enough wealth to satisfy not just the needs but also the desires of all.

As Americans became more accustomed to leisure as a normal part of life, they began to look for new experiences and entertainments. Mass entertainment occasionally bridged differences of class, race, and gender. But it could also be sharply divided. Saloons and some sporting events tended to be male preserves. Shopping and going to tea rooms and luncheonettes were more popular among women. Theaters, pubs, and clubs were often specific to particular ethnic communities or particular work groups. When the classes did meet in public spaces—as they did, for example, in city parks—there was often considerable conflict over what constituted appropriate public behavior. Elites in New York City, for example, tried to prohibit anything but quiet activities in Central Park, while working-class people wanted to use the public spaces for sports and entertainment.

Spectator Sports

Among the most important responses to the search for entertainment was the rise of organized spectator sports, especially baseball. A game much like baseball, known as "rounders" and derived from cricket, had enjoyed limited popularity in Great Britain in the early nineteenth century. Versions of the game began to appear in America in the early 1830s. By the end of the Civil War, interest in the game had grown rapidly. More than 200 amateur or semiprofessional teams and clubs existed, many of which joined a national association and proclaimed a set of standard rules. As the game grew in popularity, it offered opportunities for profit. The first salaried team, the Cincinnati Red Stockings, was formed in 1869. Other cities fielded professional teams, and in 1876 the teams banded together in the National League. A rival league, the American Association, appeared and collapsed, but in 1901 the American League emerged to replace it. And in 1903, the first modern World Series was played, in which the American League's Boston Red Sox beat the National League's Pittsburgh Pirates. By then, baseball had become an important business and a national preoccupation.

Baseball had great appeal to working-class males. The second most popular game, football, appealed at first to a more elite segment of the male population, in part because it originated in colleges and universities. The first intercollegiate football game in America occurred between Princeton and Rutgers in 1869. Early intercollegiate football bore only an indirect relation to the modern game; it was more similar to present-day rugby. By the

(©Transcendental Graphics/Getty Images)

THE AMERICAN NATIONAL GAME Long before the modern major leagues began, local baseball clubs were active throughout much of the United States, establishing the game as the "national pastime." This print of a "grand match for the championship" depicts an 1866 game at Elysian Fields, a popular park just across the river from New York City in Hoboken, New Jersey.

late 1870s, however, the game was becoming standardized and was taking on the outlines of its modern form.

Basketball was invented in 1891 in Springfield, Massachusetts, by Dr. James A. Naismith, a Canadian working as an athletic director for a local college. Boxing, which had long been a disreputable activity concentrated primarily among the urban lower classes, became by the 1880s a more popular and, in some places, more reputable sport.

Participation in the major sports was almost exclusively the province of men, but several sports emerged in which women became involved. Golf and tennis both attracted more and more relatively wealthy men and women. Bicycling and croquet also enjoyed widespread popularity in the 1890s among women as well as men. Women's colleges introduced their students to more strenuous sports as well—track, crew, swimming, and (beginning in the late 1890s) basketball.

MUSIC, THEATER, AND MOVIES

Other forms of popular entertainment also developed in the cities. Many ethnic communities maintained their own theaters, which presented plays in the native languages. Urban theaters in the heart of cities attracted a much broader audience. They introduced new entertainment forms: the musical comedy, which evolved gradually from the comic operettas of Europe; and **vaudeville**, a form of theater adapted from French models, which remained the most popular urban entertainment into the first decades of the twentieth century. Vaudeville consisted of a variety of acts (musicians, comedians, magicians, jugglers, and others) and was, at least in the beginning, inexpensive to produce. As the economic potential of vaudeville grew, some promoters, most prominently Florenz Ziegfeld of New York, staged more elaborate spectacles.

Vaudeville was also one of the few entertainment media open to black performers, who brought to it elements of the minstrel shows they had earlier developed for black audiences in the late nineteenth century. Some minstrel singers (including the most famous, Al Jolson) were white performers wearing heavy makeup (or "blackface"), but most were black. Entertainers of both races performed music based on the gospel and folk tunes of the plantation and on the jazz and ragtime of black urban communities. White and black performers also tailored their acts to prevailing prejudices, ridiculing African Americans by acting out demeaning stereotypes.

American popular entertainment was transformed with the emergence of motion picture shows. Thomas Edison and others had created the technology underpinning the motion picture in the 1880s. Soon after that, short films became available to individual viewers watching peepshows in pool halls, penny arcades, and amusement parks. Soon, larger projectors made it possible to display the images on big screens, which permitted substantial audiences to see films in theaters. By 1900, Americans were becoming attracted in large numbers to these early movies, usually plotless films of trains or waterfalls or other spectacles. The director D. W. Griffith carried the motion picture into a new era with his silent epics—*The Birth of a Nation* (1915), *Intolerance* (1916), and others—which introduced serious if notoriously racist plots and elaborate productions to filmmaking.

PATTERNS OF PUBLIC AND PRIVATE LEISURE

Particularly striking about popular entertainment in the late nineteenth and early twentieth centuries was its public quality. Many Americans spent their leisure time in places where they would find not only entertainment but also other people. Thousands of working-class New Yorkers spent evenings in dance halls, vaudeville houses, and concert halls. More affluent New Yorkers enjoyed afternoons in Central Park, where a principal attraction was seeing other people and being seen by them. Moviegoers were attracted not just by the movies themselves but also by the energy of the audiences at lavish new movie palaces, just as sports fans were drawn by the crowds as well as by the games.

Perhaps the most striking example of popular public entertainment in the early twentieth century was **Coney Island**, the famous amusement park and resort on a popular beach in Brooklyn. Luna Park, the greatest of the Coney Island attractions, opened in 1903 and provided rides, stunts, and lavish reproductions of exotic places and spectacular adventures: Japanese gardens, Venetian canals with gondoliers, a Chinese theater, a simulated trip to the moon, and reenactments of such disasters as burning buildings and earthquakes. A year later, a competing company opened Dreamland, which tried to outdo even Luna Park with a 375-foot tower, a three-ring circus, chariot races, and a Lilliputian village from *Gulliver's Travels*. The popularity of Coney Island in these years was phenomenal. Thousands of people flocked to the large resort hotels that lined the beaches. Many thousands more made day trips out from the city by train and, after 1920, subway. In 1904, the average daily attendance at Luna Park alone was 90,000 people.

Most people found Coney Island appealing in part because it provided an escape from the genteel standards that governed so much of American life at the time. In the amusement parks of Coney Island, decorum was often forgotten, and people delighted in finding themselves in situations that in any other setting would have seemed embarrassing or improper: women's skirts blown above their heads with hot air; people pummeled with water and rubber paddles by clowns; hints of sexual freedom as strangers were forced to come into physical contact with one another on rides and amusements.

Not all popular entertainment, however, involved public events. Many Americans amused themselves privately by reading novels and poetry. The so-called dime novels, cheaply bound and widely circulated, became popular after the Civil War, with detective stories, tales of the Wild West, sagas of scientific adventure, and novels of "moral uplift." Publishers also distributed sentimental novels of romance, which developed a large audience among women, as did books about animals and about young children growing up. Louisa May Alcott's *Little Women,* most of whose readers were female, sold more than 2 million copies.

THE TECHNOLOGIES OF MASS COMMUNICATION

American journalism experienced dramatic change in the decades following the Civil War. Between 1870 and 1910, the circulation of daily newspapers increased nearly ninefold, from under 3 million to more than 24 million, a rate three times as great as the rate of population increase. And while standards varied widely from one paper to another, American journalism was developing the beginnings of a professional identity. Salaries of reporters increased; many newspapers began separating the reporting of news from the expression of opinion; and newspapers themselves became important businesses.

This transformation was to a large degree a result of new technologies of communication. The emergence of national press services, for example, was a product of the telegraph, which made it possible to supply papers with news and features from around the nation and the world. By the turn of the century, important newspaper chains had emerged as well, linked together by their own internal wire services. The most powerful was owned by **William Randolph Hearst**, who by 1914 controlled nine newspapers and two magazines. New printing technologies were making possible more elaborate layouts, the publication of color pictures, and, by the end of the century, the printing of photographs. These advances not only helped publishers make their own stories more vivid, they also made it possible for them to attract more advertisers.

THE TELEPHONE

The most important new technology of communication in the late nineteenth century was the telephone, which Alexander Graham Bell had first demonstrated in 1876. In its first years, the telephone was a relatively impractical tool. Those who subscribed to telephone service had to have direct wire links to everyone else they wished to call. In 1878, the first "switchboard" opened in New Haven, Connecticut, paving the way for more practical uses of the telephone. Once there was a switchboard, a telephone subscriber needed only a line to the central telephone office from which connections could be made to any other subscriber. A new occupation—the telephone "operator"—was born. The Bell System, which controlled all American telephone service, hired young white women to work as operators, hoping that a pleasant female voice would make the experience of using the telephone, and the inconvenience of the frequent technological problems that accompanied it, less irritating to customers. Telephone signals were very weak at first, and callers could seldom reach anyone more than a few miles away. In an effort to increase the range of telephones, engineers created the "repeater," which periodically strengthened the signal as it moved over distances. By 1914, the repeaters had improved to the point that it was now practical to envision a transcontinental line.

In its early years, the telephone was an almost entirely commercial instrument. Of the nearly 7,400 telephone customers in the New York–New Jersey area in 1891, 6,000 were businesses and organizations. Even the residential telephones tended to belong to doctors or business managers.

The growing reach of the telephone in the early years of the twentieth century made the Bell System (formally named American Telephone and Telegraph, or AT&T) one of the most powerful corporations in America and a genuine monopoly. Central to its success was an early decision by executives that the company would exclusively build and own all telephone instruments and then lease them to subscribers. That made it possible for AT&T to control both the equipment and the telephone service itself, and to exclude any competitors in either field. It also gave AT&T effective control over the local telephone companies allied with it and made the nation's telephone system into an effective cartel.

HIGH CULTURE IN THE URBAN AGE

In addition to the important changes in popular culture that accompanied the rise of cities and industry, there were profound changes in the realm of "high culture." The distinction between "highbrow" and "lowbrow" culture was largely new to the industrial era. In the early nineteenth century, most cultural activities had targeted people of all classes. By the late nineteenth century, however, elites were developing a cultural and intellectual life quite separate from the popular amusements of the urban masses.

LITERATURE AND ART IN URBAN AMERICA

One of the strongest impulses in American literature was the effort to recreate urban social reality. This trend toward realism found an early voice in Stephen Crane, who—although perhaps best known for his novel of the Civil War, *The Red Badge of Courage* (1895)—created a sensation in 1893 when he published *Maggie: A Girl of the Streets,* a grim picture of urban poverty and slum life. Theodore Dreiser, Frank Norris, and Upton Sinclair were similarly drawn to social issues as themes. **Kate Chopin**, a southern writer who explored the oppressive features of traditional marriage, encountered widespread public abuse after the publication of her shocking 1899 novel, *The Awakening,* which described a young wife and mother who abandoned her family in search of personal fulfillment. William Dean Howells, in *The Rise of Silas Lapham* and other works, described what he considered the shallowness and corruption of ordinary American lifestyles.

American art through most of the nineteenth century had been overshadowed by that of Europe. By 1900, however, a number of American artists broke from Old World traditions and experimented with new styles. Winslow Homer brought a distinctive approach to his paintings of New England maritime life and other American subjects. James McNeil Whistler was one of the first Western artists to introduce Asian themes into American and European art.

By the first years of the new century, some American artists were turning decisively away from the traditional academic style, perhaps most identified in America by the portraitist John Singer Sargent. Members of the so-called **Ashcan school** produced work startling in its naturalism and stark in its portrayal of the social realities of the era. John Sloan portrayed the dreariness of American urban slums, George Bellows caught the vigor and violence of his time in paintings and drawings of prizefights, Edward Hopper explored

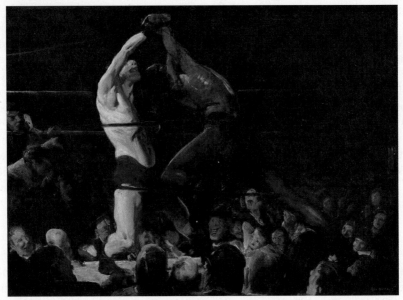

(Source: National Gallery of Art, Washington)

DEMPSEY THROUGH THE ROPES   The artist George Bellows began painting fight scenes in the first years of the twentieth century, when boxing appealed primarily to working-class audiences. By 1924, when he created a lithograph of this moment from a famous prizefight, boxing had become one of the most popular sports in America.

the starkness and loneliness of the modern city. The Ashcan artists were also among the first Americans to appreciate expressionism and abstraction; and they showed their interest in new forms in 1913 when they helped stage the famous **Armory Show** in New York City, which displayed works of the French postimpressionists and of some American moderns.

THE IMPACT OF DARWINISM

One of the most profound intellectual developments in the late nineteenth century was the widespread acceptance of the theory of evolution, associated most prominently with the English naturalist Charles Darwin. Darwin argued that the human species had evolved from earlier forms of life through a process of "natural selection." History, Darwin suggested, was not the working out of a divine plan. It was a natural process dominated by the fiercest or luckiest competitors.

The theory of evolution met widespread resistance at first from educators, theologians, and even many scientists. By the end of the century, however, the evolutionists had converted most members of the urban professional and educated classes. Even many middle-class Protestant religious leaders had accepted the doctrine, making significant alterations in theology to accommodate it. The rise of **Darwinism**, however, contributed to something unseen by most urban Americans at the time: a deep schism between the new, cosmopolitan culture of the city and the more traditional, provincial culture of some rural areas. Thus the late nineteenth century saw not only the rise of a liberal Protestantism in tune with new scientific discoveries but also the beginning of an organized Protestant fundamentalism.

Darwinism helped spawn other new intellectual currents. There was the Social Darwinism of William Graham Sumner and others, which industrialists used so enthusiastically to justify their favored position in American life. But there were also more sophisticated philosophies, among them a doctrine that became known as "pragmatism." **William James**, a Harvard psychologist, was the most prominent publicist of the new theory, although earlier intellectuals such as Charles S. Peirce and later ones such as John Dewey were also important to its development and dissemination. According to the pragmatists, modern society should rely for guidance not on inherited ideals and moral principles but on the test of scientific inquiry. No idea or institution, not even religious faith, was valid, they claimed, unless it "worked," unless it stood the test of experience.

A similar concern for scientific inquiry was influencing the social sciences. Sociologists such as Edward A. Ross and Lester Frank Ward urged applying the scientific method to the solution of social and political problems. Historians such as Frederick Jackson Turner and Charles Beard argued that economic factors more than spiritual ideals had been the governing force in historical development. John Dewey proposed a new approach to education that placed less emphasis on the rote learning of traditional knowledge and more on flexible, democratic schooling.

The implications of Darwinism also promoted the growth of anthropology and encouraged some scholars to begin examining other cultures in new ways. Some white Americans began to look at Indian society, for example, as a coherent culture with its own norms and values that were worthy of respect and preservation, even though they were different from those of white society.

Toward Universal Schooling

The growing demand for specialized skills and scientific knowledge created a growing, and changing, demand for education. The late nineteenth century, therefore, was a time of rapid expansion and reform of American schools and universities.

Free public primary and secondary education spread rapidly. By 1900, compulsory school attendance laws existed in thirty-one states and territories. Education was still far from universal. Rural areas lagged far behind urban-industrial ones in funding public education. In the South, many African Americans had no access to schools at all. But for many white men and women, educational opportunities were expanding.

Educational reformers tried to extend educational opportunities to the Indian tribes as well, in an effort to "civilize" them into white society. In the 1870s, reformers recruited small groups of Native Americans to attend Hampton Institute, a primarily black college. In 1879, they organized the Carlisle Indian Industrial School in Pennsylvania. Like many black colleges, Carlisle emphasized practical "industrial" education. Ultimately, however, these reform efforts failed, in part because they were unpopular with their intended beneficiaries.

Universities and the Growth of Science and Technology

Colleges and universities also proliferated rapidly in the late nineteenth century. The Morrill Land Grant Act of 1862, by which the federal government had donated public land to states for the establishment of colleges, led to the creation of sixty-nine "land-grant" institutions in the last decades of the century—among them the state university systems of California, Illinois, Minnesota, and Wisconsin. Other universities, including Chicago, Columbia, Harvard, Northwestern, Princeton, Syracuse, and Yale, benefited from millions of dollars contributed by business and financial titans such as Rockefeller and Carnegie. Other philanthropists founded new universities or reorganized older ones to perpetuate their family names—Vanderbilt, Johns Hopkins, Cornell, Duke, Tulane, Stanford, and others.

Universities played a vital role in the economic development of the United States in the late nineteenth century and beyond. The land-grant institutions were specifically mandated to advance knowledge in "agriculture and mechanics." From the beginning, therefore, they were committed not just to abstract knowledge but to making discoveries that would be of practical use to farmers and manufacturers. As they evolved into great state universities, they retained that tradition and became the source of many of the discoveries that helped American industry and commerce advance. Private universities emerged that served many of the same purposes: the Massachusetts Institute of Technology, founded in 1865, soon became the nation's premier engineering school; Johns Hopkins University in Baltimore, founded in 1876, did much to advance medical scholarship, as did the Rockefeller Institute for Medical Research in New York (later Rockefeller University) and the Carnegie Institution. By the early twentieth century, older and more traditional universities were beginning to form relationships with the private sector and the government, doing research that did not just advance knowledge for its own sake but that was directly applicable to practical problems of the time.

MEDICAL SCIENCE

Both the culture of and the scientific basis for medical care were changing rapidly in the early twentieth century. Most doctors were beginning to accept the new medical assumption that there were underlying causes to particular symptoms, that a symptom was not itself a disease. They were also beginning to make use of new or improved technologies—the X-ray, improved microscopes, and other diagnostic devices—that made it possible to classify, and distinguish among, different diseases. Laboratory tests could now identify infections such as typhoid and dysentery. These technologies were a critical first step toward the effective treatment of diseases.

At about the same time, pharmaceutical research began to produce some important new medicines. Aspirin was first synthesized in 1899. Other researchers experimented with chemicals that might destroy diseases in the blood, an effort that eventually led to the various forms of chemotherapy that are still widely used in treating cancer. In 1906, an American surgeon, G. W. Crile, became the first physician to use blood transfusion in treatment, which revolutionized surgery. In the past, patients often lost so much blood during operations that extensive surgery could be fatal for that reason alone. With transfusions, it became possible to conduct much longer and more elaborate operations.

The widespread acceptance by the end of the nineteenth century of the germ theory of disease had important implications. Physicians quickly discovered that exposure to germs did not by itself necessarily cause disease, and they began looking for the other factors that determined who got sick and who did not. Among the factors they eventually discovered were general health, previous medical history, diet and nutrition, and eventually genetic predisposition. The awareness of the importance of infection in spreading disease also encouraged doctors to sterilize their instruments, use surgical gloves, and otherwise purify the medical environment.

By the early twentieth century, American physicians and surgeons were generally recognized as among the best in the world, and American medical education was beginning to attract students from many other countries. These improvements in medical knowledge and training, along with improvements in sanitation and public health, did much to reduce infection and mortality in most American communities.

EDUCATION FOR WOMEN

The post–Civil War era saw an important expansion of educational opportunities for women, although such opportunities continued to lag far behind those available to men and were almost entirely denied to women of color.

Most public high schools accepted women readily, but opportunities for higher education were fewer. At the end of the Civil War, only three American colleges were coeducational. After the war, many of the land-grant colleges and universities in the Midwest and such private universities as Cornell and Wesleyan began to admit women along with men. But coeducation was less crucial to women's education in this period than was the creation of a network of women's colleges. Mount Holyoke in central Massachusetts had begun its life in 1836 as a "seminary" for women. It became a full-fledged college in the 1880s, at about the same time that entirely new female institutions were emerging: Vassar, Wellesley, Smith, Bryn Mawr, Wells, and Goucher. A few of the larger private universities created separate colleges for women on their campuses, including Barnard at Columbia and Radcliffe at Harvard.

The female college was part of an important phenomenon in the history of modern American women: the emergence of distinctive women's communities outside the family. Most faculty members and many administrators were women. And college life produced a spirit of collective identity and commitment among educated women that had important effects in later years. Most female college graduates ultimately married, but they married at a more advanced age than their non-college counterparts. A significant minority, perhaps over 25 percent, did not marry at all, but devoted themselves to careers. The growth of female higher education clearly became for some women a liberating experience, persuading them that they had roles other than those of wives and mothers to perform in their rapidly changing urban-industrial society.

CONCLUSION

The extraordinary growth of American cities in the last decades of the nineteenth century led to both great achievements and enormous problems. Cities became centers of learning, art, and commerce and produced great advances in technology, transportation, architecture, and communications. They provided their residents—and their many visitors—with varied and dazzling experiences, so much so that people increasingly left the countryside to move to the city.

But cities were also places of congestion, filth, disease, and corruption. With populations expanding too rapidly for services to keep up, most American cities in this era struggled with makeshift techniques to solve the basic problems of providing water, disposing of sewage, building roads, running public transportation, fighting fire, stopping crime, and preventing or curing disease. City governments, many of them dominated by political machines and ruled by party bosses, were often models of inefficiency and corruption, although in their informal way they also provided substantial services to the working-class and immigrant constituencies who needed them most. Yet they also managed to oversee great public projects: the building of parks, museums, opera houses, and theaters, usually in partnership with private developers.

The city brought together races, ethnic groups, and classes of extraordinary variety, from the families of great wealth that the new industrial age was creating to the vast working class, much of it consisting of immigrants, who crowded into densely packed neighborhoods divided by nationality. The city also spawned temples of consumerism: shops, boutiques, and, above all, the great department stores. And it created forums for public recreation and entertainment, including green spaces, theaters, athletic fields, amusement parks, and, later, movie palaces.

Urban life created anxiety among those who lived within the cities and among those who observed them from afar. But in fact, American cities adapted reasonably successfully over time to the great demands their growth made of them and learned to govern themselves, if not entirely honestly and efficiently, at least enough to allow them to survive and grow.

KEY TERMS/PEOPLE/PLACES/EVENTS

Armory Show 448
Ashcan school 447
city beautiful movement
  434
Coney Island 445
consumerism 441
Darwinism 448

Jacob Riis 435
Kate Chopin 447
National Consumers League
  (NCL) 442
Public Health Service 437
Tammany Hall 439
tenements 435

Theodore Dreiser 438
vaudeville 444
William James 449
William M. Tweed 439
William Randolph
  Hearst 446

RECALL AND REFLECT

1. What groups of people were most likely to move to the cities of late-nineteenth-century America, and why?
2. What was the relationship between immigration and urbanization in the late nineteenth century?
3. How did the new consumer economy affect roles and expectations for women?
4. What was Darwinism, and what was its impact on American intellectual life?

19 | FROM CRISIS TO EMPIRE

THE POLITICS OF EQUILIBRIUM
THE AGRARIAN REVOLT
THE CRISIS OF THE 1890s
STIRRINGS OF IMPERIALISM
WAR WITH SPAIN
THE REPUBLIC AS EMPIRE

LOOKING AHEAD

1. What were the major social and economic problems that beset the United States in the late nineteenth century, and how did the two major political parties respond to these problems?
2. What was Populism, what were its goals, and to what degree were these goals achieved?
3. How did the United States become an imperial power?

THE UNITED STATES APPROACHED the end of the nineteenth century as a fundamentally different nation from what it had been at the beginning of the Civil War. With rapid change came cascading social and political problems—ones the weak and conservative governments of the time showed little inclination or ability to address.

A catastrophic depression that began in 1893 devastated millions of Americans. Farmers responded to this and earlier economic downturns by creating an agrarian political movement known as Populism. American workers, facing massive unemployment, staged large and occasionally violent strikes. Not since the Civil War had American politics been so polarized and impassioned. The election of 1896, which pitted the agrarian hero William Jennings Bryan against the conservative William McKinley, was dramatic but anticlimactic. Supported by the mighty Republican Party and many eastern groups who looked with suspicion and unease at the agricultural demands coming from the West, McKinley easily triumphed.

McKinley did little in his first term in office to resolve the grievances of his time, but the economy revived nevertheless. Having largely ignored the depression, McKinley focused on another national cause: the plight of Cuba in its war with Spain. In the spring of 1898, the United States declared war on Spain and entered the conflict in Cuba, a brief but bloody war that ended with an American victory four months later. The conflict had begun in part as a way to support Cuban independence from the Spanish, but a group of fervent and influential imperialists worked to convert the war into an occasion for acquiring overseas possessions. Despite a powerful anti-imperialist movement, the acquisition of the former Spanish colonies proceeded, only to draw Americans into yet another imperial war, this one in the Philippines, where the Americans, not the Spanish, were the targets of local enmity.

THE POLITICS OF EQUILIBRIUM

The enormous social and economic changes of the late nineteenth century strained not only the nation's traditional social arrangements but its political institutions as well. Searching for stability and social justice, Americans looked to the government for leadership. Yet that government during much of this period was ill equipped to confront these new challenges. As a result, problems festered and grew.

THE PARTY SYSTEM

The most striking feature of late-nineteenth-century politics was the stability of the party system. From the end of Reconstruction until the late 1890s, the electorate was divided almost evenly between the Republicans and the Democrats. Sixteen states were solidly and consistently Republican, and fourteen states (most in the South) were solidly and consistently Democratic. Only a handful of states were usually in doubt, and they generally decided the results of national elections, often on the basis of voter turnout. The Republican Party captured the presidency in all but two of the elections of the era, but in the five presidential elections beginning in 1876, the average popular-vote margin separating the Democratic and Republican candidates was 1.5 percent. The congressional balance was similarly stable, with the Republicans generally controlling the Senate and the Democrats generally controlling the House.

Despite the relatively modest differences, most eligible Americans had strong loyalties to their chosen party. Voter turnout in presidential elections between 1860 and 1900 averaged over 78 percent of all eligible voters. Large groups of potential voters were disenfranchised in these years: women in most states and, particularly toward the end of the century, almost all blacks and some poor whites in the South. But for many adult white males, there were few restrictions on voting.

What explains this extraordinary loyalty to the two political parties? It was not that the parties took distinct positions on important public issues; their positions were similar, with a few exceptions. Party loyalties reflected other factors. Region was perhaps the most important. To white southerners, loyalty to the Democratic Party, the vehicle by which they had seceded from the Union and then triumphed over Reconstruction and preserved white supremacy, was a matter of unquestioned faith. Republican loyalties were equally intense in the North. To many, the party of Lincoln remained a bulwark against slavery and treason.

Religious and ethnic differences also shaped party loyalties. The Democratic Party attracted many Catholic voters, recent immigrants, and poorer workers in cities where Democratic political machines held power. The Republican Party appealed to northern Protestants, citizens of old stock, much of the middle class, and industrial elites. The few substantive issues on which the parties took different stands reflected their different constituencies. Republicans tended to support immigration restriction and to favor temperance legislation, which many believed would help discipline foreign-born communities. Catholics and immigrants viewed such proposals as assaults on them and their cultures, and the Democratic Party followed their lead.

Party identification, then, was usually more a reflection of cultural inclinations than a calculation of economic interest. Individuals might affiliate with a party because their parents had done so or because it was the party of their region, their church, or their ethnic group. Both parties, by twentieth- and twenty-first century standards, believed in very limited government.

THE NATIONAL GOVERNMENT

One reason the parties avoided most substantive issues was that the federal government did relatively little. Washington was responsible for delivering the mail, maintaining a military, conducting foreign policy, and collecting tariffs and taxes. It had few other responsibilities and few institutions capable of undertaking additional responsibilities even if it chose to do so.

There was one significant exception. From the end of the Civil War to the early twentieth century, the federal government administered a system of annual pensions for Union Civil War veterans and their widows, and state governments in the South acted similarly on behalf of Confederate ex-soldiers. At its peak, this pension system was making payments to a majority of the male citizens of the North and to many women as well, though African American veterans rarely applied and usually met rejection when they did. Some reformers hoped to make the system permanent and universal, others found it corrupt and expensive; by 1915, it had exceeded the cost of fighting the war. When the Civil War generation died out, the pension system died with it.

In most other respects, the United States in the late nineteenth century was a society without a modern national government. The most powerful institutions were the two political parties, the bosses and machines that dominated them, and the federal courts.

PRESIDENTS AND PATRONAGE

Presidents in the late nineteenth century had great symbolic importance, but they were unable to do very much except distribute government appointments. A new president and his tiny staff had to make almost 100,000 appointments.

It sometimes proved impossible for a president to avoid factional conflict, as the presidency of **Rutherford B. Hayes** demonstrated. By the end of his term, two groups—the **Stalwarts**, led by Roscoe Conkling of New York, and the **Half-Breeds**, captained by James G. Blaine of Maine—were competing for control of the Republican Party. Rhetorically, the Stalwarts favored traditional, professional machine politics, while the Half-Breeds favored reform. In fact, both groups were mainly interested in a larger share of patronage. Hayes tried to satisfy both and ended up satisfying neither.

The battle over patronage overshadowed all else during Hayes's unhappy presidency. His one important, substantive initiative—an effort to create a civil service system—attracted no support from either party. And his early announcement that he would not seek reelection only weakened him further.

The Republicans managed to retain the presidency in 1880 in part because they agreed on a ticket that included a Stalwart and a Half-Breed. They nominated **James A. Garfield**, a veteran congressman from Ohio and a Half-Breed, for president and Chester A. Arthur of New York, a Stalwart, for vice president. The Democrats nominated General Winfield

GETTING HOT ENOUGH FOR HIM.

(Source: Library of Congress, Prints and Photographs Division [LC-DIG-ppmsca-28490])

PRESIDENT CHESTER A. ARTHUR   Although originally a Stalwart, Arthur attempted to reform the spoils system. In this *Puck* cartoon, he is catching heat from a variety of Republican factions, including the Stalwarts and Half-Breeds.

Scott Hancock, a minor Civil War commander with no national following. Benefiting from the end of the recession of 1879, Garfield won a decisive electoral victory, although his popular-vote margin was thin.

Garfield began his presidency by defying the Stalwarts and supporting civil service reform. He soon found himself embroiled in an ugly public quarrel with Conkling and the Stalwarts. The dispute was never resolved. On July 2, 1881, only four months after his inauguration, Garfield was shot twice while standing in the Washington railroad station by an apparently deranged gunman, and unsuccessful office seeker, who shouted, "I am a Stalwart and Arthur is president now!" Garfield lingered for nearly three months before dying.

Garfield's successor, **Chester A. Arthur**, had spent his political lifetime as a devoted, skilled, and open spoilsman and a close ally of New York political boss Roscoe Conkling. But on becoming president, he tried, like Hayes and Garfield before him, to follow an independent course and even promote reform. To the dismay of the Stalwarts, Arthur kept most of Garfield's appointees in office and supported civil service reform. In 1883, Congress passed the first national civil service measure, the **Pendleton Act**, which required that some federal jobs be filled by competitive written examinations rather than patronage. Relatively few offices fell under civil service at first, but its reach steadily widened.

CLEVELAND, HARRISON, AND THE TARIFF

In the unsavory election of 1884, the Republican candidate for president was Senator James G. Blaine of Maine, known to his admirers as the "Plumed Knight" but to many others as a symbol of seamy party politics. Rather than support Blaine, a group of disgruntled "liberal Republicans," known to their critics as the "mugwumps," announced they would bolt the party and support an honest Democrat. Rising to the bait, the Democrats nominated **Grover Cleveland**, the reform governor of New York.

In a campaign filled with personal invective, what may have decided the race was the last-minute introduction of a religious controversy. Shortly before the election, a delegation of Protestant ministers called on Blaine in New York City; their spokesman, Dr. Samuel Burchard, referred to the Democrats as the party of "rum, Romanism, and rebellion." Blaine was slow to repudiate Burchard's indiscretion, and Democrats quickly spread the news that Blaine had tolerated a slander on the Catholic Church. Cleveland's narrow victory probably resulted from an unusually heavy Catholic vote for the Democrats in New York.

Grover Cleveland was respected, if not often liked, for his stern and righteous opposition to politicians, grafters, pressure groups, and Tammany Hall. He embodied an era in which few Americans believed the federal government could or should do much. Cleveland had always doubted the wisdom of protective tariffs, taxes on imported goods designed to protect domestic producers. The existing high rates, he believed, were responsible for the annual surplus in federal revenues, which was tempting Congress to pass extravagant legislation, which he frequently vetoed. In December 1887, therefore, he asked Congress to reduce the tariff rates. Democrats in the House approved a tariff reduction, but Senate Republicans defiantly passed a bill of their own, actually raising the rates as part of their broader protective impulse toward American corporations. The resulting deadlock made the tariff an issue in the election of 1888.

The Democrats renominated Cleveland and supported tariff reductions. Endorsing protection, Republicans settled on former senator **Benjamin Harrison** of Indiana, who was obscure but respectable, and the grandson of President William Henry Harrison. Cleveland won the popular vote by 100,000, but Harrison won an Electoral College majority of 233 to 168.

NEW PUBLIC ISSUES

Benjamin Harrison's record as president was little more substantial than that of his grandfather, who had died a month after taking office. Harrison harbored few visible convictions and made no effort to influence Congress. And yet during Harrison's passive administration, public opinion was beginning to force the government to confront some of the pressing social and economic issues of the day, most notably the power of trusts.

By the mid-1880s, fifteen western and southern states had adopted laws prohibiting combinations that restrained competition. But corporations found it easy to escape limitations by incorporating in states, such as New Jersey and Delaware, that offered them special privileges. If antitrust legislation was to be effective, its supporters believed, it would have to come from the national government. In July 1890, both houses of Congress passed the **Sherman Antitrust Act** almost without dissent. For over a decade after its passage, the law was unevenly enforced and steadily weakened by the courts. As of 1901, the Justice Department had instituted many antitrust suits against unions, but only fourteen against business combinations.

The Republicans were more interested in the issue they believed had won them the 1888 election: the tariff. Representative **William McKinley** of Ohio and Senator Nelson W. Aldrich of Rhode Island drafted the highest protective measure ever proposed to Congress. Known as the McKinley Tariff, it became law in October 1890. But Republican leaders apparently misinterpreted public sentiment. Many voters saw the high tariff as a way to enrich producers and starve consumers. The party suffered a stunning reversal in the 1890 congressional election. The Republicans' substantial Senate majority was slashed to 8; in the House, the party retained only 86 of the 332 seats, losing its majority in that chamber.

Nor were the Republicans able to recover over the next two years. In the presidential election of 1892, Benjamin Harrison once again supported protection. Grover Cleveland, renominated by the Democrats, once again opposed it. A new third party, the People's (or Populist) Party, with James B. Weaver as its candidate, advocated substantial economic reform. Cleveland won 277 electoral votes to Harrison's 145 and had a popular margin of 380,000. Weaver ran far behind.

The policies of Cleveland's second term were much like those of his first. Again, he supported a tariff reduction, which the House approved but the Senate weakened. Cleveland denounced the result but allowed it to become law as the Wilson-Gorman Tariff.

Public pressure had been growing since the 1880s for other reforms, among them regulation of the railroads. Farm organizations in the Midwest had persuaded several state legislatures to pass regulatory legislation in the early 1870s. But in 1886, the Supreme Court—in *Wabash, St. Louis, and Pacific Railway Co. v. Illinois,* known as the *Wabash* case— ruled one of the regulatory laws in Illinois unconstitutional. According to the Court, the law was an attempt to control interstate commerce and thus infringed on the exclusive power of Congress. Later, the courts limited the powers of the states to regulate commerce even within their own boundaries.

Effective railroad regulation, it was now clear, could come only from the federal government. Congress responded to public pressure in 1887 with the **Interstate Commerce Act**, which banned discrimination in rates between long and short hauls, required that railroads publish their rate schedules and file them with the government, and declared that all interstate rail rates must be "reasonable and just." A five-person agency, the Interstate Commerce Commission (ICC) was to administer the act. But the commissioners, like advocates of the law in Congress once it passed through their chambers, had little power on their own, relying instead on the courts to enforce their rulings. For almost twenty years after its passage, the Interstate Commerce Act, haphazardly enforced and narrowly interpreted by the courts rather like the Sherman Act, had little practical effect.

THE AGRARIAN REVOLT

No group watched the performance of the federal government in the 1880s with greater dismay than American farmers. They helped produce the Populist upheaval—one of the most powerful movements of political protest in American history.

THE GRANGERS

Farmers had been making efforts to organize politically for several decades before the 1880s. The first major farm organization was the National Grange of the Patrons of Husbandry, or **Grangers**, founded in 1867. From it emerged a network of local organizations that tried to teach new scientific agricultural techniques to its members. When the depression of 1873 caused a sharp decline in farm prices, membership rapidly increased and the direction of the organization changed. Granges in the Midwest began to organize marketing cooperatives and to promote political action to curb monopolistic practices by railroads and warehouses. At their peak, Grange supporters controlled the legislatures in most of the midwestern states. The result was the Granger Laws of the early 1870s, by which many states imposed strict regulations on railroad rates and practices. But the destruction of the new regulations by the courts, combined with the political inexperience of many Grange leaders and the return of prosperity in the late 1870s, produced a dramatic decline in the power of the association.

THE FARMERS' ALLIANCES

As early as 1875, farmers in parts of the South were banding together in **Farmers' Alliances** just as the Granges were weakening. By the 1880s, the Southern and Northwestern Alliances had more than 4 million members between them in the South, Midwest, and Great Plains, while a separate Colored Farmers' National Alliance contributed more than a million people to the movement.

Like the Granges, the Alliances formed cooperatives and other marketing mechanisms. They established stores, banks, processing plants, and other facilities to free their members from dependence on the hated furnishing merchants who kept so many farmers in debt. Some Alliance leaders, however, saw the movement in larger terms: as an effort to build a society in which economic competition might give way to cooperation. Alliance lecturers traveled throughout rural areas, lambasting the concentrated power of great corporations, railroads, and financial institutions.

Although the Alliances quickly became far more widespread than the Granges had ever been, they suffered from similar problems. Their cooperatives did not always work well, partly because of mismanagement and partly because of the strength of opposing market forces.

(©Corbis)

MARY E. LEASE The fiery Populist orator Mary E. Lease was a fixture on the Alliance lecture circuit in the 1890s. She made some 160 speeches in 1890 alone. Her critics called her the "Kansas Pythoness," but she was popular among farmers with her denunciations of banks, railroads, and intermediaries, and her famous advice to "raise less corn and more hell."

These economic frustrations helped push the movement into a new phase at the end of the 1880s: the creation of a national political organization.

In 1889, the Southern and Northwestern Alliances agreed to a loose merger. The next year the Alliances held a national convention at Ocala, Florida, and issued the so-called Ocala Demands, which were, in effect, a party platform. In the 1890 off-year elections, candidates supported by the Alliances won partial or complete control of the legislatures in twelve states. They also won six governorships, three seats in the U.S. Senate, and approximately fifty in the U.S. House of Representatives. Many of the successful Alliance candidates were Democrats who had benefited, often passively, from Alliance endorsements. But dissident farmers drew enough encouragement from the results to contemplate further political action.

Alliance leaders discussed plans for a third party at meetings in Cincinnati in May 1891 and St. Louis in February 1892. Then, in July 1892, 1,300 exultant delegates poured into

Omaha, Nebraska, to proclaim the creation of the new party, approve an official set of principles, and nominate candidates for the presidency and vice presidency. The new organization's official name was the People's Party, but the movement was more commonly referred to as **Populism**.

The election of 1892 demonstrated the potential power of the new movement. The Populist presidential candidate—James B. Weaver of Iowa, a former Greenbacker—polled more than 1 million votes. Nearly 1,500 Populist candidates won election to seats in state legislatures. The party elected three governors, five senators, and ten congressmen. It could also claim the support of many Republicans and Democrats in Congress who had been elected by appealing to Populist sentiment.

The Populist Constituency

Already, however, there were signs of the limits of Populist strength. Populism had great appeal to farmers, particularly to small farmers with little long-range economic security. But Populism failed to move much beyond that group. Its leaders made energetic efforts to include labor within the coalition by courting the Knights of Labor and adding a labor plank to its platform. But Populism never attracted significant labor support or became a truly cohesive working-class movement, in part because the economic interests of labor and the interests of farmers were often at odds.

In the South, white Populists struggled with the question of whether to accept African Americans into the party. Despite the large and important black component to the Alliance movement, most white Populists accepted the assistance of African Americans only as long as it was clear that whites would remain in control. When southern conservatives began to attack the Populists for undermining white supremacy, party leaders succumbed to such pressures as well their own racial prejudices in marginalizing or excluding black farmers from the movement. Here was a consistent pattern in southern racial politics: white elites, fearful of a biracial coalition of rural or working-class people, used race to drive a wedge between those groups, fomenting white resentment of black economic competition to undermine what might have been shared concerns.

Populist Ideas

The Populists spelled out their program first in the Ocala Demands of 1890 and then, more clearly, in the Omaha platform of 1892. They proposed a system of "subtreasuries," a network of government-owned warehouses where farmers could deposit their crops, to allow them to borrow money from the government at low rates of interest until the price of their goods went up. In addition, the Populists called for the abolition of national banks (which they believed were dangerous institutions of concentrated power), the end of absentee ownership of land, the direct election of U.S. senators (which would weaken the power of conservative state legislatures), and other devices to improve the ability of the people to influence the political process. They called as well for regulation and (after 1892) government ownership of railroads, telephones, and telegraphs. And they demanded a system of government-operated postal savings banks, a graduated income tax, the inflation of the currency, and, later, the remonetization of silver.

Some Populists were anti-Semitic, anti-intellectual, anti-eastern, and anti-urban. But bigotry was not the dominant force behind Populism. It was, rather, a serious effort to find solutions to real problems. Populists emphatically rejected the laissez-faire orthodoxies of their time, including the idea that the rights of ownership are absolute, and in fact called on the federal government to promote a dramatic redistribution of wealth and power. In short, the Populists raised one of the most overt, radical, and powerful challenges of the era to the direction in which American industrial capitalism was moving.

THE CRISIS OF THE 1890s

The agrarian protest was only one of many indications of the national political crisis emerging in the 1890s. There was a severe depression, widespread labor unrest and violence, and the continuing failure of either major party to respond to the growing distress. Grover Cleveland, who took office for the second time just as the economy was collapsing, remained convinced that any government action would be a violation of principle.

THE PANIC OF 1893

The **Panic of 1893** launched the most severe depression the nation had ever experienced. It began in March 1893, when the Philadelphia and Reading Railroad, unable to meet payments on loans, declared bankruptcy. Two months later, the National Cordage Company

(©Fotosearch/Getty Images)

COXEY'S ARMY   Jacob S. Coxey leads his "army" of unemployed men through the town of Allegheny, Pennsylvania, in 1894, en route to Washington, where he hoped to pressure Congress to approve his plans for a massive public works program to put people back to work.

failed as well. Together, these two corporate failures triggered a stock market collapse. And since many of the major New York banks were heavy investors in the market, a wave of bank failures soon began. That caused a contraction of credit, which meant that many of the new, aggressive, and loan-dependent businesses went bankrupt.

The depression reflected, among other things, the degree to which all parts of the American economy were now interconnected. And it showed how dependent the economy was on the health of the railroads, which remained the nation's most powerful corporate and financial institutions. When the railroads suffered, as they did beginning in 1893, everyone suffered.

Once the panic began, it spread with startling speed. Within six months, more than 8,000 businesses, 156 railroads, and 400 banks failed. Already low agricultural prices tumbled further. Up to 1 million workers, 20 percent of the labor force, lost their jobs. The depression was unprecedented not only in its severity but also in its persistence. Although conditions improved slightly beginning in 1895, prosperity did not fully return until 1901.

The depression produced widespread social unrest, especially among the enormous numbers of unemployed workers. In 1894, Jacob S. Coxey, an Ohio businessman and Populist, began advocating a massive public works program to create jobs for the unemployed. When it became clear that Congress was ignoring his proposals, Coxey organized a march of the unemployed (known as "**Coxey's Army**") to Washington, D.C., to present his demands to the government. Congress continued to ignore them.

To many middle-class Americans, the labor turmoil of the time—the Homestead and Pullman strikes, for example (see Chapter 17)—was a sign of a dangerous instability, perhaps even revolution. Labor radicalism, some of it real, more of it imagined by the frightened middle class, heightened the general sense of crisis among the public.

THE SILVER QUESTION

The financial panic weakened the government's monetary system. President Cleveland believed that the instability of the currency was the primary cause of the depression. The "money question," therefore, became one of the burning issues of the era.

The debate centered on what would form the basis of the dollar, what would lie behind it and give it value. Today, the value of the dollar rests on little more than public confidence in the government. But in the nineteenth century, many people believed that currency was worthless if there was not something concrete behind it—precious metal (specie), which holders of paper money could collect if they presented their currency to a bank or to the Treasury.

During most of its existence as a nation, the United States had recognized two metals—gold and silver—as a basis for the dollar, a system known as "bimetallism." In the 1870s, however, that had changed. The official ratio of the value of silver to the value of gold for purposes of creating currency (the "mint ratio") was 16 to 1: sixteen ounces of silver equaled one ounce of gold. But the actual commercial value of silver (the "market ratio") was much higher than that. Owners of silver could get more by selling it for manufacture into jewelry and other objects than they could by taking it to the mint for conversion into coins. So they stopped taking it to the mint, and the mint stopped coining silver.

In 1873, Congress passed a law that seemed simply to recognize the existing situation by officially discontinuing silver coinage. Few objected at the time. But later in the 1870s, the market value of silver fell well below the official mint ratio of 16 to 1. Silver was suddenly available for coinage again, and it soon became clear that Congress had foreclosed a potential method of expanding the currency. Before long, many Americans concluded that a conspiracy of big bankers had been responsible for the "demonetization" of silver and referred to the law as the "Crime of '73."

Two groups of Americans were especially determined to undo that crime. One consisted of the silver-mine owners, now understandably eager to have the government take their surplus silver and pay them much more than the market price. The other group was discontented farmers, who wanted an increase in the quantity of money—an inflation of the currency—as a means of raising the prices of farm products and easing payment of the farmers' debts. The inflationists, or advocates of **free silver**, demanded that the government return at once to the "free and unlimited coinage of silver" at the old ratio of 16 to 1. Congress responded weakly to these demands with the Sherman Silver Purchase Act of 1890, which required the government to purchase silver and pay for it in gold. But the government allowed only existing silver coinage. It did not allow any newly minted silver money. Whatever the economic intricacies of the issue, it boiled down to another battle between conservative supporters of corporations or the "monied interests," who preferred gold, and advocates of farmers, workers, and the "little guy," who argued for silver.

At the same time, the nation's gold reserves were steadily dropping. President Cleveland believed that the chief cause of the weakening gold reserves was the Sherman Silver Purchase Act. Early in his second administration, therefore, Congress responded to his request and repealed the Sherman Act—although only after a bitter and divisive battle that helped create a split in the Democratic Party.

"A Cross of Gold"

Republicans, watching the failure of the Democrats to deal effectively with the depression, were confident of success in 1896. Party leaders, led by the Ohio boss Marcus A. Hanna, settled on former congressman William McKinley, author of the 1890 tariff act and now governor of Ohio, as the party's presidential candidate. The tariff, they believed, should be the key issue in the campaign. But they also opposed the free coinage of silver, except by agreement with the leading commercial nations, which everyone realized was unlikely. Thirty-four delegates from the mountain and plains states walked out of the convention in protest and joined the Democratic Party.

The Democratic Convention of 1896 was unusually tumultuous. Southern and western delegates, eager for a way to compete with the Populists, were determined to seize control of the party from conservative easterners, incorporate some Populist demands into the Democratic platform—among them free silver—and nominate a pro-silver candidate.

Defenders of the gold standard seemed to dominate the debate, until **William Jennings Bryan**, a thirty-six-year-old congressman from Nebraska, mounted the podium to address the convention. His great voice echoed through the hall as he delivered what became one of the most famous political speeches in American history. The closing passage sent his audience into something close to a frenzy: "Having behind us the producing masses of this nation and the world, supported by the commercial interests, the laboring interests and the toilers everywhere, we will answer their demand for a gold standard by saying to them: 'You shall not press down upon the brow of labor this crown of thorns; you shall not crucify mankind upon a cross of gold.'" It became known as the "Cross of Gold" speech.

In the glow of Bryan's speech, the convention voted to adopt a pro-silver platform. And the following day, Bryan, as he had hoped, was nominated for president on the fifth ballot.

(Source: Library of Congress, Prints and Photographs Division [LC-USZC2-6263])

THE 1896 DEMOCRATIC TICKET   This political broadside from the 1896 election followed the nomination of William Jennings Bryan and Arthur Sewall at the Democratic National Convention in Chicago. It reflects Bryan's famous "Cross of Gold" speech and reveals how powerfully the promise of bimetallism, with its implications for the distribution of wealth and power, shaped the Democrats' message.

The choice of Bryan and the Democratic platform created a quandary for the Populists. They had expected both major parties to adopt conservative programs and nominate conservative candidates, leaving the Populists to represent the growing forces of protest. But now the Democrats had stolen much of their thunder. The Populists faced the choice of naming their own candidate and splitting the protest vote or endorsing Bryan and losing their identity as a party. Many Populists argued that "fusion" with the Democrats would destroy their party. But the majority concluded that there was no viable alternative. Amid considerable acrimony, the convention voted to nominate Bryan as the Populist candidate, although with a different running mate than the one Democrats had selected.

THE CONSERVATIVE VICTORY

The campaign of 1896 produced panic among conservatives. The business and financial community, frightened at the prospect of a Bryan victory, contributed lavishly to the Republican campaign. From his home in Canton, Ohio, McKinley conducted a traditional front-porch campaign by receiving pilgrimages of the Republican faithful, organized and paid for by Hanna.

Bryan showed no such restraint. He became the first presidential candidate in American history to stump every section of the country systematically. He traveled 18,000 miles and addressed an estimated 5 million people.

On election day, McKinley polled 271 electoral votes to Bryan's 176 and received 51.1 percent of the popular vote to Bryan's 47.7. Bryan carried the areas of the South and West where miners or struggling staple farmers predominated, but he couldn't attract workers in industrial states. The Democratic program, like that of the Populists, had been too narrow to galvanize working people and to win a national election. The Republicans also persuaded many factory workers that their program of high tariffs protected not only corporate profits but also, by extension, laborers' wages.

For the Populists and their allies, the election results were a disaster. They had gambled everything on their fusion with the Democratic Party and lost. Within months of the election, the People's Party began to dissolve.

McKinley and Recovery

The administration of William McKinley saw a return to relative calm. One reason was the exhaustion of frustrated dissenters. Another reason was the shrewd character of the McKinley administration itself, committed as it was to reassuring stability. Most important, however, was the gradual easing of the economic crisis, a development that undercut many of those who were agitating for change.

McKinley and his allies committed themselves fully to only one issue: the need for higher tariff rates. Within weeks of his inauguration, the administration won approval of the Dingley Tariff, raising duties to the highest point in American history. The administration dealt more gingerly with the explosive silver question, an issue that McKinley himself had never considered very important. He sent a commission to Europe to explore the possibility of a silver agreement with Great Britain and France. As he and everyone else anticipated, the effort produced nothing. The Republicans then enacted the Currency, or Gold Standard, Act of 1900, which confirmed the nation's commitment to gold.

And so the "battle of the standards" ended in victory for the forces of conservatism. Economic developments at the time seemed to vindicate the Republicans. Prosperity began

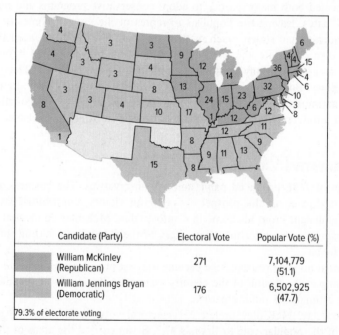

Candidate (Party)	Electoral Vote	Popular Vote (%)
William McKinley (Republican)	271	7,104,779 (51.1)
William Jennings Bryan (Democratic)	176	6,502,925 (47.7)

79.3% of electorate voting

THE ELECTION OF 1896 The results of the presidential election of 1896 revealed striking regional differentiation. William McKinley won the election by a comfortable if not enormous margin, but his victory was not broad-based. He carried all the states of the Northeast and the industrial Midwest, along with California and Oregon, but virtually nothing else. Bryan carried the entire South and almost all of the agrarian West. • *What campaign issues in 1896 helped account for the regional character of the results?*

to return in 1898. Foreign crop failures drove farm prices upward, and American business entered another cycle of expansion. Prosperity and the gold standard, it seemed, were closely allied.

But while the free-silver movement had failed, it had raised an important question for the American economy. In the quarter century before 1900, the countries of the Western world had experienced spectacular growth in productive facilities and population. Yet the supply of money had not kept pace with economic progress. Had it not been for a dramatic increase in the gold supply in the late 1890s, a result of new techniques for extracting gold from low-content ores and the discovery of huge new gold deposits in Alaska, South Africa, and Australia, Populist predictions of financial disaster might in fact have proved correct. In 1898, two and a half times as much gold was produced as in 1890, and the currency supply was soon inflated far beyond anything Bryan and the free-silver forces had anticipated.

By then, however, Bryan—like many other Americans—was becoming engaged with another major issue: the nation's growing involvement in world affairs and its increasing flirtation with **imperialism**.

STIRRINGS OF IMPERIALISM

As the nineteenth century drew to a close, many Americans hoped to translate the era's great industrial feats into global economic, political, and military power. The depression of 1893 further pushed observers to call for greater overseas trade to stimulate the economy. These expansionists—some called them "**jingoes**"—hoped to resume the course of Manifest Destiny.

THE NEW MANIFEST DESTINY

In addition to their economic and political motivations, jingoes believed that domestic tensions in the country might be resolved by a more robust foreign policy and stronger American nationalistic spirit—or even by war. It had been a generation since the Civil War, and some jingoes felt the nation's masculinity had withered in the meantime. Mass industrial wage labor, the same line of reasoning went, had turned American workers from independent producers into faceless cogs in a machine. Some critics of the woman suffrage movement thought it threatened to feminize and weaken the traditional male preserve of politics. Waves of immigration and wars of labor had divided the country. A more stout assertion of power abroad, jingoes hoped, might restore American vitality and unity.

Expansionists were also driven by competitive impulses. Americans were well aware of the imperialist fever that was raging through Europe, leading the major powers to divide much of Africa among themselves and turn eager eyes to the Far East and the Chinese Empire. (See "America in the World: Imperialism.") Some Americans feared their nation would be left out of these potential markets. Scholars and others found a philosophic justification for expansionism in Charles Darwin's theories. They contended that nations or "races," like biological species, struggled constantly for existence and that only the fittest could survive. For strong nations to dominate weak ones was, therefore, in accordance with the laws of nature.

IMPERIALISM

Empires were not, of course, new to the nineteenth century, when the United States acquired its first overseas colonies. They had existed since the early moments of recorded history, and they have continued into our own time.

But in the second half of the nineteenth century, the construction of empires took on a new form, and the word *imperialism* emerged for the first time to describe it. In many places, European powers now created colonies not by sending large numbers of migrants to settle and populate new lands, but instead by creating military, political, and business structures that allowed them to dominate and profit from the existing populations. This new imperialism changed the character of the colonizing nations, enriching them greatly and producing new classes of people whose lives were shaped by the demands of imperial business and administration. It changed the character of colonized societies even more, drawing them into the vast nexus of global industrial capitalism and introducing Western customs, institutions, and technologies to the subject peoples.

As the lure of empire grew in the West, efforts to justify it grew as well. Champions of imperialism argued that the acquisition of colonies was essential for the health, even the survival, of their own industrializing nations. Colonies were sources of raw materials vital to industrial production; they were markets for manufactured goods; and they were suppliers of cheap labor. Defenders of empire also argued that imperialism was good for the colonized people. Many saw colonization as an opportunity to export Christianity to "heathen" lands, and new missionary movements emerged in Europe and America in response. More secular apologists argued that imperialism helped bring colonized people into the modern world.

The invention of steamships, railroads, telegraphs, and other modern vehicles of transportation and communication; the construction of canals (particularly the Suez Canal, completed in 1869, and the Panama Canal, completed in 1914); the creation of new military technologies (repeating rifles, machine guns, and modern artillery)—all contributed to the ability of Western nations to reach, conquer, and control distant lands.

The greatest imperial power of the nineteenth century was Great Britain. By 1800, despite its recent loss of the colonies that became the United States, it already possessed vast territory in North America, the Caribbean, and the Pacific. In the second half of the nineteenth century, Britain greatly expanded its empire. Its most important acquisition was India, one of the largest and most populous countries in the world and a nation in which Great Britain had long exerted informal authority. In 1857, when Indians revolted against British influence, British forces brutally crushed the rebellion and established formal colonial control over India. British officials, backed by substantial military power, now governed India through a large civil service staffed mostly by people from England and Scotland but with some Indians serving in minor positions. The British invested heavily in railroads, telegraphs, canals, harbors, and agricultural improvements to enhance the economic opportunities available to them. They created schools for Indian children in an effort to draw them into British culture and make them supporters of the imperial system.

The British also extended their empire into Africa and other parts of Asia. The great

(©Time Life Pictures/Mansell/Getty Images)

THE BRITISH RAJ The Drum Corps of the Royal Fusiliers in India poses here for a formal portrait, taken in 1877. Although the drummers are British, an Indian associate is included at top left. This blending of the dominant British with subordinate Indians was characteristic of the administration of the British Empire in India—a government known as the "raj," from the Indian word for "rule."

imperial champion Cecil Rhodes expanded a small existing British colony at Capetown into a substantial colony that included much of what is now South Africa. In 1895, he added new British territories to the north, which he named Rhodesia (and which today are Zimbabwe and Zambia). Others spread British authority into Kenya, Uganda, Nigeria, and much of Egypt. British imperialists also extended the empire into East Asia, with the acquisition of Singapore, Hong Kong, Burma, and Malaya; and they built a substantial presence—although not formal colonial rule—in China.

Other European states, watching the vast expansion of the British Empire, quickly jumped into the race for colonies. France built colonies in Indochina (Vietnam and Laos), Algeria, west Africa, and Madagascar. Belgium moved into the Congo in west Africa. Germany established footholds in the Cameroons, Tanganyika, and other parts of Africa, and in the Pacific islands north of Australia. Dutch, Italian, Portuguese, Spanish, Russian, and Japanese imperialists created colonies as well in Africa, Asia, and the

Pacific—driven both by a calculation of their own commercial interests and by the frenzied competition that had developed among rival imperial powers. In 1898, the United States was drawn into the imperial race, in part inadvertently as an unanticipated result of the Spanish-American War. But the drive to acquire colonies resulted as well from the deliberate efforts of home-grown proponents of empire (among them Theodore Roosevelt), who believed that in the modern industrial-imperial world, a nation without colonies would have difficulty remaining, or becoming, a true great power. •

UNDERSTAND, ANALYZE, & EVALUATE

1. What motivated the European nations' drive for empire in the late nineteenth century?
2. Why was Great Britain so successful in acquiring its vast empire?
3. How do the imperial efforts and ambitions of the United States at the end of the nineteenth century compare with those of European powers?

The most effective apostle of imperialism was Alfred Thayer Mahan, a captain and, later, admiral in the U.S. Navy. Mahan's thesis, presented in *The Influence of Sea Power upon History* (1890) and other works, was simple: countries with sea power were the great nations of history. Effective sea power required, among other things, colonies. Mahan believed that the United States should, at the least, acquire defensive bases in the Caribbean and the Pacific and take possession of Hawaii and other Pacific islands. He feared that the United States did not have a large enough navy to play the great role he envisioned. But during the 1870s and 1880s, the government launched a shipbuilding program that by 1898 had moved the United States to fifth place among the world's naval powers, and by 1900 to third place.

HAWAII AND SAMOA

The islands of Hawaii in the mid-Pacific had been an important way station for American ships in the China trade since the early nineteenth century. By the 1880s, officers of the expanding U.S. Navy were looking covetously at Pearl Harbor on the island of Oahu as a possible permanent base for American ships. The growing number of Americans who had taken up residence on the islands also pressed for an increased American presence in Hawaii.

Settled by Polynesian people beginning in about 1500 B.C., Hawaii had developed an agricultural and fishing society in which different islands, and different communities on the same islands, each with its own chieftain, lived more or less self-sufficiently. When the first Americans arrived in Hawaii in the 1790s on merchant ships from New England, there were perhaps half a million people living there. Battles among rival communities were frequent, as chieftains tried to consolidate power over their neighbors. In 1810, after a series of such battles, King Kamehameha I established his dominance, welcomed American traders, and helped them develop a thriving trade between Hawaii and China. But Americans soon wanted more than trade. Missionaries began settling there in the early nineteenth century; and in the 1830s, William Hooper, a Boston trader, became the first of many Americans to buy land and establish a sugar plantation on the islands.

The arrival of these merchants, missionaries, and planters was devastating to traditional Hawaiian society. The newcomers inadvertently brought infectious diseases to which the Hawaiians, like the American Indians before them, were vulnerable. By the mid-nineteenth century, more than half the native population had died. The Americans brought other incursions as well. Missionaries worked to replace native religion with Christianity. Other white settlers introduced liquor, firearms, and a commercial economy, all of which eroded the traditional character of Hawaiian society. By the 1840s, American planters had spread throughout the islands, and an American settler, G. P. Judd, had become prime minister of Hawaii under King Kamehameha III, who had agreed to establish a constitutional monarchy. Judd governed Hawaii for over a decade.

In 1887, the United States negotiated a treaty with Hawaii that permitted it to open a naval base at Pearl Harbor. By then, growing sugar for export to America had become the basis of the Hawaiian economy—as a result of an 1875 agreement allowing Hawaiian sugar to enter the United States duty-free. The American-dominated sugar plantation system displaced native Hawaiians from their lands and relied heavily on Asian immigrants, whom the Americans considered more reliable and more docile than the natives.

Native Hawaiians did not accept their subordination without protest. In 1891, they elevated a powerful nationalist to the throne: **Queen Liliuokalani**, who set out to challenge the growing American control of the islands. But she remained in power only two years. In 1890, the United States had eliminated the exemption from American tariffs in Hawaiian sugar trade. The result was devastating to the economy of the islands, and American planters concluded that the only way for them to recover was to become part of the United States, and, hence, exempt from its tariffs. In 1893, they staged a revolution and called on the United States for protection. After the American minister ordered marines from a warship in Honolulu harbor to go ashore to aid the American rebels, the queen yielded her authority.

A provisional government, dominated by Americans, immediately sent a delegation to Washington to negotiate a treaty of annexation. Debate over the treaty continued until 1898, when Congress finally approved the agreement.

Three thousand miles south of Hawaii, the Samoan islands had also long served as a stopover for American ships in the Pacific trade. As American commerce with Asia increased, business groups in the United States regarded Samoa with new interest, and the American navy began eyeing the Samoan harbor at Pago Pago. In 1878, the Hayes administration extracted a treaty from Samoan leaders for an American naval station at Pago Pago.

Great Britain and Germany were also interested in the islands, and they, too, secured treaty rights from the native princes. For the next ten years, the three powers jockeyed for dominance in Samoa, finally agreeing to create a tripartite protectorate over Samoa, with the native chiefs exercising only nominal authority. The three-way arrangement failed to halt the rivalries of its members, and in 1899, the United States and Germany divided the islands between them, compensating Britain with territories elsewhere in the Pacific. The United States retained the harbor at Pago Pago.

WAR WITH SPAIN

Imperial ambitions had thus begun to stir within the United States well before the late 1890s. But a war with Spain in 1898 turned those stirrings into overt expansionism.

CONTROVERSY OVER CUBA

Spain's once-formidable empire had grown rickety but still included two prized island possessions: Cuba, ninety miles off the shores of Florida, and the Philippines, in Asia. As in many imperial holdings, the native peoples in these regions objected to the presence of European colonizers and occasionally waged insurrections. One rebellion in Cuba had ended in 1878 with Spanish rule intact. Nominal Cuban control over the economy followed, but the depression of the 1890s led Spain to withdraw even that privilege. In 1895, Cuban revolutionaries mounted a new insurrection, led by the revolutionary poet José Martí and military heroes of the earlier wars of liberation.

The rebellion soon attracted the sympathies of people in the United States. Popular newspapers reported horrific atrocities committed by the Spanish against Cuban rebels and civilians. The Spanish governor since 1896, General Valeriano Weyler, was rounding up Cubans in detention camps to isolate rebels in the countryside and then destroying agriculture to starve them out. These policies of "the Butcher" led to the deaths of tens of thousands of Cuban civilians. The conflict also imperiled the American-owned sugar plantations in Cuba and regional commerce more broadly. And ever since the articulation

YELLOW JOURNALISM

Joseph Pulitzer was a successful newspaper publisher in St. Louis, Missouri, when he traveled to New York City in 1883 to buy a struggling paper, the *New York World*. "There is room in this great and growing city," he wrote in one of his first editorials, "for a journal that is not only cheap, but bright, not only bright but large, not only large but truly democratic . . . that will serve and battle for the people with earnest sincerity." Within a year, the *World*'s daily circulation had soared from 10,000 to over 60,000. By 1886, it had reached 250,000 and was making enormous profits.

The success of Pulitzer's *World* marked the birth of what came to be known as "yellow journalism," a phrase that reportedly derived from a character in one of the *World*'s comic strips: "the Yellow Kid." Color printing in newspapers was relatively new, and yellow was the most difficult color to print. So in the beginning, the term *yellow journalism* was a comment on the new technological possibilities that Pulitzer was so eagerly embracing. Eventually, however, it came to refer to a sensationalist style of reporting and writing that spread quickly through urban America and changed the character of newspapers.

Sensationalism was not new to journalism in the late nineteenth century, of course. Political scandal sheets had been publishing lurid stories since before the American Revolution. But the yellow journalism of the 1880s and 1890s took the search for a mass audience to new levels. The *World* created one of the first Sunday editions, with lavishly colored special sections, comics, and illustrated features. It expanded coverage of sports, fashion, literature, and theater.

It pioneered large, glaring, overheated headlines that captured the eyes of people who were passing newsstands. It published exposés of political corruption. It made considerable efforts to bring drama and energy to its coverage of crime. It tried to involve readers directly in its stories (as when a *World* campaign helped raise $300,000 to build a base for the Statue of Liberty, with much of the money coming in donations of 5 or 10 cents from working-class readers). And it introduced a self-consciously populist style of writing that appealed to working-class readers. "The American people want something terse, forcible, picturesque, striking," Pulitzer said. His reporters wrote short, forceful sentences. They did not shy away from expressing sympathy or outrage. And they were not always constrained by the truth.

Pulitzer very quickly produced imitators, the most important of them the California publisher William Randolph Hearst, who in 1895 bought the *New York Journal*, cut its price to 1 cent (Pulitzer quickly followed suit), copied many of the *World*'s techniques, and within a year raised its circulation to 400,000. Hearst soon made the *Journal* the largest-circulation paper in the country, selling more than a million copies a day. Pulitzer, whose own circulation was not far behind, accused him of "pandering to the worst tastes of the prurient and the horror-loving" and "dealing in bogus news." But the *World* wasted no time before imitating the *Journal*. The competition between these two yellow journals soon drove both to new levels of sensationalism. Their success drove newspapers in other cities around the nation to copy their techniques.

The civil war in Cuba in the 1890s gave both papers their best opportunities yet for combining sensational reporting with shameless appeals to patriotism and moral outrage. They avidly published exaggerated reports of Spanish atrocities toward the Cuban rebels, fanning popular anger toward Spain. When the American battleship *Maine* mysteriously exploded in Havana harbor in 1898, both papers without evidence blamed Spanish authorities. The *Journal* offered a $50,000 reward for information leading to the conviction of those responsible for the explosion, and it crowded all other stories off its front page ("There is no other news," Hearst told his editors) to make room for such screaming headlines as THE WHOLE COUNTRY THRILLS WITH WAR FEVER and HAVANA POPULACE INSULTS THE MEMORY OF THE *MAINE* VICTIMS. In the three days following the *Maine* explosion, the *Journal* sold more than 3 million copies, a new world's record for newspaper circulation.

In the aftermath of the *Maine* episode, the more conservative press launched a spirited attack on yellow journalism. It responded in part to Hearst's boast that the conflict in Cuba was "the *Journal*'s war." He sent a cable to one of his reporters in Cuba saying: "You furnish the pictures, and I'll furnish the war." Growing numbers of critics tried to discourage yellow journalism, which "respectable" editors both deplored and feared. Some schools, libraries, and clubs began to banish the papers from their premises. But the techniques the yellow press pioneered in the 1890s helped map the way for a tradition of colorful, popular journalism, later embodied in "tabloids," some elements of which eventually found their way into television news and the Internet. •

UNDERSTAND, ANALYZE, & EVALUATE

1. Did Pulitzer's *World*, Hearst's *Journal*, and their imitators report the news or manufacture it?
2. How did the yellow press influence the public's perception of the Spanish-American War?
3. How does television news continue the tradition of yellow journalism? In what other mass media do you see the style and techniques pioneered by the yellow press?

of the Monroe Doctrine in 1823, Americans had dreamed of ridding North and South America of European colonizers. Some hoped to replace the Spanish with a heavy American presence in the region, while others, including William Jennings Bryan and other prominent Democrats and members of Congress, wished only to liberate Cuba and leave it to the Cubans.

The conflict in Cuba came at a particularly opportune moment for the newspaper publishers Joseph Pulitzer of the *New York World* and William Randolph Hearst of the *New York Journal*. In the 1890s, Hearst and Pulitzer were engaged in a ruthless circulation war, and they both sent batteries of reporters and illustrators to Cuba with orders to provide accounts of Spanish atrocities. This sort of sensationalist reporting was known as **yellow journalism**. (See "Patterns of Popular Culture: Yellow Journalism.")

Although President Cleveland worried about the potential disruptions of American trade, he did not intervene. Nor, at first, did his successor, William McKinley. Both men shared commercial and humanitarian concerns, but sought to avoid war with a European power. An irritated Theodore Roosevelt, assistant secretary of the navy, excoriated President McKinley for his un-masculine weakness, charging that he had "no more backbone than a chocolate éclair."

The situation changed in early 1898. In January, pro-Spanish Cubans rioted in Havana against the idea of a free Cuba, or *Cuba libre*, which the two American political parties had at least rhetorically supported even as successive U.S. administrations remained neutral. Thus the riots carried anti-American undertones, and President McKinley, under pressure from the popular media after unfulfilled promises from Spain, sent the **U.S.S.** *Maine* to Havana harbor to protect American citizens. On February 15, 1898, the ship exploded, killing 266 Americans. Although later investigations revealed it likely an accident, most Americans, egged on by the jingoistic press, blamed the Spanish.

For all the earlier arguments about humanity, commerce, and geopolitical strategy, the destruction of the *Maine* challenged American resolve. A Democrat in the House voted for war "to defend the honor and maintain the dignity of this republic"; a Republican sought "peace with honor." On April 25, Congress passed a resolution declaring war against the Spanish. It included the **Teller Amendment**, named for Democratic senator Henry T. Teller from Colorado, which swore off any intentions to occupy, possess, or control Cuba after a future victory against the Spanish.

"A Splendid Little War"

The American ambassador to England, John Hay, called the ensuing conflict "a splendid little war," an opinion that most Americans, except for many of the enlisted men who fought it, seemed to share. Declared in April, the **Spanish-American War** was over in August, in part because Cuban rebels had already greatly weakened the Spanish resistance, making the American intervention in many respects little more than a mopping-up exercise. Four hundred and sixty Americans were killed in battle or died of wounds, although some 5,200 others perished of malaria, dysentery, typhoid, and other diseases. Casualties among Cuban insurgents, who continued to bear the brunt of the fighting, were much higher.

American soldiers faced serious supply problems: a shortage of modern rifles and ammunition, uniforms too heavy for the warm Caribbean weather, inadequate medical services, and skimpy, almost indigestible food. The regular army numbered only 28,000 troops and officers, most of whom had experience fighting Indians but none in larger-scale warfare. That meant that, as in the Civil War, the United States had to rely heavily on National Guard units, organized by local communities and commanded for the most part by local leaders without military experience.

A significant proportion of the American invasion force consisted of black soldiers. Some were volunteer troops put together by African American communities. Others were members of the four black regiments in the regular army, who had been stationed on the frontier to protect white settlements and were now transferred east to fight in Cuba. As the black soldiers traveled through the South toward the training camps, some resisted the rigid segregation to which they were subjected. African American soldiers in Georgia deliberately made use of a "whites only" park; in Florida, they beat a soda-fountain operator for refusing to serve them; in Tampa, white provocations and black retaliation led to a nightlong riot that left thirty wounded.

Racial tensions continued in Cuba. African Americans played crucial roles in some of the important battles of the war, including the famous charge at San Juan Hill, and won many medals. Nearly half the Cuban insurgents fighting with the Americans were themselves black, including one of the leading insurgent generals, Antonio Maceo. The sight of black Cuban soldiers fighting alongside whites as equals gave African Americans a stronger sense of the injustice of their own situation.

(Source: Library of Congress, Prints and Photographs Division [LC-USZ62-57107])

AFRICAN AMERICAN CAVALRY   Substantial numbers of African Americans fought in the U.S. Army during the Spanish-American War. Although confined to all-black units, they engaged in combat alongside white units and fought bravely and effectively. This photograph shows a troop of African American cavalry in formation in Cuba. It is meant to be viewed through a stereoscope, which would create a single three-dimensional image.

SEIZING THE PHILIPPINES

The assistant secretary of the navy during the Cuban revolution was Theodore Roosevelt, an ardent Anglophile eager to see the United States join the British and other nations as imperial powers. In late February, in the wake of the *Maine* disaster and without the knowledge of his superiors, Roosevelt had sent a message to Commodore George Dewey in Hong Kong. The telegram authorized Dewey's Asiatic Squadron to engage the Spanish fleet in the Philippines should hostilities come. Once war was declared, the Navy ordered Dewey on May 1, 1898, to lead the squadron into Manila harbor, where he quickly destroyed the aging Spanish fleet. Once army reinforcements arrived, Dewey forced the colonial government to surrender Manila with hardly a shot fired. At home, Dewey was lauded as a hero despite the relatively easy time his forces had had subduing the Spanish.

THE BATTLE FOR CUBA

Cuba remained the principal focus of American military efforts. At first, the commanding general of the Army, Nelson A. Miles, planned a long period of training before actually sending troops into combat. But when a Spanish fleet under Admiral Pascual Cervera slipped past the American navy into Santiago harbor on the southern coast of Cuba, plans changed quickly. As the American Atlantic fleet bottled Cervera up in the harbor, the War Department ordered Major General William R. Shafter to assemble forces in Tampa in June and proceed to Santiago. After a chaotic and delayed mobilization, an American force of 17,000 left on June 14 on dilapidated craft. More than two weeks of sweltering heat and overcrowding stood between the men and Cuba's southern shoreline.

Once on land, Shafter was ordered to advance toward Santiago, which he planned to surround and capture. On the way, his cavalry division, now under the command of the former Confederate Major General Joseph Wheeler, met and defeated Spanish forces at Las Guásimas. Meanwhile problems of disease and supply hampered the American undertaking.

A week later, on July 1, Shafter's forces attacked El Caney and the San Juan Heights, which included San Juan Hill and Kettle Hill. El Caney took twelve hours to subdue, which meant the attack on the Heights had to proceed without expected help from those forces. Among the troops assigned to take the hills were the Rough Riders, headed by Theodore Roosevelt, who had resigned from the Navy Department to get into the war, and the all-black Ninth and Tenth Cavalry Regiments. Roosevelt's passion to join the war undoubtedly reflected the decision of his beloved father, Theodore Roosevelt Sr., not to fight in the Civil War, a source of private shame within the family that his son sought to erase.

The July 1 battles were bloody and miserable engagements, filled with logistical nightmares, hot weather, little water, and fierce Spanish resistance. Into withering fire the Rough Riders advanced up Kettle Hill. Roosevelt himself emerged unscathed, but nearly a hundred soldiers were killed or wounded. "We have won so far at a heavy cost," Roosevelt wrote at the time. "We *must* have help." The African American units in particular put themselves at great risk to cover the Rough Riders' bold, if reckless, charges. Though more than two hundred Americans lay dead by nightfall, the forces took the Heights as the Spanish retreated to Santiago. Blustery headlines back home, and later romanticization of the day's events, made a hero of Roosevelt, who with the benefit of hindsight called July "the great day of my life."

Although Shafter was now in position to assault Santiago, his army was so weakened by sickness that he feared he might have to abandon his position. But unknown to the Americans, the Spanish government had decided Santiago was lost and ordered Cervera to evacuate. On July 3, Cervera tried to escape the harbor. The waiting American squadron destroyed his entire fleet. On July 16, the commander of Spanish ground forces in Santiago ceased fighting. In a sign of things to come, the Cubans so central to the weakening of Spanish forces were not invited to participate in the ceremonies of capitulation. At about the same time, an American army under General Miles landed in Puerto Rico and occupied it against virtually no opposition. On August 12, an armistice ended the war. Under its terms, Spain recognized the independence of Cuba, ceded Puerto Rico and the Pacific island of Guam to the United States, and accepted continued American occupation of Manila pending the final disposition of the Philippines.

Puerto Rico and the United States

The island of **Puerto Rico** had been a part of the Spanish Empire since 1508. By the early seventeenth century, the native people of the island, the Arawaks, had largely disappeared as a result of infectious diseases, Spanish brutality, and poverty. Puerto Rican society developed, therefore, with a Spanish ruling class and a large African workforce for the coffee and sugar plantations that came to dominate its economy.

Puerto Rican resistance to Spanish rule began to emerge in the nineteenth century. The resistance prompted some reforms: the abolition of slavery in 1873, representation in the Spanish parliament, and other changes. Demands for independence continued to grow, and in 1898, Spain granted the island a degree of independence. But before the changes had any chance to take effect, control of Puerto Rico shifted to the United States. American military forces occupied the island during the Spanish-American War and remained in control until 1900, when the Foraker Act ended military rule and established a formal colonial government. Agitation for independence continued, and in 1917, Congress passed the Jones Act, which declared Puerto Rico to be a U.S. territory and made all Puerto Ricans American citizens.

THE SPANISH-AMERICAN WAR IN CUBA, 1898 The military conflict between the United States and Spain in Cuba was a brief affair. The Cuban rebels and an American naval blockade had already brought the Spanish to the brink of defeat. The arrival of American troops was the final blow. In the space of about a week, U.S. troops won four decisive battles in the area around Santiago in southeast Cuba. This map shows the extent of the American naval blockade, the path of American troops from Florida to Cuba, and the location of the actual fighting. • *What were the implications of the war in Cuba for Puerto Rico?*

The Puerto Rican sugar industry flourished as it took advantage of the American market that was now open to it without tariffs. As in Hawaii, Americans from the mainland began establishing large sugar plantations on the island and hiring natives to work them. The growing emphasis on sugar as a cash crop, and the transformation of many Puerto Rican farmers into paid laborers, led to a reduction in the growing of food for the island and greater reliance on imported goods. When international sugar prices were high, Puerto Rico did well. When they dropped, the island's economy sagged, pushing many plantation workers, already poor, into destitution.

THE DEBATE OVER THE PHILIPPINES

Although the annexation of Puerto Rico produced relatively little controversy, the seizure of the Philippines created an impassioned debate. Controlling a nearby Caribbean island fit reasonably comfortably into the United States' sense of itself as the dominant power in the Western Hemisphere. But to many Americans, controlling a large and densely populated territory thousands of miles away seemed ominously different.

McKinley claimed to be reluctant to support annexation. But, according to his own accounts, he came to believe there were no acceptable alternatives. Returning the Philippines to Spain would be "cowardly and dishonorable," he claimed. Turning them over to another imperialist power (France, Germany, or Britain) would be "bad business and discreditable." Granting them independence would be irresponsible because the Filipinos were "unfit for self government." The only solution was "to take them all and to educate the Filipinos, and uplift and Christianize them, and by God's grace do the very best we could by them."

The Treaty of Paris, signed in December 1898, confirmed the terms of the armistice and brought a formal end to the war. American negotiators had startled the Spanish by

(Source: Library of Congress, Prints and Photographs Division [LC-DIG-ppmsca-25453])

MEASURING UNCLE SAM FOR A NEW SUIT In this *Puck* cartoon, President McKinley is depicted as a tailor, meaning his client for a suit is large enough to accommodate the new possessions the United States obtained in the aftermath of the Spanish-American War. The stripes on Uncle Sam's pants bear the names of earlier, less controversial acquisitions, such as the Louisiana Purchase.

demanding they also cede the Philippines to the United States, but an American offer of $20 million for the islands softened their resistance. They accepted all the American terms.

In the U.S. Senate, however, resistance was fierce. During debate over ratification of the treaty, a powerful anti-imperialist movement arose to oppose acquisition of the Philippines. The anti-imperialists included some of the nation's wealthiest and most powerful figures: Andrew Carnegie, Mark Twain, Samuel Gompers, Senator John Sherman, and others. Some anti-imperialists believed that imperialism was immoral, a repudiation of America's commitment to human freedom, or a hypocritical turn for a nation that owed its own existence to liberation from distant colonial rule. Others feared "polluting" the American population by introducing Asian races into it. Industrial workers feared being undercut by a flood of cheap laborers from the new colonies. Conservatives worried about the large standing army and entangling foreign alliances they believed imperialism would require and they feared would threaten American liberties. Sugar growers and other anti-imperialists feared unwelcome competition from the new territories. The Anti-Imperialist League, established late in 1898 by upper-class Bostonians, New Yorkers, and others to fight annexation, waged a vigorous campaign against ratification of the Paris treaty. (See "Consider the Source: Platform of the Anti-Imperialist League.")

But favoring ratification was an equally varied group. There were the exuberant imperialists such as Theodore Roosevelt, who saw the acquisition of empire as a way to reinvigorate the nation. Some businessmen saw opportunities to dominate the Asian trade, and more broadly, inject capital into an economic system prone to periodic depressions and panics. Most Republicans saw partisan advantage in acquiring valuable new territories through a war fought and won by a Republican administration. Perhaps the strongest argument in favor of annexation, however, was that the United States already possessed the islands.

When anti-imperialists warned of the danger of acquiring heavily populated territories whose people might have to become citizens, the jingoes had a ready answer. The nation's long-standing policies toward Indians—treating them as dependents rather than citizens—had created a precedent for annexing land without absorbing people.

The fate of the treaty remained in doubt for weeks, until it received the unexpected support of William Jennings Bryan, a fervent anti-imperialist. He backed ratification because he hoped to move the issue out of the Senate and make it the subject of a national referendum in 1900, when he expected to be the Democratic presidential candidate again. Bryan persuaded a number of anti-imperialist Democrats to support the treaty to set up the 1900 debate. The Senate ratified it on February 6, 1899.

But Bryan miscalculated. If the election of 1900 was in fact a referendum on the Philippines, as Bryan expected, it proved beyond a doubt that the nation had decided in favor of imperialism. Once again Bryan ran against McKinley; and once again McKinley won, even more decisively than in 1896. It was not only the issue of the colonies, however, that ensured McKinley's victory. The Republicans benefited from growing prosperity—and also from the colorful personality of their vice presidential candidate, the Rough Rider Theodore Roosevelt.

THE REPUBLIC AS EMPIRE

The new American empire was small by the standards of the great imperial powers of Europe. But it embroiled the United States in the politics of both Europe and the Far East in ways the nation had tried to avoid in the past. It also drew Americans into a brutal war in the Philippines.

PLATFORM OF THE AMERICAN ANTI-IMPERIALIST LEAGUE (1899)

As part of their campaign against the annexation of the Philippines by the United States, members of the Anti-Imperialist League circulated this party platform. Here they argue that American political ideals are not compatible with imperialist actions.

We hold that the policy known as imperialism is hostile to liberty and tends toward militarism, an evil from which it has been our glory to be free. We regret that it has become necessary in the land of Washington and Lincoln to reaffirm that all men, of whatever race or color, are entitled to life, liberty, and the pursuit of happiness. We maintain that governments derive their just powers from the consent of the governed. We insist that the subjugation of any people is "criminal aggression" and open disloyalty to the distinctive principles of our Government.

We earnestly condemn the policy of the present National Administration in the Philippines. It seeks to extinguish the spirit of 1776 in those islands. We deplore the sacrifice of our soldiers and sailors, whose bravery deserves admiration even in an unjust war. We denounce the slaughter of the Filipinos as a needless horror. We protest against the extension of American sovereignty by Spanish methods.

We demand the immediate cessation of the war against liberty, begun by Spain and continued by us. We urge that Congress be promptly convened to announce to the Filipinos our purpose to concede to them the independence for which they have so long fought and which of right is theirs.

The United States have always protested against the doctrine of international law which permits the subjugation of the weak by the strong. A self-governing state cannot accept sovereignty over an unwilling people.

The United States cannot act upon the ancient heresy that might makes right.

Imperialists assume that with the destruction of self-government in the Philippines by American hands, all opposition here will cease. This is a grievous error. Much as we abhor the war of "criminal aggression" in the Philippines, greatly as we regret that the blood of the Filipinos is on American hands, we more deeply resent the betrayal of American institutions at home. The real firing line is not in the suburbs of Manila. The foe is of our own household. The attempt of 1861 was to divide the country. That of 1899 is to destroy its fundamental principles and noblest ideals.

Whether the ruthless slaughter of the Filipinos shall end next month or next year is but an incident in a contest that must go on until the Declaration of Independence and the Constitution of the United States are rescued from the hands of their betrayers. Those who dispute about standards of value while the Republic is undermined will be listened to as little as those who would wrangle about the small economies of the household while the house is on fire. The training of a great people for a century, the aspiration for liberty of a vast immigration are forces that will hurl aside those who in the delirium of conquest seek to destroy the character of our institutions.

We deny that the obligation of all citizens to support their Government in times of grave national peril applies to the present situation. If an Administration may with impunity ignore the issues upon which it was chosen, deliberately create a condition of war anywhere on the face of the globe, debauch the civil service for spoils to promote the adventure, organize a truth-suppressing censorship and demand of all citizens a suspension of judgment and their unanimous support while it chooses to continue the fighting, representative government itself is imperiled.

We propose to contribute to the defeat of any person or party that stands for the forcible subjugation of any people. We shall oppose for reelection all who in the White House or in Congress betray American liberty in pursuit of un-American gains. We still hope that both of our great political parties will support and defend the Declaration of Independence in the closing campaign of the century.

Source: Bancroft, Frederick (ed.), "Platform of the American Anti-Imperialist League," in *Speeches, Correspondence, and Political Papers of Carl Schurz, vol. 6.* New York, NY: G.P. Putnam's Sons, 1913, 77, note 1.

UNDERSTAND, ANALYZE, & EVALUATE

1. On what grounds did the Anti-Imperialist League oppose U.S. expansion, and where were these principles ratified?
2. What were the costs of imperial expansion for the United States and what losses were Filipinos to incur?
3. How did the prospect of an American empire affect the nation's democratic principles?

GOVERNING THE COLONIES

Three American dependencies—Hawaii, Alaska, and Puerto Rico—presented relatively few problems. They received territorial status, and their residents American citizenship, relatively quickly: Hawaii in 1900, Alaska in 1912, and Puerto Rico in 1917. The Navy took control of the Pacific islands of Guam and Tutuila, while it left alone some of the smallest, least populated Pacific islands now under its control. Cuba was a thornier problem. American military forces, commanded by General Leonard Wood, remained there until 1902, theoretically to prepare the island for independence. Americans built roads, schools, and hospitals; reorganized the legal, financial, and administrative systems; and introduced medical and sanitation reforms. But the United States also laid the basis for years of American economic domination of the island.

When Cuba drew up a constitution that made no reference to the United States, Congress responded by passing the Platt Amendment in 1901 and pressuring Cuba into incorporating its terms into its constitution. The Platt Amendment barred Cuba from making treaties with other nations; gave the United States the right to intervene in Cuba to preserve independence, life, and property; and required Cuba to permit American naval stations on its territory. The amendment left Cuba with only nominal political independence.

American capital made the island an American economic appendage as well. American investors poured into Cuba, buying up plantations, factories, railroads, and refineries. Resistance to "Yankee imperialism" produced intermittent revolts against the Cuban government, which at times prompted U.S. military intervention. American troops occupied the island from 1906 to 1909 after one such rebellion; they returned again in 1912 to suppress a revolt by black plantation workers. As in Puerto Rico and Hawaii, sugar production—spurred by access to the American market—increasingly dominated the island's economy and subjected it to the same cycle of booms and busts that plagued other sugar-producing participants in the U.S. economy.

THE PHILIPPINE WAR

Like other imperial powers, the United States soon discovered that local people in colonies resent their subjugation. The American experience in the Philippines began with a long and bloody war.

The conflict in the Philippines is a largely forgotten American war. It was also one of the longest, lasting from 1898 to 1902, and one of the most vicious. It involved 125,000 American troops and resulted in 4,300 American deaths. The number of Filipinos killed in the conflict has long been a matter of dispute, but it seems likely that at least 50,000 natives and perhaps hundreds of thousands died of disease, starvation, or violence. The American occupiers faced a guerrilla war in the Philippines, and soon resorted to the same brutal practices that had outraged so many Americans when Weyler had used them in the Caribbean.

The Filipinos had rebelled against Spanish rule before 1898, and as soon as they realized the Americans had come to stay, rebelled against them as well. Ably led by Emilio Aguinaldo, who claimed to head the legitimate government of the nation, Filipinos harried the American army of occupation from island to island for more than three years. At first, American commanders believed the rebels had only a small popular following. But by early 1900, General Arthur MacArthur, an American commander in the islands (and father of General Douglas MacArthur), was writing, "I have been reluctantly compelled to believe that the Filipino masses are loyal to Aguinaldo and the government which he heads."

To MacArthur and others, that realization was not a reason to abandon the colonial project, moderate American tactics, or conciliate the rebels, but rather to adopt more severe measures. Gradually, the American military effort became more systematically vicious. Captured Filipino guerrillas were treated not as prisoners of war but murderers, many

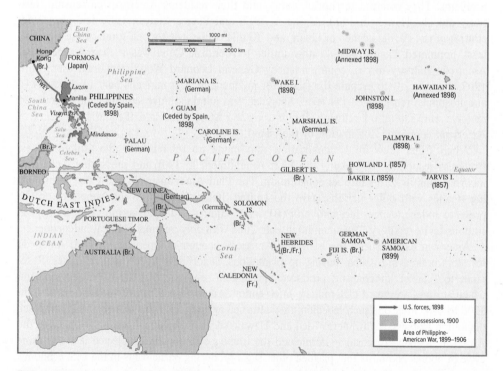

THE AMERICAN SOUTH PACIFIC EMPIRE, 1900   Except for Puerto Rico, all of the colonial acquisitions of the United States in the wake of the Spanish-American War occurred in the Pacific. The new attraction of imperialism persuaded the United States to annex Hawaii in 1898. The war itself gave America control of the Philippines, Guam, and other, smaller Spanish possessions in the Pacific. When added to the small, scattered islands that the United States had acquired as naval bases earlier in the nineteenth century, these new possessions gave the nation a far-flung Pacific empire, even if one whose total territory and population remained small by the standards of the other great empires of the age. • *What was the reaction in the United States to the acquisition of this new empire?*

summarily executed. On some islands, entire communities were evacuated, the residents forced into concentration camps while American troops destroyed their villages. A spirit of savagery grew among some American soldiers, who came to view the Filipinos as subhuman and, at times, seemed to take pleasure in arbitrarily killing them.

The racial undertones of the war—American soldiers called the Filipinos "niggers"—were particularly grating for African American troops serving in segregated units. They were hardly unaware that at home, southern states and lynch mobs were in the process of disfranchising and terrorizing black people. Some noticed a resemblance between the attitude of the American military and government toward the Filipino natives and popular attitudes toward African Americans and Native Americans.

By 1902, reports of brutality and American casualties had soured the American public on the war. But by then, the rebellion had largely exhausted itself and the occupiers had established control over most of the islands. The key to their victory was the March 1901 capture of Aguinaldo, who later signed a document urging his followers to stop fighting and declared his own allegiance to the United States in exchange for a pension. Fighting continued intermittently until as late as 1906, but American possession of the Philippines was now secure. In the summer of 1901, the military transferred authority over the islands to William Howard Taft, who became their first civilian governor and gave the Filipinos broad local autonomy. The Americans also built roads, schools, bridges, and sewers; instituted major administrative and financial reforms; and established a public health system. Filipino self-rule gradually increased, but it was not until July 4, 1946, that the islands finally gained their independence.

THE OPEN DOOR

The American acquisition of the Philippines increased the already strong U.S. interest in Asia. Americans were particularly concerned about the future of China, which provided a tempting target for exploitation by other countries. By 1900, England, France, Germany, Russia, and Japan were beginning to carve up China among themselves, pressuring the Chinese government for concessions that gave them effective control over regions of China. In some cases, they simply seized Chinese territory and claimed it as their own. Many Americans feared the process would soon cut them out of the China trade altogether.

Eager for a way to advance American interests in China without risking war, McKinley issued a statement in September 1898 saying the United States wanted access to China but no special advantages there: "Asking only the open door for ourselves, we are ready to accord the open door to others." The next year, Secretary of State John Hay translated those words into policy when he addressed identical messages—which became known as the "Open Door notes"—to England, Germany, Russia, France, Japan, and Italy. He asked that each nation with influence in China allow other nations to trade freely and equally in its sphere. The principles Hay outlined would allow the United States to do business in China without fear of interference.

Europe and Japan received the **Open Door** proposals coolly. Russia openly rejected them; the other powers claimed to accept them in principle but to be unable to act unless all the other powers agreed. Hay refused to consider this a rebuff. He boldly announced that all the powers had accepted the principles of the Open Door in "final and definitive" form and that the United States expected them to observe those principles.

No sooner had the diplomatic maneuvering over the Open Door ended than the Boxers, a nationalist Chinese martial-arts society, launched a revolt against foreigners in China.

The **Boxer Rebellion** spread widely across eastern China, targeting Westerners wherever the attackers could find them, including many Christian missionaries. But the climax of the revolt was a siege of the entire Western foreign diplomatic corps, which took refuge in the British embassy in Peking. The imperial powers, including the United States, sent an international expeditionary force into China to rescue the diplomats. In August 1900, it fought its way into the city and broke the siege.

The Boxer Rebellion became an important event for the role of the United States in China. McKinley and Hay had agreed to American participation in quelling the Boxer Rebellion in order to secure a voice in the settlement of the uprising and prevent the partition of China by the European powers. Hay now won support for his Open Door approach from England and Germany and induced the other participating powers to accept compensation from the Chinese for the damages the Boxer Rebellion had caused. Chinese territorial integrity survived at least in name, but the United States retained access to its lucrative China trade.

A MODERN MILITARY SYSTEM

The war with Spain had revealed glaring deficiencies in the American military system. Had the United States been fighting a more powerful foe, disaster might have resulted. After the war, McKinley appointed Elihu Root, an able corporate lawyer in New York, as secretary of war to supervise a major overhaul of the armed forces.

Root's reforms enlarged the regular army from 25,000 to a maximum of 100,000. They established federal military standards for the National Guard, ensuring that never again would the nation fight a war with volunteer regiments trained and equipped differently than those in the regular army. They sparked the creation of a system of officer training schools, including the Army Staff College (later the Command and General Staff School) at Fort Leavenworth, Kansas, and the Army War College in Washington. And in 1903, at Root's urging, a group called the Joint Chiefs of Staff was established to act as military advisers to the secretary of war. As a result of the new reforms, the United States entered the twentieth century with something resembling a modern military system.

CONCLUSION

For nearly three decades after the end of Reconstruction, American politics remained locked in a rigid stalemate. The electorate was almost evenly divided, and the two major parties differed on only a few issues. A series of unimposing presidents presided over this political system as symbols of its stability and passivity.

Beneath the calm surface of national politics, however, social issues were creating deep tensions: battles between employers and workers, growing resentment among American farmers facing declining prosperity, outrage at what many voters considered corruption in government and excessive power in the hands of corporate titans. When a serious depression began in 1893, these social tensions erupted into a heated debate over fundamental questions of power, wealth, and governance in the United States.

The most visible sign of the challenge to the political stalemate was the Populist movement, an uprising of American farmers demanding far-reaching changes in politics and the economy. In 1892, they created their own political party, the People's Party, which for a few years showed impressive strength. But in the climactic election of 1896, in which the

Populist hero William Jennings Bryan became the presidential nominee of both the Democratic Party and the People's Party, the Republicans won a substantial victory—and, in the process, helped create a great electoral realignment that left the Republicans with a clear majority for the next three decades.

The crises of the 1890s helped spur the United States' growing involvement in the world. In 1898, the United States intervened in a colonial war between Spain and Cuba, won a quick military victory, and signed a treaty with Spain that ceded significant territory to the Americans. A vigorous anticolonial movement failed to stop the imperial drive. But taking the overseas possessions proved easier than holding them. In the Philippines, American forces became bogged down in a brutal four-year war with Filipino rebels. The conflict soured much of the American public. The territorial expansion of 1898 proved to be short-lived, but it marked the beginning of an American global interventionism that persisted long past the lifetimes of those who initiated it.

KEY TERMS/PEOPLE/PLACES/EVENTS

Benjamin Harrison 457
Boxer Rebellion 484
Chester A. Arthur 457
Coxey's Army 463
Farmers' Alliances 459
Free silver 464
Grangers 459
Grover Cleveland 457
Half-Breeds 456
imperialism 467

Interstate Commerce Act 458
James A. Garfield 456
jingoes 467
Open Door 483
Panic of 1893 462
Pendleton Act 457
Populism 461
Puerto Rico 476
Queen Liliuokalani 470

Rutherford B. Hayes 456
Sherman Antitrust Act 458
Spanish-American War 474
Stalwarts 456
Teller Amendment 474
William Jennings Bryan 464
William McKinley 458
U.S.S. *Maine* 474
yellow journalism 473

RECALL AND REFLECT

1. How and why did the federal government attempt to regulate interstate commerce in the late nineteenth century?
2. What efforts did farmers undertake to deal with the economic problems they faced in the late nineteenth century?
3. What was the "silver question"? Why was it so important to so many Americans? How did the major political parties deal with this question?
4. How did the Spanish-American War change America's relationship with the rest of the world?
5. What were the main arguments of those who supported U.S. imperialism and those who opposed the nation's imperial efforts?

20 | THE PROGRESSIVES

THE PROGRESSIVE IMPULSE

WOMEN AND REFORM

THE ASSAULT ON THE PARTIES

SOURCES OF PROGRESSIVE REFORM

CRUSADES FOR SOCIAL ORDER AND REFORM

THEODORE ROOSEVELT AND THE MODERN PRESIDENCY

THE TROUBLED SUCCESSION

WOODROW WILSON AND THE NEW FREEDOM

LOOKING AHEAD

1. What role did women and women's organizations play in the reforms of the progressive era? How did progressive era reforms affect women?

2. What changes to politics and government did progressive reformers advocate at the local, state, and federal levels? How did government change as a result of their reform efforts?

3. How did Woodrow Wilson's progressivism differ from that of Theodore Roosevelt? In what ways was it similar to Roosevelt's?

WELL BEFORE THE END OF THE NINETEENTH CENTURY, many Americans had become convinced that rapid industrialization and urbanization had created a growing crisis. The nation's most pressing need, they claimed, was to impose order and justice on a society that seemed to be approaching chaos. By the early years of the twentieth century, this outlook had acquired a name: **progressivism**.

Not even those who called themselves progressives could agree on what the term meant, for it was a phenomenon of great scope and diversity. But despite or perhaps because of its broad character, the progressive movement generated a remarkable wave of political and social innovation. From the late nineteenth century until at least the end of World War I, progressive reformers brought into public debate such issues as the role of women in society, racial equality, the rights of labor, and the impact of immigration and cultural diversity.

Progressivism began as a series of local movements and encompassed many different efforts to improve the working of society. Slowly but steadily, these efforts became national efforts.

Ultimately it was the presidency, not the Congress, that became the most important vehicle of national reform—first under the dynamic leadership of Theodore Roosevelt and then under the disciplined, moralistic guidance of Woodrow Wilson. By the time America entered World War I in 1917, the federal government—which had exercised limited powers prior to the twentieth century—had greatly expanded its role in American life.

THE PROGRESSIVE IMPULSE

Progressives believed, as their name implies, in the idea of progress. They were optimistic that society was capable of improvement and that continued advancement was the nation's destiny. But progressives believed, too, that growth must not continue to occur recklessly, as it had in the late nineteenth century. The "natural laws" of the marketplace, and the doctrines of laissez-faire and Social Darwinism that dominated those laws, were not sufficient. Direct, purposeful human intervention was essential to ordering and bettering society. These ideas percolated in the United States as well as many other industrializing parts of the world. (See "America in the World: Social Democracy.")

Progressives did not always agree on the form their interventions should take, and the result was a variety of reform impulses. One powerful impulse was the spirit of "antimonopoly," the fear of concentrated power and the urge to limit and disperse authority and wealth. Another progressive impulse was a belief in the importance of social cohesion: the belief that individuals are part of a great web of social relationships, that each person's welfare is dependent on the welfare of society as a whole. Still another impulse was a deep faith in knowledge—in the possibilities of applying

1873
Women's Christian Temperance Union (WCTU) founded

1889
Jane Addams opens Hull House in Chicago

1893
Anti-Saloon League founded

1900
Galveston, Texas, establishes commission government

1901
McKinley assassinated; Theodore Roosevelt becomes president

1902
Northern Securities antitrust case

1906
Hepburn Railroad Regulation Act

Meat Inspection Act

1907
Financial panic and recession

1908
Taft elected president

1909
NAACP formed

Pinchot-Ballinger dispute

1911
Triangle Shirtwaist Company fire

1912
Roosevelt forms Progressive Party

Woodrow Wilson elected president

1913
Sixteenth Amendment (income tax)

Seventeenth Amendment (direct popular election of U.S. senators)

Federal Reserve Act

1914
Federal Trade Commission Act

Clayton Antitrust Act

1919
Eighteenth Amendment (prohibition)

1920
Nineteenth Amendment (woman suffrage)

SOCIAL DEMOCRACY

Enormous energy, enthusiasm, and organization drove the reform efforts in America in the late nineteenth and early twentieth centuries, much of it a result of social crises and political movements in the United States. But the "age of reform," as some have called it, was not an American phenomenon alone. It was part of a wave of social experimentation that was occurring throughout much of the industrial world. "Progressivism" in other countries influenced the social movements in the United States. American reform, in turn, had significant influence elsewhere.

Several industrializing nations adopted the term *progressivism* for their efforts—not only the United States, but also England, Germany, and France. But the term that most broadly defined the new reform energies was *social democracy*. Social democrats in many countries shared a belief in the betterment of society through the accumulation of knowledge. They favored improving the social condition of all people through reforms of the economy and government programs of social protection. And they believed that these goals could be achieved through peaceful political change, rather than through radicalism or revolution. Political parties committed to these goals emerged in several countries: the Labour Party in Britain, social democratic parties in various European nations, and the short-lived Progressive Party in the United States. Intellectuals, academics, and government officials across the world shared the knowledge they were accumulating and observed one another's social programs. American reformers at the turn of the century spent much time visiting Germany, France, Britain, Belgium, and the Netherlands, observing the

reforms in progress there; and Europeans, in turn, visited the United States. Reformers from both America and Europe were also fascinated by the advanced social experiments in Australia and, especially, New Zealand, which the American reformer Henry Demarest Lloyd once called "the political brain of the modern world." But New Zealand's dramatic experiments in factory regulation, woman suffrage, old-age pensions, progressive taxation, and labor arbitration gradually found counterparts in many other nations as well. William Allen White, a progressive journalist from Kansas, said of this time: "We were parts of one another, in the United States and Europe. Something was welding us into one social and economic whole with local political variations . . . [all] fighting a common cause."

Social democracy—or, as it was sometimes called in the United States and

(Source: Library of Congress, Prints and Photographs Division [LC-USZ62-94920])

THE PARIS EXPO, A PROGRESSIVE SYMBOL
The Paris Expositions of 1889 and 1900, symbolized by the Eiffel Tower and enormous globe, drew progressive experts as well as tourists with the vision of progress through industrial innovation. During the Expos, an international group of progressives held meetings to share ideas for bettering society.

elsewhere, social justice or the social gospel—was responsible for many public programs. Germany began a system of social insurance for its citizens in the 1880s while simultaneously undertaking a massive study of society that produced over 140 volumes of "social investigation" of the nation's life. French reformers pressed in the 1890s for factory regulation, assistance to elderly people, and progressive taxation. Britain pioneered the settlement houses in working-class areas of London—a movement that soon spread to the United States—and, like America, witnessed growing challenges to the power of monopolies at both the local and national levels.

In many countries, social democrats felt pressure from the rising worldwide labor movement and from the rise of socialist parties in many industrial countries as well. Strikes, sometimes violent, were common in France, Germany, Britain, and the United States in the late nineteenth century. The more militant workers became, the more unions seemed to grow.

Social democrats did not always welcome the rise of militant labor movements, but they took them seriously and used them to support their own efforts at reform.

The politics of social democracy represented a great shift in the character of public life all over the industrial world. Instead of battles over the privileges of aristocrats or the power of monarchs, reformers now focused on the social problems of ordinary people and attempted to improve their lot. "The politics of the future are social politics," the British reformer Joseph Chamberlain said in the 1880s, referring to efforts to deal with the problems of ordinary citizens. That belief was fueling progressive efforts across the world in the years that Americans have come to call the "progressive era." •

UNDERSTAND, ANALYZE, & EVALUATE

1. What is social democracy?
2. What progressive era reforms in American social and political life can be seen in other nations as well?

to society the principles of natural and social sciences. Most progressives believed, too, that a modern government must play an important role in the process of improving and stabilizing society.

THE MUCKRAKERS AND THE SOCIAL GOSPEL

Among the first people to articulate the new spirit of national reform were crusading journalists who began to direct public attention toward social, economic, and political injustices. Known as the **muckrakers**, after Theodore Roosevelt accused them of raking up muck through their writings, they were committed to exposing scandal, corruption, and injustice.

Their first major targets were the trusts and, particularly, the railroads, which the muckrakers considered powerful and corrupt. Exposés of the great corporate organizations began to appear as early as the 1860s, when Charles Francis Adams Jr. and others uncovered corruption among the railroad barons. Decades later, journalist Ida Tarbell produced a scorching study of the Standard Oil trust. By the turn of the century, many muckrakers were turning their attention to government and particularly to the urban political machines. Among the most influential was Lincoln Steffens, a reporter for *McClure's* magazine. His portraits of "machine government" and "boss rule" in cities, written in a tone of studied moral outrage, helped arouse sentiment for urban political reform.

THE BOSSES OF THE SENATE (1889), BY JOSEPH
KEPPLER Keppler was a popular political cartoonist of the
late nineteenth century who shared the growing concern
about the power of trusts—portrayed here as bloated,
almost reptilian figures standing menacingly over the members
of the U.S. Senate, to whose chamber the "people's entrance"
is "closed."

(Source: Library of Congress, Prints and Photographs Division
[LC-USZC4-494])

By presenting social problems to the public with indignation and moral fervor, they helped inspire other Americans to take action.

Growing outrage at social and economic injustice committed many reformers to the pursuit of **social justice**. That impulse helped create the rise of what became known as the "Social Gospel," the effort to make faith into a tool of social reform. The Social Gospel movement was chiefly concerned with redeeming the nation's cities. The Salvation Army, which began in England but soon spread to the United States, was a Christian social welfare organization with a vaguely military structure. It had recruited 3,000 "officers" and 20,000 "privates" by 1900 and was offering both material aid and spiritual service to the urban poor. In addition, many ministers, priests, and rabbis left traditional parish work to serve in troubled cities. Charles Sheldon's book *In His Steps* (1898), the story of a young minister who abandoned a comfortable post to work among those in need, sold more than 15 million copies. The Social Gospel was never the dominant element in the movement for urban reform. But the engagement of religion with reform helped bring to progressivism a powerful moral commitment to redeem the lives of even the least-favored citizens.

THE SETTLEMENT HOUSE MOVEMENT

An element of much progressive thought was the belief in the influence of the environment on individual development. Nothing produced greater distress, many urban reformers believed, than crowded immigrant neighborhoods. One response to the problems of such communities, borrowed from England, was the "settlement house." The most famous was **Hull House**, which opened in 1889 in Chicago as a result of the efforts of the social worker **Jane Addams**. It became a model for more than 400 similar institutions throughout the nation. Staffed by members of the educated middle class, settlement houses sought to help immigrant families adapt to the language and customs of their new country.

Young, mostly unmarried college women were important participants in the settlement house movement. Working in a settlement house, a protected site that served mainly women, was consistent with the widespread assumption that they needed to be sheltered from difficult environments. The clean and well-tended settlement houses were not only a model for immigrant women, but an appropriate site of social engagement for elite women as well.

The settlement houses also helped create another important institution of reform: the profession of social work. A growing number of programs for the professional training of social workers began to appear in the nation's leading universities, partly in response to the activities of the settlement houses.

THE ALLURE OF EXPERTISE

As the emergence of the social work profession suggests, progressives involved in humanitarian efforts placed a high value on knowledge and expertise. Even nonscientific problems, they believed, could be analyzed and solved scientifically. Many reformers came to believe that only enlightened experts and well-designed bureaucracies could create the stability and order America needed.

Some even spoke of the creation of a new civilization, in which the expertise of scientists and engineers could be brought to bear on the problems of the economy and society. The social scientist Thorstein Veblen, for example, proposed a new economic system in which power would reside in the hands of highly trained engineers. Only they, he argued, could fully understand the "machine process" by which modern society must be governed.

THE PROFESSIONS

The late nineteenth century saw a dramatic expansion in the number of Americans engaged in administrative and professional tasks. Industries needed managers, technicians, and accountants as well as workers. Cities required commercial, medical, legal, and educational services. New technology required scientists and engineers, who, in turn, required institutions and instructors to train them. By the turn of the century, those performing these services had come to constitute a distinct social group—what some historians have called a "new middle class."

By the early twentieth century, millions within this middle class were building organizations and establishing standards to secure their position in society. Most of all, they created the modern, organized professions. The idea of professionalism had been a frail one in America even as late as 1880, but as the demand for professional services increased, so did the pressures for reform.

Among the first to respond was the medical profession. In 1901, doctors who considered themselves trained professionals reorganized the American Medical Association (AMA) into a national professional society. By 1920, nearly two-thirds of all American doctors were members. The AMA called for strict, scientific standards for admission to the practice of medicine. State governments responded by passing laws requiring the licensing of all physicians. By 1900, medical education at a few medical schools—notably Johns Hopkins in Baltimore (founded in 1893)—compared favorably with those in the leading institutions of Europe.

By 1916, lawyers in all forty-eight states had established professional bar associations. The nation's law schools expanded greatly. Businessmen supported the creation of schools of business administration and set up their own national organizations: the National Association of Manufacturers in 1895 and the United States Chamber of Commerce in 1912. Farmers responded to the new order by forming, through the National Farm Bureau Federation, a network of agricultural organizations designed to spread scientific farming methods.

The ethos of professionalization aimed to remove the untrained and incompetent. But the admission requirements also protected those already in the professions from excessive competition and lent them prestige and status. Some professions used their entrance requirements to exclude African Americans, women, immigrants, and other "undesirables" from their ranks. Others used them simply to keep numbers down, ensuring demand for their services would remain high.

WOMEN AND THE PROFESSIONS

American women found themselves excluded from most of the emerging professions. But a substantial number of middle-class women, particularly those emerging from the new women's colleges and coeducational state universities, entered professional careers nevertheless.

A few women managed to establish themselves as physicians, lawyers, engineers, scientists, and corporate managers. Most, however, turned by necessity to those professional outlets that society considered suitable for women: settlement houses, social work, and, most important, teaching. Indeed, in the late nineteenth century, perhaps 90 percent of all professional women were teachers. For educated black women, in particular, the existence of segregated schools in the South created a substantial market for African American teachers.

Women also dominated other professional activities. Nursing had become primarily a women's field during and after the Civil War. By the early twentieth century, it was adopting professional standards. And some women entered academia, often earning advanced degrees at such predominantly male institutions as the University of Chicago, MIT, or Columbia, and then finding professional opportunities in the new and expanding women's colleges.

WOMEN AND REFORM

The prominence of women in reform movements is one of the most striking features of progressivism. In many states in the early twentieth century, women could not vote. They almost never held public office. They had footholds in only a few, usually primarily female professions and lived in a culture in which most people believed women were not suited for the public world. What, then, explains the prominent role so many women played in the reform activities of the period?

THE "NEW WOMAN"

The phenomenon of the "new woman" was a product of social and economic changes in both the private and public spheres. By the end of the nineteenth century, almost all income-producing activity had moved out of the home and into the factory or the office. At the same time, many women were having fewer children, and their children were beginning school at earlier ages and spending more time there. For wives and mothers who did not work for wages, the home was less of an all-consuming place. Hence, more and more women began looking for activities outside the domestic sphere.

Some educated women shunned marriage entirely, believing that only by remaining single could they play the roles they envisioned in the public world. Single women were among the most prominent reformers of the time. Some of these women lived alone. Others lived with other women, often in long-term relationships—some of them secretly romantic—that were known at the time as "Boston marriages." The divorce rate also rose rapidly in the late nineteenth century, from one divorce for every twenty-one marriages in 1880 to one in nine by 1916. Women initiated the majority of divorces.

THE CLUBWOMEN

Among the most visible signs of the increasing public roles of women in the late nineteenth and early twentieth centuries were women's clubs, which proliferated rapidly beginning in the 1880s and 1890s and became the vanguard of many important reforms.

The women's clubs began largely as cultural organizations to provide middle- and upper-class women with an outlet for their intellectual energies. In 1892, when women formed the General Federation of Women's Clubs, there were more than 100,000 members in nearly 500 clubs. By 1917, there were over 1 million members.

Much of what the clubs did was uncontroversial: planting trees; supporting schools, libraries, and settlement houses; building hospitals and parks. But clubwomen were also an important force in winning passage of state and ultimately federal laws that regulated the conditions of woman and child labor. They pushed government to inspect workplaces, regulate the food and drug industries, reform policies toward the Indian tribes, apply new standards to urban housing, and, perhaps most notably, outlaw the manufacture and sale of alcohol. Women's clubs were instrumental in pressuring state legislatures in most states to provide pensions to widowed or abandoned mothers with small children, a system that ultimately became absorbed into the Social Security system. In 1912, they convinced Congress to establish the Children's Bureau in the Labor Department, an agency directed to develop policies to protect children.

In many of these efforts, the clubwomen formed alliances with other women's groups, such as the Women's Trade Union League (WTUL), founded in 1903 by female union members and upper-class reformers and committed to persuading women to join unions. In addition to working on behalf of protective legislation for women, WTUL members held public meetings on behalf of female workers, raised money to support strikes, marched on picket lines, and bailed striking women out of jail.

Black women occasionally joined clubs dominated by whites. But most clubs excluded blacks, and so African Americans formed clubs of their own. Some of them affiliated with the General Federation, but most became part of the independent National Association of Colored Women. Some black clubs also took positions on issues of particular concern to African Americans, such as lynching and segregation.

WOMAN SUFFRAGE

Perhaps the largest single reform movement of the progressive era, indeed one of the largest in American history, was the fight for woman suffrage.

Throughout the late nineteenth century, many suffrage advocates argued that "natural rights" entitled them to the same rights as men—including, first and foremost, the right to vote. Elizabeth Cady Stanton, for example, wrote in 1892 of woman as "the arbiter of her own destiny . . . if we are to consider her as a citizen, as a member of a great nation, she must have the same rights as all other members." This argument challenged the views of many men and women who believed society required a distinctive female sphere, in which women would serve first and foremost as wives and mothers. A powerful antisuffrage movement emerged, dominated by men but with the active support of many women. To these critics, woman suffrage seemed a radical demand.

In the first years of the twentieth century, suffragists were becoming better organized and more politically sophisticated than their opponents. Under the leadership of Anna Howard Shaw, a Boston social worker, and Carrie Chapman Catt, a journalist from Iowa, membership in the National American Woman Suffrage Association (NAWSA) grew from about 13,000 in 1893 to over 2 million in 1917. The movement gained strength because many of its most prominent leaders began to justify suffrage in "safer," less threatening ways. Suffrage, some supporters began to argue, would not challenge the "separate sphere" in which women resided. Instead, they claimed that because women occupied a distinct

(Source: Library of Congress, Prints and Photographs Division [LC-USZ62-70382])

SUFFRAGE PAGEANT On March 3, 1913—the day before Woodrow Wilson's presidential inauguration—more than 5,000 supporters of woman suffrage staged a parade in Washington, D.C., that overshadowed Wilson's arrival in the capital. Crowds estimated at over half a million watched the parade; some of the onlookers attacked the marchers. In this photograph from the event, suffragist Florence Noyce poses as Liberty in front of the U.S. Treasury building.

sphere—because as mothers and wives and homemakers they had special experiences and special sensitivities to bring to public life—woman suffrage would bring those sensitivities to the nation's politics and thereby bolster, not weaken, domestic spaces.

In particular, many suffragists argued that enfranchising women would help the temperance movement by giving its largest group of supporters a political voice. Some suffrage advocates claimed that once women had the vote, war would become a thing of the past, since women would, by their calming, maternal influence, help curb the belligerence of men.

The principal triumphs of the suffrage movement resumed in 1910, when Washington became the first state in fourteen years to extend suffrage to women. California followed a year later, and four other western states in 1912. In 1913, Illinois became the first state east of the Mississippi to embrace woman suffrage. And in 1917 and 1918, New York and Michigan—two of the most populous states in the Union—gave women the vote. By 1919, thirty-nine states had granted women the right to vote in at least some elections, fifteen had allowed full participation. In 1920, finally, suffragists won ratification of the **Nineteenth Amendment**, which guaranteed voting rights to women throughout the nation.

To some feminists, however, the victory seemed less than complete. **Alice Paul**, head of the National Woman's Party (founded in 1916), never accepted the relatively conservative "separate sphere" justification for suffrage. She argued that the Nineteenth Amendment alone would not be sufficient to protect women's rights. Women needed more: a constitutional amendment that would provide full, legal protection for their rights and would prohibit all discrimination on the basis of gender. But Alice Paul's argument found limited favor even among many of the most important leaders of the recently triumphant suffrage crusade.

THE ASSAULT ON THE PARTIES

Most progressive goals required the involvement of the state. Only government, reformers agreed, could effectively counter the many powerful private interests that threatened the nation. But American government at the dawn of the new century was poorly adapted to meet progressive demands. Before progressives could reform society effectively, they would have to reform government itself. Many reformers believed the first step must be an assault on the dominant role political parties played in the life of the state.

EARLY ATTACKS

Attacks on party dominance had been frequent in the late nineteenth century. Greenbackism and Populism, for example, had been efforts to break the hammerlock with which the Republicans and Democrats controlled public life. The Independent Republicans (or mugwumps) had attempted to challenge the grip of partisanship.

The early assaults enjoyed some success. In the 1880s and 1890s, for example, most states adopted the secret ballot. Prior to that, the political parties themselves had printed ballots (or "tickets"), with the names of the party's candidates, and no others. They distributed the tickets to their supporters, who then simply went to the polls to deposit them in the ballot boxes. The old system had made it possible for bosses to monitor the voting behavior of their constituents. The new secret ballot, printed by the government and distributed at the polls to be filled out and deposited in secret, helped chip away at the power of the parties over the voters.

MUNICIPAL REFORM

Many progressives believed the impact of party rule was most damaging in the cities. Municipal government therefore became the first target of those working for political reform. The muckrakers were especially successful in arousing public outrage at corruption and incompetence in city politics. They struck a responsive chord among a powerful group of urban middle-class progressives, who set out to destroy the power of city bosses and their entrenched political organizations.

One of the first major successes in municipal reform came in Galveston, Texas, where the old city government proved completely unable to deal with the effects of a destructive hurricane in 1900. Capitalizing on public dismay, reformers won approval of a new city charter that replaced the mayor and council with an elected, nonpartisan commission. In 1907, Des Moines, Iowa, adopted its own version of the commission plan, and other cities soon followed.

Another approach to municipal reform was the city manager plan, by which elected officials hired an outside expert—often a professionally trained business manager or engineer—to take charge of the government. The city manager would presumably remain untainted by the corrupting influence of politics. By the end of the progressive era, almost 400 cities were operating under commissions, and another 45 employed city managers.

In most urban areas, reformers had to settle for lesser victories. Some cities made the election of mayors nonpartisan, so the parties could not choose the candidates. Or they moved them to years when no presidential or congressional races were in progress, to reduce the influence of the large turnouts that party organizations produced. Reformers tried to make city councilors run at large, to limit the influence of ward leaders and district bosses.

They tried to strengthen the power of the mayor at the expense of the city council, on the assumption that reformers were more likely to succeed in getting a sympathetic mayor elected than they were to win control of the entire council.

STATEHOUSE PROGRESSIVISM

Other progressives turned to state government as an agent for reform. They looked with particular scorn on state legislatures, whose ill-paid, relatively undistinguished members, they believed, were generally incompetent, often corrupt, and totally controlled by party bosses. Reformers began looking for ways to circumvent the boss-controlled legislatures by increasing the power of the electorate. A big victory came in 1913, when the states ratified a constitutional amendment—the seventeenth—that transferred the right to elect U.S. senators from the state legislatures to ordinary voters.

Two other important changes were proposed by Populists in the 1890s: the initiative and the referendum. The initiative allowed reformers to bypass state legislatures by submitting new legislation directly to the voters in general elections. The referendum provided a method by which actions of the legislature could be put to the electorate for approval. By 1918, more than twenty states had enacted one or both of these reforms.

The direct primary and the recall were other efforts to limit the power of parties and improve the quality of elected officials. The primary election was an attempt to remove the selection of candidates from the bosses and give it to the people. Yet in the South, it was also an effort to limit black voting, since primary voting, many white southerners believed, would be easier to control than general elections. The recall gave voters the right to remove a public official from office with a special election, which could be called after a sufficient number of citizens had signed a petition. By 1915, every state in the nation had instituted primary elections for at least some offices. The recall encountered more strenuous opposition, but a few states (such as California) adopted it as well.

The most celebrated state-level reformer was **Robert M. La Follette** of Wisconsin. Elected governor in 1900, he helped turn his state into what reformers across the nation described as a laboratory of progressivism. Under his leadership, Wisconsin progressives won approval of direct primaries, initiatives, and referendums. They regulated railroads and utilities, addressing abuses of power such as rate-fixing and collusion among railway companies. They passed laws to providing compensation for laborers injured on the job. They instituted graduated taxes on inherited fortunes, and they nearly doubled state levies on railroads and other corporate interests.

PARTIES AND INTEREST GROUPS

The reformers did not, of course, eliminate parties from American political life. But they did contribute to a decline in party influence. Evidence of their impact came, among other things, from the decline in voter turnout. In the late nineteenth century, up to 81 percent of eligible voters routinely turned out for national elections. In the early twentieth century, the figure declined markedly. In the presidential election of 1900, 73 percent of the electorate voted. By 1912, turnout had declined to about 59 percent. Never again has voter turnout reached as high as 70 percent.

Why did voter turnout decline in these years? The secret ballot was one reason. Party bosses had less ability to get voters to the polls. Illiterate voters had trouble reading the new ballots. Party bosses lost much of their authority and were unable to mobilize voters as successfully as they had in the past. The popular, highly partisan politics of the nineteenth century gave way over time to more bureaucratic government and parties and a less inclusive politics; recall the wave of disfranchisement, too, that limited the ballot for blacks and poor whites. But perhaps the most important reason for the decline of party rule and voter turnout was that other power centers were beginning to replace them. They have become known as "interest groups." Beginning late in the nineteenth century and accelerating rapidly in the twentieth century, new organizations emerged outside the party system: professional organizations, trade associations representing businesses and industries, labor organizations, farm lobbies, and many others. Social workers, the settlement house movements, women's clubs, and others learned to operate as interest groups to advance their demands without relying on parties.

SOURCES OF PROGRESSIVE REFORM

Middle-class reformers, most of them from the East, dominated the public image and much of the substance of progressivism in the late nineteenth and early twentieth centuries. But they were not alone in seeking to improve social conditions. Working-class Americans, African Americans, westerners, and even party bosses played crucial roles in advancing some of the important reforms of the era. (For historians' changing views on who the progressives were and what motivated them, see "Debating the Past: Progressivism.")

LABOR, THE MACHINE, AND REFORM

Although the American Federation of Labor, and its leader Samuel Gompers, remained largely aloof from many of the reform efforts of the time, some unions played important roles in them. Between 1911 and 1913, thanks to political pressure from labor groups such as the newly formed Union Labor Party, California passed a child labor law, a workmen's compensation law, and a limitation on working hours for women. Union pressures contributed to the passage of similar laws in many other states as well.

Party bosses sometimes allowed their machines to become vehicles of social reform. One example was New York's Tammany Hall, the nation's oldest and most notorious city machine. Its astute leader, Charles Francis Murphy, began in the early years of the twentieth century to fuse the techniques of boss rule with some of the concerns of social reformers. Tammany at times used its political power on behalf of legislation to improve working conditions, protect child laborers, and eliminate the worst abuses of the industrial economy.

In 1911, a terrible fire swept through the factory of the **Triangle Shirtwaist Company** in New York; 146 workers, most of them women, died. Many of them had been trapped inside the burning building because management had locked the emergency exits to prevent malingering. For the next three years, a state commission studied the disaster and the conditions of factories generally. In 1914, it issued a series of reports calling for major reforms in the conditions of modern labor. The report itself was a classic progressive document, based on the testimony of experts and filled with statistics and technical data. When its recommendations reached the New York legislature, its most effective supporters were two Tammany Democrats from working-class backgrounds: Senator Robert F. Wagner and Assemblyman Alfred E. Smith. With the support of Murphy and the backing of other Tammany legislators, they helped pass a series of pioneering labor laws that imposed strict regulations on factory owners and established effective mechanisms for enforcement.

PROGRESSIVISM

Until the early 1950s, most historians seemed to agree on the central characteristics of early-twentieth-century progressivism. It was just what many progressives themselves had said it was: a movement by the people to curb the power of special interests. More specifically, it was a protest by an aroused citizenry against the excessive power of urban bosses, corporate moguls, and corrupt elected officials.

In 1951, the historian George Mowry began challenging these assumptions by examining progressives in California and describing them as a small, privileged elite of business and professional figures: people who considered themselves the natural leaders of society and who were trying to recover their fading influence from the new capitalist institutions that had displaced them. Progressivism was not, in other words, a popular democratic movement but the effort of a displaced elite to restore its authority. Richard Hofstadter expanded on this idea in *The Age of Reform* (1955) by describing reformers as people afflicted by "status anxiety"—fading elites suffering not from economic but from psychological discontent.

The Mowry-Hofstadter argument soon encountered a range of challenges. Gabriel Kolko, in *The Triumph of Conservatism* (1963), rejected both the older "democratic" view of progressivism and the newer status-anxiety view. Progressive reform, he argued, was not an effort to protect the people from the corporations; it was, rather, a vehicle through which corporate leaders used the government to protect themselves from competition.

A more moderate reinterpretation came from historians embracing what would later be called the "organizational" approach to twentieth-century American history. Samuel Hays, in *The Response to Industrialism* (1957), and Robert Wiebe, in *The Search for Order* (1967), portrayed progressivism as a broad effort by businessmen, professionals, and other middle-class people to bring order and efficiency to political and economic life. In the new industrial society, economic power was increasingly concentrated in large national organizations, while social and political life remained centered primarily in local communities. Progressivism, Wiebe argued, was the effort of a "new middle class"—a class tied to the emerging national economy—to stabilize and enhance its position in society by bringing those two worlds together.

In the 1970s and 1980s, much of the scholarship on progressivism focused on discovering new groups among whom progressive ideas and efforts flourished. Historians found evidence of progressivism in the rising movement by consumers to define their interests; in the growth of reform movements among African Americans; in the changing nature of urban political machines; and in the political activism of working people and labor organizations. Some historians, in turn, found the "movement" becoming so diverse in the scholarship that they ceased to think of it as a movement at all.

Other scholars attempted to identify progressivism with broad changes in the structure and culture of politics. Richard McCormick, writing in 1981, argued that the crucial change in the progressive era was the decline of political parties and the corresponding rise of interest groups working for particular social and economic goals.

At the same time, many historians have focused on the role of women and the vast network of voluntary associations they created in shaping and promoting progressive reform. Some progressive battles, historians such as Kathryn Sklar, Ruth Rosen, Elaine Tyler May, and Linda Gordon have argued, were part of an effort by women to protect their interests within the domestic sphere in the face of jarring challenges from the new industrial world. This protective urge drew women reformers to such issues as temperance, divorce, prostitution, and the regulation of female and child labor. Other women worked to expand their own roles in the public world, particularly through their support of suffrage. The gendered interests of women reformers are, many historians insist, critical to an understanding of progressivism.

More recently, a number of historians have sought to place progressivism in a broader context. Daniel Rodgers's *Atlantic Crossings* (1998) is an important study of how European reformers shaped the goals of many American progressives. Both Michael McGerr, in *A Fierce Discontent* (2003), and Alan Dawley, in *Changing the World* (2003), see progressivism as a fundamentally moral project—McGerr, as an effort by the middle class to create order and stability, and Dawley, as an effort by groups on the left to attack social injustice. Progressivism, they argue, was not just a political movement but also an effort to remake society and reshape social relations. •

UNDERSTAND, ANALYZE, & EVALUATE

1. What is the gendered view of progressive reform advanced by historians?
2. Was progressivism a "people's" movement?

WESTERN PROGRESSIVES

The American West produced some of the most notable progressive leaders of the time: Hiram Johnson of California, George Norris of Nebraska, William Borah of Idaho, and others, almost all of whom spent at least some of their political careers in the U.S. Senate. For western states, the most important vehicle of reform was the federal government, which exercised a kind of authority in the West that it never possessed in the East. Disputes over

(Source: Library of Congress, Prints and Photographs Division [LC-USZ62-29333])

PARADE FOR VICTIMS OF THE TRIANGLE SHIRTWAIST FIRE On a rainy day in the spring of 1911, people and horses in mourning dress walked in commemoration of victims of the fire in the Triangle Shirtwaist Company. This tragedy galvanized New York legislators into passing laws to protect workers.

water, for example, almost always involved rivers and streams that crossed state lines. More significant, perhaps, the federal government exercised enormous power over the lands and resources of the western states and provided substantial subsidies to the region in the form of land grants and support for railroad and water projects. Huge areas of the West remained and still remain public lands, controlled by Washington. Much of the growth of the West was a result of federally funded dams, water projects, and other infrastructure undertakings.

AFRICAN AMERICANS AND REFORM

Most white progressives paid little attention to race or even supported segregation, although they usually rationalized it as a measure to protect imperiled groups including black people and Native Americans. But among African Americans themselves, the progressive era produced significant challenges to existing racial norms.

African Americans faced greater obstacles than any other group in seeking reform. So it was not surprising, perhaps, that so many African Americans embraced the message of Booker T. Washington in the late nineteenth century. Washington encouraged black men and women to work for immediate self-improvement rather than long-range social change. By the beginning of the twentieth century, however, a powerful challenge to the philosophy of Washington was emerging. The chief spokesperson for this new approach was **W. E. B. Du Bois**, a sociologist and historian and one of the first African Americans to receive a degree from Harvard.

In *The Souls of Black Folk* (1903), Du Bois launched an open attack on the philosophy of Washington, accusing him of encouraging white efforts to sustain segregation and of limiting the aspirations of his race. Rather than content themselves with education at trade and agricultural schools, Du Bois encouraged talented blacks to accept nothing less than a full university education and aspire to the professions. They should, above all, fight for their civil rights, not simply wait for them to be granted as a reward for patience. In 1905, Du Bois and a group of his supporters met at Niagara Falls—on the Canadian side of the

(©George Rinhart/Getty Images)

THE CRISIS   W. E. B. Du Bois founded *The Crisis*, the magazine of the NAACP, in 1910. Its object was to "show the danger of race prejudice, particularly as manifested today toward colored people." This photograph shows the magazine's office.

border because no hotel on the American side would have them—and launched what became known as the Niagara Movement. Four years later, they joined with sympathetic white progressives to form the **National Association for the Advancement of Colored People (NAACP)**. In the years that followed, the new organization worked for equal rights.

Among the many issues that engaged the NAACP and other African American organizations was lynching in the South. Among the most determined opponents of lynching were southern women, and the most effective crusader was a black woman, Ida B. Wells-Barnett, who worked both on her own, at great personal risk, and with such organizations as the National Association of Colored Women and the Women's Convention of the National Baptist Church to try to expose lynching and challenge segregation.

CRUSADES FOR SOCIAL ORDER AND REFORM

Many reformers crusaded on behalf of what they considered moral issues—working to eliminate alcohol, curb prostitution, limit divorce, and restrict immigration.

THE TEMPERANCE CRUSADE

Many progressives considered the elimination of alcohol from American life a necessary step in restoring order to society. Scarce wages vanished as male workers spent hours in saloons. Drunkenness spawned violence, and occasionally murder, within urban families. Many working-class wives and mothers hoped through temperance to reform male behavior and thus improve women's lives. Employers, too, regarded alcohol as an impediment to industrial efficiency. Workers often missed time on the job or worked ineffectively because of drunkenness. Critics of economic privilege denounced the liquor industry as one of the nation's most sinister trusts. And political reformers, who correctly looked on the saloon as one of the central institutions of the urban machine, saw an attack on drinking as part of an attack on the bosses. Out of such sentiments emerged the temperance movement.

There had been a major temperance movement before the Civil War, mobilizing large numbers of people in a crusade with strong evangelical overtones. In 1873, the movement developed new strength. Temperance advocates formed the **Women's Christian Temperance Union (WCTU)**, which was led after 1879 by Frances Willard. By 1911, it had 245,000 members and had become the single largest women's organization in American history to that point. In 1893, the Anti-Saloon League joined the movement and, along with the WCTU, began to press for the legal abolition of saloons as a step toward eradicating drinking altogether. Gradually, that demand grew to include the complete prohibition of the sale and manufacture of alcoholic beverages.

Pressure for **prohibition** grew steadily through the first decades of the new century. By 1916, nineteen states had passed prohibition laws. America's entry into World War I, which made the use of grain for alcohol seem wasteful and unnecessary, provided the last push to the advocates of prohibition. In 1917, with the support of rural fundamentalists who opposed alcohol on moral and religious grounds, progressive advocates of prohibition steered through Congress a constitutional amendment. Two years later, after ratification by every state in the nation except Connecticut and Rhode Island (with large populations of Catholic immigrants opposed to prohibition), the Eighteenth Amendment became law, to take effect in January 1920.

Immigration Restriction

Virtually all reformers agreed that the growing immigrant population had created social problems, but there was wide disagreement on how best to respond. Some progressives believed the proper approach was to help new residents adapt to American society. Others argued the only solution was to limit the flow of new arrivals.

In the first decades of the century, pressure grew to close the nation's gates. New scholarly theories argued that the introduction of immigrants into American society was polluting the nation's racial stock. One of these theories, **eugenics**, began as the science of altering the reproductive processes of plants and animals to produce new hybrids or breeds. But in the late nineteenth century, eugenicists spread the spurious belief that human inequalities were hereditary and that immigration was contributing to the multiplication of the unfit. A special federal commission of "experts," chaired by Senator William P. Dillingham of Vermont, issued a study filled with statistics and scholarly testimony. It argued that the newer immigrant groups, largely southern and eastern Europeans, had proved themselves less assimilable than earlier immigrants. Immigration, the report implied, should be restricted by nationality. Even many people who rejected these racial arguments supported limiting immigration as a way to solve such urban problems as overcrowding, unemployment, strained social services, and social unrest.

The combination of these concerns gradually won the support of some of the nation's leading progressives for limiting immigration, including former president Theodore Roosevelt. Powerful opponents—employers who saw immigration as a source of cheap labor, immigrants themselves, and their political representatives—managed to block the restriction movement for a time. But by the beginning of World War I, which itself effectively blocked immigration temporarily, the nativist tide was gaining strength.

The Dream of Socialism

Although never a force to rival or even seriously threaten the two major parties, **socialism** gained considerable strength during the early years of the twentieth century. In the election of 1900, the Socialist Party of America attracted the support of fewer than 100,000 voters. In 1912, its durable leader and perennial presidential candidate, Eugene V. Debs, received nearly 1 million ballots. Strongest in urban immigrant communities, particularly among Germans and Jews, it also attracted the loyalties of a substantial number of Protestant farmers in the South and the Midwest.

Virtually all socialists agreed on the need for basic structural changes in the economy, but they differed widely on the extent of those changes and the tactics necessary to achieve them. Some socialists endorsed the radical goals of European Marxists (a complete end to capitalism and private property); others envisioned more moderate reform that would allow small-scale private enterprise to survive but would nationalize major industries. Some believed in working for reform through electoral politics; others favored militant direct action. Among the militants was the radical labor union the **Industrial Workers of the World (IWW)**, known to opponents as the "Wobblies." Under the leadership of William "Big Bill" Haywood, the IWW advocated a single union for all workers and was one of the few labor organizations to champion the cause of unskilled workers. Many people believed the Wobblies had been responsible for dynamiting railroad lines and power stations and committing other acts of terror in the first years of the twentieth century.

Moderate socialists who advocated peaceful change through political struggle dominated the Socialist Party. They emphasized a gradual education of the public to the need for change and patient efforts within the system to enact it. But the party refused to support the nation's war effort in World War I. The growing wave of antiradicalism during the war subjected the socialists to enormous harassment and persecution, contributing to socialism's decline.

DECENTRALIZATION AND REGULATION

Most progressives retained faith in the possibilities of reform within a capitalist system. Rather than nationalize basic industries, many reformers hoped to restore the economy to a more human scale. They argued that the federal government should work to break up the largest combinations and enforce a balance between the need for size and the need for competition. This viewpoint came to be identified particularly closely with **Louis D. Brandeis**, a lawyer and later justice of the Supreme Court, who wrote in his 1913 book *Other People's Money* about the "curse of bigness." Brandeis insisted that government must regulate competition in such a way as to ensure that large combinations did not emerge.

Other progressives were less enthusiastic about the virtues of competition. More important to them was efficiency. Government, they argued, should not fight corporate growth but rather should guard against abuses of power by large institutions. It should distinguish between good trusts and bad trusts. Since economic consolidation was destined to remain a permanent feature of American society, said many progressives, a strong, modernized government should play a more active role in regulating and planning economic life. One of those who came to endorse that position (although not fully until after 1910) was **Theodore Roosevelt**, who once said: "We should enter upon a course of supervision, control, and regulation of those great corporations." Roosevelt became, for a time, the most powerful symbol of the reform impulse at the national level.

THEODORE ROOSEVELT AND THE MODERN PRESIDENCY

To a generation of progressive reformers, Theodore Roosevelt was more than an admired public figure; he was an idol. No president before, and few since, attracted such attention and devotion. Yet for all his popularity among reformers, Roosevelt was in many respects decidedly conservative. He earned his extraordinary popularity less because of the extent of reforms he championed than because he brought to his office a broad conception of its powers. He boosted the presidency into something like its modern position as the center of national political life.

THE ACCIDENTAL PRESIDENT

President William McKinley was in Buffalo, New York, in September 1901 to visit the Pan-American Exposition. He was greeting members of the public when a man named Leon Czolgosz approached McKinley with a pistol concealed in a handkerchief and shot him in the stomach. After appearing on the path to recovery, the president died of an infection about a week later. It turned out the assassin, executed the next month, was an unemployed anarchist who blamed growing federal power for the plight of working people. News of Czolgosz's politics inflamed existing vilification of anarchism and other philosophies of the left, and soon it became illegal for avowed anarchists to enter the country. Secret Service also began shadowing presidents from that time forward.

Roosevelt, at forty-two years old, became the youngest man ever to assume the presidency. "I told William McKinley that it was a mistake to nominate that wild man at Philadelphia," party boss Mark Hanna was reported to have exclaimed. "Now look, that damned cowboy is President of the United States!" Yet as president, Roosevelt rarely openly

(Source: Library of Congress, Prints and Photographs Division [LC-DIG-nclc-01130])

BOYS IN THE MINES These young boys, covered in grime and no more than twelve years old, pose for Lewis Hine outside the coal mine in Pennsylvania where they worked as "breaker boys," crawling into newly blasted areas and breaking up the loose coal. The rugged conditions in the mines were one cause of the great strike of 1902, in which Theodore Roosevelt intervened.

rebelled against the leaders of his party. He became, rather, a champion of cautious, moderate change. Reform, he believed, was a vehicle less for remaking American society than for protecting it against more radical challenges.

Roosevelt allied himself with those progressives who urged regulation (but not destruction) of the trusts, wishing to give the government the power to investigate corporations and publicize the results. Yet although Roosevelt was not a trustbuster at heart, he made a few highly publicized efforts to break up combinations. In 1902, he ordered the Justice Department to invoke the Sherman Antitrust Act against a great new railroad monopoly in the Northwest, the Northern Securities Company, a $400 million enterprise pieced together by J. P. Morgan and others. Roosevelt filed more than forty additional antitrust suits during the remainder of his presidency, but he made no serious commitment to reverse the prevailing trend toward economic concentration.

When a bitter 1902 strike by the United Mine Workers endangered coal supplies for the coming winter, Roosevelt asked both the operators and the miners to accept impartial federal arbitration. When the mine owners balked, Roosevelt threatened to send federal troops to seize the mines. The operators finally relented. Arbitrators awarded the strikers a 10 percent wage increase and a nine-hour day, although no recognition of their union—less than the miners had wanted but more than they would likely have won without Roosevelt's intervention.

THE "SQUARE DEAL"

During the 1904 campaign for the presidency, Roosevelt boasted that he had worked in the anthracite coal strike to provide everyone with a "square deal." One of his first targets after winning the election was the powerful railroad industry. The Interstate Commerce Act of 1887, establishing the Interstate Commerce Commission (ICC), had represented an early effort to regulate the industry, but over the years, the courts had sharply limited its influence. The Hepburn Railroad Regulation Act of 1906 sought to restore some regulatory authority to the government by giving the ICC power to oversee railroad rates.

Roosevelt also pressured Congress to enact the Pure Food and Drug Act, which restricted the sale of dangerous or ineffective medicines. *The Jungle*, a powerful novel published by Upton Sinclair in 1906, included appalling descriptions of conditions in the meatpacking industry. Roosevelt pushed for passage of the Meat Inspection Act, which helped eliminate many diseases once transmitted in impure meat. Starting in 1907, he proposed even more stringent reforms: an eight-hour day for workers, broader compensation for victims of industrial accidents, inheritance and income taxes, and regulation of the stock market. Conservative opposition blocked much of his agenda, widening the gulf between the president and the conservative wing of his party.

Roosevelt and the Environment

Roosevelt's aggressive policies on behalf of conservation contributed to that gulf. Using executive powers, he restricted private development on millions of acres of undeveloped government land, most of it in the West, by adding them to the previously modest national

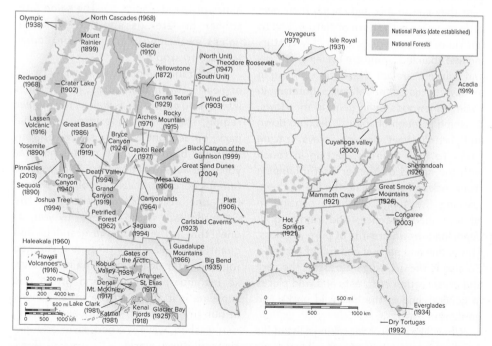

ESTABLISHMENT OF NATIONAL PARKS AND FORESTS This map illustrates the steady growth through the late nineteenth, twentieth, and twenty-first centuries of the systems of national parks and national forests in the United States. Although Theodore Roosevelt is widely and correctly remembered as a great champion of national parks and forests, the greatest expansions of these systems occurred after his presidency. • *How many new areas were added in the 1920s? Where are the most recently designated parks and forests?*

JOHN MUIR ON THE VALUE OF WILD PLACES (1901)

John Muir is often called the "father of the national parks" for his role as advocate on behalf of legislation to designate certain wilderness areas as off-limits for commercial development. In this excerpt from his book *Our National Parks*, he argues for the restorative benefits of visiting unspoiled nature.

The tendency nowadays to wander in wildernesses is delightful to see. Thousands of tired, nerve-shaken, over-civilized people are beginning to find out that going to the mountains is going home; that wildness is a necessity; and that mountain parks and reservations are useful not only as fountains of timber and irrigating rivers, but as fountains of life. Awakening from the stupefying effects of the vice of over-industry and the deadly apathy of luxury, they are trying as best they can to mix and enrich their own little ongoings with those of Nature, and to get rid of rust and disease. Briskly venturing and roaming, some are washing off sins and cobweb cares of the devil's spinning in all-day storms on mountains; sauntering in rosiny pinewoods or in gentian meadows, brushing through chaparral, bending down and parting sweet, flowery sprays; tracing rivers to their sources, getting in touch with the nerves of Mother Earth; jumping from rock to rock, feeling the life of them, learning the songs of them, panting in whole-souled exercise, and rejoicing in deep, long-drawn breaths of pure wildness. This is fine and natural and full of promise. So also is the growing interest in the care and preservation of forests and wild places in general, and in the half wild parks and gardens of towns. . . .

When, like a merchant taking a list of his goods, we take stock of our wildness, we are glad to see how much of even the most destructible kind is still unspoiled. Looking at our continent as scenery when it was all wild, lying between beautiful seas, the starry sky above it, the starry rocks beneath it, to compare its sides, the East and the West, would be like comparing the sides of a rainbow. But it is no longer equally beautiful. . . . [T]he continent's outer beauty is fast passing away, especially the plant part of it, the most destructible and most universally charming of all.

Only thirty years ago, the great Central Valley of California, five hundred miles long and fifty miles wide, was one bed of golden and purple flowers. Now it is ploughed and pastured out of existence, gone forever,—scarce a memory of it left in fence corners and along the bluffs of the streams. . . . The same fate, sooner or later, is awaiting them all, unless awakening public opinion comes forward to stop it. . . .

The Grand Cañon Reserve of Arizona, of nearly two million acres, or the most interesting part of it, as well as the Rainier region, should be made into a national park, on account of their supreme grandeur and beauty. . . . No matter how far you have wandered hitherto, or how many famous gorges and valleys you have seen, this one, the Grand Cañon of the Colorado, will seem as novel to you, as unearthly in the color and grandeur and quantity of its architecture, as if you had found it after death, on some other star; so incomparably lovely and grand and supreme is it above all the other cañons in our fire-moulded, earthquake-shaken, rain-washed, wave-washed, river and glacier sculptured world.

1. What benefits does Muir describe as a result of spending time in the "wilderness"? What maladies does Muir believe the "wilderness" will correct? How do his arguments reflect the economic and social history of his time?

2. What is Muir's purpose? Is he attempting primarily to instruct or to persuade? How does that purpose affect the tone of the writing?

Source: Library of Congress, Materials from the General Collection and Rare Book and Special Collections Division of the Library of Congress.

forest system. When conservatives in Congress restricted his authority over public lands in 1907, Roosevelt and his chief forester, Gifford Pinchot, seized all the forests and many of the water power sites still in the public domain before the bill became law.

Roosevelt was the first president to take an active interest in the new and struggling American conservation movement. In the early twentieth century, many people who considered themselves **conservationists**—including Pinchot, the first director of the U.S. Forest Service (which he helped create)—promoted policies to protect land for carefully managed development.

Roosevelt also supported public reclamation and irrigation projects. In 1902, the president backed the National Reclamation Act, which used funds raised by the sale of public lands in the West for the construction of dams, reservoirs, and canals, projects that would "reclaim" arid lands for cultivation and later provide cheap electric power.

Despite his sympathy with Pinchot's vision of conservation, Roosevelt also shared some of the concerns of the naturalists—those committed to protecting the natural beauty of the land and the health of its wildlife from human intrusion. Early in his presidency, Roosevelt spent four days camping in the Sierras with **John Muir**, the nation's leading **preservationist** and the founder of the Sierra Club. Roosevelt also added significantly to the still-young National Park System, whose purpose was to protect public land from exploitation or development. (For Muir's views on the system, see "Consider the Source: John Muir on the Value of Wild Places.")

The contending views of the early conservation movement came to a head beginning in 1906 in a controversy over the **Hetch Hetchy** Valley in Yosemite National Park—a spectacular high-walled valley popular with naturalists. But many residents of San Francisco worried about finding enough water to serve their growing population. They saw Hetch Hetchy as an ideal place for a dam, which would create a large reservoir for the city.

In 1906, San Francisco suffered a devastating earthquake and fire. Widespread sympathy for the city strengthened the case for the dam, and Roosevelt turned the decision over to Pinchot, who approved its construction.

For over a decade, a battle raged between naturalists and the advocates of the dam, a battle that consumed the energies of John Muir for the rest of his life and that eventually, many believed, led him to an early death. To Pinchot, the needs of the city were more important than the claims of preservation. Muir helped place a referendum question on the ballot in 1908, certain that the residents of the city would oppose the project. Instead, San Franciscans approved the dam by a huge margin. Construction of the dam finally began after World War I.

This setback for the naturalists was not, however, a total defeat. The fight against Hetch Hetchy helped mobilize a new coalition of people committed to preservation of wilderness.

PANIC AND RETIREMENT

Despite the flurry of reforms Roosevelt was able to enact, the government still had relatively little control over the industrial economy. That became clear in 1907, when a serious panic and recession began. Conservatives blamed Roosevelt's "mad" economic policies for the disaster. And while the president naturally disagreed, he nevertheless acted quickly to reassure business leaders that he would not interfere with their recovery efforts.

The financier J. P. Morgan helped construct a pool of the assets of several important New York banks to prop up shaky financial institutions. The key to the arrangement, Morgan told the president, was a purchase by U.S. Steel of the shares of the Tennessee Coal and Iron Company, currently held by a threatened New York bank. Morgan insisted that he needed assurances that the purchase would not prompt antitrust action. Roosevelt tacitly agreed, and the Morgan plan proceeded. Whether or not as a result, the panic soon subsided.

Roosevelt loved being president, and many people assumed that he would run for reelection in 1908, despite the long-standing tradition of presidents serving no more than two terms. But the Panic of 1907 and Roosevelt's reform efforts so alienated conservatives in his own party that he might have had difficulty winning the Republican nomination. In 1904, moreover, he had made a public promise to step down four years later. And so in 1909, Roosevelt, fifty years old, retired from public life—briefly.

THE TROUBLED SUCCESSION

William Howard Taft, who assumed the presidency in 1909, had been Theodore Roosevelt's most trusted lieutenant and his handpicked successor; progressive reformers believed him to be one of their own. But Taft was also a restrained and moderate jurist, a man with a punctilious regard for legal process. Conservatives expected him to abandon Roosevelt's aggressive use of presidential powers. By seeming acceptable to almost everyone, Taft easily won election to the White House in 1908 over William Jennings Bryan, running for the Democrats for the third time.

Four years later, however, Taft would leave office the most decisively defeated president of the twentieth century, his party deeply divided and the government in the hands of a Democratic administration for the first time in twenty years.

TAFT AND THE PROGRESSIVES

Taft's first problem arose in the opening months of the new administration, when he called Congress into special session to lower protective tariff rates, an old progressive demand. But the president made no effort to overcome the opposition of congressional Old Guard conservatives like House Speaker Joseph Cannon (R-IL), arguing that to do so would violate the constitutional doctrine of separation of powers. The result was the feeble Payne-Aldrich Tariff, which reduced tariff rates scarcely at all. Yet although he tended to refrain from railing against big business in public, Taft filed almost a hundred antitrust suits against corporations during his administration.

Then a sensational controversy breaking out late in 1909 helped destroy Taft's popularity with reformers. Many progressives had been unhappy when Taft replaced Roosevelt's secretary of the interior, James R. Garfield, an aggressive conservationist, with Richard A. Ballinger, a conservative corporate lawyer. Suspicion of Ballinger grew when he attempted to invalidate Roosevelt's removal of nearly 1 million acres of forests and mineral reserves from private development.

In the midst of this mounting concern, Louis Glavis, an Interior Department investigator, charged Ballinger with having once connived to turn over valuable public coal lands in Alaska to a private syndicate for personal profit. Glavis took the evidence to Gifford Pinchot, still director of the U.S. Forest Service and a critic of Ballinger's policies. Pinchot took the charges to the president. Taft investigated them and decided they were groundless. Unsatisfied, Pinchot leaked the story to the press and asked Congress to investigate the scandal. The president discharged Pinchot for insubordination, and the congressional committee appointed to study the controversy, dominated by Old Guard Republicans, exonerated Ballinger. But progressives throughout the country supported Pinchot. The controversy aroused as much public passion as any dispute of its time. By the time it was over, Taft had alienated the supporters of Roosevelt completely, despite his trust-busting record. Taft's shifting devotion to both the conservative and progressive impulses of the Republican Party left him popular with almost no one. To Roosevelt, he had become a tool of big business.

THE RETURN OF ROOSEVELT

During most of these controversies, Theodore Roosevelt was out of the country on a long hunting safari in Africa and an extended tour of Europe. To the American public, however, Roosevelt remained a formidable presence. His return to New York in the spring of 1910

(Source: Library of Congress, Prints and Photographs Division [LC-DIG-ppmsca-36445])

ROOSEVELT AT MISSOURI VALLEY Roosevelt's 1910 speech in Iowa was part of a swing through the Great Plains and Midwest that saw the ex-president mark his break with the Taft administration and the Republican leadership. In Kansas that summer, Roosevelt told his largely conservative audience, "The essence of any struggle for liberty has always been, and must always be to take from some one man or class of men the right to enjoy power, or wealth, or position or immunity, which has not been earned by service to his or their fellows."

was a major public event. Roosevelt insisted that he had no plans to reenter politics, but within a month he announced that he would embark on a national speaking tour before the end of the summer. Furious with Taft, he was becoming convinced that he alone was capable of reuniting the Republican Party.

The real signal of Roosevelt's decision to assume leadership of Republican reformers came in a speech he gave on September 1, 1910, in Osawatomie, Kansas. In it he outlined a set of principles, which he labeled the "**New Nationalism**," that made clear he had moved away from the cautious conservatism of his presidential years. He argued that social justice was possible only through a strong federal government whose executive acted as the "steward of the public welfare." He supported graduated income and inheritance taxes, workers' compensation for industrial accidents, regulation of the labor of women and children, tariff revision, and firmer regulation of corporations.

Spreading Insurgency

The congressional elections of 1910 provided further evidence of how far the progressive revolt had spread. In primary elections, conservative Republicans suffered defeat after defeat, while almost all the progressive incumbents were reelected. In the general election, the Democrats won control of the House of Representatives for the first time in sixteen years and gained strength in the Senate. But Roosevelt still denied any presidential ambitions and claimed his real purpose was to pressure Taft to return to progressive policies. Two events, however, changed his mind. The first, on October 27, 1911, was the announcement by the administration of a suit against U.S. Steel, which charged, among other things, that the 1907 acquisition of the Tennessee Coal and Iron Company had been illegal. Roosevelt had approved that acquisition in the midst of the 1907 panic, and he was enraged by the implication that he had acted improperly.

Roosevelt was still reluctant to become a candidate for president because Senator Robert La Follette, the Wisconsin progressive, had been working since 1911 to secure the presidential nomination for himself. But La Follette's candidacy stumbled in February 1912 when, exhausted and distraught over the illness of a daughter, he appeared to suffer a nervous breakdown during a speech in Philadelphia. Roosevelt announced his candidacy on February 22.

Roosevelt versus Taft

For all practical purposes, the campaign for the Republican nomination had now become a battle between Roosevelt and Taft. Roosevelt scored overwhelming victories in all thirteen presidential primaries. Taft, however, remained the choice of most party leaders, who controlled the nominating process.

The battle for the nomination at the Chicago convention revolved around an unusually large number of contested delegates: 254 in all. Roosevelt needed fewer than half the disputed seats to clinch the nomination. But on the eve of the convention, the Republican National Committee, controlled by the Old Guard, awarded all but 19 of them to Taft. At a rally the night before the convention opened, Roosevelt addressed 5,000 cheering supporters. "We stand at Armageddon," he told the roaring crowd, "and we battle for the Lord." The next day, he led his supporters out of the convention, and out of the party. The convention then quietly nominated Taft on the first ballot.

Roosevelt summoned his supporters back to Chicago in August for another convention, this one to launch the new Progressive Party and to nominate himself as its presidential candidate. Roosevelt approached the battle feeling, as he put it, "fit as a bull moose," thus giving his new party an enduring nickname, the **Bull Moose Party**. But Roosevelt was also aware that his cause was almost hopeless, partly because many of the insurgents who had supported him during the primaries refused to follow him out of the Republican Party. It was also because of the man the Democrats had nominated for president.

WOODROW WILSON AND THE NEW FREEDOM

The 1912 presidential contest was not simply one between conservatives and reformers. It was also one between two brands of progressivism. And it matched the two most important national leaders of the early twentieth century in an unequal contest.

WOODROW WILSON

Reform sentiment had been gaining strength within the Democratic Party as well as the Republican Party in the first years of the century. At the June 1912 Democratic Convention in Baltimore, Champ Clark, the conservative Speaker of the House, was unable to assemble the two-thirds majority necessary for nomination because of progressive opposition. Finally, on the forty-sixth ballot, **Woodrow Wilson**, the governor of New Jersey and the only genuinely progressive candidate in the race, emerged as the party's nominee.

Wilson had been a professor of political science at Princeton until 1902, when he was named president of the university. Elected governor of New Jersey in 1910, he quickly earned a national reputation for winning passage of progressive legislation. As a presidential candidate in 1912, Wilson presented a progressive program that came to be called the **New Freedom**. Roosevelt's New Nationalism supported economic concentration and using government to regulate and control it. Wilson seemed to side with those who (like Louis Brandeis) believed that bigness was both unjust and inefficient, and the proper response to monopoly was not to regulate but destroy it.

The 1912 presidential campaign was an anticlimax. Taft, resigned to defeat, barely campaigned. Roosevelt campaigned energetically, until a gunshot wound from a would-be assassin forced him to the sidelines during the last weeks before the election, but he failed to draw any significant number of Democratic progressives away from Wilson. In November, Roosevelt and Taft split the Republican vote, while Wilson held on to most Democrats and won. He received only 42 percent of the popular vote, compared with 27 percent for Roosevelt, 23 percent for Taft, and 6 percent for the socialist Eugene Debs. But in the electoral college, Wilson won 435 of the 531 votes.

THE SCHOLAR AS PRESIDENT

Wilson was a bold and forceful president. He exerted firm control over his cabinet, and he delegated real authority only to those who were loyal to him. His most powerful adviser, Colonel Edward M. House, was an ambitious Texan who held no office and whose only claim to authority was his personal intimacy with the president.

In legislative matters, Wilson skillfully welded together a coalition that would support his goals. Democratic majorities in both houses of Congress made his task easier. Wilson's first triumph as president was the fulfillment of an old Democratic (and progressive) goal: a substantial lowering of the protective tariff. The Underwood-Simmons

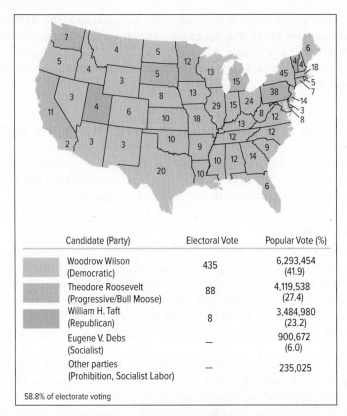

Candidate (Party)	Electoral Vote	Popular Vote (%)
Woodrow Wilson (Democratic)	435	6,293,454 (41.9)
Theodore Roosevelt (Progressive/Bull Moose)	88	4,119,538 (27.4)
William H. Taft (Republican)	8	3,484,980 (23.2)
Eugene V. Debs (Socialist)	—	900,672 (6.0)
Other parties (Prohibition, Socialist Labor)	—	235,025

58.8% of electorate voting

THE ELECTION OF 1912   The election of 1912 was one of the most unusual in American history because of the dramatic schism within the Republican Party. Two Republican presidents—William Howard Taft, the incumbent, and Theodore Roosevelt, his predecessor—ran against each other, opening the way for a victory by the Democratic candidate, Woodrow Wilson, who won with only 42 percent of the popular vote. A fourth candidate, the socialist Eugene V. Debs, received a significant 6 percent of the vote. • *What events caused the schism between Taft and Roosevelt?*

Tariff provided cuts significant enough, progressives believed, to introduce real competition into American markets and thus to help break the power of trusts. To make up for the loss of revenue under the new tariff, Congress approved a graduated income tax, which the recently adopted Sixteenth Amendment to the Constitution now permitted. This first modern federal income tax imposed a 1 percent tax on individuals and corporations earning more than $4,000 a year, with rates ranging up to 6 percent on incomes over $500,000 annually.

Wilson held Congress in session through the summer to work on a major reform of the American banking system: the Federal Reserve Act, which Congress passed and the president signed on December 23, 1913. It created twelve regional banks, each to be owned and controlled by the individual banks of its district. The regional Federal Reserve banks would hold a certain percentage of the assets of their member banks in reserve; they would use those reserves to support loans to private banks at a discounted interest rate that the Federal Reserve system would set; they would issue new, standardized paper bills called Federal Reserve notes that would become the nation's basic

(Source: Library of Congress, Prints and Photographs Division [LC-USZ62-20570])

WOODROW WILSON   Woodrow Wilson, the twenty-eighth president of the United States, was a Virginian, the first southerner to be elected president since before the Civil War, a professor of political science and later president of Princeton University, governor of New Jersey, and a progressive. His election to the presidency brought the first Democrat to the White House since 1896.

medium of trade and would be backed by the government (to this day American bills read "Federal Reserve Note" at the top). Most important, they would be able to shift funds quickly to troubled areas to meet increased demands for credit or to protect imperiled banks. Supervising and regulating the entire system was a national Federal Reserve Board, whose members were appointed by the president.

In 1914, turning to the central issue of his 1912 campaign, Wilson proposed two measures to deal with the problem of monopoly, which took shape as the Federal Trade Commission Act and the Clayton Antitrust Act. The Federal Trade Commission Act created a regulatory agency that would help businesses determine in advance whether their actions would be acceptable to the government. The agency would also have authority to launch prosecutions against "unfair trade practices," and it would have wide power to investigate corporate behavior. Wilson signed the Federal Trade Commission Bill happily, but he seemed to lose interest in the Clayton Antitrust Bill, which proposed stronger measures to break up trusts. Wilson did little to protect it from conservative assaults, which greatly weakened it.

RETREAT AND ADVANCE

By the fall of 1914, Wilson believed that the New Freedom program was essentially complete and that agitation for reform would now subside. He refused to support the movement for national woman suffrage. Deferring to southern Democrats, he condoned the reimposition of segregation in the agencies of the federal government, in contrast to Roosevelt, who had ordered the elimination of many such barriers. When congressional progressives attempted to enlist his support for new reform legislation, Wilson dismissed their proposals as unconstitutional or unnecessary.

The congressional elections of 1914, however, shattered the president's complacency. Democrats suffered major losses in Congress, and voters who in 1912 had supported the Progressive Party began returning to the Republicans. Wilson realized he would not be able to rely on a divided opposition when he ran for reelection in 1916. By the end of 1915, therefore, Wilson had begun to support a second flurry of reforms. In January 1916, he appointed Louis Brandeis to the Supreme Court, making him not only the first Jew but also the most advanced progressive to serve there. Later, Wilson supported a measure to make it easier for farmers to receive credit, and another measure creating a system of workers' compensation for federal employees.

In 1916, Wilson supported the Keating-Owen Act, which prohibited the shipment of goods produced by underage children across state lines, thus giving an expanded importance to the constitutional clause assigning Congress the task of regulating interstate commerce. The president similarly supported measures that used federal taxing authority as a vehicle for legislating social change. After the Court struck down Keating-Owen, a new law attempted to achieve the same goal by imposing a heavy tax on the products of child labor. (The Court later struck down that law too.) The Smith-Lever Act of 1914 offered matching federal grants to support agricultural extension education. Over time, these innovative uses of government overcame most of the constitutional objections and became the foundation of a long-term growth in federal power over the economy.

CONCLUSION

The powerful surge of reform efforts in the last years of the nineteenth century and the first years of the twentieth century caused many Americans to identify themselves as "progressives." That label meant many different things to many different people, but at its core was a belief that human effort and government action could improve society. By the early twentieth century, progressivism had become a powerful, transformative force in American life.

This great surge of reform eventually reached the federal government and national politics, as progressives came to believe that success required the engagement of the federal government. Two national leaders, Theodore Roosevelt and Woodrow Wilson, contributed to a period of national reform that made the government in Washington a great center of power for the first time since the Civil War, a position it has never relinquished. Progressivism did not solve the nation's problems, but it gave movements, organizations, and governments new tools to deal with them.

KEY TERMS/PEOPLE/PLACES/EVENTS

Alice Paul 494
Bull Moose Party 511
conservationists 507
eugenics 502
Hetch Hetchy 507
Hull House 490
Industrial Workers of the
  World (IWW) 502
Jane Addams 490
John Muir 507
Louis D. Brandeis 503
muckrakers 489

National Association for the
  Advancement of Colored
  People (NAACP) 501
New Freedom 511
New Nationalism 510
Nineteenth Amendment
  494
progressivism 486
prohibition 501
preservationists 507
Robert M. La Follette 496
Social Gospel 490

socialism 502
social justice 490
Theodore Roosevelt 503
Triangle Shirtwaist
  Company fire 497
W. E. B. Du Bois 500
William Howard Taft 508
Women's Christian
  Temperance Union
  (WCTU) 501
Woodrow Wilson 511

RECALL AND REFLECT

1. What "moral" crusades did progressives undertake in their efforts to reform
   the social order?
2. How did W. E. B. Du Bois's philosophy on race relations differ from that of Booker
   T. Washington?
3. What were some of the approaches progressives used to challenge the power
   and influence of corporate America?
4. What was the difference between Theodore Roosevelt's "New Nationalism"
   and Woodrow Wilson's "New Freedom"?

21 | AMERICA AND THE GREAT WAR

THE "BIG STICK": AMERICA AND THE
    WORLD, 1901–1917

THE ROAD TO WAR

"OVER THERE"

THE SEARCH FOR A NEW WORLD ORDER

A SOCIETY IN TURMOIL

LOOKING AHEAD

1. What were the most important events that led up to the United States declaring war on Germany?

2. How did U.S. participation in the Great War affect the nation's economy and society, both during the war and after the conflict ended?

3. Why did the Great War fail to become the "war to end all wars"?

THE "GREAT WAR," AS IT was known to a generation unaware that a greater war would soon follow, began in August 1914 when Austria-Hungary invaded the tiny Balkan nation of Serbia. Within weeks, however, the conflict had grown into a conflagration engaging the armies of most of the major nations of Europe.

Americans looked on with horror as the war became what many people claimed was the most savage in history. It dragged on, brutally and inconclusively, for over four years. Most Americans also believed at first that the conflict had little to do with them. They were wrong. The United States had been deeply involved in world affairs since at least the Spanish-American War, taking on increasing international commitments in the early years of the twentieth century. After nearly three years of attempting to affect the outcome of the conflict without becoming embroiled in it, then, it should not be surprising that the United States entered the war in April 1917.

For America, the war as a military struggle was brief but costly. It killed 116,000 Americans, about half succumbing to influenza and other diseases and half dying by armed violence, though these statistics didn't remotely approach losses among the other major belligerents. Viewed in the long term, the war left a mixed legacy. Economically, it stimulated a great industrial boom that would propel the country into the prosperous era that followed, yet the wartime gains for labor proved temporary. It fostered victories for progressive causes such as prohibition and woman suffrage but also accelerated immigration restriction.

Ethnic and racial minorities served in mass numbers amid the first major conscription in American history, though African Americans in particular endured second-class status in the military and found no postwar extension of political rights awaiting them upon return. Finally, although the conflict propelled the United States into the international arena, it failed to either end war or deliver a democratic world order as President Woodrow Wilson had hoped. Instead, the Great War's resolution led to two decades of global instability and ultimately an even bigger conflict.

THE "BIG STICK": AMERICA AND THE WORLD, 1901–1917

To most of the American public, foreign affairs remained largely remote in the early twentieth century. But to Theodore Roosevelt and later presidents, that remoteness made foreign affairs appealing. Overseas, the president could act with less regard for Congress and the courts.

ROOSEVELT AND "CIVILIZATION"

Theodore Roosevelt believed in using American power in the world, once citing the proverb, "Speak softly, and carry a big stick." But he had two different standards for using that power.

Roosevelt believed an important distinction existed between the "civilized" and "uncivilized" nations of the world. "Civilized" nations, as he defined them, were predominantly white and Anglo-Saxon or Teutonic; "uncivilized" nations were generally nonwhite, Latin, or Slavic. Civilized nations were also, by Roosevelt's definition, producers of industrial goods. Uncivilized nations were suppliers of raw materials and markets for industrial products. Roosevelt

1914
World War I begins
Panama Canal opened

1915
U.S. troops in Haiti
Lusitania torpedoed
Wilson supports preparedness

1916
Wilson reelected
U.S. troops in Mexico

1917
German unrestricted submarine warfare
U.S. enters World War I
Selective Service Act
War Industries Board created

1918
Sedition Act
Wilson's Fourteen Points
Armistice ends war
Paris Peace Conference

1919
Senate rejects Treaty of Versailles
Race riots in Chicago and other cities
Steel strike and other labor actions

1920
Palmer raids and Red Scare
Harding elected president

1927
Sacco and Vanzetti executed

believed that a civilized society had the right and duty to intervene in the affairs of "backward nations" to preserve order and stability—for the sake of both nations. That belief, the obligation of a "civilized" nation to police the world, was one important reason for Roosevelt's early support of the development of American sea power. By 1906, the American navy had attained a size and strength surpassed only by that of Great Britain.

Protecting the "Open Door" in Asia

In 1904, the Japanese staged a surprise attack on the Russian fleet at Port Arthur in southern Manchuria, a province of China that both Russia and Japan hoped to control. Roosevelt, hoping to prevent either nation from becoming dominant there, agreed to mediate an end to the conflict. Russia, faring badly in the war, had no choice but to agree. At a peace conference in Portsmouth, New Hampshire, in 1905, Roosevelt pressured the embattled Russians to accept Japan's territorial gains. The Japanese agreed to cease the fighting and expand no farther. At the same time, Roosevelt negotiated a secret agreement with the Japanese to ensure that the United States could continue to trade freely in the region. Roosevelt received the Nobel Peace Prize in 1906 for his mediation of what became the Treaty of Portsmouth.

In the years that followed, relations between the United States and Japan steadily deteriorated. Japan, by then the preeminent naval power in the Pacific, began to exclude American trade from many of the territories it controlled. Roosevelt took no direct action against Japan, but to be sure the Japanese government recognized the power of the United States, he sent sixteen battleships of the new American navy (known as the "Great White Fleet" because the ships were temporarily painted white for the voyage) on an unprecedented journey around the world that included a call on Japan.

THE WORLD CONSTABLE.

(Source: Library of Congress, Prints and Photographs Division [LC-DIG-ds-05213])

THE NEW DIPLOMACY This 1904 drawing by the famous *Puck* cartoonist Louis Dalrymple conveys the new image of America as a great power that Theodore Roosevelt hoped to convey. Roosevelt polices the world by dealing with "less civilized" people on the left using the "big stick" and with "civilized" nations on the right by using diplomacy.

THE IRON-FISTED NEIGHBOR

Roosevelt took a particular interest in Latin America. Embarking on a series of ventures in the Caribbean and South America, he established a pattern of American intervention in the region that would outlive his presidency.

In 1902, the government of Venezuela began to renege on debts to European bankers. Naval forces of Britain, Italy, and Germany blockaded the Venezuelan coast in response. Then German ships began to bombard a Venezuelan port. Amid rumors that Germany planned to establish a permanent base in the region, Roosevelt used the threat of American naval power to pressure the German navy to withdraw.

The incident helped persuade Roosevelt that European intrusions into Latin America could result not only from aggression but also from instability or irresponsibility (such as defaulting on debts) within the Latin American nations themselves. As a result, in 1904 he announced what came to be known as the **Roosevelt Corollary** to the Monroe Doctrine. The United States, he claimed, had the right not only to oppose European intervention in the Western Hemisphere but also to intervene in the domestic affairs of its neighbors if those neighbors proved unable to maintain order and national sovereignty on their own.

The immediate motivation for the Roosevelt Corollary, and the first opportunity for using it, was a crisis in the Dominican Republic. A revolution had toppled its corrupt and bankrupt government in 1903, but the new regime proved no better able than the old to make good on the country's $22 million in debts to European nations. Using the rationale provided by the Roosevelt Corollary, Roosevelt established, in effect, an American receivership, assuming control of Dominican customs and distributing 45 percent of the revenues to the Dominicans and the rest to foreign creditors. This arrangement lasted, in one form or another, for more than three decades.

THE PANAMA CANAL

The most celebrated foreign policy accomplishment of Roosevelt's presidency was the construction of the **Panama Canal**, which linked the Atlantic and the Pacific by creating a channel through Central America. At first, Roosevelt and many others favored a route across Nicaragua, which would permit a sea-level canal requiring no locks. But they soon turned instead to the narrow Isthmus of Panama (then part of Colombia), the site of an earlier failed effort by a French company to construct a channel. Although the Panama route was not at sea level, it was shorter than the one in Nicaragua, and construction was already about 40 percent complete. The French then lowered the price for its holdings, and the United States opted for the Panama route through Colombia.

Roosevelt dispatched John Hay, his secretary of state, to negotiate an agreement with Colombian diplomats that would allow construction to begin without delay. Under heavy American pressure, the Colombian chargé d'affaires, Tomás Herrán, signed an agreement giving the United States perpetual rights to a six-mile-wide "Canal Zone" across Colombia; in return, the United States would pay Colombia $10 million and an annual rent of $250,000. The outraged Colombian senate refused to ratify the treaty. Colombia then sent a new representative to Washington with instructions to demand at least $20 million from the Americans plus a share of the payment to the French.

Roosevelt was furious and began to look for ways to circumvent the Colombian government. Philippe Bunau-Varilla, chief engineer of the French canal project, was a ready ally.

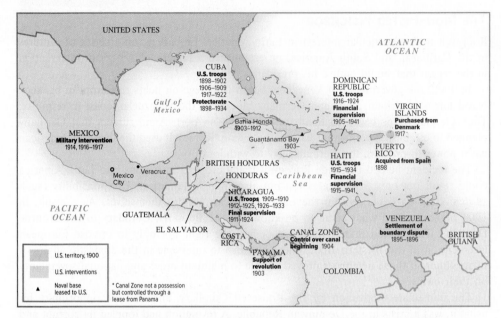

THE UNITED STATES AND LATIN AMERICA, 1895–1941 Except for Puerto Rico, the Virgin Islands, and the Canal Zone, the United States had no formal possessions in Latin America and the Caribbean in the late nineteenth century and the first half of the twentieth. But as this map reveals, the United States exercised considerable influence—both political and economic, augmented at times by military intervention—in these regions throughout this period. Note the particularly intrusive presence of the United States in the affairs of Cuba, Haiti, and the Dominican Republic—as well as the canal-related interventions in Colombia and Panama. • *What were the reasons for American intervention in Latin America?*

In 1903, with the support of the United States, he helped organize and finance a revolution in Panama. Roosevelt landed troops from the U.S.S. *Nashville* there to "maintain order." Their presence prevented Colombian forces from suppressing the rebellion, and three days later Roosevelt recognized Panama as an independent nation. The new Panamanian government quickly agreed to the terms the Colombian senate had rejected. Work on the canal proceeded rapidly, and it opened in 1914.

TAFT AND "DOLLAR DIPLOMACY"

Like his predecessor, William Howard Taft worked to advance the nation's economic interests in Latin America. But he showed little interest in Roosevelt's larger vision of world stability. Instead, Taft's secretary of state, Philander C. Knox, worked aggressively to extend American investments into less-developed regions. Critics called his policies **Dollar Diplomacy**.

The policy was particularly visible in the Caribbean. When a revolution broke out in Nicaragua in 1909, the administration quickly sided with the insurgents and sent American troops into the country to seize the customs houses. As soon as peace was restored, Knox encouraged American bankers to offer substantial loans to the new government, thus increasing Washington's financial leverage over the country. When the new pro-American government faced an insurrection less than two years later, Taft again landed American troops in Nicaragua, this time to protect the existing regime. The troops remained there for more than a decade.

Diplomacy and Morality

Woodrow Wilson entered the presidency with relatively little interest or experience in international affairs. Yet he faced international challenges of a scope and gravity unmatched by those of any president before him. In many respects, he continued—and even strengthened—the Roosevelt-Taft approach to foreign policy.

Having already seized control of the finances of the Dominican Republic in 1905, the United States established a military government there in 1916. The military occupation lasted eight years. In Haiti, Wilson landed marines in 1915 to quell a revolution during which a mob had murdered an unpopular president. American military forces remained in the country until 1934, and American officers drafted the new Haitian constitution adopted in 1918. When Wilson began to fear that the Danish West Indies might be about to fall into the hands of Germany, he bought the colony from Denmark and renamed it the Virgin Islands. Concerned about the possibility of European influence in Nicaragua, he signed a treaty with that country's government allowing for intervention to protect American interests.

Closer to the American border, the dictator Porfirio Díaz had long permitted American businessmen to establish an enormous economic presence in Mexico. In 1911, however, Díaz was overthrown by the popular leader Francisco Madero, who promised democratic reform and seemed hostile to American businesses in Mexico. The United States quietly encouraged a reactionary general, Victoriano Huerta, to depose Madero early in 1913. But when the new government under Huerta murdered Madero, Woodrow Wilson announced that he would never recognize Huerta's "government of butchers."

Wilson hoped that by refusing to recognize Huerta he could help topple the regime and bring to power the constitutionalists, now led by Venustiano Carranza. But Huerta, with the support of American business interests, established a full military dictatorship in October 1913; a few months later, one of his army officers briefly arrested several American sailors from the U.S.S. *Dolphin* who had gone ashore in Tampico. The men were immediately released, but the American admiral demanded a twenty-one-gun salute as a public display of penance. Huerta refused. Wilson used the slight as a pretext for seizing the Mexican port of Vera Cruz.

Wilson had envisioned a bloodless action, but in a clash with Mexican troops, the Americans killed 126 of the defenders and suffered 19 casualties. His show of force, however, had helped strengthen the position of the Carranza faction, which captured Mexico City in August 1914 and forced Huerta to flee the country. At last, it seemed, the crisis might be over.

But Wilson reacted angrily when Carranza, whom he had previously supported, refused to accept American guidelines for the creation of a new government, and he briefly considered throwing his support to still another aspirant to leadership: Carranza's erstwhile lieutenant **Pancho Villa**, now staking his own claim to power. When Villa's military position deteriorated, however, Wilson abandoned him and granted preliminary recognition to Carranza. Villa, angry at what he considered an American betrayal, retaliated in early 1916 by shooting sixteen American mining engineers in northern Mexico and seventeen more Americans across the border in Columbus, New Mexico.

Wilson ordered General **John J. Pershing** to lead an American expeditionary force across the Mexican border to capture Villa, who managed to elude them. Carranza's new government acquiesced to but also resented the U.S. military intrusion on Mexican soil, and on June 21, 1916, Carranza's army attacked one of Pershing's units, killing twenty-two Americans. But before a fuller war could erupt, Wilson quietly withdrew American troops from Mexico and, in March 1917, finally granted formal recognition to the Carranza regime. By now, however, Wilson's attention was turning to a far greater international crisis.

THE ROAD TO WAR

By 1914, the European nations had created an unusually precarious international system. It careened into war very quickly on the basis of what seemed to be a minor series of provocations.

The Collapse of the European Peace

The major powers of Europe were organized by 1914 in two great, competing alliances. The "Triple Entente" linked Britain, France, and Russia. The "Triple Alliance" united Germany, the Austro-Hungarian Empire, and Italy.

The conflict emerged most directly out of a controversy involving nationalist movements within the Austro-Hungarian Empire. On June 28, 1914, Archduke Franz Ferdinand, heir to the throne of the tottering empire, was assassinated while paying a state visit to Sarajevo, the capital of Bosnia, then a province of Austria-Hungary. Slavic nationalists wished to annex Bosnia to neighboring Serbia. The killer of the archduke and his wife Sophie was a Serbian nationalist.

Austria immediately blamed Serbia for the murders and issued impossible ultimatums. Russia, Serbia's Slavic ally and a seeker of greater influence in the Balkans, mobilized its armies along the border with Austria-Hungary. The Germans, faced with that provocation against their ally and concerned about a two-front war against Russia and France, declared war against both. Germany's subsequent invasion of neutral Belgium prompted Britain to declare war on Germany. By August, Austria-Hungary and Germany were fighting Russia, and Germany had charged through Belgium into France.

The coalitions soon changed in name and membership. On one side were the **Central Powers**: Germany and Austria-Hungary, joined in the fall by the Ottoman Empire. On the other side were the **Allies**, made up of Britain, France, and Russia. Hoping to seize territory from the Central Powers, Italy and Japan soon threw in their lot with the Allies.

As these changes suggest, the alliance system did not necessarily *bind* nations to act as they did. Leaders made the decision for war based on their own interests and ambitions, on the assumption that national self-defense required it, and on the erroneous belief that their objectives could be met quickly. What the alliance system did was provide a framework within which the choices for war were made. As tragic as those choices seem in retrospect, no one expected or wanted the ghastly world war that followed.

Wilson's Neutrality

Wilson called on his fellow citizens in 1914 to remain "impartial in thought as well as deed." But that was impossible. Most Americans sympathized with Britain. Lurid reports of German atrocities in Belgium and France, sometimes (but not always) exaggerated by British propagandists, strengthened American hostility toward Germany.

Economic realities also made it impossible for the United States to deal with the belligerents on equal terms. The British had imposed a naval blockade on Germany to prevent munitions and supplies from reaching the enemy. As a neutral, the United States had the right, in theory, to trade with Germany, but the British blockade made that impossible. A truly neutral response to the blockade would have been to stop trading with Britain as well. But while the United States could survive an interruption of its relatively modest trade with the Central Powers, a potential break in its much more extensive trade with the Allies posed a serious threat to American commerce. So America tacitly accepted the blockade of Germany and continued trading with Britain. By 1915, the United States had gradually transformed itself from a neutral power into the arsenal of the Allies.

The Germans, in the meantime, were resorting to a new and, in American eyes, barbaric tactic: submarine warfare. Unable to challenge British domination on the ocean's surface, the Germans announced early in 1915 that they would sink enemy vessels on sight. Months later, on May 7, a German submarine (or U-boat, from the German *Unterseeboot*) sank the British passenger liner **Lusitania** without warning, causing the deaths of 1,198 people, 128 of them Americans. The ship was carrying both passengers and munitions, but most Americans considered the attack an unprovoked act on civilians.

Wilson angrily demanded that Germany promise not to repeat such outrages, and the Germans reluctantly agreed. But early in 1916, in response to an announcement that the Allies were now arming merchant ships to sink submarines, Germany proclaimed that it would fire on such vessels without warning. A few weeks later, it attacked the unarmed French steamer *Sussex,* injuring several American passengers. Again, Wilson demanded that Germany abandon its "unlawful" tactics; again, the German government relented.

Preparedness versus Pacifism

Despite the president's increasing bellicosity in 1916, he was still far from ready to commit the United States to war. One obstacle was American domestic politics.

The question of whether America should make military and economic preparations for war sparked a heated debate between pacifists and interventionists. Wilson at first denounced the idea of an American military buildup as needless and provocative. In the fall of 1915, however, he endorsed an ambitious proposal by American military leaders for a large and rapid increase in the nation's armed forces.

Still, the peace faction wielded considerable political strength, as became clear at the Democratic National Convention in the summer of 1916. The convention became especially enthusiastic when the keynote speaker punctuated his list of the president's diplomatic achievements with the chant, "What did we do? What did we do? . . . We didn't go to war! We didn't go to war!" That speech helped produce one of the most prominent slogans of Wilson's reelection campaign: "He kept us out of war." During the campaign, Wilson did nothing to discourage those who argued that the Republican candidate, the progressive New York governor Charles Evans Hughes, was more likely than he to lead the nation into war. Wilson ultimately won reelection by fewer than 600,000 popular votes and only 23 electoral votes. But he was uncomfortable about a slogan that had aided his victory. "Any little German lieutenant," he said of the U-boat situation, "can put us into the war at any time by some calculated outrage."

Intervention

Wilson was right—but it was the German leadership that provoked him. In January 1917 Germany made a desperate gamble, declaring unrestricted submarine warfare against all maritime traffic in the hopes of defeating the Allies before Wilson could mobilize an army. Meanwhile, the German foreign secretary Arthur Zimmermann sent a telegram to the German ambassador in Mexico instructing him to offer the Mexicans a deal: if they would join a military alliance, Germany would help Mexico take back territory in the present states of Texas, New Mexico, and Arizona. By March, when Wilson released the intercepted and decoded **Zimmermann Telegram**—and after three United States ships were torpedoed by U-boats—war with Germany seemed imminent.

Although German crimes on the seas, the offer to Mexico, and threats to American commerce provided the immediate causes for war, Wilson had broader purposes in mind

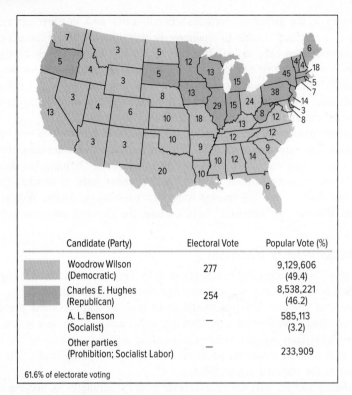

Candidate (Party)	Electoral Vote	Popular Vote (%)
Woodrow Wilson (Democratic)	277	9,129,606 (49.4)
Charles E. Hughes (Republican)	254	8,538,221 (46.2)
A. L. Benson (Socialist)	—	585,113 (3.2)
Other parties (Prohibition; Socialist Labor)	—	233,909

61.6% of electorate voting

THE ELECTION OF 1916 Woodrow Wilson had good reason to be concerned about his reelection prospects in 1916. He had won only about 42 percent of the vote in 1912, and the Republican Party—which had been divided four years earlier—was now reunited around the popular Charles Evans Hughes. In the end, Wilson won a narrow victory over Hughes with just under 50 percent of the vote and a similarly narrow margin in the electoral college. Note the striking regional character of his victory. • *How did Wilson use the war in Europe to bolster his election prospects?*

as well. The president hoped that American intervention, by earning him a seat at the postwar negotiating table, would usher in a new era. In the place of militarism, secret alliances, violence, and autocracy would come democracy, freedom of travel and commerce, open diplomacy, and self-determination.

President Wilson articulated this vision on the rainy evening of April 2, 1917, when he asked Congress for a declaration of war. German U-boat warfare had claimed American lives and treasure. The country's honor could not tolerate such affronts. But aware of divisions in public opinion, Wilson sought to invest the moment with higher meaning. The war would make the world "safe for democracy" and safeguard "the rights of mankind." America would not fight for material gain or territory, the president said, but to guarantee a future of free trade, self-governance, peace, and justice. Opposition to the war would not be tolerated. "If there should be disloyalty," he warned, "it will be dealt with with a firm hand of repression."

Wilson's view carried the session, but dissenters spoke up. Some midwesterners and southerners saw corporate profits, not honor, at stake in the Atlantic. A few pacifists, including the first woman elected to Congress, Jeannette Rankin, a Republican from Montana, argued that no war was worth the costs. Still others argued the United States should stay out of Europe's affairs. When the declaration of war finally passed on April 6, six senators and fifty representatives voted against it.

"OVER THERE"

European armies on both sides of the conflict were decimated and exhausted by the time of Woodrow Wilson's declaration of war. The Allies looked desperately to the United States for help in breaking the stalemate.

MOBILIZING THE MILITARY

By the spring of 1917, Great Britain was suffering such vast losses from German submarines that its ability to receive vital supplies from across the Atlantic was in jeopardy. Within weeks of joining the war, the United States had begun to alter the balance. A fleet of American destroyers aided the British navy in attacking the U-boats and planting antisubmarine mines in the North Sea. The results were dramatic. Losses among Allied ships dropped from nearly 900,000 tons in the month of April 1917 to 350,000 by December 1917 and 112,000 by October 1918.

Many Americans had hoped that providing naval assistance alone would be enough to end the war, but it quickly became clear that a major commitment of American ground forces would be necessary as well. Britain and France had few remaining reserves. After the Bolshevik Revolution in November 1917, a new communist government, led by V. I. Lenin, negotiated a hasty and costly peace between Russia and the Central Powers. That freed German troops to fight on the western front.

The United States did not have a large enough standing army to provide the necessary ground forces in 1917. Even amid recruitment efforts (see "Consider the Source: Race, Gender, and World War I Posters"), enlistments proved inadequate. Only a national draft could provide the needed men. Despite protests, Wilson won passage of the **Selective Service Act** in mid-May. From a prewar total of 121,000 enlisted soldiers, the army grew to more than 4 million, 2 million of whom went to France. Draftees comprised 72 percent of all American soldiers in the war—a far higher percentage than on either side of the Civil War.

The typical American soldier (or "doughboy," a term dating to the mid-nineteenth century but of mysterious origins) in the Great War was a white, single, poorly educated draftee in his early twenties. Women were barred from regular military service, but could sign up for things like nursing, clerical work, and telephone operation. As many as 400,000 African Americans joined the military, the vast majority conscripted. But this was a strict Jim Crow army. Units were segregated, white officers were in charge, and blacks generally performed menial labor. Yet two combat divisions, the Ninety-Second and Ninety-Third, were composed entirely of African American soldiers.

In training camps around the country, selectees learned how to be soldiers. They marched and drilled and practiced maneuvers. In case they weren't sure what they were fighting for, every backpack contained a copy of Wilson's war message. For the huge number of foreign-born soldiers—approaching 20 percent of the wartime army, speaking forty-six different languages—military service acted as a tool of assimilation, to the delight of nativists. Another target of assimilative energies, Native Americans, sent about twelve thousand men into the military. Meanwhile the draftees received moral instruction as well. Progressives in the government, as well as thousands of American parents, worried about the sexual purity of the soldier. One social hygiene poster implored the soldier to "Remember— the folks at home. Go back to them physically fit and morally clean. Don't allow a whore to smirch your record."

RACE, GENDER, AND WORLD WAR I POSTERS

Much can be learned about a society's values from how it handles the mobilization of the home front during wartime. Nations typically clarify the terms of citizenship and service—asking some people to fight, some to stay home and support the effort in other ways. As part of the broad national campaign to mobilize public opinion and service during World War I, American officials disseminated the two posters reproduced here. One urged enlistment, the other the purchase of war bonds.

UNDERSTAND, ANALYZE, & EVALUATE

1. How do the posters use images of women or the home to encourage either enlistment or financial support for the war?

2. What do these posters say about contemporary understandings of gender roles? What did the state and society expect from men? What did they expect from women?

3. Like almost all recruiting posters of World War I, these two depict white people—despite the fact that many African Americans and ethnic minorities served as well. What does that say about mainstream attitudes toward race and ethnicity during World War I?

(Source: Library of Congress, Prints and Photographs Division [LC-USZC4-1124])

(Source: Library of Congress, Prints and Photographs Division [LC-USZC4-9884])

The Yanks Are Coming

The United States had sent the first units of the American Expeditionary Forces (AEF) to France in June 1917 under the leadership of General John J. Pershing, but American soldiers weren't heavily implicated in the fighting until the next year. In March 1918, the Germans launched nimble thrusts into the Allied defenses. Under the French commander of Allied forces, Ferdinand Foch, Pershing's troops halted the German offensive at Cantigny and Château-Thierry. Then the American Second Division, including a brigade of marines, lost 9,800 casualties in a savage but successful fight to drive the Germans from Belleau Wood, a place that would live on in Marine Corps lore. In July the Germans attacked again, and at the Second Battle of the Marne, the Allies fought together to repulse them. Over the course of that summer, the influx of American divisions helped the Allies push the German army back roughly to its original position.

By September, with American troops plentiful and the Germans depleted, the Allies prepared to advance toward Germany. Pershing withdrew many of his divisions to the Americans' own sector on the southern edge of the front. From that position, the doughboys took the Saint-Mihiel salient, a bulge into Allied lines that the Germans had held for years. Foch then ordered Pershing's divisions to their place in the war's final Allied push, the Meuse-Argonne offensive. Beginning on September 26, more than a million American doughboys—the great majority of them seeing combat for the first time—advanced against the Germans, while to the northwest the British and French undertook coordinated campaigns. The Germans sagged but held, and something like **trench warfare** set in for a brief time.

Meanwhile Choctaw code talkers relayed messages in their native tongue to thwart German attempts to tap into American telephone lines and decipher battle orders. And black combat units, some fighting under French command, acquitted themselves honorably in the war's late battles, though white military leadership magnified their isolated failures. The Ninety-Second Division in particular suffered charges of poor martial performance as well as unwarranted rumors of rape, and authorities ultimately curtailed the mingling of black doughboys and white Frenchwomen. But the Ninety-Third's 369th Infantry or "Harlem Hell Fighters," fighting with the French, earned 170 Croix de Guerre awards for valor for their part in the war's final offensives.

In October, the push was rolling again, but those weeks of the Meuse-Argonne offensive were terrible for the Americans, with 27,000 men killed. "Those of us who still lived," wrote one doughboy, "who were able to move, in body if not in spirit, wanted to drop to our knees and implore God to stop this horrible slaughter of mankind." Slow transportation, communication glitches, the hasty training of soldiers, logistical bottlenecks, friendly fire accidents, and more generally, the growing pains of a mass American army operating overseas, all combined to generate casualties and low morale among the doughboy rank-and-file and hamper the fighting ability of the AEF. Yet by November the push had driven the Germans back, their civilian population suffering from an effective blockade, their soldiers captured by the hundreds of thousands, their U-boats more or less neutralized by a convoy system, and their rear harassed by airplane bombardment. Facing invasion, the Germans sought an armistice. Early on the morning of November 11, 1918, while men along the front were still dying, representatives of the warring parties signed an armistice in a railway car in the French forest. The four-year "war to end all wars" shuddered to a close.

AMERICA IN WORLD WAR I: THE WESTERN FRONT, 1918 These maps show the principal battles in which the United States participated in the last year of World War I. The small map on the upper right helps locate the area of conflict within the larger European landscape. The larger map at left shows the long, snaking red line of the western front in France—stretching from the border between France and southwest Germany all the way to the northeast border between Belgium and France. Along that vast line, the two sides had been engaged in murderous, inconclusive warfare for over three years by the time the Americans arrived. Beginning in the spring and summer of 1918, bolstered by reinforcements from the United States, the Allies began to win a series of important victories that finally enabled them to begin pushing the Germans back. American troops, as this map makes clear, were decisive along the southern part of the front. • *At what point did the Germans begin to consider putting an end to the war?*

The New Technology of Warfare

World War I was a proving ground for a range of new military technologies. The trench warfare that characterized the conflict was a result of the enormous destructive power of newly improved machine guns and higher-powered artillery. It was no longer feasible to send troops out into an open field, where new weaponry would slaughter them in an instant. Trenches sheltered troops while allowing limited, and usually inconclusive, fighting. But technology overtook the trenches, too, as mobile weapons—tanks and flamethrowers—proved capable of piercing entrenched positions. Most terrible of all, perhaps, new chemical weapons—poisonous mustard gas, which required troops to carry gas masks at all times—made it possible to attack entrenched soldiers without direct combat.

The new forms of technological warfare required elaborate maintenance. Faster machine guns needed more ammunition. Motorized vehicles required fuel, spare parts, and mechanics capable of servicing them. The logistical difficulties of supply became a major factor in planning tactics and strategy. Late in the war, when the Allied armies were advancing toward Germany, they frequently had to stop for days at a time to wait for their equipment to catch up with them.

(Source: National Archives and Records Administration)

LIFE IN THE TRENCHES For most British, French, German, and, to a lesser extent, American troops in France, the most debilitating part of World War I was the misery of life in the trenches. Some young men lived in these cold, wet, muddy dugouts for months, even years, surrounded by filth, sharing their space with vermin, eating mostly rotten food. Occasional attacks to try to dislodge the enemy from its trenches usually ended in failure and became the scenes of terrible slaughter.

World War I was the first conflict in which airplanes played a significant role. The planes themselves were relatively simple and not very maneuverable, but antiaircraft technology was not yet highly developed either, so their effectiveness was significant. Planes served various functions: bombing enemy lines, engaging other planes in "dogfights," and performing reconaissance.

The most modern part of the military during World War I was the navy. Battleships emerged that made use of new technologies such as turbine propulsion, hydraulic gun controls, electric light and power, wireless telegraphy, and advanced navigational aids. Submarines, which had made a brief appearance in the American Civil War, now became significant weapons (as the German U-boat campaign in 1915 and 1916 made clear). The new submarines were driven by diesel engines that were more compact than steam engines and used fuel that was less explosive than that of gasoline engines.

The new technologies were responsible for the war's truly stunning statistics of death. Russia lost 1.8 million soldiers; Germany, 2 million; France, 1.4 million; the British Empire, 1 million; Austria-Hungary, 1.5 million; Italy, 460,000. Something like 5 million civilians died under the stress of war—by violence or slower means—though the exact number is hard to know. The United States lost 116,000 soldiers, about half of those in combat, the others to disease. Some perished in the 1918 influenza pandemic that ultimately claimed an estimated 50 to 100 million lives worldwide.

Although only in the war briefly, the Americans had played a significant role in the victory. Their casualty rates in the periods of intense fighting approximated or exceeded those of their allies. The prospect of more doughboys arriving in the future surely affected the German leadership's capitulation in 1918. The British, Russian, and French contributions, of course, dwarfed the American one in sheer numbers. But Wilson's army had acquitted itself well enough to earn him a seat at the negotiating table—one of his ambitions all along.

Organizing the Economy for War

By the time the war ended, the federal government had appropriated $32 billion for war expenses—a staggering sum at the time. The entire federal budget had seldom exceeded $1 billion before 1915, and as recently as 1910 the nation's entire gross national product had been only $35 billion. To raise the money, the government relied on two devices. First, it launched a major drive to solicit loans from the American people by selling "Liberty Bonds" to the public. By 1920, the sale of bonds, accompanied by elaborate patriotic appeals, had produced $23 billion. At the same time, new taxes were bringing in an additional sum of nearly $10 billion—some of it coming from levies on the "excess profits" of corporations but much of it coming from new, steeply graduated income and inheritance taxes that ultimately rose as high as 70 percent in some brackets.

An even greater challenge was to organize the economy to meet war needs. In 1916, Wilson established the Council of National Defense, composed of members of his cabinet, and the Civilian Advisory Commission, which set up local defense councils in every state and locality. But this early administrative structure soon proved completely unworkable, and members of the council urged a more centralized approach. The administrative structure that slowly emerged was dominated by a series of "war boards," one to oversee the railroads, one to supervise fuel supplies (largely coal), another to handle food (a board that elevated to prominence the young engineer and business executive Herbert Hoover). The boards generally succeeded in meeting essential war needs without paralyzing the domestic economy.

The **War Industries Board** was created in July 1917 to coordinate government purchases of military supplies. Casually organized at first, it stumbled badly until March 1918, when Wilson restructured it and placed it under the control of Wall Street financier Bernard Baruch. He decided which factories would convert to the production of which war materials and set prices for the goods they produced. When materials were scarce, Baruch decided to whom they should go. When corporations were competing for government contracts, he chose among them.

(©Margaret Bourke-White/The LIFE Picture Collection/Getty Images)

WOMEN INDUSTRIAL WORKERS   In World War II, such women were often called "Rosie the Riveter." Their presence in these previously all-male work environments was no less startling to Americans during World War I. These women are shown working with acetylene torches to bevel armor plate for tanks. The photographer was Margaret Bourke-White, who herself broke gender boundaries as the first female photojournalist for *Life* magazine and the first female war correspondent.

Baruch viewed himself, openly and explicitly, as a partner of business; and within the WIB, businessmen themselves—the so-called dollar-a-year men, who took paid leave from their corporate jobs and worked for the government for a token salary—supervised the affairs of the private economy.

The National War Labor Board, established in April 1918, served as the final mediator of labor disputes. It pressured industry to grant important concessions to workers: an eight-hour day, the maintenance of minimal living standards, equal pay for women doing equal work, recognition of the right of unions to organize and bargain collectively. In return, it insisted that workers forgo strikes and that employers not engage in lockouts.

THE SEARCH FOR SOCIAL UNITY

Government leaders were painfully aware that public sentiment about the war was sharply divided. The most conspicuous official effort to support the war was a vast propaganda campaign orchestrated by the Committee on Public Information (CPI), under the direction of the progressive journalist George Creel. The CPI supervised the distribution of over 75 million pieces of printed material and controlled much of the information available for newspapers and magazines. Creel encouraged journalists to exercise "self-censorship" when reporting war news, and most complied by covering the war largely as the government wished. By 1918, government-distributed posters and films were offering lurid portrayals of the savagery of the Germans. In this climate, songwriters and other artists produced popular works that heavily favored the war. (See "Patterns of Popular Culture: George M. Cohan, 'Over There,' 1917.")

GEORGE M. COHAN, "OVER THERE," 1917

Music was one of the richest forms of American popular culture in the early twentieth century, much of it emanating from New York City companies in a neighborhood known as Tin Pan Alley. Lyricists and composers, eager to peddle their sheet music widely, had long captured popular attitudes toward the issues of their day. In 1915, with men dying in the Great War at a staggering rate, songwriters churned out such antimilitarist numbers as "I Didn't Raise My Boy to Be a Soldier" and "Don't Take My Darling Boy Away!"

In April 1917, however, President Wilson's demand for unanimity changed Tin Pan Alley's tune. Songs now demonized Kaiser Wilhelm II, the emperor of Germany, glorified the American doughboy and sentimentalized the home-front family. Other tunes became anthems of American confidence and strength, none more so than George M. Cohan's "Over There." Even before that hit—which became the best-known song of the war—Cohan was a leading figure in the American entertainment industry, a prolific creator and performer of Broadway productions, and the composer of hundreds of original songs, including classics such as "Yankee Doodle Boy."

Written just after Wilson's war address of April 2, "Over There" offered a jaunty soundtrack for American intervention. It was sung on the home front and in basic training; doughboys in France found it in songbooks issued by various civilian agencies. "Over There" represented a prominent strain in public culture of 1917—deeply patriotic, optimistic, and sentimental—even as many Americans worried quietly about what this new war would mean for them and their families.

Johnnie, get your gun,
Get your gun, get your gun,
Take it on the run,
On the run, on the run.
Hear them calling, you and me,
Every son of liberty.
Hurry right away,
No delay, no delay,
Make your daddy glad
To have had such a lad.
Tell your sweetheart not to pine,
To be proud her boy's in line.

Chorus
Over there, over there
Send the word, send the word over there
That the Yanks are coming,
The Yanks are coming,
The drums rum-tumming
Ev'rywhere.
So prepare, say a pray'r,
Send the word, send the word to beware.
We'll be over, we're coming over,
And we won't come back till it's over
Over there.
Johnnie get your gun,
Get your gun, get your gun,
Johnnie show the Hun
Who's a son of a gun.
Hoist the flag and let her fly,
Yankee Doodle do or die.
Pack your little kit,

Show your grit, do your bit.
Yankee Doodle fill the ranks,
From the towns and the tanks.
Make your mother proud of you,
And the old Red, White and Blue. •

(repeat chorus twice)

Source: Cohan, George M., "Over There" (public domain).

The government also suppressed dissent. CPI-financed advertisements in magazines implored citizens to report to the authorities any evidence among their neighbors of disloyalty, pessimism, or yearning for peace. The Espionage Act of 1917 gave the government new tools with which to combat spying, sabotage, or obstruction of the war effort (crimes that were often broadly defined). The Sabotage Act and the Sedition Act, both passed in 1918, expanded the meaning of the Espionage Act to make illegal *any* public expression of opposition to the war; in practice, they allowed officials to prosecute anyone who criticized the president or the government.

The most frequent targets of the new legislation were anticapitalist groups such as the Socialist Party and the Industrial Workers of the World (IWW). Many Americans had favored the repression of socialists and radicals even before the war; the wartime policies now made it possible to move against them with full legal sanction. Eugene V. Debs, the leader of the Socialist Party and an opponent of the war, was sentenced to ten years in prison in 1918. (A pardon by President Warren G. Harding freed him in 1921.) Big Bill Haywood and members of the IWW were energetically prosecuted. Only by fleeing to the Soviet Union did Haywood avoid imprisonment. In all, more than 1,500 people were arrested in 1918 for the crime of criticizing the government or the war.

State and local governments, corporations, universities, and private citizens contributed as well to the climate of repression. A cluster of citizens' groups emerged to mobilize "respectable" members of communities to root out disloyalty. The greatest target of abuse was the German American community. Most German Americans supported the American war effort once it began, but public opinion remained hostile. A campaign to purge society of all things German quickly gathered speed, at times assuming ludicrous forms. Performances of German music were frequently banned. German foods such as sauerkraut and bratwurst were renamed "liberty cabbage" and "liberty sausage." German books were removed from library shelves. Courses in the German language were dropped from school curricula. Germans were routinely fired from jobs in war industries, lest they "sabotage" important tasks.

THE SEARCH FOR A NEW WORLD ORDER

Woodrow Wilson had led the nation into war promising a just and stable peace at its conclusion. Even before the armistice, he was preparing to lead the fight for what he considered a democratic postwar settlement.

THE FOURTEEN POINTS

On January 8, 1918, Wilson appeared before Congress to present the principles for which he believed the nation was fighting. He grouped the war aims under fourteen headings, widely known as the **Fourteen Points**. They fell into three broad categories. First, Wilson's proposals contained a series of eight specific recommendations for adjusting postwar boundaries and establishing new nations to replace the defunct Austro-Hungarian and Ottoman Empires. Second, five general principles would govern international conduct in the future: freedom of the seas, open covenants instead of secret treaties, reductions in armaments, free trade, and impartial mediation of colonial claims. Finally, there was a proposal for a **League of Nations** that would help implement these new principles and territorial adjustments and resolve future controversies.

Wilson's international vision ultimately enchanted not only much of his own generation (in both America and Europe) but also members of generations to come. It reflected his belief that the world was as capable of just and efficient government as were individual nations—that once the international community accepted certain basic principles of conduct and constructed modern institutions to implement them, the world could live in peace.

Despite Wilson's confidence, leaders of the Allied powers were preparing to resist him even before the armistice was signed. Britain and France, in particular, were in no mood for a generous peace. At the same time, Wilson was encountering problems at home. In 1918, with the war almost over, Wilson tied support of his peace plans to the election of Democrats to Congress in November. Days later, the Republicans captured majorities in both houses. Domestic economic troubles, more than international issues, had been the most important factor in the voting; but the results damaged his ability to claim broad popular support for his peace plans. Wilson further antagonized the Republicans when he refused to appoint any important member of their party to the negotiating team attending the peace conference in Paris.

The Paris Peace Conference

When Wilson entered Paris on December 13, 1918, he was greeted, some claimed, by the largest crowd in the history of France. The peace conference itself, however, proved less satisfying.

The principal figures in the negotiations were the leaders of the victorious Allied nations: President Wilson; David Lloyd George, prime minister of Great Britain; Georges Clemenceau, prime minister of France; and Vittorio Orlando, prime minister of Italy.

From the beginning, Wilson's idealism competed with his counterparts' national self-interest, thirst for revenge, and fears of the unstable situation in eastern Europe and the threat of communism. Russia, whose new Bolshevik government was still fighting anti-Bolshevik counterrevolutionaries, was unrepresented in Paris. But the radical threat it seemed to pose to Western governments was never far from the minds of the delegates.

In this tense and often vindictive atmosphere, Wilson was unable to win approval of many of his broad principles or to prevent the other allies from imposing punitive reparations on Germany. Wilson did manage to win some important victories in Paris in setting boundaries and dealing with former colonies. But his most visible triumph, and the one most important to him, was the creation of a permanent international organization to oversee world affairs and prevent future wars. On January 25, 1919, the Allies voted to accept the "covenant" of the League of Nations.

The Ratification Battle

Wilson presented the Treaty of Versailles, so named for the palace outside Paris where the agreement was signed, to the Senate on July 10, 1919. But members of that chamber had many objections. Some—the so-called irreconcilables—believed that America should remain free of binding foreign entanglements. But many other opponents were principally concerned with constructing a winning issue for the Republicans in 1920. Most notable of these was Senator **Henry Cabot Lodge** of Massachusetts, the powerful chair of the Foreign Relations Committee, who loathed the president and used every possible tactic to obstruct the treaty.

Public sentiment clearly favored ratification, so at first Lodge could do little more than play for time. Gradually, however, his opposition to the treaty crystallized into a series of "reservations"—amendments to the League covenant further limiting American obligations to the organization. Wilson might still have won approval at this point if he had agreed to some relatively minor changes in the language of the treaty. But the president refused to yield.

When he realized the Senate would not budge, Wilson embarked on a grueling, cross-country speaking tour to arouse public support for the treaty. For more than three weeks, he traveled over 8,000 miles by train, speaking as often as four times a day, resting hardly at all. Finally, he reached the end of his strength. After speaking at Pueblo, Colorado, on September 25, 1919, he collapsed with severe headaches.

Canceling the rest of his itinerary, he rushed back to Washington, where, a few days later, he suffered a major stroke. For two weeks, Wilson was close to death; for six weeks more, he was so seriously ill that he was virtually unable to work. His wife and his doctor formed an almost impenetrable barrier around him, shielding the president from any official pressures that might impede his recovery.

Wilson ultimately recovered enough to resume a limited official schedule, but he was essentially an invalid for the remaining eighteen months of his presidency. His condition only intensified his tendency to view public issues in moral terms and resist any attempts at compromise. When the Foreign Relations Committee finally sent the treaty to the Senate, recommending nearly fifty amendments and reservations, Wilson refused to consider any of them. The effort to win ratification failed.

In the aftermath of this defeat, Wilson became convinced that the 1920 national election would serve as a "solemn referendum" on the League of Nations. But the efforts by Lodge and others had defeated American membership in the League for good. What was more, public interest in the peace process had begun to fade as a series of other crises claimed attention.

A SOCIETY IN TURMOIL

Even during the Paris Peace Conference, many Americans were concerned less about international matters than about turbulent events at home. Some of this unease was a legacy of the almost hysterical social atmosphere of the war years, some of it was a response to issues that surfaced after the armistice.

THE UNSTABLE ECONOMY

The war ended sooner than almost anyone had anticipated. Without warning, without planning, the nation lurched into the difficult task of economic reconversion. At first, the boom continued, but accompanied by raging inflation. Through most of 1919 and 1920, prices rose at an average of more than 15 percent a year. Finally, late in 1920, the economic bubble burst as inflation began killing the market for consumer goods. Between 1920 and 1921, the gross national product declined nearly 10 percent; 100,000 businesses went bankrupt; and nearly 5 million Americans lost their jobs.

Well before this severe recession began, labor unrest increased dramatically. The raging inflation of 1919 wiped out the modest wage gains workers had achieved during the war; many laborers were worried about job security as veterans returned to the workforce; arduous working conditions continued to be a source of discontent. Employers aggravated the resentment by using the end of the war to rescind benefits they had been forced to concede to workers in 1917 and 1918—most notably, recognition of unions. The year 1919, therefore, saw an unprecedented strike wave. In January, a walkout by shipyard workers in Seattle, Washington, evolved into a general strike that brought the entire city to a virtual standstill. In September, the Boston police force struck to demand recognition of its union. With its police off the job, Boston erupted in violence and looting. Governor Calvin Coolidge called in the National Guard to restore order and attracted national acclaim by declaring, "There is no right to strike against the public safety."

Coolidge's statement tapped into a broad middle-class hostility to unions and strikes. That hostility played a part in defeating the greatest strike of 1919: a steel strike that began in September, when 350,000 steelworkers in several Midwestern cities demanded an eight-hour day and union recognition. The long and bitter steel strike climaxed in a riot in Gary, Indiana, in which eighteen strikers were killed. Steel executives managed to keep most plants running with nonunion labor, and public opinion was so hostile to the strikers that the American Federation of Labor, at first supportive of the strike, timidly repudiated it. By January, the strike—like most of the others in 1919—had collapsed.

The Demands of African Americans

Four hundred thousand black World War I veterans came home in 1919 and marched down the main streets of cities. And then in New York and elsewhere they marched again through the streets of black neighborhoods such as Harlem, led by jazz bands and cheered by thousands of African Americans. They hoped the glory of black heroism in the war would make it impossible for white society to continue its mistreatment of African Americans.

As it turned out, the fact that black soldiers had fought in the war had almost no impact on white attitudes. Unfounded stories of black combat cowardice circulated in the popular media, reinforcing what were already entrenched prejudices. But the war profoundly affected black attitudes, accentuated African American bitterness, and increased the determination to fight for civil rights. During the war, nearly half a million blacks had migrated from the rural South to industrial cities, often enticed by northern "labor agents," who offered free transportation, in search of the factory jobs the war was generating. This was the beginning of what became known as the **Great Migration**. Large black communities arose in northern cities, part of the broader twentieth-century transformation of the black population from a generally southern rural one to a northern urban one. African American veterans in these communities helped organize the interwar civil rights movement and set precedents for activism that came later.

By 1919, the racial climate had become tense. In the South, lynchings suddenly increased. More than seventy blacks, some of them war veterans, died at the hands of white mobs in 1919 alone. In the North, black factory workers faced widespread layoffs as returning white veterans displaced them from their jobs. And as whites became convinced that black workers with lower wage demands were hurting them economically, animosity grew.

Wartime riots in East St. Louis and elsewhere were a prelude to a summer of much worse racial violence in 1919. In Chicago, a black teenager swimming in Lake Michigan on a hot July day happened to drift toward a white beach. Whites onshore allegedly stoned

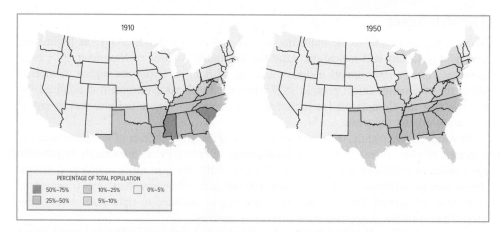

AFRICAN AMERICAN MIGRATION, 1910–1950   Two great waves of migration produced a dramatic redistribution of the African American population in the first half of the twentieth century—one around the time of World War I, the other during and after World War II. The map on the left shows the almost exclusive concentration of African Americans in the South as late as 1910. The map on the right shows both the tremendous increase of black populations in northern states by 1950, and the relative decline of black populations in parts of the South. Note in particular the changes in Mississippi and South Carolina. • *Why did the wars produce such significant migration out of the South?*

him unconscious; he sank and drowned. Angry African Americans gathered in crowds and marched into white neighborhoods to retaliate. Whites formed even larger crowds and roamed into mostly black neighborhoods. For more than a week, Chicago was virtually at war. In the end, 38 people had died—15 whites and 23 blacks—and 537 were injured. Over 1,000 people were left homeless. The Chicago riot was the worst but not the only racial violence during the so-called red summer of 1919. In all, 120 people died in such racial outbreaks in little more than three months.

Racially motivated urban riots were not new. But the 1919 riots were different in one respect: they did not just involve white people attacking blacks, but also blacks fighting back. The NAACP signaled this change by urging blacks not just to demand government protection but also to defend themselves. The poet Claude McKay, one of the major figures of what would soon be known as the Harlem Renaissance, wrote a poem after the Chicago riot called "If We Must Die":

> Like men we'll face the murderous cowardly pack.
> Pressed to the wall, dying, but fighting back.

At the same time, a black Jamaican, **Marcus Garvey**, began to attract a wide following in the United States with an ideology of black nationalism. Garvey encouraged African Americans to reject assimilation into white society and develop pride in their own race and culture. His Universal Negro Improvement Association (UNIA) launched a chain of black-owned grocery stores and pressed for the creation of other black businesses. Eventually, Garvey began urging his supporters to leave America and return to Africa, where they could create a new society of their own. In the early 1920s, the Garvey movement experienced explosive growth, but it began to decline after Garvey was indicted in 1923 on charges of business fraud. He was deported to Jamaica two years later. But the allure of black nationalism survived in black culture long after Garvey was gone.

THE RED SCARE

Many Americans regarded the industrial warfare and racial violence of 1919 as frightening omens of instability and radicalism. After the Russian Revolution of November 1917, communism was no longer simply a theory, but the basis of an important regime. Concerns about the communist threat grew in 1919 when the Bolshevik government announced the formation of the Communist International (or Comintern), whose purpose was to export revolution around the world.

In America, meanwhile, there was, in addition to the great number of imagined radicals, a modest number of real ones. These small groups of radicals were presumably responsible for a series of bombings in the spring of 1919. In April, the post office intercepted several dozen parcels addressed to leading businessmen and politicians that were triggered to explode when opened. Two months later, eight bombs exploded in eight cities within minutes of one another, suggesting a nationwide conspiracy.

The combination of strikes and the Comintern announcement produced what became known as the **Red Scare**. Nearly thirty states enacted new peacetime sedition laws imposing harsh penalties on promoters of revolution. Spontaneous acts of violence against supposed radicals occurred in some communities, and universities and other institutions tried to expel radicals from their midst. But the greatest agent of the Red Scare was the federal government. In January 1920, Attorney General A. Mitchell Palmer and his ambitious young assistant, J. Edgar Hoover, orchestrated the biggest of the **Palmer Raids**. This particular police action against alleged radical centers resulted in the arrest of more than 6,000 people, and authorities made many of the searches and arrests in 1919 and 1920 without proper warrants. Most of those arrested were ultimately released, but about 500 who were not American citizens were deported. Later in 1920, a bomb exploded on Wall Street, killing thirty-eight people. No one was ever convicted of this bombing.

The ferocity of the Red Scare gradually abated, but its effects lingered well into the 1920s. In May 1920, two Italian immigrants, **Nicola Sacco and Bartolomeo Vanzetti**, were charged with the murder of a paymaster in South Braintree, Massachusetts. The case against them was weak and suffused with nativist prejudices and fears, but because both men were confessed anarchists, they faced widespread public presumption of guilt. They were convicted and eventually sentenced to death. Over the next several years, public support for Sacco and Vanzetti grew to formidable proportions. But on August 23, 1927, amid protests in the United States and around the world, Sacco and Vanzetti, still proclaiming their innocence, died in the electric chair.

REFUTING THE RED SCARE

One result of postwar turmoil was the emergence of a vigorous defense of civil liberties that helped give new force to the Bill of Rights. The heavy-handed and often illegal actions of the federal government after the war created a powerful backlash. It destroyed the career of A. Mitchell Palmer. It almost nipped in the bud the ascent of J. Edgar Hoover. It damaged the Democratic Party. And it led to an organization committed to protecting civil liberties: the National Civil Liberties Bureau, launched in 1917, which in 1920 was renamed the American Civil Liberties Union (ACLU) and which remains a prominent institution today. At the same time, members of the Supreme Court—most notably Justices Oliver Wendell Holmes and Louis Brandeis—gradually moved to defend unpopular speech. The clash of "fighting faiths," Holmes wrote in a dissent in 1920, was best resolved "by free trade in ideas—that the best test of truth is . . . the competition of the market." This and other dissents eventually became law as other justices committed themselves to a robust defense of speech, however unpopular.

THE RETREAT FROM IDEALISM

On August 26, 1920, the Nineteenth Amendment, guaranteeing women the right to vote, became part of the Constitution. To the suffrage movement, this was the culmination of nearly a century of struggle. To many progressives, it seemed to promise new support for reform. Yet the Nineteenth Amendment marked not the beginning of a new era of progressive reform but the end of an earlier one.

Economic problems, labor unrest, racial tensions, and the intensity of the antiradicalism they helped create—all combined in the years immediately following the war to produce a general sense of disillusionment. That became particularly apparent in the election of 1920. Woodrow Wilson hoped the campaign would be a referendum on the League of Nations, and the Democratic candidates, Governor James M. Cox of Ohio and Assistant Secretary of the Navy Franklin D. Roosevelt, dutifully tried to keep Wilson's ideals alive. The Republican presidential nominee, Warren Gamaliel Harding, an obscure Ohio senator, offered a different vision. He embraced no soaring ideals, only a vague promise of a return, as he later phrased it, to "normalcy." Harding won in a landslide, with 61 percent of the popular vote and victories in every state outside the South. The party made major gains in Congress as well. To many Americans it seemed that, for better or worse, a new age had begun.

CONCLUSION

Presidents Roosevelt, Taft, and Wilson contributed to a continuation, and indeed an expansion, of America's active role in international affairs, in part as an effort to abet the growth of American capitalism and in part as an attempt to impose American ideas of morality and democracy on other parts of the world. Similar mixtures of ideals and self-interest soon guided the United States into a great world war.

For a time after the outbreak of war in Europe in 1914, most Americans—President Wilson among them—wanted nothing so much as to stay out of the conflict. But as the war dragged on and the tactics of Britain and Germany began to impinge on American trade and access to the seas, the United States found itself drawn into the conflict. In April 1917, Congress agreed to the president's request that the United States enter the war as an ally of Britain, France, and Russia.

Within a few months of the arrival of American troops in Europe, Germany agreed to an armistice and the war ended. American casualties, although not inconsiderable, were negligible compared to the millions suffered by the European combatants.

Wilson's bold and idealistic dream of a peace based on international cooperation suffered a painful death. The Treaty of Versailles, which he helped draft, contained a provision for a League of Nations, which Wilson believed could transform the international order. But the League quickly became controversial in the United States, and despite strenuous efforts by the president—which hastened his own physical collapse—the treaty was defeated in the Senate. In the aftermath of that traumatic battle, the American people turned away from Wilson and his ideals and faced a very different era.

The social experience of the war in the United States was, on the whole, dismaying to reformers. Although the war enhanced some reform efforts—most notably prohibition and woman suffrage—it also introduced an atmosphere of intolerance and repression into American life. The aftermath of the war was even more disheartening to progressives, because of both a brief but highly destabilizing recession and a wave of repression directed against labor, radicals, African Americans, and immigrants.

KEY TERMS/PEOPLE/PLACES/EVENTS

Allies 522
Central Powers 522
Dollar Diplomacy 520
Fourteen Points 534
Great Migration 536
Henry Cabot Lodge 535
John J. Pershing 521

League of Nations 534
Lusitania 523
Marcus Garvey 537
Nicola Sacco and
  Bartolomeo Vanzetti 538
Palmer Raids 538
Panama Canal 519

Pancho Villa 521
Red Scare 538
Roosevelt Corollary 519
Selective Service Act 525
trench warfare 527
War Industries Board 530
Zimmermann Telegram 524

RECALL AND REFLECT

1. Who opposed U.S. involvement in World War I and why?
2. How did the Wilson administration mobilize the nation for war?
3. What effect did the war have on race relations in the United States?
4. What were some of the ways that U.S. participation in the Great War changed American society?
5. Why did the battle over ratification of the Treaty of Versailles come to an impasse? Why did the Senate ultimately reject the treaty? What was the significance of that rejection?

22 | THE NEW ERA

THE NEW ECONOMY
THE NEW CULTURE
A CONFLICT OF CULTURES
REPUBLICAN GOVERNMENT

LOOKING AHEAD

1. How did the technological innovations of the early twentieth century affect industry and American social life of the 1920s?
2. What were some of the cultural conflicts of the 1920s, and what caused them?
3. Is the term the *New Era* a fitting description of the 1920s?

IN POPULAR CULTURE, THE 1920s are often remembered as an era of affluence, conservatism, and cultural frivolity. In reality, the decade was a time of significant, even dramatic, social, economic, and political change. The American economy not only enjoyed spectacular growth but also developed new forms of organization. Many Americans reshaped themselves to reflect the increasingly urban, industrial, consumer-oriented society of the United States. And American government experimented with new approaches to public policy. That was why contemporaries liked to refer to the 1920s as the "New Era"—an age in which America was becoming a modern nation.

At the same time, however, the decade saw the rise of a series of spirited, and at times effective, rebellions against the transformations in American life. The intense cultural conflicts that characterized the 1920s showed that much of American society remained unreconciled to the modernizing currents of the New Era.

1920

Prohibition begins

Harding elected
president

1922

Lewis's *Babbitt*

1923

Harding dies; Coolidge
becomes president

Harding administration
scandals revealed

1924

National Origins
Act passed

Coolidge elected
president

Ku Klux Klan
membership peaks

1925

Fitzgerald's *The
Great Gatsby*

Scopes trial

1927

First sound motion
picture, *The Jazz Singer*

1928

Hoover elected
president

THE NEW ECONOMY

After the recession of 1921–1922, the United States began a period of almost uninterrupted prosperity and economic expansion. Less visible at the time, but equally significant, was the survival and even growth of inequalities and imbalances.

TECHNOLOGY, ORGANIZATION, AND ECONOMIC GROWTH

No one could deny the remarkable feats of the American economy in the 1920s. The nation's manufacturing output rose by more than 60 percent. Per capita income grew by a third. Inflation was negligible. A mild recession in 1923 briefly interrupted the pattern of growth, but when it subsided early in 1924 the economy expanded with even greater vigor.

The economic boom was a result of many things, but one of the most important was technology. As a result of the development of the assembly line and other innovations, automobiles now became one of the most important industries in the nation, stimulating growth in such related industries as steel, rubber, and glass, tool companies, oil corporations, and road construction. The increased mobility that the automobile made possible increased the demand for suburban housing, fueling a boom in the construction industry.

Radio contributed as well to the economic growth. Early radio had been able to broadcast little besides pulses, which meant that radio communication could occur only through the Morse code. But with the discovery of the theory of modulation, pioneered by the Canadian scientist Reginald Fessenden, it became possible to transmit speech and music. Many people built their own radio sets at home for very little money, benefiting from the discovery that inexpensive crystals could receive signals over long distances. These "shortwave" radios, which allowed individual owners to establish contact with one another, marked the beginning of what later became known as ham radio. Once commercial broadcasting began, families flocked to buy more conventional radio sets powered by reliable vacuum tubes and capable of receiving high-quality signals over short and medium distances. By 1925, there were 2 million sets in American homes, and by the end of the 1920s, almost every family had one.

Commercial aviation developed slowly in the 1920s, beginning with the use of planes to deliver mail. On the whole, airplanes remained curiosities and sources of entertainment. But technological advances—the development of the radial engine and the creation of pressurized cabins—laid the groundwork for the great increase in commercial travel in the 1930s and beyond. Electronics, home appliances, plastics and synthetic fibers (such as nylon), aluminum, magnesium, oil, electric power, and other industries fueled by technological advances—all grew dramatically. Telephones continued to proliferate. By the late 1930s, there were approximately 25 million telephones in the United States, roughly one for every six people.

The seeds of future technological breakthroughs were also visible. In both England and America, scientists and engineers were working to transform primitive calculating machines into devices capable of performing more complicated tasks. By the early 1930s, researchers at MIT, led by Vannevar Bush, had created an instrument capable of performing a variety of complicated tasks—the first analog computer. A few years later, Howard Aiken, with financial assistance from Harvard and MIT, built a much more complex computer with memory, capable of multiplying eleven-digit numbers in three seconds.

Genetic research had begun in Austria in the mid-nineteenth century through the work of Gregor Mendel, a Catholic monk who performed experiments on the hybridization of vegetables in his monastery garden. His findings attracted little attention during his lifetime, but in the early twentieth century several investigators used them to help shape modern genetic research. Among the American pioneers was Thomas Hunt Morgan of Columbia University and, later, Cal Tech, whose experiments with fruit flies revealed how several genes could be transmitted together. He also revealed the way in which genes were arranged along the chromosome. His work helped open the path to understanding how genes could recombine—a critical discovery that led to more advanced experiments in hybridization and genetics.

Large sectors of American business accelerated their drive toward national organization and consolidation. Certain industries—notably those dependent on large-scale mass production, such as steel and automobiles—moved toward concentrating production in a few large firms. Other industries, less dependent on technology and less susceptible to great economies of scale, proved more resistant to consolidation.

The strenuous efforts by industrialists throughout the economy to find ways to curb competition reflected a strong fear of overcapacity. Even in the booming 1920s, industrialists remembered how rapid expansion and overproduction had helped produce recessions in 1893, 1907, and 1920. The great unrealized dream of the New Era was to find a way to stabilize the economy so that such collapses would never occur again.

WORKERS IN AN AGE OF CAPITAL

Despite the remarkable economic growth, more than two-thirds of the American people in 1929 lived at no better than what one major study described as the "minimum comfort level." Half of those were at or below the level of "subsistence and poverty."

American labor experienced both the successes and the failures of the 1920s. On the one hand, most workers saw their standard of living rise during the decade. Some employers adopted paternalistic techniques that came to be known as **welfare capitalism**. Henry Ford, for example, shortened the workweek, raised wages, and instituted paid vacations. By 1926,

(©ullstein bild/Getty Images)

FORD ASSEMBLY LINE   This image from the 1920s shows workers arrayed along the assembly, each of them responsible for a particular piece of the process. These were the laborers whom management tried to appease by the cultivation of welfare capitalism.

nearly 3 million industrial workers were eligible for at least modest pensions upon retirement. When labor grievances surfaced despite these efforts, workers could voice them through the so-called company unions that emerged in many industries—workers' councils and shop committees, organized by the corporations themselves. But welfare capitalism, in the end, gave workers no real control over their own fates. Company unions were feeble vehicles. And welfare capitalism survived only as long as industry prospered. After 1929, with the economy in crisis, the entire system collapsed.

Welfare capitalism affected only a relatively small number of firms in any case. Most laborers worked for employers who were interested primarily in keeping their labor costs low. Workers as a whole, therefore, received wage increases that were proportionately far below the growth of the economy. At the end of the decade, the average annual income of a worker remained below $1,500, when $1,800 was considered necessary to maintain a minimally decent standard of living. Only by relying on the combined earnings of several family members could many working-class families make ends meet.

The New Era was a bleak time for labor organization, in part because many unions themselves were relatively conservative and failed to adapt to the realities of the modern economy. The American Federation of Labor (AFL), led after Samuel Gompers's death by William Green, sought peaceful cooperation with employers and remained wedded to the concept of the craft union. In the meantime, the rapidly rising number of unskilled industrial workers received little attention from the craft unions.

But whatever the unions' weaknesses, the strength of the corporations was the principal reason for the absence of effective labor organization in the 1920s. After the turmoil of 1919, corporate leaders worked hard to spread the doctrine that a crucial element of democratic capitalism was the protection of the "open shop," where no worker could be required to join a union. The crusade for the open shop, meaningfully titled the **American Plan**, became a pretext for a harsh campaign of union-busting. As a result, union membership fell from more than 5 million in 1920 to under 3 million in 1929.

WOMEN AND MINORITIES IN THE WORKFORCE

A growing proportion of the workforce consisted of women, who were concentrated in what have since become known as "pink-collar" jobs—low-paying service occupations. Large numbers of women worked as secretaries, salesclerks, and telephone operators and in other nonmanual service capacities. Because technically such positions were not industrial jobs, the AFL and other labor organizations were uninterested in organizing these workers. Similarly, the half-million African Americans who had migrated from the rural South into the cities during the Great Migration after 1914 had few opportunities for union representation. The skilled crafts represented in the AFL usually excluded black workers. Partly as a result of that exclusion, most blacks worked in jobs in which the AFL took no interest at all—as janitors, dishwashers, garbage collectors, and domestics and in other service capacities. **A. Philip Randolph**'s **Brotherhood of Sleeping Car Porters** was one of the few important unions dominated and led by African Americans.

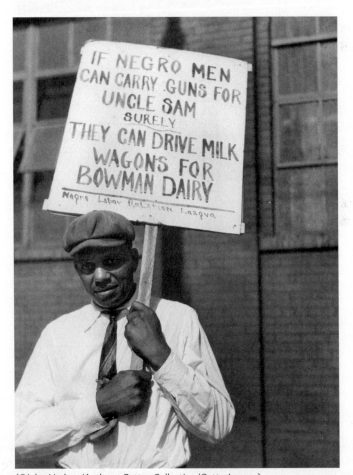

(©John Vachon/Anthony Potter Collection/Getty Images)

AFRICAN AMERICAN WORKER PROTESTING   The frail union movement among African Americans in the 1920s, led by A. Philip Randolph and others, slowly built up a constituency within the black working class. Here, an aspiring dairy worker draws attention to the unjust treatment of African American men who had demonstrated their patriotism during the war.

In the West and the Southwest, the ranks of the unskilled included considerable numbers of Asians and Hispanics. In the wake of the Chinese Exclusion Acts, Japanese immigrants increasingly replaced the Chinese in menial jobs in California. They worked on railroads, construction sites, farms, and in many other low-paying workplaces. Some Japanese

1900

1930

AREA REACHED IN:

1 hour	3 hours	┼┼┼┼┼ Railroads (1900)
		── Paved roads (1930)
2 hours	More than 3 hours	╌╌╌ Unpaved roads (1930)

BREAKING DOWN RURAL ISOLATION: THE EXPANSION OF TRAVEL HORIZONS IN OREGON, ILLINOIS This map uses the small town of Oregon, Illinois—west of Chicago—to illustrate the way in which first railroads and then automobiles reduced the isolation of rural areas in the early decades of the twentieth century. The gold and purple areas of the two maps show the territory that residents of Oregon could reach within two hours. Note how small that area was in 1900 and how much larger it was in 1930, by which time an area of over 100 square miles had become easily accessible to the town. Note, too, the significant network of paved roads in the region by 1930, few of which had existed in 1900. • *Why did automobiles do so much more than railroads to expand the travel horizons of small towns?*

managed to escape the ranks of the unskilled by forming their own small businesses or setting themselves up as truck farmers. Many of the **Issei** (Japanese immigrants) and **Nisei** (their American-born children) enjoyed significant economic success, so much so that California passed laws in 1913 and 1920 to make it more difficult for them to buy land. Other Asians, most notably Filipinos, also swelled the unskilled workforce and generated considerable hostility. Anti-Filipino riots in California beginning in 1929 helped produce legislation in 1934 virtually eliminating immigration from the Philippines.

Mexican immigrants formed a major part of the unskilled workforce throughout the Southwest and California. Nearly half a million Mexicans entered the United States in the 1920s. Most lived in California, Texas, Arizona, and New Mexico, and by 1930, most lived in cities. Large Mexican barrios grew up in Los Angeles, El Paso, San Antonio, Denver, and many other urban centers. Some of the residents found work locally in factories and shops; others traveled to mines or did migratory labor on farms but returned to the cities between jobs. Mexican workers, too, faced hostility and discrimination from the Anglo population, but there were few efforts actually to exclude them. Employers in the relatively underpopulated West needed this ready pool of low-paid and unorganized workers.

Agricultural Technology and the Plight of the Farmer

Like industry, American agriculture in the 1920s embraced new technologies. The number of tractors on American farms quadrupled during the decade, especially after they began to be powered by internal combustion engines, like automobiles, rather than by the cumbersome steam engines of the past. They helped open 35 million new acres to cultivation. Increasingly sophisticated combines and harvesters proliferated, making it possible to produce more crops with fewer workers.

Agricultural researchers worked on other innovations: the invention of hybrid corn, made possible by advances in genetic research, which became available to farmers in 1921 but was not grown in great quantities for a decade or more; and the creation of chemical fertilizers and pesticides, which also had limited use in the 1920s but proliferated quickly in the 1930s and 1940s.

The new technologies greatly increased agricultural productivity, and in fact outpaced the demand for agricultural goods. As a result, the 1920s saw substantial surpluses, a disastrous decline in food prices, and a severe drop in farmers' incomes. More than 3 million people left agriculture altogether in the course of the decade. Of those who remained, many lost ownership of their lands and had to rent instead from banks or other landlords.

In response, some farmers began to demand relief in the form of government price supports. One price-raising scheme in particular came to dominate agrarian demands: the idea of **parity**. Parity was a complicated formula for setting an adequate price for farm goods and ensuring that farmers would earn back at least their production costs no matter how the national or world agricultural market might fluctuate. Champions of parity urged high tariffs against foreign agricultural goods and a government commitment to buy surplus domestic crops at parity and sell them abroad.

The demand for parity found legislative expression in the McNary-Haugen Bill, which required the government to support prices at parity for grain, cotton, tobacco, and rice. It was introduced repeatedly. In 1926 and again in 1928, Congress approved the bill, but President Calvin Coolidge vetoed it both times.

THE NEW CULTURE

The urban and consumer-oriented culture of the 1920s helped Americans in all regions live their lives and perceive their world in increasingly similar ways. That same culture exposed them to new values. But different segments of American society experienced the new culture in different ways.

CONSUMERISM AND COMMUNICATIONS

The United States of the 1920s was a consumer society. More people than ever before could buy items not just because of need but also for convenience and pleasure. Middle-class families purchased electric refrigerators, washing machines, and vacuum cleaners. People wore wristwatches and smoked cigarettes. Women purchased cosmetics and mass-produced fashions. Above all, Americans bought automobiles. By the end of the decade, there were more than 30 million cars on American roads.

No group was more attuned to the emergence of consumerism, or more responsible for creating it, than the advertising industry. In the 1920s, partly as a result of techniques pioneered by wartime propaganda, advertising came of age. Publicists no longer simply conveyed information; they sought to identify products with a particular lifestyle. They also encouraged the public to absorb the values of promotion and salesmanship and to admire those who were effective boosters. One of the most successful books of the 1920s was *The Man Nobody Knows*, by the advertising executive Bruce Barton. It portrayed Jesus as not only a religious prophet but also a "super salesman." Barton's message, one sensitive to the new spirit of the consumer culture, was that Jesus had been concerned with living a full and rewarding life in this world and that twentieth-century men and women should do the same.

The advertising industry made good use of new vehicles of communication. Newspapers were absorbed into national chains. Mass-circulation magazines attracted broad national audiences. Movies in the 1920s became an ever more popular and powerful form of mass communication. Over 100 million people saw films in 1930, as compared to 40 million in 1922. The addition of sound to motion pictures—beginning in 1927 with the first feature-length "talkie," *The Jazz Singer* starring Al Jolson—greatly enhanced film's appeal. A series of scandals in the early 1920s led to the creation of the new Motion Picture Association, which imposed much tighter controls over the content of films. The result was safer, more conventionally acceptable films, which may in fact have broadened the appeal of movies generally. (See "America in the World: The Cinema.")

Meanwhile, the first commercial radio station in America, KDKA in Pittsburgh, began broadcasting in 1920, and the first national radio network, the National Broadcasting Company, was formed in 1927. That same year, Congress passed the Radio Act, which created a Federal Radio Commission to regulate the public airwaves used by private companies. (In 1935, it became the Federal Communications Commission, or FCC, which survives today.)

WOMEN IN THE NEW ERA

College-educated women were no longer pioneers in the 1920s. There were now two and even three generations of graduates of women's or coeducational colleges and universities, and some were making their presence felt in professional areas that in the past women had rarely penetrated. The "new professional woman" was a vivid and widely publicized figure in the 1920s.

In reality, however, most employed women were still nonprofessional, lower-class workers. Middle-class women, in the meantime, remained largely in the home, though advertising brought marketing strategies concerning gender roles and identity into the home. (See "Consider the Source: American Print Advertisements.")

The 1920s constituted a new era for middle-class women nonetheless. In particular, the decade saw a redefinition of motherhood. Shortly after World War I, John B. Watson and other behavioralists began to challenge the long-held assumption that women had an instinctive capacity for motherhood. Maternal affection was not, they claimed, sufficient preparation for child rearing. Instead, mothers should rely on the advice and assistance of experts and professionals: doctors, nurses, and trained educators.

For many middle-class women, these changes devalued what had been an important and consuming activity. Many attempted to compensate through what are often called "companionate marriages," which elevated the importance of compatibility and love between partners. Some women now openly considered their sexual relationships with their husbands not simply as a means of procreation, as earlier generations had been taught, but as important and pleasurable experiences in their own right, the culmination of romantic love.

One result of the new era for women was growing interest in birth control. The pioneer of the American birth-control movement, **Margaret Sanger**, began her career as a promoter of the diaphragm and other birth-control devices out of a concern for working-class women. She believed large families contributed to poverty and distress in poor communities. By the 1920s, she was becoming more effective in persuading middle-class women to see the benefits of birth control. Nevertheless, some birth-control devices remained illegal in many states, and abortion remained illegal nearly everywhere.

To the consternation of many longtime women reformers and progressive suffragists, some women concluded that in the New Era it was no longer necessary to maintain a rigid, Victorian female respectability. They could smoke, drink, dance, wear seductive clothes and makeup, and attend lively parties. Those assumptions were reflected in the emergence of

(©Bettmann/Corbis)

THE FLAPPER By the mid-1920s, the flapper—the young woman who challenged traditional expectations—had become not only a social type but a movement in fashion as well. Here, Catherine Dear is shown posing in a "beach costume," a fashion a long way from the rigid "respectability" of Victorian-age styles.

THE CINEMA

There is probably no cultural or commercial product more closely identified with the United States than motion pictures—or, as they are known in much of the world, the cinema. Although the technology of cinema emerged from the work of inventors in England and France as well as the United States, the production and distribution of films has been dominated by Americans almost from the start. The United States was the first nation to create a film "industry," and it did so at a scale vaster than that of any other country. With 700 feature films a year in the 1920s, Hollywood produced ten times as many movies as any other nation; and even then, its films were dominating not only the huge American market but much of the world's market as well. Seventy percent of the films seen in France, 80 percent of those seen in Latin America, and 95 percent of the movies viewed in Canada and Great Britain were produced in the United States in the 1920s. As early as the 1930s, the penetration of other nations by American movies was already troubling many governments. The Soviet Union responded to the popularity of Walt Disney's Mickey Mouse cartoons by inventing a cartoon hero of its own—a porcupine, designed to entertain in a way consistent with socialist values and not the capitalist ones they believed Hollywood conveyed. During World War II, American films were banned in occupied France, prompting some antifascist dissidents to screen such American films as Frank Capra's *Mr. Smith Goes to Washington* in protest.

American dominance was a result in part of World War I and its aftermath, which debilitated European filmmaking just as movie production was growing in the United States. By 1915, the United States had gained complete control of its own vast market and had so saturated it with movie theaters that by the end of World War I, half the world's theaters were in America. Two decades later, after an expansion of movie houses in other nations, the United States continued to have over 40 percent of the world's cinemas. And while the spread of theaters through other areas of the world helped launch film industries in many other countries, it also increased the market (and the appetite) for American films and strengthened American supremacy in their production. "The sun, it now appears," the *Saturday Evening Post* commented in the mid-1920s, "never sets on the British Empire and the American motion picture." Movies were then, and perhaps remain still, America's most influential cultural export. Even American popular music, which has enormous global reach, faces more significant local competition than American movies do in most parts of the world.

Despite this American dominance, however, filmmaking has flourished—and continues to flourish—in many countries around the world. India's fabled Bollywood, for example, produces an enormous number of movies for its domestic market—almost as many as the American industry creates—although few of them are widely exported. This global cinema has had a significant impact on American filmmaking. The small British film industry had a strong early influence on American movies, partly because of the quality and originality of British films and partly because of the emigration of talented actors, directors, and screenwriters to the United States. The great Alfred Hitchcock, for example, made his first films in London before moving to Hollywood, where he spent the rest of his long career. After World War II, French "new wave" cinema helped spawn a new generation of highly individualistic directors in the United States. Filmmakers from Germany, Italy, Sweden, the Netherlands, Japan, Spain, Australia, India, and Hong Kong had enormous influence on Hollywood, and over time perhaps even greater influence on the large and growing "independent film" movement in the United States.

In recent decades, as new technologies and new styles have transformed films around the world, the American movie industry has continued to dominate global cinema. But national boundaries no longer adequately describe moviemaking in the twenty-first century. It is becoming as truly global as other commercial ventures. "American" films today are often produced abroad, often have non-American directors and actors, and are often paid for with international financing. Hollywood still dominates worldwide filmmaking, but Hollywood itself is now an increasingly global community. •

(©Hulton Deutsch/Corbis Historical/Getty Images)

VALENTINO The popularity of the film star Rudolph Valentino among American women was one of the most striking cultural phenomena of the 1920s. Valentino was slight and delicate, not at all like the conventional image of "manliness." But he developed an enormous following among women, in part—as this poster is obviously intended to suggest—by baring his body onscreen. Valentino was Italian, which made him seem somehow strange and foreign to many old-stock Americans, and he was almost always cast in exotic roles, never as an American. His sudden death in 1926 (at the age of 31) created enormous outpourings of grief among many American women.

UNDERSTAND, ANALYZE, & EVALUATE

1. Did American movies, as the Soviet Union claimed in the 1930s, promote capitalism?
2. Why has the American movie industry continued to dominate global cinema?

flappers—modern women whose liberated lifestyle found expression in dress, hairstyle, speech, and behavior. The flapper lifestyle had a particular impact on urban lower-middle-class and working-class single women, who were filling new jobs in industry and the service sector. At night, such women flocked to clubs and dance halls in search of excitement and companionship. Many more affluent women soon began to copy the flapper style.

Despite all the changes, most women remained highly dependent on men and relatively powerless when men exploited that dependence. The National Woman's Party, under the leadership of Alice Paul, attempted to fight that powerlessness through its campaign for the Equal Rights Amendment, although it found little support in Congress. Responding to the suffrage victory, women organized the League of Women Voters and the women's auxiliaries of both the Democratic and Republican Parties. Female-dominated consumer groups grew rapidly and increased the range and energy of their efforts.

AMERICAN PRINT ADVERTISEMENTS

Companies advertised their products before millions of Americans in the expanding consumer marketplace of the 1920s. Radio and magazines were key venues for reaching the masses, and advertisers began focusing as much on the persuasive power of identity and lifestyle as the quality of the products themselves. This Procter & Gamble ad, appearing in 1928, peddled Ivory Soap to American women.

Your hands *can* keep their good looks *even though they work in the kitchen*

She is a heroine who does all her own housework; but she seems a genius whose hands never show it.

The question women ask every day is, "Can I do dishes, wash clothes and clean house, and still have hands that do not confess it?"

Millions of women answer "Yes."

You can surprise these women in the midst of any one of a dozen soap-and-water tasks and their hands seem by some miracle to have kept their fine, smooth whiteness through it all.

But it is not really a miracle—it is just Ivory Soap.

Here is what some of these women have written:

"The neighbors thought my mother extravagant for buying what they called 'toilet soap' for dishwashing and laundering purposes, but she suffered a great deal with soreness of her hands, and Ivory was the only soap that did not cause suffering. She was not able to hire the washing done so she did the next best thing—used the soap that caused no irritation."
—Mrs. E. H., Elkton, Md.

"Nothing to injure delicate skin"

"I have been using your Ivory Soap for 40 years. There is no other like it—I have tried many of the floating imitations but Ivory is the only soap with great cleansing quality and at the same time nothing to injure delicate skin. I use it exclusively for dishwashing."
—Mrs. I. W. R., Easton, Md.

"There are many other soaps cheaper and very cleansing, but, oh, so hard on the hands, while a daily use of Ivory leaves the hands soft and white. This is of great importance to mothers with young babies, who find it necessary to do the daily washings and tend the baby too. Their hands must be soft to rub the tender skin."
—Mrs. E. R. L., Emeryville, Cal.

You have probably used Ivory for toilet purposes, so you know it is pure and safe. You have used it for fine laundry and found that it harms nothing that can stand the touch of water. Now we suggest that you use it for dishes and general laundry and cleaning, because it cleanses thoroughly while it saves your hands.

Whatever the soap, remember it is the *suds* that do the work. And Ivory of course is famous for its suds, as women who do all their work with it enthusiastically testify.

Use Ivory for all your soap-and-water tasks —try your very next washing with Ivory —see if your hands do not keep their beauty all through the day.

Baby's underclothes need this special attention

If baby's diapers, bands and shirts are rough, or if they are not thoroughly cleansed, or if unrinsed soap is left in them, skin irritation is almost certain to result.

If you will make sure that all of baby's garments are washed with Ivory (cake or flakes), the likelihood of irritation will be greatly lessened. In the first place Ivory is pure—this is extremely important. Second, Ivory, mild as it is, cleanses thoroughly and rinses out completely, leaving the tiny garments in a perfectly sanitary condition and so soft that chafing becomes practically impossible.

Because of its convenient form, the use of Ivory Flakes for baby clothes saves both time and labor. A brief soaking in warm Ivory suds before the final washing quickens the cleansing and purifying process.

Ivory Flakes *for a very special need*— a sample—FREE

If you have a particularly precious garment that requires the most careful treatment, and you have made certain that it will stand the touch of pure water, let us send you a sample of Ivory Flakes for this particular purpose. With the sample will come also a beautifully illustrated booklet, "The Care of Lovely Garments," which is a veritable encyclopedia of laundering information. Address a postcard or letter to Section 12-JF, Department of Home Economics, Procter & Gamble, Cincinnati, O.
PROCTER & GAMBLE

I V O R Y   S O A P

© 1928, by The Procter & Gamble Co., Cincinnati

99 44/100 % PURE
IT FLOATS

FLAKES   CAKES

(©Apic/Hulton Archive/Getty Images)

1. What sort of lifestyle does the image suggest might come with using Ivory Soap?
2. What do the main heading and smaller print indicate would be proper or common roles for women?

3. Does the combination of image and text send a progressive message or a conservative one? Does it trade in the flapper aesthetic or something more traditional?
4. To what groups of women does the advertisement seem aimed? Who are the judges of "good looks" suggested by the text?

Source: Duke University Libraries Hartman Center.

Women activists won a brief triumph in 1921 when they helped secure passage of the Sheppard-Towner Act, which provided federal funds to states to establish prenatal and child health-care programs. From the start, however, the act produced controversy. Alice Paul and her supporters opposed the measure, complaining that it classified all women as mothers. More important, the American Medical Association fought Sheppard-Towner, warning that it would introduce untrained outsiders into the health-care field. In 1929, no longer worried about women voting as a bloc, Congress terminated the program.

THE DISENCHANTED

The generation that lived through (and in many cases fought in) the Great War quickly came to see the conflict as a useless waste of lives lost for no purpose. For some young people in the 1920s, disenchantment with the war contributed to a growing disenchantment with the United States. The newly prosperous and consumer-driven era they encountered seemed meaningless and vulgar to many artists and intellectuals in particular. As a result, they came to view their own culture with contempt. Rather than trying to influence and reform their society, they isolated themselves from it and embarked on a restless search for personal fulfillment. The American writer Gertrude Stein once referred to the young Americans emerging from World War I as a **Lost Generation**, though they faced a consistent counternarrative, pushed by veterans' groups and others, that emphasized the war's ennobling and even glorious character.

Among the artists and intellectuals of the 1920s who experienced disenchantment with modern America was the Baltimore journalist H. L. Mencken, who delighted in ridiculing religion, politics, the arts, even democracy itself. Sinclair Lewis published a series of novels—*Main Street* (1920), *Babbitt* (1922), *Arrowsmith* (1925), and others—in which he lashed out at one aspect of modern bourgeois society after another. Intellectuals of the 1920s claimed to reject the "success ethic" they believed dominated American life. The novelist F. Scott Fitzgerald, for example, attacked the American obsession with material success in *The Great Gatsby* (1925). The roster of important American writers active in the 1920s may have no equal in any other period. It included Fitzgerald, Lewis, Ernest Hemingway, Thomas Wolfe, John Dos Passos, Ezra Pound, T. S. Eliot, Gertrude Stein, Edna Ferber, William Faulkner, Eugene O'Neill, and a remarkable group of African American artists. In New York City, a new generation of black intellectuals created a flourishing artistic life widely described as the **Harlem Renaissance**. The Harlem poets, novelists, and artists drew heavily from their African roots in an effort to prove the richness of their own racial heritage and assert resistance against white racism and stereotyping. The ethos was captured in a single sentence by the author **Langston Hughes**: "I am a Negro—and beautiful."

Other black writers in Harlem and elsewhere—James Weldon Johnson, Countee Cullen, Zora Neale Hurston, Claude McKay, Alain Locke—as well as black artists and musicians helped establish a thriving and at times highly politicized culture.

A CONFLICT OF CULTURES

The modern, secular culture of the 1920s did not go unchallenged. It grew up alongside an older, more traditional culture, with which it continually and often bitterly competed.

PROHIBITION

When the prohibition of the sale and manufacture of alcohol went into effect in January 1920, it had the support of most members of the middle class and most of those who considered themselves progressives. Within a year, however, it had become clear that the "noble experiment," as its defenders called it, was not working well. At first, prohibition did substantially reduce drinking in most parts of the country. But it also produced conspicuous and growing violations. Before long, it was almost as easy to acquire illegal alcohol in many parts of the country as it had once been to acquire legal alcohol. And since an enormous, lucrative industry was now barred to legitimate businessmen, organized crime took it over.

Many middle-class progressives who had originally supported prohibition soon soured on the experiment. But a constituency of largely rural Protestant Americans continued vehemently to defend it. To them, prohibition represented the effort of an older America to protect traditional notions of morality. Drinking, which they associated with the modern city and Catholic immigrants, became a symbol of the new culture they believed was displacing them.

As the decade proceeded, opponents of prohibition (or "wets") gained steadily in influence. Not until 1933, however, when the Great Depression added weight to their appeals, were they finally able to challenge the "drys" effectively and win repeal of the Eighteenth Amendment.

NATIVISM AND THE KLAN

Agitation for a curb on foreign immigration had begun in the nineteenth century and, as with prohibition, had gathered strength in the years before the war largely because of the support of middle-class progressives. In the years immediately following the war, as immigration's association with radicalism intensified and migration from Europe resumed, popular sentiment on behalf of restriction grew rapidly.

In 1921, Congress passed an emergency immigration act, establishing a quota system by which annual immigration from any country could not exceed 3 percent of the number of persons of that nationality who had been in the United States in 1910. The new law cut immigration from 800,000 to 300,000 in any single year, but the nativists remained unsatisfied. The **National Origins Act of 1924** banned immigration from East Asia entirely and reduced the quota for Europeans from 3 to 2 percent. The quota would be based, moreover, not on the 1910 statistics but on the census of 1890, a year in which there had been far fewer southern and eastern Europeans in the country. What new immigration there was, in other words, would heavily favor northwestern Europeans. Five years later, a further restriction set a rigid limit of 150,000 immigrants a year. In the years that followed, immigration officials seldom permitted even half that number actually to enter the country.

To defenders of an older, more provincial America, the growth of large communities of foreign peoples, alien in speech, habits, and values, came to seem a direct threat to their own embattled way of life. Among other things, this nativism helped revitalize the **Ku Klux Klan** as a major force in American society. The first Klan, founded during Reconstruction, had died in the 1870s. But in 1915, a new group of white southerners met on Stone Mountain near Atlanta and established a modern version of the society. Nativist passions had swelled in Georgia and elsewhere in response to the case of Leo Frank, a Jewish factory manager in Atlanta convicted in 1914 on flimsy evidence of murdering a female employee; a mob stormed Frank's jail and lynched him. The premiere, also in Atlanta, of D. W. Griffith's film *The Birth of a Nation*, which glorified the early Klan, also helped inspire white southerners to form a new one.

At first the new Klan, like the old, was largely concerned with intimidating blacks. After World War I, however, concern about blacks gradually became secondary to concern about Catholics, Jews, and foreigners. At that point, membership in the Klan expanded rapidly and dramatically, not just in the small towns and rural areas of the South but in industrial cities in the North and Midwest as well. By 1924, there were reportedly 4 million members, including many women, organized in separate, parallel units. The largest state Klan was not in the South but in Indiana. Beginning in 1925, a series of scandals involving the organization's leaders precipitated a slow but steady decline in the Klan's influence.

Most Klan units (or "klaverns") tried to present their members as patriots and defenders of morality, and some did nothing more menacing than stage occasional parades and rallies. Often, however, the Klan also operated as a brutal, even violent, opponent of "alien" groups. Klansmen systematically terrorized blacks, Jews, Catholics, and foreigners. At times, they engaged in public whipping, tarring and feathering, arson, and lynching. What the Klan feared, however, was not simply "foreign" or "racially impure" groups, but anyone who posed a challenge to traditional values.

RELIGIOUS FUNDAMENTALISM

Another cultural controversy of the 1920s involved the place of religion in contemporary society. By 1921, American Protestantism was already divided into two warring camps. On one side stood the modernists: mostly urban, middle-class people who were attempting to adapt religion to the teachings of modern science and the secularizing forces of their society. On the other side stood the fundamentalists: largely though not exclusively rural men and women fighting to preserve traditional faith and to maintain the centrality of religion in American life. The fundamentalists insisted the Bible was to be interpreted literally. Above all, they opposed the teachings of Charles Darwin, whose theory of evolution had openly challenged the biblical story of Creation. Evangelical fundamentalists sought to spread their doctrine widely through revival meetings. The leading evangelist of the age, Billy Sunday, attracted huge crowds across the country with his fiery delivery, moral certitude, and plain exhortations to follow the Bible or face eternal damnation.

By the mid-1920s, to the great alarm of modernists, fundamentalist demands to forbid the teaching of evolution in public schools were gaining political strength in some states. In Tennessee in March 1925, the legislature adopted a measure making it illegal for any public school teacher "to teach any theory that denies the story of the divine creation of man as taught in the Bible."

The Tennessee law caught the attention of the fledgling American Civil Liberties Union (ACLU), founded in 1917 to defend pacifists, radicals, and conscientious objectors during World War I. The ACLU offered free counsel to any Tennessee educator willing to defy the law and become the defendant in a test case. A twenty-four-year-old biology teacher in the town of Dayton, John T. Scopes, agreed to have himself arrested. When the ACLU decided to send the famous attorney Clarence Darrow to defend Scopes, the aging William Jennings Bryan, now an important fundamentalist spokesman, announced he would travel to Dayton to assist the prosecution. Journalists from across the country flocked to Tennessee. Scopes had, of course, deliberately violated the law, and a verdict of guilty was a foregone conclusion, especially when the judge refused to permit "expert" testimony by evolution scholars. Scopes was fined $100, but the case was ultimately dismissed in a higher court because of a technicality. Nevertheless, Darrow scored an important victory for the modernists by calling Bryan himself to the stand to testify as an "expert on the Bible." In the course of the cross-examination, which was broadcast by radio to much of the nation, Darrow made Bryan's defense of biblical truths appear stubborn and finally maneuvered him into admitting the possibility that religious dogma was open to interpretation.

The **Scopes trial** put fundamentalists on the defensive. It discouraged many of them from participating openly in politics. But it did not resolve the conflict between fundamentalists and modernists, which continued to smolder.

THE DEMOCRATS' ORDEAL

The anguish of provincial Americans attempting to defend an embattled way of life proved particularly troubling to the Democratic Party during the 1920s. The Democrats consisted of a diverse coalition of interest groups, including prohibitionists, Klansmen, fundamentalists, and most white southerners on one side, and Catholics, urban workers, and immigrants on the other.

At the 1924 Democratic National Convention in New York City, a bitter conflict broke out over the platform when the party's urban wing attempted to win approval of planks calling for the repeal of prohibition and a denunciation of the Klan. Both planks narrowly failed. Even more damaging to the party was a deadlock in the balloting for a presidential candidate. Urban Democrats supported Alfred E. Smith, the Irish Catholic governor of New York; rural Democrats backed William McAdoo, Woodrow Wilson's Treasury secretary, who had skillfully positioned himself to win the support of southern and western delegates suspicious of modern urban life but whose reputation had been tarnished by a series of scandals resulting from his work as an attorney for an unsavory oil tycoon. For 103 ballots, the convention dragged on, with Smith supporters chanting "No oil on Al," until finally both Smith and McAdoo withdrew. The party settled on a compromise: the corporate lawyer John W. Davis, who lost decisively to Calvin Coolidge.

A similar schism plagued the Democrats again in 1928, when Al Smith finally secured his party's nomination for president. He was not, however, able to unite his divided party, in part because of widespread anti-Catholic sentiment especially in the South. He was the first Democrat since the Civil War not to carry the entire South. Elsewhere, he carried no states at all except Massachusetts and Rhode Island. Smith's opponent, and the victor in the presidential election, was a man who personified the modern, prosperous, middle-class society of the New Era: Herbert Hoover.

REPUBLICAN GOVERNMENT

For twelve years, beginning in 1921, both the presidency and the Congress rested in the hands of the Republican Party. For most of those years, the federal government enjoyed a warm and supportive relationship with the American business community. Yet the government of the New Era was less passive than critics often described. It attempted to serve in many respects as an agent of economic change.

The Republican administrations also played an active role in world affairs. Far from the "isolationists" their critics later called them, the governments of the 1920s did not sit idly by as the terms of one world war continued to reverberate and the specter of a second one loomed.

THE HARDING ADMINISTRATION

Warren G. Harding was elected to the presidency in 1920. An undistinguished senator from Ohio, he had received the Republican presidential nomination as a result of an agreement among leaders of his party, who considered him, as one noted, a "good second-rater." Harding appointed distinguished men to some important cabinet offices and attempted to stabilize the nation's troubled foreign policy. But he seemed baffled by his responsibilities, as if he recognized his unfitness. "I am a man of limited talents from a small town," he reportedly told friends on one occasion. "I don't seem to grasp that I am President." Harding's intellectual limits were compounded by his penchant for gambling, illegal alcohol, and attractive women.

By the time the Harding administration took office in 1921, American membership in the League of Nations was no longer a realistic possibility. But Secretary of State Charles Evans Hughes wanted to find a replacement for the League as a guarantor of world peace and stability.

The most important effort was the Washington Conference of 1921—an attempt to prevent a destabilizing naval armaments race among the United States, Britain, and Japan. Hughes proposed a plan for dramatic reductions in the fleets of all three nations and a ten-year moratorium on the construction of large warships. To the surprise of almost everyone, the conference ultimately agreed to accept most of Hughes's terms. The Five-Power Pact of February 1922 established limits for total naval tonnage and a ratio of armaments among the signatories. For every 5 tons of American and British warships, Japan would maintain 3 and France and Italy 1.75 each.

When the French foreign minister, Aristide Briand, asked the United States in 1927 to join an alliance against Germany, Secretary of State Frank Kellogg (who had replaced Hughes in 1925) proposed instead a multilateral treaty outlawing war as an instrument of national policy. Fourteen nations signed the agreement in Paris on August 27, 1928, amid wide international acclaim. Forty-eight other nations later joined the Kellogg-Briand Pact. It contained no instruments of enforcement.

Back at home, Harding lacked the strength to abandon the party hacks who had helped give him power. One of them, Ohio party boss Harry Daugherty, he appointed attorney general. Another, New Mexico senator Albert B. Fall, he made secretary of the interior. Members of the so-called Ohio Gang filled important offices throughout the administration. Unknown to the public, Daugherty, Fall, and others were engaged in fraud and corruption. The most spectacular scandal involved the rich naval oil reserves at **Teapot Dome**, Wyoming, and Elk Hills, California. At the urging of Fall, Harding transferred control of those reserves from the Navy Department to the Interior Department. Fall then secretly leased them to two wealthy businessmen and received in return nearly half a million dollars in "loans" to ease his private financial troubles. Fall was ultimately convicted of bribery and sentenced to a year in prison. Harry Daugherty barely avoided a similar fate for his part in another scandal.

In the summer of 1923, only months before Senate investigations and press revelations brought the scandals to light, a tired and depressed Harding left Washington for a speaking tour in the West. In Seattle late in July, he complained of severe pain, which his doctors wrongly diagnosed as food poisoning. A few days later, in San Francisco, he died. He had suffered two major heart attacks.

The Coolidge Administration

Calvin Coolidge succeeded Harding in the presidency. Where Harding was genial, garrulous, and debauched, Coolidge was dour, silent, even puritanical. Elected governor of Massachusetts in 1919, Coolidge had won national attention with his tough response to the Boston police strike that year. That was enough to make him his party's vice presidential nominee in 1920. Three years later, after Harding's death, he took the oath of office from his father, a justice of the peace, by the light of a kerosene lamp.

If anything, Coolidge was even less active as president than Harding, partly as a result of his conviction that government should interfere as little as possible in the life of the nation. In 1924, he received his party's presidential nomination virtually unopposed. Running against John W. Davis, he won a comfortable victory: 54 percent of the popular vote and 382 of the 531 electoral votes. Coolidge probably could have won renomination and reelection in 1928. Instead, in characteristically understated fashion, he walked into a press room one day and handed each reporter a slip of paper containing a single sentence: "I do not choose to run for president in 1928."

In between, Coolidge governed amid the lingering economic fallout of the Great War. The first responsibility of diplomacy, Hughes, Kellogg, and others agreed, was to ensure that American overseas trade faced no obstacles. The Allied powers of Europe were struggling to repay $11 billion in loans they had contracted with the United States during and shortly after the war. At the same time, Germany was attempting to pay the reparations levied by the Allies. The United States stepped in with a solution.

Charles G. Dawes, an American banker who became vice president under Coolidge in 1925, negotiated an agreement in 1924 among France, Britain, Germany, and the United States. Under the **Dawes Plan**, American banks would provide enormous loans to Germany, which would use that money to pay reparations to France and Britain; Britain and France would agree to reduce the amount of those payments and, in turn, use those funds (as well as the large loans they themselves were receiving from American banks) to repay war debts to the United States. One historian said of this circular plan, "It would have made equal sense for the U.S. to have taken the money out of one drawer in the Treasury and put it into another." None of this activity led to economic recovery in Europe. Rather, the flow of funds was able to continue only by virtue of the growing debts the European nations were acquiring to American banks and corporations. The American economic involvement in Europe continued to expand until the worldwide depression shattered the system in 1931.

During the 1920s, American military forces maintained a presence in Nicaragua, Panama, and several other countries in the region, while U.S. investments in Latin America more than doubled. American banks offered large loans to Latin American governments, just as in Europe; and as with the Europeans, the Latin Americans had difficulty earning the money to repay them in the face of the formidable U.S. tariff barrier.

Government and Business

However passive the New Era presidents may have been, much of the federal government worked effectively and efficiently during the 1920s to adapt public policy to the widely accepted goal of the time: helping business and industry to operate with maximum efficiency and productivity. The close relationship between the private sector and the federal government forged during World War I continued. Secretary of the Treasury Andrew Mellon, a wealthy steel and aluminum tycoon, worked to achieve substantial reductions in taxes on corporate profits, personal incomes, and inheritances. Largely because of his efforts, Congress cut them all by more than half. Mellon also worked closely with President Coolidge after 1924 on a series of measures to trim dramatically the already modest federal budget, even managing to retire half the nation's World War I debt.

The most prominent member of the cabinet was Commerce Secretary **Herbert Hoover**. During his eight years in the Commerce Department, Hoover constantly encouraged voluntary cooperation in the private sector as the best avenue to stability. But the idea of voluntarism did not require that the government remain passive; on the contrary, public institutions, Hoover believed, had a duty to play an active role in creating the new, cooperative order. Above all, Hoover became the champion of the concept of business "associationalism"—a concept that envisioned the creation of national organizations of businessmen in particular industries. Through these trade associations, private entrepreneurs could, Hoover believed, study and stabilize their industries and promote efficiency in production and marketing.

Many progressives derived encouragement from the election of Herbert Hoover to the presidency in 1928. Hoover easily defeated Al Smith, the Democratic candidate. And he entered office promising bold new efforts to solve the nation's remaining economic problems. But Hoover had few opportunities to prove himself. Less than a year after his inauguration, the nation plunged into the severest and most prolonged economic crisis in its history—a crisis that brought many of the optimistic assumptions of the New Era crashing down and launched the nation into a period of unprecedented social innovation and reform.

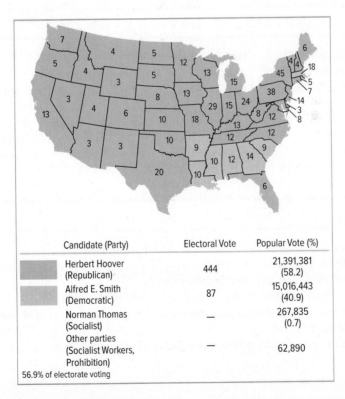

	Candidate (Party)	Electoral Vote	Popular Vote (%)
	Herbert Hoover (Republican)	444	21,391,381 (58.2)
	Alfred E. Smith (Democratic)	87	15,016,443 (40.9)
	Norman Thomas (Socialist)	—	267,835 (0.7)
	Other parties (Socialist Workers, Prohibition)	—	62,890

56.9% of electorate voting

THE ELECTION OF 1928   The election of 1928 was highly one-sided. Herbert Hoover won over 58 percent of the popular vote to Alfred Smith's 41 percent. Smith carried only Massachusetts, Rhode Island, and some traditionally Democratic states in the South. • *Why did Smith do so poorly even in some parts of the South?*

CONCLUSION

The remarkable prosperity of the 1920s shaped much of what exuberant contemporaries liked to call the "New Era." In the years after World War I, America built a vibrant and extensive national culture. Its middle class moved increasingly into the embrace of the growing consumer culture. Politics were reorganized around the needs of a booming, interdependent industrial economy, undermining many of the reform crusades of the previous generation but also creating new institutions to help promote economic growth and stability.

Beneath the glittering surface of the New Era, however, were great controversies and injustices. Although the prosperity of the 1920s spread more widely than at any time in the nation's industrial history, more than half the population failed to achieve any real benefits from the growth. A new, optimistic, secular culture attracted millions of urban middle-class people, even as many other Americans looked at it with alarm and fought it with great fervor. The unprepossessing conservative presidents of the era suggested a time of stability, but in fact few eras in modern American history have seen so much political and cultural conflict.

The 1920s ended in a catastrophic economic crash that has colored the image of those years ever since. The crises of the 1930s should not obscure the real achievements of the New Era economy. Neither, however, should the prosperity of the 1920s obscure the inequity and instability in those years that helped produce the difficult years to come.

KEY TERMS/PEOPLE/PLACES/EVENTS

A. Philip Randolph 545
American Plan 544
Brotherhood of Sleeping
  Car Porters 545
Calvin Coolidge 558
Dawes Plan 558
flappers 551
Harlem Renaissance 553

Herbert Hoover 559
Issei 547
Ku Klux Klan 555
Langston Hughes 553
Lost Generation 553
Margaret Sanger 549
National Origins Act
  of 1924 554

Nisei 547
parity 547
Scopes trial 556
Teapot Dome 557
The Jazz Singer 548
Warren G. Harding 557
welfare capitalism 543

RECALL AND REFLECT

1. What was the impact of the automobile on American life?
2. How did labor fare during the 1920s? What particular problems did female, black, immigrant, and unskilled laborers face?
3. How did religion respond to the consumer culture of the 1920s?
4. What was the myth and what was the reality of the new professional woman of the 1920s?
5. What was the nature and extent of the nativism of the 1920s?

23 | THE GREAT DEPRESSION

THE COMING OF THE DEPRESSION
THE AMERICAN PEOPLE IN HARD TIMES
THE DEPRESSION AND AMERICAN CULTURE
THE ORDEAL OF HERBERT HOOVER

LOOKING AHEAD

1. What were some of the causes of the Great Depression? What made it so severe, and why did it last so long?
2. What was the impact of the Depression on farmers, minorities, and women?
3. How did President Hoover and his administration try to deal with the Depression? What was the result of those efforts?

"WE IN AMERICA TODAY," presidential candidate Herbert Hoover proclaimed in August 1928, "are nearer to the final triumph over poverty than ever before in the history of any land. The poorhouse is vanishing from among us." Only fifteen months later, those words would return to haunt him, as the nation plunged into the severest and most prolonged economic depression in its history—a depression that continued in one form or another for a full decade, not only in the United States but throughout much of the world.

The Depression reached into every area of economic and social life. It destroyed the bull market of the 1920s, drove stock prices into a long decline, halted the investment in industrial plants and infrastructure that had helped fuel economic growth, and jeopardized the national banking system. Worst of all, from the perspective of many citizens, it created massive unemployment, which at times approached a full quarter of the workforce.

In the midst of this crisis, President Hoover used the tools of the federal government to address economic problems more aggressively than any president before him. But even these measures were overwhelmed by the Depression. And Hoover refused to consider steps that he believed betrayed basic principles of American life, particularly the rights and responsibilities of individuals. Faith in individualism had been strong throughout American history, but the scale of the Depression called it into question, undermined Hoover's reputation, and eventually led to major shifts in American political and economic life.

THE COMING OF THE DEPRESSION

The sudden financial collapse in 1929 came as an especially severe shock because it followed so closely an era of remarkable stock market performance. In February 1928, stock prices began a steady ascent that continued, with only a few temporary lapses, for a year and a half. Between May 1928 and September 1929, the average price of stocks rose over 40 percent. Trading mushroomed from 2 or 3 million shares a day to over 5 million, and at times to as many as 10 or 12 million. In short, a widespread speculative fever grew steadily more intense, particularly once brokerage firms began encouraging the mania by offering easy credit to those buying stocks.

THE GREAT CRASH

In the autumn of 1929, the market began to fall apart. On October 29, "Black Tuesday," after a week of growing instability, all efforts to save the market failed. Sixteen million shares of stock were traded; the industrial index dropped 43 points (or nearly 10 percent), wiping out all the gains of the previous year; stocks in many companies became virtually worthless. Within a month, stocks had lost half their September value, and despite occasional, short-lived rallies, they continued to decline for several years after that.

Popular folklore has established the stock market crash as the beginning, and even the cause, of the **Great Depression**. Although October 1929 might have been the most visible early sign of the crisis, the Depression had earlier beginnings and other causes.

CAUSES OF THE DEPRESSION

Economists and historians have argued for decades about the causes of the Great Depression. But most agree that what was

1) lack of diversification
2) maldistribution of pp
3) credit structure   4) international trade

remarkable about the crisis is not that it occurred but that it was so severe and lasted so long. If they agree on little else, most observers attribute that severity and length to several factors.

One was a lack of diversification in the American economy in the 1920s. Prosperity had depended excessively on a few basic industries, notably construction and automobiles, which in the late 1920s began to decline. Expenditures on construction fell from $11 billion in 1926 to under $9 billion in 1929. Automobile sales fell by more than a third in the first nine months of 1929. Newer industries were emerging to take up the slack—among them petroleum, chemicals, electronics, and plastics—but none had developed enough strength to compensate for this decline.

A second important factor was the maldistribution of purchasing power and, as a result, a weakness in consumer demand. As industrial and agricultural production increased, the proportion of the profits going to potential consumers was too small to create an adequate market for the goods the economy was producing. Even in 1929, after nearly a decade of economic growth, more than half the families in America lived on the edge of or below the minimum subsistence level.

A third major problem was the credit structure of the economy. Farmers were deeply in debt, and crop prices were too low to allow them to pay off what they owed. Small banks were in constant trouble as their customers defaulted on loans; large banks were in trouble, too. Although most American bankers were very conservative, some of the nation's biggest banks were investing recklessly in the stock market or making unwise loans. When the market crashed and the loans went bad, some banks failed and others made the crisis worse by contracting already scarce credit and calling in loans that borrowers could not pay.

A fourth factor was America's position in international trade. Late in the 1920s, European demand for American goods began to decline, partly because European industry and agriculture were becoming more productive and partly because some European nations were having financial difficulties of their own. But it was also because the European economy was being destabilized by the international debt structure that had emerged in the aftermath of World War I.

This debt structure, therefore, was a fifth factor contributing to the Depression. When the war came to an end in 1918, all the European nations that had been allied with the United States owed large sums of money to American banks, sums much too large to be repaid out of their shattered economies, which is partly why the Allies had insisted on reparation payments from Germany and Austria. Reparations, they believed, would provide them with a way to pay off their own debts. But Germany and Austria were no more able to pay the reparations than the Allies were able to pay their debts.

The American government refused to forgive or reduce the debts. Instead, American banks began making large loans to European governments, which used them to pay off their earlier loans. Thus debts (and reparations) were being paid only by piling up new and greater debts. At the same time, American protective tariffs were making it difficult for Europeans to sell their goods in American markets. Without any source of foreign exchange with which to repay their loans, they began to default. The collapse of the international credit structure was one of the reasons the Depression spread to Europe after 1931. (See "America in the World: The Global Depression.")

THE GLOBAL DEPRESSION 1929-1941

The Great Depression began in the United States. But it did not end there. The American economy was the largest in the world, and its collapse sent shock waves across the globe. By 1931, the American depression had become a world depression, with important implications for the course of global history.

The origins of the worldwide depression lay in the pattern of debts that had emerged during and after World War I, when the United States loaned billions of dollars to European nations. In 1931, with American banks staggering and in many cases collapsing, large banks in New York began desperately calling in their loans from Germany and Austria. That precipitated the collapse of one of Austria's largest banks, which in turn created panic through much of central Europe. The economic collapse in Germany and Austria meant that those nations could not continue paying reparations to Britain and France (required by the Treaty of Versailles of 1919), which meant in turn that Britain and France could not continue paying off their loans to the United States. This spreading financial crisis was accompanied by a dramatic contraction of international trade, precipitated in part by the Hawley-Smoot Tariff in the United States, which established the highest import duties in history and stifled much global commerce. Depressed agricultural prices—a result of worldwide overproduction—also contributed to the downturn. By 1932, worldwide industrial production had declined by more than one-third, and world trade had plummeted by nearly two-thirds. By 1933, 30 million people in industrial nations were unemployed, five times the number of four years before.

But the Depression was not confined to industrial nations. Imperialism and

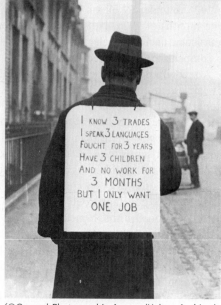

(©General Photographic Agency/Hulton Archive/ Getty Images)

LOOKING FOR WORK IN LONDON, 1935 An unemployed London man wears a sign that seems designed to convince passersby that he is an educated, respectable person despite his present circumstances.

industrialization had drawn almost all regions of the world into the international industrial economy. Colonies and nations in Africa, Asia, and South America—critically dependent on exporting raw materials and agricultural goods to industrial countries—experienced a collapse in demand for their products and thus rising levels of poverty and unemployment. Some nations, among them the Soviet Union and China, remained relatively unconnected to the global economy and suffered relatively little from the Great Depression. But in most parts of the world, the Depression caused tremendous social and economic hardship.

It also created political turmoil. Among the countries hardest hit by the Depression was Germany, where industrial production declined by 50 percent and unemployment reached 35 percent in the early 1930s. The desperate economic conditions there contributed greatly to the rise of the Nazi Party and its leader, Adolf Hitler, who became chancellor in 1933. Japan suffered as well, dependent as it was on world trade to sustain its growing industrial economy and purchase essential commodities for its needs at home. And in Japan, as in Germany, economic troubles produced political turmoil and aided the rise of a new militaristic regime. In Italy, the fascist government of Benito Mussolini, which had first taken power in the 1920s, also saw militarization and territorial expansion as a way out of economic difficulties.

In other nations, governments sought solutions to the Depression through reform of their domestic economies. Among the most common responses to the Depression around the world was substantial government investment in public works, such as roads, bridges, dams, public buildings, and other large projects. Among the nations that adopted this approach—in addition to the United States—were Britain, France, Germany, Italy, and the Soviet Union. Another response was the expansion of government-funded relief for the unemployed. All the industrial countries of the world experimented with various forms of relief, often borrowing ideas from one another. And the Depression helped create new approaches to economics, in the face of the apparent failure of classical models of economic behavior to explain, or provide solutions to, the crisis. The British economist John Maynard Keynes revolutionized economic thought in much of the world. His 1936 book *The General Theory of Employment, Interest, and Money* created a sensation by arguing that the Depression was a result not of declining production but of inadequate consumer demand. Governments, he said, could stimulate their economies by growing the money supply and creating investment through a combination of lowering interest rates and increasing public spending. Keynesianism, as Keynes's theories became known, began to have an impact in the United States in 1938, and in much of the rest of the world in subsequent years.

The Great Depression was an important turning point not only in American history but also in the history of the twentieth-century world. It transformed ideas of public policy and economics in many nations. It toppled old regimes and created new ones. And perhaps above all, it was a major factor in the coming of World War II. •

UNDERSTAND, ANALYZE, & EVALUATE

1. How did the 1919 Treaty of Versailles and the Hawley-Smoot Tariff contribute to the global depression of the 1930s?
2. How did the governments of European nations respond to the Depression?
3. What effect did the global depression have on economic theory?

PROGRESS OF THE DEPRESSION

The stock market crash of 1929 did not so much cause the Depression, then, as help trigger a chain of events that exposed larger weaknesses in the American economy. During the next three years, the crisis grew.

The most serious problem at first was the collapse of much of the banking system. Between 1930 and 1933, over 9,000 American banks either went bankrupt or closed their doors to avoid bankruptcy. Partly as a result of these banking closures, the nation's money supply shrank by perhaps a third between 1930 and 1933, which caused a decline in purchasing power and thus deflation. Manufacturers and merchants began reducing prices, cutting back on production, and laying off workers. Some economists argue that a severe depression could have been avoided if the Federal Reserve system had acted responsibly. But late in 1931, in a misguided effort to build international confidence in the dollar, it raised interest rates, which contracted the money supply even further.

The American gross national product plummeted from over $104 billion in 1929 to $76.4 billion in 1932, a 25 percent decline in three years. By 1932, according to relatively crude estimates, 25 percent of the American workforce was unemployed. (Some argue the figure was even higher.) For the rest of the decade, unemployment averaged nearly 20 percent, never dropping below 15 percent. Up to another one-third of the workforce was "underemployed"–experiencing major reductions in wages, hours, or both.

THE AMERICAN PEOPLE IN HARD TIMES

Someone asked the economist John Maynard Keynes in the 1930s whether he was aware of any historical era comparable to the Great Depression. "Yes," Keynes replied. "It was called the Dark Ages, and it lasted 400 years." The Depression was far shorter, but it brought unprecedented economic despair to the United States and much of the Western world.

UNEMPLOYMENT AND RELIEF

In the industrial Northeast and Midwest, cities were virtually paralyzed by unemployment. Cleveland, Ohio, for example, had an unemployment rate of 50 percent in 1932; Akron, 60 percent; Toledo, 80 percent. Unemployed workers walked through the streets day after day looking for jobs that did not exist. An increasing number of families turned to state and local public relief systems, just to be able to eat. But those systems, which in the 1920s had served only a small number of indigents, were totally unequipped to handle the heavy new demands. In many cities, therefore, relief simply collapsed. Private charities attempted to supplement the public relief efforts, but the problem was far beyond their capabilities as well.

In rural areas, conditions were often worse. Farm income declined by 60 percent between 1929 and 1932. A third of all American farmers lost their land. In addition, a large area of agricultural settlement in the Great Plains suffered from one of the worst droughts in the history of the nation. Beginning in 1930, the region that came to be known as the "Dust Bowl," which stretched north from Texas into the Dakotas, experienced a steady decline in rainfall and an accompanying increase in heat. The drought continued for a decade, turning what had once been fertile farm regions into virtual deserts. Severe winds blew dust across the eastern United States.

Many farmers, like the urban unemployed, left their homes in search of work. In the South, in particular, many dispossessed farmers, black and white, simply wandered from town to town, hoping to find jobs or handouts. Hundreds of thousands of families from the Dust Bowl (often known collectively as "Okies," though not all came from Oklahoma) traveled to California and other states, where they found conditions little better than those they had left. Many worked as agricultural migrants, traveling from farm to farm, picking fruit and other crops at starvation wages.

(©Bettmann/Getty Images)

THE HUNGRY Hundreds of men wait to be fed outside the Municipal Lodging House in New York City.

AFRICAN AMERICANS AND THE DEPRESSION

African Americans were among the groups least aided by the prosperity of the 1920s and most devastated by the hardships of the Great Depression. As the crisis began, over half of all black Americans still lived in the South. Most were farmers. The collapse of prices for cotton and other staple crops left some with no income at all. Many left the land altogether, either by choice or because they had been evicted by landlords who no longer found sharecropping profitable. Some migrated to southern cities. But there, unemployed whites believed they had first claim to what work there was, and some now began displacing African Americans as janitors, street cleaners, and domestic servants. By 1932, over half the blacks in the South were unemployed.

Unsurprisingly, therefore, many black southerners—perhaps 400,000 in all—left the South in the 1930s and journeyed to the cities of the North, where conditions were little better. In New York, black unemployment was nearly 50 percent, in other cities, it was higher. Two million African Americans—half the total black population of the country—were on some form of relief by 1932.

Traditional patterns of segregation and disfranchisement in the South survived the Depression largely unchallenged, while a few particularly notorious examples of racism did attract the attention of the nation. The most celebrated was the Scottsboro case. In March 1931, nine young black men, all but one teenagers, were taken off a freight train in northern Alabama (in a small town near Scottsboro) and arrested for vagrancy and disorder. Later, two white women who had also been riding the train accused them of rape. In fact, there was overwhelming evidence, medical and otherwise, that the women had not been raped

(©Bettmann/Getty Images)

DUST STORM, SOUTHWEST PLAINS, 1937   The dust storms of the 1930s were a terrifying experience for all who lived through them. Resembling a black wall sweeping in from the western horizon, such a storm engulfed farms and towns alike, blotting out the light of the sun and covering everything with a fine dirt.

at all; they may have made their accusations out of fear of being arrested themselves. Nevertheless, an all-white jury in Alabama (blacks were routinely barred from jury rolls) quickly convicted all nine of the "Scottsboro boys," as they were known to both friends and foes, and sentenced eight of them to death.

The Supreme Court overturned the convictions in 1932, and a series of new trials began. The International Labor Defense, an organization associated with the Communist Party, came to the aid of the accused youths and began to publicize the case. Meanwhile one of the accusers recanted her testimony. Although the juries who sat on the case never acquitted any of the defendants, all of the accused eventually saw their charges dropped or sentences suspended, though the last of the Scottsboro defendants did not leave prison until 1950.

Hispanics and Asians in Depression America

Similar patterns of discrimination confronted many Mexicans and Mexican Americans. The Hispanic population of the United States had been growing steadily since early in the century, largely in California and other areas of the Southwest. Chicanos (Mexican Americans) filled many of the same menial jobs there that blacks had traditionally filled in other regions. Some farmed small, marginal tracts, others became agricultural migrants. It had always been a precarious existence, and the Depression made things significantly worse. Unemployed whites in the Southwest demanded jobs held by Hispanics, jobs that whites had previously considered beneath them. Thus Mexican unemployment rose quickly to levels far higher than those for whites. Some officials arbitrarily removed Mexicans from relief rolls or simply rounded up and deported them. Perhaps half a million Chicanos left the United States for Mexico in the first years of the Depression.

There were occasional signs of organized resistance by Mexican Americans themselves, most notably in California, where some formed a union of migrant farmworkers. But harsh repression by local growers and public authorities prevented such organizations from having much impact. As a result, many Hispanics began to migrate to cities such as Los Angeles, where they lived in poverty comparable to that of urban blacks in the South and Northeast.

For Asian Americans, too, the Depression reinforced long-standing patterns of discrimination and economic marginalization. In California, with the largest Japanese American and Chinese American populations, educated Asians had always found it difficult, if not impossible, to move into mainstream professions. Japanese American college graduates often found themselves working in family fruit stands. For those who found jobs in the industrial or service economy, employment was precarious. Like blacks and Hispanics, Asians often lost jobs to white Americans desperate for work. Japanese farmworkers suffered from the increasing competition for even these low-paying jobs with white migrants from the Great Plains.

The overwhelming majority of Chinese Americans worked, as they had for many years, in Chinese-owned laundries and restaurants. Those who moved outside the Asian community could rarely find jobs above the entry level. Chinese women, for example, might find work as stock girls in department stores but almost never as salesclerks. Educated Chinese men and women could hope for virtually no professional opportunities outside the world of Chinatowns.

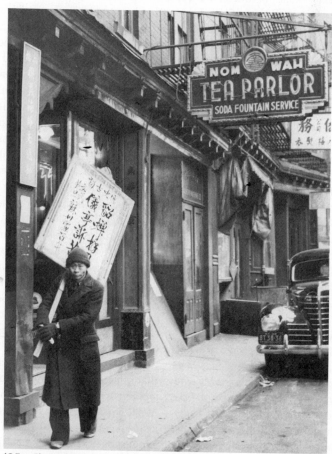

(©Fox Photos/Hulton Archive/Getty Images)

CHINATOWN, NEW YORK CITY   A Chinese man carries a signboard through the streets of New York City's Chinatown bearing the latest news of the war between China and Japan, which in 1938 was well under way. Chinese Americans had the dual challenge in the 1930s of dealing both with large-scale unemployment and with continuing news of catastrophe from China, where most still had family members.

MR. TARVER REMEMBERS THE GREAT DEPRESSION (1940)

The Federal Writers' Project (FWP) was a New Deal program that employed authors and researchers during the Great Depression. Participants produced tourist guidebooks, ethnographies, oral histories, and many other kinds of documents. In 1940, an FWP writer interviewed a bank employee named Mr. Tarver.

Yes, I really went through the depression. [. . .] "There were thousands who went down during the panic—lost fortunes, homes, business, and in fact everything. Some have survived, and many never will. A great many were too old to begin building up again. In the kind of work I'm in I have been in position to know some of the devastating effects of it, and it certainly gets on your sympathy.

"I guess you would say I am recovering from it. When I say that though, I'm not boasting, but I'm deeply grateful for the good fortunes that have came my way. Then, too, I feel under everlasting obligations to some of my friends who have helped me to get where I am.

"I had not accumulated a great deal at the time of the panic, but I did have some savings and a good job. That was the trouble, my savings and my job went at the same time. Now that was real trouble. Nobody but my wife and I knew just what we did go through. [. . .]

I was making a fine salary, had a growing savings account, and a host of friends, and no serious troubles to worry about. My wife is just the smartest, thriftiest person you have ever seen. To her I owe a lot of my successes. She is fine with her needle and crocheting, and you never saw her idle. She made all her spending money that way. Even now since we have been in Washington she keeps it up. And her fruit cake! People here rave about it. She cooks an enormous

amount of it every Christmas and sells it for a big profit. She can't fill all the orders she gets. She is very resourceful and right now, if I were to die and not leave her a thing, she would manage some way. One of my hobbies was gardening and it proved to be a profitable one too. This place we rented had a fine garden spot, the finest in Dublin, so every one said. I worked in it early every morning and in the afternoon after banking hours. I sold lots of vegetables, and relied a lot on them—especially the early variety that brought a good price." [. . .]

"One morning we three were at the breakfast table when the phone rang. It was one of the fellows who worked at the bank.

"Tarver, he said, 'have you heard the news?'

"'What news? No, I haven't heard any news,' said I. What's it all about?'

"'Well,' he said, "hurry on down and see.'

"If you will excuse the expression, when he said that, the seat of my britches almost dropped out. I felt like it meant trouble of some kind. I had had a terrible feeling of uneasiness over the bank for some time. Banks had been closing all over the country. There had been a run on our bank some time previous to that, but we tided that over, and since then it had seemed stronger than ever.

"I hurried down and, sure enough, in front of the bank, there stood a crowd of employees, as blank expressions on their faces as I've ever seen. They were too dumbfounded to be excited even.

"The bank was closed and a notice to that effect on the door. We stood there just looking at each other until finally one said, 'Well, boys, guess we had better go on the inside and see if we can find out what it's all about. I guess there goes our jobs.'

[. . .] "Just as I was getting in the dumps about a regular job, I was notified to report at once, to act as assistant receiver for a defunct bank in Florida. They were feeling the depression there even more than we were in Georgia, and banks were closing every day.

[. . .] "Banks were still closing until it was hard to get enough receivers for them. Oh, we did work. Banks in neighboring towns were added to our work until we were liquidating six banks at one time, all in different places. I had to have another car then but was lucky to pick up a good used car almost at my own price. People had lost their cars as well as their homes, so it was no trouble to buy a good used one. Sometimes I would ride to all six of these banks in one day and when night came I would be completely given out. I couldn't stop even then, for there was scarcely a night that we didn't work."

UNDERSTAND, ANALYZE, & EVALUATE

1. Why was Mr. Tarver doubly affected by the banking crisis of the Great Depression? How did Mr. and Mrs. Tarver compensate for their losses in the job market?

2. How might the Great Depression have shaped the outlook of Mr. and Mrs. Tarver on work, leisure, and consumption for years, if not decades, to come?

Source: Mr. W. W. Tarver (White), Finance Officer in U.S. Treasury (Bank Conservator), 5001 Nebraska Ave., N.W., Washington, D.C., interviewed by Bradley. Library of Congress, *American Life Histories: Manuscripts from the Federal Writers' Project, 1936–1940*. http://memory.loc.gov/cgi bin/query/r?ammem/wpa:@field%28DOCID+@lit%28wpa112060215%29%29

WOMEN AND FAMILIES IN THE GREAT DEPRESSION

The economic crisis strengthened the widespread belief that a woman's proper place was in the home. Many men and women believed that with employment so scarce, what work there was should go to men and that no woman whose husband was employed should accept a job. Indeed, from 1932 until 1937, it was illegal for more than one member of a family to hold a federal civil service job.

But the widespread assumption that married women, at least, should not work outside the home did not stop them from doing so. Both single and married women worked in the 1930s because they or their families needed the money. Some women did small jobs at home or sold food or goods to make ends meet. (See "Consider the Source: Mr. Tarver Remembers the Great Depression.") By the end of the Depression, 25 percent more women were working for wages than had been doing so at the beginning, despite considerable obstacles. Professional opportunities for women declined because unemployed men began moving into professions that had previously been considered women's fields. Female industrial workers were more likely to be laid off or to experience wage reductions than their male counterparts. But white women also had certain advantages in the workplace. The nonprofessional jobs that women traditionally held—salesclerks, stenographers, and other service positions—were less likely to disappear than the predominantly male jobs in heavy industry.

Black women suffered massive unemployment, particularly in the South, because of a great reduction of domestic service jobs. As many as half of all black working women lost their jobs in the 1930s. Even so, at the end of the 1930s, 38 percent of black women were employed, as compared with 24 percent of white women, mirroring the broader historical pattern that economic necessity drove married and unmarried black women into the workforce at a higher rate than white women.

The Depression also worked to erode the strength of many family units. There was a decline in the divorce rate, but largely because divorce was expensive. More common was the informal breakup of families, particularly the desertion of families by unemployed men trying to escape the humiliation of being unable to earn a living. The marriage rate and the birthrate both declined for the first time since the early nineteenth century.

THE DEPRESSION AND AMERICAN CULTURE

The Great Depression was a traumatic experience for millions of Americans. Out of the crisis emerged probing criticisms of American life. But the Depression also produced powerful confirmations of more traditional values and reinforced many traditional goals. There was not one Depression culture, but many.

DEPRESSION VALUES

Prosperity and industrial growth had done much to shape American values in the 1920s. Yet even when hard times came, American social values seemed to change relatively little in response to the Depression. Instead, many people responded to hard times by redoubling their commitment to familiar ideas and goals. The Depression did not destroy the success ethic.

The survival of the ideals of work and individual responsibility was evident in many ways, not least in the reactions of those traumatized by unemployment. Some expressed anger and struck out at the economic system. Many, however, seemed to blame themselves. At the same time, millions responded eagerly to reassurances that they could, through their own efforts, restore themselves to prosperity. **Dale Carnegie**'s *How to Win Friends and Influence People* (1936), a self-help manual preaching individual initiative, was one of the best-selling books of the decade.

Yet the most popular cultural products of the 1930s diverted attention away from the Depression. And they came to Americans primarily through the two most powerful instruments of popular culture in the 1930s—radio and the movies. (For another powerful vehicle of escapist culture, see "Patterns of Popular Culture: The Golden Age of Comic Books.")

RADIO

Almost every American family had a radio in the 1930s. Even in remote rural areas without access to electricity, many families purchased radios and hooked them up to car batteries when they wished to listen.

Radio was often a community experience. Young people would place radios on their front porches and invite friends by to listen, talk, or dance. In poor urban neighborhoods, people would gather on a street or in a backyard to hear sporting events or concerts. Within families, the radio often drew parents and children together to listen to favorite programs.

Although radio stations occasionally carried provocative programs, the staple of broadcasting was escapism, including comedies such as *Amos 'n' Andy* (with its demeaning picture of urban blacks) and adventures such as *Superman, Dick Tracy*, and *The Lone Ranger*. Radio brought a new kind of comedy to a wide audience. Jack Benny, George Burns and Gracie Allen, and other masters of elaborately timed repartee began to develop broad followings. Soap operas were enormously popular escapist entertainment in which emotionally charged stories unfolded on a daily or weekly basis. These radio dramas were generally sponsored by soap companies, whose advertising was targeted at women who were alone in the house during the day.

Radio provided Americans with their first direct access to important public events. On-air coverage of news and sports expanded rapidly to meet the demand. Radio carried some of the most dramatic moments of the 1930s: the World Series, the Academy Awards, political conventions. When the German dirigible *Hindenburg* crashed in flames in Lakehurst, New Jersey, in 1937, it produced an enormous national reaction largely because of the live radio account by a broadcaster, overcome with emotion, who cried out, "Oh the humanity! Oh the humanity!" The actor-director Orson Welles created another memorable event on Halloween night, 1938, when he broadcast a radio play about aliens landing in central New Jersey who had set off toward New York armed with terrible weapons. The play took the form of a news broadcast, and it created panic among some people who believed the events were real.

THE MOVIES

In the first years of the Depression, movie attendance dropped significantly. By the mid-1930s, however, most Americans had resumed their moviegoing habits in part because the movies (now with sound and, by the end of the decade, color) were becoming more appealing.

Hollywood continued to exercise tight control over its products in the 1930s through its resilient censor Will Hays, who ensured that most movies carried no sensational or controversial messages. The studio system—through which a few large movie companies exercised iron control over actors, writers, and directors—also worked to ensure that Hollywood films avoided controversy.

Neither the censor nor the studio system, however, could completely prevent films from exploring social questions. There were many serious films that portrayed the problems of the Depression, including King Vidor's *Our Daily Bread* (1932) and John Ford's adaptation of *The Grapes of Wrath* (1940). Gangster movies such as *Little Caesar* (1930) and *The Public Enemy* (1931) portrayed a dark, gritty, violent world with which few Americans were familiar, but their desperate stories were popular with those engaged in their own struggles.

But the most effective presentation of a social message came from the Italian-born director **Frank Capra**. Capra had a deep love for his adopted country, and he translated that love into a vaguely populistic admiration for ordinary people. He contrasted the decency of small-town America and the common man with what he considered the opportunism of the city and the capitalist marketplace. In *Mr. Deeds Goes to Town* (1936), a simple man from a small town inherits a large fortune, moves to the city, and—not liking the greed and dishonesty he finds there—gives the money away and moves back home. In *Mr. Smith Goes to Washington* (1939), a decent man from a western state is elected to the U.S. Senate, refuses to join in the self-interested politics of Washington, and dramatically exposes the corruption and selfishness of his colleagues. Capra's popular films helped audiences in the 1930s find solace in a vision of an imagined American past of warmth, goodness, and honesty.

More often, however, the commercial films of the 1930s, like most radio programs, were deliberately and explicitly escapist: lavish musicals such as *Gold Diggers of 1933*, "screwball" comedies such as Capra's *It Happened One Night*, or the films of the Marx Brothers, pictures designed to divert audiences from their troubles and indulge fantasies about easy wealth.

The 1930s were the first years of Walt Disney's long reign as the champion of animation and children's entertainment. After producing cartoon shorts for theaters in the late 1920s, many of them starring the newly created character Mickey Mouse, Disney began to produce feature-length animated films, starting in 1937 with *Snow White*. Other enormously popular movies of the 1930s were adaptations of popular novels, such as *The Wizard of Oz* and *Gone with the Wind*, both released in 1939.

THE GOLDEN AGE OF COMIC BOOKS

In the troubled years of the Great Depression (and later, World War II), many Americans sought release from their anxieties in fantasy. Movies, plays, books, radio shows, and other diversions drew people out of their own lives and into a safer or more glamorous or more exciting world. Beginning in 1938, one of the most popular forms of escape for many young Americans was the comic book.

In February 1935, Malcolm Wheeler-Nicholson founded the first comics magazine—what we now know as the "comic book"—titled *New Fun*. It was not successful, but Wheeler founded the company Detective Comics. He began in 1937 to design a new magazine called *Action Comics*. Wheeler ran out of money before he could publish anything, but the company continued without him. In 1938, the first issue of *Action Comics* appeared with a startling and controversial cover—a powerful man in a skintight suit lifting a car over his head. His name was Superman, and he became the most popular cartoon character of all time.

Within a year, Superman had a comic book named after him, which was selling over 1.2 million copies each issue. By 1940, there was a popular Superman radio show, introduced by a breathless announcer crying, "It's a bird! It's a plane! It's . . . Superman!" Soon, other publishers began developing new *superheroes* (a term invented by the creators of Superman) to capitalize on this growing popular appetite. In 1939, a second great comic book publisher appeared—Marvel Comics.

By the early 1940s, Superman had been joined by other superheroes: the Human Torch, the Sub-Mariner, Batman, the Flash, and Wonder Woman, a character created in part to signal the importance of women to the war effort.

It is not hard to imagine why superheroes would be so appealing to Americans in the 1930s and 1940s—particularly to the teenage boys who were the largest single purchasers of comic books. Superman and other superheroes were idealized versions of the ideal boy—smart, good, "the perfect Boy Scout," as one fan put it. But they were also all-powerful, capable of righting wrong and preventing catastrophe. As the national economy faltered, comic book heroes modeled patriotic pride, resilience, and optimism. They operated with moral certainty when so much was uncertain. At a time of suffering, superheroes offered escape.

Many of the early comic book writers were young Jewish men, conscious of their outsider status in an American culture not yet wholly open to them. Almost all the characters they created had alter egos, identities they used while living within the normal world. Superman was Clark Kent, a "mild-mannered reporter." Batman was Bruce Wayne, a wealthy heir. All were part of mainstream American society, and they expressed in part the outsider's dream of assimilation. The superheroes themselves were outsiders too, but outsiders endowed with special powers and abilities unavailable to ordinary people.

In the last years of the Depression, the comic superheroes began battling the Axis powers. Marvel's Human Torch and Sub-Mariner joined forces against the German navy. Superman fought spies and

(©Hulton Archive/Getty Images)

SUPERMAN The most popular action figure in the history of comic books was Superman, whose superhuman powers were particularly appealing fantasies to Americans suffering through the Depression and, later, World War II.

saboteurs at home. Captain America, a new character created in March 1941, was a frail young man rejected by the army who, after being given a secret serum by a military doctor, became extraordinarily powerful. The cover of the first issue of *Captain America* showed the title character punching Adolf Hitler in his headquarters in Germany.

The end of the war was also the end of this first golden age of American comic books. New comic books emphasized romance, mild sexuality, and, over time, violence and cruelty. But comic books never surpassed the heights of popularity they attained during the Depression and World War II. •

UNDERSTAND, ANALYZE, & EVALUATE

1. What could comic books offer readers suffering through the crisis of the Great Depression?
2. How and why have comic book superheroes changed over time?

Hollywood did little to challenge the conventions of popular culture on issues of gender and race. Women in movies were portrayed overwhelmingly as wives, mothers, or attractive flirts. Mae West portrayed herself in a series of successful films as an overtly sexual woman manipulating men through her attractiveness. Few films included important African American characters. Most black men and women on the silver screen were portrayed as servants or farmhands or entertainers, or had their history as enslaved peoples romanticized for white audiences.

LITERATURE AND JOURNALISM

Much literature and journalism in the 1930s dealt directly or indirectly with the tremendous disillusionment, and the increasing radicalism, of the time.

Not all literature, of course, was challenging or controversial. The most popular books and magazines of the 1930s, in fact, were as escapist and romantic as many radio shows and movies. Two of the best-selling novels of the decade were romantic sagas set in earlier eras: Margaret Mitchell's *Gone with the Wind* (1936) and Hervey Allen's *Anthony Adverse* (1933). Leading magazines focused more on fashions, stunts, scenery, and the arts than on the social conditions of the nation. The new and enormously popular photographic journal *Life* **magazine**, first published in 1936, had the largest readership of any publication in the United States other than *Reader's Digest*. It devoted some attention to politics and the economic conditions of the Depression, but it was best known for stunning photographs

(©Silver Screen Collection/Moviepix/Getty Images)

THE WIZARD OF OZ Whatever contemporary political messages L. Frank Baum may have embedded in his 1900 novel, *The Wizard of Oz*, the 1939 cinematic version featured memorable characters shot in vivid Technicolor. Dorothy, the Tin Man, the Cowardly Lion, the Scarecrow, and the Wicked Witch of the West, shown here, offered escapist fantasy for mass audiences during the Great Depression.

of sporting and theater events, natural landscapes, and public projects. One of its most popular features was "*Life* Goes to a Party," which took the chatty social columns of daily newspapers and turned them into glossy photographic glimpses of the rich and famous but also ordinary people at lavish parties.

Other Depression writing, however, frankly challenged the dominant values of American popular culture. Some of the most significant literature offered portraits of the harshness and emptiness of American life: **John Dos Passos**'s *U.S.A.* trilogy (1930–1936), which attacked what he considered the materialistic madness of American culture; **Richard Wright**'s *Native Son* (1940), the story of a young African American man broken by racial oppression; Nathanael West's *Miss Lonelyhearts* (1933), the story of an advice columnist overwhelmed by the sadness he encounters in the lives of those who consult him; Jack Conroy's *The Disinherited* (1933), a harsh portrait of the lives of coal miners; and James T. Farrell's *Studs Lonigan* (1932), the tale of a lost, hardened working-class youth. Perhaps the best-known depiction of Depression-era life is **John Steinbeck**'s *The Grapes of Wrath* (1939). The novel's main characters are the Joad family, migrants from the **Dust Bowl** to California who encounter an unending string of calamities and failures. Their story offers a critique of the exploitative features of agrarian life in the West, as well as a tribute to the fortitude of the community the Joads represent.

THE POPULAR FRONT AND THE LEFT

The American Communist Party (CPUSA), a relatively small organization in the early twentieth century, gained credibility during the Great Depression as the capitalist system's flaws were exposed. Meanwhile, in 1935 the Soviet Union called for a **Popular Front** against fascism, which materialized in the United States as a broad coalition of groups on the left. In this environment of cooperation, the Soviet party leader **Josef Stalin** and the CPUSA softened their attitude toward President Franklin Roosevelt (elected in 1932), hoping that he would become an ally against fascism in Germany. The Popular Front formed loose alliances with progressive groups, and it praised even some strong anticommunists such as the labor leader John L. Lewis. The CPUSA flourished under these conditions, adding tens of thousands of members, though not all members of the Popular Front considered themselves communists. But in its heyday, the antifascist movement enhanced the reputation and influence of the Communist Party while also helping collapse some of the divisions on the American left. For a time, communists, civil rights activists, labor leaders, and liberals united around the Popular Front's cause.

One of the key events of the mid-1930s that rallied the American left was the **Spanish Civil War**. The war pitted the forces supporting Francisco Franco, who received aid from the fascists Hitler and Mussolini, against the republican government of Spain. A substantial group of young Americans—more than 3,000 in all—formed the **Abraham Lincoln Brigade** and traveled to Spain to fight an ultimately losing battle against fascism on the side of the republicans. The CPUSA was instrumental in creating the Lincoln Brigade and directed many of its activities.

The American Communist Party was active as well in organizing the unemployed in the early 1930s, and it staged a hunger march in Washington, D.C., in 1931. Party members were among the most effective union organizers in some industries. And the party was virtually alone among political organizations in taking a firm stand in favor of racial justice.

(©Daily Express/Hulton Archive/Getty Images)

THE SPANISH CIVIL WAR Many Americans took up arms to help the republican forces fight against Franco and his army. The novelist Ernest Hemingway joined them in Spain as a reporter and supporter of the republicans. He spent much of his time talking with both American and Spanish troops as well as (in this image) the Dutch filmmaker Joris Ivens. His novel *For Whom the Bell Tolls* was inspired by his experience in the civil war.

Its active defense of the Scottsboro defendants was but one example of its efforts to ally itself with the aspirations of African Americans.

The CPUSA was not, however, the open, patriotic organization it tried to project. It was always under the close and rigid supervision of the Soviet Union. The subordination of the party leadership to the Russians was most clearly demonstrated in 1939, when Stalin signed a nonaggression pact with Nazi Germany. Moscow sent orders to the American Communist Party to abandon the Popular Front and return to its old stance of harsh criticism of American liberals. Communist Party leaders in the United States immediately obeyed, though thousands of disillusioned members left the party as a result.

The Socialist Party of America, under the leadership of Norman Thomas, also cited the economic crisis as evidence of the failure of capitalism and sought vigorously to win public support for its own political program. Among other things, it attempted to mobilize support among the rural poor. The Southern Tenant Farmers Union (STFU), supported by the party and organized by a young socialist, H. L. Mitchell, attempted to create a biracial coalition of sharecroppers, tenant farmers, and others to demand economic reform. Neither the STFU nor the party itself, however, made any real progress toward establishing socialism as a major force in American politics.

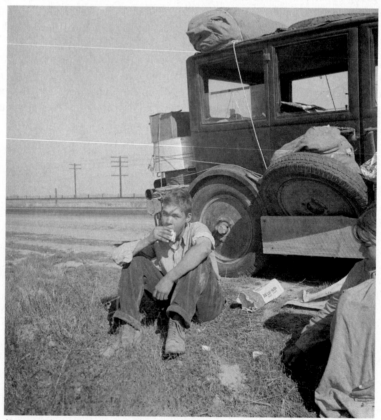

(Source: Library of Congress, Prints and Photographs Division [LC-USF34-009872-E])

MIGRANT FAMILY This photograph by the Great Depression photographer Dorothea Lange portrays the son of an Oklahoma family of migrants on a roadside in California. It suggests the plight of hundreds of thousands of families who fled the regions affected by drought in the 1930s—a devastation that became known as the Dust Bowl.

While the left was broadening its appeal in the 1930s, antiradicalism remained a powerful force. Hostility toward the Communist Party, in particular, was intense at many levels of government. Congressional committees chaired by Hamilton Fish of New York and Martin Dies of Texas investigated communist influence wherever they could find or imagine it. White southerners tried to drive communist organizers out of the countryside, just as growers in California and elsewhere tried unsuccessfully to keep communists from organizing Mexican American and other workers.

At few times before in American history, and few since, did being part of the left seem so respectable and even conventional among workers, intellectuals, and others. The 1930s witnessed an impressive, if temporary, widening of the ideological range of mainstream art and politics. The Roosevelt administration's New Deal, for example, sponsored artistic work through the Works Projects Administration that was frankly challenging to the capitalist norms of the 1920s. The filmmaker Pare Lorentz, with funding from New Deal agencies, made two powerful documentaries—*The Plow That Broke the Plains* (1936) and *The River* (1937)—that combined a celebration of New Deal programs with a harsh critique of industrial capitalism's exploitation of people and the environment.

Other New Deal-sponsored artists sought to reveal the harshness of poverty and the human cost of social neglect. Notable among them were numerous documentary photographers, many of them employed by the Farm Security Administration, who traveled through rural areas recording the ravaged nature of agricultural life. They included some of the great photographers of their era—Dorothea Lange, Margaret Bourke-White, Arthur Rothstein, Russell Lee, Walker Evans, Ben Shahn, and others. Writers, too, devoted themselves to exposing social injustice, some of them working through the New Deal's Federal Writers' Project and Federal Art Project.

THE ORDEAL OF HERBERT HOOVER

Herbert Hoover began his presidency in March 1929 believing, like most Americans, that the nation faced a bright and prosperous future. For the first six months of his administration, he attempted to expand the associational policies he had advocated for eight years as secretary of commerce. The economic crisis that began before the year was out forced Hoover to deal with a new set of problems. But he tended to rely on principles that had always governed his public life.

THE HOOVER PROGRAM

Hoover first responded to the Depression by attempting to restore public confidence in the economy. "The fundamental business of this country, that is, production and distribution of commodities," he said in 1930, "is on a sound and prosperous basis." He then summoned leaders of business, labor, and agriculture to the White House and urged them to adopt a program of voluntary cooperation for recovery. He implored businessmen not to cut production or lay off workers; he talked labor leaders into forgoing demands for higher wages or better hours. But by mid-1931, economic conditions had deteriorated so much that the structure of voluntary cooperation had collapsed.

Hoover also attempted to use government spending as a tool for fighting the Depression. The president proposed to Congress a significant increase ($423 million) in federal public works programs, and he encouraged state and local governments to fund public construction.

But the spending was not nearly enough. And when economic conditions worsened, he became less willing to increase spending, worrying instead about keeping the budget balanced.

Even before the stock market crash, Hoover had begun to construct a program to assist the troubled agricultural economy. In April 1929, he proposed the **Agricultural Marketing Act**, which established the first major government program to help farmers maintain prices. A federally sponsored Farm Board would make loans to national marketing cooperatives or establish corporations to buy surpluses and thus raise prices. At the same time, Hoover attempted to protect American farmers from international competition by raising agricultural tariffs. The **Hawley-Smoot Tariff** of 1930 increased protection on seventy-five farm products. But neither the Agricultural Marketing Act nor the Hawley-Smoot Tariff ultimately helped American farmers significantly. Agricultural surpluses, combined with declining consumption, kept the farm economy in crisis.

By the spring of 1931, Herbert Hoover's political position had deteriorated considerably. In the 1930 congressional elections, Democrats won control of the House and made substantial inroads in the Senate. Many Americans blamed the president personally for the crisis and attached the name "**Hoovervilles**" to the shantytowns unemployed people established on the outskirts of cities. Democrats urged the president to support more vigorous programs of relief and public spending. Hoover, instead, seized on a slight improvement in economic conditions early in 1931 as proof that his policies were working. The international financial panic of the spring of 1931 destroyed that illusion.

By the time Congress convened in December 1931, conditions had grown so desperate that Hoover supported a series of measures designed to keep endangered banks afloat and protect homeowners from foreclosure on their mortgages. Most important was a bill passed in January 1932 establishing the **Reconstruction Finance Corporation (RFC)**, a government agency to provide federal loans to troubled banks, railroads, and other businesses. Unlike some earlier Hoover programs, the RFC operated on a large scale. In 1932, it had a budget of $1.5 billion for public works alone.

That was a large sum, but the RFC did not spend all of it. The new agency lent funds only to financial institutions with sufficient collateral, so much of its money went to large banks and corporations. At Hoover's insistence, it helped finance only those public works projects that promised ultimately to pay for themselves—toll bridges, public housing, and others. So although the RFC represented a more energetic attempt by the federal government to stabilize the economy, it failed to have a major impact on the Depression.

Popular Protest

For the first several years of the Depression, most Americans were either too stunned or too confused to raise much effective protest. By the middle of 1932, however, dissident voices began to be heard.

In the summer of 1932, a group of unhappy farm owners gathered in Des Moines, Iowa, to establish a new organization: the Farmers' Holiday Association, which endorsed the withholding of farm products from the market—in effect a farmers' strike. The strike began in August in western Iowa, spread briefly to a few neighboring areas, and succeeded in blockading several markets. But in the end, it dissolved in failure.

A more celebrated protest movement emerged from American veterans. In 1924, Congress had approved the payment of a $1,000 bonus in 1945 to all those who had served in World War I. By 1932, however, many veterans were demanding that the bonus be paid immediately. Hoover, concerned about balancing the budget, rejected their appeal. In June, more than

20,000 veterans, members of the self-proclaimed Bonus Expeditionary Force, or "**Bonus Army**," marched into Washington, built crude camps around the city, and promised to stay until Congress approved legislation to pay the bonus. Some of the veterans departed in July after Congress had voted down their proposal. Many, however, remained in Washington.

Their continued presence in Washington embarrassed President Hoover. Finally, in mid-July, he ordered police to clear the marchers out of several abandoned federal buildings in which they had been staying. A few marchers threw rocks at the police. Someone opened fire, and two veterans fell dead. Hoover called the incident evidence of uncontrolled violence and radicalism and ordered the U.S. Army to assist the police in clearing out the buildings.

General Douglas MacArthur, the army chief of staff, carried out the mission himself and greatly exceeded the president's orders. He led the Third Cavalry, two infantry regiments, a machine-gun detachment, and six tanks down Pennsylvania Avenue in pursuit of

(©Bettmann/Getty Images)

CLEARING OUT THE BONUS MARCHERS In July 1932, President Hoover ordered the Washington, D.C., police to evict the Bonus Marchers from some of the public buildings and land they had been occupying. After a series of skirmishes between police and the protesters, Hoover ordered the U.S. Army to complete the eviction.

the Bonus Army. The veterans fled in terror. MacArthur followed them across the Anacostia River, where he ordered the soldiers to burn their tent city to the ground. More than 100 marchers were injured.

The incident dealt another blow to Hoover's already battered political standing. The "Great Engineer," the personification of the optimistic 1920s, had become a symbol of the nation's failure to deal effectively with its startling reversal of fortune.

HOOVER AND THE WORLD CRISIS

By 1931, the world financial crisis had produced a rising nationalism in Europe and Japan. It soon toppled some existing political leaders and replaced them with powerful, belligerent governments committed to expansion. Herbert Hoover thus confronted the beginning of a process that would ultimately lead to war.

In Latin America, Hoover tried to repair some of the damage done by earlier American policies. He made a ten-week goodwill tour through Latin America before his inauguration. Once in office, he generally abstained from intervening in the internal affairs of neighboring nations and moved to withdraw American troops from Nicaragua and Haiti. He also announced a new policy: America would grant diplomatic recognition to any sitting government in the region without questioning the means it had used to obtain power. He even repudiated the Theodore Roosevelt Corollary to the Monroe Doctrine by refusing to permit American intervention when several Latin American countries defaulted on debt obligations in October 1931.

In Europe, the administration enjoyed few successes. When Hoover's proposed moratorium on debts failed to produce financial stability, he refused to cancel all war debts to the United States as many economists advised him to do. Several European nations promptly went into default. Efforts to extend the 1921 limits on naval construction fell victim to French and British fears of German and Japanese militarism.

(©Instituto Nazionale Luce/Alinari Archives/Getty Images)

HITLER AND MUSSOLINI IN BERLIN The German and Italian dictators (shown here reviewing Nazi troops in Berlin in the mid-1930s) acted publicly as if they were equals. Privately, Hitler treated Mussolini with contempt, and Mussolini complained constantly of being a junior partner in the relationship.

The ineffectiveness of American diplomacy in Europe was particularly troubling in light of the rise of **fascism**, an ideology that rejected democratic forms of government in favor of concentrated state power under a dictator. **Benito Mussolini**'s Fascist Party had been in control of Italy since the early 1920s and had become increasingly nationalistic and militaristic. Still more ominous was the growing power of the **National Socialist (or Nazi) Party** in Germany. By the late 1920s, the Weimar Republic, the nation's government since the end of World War I, had been largely discredited by, among other things, a ruinous inflation. **Adolf Hitler**, the leader of the Nazis, grew rapidly in popular favor and took power in 1933. He believed in, among other things, the genetic superiority of the Aryan (German) people and in extending German territory to provide *Lebensraum* (living space) for what he called the German "master race." He displayed a pathological anti-Semitism and a passionate militarism.

More immediately alarming to the Hoover administration was a major crisis in Asia—another early step toward World War II. The Japanese, suffering from an economic depression of their own, were concerned about the increasing power of the Soviet Union and about the insistence of the Chinese leader Chiang Kai-shek on expanding his government's power in Manchuria, officially a part of China but over which the Japanese had maintained informal economic control since 1905. In 1931, Japan's military leaders staged what was, in effect, a coup in Tokyo. Shortly after that, a railroad explosion in southern Manchuria, likely set by Japanese soldiers (and known as the "Mukden Incident"), served as a pretext for a Japanese invasion of northern Manchuria. They had conquered the region by the end of the year. Secretary of State Henry Stimson issued stern warnings to the Japanese but to no avail. Early in 1932, Japan moved farther into China, attacking the city of Shanghai and killing thousands of civilians.

THE ELECTION OF 1932

As the 1932 presidential election approached, few people doubted the outcome. The Republican Party dutifully renominated Herbert Hoover for a second term of office, but few delegates believed he could win. The Democrats, in the meantime, gathered in Chicago to nominate the governor of New York, **Franklin Delano Roosevelt**.

Roosevelt had been a well-known figure in the party for many years already. A Hudson Valley aristocrat, a distant cousin of Theodore Roosevelt, and a handsome, charming young man, he progressed rapidly from a seat in the New York State legislature to a position as assistant secretary of the navy during World War I to his party's vice presidential nomination in 1920 with James M. Cox. Less than a year later, he was stricken with polio. Although he never regained use of his legs, and could walk only by using crutches and braces, he built up sufficient physical strength to return to politics in 1928. When Al Smith received the Democratic nomination for president that year, Roosevelt was elected to succeed him as governor. In 1930, he easily won reelection.

Roosevelt worked no miracles in New York, but he did initiate enough government assistance to be able to present himself as a more imaginative leader than Hoover. In national politics, he avoided divisive cultural issues and emphasized the economic grievances that most Democrats shared. As a result, he was able to assemble a broad coalition within the party and win its nomination. In a dramatic break with tradition, he flew to Chicago to address the Democratic National Convention in person and accept the nomination. In the course of his acceptance speech, Roosevelt made a ringing promise: "I pledge you, I pledge myself, to a new deal for the American people." Neither then nor in the subsequent campaign did Roosevelt give much indication of what that program would be. But Herbert Hoover's unpopularity virtually ensured Roosevelt's election.

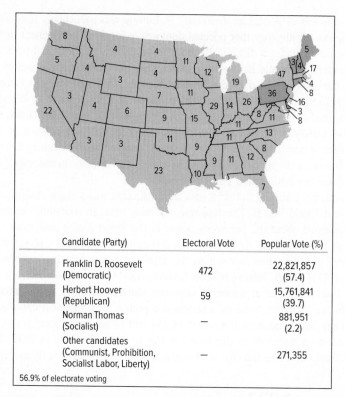

Candidate (Party)	Electoral Vote	Popular Vote (%)
Franklin D. Roosevelt (Democratic)	472	22,821,857 (57.4)
Herbert Hoover (Republican)	59	15,761,841 (39.7)
Norman Thomas (Socialist)	—	881,951 (2.2)
Other candidates (Communist, Prohibition, Socialist Labor, Liberty)	—	271,355

56.9% of electorate voting

THE ELECTION OF 1932   Like the election of 1928, the election of 1932 was exceptionally one-sided. But this time, the landslide favored the Democratic candidate, Franklin Roosevelt, who overwhelmed Herbert Hoover in all regions of the country except New England. Roosevelt obviously benefited from disillusionment with Hoover's response to the Great Depression. • *But what characteristics of Roosevelt himself contributed to his victory?*

Roosevelt won by a landslide, receiving 57.4 percent of the popular vote to Hoover's 39.7, and carried every state except Delaware, Pennsylvania, Connecticut, Vermont, New Hampshire, and Maine. Democrats won large majorities in both houses of Congress. It was a convincing mandate, but it was not yet clear what Roosevelt intended to do with it.

THE "INTERREGNUM"

The period between the election and the inauguration, which in the early 1930s lasted more than four months, was a season of growing economic crisis. Presidents-elect traditionally do not involve themselves directly in government. But in a series of brittle exchanges, Hoover tried to exact a pledge from the incoming Roosevelt to maintain policies of economic orthodoxy. Roosevelt genially refused.

In February, only a month before the inauguration, a new crisis developed when the collapse of the American banking system suddenly and rapidly accelerated. Depositors withdrew their money in panic; and one bank after another closed its doors and declared bankruptcy. Hoover again asked Roosevelt to give prompt public assurances that there would be no tinkering with the currency, no heavy borrowing, no unbalancing of the budget. Roosevelt again refused.

March 4, 1933, was, therefore, a day of both economic crisis and considerable personal bitterness. On that morning, Herbert Hoover rode glumly down Pennsylvania Avenue with a beaming, buoyant Franklin Roosevelt, who would shortly be sworn in as the thirty-second president of the United States.

CONCLUSION

The Great Depression changed many things in American life. It created unemployment unprecedented in the nation's history. It put enormous pressures on families, communities, state and local governments, and Washington. The innovative but ultimately failed presidency of Herbert Hoover was unable to produce policies capable of dealing with the crisis. In the nation's politics and culture, there were strong currents of radicalism and protest, and many middle-class Americans came to fear that a revolution might be approaching.

In reality, while the Great Depression shook much of American society and culture, it actually toppled very little. The capitalist system survived, damaged for a time but never truly threatened. The values of materialism and personal responsibility were shaken but never overturned. The American people in the 1930s were more receptive than they had been in the 1920s to evocations of community, generosity, and the dignity of common people. They were more open to experiments in government and business and even private lives than they had been in earlier years. But for most Americans, belief in the "American way of life" remained strong throughout the long years of economic despair.

KEY TERMS/PEOPLE/PLACES/EVENTS

Abraham Lincoln
  Brigade 577
Adolf Hitler 583
Agricultural Marketing
  Act 580
Benito Mussolini 583
Bonus Army 581
Dale Carnegie 572
Dust Bowl 576
fascism 583

Frank Capra 573
Franklin Delano
  Roosevelt 583
Great Depression 562
Hawley-Smoot Tariff 580
Hindenburg 573
Hoovervilles 580
John Dos Passos 576
John Steinbeck 576
Josef Stalin 577

Life magazine 575
National Socialist (Nazi)
  Party 583
Okies 566
Popular Front 577
Reconstruction Finance
  Corporation (RFC) 580
Richard Wright 576
Scottsboro case 567
Spanish Civil War 577

RECALL AND REFLECT

1. Was the 1929 stock market crash the cause of the Depression? Why or why not?
2. How did farmers fare during the Depression? What environmental conditions contributed to their plight?
3. How did popular entertainment and the arts respond to the needs of Depression-era audiences?
4. What popular protests arose in response to the Depression? How successful were these protests?
5. How did Hoover's political beliefs affect his attempt to deal with the economic crisis of the Depression?

24 | THE NEW DEAL ERA

LAUNCHING THE NEW DEAL
THE NEW DEAL IN TRANSITION
THE NEW DEAL IN DISARRAY
ISOLATION AND INTERNATIONALISM
LIMITS AND LEGACIES OF THE NEW DEAL

LOOKING AHEAD

1. What emergency measures did Franklin Delano Roosevelt (FDR) take in his first hundred days as president?
2. Who were the major critics of FDR's New Deal, and how did their criticisms influence FDR's "Second New Deal"?
3. What were the principal achievements of the Second New Deal in 1935?
4. How did the economic crisis of the worldwide Great Depression help create new political orders in many nations?

DURING HIS TWELVE YEARS IN OFFICE, Franklin Roosevelt became more central to the life of the nation than any president had ever been. Simmering tensions around the world exploded into a catastrophic war, one that ultimately enveloped the United States and millions upon millions of its citizens. Meanwhile he faced the worst economic crisis in American history. His administration constructed a series of reforms (the New Deal) that fundamentally altered the federal government and its relationship to society.

Roosevelt never had a single, guiding philosophy for his programs but rather experimented with all manner of reforms to relieve suffering, stabilize the economy, and prevent comparable catastrophes in the future. Nevertheless, the New Deal did change across its two major phases, becoming more anticorporate and more focused on making long-term structural changes to the national economy and people's personal welfare. By the end of the 1930s, the Roosevelt administration had galvanized a powerful coalition within the Democratic Party that would dominate American politics for most of the next thirty years and had generated the beginnings of a new liberal ideology that would drive reform efforts for decades.

Despite its successes, Roosevelt's New Deal did not end the Great Depression. Near the close of Roosevelt's second term in 1940, many of the basic problems of the Depression remained unsolved. The persistence of those problems fueled attacks from dissident groups on the right and the left, some of them of considerable size and strength. These critics mobilized in the business world and outside the conventional party system to promote alternative paths to recovery. Factions with the Democratic Party, mainly conservative southerners, turned against Roosevelt's policies, joined with Republicans, and helped forge a conservative coalition in Congress that thwarted many of his goals. Only the preparations for World War II in 1940 and 1941 succeeded in ending the Great Depression. Although the New Deal ended with the war, some of its initiatives and philosophies, and the criticisms they provoked, would combine to create the broad outlines of the political world we know today.

LAUNCHING THE NEW DEAL

Roosevelt's first task upon taking office was to alleviate the panic that was creating chaos in the financial system. He did so in part by force of personality and in part by rapidly constructing an ambitious and diverse program of legislation. These laws would collectively come to be known by the term Roosevelt had used during the campaign: the **New Deal**.

RESTORING CONFIDENCE

Much of Roosevelt's early success was a result of his ebullient personality. He was the first president to make regular use of the radio. His **fireside chats**, during which he explained in simple terms his programs and plans to the people, helped build confidence in the administration. But Roosevelt could not rely on image alone. On March 6, two days after taking office, he issued a proclamation closing all banks for four days until Congress could meet in special session to consider banking reform legislation. So great was the panic about bank failures that the "bank holiday," as the president euphemistically described it, created a general sense of relief and hope.

TIME LINE

1931
Japan invades Manchuria

1933
"First New Deal" legislation

Prohibition ends

U.S. recognizes Soviet Union

Good Neighbor Policy

1934
American Liberty League founded

Long's Share-Our-Wealth Society established

1935
Supreme Court invalidates NRA

"Second New Deal" legislation, including Social Security and Wagner Acts

Lewis breaks with AFL

1936
Supreme Court invalidates Agricultural Adjustment Act

CIO established

Roosevelt reelected

Sit-down strikes

1937
Roosevelt's "Court-packing" plan

Supreme Court upholds Wagner Act

Severe recession

FDR's "quarantine speech"

1938
Fair Labor Standards Act

Munich Conference

1939
Nazi/USSR pact

Germany invades Poland

Three days later, Roosevelt sent to Congress the Emergency Banking Act, a generally conservative bill designed primarily to protect the larger banks from being dragged down by the weakness of smaller ones. The bill provided for Treasury Department inspection of all banks before they would be allowed to reopen. It also provided federal assistance to some troubled institutions and a thorough reorganization of those banks in the greatest difficulty. Congress passed the bill within a few hours of its introduction. Whatever else the new law accomplished, it helped dispel panic. Three-quarters of the banks in the Federal Reserve system reopened within the next three days, and $1 billion in hoarded currency and gold flowed back into them within a month. The immediate banking crisis was over.

On the morning after passage of the Emergency Banking Act, Roosevelt sent to Congress another measure—the Economy Act—designed to convince the public (and especially the business community) that the federal government was in safe, responsible hands. The act proposed to balance the federal budget by cutting the salaries of government employees and reducing pensions to veterans by as much as 15 percent. Like the banking bill, this one passed through Congress almost instantly, even though the cost cutting reduced the growth of the economy. Roosevelt then signed the Glass-Steagall Act of June 1933, which gave the government authority to curb irresponsible speculation by banks. More important, perhaps, it established the **Federal Deposit Insurance Corporation (FDIC)**, which guaranteed all bank deposits up to $2,500. Even if a bank should fail, small depositors would be able to recover their money.

To restore confidence in the stock market, Congress passed the so-called Truth in Securities Act of 1933, requiring corporations issuing new securities to provide full and accurate information about them to the public. In June 1934, another act established the **Securities and Exchange Commission (SEC)** to police the stock market. Roosevelt also signed a bill to legalize the manufacture and sale of beer with a 3.2 percent alcohol content—an interim measure pending the repeal of prohibition, for which a constitutional amendment (the Twenty-First) was already in process. The amendment was ratified later in 1933.

AGRICULTURAL ADJUSTMENT

These initial actions bought time for more comprehensive programs. The first was the **Agricultural Adjustment Act**, which Congress passed in May 1933. Under the provisions of the act, producers of seven basic commodities (wheat, cotton, corn, hogs, rice, tobacco, and dairy products) would impose production limits on their crops in order to keep the prices they could charge for those crops up. The government, through the Agricultural Adjustment Administration (AAA), would then tell individual farmers how much they should produce and would pay them subsidies for leaving some of their land idle. A tax on food processing (for example, the milling of wheat) would provide the funds for the new payments.

The AAA helped bring about a rise in prices for farm commodities in the years after 1933. Gross farm income increased by half in the first three years of the New Deal, and the agricultural economy as a whole emerged from the 1930s more stable and prosperous than it had been in many years. The AAA did, however, favor larger farmers over smaller ones. By distributing payments to landowners, not those who worked the land, the government allowed planters to reduce their acreage and cultivation output. This could mean evicting tenants and sharecroppers and firing field hands.

In January 1936, the Supreme Court struck down crucial provisions of the AAA, argu-ing that the government had no constitutional authority to require farmers to limit produc-tion. But within a few weeks, the administration had secured passage of new legislation (the Soil Conservation and Domestic Allotment Act), which permitted the government to pay farmers to reduce production to "conserve soil," prevent erosion, and accomplish other secondary goals.

The administration launched several efforts to assist poor farmers as well. The Resettlement Administration, established in 1935, and its successor, the **Farm Security Administration**, created in 1937, provided loans to help farmers cultivating submarginal soil to relocate to better lands. But the programs moved no more than a few thousand farmers. More effective was the Rural Electrification Administration, created in 1935, which worked to make electric power available for the first time to thousands of farmers through utility cooperatives.

INDUSTRIAL RECOVERY

Since 1931, leaders of the U.S. Chamber of Commerce and many others had been urging the government to adopt an antideflation program that would permit trade associations to cooperate in stabilizing prices within their industries. Existing antitrust laws clearly forbade such practices, and Herbert Hoover had refused to endorse suspension of the laws. The Roosevelt administra-tion was more receptive. In exchange for relaxing antitrust protections, however, New Dealers insisted on other provisions. Business leaders would have to recognize workers' right to bargain collectively through unions and ensure the incomes of workers would rise along with prices. And to help create jobs and increase consumer buying power, the administration added a major program of public works spending. The result of these and many other impulses was the National Industrial Recovery Act, which Congress passed in June 1933.

At its center was a new federal agency, the **National Recovery Administration (NRA)**, under the direction of Hugh S. Johnson. Johnson called on every business establishment in the nation to accept a temporary "blanket code": a minimum wage of between 30 and 40 cents an hour, a maximum workweek of thirty-five to forty hours, and the abolition of child labor. At the same time, Johnson negotiated another, more specific set of codes with leaders of the nation's major industries. These industrial codes set floors below which no company would lower prices or wages in its search for a competitive advantage, and they included provisions for maintaining employment and production. He quickly won agreements from almost every major industry in the country.

From the beginning, however, the NRA stumbled. The codes themselves were hastily and often poorly written. Large producers consistently dominated the code-writing process and ensured that the new regulations would work to their advantage and to the disadvantage of smaller firms. And the codes at times did more than simply set floors under prices; they actively and artificially raised them, sometimes to levels higher than buyers in the market could afford.

Other NRA goals also worked against recovery. Section 7(a) of the National Industrial Recovery Act promised workers the right to form unions and engage in collective bargaining and encouraged many workers to join unions for the first time. But Section 7(a) contained no enforcement mechanisms. The Public Works Administration (PWA), established to administer the National Industrial Recovery Act's spending programs, only gradually allowed the $3.3 billion in public works funds to trickle out.

Perhaps the clearest evidence of the NRA's failure was that industrial production actually declined in the months after the agency's establishment, despite the rise in prices that the codes

(©MPI/Archive Photos/Getty Images)

THE NRA (1933)   This cartoon by Clifford Berryman praised the spirit of cooperation between industry and labor that the National Recovery Administration was supposed to cultivate. It also lent visual expression to the magnified power, reach, confidence, and perhaps benevolence of the federal government in the early days of the New Deal.

had helped create. The NRA failed to increase the buying power for consumers, who were still reeling from unemployment or underemployment, which made the higher prices an obstacle to growth. By the spring of 1934, the NRA was besieged by criticism. That fall, Roosevelt pressured Johnson to resign and established a new board of directors to oversee the NRA.

Then in 1935, the Supreme Court intervened with a case involving alleged NRA code violations by the Schechter brothers, who operated a wholesale poultry business confined to Brooklyn, New York. The Court ruled unanimously that the Schechters were not engaged in interstate commerce (and thus not subject to federal regulation) and, further, that Congress had unconstitutionally delegated legislative power to the president to draft the NRA codes. The justices struck down the legislation establishing the agency. Roosevelt denounced the justices for their "horse-and-buggy" interpretation of the interstate commerce clause. He was rightly concerned, for the reasoning in the Schechter case threatened many other New Deal programs as well.

REGIONAL PLANNING

The AAA and the NRA largely reflected the beliefs of New Dealers who favored economic planning but wanted private interests (farmers or business leaders) to dominate the planning process.

But other reformers believed that the government itself should be the chief planning agent in the economy. Their most conspicuous success was an unprecedented experiment in regional planning: the **Tennessee Valley Authority (TVA)**.

Progressive reformers had agitated for years for public development of the nation's water resources as a source of cheap electric power. In particular, they had urged completion of a great dam at Muscle Shoals on the Tennessee River in Alabama—a dam begun during World War I but left unfinished when the war ended. But opposition from the utilities companies had blocked further progress on the dam.

In 1932, however, the great electricity empire of Samuel Insull collapsed spectacularly amid widely publicized exposés of corruption. Hostility to the utilities soon grew so intense that the companies were no longer able to block the public power movement. The result was legislation, supported by the president and enacted by Congress in May 1933, creating the Tennessee Valley Authority. The TVA was authorized to complete the dam at Muscle Shoals and build other dams in the region, and to generate and sell electricity from them to the public at reasonable rates. It was also intended to encourage the growth of local industries, supervise a substantial program of reforestation, and help farmers improve productivity.

Opposition by conservatives ultimately blocked many of the ambitious social planning projects proposed by the more visionary TVA administrators, but the Authority revitalized the region in numerous ways. By manipulating the flow of water, it made rivers more navigable, virtually eliminated flooding in the region, and provided electricity to thousands who had never before had it. Throughout the country, largely because of the yardstick

THE TENNESSEE VALLEY AUTHORITY The Tennessee Valley Authority was one of the largest experiments in government-funded public works and regional planning in American history to that point. The federal government had helped fund many projects in its history—canals, turnpikes, railroads, bridges, dams, and others. But never before had it undertaken a project of such great scope, and never before had it maintained such close control and ownership over the public works it helped create. This map illustrates the broad reach of the TVA within the Tennessee Valley region, which spanned seven states. TVA dams throughout the region helped control floods and also provided a source of hydroelectric power, which the government sold to consumers. Note the dam near Muscle Shoals, Alabama, in the bottom left of the map. It was begun during World War I, and efforts to revive it in the 1920s helped create the momentum that produced the TVA. • *Why were progressives so eager to see the government enter the business of hydroelectric power in the 1920s?*

provided by the TVA's cheap production of electricity, private power rates declined. Even so, the Tennessee Valley remained a generally impoverished region despite the TVA's efforts.

THE GROWTH OF FEDERAL RELIEF

The Roosevelt administration did not consider relief to the unemployed its most important task, but it recognized the necessity of doing something to help impoverished Americans survive until the government could revive the economy to the point where relief might not be necessary. Among Roosevelt's first acts as president was the establishment of the Federal Emergency Relief Administration (FERA), which provided cash grants to states to prop up bankrupt relief agencies. To administer the program, he chose the director of the New York State relief agency, Harry Hopkins. Both Hopkins and Roosevelt had misgivings about establishing a government "dole," or handout, but felt more comfortable with work relief. Thus when it became clear that the FERA grants were not enough, the administration established a second program: the Civil Works Administration (CWA), which put more than 4 million people to work on temporary projects between November 1933 and April 1934. Some of the projects were of lasting value, such as the construction of roads, schools, and parks; others were little more than make-work. To Hopkins, however, the important things were pumping money into the economy and providing assistance to people with nowhere else to turn.

Roosevelt's favorite relief project was the **Civilian Conservation Corps (CCC)**. The CCC created camps in national parks and forests and in other rural and wilderness settings. There, young unemployed men from the cities worked in a semimilitary environment on such projects as planting trees, building reservoirs, developing parks, and improving agricultural irrigation.

Mortgage relief was a pressing need for millions of farm owners and homeowners. The Farm Credit Administration, which within two years refinanced one-fifth of all farm mortgages in the United States, was one response to that problem. The Frazier-Lemke Farm Bankruptcy Act of 1933 was another. It enabled some farmers to regain their land even after the foreclosure of their mortgages. Despite such efforts, however, 25 percent of all American farm owners had lost their land by 1934. Homeowners were similarly troubled, and in June 1933 the administration established the Home Owners' Loan Corporation, which by 1936 had refinanced the mortgages of more than 1 million householders. A year later, Congress established the Federal Housing Administration to insure mortgages for new construction and home repairs.

THE NEW DEAL IN TRANSITION

Seldom has an American president enjoyed such remarkable popularity as Franklin Roosevelt did during his first two years in office. But by early 1935, the New Deal faced fierce public criticism. (For reverberations of such praise and condemnation in the historical scholarship on Roosevelt, see "Debating the Past: The New Deal.") In the spring of 1935, partly in response to these growing attacks, Roosevelt launched an ambitious new program of legislation that has often been called the "Second New Deal."

THE CONSERVATIVE CRITICISM OF THE NEW DEAL

Despite his great popularity, Franklin Roosevelt had many conservative critics. Some of them detested him so bitterly that they would refuse to say his name, calling him "that man." Those critics included businessmen, financiers, and wealthy members of society.

Roosevelt himself was among the most aristocratic presidents in American history. But he became the enemy of the very world that he came from. He was an alumnus of Harvard University, but the university president barely spoke to him when he went there to give a speech. He was, as many members of the American elite called him, a "traitor to his class." But even greater hatred came from conservative businessmen and financiers, who correctly accused New Dealers of imposing new regulations on the business and financial worlds. His critics were also infuriated by new taxes imposed by Roosevelt, even though high taxation reached only a few wealthy people.

The hatred of Roosevelt from conservatives took many forms. In 1935, a "whispering campaign" emerged from a New Deal effort to regulate the public utility industry. Stories circulated that the president was a drug addict, that he was insane, and that he was surrounded by psychiatrists. Hamilton Fish Jr., a conservative member of Congress, said on the floor of the House of Representatives that "whom the gods would destroy, they make first mad."

Others leveled ideological critiques. Walter Lippmann, a revered columnist, complained that Roosevelt was moving away from the nation's traditions. "We belong to a generation that has lost its way," he wrote. "Unable to develop the great truths which it inherited from the emancipators, it has returned to the heresies of absolutism, authority, and the domination of men by men." Lippmann and others charged that Roosevelt had become attracted to fascism and communism, with their dangerous investment of power in the government, instead of protecting the freedom of individuals.

Lewis Douglas, Roosevelt's first budget director, resigned in response to the president's determination to spend deficit funds to help provide relief to the unemployed. Al Smith, the former New York governor and twice the Democratic candidate, also turned against the president, partly because he considered the New Deal much too far to the left. However, for the most part, the New Deal lacked a clear ideology and, instead, experimented in many ways, some that conservatives found offensive.

Conservative business leaders were the most committed leaders of the attack on the New Deal. They formed an organization called the **Liberty League**, led by the Du Pont family, owners of the nation's largest chemical company. Its goal was to arouse public opposition to what its members called the "dictatorial" policies of the New Deal and to what they considered its attacks on free enterprise. It was led by John Jacob Raskob, a former head of the Democratic National Committee, former director of General Motors, and a trustee of Du Pont, who had abandoned the Democratic Party and joined the League. The League reached a peak of 125,000 members in 1936. It also recruited college students from 345 institutions, gaining over 10,000 members. Many followers were northeastern industrialists. The League described itself as a "nonpartisan organization founded to defend the Constitution and defend the rights and liberties guaranteed by that Constitution." Its purpose was

> to teach the necessity of respect for the rights of persons and property as fundamental to every form of government . . . to teach the duty of government, to encourage and protect individual and group initiative and enterprise, to foster the right to work, earn, save and acquire property, and to preserve the ownership and lawful use of property when acquired.

The Liberty League attracted considerable attention, but it had relatively little impact on the New Deal. Its leaders tried to remain nonpartisan, even though its members were staunchly anti-Roosevelt. They became a target for the president's 1936 reelection campaign. Soon after Roosevelt's landslide victory, the League dissolved. Hatred of Roosevelt did not disappear, but there was little organized opposition after 1936.

THE NEW DEAL

Contemporaries of Franklin Roosevelt debated the impact of the New Deal with ferocious intensity. Conservatives complained of a menacing tyranny of the state. Liberals celebrated the New Deal's progressive achievements. Some people on the left charged that the reforms of the 1930s were largely cosmetic and ignored the nation's fundamental problems. Although the conservative critique found relatively little scholarly expression until many years after Roosevelt's death, the liberal and left positions continued for decades to shape the way historians described the Roosevelt administration.

The dominant view from the beginning was an approving liberal interpretation, and its most important early voice was that of Arthur M. Schlesinger Jr. He argued in the three volumes of *The Age of Roosevelt* (1957–1960) that the New Deal marked a continuation of the long struggle between public power and private interests, a struggle Roosevelt had moved to a new level. Workers, farmers, consumers, and others now had much more protection than they had enjoyed in the past.

At almost the same time, however, other historians were offering more qualified assessments of the New Deal, although they remained securely within the liberal framework. Richard Hofstadter argued in 1955 that the New Deal gave American liberalism a "social-democratic tinge that had never before been present in American reform movements," but that its highly pragmatic approach lacked a central, guiding philosophy. James MacGregor Burns argued in 1956 that Roosevelt failed to make full use of his potential as a leader.

William Leuchtenburg's *Franklin D. Roosevelt and the New Deal* (1963) was the first systematic "revisionist" interpretation. Leuchtenburg challenged the views of earlier scholars who had proclaimed the New Deal a "revolution" in social policy. Leuchtenburg could muster only enough enthusiasm to call it a "halfway revolution," one that helped some previously disadvantaged groups (most notably farmers and workers) but that did little or nothing for many others (African Americans, sharecroppers, the urban poor).

Harsher criticisms soon emerged. Barton Bernstein in a 1968 essay concluded that the New Deal had saved capitalism, but at the expense of the least powerful. Ronald Radosh, Paul Conkin, and, later, Thomas Ferguson and Colin Gordon expanded on these criticisms. The New Deal, they contended, was part of the twentieth-century tradition of "corporate liberalism"—a tradition in which reform is closely wedded to the needs and interests of capitalism.

Most scholars in the 1980s and 1990s, however, seemed largely to have accepted the revised liberal view: that the New Deal was a significant and valuable chapter in the history of reform, but one that worked within rigid, occasionally crippling limits. Much of that work on the New Deal, therefore, focused on the constraints it faced. Some scholars (notably the sociologist Theda Skocpol) emphasized the issue of "state capacity"—the absence of a government bureaucracy with sufficient strength and expertise to shape or administer many programs. James T. Patterson, Barry Karl, Mark Leff, and others stressed the political constraints the New Deal encountered—the conservative inhibitions about government that remained strong in Congress and among the public. Frank Freidel, Ellis Hawley, Herbert Stein, and many others pointed as well to the ideological constraints affecting Franklin Roosevelt and his supporters—the limits of their own understanding of their time. Alan Brinkley, in *The End of Reform* (1995), described an ideological shift within New Deal liberalism that marginalized older concerns about wealth and monopoly power and replaced them with consumer-oriented Keynesianism. David Kennedy, in *Freedom from Fear* (1999), by contrast argued that the more aggressively anticapitalist measures of the early New Deal actually hampered recovery. Only when Roosevelt embraced the power of the market did prosperity begin to return.

The conservative attacks on the New Deal in the 2000s provided a newly powerful alternative view. A group of conservatives—among them Amity Schlaes and Burton Folsom—attacked the New Deal as a failure that created a vast bureaucracy and caused the Depression to last longer than it had to. Other scholarship has examined such conservative critiques against the New Deal in its own time. Kim Phillips-Fein (2009) wrote about businessmen's "crusade" against Roosevelt's programs, and Kevin Kruse (2015) attributed America's postwar religiosity not to the Cold War but to a concerted and successful effort by those corporate antagonists to mobilize opposition to the New Deal as a threat to "freedom under God."

The phrase "New Deal liberalism" has come in the postwar era to seem synonymous with modern ideas of aggressive federal management of the economy, elaborate welfare systems, a powerful bureaucracy, and large-scale government spending. But many historians of the New Deal would argue that the modern idea of New Deal liberalism bears only a limited relationship to the ideas that New Dealers themselves embraced. •

UNDERSTAND, ANALYZE, & EVALUATE

1. How has the scholarly understanding of the New Deal changed over time?
2. Did the New Deal save capitalism? If so, how and why?

THE POPULIST CRITICISM OF THE NEW DEAL

Roosevelt's policies also generated criticism from the far left. The Communist Party, the Socialist Party, and other radical and semiradical organizations were at times harshly critical of the New Deal. But like the conservatives, they failed to attract genuine mass support.

More menacing to the New Deal than either the far right or the far left was a group of dissident political movements that defied easy ideological classification. Some gained substantial public support within particular states and regions. And three men succeeded in mobilizing genuinely national followings. Dr. Francis E. Townsend, an elderly California physician, rose from obscurity to lead a movement of more than 5 million members with his plan for federal pensions for older adults. According to the **Townsend Plan**, all Americans over the age of sixty would receive monthly government pensions of $200, provided they retired (thus freeing jobs for younger, unemployed Americans) and spent the money in full each month (which would pump needed funds into the economy). By 1935, the Townsend Plan had attracted the support of many older men and women.

Father **Charles E. Coughlin**, a Catholic priest in the Detroit suburb of Royal Oak, Michigan, achieved even greater renown through his weekly national radio sermons. He proposed a series of monetary reforms—remonetization of silver, issuing of greenbacks, and nationalization of the banking system—that he insisted would restore prosperity and ensure economic justice. At first a warm supporter of Roosevelt, Coughlin had become disheartened by late 1934 by what he claimed was the president's failure to deal harshly enough with the "money powers." In the spring of 1935, he established his own political organization, the National Union for Social Justice.

Most alarming to the administration was the growing national popularity of Senator **Huey P. Long** of Louisiana. Long had risen to power in his home state through his strident attacks on the banks, oil companies, and utilities and on the conservative political oligarchy allied with them. Elected governor in 1928, he launched an assault on his opponents so thorough and forceful they were soon left with virtually no political power. But he also maintained the overwhelming support of the Louisiana electorate, in part because of his flamboyant personality and in part because of his solid record of conventional progressive accomplishments: building roads, schools, and hospitals; revising the tax codes; distributing free textbooks; lowering utility rates. Barred by law from succeeding himself as governor, he ran in 1930 for a seat in the U.S. Senate and won easily.

Long, like Coughlin, supported Franklin Roosevelt for president in 1932. But within six months of Roosevelt's inauguration, Long had broken with the president. As an alternative to the New Deal, he advocated a drastic program of wealth redistribution, a program he ultimately named the Share-Our-Wealth Plan. The government, he claimed, could end the

(©Fotosearch/Archive Photos/Getty Images)

HUEY LONG Few public speakers could inflame a crowd more effectively than Huey Long of Louisiana, known to many as "the Kingfish" (a nickname borrowed from a scheming character on the popular radio show *Amos 'n' Andy*). It was Long's effective use of radio, however, that contributed most directly to his spreading national popularity in the early 1930s.

Depression easily by using the tax system to confiscate the surplus riches of the wealthiest men and women in America and distribute these surpluses to the rest of the population. That would, he claimed, allow the government to guarantee every family a minimum "homestead" worth $5,000 and an annual wage of $2,500. In 1934, Long established his own national organization: the Share-Our-Wealth Society, which soon attracted a large following through much of the nation. A poll by the Democratic National Committee in the spring of 1935 disclosed that Long might attract more than 10 percent of the vote if he ran as a third-party candidate, possibly enough to tip a close election to the Republicans.

Members of the Roosevelt administration considered dissident movements—and the broad popular discontent they represented—a genuine threat. An increasing number of advisers were warning Roosevelt that he would have to do something dramatic to counter their strength.

THE "SECOND NEW DEAL"

Roosevelt launched the so-called **Second New Deal** in the spring of 1935 in response both to growing political pressures and to the continuing economic crisis. The new proposals represented a shift in the emphasis of New Deal policy. Perhaps the most conspicuous change was in the administration's attitude toward big business. Symbolically at least, the president was now willing to attack corporate interests openly. In March, for example, he proposed to Congress an act designed to break up the great utility holding companies. The Holding Company Act of 1935 was the result, although furious lobbying by the utilities led to amendments that sharply limited its effects.

Equally alarming to affluent Americans was a series of tax reforms proposed by the president in 1935. Apparently designed to undercut the appeal of Huey Long's Share-Our-Wealth Plan, the Roosevelt proposals called for establishing the highest and most progressive peacetime tax rates in history—although the actual impact of these rates was limited.

The Supreme Court decision in 1935 to strike down the National Industrial Recovery Act also invalidated Section 7(a) of the act, which had guaranteed workers the right to organize and bargain collectively. A group of progressives in Congress, led by Senator Robert E. Wagner of New York, introduced what became the National Labor Relations Act of 1935. The new law, popularly known as the Wagner Act, provided workers with a crucial enforcement mechanism missing from the 1933 law: the **National Labor Relations Board (NLRB)**, which would have power to compel employers to recognize and bargain with legitimate unions. The president was not entirely happy with the bill, but he signed it anyway. That was largely because American workers themselves had by 1935 become so important and vigorous a force that Roosevelt realized his own political future would depend in part on responding to their demands.

LABOR MILITANCY

The emergence of a powerful trade union movement in the 1930s occurred partly in response to government efforts to enhance the power of unions. It was also a result of the increased militancy of American workers after a lull during the 1920s. Business leaders and industrialists lost (at least temporarily) the ability to control government policies. Equally important, new and more powerful labor organizations emerged.

The American Federation of Labor (AFL) remained committed to the idea of the craft union: organizing workers on the basis of their skills. But that concept had little to offer unskilled laborers, who now constituted the bulk of the industrial workforce. During the 1930s, therefore, a newer concept of labor organization challenged the craft union ideal: industrial unionism.

Advocates of this approach argued that all workers in a particular industry should be organized in a single union, regardless of what functions the workers performed. So united, workers would greatly increase their power.

Leaders of the AFL craft unions for the most part opposed the new concept. But industrial unionism found a number of important advocates, most prominent among them **John L. Lewis**, the leader of the United Mine Workers. At first, Lewis and his allies attempted to work within the AFL, but friction between the new industrial organizations Lewis was promoting and the older craft unions grew. At the 1935 AFL convention, Lewis became embroiled in a series of angry confrontations with craft union leaders before finally walking out. A few weeks later, he created the Committee on Industrial Organization. When the AFL expelled the new committee and all the industrial unions it represented, Lewis renamed the committee the **Congress of Industrial Organizations (CIO)** and became its first president.

The CIO expanded the constituency of the labor movement. It was more receptive to women and African Americans than the AFL had been, in part because CIO organizing drives targeted previously unorganized industries (textiles, laundries, tobacco factories, and others) where women and minorities constituted much of the workforce. The CIO was also more militant than the AFL. By the time of the 1936 schism, it was already engaged in major organizing battles in the automobile and steel industries.

Organizing Battles

The United Auto Workers (UAW) gradually emerged preeminent in the early and mid-1930s. Although it was gaining recruits, it was making little progress in winning recognition from the corporations. In December 1936, however, autoworkers employed a controversial and effective new technique for challenging corporate opposition: the **sit-down strike**. Employees in several General Motors plants in Detroit simply sat down inside the plants, refusing either to work or to leave, thus preventing the company from using strikebreakers. The tactic spread to other locations, and by February 1937, strikers had occupied seventeen GM plants. The strikers ignored court orders and local police efforts to force them to vacate the buildings. When Michigan's governor refused to call up the National Guard to clear out the strikers, and when the federal government also refused to intervene on behalf of employers, General Motors relented. In February 1937, it became the first major manufacturer to recognize the UAW. Other automobile companies soon did the same.

In the steel industry, the battle for unionization was less easily won. In 1936, the Steel Workers Organizing Committee (SWOC), later the United Steelworkers of America, began a major organizing drive involving thousands of workers and frequent strikes. In March 1937, to the surprise of almost everyone, United States Steel, the giant of the industry, recognized the union rather than risk a costly strike. But the smaller companies, known collectively as "Little Steel," were less accommodating. On Memorial Day 1937, striking workers from Republic Steel gathered with their families for a picnic and demonstration in south Chicago. When they attempted to march peacefully and legally toward the steel plant, police opened fire on them. Ten demonstrators were killed; another ninety were wounded. Despite a public outcry against the "Memorial Day Massacre," the harsh tactics of Little Steel companies succeeded. The 1937 strike failed.

But the victory of Little Steel was among the last gasps of the kind of brutal strikebreaking that had proven effective in the past. In 1937 alone, there were 4,720 strikes, over 80 percent of them settled in favor of the unions. By the end of the year, more than 8 million workers were members of unions recognized as official bargaining units by employers (as compared with

(©Carl Linde/AP Photo)

THE "MEMORIAL DAY MASSACRE" The bitterness of the labor struggles of the 1930s was nowhere more evident than in Chicago in 1937, when striking workers attempting to march on a Republic Steel plant were brutally attacked by Chicago police, who used clubs, tear gas, and guns to turn away the marchers. Ten strikers were killed and many others were injured.

3 million in 1932). By 1941, that number had expanded to 10 million and included the workers of Little Steel, whose employers had finally recognized the SWOC.

SOCIAL SECURITY

From the first moments of the New Deal, important members of the administration had been lobbying for a system of federally sponsored social insurance for elderly people and those who were unemployed—not just for humanitarian reasons, but also to keep those groups active in the nation's economy. In 1935, Roosevelt gave public support to what became the **Social Security Act**, which Congress passed the same year. It established several distinct programs. For older people, there were two types of assistance. Those who were presently destitute could receive up to $15 a month in federal assistance. More important for the future, many Americans presently working were incorporated into a pension system, to which they and their employers would contribute through a payroll tax. These funds would provide them with an income on retirement, though initially these pension payments would provide only $10 to $85 a month to recipients. And at first, payment was not to be distributed until 1942. But public pressure pushed the payment date back to 1937. Broad categories of workers (including domestic servants and agricultural laborers, often women or racial minorities) were excluded from the program. But the act was a crucial first step in building the nation's most important social program for retired Americans.

In addition, the Social Security Act created a system of unemployment insurance that employers alone would finance. It also established a system of federal aid to people with disabilities and a program of aid to dependent children.

The framers of the Social Security Act wanted to create a system of "insurance," not "welfare." And the largest programs (old-age pensions and unemployment insurance) were in many ways similar to private insurance programs. But the act also provided considerable direct assistance based on need—to low-income aging adults, to those with disabilities, to dependent children and their mothers. These groups were widely perceived to be small and genuinely unable to support themselves. But in later generations, the programs for these groups would expand until they assumed dimensions planners of Social Security had not foreseen.

New Directions in Relief

Social Security was designed primarily to fulfill long-range goals. But millions of unemployed Americans had immediate needs. To help them, the Roosevelt administration established in 1935 the **Works Progress Administration (WPA)**. Like the Civil Works Administration and other earlier efforts, the WPA established a system of work relief for the unemployed. But it was much bigger than the earlier agencies.

Under the direction of **Harry Hopkins**, the WPA was responsible for building or renovating 110,000 public buildings and for constructing almost 600 airports, more than 500,000 miles of roads, and over 100,000 bridges. In the process, the WPA kept an average of 2.1 million workers employed and pumped needed money into the economy.

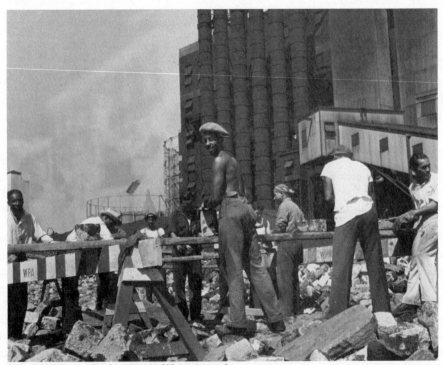

(©Joseph Schwartz/Corbis Historical/Getty Images)

WPA WORKERS ON THE JOB The Works Progress Administration funded an enormous variety of work projects to provide jobs for unemployed individuals. The majority of WPA employees, however, worked on construction sites.

The WPA also displayed remarkable flexibility and imagination. The Federal Writers' Project of the WPA, for example, gave unemployed writers a chance to do their work and receive a government salary. The Federal Art Project, similarly, helped painters, sculptors, and others continue their careers. The Federal Music Project and the Federal Theatre Project oversaw the production of concerts and plays, creating work for unemployed musicians, actors, and directors. Other relief agencies emerged alongside the WPA. The National Youth Administration (NYA) provided work and scholarship assistance to men and women of high school and college age. The Emergency Housing Division of the Public Works Administration began federal sponsorship of public housing.

The new welfare system dealt with men and women in very different ways. For men, the government concentrated mainly on work relief, including the CCC, the CWA, and the WPA. The principal government aid to women was not work relief but cash assistance—most notably through the Aid to Dependent Children program of Social Security, which was designed largely to assist single mothers. This disparity in treatment reflected a widespread assumption that men should constitute the bulk of the paid workforce. Yet millions of women were already employed by the 1930s.

THE 1936 "REFERENDUM"

By the middle of 1936—with the economy visibly reviving—there could be little doubt that Roosevelt would win a second term. The Republican Party nominated the moderate governor of Kansas, Alf M. Landon, who waged a relatively dull campaign. Roosevelt's dissident challengers now appeared powerless. One reason was the assassination of their most effective leader, Huey Long, in Louisiana in September 1935. Another reason was the ill-fated alliance among Father Coughlin, Dr. Townsend, and Gerald L. K. Smith (an intemperate henchman of Huey Long), who joined forces that summer to establish a new political movement—the Union Party, which nominated an undistinguished North Dakota congressman, William Lemke.

The result was the greatest landslide in American history to that point. Roosevelt polled just under 61 percent of the vote to Landon's 36 percent and carried every state except Maine and Vermont. The Democrats increased their already large majorities in both houses of Congress.

The election results demonstrated the party realignment that the New Deal had produced. The Democrats now controlled a broad coalition of western and southern farmers, the urban working classes, the poor and unemployed, and white southerners, as well as traditional progressives and committed new liberals. New Deal aid flowing to black communities in northern cities helped pry that constituency from the Republican column. The resulting coalition constituted a substantial majority of the electorate. It would be decades before the Republican Party could again create a lasting majority coalition of its own.

THE NEW DEAL IN DISARRAY

Roosevelt emerged from the 1936 election at the zenith of his popularity. Within months, however, the New Deal was mired in serious new difficulties.

THE COURT FIGHT

The 1936 mandate, Franklin Roosevelt believed, made it possible for him to do something about the Supreme Court. No program of reform, he believed, could long survive the conservative justices, who had already struck down the NRA and the AAA.

In February 1937, Roosevelt sent a surprise message to Capitol Hill proposing an overhaul of the federal court system. Included among the many provisions was one to add up to six new justices to the Supreme Court. The courts were "overworked," the president claimed, and needed additional manpower and younger blood to enable them to cope with their increasing burdens. But Roosevelt's real purpose was to give himself the opportunity to appoint new, liberal justices and change the ideological balance of the Court.

Conservatives were outraged at the "**Court-packing plan**," and even many Roosevelt supporters were disturbed by it. Still, Roosevelt might well have persuaded Congress to approve at least a compromise measure had not the Supreme Court itself intervened. Of the nine justices, three reliably supported the New Deal, and four reliably opposed it. Of the remaining two, Chief Justice Charles Evans Hughes often sided with the progressives, and Associate Justice Owen J. Roberts usually voted with the conservatives. On March 29, 1937, Roberts, Hughes, and the three progressive justices voted together to uphold a state minimum-wage law—in the case of *West Coast Hotel v. Parrish*—thus reversing a 5-to-4 decision of the previous year invalidating a similar law. Two weeks later, again by a 5-to-4 margin, the Court upheld the Wagner Act, and in May it validated the Social Security Act. Whatever the reasons for the decisions, the Court's newly moderate position made the Court-packing bill seem unnecessary. Congress ultimately defeated it.

On one level, Franklin Roosevelt had achieved a victory. The Court was no longer an obstacle to New Deal reforms. But the Court-packing episode politically damaged the administration. From 1937 on, southern Democrats and other conservatives voted against Roosevelt's measures much more often than they had in the past.

RETRENCHMENT AND RECESSION

By the summer of 1937, the national income—which had dropped from $82 billion in 1929 to $40 billion in 1932—had risen to nearly $72 billion. Other economic indices showed similar advances. Roosevelt seized on these improvements as justification for trying to balance the federal budget. Between January and August 1937, he cut the WPA in half, laying off 1.5 million relief workers. A few weeks later, the fragile boom collapsed. An important index of industrial production dropped dramatically from August 1937 to May 1938. Four million additional workers lost their jobs. Economic conditions were soon almost as bad as they had been in the bleak days of 1932–1933.

The recession of 1937, known to the president's critics as the "Roosevelt recession," was a result of many factors. But to many observers at the time, it seemed to be a direct result of the administration's unwise decision to reduce spending. And so in April 1938, the president asked Congress for an emergency appropriation of $5 billion for public works and relief programs, and government funds soon began pouring into the economy once again. Within a few months, another tentative recovery seemed to be under way.

At about the same time, Roosevelt sent a stinging message to Congress, vehemently denouncing what he called an "unjustifiable concentration of economic power" and asking for the creation of a commission to consider major reforms in the antitrust laws. In response, Congress established the Temporary National Economic Committee (TNEC), whose members included representatives of both houses of Congress and officials from several executive agencies. Later in 1938, the administration successfully supported one of its most ambitious pieces of labor legislation, the Fair Labor Standards Act, which for the first time established a national minimum wage and a forty-hour workweek and which also placed strict limits on child labor.

Despite these achievements, however, by the end of 1938 the New Deal had essentially come to an end. Congressional opposition now made it difficult for the president to enact any major new programs. But more important, perhaps, the threat of world crisis hung heavy in the political atmosphere, and Roosevelt was gradually growing more concerned with persuading a reluctant nation to prepare for war than with pursuing new avenues of reform.

ISOLATIONISM AND INTERNATIONALISM

Alongside the deep economic crises Franklin Roosevelt faced, his administration had to deal as well with the effects of a decaying international structure. Those problems owed to continuing fallout from the Great War and confronted Roosevelt from the time he took office.

DEPRESSION DIPLOMACY

When Roosevelt entered office in 1933, the Depression was worldwide. The struggles of American banks had led them to call in loans to the former Central Powers, which spurred the collapse of financial institutions in Germany and Austria and thus their payment of reparations to the Allies. Roosevelt broke with his predecessor on the American role in this system. The Hoover administration had worked to settle the issue of war debts through international agreement. Roosevelt abandoned that effort, signing a bill in April 1934 that prohibited American banks from making loans to any nation in default on its debts. The legislation ended the old, circular system by which debt payments continued only by virtue of increasing American loans. Within months, war-debt payments from every nation except Finland stopped for good.

Roosevelt also parted company with Hoover on the question of the money supply, which pivoted around whether that supply should be backed only by gold. Hoover had firmly argued that reinforcing the gold standard would stabilize the American economy. Roosevelt countered that a fluid money supply would stabilize falling prices and allow the Federal Reserve to more freely provide emergency relief to banks. Though he did not explicitly make the connection, his argument here echoed Populist advocacy of bimetallism in the 1890s as an economic stabilizer. Joining many European countries, he effectively took the United States off the gold standard in April 1933.

Sixteen years after the Bolshevik Revolution of 1917, the American government still had not officially recognized the government of the Soviet Union. But a growing number of influential Americans were urging a change in policy—largely because the Soviet Union appeared to be a possible source of trade. Soviet leader Josef Stalin was hoping for American cooperation in containing Japan. In November 1933, the United States and the Soviet Union agreed to open formal diplomatic exchange. Relations with the Soviet Union, however, soon soured. American trade failed to establish a foothold in Russia, disappointing hopes in the United States. The American government did little to reassure the Soviets that it was interested in stopping Japanese expansion in Asia, dousing expectations in Russia. By the end of 1934, the Soviet Union and the United States were once again viewing each other with considerable mistrust.

The Roosevelt administration was also taking a new approach toward Latin America, an approach that became known as the **Good Neighbor Policy** and that expanded on the changes the Hoover administration had made. At an Inter-American Conference in Montevideo,

Uruguay, in December 1933, Secretary of State Cordell Hull signed a formal convention declaring: "No state has the right to intervene in the internal or external affairs of another."

THE RISE OF ISOLATIONISM

With the international system of the 1920s now beyond repair, the United States faced a choice between more active efforts to stabilize the world or more energetic attempts to isolate itself from it. Many Americans chose isolation. Support for **isolationism** emerged from many quarters. Some Wilsonian internationalists had grown disillusioned with the League of Nations and its inability to stop Japanese aggression in Asia. Other Americans argued that the American role in the Great War was a result of Wall Street and munitions makers; most of the public, according to new polling data, believed intervention in the war had been an error. An investigation by a Senate committee chaired by Senator Gerald Nye of North Dakota claimed to have produced evidence of exorbitant profiteering and tax evasion by many corporations during the war, and it suggested that bankers had pressured Wilson to intervene in the war so as to protect their loans abroad. (Few historians now lend much credence to these charges.)

Roosevelt continued to hope for at least a modest American role in maintaining world peace. In 1935, he proposed to the Senate a treaty to make the United States a member of the World Court—a largely symbolic gesture. Isolationists led by Father Coughlin and William Randolph Hearst aroused popular opposition to the agreement, and the Senate voted it down.

In the summer of 1935, Benito Mussolini's Italy was preparing to invade Ethiopia. Fearing the invasion would provoke a new European war, American legislators tried to prevent the United States from being dragged into the conflict. The Neutrality Act of 1935 established a mandatory arms embargo against both sides in any military conflict and warned American citizens against traveling on the ships of warring nations. Thus, isolationists believed, the "protection of neutral rights" could not again become an excuse for American intervention in war. A 1937 law established the so-called cash-and-carry policy, by which warring nations could purchase only nonmilitary goods from the United States and could do so only by paying cash and shipping their purchases themselves. Collectively these laws were known as the **Neutrality Acts**.

Isolationist sentiment showed its strength again in 1936 in response to the start of the Spanish Civil War. While more than 3,000 Americans had joined the Lincoln Brigade to fight on the side of the republican government's forces, the U.S. government joined with Britain and France in an agreement to offer no assistance to either side. With material support from Hitler and Mussolini, Franco's forces were able to take full control of Spain by 1939.

In the summer of 1937, Japan intensified its six-year-old assault on the northern Chinese region of Manchuria, widening its attack to encompass a large part of southern China, including most of the port cities. China's vulnerability stemmed in part from its own civil war between Chiang Kai-shek's nationalist party and Mao Zedong's Chinese Communist Party, but the two sides settled on an uneasy truce to fight the invaders together. In a speech in Chicago in October 1937, Roosevelt warned that Japanese and other aggressors should be "quarantined" by the international community to prevent the contagion of war from spreading. He was deliberately vague about what such a quarantine would mean. Even so, public response to the speech was hostile, and Roosevelt drew back. On December 12, 1937, Japanese aviators bombed and sank the U.S. gunboat *Panay*, almost certainly deliberately, as it sailed the Yangtze River in China. But so reluctant was the Roosevelt administration to antagonize the isolationists that the United States eagerly seized on Japanese claims that the bombing had been an accident and accepted Japan's apologies.

THE FAILURE OF MUNICH

In 1936, Hitler had moved the revived German army into the Rhineland, rearming an area that had been off-limits to German troops since World War I. In March 1938, German forces marched without opposition into Austria, and Hitler proclaimed a union (or *Anschluss*) between Austria, his native land, and Germany, his adopted one. Neither in America nor in most of Europe was there much more than a murmur of opposition.

Germany had by now occupied territory surrounding three sides of western Czechoslovakia, a region Hitler dreamed of annexing. In September 1938, he demanded that Czechoslovakia cede him the Sudetenland, a part of Czechoslovakia in which many ethnic Germans lived. Although Czechoslovakia was prepared to fight to stop Hitler, it needed assistance from other nations. But most Western governments, including the United States, were willing to pay almost any price to settle the crisis peacefully. On September 29, Hitler met with the leaders of France and Great Britain at Munich in an effort to resolve the crisis. The French and British agreed to accept the German demands in Czechoslovakia in return for Hitler's promise to expand no farther. Americans watched these events nervously.

The Munich agreement, which Roosevelt supported at the time, was the most prominent element of a policy that came to be known as **appeasement** and that came to be identified

(©Everett Historical/Shutterstock)

1936 NUREMBERG RALLY The Nazi Party held rallies at Nuremberg in the 1930s to celebrate German military strength, project Adolf Hitler's authority, and deliver political speeches. The gatherings also generated material for propaganda films, including Leni Riefenstahl's *Triumph of the Will*. Here German soldiers assembled for the 1936 event.

(not altogether fairly) with British prime minister Neville Chamberlain. Whoever was to blame, the policy was a failure. In March 1939, Hitler occupied the remaining areas of Czechoslovakia, violating the Munich agreement. And in April, he began issuing threats against Poland.

At that point, both Britain and France assured the Polish government that they would come to its assistance in case of invasion. They even tried, too late, to draw the Soviet Union into a mutual defense agreement. But the Soviet leader **Josef Stalin**, who had not even been invited to the Munich Conference, had decided he could expect no protection from the West. He signed a nonaggression pact with Hitler in August 1939, freeing the Germans (for now) from the danger of a two-front war. Shortly after that, Hitler staged an incident on the Polish border to allow him to claim that Germany had been attacked, and on September 1, 1939, he launched a full-scale invasion of Poland. Britain and France, true to their pledges, declared war on Germany two days later. World War II, already under way in Asia, had begun in Europe.

LIMITS AND LEGACIES OF THE NEW DEAL

While the embers of war began burning in Asia and Europe, the New Deal made major changes in American government, some of them still controversial today. It also left important problems unaddressed.

African Americans and the New Deal

The New Deal was not hostile to black aspirations. **Eleanor Roosevelt** spoke throughout the 1930s and beyond on behalf of racial justice and put continuing pressure on her husband and others in the federal government to ease discrimination against blacks. (See "Consider the Source: Eleanor Roosevelt on Civil Rights.") The president himself appointed a number of African Americans to significant second-level positions in his administration, creating an informal network of officeholders that became known as the "Black Cabinet." Eleanor Roosevelt, Interior Secretary Harold Ickes, and WPA Director Harry Hopkins all made efforts to ensure that New Deal relief programs did not exclude blacks. By 1935 an estimated 30 percent of all African Americans were receiving some form of government assistance, even amid persistent racial discrimination against people of color by local administrators of aid. One result was a historic change in black electoral behavior. As late as 1932, most black Americans were voting Republican, as they had since the Civil War. By 1936, more than 90 percent were voting Democratic.

African Americans supported Franklin Roosevelt, but they had few illusions that the New Deal represented a major turning point in American race relations. The president was, for example, never willing to risk losing the support of southern Democrats by supporting legislation to make lynching a federal crime or to ban the poll tax, one of the most potent tools keeping blacks from voting.

New Deal relief agencies did not challenge, and indeed reinforced, existing patterns of discrimination. The CCC established separate black camps. The NRA codes tolerated paying blacks less than whites doing the same jobs. The WPA routinely relegated African American and Hispanic workers to the least-skilled and lowest-paying jobs. When funding ebbed, African Americans, like women, were among the first to be dismissed.

The New Deal was not hostile to African Americans, and it made some contributions to their progress. But it never made racial justice a significant part of its agenda.

The New Deal and the "Indian Problem"

New Deal policy toward the Indian tribes marked a significant break from earlier approaches, largely because of the efforts of the commissioner of Indian affairs, **John Collier**. Collier was greatly influenced by the work of twentieth-century anthropologists who advanced the idea of cultural relativism, the theory that every culture should be accepted and respected on its own terms.

Collier wanted to reverse the pressures on Native Americans to assimilate and instead allow them to remain Indians. He effectively promoted the Indian Reorganization Act (1934) that restored to the tribes the right to own land collectively and elect tribal governments. In the thirteen years after passage of the bill, tribal land increased by nearly 4 million acres, and Indian agricultural income increased from under $2 million in 1934 to over $49 million in 1947. Even with the redistribution of lands under the 1934 act, however, Indians continued to possess, for the most part, only territory whites did not want, much of it arid, some of it desert. And as a group, they continued to constitute the poorest segment of the population.

Women and the New Deal

Symbolically at least, the New Deal marked a breakthrough in the role of women in public life. Roosevelt appointed the first female member of the cabinet in the nation's history: Secretary of Labor **Frances Perkins**. He also named more than 100 other women to positions at lower levels of the federal bureaucracy. But the administration was concerned not so much about achieving gender equality as about obtaining special protections for women.

(©George Rinhart/Corbis Historical/Getty Images)

ELEANOR ROOSEVELT First Lady Eleanor Roosevelt was among the first women to play an important role in politics and government. She oversaw Franklin Roosevelt's political campaigns before he became president as well as developing an important career of her own working on social programs in New York. When she moved to the White House, she championed human rights issues. In this photograph she is on the way to inspect a Washington, D.C., jail that had a reputation for being overcrowded and obsolete.

CONSIDER THE SOURCE

ELEANOR ROOSEVELT ON CIVIL RIGHTS (1942)

Although written in the context of World War II, this article in *The New Republic* captures Eleanor Roosevelt's dedication to the causes of racial and religious equality. Published on May 11, 1942, "Race, Religion, and Prejudice" referred to existing immigration laws and grappled with their place, and the place of stateside racial discrimination, in the evolving political philosophy of twentieth-century liberalism.

We have had a definite policy toward the Chinese and Japanese who wished to enter our country for many years, and I doubt very much if after this war is over we can differentiate between the peoples of Europe, the Near East and the Far East.

Perhaps the simplest way of facing the problem in the future is to say that we are fighting for freedom, and one of the freedoms we must establish is freedom from discrimination among the peoples of the world, either because of race, or of color, or of religion.

The people of the world have suddenly begun to stir and they seem to feel that in the future we should look upon each other as fellow human beings, judged by our acts, by our abilities, by our development, and not by any less fundamental differences.

Here in our own country we have any number of attitudes which have become habits and which constitute our approach to the Jewish people, the Japanese and Chinese people, the Italian people, and above all, to the Negro people in our midst.

Perhaps because the Negroes are our largest minority, our attitude towards them will have to be faced first of all. I keep on repeating that the way to face this situation is by being completely realistic. We cannot force people to accept friends for whom they have no liking, but living in a democracy it is entirely reasonable to demand that every citizen of that democracy enjoy the fundamental rights of a citizen.

Over and over again, I have stressed the rights of every citizen:

Equality before the law.
Equality of education.
Equality to hold a job according to his ability.
Equality of participation through the ballot in the government.

These are inherent rights in a democracy, and I do not see how we can fight this war and deny these rights to any citizen in our own land.

The other relationships will gradually settle themselves once these major things are part of our accepted philosophy.

It seems trite to say to the Negro, you must have patience, when he has had patience so long; you must not expect miracles overnight, when he can look back to the years of slavery and say-how many nights! he has waited for justice. Nevertheless, it is what we must continue to say in the interests of our government as a whole and of the Negro people; but that does not mean that we must sit idle and do nothing. We must keep moving forward steadily, removing restrictions which have no sense, and fighting prejudice. If we are wise we will do this where it is easiest to do it first, and watch it spread gradually to places where the old prejudices are slow to disappear.

There is now a great group of educated Negroes who can become leaders among their people, who can teach them the value of things of the mind and who qualify as the best in any field of endeavor. With these men and women it is impossible to think of any barriers of inferiority, but differences there are and always will be, and that is why on both sides there must be tact and patience and an effort at real understanding. Above everything else, no action must be taken which can cause so much bitterness that the whole liberalizing effort may be set back over a period of many years.

UNDERSTAND, ANALYZE, & EVALUATE

1. What exactly was Eleanor Roosevelt calling for in this piece?

2. What seem to have been her attitudes toward Americans who harbored racial or religious prejudice?
3. How might African American civil rights activists have reacted to the last two paragraphs?
4. What were the dangers, to Roosevelt, of reforming race relations too quickly?

Roosevelt, Eleanor, "Race, Religion and Prejudice," *The New Republic*, May 11, 1942, 630. Copyright ©1942 by The Eleanor Roosevelt Literary Estate. All rights reserved. Used with permission.

The New Deal generally supported the widespread belief that in hard times women should withdraw from the workplace to open jobs for men. New Deal relief agencies offered relatively little employment for women. The Social Security program excluded domestic servants, waitresses, and other predominantly female occupations.

Repeating its handling of racial justice, the New Deal was not actively hostile to feminist aspirations, but it accepted prevailing cultural norms. There was not yet sufficient political pressure from women themselves to persuade the administration to do otherwise. Indeed, some of the most important supporters of policies that reinforced traditional gender roles (such as Social Security) were themselves women.

THE NEW DEAL AND THE WEST

One part of American society that did receive special attention from the New Deal was the American West. That region received more government funds per capita through relief programs than any other.

Except for the TVA, the largest New Deal public works programs—the great dams and power stations—were mainly in the West, both because the best locations for such facilities were there and because the West had the greatest need for new sources of water and power. The Grand Coulee Dam on the Columbia River was the largest public works project in American history to that point, and it provided cheap electric power for much of the Northwest. Its construction, and that of other, smaller dams and water projects, created a basis for economic development in the region. Without this enormous public investment by the federal government, much of the economic growth that transformed the West after World War II would have been much more difficult.

THE NEW DEAL, THE ECONOMY, AND POLITICS

The most frequent criticisms of the New Deal involve its failure to revive or reform the American economy. New Dealers never fully recognized the value of government spending as a vehicle for recovery. The economic boom sparked by World War II—not the New Deal—finally ended the crisis.

Nevertheless, the New Deal did have a number of important and lasting effects on the American economy. It helped elevate new groups—workers and farmers in particular—to positions from which they could at times challenge the power of the corporations. It increased the regulatory functions of the federal government in ways that helped stabilize previously troubled areas of the economy: the stock market, the banking system, and others. These and other tools for promoting and regulating economic growth would expand in the postwar years.

The New Deal also created the rudiments of the American welfare state through its many relief programs and, above all, through the Social Security system. The conservative inhibitions New Dealers brought to this task ensured that the welfare system did not solve the problem of poverty, would reinforce some traditional patterns of gender and racial discrimination, and would be expensive and cumbersome to administer. But for all its limits, the new system marked a historic break with the federal government's traditional reluctance to offer public assistance to its neediest citizens.

Finally, the New Deal had a dramatic effect on the character of American politics. It took a weak and divided Democratic Party, which had been a minority force in American politics for many decades, and turned it into a mighty coalition that would dominate national party competition for more than thirty years. It turned the attention of many voters away from some of the controversial cultural issues that had preoccupied them in the 1920s and awakened an interest in economic matters of direct importance to the lives of citizens.

CONCLUSION

From the time of Franklin Roosevelt's inauguration in 1933 to the beginning of World War II eight years later, the federal government engaged in a broad and diverse series of experiments designed to relieve the distress of unemployment and poverty; to stabilize the economy; to prevent future crises; and to bring the Great Depression itself to an end. It had only partial success in all those efforts.

Unemployment and poverty remained high throughout the New Deal, although many federal programs provided assistance to millions of people who would otherwise have had none. The structure of the American economy remained essentially the same as it had been in earlier years, but by the end of the New Deal there were some important new regulatory agencies in Washington—and an important new role for organized labor. The New Deal failed to end the Great Depression. However, some of its policies kept the Depression from getting worse; others helped alleviate the suffering of people caught in its grip; and still others pointed the way toward more effective economic policies in the future.

Perhaps the most important legacy of the New Deal was to create a sense of possibilities among many Americans. The New Deal persuaded many citizens that the fortunes of individuals need not be left entirely to chance or to the workings of an unregulated market. Many Americans, Republicans and Democrats alike, emerged from the 1930s convinced that individuals deserved some protections from the unpredictability and instability of the modern economy. Various parts of the Roosevelt reforms persisted amid broad bipartisan support. The New Deal, for all its limitations, had demonstrated the value of enlisting government in the effort to provide for the welfare of the citizenry.

KEY TERMS/PEOPLE/PLACES/EVENTS

Agricultural Adjustment
  Administration (AAA) 588
appeasement 605
Charles E. Coughlin 595
Civilian Conservation
  Corps (CCC) 592
Congress of Industrial
  Organizations (CIO) 598
Court-packing plan 602
Eleanor Roosevelt 606
Farm Security
  Administration 589
Federal Deposit Insurance
  Corporation (FDIC) 588

fireside chats 587
Frances Perkins 607
Good Neighbor Policy 603
Harry Hopkins 600
Huey P. Long 596
isolationism 604
John Collier 607
John L. Lewis 598
Josef Stalin 606
Liberty League 593
National Labor Relations
  Board (NLRB) 597
National Recovery
  Administration (NRA) 589

Neutrality Acts 604
New Deal 587
Second New Deal 597
Securities and Exchange
  Commission (SEC) 588
sit-down strike 598
Social Security Act 599
Tennessee Valley
  Authority (TVA) 591
Townsend Plan 595
Works Progress
  Administration (WPA) 600

RECALL AND REFLECT

1. What New Deal programs were aimed at agricultural and industrial recovery, and what was the effect of the programs in both areas?
2. What criticisms did critics on both the right and the left level at the New Deal? How did FDR and his administration respond to these criticisms?
3. What gains did organized labor make during the 1930s?
4. What was the impact of the New Deal on women?

25 | AMERICA IN A WORLD AT WAR

FROM NEUTRALITY TO INTERVENTION
WAR ON TWO FRONTS
THE AMERICAN ECONOMY IN WARTIME
RACE AND ETHNICITY IN WARTIME AMERICA
ANXIETY AND AFFLUENCE IN WARTIME CULTURE
THE DEFEAT OF THE AXIS

LOOKING AHEAD

1. What was the impact of the war on the U.S. economy?
2. How was the military experience of the United States in World War II different in Europe and the Pacific?
3. How did the war affect life on the home front, especially for women, organized labor, and minorities?

THE ARCHITECTS OF AMERICAN FOREIGN POLICY in the years after 1918 attempted something that ultimately proved impossible. They were determined to be a major power in the world, extend the nation's trade, and influence other nations in ways beneficial to American interests while also staying completely free of alliances and international agreements. The United States would not join the League of Nations or the World Court. It would operate powerfully—and alone.

But forces were at work that would gradually push the United States into greater engagement with other nations. The economic disarray that the Great Depression created around the globe, the rise of totalitarian regimes, the expansionist ambitions of powerful new leaders—all worked to destroy the uneasy stability of the international system. America's own interests, economic and otherwise, were now imperiled. And America's go-it-alone foreign policy seemed powerless to change the course of events.

Franklin Roosevelt tried throughout the later years of the 1930s to nudge the American people into a greater involvement in international affairs. In particular, he tried to cultivate support for taking a more forceful stand against dictatorship and aggression. A powerful isolationist movement helped stymie him for a time, even after war broke out in Europe, Asia, and Africa. Gradually, however, public opinion shifted toward support of one side in that fight. Then, a direct attack on American forces eliminated the last elements of uncertainty and drove the United States into the greatest and most terrible conflict in human history.

FROM NEUTRALITY TO INTERVENTION

"This nation will remain a neutral nation," Roosevelt declared shortly after the hostilities began in Europe, "but I cannot ask that every American remain neutral in thought as well." There was never any question that he and the majority of people favored Britain, France, and the other Allied nations over the Axis (Germany, Italy, and soon, Japan). The question was how much the United States was prepared to do to help.

Neutrality Tested

At the very least, Roosevelt believed, the United States should make armaments available to the Allied armies to counter the military advantage the large German munitions industry gave Adolf Hitler. In September 1939, he asked Congress to revise the Neutrality Acts and lift the arms embargo against any nation engaged in war. Congress maintained the prohibition on American ships entering war zones, but the 1939 law did permit belligerents to purchase arms on the same cash-and-carry basis that the earlier Neutrality Acts had established for the sale of nonmilitary materials.

After the German armies quickly subdued Poland, the war in Europe settled into a long, quiet lull that lasted through the winter and spring. But in the spring of 1940, Germany launched a massive invasion, known as a "blitzkrieg" (lightning war), to the west. Hitler slashed into Denmark and Norway, then the Netherlands and Belgium, and finally drove deep into the heart of France. On June 10, Mussolini invaded France from

TIME LINE

1940
Tripartite Pact
America First Committee
FDR reelected
Destroyers-for-Bases Deal

1941
Lend-lease
Atlantic Charter
Pearl Harbor
U.S enters WWII

1942
Battle of Midway
Campaign in North Africa
Japanese Americans interned
Manhattan Project begins
CORE founded

1943
Americans capture Guadalcanal
Allied invasion of Italy
Soviet victory at Stalingrad

1944
Allies invade Normandy
Roosevelt reelected
Americans capture Philippines

1945
Roosevelt dies; Truman becomes president
Germany surrenders
U.S. drops atomic bombs on Hiroshima, Nagasaki
Japan surrenders

the south. On June 22, France fell, and Nazi troops marched into Paris. A new French government assembled in Vichy, a regime largely controlled by the German occupiers. In all of Europe, only the shattered remnants of the British and French armies—daringly rescued from the beaches of Dunkirk by a hastily organized armada of English boats, trawlers, and yachts—remained to oppose the Axis forces.

On May 16, in the midst of the offensive, Roosevelt asked Congress for and quickly received an additional $1 billion for defense. That was one day after **Winston Churchill**, the new British prime minister, sent Roosevelt the first of many requests for armaments, without which, he insisted, Britain could not long survive. Some Americans argued that the British plight was already hopeless, that any aid to the English was a wasted effort. But the president was determined to make war materials available to Britain. Roosevelt even circumvented the cash-and-carry provisions of the Neutrality Acts by giving Britain fifty American destroyers, most left over from World War I, in return for the right to build American bases on British territory in the Caribbean. He also facilitated the transfer of new airplanes purchased by the American military for sale to the British.

Roosevelt was able to take such steps in part because of a major shift in American public opinion. By July 1940, polls showed more than 66 percent of the public believing Germany posed a direct threat to the United States. As a result, Congress was more willing to permit expanded assistance to the Allies, and even authorized the first peacetime military draft in American history.

(©Daily Mail/Rex/Alamy)

THE BLITZ, LONDON   The German *Luftwaffe* terrorized London and other British cities in 1940–1941 and again late in the war by bombing civilian areas indiscriminately in an effort to break the spirit of the English people. The effort failed, and the fortitude of the British did much to arouse American support for their cause. St. Paul's Cathedral, largely undamaged throughout the raids, looms in the background of this photograph, as other buildings crumble under the force of German bombs.

But a powerful new isolationist lobby—the America First Committee, whose members included such prominent Americans as Charles Lindbergh and Senators Gerald Nye and Burton Wheeler—joined the debate over American policy toward the war. The lobby had at least the indirect support of a large proportion of the Republican Party. Through the summer and fall of 1940, the debate was complicated by a presidential campaign.

THE CAMPAIGN OF 1940

The biggest political question of 1940 was whether Franklin Roosevelt would break tradition and run for an unprecedented third term. The president did not reveal his wishes, but by refusing to withdraw from the contest, he made it impossible for rival Democrats to establish a claim to the nomination. And when, just before the Democratic National Convention in July, he let it be known that he would accept a "draft" from his party, the issue was virtually settled. The Democrats quickly renominated him and even swallowed his choice for vice president: Agriculture Secretary Henry A. Wallace, a man too liberal and controversial for the taste of many party leaders.

The Republicans nominated a politically inexperienced Indiana businessman, Wendell Willkie, who benefited from a powerful grassroots movement as well as strong support from the magazines *Time* and *Life*. The Republicans took positions little different from Roosevelt's: they would keep the country out of war but extend generous assistance to the Allies. Willkie was a vigorous campaigner and managed to evoke more public enthusiasm than any Republican candidate in decades. But Roosevelt still won decisively. He received 55 percent of the popular vote to Willkie's 45 percent, and 449 electoral votes to Willkie's 82.

NEUTRALITY ABANDONED

In the last months of 1940, Roosevelt began to make subtle changes to the American role in the war. Great Britain was virtually bankrupt and could no longer meet the cash-and-carry requirements imposed by the Neutrality Acts. The president therefore, proposed a new system for supplying Britain: "**lend-lease.**" It would allow the federal government not only to sell but also to lend or lease armaments to any nation deemed "pivotal to the defense of the United States." In other words, America could funnel weapons to the British on the basis of no more than Britain's promise to return them when the war was over. Congress enacted the bill by wide margins in March 1941.

In a repeat of the events leading up to American intervention in World War I, attacks by German submarines had made shipping lanes in the Atlantic extremely dangerous. The British navy was losing vessels more rapidly than it could replace them and finding it difficult to transport materials from America. Roosevelt argued that the western Atlantic was a neutral zone and therefore eligible for patrolling by American ships. By July 1941, the navy was ranging as far east as Iceland.

At first, Germany did little to challenge these American actions. By September 1941, however, the situation had changed. In violation of their nonaggression pact, Nazi forces had invaded the Soviet Union in June of that year. When the Soviets did not surrender as many predicted, Roosevelt persuaded Congress to extend lend-lease privileges to them. Now American industry was providing vital assistance to Hitler's foes on two fronts, and the American navy was protecting the flow of those goods to Europe. In September, Nazi submarines began a concerted torpedo campaign against American vessels. Roosevelt ordered U.S. ships to fire on German submarines "on sight." In October, Hitler's submarines hit two American destroyers and sank one of them, the *Reuben James*, killing many American sailors. Congress quickly voted to allow the United States to arm its merchant vessels and receive escort all the way into belligerent ports. The United States was now in effect engaged in a naval war against Germany. Meanwhile, Roosevelt met with Churchill to issue a statement of shared goals known as the **Atlantic Charter**. In August 1941, the two nations called for a new world order based on self-determination, economic cooperation, and antimilitarism.

THE ROAD TO PEARL HARBOR

Events in the Pacific would draw America directly into the conflict. In September 1940, the Japanese signed the Tripartite Pact, a loose defensive alliance with Germany and Italy, although the European Axis powers never developed a strong relationship with Japan.

Meanwhile the Japanese were still at war with China and expanding into other parts of Asia. After the fall of France, Japan marched into French Indochina and seized the capital of Vietnam in July 1941. The Roosevelt administration responded by making it impossible for the Japanese to buy American oil and by freezing all Japanese assets in the United States, severely limiting Japan's ability to purchase needed American supplies. Japan then eyed the oil-rich Dutch East Indies (present-day Indonesia). Codebreakers in the United States knew of those ambitions and warned Japan against further aggression. Subsequent negotiations to defuse the hostilities went nowhere. Either Tokyo would have to repair relations with the United States to restore the flow of oil and other supplies or find those supplies elsewhere, most notably by seizing British and Dutch possessions in the Pacific. A sense of which direction things were headed came in October, when militants in Tokyo forced the moderate prime minister out of office and replaced him with the leader of the war party, General **Hideki Tojo**.

By late November, the State Department had given up on the possibility of a peaceful settlement. American intelligence had decoded Japanese messages that made clear an attack was imminent, but Washington did not know where. Most officials continued to believe the Japanese would move first against British or Dutch possessions. A combination of confusion, miscalculation, and underestimation of the Japanese military caused the government to overlook indications that Japan intended an assault on American forces.

At 7:55 A.M. on Sunday, December 7, 1941, the first of two waves of Japanese bombers attacked the U.S. naval base in Hawaii at **Pearl Harbor**, part of a coordinated pattern of attacks against American and British holdings in Asia. Within two hours, more than 2,400 soldiers and sailors died, and another 1,000 were injured. The United States lost 8 battleships, 3 cruisers, 4 other vessels, 188 airplanes, and several vital shore installations, although by a fortunate accident, no American aircraft carriers—the heart of the Pacific Fleet—had been at Pearl Harbor. The Japanese suffered only light losses.

American forces were now greatly diminished in the Pacific. Nevertheless, the raid on Hawaii unified the American people behind war. On December 8, after a stirring speech by the president, all but one member of Congress voted to approve a declaration of war against Japan. Three days later, Germany and Italy, Japan's European allies, declared war on the United States. On the same day, December 11, Congress reciprocated without a dissenting vote.

(©GL Archive/Alamy)

PEARL HARBOR, DECEMBER 7, 1941 At least seven aerial torpedoes and two bombs struck the battleship U.S.S. *West Virginia* on that fateful morning. Repair workers discovered 66 bodies of *West Virginia* crewmembers. After it was restored to fighting condition, the ship reentered the war and participated in the Battles of Iwo Jima and Okinawa.

WAR ON TWO FRONTS

Whatever political disagreements and social tensions there may have been among the American people during World War II, there was striking unity of opinion about the conflict itself. But unity and confidence faced severe tests in the first, troubled months of 1942.

CONTAINING THE JAPANESE

Ten hours after the strike at Pearl Harbor, Japanese airplanes attacked American airfields at Manila in the Philippines, destroying much of America's remaining air power in the Pacific. Three days later, Guam, an American possession, fell. Wake Island and Hong Kong followed. The great British fortress of Singapore in Malaya surrendered in February 1942, the Dutch East Indies in March, and Burma in April. In the Philippines, exhausted Filipino and American troops gave up their defense of the islands on May 6. The American commander, General Douglas MacArthur, vowed as he left, "I shall return."

American strategists planned two broad offensives to turn the tide against the Japanese. One, under the command of MacArthur, would move north from Australia, through New Guinea, and eventually to the Philippines. The other, under Admiral Chester Nimitz, would move west from Hawaii toward major Japanese island outposts in the central Pacific. Ultimately, strategists predicted, the two offensives would come together to invade Japan.

The Allies achieved their first important victory in the Battle of the Coral Sea, just northeast of Australia, on May 7-8, 1942, when American forces turned back the previously unstoppable Japanese navy. An even more important turning point occurred a month later northwest of Hawaii, near the small American outpost at Midway Island. There, after an enormous four-day battle (June 3-6, 1942), the American navy, despite terrible losses, regained control of the central Pacific. The United States destroyed four Japanese aircraft carriers without losing one of its own.

The Americans took the offensive several months later in the southern Solomon Islands, to the east of New Guinea. In August 1942, American forces assaulted three of the islands: Gavutu, Tulagi, and Guadalcanal. A struggle of terrible ferocity continued at **Guadalcanal** for six months, inflicting heavy losses on both sides. In the end, however, the Japanese were forced to abandon the island—and with it their last chance of launching an effective offensive to the south. The Americans, with aid from Australians and New Zealanders, now began the slow, arduous process of moving toward the Philippines and Japan itself.

Holding Off the Germans

In the European theater, the United States fought in cooperation with, among others, Britain and the exiled "Free French" forces in the west, and tried also to placate its new ally, the Soviet Union, now fighting Hitler in the east and desperate for the opening of other fronts against Germany. The army chief of staff, General George C. Marshall, supported a plan for a major Allied invasion of France across the English Channel in the spring of 1943, and he placed the little-known General **Dwight D. Eisenhower** in charge of planning the operation. The Soviet Union wanted the Allied invasion to begin at the earliest possible moment. But the British wanted to prioritize a series of Allied offensives around the edges of the Nazi empire in northern Africa and southern Europe before undertaking the invasion of France.

Roosevelt ultimately decided to support the British plan, in part because he was eager to get American forces into combat quickly and knew a cross-channel invasion would take a long time to prepare. At the end of October 1942, the British opened a counteroffensive against General Erwin Rommel and Nazi forces in northern Africa threatening the Suez Canal. In a major battle at El Alamein, they forced the Germans to retreat from Egypt. In early November, British and American troops landed at Oran and Algiers in Algeria and at Casablanca in Morocco—areas under the Nazi-controlled French Vichy government—and began moving east toward Rommel. The Germans threw the full weight of their forces in Africa against the inexperienced Americans and inflicted a serious defeat on them at the Kasserine Pass in Tunisia. General George S. Patton, however, regrouped and began an effective counteroffensive. With the help of Allied air and naval power and of British forces attacking from the east under Field Marshall Bernard Montgomery, victor at El Alamein, the offensive finally drove the Germans from Africa in May 1943.

The North African campaign had tied up a large proportion of Allied resources, postponing the planned May 1943 cross-channel invasion of France amid angry complaints from Soviet leader Josef Stalin. By now, however, the threat of a Soviet collapse seemed much diminished, for during the winter of 1942-1943, the Red Army had successfully held off a major German assault at Stalingrad in southern Russia. Hitler had committed such enormous forces to the battle, and had suffered such appalling losses, that he could not continue his eastern offensive.

WORLD WAR II IN NORTH AFRICA AND ITALY: THE ALLIED COUNTEROFFENSIVE, 1942-1943
The United States and Great Britain understood from the beginning that an invasion of France across the English Channel would eventually be necessary for a victory in the European war. In the meantime, however, they fought the Axis forces in North Africa, and in the spring of 1943 they began an invasion across the Mediterranean into Italy. This map shows the points along the coast of North Africa where Allied forces landed in 1942, moving east from Morocco and Algeria and west from Egypt. The two armies met in Tunisia and crossed to Italy from there. • *Why were America and Britain reluctant to launch the cross-channel invasion in 1942 or 1943?*

The Soviet successes persuaded Roosevelt to agree, in a January 1943 meeting with Churchill in Casablanca, to a British plan for an Allied invasion of Sicily. Churchill wished to knock Italy out of the war and draw in German divisions that might otherwise be stationed in France. On the night of July 9-10, 1943, American and British armies landed in southeastern Sicily. Thirty-eight days later, they had conquered the island and were moving onto the mainland. Mussolini's government collapsed and the dictator fled north toward Germany, only to be captured later by Italian insurgents and hanged. His successor, Pietro Badoglio, quickly committed Italy to the Allies. Germany nonetheless moved eight divisions into Italy and established a powerful defensive line south of Rome. The Allied offensive, which began on September 3, 1943, got bogged down at that line. Not until May 1944 did the Allies break through the German defenses to resume their northward advance. On June 4, 1944, they captured Rome.

AMERICA AND THE HOLOCAUST

In the midst of this intensive fighting, the leaders of the American government confronted one of history's great tragedies: the Nazi campaign to exterminate the Jews of Europe, which became known as the **Holocaust**. As early as 1942, high officials in Washington had incontrovertible evidence that Hitler's forces were rounding up Jews and others (including Poles, homosexuals, and communists) from all over Europe, transporting them to concentration camps in eastern Germany and Poland, and systematically murdering them.

The death toll would ultimately reach 6 million Jews and at least 4 million others. News of the atrocities soon reached the public as well, and pressure began to build for an Allied effort to end the killing or at least to rescue some of the surviving Jews.

The American government consistently resisted almost all such demands. Although by mid-1944 Allied bombers were flying missions within a few miles of the most notorious death camp, at Auschwitz in Poland, the War Department argued that sending planes to destroy the crematoria was unfeasible. American officials also refused to destroy railroad lines leading to the camp. And the United States resisted pleas that it admit large numbers of Jewish refugees attempting to escape Europe.

More forceful action by the United States, and Britain, which was even less amenable to Jewish requests for assistance, might have saved at least some lives. That they did not take such action, it seems clear in retrospect, constituted an abject moral failure. But policymakers justified their inaction by insisting that they needed to focus exclusively on the larger goal of winning the war. Any diversion of energy and attention to other purposes, they maintained, would distract them from the overriding goal of victory.

(©Bettmann/Getty Images)

THE ST. LOUIS Many people consider the fate of the German liner *St. Louis* to be a powerful symbol of the indifference of the United States and other nations to the fate of European Jews during the Holocaust, even though its forlorn journey preceded both the beginning of World War II and the beginning of systematic extermination of Jews by the Nazi regime. The *St. Louis* carried a group of over 900 Jews fleeing from Germany in 1939, carrying exit visas of dubious legality cynically sold to them by members of Hitler's Gestapo. It became a ship without a port as it sailed from country to country—Mexico, Paraguay, Argentina, Costa Rica, and Cuba—where its passengers were refused entry time and again. Most of the passengers were hoping for a haven in the United States, but the American State Department refused to allow the ship even to dock as it sailed up the American eastern seaboard. Eventually, the *St. Louis* returned to Europe and distributed its passengers among Britain, France, Holland, and Belgium (where this photograph was taken, showing refugees smiling and waving as they prepared to disembark in Antwerp in June 1939). Less than a year later, all those nations except Britain fell under Nazi control.

THE SOLDIER'S EXPERIENCE

The Americans fighting in two theaters represented a cross-section of the country. Conscription helped fill a military force of 16 million that included the vast majority of draft-age men. They came from every ethnic and racial group and all of the communities—Italians, Jews, Russians, Greeks, and many more—largely cut off from new immigration since 1924. Although known later as "the good war," there was nothing good about it to many American GIs. They collectively experienced searing heat, numbing cold, bad food, miserable living conditions, years-long separation from families, and of course the terrors of combat.

Very different war experiences awaited pilots and infantrymen, officers and grunts, generals and nurses. The same was true of white GIs and soldiers of color. During World War II, military leadership consigned African Americans to the most menial assignments, keeping them in segregated training camps and units, and barring them entirely from the Marine Corps and the Army Air Force. In some of the partially integrated army bases—Fort Dix, New Jersey, for example—riots broke out when black soldiers protested mistreatment and segregation. Yet there were signs of change. By the end of the war, the number of black servicemen had increased to almost a million. African Americans were allowed to serve on ships with white sailors, and more black units were sent into combat.

Approximately 25,000 Native Americans served in the military during World War II. Many saw combat, including Ira Hayes, one of the flag-raisers in the famous photograph of Marines on Iwo Jima. Others (mostly Navajo) became military "code talkers," speaking their own language over the radio and the telephones to confound enemy attempts at intelligence-gathering. The war had important effects on the Indians who served in the military. It brought them into intimate contact, often for the first time, with white society, and it awakened among some of them a taste for the material benefits of life in capitalist America. Some never returned to the reservations but chose to remain in the non-Indian world and assimilate to its ways.

A higher proportion of Chinese Americans (22 percent of all adult males) was drafted than that of any other national group, and the entire Chinese community in most cities worked hard and conspicuously for the war effort. And Japanese Americans, eager to prove their patriotism amid vicious prejudice and ultimately internment, fought against the Germans with the 442nd Regiment. Their ranks included future senator Daniel Inouye, who had undergone harrowing experiences as a teenaged medical volunteer at Pearl Harbor on December 7.

The GIs' most faithful chronicler was the beloved war correspondent Ernie Pyle, who spun tales of everyday life, individual personalities, and occasionally tragedy to a stateside audience of millions. Pyle believed no one at home, in part because of censorship, saw the war as he and the soldiers did. After a Japanese sniper killed Pyle in April 1945, GIs found an unfinished column in his pocket. "You didn't see him lying so grotesque and pasty beside the gravel road in France," he wrote of the generic dead soldier. "We saw him, saw him by the multiple thousands. That's the difference."

THE AMERICAN ECONOMY IN WARTIME

Not since the Civil War had the United States been involved in so prolonged and consuming a military experience as World War II. American armed forces engaged in combat around the globe for nearly four years. Stateside changes, in the meantime, reached into every corner of the nation.

PROSPERITY AND THE RIGHTS OF LABOR

World War II had a profound impact on American domestic life by ending the Great Depression. By the middle of 1941, the economic problems of the 1930s—unemployment, deflation, industrial sluggishness—had vanished before the great wave of wartime industrial expansion.

The most important catalyst of the new prosperity was government spending, which after 1939 was pumping more money into the economy each year than had all the New Deal relief agencies combined. In 1939, the federal budget had been $9 billion, the highest in American peacetime history. By 1945, it had risen to $100 billion. Largely as a result, the gross national product soared: from $91 billion in 1939 to $166 billion in 1945. Personal incomes in some regions grew by as much as 100 percent or more.

The West Coast, naturally, became the launching point for the war against Japan, and the government created large manufacturing facilities in California and elsewhere to serve the needs of the military. Altogether, the government made almost $40 billion worth of wartime capital investments (factories, military and transportation facilities, highways, power plants) in the West, more than in any other region. By the end of the war, the Pacific Coast had become the center of a growing American aircraft industry and an important shipbuilding center. Los Angeles, formerly a medium-sized city notable for its film industry, now became a major industrial center as well.

The war created a serious labor shortage. The armed forces took more than 16 million men and women out of the civilian workforce at the same time that the demand for labor was rising rapidly. Nevertheless, the supply of workers increased by almost 20 percent during the war—largely through the employment of many people previously considered inappropriate for the workforce: the young or elderly, minorities, and several million women.

The war gave a substantial boost to union membership, which rose from about 10.5 million in 1941 to over 13 million in 1945. That was in part a result of labor's "maintenance-of-membership" agreement with the government, which ensured that the thousands of new workers pouring into unionized defense plants would be automatically enrolled in the unions. But the government also managed to win two important concessions from union leaders. One was the "no-strike" pledge, by which unions agreed not to stop production in wartime. Another was the so-called Little Steel formula, which set a 15 percent limit on wage increases.

Despite the no-strike pledge, nearly 15,000 work stoppages took place during the war, mostly wildcat strikes (strikes not authorized by the union leadership). When the United Mine Workers defied the government by striking in May 1943, Congress reacted by passing, over Roosevelt's veto, the Smith-Connally Act (the War Labor Disputes Act), which required that unions wait thirty days before striking and which empowered the president to seize a struck war plant. In the meantime, public animosity toward labor rose rapidly, and some states passed laws to limit union power.

STABILIZING THE BOOM AND MOBILIZING PRODUCTION

The fear of deflation, the central concern of the 1930s, gave way during the war to a fear of inflation, particularly after prices rose 25 percent in the two years before Pearl Harbor. Fighting inflation was the task of the **Office of Price Administration (OPA)**, which helped moderate what had been a serious problem during World War I. Even so, the agency was never popular. Black-marketing and overcharging grew in proportions far beyond the OPA's policing capacity.

From 1941 to 1945, the federal government spent a total of $321 billion—twice as much as it had spent in the entire 150 years of its existence as a nation to that point, and ten times as much as the cost of World War I. The national debt rose from $49 billion in 1941 to $259 billion in 1945. The government borrowed about half the revenues it needed by selling $100 billion worth of bonds. Much of the rest it raised by radically increasing income-tax rates, through the Revenue Act of 1942. To simplify collection, Congress enacted a withholding system of payroll deductions in 1943.

In January 1942, to mobilize the wartime economy, the president created the War Production Board (WPB). Throughout its troubled history, the WPB was never able to win complete control over military purchases; the army and navy often circumvented the board. Nor was it able to satisfy the complaints of small business, which griped that most contracts went to large corporations. Gradually, the president transferred much of the WPB's authority to a new office located within the White House: the Office of War Mobilization (OWM). But the OWM was only slightly more successful than the WPB.

Despite the administrative problems, however, the war economy managed to meet almost all of the nation's critical war needs. By the beginning of 1944, American factories were, in fact, producing more than the government needed. Their output doubled that of all the Axis countries combined.

WARTIME SCIENCE AND TECHNOLOGY

More than any previous American war, World War II was a watershed for technological and scientific innovation, partly because the American government poured substantial funds into research and development beginning in 1940. In that year, the government created the National Defense Research Committee (which later became the Office of Scientific Research and Development). By the end of the war, the new agency had spent more than $100 million on research, more than four times the amount spent by the government on military research and development in the previous forty years.

In the first years of the war, all the technological advantages seemed to lie with the Germans and Japanese. Germany had made great advances in tanks and other mechanized armor in the 1930s, particularly during the Spanish Civil War, when it helped arm Franco's forces. German submarine technology surpassed British and American capabilities in 1940. Japan had developed extraordinary naval–air technology, as indicated by the successful raid on Pearl Harbor.

But Britain and America had advantages of their own. American techniques of mass production such as automotive assembly lines were converted efficiently to military production in 1941 and 1942 and soon began producing airplanes, ships, tanks, and other armaments in numbers far beyond what the Germans and Japanese could reach. Allied scientists and engineers moved quickly as well to improve Anglo-American aviation and naval technology, particularly submarines and tanks. By late 1942, Allied weaponry was at least as advanced as, and more plentiful than, that of the enemy. The Allies likewise enjoyed superiority in radar technology and developed effective naval mine detection systems.

Anglo-American antiaircraft technology, on land and on sea, also improved, but never to the point where it could defeat bombing raids altogether. Germany made substantial advances in the development of rocket technology in the early years of the war and managed to launch some rocket-propelled bombs (V1s and V2s) across the English Channel, aimed at London. The psychological effects of the rockets on the British people were considerable. But the Germans were never able to build enough rockets to make a real difference in the balance of military power.

Beginning in 1942, British and American forces seized the advantage in the air war by producing new and powerful four-engine bombing aircraft in great numbers. At higher altitudes and with new navigation systems, they were able to conduct extensive bombing missions over Germany (and, later, Japan) with much less danger of being shot down. The Allies also benefited from a radio device that sent a sonic message to airplanes to tell them when they were within 20 yards of their targets, first introduced in December 1942.

The area in which the Allies had perhaps the greatest advantage was the gathering of intelligence, much of it through Britain's top-secret Ultra project. Some of the benefits the Allies enjoyed came from the capture of German and Japanese intelligence devices. More important, however, were the efforts of cryptologists, or code breakers. Much of Germany's coded communication ran through the so-called Enigma machine, which constantly changed the coding systems it used. In the first months of the war, Polish intelligence had developed an electromechanical computer. It was called the "Bombe," and it could decipher some Enigma messages. After the fall of Poland, British scientists, led by the computer pioneer Alan Turing, took the Bombe and greatly improved it. On April 15, 1940, the new, improved high-speed Bombe deciphered a series of German messages within hours rather than days. A few weeks later, it began decrypting German messages at the rate of 1,000 a day, providing the British (and, later, the Americans) with a constant flow of information about enemy operations throughout the war. British scientists working for the intelligence services, meanwhile, built the first real programmable, digital computer—the Colossus II, which became operational less than a week before the beginning of the Normandy invasion and which could decipher an enormous number of intercepted German messages almost instantly. The United States similarly developed the ability to crack a Japanese coding system.

RACE AND ETHNICITY IN WARTIME AMERICA

The war loosened many traditional barriers that had restricted the lives of minorities and women. There was so much demand for fighting men, so much demand for labor, and so much fluidity and mobility that the social and cultural barriers could not survive intact.

MINORITY GROUPS AND THE WAR EFFORT

In the summer of 1941, A. Philip Randolph, president of the mostly African American Brotherhood of Sleeping Car Porters Union, began to insist that the government require companies receiving defense contracts to integrate their workforces. To mobilize support for the demand, Randolph planned a massive march on Washington. The threat led Roosevelt to promise to establish what became the Fair Employment Practices Commission (FEPC) to investigate discrimination against African Americans in war industries.

The need for labor in war plants greatly increased the migration of African Americans from the rural South into industrial cities. The migration improved the economic conditions of many African Americans. But it also created urban tensions and occasional violence. A terrible race riot in Detroit in 1943 killed thirty-four people, twenty-five of them black.

Despite such tensions, leading black organizations redoubled their efforts to challenge segregation. The **Congress of Racial Equality (CORE)**, organized in 1942, mobilized popular resistance to discrimination in a way that the older, more conservative organizations had never done. Randolph, Bayard Rustin, James Farmer, and other, younger African American leaders helped organize sit-ins and demonstrations in segregated theaters and restaurants. CORE also organized "freedom rides" to desegregate buses and bus terminals. Though often unsuccessful, these efforts strengthened a culture of civil rights activism in the black community.

Leaders called their stateside movement, together with the participation of almost a million black people in the military, the "double-V" campaign—victory at home over racism, abroad over fascism.

The war had important effects, too, on the Native Americans who stayed on the reservations. Little war work reached the tribes. Government subsidies dwindled. Talented young people left the reservations to serve in the military or work in war production, creating workforce shortages in some tribes. The wartime emphasis on national unity undermined support for the revitalization of tribal autonomy that the Indian Reorganization Act of 1934 had launched. New pressures emerged to eliminate the reservation system and to require the tribes to assimilate into white society. The pressures were so severe that John Collier, the energetic director of the Bureau of Indian Affairs who had done so much to promote the reinvigoration of the reservations, resigned in 1945.

Large numbers of Mexican workers entered the United States in response to wartime labor shortages on the Pacific Coast and in the Southwest. The American and Mexican governments agreed in 1942 to a program by which *braceros* (contract laborers) would be admitted to the United States for a limited time. Some worked as migrant farm laborers, but many Mexicans were able for the first time to find factory jobs. They formed the second-largest group of migrants (after African Americans) to U.S. cities in the 1940s. They concentrated mainly in the West but established significant Mexican communities in Chicago, Detroit, and other industrial cities.

The sudden expansion of Mexican American neighborhoods created tensions and occasional conflict. Anglo residents of Los Angeles became alarmed at the activities of Mexican American teenagers, many of whom joined street gangs (*pachucos*). Some wore long, loose jackets with padded shoulders, baggy pants tied at the ankles ("**zoot suits**"), long watch chains, broad-brimmed hats, and greased, ducktail hairstyles. At a time when fabric had been rationed for the war effort, some white people wrongly interpreted the zoot suits to mean Mexican Americans were unsupportive of the war effort—a great number served in the wartime army. But in June 1943, animosity toward the zoot-suiters, driven partly by ethnic prejudice and partly by the apparent disregard of rationing, produced a four-day riot in Los Angeles. Anglo sailors in Long Beach invaded Mexican American communities and attacked zoot-suiters. The police did little to restrain the sailors, who grabbed Hispanic teenagers, tore off and burned their clothes, cut off their ducktails, and beat them. When Mexicans tried to fight back, the police moved in and arrested them. In the aftermath of the "zoot-suit riots," Los Angeles passed a law prohibiting the outfit.

The Internment of Japanese Americans

After the attack on Pearl Harbor, government propaganda and popular culture combined to create an image of the Japanese as a devious, malign, and savage people. (See "Consider the Source: The Face of the Enemy.")

This racial animosity soon extended to Americans of Japanese descent. There were not many Japanese Americans in the United States—about 127,000, most of them concentrated in a few areas in California. About one-third were unnaturalized first-generation immigrants (Issei); two-thirds were naturalized or native-born citizens of the United States (Nisei). Because they generally kept to themselves and preserved traditional cultural patterns, it was easy for Anglo Americans to imagine wrongly that the Japanese Americans were engaged in conspiracies on behalf of their ancestral homeland.

CONSIDER THE SOURCE

THE FACE OF THE ENEMY

During World War II, illustrators used caricature, symbolism, exaggeration, and juxtaposition to mobilize public opinion and behavior. The Japanese were frequent objects of such representation. Early in the war, an artist working under the auspices of the Work Projects Administration (WPA, formerly the Works Progress Administration) produced the poster "Salvage Scrap to Blast the Jap." The second image, Arthur Szyk's cover for *Collier's* magazine in December 1942, depicts the Japanese prime minister Hideki Tojo.

UNDERSTAND, ANALYZE, & EVALUATE

1. The Americans and Japanese are represented by different animals in the WPA poster. What do those choices suggest about how people in the United States viewed the character of the two nations?

2. What event is artist Arthur Szyk depicting in the cartoon on the *Collier's* cover? What evidence can you find in the cartoon to support your choice?

(Source: Library of Congress, Prints and Photographs Division [LC-USZC2-1109])

U.S. NAVY POSTER "SALVAGE SCRAP TO BLAST THE JAP"

(©akg-images/Newscom)

ARTHUR SZYK, COLLIER'S COVER, DECEMBER 12, 1942

In February 1942, in response to pressure from military officials and political leaders on the West Coast (including California attorney general Earl Warren) and recommendations from the War Department, the president authorized the army to "intern" the Japanese Americans. The move rested entirely on the assumption that Japanese people harbored characteristics that would make it impossible to tell the guilty from the innocent. So despite the lack of evidence that military necessity required it, and in one of the most extreme cases of racial profiling in American history, more than 100,000 people (Issei and Nisei alike) were rounded up, told to dispose of their property however they could (which often meant abandoning it), and taken to what the government euphemistically called **relocation centers**. In fact, they were facilities little different from prisons, many of them located in the western mountains and desert. A group of innocent people, many of them citizens of the United States, were forced to spend up to three years in grim, debilitating isolation, barred from lucrative employment, provided with only minimal medical care, and deprived of decent schools for their children. The Supreme Court upheld the internment in the 1944 *Korematsu v. U.S.* decision, in part based on evidence from the War Department that later investigation showed had been deliberately stripped of racist language, leaving only the logic of military necessity. Although most of the Japanese Americans were released later that year, they were unable to win any significant compensation for their losses until Congress finally acted in the 1980s. And it was not until June 2018 that the Supreme Court explicitly repudiated the *Korematsu* decision, though that overruling came in the course of upholding President Donald Trump's travel ban on citizens of several predominantly Muslim countries. Critics of the administration quickly pointed out the irony of the Court tossing out *Korematsu* while simultaneously upholding its spirit, in their view, by sanctioning the travel ban.

CHINESE AMERICANS AND THE WAR

At the same time that the war undermined the position of Japanese Americans, the American alliance with China during World War II significantly enhanced both the legal and social status of Chinese Americans. In 1943, partly to improve relations with the government of China, Congress repealed the Chinese Exclusion Act, which had barred almost all Chinese immigration since its renewal in 1892. The new quota for Chinese immigrants was minuscule (105 a year), but a substantial number of Chinese women managed to gain entry into the country through other provisions covering war brides and fiancées. Over 4,000 Chinese women entered the United States in the first three years after the war. Permanent residents of Chinese descent were finally permitted to become citizens.

Racial animosity toward the Chinese did not disappear, but it did decline—in part because government propaganda and popular culture presented positive images of the Chinese to contrast them with the Japanese and in part because Chinese Americans, like African Americans and other previously marginal groups, began taking jobs in war plants and other areas suffering from labor shortages.

ANXIETY AND AFFLUENCE IN WARTIME CULTURE

The war created considerable anxiety in American lives. Families worried about loved ones at the front, and as the war continued, many mourned relatives who had died in combat. Women struggled to support families in the absence of husbands and fathers. Businesses and communities struggled with shortages of goods and labor.

But the abundance of the war years also created a striking buoyancy in American life. Suddenly people had money to spend again, and despite the many shortages, at least some things to spend it on. In fact, consumerism became, as it had in the 1920s, one of the most powerful forces in American culture.

HOME-FRONT LIFE AND CULTURE

As part of the consumerist resurgence of the war years, Americans spent millions of dollars and hours on entertainment and leisure. Audiences equal to about half the nation's population attended movies each week. Radio ownership increased, and pictorial magazines such as *Life* flourished. Dance halls were packed with young people drawn to the seductive music of bands. Soldiers and sailors home on leave, or awaiting shipment abroad, were special fans of the dances, which became to many of them a symbol of the life they were leaving and fighting to protect. The most popular music was the relatively new jazz form known as swing, which had emerged from the black musical imagination. Bandleaders such as Duke Ellington, who was African American, and Benny Goodman were among the most recognized figures in popular culture, rivaling movie stars.

Much of what Americans read, heard, and saw during the war was managed by the government and military. At the center of the government's propaganda effort was the **Office of War Information (OWI)**. The OWI issued posters, ran magazine advertisements, and produced documentary films. These materials urged ordinary Americans to do their part—buy war bonds, conserve household resources, keep quiet about troop movements.

Government and military officials, meanwhile, censored the reports that journalists filed from the war zone. Correspondents happily refrained from printing anything that might compromise military strategy or effectiveness—they wanted the United States to win too, after all. But Roosevelt and others also believed that gory or depressing war news would sap the public's will, especially in the first two years of the war. It wasn't until September 1943 that officials allowed an image of American dead to appear in print. Federal officials had changed their minds, deciding that slightly more graphic war coverage would awaken a public growing complacent about the sacrifices being made on its behalf.

Hollywood films about the war—and there were hundreds of them—offered a relatively sanitized picture of the conflict. Whether of their own volition or in consultation with military officials, movie producers usually offered a picture of the soldier in line with journalistic reports and government propaganda. In many "platoon films," death came quickly and without blood and guts. Soldiers behaved courageously, missed home, and found maturity (rather than breakdown) through combat. Blacks didn't typically appear in these platoons—true to the reality of a Jim Crow army—but many other white ethnic groups did. In fact, a central point of many wartime pictures, as well as OWI propaganda posters, was that Jews, Polish Americans, Italian Americans, and other groups largely barred by the 1924 immigration restriction had become assimilated contributors to the American military machine. The upshot of all this was a wartime popular culture saturated with combat imagery but which kept some of the worst realities of war obscured, as Ernie Pyle lamented in 1945.

LOVE, FAMILY, AND SEXUALITY IN WARTIME

For men at the front, the image of home both served as a motivational symbol and helped soften the rigors of combat. Letters and mementos from loved ones sustained the morale of millions of service members. They dreamed of music, food, movies, and other material comforts. Many also dreamed of women—wives and girlfriends, but also movie stars and entertainers, who became the source of one of the most popular icons of the front: the pinup. Sailors pasted pinups inside their lockers. Infantrymen carried them (along with pictures of wives, mothers, and girlfriends) in their knapsacks. Fighter pilots gave their planes female names and painted bathing beauties on their nose cones.

For the servicemen who remained in America, and for soldiers and sailors in cities far from home in particular, the company of friendly, "wholesome" women was, the military believed, critical to sustaining morale. The branches of the **United Service Organization (USO)** recruited thousands of young women to serve as hostesses in their clubs. They were expected to dress nicely, dance well, and chat happily with lonely men. Other women joined "dance brigades," traveling by bus to military bases for social evenings with servicemen. The "USO girls" and the members of the dance brigades were forbidden to have any contact with men except at parties at the clubs or during dances. Such regulations were of course often violated. The military took elaborate measures to root out gay men and lesbians from their ranks, vigilantly searching for evidence of homosexuality and unceremoniously dismissing gay people with undesirable discharges. Still, homosexual encounters did occur among and between soldiers. Meanwhile the services quietly tolerated illicit heterosexual activity, which they believed were temporary, natural, and, for many men, necessary.

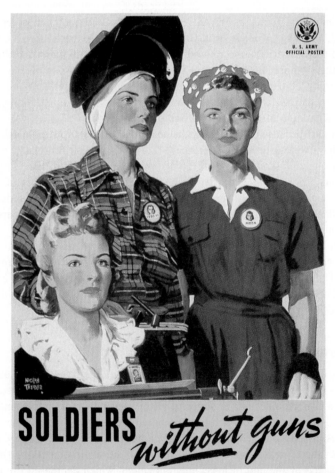

(Source: Library of Congress, Prints and Photographs Division [LC-USZC4-1047])

WOMEN AT WAR Many American women enlisted in the army and navy women's corps during World War II, but an equally important contribution to the war effort was their work in factories and offices—often in jobs that would have been considered inappropriate for them in peacetime but that they were now encouraged to assume because of the absence of so many men.

Wartime families also experienced change. The number of women in the workforce increased by nearly 60 percent during the war, as many women replaced male industrial workers serving in the military. These new wage-earning women, on the whole, were older and more likely to be married than most who had entered the workforce in the past.

Many factory owners continued to categorize jobs by gender, reserving the most lucrative positions for men. Female work, like male work, was also categorized by race: black women were usually assigned more menial tasks, and paid at a lower rate, than their white counterparts. But some women began to take on heavy industrial jobs that had long been considered "men's work." The famous wartime image of "**Rosie the Riveter**" symbolized the new importance of the female industrial worker. Women joined unions in substantial numbers and helped erode at least some of the prejudice, including the prejudice against mothers working, that had previously kept many of them from paid employment.

Most women workers during the war, however, were employed not in factories but in service-sector jobs. Above all, they worked for the government, whose bureaucratic needs expanded dramatically alongside its military and industrial needs. Even within the military, which enlisted substantial numbers of women as WAACs (army) and WAVEs (navy), most female work was clerical. But thousands of women, as in Britain, worked for the armed forces cracking enemy codes, though their service was secret and not known about until many decades later.

Many mothers whose husbands were in the military had to combine work with child care. The scarcity of child-care facilities or other community services meant that some working women had no choice but to leave young children at home alone, or locked in cars in factory parking lots, or with relatives or neighbors.

Perhaps in part because of the family dislocations of the war, juvenile crime rose markedly. Young boys were arrested at increasing rates for car theft, burglary, vandalism, and vagrancy. For many children, however, the distinctive experience of the war years was not crime but work. More than a third of all teenagers between the ages of fourteen and eighteen were employed during the last years of the war, causing some reduction in high school enrollments. And lots of children, finally, internalized terrible fears about what might be happening to their fathers or loved ones overseas.

The return of prosperity helped increase the marriage rate and lower the age at which people married, but many marriages were unable to survive the pressures of wartime separation. The divorce rate rose rapidly. Even so, the rise in the birthrate that accompanied the increase in marriages was the first sign of what would become the great postwar "baby boom."

The Growth of Wartime Conservatism

Late in 1943, Franklin Roosevelt publicly suggested that "Dr. New Deal," as he called it, had served its purpose and should give way to "Dr. Win-the-War." The statement reflected the president's own genuine shift in concern: victory was now more important than reform. But it reflected, too, the political reality that had emerged during the first two years of war.

The greatest assault on New Deal reforms came from conservatives in Congress, who seized on the war as reason to dismantle many of the achievements of the New Deal. They were assisted by the end of mass unemployment, which decreased the need for such relief programs as the Civilian Conservation Corps and the Works Progress Administration (both of which Congress abolished). They were assisted, too, by their own increasing numbers. In the congressional elections of 1942, Republicans gained 47 seats in the House and 10 in the Senate.

Republicans approached the 1944 election determined to exploit what they believed was resentment of wartime regimentation and Democratic reform. They nominated as their candidate the young and vigorous governor of New York, Thomas E. Dewey. Roosevelt was unopposed within his party, but Democratic leaders pressured him to abandon Vice President Henry Wallace, an advanced New Dealer and hero of the labor movement. Roosevelt agreed to replace him with a more moderate figure, Senator **Harry S. Truman** of Missouri. Truman had won acclaim as chair of the Senate War Investigating Committee, which compiled an impressive record uncovering waste and corruption in wartime production.

The election revolved around domestic economic issues and, indirectly, the president's health. He was in fact gravely ill, suffering from, among other things, advanced arteriosclerosis. But the campaign seemed momentarily to revive him. Roosevelt made strenuous public appearances late in October, which dispelled popular doubts about his health and ensured his reelection. He captured 53.5 percent of the popular vote to Dewey's 46 percent, and 432 electoral votes to Dewey's 99. Democrats lost 1 seat in the Senate, gained 20 in the House, and maintained control of both.

THE DEFEAT OF THE AXIS

By the middle of 1943, America and its allies had succeeded in stopping the Axis advance in both Europe and the Pacific. In the next two years, the Allies themselves seized the offensive and launched a series of powerful drives that led to victory.

THE EUROPEAN OFFENSIVE

By early 1944, American and British bombers were attacking German industrial installations and other targets almost around the clock, drastically cutting production and impeding transportation. A February 1945 incendiary raid on Dresden created a great firestorm that

(©Robert F. Sargent/US Coast Guard/The LIFE Picture Collection/Getty Images)

THE NORMANDY INVASION This photograph, taken from a landing craft, shows American troops wading ashore and onto the Normandy beaches, where one of the decisive battles of World War II was taking shape. The invasion was launched despite threatening weather and rough seas.

destroyed three-fourths of the previously undamaged city and killed approximately 135,000 people, almost all civilians.

An enormous offensive force had been gathering in Britain for two years before the spring of 1944: almost 3 million troops and perhaps the greatest array of naval vessels and armaments ever assembled in one place. On the morning of June 6, 1944 (**D-Day**), this vast invasion force moved into action. The landing came not at the narrowest part of the English Channel, where the Germans had expected and prepared for it, but along sixty miles of the Cotentin Peninsula on the coast of Normandy. While airplanes and battleships offshore bombarded the Nazi defenses, 4,000 vessels landed American, British, Canadian, and other troops and supplies on the beaches. (Three divisions of paratroopers had been dropped behind the German lines the night before.) Fighting was intense along the beach. The superior manpower and equipment of the Allied forces gradually prevailed, though at horrible cost. Within a week, the German forces had been dislodged from virtually the entire Normandy coast.

WORLD WAR II IN EUROPE: THE ALLIED COUNTEROFFENSIVE, 1943-1945 This map illustrates the final, climactic movements in the war in Europe—the two great offensives against Germany that began in 1943 and culminated in 1945. The armies of the Soviet Union, having halted the Germans at Stalingrad and Moscow, swept across eastern Europe toward Germany. From the west and the south, American, British, and other Allied forces moved toward Germany through Italy and, after Normandy in June 1944, through France. The two offensives met in Berlin in May 1945. • *Given the history of animosity between the Americans and Soviets, what consequences might have followed from this final positioning of the Allied forces?*

(©Alexander Vorontsov/Keystone/Hulton Archive/Getty Images)

AUSCHWITZ, DECEMBER 1944 This photograph, taken near the end of World War II, shows a group of imprisoned children behind a barbed wire fence in one of the most notorious Nazi concentration camps. A month later, the Soviets reached Auschwitz and liberated the remaining prisoners, though most had been forced to evacuate by the retreating Nazis. Thousands of people met their deaths during those marches.

For the next month, progress remained slow. But in late July, in the Battle of Saint-Lô, General Omar Bradley's First Army smashed through the German lines. George S. Patton's Third Army, spearheaded by heavy tank attacks, then moved through the hole Bradley had created and began a drive into the heart of France. On August 25, Free French forces arrived in Paris and liberated the city from four years of German occupation. By mid-September the Allied armies had driven the Germans almost entirely out of France and Belgium.

The great Allied drive came to a halt, however, at the Rhine River against a firm line of Nazi defenses. In mid-December, German forces struck in desperation along fifty miles of front in the Ardennes Forest. In the **Battle of the Bulge** (named for a large bulge that appeared in the American lines as the Germans pressed forward), they drove fifty-five miles toward Antwerp before they were finally stopped at Bastogne. It was the last major battle on the western front.

While the Allies fought their way through France, Soviet forces swept westward into central Europe and the Balkans. In late January 1945, the Russians launched a great offensive toward the Oder River, inside Germany. By early spring, they were ready to launch a final assault against Berlin. General Omar Bradley, in the meantime, was pushing toward the Rhine from the west. Early in March, Bradley's forces captured the city of Cologne, on the river's west bank. The next day, they discovered and seized an undamaged bridge over the river at Remagen. Allied troops were soon pouring across the Rhine. In the following weeks, the British commander Montgomery, with a million troops, pushed into Germany in the north while Bradley's army, sweeping through central Germany, completed the encirclement of 300,000 German soldiers in the Ruhr region.

The German resistance was now broken on both fronts. American forces were moving eastward faster than they had anticipated and could have beaten the Russians to Berlin and Prague. Instead, the American and British high commands decided to halt the advance along the Elbe River in central Germany to await the Russians. That decision enabled the Soviets to occupy eastern Germany and Czechoslovakia.

On April 30, with Soviet forces on the outskirts of Berlin, Adolf Hitler killed himself in his bunker in the capital. And on May 8, 1945, the remaining German forces surrendered unconditionally. During the drive and in the days and weeks that followed, Allied troops discovered heartbreaking confirmation of earlier reports of Nazi mass murder.

The Pacific Offensive

In February 1944, American naval forces under Admiral Chester Nimitz won a series of victories in the Marshall Islands and cracked the outer perimeter of the Japanese Empire. Within a month, the navy had destroyed other vital Japanese bastions. American submarines, in the meantime, were decimating Japanese shipping and crippling Japan's domestic economy.

America's principal ally in Asia was China. To assist the Chinese forces, the army sent General Joseph W. Stilwell to help provide critical supplies to China by a land route through India and across the Himalayas. It was a brutal task, but in the fall of 1944, Stilwell's forces succeeded in constructing a road and pipelines across the mountains into China. More dangerously, the Japanese were also threatening the wartime capital of China in Chungking. Chiang Kai-shek, the Chinese premier, was reluctant to use his troops against the Japanese and seemed more concerned with attacking Chinese communists, who were also fighting the Japanese. After Stilwell left China, his successors continued to have trouble prodding Chiang to confront the Japanese.

The decisive battles of the Pacific war occurred not in China but at sea. In mid-June 1944, an enormous American armada struck the heavily fortified Mariana Islands and, after some of the bloodiest operations of the war, captured Tinian, Guam, and Saipan. On October 20, General MacArthur's troops landed on Leyte Island in the Philippines. The Japanese now deployed virtually their entire fleet against the Allied invaders in three major encounters, which together constituted the decisive Battle of Leyte Gulf, the largest naval engagement in history. American forces held off the Japanese onslaught and sank four Japanese carriers, all but destroying Japan's capacity to continue a serious naval war. In February 1945, American marines seized the tiny volcanic island of Iwo Jima, just 750 miles from Tokyo, but only after the most deadly battle in the history of the Marine Corps.

The battle for **Okinawa**, an island only 370 miles south of Japan, gave evidence of the strength of the Japanese resistance in these last desperate days. Week after week, the Japanese sent kamikaze (suicide) planes against American and British ships, sacrificing

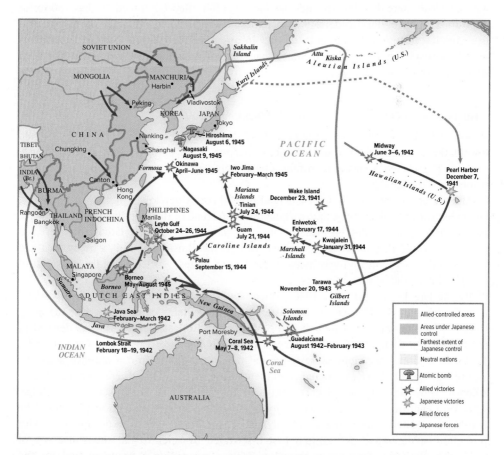

WORLD WAR II IN THE PACIFIC This map illustrates the changing fortunes of the two combatants in the Pacific phase of World War II. The long red line stretching from Burma around to Manchuria represents the eastern boundary of the vast areas of the Pacific that had fallen under Japanese control by the summer of 1942. The blue lines illustrate the advance of American forces in the Pacific beginning in May 1942 and accelerating in 1943 and after. The American advance was a result of two separate offensives—one in the central Pacific, under the command of Chester Nimitz, which moved west from Hawaii; and the other, under the command of Douglas MacArthur, which moved north from Australia. By the summer of 1945, American forces were approaching the Japanese mainland and bombing Tokyo itself. The dropping of two American atomic bombs, on Hiroshima and Nagasaki, finally brought the war to an end. • *What might the Soviet Union have hoped to gain by entering the Pacific war in August 1945, at the very end of the conflict, as shown in the upper-left corner of the map?*

3,500 of them while inflicting great damage. Japanese troops on shore launched desperate nighttime attacks on the American lines. The United States and its allies suffered nearly 50,000 casualties before finally capturing Okinawa in late June 1945. Over 100,000 Japanese, a huge percentage of the force, died in the siege.

It seemed likely that the same kind of bitter fighting would await the Americans when they invaded Japan. But there were also some signs early in 1945 that such an invasion might not be necessary. The Japanese had almost no ships or planes left with which to fight. The firebombing of Tokyo in March, in which American bombers dropped napalm on the city and created a firestorm in which over 80,000 people died, further weakened the Japanese will to resist. Moderate Japanese leaders, who had long since concluded the war was lost, were looking to end the fighting. But they continued to face powerful opposition from military leaders. Whether the moderates could ultimately have prevailed is a question historians continue to debate. In any case, their efforts became superfluous in August 1945, when the United States made use of a terrible new weapon it had been developing throughout the war.

THE MANHATTAN PROJECT AND ATOMIC WARFARE

Reports had reached the United States in 1939 that Nazi scientists had taken the first step toward the creation of an atomic bomb, a weapon more powerful than any previously devised. The United States and Britain immediately began a race to develop the weapon before the Germans did.

The search for the new weapon emerged from theories developed by atomic physicists, beginning early in the century, and particularly from some of the founding ideas of modern physics developed by Albert Einstein. Einstein's famous theory of relativity had revealed that matter could be converted into tremendous energy. Einstein himself, who by then had left his native Germany and was living in the United States, warned Franklin Roosevelt of German interest in atomic weapons.

By the late 1930s and early 1940s, scientists at American universities were working to catch up with the Germans. Soon after the United States entered the war, the army took over the research and named it the **Manhattan Project**, because it was devised in the Manhattan Engineer District Office of the Army Corps of Engineers. Over the next three years, the government secretly poured nearly $2 billion into a massive scientific and technological effort conducted at hidden laboratories in Oak Ridge, Tennessee; Los Alamos, New Mexico; Hanford, Washington; and other sites. Scientists in Oak Ridge, who were charged with finding a way to create a nuclear chain reaction that could be feasibly replicated within the confined space of a bomb, began experimenting with plutonium—a derivative of uranium first discovered by scientists at the University of California-Berkeley. Plutonium proved capable of providing a practical fuel for the weapon. Scientists in Los Alamos, under the direction of J. Robert Oppenheimer, were charged with the construction of the actual atomic bomb.

By 1944, despite many unforeseen problems, the Manhattan Project scientists pushed ahead much faster than anyone had predicted. Even so, the war in Europe ended before they were ready to test the first weapon. Just before dawn on July 16, 1945, in the desert near Alamogordo, New Mexico, the scientists gathered to witness the first atomic explosion in history: the detonation of a plutonium-fueled bomb that scientists had named Trinity. The explosion—a blinding flash of light, perhaps brighter than any ever before seen on earth, followed by a huge, billowing mushroom cloud—created a vast crater in the barren desert. Watching the test, Oppenheimer was reminded of a passage from Hindu scripture: "I am become death, the destroyer of worlds."

News of the explosion reached President Harry S. Truman, who had taken office in April on the death of Roosevelt, in Potsdam, Germany, where he was attending a conference of Allied leaders. Along with the British, he issued an ultimatum to the Japanese demanding they surrender by August 3 or face utter devastation. When the Japanese failed to meet the deadline, Truman ordered the air force to use the new atomic weapons against Japan.

Controversy has continued for decades over whether Truman's decision to use the bombs was justified and what his motives were. Some have argued that the atomic attack was unnecessary—that had the United States agreed to the survival of the emperor before the bombs were used (which it ultimately did agree to after the bombings), or had it waited only a few more weeks, the Japanese would have surrendered. Others argue that nothing less than the atomic bombs could have persuaded the Japanese to surrender without a costly American invasion. (See "Debating the Past: The Decision to Drop the Atomic Bomb.")

Most of the nation's military and political leaders, however, seemed little concerned about such matters. Truman, who had not even known of the existence of the Manhattan Project until he became president, made what he apparently believed to be a simple military decision. A weapon was available that would end the war quickly; he could see no reason not to use it.

On August 6, 1945, an American B-29, the *Enola Gay*, dropped an atomic weapon on the Japanese industrial center at **Hiroshima**. With a single bomb, the United States completely incinerated a four-square-mile area at the center of the city. More than 80,000 civilians died, according to later American estimates. Many more suffered the crippling effects of radioactive fallout or passed on those effects to their children in the form of birth defects.

The Japanese government, stunned by the attack, was at first unable to agree on a response. Two days later, on August 8, the Soviet Union declared war on Japan. And the following day, another American plane dropped another atomic weapon—this time on the city of Nagasaki—inflicting 100,000 deaths and terrible damage on yet another community. Finally, the emperor intervened to break the stalemate in the cabinet, and on August 14 the government announced it was ready to give up. On September 2, 1945, on board the American battleship *Missouri*, anchored in Tokyo Bay, Japanese officials signed the articles of surrender.

The most destructive war in human history had come to an end, and the United States had emerged from it not only victorious but also in a position of unprecedented power, influence, and prestige. It was a victory, however, that few could greet with unambiguous joy. Fourteen million combatants had died in the struggle. Fifty million or more civilians may have perished, making World War II by far the deadliest war in history. The United States had suffered only light casualties in comparison with some other nations (and particularly in comparison with Russia and Germany), but the cost had still been high: more than 400,000 dead, almost 700,000 injured. And the world continued to face an uncertain future, menaced by the threat of nuclear warfare and by an emerging antagonism between the world's two strongest nations—the United States and the Soviet Union—that would darken the peace for many decades to come.

THE DECISION TO DROP THE ATOMIC BOMB

There has been continuing disagreement since 1945 among historians—and many others—about how to explain and evaluate President Truman's decision to use the atomic bomb against Japan.

Truman himself, both at the time and in his 1955 memoirs, insisted that the decision was a simple and straightforward one. Japan was not ready to surrender in the summer of 1945. The alternative to using atomic weapons, he claimed, was an American invasion of mainland Japan that might have cost hundreds of thousands of American lives. Secretary of War Henry Stimson made the same argument, known as the "orthodox" one, in a 1947 piece in *Harper's Magazine*. That view received considerable support from historians. Herbert Feis argued in *The Atomic Bomb and the End of World War II* (1966) that Truman made his decision on purely military grounds—to ensure a speedy American victory.

(©Bettmann/Getty Images)

NAGASAKI SURVIVORS A Japanese woman and child look grimly at a photographer as they hold pieces of bread in the aftermath of the dropping of the second American atomic bomb—this one on Nagasaki.

Others strongly disagreed. As early as 1948, British physicist P. M. S. Blackett wrote in *Fear, War, and the Bomb* that the destruction of Hiroshima and Nagasaki was "not so much the last military act of the second World War as the first major operation of the cold diplomatic war with Russia." The most important "revisionist" critic of Truman's decision is the historian Gar Alperovitz, the author of two influential books on the subject: *Atomic Diplomacy: Hiroshima and Potsdam* (1965) and *The Decision to Use the Atomic Bomb* (1995). Alperovitz dismissed the argument that the bomb was used to shorten the war and save lives. Japan was likely to have surrendered soon even if the bomb had not been used, he claimed. Instead, he argued, the United States used the bomb less to influence Japan than for what he called "atomic diplomacy"—to intimidate the Soviet Union and "make Russia more manageable in Europe." In *A World Destroyed: The Atomic Bomb and the Grand Alliance* (1975), Martin Sherwin agreed that the bombs carried diplomatic value but also granted the orthodox position that Truman dropped them to end the war quickly.

Other critics of the Truman administration suggested that race played a role in the decision to drop atomic weapons on Japan. These include John Dower's *War Without Mercy: Race and Power in the Pacific War* (1986), Ronald Takaki's *Hiroshima: Why America Dropped the Atomic Bomb* (1995), and Tsuyoshi Hasegawa's *Racing the Enemy: Stalin, Truman, and the Surrender of Japan* (2005). These writers contend that American visions of the Japanese as almost subhuman animated not only Hiroshima and Nagasaki but also the broader character of the war in the Pacific. But there is much disagreement within the revisionist camp. Takaki and Hasegawa agreed with Alperovitz, for instance, that anti-Soviet impulses motivated the deployment of the bomb, but they parted company over other matters including race. Alperovitz wrote that it is "all but impossible to find specific evidence that racism was an important factor in the decision to attack Hiroshima and Nagasaki."

Orthodox scholars, in turn, reasserted their opposition to Alperovitz's idea of "atomic diplomacy" in the 1990s and 2000s with a similar charge: that revisionist scholars misread the evidence or wrote before the release of important new documents. Declassified reports suggested the United States knew in 1945 that Japan was readying itself for an American invasion. Two scholars, Robert H. Ferrell, in *Harry S. Truman: A Life* (1994) and *Harry S. Truman and the Cold War Revisionists* (2006), as well as Alonzo L. Hamby, in *Man of the People* (1995), defended Truman's decision to drop the bomb on military grounds. They cited Japan's unwillingness to surrender and Truman's belief that an invasion would be costly, thus denying the place of atomic diplomacy in the attacks. "One consideration weighed most heavily on Truman," Hamby concluded. "The longer the war lasted, the more Americans killed." In *The Most Controversial Decision: Truman, the Atomic Bombs, and the Defeat of Japan* (2011), Wilson Miscamble likewise called it a "myth" that Japan was ready to give up before Hiroshima and Nagasaki.

The debate over Truman's decision to drop the bomb has generated bitter and even personal exchanges, because at their heart, those exchanges pivot around a wrenching and divisive question: Were Hiroshima and Nagasaki brutal, unnecessary tragedies that killed thousands of innocent people, or terrible but justifiable acts that shortened a war and saved many thousands more? •

UNDERSTAND, ANALYZE, & EVALUATE

1. The United States dropped two atomic bombs on Japan, one on Hiroshima and the other on Nagasaki. Was dropping the bomb on Hiroshima necessary? Was it justifiable? Do the reasons for dropping the bomb on Hiroshima apply equally to the bombing of Nagasaki?
2. How might the war in the Pacific have been different if the United States had decided not to drop the bombs?

CONCLUSION

The United States played a critical role in the war against Germany and Italy. It defeated Imperial Japan in the Pacific largely alone. But America's contributions to and sacrifices in the war paled next to those of its most important allies. Britain, France, and, above all, the Soviet Union, paid a staggering price—in lives, treasure, and social unity—that had no counterpart in the United States. Most American citizens in the United States experienced a booming prosperity and only modest privations during the four years of American involvement in the conflict. There were, of course, jarring social changes during the war that even prosperity could not entirely offset: shortages, restrictions, regulations, family dislocations, and, perhaps most of all, the absence of millions of men and considerable numbers of women who went overseas.

American fighting men and women, of course, had very different experiences from those of the people who remained at home. They endured tremendous hardships, substantial casualties, and much fear and loneliness. They fought effectively and bravely. They helped liberate North Africa and Italy from German occupation. And in June 1944, they joined British, French, and other forces in a successful invasion of France. It led less than a year later to the destruction of the Nazi regime and the end of the European war. In the Pacific, Americans turned back the Japanese offensive through a series of difficult naval and land battles. Ultimately, however, it was not only the American army and navy that brought the war against Japan to a close. It was the unleashing of the most destructive weapon ever created—the atomic bomb—on the people of Japan that finally persuaded the leaders of that nation to surrender.

KEY TERMS/PEOPLE/PLACES/EVENTS

Atlantic Charter 616
Battle of the Bulge 634
braceros 625
Congress of Racial
   Equality (CORE) 624
D-Day 632
Dwight D. Eisenhower 618
Guadalcanal 618
Harry S. Truman 631
Hideki Tojo 616

Hiroshima 637
Holocaust 619
Korematsu v. U.S. 627
lend-lease 615
Manhattan Project 636
Office of Price
   Administration (OPA) 622
Office of War Information
   (OWI) 628
Okinawa 635

Pearl Harbor 616
relocation centers 627
Rosie the Riveter 630
United Service
   Organization (USO) 629
Winston Churchill 614
zoot suits 625

RECALL AND REFLECT

1. List some of the measures that the federal government took to mobilize the nation for the war effort.
2. How did advances in technology affect the course of the military conflict?
3. How did the United States contribute to the Allied victory in Europe? How important were America's allies? Which allies were most important?
4. How did the war affect U.S. society—women, workers, African Americans, Japanese Americans, and immigrants?
5. Why did the United States bomb civilians in Japan and Europe in the last years of the war?

26 THE COLD WAR

ORIGINS OF THE COLD WAR
THE COLLAPSE OF THE PEACE
AMERICA AFTER THE WAR
THE KOREAN WAR
THE CRUSADE AGAINST SUBVERSION

LOOKING AHEAD

1. What made the growing tension between the United States and the Soviet Union evolve into the Cold War?
2. What is the theory of containment, and how did it drive U.S. foreign policy and foreign interventions in the postwar era?
3. Why did the U.S. government and the American people believe that there was a threat of internal communist subversion?

LONG BEFORE WORLD WAR II ENDED, there were signs of tension between the United States and the Soviet Union. Since 1917, the two states had been suspicious of and opposed to the ideology of the other. Then they were forced into alliance by their mutual antagonism toward the Axis powers, but it infuriated Josef Stalin that the other Allies waited so long to invade mainland Europe. Sensing that hostilities between the two powers might resume after the war, and betting that boots on the ground would translate into influence, both sides sought to occupy as much Nazi territory as possible.

Once the fighting was over, those tensions grew to create what became known as the "Cold War"—a long and dangerous rivalry between the two former allies that would cast its shadow over international affairs and American domestic life for more than four decades. The Cold War took shape gradually over a five-year period, during which the relationship between the United States and the Soviet Union deteriorated and the United States crafted a new structure for American foreign policy—known as "containment"—that sought to keep communism from expanding.

Ideological differences between capitalism and communism laced the rivalry with a vocabulary of fear and difference. Yet both sides ultimately fought for something similar, something deeper, and something up for grabs in an era of decolonization—power and credibility around the world and security at home. Sometimes their ideologies led the two sides to pursue such ends very differently. At other times, they behaved similarly. But both sought economic markets, access to resources, military alliances, and above all, to bolster the strength and influence of their states.

ORIGINS OF THE COLD WAR

Few issues in twentieth-century American history have aroused more debate than the origins of the Cold War. Some have claimed that Soviet duplicity and expansionism created the international tensions; others, that American provocations and global ambitions were at least equally to blame. (See "Debating the Past: The Cold War.")

SOURCES OF SOVIET–AMERICAN TENSION

For a time, the rivalry between the United States and the Soviet Union rested on a fundamental difference in the ways the great powers envisioned the postwar world. One vision, first openly outlined in the Atlantic Charter in 1941, was a world in which nations abandoned their traditional beliefs in military alliances and spheres of influence and governed their relations with one another through democratic processes, with an international organization serving as the arbiter of disputes and the protector of every nation's right of self-determination. At least in theory, that vision appealed to many Americans, including Franklin Roosevelt.

The other vision was that of the Soviet Union and, to some extent, Great Britain. Both Josef Stalin and Winston Churchill had signed the Atlantic Charter. But Churchill had always been uneasy about the implications of self-determination for Britain's own enormous empire. And the Soviet Union was eager to create a secure sphere for itself in Central and Eastern Europe as protection against possible future aggression from the West. Both Churchill and Stalin, therefore, tended to envision a postwar structure vaguely similar to the traditional European balance of power, in which the great powers would control areas of strategic interest to them.

TIME LINE

1945
Yalta and Potsdam Conferences

United Nations founded

1946
Atomic Energy Commission established

1947
Truman Doctrine

Marshall Plan proposed

National Security Act

Taft-Hartley Act

1948
Berlin blockade

Truman elected president

1949
NATO established

Soviet Union explodes A-bomb

Mao victorious in China

Hiss case begins

1950
NSC-68

Korean War begins

1951
Truman fires MacArthur

McCarthy's anticommunism campaign begins

1952
American occupation of Japan ends

Eisenhower elected president

THE COLD WAR

For more than a decade after the beginning of the Cold War, few historians saw any reason to challenge the official American interpretation of its origins: the breakdown of relations between the United States and the Soviet Union was a direct result of Soviet expansionism and of Stalin's violation of wartime agreements forged at Yalta and Potsdam. The Soviet imposition of communist regimes in Eastern Europe was part of a larger ideological design to spread communism throughout the world. American policy was the logical and necessary response: a firm commitment to oppose Soviet expansionism and to keep American forces in a continual state of readiness.

Disillusionment with official justifications for the Cold War began to find expression even in the late 1950s, when anticommunist sentiment in America remained pervasive. William Appleman Williams's *The Tragedy of American Diplomacy* (1959) insisted that the Cold War was simply the most recent version of a consistent American effort in the twentieth century to preserve an "open door" for American trade in world markets. The confrontation with the Soviet Union, he argued, was less a response to Soviet aggressive designs than an expression of the American belief in capitalist expansion.

As the Vietnam War grew larger and more unpopular in the 1960s, the scholarly critique of the Cold War gained intensity. Walter LaFeber's *America, Russia, and the Cold War*, first published in 1967, maintained that America's supposedly idealistic internationalism at the close of the war was in reality an effort to ensure a postwar order shaped in the American image—with every nation open to American influence and trade. That was why the United States was so apt to misinterpret Soviet policy, much of which reflected a commitment to ensure the security of the Soviet Union itself, as part of a larger aggressive design.

The revisionist interpretations of the Cold War ultimately produced a reaction of their own: what has come to be known as "postrevisionist" scholarship. The most important work in this school attempted to strike a balance between orthodoxy and revisionism and to identify areas of blame and patterns of misconceptions on both sides of the conflict. An important statement of this approach was John Lewis Gaddis's *The United States and the Cold War, 1941–1947* (1972), which argued that "neither side can bear sole responsibility for the onset of the Cold War." Both sides had limited options, given their own political constraints and preconceptions. Other postrevisionist works—by Thomas G. Paterson, Melvyn Leffler, William Taubman, and others—have elaborated on ways in which the United States and the Soviet Union acted in response to genuine, if not necessarily accurate, beliefs about the intentions of the other. "The United States and the Soviet Union were doomed to be antagonists," Ernest May wrote in 1984. "There probably was never any real possibility that the post-1945 relationship could be anything but hostility verging on conflict."

Since the fall of the Soviet Union in 1991, scholars have had access to newly released Russian archives that have enriched the way historians view the Cold War. Those records have shown Soviet ambitions under Stalin in particular to be more tied to strategic and security concerns than to ideological motivations. John Lewis Gaddis, in *We Now Know: Rethinking Cold War History* (1998) and *The Cold War* (2005), portrays a Cold War somewhat more dangerous than his own earlier studies, and those of many other scholars, had portrayed; and he argues that the strong anticommunist positions of Margaret Thatcher, Ronald Reagan, and Pope John Paul II had a larger impact on the weakening of the Soviet Union than was previously understood. Odd Arne Westad, in *The Global Cold War* (2005) and *The Cold War: A World History* (2017), roots the origins of instability in the so-called Third World in the frequent interventions of both the Soviet Union and the United States in the Cold War era. He argues that the conflict reached into every corner of the globe, fueling ideological divides and terrible violence that reverberate to this day. •

UNDERSTAND, ANALYZE, & EVALUATE

1. What are the orthodox, revisionist, and postrevisionist arguments concerning the origins of the Cold War?
2. Was the Cold War inevitable?

But as World War II raged, and even more so as it ended, it became clear that such visions were outdated. The twentieth century had witnessed the diminution or collapse of several major empires—the German, Austro-Hungarian, Ottoman, Italian, Japanese, British, and French. Those upheavals left the Soviets and Americans as the two primary world powers, a situation more dangerous for both parties than one in which strength was spread across various empires that might be played off against one another. As empires shrunk or dissolved, millions of people eventually broke free of the control of distant states. These forces—what historians call decolonization—merged to create an increasingly bipolar world where the United States and the Soviet Union would compete for influence and power, often in places not previously thought to implicate the security of either state. The Cold War ultimately boiled down to that—the search for security and power in a perilous world.

Wartime Diplomacy

Serious strains began to develop in the alliance with the Soviet Union in January 1943, when Roosevelt and Churchill met in Casablanca, Morocco, to discuss Allied strategy. The two leaders could not accept Stalin's most important demand—the immediate opening of a second front in Western Europe to help the Soviet Red Army fight off a German invasion. But they tried to reassure Stalin by announcing that they would accept nothing less than the unconditional surrender of the Axis powers. They would not negotiate a separate peace with Hitler and leave the Soviets to fight alone.

In November 1943, Roosevelt and Churchill traveled to Tehran, Iran, for their first meeting with Stalin. By now, however, Roosevelt's most effective bargaining tool—Stalin's need for American assistance against Germany—had been largely removed. The German advance against Russia had been halted, and Soviet forces were launching their own westward offensive. Nevertheless, the Tehran Conference seemed in most respects a success. Stalin agreed to an American request that the Soviet Union enter the war in the Pacific soon after the end of hostilities in Europe. Roosevelt, in turn, promised that an Anglo–American second front would be established within six months.

On other matters, however, the origins of future disagreements were already visible. Most important was the question of Poland. Roosevelt and Churchill were willing to agree to a movement of the Soviet border westward, allowing Stalin to annex some historically Polish territory. But they differed sharply on the nature of the postwar government in the portion of Poland that would remain independent. Roosevelt and Churchill supported the claims of the Polish government-in-exile that had been functioning in London since 1940. Stalin wished to install another, pro-communist exiled government that had spent the war in Lublin, in the Soviet Union. The three Allied leaders left the Tehran Conference with the issue of the Polish government unresolved.

YALTA

More than a year later, in February 1945, Roosevelt joined Churchill and Stalin again, for a peace conference in the Soviet city of Yalta. In return for Stalin's renewed promise to enter the Pacific war, Roosevelt agreed that the Soviet Union should receive some of the Pacific territory that Russia had lost in the 1904–1905 Russo-Japanese War.

The negotiators also agreed to a plan for a new international organization, one that had been hammered out during the previous summer at a conference in Washington, D.C. The new **United Nations** would contain a General Assembly, in which every member would be represented, and a Security Council, with permanent representatives of the five major powers (the United States, Britain, France, the Soviet Union, and China), each of which would have veto power. The Security Council would also have temporary delegates from several other nations. These agreements became the basis of the UN charter, drafted at a conference of fifty nations beginning April 25, 1945, in San Francisco. In sharp contrast to the American rejection of the League of Nations a generation before, the U.S. Senate ratified the charter in July by a vote of 80 to 2. It was, many internationalists believed, a second chance to create a stable world order.

On other issues, however, the **Yalta Conference** produced no real accord. Basic disagreement remained about the postwar Polish government. Stalin, whose armies now occupied Poland, had already installed a government composed of the pro-communist Lublin Poles. Roosevelt and Churchill insisted that the pro-Western London Poles must be allowed a place in the Warsaw regime. Roosevelt envisioned a government based on free, democratic elections, which both he and Stalin recognized the pro-Western forces would win. Stalin agreed only to a vague compromise by which an unspecified number of pro-Western Poles would be granted a place in the government. He said he would hold "free and unfettered elections" in Poland on an unspecified future date. They did not happen until 1989.

Nor was there agreement about Germany. Roosevelt seemed to want a reconstructed Germany. Stalin wanted to impose heavy reparations on Germany and to ensure a permanent dismemberment of the nation. The final agreement was, like the Polish accord, vague and unstable. The decision on reparations would be referred to a future commission. The United States, Great Britain, France, and the Soviet Union would each control its own "zone of occupation" in Germany—the zones to be determined by the position of troops at the end of the war. Berlin, the German capital, was already well inside the Soviet zone, but because of its symbolic importance, it would itself be divided into four occupied sectors. At an unspecified date, Germany would be reunited. As for the rest of Europe, the conference produced a murky accord on the establishment

(©Bettmann/Getty Images)

YALTA, 1945 Churchill (left) and Stalin (right) were shocked at the physical appearance of Franklin Roosevelt (center) when he arrived for their critical meeting at Yalta. Roosevelt had enough energy to perform capably at the conference, but he was in fact gravely ill. Two months later, not long after he gave Congress what turned out to be an unrealistically optimistic report on the prospects for postwar peace, Roosevelt died.

of governments "broadly representative of all democratic elements" and "responsible to the will of the people."

The Yalta accords, in other words, were less a settlement of postwar issues than a set of loose principles that sidestepped the most difficult questions. Roosevelt, Churchill, and Stalin returned home from the conference, each apparently convinced that he had signed an important agreement. But the Soviet interpretation of the accords differed so sharply from the Anglo–American interpretation that the illusion endured only briefly. In the weeks following the Yalta Conference, Roosevelt watched with growing alarm as the Soviet Union moved systematically to establish pro-communist governments in one Central or Eastern European nation after another and as Stalin refused to make the changes in Poland that the president believed he had promised. Still hoping the differences could be settled, Roosevelt left Washington early in the spring for a vacation at his retreat in Warm Springs, Georgia. There, on April 12, 1945, he suffered a massive stroke and died.

THE COLLAPSE OF THE PEACE

The new president, Harry S. Truman, had almost no familiarity with international issues. Nor did he share Roosevelt's apparent faith in Soviet flexibility. Truman sided with the many people in the government who considered the Soviet Union fundamentally untrustworthy and viewed Stalin himself with suspicion and even hatred.

THE FAILURE OF POTSDAM

Truman had been in office only a few days before he decided to "get tough" with the Soviet Union. On April 23, he met with Soviet foreign minister Molotov and sharply chastised him for violations of the Yalta accords. In fact, Truman had little leverage. Russian forces already occupied Poland and much of the rest of Central and Eastern Europe.

Germany was already divided among the Allies. The United States was still engaged in a war in the Pacific and was neither able nor willing to enter into a renewed conflict in Europe. Truman insisted that the United States should be able to get "85 percent" of what it wanted, but he was ultimately forced to settle for much less.

He conceded first on Poland. When Stalin made a few minor concessions to the pro-Western exiles, Truman recognized the Warsaw government, hoping that noncommunist forces might gradually expand their influence there. (Until the 1980s, they did not.) To settle other questions, Truman met in July at Potsdam, in Russian-occupied Germany, with Stalin and Churchill (who, after elections in Britain in the midst of the talks, was replaced as prime minister by Clement Attlee). Truman reluctantly accepted the adjustments of the Polish–German border that Stalin had long demanded. He refused, however, to permit the Russians to claim any reparations from the American, French, and British zones of Germany. This stance effectively confirmed that Germany would remain divided. The western zones ultimately united into one nation, friendly to the United States, and the Russian zone survived as another nation, with a pro-Soviet, communist government.

THE CHINA PROBLEM AND JAPAN

American hopes for an open, peaceful world policed by the great powers required a strong, independent China. But those hopes faced a major obstacle: the Chinese government of Chiang Kai-shek. Chiang was generally friendly to the United States, but his government was corrupt and incompetent, with feeble popular support. Ever since 1927, the nationalist government he headed had been engaged in a bitter rivalry with the communist armies of **Mao Zedong**. By 1945, Mao controlled a quarter of the population.

Some Americans urged the government to try to find a third force as an alternative to Chiang and Mao. Truman, however, decided reluctantly that he had no choice but to continue supporting Chiang. For the next several years, the United States continued to pump money and weapons to Chiang, even as it was becoming clear that the cause was lost. The situation foreshadowed a looming question throughout the Cold War: how far should American leaders go to support anticommunist alternatives around the world, especially when those alternative forces contained their own deep flaws? The Truman administration badly wanted to keep Mao from power in China, but the president was not prepared to intervene militarily to save the nationalist regime.

Instead, the American government began to consider an alternative to China as the strong, pro-Western force in Asia: a revived Japan. Abandoning the strict occupation policies of the first years after the war (when General **Douglas MacArthur** had governed the defeated nation), the United States lifted restrictions on industrial development and encouraged rapid economic growth in Japan. The vision of an open, united world was giving way in Asia, as it was in Europe, to an acceptance of a divided world with a strong pro-American sphere of influence.

THE CONTAINMENT DOCTRINE

By the end of 1945, a new American foreign policy was slowly emerging. It became known as **containment**. Rather than attempting to create a unified world or destroy communism where it already existed, the United States and its allies would work to prevent Soviet expansion. American leaders almost always assumed the communists sought to spread their ideology in a global revolution and that all communist states were conspiring together to make it happen. Both assumptions, it is clear with hindsight, were problematic. Global revolution and lock-step communist alliances may have been long-term hopes. But Stalin, for his part, put the survival of himself and his regime above all other priorities, and tended to view communist allies more as vehicles for promoting the interests of the Soviet state than as ideological partners. This thirst for security had already led Stalin to murder or exile millions of his own citizens in the purges of the 1930s. Now, fearing capitalist encirclement, he projected that ruthless worldview outward.

But American leaders at the time saw their adversary not as an insecure paranoiac but as an ideologically driven expansionist, and they perceived evidence for that view in Europe and Asia in 1946. In Turkey, Stalin sought control over the vital sea lanes to the Mediterranean, though he harbored no particular hope for communist revolution there. In Greece, communist forces were threatening the pro-Western government, and the British had announced they could no longer provide assistance. And Soviet troops continued to occupy parts of Iran past dates earlier agreed upon. Faced with these challenges, Truman enunciated a firm new policy. In doing so, he drew from the ideas of the American diplomat George F. Kennan, who had warned not long after the war that the only viable American response to Soviet power was "a long-term, patient but firm and vigilant containment of Russian expansive tendencies." On March 12, 1947, Truman appeared before Congress and used Kennan's warnings as the basis of what became known as the **Truman Doctrine**. "I believe," he argued, "that it must be the policy of the United States to support free peoples who are resisting attempted subjugation by armed minorities or by outside pressures." In the same speech, he requested $400 million for aid to Greece and Turkey, which Congress quickly approved.

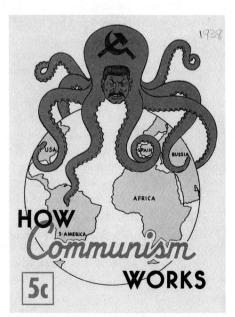

(Source: Rare Book and Special Collections Division, The Library of Congress)

HOW COMMUNISM WORKS This image and many others like it depicted Stalin as a dangerous expansionist, and communism as an insidious force threatening to take over the world.

The American commitment ultimately helped reduce Soviet pressure on Turkey and helped the Greek government defeat the communist insurgents. In the process, containment became a basis for American policy that survived for more than forty years.

THE CONSERVATIVE OPPOSITION TO CONTAINMENT

The containment doctrine attracted broad, bipartisan support for dealing with the Cold War. But not everyone believed containment was the right way to deal with communism. Some Americans on the left believed that it was an unnecessarily belligerent approach to the Soviet Union and that the United States could have made peace with the Russians. Wider opposition to containment came from conservative Americans, who thought it too weak a response to communism—that, indeed, it was a kind of appeasement.

Among the conservatives who disdained containment were members of an anticommunist organization known as the **John Birch Society**. Its leader was Robert Welch, a man so fearful of communism that he believed that some of the most important leaders of American government were trying to undermine the United States and collaborating with the Soviets. Welch presented his opposition in *The Blue Book of the John Birch Society*, in which he argued that much of the American government was riddled with treason. "For years," he wrote, "we have been taken steadily down the road to Communism by steps supposedly designed . . . as ways of *fighting* Communism." Instead, he argued, it was communist Americans themselves who were undermining the nation. "Both the U.S. and Soviet governments are controlled by the same furtive conspiratorial cabal of internationalists, greedy bankers, and corrupt politicians," Welch wrote. "If left unexposed, the traitors inside the U.S. government would betray the country's sovereignty to the United Nations for a collectivist New World Order, managed by a 'one-world' socialist government." Among the results of treason, Welch claimed, was the creation of the United Nations and other international institutions. Many Americans considered the John Birch Society an extremist organization, but the belief that communism was the greatest danger facing the United States was widely supported.

The opposition to containment reached some of the highest levels of government. John Foster Dulles, who would soon become secretary of state in the Eisenhower administration, wrote the foreign policy plank in the Republican platform in 1952. "We charge that the leaders of the Administration in power lost the peace so dearly earned by World War II," Dulles charged. "They abandoned friendly nations such as Latvia, Lithuania, Estonia, Poland, and Czechoslovakia." Containment, they argued, was a policy of weakness that had allowed the communists to take over much of the world. Instead, those who opposed containment called for what was known as "rollback." Instead of containing communism, the United States should be pushing back the borders of communism, despite the possibility of another war. President Dwight Eisenhower, however, elected in 1952, did not share Dulles's faith in rollback. The government abided by the containment strategy throughout the 1950s and beyond— despite the fevered opposition to what some still considered to be treason.

THE MARSHALL PLAN

An integral part of the containment policy was a proposal to aid in the economic recon- struction of Western Europe. There were many motives: humanitarian concern for the European people; a fear that Europe would remain an economic drain on the United States if not quickly rebuilt; and a desire for a strong European market for American goods.

But above all, American policymakers believed that unless something could be done to strengthen the shaky pro-American governments in Western Europe, those governments might fall under the control of domestic communist parties.

In June 1947, Secretary of State George C. Marshall announced a plan to provide economic assistance to all European nations (including the Soviet Union) that would join in drafting a program for recovery. Although Russia and its Eastern satellites predictably rejected the plan, sixteen Western European nations eagerly participated. Opposition from isolationists in the United States largely vanished after a sudden coup in Czechoslovakia in February 1948 established a Soviet-dominated communist government. In April, Congress approved the creation of the Economic Cooperation Administration, the agency that would administer the **Marshall Plan**, as it became known. Over the next three years, the Marshall Plan channeled $13 billion of American aid into Europe, helping spark a substantial economic revival. By the end of 1950, European industrial production had risen 64 percent, communist strength in the member nations had declined, and opportunities for American trade had revived.

Mobilization at Home

In 1948, at the president's request, Congress approved a new military draft and revived the Selective Service System. In the meantime, the United States, having failed to reach agreement with the Soviet Union on international control of nuclear weapons, redoubled its own efforts in atomic research, elevating nuclear weaponry to a central place in its military arsenal. The Atomic Energy Commission, established in 1946, became the supervisory body charged with overseeing all nuclear research, civilian and military alike. And in 1950, the Truman administration approved the development of the new hydrogen bomb, a nuclear weapon far more powerful than those used in 1945.

The National Security Act of 1947 reshaped the nation's military and diplomatic institutions. A new Department of Defense would oversee all branches of the armed services, combining functions previously performed separately by the War and Navy Departments. A National Security Council (NSC), operating out of the White House, would govern foreign and military policy. The **Central Intelligence Agency (CIA)** would replace the wartime Office of Strategic Services and would be responsible for collecting information through open and covert methods. As the Cold War continued, the CIA would also engage in secret political and military operations on behalf of American interests. The National Security Act, in other words, gave the president expanded powers with which to pursue the nation's international goals.

The Road to NATO

The United States also moved to strengthen the military capabilities of Western Europe. Convinced that a reconstructed Germany was essential to the needs of the West, Truman reached an agreement with Britain and France to merge the three western zones of occupation into a new West German republic (which would include the three non-Soviet sectors of Berlin, even though that city lay within the Soviet zone). Stalin responded quickly. On June 24, 1948, he imposed a tight blockade around the western sectors of Berlin. If Germany was to be officially divided, Stalin was implying, then the country's Western government would have to abandon the capital city in the heart of the Soviet-controlled eastern zone. Truman refused to do so. Unwilling to risk war through a military challenge to the blockade, he ordered a massive airlift to supply the western half of Berlin with food, fuel, and other needed goods. The airlift continued for more than ten months, transporting nearly 2.5 million tons of food and other material, keeping a city of 2 million people alive. In the spring of 1949, Stalin lifted the now ineffective blockade. And in October, the division of Germany into two nations—the Federal Republic in the west (with its new capital in Bonn) and the Democratic Republic in the east (with its capital in East Berlin)—became official.

The crisis in Berlin accelerated the consolidation of what was already in effect an alliance among the United States and the countries of Western Europe. On April 4, 1949, twelve nations signed an agreement establishing the **North Atlantic Treaty Organization (NATO)**,

DIVIDED EUROPE AFTER WORLD WAR II This map shows the sharp division that emerged in Europe after World War II between the area under the control of the Soviet Union and the area allied with the United States. In the east, Soviet domination extended into all the nations shaded brown—including the eastern part of Germany. In the west and south, the green-shaded nations were allied with the United States as members of the North Atlantic Treaty Organization (NATO). The countries shaded gold were aligned with neither of the two superpowers. The small map in the upper right shows the division of Berlin among the various occupying powers at the end of the war. Eventually, the American, British, and French sectors were combined to create West Berlin, a city governed by West Germany but entirely surrounded by communist East Germany. The airplane icons represent the airlift of supplies ordered by President Truman into the blockaded zones of West Berlin beginning in June 1948. • *How did the West prevent East Germany from absorbing West Berlin?*

declaring that an armed attack against one member would be considered an attack against all. The NATO countries would, moreover, maintain a standing military force in Europe to defend against what they believed was the threat of a Soviet invasion. The formation of NATO eventually spurred the Soviet Union to create an alliance of its own with the communist governments in Eastern Europe, formalized in 1955 by the **Warsaw Pact**.

Reevaluating Cold War Policy

In September 1949, the Soviet Union successfully exploded its first atomic weapon. The Russian nuclear capacity came years earlier than predicted, shocking and frightening many Americans. So did the collapse of Chiang Kai-shek's nationalist government in China, which occurred with startling speed in the last months of 1949. Chiang fled with his political allies and the remnants of his army to the offshore island of Formosa (Taiwan), and the entire Chinese mainland came under the control of a communist government led by Mao Zedong that many Americans believed to be an extension of the Soviet Union. The United States refused to recognize the new communist regime.

The fall of China accelerated the fear of communism and persuaded many Americans that the defeat was a result of weakness or even treason. As a result, American friends of China formed what came to be known as the China Lobby. Among its eminent leaders were members of Congress, high-level military figures, and powerful journalists. They believed that the United States had not done enough to prevent the communists from taking over mainland China. The failure persuaded many Americans that the government—particularly members of the State Department—was responsible.

In this atmosphere of escalating crisis, Truman called for a thorough review of American foreign policy. The result, a National Security Council report, issued in 1950 and commonly known as **NSC-68**, outlined a shift in the American position. The first statements of the containment doctrine—the writings of George Kennan, the Truman Doctrine speech—had made distinctions between areas of vital interest to the United States and areas of less importance to the nation's foreign policy. The containment doctrine also called for sharing the military burden of protecting the Western nations. But NSC-68 argued that the United States could no longer rely on other nations to take the initiative in resisting communism. It must move on its own to stop communist expansion virtually anywhere it occurred, regardless of the intrinsic strategic or economic value of the lands in question. To make this happen, the document called for a permanent expansion of American military power, with a defense budget almost four times the previously projected figure.

AMERICA AFTER THE WAR

The crises overseas were not the only frustrations the American people encountered after the war. The nation also faced serious, if short-lived, economic difficulties in adapting to peace. And it suffered from an exceptionally heated political climate that produced a new wave of insecurity and repression.

The Problems of Reconversion

Despite widespread predictions that the end of the war would return America to depression conditions, economic growth continued after 1945. Pent-up consumer demand from workers who had accumulated substantial savings during the war helped spur the boom. So did a

$6 billion tax cut. The Servicemen's Readjustment Act of 1944, better known as the **GI Bill** of Rights, provided housing, education, and job-training subsidies to veterans and increased spending even further.

The GI Bill expressed the progressive hopes of many Americans who wanted to see the government do more to assist its citizens. But it also expressed some of the enduring inequalities in American life. Few GI Bill benefits were available to women, even though many women had assisted the war effort in important ways. And while the GI Bill itself did not discriminate against African Americans, its provisions giving local governments jurisdiction allowed southern states, in particular, to deny or limit benefits to black veterans.

The flood of consumer demand contributed to more than two years of inflation, during which prices rose at annual rates of 14 to 15 percent. Compounding the economic difficulties was a sharp rise in labor unrest. By the end of 1945, major strikes had occurred in the automobile, electrical, and steel industries. In April 1946, John L. Lewis led the United Mine Workers out on strike, shutting down the coal fields for forty days. Truman finally forced coal production to resume by ordering government seizure of the mines. But in the process, he pressured mine owners to grant the union most of its demands. Almost simultaneously, the nation's railroads suffered a total shutdown—the first in the nation's history—as two major unions walked out on strike. By threatening to use the army to run the trains, Truman pressured the strikers back to work after only a few days.

Reconversion was particularly difficult for the millions of women and minorities who had entered the workforce during the war. With veterans returning home, employers tended to push women, African Americans, Hispanics, and others out of the plants to make room for white males. Some war workers, particularly women, left the workforce voluntarily, out of a desire to return to their former domestic lives. But a large majority of women workers and virtually all black and Hispanic males wanted to continue working. Postwar inflation, the pressure of a growing high-consumption society, a rising divorce rate that left many women responsible for their own economic well-being—all combined to create a high demand for paid employment among women. As women workers found themselves excluded from industrial jobs, therefore, they moved increasingly into other areas of the economy, above all the service sector.

The Fair Deal Rejected

Days after the Japanese surrender, Truman submitted to Congress a twenty-one-point domestic program he later named the **Fair Deal**. It called for an expansion of Social Security benefits, the raising of the legal minimum wage from 40 to 65 cents an hour, a program to ensure full employment through aggressive use of federal spending and investment, a permanent Fair Employment Practices Act, public housing and slum clearance, long-range environmental and public works planning, and government promotion of scientific research. Weeks later he added other proposals: federal aid to education, government health insurance and prepaid medical care, funding for the St. Lawrence Seaway, and nationalization of atomic energy.

But most of Truman's programs fell victim to the same public and congressional conservatism that had crippled the last years of the New Deal. Indeed, that conservatism seemed to be intensifying, as the November 1946 congressional elections suggested. Using the simple but devastating slogan "Had Enough?" the Republican Party won control of both houses of Congress, which quickly moved to reduce government spending and chip away at New Deal reforms. Its most notable action was its assault on the Wagner Act of 1935, in the form of the Labor-Management Relations Act of 1947, better known as the

Taft-Hartley Act. It outlawed the closed shop, a workplace in which no one can be hired without first being a member of a union. And although it continued to permit the creation of union shops, in which workers must join a union *after* being hired, it allowed states to pass "right-to-work" laws prohibiting even that. The Taft-Hartley Act also empowered the president to call for a ten-week "cooling-off" period before a strike by issuing an injunction against any work stoppage that endangered national safety or health. Outraged workers and union leaders denounced the measure as a "slave labor bill." Truman vetoed it. But both houses easily overruled him the same day. The Taft-Hartley Act did not destroy the labor movement, but it did damage weaker unions in relatively lightly organized industries such as chemicals and textiles, and it made much more difficult the organizing of workers who had never been union members at all, especially in the South and the West.

THE ELECTION OF 1948

Truman and his advisers believed that the American public was not ready to abandon the achievements of the New Deal, despite the 1946 election results. As they planned their strategy for the 1948 campaign, therefore, they hoped to appeal to enduring Democratic loyalties. Throughout 1948, Truman proposed one reform measure after another (including, on February 2, the first major civil rights bill of the century). To no one's surprise, Congress ignored or defeated them all, but the president was building campaign issues for the fall.

There remained, however, the problems of Truman's personal unpopularity—the assumption among much of the electorate that he lacked stature and that his administration was weak and inept—and the deep divisions within the Democratic Party. At the Democratic National Convention that summer, two factions abandoned the party altogether. Angered by Truman's proposed civil rights bill and by the approval at the convention of a civil rights plank in the platform (engineered by Hubert Humphrey, the reform mayor of Minneapolis), some southern conservatives walked out and formed the States' Rights Democratic (or "Dixiecrat") Party, with Governor Strom Thurmond of South Carolina as its nominee. At the same time, some members of the party's left wing—contemptuous of what they considered Truman's ineffectual leadership and his excessively confrontational stance toward the Soviet Union—joined the new Progressive Party, whose candidate was Henry A. Wallace.

Many Democratic liberals who were unhappy with Truman were unwilling to leave the party. The Americans for Democratic Action (ADA), a coalition of anticommunist liberals, tried to entice Dwight D. Eisenhower, the popular war hero, to contest the nomination. Only after Eisenhower refused did liberals concede the nomination to Truman. The Republicans, in the meantime, once again nominated Governor Thomas E. Dewey of New York. Austere, dignified, and competent, he seemed to offer an unbeatable alternative to the president.

Only Truman seemed to believe he could win. As the campaign gathered momentum, he became more and more aggressive, turning the fire away from himself and toward Dewey and the "do-nothing, good-for-nothing" Republican Congress, which was, he told voters, responsible for fueling inflation and abandoning workers and common people. To dramatize his point, he called Congress into special session in July to give it a chance, he said, to enact the liberal measures the Republicans had recently written into their platform. Congress met for two weeks and, predictably, managed to pass almost nothing.

On election night, to the surprise of almost everyone, Truman won a narrow but decisive and dramatic victory: 49.5 percent of the popular vote to Dewey's 45.1 percent (with the two splinter parties dividing the small remainder evenly between them), and an electoral margin of 303 to 189. Democrats regained both houses of Congress by substantial margins.

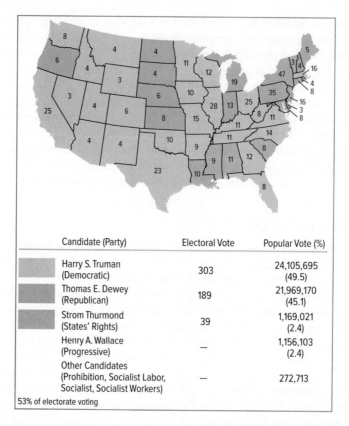

Candidate (Party)	Electoral Vote	Popular Vote (%)
Harry S. Truman (Democratic)	303	24,105,695 (49.5)
Thomas E. Dewey (Republican)	189	21,969,170 (45.1)
Strom Thurmond (States' Rights)	39	1,169,021 (2.4)
Henry A. Wallace (Progressive)	–	1,156,103 (2.4)
Other Candidates (Prohibition, Socialist Labor, Socialist, Socialist Workers)	–	272,713

53% of electorate voting

THE ELECTION OF 1948 Despite the widespread expectation that the Republican candidate, Thomas Dewey, would easily defeat Truman in 1948, the president in fact won a substantial reelection victory that year. This map shows the broad geographic reach of Truman's victory. Dewey swept most of the Northeast, but Truman dominated almost everywhere else. Strom Thurmond, the States' Rights candidate, carried four states in the South. • *What prompted Thurmond to desert the Democratic Party and run for president on his own?*

THE FAIR DEAL REVIVED

With the support of his party in Congress, Truman's Fair Deal reform won some important victories. Congress raised the legal minimum wage from 40 cents to 75 cents an hour. It approved an important expansion of the Social Security system, increasing benefits by 75 percent and extending them to 10 million additional people. And it passed the National Housing Act of 1949, which provided for the construction of 810,000 units of low-income housing accompanied by long-term rent subsidies.

But on other issues—national health insurance and aid to education, among them—Truman made little progress. Nor was he able to persuade Congress to accept the civil rights legislation he proposed in 1949, legislation that would make lynching a federal crime, provide federal protection of black voting rights, abolish the poll tax, and establish a new Fair Employment Practices Commission to curb discrimination in hiring. Southern Democrats filibustered to kill the bill.

Undeterred, Truman proceeded on his own to battle several forms of racial discrimination. He ordered an end to discrimination in the hiring of government employees. He began to dismantle segregation within the armed forces. And he allowed the Justice Department to become actively involved in court battles against discriminatory statutes. The Supreme Court, in the meantime, signaled its own growing awareness of the issue by ruling, in *Shelley v. Kraemer* (1948), that courts could not be used to enforce private "covenants" meant to bar African Americans from residential neighborhoods.

THE NUCLEAR AGE

Looming over the many struggles of the postwar years were images of the terrible mushroom clouds that had risen over Alamogordo in July 1945 and then over the Japanese cities of Hiroshima and Nagasaki. Americans greeted these new instruments of destruction with fear and awe but also expectation. Postwar culture was torn between a dark image of the nuclear war that many Americans feared would result from the rivalry with the Soviet Union, and the bright image of a dazzling technological future that atomic power might help produce.

The fear of nuclear weapons appeared widely in popular culture, but it was often disguised. The late 1940s and early 1950s were the heyday of *film noir*, a kind of filmmaking that originated in France and had been named for the dark lighting characteristic of the genre. American *film noir* portrayed the loneliness of individuals in an impersonal world—a staple of American culture for many decades—but also suggested the menacing character of the age, the looming possibility of vast destruction. Sometimes, popular fears addressed nuclear fear explicitly—for example, the celebrated television show of the 1950s and early 1960s,

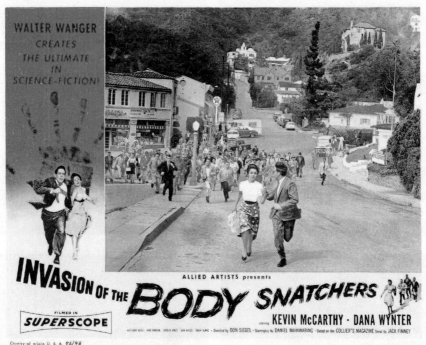

(©Allied Artists/Kobal/REX/Shutterstock)

INVASION OF THE BODY SNATCHERS This 1955 movie was one of many in the decade that imagined dangerous, mysterious invasions or transformations as allegories for the lurking menace of communism. The film told the story of a small town under attack from extraterrestrial, plant-like pods that replicate the townspeople, forming heartless, cold imposters rather like the stereotypical brainwashed communists.

CONSIDER THE SOURCE

"BERT THE TURTLE (*DUCK AND COVER*)" (1952)

Millions of American schoolchildren watched the 1952 film *Duck and Cover*, issued by the Federal Civil Defense Administration. It featured the animated character Bert the Turtle and a jaunty song whose lyrics are below. The filmmakers used the character to educate children on how to protect themselves during a nuclear attack. Live action sequences showed air-raid sirens and children diving under desks but noted that some attacks might come without warning. Students should "be like Bert! When there is a flash, duck and cover and do it fast!" Desks might seem inadequate protection against an atomic bomb, and indeed, the film has been widely mocked as falsely reassuring Cold War propaganda. But the experiences of survivors in Hiroshima and Nagasaki

There was a turtle by the name of Bert
And Bert the Turtle was very alert
When danger threatened him he never got hurt
He knew just what to do
He'd duck and cover, duck and cover

He did what we all must learn to do

You, and you, and you, and you

Duck and cover!

(Source: U.S. Office for Emergency Management. Office of Civilian Defense. 5/20/1941-6/30/1945/ NARA (38174))

suggested that people outside a certain radius from ground zero could indeed minimize burns and blindness by shielding themselves. In fact, well into the twenty-first century, American officials recommended people take cover and seek shelter in the event of a nuclear terrorist attack.

Source: Federal Civil Defense Administration

UNDERSTAND, ANALYZE, & EVALUATE

1. What are the main messages of this song?
2. In the context of Cold War America, would "Bert the Turtle" frighten or reassure schoolchildren?
3. How could this song and the film be considered propaganda?

The Twilight Zone, which featured dramatic portrayals of the aftermath of nuclear war, or postwar comic books, which depicted powerful superheroes saving the world from destruction.

Such images resonated with the public because awareness of nuclear weapons was increasingly built into their daily lives. Schools and office buildings held regular air-raid drills to prepare people for the possibility of nuclear attack. (See "Consider the Source: Bert the Turtle [*Duck and Cover*].") Radio stations regularly tested the Emergency Broadcast System, which stood in readiness for war. Fallout shelters stocked with water and canned goods sprang up in public buildings and private homes. Though few Americans went about their daily lives in a state of panic, anxiety simmered below the surface.

And yet, the United States was also an exuberant nation in these years, dazzled by its own prosperity and excited by the technological innovations transforming the nation, including nuclear power. The same scientific knowledge that could destroy the world, many believed, might also lead it into a glimmering future. The *New York Times*, only days after Hiroshima, expressed its own rosy view of the nuclear future: "This new knowledge . . . can bring to this earth not death but life, not tyranny and cruelty, but a divine freedom."

That kind of optimism soon became widespread. The "secret of the atom," many Americans predicted, would bring "prosperity and a more complete life." A public opinion poll late in 1948 revealed that approximately two-thirds of those questioned believed that, "in the long run," atomic energy would "do more good than harm." Nuclear power plants began to spring up in many areas of the country and were welcomed as the source of cheap and unlimited electricity, their potential dangers scarcely discussed by those who celebrated their creation.

THE KOREAN WAR

Though the Cold War started in Europe, it quickly spread to Asia. On June 24, 1950, the armies of communist North Korea swept across their southern border and invaded the pro-Western half of the Korean peninsula. Within days, they had occupied much of South Korea, including Seoul, its capital. True to the dictates of containment, the United States almost immediately committed itself to the conflict.

THE DIVIDED PENINSULA

When World War II ended, both the United States and the Soviet Union had troops in Korea fighting the Japanese, and neither army was willing to leave. Instead, they divided the nation, supposedly temporarily, along the 38th parallel. The Russians finally departed in 1949, leaving behind a communist government in the north with a strong, Soviet-equipped army. The Americans left a few months later, handing control to the pro-Western government of **Syngman Rhee**. Anticommunist but not reliably democratic, he used his relatively small military primarily to suppress internal opposition.

The relative weakness of South Korea offered a strong temptation to nationalists in the North Korean government who wanted to reunite the country, particularly after the American government implied that it did not consider Korea within its own "defense perimeter." Josef Stalin did, however, view Korea as important to Soviet security, and he approved of North Korean leader Kim Il Sung's decision to launch the invasion. Once again, Stalin's priorities were strategic more than ideological. He held only dim hopes of socialism taking hold on the peninsula but feared that an American-backed South Korean offensive might put a unified pro-Western government at his doorstep. But these distinctions are more apparent in retrospect than they were at the time. To alarmed American leaders, Korea seemed evidence of an ongoing communist crusade to spread itself around the world.

Almost immediately, on June 27, 1950, the president ordered limited American military assistance to South Korea, and on the same day he appealed to the United Nations to intervene. The Soviet Union was boycotting the Security Council at the time (to protest the council's refusal to recognize the new communist government of China) and was thus unable to exercise its veto power. As a result, American delegates were able to win UN agreement to a resolution calling for international assistance to the Rhee government. On June 30, the United States ordered its own ground forces into Korea, and Truman appointed General Douglas MacArthur to command the UN operations there. Several other nations provided assistance and troops, but the "UN" armies were overwhelmingly American.

After a surprise American invasion at Inchon in September had routed the North Korean forces from the south and sent them back across the 38th parallel, Truman gave MacArthur permission to pursue the communists into their own territory. Hoping now to create "a unified, independent and democratic Korea," the president had moved beyond simple containment to an attempted rollback of communist power.

FROM INVASION TO STALEMATE

For several weeks, MacArthur's invasion of North Korea proceeded smoothly. On October 19, the capital, Pyongyang, fell to the UN forces. Victory seemed near, until the Chinese government, alarmed by the movement of American forces toward its border, intervened.

In early November, eight divisions of the Chinese army entered the war. The UN offensive stalled and then collapsed. Through December 1950, outnumbered American forces were forced into a rapid, bitter retreat in numbingly cold temperatures. Within weeks, communist forces had pushed the Americans back below the 38th parallel once again and recaptured the South Korean capital of Seoul. By mid-January 1951 the rout had ceased, and by March the UN armies had regained much of the territory they had recently lost, taking back Seoul and pushing the communists north of the 38th parallel for the second time. With that, the war turned into a protracted stalemate.

From the start, Truman had been determined to avoid a direct conflict with China, which he feared might lead to a new world war. Once China entered the war, he began seeking a negotiated solution to the struggle. But General MacArthur had ideas of his own.

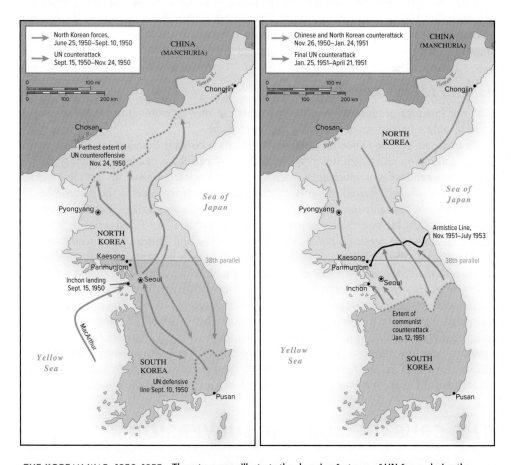

THE KOREAN WAR, 1950-1953 These two maps illustrate the changing fortunes of UN forces during the 1950–1953 Korean War. The map at the left shows the extent of the North Korean invasion of South Korea in 1950. Communist forces for a time controlled all of Korea except a small area around Pusan in the southeast. On September 15, 1950, UN troops under Douglas MacArthur landed in force at Inchon and soon drove the North Koreans back across the border. MacArthur then pursued the North Koreans well into their own territory. The map at right shows the very different circumstances once the Chinese entered the war in November 1950. Chinese forces drove the UN army back below the 38th parallel and, briefly, deep into South Korea, below Seoul. The UN troops fought back to the prewar border between North and South Korea late in 1951, when the war bogged down into a stalemate that continued for a year and a half. • *How did the Korean War reveal the broader character, dangers, and strategies of the Cold War?*

The United States was really fighting the Chinese, MacArthur argued. It should, therefore, attack China itself, if not through an actual invasion, then at least by bombing communist forces massing north of the Chinese border with conventional or even atomic weapons. In March 1951, he indicated his unhappiness with Truman's reluctance to invade China. In a public letter to House Republican Leader Joseph W. Martin, he concluded: "There is no substitute for victory." His position had wide popular support. Yet the release of the Martin letter struck the president as intolerable insubordination. On April 11, 1951, he relieved MacArthur of his command.

Sixty-nine percent of the American people supported MacArthur, a Gallup poll reported. When the general returned to the United States later in 1951, he was greeted with wild enthusiasm. Criticism of Truman finally abated somewhat when a number of prominent military figures, including General Omar Bradley, publicly supported the president's decision. But substantial hostility toward Truman remained. In the meantime, the Korean stalemate continued. Negotiations between the opposing forces began at Panmunjom in July 1951, but the talks—and the war—dragged on until 1953.

LIMITED MOBILIZATION

The war in Korea produced only a limited American military commitment abroad. It also created only a limited economic mobilization at home.

Truman set up the Office of Defense Mobilization to fight inflation by holding down prices and discouraging high union wage demands. When these cautious regulatory efforts failed, the president took more drastic action. Railroad workers walked off the job in 1951, and Truman, who considered the workers' demands inflationary, ordered the government to take control of the railroads. In 1952, during a nationwide steel strike, Truman seized the steel mills, citing his powers as commander in chief. But in a 6-to-3 decision, the Supreme Court ruled that the president had exceeded his authority, and Truman was forced to relent.

The Korean War significantly boosted economic growth by pumping new government funds into the economy. But the war had other, less welcome effects. It came at a time of rising insecurity about America's position in the world and intensified anxiety about communism. As the long stalemate continued, producing 140,000 American dead and wounded, frustration turned to anger. The United States, which had recently won the greatest war in history, seemed unable to conclude what many Americans considered a minor border skirmish in a small country. They began to believe that something must be deeply wrong—not only in Korea but within the United States as well. Such fears contributed to the rise of the second major campaign of the century against domestic communism.

THE CRUSADE AGAINST SUBVERSION

Why did the American people develop a growing fear of internal communist subversion, a fear that by the early 1950s occasionally reached the point of hysteria?

One factor was obvious: communism was not an imagined enemy. It took tangible shape in Josef Stalin and the Soviet Union. Adding to the concern were the Korean stalemate, the "loss" of China, and the Soviet development of an atomic bomb. Searching for someone to blame, many began to believe that there was a communist conspiracy within American borders. But there were other factors as well, rooted in events in American domestic politics.

HUAC and Alger Hiss

Much of the anticommunist furor emerged out of the search by Republicans for an issue with which to attack the Democrats, and out of the efforts of the Democrats to take that issue away from them. Beginning in 1947, the **House Un-American Activities Committee (HUAC)** held widely publicized investigations to prove that, under Democratic rule, the government had tolerated if not actually encouraged communist subversion. The committee turned first to the movie industry, arguing that communists had infiltrated Hollywood and tainted American films with propaganda. Writers and producers, some of them former communists, were called to testify; and when some of them (the "Hollywood Ten") refused to answer questions about their political beliefs and those of their colleagues, they were sent to jail for contempt. Others were barred from employment in the industry when Hollywood, attempting to protect its public image, adopted a "blacklist" of those of "suspicious loyalty."

More alarming to the public was HUAC's investigation into charges of disloyalty leveled against **Alger Hiss**, a former high-ranking member of the State Department. In 1948, Whittaker Chambers, a former communist agent, now a conservative editor at *Time* magazine, told the committee that Hiss had passed classified State Department documents to him in 1937 and 1938. When Hiss sued him for slander, Chambers produced microfilms of the documents (called the "pumpkin papers," because Chambers had kept them hidden in a pumpkin in his vegetable garden). Hiss could not be tried for espionage because of the statute of limitations, which protects individuals from prosecution for most crimes after seven years have passed. But largely because of the relentless efforts of Richard M. Nixon, a first-term congressman from California and a member of HUAC, Hiss was convicted of perjury and served several years in prison. The Hiss case not only discredited a prominent young diplomat, it also cast suspicion on a generation of liberal Democrats. And it transformed Nixon into a national figure and helped him win a Senate seat in 1950.

The Federal Loyalty Program and the Rosenberg Case

Partly to protect itself against Republican attacks and partly to encourage support for the president's foreign policy initiatives, the Truman administration in 1947 initiated a widely publicized program to review the loyalty of federal employees. By 1951, more than 2,000 government employees had resigned under pressure and 212 had been dismissed.

The Federal Employee Loyalty Program helped launch a major assault on subversion throughout the government and beyond. The attorney general established a widely cited list of supposedly subversive organizations. The director of the Federal Bureau of Investigation (FBI), J. Edgar Hoover, investigated and harassed alleged radicals. In 1950, Congress passed the McCarran Internal Security Act, which, among other restrictions on "subversive" activity, required that all communist organizations register with the government and publish their records. Congress easily overrode Truman's veto of the bill.

The successful Soviet detonation of an atomic bomb in 1949 suggested to some that there had been a conspiracy to pass American atomic secrets to the Russians. In 1950, Klaus Fuchs, a young British scientist, seemed to confirm those fears when he testified that he had delivered to the Russians details of the bomb's manufacture. The case ultimately moved to an obscure New York couple, **Julius and Ethel Rosenberg**, members of the Communist Party. The government claimed the Rosenbergs had received secret information from Ethel's brother, a machinist on the Manhattan Project in New Mexico, and had passed it on to the Soviet Union through other agents (including Fuchs). The Rosenbergs were convicted and, on April 5, 1951, sentenced to death. After two years of appeals and public protests, they died in the electric chair on June 19, 1953. Historians now believe that Julius—but not Ethel—was guilty as charged.

All these factors—the HUAC investigations, the Hiss trial, the loyalty investigations, the McCarran Act, the Rosenberg case—combined with other concerns by the early 1950s to create a fear of communist subversion that seemed to grip the country. State and local governments, the judiciary, schools and universities, labor unions—all sought to purge themselves of real or imagined subversives. It was a climate that made possible the rise of an extraordinary public figure.

McCarthyism

Joseph McCarthy was an undistinguished first-term Republican senator from Wisconsin until, in February 1950, in the midst of a speech in Wheeling, West Virginia, he lifted up a sheet of paper and claimed to "hold in my hand" a list of 205 known communists currently working in the American State Department. No person of comparable stature had ever made so bold a charge against the federal government. In the months to come,

(©REX/Shutterstock)

MCCARTHY TESTIFIES IN THE SENATE, MARCH 1950 One of the first consequences of Senator Joseph McCarthy's speech in West Virginia was the creation of a subcommittee of the Senate Foreign Relations Committee to investigate his charges. Although the committee chairman, Democrat Millard Tydings of Maryland, thought McCarthy's infamous list a "hoax," it was from this platform that the senator leveled many of his early accusations of communist State Department infiltration.

as McCarthy repeated and expanded on his accusations, he emerged as the nation's most prominent leader of the crusade against domestic subversion.

Within weeks of his charges against the State Department, McCarthy leveled accusations at other agencies. After 1952, with the Republicans in control of the Senate and McCarthy now the chair of a special subcommittee, he conducted highly publicized investigations of alleged subversion in many areas of the government. McCarthy never produced conclusive evidence that any federal employee was a communist. But a growing constituency adored him nevertheless for his coarse assaults on a government establishment that many considered arrogant, effete, even traitorous. Republicans, in particular, rallied to his claims that the Democrats had been responsible for "twenty years of treason" and that only a change of parties could rid the country of subversion.

McCarthy, in short, provided his followers with an issue into which they could channel a wide range of resentments: fear of communism, animosity toward east coast intellectual foreign policy elites, and frustrated partisan ambitions. Homophobia and racism, too, coursed through the anticommunist crusade. President Truman and many others used phrases like "parlor pinks" to describe communists, suggesting that depraved sexual behaviors accompanied or signaled depraved political philosophies. Opponents of equality for African Americans, as well, increasingly blamed southern civil rights activity on "outside agitators," widely understood to mean communists. Thus McCarthyism and anticommunism more broadly gave their prophets a venue and vocabulary for expressing other frustrations and prejudices.

For a time, McCarthy intimidated all but a few people from opposing him. Even the highly popular Dwight D. Eisenhower, running for president in 1952, did not speak out against him, although he disliked McCarthy's tactics and was outraged at, among other things, McCarthy's attacks on General George Marshall. Eventually his assaults against such respected figures and institutions drove McCarthy from popular favor—but not before "**McCarthyism**" came to define an era of hysterical and often unfounded accusations.

The Republican Revival

Public frustration over the stalemate in Korea and popular fears of internal subversion combined to make 1952 a bad year for the Democratic Party. Truman, now deeply unpopular, withdrew from the presidential contest. The party united instead behind Governor Adlai E. Stevenson of Illinois. Stevenson's dignity, wit, and eloquence made him a beloved figure to many liberals and intellectuals. But those same qualities seemed only to fuel Republican charges that Stevenson lacked the strength or the will to combat communism sufficiently.

Stevenson's greatest problem, however, was the Republican candidate opposing him. Rejecting the efforts of conservatives to nominate Robert Taft or Douglas MacArthur, the Republicans turned to a man who had no previous identification with the party: General Dwight D. Eisenhower—military hero, commander of NATO, president of Columbia University—who won nomination on the first ballot. He chose as his running mate the young California senator who had gained national prominence through his crusade against Alger Hiss: Richard M. Nixon.

In the fall campaign, Eisenhower attracted support through his geniality and his statesmanlike pledges to settle the Korean conflict. Nixon, after surviving early accusations of financial improprieties, which he effectively neutralized in a famous television address, the Checkers speech, exploited the issue of domestic anticommunism by attacking the Democrats for "cowardice" and "appeasement." The response at the polls was overwhelming.

Eisenhower won both a popular and an electoral landslide: 55 percent of the popular vote to Stevenson's 44 percent, 442 electoral votes to Stevenson's 89. Republicans gained control of both houses of Congress for the first time since 1946.

CONCLUSION

Even during World War II, when the United States and the Soviet Union were allies, it was evident to leaders in both nations that America and Russia had quite different visions of what the postwar world should look like. Very quickly after the war ended, the relationship between the world's greatest powers soured. Americans came to believe that the Soviet Union, like Hitler's Germany, harbored dangerous expansionist ambitions. Soviets came to believe that the United States was trying to protect its own dominance in the world by encircling the Soviet Union. The result of these tensions by the end of the 1940s was the Cold War.

In the early years of the rivalry, the United States constructed a series of policies designed to prevent both war and Soviet aggression. It helped rebuild the shattered economies of Western Europe through the Marshall Plan, to stabilize those nations and prevent them from becoming communist. America embraced a new foreign policy—known as containment—that committed it to keeping the Soviet Union from expanding its influence further into the world. The United States and Western Europe formed a strong and enduring alliance, NATO, to defend Europe against possible Soviet advances.

In 1950, the armed forces of communist North Korea launched an invasion of noncommunist South Korea. To many Americans, the conflict seemed a test of American resolve. The Korean War was long, costly, and unpopular, with many military setbacks and frustrations. In the end, however, the United States—working through the United Nations—managed to drive the North Koreans out of South Korea and restore the original division of the peninsula.

The Korean War hardened American foreign policy into a much more rigidly anticommunist form. It undermined the Truman administration, and the Democratic Party, and helped strengthen conservatives and Republicans. It greatly bolstered an already powerful crusade against communists, and those believed to be communists, within the United States—a crusade often known as McCarthyism, because of the notoriety of Senator Joseph McCarthy of Wisconsin, the most celebrated leader of the effort.

America after World War II was indisputably the wealthiest and most powerful nation in the world. But in the harsh climate of the Cold War, neither wealth nor power could dispel deep anxieties and bitter divisions.

KEY TERMS/PEOPLE/PLACES/EVENTS

Alger Hiss 663
Central Intelligence
  Agency (CIA) 651
Cold War 642
containment 648
Douglas MacArthur
  648
Fair Deal 654
GI Bill 654

House Un-American
  Activities Committee
  (HUAC) 663
John Birch Society 650
Julius and Ethel
  Rosenberg 663
Mao Zedong 648
Marshall Plan 651
McCarthyism 665

North Atlantic Treaty
  Organization (NATO) 652
NSC-68 653
Syngman Rhee 660
Taft-Hartley Act 655
Truman Doctrine 649
United Nations 646
Warsaw Pact 653
Yalta Conference 646

RECALL AND REFLECT

1. How did American diplomats plan for the postwar world and settle postwar issues? How did opposing visions of the postwar world order thwart those efforts?
2. How did postwar economic problems affect American politics and society?
3. Why did the United States become involved in the war in Korea? What was the result of U.S. involvement in that war?
4. Why did the fear of communism at home reach such great proportions? What events helped fan that fear?

27

THE AFFLUENT SOCIETY

THE ECONOMIC "MIRACLE"

THE EXPLOSION OF SCIENCE
AND TECHNOLOGY

PEOPLE OF PLENTY

THE OTHER AMERICA

THE RISE OF THE CIVIL RIGHTS MOVEMENT

EISENHOWER REPUBLICANISM

EISENHOWER, DULLES, AND THE COLD WAR

LOOKING AHEAD

1. Why did the U.S. economy experience such a boom in the late 1950s and early 1960s? How did this boom affect American society?

2. Who constituted the "other America"—those who failed to share in the economic prosperity and affluence of the postwar era? Why were they left out?

3. What was the response to the Supreme Court decision in *Brown v. Board of Education*? How did the Court's decision affect African Americans and the early civil rights movement? How did it affect white southerners?

4. What policy guided foreign affairs under Eisenhower, and how was that policy implemented around the world?

IF AMERICA EXPERIENCED A GOLDEN age in the 1950s and early 1960s, as many Americans believed at the time and many continue to do so today, it was largely a result of two developments. One was a booming national prosperity, which profoundly altered the social, economic, and even physical landscape of the United States. More Americans had more money than ever before, and this new level of wealth fueled a rise in popular consumption unrivaled in the nation's history.

The other was the continuing struggle against communism, which created considerable anxiety but also encouraged many Americans to look even more approvingly at their own society. As communist powers like the Soviet Union and smaller nations like Cuba staked an increasingly defiant posture against democracy, American leaders responded by building up the nuclear arsenal and fashioning a muscular foreign policy that promised to counter the spread of communism around the globe. These escalating international tensions triggered anxiety at home, however, and prompted lawmakers to search desperately for communists and turncoats that may be living among them. They also motivated everyday citizens to find comfort by celebrating family life and the material abundance that the American way of life supposedly made possible.

But if these powerful forces created a popular sense of national purpose and self-satisfaction, it was far from universal. The poor and the marginalized were largely forgotten while African Americans and other citizens of color were effectively blocked from participating in them. These forces also helped blind many Americans to serious problems brimming at home, such as racism and high rates of poverty among many rural and urban communities, and they helped set the stage for civil rights protests that shook the country in the mid-twentieth century.

THE ECONOMIC "MIRACLE"

Perhaps the most striking feature of American society in the 1950s and early 1960s was the booming economic growth that made even the heady 1920s seem pale by comparison. It was a better-balanced and more widely distributed prosperity than that of thirty years earlier. But it was far from universal.

ECONOMIC GROWTH

By 1949, despite the continuing problems of postwar reconversion, an economic expansion had begun that would continue with only brief interruptions for almost twenty years.

The causes of this growth were varied. Part of it came from Americans throwing off the emotional shackles of the Great Depression. Buoyed by victory in the world war, Americans again began to believe in a brighter future and they invested heavily in it. Politicians led the way by committing

TIME LINE

1947
Levittown construction begins

1953
Korean War ends

1954
Brown v. Board of Education
Army–McCarthy hearings

1955
Montgomery bus boycott

1956
Federal Highway Act
Eisenhower reelected
Suez crisis

1957
Sputnik launched
Kerouac's *On the Road*
Little Rock desegregation crisis

1959
Castro seizes power in Cuba

1960
U-2 incident
Eisenhower's farewell address

1961
First American in space
U.S. severs diplomatic relations with Cuba

1969
Americans land on moon

near-record levels of public money to accelerate the growth of different facets of the economy. As it had during the Great Depression and World War II, government spending stimulated rapid economic progress. Millions of dollars flowed to public schools and housing, veterans' benefits, welfare, interstate highways, and the especially the military.

The results were impressive. Between 1945 and 1960, the gross national product grew by a staggering 250 percent, from $200 billion to over $500 billion. Unemployment remained at about 5 percent or lower throughout the 1950s and early 1960s. Inflation, in the meantime, hovered around 3 percent a year or less. Economic growth actually peaked during the first half of the 1950s, when the government upped its military spending to fight the Korean War. Additionally, trade agreements forged immediately after the war opened new and profitable markets for goods and services like no other time before. Virtually untouched by the destruction of war, U.S. manufacturing and services reaped the initial rewards of international trade.

The rising economy inspired confidence in the future for many Americans. Not surprisingly, the national birthrate jumped, replacing a long pattern of decline with what is now commonly called the **Baby Boom**. It began during World War II and peaked in 1957. The nation's population rose almost 20 percent in this decade, from 150 million in 1950 to 179 million in 1960, which in turn boosted consumer demand and spending and further contributed to the expanding economy.

Many parents sought to raise their growing families in the suburbs, a critical reason for the 47 percent increase in the suburban population during the 1950s. Related sectors of the economy expanded as well. The number of privately owned cars, for example,

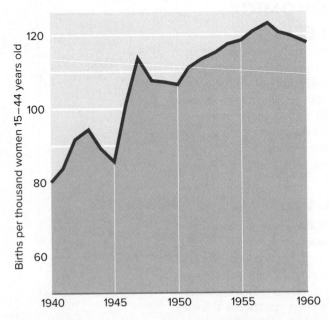

THE AMERICAN BIRTHRATE, 1940–1960   This chart shows how the American birthrate grew rapidly during and after World War II (following a long period of decline in the 1930s) to produce what became known as the "Baby Boom." At the peak of the Baby Boom, during the 1950s, the nation's population grew by 20 percent. • *What impact did the Baby Boom have on the nation's economy?*

more than doubled in a decade. The housing industry boomed. And road construction suddenly jumped.

The combination of post–WWII economic growth, rising rates of government spending, and surging population increase led to a renewed American prosperity. And while not every American—especially black, Hispanic, and Native American—shared equally in that prosperity, the average American in 1960 still had over 20 percent more purchasing power than in 1945 and more than twice as much as during the prosperous 1920s. By 1960, the American people had achieved the highest standard of living of any society in the history of the world.

The Rise of the Modern West

No region experienced more dramatic changes than the American West. Its population expanded dramatically; its cities boomed; its industrial economy flourished. By the 1960s, the West contained some of the most important industrial and cultural centers in the nation.

As during World War II, federal spending and investment powered much of the growth of the West. Funding from Washington made possible the construction of new dams, power stations, highways, and irrigation projects. Massive military contracts continued to flow to factories in California and Texas, as they had during the war. The increasing number of automobiles created new demand for petroleum, which led to the swift expansion in the number oil fields and refineries in Texas and Colorado and the development of Houston, Dallas, Denver, and other key cities.

State legislatures also fueled growth by investing heavily in higher education. The University of Texas and University of California systems, in particular, became among the largest universities in the country and established themselves as national leaders in medical, aerospace, petroleum, and computer research—which helped attract technology-intensive industries to the region.

Climate also contributed to growth in the West. Southern California, Nevada, and Arizona, in particular, attracted many migrants from the East because of their warm, dry climates. Symbolizing the rise of the West in the postwar era was the city of Los Angeles. More than 10 percent of all new businesses in the United States between 1945 and 1950 began in Los Angeles. And its population soared by over 50 percent between 1940 and 1960.

Capital and Labor

Booming corporations were reluctant to allow strikes to interfere with their operations; and since the most important labor unions were now so large and entrenched that they could not easily be suppressed or intimidated, leaders of large businesses made important concessions to them. By the mid-1950s, factory wages in most industries had risen substantially, to an average of $80 per week. In December 1955, the American Federation of Labor and the Congress of Industrial Organizations ended their twenty-year rivalry and merged to create the powerful **AFL-CIO**, under the leadership of George Meany.

But labor success also bred stagnation and corruption in some union bureaucracies. In 1957, the powerful Teamsters Union became the subject of a congressional inquiry, and its president, David Beck, was charged with the misappropriation of union funds. Beck ultimately stepped down to be replaced by Jimmy Hoffa, whom government investigators pursued for nearly a decade before finally winning a conviction against him in 1964 for jury tampering. The United Mine Workers, similarly, became tainted by violence and charges of corruption.

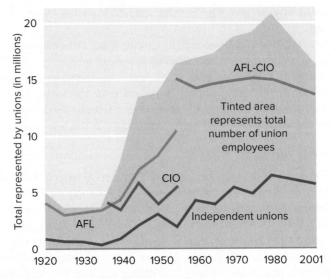

WORKERS REPRESENTED BY UNIONS, 1920–2001 This chart shows the number of workers represented by unions over an eighty-year period. Note the dramatic rise in the unionized workforce during the 1930s and 1940s, the slower but still significant rise in the 1960s and 1970s, and the steady decline that began in the 1980s. The chart, in fact, understates the decline of unionized labor in the postwar era, since it shows union membership in absolute numbers and not as a percentage of the rapidly growing workforce. • *Why did the total number of union members continue to rise in the 1970s, despite a plateau in AFL-CIO membership?*

THE EXPLOSION OF SCIENCE AND TECHNOLOGY

In 1961, *Time* magazine selected as its "man of the year" not a specific person but "the American Scientist." The choice was an indication of the widespread fascination with which Americans in the age of atomic power viewed science and technology.

MEDICAL BREAKTHROUGHS

The twentieth century saw greater progress in the development of medical science than had occurred in all the centuries before it. Much of it was concentrated during and after World War II. Especially important was the development of new antibacterial drugs capable of fighting infections that had once been all but untreatable.

To be sure, the development of antibiotics originated in the discoveries of Louis Pasteur and Jules-Francois Joubert. Working in France in the 1870s, they produced the first conclusive evidence that virulent bacterial infections could be defeated by other, more ordinary bacteria. Using their discoveries, the English physician Joseph Lister revealed the value of antiseptic solutions in preventing infection during surgery several years later.

But the practical use of antibacterial agents to combat disease did not begin until many decades later. In the 1930s, scientists in Germany, France, and England demonstrated the power of so-called sulfa drugs—drugs derived from an antibacterial agent known as sulfanilamide—which could be used effectively to treat streptococcal blood infections. New sulfa drugs were soon being developed at an astonishing rate and continuously improved; they were enormously successful in treating what had once been a major cause of death.

In the meantime, in 1928, Alexander Fleming, an English medical researcher, accidentally discovered the antibacterial properties of an organism that he named penicillin, after the mold (*pencillium notatum*) from which it was attained. There was little progress in using penicillin to treat human illness, however, until a group of researchers at Oxford University, directed by Howard Florey and Ernest Chain, learned how to produce stable, potent penicillin in sizable enough quantities to make it a practical weapon against bacterial disease. The first human trials of the new drug, in 1941, were dramatically successful, but progress toward the mass availability of penicillin was stalled in England because of World War II. American laboratories further developed methods for the mass production and commercial distribution of penicillin, which became widely available to doctors and hospitals around the world by 1948. Since then, a wide range of new antibiotics of highly specific character have been developed so that bacterial infections are now among the most successfully treated of all human illnesses.

Immunization—the development of vaccines that can protect humans from contracting both bacterial and viral diseases—also progressed dramatically. The first great immunological triumph was the development of the smallpox vaccine by the English researcher Edward Jenner in the late eighteenth century. A vaccine effective against typhoid was developed by an English bacteriologist, Almroth Wright, in 1897 and was in wide use by World War I. Vaccination against tetanus became widespread just before and during World War II. Medical scientists also developed a vaccine against another major killer, tuberculosis, in the 1920s; but controversy over its safety stalled its adoption, particularly in the United States, for many years. It was not widely used in America until after World War II, when it largely eliminated tuberculosis until a limited recurrence began in the 1990s.

Viruses are much more difficult to prevent and treat than bacterial infections, and progress toward vaccines against viral infections—except for smallpox—was relatively slow. Not until the 1930s, when scientists discovered how to grow viruses in tissue cultures, could researchers study them with any real effectiveness. Gradually, they discovered how to produce forms of a virus capable of triggering antibodies that would protect vaccinated people from contracting disease. An effective vaccine against yellow fever was developed in the late 1930s, and one against influenza—one of the great killers of the early twentieth century—appeared in 1945.

A major postwar triumph in medicine was the development of a vaccine against polio, which for decades had killed or crippled thousands of children and adults (among them President Franklin Roosevelt). The federal government provided the vaccine, developed by American scientist Jonas Salk, for free beginning in 1955. After 1960, an oral vaccine developed by Albert Sabin—usually administered in a sugar cube—made widespread vaccination even easier. By the early 1960s, these vaccines had virtually eliminated polio from American life and from much of the rest of the world.

These new drugs and vaccines drove down both infant mortality and the death rate among young children in the first twenty-five years after the war. They also helped raise the average life expectancy for that same period by five years, to seventy-one. While these medical advances have saved millions, however, their overuse in the decades that followed created a new round of contemporary problems. Indeed, the overuse of antibacterial agents has slowly led to genetic mutations in once-controlled diseases. New "super bugs" resist traditional treatment, and their defeat represents the next great challenge of the medical field.

PESTICIDES

Scientists also developed new kinds of chemical pesticides to protect crops from destruction by insects and to protect humans from such insect-carried diseases as typhus and malaria. Perhaps the most famous of the new pesticides was dichlorodiphenyltrichloro-ethane, generally known as DDT, a compound discovered in 1939 by the Swiss chemist Paul Muller. He had discovered that although DDT seemed harmless to human beings and other mammals, it was extremely toxic to insects. American scientists learned of Muller's discovery in 1942, just as the army was grappling with the insect-borne tropical diseases—especially malaria and typhus—that threatened American soldiers.

DDT was first used on a large scale in Italy in 1943-1944 during a typhus outbreak, which it quickly helped end. Soon DDT was being sprayed in mosquito-infested areas of Pacific islands where American troops were fighting the Japanese. The incidence of malaria dropped precipitously. DDT quickly gained a reputation as a miraculous tool for controlling insects, and it undoubtedly saved thousands of lives. Only later did it become evident that DDT had long-term toxic effects on animals and humans.

POSTWAR ELECTRONIC RESEARCH

The 1940s and 1950s saw dramatic new developments in electronic technology. Researchers in the 1940s produced the first commercially viable televisions and created a technology that made it possible to broadcast programming over large areas. In the late 1950s, scientists at Radio Corporation of America, better known as RCA, developed color television, which first became widely available in the early 1960s.

In 1948, Bell Labs, the research arm of AT&T, produced the first transistor, a solid-state device capable of amplifying electrical signals that was much smaller and more efficient than the cumbersome vacuum tubes that had powered most electronic equipment up until that time. Transistors made possible the miniaturization of many devices (radios, televisions, audio equipment, hearing aids) and also led to advances in modern aviation, weaponry, and satellites. They contributed as well to another major breakthrough in electronics: the development of integrated circuitry in the late 1950s.

Integrated circuits combined a number of once-separate electronic elements (transistors, resistors, diodes) and embedded them into a single, microscopically small device. Suddenly the construction of faster and more compact electronic machines—like the computer— became possible.

POSTWAR COMPUTER TECHNOLOGY

Prior to the 1950s, computers had been constructed mainly to perform complicated mathematical tasks, such as breaking military codes. In the 1950s, they began to perform commercial functions for the first time.

The first significant computer of the 1950s was the Universal Automatic Computer (or UNIVAC), which was developed initially for the U.S. Bureau of the Census by the Remington Rand Company. It was able to handle both alphabetical and numerical information easily. It used tape storage and could perform calculations and other functions much faster than its predecessor, the Electronic Numerical Integrator and Computer. Searching for a larger market for its very expensive new device, Remington Rand arranged to use a UNIVAC to predict the results of the 1952 election for CBS television news. Analyzing early voting results, the UNIVAC accurately predicted an enormous landslide victory for Eisenhower over Stevenson. Few Americans had ever heard of a computer before that night, and the UNIVAC's television debut was a breakthrough in public awareness of computer technology.

The UNIVAC and its technology was not much used outside of government circles until the mid-1950s, when the International Business Machines Company (IBM) successfully introduced its first major data-processing computers and marketed them aggressively to businesses in the United States and abroad. Pouring money into research and development of computers made IBM into the worldwide leader in computers for many years, until the emergence of Apple in the late twentieth century.

BOMBS, ROCKETS, AND MISSILES

In 1952, the United States successfully detonated the first hydrogen bomb. The Soviet Union quickly followed suit and tested one a year later. Unlike the plutonium and uranium bombs developed during World War II, the hydrogen bomb derives its vastly greater power not from fission (the splitting of atoms) but fusion (the joining together of lighter atomic elements with heavier ones).

The hydrogen bomb reignited a stalled scientific project in both the United States and the Soviet Union: the effort to develop unmanned rockets and missiles capable of carrying this new and more deadly weapon to its target. These projectiles were to fly on their own power, unaided by any aircraft. Both nations funneled money and manpower to create them. The United States had a decided advantage in this international competition, benefiting from the emigration during World War II of some of Germany's top rocket scientists.

In the United States, early missile research, conducted almost entirely by the newly formed air force, quickly produced rockets capable of traveling several hundred miles. But American and Soviet scientists struggled to build longer-range missiles that were capable of traveling through space and across oceans and continents to reach distant targets. These were dubbed **intercontinental ballistic missiles (ICBMs)**. American scientists experimented in the 1950s first with the Atlas and then the Titan ICBM. Despite some early limited successes, the difficulty of massing sufficient stable fuel to provide the tremendous power needed to launch and then propel missiles far beyond the atmosphere choked progress. By 1958, however, scientists had created a solid fuel to replace the volatile liquid fuels of the early missiles and a miniaturized guidance systems capable of ensuring that missiles could travel to reasonably precise destinations. Within a few years, a new generation of missile capable of traveling several thousand miles, known as the Minuteman, became the basis of the American atomic weapons arsenal. American scientists also pioneered a nuclear missile capable of being carried and fired by submarines—the Polaris, which is launched from below the surface of the ocean by compressed air and fires its engines only after it surfaces. A Polaris was first successfully fired from underwater in 1960.

THE SPACE PROGRAM

The origins of the American space program traces most directly to a dramatic event in 1957, when the Soviet Union announced that it had launched an earth-orbiting satellite—*Sputnik*—into outer space. The United States had yet to perform any similar feat, and the American government (and much of American society) reacted with alarm. Almost overnight, Washington demanded and generously funded efforts to improve scientific education in the schools, to create more research laboratories, and, above all, to speed the development of America's own exploration of outer space. The United States launched its own first satellite, *Explorer I*, in January 1958.

The centerpiece of space exploration, however, soon became the manned space program, established in 1958 along with a new agency, the National Aeronautics and Space Administration (NASA). The first American space pilots, or "astronauts," quickly became national heroes. On May 5, 1961, Alan Shepard became the first American launched into space. But his short

(Source: NASA)

MOON WALK Edwin ("Buzz") Aldrin is photographed by his fellow astronaut Neil Armstrong in July 1969, when they became the first humans to set foot on the surface of the moon.

suborbital flight came several months after a Soviet "cosmonaut," Yuri Gagarin, had made a flight in which he had actually orbited the earth. On February 2, 1962, John Glenn (later a U.S. senator from Ohio) became the first American to orbit the globe. NASA later introduced the Gemini program, whose spacecraft could carry two astronauts at once.

These early successes led to the creation of the **Apollo program**, whose purpose was to land astronauts on the moon. It suffered catastrophic setbacks, most notably a fire in January 1967 that killed three astronauts during a training session. But on July 20, 1969, Neil Armstrong, Edwin "Buzz" Aldrin, and Michael Collins successfully traveled in a space capsule into orbit around the moon. Armstrong and Aldrin then detached a smaller craft from the capsule, landed on the surface of the moon, and became the first humans to walk on a celestial body other than earth. It sparked a national celebration. Six more lunar missions followed, the last in 1972.

Eventually, the space program became a relatively modest effort to make travel in near-space easier and more practical through the development of the "space shuttle," an airplane-like vehicle launched by a missile but capable of both navigating in space and landing on earth much like a conventional aircraft. The first space shuttle was successfully launched in 1982. One shuttle, *Challenger*, exploded in January 1986 shortly after takeoff, killing all seven astronauts including Ronald McNair, one of America's first black astronauts. The tragedy stalled the program for two years. Missions resumed in the late 1980s, but problems remained, as illustrated by the explosion of the space shuttle *Columbia* during reentry in 2003. The space shuttle was used to launch and repair communications satellites and to insert the Hubble Space Telescope into orbit in 1990 (and to repair its flawed lens on several occasions, including in 2009). The space shuttle program officially ended in 2011.

PEOPLE OF PLENTY

Among the most striking social developments of the postwar era was the rapid extension of a middle-class lifestyle and outlook to an expanding portion of the population. The historian David Potter published an influential examination of "economic abundance and American character" in 1954. He called it *People of Plenty*. For the American middle class in the 1950s, especially among whites, it seemed an appropriate label.

THE CONSUMER CULTURE

At the center of middle-class culture in the 1950s was a growing preoccupation with consumer goods—a result of increased prosperity, suburbanization, greater variety and availability of products, and the skillfulness of advertisers in exciting demand for what they sold. Making many of these purchases possible as well was the modern expansion of consumer credit, which jumped by 800 percent between 1945 and 1957 through the development of credit cards, revolving charge accounts, and easy-payment plans. Americans now snapped up new products such as dishwashers, garbage disposals, television, and stereos. No good was more popular than the automobile and Detroit responded by turning out ever-flashier styling and accessories.

Because consumer goods were so often marketed and advertised nationally, the 1950s were notable for the rapid spread of national consumer crazes. For example, children, adolescents, and even some adults became entranced in the late 1950s with the hula hoop—a large plastic ring kept spinning around the waist. The popularity of the Walt Disney–produced children's television show *The Mickey Mouse Club* created a widespread demand for Mickey Mouse watches and hats and contributed to the stunning success of Disneyland, an amusement park near Los Angeles that re-created many of the characters and events of Disney entertainment programs.

THE SUBURBAN NATION

A third of the nation's population lived in suburbs by 1960—a result not only of increased affluence but of important innovations in home building, which made single-family houses affordable to millions of new people. The most famous of the suburban developers, William Levitt, built low-cost, mass-produced houses in large suburban developments known as "**Levittowns.**" These types of relatively inexpensive developments popped up in New York, New Jersey, and Pennsylvania and eventually throughout the country.

Why did so many Americans want to move to the suburbs? One reason was the enormous importance postwar Americans placed on family life after soldiers returned from World War II. Suburbs provided families with larger homes than they could find or afford in the cities and thus made it easier to raise larger numbers of children. The suburbs provided privacy and a sense of security from the noise and supposed dangers of urban living. They offered space for new consumer goods—the appliances, cars, boats, outdoor furniture, and other products that many middle-class Americans craved.

Another factor motivating white Americans in particular to move to the suburbs was race. Most suburbs were essentially restricted to white inhabitants—both because relatively few African Americans could afford to live in them and because formal and informal barriers kept even prosperous blacks out of all but a few. Some suburban communities, for example, carried restrictive convenants that prohibited property owners from renting or selling to blacks. In an era when the black population of most cities was rapidly growing, many white families fled to the suburbs in part to escape the integration of urban neighborhoods and schools.

THE SUBURBAN FAMILY

For professional men who tended to work in the city, at some distance from their homes, suburban life generally meant a rigid division between their working and personal worlds. For many middle-class women, it meant an increased isolation from the workplace. Middle-class husbands often considered it demeaning for their wives to be employed. And many women themselves shied away from the workplace when they could afford to, in part because of prevailing ideas about motherhood popularized by such widely consulted books as Dr. Benjamin Spock's *Baby and Child Care*. First published in 1946, it strongly advised women to devote themselves strictly to child-rearing. "Stay-at-home" mothers presumably raised healthier, more disciplined children. Other factors included the practice of many professional schools—law, medicine, business—to deny admissions to women.

Some women, however, had to balance these domestic pressures against other, contradictory ones. As expectations of material comfort rose, many middle-class families needed a second income to maintain the standard of living they desired. Consequently, the number of married women working outside the home actually increased in the postwar years. By 1960, nearly a third of all married women were part of the paid workforce.

THE BIRTH OF TELEVISION

During the 1950s, television quickly emerged as perhaps the most powerful medium of mass communication in history. Experiments in broadcasting pictures (along with sound) had begun as early as the 1920s, but commercial television began only shortly after World War II. Its growth was phenomenally rapid. In 1946, there were only 17,000 sets in the country; by 1957, there were 40 million—almost as many television sets as there were families. More people had television sets, according to one report, than had refrigerators.

The television industry emerged directly out of the radio industry, and all three of the major networks—the National Broadcasting Company, the Columbia Broadcasting System, and the American Broadcasting Company—had started as radio companies. Advertising drove the television business. The need to attract advertisers determined most programming decisions; and in the early days of television, corporate sponsors often played a direct role in determining the content of programs. Many early television shows bore the names of the corporations that were paying for them: the *General Electric Theater*, the *Chrysler Theatre*, and the *Camel News Caravan*. Some daytime serials (known as "soap operas," because their sponsors were almost always companies making household goods targeted at women) were actually written and produced by Procter & Gamble and other companies.

By the late 1950s, television news had replaced newspapers, magazines, and radios as the nation's most important vehicle of information. Television advertising helped create a vast market for new fashions and products. Televised athletic events made college and professional sports one of the most important sources of entertainment and one of the biggest businesses in America by the 1970s. And television entertainment programming—almost all of it controlled by the three national networks and their corporate sponsors—replaced movies and radio as the principal source of diversion for American families.

Much of the programming of the 1950s and early 1960s created a common image of American life—predominantly white, middle class, and suburban. Most popular were the situation comedies, featuring families in which, as the title of one of the most successful shows put it, *Father Knows Best*, and women were mothers and housewives striving to serve their children and please their husbands. Another top comedy, *I Love Lucy*, featured women in conventional roles but also tried to expand them, often in hilarious ways. *I Love Lucy* both idealized and poked fun at conventional domestic life. (See "Patterns of Popular Culture: Lucy and Desi.")

Yet television also could create conditions that could accentuate social conflict. Even those unable to share in the affluence of the era could, through television, acquire a vivid picture of how the rest of their society lived. While television was celebrating the white middle class, it was also showing glimpses of the alienation and powerlessness of groups who felt excluded from the world it portrayed. And television news conveyed with unprecedented power the social upheavals that gradually spread beginning in the late 1950s.

Travel, Outdoor Recreation, and Environmentalism

Although the idea of a paid vacation for American workers, and the connection of that idea with travel, had entered American culture beginning in the 1920s, it was not until the postwar years that vacation travel became truly widespread among middle-income Americans. The construction of the interstate highway system contributed dramatically to the growth of travel. So did the increasing affluence of workers. Even in the 1950s, there was a healthy market for vacation vehicles—trailers and small vans. That market grew steadily larger in subsequent decades. But the urge to travel was also an expression of some of the same impulses that produced suburbs: a desire to escape the crowding and stress of densely populated areas and find a place where it was possible to experience the natural world.

Nowhere was this surge in travel and recreation more visible than in national parks, which underwent a surge in attendance in the 1950s. People who traveled to national parks did so for many reasons—some to hike and camp, others to fish and hunt, and still others simply to see the extraordinary landscape. But whatever their motives, most visitors came in search of an experience in the wilderness. The importance of that search became clear in the early 1950s with the fight to preserve **Echo Park**.

Echo Park is a spectacular valley in the Dinosaur National Monument, on the border between Utah and Colorado and near the southern border of Wyoming. In the early 1950s, the federal government's Bureau of Reclamation—which encouraged irrigation, electric power, and water supplies—proposed building a dam across the Green River, which runs through Echo Valley, to create a lake for recreation and a source of hydroelectric power. The American environmental movement had been relatively quiet since its searing defeat early in the century in its effort to stop a similar dam in the Hetch Hetchy Valley at Yosemite National Park. But the Echo Park proposal helped rouse it from its slumber.

In 1950, Bernard DeVoto—a well-known writer and a great champion of the American West—published an essay in the *Saturday Evening Post* titled "Shall We Let Them Ruin Our National Parks?" It had a sensational impact, arousing opposition to the Echo Valley dam from many areas of the country. The Sierra Club, relatively obscure in previous decades, sprang into action. The controversy helped elevate a new and aggressive leader, David Brower, who eventually transformed the club into one of the nation's leading environmental organizations. By the mid-1950s, a large coalition of environmentalists, naturalists, and wilderness vacationers had mobilized in opposition to the dam, and in 1956, Congress—bowing to public

LUCY AND DESI

The most popular show in the early history of network television began as an effort by a young comedian to strengthen her troubled marriage. In 1950, Lucille Ball was performing in a popular weekly CBS radio comedy, *My Favorite Husband*, in which she portrayed a slightly zany housewife who tangled frequently with her banker husband, played by Richard Denning. The network proposed to transfer the show from radio to television. Lucy said she would do so only if she could replace Denning with her real-life husband of

(©CBS-TV/Kobal/REX/Shutterstock)

LUCY AT HOME Although Lucy and Desi at first portrayed a childless, ethnically mixed couple living in a Manhattan apartment, many of the comic situations in the early years of the show were purely domestic. Here, Lucy, wearing an apron, deals with one of her many household predicaments with the extraordinary physical comedy that was part of her great success. Desi, watching skeptically, played a buttoned-down bandleader to Lucy's zaniness.

ten years, Desi Arnaz—a Cuban-born bandleader whose almost constant traveling was putting a strain on their marriage. Network officials tried in vain to talk her out of the idea. Arnaz had no acting experience, they told her. Lucy herself recognized another reason for their reluctance: the radicalism of portraying an ethnically mixed marriage on the air. But she held her ground.

On Monday, October 15, 1951, the first episode of *I Love Lucy* was broadcast over CBS. Desi Arnaz played Ricky Ricardo, a Cuban bandleader and singer who spoke, at times, with a comically exaggerated Latin accent. Lucille Ball was Lucy Ricardo, his stage-struck and slightly dizzy wife. Performing with them were William Frawley and Vivian Vance, who played their neighbors and close friends, Fred and Ethel Mertz. In the premiere episode, "The Girls Want to Go to a Nightclub," Ricky and Fred want to go to a boxing match on the night of Fred and Ethel's anniversary, while the wives are arranging an evening at a nightclub.

The opening episode contained many of the elements that characterized the show throughout its long run and ensured its extraordinary success: the remarkable chemistry among the four principal actors, the unexpected comedic talent of Desi Arnaz, and most of all the brilliance of Lucille Ball. She was a master of physical comedy, and many of her funniest moments involved scenes of absurdly incongruous situations (Lucy working an assembly line, Lucy stomping grapes in Italy). Her characteristic yowl of frustration became one of the most familiar sounds in American culture. She was a beautiful woman, but she never hesitated to make herself look ridiculous. "She was everywoman," her long-time writer Jess Oppenheim once wrote; "her little expressions and inflections stimulated the shock of recognition in the audience."

But it was not just the great talents of its cast that made *I Love Lucy* such a phenomenon. It was the skill of its writers in evoking some of the most common experiences and desires of television viewers in the 1950s. Lucy, in particular, mined the frustrations of domestic life for all they were worth, constantly engaging in zany and hilarious schemes to break into show business or somehow expand her world. The husbands wanted calm and conventional domestic lives—and time to themselves for conspicuously male activities: boxing, fishing, baseball. In the first seasons, the fictional couples lived as neighbors, without children, in a Manhattan apartment building. Later, Lucy had a child and they all moved to the suburbs. (The show used Lucy's real-life pregnancy on the air; and on January 19, 1953—only hours after Lucille Ball gave birth to her real son and second child—CBS aired a previously filmed episode of the fictional Lucy giving birth to a fictional son, "Little Ricky" Ricardo.)

Lucille Ball remained a major television star for nearly twenty years after *I Love Lucy* (and its successor, *The Lucille Ball–Desi Arnaz Comedy Hour*) left the air in 1960. Desi Arnaz, whom Lucy divorced in 1960, remained for a time one of Hollywood's most powerful and successful studio executives as the head of Desilu Productions. And nearly seventy years after the first episode of *I Love Lucy* aired, the series remains extraordinarily popular all over the world—shown so frequently in reruns that in some American cities it is sometimes possible to see six Lucy episodes in a single evening. "People identified with the Ricardos," Lucille Ball once said, "because we had the same problems they had. We just took ordinary situations and exaggerated them." •

UNDERSTAND, ANALYZE, & EVALUATE

1. In what ways did *I Love Lucy* reflect American society and family life of the 1950s?
2. How have television situation comedies since *I Love Lucy* copied the formula for success established by that program? Do you see elements of the *I Love Lucy* pattern in today's situation comedies?
3. Why do you think *I Love Lucy* has continued to be so popular, both in the United States and throughout the world?

pressure—blocked the project and preserved Echo Park in its natural state. The controversy was a major victory for those who wished to preserve the sanctity of the national parks and it was an important spur to the dawning of modern environmental consciousness.

ORGANIZED SOCIETY AND ITS DETRACTORS

Large-scale organizations and bureaucracies increased their influence over American life in the postwar era, as they had been doing for many decades before. White-collar workers came to outnumber blue-collar laborers for the first time, and an increasing proportion of them worked in corporate settings with rigid hierarchical structures. Industrial workers also confronted large bureaucracies both in the workplace and in their own unions.

The debilitating impact of bureaucratic life on the individual became one of the central themes of popular and scholarly debate. William H. Whyte, Jr., produced one of the most widely discussed books of the decade: *The Organization Man* (1956), which attempted to describe the special mentality of the worker in a large bureaucratic setting. Self-reliance, Whyte claimed, was losing place to conformity and the ability to "get along" and "work as a team." The sociologist David Riesman made similar observations in *The Lonely Crowd* (1950), in which he argued that the traditional "inner-directed man," who judged himself on the basis of his own values and the esteem of his family, was giving way to a new "other-directed man," more concerned with winning the approval of his boss and the larger organization or community.

Novelists, too, expressed misgivings about the impersonality of modern society. Saul Bellow produced a series of novels—*The Adventures of Augie March* (1953), *Seize the Day* (1956), *Herzog* (1964), and many others—that chronicled the difficulties of American Jewish men in finding fulfillment in modern urban America. J. D. Salinger wrote in *The Catcher in the Rye* (1951) of a prep-school student, Holden Caulfield, who is unable to find any area of society—school, family, friends, city—in which he can feel secure or committed.

THE BEATS AND THE RESTLESS CULTURE OF YOUTH

The most derisive critics of bureaucracy and middle-class society were a group of young poets, writers, and artists known as the "**Beats**" and often called "beatniks" by disapproving critics. They wrote harsh critiques of what they considered the sterility and conformity of American life, the meaninglessness of American politics, and the banality of popular culture. Jack Kerouac produced the most popular document of the Beat Generation in his novel *On the Road* (1957), an account of a cross-country automobile trip that depicts the rootless, iconoclastic lifestyle of Kerouac and his friends.

The culture of alienation that the Beats so vividly represented had counterparts even in ordinary middle-class behavior: teenage rebelliousness toward parents, youthful fascination with fast cars and motorcycles, and increasing sexual activity, assisted by the greater availability of birth-control devices. The popularity of James Dean, who starred in *Rebel Without a Cause* (1955), *East of Eden* (1955), and *Giant* (1956), was a particularly vivid sign of youth culture in the 1950s. Both in the roles he played (moody, alienated teenagers and young men with a streak of self-destructive violence) and in the way he lived his own life (he died in 1955, at the age of 24, in an automobile accident), Dean became an icon of the unfocused rebelliousness of American youth in his time.

For middle-class adults in the 1950s, Dean was less an icon of cool than a symbol of "juvenile delinquency." In both politics and popular culture, dire warnings surfaced about the growing criminality of American youth. The 1955 film *Blackboard Jungle*, for example, was a frightening depiction of crime and violence in city schools. Scholarly studies, presidential commissions, and journalistic exposés all contributed to the sense of alarm about the spread of delinquency—although in fact, youth crime did not dramatically increase in the 1950s.

Rock 'n' Roll

One of the most important cultural developments of the 1950s was the birth of rock 'n' roll—and the enormous popularity of the greatest early rock star, Elvis Presley. Presley became a symbol of a youthful determination to push at the borders of the conventional and the acceptable. His sultry good looks, his self-conscious effort to dress in the vaguely rebellious style of urban gangs (motorcycle jackets and slicked-back hair, even though Presley himself was a product of the conservative rural South), and, most of all, the open sexuality of his music and his public performances all made him wildly popular among young Americans in the 1950s. His first great hit, "Heartbreak Hotel," established him as a national phenomenon in 1956, and he remained a powerful figure in American popular culture well after his death in 1977.

Presley's music, like that of many early white rock musicians, drew heavily from black rhythm and blues traditions. Sam Phillips, a record promoter who had recorded some of the important black R&B musicians of his time, reportedly said in the early 1950s: "If I could find a white man with a Negro sound, I could make a billion dollars." Soon after that, he found Presley. But there were others as well—among them Buddy Holly and Bill Haley

(©Hulton Archive/Getty Images)

ELVIS This photograph of the musician in performance is from very early in his career.

(whose 1955 song "Rock Around the Clock," used in the film *Blackboard Jungle*, announced the arrival of rock 'n' roll to millions of young people)—who were closely connected to African American musical traditions. Rock drew from other sources, too: from country western music (another strong influence on Presley), from gospel music, even from jazz.

The 1950s also saw African American bands and singers grow in popularity among both black and white audiences. Chuck Berry, Little Richard, B. B. King, Chubby Checker, the Temptations, the Miracles, the Supremes, and others—many of them recorded by the black producer Berry Gordy, the founder and president of Motown Records in Detroit—never rivaled Presley in their popularity among white youths but did develop significant multiracial audiences of their own.

The rapid rise of rock owed a great deal to innovations in radio and television programming. By the 1950s, radio stations no longer felt obliged to present mostly live programming—especially once television took over many of the entertainment functions radio had once performed. Instead, many radio stations devoted themselves almost entirely to playing recorded music. Early in the 1950s, a new breed of radio announcers, known as "disk jockeys" or "djs" for the record disks they played, began to create programming aimed specifically at young fans of rock music; and when their programs became enormously successful, other stations quickly followed suit. *American Bandstand*, which began airing in 1957, was a televised showcase for rock 'n' roll hits in which a live audience danced to recorded music. The program helped spread the popularity of rock—and made its host, Dick Clark, one of the best-known figures among young Americans.

Radio and television were important to the recording industry, of course, because they encouraged the rapidly increasing sale of records in the mid- and late 1950s, especially in the inexpensive and popular 45 rpm format—small disks that contained one song on each side and turned at the rate of 45 revolutions per minute. Also important were jukeboxes, which played individual songs on 45s and became stock items in soda fountains, diners, bars, and other places where young people congregated. Sales of records increased from $182 million to $521 million between 1954 and 1960. So eager were record promoters to get their songs on the air that they routinely made secret payments to station owners and disk jockeys to encourage them to showcase their artists. These payments, which became known as "payola," produced a series of scandals when they were exposed in the late 1950s and early 1960s.

THE OTHER AMERICA

It was relatively easy for white middle-class Americans in the 1950s to believe that the world of economic growth, personal affluence, and cultural homogeneity was universal and that their values and assumptions were ones that other Americans shared. But such beliefs were false. Large groups of Americans remained outside the circle of abundance and shared neither in the affluence of the middle class nor many of its values.

ON THE MARGINS OF THE AFFLUENT SOCIETY

In 1962, the socialist writer Michael Harrington published a celebrated book called *The Other America*, which chronicled the continuing existence of poverty in the United States.

The great economic expansion of the postwar years reduced poverty dramatically but did not eliminate it. In 1960, at any given moment, more than a fifth of all American families (over 30 million people) continued to live below what the government defined as the poverty line (down from a third of all families fifteen years before). Many millions more lived just above the official poverty line, but with incomes that gave them little comfort and no security.

Most of the poor—up to 80 percent—experienced poverty intermittently and temporarily. But approximately 20 percent were people for whom poverty was a continuous, often inescapable reality. That included approximately half the nation's elderly population and a significant proportion of African Americans and Hispanics. Native Americans constituted the single poorest group in the country.

This "hard-core" poverty rebuked the popular assumption that "a rising tide lifts all boats." It was a poverty that the growing prosperity of the postwar era seemed to affect hardly at all, a poverty, as Harrington observed, that appeared "impervious to hope."

RURAL POVERTY

Among those on the margins of the affluent society were many rural Americans. In 1948, farmers had received 8.9 percent of the national income; in 1956, they received only 4.1 percent. In part, this decline reflected the steadily shrinking farm population; in 1956 alone, nearly 10 percent of the rural population moved into or was absorbed by cities. But it also reflected declining farm prices. Because of enormous surpluses in basic staples, prices fell 33 percent in those years, even though national income as a whole rose 50 percent at the same time. The surpluses were the result of higher yields per acre as well as increases in the amount of acreage under production, a function of the widespread use of tractors.

Sharecroppers and tenant farmers (most of them African American) continued to live at or below subsistence levels throughout the rural South—largely because of the mechanization of cotton picking after 1944 and the development of synthetic fibers that reduced demand for cotton. (Two-thirds of the cotton acreage went out of production between 1930 and 1960.) Migrant farmworkers, a group concentrated especially in the West and Southwest and heavily composed of Mexican Americans and Asian Americans, lived in similarly dire circumstances. In rural areas without much commercial agriculture—such as the Appalachian region in the East, where the decline of the coal economy reduced the one significant source of support for the region—whole communities lived in desperate poverty, increasingly cut off from the market economy. All these groups were vulnerable to malnutrition and even starvation.

THE INNER CITIES

As prospering white families moved from cities to suburbs in vast numbers, more and more inner-city neighborhoods became repositories for the poor—"ghettoes" from which there was no easy escape. The growth of these neighborhoods owed much to a vast migration of African Americans out of the countryside and into industrial cities. Not all these black migrants were poor, and many found in the city routes to economic progress similar to those of whites. But urban African Americans were substantially more likely to live in poverty than most other groups, in part because of the persistent patterns of discrimination that denied them any real opportunities.

More than 3 million black men and women moved from the South to northern cities between 1940 and 1960. Chicago, Detroit, Cleveland, New York, and other eastern and midwestern industrial cities experienced a major expansion of their black populations at the same time many whites were leaving cities.

Similar migrations from Mexico and Puerto Rico expanded Hispanic neighborhoods in many American cities. Between 1940 and 1960, nearly a million Puerto Ricans moved into American cities, especially New York. Mexican workers crossed the borders into Texas and California and swelled the already substantial Latino communities of such cities as San Antonio, Houston, San Diego, and Los Angeles (which by 1960 had the largest Mexican American population of any city, approximately 500,000 people). Many of these Americans also struggled to make it into the middle-class.

Inner cities filled up with poorer minority residents at the same time that the unskilled industrial jobs they sought diminished. Employers were moving factories and mills from old industrial cities to new locations in suburban and rural areas, smaller cities, and even abroad—places where the costs of labor were lower. Even in the factories that remained, automation reduced the number of unskilled jobs. The economic opportunities that had helped earlier immigrant groups to rise up from poverty were simply unavailable to many of the postwar migrants. Racial discrimination in hiring, education, and housing further hampered many members of these communities as they strove to escape poverty.

THE RISE OF THE CIVIL RIGHTS MOVEMENT

Ever since the end of Reconstruction, there was never a time when African Americans were not pushing to preserve their freedoms and defeat those who would snatch them away. The long battle for black liberty in the modern era came to a head in the 1950s and 1960s, forcing white Americans to recast their understanding about the meaning of citizenships and the moral wrong of segregation.

THE *BROWN* DECISION AND "MASSIVE RESISTANCE"

On May 17, 1954, the Supreme Court announced its decision in the case of *Brown v. Board of Education of Topeka*. In considering the legal segregation of a Kansas public school system, the Court rejected its own 1896 *Plessy v. Ferguson* decision, which had ruled that communities could provide African Americans with separate facilities as long as the facilities were equal to those of whites. The *Brown* decision declared that segregating public schools on the basis of race was unconstitutional. The justices argued that school segregation inflicted unacceptable damage on those it affected, regardless of the relative quality of the separate schools. Chief Justice Earl Warren explained the unanimous opinion of his colleagues: "We conclude that in the field of public education the doctrine of 'separate but equal' has no place. Separate educational facilities are inherently unequal." The following year, the Court issued another decision (known as *Brown II*) to provide rules for implementing the 1954 order. It ruled that communities must work to desegregate their schools "with all deliberate speed," but it set no timetable and left specific decisions up to lower courts.

Some communities, such as Washington, D.C., complied relatively quickly and quietly. But they were rare. More than 100 southern members of Congress signed a 1956 "manifesto" denouncing the *Brown* decision and urging their constituents to defy it. Most did, embarking on campaigns of "massive resistance" to obstruct and delay any effort to mix black and white students in public schools. Southern governors, mayors, local school boards, and White Citizens Councils—groups of local whites dedicated to preserving

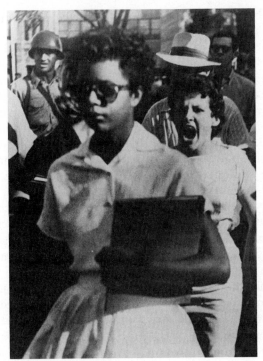

(©Everett Collection/SuperStock)

LITTLE ROCK, 1957 African American student Elizabeth Eckford passes by jeering whites on her way to Little Rock Central High School, newly integrated by federal court order.

segregation—worked feverishly to block desegregation. By the fall of 1957, only 684 of 3,000 affected school districts in the South had even begun to integrate their schools.

The Eisenhower administration was reluctant to join the battle over desegregation. But in September 1957, it faced a case of direct state defiance of federal authority and felt compelled to act. Federal courts had ordered the desegregation of Central High School in Little Rock, Arkansas. But Governor Orval Faubus disagreed and argued in public that his authority superseded that of the court on matters of local public education. Ignoring pleas for cooperation from Washington, the governor looked the other way when a violent white mob attempted to stop eight black students from entering Central High by surrounding the school and blockading its doors. He then ordered the Arkansas National Guard to turn away the black students. Eisenhower responded swiftly and angrily, federalizing the National Guard and ordering them to enforce the court's decision and sending in battle-hardened troops from the famed 101st Airborne Division to ensure full compliance. Only then did Central High School admit its first black students.

THE EXPANDING MOVEMENT

The *Brown* decision sparked a growing number of popular challenges to other forms of segregation in the South. On December 1, 1955, forty-two-year-old **Rosa Parks**, an African American seamstress, was arrested in Montgomery, Alabama, when she refused to give up her seat on a city bus to a white passenger as required by the Jim Crow laws throughout most of the South. Her arrest ignited outrage in the city's African American community and set in motion plans for a boycott.

Almost immediately the Woman's Political Committee jumped into action. Begun after World War II in Montgomery as a benevolent organization for middle-class black women, it sponsored voter registration drives, campaigns to raise awareness of sexual assault against black women, and publicly opposed segregated seating on buses. The night of Parks's arrest, President Joanne Robinson, an English professor at nearby Alabama State University, printed and distributed hundreds of fliers calling for the boycott and instructing blacks how to get to work the next day. Their work drew on earlier efforts of black boycotts in the South, such as the one in Mississippi protesting segregated public restrooms in service stations and in 1953 in Baton Rouge, Louisiana, against segregated buses.

Parks's arrest was no random event. Black leaders for years had schemed about how to upset the laws dictating segregated bus transportation. They had carefully selected Parks, the secretary for the local chapter of NAACP and a pillar of the black community, and coached her how to act. Nor was this the first arrest of a black women from Montgomery refusing to sit in the back of the bus. Others had already broken the law and been fined. Most dramatically, nine months before the Parks incident **Claudette Colvin**, a fifteen-year-old, sat in front, ignored the bus driver's command to move back, and squared off against two police officers. After she refused to leave the bus, they handcuffed her and hauled her off to jail. Colvin would later become a lead plaintiff in *Browder v. Gayle*, the federal case that would overturn bus segregation laws in Montgomery in 1956 and, along with the boycott, compel buses to abandon their discriminatory policies.

Formal organization of the boycott fell to the newly formed Montgomery Improvement Organization and its president, twenty-six-year-old Baptist pastor, **Martin Luther King Jr.** Son of a prominent Atlanta minister, a powerful orator, brilliant intellectual, and talented community leader, King had just accepted a call to serve as pastor of Montgomery's most influential black house of worship, Dexter Avenue Baptist church, in 1954. His prodigious gifts and newcomer status—meaning that local police and white politicians had had little time to threaten and terrorize him—made him the perfect candidate to lead.

King based his approach to civil rights protest on the doctrine of nonviolent resistance to injustice, even in the face of direct attack. Never should he return a punch or an insult but instead seek to love his enemy and peacefully persuade him to change his ways. His approach to racial struggle injected it with a new dimension of moral power that helped him recruit supporters and eventually win over onetime segregationists and capture the moral high ground for his supporters. For the next thirteen years—as leader of the Southern Christian Leadership Conference (SCLC), an interracial group he founded shortly after the boycott—he was the most influential and most widely admired black leader in the country. The popular movement he came to represent soon spread throughout the South and the country.

CAUSES OF THE CIVIL RIGHTS MOVEMENT

Several factors contributed to the rise of African American protest in the postwar years. In addition to the role of pathbreaking legal decisions such as *Brown* and *Browder v. Gayle* and local community activism often sparked by the work of black women, the legacy of World War II was critical. Many black women and men had served directly in the military or worked in industrial plants supporting the war effort. They had joined an effort to end totalitarianism and the suppression of freedom abroad and frequently labored side by side with whites—only to confront blatant discrimination once again when they returned home after the war. Veterans in particular demanded the same liberties and opportunities they had enjoyed in the service and refused to accept living under segregation's grip.

Another factor was the growth of an urban black middle class, which had been developing for decades and began to flourish after the war. Much of the impetus for the civil rights movement came from the leaders of these communities—ministers like Martin Luther King Jr., but also educators and professionals. Much of it came as well from students at black colleges and universities, which had expanded significantly and taught students about the history of discrimination and revolution. These younger African Americans frequently put themselves on the front lines of the struggle.

Television and other forms of popular culture also played a role in the rising consciousness of racism. More than any previous generation, postwar blacks had constant, vivid reminders of how the white majority lived—of the world from which they were effectively excluded. Television also conveyed the activities of demonstrators to a national audience, ensuring that activism in one community would inspire similar protests in others. It gave the movement a national character and momentum.

Other forces mobilized many white Americans to support the movement once it began. The Cold War made racial injustice an embarrassment to Americans trying to present their nation as a model to the world. Political mobilization of northern blacks created a valuable voting bloc within the Democratic Party. Politicians from northern industrial states especially could not ignore their views. Labor unions with powerful black memberships mobilized to help the movement, providing public support and funding.

Still becoming organized and gathering steam in the 1950s, the civil rights movement would shortly emerge as the most powerful social revolution of the twentieth century.

EISENHOWER REPUBLICANISM

Dwight D. Eisenhower was the least experienced politician to serve in the White House in the twentieth century. He was also among the most popular and politically successful presidents of the postwar era. At home, he pursued essentially moderate policies, avoiding most new initiatives but accepting the work of earlier reformers. Abroad, he continued and even intensified American commitments to oppose communism but also brought a measure of restraint that his successors did not always match.

"WHAT WAS GOOD FOR . . . GENERAL MOTORS"

The first Republican administration in twenty years staffed itself with men drawn from the same quarter as those who had staffed Republican administrations in the 1920s: the business community. But by the 1950s, many business leaders had acquired a social and political outlook very different from that of their predecessors. Above all, many had reconciled themselves to at least the broad outlines of the Keynesian welfare state, named after the famed Great Depression economist John Maynard Keynes and launched during the New Deal. Indeed, some corporate leaders had come to see it as something that actually benefited them—by helping maintain social order, by increasing mass purchasing power, and by stabilizing labor relations.

To his cabinet, Eisenhower appointed wealthy corporate lawyers and business executives who were unapologetic about their backgrounds. Charles Wilson, president of General Motors, assured senators considering his nomination for secretary of defense that "what was good for our country was good for General Motors, and vice versa."

Eisenhower encouraged private enterprise. He supported the private rather than public development of natural resources. To the chagrin of farmers, he lowered federal support for farm prices. He also removed the last limited wage and price controls maintained by the Truman administration, opposed the creation of new social service programs such as national health insurance, and strove constantly to reduce federal expenditures (even during the recession of 1958) and balance the budget. He ended 1960, his last full year in office, with a $1 billion budget surplus.

The Survival of the Welfare State

While the president took few new initiatives in domestic policy, he steadily resisted conservative pressure to dismantle the welfare policies of the New Deal. Indeed, during his term he agreed to extend the Social Security system to an additional 10 million people and unemployment compensation to an additional 4 million, and he approved an increase to the minimum hourly wage from 75 cents to one dollar. One of the most significant legislative accomplishments of the Eisenhower administration was the **Federal Highway Act of 1956**, which authorized $25 billion for a ten-year project that built over 40,000 miles of interstate highways—the largest public works project in American history to that point. The program was funded through a highway "trust fund," whose revenues would come from new taxes on the purchase of fuel, automobiles, trucks, and tires.

In 1956, Eisenhower ran for a second term on the Republican ticket, even though he had suffered a serious heart attack the previous year. With Adlai Stevenson opposing him once again, he won by another, even greater, landslide, receiving 57.6 percent of the popular vote and 457 electoral votes to Stevenson's 73. Democrats retained control of both houses of Congress they had won back in 1954. In 1958—even during a serious recession—they increased that control by substantial margins.

The Decline of McCarthyism

The Eisenhower administration did little in its first years in office to discourage the anti-communist furor that had gripped the nation. By 1954, however, what came to be known as McCarthyism began to become increasingly unpopular.

During the first year of the Eisenhower administration, McCarthy continued to operate with impunity. But in January 1954, he attacked Secretary of the Army Robert Stevens and the armed services in general, claiming that communists had intruded into the military. At that point, the administration and influential members of Congress organized a special investigation of the charges, the **Army-McCarthy hearings**, which were among the first congressional hearings to be nationally televised. Watching McCarthy in action—bullying witnesses, hurling groundless and often cruel accusations, evading issues—much of the public turned on him and began to see him as a villain, even a buffoon. In December 1954, the Senate voted 67 to 22 to condemn him for "conduct unbecoming a senator." Three years later, he died—a victim, apparently, of complications arising from alcoholism. The Red Scare did not die with McCarthy, but its intensity began to decline.

EISENHOWER, DULLES, AND THE COLD WAR

The threat of nuclear war created a sense of high anxiety in international relations in the 1950s. But the nuclear threat also encouraged both superpowers to edge away from direct confrontations. Indeed, the attention of both the United States and the Soviet Union began to turn instead to the rapidly growing instability in the Third World.

DULLES AND "MASSIVE RETALIATION"

Secretary of State **John Foster Dulles** was the most important figure in the Eisenhower administration next to the president himself. He was an aristocratic corporate lawyer with a stern moral revulsion to communism. He entered office denouncing the containment policies of the Truman years as excessively passive, arguing that the United States should pursue an active program of "liberation," which would lead to a "rollback" of communist expansion. Once in power, however, he had to defer to the more moderate views of the president himself.

The most prominent of Dulles's innovations was the policy of "massive retaliation," which he announced early in 1954. The United States would, he explained, respond to communist threats to its allies in part by relying on "the deterrent of massive retaliatory power," by which he clearly meant nuclear weapons. In part, the new doctrines reflected Dulles's inclination for tense confrontations, an approach he once defined as **brinksmanship**—pushing the Soviet Union to the brink of war in order to exact concessions. But the real force behind the massive-retaliation policy was economics. With pressure growing both in and out of government for a reduction in American military expenditures, an increasing reliance on atomic weapons seemed to promise, as some advocates put it, "more bang for the buck."

FRANCE, AMERICA, AND VIETNAM

On July 27, 1953, negotiators at Panmunjom finally signed an agreement ending the hostilities in Korea. Each antagonist was to withdraw its troops a mile and a half from the existing battle line, which ran roughly along the 38th parallel, the prewar border between North and South Korea. A conference in Geneva was to consider means by which to reunite the nation peacefully—although in fact that 1954 meeting produced no agreement and left the cease-fire line in place as the apparently permanent border between the two countries into the twenty-first century.

Almost simultaneously, however, the United States was entering into a long, bitter struggle in Southeast Asia. Ever since 1945, France had been attempting to restore its authority over Vietnam, its one-time colony, which it had been forced to abandon to the Japanese during World War II. Opposing the French, however, were the powerful nationalist forces of **Ho Chi Minh**, determined to win independence for their nation. Ho had hoped for American support in 1945, on the basis of the anticolonial rhetoric of the Atlantic Charter and Franklin Roosevelt's speeches, and also because he had received support from American intelligence forces during World War II while fighting the Japanese. But because he was not only a nationalist but also a communist, the Truman administration ignored him and supported the French, one of America's most important Cold War allies. Ho Chi Minh launched a war of national liberation against the French in 1946.

By 1954, Ho was receiving aid from communist China and the Soviet Union. America, in the meantime, had been paying most of the costs of France's ineffective military campaign in Vietnam since 1950. Early in 1954, 12,000 French troops became surrounded in a disastrous siege at the village of Dien Bien Phu. Only American intervention, it was clear, could prevent the total collapse of the French military effort. Yet despite the urgings of Secretary of State Dulles, Vice President Nixon, and others, Eisenhower refused to permit direct American military intervention in Vietnam, claiming that neither Congress nor America's other allies would support such action.

Without American aid, the French defense of Dien Bien Phu finally collapsed on May 7, 1954, and France soon abandoned Vietnam. The French agreed to a settlement of the conflict at the same international conference in Geneva that was considering the Korean settlement. The Geneva accords on Vietnam of July 1954 established a supposedly temporary division of the country along the 17th parallel. The north would be governed by Ho Chi Minh, the south by a pro-Western regime. Democratic elections would reunite the nation in 1956. The agreement marked the end of the French commitment to Vietnam and the beginning of an expanded American presence there. The United States helped establish a pro-American government in the south, headed by Ngo Dinh Diem, a member of his country's Roman Catholic minority. Because he enjoyed the full military backing of the American government, Diem acted ruthlessly, refusing, for example, to permit the 1956 popular elections when he realized he would lose.

COLD WAR CRISES

American foreign policymakers in the 1950s were challenged by both real and imagined crises in far-flung areas of the world. Among them were a series of crises in the Middle East, a region in which the United States had been little involved until after World War II.

On May 14, 1948, after years of Zionist efforts and a decision by the new United Nations, the nation of Israel proclaimed its independence. President Truman recognized the new Jewish homeland the next day. But the creation of Israel, while resolving some conflicts, created others. Palestinian Arabs, unwilling to accept being displaced from what they considered their own country, joined with Israel's Arab neighbors and fought determinedly against the new state in 1948–the first of several Arab–Israeli wars.

Committed as the American government was to Israel, it was also concerned about the stability and friendliness of the Arab regimes in the oil-rich Middle East, where American petroleum companies had major investments. Thus the United States reacted with alarm as it watched Mohammed Mossadegh, the nationalist prime minister of Iran, begin to resist the presence of Western corporations in his nation in the early 1950s. In 1953, the American CIA joined forces with conservative Iranian military leaders to engineer a coup that drove Mossadegh from office. To replace him, the CIA helped elevate the young shah of Iran, Mohammed Reza Pahlevi, from his position as token constitutional monarch to that of virtually absolute ruler. The shah remained closely tied to the United States for the next twenty-five years.

The U.S. State Department was less effective in influencing the nationalist government of Egypt, under the leadership of General Gamal Abdel Nasser. He began to develop a trade relationship with the Soviet Union in the early 1950s. In 1956, to punish Nasser for his friendliness toward the communists, Dulles withdrew American offers to assist in building the Aswan Dam across the Nile. A week later, Nasser retaliated by seizing control of the Suez Canal from the British, saying that he would use the income from it to build the dam himself.

On October 29, 1956, Israeli forces attacked Egypt. The next day the British and French landed troops in the Suez to drive the Egyptians from the canal. Dulles and Eisenhower feared that the Suez crisis would drive the Arab states toward the Soviet Union and precipitate a new world war. By refusing to support the invasion, and by joining in a UN denunciation of it, the United States helped pressure the French and British to withdraw and persuaded Israel to agree to a truce with Egypt.

Cold War concerns affected American relations in Latin America as well. In 1954, the Eisenhower administration ordered the CIA to help topple the new, leftist government of Jacobo Arbenz Guzmán in Guatemala, a regime that Dulles (responding in part to the requests of the United Fruit Company, a major investor in Guatemala) argued was potentially communist.

No nation in the region had been more closely tied to America than Cuba. Its leader, Fulgencio Batista, had ruled as a military dictator since 1952, when American assistance helped him topple a more moderate government. Cuba's relatively prosperous economy had become a virtual colony of American corporations, which controlled almost all the island's natural resources and had cornered over half the vital sugar crop. American organized-crime syndicates controlled much of Havana's lucrative hotel and nightlife business. In 1957, a popular movement of resistance to the Batista regime began to gather strength under the leadership of **Fidel Castro**. On January 1, 1959, as Batista fled to exile in Spain, Castro marched into Havana and established a new government.

Castro soon began implementing policies of land reform and expropriating foreign-owned businesses and resources. He established himself as a dictator by canceling promised elections and jailing or killing political rivals and critics. When Castro began accepting assistance from the Soviet Union in 1960, the United States cut back the "quota" by which Cuba could export sugar to America at a favored price. Early in 1961, as one of its last acts, the Eisenhower administration severed diplomatic relations with Castro. Isolated by the United States, Castro soon cemented an alliance with the Soviet Union.

(©Bettmann/Getty Images)

THE CUBAN REVOLUTION Fidel Castro (standing at center) is shown here in the Cuban jungle in 1957 with a small group of his staff and soldiers. Two years later, Castro's forces toppled the U.S.-backed Batista government and elevated Castro to the nation's leadership, where he remained for almost fifty years.

CONSIDER THE SOURCE

EISENHOWER WARNS OF THE MILITARY–INDUSTRIAL COMPLEX (1961)

In the tradition of outgoing presidents, Eisenhower delivered a "farewell address" that offered a summary of his accomplishments and vision for the future of the country. He warned of a growing "military–industrial complex" that, if left unchecked, would drive the nation's economy and politics.

Good evening, my fellow Americans. [. . .] This evening I come to you with a message of leave-taking and farewell, and to share a few final thoughts with you, my countrymen. Like every other citizen, I wish the new President, and all who will labor with him, Godspeed. I pray that the coming years will be blessed with peace and prosperity for all. [. . .]

America is today the strongest, the most influential, and most productive nation in the world. Understandably proud of this pre-eminence, we yet realize that America's leadership and prestige depend, not merely upon our unmatched material progress, riches and military strength, but on how we use our power in the interests of world peace and human betterment. [. . .]

A vital element in keeping the peace is our military establishment. Our arms must be mighty, ready for instant action, so that no potential aggressor may be tempted to risk his own destruction. Our military organization today bears little relation to that known by any of my predecessors in peacetime, or, indeed, by the fighting men of World War II or Korea. [. . .]

Now this conjunction of an immense military establishment and a large arms industry is new in the American experience. The total influence—economic, political, even spiritual—is felt in every city, every Statehouse, every office of the Federal government. We recognize the imperative need for this development. Yet we must not fail to comprehend its grave implications. Our toil, resources, and livelihood are all involved. So is the very structure of our society.

In the councils of government, we must guard against the acquisition of unwarranted influence, whether sought or unsought, by the military–industrial complex. The potential for the disastrous rise of misplaced power exists and will persist. We must never let the weight of this combination endanger our liberties or democratic processes. We should take nothing for granted. Only an alert and knowledgeable citizenry can compel the proper meshing of the huge industrial and military machinery of defense with our peaceful methods and goals, so that security and liberty may prosper together.

Akin to, and largely responsible for the sweeping changes in our industrial-military posture, has been the technological revolution during recent decades. In this revolution, research has become central, it also becomes more formalized, complex, and costly. A steadily increasing share is conducted for, by, or at the direction of, the Federal government.

Today, the solitary inventor, tinkering in his shop, has been overshadowed by task forces of scientists in laboratories and testing fields. In the same fashion, the free university, historically the fountainhead of free ideas and scientific discovery, has experienced a revolution in the conduct of research. Partly because of the huge costs involved, a government contract becomes virtually a substitute for intellectual curiosity. For every old blackboard there are now hundreds of new electronic computers. The prospect of domination of the nation's scholars by Federal employment, project allocations, and the power of money is ever present—and is gravely to be regarded.

Yet, in holding scientific research and discovery in respect, as we should, we must also be alert to the equal and opposite danger that public policy could itself become the captive of a scientific-technological elite.

It is the task of statesmanship to mold, to balance, and to integrate these and other forces, new and old, within the principles of our democratic system—ever aiming toward the supreme goals of our free society.

...As we peer into society's future, we—you and I, and our government—must avoid the impulse to live only for today, plundering for our own ease and convenience the precious resources of tomorrow. We cannot mortgage the material assets of our grandchildren without risking the loss also of their political and spiritual heritage. We want democracy to survive for all generations to come, not to become the insolvent phantom of tomorrow. [. . .]

Disarmament, with mutual honor and confidence, is a continuing imperative. Together we must learn how to compose differences, not with arms, but with intellect and decent purpose. Because this need is so sharp and apparent, I confess that I lay down my official responsibilities in this field with a definite sense of disappointment. As one who has witnessed the horror and the lingering sadness of war, as one who knows that another war could utterly destroy this civilization which has been so slowly and painfully built over thousands of years, I wish I could say tonight that a lasting peace is in sight. [. . .]

You and I, my fellow citizens, need to be strong in our faith that all nations, under God, will reach the goal of peace with justice. May we be ever unswerving in devotion to principle, confident but humble with power, diligent in pursuit of the Nations' great goals. [. . .]

Now, on Friday noon, I am to become a private citizen. I am proud to do so. I look forward to it.

Thank you, and good night.

UNDERSTAND, ANALYZE, & EVALUATE

1. What specifically was the military–industrial complex, and how did it support American postwar prosperity? How did it change the relationship between knowledge, industrial production, and defense?
2. What dangers for American political traditions did Eisenhower foresee? What economic dangers did he envision for future generations of Americans?

Source: Farewell address by President Dwight D. Eisenhower, January 17, 1961; Final TV Talk 1/17/61 (1), Box 38, Speech Series, Papers of Dwight D. Eisenhower as President, 1953–61, Eisenhower Library; National Archives and Records Administration [Public Domain].

THE U-2 CRISIS

Although the problems of the developing world were moving slowly toward the center of American foreign policy, the direct relationship with the Soviet Union and the effort to resist communist expansion in Europe remained the principal foreign policy concerns of the Eisenhower administration. Relations between the Soviet Union and the West soured further in 1956 in response to the Hungarian Revolution. Hungarian dissidents had launched a popular uprising in November to demand democratic reforms. Before the month was out, Soviet tanks and troops rolled into Budapest to crush the uprising and restore an orthodox, pro-Soviet regime.

In November 1958, Nikita Khrushchev, who had become leader of the Soviet Union upon Josef Stalin's death in 1953, renewed the demands of his predecessors that the NATO powers abandon West Berlin. When the United States and its allies predictably refused,

Khrushchev suggested that he and Eisenhower discuss the issue personally, both in visits to each other's countries and at a summit meeting in Paris in 1960. The United States agreed. Khrushchev's 1959 visit to America produced a cool but polite public response. Plans proceeded for the summit conference and for Eisenhower's visit to Moscow shortly thereafter. Only days before the Paris meeting, however, the Soviet Union announced that it had shot down an American U-2, a high-altitude spy plane, over Russian territory. Its pilot, Francis Gary Powers, was in captivity. Khrushchev lashed out angrily at the American incursion into Soviet airspace, breaking up the Paris summit almost before it could begin and withdrawing his invitation to Eisenhower to visit the Soviet Union. The Soviets convicted Powers of espionage (he was later exchanged for a Soviet spy), and the **U-2 crisis** ratcheted up mistrust on both sides.

After eight years in office, Eisenhower had failed to eliminate, and in some respects had actually increased, the tensions between the United States and the Soviet Union. Yet Eisenhower had also brought to the Cold War his own sense of the limits of American power. He had resisted military intervention in Vietnam, but he could not find a solution to Vietnam's likely slide into communism. And he had placed a measure of restraint on those who urged the creation of an enormous American military establishment. In his farewell address in January 1961, he warned of the "unwarranted influence" of a vast "military–industrial complex." (See "Consider the Source: Eisenhower Warns of the Military–Industrial Complex.") His caution, in both domestic and international affairs, stood in marked contrast to the attitudes of his successors, who argued that the United States must act more boldly and aggressively on behalf of its goals at home and abroad.

CONCLUSION

The booming economic growth of the 1950s—and the anxiety over the Cold War that formed a backdrop to it—shaped the politics and the culture of the decade. For most Americans, the 1950s were years of increasing personal prosperity. Sales of private homes increased dramatically; suburbs grew precipitously; young families had children at an astounding rate—creating what came to be known as the postwar "Baby Boom." After the end of the divisive Korean War, the nation's politics entered a period of relative calm, symbolized by the genial presence in the White House of General Dwight D. Eisenhower, who provided moderate and undemanding leadership through most of the decade.

The nation's culture, too, helped create a broad sense of stability and calm. Television, which emerged in the 1950s as the most powerful medium of mass culture, presented largely uncontroversial programming dominated by middle-class images and traditional values. Movies, theater, popular magazines, and newspapers all contributed to a broad sense of well-being.

But the 1950s were not, in the end, as calm and contented as the politics and popular culture of the time suggested. A powerful youth culture emerged in these years, displaying a considerable level of restiveness and even disillusionment. African Americans and other minorities who did not share in the economic boom equally with whites began to escalate their protests against segregation and inequality. The continuing existence of widespread poverty among large groups of Americans attracted increasing attention as the decade progressed. These pulsing anxieties, combined with frustration over the continuing tensions of the Cold War, eventually produced a growing sense of impatience with the calm, placid public culture of the time. That was a powerful reason for the growing desire for political action and social innovation as the 1960s began.

KEY TERMS/PEOPLE/PLACES/EVENTS

AFL-CIO 671
Apollo program 676
Army–McCarthy
 hearings 690
Baby Boom 670
Beats 682
brinksmanship 691
Browder v. Gayle 688
*Brown v. Board of Education
 of Topeka* 686

Claudette Colvin 688
Echo Park 679
Federal Highway Act
 of 1956 690
Fidel Castro 693
Ho Chi Minh 691
intercontinental ballistic
 missiles (ICBM) 675
John Foster Dulles 691
Levittowns 677

Martin Luther King Jr. 688
Rosa Parks 687
Sputnik 675
The Other America 684
U-2 crisis 696

RECALL AND REFLECT

1. How did the economic boom of the postwar era change American lifestyles?
2. What were some of the significant scientific and technological breakthroughs, especially in medicine, chemistry, electronics, weaponry, and space exploration, of the 1950s and 1960s? How did these developments affect American life?
3. How did the increasing popularity of the automobile change the American landscape and American society?
4. Why did the struggle for black freedom accelerate in the postwar years?

28 | THE TURBULENT SIXTIES

LOOKING AHEAD

1. What was the domestic reform agenda of Kennedy's New Frontier, and how did Johnson's Great Society programs expand on that agenda?
2. Why did the civil rights movement become increasingly assertive and militant over the course of the 1960s?
3. In what ways did the liberal politics and domestic agenda of the 1960s ignite the rise of the modern conservative movement?

IN THE LATE 1950s, few predicted that sweeping political protests were coming. The economic prosperity of the postwar years had left more Americans better off than ever before. Popular culture, especially television, portrayed a contented, smiling people enjoying the highest standard of living of any generation of Americans. And indeed the 1960s dawned with political leaders confidently attacking social and international problems within a traditional framework of modern liberalism.

Yet just beneath the apparently placid surface of American society in the 1950s smoldered the embers of social revolution. Segregation and sexism, among other social ills, had made a mockery of any notion of a content and unified citizenry during the Truman and Eisenhower administrations. Large-scale public battles would soon erupt over the meaning of citizenship and freedom that would ultimately make the 1960s one of the most turbulent and divisive eras of the twentieth century.

At the heart of some of those battles would be one of the most traumatic foreign policy experiences in the nation's history, the war in Vietnam. Though far less damaging in material and human terms to Americans than to the Vietnamese, the war generated great division and discord. What began as a relatively quiet, small, and popular intervention consonant with established Cold War policy ended up stimulating the mobilization of the biggest antiwar movement in American history, ending a presidency, and putting limits on what subsequent administrations felt they could do abroad for decades.

EXPANDING THE LIBERAL STATE

Those who yearned for a more active government in the late 1950s, and who accused the Eisenhower administration of failing to address racial inequality and other social problems, hoped for vigorous new leadership from the next presidents. The two men who served in the White House through most of the 1960s—**John Kennedy** and **Lyndon Johnson**—promised just that and seemed for a time to embody these hopes.

JOHN KENNEDY

The campaign of 1960 produced two candidates with differing visions of the role of government in society. Eisenhower's vice president, Richard Nixon, easily scooped up the Republican nomination by pledging only moderate governmental action on social reform. The Democrats, in the meantime, emerged from a spirited primary campaign united, although somewhat uneasily, behind John Fitzgerald Kennedy, a senator from Massachusetts who had narrowly missed being the party's vice presidential candidate in 1956. He hinted at making robust changes to society, especially in matters of welfare and civil rights.

John Kennedy came from a family of great wealth and influence. His father, the powerful and highly controversial Joseph P. Kennedy, was a former American ambassador to Britain. Unlike Nixon, Kennedy based his campaign "on the single assumption that the American people are uneasy at the present drift in our national course." But nearly as important as his politics was his carefully managed public image, which helped him win popular support. Handsome, a war hero, and married to socialite Jacqueline Bouvier Kennedy who was pregnant with their second child during the presidential campaign, he was at ease on

TIME LINE

1960
Kennedy elected president

1961
Freedom rides
Bay of Pigs
Berlin Wall erected

1962
Cuban missile crisis

1963
March on Washington
Kennedy assassinated; Johnson becomes president
Civil rights demonstrations in Birmingham

1964
Johnson launches war on poverty
Civil Rights Act
Gulf of Tonkin Resolution
Johnson elected president

1965
Malcolm X assassinated
Voting Rights Act
U.S. troops in Vietnam
Racial violence in Watts

1967
Antiwar movement grows
Racial violence in Detroit

1968
Tet offensive
Martin Luther King Jr. assassinated
Robert Kennedy assassinated
Nixon elected president

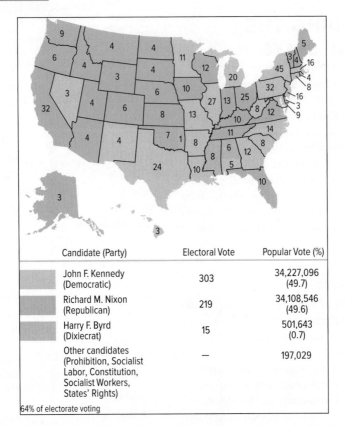

Candidate (Party)	Electoral Vote	Popular Vote (%)
John F. Kennedy (Democratic)	303	34,227,096 (49.7)
Richard M. Nixon (Republican)	219	34,108,546 (49.6)
Harry F. Byrd (Dixiecrat)	15	501,643 (0.7)
Other candidates (Prohibition, Socialist Labor, Constitution, Socialist Workers, States' Rights)	—	197,029

64% of electorate voting

THE ELECTION OF 1960   The election of 1960 was, in the popular vote at least, one of the closest in American history. John Kennedy's margin over Richard Nixon was less than one-third of 1 percent of the total national vote, but greater in the electoral college. Note the distribution of electoral strength of the two candidates. Kennedy was strong in the industrial Northeast and the largest industrial states of the Midwest, and he retained at least a portion of his party's traditional strength in the South and Southwest. But Nixon made significant inroads into the upper South, carried Florida, and swept most of the plains and mountain states. · *What was the significance of this distribution of strength to the future of the two parties?*

stump and in front of the camera. Indeed, he regularly appeared on television talk shows before and during his run for president, and these appearances helped the American people look beyond his perceived weaknesses. He overcame doubts about his youth (he turned forty-three in 1960) and religion (he was only the second Catholic ever to secure a major party presidential nomination) to win with a tiny plurality of the popular vote (49.7 percent to Nixon's 49.6 percent) and only a slightly more comfortable electoral majority (303 to 219).

Kennedy had campaigned promising a set of domestic reforms that he dubbed the **"New Frontier."** He entreated Americans to join him and become "pioneers" dedicated to forging a new America that provided health care to elderly and poor individuals, lower tax rates, economic aid for rural counties mired in poverty, and better funding for education. He also asked that they seek to end segregation. But his razor-thin popular mandate and a Congress dominated by a coalition of Republicans and conservative Democrats frustrated many of his hopes. Indeed, his most ambitious social programs came into being only under his successor.

More than any other president of the century (except perhaps the two Roosevelts and, later, Ronald Reagan), Kennedy made his own personality an integral part of his presidency and a focus of national attention. Nothing illustrated this more clearly than the public's outpouring of grief and sorrow following the tragedy of November 22, 1963. In Texas for a series of political appearances, the president was riding in a motorcade with his wife Jacqueline, Texas governor John Connally, and Connally's wife Nellie when shots rang out. Two bullets struck the president—one in the throat, the other in the head. Secret Service agents sped him to a nearby hospital, where minutes later he was pronounced dead. Lee Harvey Oswald—a young man who had spent time in the Soviet Union and, later, in Cuba—was arrested for the crime. Later that day Oswald was mysteriously murdered by a Dallas nightclub owner, Jack Ruby, as he was being moved from one jail to another. Most Americans at the time accepted the conclusions of a federal commission appointed by President Johnson to investigate the assassination. The commission, chaired by Supreme Court Chief Justice Earl Warren, found that both Oswald and Ruby had acted alone and there was no larger conspiracy. In later years, however, many Americans came to believe that the Warren Commission report had ignored evidence of a wider conspiracy behind the murders. Controversy over the assassination continues still.

LYNDON JOHNSON

The Kennedy assassination was a national trauma—a defining event for almost everyone old enough to be aware of it. At the time, however, much of the country took great comfort in the personality and performance of Kennedy's successor in the White House, Lyndon Baines Johnson. Johnson was a native of the hill country of west Texas and had risen from bitter poverty to become majority leader of the U.S. Senate by dint of extraordinary, even obsessive, effort and ambition. Having failed to win the Democratic nomination for president in 1960, he surprised many who knew him by agreeing to accept the vice presidential nomination on the ticket with Kennedy. The events in Dallas thrust him into the White House.

Johnson's first year in office was, by necessity, dominated by the campaign for reelection. There was little doubt that he would win—particularly after the Republican Party nominated the very conservative Senator Barry Goldwater of Arizona. In the November 1964 election, the president received a larger plurality, over 61 percent, than any candidate before or since. Goldwater, with his hard-line stance against communism and government expansion, managed to carry only his home state of Arizona and five states in the Deep South. Nevertheless, the failed Goldwater campaign mobilized many right-wing activists who would in later years propel the growth of conservative political strength for decades to come.

Johnson's rough-edged, even crude, personality could hardly have been more different from Kennedy's urbane manner. But like Kennedy, Johnson was a man who believed in the active use of power. Between 1963 and 1966, he compiled the most impressive legislative record of any president since Franklin Roosevelt. How did he do it? Following the death of Kennedy, the grieving public embraced many of his New Frontier proposals almost as a form of tribute to their fallen leader. Building on this popular approval for domestic reform, and benefiting from the vocal support of civil rights leaders like Martin Luther King Jr., Johnson introduced a series of social programs far more comprehensive and far-reaching than anything Kennedy had articulated. He called them the **"Great Society."** Record Democratic majorities in both houses of Congress, several

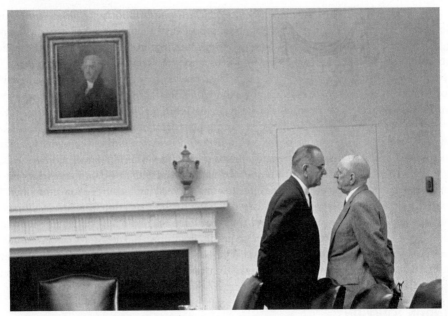

(Source: Lyndon Baines Johnson Library)

THE JOHNSON TREATMENT Lyndon Johnson was legendary for his powers of persuasion—for a combination of charm and intimidation that often worked on even the most experienced politicians. He is shown here in the Oval Office meeting with his old friend Senator Richard Russell of Georgia and demonstrating one of his most powerful and unsettling techniques: moving so close to the person with whom he was talking as to be almost touching him.

of whose members had been swept on Johnson's coattails, ensured that the president would be able to fulfill many of his legislative goals. And for those members of Congress who stood in the president's way, Johnson employed the same sort of skillful and aggressive lobbying that had previously made him such an effective majority leader in the House of Representatives.

THE ASSAULT ON POVERTY

For the first time since the New Deal, the federal government took steps in the 1960s to create important new social welfare programs. The most significant of these was **Medicare**, which provides federal aid to elderly individuals for medical expenses. Its enactment in 1965 came at the end of a bitter twenty-year debate between those who believed in the concept of national health assistance and those who denounced it as "socialized medicine." But Medicare pacified many critics. For one thing, it avoided the stigma of "welfare" by making Medicare benefits available to all older Americans, regardless of need (just as Social Security had done with pensions). That created a large middle-class constituency for the program. It also defused the opposition of the medical community by allowing doctors serving Medicare patients to practice privately and (at first) to charge their normal fees; Medicare simply shifted responsibility for paying those fees from the patient to the government. In 1966, Johnson steered to passage the **Medicaid** program, which extended federal medical assistance to welfare recipients and other indigent people of all ages.

Medicare and Medicaid were early steps in a much larger assault on poverty—one that Kennedy had been planning in the last months of his life and that Johnson launched only weeks after taking office. The centerpiece of this "war on poverty," as Johnson called it, was the Office of Economic Opportunity (OEO), which created an array of new educational, employment, housing, and health-care programs. Yet the OEO was controversial from the start, in part because of its commitment to the idea of "Community Action."

Community Action was an effort to involve members of poor communities themselves in the planning and administration of the programs designed to help them. The **Community Action programs** provided jobs for many poor people and gave them valuable experience in administrative and political work. But despite its achievements, the Community Action approach proved impossible to sustain. Administrative failures damaged the program. So did the apparent excesses of a few agencies, which damaged the popular image of the Community Action programs and indeed the war on poverty as a whole.

The OEO spent nearly $3 billion during its first two years of existence, and it helped reduce poverty in some areas. But it fell far short of eliminating poverty altogether. That was in part because of the weaknesses of the programs themselves and in part because funding for them, inadequate from the beginning, dwindled as the years passed and a costly war in Southeast Asia became the nation's first priority.

Cities, Schools, and Immigration

Closely tied to the antipoverty program were federal efforts to revitalize decaying cities and strengthen the nation's schools. The Housing Act of 1961, passed under the Kennedy administration, offered $4.9 billion in federal grants to cities for the preservation of open spaces, the development of mass-transit systems, and the subsidization of middle-income housing. In 1966, Johnson established a new cabinet agency, the Department of Housing and Urban Development (whose first secretary, Robert Weaver, was the first African American ever to serve in the cabinet). Johnson also inaugurated the Model Cities Program, which offered federal subsidies for urban redevelopment pilot programs.

Kennedy had fought for federal aid to public education, but he had failed to overcome two important obstacles. Many Americans feared that aid to education was the first step toward federal control of the schools, and Catholics insisted that federal assistance must extend to parochial as well as public schools. Johnson managed to circumvent both objections with the Elementary and Secondary Education Act of 1965 and a series of subsequent measures. The bills extended aid to all types of schools and based the aid on the economic conditions of the students, not on the needs of the schools themselves.

The Johnson administration also supported the **Immigration Act of 1965**, one of the most important pieces of legislation of the 1960s. For decades since the 1920s, the law maintained a strict limit on the number of newcomers admitted to the country each year (170,000). But the 1965 act eliminated the "national origins" system established in the 1920s, which gave preference to immigrants from northern Europe over those from other parts of the world. It continued to restrict immigration from some parts of Latin America, but it allowed people from all parts of Europe, Asia, and Africa to enter the United States on an equal basis. By the early 1970s, the character of American immigration had changed dramatically. The numbers of immigrants grew significantly, with members of new national groups—and particularly large groups of Asians—entering the United States and transforming the character of the American population.

LEGACIES OF THE GREAT SOCIETY

Taken together, the Great Society reforms significantly increased federal spending. For a time, rising tax revenues from the growing economy nearly compensated for the new expenditures. In 1964, Johnson managed to win passage of the $11.5 billion tax cut that Kennedy had first proposed in 1962. The cut increased the federal deficit, but substantial economic growth over the next several years made up for much of the revenue initially lost. As Great Society programs began to multiply, however—particularly as they began to compete with the escalating costs of America's military ventures—the federal budget rapidly outpaced increases in revenues. In 1961, the federal government had spent $94.4 billion. By 1970, that sum had risen to $196.6 billion.

The high costs of the Great Society, and the failures of some of it, eventually weakened the popularity of the federal efforts to solve social problems. But the Great Society was also responsible for some remarkable achievements. It significantly reduced hunger in America. It made medical care available to millions of elderly and poor people who would otherwise have had great difficulty affording it. It contributed to the greatest reduction in poverty in American history. In 1959, according to the most widely accepted estimates, 21 percent of the American people lived below the officially established poverty line (a level that did not survive for very long). Ten years later, only 12 percent remained below that line. Some of that progress was a result of economic growth, but much of it was a direct result of Great Society programs.

THE BATTLE FOR RACIAL EQUALITY

By the early 1960s, African Americans forced issues of racial justice and equality to the forefront of American politics. While scholars debate the origins and legacies of the modern civil rights movement, none challenge how deeply it influenced the nation's history in the late twentieth century. (See "Debating the Past: The Civil Rights Movement.")

EXPANDING PROTESTS

John Kennedy was sympathetic to the cause of racial justice, but he was far from a committed crusader. Like presidents before him, he feared alienating southern voters and powerful southern Democrats in Congress. His administration, like Eisenhower's, hoped to contain the racial problem by enforcing existing laws and using executive orders—not proposing new legislation. That reluctance would not last very long, however.

The pressure for change was growing uncontainable even before Kennedy took office. Throughout the 1950s, African Americans in southern cities had grown increasingly active in opposing discrimination. They demanded progress in housing, jobs, and education. The Montgomery bus boycott from 1955 to 1956 showcased the resolve and ability of southern blacks to fight against segregation. Protests grew in the early 1960s, mainly centered in the South. In February 1960, black college students in Greensboro, North Carolina, staged a sit-in at a segregated Woolworth's lunch counter; and in the following months, similar demonstrations spread throughout the former states of the Confederacy, forcing many merchants to integrate their facilities. In the fall of 1960, some of those who had participated in the sit-ins formed the Student Nonviolent Coordinating Committee (SNCC)—a student branch of Martin Luther King Jr.'s Southern Christian Leadership Conference dedicated to defeating the color line through campaigns of nonviolent action.

In 1961, an interracial group of students, working with the Congress of Racial Equality (CORE), began what they called "**freedom rides**." Traveling by bus throughout the South, they tried to force the desegregation of bus stations. Their activism infuriated segregationists and functioned like a call to arms for many of them. On Mother's Day in 1961 in Anniston, Alabama, Klansmen stormed the Greyhound Station once word got out that freedom riders were in town. The alert bus driver pulled away before the angry mob could sack the bus, but attackers still managed to slit the tires. Just outside of town the tires blew and the bus came to a complete stop, where infuriated Klansmen tracked it down and renewed their assault. They firebombed the bus and blocked the doors, hoping to burn the passengers alive. But riders pushed their way outside, where the Klansmen began to beat them with bricks, clubs, and iron pipes. Only warning shots fired by a highway patrol officer in plainclothes who was secretly riding with the bus scattered the crowd and saved the riders. Widely covered in the press, the bus bombing actually encouraged new waves of civil rights protesters to become freedom riders. They met similar savagery in Birmingham and Montgomery, prompting Attorney General Robert Kennedy to dispatch federal marshals to help keep the peace and order the integration of all bus and train stations serving interstate travel.

Even more dramatic and bloody events in the Deep South in 1963 propelled the movement to the forefront of the nation's conscience. In April, Martin Luther King Jr. helped launch a series of nonviolent demonstrations in Birmingham, Alabama. Police Commissioner Eugene "Bull" Connor personally supervised a brutal effort to break up the peaceful marches, arresting hundreds of demonstrators and using attack dogs, tear gas, electric cattle prods, and fire hoses—at times even against small children—in full view of television cameras that broadcast images nationally. Two months later, on June 11, Governor George Wallace stood in the doorway of the Foster Auditorium at the University of Alabama, his alma mater, to block the court-ordered enrollment of two black students, Vivian Malone and James Hood. It was a tense standoff, carried live by the television networks. The stakes were high because Wallace was quickly becoming the face of resistance to integration in the South. At his inauguration in Montgomery earlier in January, he had catapulted to national prominence by urging southerners to resist federal encroachment and reject the Kennedy administration's attempts at desegregation. In the most famous line from his speech, Wallace had declared that "In the name of the greatest people that have ever trod this earth, I draw the line in the dust and toss the gauntlet before the feet of tyranny and I say segregation today, segregation tomorrow, segregation forever." But even while he relished the spotlight in Tuscaloosa, the governor knew that he was not going to win this particular battle. Indeed, he quickly stepped aside after President Kennedy federalized the Alabama National Guard to ensure integration.

Later that day, the president addressed the nation on live television and made his most forceful statement to date for his support for civil rights. Kennedy told his viewers, "It ought to be possible for American consumers of any color to receive equal service in places of public accommodation, such as hotels and restaurants and theaters and retail stores, without being forced to resort to demonstrations in the street, and it ought to be possible for American citizens of any color to register and to vote in a free election without interference or fear of reprisal." Tragically, only several hours later the NAACP official and key leader of the movement in Mississippi, Medgar Evers, was gunned down in his driveway by white supremacist Byron De La Beckwith.

A National Commitment

The events in Alabama and Mississippi were a warning to the president that he could no longer avoid the issue of race. Days after delivering his civil rights address and the murder of Evers, he introduced new legislative proposals prohibiting segregation in "public accommodations" (stores, restaurants, theaters, hotels), barring discrimination

THE CIVIL RIGHTS MOVEMENT

The civil rights movement was one of the most important events in the modern history of the United States. It helped force the dismantling of legalized segregation and disenfranchisement of African Americans and also served as a model for other groups mobilizing to demand dignity and rights. And like all important events in history, it has produced scholarship that examines the movement in a number of different ways.

The early histories of the civil rights movement remain widely accepted. They rest on a heroic narrative of moral purpose and personal courage by which great men and women inspired ordinary people to rise up and struggle for their rights. This narrative generally begins with the *Brown* decision of 1954 and the Montgomery bus boycott of 1955, continues through the civil rights campaigns of the early 1960s, and culminates in the Civil Rights Acts of 1964 and 1965. Among the central events in this narrative are the March on Washington of 1963, with Martin Luther King Jr.'s famous "I Have a Dream" speech, and the assassination of King in 1968, which has often symbolized the end of the movement and the beginning of a different, more complicated period of the black freedom struggle. The key element of these narratives is the central importance to the movement of a few great leaders, most notably King himself. Among the best examples of this narrative are Taylor Branch's powerful studies of the life and struggles of King, *Parting the Waters* (1988), *Pillar of Fire* (1998), and *At Canaan's Edge* (2006), as well as David Garrow's important study, *Bearing the Cross* (1986).

Few historians would deny the importance of King and other leaders to the successes of the civil rights movement. But a number of scholars have argued that the leader-centered narrative obscures the vital contributions of ordinary people in communities throughout the South, and the nation, to the struggle. John Dittmer's *Local People: The Struggle for Civil Rights in Mississippi* (1994) and Charles Payne's *I've Got the Light of Freedom* (1995) both examine the day-to-day work of the movement's rank and file in the early 1960s and argue that their efforts were at least as important as those of King and other leaders. The national leadership helped bring visibility to these struggles, but King and his circle were usually present only briefly, if at all, for the actual work of communities in challenging segregation. Only by understanding the local origins of the movement, these and other scholars argue, can we understand its true character.

Scholars also disagree about the time frame of the movement. Rather than beginning the story in 1954 or 1955 (as in Robert Weisbrot's 1991 synthesis *Freedom Bound* or in William Chafe's 1981 local study *Civilities and Civil Rights*, which examined the Greensboro sit-ins of 1961), a number of scholars have tried to move the story into both earlier periods and later ones. Robin Kelly's *Race Rebels* (1994) emphasizes the important contributions of working-class African Americans, some of them allied for a time with the Communist Party, to the undermining of racist assumptions starting in the 1930s. These activists organized some of the earliest civil rights demonstrations— sit-ins, marches, and other efforts to challenge segregation—well before the

(©Carl Iwasaki/The LIFE Images Collection/Getty Images)

BROWN V. BOARD OF EDUCATION This photograph, taken for an Atlanta newspaper, illustrated the long and dangerous walk that Linda Brown, one of the plaintiffs in the famous desegregation case that ultimately reached the Supreme Court, had to travel each day on her way to a segregated school in Topeka, Kansas. An all-white school was located close to her home, but to reach the black school she had to attend required a long walk and a long bus ride each day. Not only does the picture illustrate the difficulties segregation created for Linda Brown, it was also part of a broad publicity campaign launched by the supporters of the case.

conventional dates for the beginning of the movement. Gail O'Brien's *The Color of the Law* (1999) examines a 1946 "race riot" in Columbia, Tennessee, arguing for its importance as a signal of the early growth of African American militancy and the movement of that militancy from the streets into the legal system.

Other scholars have looked beyond the 1960s and have incorporated events outside the orbit of the formal "movement" to explain the history of the civil rights struggle. A growing literature on northern, urban, and relatively radical activists has suggested that focusing too much on mainstream leaders and the celebrated efforts in the South in the 1960s diverts our view from the equally important challenges facing northern African Americans and the very different tactics and strategies that

they often chose to pursue their goals. Thomas Sugre makes this point in his *Origins of the Urban Crisis: Race and Poverty in Postwar Detroit* (1988). The enormous attention historians have given to the life and legacy of Malcolm X—among them Alex Haley's influential *Autobiography of Malcolm X* (1965), Michael Eric Dyson's *Making Malcolm* (1996), and Manning Marable's important biography, *Malcolm X: A Life of Reinvention* (2012)— is also an example of the growing focus on ideas of black power, as is the increasing attention scholars like Hassan Jeffries in *Bloody Lowndes: Civil Right and Black Power in Alabama's Black Belt* (2010) have given to black radicalism and such militant groups as the Black Panthers. Other literature has extended the civil rights struggle even further. Carol Anderson, in *Eyes Off the Prize: The United Nations and the African American Struggle for Civil Rights, 1945–1955* (2003) and Mary Dudziak, in *Cold War Civil Rights: Race and the Image of American Democracy* (2011) offer international perspectives on the movement. Others have brought into focus such issues as the highly disproportionate number of African Americans sentenced to death within the criminal justice system. Randall Kennedy's *Race, Crime, and the Law* (1997), Michelle Alexander's *The New Jim Crow: Mass Incarceration in the Age of Color Blindness* (2012), and Bryan Stevenson's *Just Mercy: A Story of Justice and Redemption* (2014) are particularly important studies of this issue.

Even *Brown v. Board of Education* (1954), the great landmark of the legal challenge to segregation, has been subject to reexamination. Richard Kluger's narrative history of the *Brown* decision, *Simple Justice* (1975), is a classic statement of the traditional view of *Brown* as a triumph over injustice. But others have been less certain of the dramatic success of the ruling. James T. Patterson's *Brown v. Board of Education: A Civil Rights Milestone and Its Troubled Legacy* (2001) argues that the *Brown* decision long preceded any national consensus on the need to end segregation and that its impact was far less decisive than earlier scholars have suggested. Michael Klarman's *From Jim Crow to Civil Rights* (2004) examines the role of the Supreme Court in advancing civil rights and suggests, among other things, that the *Brown* decision may actually have retarded racial progress in the South for a time because of the enormous backlash it created. Charles Ogletree's *All Deliberate Speed* (2004) and Derrick Bell's *Silent Covenants* (2004) both argue that the Court's decision did not provide an effective enforcement mechanism for desegregation and in many other ways failed to support measures that would have made school desegregation a reality. Stephen Tuck's *We Ain't What We Ought to Be: The Black Freedom Struggle from Emancipation to Obama* (2011)

concludes his broad narrative about the road to racial equality by focusing on the continued activism of African Americans into the present.

As the literature on the African American freedom struggles of the twentieth century has grown, historians have begun to speak of civil rights *movements*, rather than a single, cohesive movement. •

UNDERSTAND, ANALYZE, & EVALUATE

1. If historians now speak of plural civil rights *movements*, what are these movements?
2. Why are the contributions of local grassroots workers so often overlooked, in studies of the civil rights movement as well as in accounts of other great events in American history?

in employment, and increasing the power of the government to file suits on behalf of school integration. These proposals would eventually become key elements of the Civil Rights Act of 1964.

To generate support for Kennedy's legislation, and to dramatize the power of the growing movement, more than 200,000 demonstrators marched on the Mall in Washington, D.C., in August 1963 and gathered before the Lincoln Memorial for the largest civil rights demonstration in the nation's history to that point. Martin Luther King Jr., in one of the greatest speeches of American politics, "I Have a Dream," set the movement in historical perspective and called upon the nation to fulfill its moral obligations to all of its citizens and usher in a new era of full equality.

Joining King on the dais that day was twenty-three-year-old John Lewis, chair of the Student Nonviolent Coordinating Committee and a key organizer of the march who had grown up the son of sharecroppers in Pike County, Alabama. As a freedom rider in 1961 he had faced angry mobs in Montgomery and been attacked by them. Now looking back to the birth of the country, Lewis begged Americans to join him in "this great revolution that is sweeping this nation. Get in and stay in the streets of every city, every village and hamlet of this nation until true freedom comes, until the revolution of 1776 is complete." No longer would there be any pause in the push for freedom, he continued. "They're talking about slow down and stop. We will not stop. . . . If we do not get meaningful legislation out of this Congress, the time will come when we will not confine our marching to Washington." The protest, however, would always be a public statement of nonviolence and profession of faith in the ability of the nation to progress to a higher state of equality and justice. "But we will march with the spirit of love and with the spirit of dignity that we have shown here today. By the force of our demands, our determination, and our numbers,

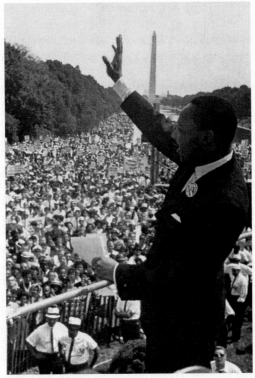

(©AP Photo)

MARTIN LUTHER KING JR. IN WASHINGTON Moments after completing his memorable speech during the August 1963 March on Washington, King waves to the vast and enthusiastic crowd that had gathered in front of the Lincoln Memorial to demand "equality and jobs."

we shall splinter the segregated South into a thousand pieces and put them together in the image of God and democracy. We must say: 'Wake up America! Wake up!' For we cannot stop, and we will not and cannot be patient."

The assassination of President Kennedy three months later gave new impetus to civil rights legislation. The ambitious measure that Kennedy had proposed in June 1963 was stalled in the Senate after having passed through the House of Representatives with relative ease. Early in 1964, however, after Lyndon Johnson had applied both public and private pressure, supporters of the measure finally mustered the two-thirds majority necessary to end a filibuster by southern senators, and the Senate passed the most important civil rights bill of the twentieth century.

THE BATTLE FOR VOTING RIGHTS

With the passage of the Civil Rights Act of 1964 and banning of segregation in public spaces, leaders of the movement shifted focus to another area of racial discrimination: voting rights. Beginning in the late nineteenth century, southern legislatures had successfully disfranchised blacks and many poor whites through a variety of means. Some were straightforward: politicians modified state constitutions and passed laws that blocked access to the ballot box. Others were more creative but no less effective: they required literacy tests with intentionally confusing and unanswerable questions, assessed poll taxes, and made it difficult to met residency requirements. These measures produced dramatic results: in 1940, only 3 percent of southern blacks were registered to vote. That number moved up slowly in response to civil rights activism, to 16.8 percent in 1950 and almost 29 percent in 1960. But in some parts of the South, few blacks ever voted.

During the summer of 1964, thousands of civil rights workers, black and white, northern and southern, spread throughout the South but primarily into Mississippi to work on behalf of black voter registration and participation. The state was a logical choice to make a stand for voting rights: it had long been a flashpoint in the struggle for equality, and only 6.7 percent of its eligible black voters were registered in 1962, the lowest percentage in America. The campaign was known as **"Freedom Summer,"** and it met with stiff resistance from local whites. Activists faced harassment, beatings, arrest, and jail. Their churches were bombed, their cars shot at. Three of the first freedom workers to arrive in the South—two whites, Andrew Goodman and Michael Schwerner, and one African American, James Chaney—were murdered in June. The men had been arrested in Philadelphia, Mississippi, and the local sheriff released them at night. Local Klansmen overtook their car as they drove away, shot all three, and hid their bodies in a nearby earthen dam where the FBI, called in by an infuriated Attorney General Robert Kennedy, found them six weeks later. During the search, federal officials turned up eight other bodies, all African American, who had apparently been murdered as well.

Freedom Summer also helped birth the Mississippi Freedom Democratic Party (MFDP). It was a natural outgrowth of the voting rights campaign, offering an integrated alternative to the whites-only state Democratic Party organization. Under the leadership of Fannie Lou Hamer and others, the MFDP challenged the regular party's right to its seats at the Democratic National Convention that summer. Hamer, appearing before the Credentials Committee and televised live by NBC News, spoke stirringly about growing up poor and black in Mississippi and enduring brutal sexual assaults as she tried to vote. (See "Consider the Source: Fannie Lou Hamer on the Struggle for Voting Rights.") Her testimony and unrelenting demand for proper representation within her state's delegation caused a stir among the national Democratic Party. President Johnson, with King's help, managed to broker a compromise by which members of the MFDP could be seated as observers, without formal power but with a promise of future party reforms, while the regular party leadership retained its official standing. Many MFDP members rejected the agreement and left the convention embittered.

A year later, on Sunday, March 7, 1965, John Lewis and Rev. Hosea Williams helped organize a major voting rights march in Selma, Alabama. Selma Sheriff Jim Clark led local police, some on horseback, others armed with shotguns, billy clubs, and tear gas canisters, in a vicious attack on the demonstrators as they attempted to cross the Edmund Pettus Bridge and make their way to the state capital of Montgomery. Bloody Sunday, as the day came to be known, sparked national outrage and helped push Lyndon Johnson to win passage of the **Voting Rights Act of 1965,** which provided federal protection to African Americans attempting to exercise their right to the ballot. But important as such gains were, they failed to satisfy the rapidly rising expectations of civil rights activists nationally as the focus of the movement began to move from political to economic issues and to include the North.

THE CHANGING MOVEMENT

By the mid-1960s, the scope of the movement became more national and city-based. Given that in 1966 about 45 percent of all blacks lived outside the South, many in urban neighborhoods, it was hardly surprising. Indeed, the publicity of the civil rights movement in the South intensified civil rights efforts in northern cities, where black leaders had labored for decades to alleviate discriminatory practices. While black northerners typically enjoyed a greater range of freedom in the practice of daily life and were not subject to the same discriminatory state laws that marred the South, they still battled harsh local customs and municipal codes that placed a strict color line around where they could live, work, travel, and play.

A symbol of the movement's new direction, and of the problems it would cause, was a major campaign in the summer of 1966 in Chicago, in which King played a prominent role. Organizers of the Chicago campaign hoped to direct the nation's attention to housing and employment discrimination in northern industrial cities. But the Chicago campaign evoked vicious and at times violent opposition from white residents and failed to attract wide attention or support in the way events in the South had done.

Many African American leaders (and their white supporters), having struggled in relative obscurity in the 1940s and 1950s, now began to move the battle against job discrimination to a new level. They argued that the only way for employers to prove they were not discriminating against African Americans was to demonstrate that they were indeed hiring minorities. If necessary, they should adopt positive measures to recruit minorities. Lyndon Johnson gave his support to this concept of **affirmative action** in 1965. Over the next decade, affirmative action guidelines gradually extended to virtually all institutions doing business with or receiving funds from the federal government (including schools and universities)— and to many others as well. Discrimination based on gender also began to receive federal interest. When "sex" was added at the last minute to Title VII of the 1964 Civil Rights Act, many thought it was an attempt to kill the bill. Regardless, the result added federal authority to begin dismantling the entrenched discrimination of women in the workplace and higher education.

Urban Violence

Well before the Chicago campaign, the problem of urban poverty and violence had flared and captured national prominence. In July 1964 in Harlem, New York City, a police shooting death of a fifteen-year-old black student set off six days of rioting that left 1 dead, 118 injured, and 465 arrested. Yet the most serious race riot since the end of World War II occurred the following summer in the Watts section of Los Angeles. In the midst of a traffic arrest, a white police officer struck a protesting black bystander with his club. The incident triggered a storm of anger and a week of violence. Thirty-four people died during the uprising, which was eventually quelled by the National Guard. In the summer of 1966, forty-three additional outbreaks occurred, the most serious in Chicago and Cleveland. And in the summer of 1967, eight major disorders took place, including the largest of them all—a racial clash in Detroit in which forty-three people died.

Televised images of the violence alarmed millions of Americans and set off a round of soul-searching among politicians and civil rights activists. What was the solution to the violence? A special Commission on Civil Disorders, ordered by President Johnson in response to the riots, issued a celebrated report in the spring of 1968 recommending massive spending to eliminate the abysmal conditions of the ghettoes. To many white Americans, however, the riots exposed the need for stern measures to stop violence and lawlessness. But to some black Americans, the time was ripe for a more aggressive attack on segregation.

FANNIE LOU HAMER ON THE STRUGGLE FOR VOTING RIGHTS (1964)

Fannie Lou Hamer shone a harsh spotlight on racial terror in her native state of Mississippi during her speech before the Credentials Committee of the Democratic National Convention in Atlantic City, New Jersey, in August 1964. With this testimony, Hamer tried—unsuccessfully—to unseat the all-white Mississippi delegation and seat members of the Mississippi Freedom Democratic Party (MFDP). Four years later, the MFDP succeeded in winning seats at the Convention.

Mr. Chairman, and to the Credentials Committee, my name is Mrs. Fannie Lou Hamer, and I live at 626 East Lafayette Street, Ruleville, Mississippi, Sunflower County, the home of Senator James O. Eastland, and Senator Stennis.

It was the 31st of August in 1962 that eighteen of us traveled twenty-six miles to the county courthouse in Indianola to try to register to become first-class citizens.

We was met in Indianola by policemen, Highway Patrolmen, and they only allowed two of us in to take the literacy test at the time. After we had taken this test and started back to Ruleville, we was held up by the City Police and the State Highway Patrolmen and carried back to Indianola where the bus driver was charged that day with driving a bus the wrong color.

After we paid the fine among us, we continued on to Ruleville, and Reverend Jeff Sunny carried me four miles in the rural area where I had worked as a timekeeper and sharecropper for eighteen years. I was met there by my children, who told me that the plantation owner was angry because I had gone down to try to register.

After they told me, my husband came, and said the plantation owner was raising Cain because I had tried to register. Before he quit talking the plantation owner came and said, "Fannie Lou, do you know—did Pap tell you what I said?"

And I said, "Yes, sir."

He said, "Well I mean that." He said, "If you don't go down and withdraw your registration, you will have to leave." Said, "Then if you go down and withdraw," said, "you still might have to go because we are not ready for that in Mississippi."

And I addressed him and told him and said, "I didn't try to register for you. I tried to register for myself."

I had to leave that same night.

On the 10th of September 1962, sixteen bullets was fired into the home of Mr. and Mrs. Robert Tucker for me. That same night two girls were shot in Ruleville, Mississippi. Also Mr. Joe McDonald's house was shot in.

And June the 9th, 1963, I had attended a voter registration workshop; was returning back to Mississippi. Ten of us was traveling by the Continental Trailway bus. When we got to Winona, Mississippi, which is Montgomery County, four of the people got off to use the washroom, and two of the people—to use the restaurant—two of the people wanted to use the washroom.

The four people that had gone in to use the restaurant was ordered out. During this time I was on the bus. But when I looked through the window and saw they had rushed out I got off of the bus to see what had happened. And one of the ladies said, "It was a State Highway Patrolman and a Chief of Police ordered us out."

I got back on the bus and one of the persons had used the washroom got back on the bus, too.

As soon as I was seated on the bus, I saw when they began to get the five people in a highway patrolman's car. I stepped off of the bus to see what was happening and somebody screamed from the car that the five workers was in and said, "Get that one there." When I went to get in the car, when the man told me I was under arrest, he kicked me.

I was carried to the county jail and put in the booking room. They left some of the people in the booking room and began to place us in cells. I was placed in a cell with a young woman called Miss Ivesta Simpson. After I was placed in the cell I began to hear sounds of licks and screams, I could hear the sounds of licks and horrible screams. And I could hear somebody say, "Can you say, 'yes, sir,' nigger? Can you say 'yes, sir'?"

And they would say other horrible names.

She would say, "Yes, I can say 'yes, sir.'"

"So, well, say it."

She said, "I don't know you well enough."

They beat her, I don't know how long. And after a while she began to pray, and asked God to have mercy on those people.

And it wasn't too long before three white men came to my cell. One of these men was a State Highway Patrolman and he asked me where I was from. I told him Ruleville and he said, "We are going to check this."

They left my cell and it wasn't too long before they came back. He said, "You are from Ruleville all right," and he used a curse word. And he said, "We are going to make you wish you was dead."

I was carried out of that cell into another cell where they had two Negro prisoners. The State Highway Patrolmen ordered the first Negro to take the blackjack.

The first Negro prisoner ordered me, by orders from the State Highway Patrolman, for me to lay down on a bunk bed on my face.

I laid on my face and the first Negro began to beat. I was beat by the first Negro until he was exhausted. I was holding my hands behind me at that time on my left side, because I suffered from polio when I was six years old.

After the first Negro had beat until he was exhausted, the State Highway Patrolman ordered the second Negro to take the blackjack.

The second Negro began to beat and I began to work my feet, and the State Highway Patrolman ordered the first Negro who had beat me to sit on my feet—to keep me from working my feet. I began to scream and one white man got up and began to beat me in my head and tell me to hush.

One white man—my dress had worked up high—he walked over and pulled my dress—I pulled my dress down and he pulled my dress back up.

I was in jail when Medgar Evers was murdered.

All of this is on account of we want to register, to become first-class citizens. And if the Freedom Democratic Party is not seated now, I question America. Is this America, the land of the free and the home of the brave, where we have to sleep with our telephones off the hooks because our lives be threatened daily, because we want to live as decent human beings, in America?

Thank you.

UNDERSTAND, ANALYZE, & EVALUATE

1. What tactics were used to prevent Hamer from registering to vote?
2. Why did the Highway Patrolmen choose black prisoners to beat Hamer?
3. When the television networks broadcast this speech, the level of public support for the Mississippi Freedom Democratic Party rose sharply. What aspects of Hamer's speech were so effective?

Source: Fannie Lou Hamer, "Testimony Before the Credentials Committee," Democratic National Convention, August 22, 1964. Copyright ©1964 by Fannie Lou Hamer. All rights reserved. Used with permission.

BLACK POWER

Disillusioned with the ideal of peaceful change through cooperation with whites, an increasing number of African Americans turned to a new approach to solving racial conflict and promoting civil rights: the philosophy of **black power**. Black power meant many different things. But in all its forms, it suggested a shift away from the goals of assimilation and toward increased awareness of racial distinctiveness and the promotion of black-run institutions.

Perhaps the most enduring impact of the black-power ideology was a social and psychological one: instilling racial pride in African Americans. But black power took political forms as well, and it created a deep schism within the civil rights movement. Traditional black organizations that emphasized cooperation with sympathetic whites—groups such as the NAACP, the Urban League, and King's Southern Christian Leadership Conference— now faced competition from more radical groups. The Student Nonviolent Coordinating Committee and the Congress of Racial Equality had both begun as relatively moderate interracial organizations. By the mid-1960s, however, these and other groups were calling for more radical and occasionally even violent action against white racism and were openly rejecting the approaches of older, more established black leaders.

The most radical expressions of the black-power idea came from such revolutionary organizations as the Black Panthers. Formed in Oakland, California, in the fall of 1966 by Huey Newton and Bobby Seale, the Black Panthers originally aimed to curb what it saw as the problem of police mistreatment of black citizens. Armed Panthers, often uniformed in close-fitting leather jackets and black berets, closely monitored police patrols and promised to intervene in acts of police brutality. Images of Black Panthers marching and shouting "Off the Pigs" stunned many white Americans who associated civil rights protests with nonviolent marches and sit-ins. At the height of its popularity in the early 1970s, the Panthers had chapters in over sixty cities and thousands of members. Importantly, the Panthers spreading popularity was not simply a fact of their militant image. Rather, they also grew because of their efforts to improve local communities—bettering schools, opening health clinics, and providing food for the hungry. Indeed, their Ten-Point program, which functioned as a public declaration of their core principles, included calls for freedom as well as full employment, acceptable housing, clothing, justice and peace. They also actively recruited and promoted women into high-ranking and visible leadership posts, uncommon among most civil rights groups at the time.

Similar to the Black Panthers, the Nation of Islam preached a radical form of black power. It openly denounced whites as "devils" and appealed to African Americans to embrace its version of Islamic faith and work for complete racial separation. The most celebrated of the "Black Muslims," as the media often termed them, was Malcolm Little. Born in Boston in 1925, imprisoned at age twenty for larceny, he discovered the Nation of Islam while behind bars and adopted the name **Malcolm X** —"X" to denote his lost African surname. Upon his release, he rose quickly through the ranks by advocating a fiery brand of black separatism, even encouraging black Americans to move to Africa. He brashly challenged the leadership and legacy of the modern civil rights movement, which he claimed capitulated too quickly to the fears of white Americans and didn't do enough to promote black communities. A captivating speaker who packed auditoriums and halls around the country, he offered a stark alternative to King's vision of nonviolent social reform, urging black Americans to defend themselves when threatened or struck and not shy away from physical violence as a source of protest. His popularity captured a rising frustration among many young blacks about the pace of change in the pursuit of racial equality.

Malcolm X had a change of heart in 1964, however, and left the Nation of Islam and founded the Muslim Mosque, Inc., and the Organization of Afro-American Unity, which he hoped would allow him to work more cooperatively with other civil rights leaders. He soon became a Sunni Muslim and, after a pilgrimage to Mecca, espoused a new hope that racial problems could be overcome through nonviolent means and with the full support of whites. He died in 1965 when gunmen, possibly under orders from rivals within the Nation of Islam, assassinated him. But he remained a major figure in many African American communities long after his death, attaining a stature near comparable to that of Martin Luther King Jr.

"FLEXIBLE RESPONSE" AND THE COLD WAR

In international affairs as much as in domestic reform, the optimistic liberalism of the Kennedy and Johnson administrations dictated a more active and aggressive approach to dealing with the nation's problems than that of the 1950s.

DIVERSIFYING FOREIGN POLICY

The Kennedy administration entered office convinced that the United States needed to be able to counter communist aggression in more flexible ways than the atomic-weapons-oriented defense strategy of the Eisenhower years. In particular, Kennedy was unsatisfied with the nation's ability to meet communist threats in the Third World, areas in which, Kennedy believed, the real struggle against communism would be waged in the future. He gave enthusiastic support to the expansion of the Special Forces (or "Green Berets"), soldiers trained specifically to fight guerrilla conflicts and other limited wars.

Kennedy also favored expanding American influence through peaceful means. To repair badly deteriorating relationships in Latin America, he proposed an "Alliance for Progress," a series of projects for peaceful development and stabilization of the nations of that region. Kennedy also inaugurated the Agency for International Development (AID) to coordinate foreign aid. And he established what became one of his most popular innovations: the Peace Corps, which sent young American volunteers abroad to work in developing areas. But these programs served the broader Cold War strategy of anticommunist containment. By nurturing good will toward the United States, they aimed to maximize American access to natural resources, cultivate commercial markets, expand geopolitical influence, and above all, counter comparable communist efforts in the developing world and deprive the Soviet Union of potential allies.

Yet one of the first foreign policy ventures of the Kennedy administration was a military one, a disastrous assault on the Castro government in Cuba. The Eisenhower administration had started the project, and by the time Kennedy took office, the CIA had been working for months to train a small army of anti-Castro Cuban exiles. On April 17, 1961, with the approval of the new president, 2,000 of the armed exiles landed at the **Bay of Pigs** in Cuba, expecting American air support and then a spontaneous uprising by the Cuban people. They received neither. At the last minute, as it became clear that things were going badly, Kennedy withdrew the air support, fearful of involving the United States too directly in the invasion. Nor did the expected uprising occur. Instead, well-armed Castro forces easily crushed the invaders, and within two days the entire mission had collapsed.

CONFRONTATIONS WITH THE SOVIET UNION

In the grim aftermath of the Bay of Pigs, Kennedy traveled to Vienna in June 1961 for his first meeting with Soviet Premier Nikita Khrushchev. Their frosty exchange of views did little to reduce strains between the two nations—nor did Khrushchev's veiled threat of war unless the United States ceased to support a noncommunist West Berlin in the heart of East Germany.

Khrushchev was particularly unhappy about the mass exodus of residents of East Germany to the West through the easily traversed border in the center of Berlin. But he ultimately found a method short of war to stop it. Just before dawn on August 13, 1961, the East German government, complying with directives from Moscow, constructed a wall between East and West Berlin. Guards fired on those who continued to try to escape. For nearly thirty years, the Berlin Wall served as the most potent physical symbol of the conflict between the communist and noncommunist worlds.

The rising tensions culminated the following October in the most dangerous moment of the Cold War—the **Cuban missile crisis**. During the summer of 1962, American intelligence agencies became aware of the arrival of a new wave of Soviet technicians and equipment in Cuba and of military construction in progress. On October 14, aerial reconnaissance photos produced clear evidence that the Soviets were constructing sites on the island for offensive nuclear weapons. To the Soviets, placing missiles in Cuba probably seemed a reasonable—and relatively inexpensive—way to counter the presence of American missiles in Turkey (and a way to deter any future American invasion of Cuba). But to Kennedy and most other Americans, the missile sites represented an act of naked aggression by the Soviets toward the United States. Almost immediately, the president—working with a special executive committee assembled to deal with the crisis—decided that the weapons must go. On October 22, he ordered a naval and air blockade around Cuba, a "quarantine" against all offensive weapons. Preparations were under way for an American air attack on the missile sites when, late in the evening of October 26, Kennedy received a message from Khrushchev implying that the Soviet Union would remove the missile bases in exchange for an American pledge not to invade Cuba. The president agreed. And, in secret, Kennedy agreed to withdraw the missiles from Turkey in what is now called the Kennedy-Khrushchev Pact. The resolution of the conflict was a political victory for Kennedy, and in an effort to avoid the threat of war again, the two leaders established a Moscow–Washington hotline that created a direct link between the nuclear nations. The improved dialogue between the nuclear superpowers also paved the way for the Nuclear Test Ban Treaty of 1963, which banned atmospheric tests.

JOHNSON AND THE WORLD

Lyndon Johnson entered the presidency with little prior experience in international affairs. He was eager, therefore, not only to continue the flexible response policies of his predecessor but also to prove quickly that he, too, was a strong and forceful leader.

An internal rebellion in the Dominican Republic gave him an opportunity to do so. A 1961 assassination had toppled the dictatorship of General Rafael Trujillo, and for the next four years various factions in the country had struggled for dominance. In the spring of 1965, a conservative regime began to collapse in the face of a revolt by a broad range of groups on behalf of the left-wing nationalist Juan Bosch. Arguing without evidence that Bosch planned to establish a pro-Castro communist regime, Johnson dispatched 30,000 American troops to quell the disorder. Only after a conservative candidate defeated Bosch in a 1966 election were the forces withdrawn.

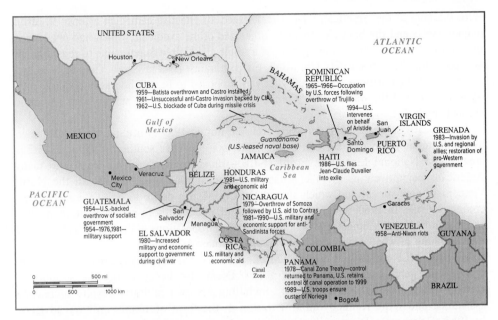

THE UNITED STATES IN LATIN AMERICA, 1954-2006 The Cold War greatly increased the readiness of the United States to intervene in the affairs of its Latin American neighbors. This map presents the many times and ways in which Washington ordered interventions in Central America, the Caribbean, and the northern nations of South America. During much of this period, the interventions were driven by Cold War concerns—by fears that communists might take over nations near the United States as they had taken over Cuba in the early 1960s. • *What other interests motivated the United States to exert influence in Latin America even after the end of the Cold War?*

From Johnson's first moments in office, however, his foreign policy was almost totally dominated by the bitter war in Vietnam and by the expanding involvement of the United States there.

THE AGONY OF VIETNAM

George Kennan, who helped devise the containment doctrine in the name of which America went to war in Vietnam, once called the conflict "the most disastrous of all America's undertakings over the whole 200 years of its history." Yet at first, the conflict in Vietnam seemed simply one more foreign struggle on the periphery of the Cold War.

AMERICA AND DIEM

Having thrown its support to the new leader of South Vietnam, Ngo Dinh Diem, in the aftermath of the 1954 Geneva accords, and having supported Diem in his refusal to hold the elections in 1956 that the accords had required, the United States found itself drawn steadily deeper into the unstable politics of this fractious new nation.

Diem, an aristocratic Catholic from central Vietnam and an outsider in the south, was also a hard-line nationalist uncontaminated by any collaboration with the French and bent on shoring up the authority of his regime. And he was, for a time, apparently successful.

With the help of the American CIA, Diem waged an effective campaign against powerful religious sects and the South Vietnamese organized crime syndicate, which had challenged the authority of the central government. As a result, the United States came to regard Diem as a powerful alternative to Ho Chi Minh, his communist rival in North Vietnam who had come to rule the northern regions of what was supposed to be a temporarily divided country at the close of the war with the French in 1954. America threw military and economic aid at Diem's feet.

Diem's early successes in suppressing sects led him in 1959 to begin a similar campaign to eliminate supporters of Ho Chi Minh in the south. Those southern communists thus created the National Liberation Front (NLF)—whose soldiers became known to many Americans pejoratively as the **Viet Cong**—an organization closely allied with the North Vietnamese government and which shared Ho Chi Minh's desire to unify Vietnam under communist rule. In 1960, under orders from Hanoi, and with both material and manpower support from North Vietnam, the NLF began military operations in the south. This marked the beginning of what Americans know as the Vietnam War.

By 1961, NLF forces had established effective control over many areas of the countryside and were threatening Diem's power. Diem also began losing the support of many other groups in South Vietnam, including his own military, despite increasing assistance under the Kennedy administration in the form of 16,000 military advisers. In 1963, a desperate Diem regime precipitated a major crisis by trying to repress the South Vietnamese Buddhists in an effort to limit political dissent. The Buddhists staged enormous antigovernment demonstrations. One of them saw a monk sit cross-legged in downtown Saigon, douse himself with gasoline, and set himself on fire—in full view of photographers and television cameras. Later, other Buddhists burned themselves in other areas.

Alarmed American officials pressured Diem to reform his now tottering government, but the president made no significant concessions. As a result, in the fall of 1963, Kennedy gave his approval to a plot by a group of South Vietnamese generals to topple Diem. In early November 1963, the generals staged the coup, assassinated Diem along with his brother Ngo Dinh Nhu (killings the United States had not wanted or expected), and established the first of a series of new governments that were, for over three years, even less stable than the one they had overthrown. A few weeks after the coup, John Kennedy was assassinated.

From Aid to Intervention

Lyndon Johnson inherited what was already a substantial American commitment to the survival of an anticommunist South Vietnam. During his first months in office, he expanded the American involvement in Vietnam only slightly, sending an additional 5,000 military advisers there and preparing to send 5,000 more. Then, early in August 1964, the president announced that American destroyers on patrol in international waters in the Gulf of Tonkin had been attacked by North Vietnamese torpedo boats. Later information raised serious doubts as to whether the administration reported the attacks accurately. At the time, however, virtually no one questioned Johnson's portrayal of the incident as a serious act of aggression. By a vote of 416 to 0 in the House and 88 to 2 in the Senate, Congress hurriedly passed the **Gulf of Tonkin Resolution**, which authorized the president to "take all necessary measures" to protect American forces and "prevent further aggression" in Southeast Asia. The resolution became, in Johnson's view at least, an open-ended legal authorization for escalation of the conflict, though at the time the president had little desire to see Vietnam erupt into a larger war.

With the South Vietnamese leadership still in disarray and communist military pressure growing stronger, more and more of the burden of opposition to the Viet Cong fell on the United States. In February 1965, after communist forces attacked an American military base at Pleiku, Johnson ordered American bombings of the north, in an attempt to destroy the depots and transportation lines responsible for the flow of North Vietnamese soldiers and supplies into South Vietnam. The bombing continued intermittently until 1972. A month later, in March 1965, two battalions of American marines landed at Da Nang in South Vietnam, bringing the total American troop strength to over 100,000.

Four months later, the president announced that American soldiers would now begin playing an active role in the conflict. By the end of the year, there were more than 180,000 American combat troops in Vietnam; in 1966, that number doubled; and by the end of 1967, over 500,000 American soldiers fought there. In the meantime, the air war intensified. By the spring of 1966, more than 4,000 Americans and an unknown number of Vietnamese had been killed.

The Quagmire

Central to the American war effort in Vietnam was a strategy known as "attrition," premised on the belief that the United States could inflict more damage on the enemy than the enemy could absorb. But the attrition strategy failed because the North Vietnamese, believing that they were fighting a war for national independence, were willing to commit many more soldiers and resources to the conflict than the United States had predicted. Increasing numbers of North Vietnamese fighters joined the Viet Cong, making their way through neutral Laos and Cambodia and delivering military supplies via what became known as the Ho Chi Minh trail. The emphasis on attrition, which invited the "body count" of enemy dead as one of the main measures of progress, had tragic consequences for the people of South Vietnam. The Vietnam War featured blurry lines between villages and battlefields, between civilians and soldiers. Most Americans worked diligently to avoid killing noncombatants, but returning fire or calling in airstrikes often led to that result, and commanders were encouraged by the attrition strategy to count all dead as enemy dead. In rare cases, most notoriously during the **My Lai massacre**, American soldiers deliberately murdered civilians believed to have harbored the Viet Cong, who themselves often came from or could blend into the villages of South Vietnam.

The United States also failed in expecting its bombing of the north to eliminate the communists' war-making capacity. North Vietnam was not a modern industrial society, and it had relatively few of the sorts of targets against which bombing is effective. The North Vietnamese also responded to the bombing with great ingenuity. They created a network of underground tunnels, shops, and factories. The North Vietnamese also were provided substantial aid from the Soviet Union and China. They continually moved the Ho Chi Minh Trail to make it elusive to American bombers. Far from breaking the north's resolve, the bombing seemed actually to strengthen popular commitment to the war.

Another important part of the American strategy was the "pacification" program, whose purpose was to push the Viet Cong from particular regions and then "pacify"

THE WAR IN VIETNAM AND INDOCHINA, 1964–1975 Much of the Vietnam War was fought in small engagements in widely scattered areas and did not conform to traditional notions of combat. But as this map shows, there were traditional battles and invasions and supply routes as well. The red arrows in the middle of the map show the general path of the Ho Chi Minh Trail, the main supply route by which North Vietnam supplied its troops and allies in the south. The blue arrow in southern South Vietnam indicates the point at which American troops invaded Cambodia in 1970. • *What is there in the geography of Indochina, as presented on this map, that helps explain the great difficulty the American military had in securing South Vietnam against communist attacks?*

those regions by winning the "hearts and minds" of the people. Routing the Viet Cong was often possible, but the subsequent pacification was more difficult. Gradually, the pacification program gave way to a more heavy-handed relocation strategy, through which American troops uprooted villagers from their homes, sent them fleeing to refugee camps or into the cities (producing by 1967 more than 3 million refugees), and then destroyed the vacated villages and surrounding countryside. "It became necessary to destroy the village in order to save it," an American military official famously said of one such action, thus revealing the flawed assumptions of the pacification program.

As the war dragged on and victory remained elusive, some American officers and officials urged the president to expand the military efforts. But Johnson resisted—in part because he remembered the Korean War. He feared drawing China directly into the Vietnam War, and he was beginning to encounter obstacles and frustrations at home.

THE WAR AT HOME

Few Americans, and even fewer influential ones, had protested the American involvement in Vietnam as late as the end of 1965. But as the war dragged on inconclusively, political support for it began to erode.

By the end of 1967, American students opposed to the war (and to the military draft) had become a significant political force. Enormous peace marches in New York, Washington, D.C., and other cities drew broad public attention to the antiwar movement. (Music also raised awareness; see "Patterns of Popular Culture: The Folk-Music Revival.") In the meantime, a growing number of journalists, particularly reporters who had spent time in Vietnam, helped sustain the movement with their frank revelations about the brutality and apparent futility of the war. Later, some critics would blame the media for such reporting, but many of them had gone to Vietnam in the early 1960s believing in the American fight there and only wishing to see it conducted more effectively.

Senator J. William Fulbright of Arkansas, chair of the Senate Foreign Relations Committee, also turned against the war and in January 1966 began to stage highly publicized and occasionally televised congressional hearings to air criticisms of it. Other members of Congress joined Fulbright in opposing Johnson's policies—including, in 1967, Robert F. Kennedy, brother of the slain president, now a senator from New York. Even within the administration, the consensus seemed to be crumbling. Robert McNamara, who had done much to help extend the initial American involvement in Vietnam, quietly left the government, disillusioned, in 1968. His successor as secretary of defense, Clark Clifford, became a quiet but powerful voice within the administration on behalf of a cautious scaling down of the commitment.

In the meantime, Johnson's commitment to fighting the war while continuing his Great Society reforms helped cause a rise in inflation, from the 2 percent level it had occupied through most of the early 1960s to 3 percent in 1967, 4 percent in 1968, and 6 percent in 1969. In August 1967, Johnson asked Congress for a tax increase to avoid even more ruinous inflation. In return, congressional conservatives demanded a $6 billion reduction in the funding for Great Society programs. The president accepted the reduction as a way to mollify congressional conservatives unnerved by economic troubles and critical of social welfare programs.

THE FOLK-MUSIC REVIVAL

Two impulses of the 1960s—the renewed interest among young people in the politics of the left, and the search for an "authentic" alternative to what many considered the artificial, consumerist culture of modern America—helped produce the revived popularity of folk music in that turbulent era. Although the harder music of rock 'n' roll was more visible and more popular in the 1960s, folk music more clearly expressed many of the political ideas and aspirations that were welling up in the youth culture of the time.

The folk-music tradition, like most American musical traditions, had many roots. It drew from some of the black musical traditions of the South, and from the white country music of Appalachia. And it drew most immediately from a style of music developed by musicians associated with the Communist Party's Popular Front in the 1930s. Woody Guthrie, Pete Seeger, the Weavers, and others whose music would become popular again in the 1960s began their careers singing in Popular Front and union rallies during the Great Depression. Their music, like the Popular Front itself, set out to seem entirely American, rooted in the nation's folk traditions.

Folk music remained alive in the 1940s and 1950s, but it had only a modest popular following. Pete Seeger and the Weavers continued to perform and to attract attention on college campuses. Harry Belafonte and the Kingston Trio recorded slick, pop versions of folk songs in an effort to bring them to mass audiences. In 1952, Folkway Records released the *Anthology of American Folk Music*, a collection of eighty-four performances recorded in the 1920s and 1930s that became an inspiration and an important source of material to many younger folk musicians. Folk-music festivals—at Berkeley, Newport, and Chicago—began to proliferate beginning in 1959. And an important community of folk musicians lived and performed together in the 1950s and early 1960s in New York City's Greenwich Village.

As the politics of the 1960s became more heated, it was folk music that most directly reflected their new values and concerns. Peter, Paul, and Mary—although only intermittently political—became icons to much of the New Left, beginning with their 1962 recording of "If I Had a Hammer," a song first performed at Communist Party rallies in the 1940s by Pete Seeger and the Weavers. Bob Dylan, whose own politics were never wholly clear to the public, had a large impact on the 1960s left, even inadvertently providing a name to the most radical offshoot of Students for a Democratic Society (SDS), the Weathermen, who named themselves after a line from one of his songs: "You don't need a weatherman to know which way the wind blows."* Joan Baez, whose politics were no secret to anyone, was actively engaged in the antiwar movement and was arrested several times for participating in militant protests.

But it was not just the overt political messages of folk musicians that made them so important to young Americans in the 1960s. In addition, folk was a kind of music that seemed to reflect the "authenticity" the youth culture was attempting to find. In truth, neither the musicians themselves nor the young Americans attracted to them had much real connection with the traditions they were trying to evoke.

(©John Orris/New York Times Co./Getty Images)

COFFEEHOUSE MUSIC The Feejon Coffee House in Manhattan was popular among young writers, poets, and others in the late 1950s, in part because it was a gathering place for folk musicians, two of whom are shown here performing at right.

The audiences for folk music—a product of rural and working-class traditions—were overwhelmingly urban, middle-class people. But the message of folk music—that there was a "real" America rooted in values of sharing and community, hidden beneath the crass commercialism of modern culture—resonated with the yearnings of many people in the 1960s (and beyond) for an alternative to their own troubled world. When young audiences responded to Woody Guthrie's famous ballad "This Land Is Your Land," they were expressing a hope for a different America—more democratic, more honest, and more natural than the land they knew. •

UNDERSTAND, ANALYZE, & EVALUATE

1. What did folk music, with roots in the musical traditions of blacks, rural folk, and working-class people, offer that made it so appealing to and popular with urban, middle-class audiences?

2. What similarities between the 1930s and the 1960s might help explain the popularity of folk music during both those decades?

3. What musical style or form today continues the folk-music tradition of expressing a political message and reflecting the search for "authenticity"?

THE TRAUMAS OF 1968

By the end of 1967, the twin crises of the war in Vietnam and the deteriorating racial situation at home had produced great social and political tensions. In the course of 1968, those tensions burst to the surface and seemed to threaten national chaos. (The year 1968 was turbulent elsewhere in the world as well; see "America in the World: 1968.")

1968

The year 1968 was one of the most turbulent in the postwar history of the United States. Much of what made it so traumatic were specifically American events—the growing controversy over the war in Vietnam, the assassinations of Martin Luther King Jr. and Robert Kennedy, racial unrest across the nation's cities, student protests on campuses throughout America. But the turmoil of 1968 was not confined to the United States. There were tremendous upheavals in many parts of the globe that year.

The most common form of turbulence around the world in 1968 was student unrest. In France, a student uprising in May far exceeded in size and ferocity anything that occurred in the United States. It attracted the support of French workers and briefly paralyzed Paris and other cities. It contributed to the downfall of the government of Charles de Gaulle a year later. In England, Ireland, Germany, Italy, the Netherlands, Mexico, Canada, Japan, and South Korea, students and other young people demonstrated in great numbers, and at times with violence, against governments, universities, and other structures of authority. Elsewhere, there was more widespread protest, as in Czechoslovakia, where hundreds of thousands of citizens took to the streets in support of what became known as "Prague Spring." It caused a demand for greater democracy and a repudiation of many of the oppressive rules and structures imposed on the nation by its Soviet-dominated communist regimes. Russian tanks rolled into the city to crush the uprising.

Many people have tried to explain why so much instability emerged in so many nations at the same time. One factor that

contributed to the worldwide turbulence of 1968 was simple numbers. The postwar Baby Boom had created a very large age cohort in many nations, and by the late 1960s it was coming of age. In the industrial West, the sheer size of the new generation produced a tripling of the number of people attending colleges and universities. In fewer than twenty years it also created a heightened sense of the power of youth. The long period of postwar prosperity and relative peace in which this generation had grown up contributed to heightened expectations of what the world should offer them—and a greater level of impatience than previous generations had demonstrated with the obstacles that stood in the way of their hopes. A new global youth culture emerged that was in many ways at odds with the dominant culture of older generations. It valued nonconformity, personal freedom, and even rebellion.

A second force contributing to the widespread turbulence of 1968 was the power of global media. Satellite communication introduced in the early 1960s made it possible to transmit live news across the world. Videotape technology and the creation of lightweight portable television cameras enabled media organizations to respond to events much more quickly and flexibly than in the past. The audience for these televised images was by now global and enormous, particularly in industrial nations but even in the poorest areas of the world. Protests in one country were suddenly capable of inspiring protests in others. Demonstrators in Paris, for example, spoke openly of how campus protests in the United States in 1968—for example, the student uprising at Columbia University in New York the previous month—had helped motivate French students to rise up as well. Just as American students were protesting against what they considered antiquated, paternalistic features of their own universities, French students demanded an end to the rigid, autocratic character of their own academic world.

In most parts of the world, the 1968 uprisings came and went without fundamentally altering institutions and systems. But many changes came in the wake of these protests. Universities around the globe undertook significant reforms. Religious observance in mainstream churches and synagogues in the West declined dramatically after 1968. New concepts of personal freedom gained legitimacy, helping to inspire social movements in the years that followed—among them the dramatic growth of feminism in many parts of the world and the emergence of the gay and lesbian rights movement. The events of 1968 did not produce a revolution in the United States or in most of the rest of the world, but it did help launch a period of dramatic social, cultural, and political changes that affected the peoples of many nations. •

UNDERSTAND, ANALYZE, & EVALUATE

1. What factors combined to produce the turbulence that resulted in the uprisings of 1968?
2. Did the demonstrators of 1968 succeed or fail to achieve their objectives? What were the long-term effects of the 1968 uprisings?

THE TET OFFENSIVE

On January 31, 1968, the first day of the Vietnamese New Year (Tet), communist forces launched an enormous, concerted attack on American strongholds throughout South Vietnam. A few cities, most notably Hue, fell temporarily to the communists. But what made the **Tet offensive** so shocking to the American people, who saw vivid reports of it on television, was the sight of communist forces in the heart of Saigon, setting off bombs, shooting down South Vietnamese officials and troops, and holding down fortified areas (including, briefly, the American embassy). The Tet offensive also suggested to the American public something of the brutality of the fighting in Vietnam. In the midst of the fighting, television cameras recorded the sight of a South Vietnamese officer shooting a captured and defenseless young Viet Cong soldier in the head in the streets of Saigon.

American forces soon dislodged the Viet Cong from most of the positions they had seized. And during the battle they had inflicted enormous casualties on the communists and permanently depleted the ranks of the NLF, forcing North Vietnamese troops to take on a much larger share of the subsequent fighting. But such accomplishments registered little with the American people, who felt betrayed by an administration that had sworn the war was nearly over and the enemy was on his heels. Tet may have been a military victory for the United States, but it was a political defeat for the administration.

In the following weeks, opposition to the war grew substantially. Leading newspapers and magazines, television commentators, and mainstream politicians began taking public stands against the conflict. Public opposition to the war almost doubled, and Johnson's personal popularity rating slid to 35 percent, the lowest of any president since Harry Truman.

THE POLITICAL CHALLENGE

Beginning in the summer of 1967, dissident Democrats tried to mobilize support behind an antiwar candidate who would challenge Lyndon Johnson in the 1968 primaries.

When Robert Kennedy turned them down, they recruited Senator Eugene McCarthy of Minnesota. A brilliantly orchestrated campaign by young volunteers in the New Hampshire primary produced a startling showing by McCarthy in March; he nearly defeated the president.

A few days later, Robert Kennedy did an about-face and entered the campaign, embittering many McCarthy supporters but bringing his own substantial strength among minorities, poor people, and workers to the antiwar cause. With Kennedy now in the race, polls showed the president trailing badly in the next scheduled primary, in Wisconsin. And so Johnson adjusted. On March 31, 1968, Johnson went on television to announce a limited halt in the bombing of North Vietnam—his first major concession to the antiwar forces and a major departure from his normally hawkish policies. And then, stunningly, Johnson declared that he was withdrawing from the presidential contest.

In the aftermath of Johnson's withdrawal, Robert Kennedy quickly established himself as the champion of the Democratic primaries, winning one election after another. In the meantime, however, Vice President Hubert Humphrey, with the support of President Johnson, entered the contest and began to attract the support of party leaders and of the many delegations that were selected not by popular primaries but by state party organizations. He soon overtook Kennedy as the front-runner in the race.

ASSASSINATIONS AND POLITICS

On April 4, Martin Luther King Jr., who had traveled to Memphis, Tennessee, to lend his support to striking black sanitation workers in the city, was shot and killed while standing on the balcony of his motel. The assassin, James Earl Ray, who was captured two months later in London, had no apparent motive. Subsequent evidence suggested that he had been hired by others to do the killing, but he himself never revealed the identity of his alleged employers.

King's murder produced a great outpouring of grief. Among some African Americans, it also produced anger. In the days after the assassination, major riots broke out in more than sixty American cities. Forty-three people died.

Tragedy struck again only two months later. Late in the night of June 6, Robert Kennedy appeared in the ballroom of a Los Angeles hotel to acknowledge his victory in that day's California primary. As he left the ballroom after his speech, Sirhan Sirhan, a young Palestinian apparently enraged by pro-Israeli remarks Kennedy had recently made, emerged from a crowd and shot him in the head. Early the next morning, Kennedy died. The shock of this second death of a national politician in two months—and only five years after the assassination of John Kennedy—cast a pall over the remainder of the presidential campaign.

When the Democrats finally gathered in Chicago in August, for a convention in which Hubert Humphrey was now the only real contender, even the most optimistic observers predicted turbulence. Inside the hall, delegates bitterly debated an antiwar plank in the party platform that both Kennedy and McCarthy supporters favored. Miles away, in a downtown park, thousands of antiwar protesters staged demonstrations. On the third night of the convention, as the delegates began their balloting on the now virtually inevitable nomination of Hubert Humphrey, demonstrators and police clashed in a bloody riot in the streets of Chicago. Hundreds of protesters were injured as police attempted to disperse them with tear gas and billy clubs. Aware that the violence was being televised to the nation, the demonstrators taunted the authorities with the chant, "The whole world is watching!" And Hubert Humphrey, who had spent years dreaming of becoming his party's candidate for president, finally got the nomination but from a badly fractured party that would make it difficult for him to manage his campaign.

THE CONSERVATIVE RESPONSE

The turbulent events of 1968 persuaded some observers that American society was in the throes of revolutionary change leading to the creation of a better society. In fact, however, the response of many Americans to the turmoil was to question the social changes of the prior decade and take a conservative political turn.

The most visible sign of the conservative backlash was the surprising success of the campaign of segregationist George Wallace for the presidency. In 1968, the former Alabama governor became a third-party candidate for president, basing his campaign on a host of conservative grievances. He denounced the forced busing of students to achieve racial integration in public schools, the proliferation of government regulations and social programs, and what he called the permissiveness of authorities toward crime, race riots, and antiwar demonstrations. There was never any serious chance that Wallace

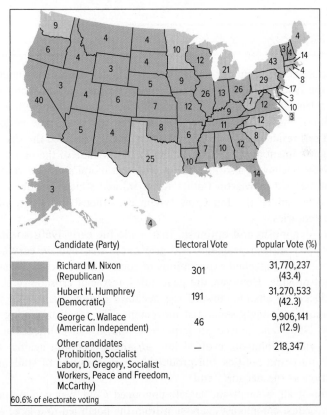

Candidate (Party)	Electoral Vote	Popular Vote (%)
Richard M. Nixon (Republican)	301	31,770,237 (43.4)
Hubert H. Humphrey (Democratic)	191	31,270,533 (42.3)
George C. Wallace (American Independent)	46	9,906,141 (12.9)
Other candidates (Prohibition, Socialist Labor, D. Gregory, Socialist Workers, Peace and Freedom, McCarthy)	—	218,347

60.6% of electorate voting

THE ELECTION OF 1968 The 1968 presidential election, which Richard Nixon won, was almost as close as the election of 1960, which he lost. Nixon might have won a more substantial victory had it not been for the independent candidacy of Governor George C. Wallace, who attracted many of the same conservative voters to whom Nixon appealed. • *How does the distribution of Democratic and Republican strength in this election compare to that in 1960?*

would win the election, but his standing in the polls rose at times to over 20 percent. He also earned the approval of many in his state, who reelected him as governor in 1970 and then for two more terms.

At the same time, a more effective effort to mobilize the conservative middle in favor of order and stability was under way within the Republican Party. **Richard Nixon**, whose political career had seemed dead after his losses in the presidential race of 1960 and a California gubernatorial campaign two years later, reemerged as the spokesperson for what he called the "silent majority." By offering a vision of stability, law and order, government retrenchment, and "peace with honor" in Vietnam, he easily captured the nomination of his party for the presidency. And despite a last-minute surge by Humphrey, he hung on to eke out a victory almost as narrow as his defeat in 1960. In the three-way race for the presidency, Nixon netted 43.4 percent of the popular vote to Humphrey's 42.3 percent (a margin of only about 500,000 votes), and 301 electoral votes to Humphrey's 191. George Wallace, who like most third-party candidates faded in the last weeks of the campaign, still managed to poll 12.9 percent of the popular vote and to carry five southern states with a total of 46 electoral ballots. Nixon had hardly won a decisive political mandate. But the election made clear that a majority of the American electorate was more interested in restoring stability than in promoting social change.

CONCLUSION

Perhaps no decade of the twentieth century created more powerful and enduring images in America than the 1960s. It began with the election—and then the traumatic assassination—of a young president, John Kennedy, who captured the imagination of millions and seemed to symbolize the rising idealism of the time. It produced a dramatic period of political innovation, led by President Lyndon Johnson, who greatly expanded the size and functions of the federal government and its responsibility for the welfare of the nation's citizens. He called it the Great Society. It also included a profound moral and legal revolution in matters of racial justice led by Martin Luther King, Jr., and which included two major civil rights acts that dismantled the Jim Crow system constructed in the late nineteenth and early twentieth centuries.

The spirit of dynamism and optimism that made the early 1960s so productive also helped bring to the surface problems and grievances that had no easy solutions. The civil rights movement awakened expectations of social and economic equality that laws alone could not provide. However, the peaceful, interracial crusade of the early 1960s gradually produced an offshoot toward the decade's end—a much more militant, confrontational, and increasingly separatist movement. The idealism among white youths that began the 1960s, and played an important role in the political success of John Kennedy and Lyndon Johnson, evolved into an angry rebellion against many aspects of American culture and politics and produced a large upsurge of student protest that rocked the nation at the decade's end.

Perhaps most of all, a small and largely unnoticed Cold War commitment to defend South Vietnam against communist aggression from the north led to a large and disastrous war that destroyed the presidency of Lyndon Johnson, sent thousands of young men and women to their deaths, and showed no signs of producing a victory. A decade that began with high hopes and soaring ideals ended with division and deep disillusionment.

KEY TERMS/PEOPLE/PLACES/EVENTS

affirmative action 711
Bay of Pigs 715
black power 714
Community Action
  programs 703
Cuban missile crisis 716
freedom rides 704
Freedom Summer 710
Great Society 701

Gulf of Tonkin
  Resolution 718
Immigration Act
  of 1965 703
John Kennedy 699
Lyndon Johnson 699
Malcolm X 714
Medicaid 702
Medicare 702

My Lai massacre 719
New Frontier 700
Richard Nixon 728
Tet offensive 725
Viet Cong (National
  Liberation Front) 718
Voting Rights Act
  of 1965 710

RECALL AND REFLECT

1. What were the political effects of John Kennedy's assassination?
2. How did increasing radicalism affect the successes and the setbacks of the civil rights movement?
3. What was the military strategy of the United States in Vietnam? What were the U.S. aims in that conflict? Why did the United States ultimately fail in Vietnam?
4. What accounted for growing opposition to the war in Vietnam?
5. What events made 1968 such a turbulent year both in the United States and elsewhere in the world? How did these events affect U.S. politics?

29 | THE CRISIS OF AUTHORITY

THE YOUTH CULTURE

THE MOBILIZATION OF MINORITIES

WOMEN AND SOCIAL CHANGE

ENVIRONMENTALISM IN A TURBULENT SOCIETY

NIXON, KISSINGER, AND THE VIETNAM WAR

NIXON, KISSINGER, AND THE WORLD

POLITICS AND ECONOMICS IN THE NIXON YEARS

THE WATERGATE CRISIS

LOOKING AHEAD

1. What were some of the characteristics of the social and cultural revolutions of the 1960s and 1970s?

2. How did the U.S. strategy in Vietnam change under Nixon? What was the result of the change in strategy?

3. What was the Watergate scandal and how did it affect the presidency?

THE 1960 AND 1970s SHOOK traditional foundations of stability and order in America. Long-cherished political assumptions about what was "normal" came under sharp attack. The rising death tolls of soldiers fighting in the Vietnam War and the failure of leaders to communicate effectively and truthfully about the progress of the war triggered a crisis of public trust in the military and the federal government. At the same time, the African American freedom movement cracked open the evil edifice of Jim Crow and inspired other Americans to demand the enjoyment and protection of their own civil liberties. Latinos, Indians, prisoners, gays, and women accelerated their own quests for full citizenship and in the process upturned decades-old assumptions about who could and could not enjoy the basic menu of constitutional rights.

Not surprisingly, many Americans who openly questioned the "rights movement" looked for a measure of relief from their candidates for president in 1968. The election of Richard Nixon, then, was the result not only of the unpopularity of Lyndon Johnson and the Vietnam War but also Nixon's perceived commitment to rejecting what many saw as an assault on

American society itself. And indeed Nixon projected an image of stern dedication to traditional values and promised a return to law and order. But nothing was as it seemed. Nixon's presidency would unravel because of lies he and his staff repeatedly told to the American public. Ironically, his time in office and eventual resignation would leave the country with even greater levels of political crisis and popular mistrust in traditional institutions than when he first entered the White House.

THE YOUTH CULTURE

Many conservatives in the 1960s and 1970s were alarmed by what they saw as a pattern of social and cultural anger by younger Americans. The protesters gave vent to two related impulses. One, emerging from the political left, was to create a great new community of "the people," which would rise up to break the traditional power of elites and force the nation to end the war, pursue racial and economic justice, and transform its political life. The other, at least equally powerful impulse was the vision of personal "liberation." It found expression in part through the efforts of many groups—African Americans, Indians, Hispanics, women, gay people, and others—to define and assert themselves and make demands on the larger society. It also found expression through the efforts of individuals to create a new culture—one that would allow them to escape from what some considered the dehumanizing pressures of the modern "technocracy."

THE NEW LEFT

Among the products of the racial crisis and the war in Vietnam was a radicalization of many American students. In the course of the 1960s, they formed what became known as the New Left. In 1962, a group of students (most of them white and many of

TIME LINE

1963
Friedan's *The Feminine Mystique*

1964
Free Speech Movement begins

1966
National Organization for Women formed

1968
Turmoil in universities

1969
Rock concert in Woodstock, NY

1970
Cambodian incursion
Kent State and Jackson State shootings

1971
Pentagon Papers published
Nixon imposes wage–price controls

1972
Nixon visits China
SALT I
"Christmas bombing" of North Vietnam
Watergate burglary
Nixon reelected

1973
U.S. withdraws from Vietnam
Arab oil embargo
Agnew resigns
Supreme Court decides *Roe v. Wade*

1974
Nixon resigns; Ford becomes president

1975
South Vietnam falls

CONSIDER THE SOURCE

DEMANDS OF THE NEW YORK HIGH SCHOOL STUDENT UNION (1970)

Like high school students across the country, young New Yorkers formed a union and demanded reform in the city's school system. Their demands from 1970 reflected the growing call among young Americans for greater control over public institutions and leaders and a new focus on the needs and aspirations of historically disadvantaged groups.

1—No suspensions, involuntary transfers, exclusion from classes, detention, harassment of students. Due process for students.

2—No cops in schools, no narcos, security guards, plain clothesmen, informers.

3—No program cards, hall checks, ID's, passes.

4—An end to commercial and general diplomas, one diploma for every student upon graduation.

5—Open admissions to colleges, a college education free for everyone who wants one.

6—Jobs and housing for every student who wants them on graduating, dropping out, or leaving home. The army is not a decent job.

7—No military recruiting in schools, no military assemblies, literature, no sending names to draft boards or recruiters. An immediate end to the draft.

8—Black and Latin departments controlled by Black and Latin students.

9—Community control of the schools and every other community facility. Students are part of the community.

10—POWER! Student control of curriculum, publications, assemblies, clubs, student government, dress, etc. The right to organize politically.

11—We support the fifteen points of the Black and Puerto Rican Citywide HS Council.

UNDERSTAND, ANALYZE, & EVALUATE

1. What might have inspired the students' demand for "due process"? What other evidence of an anti-authoritarian sentiment can you detect here?

2. How did the civil rights and the black power movements shape this Student Union? What are some of the rights movements covered in this chapter that were *not* reflected in this statement?

3. What role did the Vietnam War play for these students—what made this a possibly quite personal issue?

Source: *New York High School Free Press (an underground newspaper)*, No. 8, reprinted in John Birmingham, *Our Time Is Now: Notes from the High School Underground*, New York: Praeger, 1970, 178.

them from the University of Michigan) gathered in Michigan to form **Students for a Democratic Society (SDS)**, which became the most prominent organization of the New Left. Their declaration of beliefs, the Port Huron Statement, expressed their disillusionment with the society they had inherited and their determination to build a new politics. In the following years, SDS became the leading organization of student radicalism.

Since most members of the New Left were students, much of their radicalism centered for a time on issues related to the modern university. A 1964 dispute at the University of California at Berkeley over the rights of students to engage in political activities on campus—the Free Speech Movement—was the first major outburst of what was to be nearly a decade of campus turmoil. Berkeley's most prominent Free Speech leader, Mario Savio, seized national attention during a protest in December that landed him and about 800 others in jail. The twenty-two-year-old portrayed the Berkeley administration—and by extension, America's political establishment—as out of touch with student's aspirations and heartlessly treating them as "raw material" for corporate America. The only response was to rebel and break this "machine."

The antiwar movement greatly inflamed and expanded the challenge to the universities, and beginning in 1968, campus demonstrations, riots, and building seizures became almost commonplace. At Columbia University in New York, students seized the offices of the president and others and occupied them for several days until local police forcibly ejected them. Over the next several years, hardly any major university was immune to some level of disruption. Small groups of especially dogmatic radicals—among them the "Weathermen," an offshoot of SDS—were responsible for a few cases of arson and bombing that destroyed campus buildings and claimed several lives. Protests also erupted in high schools, where students voiced similar demands for greater control over the curriculum on the subjects taught to them and over disciplinary policy. (See "Consider the Source: Demands of the New York High School Student Union.")

Not many people accepted the radical political philosophy of the New Left. But many supported the position of SDS and other groups on particular issues, and above all on the Vietnam War. Between 1967 and 1969, student activists organized some of the largest political demonstrations in American history to protest American military involvement in the Southeast Asian conflict.

A related issue that helped fuel the antiwar movement was opposition to the military draft. The gradual abolition of many traditional deferments—for graduate students, teachers, husbands, fathers, and others—swelled the ranks of those faced with conscription (and thus likely to oppose it). Of the almost 2 million drafted, about 7,000 draft-age Americans simply refused induction, accepting what were occasionally long terms in jail as a result. Thousands of others draftees fled to Canada, Sweden, and elsewhere, where they were joined by deserters directly from the armed forces.

The Counterculture

Closely related to the New Left was a new youth culture openly scornful of the values and conventions of middle-class society. The most visible characteristic of the **counterculture**, as it became known, was a change in personal styles. As if to display their contempt for conventional standards, young Americans flaunted long hair, shabby or flamboyant clothing, and a rebellious disdain for traditional speech and decorum. Also important to the counterculture was a new, more permissive view of sex and drugs.

Like the New Left, the counterculture challenged modern American society, attacking what it claimed was its banality, its hollowness, its artificiality, and its isolation from nature. The most committed adherents of the counterculture—the hippies, who came to dominate the Haight-Ashbury neighborhood of San Francisco and other places, and the social dropouts, many of whom retreated to rural communes—rejected modern society altogether and attempted to find refuge in a simpler, more natural existence. But even those whose commitment to the counterculture was less intense shared the idea of personal fulfillment through rejecting the inhibitions and conventions of middle-class culture and giving fuller expression to personal instinct and desire.

The counterculture was only an exaggerated expression of impulses coursing through the larger society. Long hair and outlandish clothing became the badge not only of hippies and radicals but of an entire generation. The widespread use of marijuana, the freer attitudes toward sex, the iconoclastic (and often obscene) language—all spread far beyond the true devotees of the counterculture.

One of the most powerful elements of the new youth society was rock music. Its growing influence in the 1960s was a result in part of the phenomenal popularity of the Beatles, the English group whose first visit to the United States in 1964 created a remarkable sensation. For a time, most rock musicians—like most popular musicians before them—concentrated largely on uncontroversial romantic themes. By the late 1960s, however, rock had begun to reflect many of the new iconoclastic values of its time. The Beatles, for example, abandoned their once simple and seemingly innocent style for a new, experimental, even mystical approach that reflected the growing popular fascination with drugs and Eastern religions. Other groups, such as the Rolling Stones, turned even more openly to themes of anger, frustration, and rebellion. Many popular musicians used their music to express explicit political radicalism as well—especially some of the leading folk singers of the era, such as Bob Dylan and Joan Baez. Rock's driving rhythms, its undisguised sensuality, its often harsh and angry tone—all made it an appropriate vehicle for expressing the themes of the social and political unrest of the late 1960s.

A powerful symbol of the fusion of rock music and the counterculture was the massive music festival at **Woodstock**, New York, in the summer of 1969, where 400,000 people gathered on a farm for nearly a week. Despite heavy rain, mud, inadequate facilities, and impossible crowding, the attendees remained peaceful and harmonious. Champions of the counterculture spoke rhapsodically at the time of how Woodstock represented the birth of a new youth culture, the "Woodstock nation." Four months later, however, another large rock concert—at the

(©Don Hogan Charles/The New York Times Photo Archives/Redux)

WOODSTOCK In the summer of 1969, more than 400,000 people gathered for a music festival on a farm near Woodstock, New York. The gathering became a symbol of the youth movement of the sixties.

Altamont racetrack near San Francisco, featuring the Rolling Stones and attended by 300,000 people—exposed a darker side of the youth culture. Altamont became a brutal and violent event at which four people died, several accidentally or from drug overdoses but one because of injuries inflicted by members of a Hells Angels motorcycle gang, who were ostensibly serving as security guards at the concert and who brutally beat and stabbed a number of people.

THE MOBILIZATION OF MINORITIES

The growth of African American protest encouraged other minorities to assert themselves and demand redress of their grievances. For Indians, Hispanic Americans, gay men and lesbians, and others, the late 1960s and 1970s were a time of growing self-expression and political activism.

SEEDS OF NATIVE AMERICAN MILITANCY

Few minorities had deeper or more justifiable grievances against the prevailing culture than did American Indians—or Native Americans, as they began defiantly to call themselves in the 1960s. Indians were the least prosperous, least healthy, and least stable ethnic group in the nation. And while African Americans attracted the attention (for good or for ill) of many whites, Indians for years had remained largely ignored.

For much of the postwar era, federal tribal policies tried to incorporate Indians into mainstream American society whether Indians wanted to assimilate or not. Two laws passed in 1953 established the basis of this policy, which became known as "termination." Through termination, the federal government withdrew all official recognition of the tribes as legal entities; they were no longer administratively separate from state governments and were subject to the same local jurisdictions as non–Native American residents. At the same time, the government encouraged Indians to assimilate into the white world and worked to funnel Native Americans into cities, where, presumably, they would adapt themselves to the larger society and lose their cultural distinctiveness.

Despite some individual successes, the new policies were a disastrous failure on the whole. Indians themselves fought so bitterly against these policies that in 1958, the Eisenhower administration barred further terminations. In the meantime, the struggle against termination mobilized a new generation of Indian militants and breathed life into the principal Native American organization, the National Congress of American Indians, which had been created in 1944.

The Democratic administrations of the 1960s made no effort to revive termination. Instead, they made modest efforts to restore at least some degree of tribal autonomy such as funneling Office of Economic Opportunity money to tribal organizations through the Community Action programs. In the meantime, the tribes themselves began to fight for greater self-determination. The new militancy benefited from the rapid increase in the Indian population, which was growing much faster than that of the rest of the nation (nearly doubling between 1950 and 1970 to a total of about 800,000).

THE INDIAN CIVIL RIGHTS MOVEMENT

In 1961, more than 400 members from sixty-seven tribes gathered in Chicago and issued the Declaration of Indian Purpose, which stressed the "right to choose our own way of life" and the "responsibility of preserving our precious heritage." Another example of a growing

Indian self-consciousness, the National Indian Youth Council, created in the aftermath of the 1961 Chicago meeting, promoted the idea of Indian nationalism and intertribal unity. In 1968, a group of young, militant Indians established the **American Indian Movement (AIM)**, which drew support from urban areas and reservations alike.

The new activism produced results. In 1968, Congress passed the **Indian Civil Rights Act**. It guaranteed reservation Indians protections by the Bill of Rights, but also recognized the legitimacy of tribal laws within the reservations. In 1968, Indian fishermen, citing old treaty rights, clashed with Washington State officials on the Columbia River and in Puget Sound. The following year, members of several tribes occupied the abandoned federal prison on Alcatraz Island in San Francisco Bay, claiming the site "by right of discovery."

In response, the Nixon administration appointed Louis Bruce, a Mohawk-Sioux, as commissioner of Indian affairs in 1969; and in 1970, the president promised both increased tribal self-determination and an increase in federal aid. But the protests continued. In November 1972, nearly a thousand demonstrators, most of them Lakota Sioux, forcibly occupied the building of the Bureau of Indian Affairs in Washington, D.C., for six days. In February 1973, members of AIM seized the town of Wounded Knee, South Dakota, the site of the 1890 massacre of Sioux by federal troops. For two months, they occupied the town, demanding that the government honor its long-forgotten treaty obligations.

The Indian civil rights movement, like other civil rights movements of the same time, fell far short of winning full equality for Native Americans. But it helped the tribes win a series of new legal rights and protections that, together, gave them a stronger position than they had enjoyed at any previous time in the twentieth century.

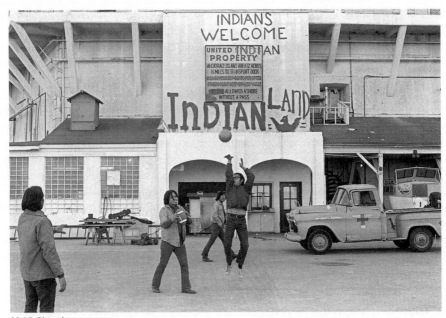

(©AP Photo)

THE OCCUPATION OF ALCATRAZ Alcatraz, an island in San Francisco Bay, once housed a large federal prison that by the late 1960s had been abandoned. In 1969, a group of Indian activists occupied the island and claimed it as Indian land—precipitating a long standoff with authorities.

Latino Activism

The fastest-growing minority group in the United States in the 1970s was Latinos, or Hispanic Americans. Large numbers of Mexicans had entered the country during World War II in response to the wartime labor shortage, and many had remained in the cities of the Southwest and the Pacific Coast. By 1960, Los Angeles had a bigger Mexican population than any place except Mexico City.

But the greatest expansion in the Latino population of the United States was yet to come. In 1960, the census reported slightly more than 3 million Latinos living in the United States. By 1970, that number had grown to 9 million and by 2000 to 35 million. By 2010, the number passed 50 million. Hispanics constituted more than a third of all legal immigrants to the United States after 1960.

Large numbers of Puerto Ricans (who were entitled to American citizenship by birth) migrated to eastern urban areas, particularly New York City, where they formed one of the poorest communities in the city. South Florida's substantial Cuban population began with a wave of middle-class refugees fleeing the Castro regime in the early 1960s. These first Cuban migrants quickly established themselves as a successful and highly assimilated part of Miami's middle class. In 1980, a second, much poorer wave of Cuban immigrants—the so-called Marielitos, named for the port from which they left Cuba—arrived in Florida when Castro temporarily relaxed exit restrictions. Later in the 1980s, large numbers of immigrants (both legal and illegal) began to arrive from Central and South America—from Guatemala, Nicaragua, El Salvador, Peru, and other countries.

(©Michael Rougier/The LIFE Images Collection/Getty Images)

KENNEDY AND CHÁVEZ César Chávez, leader of the United Farm Workers, endured a hunger strike in 1968 in the spirit of nonviolent protest against the treatment of field workers. Robert F. Kennedy, just beginning his campaign for the presidency, visited the union leader to show his support. At this point, Chávez had been fasting for several weeks.

Like African Americans and Indians, many Latinos responded to the highly charged climate of the 1960s by strengthening their ethnic identification and by organizing for political and economic power. Affluent Hispanics in Miami filled influential positions in the professions and local government; in the Southwest, Latino voters elected Mexican Americans to seats in Congress and to governorships. A Mexican American political organization, La Raza Unida, exercised influence in Southern California and elsewhere in the Southwest in the 1970s and beyond. One of the most visible efforts to organize Hispanics occurred in California, where an Arizona-born farmworker of Mexican descent, **César Chávez**, created an effective union of largely Mexican itinerant farmworkers: the United Farm Workers (UFW).

For most Latinos, however, the path to economic and political power was more difficult. Mexican Americans and others were slow to develop political influence in proportion to their numbers. In the meantime, Latinos formed one of the poorest segments of the U.S. population.

Gay Liberation

Another important liberation movement to emerge in the 1960s was the effort by gay men and lesbians to win political and economic rights and social acceptance. Homosexuality has been a generally unacknowledged reality throughout Western civilization. Nonheterosexual men and women were forced for generations to suppress their sexual orientation, to exercise it surreptitiously, or to live within isolated and often persecuted communities. But by the late 1960s, the liberating impulses that had affected other groups helped mobilize gay men and lesbians to fight for their own rights.

On June 27, 1969, police officers raided the Stonewall Inn, a gay nightclub in New York City's Greenwich Village, and began arresting patrons simply for frequenting the place. The raid was not unusual, but the response was. Gay onlookers taunted the police and then attacked them. Someone started a blaze in the Stonewall Inn itself, almost trapping the police inside. Rioting continued throughout Greenwich Village (the center of New York's gay community) through much of the night.

The **Stonewall Riot** marked the growth of the gay liberation movement—one of the most controversial challenges to traditional values and assumptions of its time. New organizations—among them the Gay Liberation Front, founded in New York in 1969—sprang up around the country. Public discussion and mainstream media coverage of homosexuality, long subject to an unofficial ban, quickly and dramatically increased. Gay activists had some success in challenging the long-standing assumption that homosexuality was aberrant behavior; many argued that no sexual preference was any more normal than another. One victory came when the American Psychiatric Association stopped categorizing homosexuality as a mental illness in 1974.

Most of all, however, the gay liberation movement transformed the outlook of many gay men and lesbians themselves. It helped them "come out," express their sexual orientation openly and unapologetically, and demand from society a recognition that gay relationships could be as significant and worthy of respect as heterosexual ones. By the early 1980s, the gay liberation movement had made remarkable strides. Even the ravages of the AIDS epidemic, which, in the beginning at least, affected the gay community more disastrously than any other group, failed to halt the growth of gay liberation. Indeed, it not only strengthened the gay community, but it also helped Americans understand and humanize those suffering, which in turn slowly led to increased acceptance.

WOMEN AND SOCIAL CHANGE

Women constitute over 50 percent of the U.S. population. But during the 1960s and 1970s, many women began to identify with minority groups as they renewed demands for a liberation of their own.

MODERN FEMINISM

The 1963 publication of **Betty Friedan**'s *The Feminine Mystique* is often cited as one of the first events of modern women's liberation. A writer for women's magazines in the 1950s, Friedan traveled around the country interviewing women who had graduated with her from Smith College in 1947. Most of these women were living out the dream that postwar American society had promised them: they were affluent wives and mothers living in comfortable suburbs. And yet many of them were deeply frustrated and unhappy, with no outlets for their intelligence, talent, and education. Friedan's book did not so much cause the revival of feminism as help give voice to a movement that was already stirring.

By the time *The Feminine Mystique* appeared, President Kennedy had already established the President's Commission on the Status of Women, which brought national attention to sexual discrimination. Also in 1963, the Kennedy administration helped win passage of the Equal Pay Act, which barred the pervasive practice of paying women less than men for the same work in some fields. A year later, Congress incorporated into the Civil Rights Act of 1964 an amendment—Title VII—that extended to women many of the same legal protections against discrimination that were being extended to African Americans and other minorities.

In 1966, Friedan joined with other feminists to create the **National Organization for Women (NOW)**, which was to become the nation's largest and most influential feminist organization. The founders had grown frustrated by the slow pace of change for women.

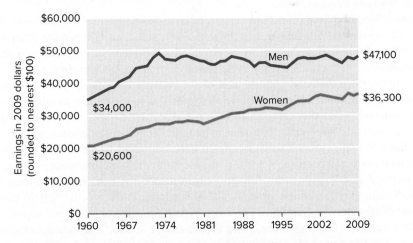

Note: People 15 years old and older beginning in 1980 and people 14 years old and older as of the following year for previous years. Before 1989, data are for civilian workers only.
(Source: U.S. Census Bureau, Current Population Survey, 1961 to 2009 Annual Social and Economic Supplements)

MEDIAN EARNINGS BY GENDER, 1960–2009   U.S. Census Bureau data comparing the median earnings of full-time, year-round workers show changes in the gender wage gap over time. • *If the Equal Pay Act barred employers from paying women less than men for the same work, what factors might account for the differences in median earnings of men and women?*

They intended to be an advocacy group for women of all colors that pressured the government to vigorously enforce the new antidiscrimination laws and expose negligent employers. NOW also intended to promote full equality for women by boosting the number of women in colleges and universities, professional schools, politics, and business. No longer should the majority of working women be found performing domestic labor.

By the late 1960s, younger, white, educated women began to push for new and more radical feminist demands. Many drew inspiration from the New Left and the counterculture and were involved in the civil rights movement or antiwar crusade. Some had found that even within those movements, they faced discrimination and exclusion because of their gender.

In its most radical form, this new feminism rejected the whole notion of marriage, family, and even heterosexual relationships (a vehicle, some women claimed, of male domination). While only a few women embraced such extremes, by the early 1970s large numbers were coming to see themselves as an exploited group united against oppression with a culture of their own. In cities and towns across the country, feminists opened women's bookstores, bars, and coffee shops and founded feminist newspapers and magazines. They also created women's health clinics, centers to assist victims of rape and abuse, day-care centers, and, particularly after 1973, abortion clinics.

Expanding Achievements

In 1971, the government extended its affirmative action guidelines to include women—linking sexism with racism as an officially acknowledged social problem. Women made rapid progress, in the meantime, in their efforts to move into the economic and political mainstream. The nation's all-male educational institutions began to crack open their doors to women. (Princeton and Yale did so in 1969, and many others soon did the same.) In 1972, Congress approved legislation (known as Title IX) requiring universities to support male and female athletic programs at equal levels.

Women were also becoming an important force in business and the professions. Nearly half of all married women held jobs by the mid-1970s, and almost 90 percent of all women with college degrees worked. The two-career family, in which both the husband and the wife maintained active professional lives, slowly became a widely accepted middle-class norm. (It had been common within much of the working class for decades.) There were also important symbolic changes, such as the refusal of many women to adopt their husbands' surnames when they married and the use of the term "Ms." in place of "Mrs." or "Miss" to signal the irrelevance of a woman's marital status in the professional world.

By the mid-1980s, women were serving in both houses of Congress, on the Supreme Court, in numerous federal cabinet positions, as governors of several states, and in many other political positions. In 1981, Ronald Reagan named the first female Supreme Court justice, Sandra Day O'Connor. In 1984, the Democratic Party was the first to choose a woman, Representative Geraldine Ferraro of New York, as its vice presidential candidate. In academia, women were expanding their presence in traditional scholarly fields; they were also creating new fields—women's and gender studies, which in the 1980s and 1990s were among the fastest-growing areas of American scholarship.

In 1972, Congress approved the Equal Rights Amendment (ERA) to the Constitution and sent it to the states. For a while, ratification seemed almost certain. By the late 1970s, however, the momentum behind the amendment had died because of a rising chorus of objections to it from people (including many antifeminist women) who feared that it would disrupt traditional social patterns. In 1982, the ten years allotted for ratification expired.

THE ABORTION ISSUE

A major goal of American feminists since the 1920s has been to win greater control of their own sexual and reproductive lives, and in the 1970s feminists made a number of strides toward that goal. They fostered awareness of and responses to the problems of rape, sexual abuse, and domestic abuse. They countered resistance to contraceptives and helped women gain greater access to birth-control information, pills, and devices. And they lead the "pro-choice" movement on the heated issue of abortion.

Abortion had once been legal in much of the United States, but by the beginning of the twentieth century, it was banned by statute in most of the country and remained so into the 1960s. Nonetheless, many abortions continued to be performed quietly, and often dangerously, out of sight of the law. Responding to pressure from women's rights groups, several states had abandoned restrictions on abortion by the end of the 1960s. The challenge to abortion laws reached the Supreme Court in 1973, with *Roe v. Wade*. The Court's decision, based on an implied but not specified "right to privacy" first protected by the Court only a few years earlier in *Griswold v. Connecticut*, invalidated all laws prohibiting abortion during the "first trimester"—the first three months of pregnancy. But even then, the issue remained far from settled.

ENVIRONMENTALISM IN A TURBULENT SOCIETY

Like feminism, environmentalism entered the 1960s with a long history but relatively little public support. Also like feminism, environmentalism profited from the turbulence of the era and emerged by the 1970s as a powerful force in American life. The rise of this new movement was in part a result of the intensifying level of environmental degradation in advanced industrial societies of the late twentieth century. It was a result, too, of the growth of ecology, a science that provided environmentalists with new and powerful arguments.

THE NEW SCIENCE OF ECOLOGY

Until the mid-twentieth century, most people who considered themselves environmentalists based their commitment on aesthetic or moral grounds. They wanted to preserve nature because it was too beautiful to despoil, because it was a mark of divinity on the world, or because it permitted humans a spiritual experience that would otherwise be unavailable to them. Other groups took their cue from the late President Theodore Roosevelt. These conservationists wanted to protect the environment for use in outdoor activities like camping and hunting. In the course of the twentieth century, however, scientists in much of the world began to create a new rationale for environmentalism. They called it ecology.

Ecology is the science of the interrelatedness of the natural world. It addresses such problems as air and water pollution, the destruction of forests, the extinction of species, and toxic wastes, which are not separate, isolated problems. All elements of the earth's environment are intimately and delicately linked. Damaging any one of those elements, therefore, risks damaging all the others.

Among the early contributions to popular knowledge of ecology was the work of writer and naturalist Aldo Leopold. During a career in forest management, Leopold sought to apply the new scientific findings on ecology to his interactions with the natural world.

And in 1949, he published a classic of environmental literature, *The Sand County Almanac*, in which he argued that humans had a responsibility to understand and maintain the balance of nature, that they should behave in the natural world according to a code that he called the "land ethic." By then, the science of ecology was spreading widely in the scientific community. Among the findings of ecologists were such now-common ideas as the "food chain," the "ecosystem," "biodiversity," and "endangered species." **Rachel Carson**'s sensational 1962 book, *Silent Spring*, which revealed the dangers of pesticides, was based solidly on the ideas of ecologists and did at least as much as Leopold's work to introduce those ideas to a larger public.

ENVIRONMENTAL ADVOCACY

Among the major environmental organizations were the Wilderness Society, the Sierra Club, the National Audubon Society, the Nature Conservancy, the National Wildlife Federation, and the National Parks and Conservation Association. All of these organizations predated the rise of modern ecological science, but the growth of environmental threats and scientific efforts to address them kept these organizations engaged like never before. They found allies among such groups as the American Civil Liberties Union, the League of Women Voters, the National Council of Churches, and even the AFL-CIO.

Out of these organizations emerged a new generation of environmental activists able to contribute to the legal and political battles of the movement. Scientists provided the necessary data. Lawyers fought battles with government agencies and in the courts.

Many other forces contributed to what became the environmental movement. Lady Bird Johnson, the first lady, helped raise public awareness of the landscape with her energetic "beautification" campaign in the mid-1960s—a campaign unconnected to any ecological concepts, but one that reflected a growing popular dismay at the despoiling of the landscape by rapid economic growth. Members of the counterculture contributed to environmental awareness with their romanticization of the natural world and their repudiation of the "technocracy."

But perhaps the greatest force behind environmentalism was the condition of the environment itself. By the 1960s, the damage to the natural world from postwar population and economic growth was becoming hard to ignore. Water pollution—which had been a problem in some areas of the country for many decades—was becoming so widespread that almost every major city was dealing with the unpleasant sight and odor, as well as the health risks, of polluted rivers and lakes. In Cleveland, Ohio, for example, the Cuyahoga River actually burst into flame from time to time from the petroleum waste being dumped into it; the city declared the river an official fire hazard.

Perhaps more alarming was the growing awareness that the air itself was becoming unhealthy, that toxic fumes from factories, power plants, and, most of all, automobiles were poisoning the atmosphere. Weather forecasts and official atmospheric information began to refer to "smog" levels—using a relatively new word formed from a combination of "smoke" and "fog," which became an almost perpetual fact of daily life in such cities as Los Angeles and Denver. In 1969, a damaged oil-well platform off Santa Barbara, California, spewed hundreds of thousands of gallons of crude oil into the ocean just off the popular beaches of this affluent city. This oil spill had a tremendous impact on the environmental consciousness of millions of Americans. Another, much larger spill—indeed, the largest in American history—occurred off the coast of Alaska in 1989 when the giant tanker *Exxon Valdez* hit a reef in Prince William Sound. The damage it caused to the nearby shoreline and wildlife also greatly increased environmental consciousness. In April 2010, the Deepwater Horizon oil rig exploded forty-one miles off the Louisiana coast, killing eleven. Over the next three months, chemical dispersants used to control the spill and 5 million gallons of crude oil spread into the Gulf of Mexico, destroying sea life and damaging the coastline. The long-term effects are still unknown.

Environmentalists brought to public attention many long-term dangers and helped create a broad and powerful movement.

EARTH DAY AND BEYOND

On April 22, 1970, people all over the United States participated in the first **Earth Day**. Originally proposed by Wisconsin senator Gaylord Nelson as a series of teach-ins on college campuses, Earth Day gradually took on a much larger life. Carefully managed by people who wanted to avoid associations with the radical left, it had a less threatening quality than antiwar demonstrations and civil rights rallies seemed to have. According to some estimates, over 20 million Americans participated in Earth Day observances, making Earth Day, possibly, the largest single demonstration in the nation's history.

The cautious, centrist character of Earth Day and related efforts to popularize environmentalism helped create a movement that was for a time less divisive than other, more controversial causes. Gradually, environmentalism became more than simply a series of demonstrations and protests. It became part of the consciousness of the vast majority of Americans—absorbed into popular culture, built into primary and secondary education, and endorsed by almost all politicians (even if many of them actually opposed some environmental goals).

It also became part of the fabric of public policy. In 1970, Congress passed and President Nixon signed the National Environmental Protection Act, which created a new agency—the Environmental Protection Agency—to enforce antipollution standards on businesses and consumers. The Clean Air Act, also passed in 1970, and the Clean Water Act, passed in 1972, became additional tools in the government's arsenal of weapons against environmental degradation.

Different administrations displayed varying levels of support for environmental goals, and new environmental problems continued to emerge even as older ones sometimes found solutions. Environmentalism became simultaneously a movement, a set of public policies, and a broad national ideal—and it was the combination of all those aspects that made it a powerful force in American life.

NIXON, KISSINGER, AND THE VIETNAM WAR

Richard Nixon assumed office in 1969 committed not only to restoring stability at home but also to creating a new and stabler order in the world. Central to his hopes for international stability was a resolution of the stalemate in Vietnam. Yet the new president felt no freer than his predecessor to abandon the American commitment there.

VIETNAMIZATION

Despite Nixon's own deep interest in international affairs, he brought with him into government a man who at times seemed to overshadow the president himself in the conduct of diplomacy: Henry Kissinger, a Harvard professor whom Nixon appointed as his special assistant for national security affairs. Kissinger quickly established dominance over

Secretary of State William Rogers and Secretary of Defense Melvin Laird. Together, Nixon and Kissinger set out to find an acceptable solution to the stalemate in Vietnam.

The new Vietnam policy moved along several fronts. One was the move to "Vietnamize" the conflict—that is, train and equip the South Vietnamese military to assume the burden of combat in place of American forces. In the fall of 1969, Nixon announced the withdrawal of 60,000 American ground troops from Vietnam. By the fall of 1972, relatively few American soldiers remained in Indochina. From a peak of more than 540,000 in 1969, the number had dwindled to about 60,000.

Vietnamization produced some immediate short-term benefits. As the number of Americans called up for the draft decreased, opposition to the war quieted for a time. The shift in combat responsibility to the South Vietnamese military, however, did nothing to break the stalemate in the negotiations with the North Vietnamese in Paris. The new administration decided that new military pressures would be necessary to do that.

ESCALATION

By the end of 1969, Nixon and Kissinger had decided that the most effective way to tip the military balance in South Vietnam's favor was to destroy bases in Cambodia and Laos that the U.S. military believed were the launching points for many communist attacks. (Laos, Cambodia, and Vietnam are neighboring states in the peninsula of Indochina.) Very early in his presidency, Nixon secretly ordered the air force to bomb these bases. On April 30, 1970, the president announced that he was sending U.S. ground troops across the border into Cambodia to destroy them.

Literally overnight, the Cambodian invasion restored the dwindling antiwar movement to life. The first days of May saw widespread and vocal antiwar demonstrations. A mood of crisis was already mounting when, on May 4, four college students were killed and nine injured after members of the National Guard opened fire on antiwar demonstrators at Kent State University in Ohio. Ten days later, police killed two African American students at Jackson State University in Mississippi during a demonstration there.

The clamor against the war spread into the government and the press. Congress angrily repealed the Gulf of Tonkin Resolution in December. Then, in June 1971, first the *New York Times* and later other newspapers began publishing excerpts from a secret study of the war prepared by the Defense Department during the Johnson administration. The so-called Pentagon Papers were leaked to the press by former Defense official Daniel Ellsberg. They provided evidence the government had been dishonest, both in reporting the military progress of the war and in explaining its own motives for American involvement. The administration went to court to suppress the documents, but the Supreme Court ruled that the press had the right to publish them.

Morale and discipline among American troops in Vietnam were rapidly deteriorating in the waning years of the war. After the 1968 massacre near My Lai came to light, Lieutenant William Calley was tried and convicted in 1971 of the murder of unarmed South Vietnamese civilians (he was soon pardoned and released). The case attracted wide public attention to the dehumanizing impact of the war on Americans and the far more tragic consequences of that dehumanization for the Vietnamese. Somewhat less publicized though still visible were other, more widespread problems among American troops in Vietnam: desertion, drug addiction, racism, refusal to obey orders, even the killing of unpopular officers by enlisted men.

By 1971, polls indicated that nearly two-thirds of Americans supported withdrawal from Vietnam. President Nixon, however, believed that a defeat in Vietnam would cause unacceptable damage to the nation's credibility. The FBI, the CIA, the White House itself, and other federal agencies increased their efforts to discredit and harass antiwar and radical groups, often through illegal means.

In Indochina, meanwhile, the fighting raged on. American bombing in Vietnam and Cambodia increased. In March 1972, the North Vietnamese mounted their biggest offensive since 1968 (the so-called Easter offensive). American and South Vietnamese forces managed to halt the communist advance, but it was clear that without American support, the South Vietnamese would not have succeeded. At the same time, Nixon ordered American planes to bomb targets near Hanoi, the capital of North Vietnam, and Haiphong, its principal port, and called for the mining of seven North Vietnamese harbors.

THE END OF THE WAR

As the 1972 presidential election approached, the administration stepped up its effort to produce a breakthrough in negotiations with the North Vietnamese. In April, the president dropped his longtime insistence on the removal of North Vietnamese troops from the south before any American withdrawal. Meanwhile, Henry Kissinger met privately in Paris with the North Vietnamese foreign secretary, Le Duc Tho, to work out terms for a cease-fire. On October 26, only days before the presidential election, Kissinger announced that "peace is at hand."

Several weeks later (after the election), negotiations broke down once again. Although both the American and North Vietnamese governments were ready to accept the Kissinger–Tho plan for a cease-fire, President Nguyen Van Thieu of South Vietnam balked, still insisting on a full withdrawal of North Vietnamese forces from the south. Kissinger tried to win additional concessions from the communists to meet Thieu's objections, but on December 16 talks broke off.

The next day, December 17, American B-52s began the heaviest and most destructive air raids of the entire war on Hanoi, Haiphong, and other North Vietnamese targets. Civilian casualties were high, and fifteen American B-52s were shot down by the North Vietnamese. In the entire war to that point, the United States had lost only one of the giant bombers. On December 30, Nixon terminated the "Christmas bombing." The United States and the North Vietnamese returned to the conference table, and on January 27, 1973, they signed the Paris Peace Accord, an "agreement on ending the war and restoring peace in Vietnam." Nixon claimed that the Christmas bombing had forced the North Vietnamese to relent and allowed Americans to secure "peace with honor." At least equally important, however, was the enormous American pressure on Thieu to accept the cease-fire.

The terms of the Paris Peace Accord were little different from those Kissinger and Thieu had accepted in principle a few months before. Nor were they much different from the peace plan Johnson had proposed in 1968. The Paris Accord specified that there would be an immediate cease-fire. The Thieu regime would survive in South Vietnam, but North Vietnamese forces in the south would not have to withdraw. The North Vietnamese would release several hundred American prisoners of war. An undefined committee would work out a permanent settlement.

DEFEAT IN INDOCHINA

American forces were hardly out of Indochina before the Paris accords began to collapse. In March 1975, the North Vietnamese launched a full-scale offensive against the now greatly weakened forces of South Vietnam. Thieu appealed to Washington for assistance. The president (now Gerald Ford) appealed to Congress for additional funding; Congress refused.

(©AP Photo)

THE EVACUATION OF SAIGON A harried U.S. official struggles to keep panicking Vietnamese from boarding an already overpacked helicopter on the roof of the U.S. embassy in Saigon. The hurried evacuation of Americans took place only hours before the arrival of North Vietnamese troops, signaling the final defeat of South Vietnam.

Late in April 1975, communist forces marched into Saigon, shortly after officials of the Thieu regime and the staff of the American embassy had fled the country in humiliating disarray. The communist forces quickly occupied the capital, renamed it Ho Chi Minh City, and began the process of reuniting Vietnam under the government based in Hanoi. At about the same time, the Lon Nol regime in Cambodia fell to the murderous forces of the Khmer Rouge—whose brutal policies led to the death of more than a third of the country's people over the next several years.

Such were the dismal results of three decades of support for an anticommunist South Vietnam and almost ten years of direct American military involvement. More than 1.2 million Vietnamese soldiers had died in combat, along with countless civilians throughout the region. A beautiful land had been ravaged, its agrarian economy left in ruins. Until an economic revival began in the early 1990s, Vietnam remained one of the poorest nations in the world. The United States had paid a heavy price as well. The war had cost the nation almost $150 billion in direct costs and much more indirectly. It had resulted in the deaths of over 58,000 young Americans and the injury of 300,000 more. And the nation had suffered a blow to its confidence and self-esteem from which it did not soon recover.

NIXON, KISSINGER, AND THE WORLD

The continuing war in Vietnam provided an unhappy backdrop to what Nixon considered his larger mission in world affairs: the construction of a new international order. The president had become convinced that the old assumptions of a "bipolar" world—in which the United States and the Soviet Union were the only real great powers—were now obsolete. America must adapt to the new "multipolar" international structure, in which China, Japan, Western Europe, and the Middle East were becoming major, independent forces. Nixon had a considerable advantage over many other politicians in changing the assumptions behind American foreign policy. His long anticommunist record gave him credibility among many conservatives for his effort to transform American relations with communist China and the Soviet Union.

THE CHINA INITIATIVE AND SOVIET–AMERICAN DÉTENTE

For more than twenty years, ever since the fall of Chiang Kai-shek in 1949, the United States had treated China, the most populous nation on earth, as if it did not exist. Instead, America recognized the regime-in-exile on the small island of Taiwan as the legitimate government of China. Nixon and Kissinger wanted to forge a new relationship with the Chinese communists, in large part to strengthen them as a counterbalance to the Soviet Union. The Chinese, for their part, were eager to end China's own isolation from the international arena.

In July 1971, Nixon sent Henry Kissinger on a secret mission to Beijing. When Kissinger returned, the president made the startling announcement that he would visit China himself within the next few months. That fall, with American approval, the United Nations admitted

(©Universal Images Group/Getty Images)

NIXON IN CHINA President Nixon's 1972 visit to China was an important step in normalizing relations between the United States and the People's Republic of China. Here, Nixon toasts the developing relationship with Prime Minister Zhou Enlai.

THE END OF COLONIALISM

On July 4, 1946, less than a year after the close of World War II, a ceremony in Manila marked what Senator Millard Tydings of Maryland called "one of the most unprecedented, most idealistic, and most far-reaching events in all recorded history." On that day, the United States voluntarily ended nearly five decades of colonial control of the Philippines, which it had acquired as part of the spoils from the 1898 Spanish-American War. Philippine independence was only a small part of a dramatic change in the political structure of the world. The close of World War II marked not only the defeat of fascism in Germany, Italy, and Japan, but also the beginning of the end of the formal system of imperialism that European powers had maintained for centuries. The repudiation of colonialism was driven in part by the heightened belief in democracy and self-determination that the war helped strengthen through much of the world. It was also driven by the weakness of the European powers after World War II and their inability to sustain control over their increasingly restive colonies. Like most great geopolitical changes, the drive for colonial independence was turbulent and often violent.

The United States had been a latecomer to the imperialist system. But even its peaceful divestiture of the Philippines reflected the challenges many imperial powers and postcolonial nations faced in renegotiating colonial relationships. America was not quite as ready to cede military presence and economic influence in the region as it was to give up political responsibility over the islands. Philippine independence came with important caveats: that the United States maintained control of Fillipino military bases and that required (through the Bell Trade Act, passed by Congress in 1946) that the Philippines not engage in any direct economic competition with the United States and that it revise its constitution to allow American interests free and unfettered access to the nation's natural resources. Many Filipinos argue that their nation did not achieve full independence until 1991, when the Philippine Senate refused to ratify a treaty that would have extended the American lease on the Subic Bay naval base (once the largest U.S. Navy installation in the Pacific). A year later, the United States closed the base and left, marking the first time in 400 years that the Philippines (once a Spanish possession) was not home to a foreign military power.

Britain's imperial holdings were the vastest in the world, and the existence of the British Empire was deeply embedded in the country's economic life and national self-image. But it, too, withdrew from most of its colonies in the decades after World War II—beginning in 1947 with its largest and most important colony, India. The British Raj—as the colonial government was known—withdrew from South Asia in response to a growing independence movement on the subcontinent. As often happened as colonial rule ended, suppressed conflicts in the native population quickly emerged—in the case of India, between Hindus and Muslims. The price of Indian independence, therefore, was the partition of the country into India and Pakistan (and, several decades later, Bangladesh).

A year later, the British gave up their World War I mandate of Palestine (ceding the territory to the United Nations and allowing for the creation of Israel) as well as many of its holdings in Southeast Asia, including Burma and Ceylon. Malaya followed in 1957 and Singapore in 1965. In 1982, Britain passed the Canada Act, effectively severing Canada from the United Kingdom and culminating a move toward full Canadian self-government that had begun several decades earlier. In 1997, England returned one of its last important overseas territories, Hong Kong, to the control of China, bringing nearly to an end the era of the British Empire.

The dissolution of the British Empire did not always proceed smoothly. The Suez Crisis of 1956, in which the combined efforts of Britain, France, and Israel failed to halt Egypt's nationalization of the Suez Canal, dealt a decisive blow to Britain's status as a major power in the Middle East. In 1982, Britain's dispute over the tiny Falkland Islands erupted into war with Argentina, which claimed the islands (just off its coast) as its own. After the deaths of 258 British and 649 Argentine soldiers, Britain maintained its control of the Falklands, although Argentina continues to assert its right to the islands.

Despite these controversies, the dissolution of the British Empire proceeded relatively smoothly compared to the experience of the French, who became engaged in several major conflicts after 1945. In late 1946, Vietnamese nationalists rose up against the French colonial government that had recently reoccupied the region after the defeat of Japan in World War II. France's effort to keep Vietnam culminated in its defeat at Dien Bien Phu in 1954 and its subsequent withdrawal from Indochina. France also became embroiled in, and tried to suppress by force, a number of other violent colonial uprisings—in Madagascar, Cameroon, and, most notably, Algeria. The Algerian War (1954–1962) was a particularly bloody and costly conflict, taking on aspects of a civil war and involving guerrilla warfare, torture, acts of terrorism,

and, eventually, the collapse of the French government in 1958. Algeria ultimately won its independence.

The end of the colonial system had a great impact on Africa. European powers had carved up almost all of sub-Saharan Africa in the nineteenth century. In the decades after World War II, almost all the African colonies won their independence, even if not always easily: Morocco (1956), Ghana (1957), the Congo (1960), Nigeria (1960), Uganda (1962), Kenya (1963), and Gambia (1965). African nationalism was troubled for decades by political instability and, in some countries, extreme poverty. The Caribbean also saw many new independent nations born in the postwar era, including Jamaica (1961), Trinidad and Tobago (1962), Barbados (1966), and Guyana (1966).

The most recent epicenter of independence movements has been in the lands that used to comprise the Soviet Union. A long and costly war in Afghanistan began in the 1970s as the Soviet Union struggled to retain control of the nation in the face of powerful local insurgencies. The war was one of the principal factors in the unraveling of the Soviet Empire that began in 1991. Many of the former Soviet republics—which considered themselves colonies of Russia—soon separated from Russia and became independent nations. These included Estonia, Latvia, and Lithuania, the formerly independent Baltic nations seized by the Soviet Union during World War II. Other former Soviet possessions that became independent nations included Ukraine, Moldova, Armenia, Georgia, Azerbaijan, Kazakhstan, Uzbekistan, Tajikistan, and Turkmenistan. Russia continues to deal with the problems of empire. A vicious conflict with Chechnya, an Islamic area of Russia insisting on independence, created terror and instability for years.

The end of colonialism was one of the most epochal global changes of the last several centuries—a change that brought to an end a system that was based on the assumption of European (and American) superiority over other peoples. Yet although formal colonialism came to an end in the post–World War II era, other aspects of imperialism did not. Many former colonies, which comprise much of the nonindustrialized world, still struggle with the indirect exercise of economic power that wealthy nations continue to exert over them. •

UNDERSTAND, ANALYZE, & EVALUATE

1. How did the experience of World War II contribute to the end of colonialism?
2. What have been the effects of colonialism—and the end of colonialism—on Africa? Why have the effects been so pronounced on that continent, more so than in other areas of the world?

the communist government of China and expelled the representatives of the Taiwan regime. Finally, in February 1972, Nixon paid a formal visit to China. It erased much of the deep animosity between the United States and the Chinese communists. Nixon did not yet formally recognize the communist regime, but in 1972 the United States and China began low-level diplomatic relations.

The initiatives in China coincided with an effort by the Nixon administration to improve relations with the Soviet Union, an initiative known by the French word **détente**, which favored diplomacy over militarism though with the same end goals of containing communism and ensuring American security. In 1971, American and Soviet diplomats produced the first Strategic Arms Limitation Treaty (SALT I), which froze the arsenals of some nuclear missiles on both sides at present levels. In May of that year, the president traveled to Moscow to sign the agreement. The next year, the Soviet premier, Leonid Brezhnev, visited Washington.

Dealing with the "Third World"

The policies of rapprochement with communist China and détente with the Soviet Union reflected Nixon's and Kissinger's belief in the importance of stable relationships among the great powers. But, as America's experience in Vietnam already illustrated, the vast areas of the globe unaligned with either superpower—what became known in the 1950s as the Third World—remained volatile and dangerous sites of international tension. In many cases such tension arose *because* of the Cold War proxy battles carried out in those regions. Since the end of World War I, the United States and the European powers had lost or withdrawn control over former colonies. The result was a number of newly independent but economically fragile and politically unstable nations around the world. (See "America in the World: The End of Colonialism.")

The Nixon-Kissinger policy toward the Third World tried to maintain the status quo without involving the United States too deeply in local disputes. In 1969 and 1970, the president described what became known as the **Nixon Doctrine**, by which the United States would "participate in the defense and development of allies and friends" but would leave the "basic responsibility" for the future of those "friends" to the nations themselves. In practice, the Nixon Doctrine meant a declining American interest in contributing to Third World development. There was also a growing contempt for the United Nations, where underdeveloped nations were gaining influence through their sheer numbers. And there was increasing American support for authoritarian regimes attempting to withstand radical challenges from within.

In 1970, for example, the CIA poured substantial funds into Chile to help support the government against a communist challenge. When the Marxist candidate for president, Salvador Allende, came to power through an open election despite American efforts, the United States began funneling more money to opposition forces in Chile to help destabilize the new government. In 1973, a military junta seized power from Allende, who was subsequently murdered. The United States developed a friendly relationship with the new, repressive military government of General Augusto Pinochet.

In the Middle East, conditions grew more volatile in the aftermath of a 1967 war in which Israel had occupied substantial new territories, dislodging many Palestinian Arabs from their homes. The refugees were a source of considerable instability in Jordan, Lebanon, and the other surrounding countries into which they moved. In October 1973, on the Jewish high holy day of Yom Kippur, Egyptian and Syrian forces attacked Israel. For ten days, the Israelis struggled to recover from the surprise attack. Finally, they launched an effective counteroffensive against Egyptian forces in the Sinai. At that point, the United States intervened, supporting Israel but placing heavy pressure on that country to accept a cease-fire rather than press its advantage.

The Yom Kippur War demonstrated the growing dependence of the United States and its allies on Arab oil. A brief but painful embargo in 1973–1974 by the Arab members of the Organization of the Petroleum Exporting Companies (OPEC) against the United States and other allies that supported Israel provided an ominous warning of the costs of dependence on foreign oil. It also prompted Congress to pass fuel economy standards, requiring automakers to raise average mileage from 13.5 miles per gallon to 27. (The standard has since been raised to 54.5 mpg by 2025.)

POLITICS AND ECONOMICS IN THE NIXON YEARS

Nixon ran for president in 1968, promising a return to more conservative social and economic policies and a restoration of law and order. Once he was in office, however, his domestic policies ironically continued and even expanded some liberal initiatives of the previous two administrations.

DOMESTIC INITIATIVES

Many of Nixon's domestic policies were a response to what he believed to be the demands of his constituency—the "**silent majority**" of conservative, mostly middle-class people who, he believed, wanted to reduce federal interference in local affairs. He tried, unsuccessfully, to persuade Congress to pass legislation prohibiting school desegregation through the use of forced busing. He was, however, able to protect school districts that ignored court orders to integrate by forbidding the Department of Health, Education, and Welfare (now called the Department of Health and Human Services) from cutting their federal funding. At the same time, he began to reduce or dismantle many of the social programs of the Great Society and the New Frontier. In 1973, he abolished the Office of Economic Opportunity— a centerpiece of the antipoverty program of the Johnson years.

Yet Nixon's domestic policies had progressive and creative elements as well. He signed legislation creating the Environmental Protection Agency and establishing the most stringent environmental regulations in the nation's history. He ordered the first affirmative action program for workers on federally funded projects. One of the administration's boldest efforts was an attempt to overhaul the nation's welfare system. Nixon proposed replacing the existing system with what he called the Family Assistance Plan (FAP). It would, in effect, have created a guaranteed annual income for all Americans: $1,600 in federal grants, which could be supplemented by outside earnings up to $4,000. The FAP won approval in the House in 1970, but the bill failed in the Senate. Nixon also became the first president since Truman to propose a plan for national health insurance, which likewise made no progress in Congress.

FROM THE WARREN COURT TO THE NIXON COURT

Of all the liberal institutions that aroused the enmity of the conservative silent majority in the 1950s and 1960s, none evoked more anger and bitterness than the Supreme Court under Chief Justice Earl Warren. The Warren Court's rulings on racial matters disrupted traditional social patterns in both the North and the South. Its defense of civil liberties directly contributed to the increase in crime, disorder, and moral decay in the eyes of many Americans. In *Roth v. United States* (1957), the Court sharply limited the authority of local governments to curb pornography. In *Engel v. Vitale* (1962), the Court ruled that prayers in public schools were unconstitutional, sparking outrage among religious fundamentalists and others. In a series of other decisions, the Court greatly strengthened the civil rights of criminal defendants and, many Americans believed, greatly weakened the power of law enforcement officials to do their jobs. For example, in *Gideon v. Wainwright* (1963), the Court ruled that every felony defendant was entitled to a lawyer, regardless of his or her ability to pay. In *Escobedo v. Illinois* (1964), it ruled that a defendant must be allowed access to a lawyer before questioning by police. In *Miranda v. Arizona* (1966), the Court confirmed the obligation of authorities to inform a criminal suspect that he or she has the right to remain silent and to be represented by an attorney. By 1968, the Warren Court had become the scorn of Americans who felt the United States had shifted too far toward helping poor, dispossessed, and criminal individuals at the expense of the middle class.

Their complaints caught the ear of the president and he promised to give the Court a more conservative cast. When Chief Justice Earl Warren retired early in 1969, Nixon swiftly replaced him with a federal appeals court judge of conservative leanings, Warren Burger. But after watching the Senate reject his nominees for the next vacancy on the court on the basis of either political extremism or an unimpressive legal career, Nixon carefully selected more moderate candidates with impeccable resumes: Harry Blackmun, an esteemed jurist from Minnesota; Lewis F. Powell Jr., a respected lawyer from Virginia; and William Rehnquist, a member of the Nixon Justice Department.

The new Court, however, fell far short of what the president and many conservatives had expected. Rather than retreating from its commitment to social reform or reversing earlier decisions, the Court continued to expand protections for individual liberties. In *Swann v. Charlotte-Mecklenburg Board of Education* (1971), it ruled in favor of forced busing to achieve racial balance in schools. Despite intense and occasionally violent opposition by local communities as diverse as Boston and Louisville, the judicial commitment to integration was not overturned. In *Furman v. Georgia* (1972), the Court ruled that the death penalty had been imposed in a way that was illegal. It forced states to retool their capital punishment laws to ensure that the death penalty was not imposed arbitrarily and instead was determined in a fair and nondiscriminatory manner. In *Roe v. Wade* (1973), one of the most controversial decisions in the Court's modern history, it struck down laws forbidding abortions in the first three months of pregnancy and ruled that the right to an abortion was constitutionally protected.

In other decisions, however, the Burger Court did demonstrate a more conservative temperament than the Warren Court had shown. Although the justices approved busing as a tool for achieving integration, they rejected, in *Milliken v. Bradley* (1974), a plan to transfer students across municipal lines (in this case, between Detroit and its suburbs) to achieve racial balance. While the Court upheld the principle of affirmative action in its celebrated 1978 decision, *Bakke v. Board of Regents of California*, it established restrictive new guidelines for such programs in the future. In *Stone v. Powell* (1976), the Court agreed to certain limits on the right of a defendant to appeal a state conviction to the federal judiciary.

THE 1972 LANDSLIDE

Nixon entered the presidential race in 1972 with substantial strength. His energetic reelection committee had collected enormous sums of money. The president himself used the powers of incumbency to strengthen his political standing among conservatives by challenging some civil rights legislation. And Nixon's foreign policy successes, especially his trip to China, increased his stature in the eyes of the nation.

The Republican Nixon was most fortunate in 1972, however, in his Democratic opposition. George Wallace, partly at Nixon's urging, entered the Democratic primaries and helped divide the party. Now renouncing his past support of segregation but voicing opposition to forced busing as a means to desegregate public schools, Wallace began to woo Democratic voters and set up a battle for the nomination against the party's more liberal wing. But after being shot by a would-be assassin during a campaign rally in a Maryland shopping mall, Wallace was left paralyzed from the waist down and withdrew from the campaign. His departure left the conservative leaders of the Democratic Party in disarray and paved the way for the most liberal factions to establish their candidate, Senator George S. McGovern of South Dakota, as the front-runner for the nomination. An outspoken critic of the Vietnam War and a forceful advocate of liberal positions on many social and economic issues, McGovern profited greatly from party reforms (which he himself had helped draft) that gave increased influence to women, minorities, and young people in the selection of the Democratic ticket. In the process, the McGovern campaign came to be tarred with aspects of the turbulent 1960s that many middle-class Americans were eager to reject.

On election day, Nixon won reelection by one of the largest margins in history: 60.7 percent of the popular vote to McGovern's 37.5 percent and an electoral margin of 520 to 17. The Democratic candidate carried only Massachusetts and the District of Columbia. But serious problems, some beyond the president's control and others of his own making, lurked in the wings.

THE TROUBLED ECONOMY

Although it was a political scandal that would ultimately destroy the Nixon presidency, the most important issue of the early 1970s was the beginning of a long-term transformation of the American economy. For three decades, that economy had been the envy of the world.

In fact, however, America's prosperity rested in part on several artificial conditions that were rapidly disappearing by the late 1960s.

The most immediate change was the end of the nation's easy access to cheap raw materials, a change that became a major cause of the serious inflation that plagued the economy through much of the 1970s. For many years, OPEC had operated as an informal bargaining unit for the sale of oil by Third World nations but had seldom managed to exercise any real strength. But in the early 1970s, OPEC began to use its oil both as an economic tool and as a political weapon. In 1973, in the midst of the Yom Kippur War, Arab members of OPEC announced that they would no longer ship petroleum to nations supporting Israel—that is, to the United States and its allies in Western Europe. At about the same time, the OPEC nations agreed to raise their prices 500 percent (from $3 to $15 a barrel). These twin shocks produced momentary economic chaos in the West. The United States suffered its first fuel shortage since World War II. And although the crisis eased a few months later, the price of energy continued to rise.

Another, longer-term change in the American economy was the transformation of the nation's manufacturing sector. Ever since World War II, American industry had enjoyed relatively little competition from the rest of the world. By the end of the 1960s, however, both Western Europe and Japan had recovered from the damage their manufacturing sectors had absorbed during World War II. By the early 1970s, they were providing stiff competition to American firms in the sale of automobiles, steel, and many other products, both in world markets and within the United States. Some American corporations failed. Others restructured themselves to become more competitive again in world markets but in the process closed many older plants and eliminated hundreds of thousands of once-lucrative manufacturing jobs. The high-wage, high-employment industrial economy that had been a central fact of American life since the 1940s was gradually disappearing.

The Nixon Response

Nixon's initial answer to these mounting economic problems was a conventional anti-inflationary one. He reduced federal spending and raised taxes, producing a modest budget surplus in 1969. But when those policies proved difficult to sustain, Nixon turned increasingly to control of the currency. Placing conservative economists at the head of the Federal Reserve Board, he ensured sharply higher interest rates and a contraction of the money supply. Even so, the cost of living rose a cumulative 15 percent during Nixon's first two and a half years in office. Economic growth, in the meantime, declined.

In the summer of 1971, Nixon imposed a ninety-day freeze on all wages and prices at their existing levels. Then, in November, he launched the second phase of his economic plan: mandatory guidelines for some wage and price increases, to be administered by a federal agency. Inflation subsided temporarily, but the recession continued. Fearful that the recession would be more damaging than inflation in an election year, the administration reversed itself late in 1971: interest rates were allowed to drop sharply, and government spending increased—producing the largest budget deficit since World War II. The new tactics helped revive the economy in the short term, but inflation rose substantially. In 1973, prices rose 9 percent; in 1974, after the Arab oil embargo and the OPEC price increases, they rose 12 percent—the highest rate since shortly after World War II. The new energy crisis, in the meantime, was quickly becoming a national preoccupation. But while Nixon talked often about the need to achieve "energy independence," he offered few concrete proposals.

THE WATERGATE CRISIS

Although economic problems greatly concerned the American people in the 1970s, another stunning development preoccupied the nation beginning early in 1973: the fall of Richard Nixon. Scholars wrangle over the exact origins and legacies of Nixon's fall from grace, but they widely agree that the president's demise was in part a result of the turbulent climate of the early 1970s. It was also a result of his own reckless personality, disregard for the constitutional limits placed on his power, and overpowering fear that he and the nation faced grave dangers from radicals and dissidents openly challenging his policies.

THE SCANDALS

Early on the morning of June 17, 1972, police arrested five men who had broken into the headquarters of the Democratic National Committee in the **Watergate** office building in Washington, D.C. Two others were seized a short time later and charged with supervising the break-in. When reporters for the *Washington Post* began researching the backgrounds of the culprits, they discovered that among those involved in the burglary were former employees of the Committee for the Re-Election of the President (CRP). One of them had worked in the White House itself. They had, moreover, been paid for the break-in from a secret fund of Nixon's reelection committee—a fund controlled by members of the White House staff, among others.

Public interest in the disclosures grew slowly in the last months of 1972. Early in 1973, however, the Watergate burglars went on trial; and under prodding from federal judge John J. Sirica, one of the defendants, James W. McCord, agreed to cooperate both with the grand jury and with a special Senate investigating committee recently established under Senator Sam J. Ervin of North Carolina. McCord's testimony opened a floodgate of confessions, and for months a parade of White House and campaign officials exposed one illegality after another. Foremost among them was a member of the inner circle of the White House, John Dean, counsel to the president, who had warned Nixon that the Watergate affair was a "cancer on the presidency" and who later leveled allegations against Nixon himself.

Two different sets of scandals emerged from the investigations. One was a general pattern of abuses of power involving both the White House and the Nixon campaign committee, which included, but was not limited to, the Watergate break-in. The other scandal, and the one that became the major focus of public attention for nearly two years, was the way in which the administration tried to manage the investigations of the Watergate break-in and other abuses—a pattern of behavior that became known as the "cover-up." There was never any conclusive evidence that the president had planned or approved the burglary in advance. But there was mounting evidence that he had been involved in illegal efforts to obstruct investigations of the episode. (See "Debating the Past: Watergate.")

Nixon accepted the departure of members of his administration implicated in the scandals. But the president continued to insist on his own innocence. There the matter might have rested had it not been for the disclosure during the Senate hearings of a White House taping system that had recorded virtually every conversation in the president's office during the period in question. All those investigating the scandals sought access to the tapes. Nixon, pleading "executive privilege," refused to release them. A special prosecutor appointed by the president to handle the Watergate cases, Harvard law professor Archibald Cox, took Nixon to court in October 1973 in an effort to force him to relinquish the recordings.

WATERGATE

Forty-two years after Watergate—one of the most famous political scandals in American history—historians and others continue to argue about its causes and significance. Their interpretations tend to fall into several broad categories.

One argument emphasizes the evolution of the institution of the presidency over time and sees Watergate as the result of a much larger pattern of presidential usurpations of power that stretched back at least several decades. Arthur M. Schlesinger Jr. helped develop this line of reasoning in his 1973 book *The Imperial Presidency*, which argues that ever since World War II, Americans have believed that the nation was in a state of permanent crisis—threatened from abroad by the menace of communism and from within by the danger of insufficient will. A succession of presidents believed in the urgency of this crisis, and in their duty to take whatever measures might be necessary to combat it. That led them gradually to usurp more and more power from Congress, from the courts, and from the public. Initially, this expansion of presidential power came in the realm of international affairs. It included covert and at times illegal activities overseas. Gradually, presidents began to look for ways to circumvent constraints in domestic matters as well. Nixon's actions in the Watergate crisis were, in other words, a culmination of this long and steady expansion of covert presidential power. Jonathan Schell, in *The Time of Illusion* (1975), offers a variation of this argument, tying the crisis of the presidency to the pressure that nuclear weapons place on presidents to protect the nation's—and their own—"credibility." Historians today rarely stake their understanding of Nixon's downfall on this particular view of government and society, preferring instead to treat this notion of a society in an unending crisis as one of many orientations that motivated Nixon to see himself engaged in a battle to preserve American values and empowered him to take strong and illegal measures to win.

Another explanation of Watergate emphasizes the difficult social and political environment of the late 1960s and early 1970s. Nixon entered office, according to this view, facing an unprecedentedly radical opposition that would stop at nothing to discredit the war and destroy his authority. He found himself, therefore, drawn into taking similarly desperate measures of his own to defend himself. Nixon made this argument in his own 1978 memoirs:

> Now that this season of mindless terror has fortunately passed, it is difficult—perhaps impossible—to convey a sense of the pressures that were influencing my actions and reactions during this period, but it was this epidemic of unprecedented domestic terrorism that prompted our efforts to discover the best means by which to deal with this new phenomenon of highly organized and highly skilled revolutionaries dedicated to the violent destruction of our democratic system.[*]

The historian Herbert Parmet echoes parts of this argument in *Richard Nixon and His America* (1990). Stephen Ambrose offers a more muted version of the same view in *Richard Nixon* (1989). Though this particular form of

[*]*RN: The Memoirs of Richard Nixon*, New York: Grosset & Dunlap, 1978.

analysis has not been popular of late, Evan Thomas in *Being Nixon: A Man Divided* (2016), offers a compelling portrait of how Nixon viewed his presidency as a war between his values and those who would undermine him.

Most of those who have written about Watergate, however, search for the explanation not in institutional or social forces but in the personalities of the people involved and, most notably, in the personality of Richard Nixon. Even many of those who have developed structural explanations (Schlesinger, Schell, and Ambrose, for example) return eventually to Nixon himself as the most important explanation for Watergate. Others begin there, perhaps most notably Stanley I. Kutler, in *The Wars of Watergate* (1990) and, later, *Abuse of Power* (1997), in which he presents extensive excerpts from conversations about Watergate taped in the Nixon White House. Kutler emphasizes Nixon's lifelong resort to vicious political tactics and his long-standing belief that he was a special target of unscrupulous enemies and had to "get" them before they got him. Watergate was rooted, Kutler argues, "in the personality and history of Nixon himself." A "corrosive hatred," he claims, "decisively shaped Nixon's own behavior, his career, and eventually his historical standing." This focus on Nixon's personality continues to be the subject of excellent studies, now aided by the declassification of presidential documents, including those by Tim Wiener, *One Man Against the World: The Tragedy of Richard Nixon* (2016) and John Farrell, *Richard Nixon: The Life* (2017). •

UNDERSTAND, ANALYZE, & EVALUATE

1. For scholars who cite social and institutional forces as explanations for Watergate, what are these forces? How did they contribute to the Watergate scandal?
2. Most scholars see Nixon himself as the party most responsible for Watergate. How did Nixon's personality contribute to both his rise to power as president and his downfall as a result of Watergate?
3. What have been the lasting effects of Watergate on the public's perception of the presidency and the government?

Nixon summarily fired Cox only to suffer the humiliation of watching both Attorney General Elliot Richardson and his deputy resign in protest. This "Saturday night massacre," as it was called, quickly backfired on Nixon. Public pressure forced him to appoint a new special prosecutor, Texas attorney Leon Jaworski, who proved just as determined as Cox to subpoena the tapes. And an outraged Congress set in motion an investigation by the House of Representatives into the possibility of impeachment.

THE FALL OF RICHARD NIXON

Nixon's situation deteriorated further in the following months. Late in 1973, Vice President Spiro Agnew became embroiled in a scandal of his own when evidence surfaced that he had accepted bribes and kickbacks while serving as governor of Maryland and even as vice president. In return for a Justice Department agreement not to prosecute the case, Agnew pleaded no contest to a lesser charge of income-tax evasion and resigned from the government. With the controversial Agnew no longer in line to succeed to the presidency, the prospect of removing Nixon from the White House became less worrisome to his opponents. The new vice president was House Minority Leader Gerald Ford, an amiable and popular Michigan congressman.

The impeachment investigation quickly gathered momentum. In April 1974, in an effort to head off further subpoenas of the tapes, the president released transcripts of a number of relevant conversations, claiming that they proved his innocence. Investigators and much of the public felt otherwise. Even these edited tapes seemed to suggest Nixon's complicity in the cover-up. In July, the crisis reached a climax. First the Supreme Court ruled unanimously, in *United States v. Richard M. Nixon*, that the president must relinquish the tapes to Special Prosecutor Jaworski. Days later, the House Judiciary Committee voted to recommend three articles of impeachment.

Even without additional evidence, Nixon might well have been impeached by the full House and convicted by the Senate. Early in August, however, he provided at last the "smoking gun"—the concrete proof of his guilt—that his defenders had long contended was missing from the case against him. Among the tapes that the Supreme Court compelled Nixon to relinquish were several that offered apparently incontrovertible evidence of his involvement in the Watergate cover-up. Only three days after the burglary, the recordings disclosed, the president had ordered the FBI to stop investigating the break-in. Impeachment and conviction now seemed inevitable.

Barbara Jordan, a thirty-eight-year-old, second-term congresswoman from Houston, Texas, and the first black women from the state to ever serve in the House of Representatives, boldly set the stage for impeachment. Speaking on July 25 as a member of the House Judiciary Committee, she passionately addressed her colleagues and a rapt national audience watching on television on the severity of Nixon's malfeasance and the pressing need to impeach him. Identifying herself as "an inquisitor," she confessed that she could not "sit here and be an idle spectator to the diminution, the subversion, the destruction, of the Constitution." Impeachment, she intoned, "is designed to 'bridle' the Executive if he engages in excesses." Quoting James Madison from the Federalist Papers, she reminded her audience that impeachment "is designed as a method of national inquest into the conduct of public men" and that

(©Bettmann/Getty Images)

NIXON'S FAREWELL Only moments before, Nixon had been in tears, saying good-bye to his staff in the East Room of the White House. But as he boarded a helicopter to begin his trip home to California shortly after resigning as president, he flashed his trademark "victory" sign to the crowd on the White House lawn.

"the framers confided in the Congress the power if need be, to remove the President in order to strike a delicate balance between a President swollen with power and grown tyrannical, and preservation of the independence of the Executive." After reviewing the president's crimes, she closed with a flourish. "If the impeachment provision in the Constitution of the United States will not reach the offenses charged here, then perhaps that 18th-century Constitution should be abandoned to a 20th-century paper shredder!"

For several days, Nixon cloistered himself in the White House. Finally, on August 8, 1974, he announced his resignation—the first president in American history ever to do so. At noon the next day, while Nixon and his family flew west to their home in California, **Gerald R. Ford** took the oath of office as president.

Many Americans expressed relief and exhilaration that, as the new president put it, "our long national nightmare is over." But the wave of good feeling could not obscure the deeper and more lasting damage of the Watergate crisis. In a society in which distrust of leaders and institutions of authority was already widespread, the fall of Richard Nixon confirmed for many Americans their most cynical assumptions about the untrustworthy character of American public life.

CONCLUSION

The victory of Richard Nixon in the 1968 presidential election represented a popular repudiation of turbulence and radicalism. It was a call for a restoration of order and stability. But order and stability were not the dominant characteristics of Nixon's troubled years in office. Nixon entered office when the political left and the counterculture were approaching the peak of their influence. American culture and society in the late 1960s and early 1970s were shaped decisively by, and were deeply divided over, the challenges by young people to the prevailing social norms. These were also the years in which a host of new liberation movements joined the drive for racial equality and when, above all, women mobilized effectively to demand changes in the way society treated gender differences.

Nixon had run for office attacking the failure of his predecessor to end the war in Vietnam. But for four years under his presidency, the war—and the protests against it—continued and even in some respects escalated. The division of opinion over the war was as deep as any of the other divisions in national life. It continued to poison the nation's politics and social fabric until the American role in the conflict finally shuddered to a close in 1973.

But much of the controversy and division in the 1970s was a product of the Nixon presidency itself. Nixon was in many ways a dynamic and even visionary leader, who proposed some important domestic reforms and who made important changes in American foreign policy, most notably making overtures to communist China and forging détente with the Soviet Union. He was also, however, a devious, secretive man whose White House became engaged in a series of covert activities that produced the most dramatic political scandal in American history. Watergate, as it was called, preoccupied much of the nation for nearly two years beginning in 1972; and ultimately, in the summer of 1974, the scandal forced Richard Nixon—who had been reelected to office only two years before by one of the largest majorities in modern history—to become the first president in American history to resign. Nixon was elected to lead the nation out of a war it no longer wanted, but his shameful exit from office and the ongoing Vietnam War continued to damage the nation's self-confidence and trust in government.

KEY TERMS/PEOPLE/PLACES/EVENTS

American Indian Movement (AIM) 736
Betty Friedan 739
César Chávez 738
counterculture 733
détente 750
Earth Day 743

Gerald R. Ford 759
Indian Civil Rights Act 736
National Organization for Women (NOW) 739
Nixon Doctrine 750
Rachel Carson 742
Roe v. Wade 741

silent majority 751
Stonewall Riot 738
Students for a Democratic Society (SDS) 732
Vietnamization 744
Watergate 755
Woodstock 734

RECALL AND REFLECT

1. What was the New Left? How was it related to the counterculture?
2. How did ethnic minorities, especially Native Americans and Latinos, challenge the status quo in the 1970s?
3. What were the objectives of the new feminism of the 1970s? What gains did women achieve in this era? What setbacks did the feminist movement experience?
4. What was the "Nixon Doctrine"? How did this doctrine play out in foreign policy?
5. What was the effect of Nixon's policies on the U.S. economy? What was Nixon's response to escalating economic difficulties?

30

FROM "THE AGE OF LIMITS" TO THE AGE OF REAGAN

POLITICS AND DIPLOMACY AFTER WATERGATE

THE RISE OF THE NEW CONSERVATIVE MOVEMENT

THE "REAGAN REVOLUTION"

THE WANING OF THE COLD WAR

LOOKING AHEAD

1. What economic and energy problems plagued the presidencies of Gerald Ford and Jimmy Carter? How did Ford and Carter attempt to deal with these problems?
2. What was the "New Right," and what effect did its rise have on American politics?
3. What was Reaganomics, and how did this policy affect the national economy?

THE FRUSTRATIONS OF THE EARLY 1970s—the defeat in Vietnam, the Watergate crisis, the decay of the American economy—inflicted damaging blows to the confident, optimistic nationalism that had characterized so much of the postwar era. Nixon's resignation in particular left Americans wondering if they could ever fully trust their government. And Americans battling to overcome generations of segregation were unsure how far the country would go to recognize and protect their freedoms.

Some Americans responded to these problems by announcing the arrival of an "age of limits," in which Americans would have to learn to live with lowered expectations for prosperity and global stature. By the end of the decade, however, another response was gaining strength—one that combined a steady retreat from some of the heady liberal visions of the 1960s with a reinforced commitment to traditional ideas of economic growth, international power, and American virtue.

1974

"Stagflation"

Ford pardons Nixon

1976

Carter elected
president

1977

Panama Canal
treaties signed

Apple introduces first
personal computer

1978–1979

Camp David accords

American hostages in
Iran

1980

U.S. boycotts Moscow
Olympics

Soviet Union invades
Afghanistan

Reagan elected president

U.S. and China restore
relations

1981

Three Mile Island
nuclear accident

American hostages in
Iran released

1982

Reagan wins tax and
budget cuts

Severe recession

1983

AIDS first reported in U.S.

U.S. invades Grenada

1984

Reagan reelected

1985

Reagan and
Gorbachev meet

1986

Iran-Contra scandal
revealed

1988

George H. W. Bush
elected president

1989

Berlin Wall dismantled

1990

Communist regimes
collapse

Iraq invades Kuwait

U.S. troops in Panama

1991

Collapse of Soviet regime

Persian Gulf War

1992

Los Angeles race riots

Clinton elected
president

POLITICS AND DIPLOMACY AFTER WATERGATE

In the aftermath of Richard Nixon's shameful departure from office, many Americans wondered whether faith in the presidency, and in the government as a whole, could ever be restored. The administrations of the two presidents who succeeded Nixon did little to answer those questions.

THE FORD CUSTODIANSHIP

Gerald R. Ford inherited the presidency under difficult circumstances. He desperately tried to rebuild confidence in government in the wake of the Watergate scandals and to restore prosperity in the face of major economic difficulties. Unfortunately, he met with little success on either account.

The new president's effort to establish himself as a symbol of political integrity suffered a setback only a month after he took office, when he granted Richard Nixon "a full, free, and absolute pardon" for any crimes he may have committed during his presidency. It was a gutsy move designed to get Americans past the trauma of Watergate. But the pardon angered Congress and a public eager to see Nixon face criminal charges and caused a sharp decline in Ford's popularity from which he never fully recovered. Indeed, it was a key reason for his failure to win reelection two years later. Nevertheless, most Americans considered Ford a decent man; his honesty and amiability did much to reduce the bitterness and acrimony of the Watergate years. Twenty-five years later, in recognition of the political resolution required by Ford to issue the pardon, the John F. Kennedy Center awarded him its Profile in Courage Award.

The Ford administration enjoyed far less success in its effort to solve the problems of the economy. Central to the economic problems was the continuing energy crisis. In the aftermath of the Arab oil embargo of 1973, the OPEC cartel raised the price of oil—by 400 percent in 1974 alone—and the price of goods and services that were dependent on oil rose in response. To curb inflation, the president called for largely ineffective voluntary efforts. After supporting high interest rates, opposing increased federal spending (through liberal use of his veto power), and resisting pressures for a tax reduction, Ford had to deal with a confounding economic mix of rising unemployment, high inflation, and slowing economic growth in 1974 and 1975 known as **stagflation**. While it occurred only during this two-year period, it was synonymous with most of the economic troubles of the seventies.

Ford retained Henry Kissinger as secretary of state and generally continued the foreign policies of the Nixon years. Late in 1974, Ford met with Leonid Brezhnev, the leader of the Soviet Union, at Vladivostok in Siberia and signed an arms control accord. Meanwhile, in the Middle East, Henry Kissinger helped produce a new accord by which Israel agreed to return large portions of the occupied Sinai to Egypt. The two nations pledged not to resolve future differences by force.

As the 1976 presidential election approached, Ford's policies came under increasing attack from both the right and the left. In the Republican primary campaign, Ford faced a powerful challenge from former California governor Ronald Reagan, leader of the party's

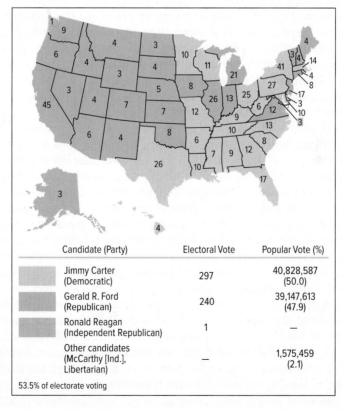

Candidate (Party)	Electoral Vote	Popular Vote (%)
Jimmy Carter (Democratic)	297	40,828,587 (50.0)
Gerald R. Ford (Republican)	240	39,147,613 (47.9)
Ronald Reagan (Independent Republican)	1	—
Other candidates (McCarthy [Ind.], Libertarian)	—	1,575,459 (2.1)

53.5% of electorate voting

THE ELECTION OF 1976 Jimmy Carter, a former governor of Georgia, swept the South in the 1976 election and carried enough of the industrial states of the Northeast and Midwest to win a narrow victory over President Gerald R. Ford. His showing indicated the importance to the Democratic Party of having a candidate capable of attracting support in the South, which was becoming increasingly Republican by the 1970s. • *What drove so many southerners into the Republican Party?*

conservative wing, who spoke for many Americans on the right who opposed any agreements with communists. The president barely survived the assault to win his party's nomination. The Democrats, in the meantime, were gradually uniting behind a new and until recently almost entirely unknown candidate: **Jimmy Carter**, a former governor of Georgia who appealed to the general unhappiness with Washington by offering honesty, piety, and an outsider's skepticism of the federal government. Unhappiness with the economy and a general disenchantment with Ford enabled the Democrat to win a narrow victory. Carter received 50 percent of the popular vote to Ford's 47.9 percent and 297 electoral votes to Ford's 240.

The Trials of Jimmy Carter

Like Ford, Jimmy Carter assumed the presidency at a moment when the nation faced problems of staggering complexity and difficulty. But Carter seemed at times to make his predicament worse by a style of leadership that many Americans considered self-righteous and inflexible.

Carter devoted much of his time to the problems of energy and the economy. Entering office in the midst of a recession, he moved first to reduce unemployment by raising public spending and cutting federal taxes. Unemployment declined, but inflation soared—mostly because of the continuing, sharp increases in energy prices by OPEC. During Carter's last two years in office, retail prices rose at over a 10 percent annual rate. Like Nixon and Ford before him, Carter responded with a combination of tight money and calls for voluntary restraint. Determined to stop inflation, he appointed conservative economists to head the Federal Reserve Board, which helped push interest rates to the highest levels in American history; at times, they exceeded 20 percent.

In the summer of 1979, instability in the Middle East produced a second major fuel shortage in the United States. In the midst of the crisis, OPEC announced another major price increase. Faced with increasing pressure to act, Carter went to Camp David, the presidential retreat in the Maryland mountains. Ten days later, he emerged to deliver a remarkable television address. It included a series of proposals for resolving the energy crisis. But it was most notable for Carter's bleak assessment of the national condition and his remarkable claim that there was a "crisis of confidence" that had struck "at the very heart and soul of our national will." The address became known as the "malaise" speech (although Carter himself had never used that word), and it helped fuel charges that the president was trying to blame his own problems on the American people. Carter's sudden firing of several members of his cabinet a few days later only deepened his political dilemma.

While the president struggled to find the right strategy to correct the economy, he championed a steady course on civil rights. Black and Latino voters had helped him win the White House and Carter never forgot it. Building on his longstanding commitment to full equality for all Americans, he zealously defended modern civil rights acts. He built a senior leadership team that included the first black female cabinet member (Patricia Roberts Harris), ambassador to the United Nations (Andrew Young), and head of the Civil Rights Division of the Department of Justice (Drew Days). He appointed more women, Latinos, and blacks as federal judges than all former administrations combined. Carter also expanded funding for historically black colleges and universities and defended federal policies on affirmative action. Although he failed to significantly improve employment, housing, and health-care policies for poor minority Americans, Carter was still a strong advocate for them.

HUMAN RIGHTS AND NATIONAL INTERESTS

Among Jimmy Carter's most frequent campaign promises was a new American foreign policy based partly on the defense of "human rights." Carter spoke out sharply about human rights violations in many countries (including, most prominently, the Soviet Union). But the administration also focused on more traditional concerns. Carter completed negotiations begun several years earlier on a pair of treaties to turn over control of the Panama Canal to the government of Panama. After an acrimonious debate, the Senate ratified the treaties by 68 to 32, only one vote more than the necessary two-thirds majority.

Carter's greatest success was in arranging a peace treaty between Egypt and Israel. Middle East negotiations had seemed hopelessly stalled until Egyptian president Anwar Sadat accepted an invitation in November 1977 from Prime Minister Menachem Begin to visit Israel. In Tel Aviv, he announced that Egypt was now willing to accept the state of Israel as a legitimate political entity.

When talks between Israeli and Egyptian negotiators stalled, Carter invited Sadat and Begin to a summit conference at Camp David in September 1978 and persuaded them to remain there for two weeks. On September 17, Carter escorted the two leaders into the White House to announce an agreement on a "framework" for an Egyptian–Israeli peace treaty, known as the **Camp David accords**. On March 26, 1979, Begin and Sadat returned together to the White House to sign a formal peace treaty between their two nations.

In the meantime, Carter continued trying to improve relations with China and the Soviet Union. He responded eagerly to the overtures of Deng Xiaoping, the new Chinese leader attempting to open his nation to the outside world. On December 15, 1978, Washington and Beijing announced the resumption of formal diplomatic relations. A few months later, Carter traveled to Vienna to meet with the aging and ailing Brezhnev to finish drafting the new Strategic Arms Limitations Treaty II (SALT II) arms control agreement, which set limits on the number of long-range missiles, bombers, and nuclear warheads on each side. Almost immediately, however, SALT II met with fierce conservative opposition in the U.S. Senate. The agreement was never ratified.

THE YEAR OF THE HOSTAGES

Since the early 1950s, the United States had provided political support and, more recently, massive military assistance to the government of the shah of Iran, hoping to make his nation a bulwark against Soviet expansion in the Middle East. By 1979, however, the shah was in deep trouble with his own people. Many Iranians resented the repressive, authoritarian tactics through which the shah had maintained his autocratic rule. At the same time, Islamic clergy (and much of the fiercely religious populace) opposed his efforts to modernize and Westernize Iranian society. The combination of resentments fueled a powerful revolutionary movement, which forced the shah to flee the country in January 1979.

By late 1979, power in Iran resided with a zealous religious leader, the **Ayatollah Ruhollah Khomeini**, who was fiercely anti-Western and anti-American. In late October 1979, the deposed shah arrived in New York to be treated for cancer. Days later, on November 4, an armed crowd stormed the American embassy in Tehran, seized the diplomats and military personnel inside, and demanded the return of the shah to Iran in exchange for their freedom. Fifty-three Americans remained hostages in the embassy for over a year.

Only weeks after the hostage seizure, on December 27, 1979, Soviet troops invaded Afghanistan, the mountainous Islamic nation lying between the Soviet Union and Iran. The Soviet Union had been a power in Afghanistan for years and the dominant force since

April 1978; a rebellion by radical Islamic guerrilla groups threatened the new Soviet-backed government. But while some observers claimed that the Soviet invasion was a Russian attempt to secure the status quo, Carter claimed it was a Russian "stepping stone to their possible control over much of the world's oil supplies" and the "gravest threat to world peace since World War II." Carter angrily imposed a series of economic sanctions on the Russians, canceled American participation in the 1980 summer Olympic Games in Moscow, and announced the withdrawal of SALT II from Senate consideration.

THE RISE OF THE NEW CONSERVATIVE MOVEMENT

The jarring social and economic changes in American life in the 1960s and 1970s provided the political right with its most important opportunity in generations to recapture a dominant position of political authority in American life.

THE SUNBELT AND ITS POLITICS

One of the most widely discussed demographic phenomena of the 1970s was the rise of what became known as the **Sunbelt**—the states of the Southeast and the Southwest. By 1980, the population of the Sunbelt had risen to exceed that of the older industrial regions of the North and the East, which gave the region newfound political power through an increased number of members of the House of Representative. This shift of people and politics directly contributed to the explosive growth of the modern conservative movement.

The strong Populist traditions in the South and the West helped produce opposition to the growth of government and resentment of the proliferating regulations and restrictions. Many of those regulations and restrictions—environmental laws, land-use restrictions, and other laws—affected the West more than any other region.

In the late 1970s, for example, a small movement arose to roll back environmental laws and policies governing and protecting western lands. Nicknamed the **Sagebrush Rebellion** for the shrub common to the mountainous region of the West, its advocates aimed to privatize large swaths of federal land or transfer ownership of them to the states so that they could be opened for commercial development, including mining. While none of the goals of the Sagebrush Rebellion were achieved, it showcased a building popular appetite for local control over politics and land.

The growth of suburbs also fueled a burgeoning spirit of localism and suspicion of federal intervention in the conduct of everyday life. Indeed, beginning in the 1950s but accelerating in the 1960s and 1970s, some of the most conservative communities developed in the suburbs ringing major Sunbelt cities like Dallas, Phoenix, and Los Angeles. The new suburbanites—often but not always white and middle class—hoped to escape rising crime rates and struggling public schools in urban areas. Some also desired to bring up their children in insular communities with others of their own race and class.

RELIGIOUS REVIVALISM

Mainstream denominations within Christianity began to decline or grow very slowly after World War II. The political and social tumult of the 1960s deepened this trend by firing suspicion of traditional authority, both civil and religious. But it also fueled a spiritual revival.

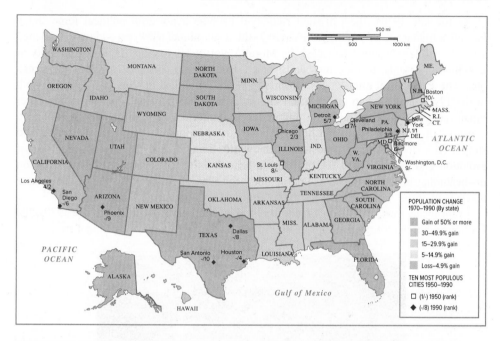

GROWTH OF THE SUNBELT, 1970-1990 One of the most important demographic changes of the last decades of the twentieth century was the shift of population out of traditional population centers in the Northeast and Midwest and toward the states of the so-called Sunbelt—most notably the Southwest and the Pacific Coast. This map gives a dramatic illustration of the changing concentration of population between 1970 and 1990. The orange states are those that lost population, while the purple and blue states are those that made significant gains (30 percent or more). • *What was the impact of this population shift on the politics of the 1980s?*

Seeking to cast off familiar conventions of worship, Americans sought new forms of spiritual experience that promised fresh understandings of the divine and new communities. It led to the rise of alternative movements and unorthodox faiths: the Church of Scientology; the Unification Church of the Reverend Sun Myung Moon; and even the tragic People's Temple, many of whom committed mass suicide in their jungle retreat in Guyana in 1978. But most importantly it inspired the growth of modern evangelical Christianity.

Evangelicals share a belief in being "born again" through direct communication with Jesus. Evangelical Christianity, with its emphasis on personal conversion and salvation, has roots in American religious history extending as far back as the eighteenth century. In its modern form, it became increasingly visible during the early 1950s when evangelicals such as Billy Graham and Pentecostals such as Oral Roberts began to attract huge national and international audiences for their energetic revivals. In the following decades, evangelical Christians became even more visible, printing their own newspapers and founding their own radio stations and television networks. Three modern presidents—Jimmy Carter, Bill Clinton, and George W. Bush—and more than 70 million Americans today openly identify themselves as evangelicals.

Some evangelical Christians, following the path of religious civil rights leaders like Rev. Martin Luther King, worked tirelessly to promote racial and economic justice and world peace. But many others had a different political focus, aimed at preserving the traditional values that they believed were being eroded by the new youth culture and progressive movements. This group became known as the "Christian right."

By the late 1970s, the Christian right had become a powerful political force. Jerry Falwell, a fundamentalist minister in Virginia with a substantial television audience, launched a highly visible movement he called the Moral Majority. He founded Liberty University in Lynchburg, Virginia, to train men and women according to conservative Christian principles. The Pentecostal minister Pat Robertson began a political movement of his own and, in the 1990s, launched an organization known as the **Christian Coalition**. These and other organizations of the Christian right opposed federal interference in local affairs; denounced abortion, divorce, feminism, and homosexuality; defended unrestricted free enterprise; and supported a strong American posture in the world. Some denied the scientific doctrine of evolution and instead urged the teaching in schools of the biblical story of the Creation or—beginning in the early twenty-first century—the idea of "intelligent design." Their goal was a new era in which "Christian values" once again dominated American life.

Evangelicals were not the only Christians to back conservative causes. In the 1970s, the Catholic Church also began to insert itself more directly into politics, making a strong case

(©Mark Meyer/The LIFE Images Collection/Getty Images)

NEW SPIRITUAL LEADERS Rev. Jerry Falwell, a Baptist minister and pioneer in Christian television and radio, founded the Moral Majority in 1979 to inject evangelical values into the political mainstream. It was a key component of the Christian Coalition that helped elected Ronald Reagan to the White House.

for what it called "traditional values" as well. The Church fought most aggressively against abortion, joining evangelicals in the "right to life" movement. Not all Catholics were or are conservatives; indeed, many priests and parishioners took strong liberal positions. But in the political world, Catholics became strong allies of evangelicals on most issues.

Mormons, too, became active members of the Christian right. For many years, Mormons did not publicize their conservatism. But like Catholics, many began to take openly conservative stances in the 1970s on some of the most controversial battles of the time. Some of these Mormons, wealthy and successful businesspeople, became powerful conservative politicians in various parts of the country. In 2012, Republican Mitt Romney was the first Mormon to secure his party's nomination for the presidency.

THE EMERGENCE OF THE NEW RIGHT

Religious issues were only a part—although an important part—of what became known as the **New Right**—a diverse but powerful movement that enjoyed rapid growth in the 1970s and early 1980s. It had begun to take shape after the 1964 election, in which Republican Barry Goldwater had suffered his shattering defeat. Energetic organizers responded to that disaster by building a new and powerful set of right-wing institutions to help conservatives campaign more effectively in the future. Among their innovations was the creation of a direct-mail operation that ultimately reached millions of conservative voters. Beginning in the 1970s, largely because of these organizational advances, conservatives found themselves almost always better funded and organized than their opponents. By the late 1970s, there were right-wing think tanks, consulting firms, lobbyists, foundations, and colleges and universities. Conservatives also succeeded in developing systems to raise money, mobilize activists, and project their ideas to a broad audience. Evangelicals such as Pat Robertson used cable television to reach the conservative faithful. Conservative radio hosts such as Rush Limbaugh created shows that attracted a vast national audience.

Another factor in the revival of the right was the emergence in the late 1960s and early 1970s of **Ronald Reagan**. Once a moderately successful actor, he had moved into politics in the early 1960s and in 1964 delivered a memorable television speech on behalf of Goldwater. After Goldwater's defeat, Reagan worked quickly to seize the leadership of the conservative wing of the party. In 1966, with the support of a group of wealthy conservatives, he won the first of two terms as governor of California.

The presidency of Gerald Ford also played an important role in the rise of conservatism. Ford, probably without realizing it, touched on some of the right's rawest nerves. He appointed as vice president Nelson Rockefeller, the liberal Republican governor of New York and an heir to one of America's great fortunes; many conservatives had been demonizing Rockefeller and his family for more than twenty years. Ford proposed an amnesty program for draft resisters, embraced the hated Nixon–Kissinger policies of détente, presided over the fall of Vietnam, and agreed to cede the Panama Canal to Panama. When Reagan challenged Ford in the 1976 Republican primaries, the president survived, barely, only by dumping Nelson Rockefeller from the ticket and replacing him with Kansas senator Robert Dole, a steadfast conservative. He also agreed to a platform largely written by conservatives.

THE TAX REVOLT

At least equally important to the success of the New Right was a new and potent conservative issue: the tax revolt. It had its public beginnings in 1978, when Howard Jarvis, a conservative activist in California, launched Proposition 13, a referendum question on the state ballot rolling back property tax rates. Because property taxes were the most important source of funding for schools, the passage of Proposition 13 began the slow deterioration of much of the California education system. Similar antitax movements soon began in other states and eventually spread to national politics.

In Proposition 13 and similar initiatives, members of the right succeeded in separating the issue of taxes from the issue of what taxes supported. Instead of attacking popular programs such as Social Security, they attacked taxes themselves and argued that much of the money government raised through taxes was wasted. Virtually no one liked to pay taxes, and as the economy grew weaker and the relative burden of paying taxes grew heavier, that resentment naturally rose.

THE CAMPAIGN OF 1980

By the time of the crises in Iran and Afghanistan, Jimmy Carter was in desperate political trouble–his standing in popularity polls was lower than that of any president in history. Senator Edward Kennedy, younger brother of John and Robert Kennedy, challenged him in the primaries. And while Carter managed to withstand the confrontation and win his party's nomination, his campaign aroused little popular enthusiasm. The stage was set for sweeping political change.

The Republican Party, in the meantime, rallied enthusiastically behind the man who, four years earlier, had nearly stolen the nomination from Gerald Ford. Ronald Reagan was

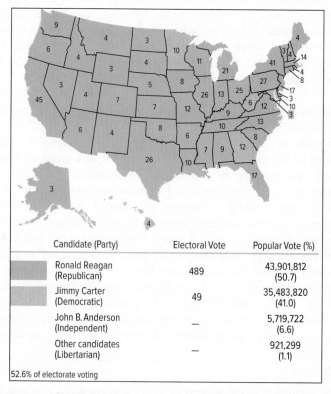

Candidate (Party)	Electoral Vote	Popular Vote (%)
Ronald Reagan (Republican)	489	43,901,812 (50.7)
Jimmy Carter (Democratic)	49	35,483,820 (41.0)
John B. Anderson (Independent)	–	5,719,722 (6.6)
Other candidates (Libertarian)	–	921,299 (1.1)

52.6% of electorate voting

THE ELECTION OF 1980   Although Ronald Reagan won only slightly more than half of the popular vote in the 1980 presidential election, his electoral majority was overwhelming—a reflection to a large degree of the deep unpopularity of President Jimmy Carter in 1980. • *What had made Carter so unpopular?*

a sharp critic of the excesses of the federal government. He linked his campaign to the spreading tax revolt by promising substantial tax cuts. He claimed that he would restore America's standing as the greatest economic and military power in the world, tapping into the public's frustration over a flagging economy and the fact that American citizens remained hostages in Iran.

On election day 1980, the anniversary of the seizure of the hostages in Iran, Reagan swept to victory, winning 51 percent of the vote to 41 percent for Jimmy Carter and 7 percent for John Anderson—a moderate Republican congressman from Illinois who had mounted an independent campaign. The Republican Party won control of the Senate for the first time since 1952; and although the Democrats retained a modest majority in the House, the lower chamber, too, seemed firmly in the hands of conservatives.

On the day of Reagan's inauguration, the American hostages in Iran were released after their 444-day ordeal. The government of Iran, desperate for funds to support its floundering war against neighboring Iraq, had ordered the hostages freed in return for a release of billions in Iranian assets that the Carter administration had frozen in American banks. Americans welcomed the hostages home with demonstrations of joy and patriotism seldom seen since the end of World War II. But while the celebration in 1945 had marked a great American triumph, the euphoria in 1981 marked something quite different—a troubled nation grasping for reassurance. Ronald Reagan set out to provide it.

THE "REAGAN REVOLUTION"

Ronald Reagan assumed the presidency in January 1981, promising a revolution in government more fundamental than any since the New Deal of fifty years before. (See "Consider the Source: Ronald Reagan on the Role of Government.") While his eight years in office produced a significant shift in public policy, they brought nothing so fundamental as many of his supporters had hoped or his opponents had feared. But Reagan succeeded brilliantly in making his own engaging personality the central fact of American politics in the 1980s. He also benefited from the power of the diverse coalition that had united behind him.

THE REAGAN COALITION

The Reagan coalition included a relatively small but highly influential group of wealthy Americans firmly committed to capitalism with little to no interference by the government. Reagan courted these free-market conservatives carefully and effectively, and in the end it was their interests his administration most effectively served. They believed that the "market" offered the best solutions to most problems, and they shared a deep hostility to most (although not all) government interference in markets. Central to this group's agenda in the 1980s was opposition to what it scorned as the "redistributive" economic politics of the government (especially its highly progressive tax structure) and hostility to the rise of what they believed were "antibusiness" government regulations. "Smaller government" was one of their favorite mantras.

A second element of the Reagan coalition consisted of a small but influential group of intellectuals commonly known as **neoconservatives**, who gave to the right something it had not had in many years—a firm base among "opinion leaders," people with access to the most influential public forums of ideas. Many of these people had once been liberals and, before that, socialists. But during the turmoil of the 1960s, they had become alarmed by

CONSIDER THE SOURCE

RONALD REAGAN ON THE ROLE OF GOVERNMENT (1981)

In this excerpt from his first inaugural address, on January 20, 1981, Ronald Reagan laid out his central vision for the role of government in society. Questioning the ability of government to solve society's social and economic ills, Reagan argued that the key to the nation's future lay in reducing the role of government in everyday life.

The economic ills we suffer have come upon us over several decades. They will not go away in days, weeks, or months, but they will go away. They will go away because we as Americans have the capacity now, as we've had in the past, to do whatever needs to be done to preserve this last and greatest bastion of freedom.

In this present crisis, government is not the solution to our problem; government is the problem. From time to time we've been tempted to believe that society has become too complex to be managed by self-rule, that government by an elite group is superior to government for, by, and of the people. Well, if no one among us is capable of governing himself, then who among us has the capacity to govern someone else? All of us together, in and out of government, must bear the burden. The solutions we seek must be equitable, with no one group singled out to pay a higher price.

We hear much of special interest groups. Well, our concern must be for a special interest group that has been too long neglected. It knows no sectional boundaries or ethnic and racial divisions, and it crosses political party lines. It is made up of men and women who raise our food, patrol our streets, man our mines and factories, teach our children, keep our homes, and heal us when we're sick—professionals, industrialists, shopkeepers, clerks, cabbies, and truck drivers. They are, in short, "We the people," this breed called Americans.

Well, this administration's objective will be a healthy, vigorous, growing economy that provides equal opportunities for all Americans with no barriers born of bigotry or discrimination. Putting America back to work means putting all Americans back to work. Ending inflation means freeing all Americans from the terror of runaway living costs. All must share in the productive work of this "new beginning," and all must share in the bounty of a revived economy. With the idealism and fair play which are the core of our system and our strength, we can have a strong and prosperous America, at peace with itself and the world.

So, as we begin, let us take inventory. We are a nation that has a government—not the other way around. And this makes us special among the nations of the Earth. Our government has no power except that granted it by the people. It is time to check and reverse the growth of government, which shows signs of having grown beyond the consent of the governed.

It is my intention to curb the size and influence of the Federal establishment and to demand recognition of the distinction between the powers granted to the Federal Government and those reserved to the States or to the people. All of us need to be reminded that the Federal Government did not create the States; the States created the Federal Government.

Now, so there will be no misunderstanding, it's not my intention to do away with government. It is rather to make it work—work with us, not over us; to stand by our side, not ride on our back. Government can and must provide opportunity, not smother it; foster productivity, not stifle it.

If we look to the answer as to why for so many years we achieved so much, prospered as no other people on Earth, it was because here in this land we unleashed the energy and individual genius of man to a greater extent than has ever been done before. Freedom and the dignity of the individual have been more available and assured here than in any other place on Earth. The price for this freedom at times has been high, but we have never been unwilling to pay that price.

It is no coincidence that our present troubles parallel and are proportionate to the intervention and intrusion in our lives that result from unnecessary and excessive growth of government. It is time for us to realize that we're too great a nation to limit ourselves to small dreams. We're not, as some would have us believe, doomed to an inevitable decline. I do not believe in a fate that will fall on us no matter what we do. I do believe in a fate that will fall on us if we do nothing. So, with all the creative energy at our command, let us begin an era of national renewal. Let us renew our determination, our courage, and our strength. And let us renew our faith and our hope.

UNDERSTAND, ANALYZE, & EVALUATE

1. What does Reagan mean when he says, in the opening lines of the second paragraph, that "government is the problem"?
2. Why did Reagan's call for a curb on the government's role in society and the economy strike such a popular chord in the 1980s?
3. According to Reagan, who has been treated unfairly under the previous administration? Whom are the disadvantaged?

Source: The Ronald Reagan Presidential Library, National Archives and Records Administration, www.reagan.utexas.edu/archives/speeches/1981/12081a.htm

what they considered a dangerous and destructive radicalism. Neoconservatives were sympathetic to the complaints and demands of capitalists, but their principal concern was to reassert legitimate authority and reaffirm Western democratic, anticommunist values and commitments. They considered themselves soldiers in a battle to "win back the culture"— from the crass, radical ideas that had polluted it.

Neoconservatives also strongly dissented from the new foreign policy orthodoxies of liberals and the left in the aftermath of the Vietnam War. These self-proclaimed "defense hawks" utterly rejected the idea that America should be a less interventionist nation, that it should work to ease tensions with the Soviet Union, and that it should tolerate radical regimes. Instead, they argued for an escalation of the Cold War as part of an effort to destabilize the Soviet Union. They insisted that the Vietnam War was an appropriate American commitment and that its abandonment was a terrible mistake. They believed that the United States had a special role to play in the world and should be willing to use military intervention to secure its vision. These ideas strongly influenced the foreign policy of the Reagan administration. The same ideas (and some of the same people) resurfaced in the early twenty-first century to help shape the international policies of the George W. Bush administration.

Free-market conservatives and neoconservatives formed an uneasy alliance with the broad grassroots conservative movement to collectively create the New Right. All shared a fundamental distrust of the "eastern establishment" that supposedly ruled Washington: a suspicion of its motives and goals and a sense that it exercised a dangerous, secret power in American life. Grassroots conservatives also feared living in a world where distant, secretive forces controlled society and threatened individual freedom and community autonomy—a point of view that could have turned them against the elite leaders who led the free-market conservatives and the neoconservatives. It was a testament to

Ronald Reagan's political skills and personal charm that he was able to generate enthusiastic support from all of these factions.

REAGAN IN THE WHITE HOUSE

Even many people who disagreed with Reagan's policies found themselves drawn to his attractive and carefully honed public image. He was sixty-nine upon taking office and was the oldest man to serve as president, until the inauguration of the seventy-year-old Donald Trump in 2017. But through most of his presidency, he appeared to be vigorous, resilient, even youthful. When wounded in an assassination attempt in 1981, he joked with doctors on his way into surgery and appeared to bounce back from the ordeal with remarkable speed. Even when things went wrong, as they often did, the blame seldom seemed to attach to Reagan himself (inspiring some Democrats to refer to him as the "Teflon president").

Reagan was not much involved in the day-to-day affairs of running the government; he surrounded himself with tough, energetic administrators who insulated him from many of the pressures of the office and who apparently relied on him largely for general guidance, not specific decisions. At times, the president revealed a startling ignorance about the nature of his own policies or the actions of his subordinates. But Reagan did make active use of his office to generate public support for his administration's programs.

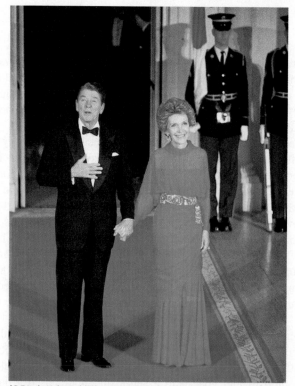

(©Dirck Halstead/The LIFE Images Collection/Getty Images)

RONALD AND NANCY REAGAN The president and the first lady greet guests at a White House social event. Nancy Reagan was committed to making the White House, and her husband's presidency, seem more glamorous than those of most recent administrations. But she also played an important, if usually quiet, policy role in the administration.

"Supply-Side" Economics

Reagan's 1980 campaign for the presidency had promised to restore the economy to health by a bold experiment that became known as "supply-side"—or, to its critics, "trickle-down"—economics. Eventually, it was called **Reaganomics**. Supply-side economics operated from the assumption that the woes of the American economy were in large part a result of excessive taxation, which left inadequate capital available to investors to stimulate growth. The solution, therefore, was to reduce taxes, with particularly generous benefits to corporations and wealthy individuals, in order to encourage new investments.

In its first months in office, the new administration hastily assembled a legislative program based on the supply-side idea. It proposed $40 billion in budget reductions and managed to win congressional approval of almost all of them. In addition, the president proposed a bold three-year, 30 percent reduction on both individual and corporate tax rates. In the summer of 1981, Congress passed it, too, after lowering the reductions to 25 percent. Reagan owed his legislative success to a disciplined Republican majority in the Senate and a Democratic majority in the House that was weak and riddled with defectors.

Reagan appointees in the executive branch of government aimed to reduce the role of government in American economic life. **Deregulation**, an idea many Democrats had begun to embrace in the Carter years, became almost a religion in the Reagan administration, especially in its environmental policies. Secretary of the Interior James Watt, a major figure in the Sagebrush Rebellion, opened up public lands and water to development and led a charge to reverse older conservationist policies. The administration ultimately permitted coal, gas, and oil corporations to prospect and develop millions of acres of federal land. Anne Gorsuch, director of the Environmental Protection Agency, slashed its budget by about 25 percent and relaxed or eliminated enforcement against polluters. She eventually resigned amid accusations that she mismanaged the $1.6 billion superfund dedicated for the cleanup of toxic waste sites. Despite his deregulation focus, Reagan signed the Montreal Protocol in 1987, an international treaty committing nations to reducing the production of harmful substances shown to deplete the ozone. And during his term of office he designated more than 10 million acres across twenty-seven states as federal wilderness.

By early 1982, the nation had sunk into a severe recession. The Reagan economic program was not directly to blame for the problems, but neither did it offer a quick solution. During 1982, unemployment reached 11 percent, one of the highest levels since the 1930s. But before the recession could do great damage to Reagan, the economy recovered more rapidly and impressively than almost anyone had expected. By late 1983, unemployment had fallen to 8.2 percent, and it declined steadily for several years after that. The gross national product (GNP) grew 3.6 percent in a year, the largest increase since the mid-1970s. Inflation fell below 5 percent. The economy continued to grow, and both inflation and unemployment remained low through most of the decade.

The recovery was a result of many things. Prior years of tight money policies by the Federal Reserve Board had helped lower inflation; perhaps equally important, the Fed had lowered interest rates early in 1983 in response to the recession. A worldwide "energy glut" and the virtual collapse of the OPEC cartel had produced at least a temporary end to the inflationary pressures of spiraling fuel costs. Gas prices now came down. At the same time, the federal government began to pump more money into the economy, especially in research and development for businesses. As a result of this "deficit spending" (when the government spends more money than it takes in and thus incurs a deficit in its budget), business investment and consumer spending increased. The stock market rose up from its doldrums of the 1970s and began a sustained and historic boom. In August 1982, the Dow Jones Industrial Average stood at 777. Five years later it had passed 2,000. Despite a frightening crash in the fall of 1987, the market continued to grow for more than another decade.

THE FISCAL CRISIS

The economic revival did little at first to reduce the staggering, and to many Americans alarming, federal budget deficits (the gap between revenue and spending in a single year) or to slow the growth in the national debt (the debt the nation accumulates over time to pay its bills). By the mid-1980s, this growing fiscal crisis had become one of the central issues in American politics. Having entered office promising a balanced budget within four years, Reagan presided over record budget deficits and accumulated more debt in his eight years in office than the American government had accumulated in its entire previous history. Before the 1980s, the highest single-year budget deficit in American history had been $66 billion (in 1976). Throughout the 1980s, the annual budget deficit consistently exceeded $100 billion. (The deficit peaked in 1991 at $268 billion.) The national debt rose from $907 billion in 1980 to nearly $3.5 trillion by 1991. Much larger deficits—and debt—were soon to come.

The enormous deficits had many causes. The budget suffered from steep increases in the costs of "entitlement" programs (especially both Social Security and Medicare), a result of the aging of the population and dramatic increases in the cost of health care. The 1981 tax cuts, the largest in American history, also contributed to the deficit. The massive increase in military spending on which the Reagan administration insisted added much more to the federal budget than its cuts in domestic spending removed.

In the face of these deficits, the administration proposed further cuts in "discretionary" domestic spending, which included many programs aimed at the poorest (and politically weakest) Americans. By the end of Reagan's third year in office, funding for domestic programs had been cut nearly as far as Congress (and, apparently, the public) was willing to tolerate, and still no end to the rising deficit was in sight. By the late 1980s, many fiscal conservatives were calling for a constitutional amendment mandating a balanced budget—a provision the president himself claimed to support. But Congress never approved the amendment.

Reagan's policies of reduced government hurt the very poor. In his enthusiasm to minimize the scope and power of the federal government in daily life and trim the budget, he reversed decades of Washington-led efforts to revitalize and improve local communities. During his eight years in the White House, Reagan cut federal assistance to state and municipal governments by about 60 percent. He slashed funds for public transportation, job training, legal services for the poor, and the Community Development Block Grant Program. America's largest cities felt the biggest pinch: federal aid fell from 22 percent of their overall budgets to 6 percent. Housing for the poor was hit especially hard. The president aimed to increase the nation's reliance on the private market to house the indigent. And so he sliced in half the budget for public housing and Section 8 housing, where the government subsidizes private landlords to rent to low-income individuals. He also reduced the budget for the Department of Housing and Urban Development from $32 billion to $7.5 billion. Not surprisingly, rates of homelessness skyrocketed to over 2 million by the time the president left office.

REAGAN AND THE WORLD

Relations with the Soviet Union, which had been steadily deteriorating in the last years of the Carter administration, grew still chillier in the first years of the Reagan presidency. The president spoke harshly of the Soviet regime (which he once called the "evil empire"), accusing it of sponsoring world terrorism and declaring that any armaments negotiations must be linked to negotiations on Soviet behavior in other areas. Although the president had long denounced the SALT II arms control treaty as unfavorable to the United States, he continued to honor its provisions. But the president proposed the most ambitious (and potentially most expensive) new military program in many years: the **Strategic Defense Initiative (SDI)**, widely known as "Star Wars" after the popular movie of that name. Reagan claimed that SDI, through the use of lasers and satellites, could provide an effective shield against incoming missiles and thus make nuclear war obsolete. The Soviet Union claimed that the new program would elevate the arms race to new and more dangerous levels and insisted that any arms control agreement should begin with an American abandonment of SDI.

The escalation of Cold War tensions and the slowing of arms control initiatives helped produce an important popular movement in Europe and the United States calling for a "nuclear freeze," an agreement between the two superpowers not to expand their atomic arsenals. In what many at the time believed was the largest mass demonstration in American history, nearly a million people rallied in New York City's Central Park in 1982 to support the freeze. Perhaps partly in response to this growing pressure, the administration began tentative efforts to revive arms control negotiations in 1983.

The administration created a new policy known as the **Reagan Doctrine**, designed to help resist communism and anti-Americanism in the Third World. The United States sent soldiers and money to aid guerrillas and resistance movements in countries with anti-American governments—among them Grenada, El Salvador, and Nicaragua. But Reagan generally backed away from more serious warfare. In 1982, when the Israeli army invaded Lebanon, American peacekeeping forces entered Beirut to stabilize the nation. But when a terrorist bombing of a U.S. military barracks in Beirut led to the death of 241 marines, Reagan quickly withdrew the American forces.

Reagan approached the campaign of 1984 at the head of a united Republican Party firmly committed to his candidacy. The Democrats nominated Carter's vice president, Walter Mondale. Mondale brought momentary excitement to the Democratic campaign by selecting a woman, Representative Geraldine Ferraro of New York, to be his running mate and the first female candidate ever to appear on a national ticket. But Reagan's triumphant campaign scarcely took note of his opponents and spoke instead of what he claimed was the remarkable revival of American fortunes and spirits under his leadership, or what he sometimes called "Morning in America." He won 59 percent of the vote and carried every state but Mondale's native Minnesota and the District of Columbia.

THE WANING OF THE COLD WAR

Many factors contributed to the collapse of the Soviet Empire. The long, stalemated war in Afghanistan proved at least as disastrous to the Soviet Union as the Vietnam War had been to America. The government in Moscow failed to address a long-term economic decline in the Soviet republics and the Eastern-bloc nations. Restiveness with the heavy-handed policies of communist police states was growing throughout much of the Soviet Empire. But the most visible factor at the time was the emergence of **Mikhail Gorbachev**, who succeeded to the leadership of the Soviet Union in 1985 and, to the surprise of almost everyone (probably including himself), very quickly became the most revolutionary figure in world politics in decades.

THE FALL OF THE SOVIET UNION

Gorbachev transformed Soviet politics with two dramatic new initiatives: *glasnost* (open-ness), the dismantling of many of the repressive mechanisms that had been conspicuous features of Soviet life for over half a century, and *perestroika* (reform), an effort to restructure the rigid and unproductive Soviet economy by introducing, among other things, such elements of capitalism as private ownership and the profit motive. He also began to transform Soviet foreign policy.

The severe economic problems at home evidently convinced Gorbachev that the Soviet Union could no longer sustain its extended commitments around the world. As early as 1987, he began reducing the Soviet presence in Eastern Europe. And in 1989, in the space of a few months, every communist state in Europe—Poland, Hungary, Czechoslovakia, Bulgaria, Romania, East Germany, Yugoslavia, and Albania—either overthrew its government or forced it to transform itself into an essentially noncommunist (and in some cases, actively anticommunist) regime. Perhaps the most dramatic event of this extraordinary revolution was the tearing down of the infamous Berlin Wall.

Not all international protests against communism were so successful. In May 1989, students in China launched a mass movement calling for greater democratization. But in June, hard-line leaders seized control of the government and sent military forces to crush the uprising. The result was a bloody massacre on June 3, 1989, in **Tiananmen Square** in Beijing, in which an unknown number of demonstrators died. The assault crushed the democracy movement and restored hard-liners to power. It did not, however, stop China's efforts to modernize and even Westernize its economy.

But China was an exception to the widespread movement toward democratization. Early in 1990, the government of South Africa, long an international pariah for its rigid enforcement

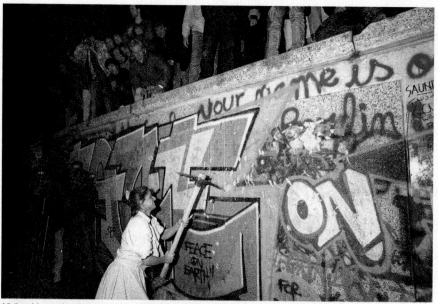

(©Sueddeutsche Zeitung Photo/Alamy)

THE FALL OF THE BERLIN WALL The Berlin Wall is widely considered to have "fallen" on November 9, 1989. Starting on that date and in the days and weeks that followed, people used sledgehammers and picks to tear down the wall, often keeping the broken pieces as souvenirs of this symbolic conclusion of the Cold War.

of "apartheid" (a system designed to protect white supremacy, much like the Jim Crow system had done in the American South) legalized the chief black party in the nation, the African National Congress (ANC), which had been banned for decades. The government also released from prison the leader of the ANC, **Nelson Mandela**, who had been in jail for twenty-seven years. Over the next several years, the South African government repealed its apartheid laws. And in 1994, there were national elections in which all South Africans could participate. As a result, Nelson Mandela became the first black president of South Africa.

In 1991, communism began to collapse in the Soviet Union itself. An unsuccessful coup by hard-line Soviet leaders on August 19 precipitated a dramatic unraveling of communist power. Within days, the coup itself collapsed in the face of resistance from the public and crucial elements within the military. By the end of August, many of the republics of the Soviet Union had declared independence; the Soviet government was clearly powerless to stop the fragmentation. Gorbachev himself finally resigned as leader of the now virtually powerless Communist Party and Soviet government, and the Soviet Union itself ceased to exist.

The last years of the Reagan administration coincided with the first years of the Gorbachev regime; and while Reagan was skeptical of Gorbachev at first, he gradually became convinced that the Soviet leader was sincere in his desire for reform. In 1988, the two superpowers signed a treaty eliminating American and Soviet intermediate-range nuclear forces (INF) from Europe—the most significant arms control agreement of the nuclear age. At about the same time, Gorbachev ended the Soviet Union's long and frustrating military involvement in Afghanistan.

THE FADING OF THE REAGAN REVOLUTION

For a time, the dramatic changes around the world and Reagan's personal popularity deflected attention from a series of scandals that might well have destroyed another administration, including revelations of illegal and ethical lapses in the Environmental Protection Agency, the CIA, the Department of Defense, the Department of Labor, the Department of Justice, and the Department of Housing and Urban Development. A more serious scandal emerged within the savings and loan industry, which the Reagan administration had helped deregulate in the early 1980s. By the end of the decade, the industry was in chaos, and the government was forced to step in to prevent a complete collapse. The cost of the debacle to the public eventually ran to more than half a trillion dollars.

But the most politically damaging scandal of the Reagan years came to light in November 1986, when the White House conceded that it had sold weapons to the revolutionary government of Iran as part of a largely unsuccessful effort to secure the release of several Americans being held hostage. Even more damaging was the revelation that some of the money from the arms deal with Iran had been covertly and illegally funneled into a fund to aid the Contras, a loose group of commandos who fought against the anti-American government after the 1979 revolution in Nicaragua.

In the months that followed, aggressive reporting and a series of congressional hearings exposed a widespread pattern of covert activities orchestrated by the White House and dedicated to advancing the administration's foreign policy aims through secret and at times illegal means. Reagan's zeal for eliminating communism lay at the heart of the **Iran–Contra scandal**, as it came to be known. Under the president's directive, the CIA had long trained anticommunist fighters around the globe. But Reagan's hands were tied in Nicaragua after the Democrat-controlled Congress passed the Boland Amendment, which severely restricted the CIA and Department of Defense from operating there and prompted senior staff to devise a way around the restriction. The Iran–Contra scandal did serious damage to the Reagan presidency—even though the investigations never tied the president himself to the most serious violations of the law. Most of the highest-ranking Reagan officials indicted or found guilty were either pardoned by future president George H. W. Bush or released on a legal technicality, some after serving a stint in jail.

THE PRESIDENCY OF GEORGE H. W. BUSH

The fraying of the Reagan administration helped the Democrats regain control of the U.S. Senate in 1986 and fueled hopes in the party for a presidential victory in 1988. Michael Dukakis, a three-term governor of Massachusetts, eventually captured the nomination. Vice President **George H. W. Bush** was the largely unopposed Republican candidate. Neither candidate, however, succeeded in whipping up much public enthusiasm.

Beginning at the Republican National Convention, Bush made his campaign a long, relentless attack on Dukakis, tying him to all the unpopular social and cultural stances Americans had come to identify with "liberals" since the 1960s. Bush won a substantial victory in November: 54 percent of the popular vote to Dukakis's 46 percent, and 426 electoral votes to Dukakis's 112. But Bush carried few Republicans into office with him; the Democrats retained secure majorities in both houses of Congress. His victory over Dukakis reflected his subdued, traditional, unthreatening image and years of decorated military and public service. While in the White House, Americans strongly supported him at first because of beneficial turns of international events during his tenure, including most notably the fall of the Berlin Wall, the signing of significant arms agreements with the Soviet Union, and ultimately the Soviet Union's collapse altogether. Equally important were successful military actions in Panama and the prosecution of the Persian Gulf War (see below).

On domestic issues, the Bush administration was less successful. It inherited a staggering burden of debt and a federal deficit that had been growing dramatically for nearly a decade. Constantly concerned about shoring up support from the right wing of his own party, Bush aggressively opposed current laws governing abortion and affirmative action, but his efforts severely damaged his ability to work with the Democratic Congress.

Despite this political stalemate, Congress and the White House managed on occasion to agree on significant measures. In 1990, the president agreed to a significant tax increase as part of a multiyear "budget package" designed to reduce the deficit—thus violating his own 1988 campaign pledge of "no new taxes." But the most serious domestic problem facing the Bush administration was one for which neither the president nor Congress had any answer: a recession that began late in 1990 and became more serious in 1991 and 1992.

THE GULF WAR

The fall of the Soviet Union left the United States in the unanticipated position of being the only real superpower in the world. It forced the Bush administration to consider what to do with America's formidable political and military power.

The events of 1989–1991 suggested two possible answers. One was that the United States would reduce its military strength dramatically and concentrate its energies and resources on pressing domestic problems. The other was that America would continue to use its power actively, not to fight communism but to defend its regional and economic interests.

The answer came quickly. In 1989, the administration ordered an invasion of Panama, which overthrew the unpopular military leader Manuel Noriega (under indictment in the United States for drug trafficking) and replaced him with an elected, pro-American regime. And in 1990, that same impulse drew the United States into the turbulent politics of the Middle East.

On August 2, 1990, the armed forces of Iraq invaded and quickly overwhelmed the emirate of Kuwait, the small oil-rich neighbor of Iraq. **Saddam Hussein**, the militaristic leader of Iraq, soon announced that he was annexing Kuwait. The Bush administration soon agreed to lead other nations in a campaign to force Iraq out of Kuwait—through the pressure of economic sanctions if possible, through military force if necessary. Within a few weeks, Bush had persuaded virtually every important government in the world, including the Soviet Union and almost all the Arab and Islamic states, to join in a United Nations–sanctioned trade embargo of Iraq.

At the same time, the United States and its allies (including the British, French, Egyptians, and Saudis) began deploying a large military force along the border between Kuwait and Saudi Arabia, a force that ultimately reached 690,000 troops (425,000 of them American). And on January 16, American and allied air forces began a massive bombardment of Iraqi troops in Kuwait and of military and industrial installations in Iraq itself.

The allied bombing continued for six weeks. On February 23, allied (primarily American) forces under the command of General Norman Schwarzkopf began a major ground offensive to the north of the Iraqi forces. The allied armies encountered almost no resistance and suffered only light casualties (141 fatalities). Estimates of Iraqi deaths in the war were 100,000 or more. On February 28, Iraq announced its acceptance of allied terms for a cease-fire, and the brief Persian Gulf War was over.

The Election of 1992

President Bush's popularity reached a record high in the immediate aftermath of the Gulf War. But the glow of that victory faded quickly as the recession worsened in late 1991. That gave **Bill Clinton**, the young two-term Democratic governor of Arkansas, an opportunity to emerge as the early front-runner. Clinton survived a bruising primary campaign and a series of damaging personal controversies to win his party's nomination.

Complicating the campaign was the emergence of Ross Perot, a blunt, forthright Texas billionaire who became an independent candidate by tapping popular resentment of the federal bureaucracy and by promising tough, uncompromising leadership to deal with the fiscal crisis. At several moments in the spring, Perot led both Bush and Clinton in public opinion polls. But in July, as he began to face hostile scrutiny from the media, he abruptly withdrew from the race. Early in October, he reentered and soon regained much (although never all) of his early support.

After a campaign in which the economy was the principal issue, Clinton won a clear, but hardly overwhelming, victory over Bush and Perot. He received 43 percent of the vote in the three-way race, to the president's 38 percent and Perot's 19 percent (the best showing for a third-party or independent candidate since Theodore Roosevelt in 1912). Clinton won 370 electoral votes to Bush's 168; Perot won none. Democrats also retained control of both houses of Congress. Republicans would have to wait eight years to reclaim the White House, when Bush's son—George W. Bush–would win the presidency.

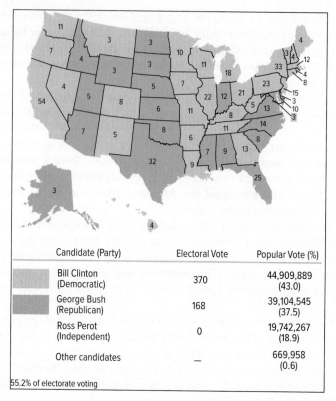

	Candidate (Party)	Electoral Vote	Popular Vote (%)
	Bill Clinton (Democratic)	370	44,909,889 (43.0)
	George Bush (Republican)	168	39,104,545 (37.5)
	Ross Perot (Independent)	0	19,742,267 (18.9)
	Other candidates	—	669,958 (0.6)

55.2% of electorate voting

THE ELECTION OF 1992 In the 1992 election, for the first time since 1976, a Democrat captured the White House. And although the third-party candidacy of Ross Perot deprived Bill Clinton of an absolute majority, he nevertheless defeated George Bush by a decisive margin in both the popular and electoral votes. • *What factors had eroded President Bush's once-broad popularity by 1992? What explained the strong showing of Ross Perot?*

CONCLUSION

America in the late 1970s was, by the standards of its own recent history, an unusually troubled nation—numbed by the Watergate scandals, the fall of Vietnam, and perhaps most of all the nation's increasing economic difficulties. The unhappy presidencies of Gerald Ford and Jimmy Carter provided little relief from these accumulating problems and anxieties. Indeed, in the last year of the Carter presidency, the nation's future seemed particularly bleak in light of severe economic problems, a traumatic seizure of American hostages in Iran, and a Soviet invasion of Afghanistan.

In the midst of these problems, American conservatives slowly and steadily prepared for a political revolution. A coalition of disparate but impassioned groups on the right—including a large movement known as the "New Right," with vaguely Populist impulses—gained strength from the nation's troubles and from their own success in winning support for a broad-ranging revolt against taxes. Their efforts culminated in the election of 1980, when Ronald Reagan became the most conservative man in at least sixty years to be elected president of the United States.

Reagan's first term was a dramatic contrast to the troubled presidencies that had preceded it and signaled a reversal or at least a modification of ruling economic and social policies.

He won substantial victories in Congress (cutting taxes, reducing spending on domestic programs, building up the military). Perhaps equally important, he made his own engaging personality one of the central political forces in national life. Easily reelected in 1984, he seemed to have solidified the conservative grip on national political life. In his second term, however, a series of scandals and misadventures—and the president's own declining energy—limited the administration's effectiveness. Nevertheless, Reagan's personal popularity remained high, and the economy continued to prosper—factors that propelled his vice president, George H. W. Bush, to succeed him in 1989.

Bush's presidency was not as successful as Reagan's had been, and the perception of his disengagement with and inability to solve the nation's growing economic problems contributed to Bush's defeat in 1992. But a colossal historic event overshadowed most domestic concerns during Bush's term in office: the collapse of the Soviet Union and the fall of communist regimes all over Europe. The United States was to some degree a dazzled observer of this process. The end of the Cold War also propelled the United States into the possession of unchallenged global preeminence—and drew it increasingly into the role of international arbiter and peacemaker. The Gulf War of 1991 was the most dramatic example of the new global role the United States would now increasingly assume as the world's only true superpower.

KEY TERMS/PEOPLE/PLACES/EVENTS

Ayatollah Ruhollah
  Khomeini 765
Bill Clinton 781
Camp David accords 765
Christian Coalition 768
deregulation 775
George H. W. Bush 780
Gerald R. Ford 762

Iran–Contra scandal 779
Jimmy Carter 764
Mikhail Gorbachev 777
Nelson Mandela 779
neoconservatives 771
New Right 769
Reagan Doctrine 777
Reaganomics 775

Ronald Reagan 769
Saddam Hussein 781
Sagebrush Rebellion 766
stagflation 763
Strategic Defense Initiative
  (SDI) 777
Sunbelt 766
Tiananmen Square 778

RECALL AND REFLECT

1. Why were the Ford and Carter presidencies unable to repair the damage done to the reputation of the presidency by the Watergate scandal and Nixon's resignation?
2. Why did the American electorate become increasingly conservative during the 1970s and 1980s? What are some examples that testify to this increasing conservatism?
3. What philosophy guided foreign policy under Reagan? How did the rise of Mikhail Gorbachev alter Reagan's foreign policy toward the Soviet Union?

31 | THE AGE OF GLOBALIZATION

A RESURGENCE OF PARTISANSHIP

SCIENCE AND TECHNOLOGY
IN THE NEW ECONOMY

A CHANGING SOCIETY

AMERICA IN THE WORLD

LOOKING AHEAD

1. How did increasing partisanship affect governing during the late 1900s and early 2000s? How does it continue to affect the relationship between the president and Congress?
2. How did the growth of the "new economy" affect how Americans worked and lived?
3. How was the American population changing at the turn of the century? What characterized it, and what key challenges does it pose?
4. How did the terrorist attack of September 11, 2001, affect the United States and begin a new era in American foreign policy?

ON AN EARLY TUESDAY MORNING IN 2001, a commercial airliner crashed into the side of one of two tallest buildings in New York, the North Tower of the World Trade Center. Within thirty minutes, another commercial airliner struck the South Tower. Before the steel girders in both towers buckled and collapsed from the tremendous heat of the burning wreckage, Americans learned of even more disasters. A plane flew into the Pentagon in Washington, D.C., and another crashed a few hundred miles away in a field not far from Pittsburgh, after passengers apparently seized the cockpit and prevented the hijackers from reaching their unknown target. In these four, almost simultaneous, catastrophes, nearly 3,000 people died.

The events of September 11 and their aftermath sparked significant changes in American life. And yet there was at least one great continuity between the world of the 1990s and the world that seemed to begin on September 11, 2001. The United States in the last years of the twentieth century and the first decades of the twenty-first, more than at any other time in its history, was becoming more and more deeply entwined in a new age of globalism—an age that combined great promise with great peril.

A RESURGENCE OF PARTISANSHIP

When Bill Clinton took the presidential oath of office in January 1993, little did he realize that partisan politics would become a crippling problem for his administration and the country in general. While partisanship had always been a steady factor of modern American political life, the turn of the twenty-first century showcased new levels of mistrust and bitter splits between the parties that fundamentally affected how the White House and Congress functioned. Clinton and the presidents to follow would find it extraordinarily difficult to engineer change on the significant issues of the day through the legislative process when the opposing party held majorities in Congress. Fewer members of Congress were willing to work out solutions that required bipartisanship, preferring to have no bill at all rather than one that required them to compromise. The inability of politicians to find middle ground between contrasting bills and initiatives gummed up the machinery of the federal government and even brought it to the brink of a shutdown on more than one occasion. At times the impasse occurred within a party, such as conservative Republicans refusing to negotiate with moderate members of their party on matters of higher taxes, raising the national debt ceiling, or supporting national health insurance.

LAUNCHING THE CLINTON PRESIDENCY

Bill Clinton entered office as the first Democratic president since Jimmy Carter and the first self-proclaimed "activist" president, meaning a president seeking to expand the active role of the federal government in solving social problems, since Lyndon Johnson. Indeed, his domestic agenda was more liberal and ambitious than that of any president since the 1960s. But Clinton also

1992
Bill Clinton elected

1993
NAFTA ratified

1995
Government shutdown

1996
Welfare reform passed

Defense of Marriage Act

Clinton reelected

1998
Lewinsky scandal breaks

Clinton impeached by House

1999
Clinton acquitted by Senate

2000
George W. Bush wins contested election

2001
9/11 attacks

U.S. defeats Taliban regime in Afghanistan

2003
U.S. invades Iraq

2004
Abu Ghraib scandal

Bush reelected

2005
Hurricane Katrina

2007
"Tea Party" fields candidates

Troop "surge" in Iraq

Mortgage crisis

2008
The Great Recession

Obama elected nation's first African American president

2010
Affordable Care Act signed

Deepwater Horizon (BP) oil spill

2012
Obama reelected

Sandy Hook school shooting

2015
Obergefell v. Hodges

2016
Trump elected

had significant political weaknesses. Having won the vote of well under half the electorate, he had no powerful mandate for change.

The new administration began with a series of missteps and misfortunes in its first months. The president's effort to end the longtime ban on gay men and lesbians serving in the military met with ferocious resistance, and he was forced to settle for a compromise known as "Don't Ask, Don't Tell," which forbade recruiters to *ask* recruits about their sexual preferences but also forbade servicemen and servicewomen to *tell* about or reveal them. Several of his early appointments became so controversial he had to withdraw them. Then Vince Foster, a longtime friend of the president who served as a deputy White House counsel and previous legal partner of First Lady **Hillary Rodham Clinton**, committed suicide in the summer of 1993. His death sparked an escalating inquiry into the Clinton's banking and real estate ventures with the Whitewater Development Corporation back in Arkansas the early 1980s. The Office of the Independent Counsel began examining these issues in what became known as the Whitewater affair in 1998 and only cleared the Clintons of wrongdoing in 2000.

Despite its many problems, the Clinton administration scored important achievements in its first year. The president narrowly won approval of a budget that marked a significant turn away from some of the policies of the Reagan–Bush years, especially the focus on reducing personal and corporate taxes. It included a substantial tax increase on the wealthiest Americans, a sizable reduction in many areas of government spending, and a major expansion of tax credits to low-income working people. He also passed the popular Family and Medical Leave Act, which permitted employees to take up to four months of unpaid maternity leave or leave to care for an infant or sick family member.

Clinton was a committed advocate of free trade. After a long and difficult battle against, among others, Ross Perot, the AFL-CIO, and many Democrats in Congress, he secured passage of the North American Free Trade Agreement (NAFTA), which eliminated most trade barriers among the United States, Canada, and Mexico. Later he won approval to sign a global accord that created the World Trade Organization (WTO), an international organization charged with negotiating agreements and settling disputes among its members.

The president's most notable and ambitious initiative was a major reform of the nation's health-care system. Early in 1993, he appointed a task force chaired by the first lady. It proposed a sweeping reform designed to guarantee coverage to every American and hold down the costs of medical care. But substantial opposition from those who believed the reform would transfer too much power to the government ultimately doomed the plan. The foreign policy of the Clinton administration was at first cautious and tentative. Yugoslavia, a nation created after World War I out of a group of small Balkan countries, dissolved again into several different countries in the wake of the 1989 collapse of its communist government. Bosnia was among the new nations, and it quickly became embroiled in a bloody civil war between its two major ethnic groups: one Muslim, the other Serbian and Christian, backed by the neighboring Serbian republic. All efforts by the other European nations and the United States to negotiate an end to the struggle failed until 1995, when the American negotiator Richard Holbrooke finally brought the warring parties together and crafted an agreement to partition Bosnia.

REPUBLICAN WINS AND LOSSES

The trials of the Clinton administration, and the failure of health-care reform in particular, proved damaging to the Democratic Party as it faced the congressional elections of 1994. Many Americans began to grow distrustful of the president and suspicious of his liberal policy goals. They looked for alternatives. For the first time in over forty years, Republicans, promising to counter Clinton and implement a Reagan-style conservative agenda, gained control of both houses of Congress.

Republicans interpreted their resounding victory at the polls as permission to fundamentally change American politics, Throughout 1995, the Republican Congress, under the leadership of House Speaker Newt Gingrich, worked feverishly to build an ambitious legislative program that they dubbed the "Contract with America." The Republicans proposed a series of measures to transfer important powers from the federal government to the states; pushed for dramatic reductions in federal spending, including a major restructuring of the Medicare program, to reduce costs; and attempted to scale back a wide range of federal regulatory functions.

President Clinton responded to the 1994 election results by shifting his own activist agenda conspicuously to the political center—announcing his own plan to cut taxes and balance the budget. But any compromise between the president and Congress was still very difficult. In November 1995 and again in January 1996, the federal government literally shut down for several days because Clinton and Congress could not agree on a budget. Utterly convinced that voters wholeheartedly embraced their aggressive conservative agenda, Republican leaders daringly refused to pass a "continuing resolution" (to allow government operations to continue during negotiations) in hopes of pressuring the president to agree to their terms. That proved to be an epic political blunder. Public opinion turned quickly and powerfully against the Republican leadership and much of its agenda. Newt Gingrich emerged as one of the most unpopular political leaders in the nation, while President Clinton slowly improved his standing in public opinion polls.

By the time the 1996 campaign began in earnest, President Clinton was in a commanding position to win reelection. Unopposed for the Democratic nomination, he faced a Republican opponent—Senator Robert Dole of Kansas—who inspired little enthusiasm even within his own party. Clinton benefited from the disastrous errors by congressional Republicans in 1995 and early 1996. But his greatest strength came from the remarkable success of the American economy and the marked reduction in the federal deficit. Like Reagan in 1984, he could campaign as the champion of peace, prosperity, and national well-being.

In a flurry of activity in the spring and summer of 1996, Congress passed several important bills. The most dramatic was a welfare reform bill that ended the fifty-year federal guarantee of assistance to families with dependent children and turned most of the responsibility for allocating federal welfare funds to the states. Most of all, it shifted the bulk of welfare benefits away from those without jobs and toward low-wage workers.

CLINTON TRIUMPHANT AND EMBATTLED

Clinton handily won reelection, becoming the first Democrat since Franklin Roosevelt to win two terms as president. Congressional Democrats, however, failed to gain a majority in the House and Senate. Clinton worked effectively with the Republican leadership on the shared goal of a balanced budget, which passed with much fanfare late in 1997. By the end of 1998, the federal budget was generating its first surplus in thirty years.

Clinton's renewed popularity was critical to his political survival in the turbulent year that followed, when the most serious crisis of his presidency suddenly erupted. Clinton had been the target of accusations of corruption and scandal since his first weeks in office: the investigation into Whitewater, charges of corruption against members of his cabinet and staff, accusations of illegalities in financing his 1996 campaign, and a civil suit for sexual harassment filed early in his first term by a former Arkansas state employee, Paula Jones.

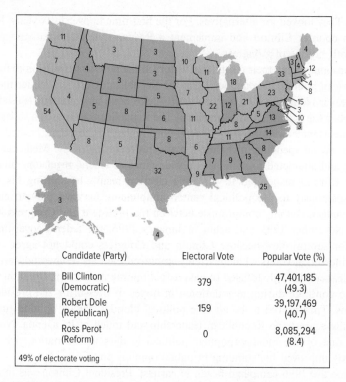

Candidate (Party)	Electoral Vote	Popular Vote (%)
Bill Clinton (Democratic)	379	47,401,185 (49.3)
Robert Dole (Republican)	159	39,197,469 (40.7)
Ross Perot (Reform)	0	8,085,294 (8.4)

49% of electorate voting

THE ELECTION OF 1996 Ross Perot received many fewer votes in 1996 than he had in 1992, and President Clinton came much closer than he had four years earlier to winning a majority of the popular vote. Once again, Clinton defeated his Republican opponent, this time Robert Dole, by a decisive margin in both the popular and electoral votes. • *After the 1994 Republican landslide in the congressional elections, Bill Clinton had seemed permanently weakened. What explains his political revival?*

In early 1998, inquiries associated with the Paula Jones case led to charges that the president had had a sexual relationship with a twenty-two-year-old White House intern, Monica Lewinsky. The most damaging charge was that he had lied about it in a sworn statement given as part of his deposition before Jones's attorneys. Those revelations produced a new investigation by the independent counsel in the Whitewater case, Kenneth Starr, who was a former judge and official in the Reagan Justice Department.

Clinton forcefully denied the charges and a majority of the public strongly backed him. His popularity soared to record levels and remained high throughout the year that followed. In the meantime, a federal judge dismissed the Paula Jones case.

But the scandal revived again with great force in August 1998, when Lewinsky struck a deal with the independent counsel and testified about her relationship with Clinton. Starr then subpoenaed Clinton himself, who—faced with the prospect of speaking to a grand jury—finally admitted that he and Lewinsky had had what he called an "improper relationship." A few weeks later, Starr submitted a lengthy and salacious report to Congress on the results of his investigation, recommending that Congress impeach the president.

IMPEACHMENT, ACQUITTAL, AND RESURGENCE

On December 19, 1998, the House, voting on strictly partisan lines, narrowly approved two counts of impeachment: perjury and obstructing justice. The matter then moved to the Senate, where a trial of the president—the first since the trial of Andrew Johnson in 1868—began in early January. It ended with a decisive acquittal of the president. Neither of the charges attracted even a majority of the votes, let alone the two-thirds necessary for conviction.

Still, the trial dampened public support for the president and stiffened congressional opposition to any of his initiatives. Indeed, the last two years of the Clinton presidency were relatively quiet. The president had no real hope of major domestic achievements in the face of a hostile Republican Congress. Overseas, however, he was more active.

In 1999, the president faced another crisis in the Balkans. This time, the conflict involved a province of Serbian-dominated Yugoslavia—Kosovo—most of whose residents were Albanian Muslims. A savage civil war erupted there in 1998 between Kosovo nationalists and Serbians. In May 1999, NATO forces—dominated and led by the United States—began a major bombing campaign against the Serbians, which after little more than a week led the leader of Yugoslavia, Slobodan Milosevic, to agree to a cease-fire. Serbian troops withdrew from Kosovo entirely, replaced by NATO peacekeeping forces. A precarious peace returned to the region.

Buoyed by his success in Europe and a rising economy, Clinton actually finished his eight years in office with his popularity higher than it had been when he had begun. No president in the years since has experienced the same approval ratings. Indeed, despite politicians' use of new technology and polling data to connect with the public, the relationship between the elected and the voter has steadily deteriorated.

THE ELECTION OF 2000

The 2000 presidential election was one of the most extraordinary in American history—not because of the campaign that preceded it but because of the sensational controversy over its results, which preoccupied the nation for more than five weeks after the actual voting.

On the ballot in November 2000 were Republican **George W. Bush**, son of the former president and a second-term governor of Texas, and Democrat Al Gore, former Tennessee senator and vice president under Clinton. Both men ran cautious, centrist campaigns. Gore won the national popular vote by the thin margin of about 540,000 votes out of about 100 million cast (a difference of 0.5 percent). But on election night, both candidates remained short of the 270 electoral votes needed for victory because the Florida results were too close to call.

After a mandatory recount over the next two days, Bush led Gore in the state by fewer than 300 votes. That total was in serious question, however, because many of the ballots cast were old-fashioned punch cards that had failed to conclusively register the choice of many voters. Instead, Florida election officials confronted cards whose holes were not cleanly punched through, leaving only a "hanging chad" or incompletely torn corner of paper for them to interpret voter intent. The Gore campaign asked for hand recounts in three critical counties, which the Florida Supreme Court unanimously supported.

The battle over the ballots continued between the candidates in the news and the courts until the U.S. Supreme Court decided *Bush v. Gore* on December 12. Voting 5 to 4 along ideological lines, the conservative majority ruled that the Florida Supreme Court's order for a recount was unconstitutional; they insisted that according to U.S. Code any revised recount order be completed by December 12 (the same day that the ruling was issued and therefore impossible to execute); and they argued that the standards for evaluating punch-card ballots were too arbitrary and unfair to withstand constitutional scrutiny. The hand recount could not proceed, and Bush's victory in Florida—and thus nationally—stood.

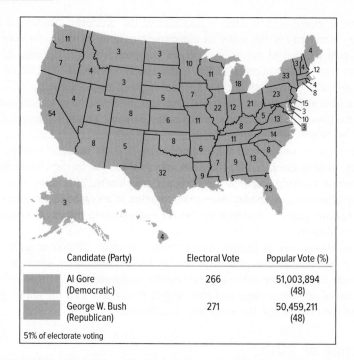

Candidate (Party)	Electoral Vote	Popular Vote (%)
Al Gore (Democratic)	266	51,003,894 (48)
George W. Bush (Republican)	271	50,459,211 (48)

51% of electorate voting

THE ELECTION OF 2000 The 2000 presidential election was one of the closest and most controversial in American history. It also starkly revealed a new pattern of party strength, which had been developing over the previous decade. Democrats swept the Northeast and most of the industrial Midwest and carried all the states of the Pacific Coast. Republicans swept the South, the plains states, and the mountain states (with the exception of New Mexico) and held on to a few traditional Republican strongholds in the Midwest. • *Compare this map to those of earlier elections, in particular the election of 1896 (Chapter 19). How did the pattern of party support change over the course of the twentieth century?*

In the congressional races, Republicans maintained control of the House of Representatives by a scant five seats, while the Senate split evenly between Democrats and Republicans. Among the victors in the Senate races was former first lady Hillary Rodham Clinton, who won in New York.

THE PRESIDENCY OF GEORGE W. BUSH

George W. Bush assumed the presidency in January 2001 burdened by both the controversies surrounding his election and the widespread perception that he was ill-prepared for the office. Nevertheless, Bush moved forcefully to enact an ambitious and controversial agenda. He won passage of the largest tax cut in American history—$1.35 trillion. Critics noted that the cuts went disproportionately to wealthy Americans, reflecting the view of White House economists that the best way to ensure growth was to put money into the hands of people most likely to invest it. He also scored a victory when Congress passed the No Child Left Behind bill, tying federal funding in schools to the success of students in taking standardized tests.

After the devastating terrorist attacks of 9/11, Bush was compelled to focus his energies on national security and foreign affairs. His tough, aggressive, and resolute stance against terrorism won him the admiration of many Americans for most of his first term. Even the Iraq War, which began in 2003 and initially enjoyed widespread backing, helped sustain his popularity for a time.

As the 2004 election approached, Karl Rove, the president's political adviser, encouraged the administration to take increasingly conservative positions to mobilize the party's conservative constituency. The electorate was divided almost evenly throughout the campaign, and in the end turnout proved decisive. Although the Democrats turned out in much higher numbers than they had in 2000, the increase in the Republican vote was even larger. Bush won a narrow victory, with 51 percent of the popular vote and an electoral vote margin of 35.

The 2004 election was one of the last successful moments in the Bush administration. Perhaps most damaging to Bush's popularity was the political fallout from Hurricane Katrina, which on August 29, 2005, smashed into 400 miles of the Gulf coast of Louisiana and Mississippi with winds of up to 125 mph and a storm surge topping 27 feet. It collapsed levees, swamped drainage canals, and flooded entire neighborhoods. Katrina caused nearly $100 billion in damages, killed more than 1,000 people, displaced over 400,000 others, and left the city of New Orleans in a state of near-ruin. During the early days of the crisis, however, federal help was slow in coming and President Bush remained on his private ranch in Texas, enjoying a vacation that had already stretched to nearly a month by the time Katrina hit. Flying back to Washington on August 30, Bush surveyed the destruction from the air and was photographed while peering sadly out of a window. Though Bush would eventually visit the damaged areas in person and direct millions of dollars in relief and aid to the hardest hit communities, he never shed the image of being indifferent to the plight of others nor the reputation of being painfully slow to respond.

The public's turn against the war in Iraq also contributed to Bush's declining approval ratings during his second term. Other factors in his growing unpopularity were scandals in the Justice Department and revelations of violations of civil liberties and brutal interviewing tactics used against suspected terrorists. Finally, unemployment rose and average household income fell during his presidency, and the economy suffered a disastrous financial crisis beginning in early 2008. Not surprisingly, Bush failed to accomplish his two major domestic policy goals in his second term, immigration reform and privatizing much of social security.

Bush managed some significant victories despite these setbacks. He won confirmation of two justices that he proposed for the Supreme Court: John Roberts, who succeeded William Rehnquist as chief justice, and Samuel Alito, who succeeded the retiring Sandra Day O'Connor. Both were fierce conservatives, inspiring hopes among some and fears among others that the Court would veer more sharply to the political right.

The Election of 2008

The 2008 presidential election was the first since 1952 that did not include an incumbent president or vice president. Both parties began the campaign with large fields of candidates, but by the spring of 2008 the contest had narrowed considerably. Republican Senator John McCain of Arizona emerged from the early primaries with the nomination ensured. In the Democratic race, the primaries quickly eliminated all but two candidates: Senator Hillary Rodham Clinton of New York, the former first lady, and Senator **Barack Obama** of Illinois, a young, charismatic politician and the son of an African father and a white American mother. As the first woman and the first African American to have a realistic chance of being elected president, Clinton and Obama attracted great enthusiasm. The passions driving both campaigns led to a primary contest that lasted much longer than usual. Not until the last primaries in June was it clear that Obama would be the nominee.

As the nomination campaigns were heating up in early 2008, the nation confronted its worst financial crisis since the Great Depression. The problem had several causes. Since the repeal in 1999 of the Glass-Steagall Act that had mandated layers of government oversight designed to catch fraud or risky investment strategies, financial institutions had been experimenting with new and risky credit instruments intended to make borrowing easier and cheaper. One such instrument, called an adjustable rate mortgage (ARM), offered homebuyers mortgages with low interest rates that would "adjust" upward in later years. Another, the "jumbo loan," extended credit that exceeded conforming loan limits to people with uncertain financial means to pay the loans back. These instruments, coupled with lax monitoring of the mortgage industry as a whole, allowed millions of people to take on large and risky mortgages to purchase homes, causing a "housing bubble"–a rapid rise in housing prices fueled by high demand. Banks offset their risks by bundling mortgages into mortgage-backed securities (MBSs), which other banks and financial firms invested heavily in. The housing bubble eventually burst. The price of homes soon leveled off and even dipped. Homeowners with ARMs saw their loans' higher rates grow beyond what they could afford, while their home's market values sunk below the value of the mortgage itself. Unable to pay off their loans, they defaulted and banks took possession of their properties; foreclosures skyrocketed across the country. Compounding the collapse of the housing bubble, the MBSs based on those loans failed as well, causing many of the nation's largest banks to teeter on the brink of collapse. Their creditors and the federal government forced them to merge with or be purchased by other, more solvent banks as a way to protect customers.

This so-called **Great Recession of 2008**, sparked by the loan crisis, pushed down wages and triggered widespread job layoffs. The increased unemployment rate further accelerated the downward economic spiral. Many Americans simply could not meet basic financial obligations such as the repayment of home, car, or school loans or credit card debt. There was also less money available for investing, stalling the potential for economic growth. Blue-collar and trades workers, manufacturers, and the poor were hardest hit by the crisis. Popular anger surfaced in art, literature, and especially contemporary music. Rap, one of the newest and most successful forms of popular music, chronicled lives of despair and called for economic change. (See "Patterns of Popular Culture: Rap.")

By mid-September 2008, the economy seemed to be spinning out of control. Secretary of the Treasury Henry Paulson, supported by other economic leaders, stepped in. He proposed a massive use of federal funds to help the government bail out banks that were failing. Both the Bush administration and eventually the Obama administration won congressional support for $750 billion in the form of the Troubled Asset Relief Program (TARP) to shore up the tottering financial institutions. The bailout kept the economy from collapsing, but it remained very weak for several years, with exceptionally high unemployment rates.

This extraordinary crisis formed the backdrop against which the two presidential candidates fought out the last two months of their campaign. Neither offered clear or convincing solutions to the crisis, but most voters came to believe that Obama would likely be a better steward of the economy than McCain. Obama benefited both from the unpopularity of George W. Bush and from his success at persuading voters that McCain would continue Bush's policies. Obama held on to–and indeed increased–his lead through late September and October, helped by a heavily financed and highly disciplined campaign.

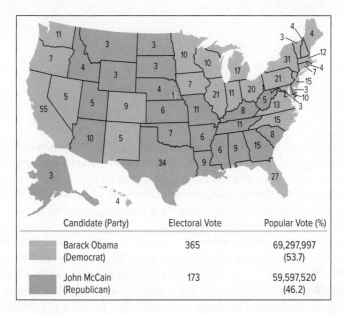

Candidate (Party)	Electoral Vote	Popular Vote (%)
Barack Obama (Democrat)	365	69,297,997 (53.7)
John McCain (Republican)	173	59,597,520 (46.2)

THE ELECTION OF 2008 The election of 2008 produced a decisive victory for Barack Obama. Democrats won majorities in both the House and the Senate, only to see the Republicans win a majority of the House two years later. • *Compare this map to the election of 2000 map. Which states did Bush win that went to Obama in 2008?*

On November 4, 2008, Barack Obama won the popular vote 53 percent to 46 percent and the electoral vote by an even larger margin. Obama became the first Democratic candidate since Lyndon Johnson to score such a decisive victory.

Obama and His Opponents

The global exuberance that Obama's election created in 2008 did not linger for long. The first two years of his presidency coincided with the worst period of the economic crisis. But large supportive Democratic majorities in both houses of Congress strengthened Obama's ability to enact broad reforms. During those years, Obama passed a stimulus package of $800 billion to support state and local budgets, public works, and other investments that he hoped would generate economic growth. He and his congressional allies also succeeded in passing significant financial regulations that were designed to avoid another crisis like the one that began in 2008. His signature achievement was the passage of the **Affordable Care Act**, a broad health-care bill aimed to give almost all Americans access to insurance, regardless of their means. Yet Obama's legislation, and especially his health-care initiative, triggered fear among many Republicans about a federal government becoming too powerful and overstepping its limits. Indeed, only one Republican member of Congress supported the health-care bill. For Obama, who had built much of his presidential bid around the idea of bipartisanship and conciliation, the polarization of the two parties was a significant setback. Many Republican states' attorneys sued to stop the health bill. Judges were divided as to whether the bill was constitutional, and only favorable rulings by the Supreme Court in June 2012 and 2015 preserved it.

The 2010 midterm congressional campaigns were dominated by the emergence of the **Tea Party movement**, a vigorous conservative effort to reduce the national debt, lower taxes, and limit the role of government. This broad movement attracted mostly white men and women, largely from the middle class. Tea Party members viewed Obama and his peers as

RAP

The long musical lineage of rap includes elements of the disco and street funk of the 1970s; of the fast-talking jive of black radio DJs in the 1950s; of the onstage patter of Cab Calloway and other African American stars of the first half of the twentieth century. It contains reminders of tap and break dancing—even of the boxing-ring poetry of Muhammad Ali.

Rap's most important element is its words. Rap is as much a form of language as a form of music. It bears a distant resemblance to some traditions of African American pulpit oratory, which also included forms of spoken song. It draws from some of the verbal traditions of urban black street life, including the "dozens"—a ritualized trading of insults particularly popular among young black men.

But rap is also the product of a distinctive place and time: the South Bronx in the 1970s and 1980s and the hip-hop culture that was born there and that soon dominated the appearance and public behavior of many young black males. "Hip hop is how you walk, talk, live, see, act, feel," said one Bronx hip-hopper. Some elements of hip-hop culture faded, and by the 1990s the most popular element of hip-hop culture was rap, which had by then been developing for nearly twenty years.

Beginning in the early 1970s, Bronx DJs began setting up their equipment on neighborhood streets and staging block parties, where they not only played records but also put on shows of their own—performances that featured spoken rhymes, jazzy phrases, and pointed comments about the audience, the neighborhood, and themselves.

Gradually, the DJs began to bring "rappers" into shows—young men who developed the DJ style into a much more elaborate form of performance, usually accompanied by dancing. As rap grew more popular in the inner city, record promoters began signing some of its new stars. In 1979, the Sugarhill Gang's "Rapper's Delight" became the first rap single to be played on mainstream commercial radio and the first to become a major hit. In the early 1980s, Run-DMC became the first national rap superstars. From there, rap moved quickly to become one of the most popular and commercially successful forms of popular music. In the 1990s and early 2000s, rap recordings routinely sold millions of copies.

Rap has taken many forms. There have been white rappers (Eminem, House of Pain), female rappers (Missy Elliott, Queen Latifah), even religious rappers and children's rappers. But it has always been primarily a product of the young male culture of the inner city, and some of the most successful rap has conveyed the frustration and anger that these men have felt about their lives—"a voice for the oppressed people," one rap artist said, "that in many other ways don't have a voice." In 1982, the rap group Grandmaster Flash and the Furious Five released a rap called "The Message," a searing description of the ghetto and the lack of educational and economic opportunities.

In the late 1980s, the Compton and Watts neighborhoods of Los Angeles—two of the most distressed minority communities in the city—produced their own style, known as West Coast rap, with such groups

(left: ©PAN Photo Agency/Shutterstock; right: ©MediaPunch/REX/Shutterstock)

SEAN "P. DIDDY" COMBS Testifying to the continued popularity of rap, Sean "P. Diddy" Combs smashed records for successful artists in 2017. Rapper, songwriter, record producer, film director, entrepreneur, and fashion designer, Combs's net worth totals $820 million. *Forbes* lists him as the most influential rapper of his time.

as Ice Cube, Ice-T, Tupac Shakur, and Snoop Doggy Dog. West Coast rap often had a harsh, angry character, and at its extremes (the so-called gangsta' rap), it could be strikingly violent and highly provocative. Scandals erupted over controversial lyrics— Ice-T's "Cop Killer," which some critics believed advocated murdering police; and the sexually explicit lyrics of 2 Live Crew and other groups, which critics accused of advocating violence against women.

But it was not just the lyrics that caused the furor. Rap artists were almost all products of tough inner-city neighborhoods, and the rough-edged styles many took with them into the public eye made many people uncomfortable. Some rappers got caught up in highly publicized trouble with the law. Several—including two of rap's biggest stars, Tupac Shakur and Notorious B.I.G.— were murdered. The business of rap, particularly the confrontational business style of Death Row Records (founded by Dr. Dre, a veteran of the first major West Coast rap group NWA), was a source of public controversy as well.

But rap is undeniably lucrative. The wealthiest artists are the most creative business minds. Kanye West invested in all aspects of the music industry. So did Sean "P. Diddy" Combs, who also started a popular clothing line bearing his name, a TV network, "Revolt TV," and designer brands of

tequila and bottled water. His net worth was estimated at $820 million in 2017, tops among rappers.

Controversies at times unfairly dominated the image of rap as a whole. Some rap is angry and cruel, as are many of the realities of the world from which it comes. But much of it is explicitly positive, some of it deliberately gentle. Chuck D, who founded Public Enemy in the mid-1980s, exhorted young black men to avoid drugs and crime, to take responsibility for their families, to get an education. More recently, St. Louis–based artist and rapper Tef Poe traveled to sites of public protests following the police shooting of unarmed black men to spread a message of peace and social activism. He has penned essays in *Time* magazine and addressed the United Nations on the need for young and old to engage in politics to improve society. And the form, if not the content, of the original rappers has spread widely through American culture. Rap came to dominate the music charts in America, and its styles made their way onto *Sesame Street* and other children's shows, into television commercials, Hollywood films, and the everyday language of millions of people, young and old, black and white. It became another of the arresting, innovative African American musical traditions that have shaped American culture for more than a century. •

1. What other African American musical forms have helped shape American popular culture?
2. If rap is so closely associated with the inner-city culture where it originated, what accounts for its widespread popularity and commercial success? What other forms or styles of popular music enjoy a popularity that extends far beyond its cultural origins?
3. Do you think rap's popularity will endure? Why or why not?

dangerous enemies to a stronger, more prosperous America. They helped send a large majority of anti-Obama Republicans to the House and reduced the majority of Democrats in the Senate. For the next two years, President Obama struggled to get proposals passed by Congress because nearly every Republican summarily rejected them.

In September 2011, another movement emerged—**Occupy Wall Street (OWS)**. But this movement preached a radically different agenda than the Tea Party movement. Significantly smaller and younger than the Tea Party, OWS argued for stricter financial regulation, progressive taxation, stronger support for unions, more resources to reduce unemployment, assaults on economic inequality, and the end of what it believed were unnecessary and failed wars. Its rallying cry was "We are the 99%," referring to the growing gap of income equality between the richest 1 percent and the rest of Americans. They symbolically demonstrated their grievances by camping in Zuccotti Park in the Wall Street area of lower Manhattan. Soon after, similar demonstrations took place in many other places in the United States and around the world. OWS, never a broad-based popular movement, quickly lost steam and was largely extinguished by 2013. Yet it served as an emblem of popular concern over the unsteady recent history of the economy and the ability of politicians to solve crises in general.

(Source: Official White House Photo by Pete Souza)

FIGHTING TERRORISM President Barack Obama and Vice President Joe Biden, along with members of the national security team, receive an update on the mission against Osama bin Laden in the Situation Room of the White House, May 1, 2011. The next day a team of U.S. Navy Seals killed bin Laden, concluding a near ten-year search for the mastermind of the 9/11 attack on America.

Obama and the Challenge of Governing

The election of 2012–the most expensive campaign in history–pitted President Obama against Mitt Romney, a former governor of Massachusetts. The race was up in the air until the very end, and enormous amounts of campaign money and effort flooded into the few states that were still up for grabs–among them Ohio, Virginia, Florida, Wisconsin, Iowa, and New Hampshire. On election night, it became clear that these states had tilted toward Obama in the last few days. The Democrats also won several new senators, giving the party a majority. The House of Representatives remained Republican, but the majority was now smaller.

The political gridlock of Obama's presidency continued after his reelection. Many of his initiatives faced serious obstacles or simply did not come to pass. A major disappointment for Obama and his supporters involved the failure to enact meaningful gun-control measures despite a series of horrific shootings occurring during his terms in office, including the shooting of twenty children and six adults at the Sandy Hook Elementary School in Newtown, Connecticut, on December 14, 2012. The National Rifle Association and the conservative wing of the Republican Party successfully warded off more than 100 attempts at introducing gun-control measures, and indeed gun sales spiked after each mass shooting.

The gridlock of the House also dashed any hopes President Obama had of gaining a deal on immigration. While he had moved aggressively to deport illegal immigrants with criminal records during his presidency, Obama also defended the essential dignity of all immigrants and highlighted their historical accomplishments in America. He now hoped to pass legislation protecting those who had lived here for long periods even if they originally entered America illegally. On June 27, 2013, the Senate, in a rare show of bipartisanship, passed a comprehensive package of provisions, including a path to U.S. citizenship for illegal immigrants already in the country. But powerful conservative Republican opposition in the House, based largely on the idea that illegal immigrants should not be granted citizenship, doomed the bill and it died in Congress. Obama responded by issuing an executive order that would delay the deportation of some immigrants, much as he had issued an executive order in 2012 protecting "dreamers" or people brought to the country illegally as children. Republicans decried what they saw as presidential overreach, and a federal judge ruled against it.

The fate of the immigration bill embodied the challenge of governing for Obama. He had whipped up popular support for a bill tackling a pressing social issue and rallied the Senate to pass it–only to see it die in the Republican-controlled House. As Clinton and Bush had before him, Obama confronted the painful realities of political leadership in modern America, where fealty to political ideology often trumped the desire to compromise with a member of the opposite party or even with those in the same party.

The Election of 2016 and President Trump

The turmoil of the 2016 presidential election overshadowed much of Obama's last year in office. Hillary Clinton, the formidable and highly experienced Democratic candidate, slugged it out with the surprise Republican nominee, **Donald Trump**. Trump, a real estate tycoon from Manhattan with no formal experience in government, had bested a strong slate of opponents during the primary by promising to "Make America Great Again" and undo or severely restrict many of Obama's policy initiatives. Campaigning to lower personal and corporate taxes, repeal and replace the Affordable Care Act, limit Muslim entry into the country, build a wall along the Mexico–U.S. border to stop illegal immigrants, roll back environmental regulations, and bolster the military, Trump appealed to voters who identified as conservatives as well as a sizable number of moderates, many of whom were dissatisfied with the status quo or viewed Hillary Clinton as untrustworthy. An emerging group of far-right white nationalists dubbed the "alt-right" also contributed to his victory. But his biggest surprise was narrowly beating Clinton, whom pundits had widely projected to become the first woman to occupy the White House. Trump lost the popular vote by nearly 2.9 million but earned 304 electoral votes to Clinton's 227. The Republican Party also retained majorities, though slim, in both the Senate and the House.

Trump's success, however, was not without controversy. Allegations that the Russian government officials had interfered with the election in favor of Trump—hacking into the e-mail accounts of the Democratic National Committee and dumping the politically damaging contents onto WikiLeaks, for example—clouded the results. In early May of his first year in office, Trump abruptly fired the FBI director, James Comey, allegedly because Comey refused to stop probes into the role of the Russians in the election, thereby giving rise to a portrayal of him as an autocratic leader. Later the same month, the Department of Justice appointed a special investigator to analyze the possibility that members of Trump's campaign staff had unsanctioned contacts or ties with representatives of the Russian government.

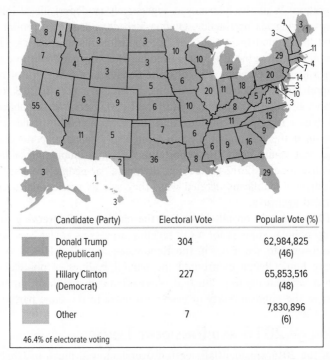

Candidate (Party)	Electoral Vote	Popular Vote (%)
Donald Trump (Republican)	304	62,984,825 (46)
Hillary Clinton (Democrat)	227	65,853,516 (48)
Other	7	7,830,896 (6)

46.4% of electorate voting

THE ELECTION OF 2016 The outcome of the 2016 presidential election was a surprise to pundits and pollsters alike. Hillary Clinton was the constant front-runner throughout much of the last weeks of the campaign. She was predicted to win, though in a close race. But Trump picked up states that traditionally voted for a Democrat in the race for the White House, including Pennsylvania, Florida, and Michigan, and won the electoral college while losing the popular vote. The race revealed a stark pattern of geographic partisanship, where voters in the South and much of the Midwest cast their ballot for Trump while those living on the West Coast and the northern half of the East Coast pledged their loyalty to Clinton. • *Compare this map to that of the election of 2000 earlier in this chapter.*
• *How did the pattern of party support change over the course of the twentieth century?*
• *What does the change—or lack of it—suggest about the state of party politics today?*

Despite the turmoil surrounding the early days of his presidency, Trump has moved aggressively if with limited success to deliver on campaign promises. His budget included tax cuts for all Americans, especially the wealthy and business owners, and a boost for the military. He worked closely with Republicans to replace the Affordable Care Act, though their efforts have failed to date. And he issued a temporary ban on Muslim immigration from countries with proven records of terrorism, only to have it rejected in federal court.

Like his predecessors in the White House, Trump is discovering the perils of governing in an era of intensely partisan politics. He struggles to reach deals with Democrats and even hold the support of members of his own party. Compounding his difficulty is his lack of experience in elected office and propensity to share his antipathies and political opinions via Twitter. His ability to "Make America Great Again" may well depend on reaching across the political divide, compromising on policy goals with political foes, and disciplining his messages to the American public.

SCIENCE AND TECHNOLOGY IN THE NEW ECONOMY

The last three decades have seen remarkable changes in American life—some a result of the end of the Cold War, some the changing character of the American population, and some a product of a rapidly evolving culture. But most of these changes were at least in part a product of the dramatic transformation of American trade and industry. Indeed, this "new economy" represented a profound shift in the nation's financial history. Throughout much of the twentieth century, manufacturing had powered the nation's economy. Making cars, rubber, steel, and airplanes, for example, had provided many workers with steady jobs and decent wages and benefits as well as entry into the middle class. But in the face of the sluggish growth and persistent inflation of the last decades of the 1900s, many American corporations began making drastic changes in the way they ran their businesses. They invested heavily in new technology to make themselves more efficient and productive and, more significantly, slashed their labor costs, which were among the highest in the world and which many economists and business leaders believed had made the United States uncompetitive against the emerging economies that relied on low-wage workers. Businesses now took a much harder line against unions. And nonunion companies became more successful in staving off unionization drives. Some companies actually moved their operations to areas of the country where unions were weak and wages low—the American South and Midwest in particular. Others simply relocated much of their production out of the United States, to such nations as Mexico and China, where there were large pools of unorganized cheap labor.

At the same time, the digital revolution took hold. The rapid development of the personal computer and the Internet profoundly reshaped how companies operated and organized themselves, rewarding in particular college-educated workers skilled in software design and application. It also redefined how people communicated, worked, shopped, and spent their free time.

The Digital Revolution

The dramatic growth in the use of computers and other digital devices was among the most significant innovations of the late twentieth and early twenty-first centuries. In 1947, Bell Labs invented the transistor, which has continued to develop and is the foundation of almost all electronic devices. The creation of the microprocessor (a specially designed collection of transistors) was first introduced in 1971 by Intel and it represented a notable advance in computational speed, energy use, and size. In 1975, Ed Roberts introduced the Altair 8800, the world's first "minicomputer," and later a personal computer or "PC." The Apple Computer Company followed by producing the Apple I desktop computer shortly thereafter in 1976 for $666, making it the first computer widely available to the public. Several years later, International Business Machines (IBM) launched its first PC, with an operating system designed by Microsoft, then a small outside developer. Over time Microsoft would overshadow IBM, as its operating systems and software became integral to most PCs with the notable exception of Apple's Mac OS (Operating System), which is preferred by professionals in the audio and visual professions. In 2007, Apple transformed personal computing with the introduction of the iPhone, combining the features of a phone, media player, and search engine in a handheld device with a novel touchscreen interface.

THE INTERNET

Out of the computer revolution emerged another dramatic source of information and communication: the Internet—a vast, geographically far-flung network of computers that allows people to communicate with others all over the world. It began in 1963, in the U.S. government's Advanced Research Projects Agency (ARPA), which funneled federal funds into scientific research projects. In the early 1960s, J. C. R. Licklider, the head of ARPA's Information Processing Techniques Office, launched a program to link together computers over large distances and create an electronic network. It was known as ARPANET.

ARPANET developed quickly because of two new technologies. The first was a system for transmitting large quantities of data in "packets." The second was the development of the Transmission Control Protocol/Internet Protocol (TCP/IP), which not only provided a way to assign addresses to machines and networks but also provided protection against lost data packets on the network.

(©Iain Masterton/Alamy)

TWENTY-FOUR-HOUR NEWS CYCLE The digital revolution has contributed to a vast change in the reporting of news events and political commentary. Politicians now have much less control over how their messages are transmitted and received.

In the early 1980s, the Defense Department, an early partner in the development of ARPANET, withdrew from the project for security reasons. The network, soon renamed the Internet, was then free to develop independently. In 1989, Tim Berners-Lee, a British scientist working at a laboratory in Geneva, introduced the World Wide Web, which helped establish an orderly system for both the distribution and retrieval of electronic information over the Internet. The growth in computer usage was remarkable. In 1971, ARPANET had linked twenty-three computers. By 2012, there were well over a billion computers in use in the world (and many more now-obsolete ones). Virtually all of them are connected to the Internet either with a physical connection or wireless (WiFi) connections that became available to the public in 1997.

The development of the Internet, along with the emergence of the computer industry and digital technology, made possible an enormous range of new products and services that quickly became central to economic life: digital music, video, and cameras; iPods, smartphones, and tablets; and Facebook, Instagram, YouTube, and Google. These modern industries employed hundreds of thousands of people (many of them from outside the United States) and created new consumer needs and appetites.

Breakthroughs in Genetics

Computers helped create new scientific breakthroughs in genetics. Early discoveries in genetics by Gregor Mendel, Thomas Hunt Morgan, and others laid the groundwork for more dramatic breakthroughs—the discovery of DNA by the British scientists Oswald Avery, Colin MacLeod, and Maclyn McCarty in 1944; and in 1953, the dramatic discovery by the American biochemist James Watson and the British biophysicist Francis Crick of the double-helix structure of DNA, and thus of the key to identifying genetic codes. From these discoveries emerged the new science—and, ultimately, the new industry—of genetic engineering, through which new medical treatments and new techniques for hybridization of plants and animals have already become possible.

Scientists began to identify specific genes in humans and other living things. But the identification of genes was painfully slow; and in 1989, in an effort to accelerate the process, the federal government appropriated $3 billion to fund the National Center for the Human Genome. The Human Genome Project formally began its mission to identify and classify all of the more than 20,000 genes in 1990 and declared its work complete in 2003.

But genetic research was (and continues to be) a source of great controversy. Many people feared that the new science might alter aspects of human life that previously seemed beyond human control. Some critics opposed genetic research on religious grounds, seeing it as an interference with "God's plan" for human nature. Still others complained that it equipped humans with immoral powers such that, for example, parents could "design" their children and "order" certain desirable traits. And a particularly heated controversy emerged over the ways in which scientists obtained genetic material. One of the most promising sources of genetic research comes from stem cell material from human embryos, but the research deeply offends those who believe that the embryo is an early-aged human life deserving of protection from harm. In 2001, President Bush issued an executive order banning federal funding of research using new sources of human stem cells. President Obama reversed the order in 2009, and in 2016 he signed the 21st Century Cures Act. The Cures Act promotes the acceleration of research on a number of fronts, including stem cell research into cell therapies that could heal damaged tissues and organs.

A CHANGING SOCIETY

The American population changed dramatically in the late twentieth and early twenty-first centuries. It grew larger, older, and more racially and ethnically diverse. It debated the success and scope of earlier landmark events, such as the civil rights movement and the Supreme Court's affirmation of a woman's right to an abortion. At the same time, the nation's citizenry confronted powerful new challenges, such as the spread of AIDS, the debate over gay rights and same-sex marriage, the prospect of dwindling natural resources, and extreme weather events and their relationship to climate change.

A SHIFTING POPULATION

Decreasing birthrates and growing life spans contributed to one of the most important characteristics of the American population in the early twenty-first century: its increasing agedness. The enormous Baby-Boom generation—people born in the first ten years after World War II—drove the median age steadily upward (from thirty-four in 1996 to thirty-eight in 2015 to a projected forty-two by 2065). It had important implications for the workforce. In the last twenty years of the twentieth century, the number of people aged twenty-five to fifty-four (known statistically as the "prime workforce") grew by over 26 million. In the first fifteen years of the twenty-first century, the number of American-born workers in that age group

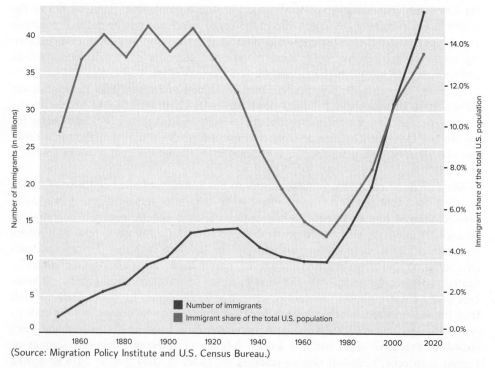

(Source: Migration Policy Institute and U.S. Census Bureau.)

U.S. IMMIGRANT POPULATION AND SHARE OVER TIME, 1850–PRESENT This chart shows the tremendous increase in immigration to the United States in the decades since the Immigration Reform Act of 1965. • *At what point since 1850 was the immigrant share of the total U.S. population highest? When was the last time that the immigrant share was at its current level?*

grew very little. This combination of fewer Americans working and more of them retired put enormous stress on the Social Security and Medicare systems to continue to fulfill their financial obligations.

The slowing growth of the native-born population, and the workforce shortages it helped create, was one reason for the rapid growth of immigration. In 2015, the number of foreign-born residents of the United States was the highest in American history—more than 43.3 million people or 13.5 percent of the entire population. These immigrants came from a wider variety of backgrounds than ever before, largely the result of the 1965 Immigration Reform Act, which eliminated national origins as a criterion for admission. The growing presence of the foreign-born contributed to a significant drop in the percentage of white residents in the United States—from 90 percent in 1965 to 76.9 percent in 2016. (Relative to overall population, non-Hispanic whites constituted just over 61 percent in 2016.) Latinos and Asians were by far the largest groups of immigrants in these years. But others came in significant numbers from Africa, the Middle East, Russia, and eastern Europe.

African Americans in the Post–Civil Rights Era

The civil rights movement and other liberal efforts of the 1960s had two very different effects on African Americans. On one hand, they increased opportunities for advancement to those in a position to take advantage of them. And they helped make possible the election of the first black American to the White House, an event unthinkable to all but the most optimistic freedom fighter during the King years. On the other hand, as the industrial economy declined and government services dwindled, there was a growing sense of helplessness and despair among large groups of the poor who continued to find themselves barred from upward mobility.

By the early twenty-first century, the black middle class constituted over half of the African American population; its progress was remarkable in the decades after the high point of the civil rights movement. African American families moved into more affluent urban communities and, in many cases, into suburbs—at times as neighbors of whites, more often into predominantly black communities. The percentage of black high school graduates going on to college was virtually the same as that of white high school graduates by the early twenty-first century (although a smaller proportion of blacks than whites completed high school). And African Americans were making rapid strides in many professions. A generation earlier, they had been barred from many jobs because of segregation. Over half of all employed African Americans in the United States had skilled white-collar jobs in 2010. There were few areas of American life from which blacks were entirely excluded.

But the rise of the black middle class also accentuated the increasingly desperate plight of less fortunate African Americans. Economic growth and the activist programs of the 1960s and beyond had never reached them in great numbers. For the school year 2012–2013, only 59 percent of black male youth graduated from high school, compared with 65 percent Latino male and 80 percent white male. In 2015, a quarter of the nation's black population was categorized as still living below the federal poverty rate, more than double that of whites. And since 1970, the percentage of black children living in poverty has rarely dipped below one-third. Black children today are three times more likely to be in poverty than white children. The black family structure changed as well from the dislocations of poverty. There was an increase in the number of single-parent black households. In 1970, 59 percent of all black children under eighteen years old lived with both their parents (already down from 70 percent a decade earlier). In 2016, only 38.7 percent of black children lived in such households, compared to 74.3 percent of white children.

Poorer African Americans were also disadvantaged by many other factors in the changing social and economic climate of the late twentieth and early twenty-first centuries. Among them was Clinton's revision of federal welfare policies and a growing impatience with affirmative action. There was also a steady decline in the number of unskilled jobs in the economy. Not surprisingly, then, many blacks openly questioned the long-term successes of the civil rights movement. A steady rise in the rate of the incarceration of young black men—indeed, perhaps one out of four black men will go to prison in the course of their lifetimes—prompted calls for better schools and intervention programs as well as a review of the justice system as a whole. Signs of popular despair surfaced during moments of racial tension, especially after the use of questionable policing tactics left black men dead, as in the case of Eric Garner in New York City in July 2014, eighteen-year-old Michael Brown in Ferguson, Missouri, in August 2014, Freddie Gray in Baltimore in April 2015, and Alton Sterling in Baton Rouge in July 2016. These highly publicized cases gave rise to the Black Lives Movement, dedicated to drawing attention to the history of questionable treatment of blacks by police and calling for formal inquiries into the killing of black men by law enforcement. It sparked national protests in cities across America, in which thousands of blacks took to the streets, demanding fairer treatment by local police and decrying a lack of racial respect between Americans of different colors.

The Abortion Debate

Conservatives became more assertive about challenging feminist causes in the late twentieth and early twenty-first centuries. Leaders of the New Right campaigned successfully against the proposed Equal Rights Amendment to the Constitution. And they won a series of legislative and judicial efforts to restrict access to abortion.

For abortion rights or "pro-choice" advocates, the Supreme Court's decision in *Roe v. Wade* (1973) had seemed to settle the question. But at the same time, critics of abortion began to build a powerful grassroots movement. These "pro-life" or "right-to-life" advocates objected to abortion on religious and moral grounds, arguing that human life was sacred from the moment of conception and that abortion itself was murder; Catholics, Mormons, and evangelical Christians passionately supported this position. The opposition of other anti-abortion activists often had less to do with religion than with their commitment to traditional morality and notions of family and gender relations. They viewed abortion as one of several assaults by feminists and their supporters on the conventional roles of women as wives, mothers, and moral guardians of the household.

Although the right-to-life movement was persistent in its demand for a reversal of *Roe v. Wade* or, barring that, a constitutional amendment banning abortion, it also attacked abortion rights in more limited ways and at their most vulnerable points. State legislatures enacted more than 1,000 restrictions in the period between 1973 and 2015, including limits on insurance coverage and on certain procedures and medications as well as imposing waiting periods, state-mandated counseling, parental consent, and tough requirements for abortion facilities. Congress passed several laws that affected abortion services, among them the Hyde Amendment—named for its chief sponsor, Rep. Henry Hyde of Illinois—that prohibited the use of federal funds for abortions except in the case of incest, rape, or threat to the mother's life. It also brought into law the Partial Birth Abortion Ban Act that banned a medical procedure called intact dilation and extraction. Presidents Reagan, Bush, and Trump were able to affect abortion policy not only by signing such laws, but also by appointing judges, health agency directors, and law enforcement officials who acted to promote a pro-life agenda.

The pro-choice movement was in many parts of the country at least as strong as, and in some areas much stronger than, the right-to-life movement. Their legislative victories included the Freedom of Access to Clinic Entrances Act (1993), which responded to the aggressive and sometimes lethal tactics of abortion protestors against abortion providers and their patients while also allowing for peaceful protests. Presidents Clinton and Obama made pro-choice appointments and supported family planning initiatives that their predecessors had curtailed. However, in order to gain support for his health-care initiative, Obama signed an order stating that the Affordable Care Act would maintain current Hyde Amendment restrictions and prohibit the use of federal funds for abortions. With the election of Donald Trump and fears of a rollback in women's reproductive rights, the feminist movement experienced a surge in activism, focusing on issues that include but are not limited to reproductive health. The Women's March on Washington, held the day after the Trump inauguration and encompassing over 650 marches across the country, has been estimated as the largest single-day demonstration in U.S. history. Planned Parenthood and NARAL (National Association for the Repeal of Abortion Laws) Pro-Choice America, among other progressive causes, saw their membership and donations spike in the aftermath of the election.

AIDS AND MODERN AMERICA

Two new and deadly epidemics ravaged many American towns and cities beginning in the 1980s. One was a dramatic increase in drug use, which penetrated nearly every community in the nation. The enormous demand for drugs, and particularly for "crack" cocaine in the late 1980s and early 1990s, spawned what was in effect a multibillion-dollar industry. Drug use declined significantly among middle-class people beginning in the late 1980s, largely because of educational campaigns, but the epidemic declined much more slowly in the poor urban neighborhoods, where it was doing the most severe damage. Yet drug abuse has never gone away. Indeed, death rates from drug overdoses have increased almost every year since 1980. More recently, widespread usage of heroin and other opioids (typically prescription painkillers) has spiked drug overdose deaths to a record high in 2016, to over 59.000. And nearly half of all federal inmates are currently serving time for drug-related offenses.

The drug epidemic facilitated the rapid spread of a new and lethal disease first documented in 1981 and soon named **AIDS** (acquired immune deficiency syndrome). AIDS is the product of the human immunodeficiency virus (HIV), which is transmitted by the exchange of body fluids (blood or semen) as can easily happen when individuals share hypodermic needles during intravenous drug usage or have unprotected sex. The virus gradually destroys the body's immune system and makes its victims highly vulnerable to a number of diseases (particularly to various forms of cancer and pneumonia) to which they would otherwise have a natural resistance.

During the early history of the disease, those infected with the virus (that is, those who identified as "HIV-positive") and became ill were almost certain to die. The first American victims of AIDS (and for many years the group among whom cases remained the most numerous) were gay, usually men. But by the late 1980s, as the gay community began to implement aggressive education and intervention programs, the most rapid increase in the spread of the disease occurred among heterosexuals, many of them intravenous drug users sharing needles.

In the mid-1990s, AIDS researchers, after years of frustration, finally began discovering effective treatments for the disease. By taking a combination of powerful drugs on a rigorous schedule, among them a group known as protease inhibitors, even people with advanced cases of AIDS experienced dramatic improvement—so much so that in many cases there were no measurable quantities of the virus left in their bloodstreams. Currently a diagnosis of AIDS is not the near-certain death sentence it was in the late nineties; rather, new medication regimes permit those living with AIDS to successfully manage the disease and live mostly normal lives. Every president has steadily increased federal funding for AIDS research and education and for the care of individuals living with AIDS, both domestically and abroad. President George W. Bush provided $15 billion to fight AIDS in Africa, where the epidemic was rampant and the poor had little access to drugs. In the budget for 2017, President Obama called for $30.4 billion to combat AIDS.

The Centers for Disease Control and Prevention (CDC) estimates that 1.1 million Americans currently suffer from AIDS, nearly one in seven not even realizing that they are infected. But the United States represents only a tiny proportion of the worldwide total of people afflicted with HIV, an estimated 36.7 million people at the end of 2015 (when the last census was taken). Over two-thirds of those cases are concentrated in Africa.

Gay Americans and Same-Sex Marriage

In the late twentieth century, inspired in part by the success of AIDS activists in winning political support and funding, many gay men and lesbians began to lobby for greater protections under the law, particularly the right to marry. Until the 1990s, the issue of same-sex marriage was not a national political issue. But in 1993, Hawaii's Supreme Court ruled in *Baehr v. Lewin* that the state needed a compelling reason to bar same-sex marriage. In response, Congress easily passed the **Defense of Marriage Act (DOMA)** in 1996 with rare bipartisan support. President Clinton signed it into law. DOMA exempted states from being required to recognize same-sex marriages from other states. It also defined marriage as being between a man and a woman and denied same-sex married couples the ability to be classified as "spouses" for federal purposes, such as the filing of joint tax returns, Social Security survivor benefit claims, adoption papers, and immigration applications. Gay rights activists identified more than 1,000 protections and responsibilities of marriage denied them by DOMA. Thirty states quickly followed suit with similar laws.

Almost immediately, gay men and lesbians and their supporters took to the courts in protest. They typically argued that DOMA and related state laws violated the Equal Protection Clause of the Fourteenth Amendment of the U.S. Constitution. They gained many victories. By 2013, eleven states had passed new legislation making same-sex marriage legal. That year as well the U.S. Supreme Court struck down the section of DOMA defining marriage as being between two people of the opposite sex, so that all married couples living in states where same-sex marriage is legal are classified as spouses by the federal government. The tide against same-sex marriage appeared to be turning.

Driving the radical change in the legal status of same-sex marriage, in addition to the guidance and political savvy of its advocates, was a profound shift in public opinion about the issue. Indeed, broad popular support for same-sex marriage grew steadily since the end of the twentieth century, primarily among younger generations of Americans. Still, there was no national consensus about the legality of same-sex marriage, and many southern and midwestern states had laws on the books preventing same-sex marriage or were engaged in heated legal battles over it. For example, in January 2015 in Alabama, a federal judge ruled in favor of same-sex marriage. (See "Consider the Source: Same-Sex Marriage, 2015.") But less than two months later, Alabama's Supreme Court, by a vote of 7 to 1, forbade county officials from issuing a marriage license to any same-sex couple. Ultimately a decision in June by the U.S. Supreme Court broke the legal stalement and compelled Alabama (and all states with gay marriage bans) to issue the licenses. In *Obergefell v. Hodges*, the Court, in a 5-to-4 decision, ruled that the U.S. Constitution guaranteed same-sex couples the fundamental right to marry. Writing for the majority, Justice Anthony Kennedy proclaimed that "No longer may this liberty be denied."

The issue of sexual orientation and citizenship, however, is far from settled. The rights of gay, transgendered, and bisexual Americans are currently being debated in courtrooms and statehouses across the country. Their ability to live free from discrimination typically depends on where they reside; different states practice different statutes because there are few federal laws binding all states to a uniform standard. Indeed, there is no federal law barring a person from being dismissed or denied employment because of sexual orientation. In July 2017, President Trump, in a reversal of policy under President Obama, announced his intention to ban transgendered men and women from serving in the military, although many were already in uniform and serving with distinction. As with the matter of same-sex marriage, the rights of gay, transgendered, and bisexual Americans will likely be settled by the Supreme Court.

THE CONTEMPORARY ENVIRONMENTAL MOVEMENT

The environmental movement in the United States continued to expand in the decades after the 1980s. It drew inspiration from the older international environmental movement, which organized in the 1960s and steadily grew in political power. (See "America in the World: The Global Environmental Movement.") After the first Earth Day, domestic environmental issues gained increasing attention and support. Although the federal government displayed only intermittent interest in the subject, environmentalists won a series of significant battles, mostly at the local level. They blocked the construction of roads, airports, and other projects that they claimed would be ecologically dangerous, taking advantage of new legislation protecting endangered species and environmentally fragile regions.

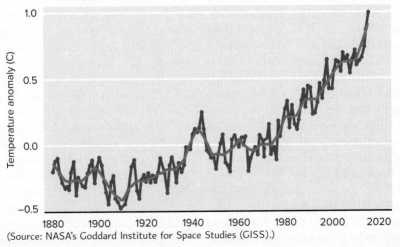

(Source: NASA's Goddard Institute for Space Studies (GISS).)

RISING GLOBAL TEMPERATURES This graph of the Global Land-Ocean Temperature Index from NASA's Goddard Institute for Space Studies illustrates the change in global surface temperature relative to 1951–1980 average temperatures.

CONSIDER THE SOURCE

SAME-SEX MARRIAGE, 2015

The debate over the right of people of the same sex to marry legally and enjoy the full range of benefits accorded to married couples under federal and state law hit a fever pitch in early January 2015.

Nearly four years earlier, Cari Searcy and Kimberly McKeand, a same-sex couple who were legally married in California under that state's laws, wanted Searcy to be able to adopt McKeand's eight-year-old biological son under a provision of Alabama's adoption code that allows a person to adopt her "spouse's child." But Searcy's petition was denied in December 2011 based on the Alabama Sanctity of Marriage Amendment and the closely related Alabama Marriage Protection Act. Both laws declared that "Marriage is inherently a unique relationship between a man and a woman," that "No marriage license shall be issued in the State of Alabama to parties of the same sex," and that "The State of Alabama shall not recognize as valid any marriage of parties of the same sex that occurred or was alleged to have occurred as a result of the law of any jurisdiction regardless of whether a marriage license was issued." Therefore, because Alabama does not recognize the legality of same-sex plaintiffs' marriage, Searcy failed to qualify as a "spouse" for adoption purposes. Searcy appealed the denial of her adoption petition to the Alabama Court of Civil Appeals, which ruled against her and affirmed the decision of the probate court.

In federal court, Searcy sued the attorney general of Alabama, Luther Strange, and sought to declare these two Alabama state laws unconstitutional on the grounds that they violated the due-process clause and equal protection clause of the Fourteenth Amendment. Callie Granade, a federal judge for the U.S. District Court in Alabama (Southern Division), agreed in January 2015. She ordered the state to begin to issue marriage licenses to same-sex couples immediately, though the order was delayed while Attorney General

Strange appealed to the U.S. Supreme Court for a stay. But once the High Court refused to hear the case, on February 9, Granade's order took effect. Some counties obliged, but others didn't, heeding the encouragement of Alabama's Supreme Court justice, Roy Moore, to ignore the federal ruling. Then, in March 2015, the state's Supreme Court ruled 7 to 1 that all probate justices (county officials charged with the management of marriage licenses) must cease issuing marriage licenses to same-sex couples. In June, the U.S. Supreme Court ruled that gay marriage bans such as Alabama's were unconstitutional.

In the following excerpt from Judge Granade's ruling, she clarifies why she ruled in favor of same-sex marriage.

Defendant contends that Alabama has a legitimate interest in protecting the ties between children and their biological parents and other biological kin. However, the Court finds that the laws in question are not narrowly tailored to fulfill the reported interest. The Attorney General does not explain how allowing or recognizing same-sex marriage between two consenting adults will prevent heterosexual parents or other biological kin from caring for their biological children. He proffers no justification for why it is that the provisions in question single out same-sex couples and prohibit them, and them alone, from marrying in order to meet that goal. Alabama does not exclude from marriage any other couples who are either unwilling or unable to biologically procreate. There is no law prohibiting infertile couples, elderly couples, or couples who do not wish to procreate from marrying. Nor does the state prohibit recognition of marriages between such couples from other states. The attorney general fails to demonstrate any rational, much less compelling, link between its prohibition and non-recognition of same-sex marriage and its goal of having more children raised in the biological family structure the state wishes to promote. There has been no evidence presented that these marriage laws have any effect on the choices of couples to have or raise children, whether they are same-sex couples or opposite-sex couples. In sum, the laws in question are an irrational way of promoting biological relationships in Alabama. . . .

If anything, Alabama's prohibition of same-sex marriage detracts from its goal of promoting optimal environments for children. Those children currently being raised by same-sex parents in Alabama are just as worthy of protection and recognition by the State as are the children being raised by opposite-sex parents. Yet Alabama's Sanctity laws harms the children of same-sex couples for the same reasons that the [U.S.] Supreme Court found that the Defense of Marriage Act harmed the children of same-sex couples. Such a law "humiliates . . . thousands of children now being raised by same-sex couples. The law in question makes it even more difficult for the children to understand the integrity and closeness of their own family and its concord with other families in their community and in their daily lives." [Windsor, 133 S. Ct. at 2694] Alabama's prohibition and non-recognition of same-sex marriage "also brings financial harm to children of same-sex couples," [id at 2695] because it denies the families of these children a panoply of benefits that the State and the federal government offer to families who are legally wed. Additionally, these laws further injures those children of all couples who are themselves gay or lesbian, and who will grow up knowing that Alabama does not believe they are as capable of creating a family as their heterosexual friends.

For all of these reasons, the court finds that Alabama's marriage laws violate the Due Process Clause and Equal Protection Clause of the Fourteenth Amendment to the United States Constitution.

UNDERSTAND, ANALYZE, & EVALUATE

1. How does Judge Granade's ruling reflect—or not reflect—changing popular attitudes toward gay men and lesbians?
2. How is the definition of a "family" being redefined?
3. In what ways do the actions of Judge Roy Moore and the Alabama Supreme Court evoke tensions between the state and civil rights protesters of the 1950s and 1960s? Or are the civil rights of black Americans and gay and lesbian Americans two very different issues?
4. In his dissenting opinion in *Obergefell v. Hodges*, Supreme Court Justice John Roberts said, "The fundamental right to marry does not include a right to make a state change its definition of marriage." What does the decision in *Searcy v. Strange* have to say about the state's definition of marriage?

Source: *Searcy v. Strange*, Civil Action No. 14-0208-CG-N (S.D. Ala. Jan. 25, 2015), https://scholar.google.com/scholar_case?case=14084561318965877067&hl=en&as_sdt=6&as_vis=1&oi=scholarr (accessed March 19, 2015).

In the late 1980s, the environmental movement began to mobilize around a new and ominous challenge—"global warming." Many scientists argued that a steady rise in the earth's temperature and corresponding climate changes could be linked to CO_2 emissions from the burning of fossil fuels (most notably coal and oil). Although these findings were disputed, by the early twenty-first century a growing consensus began to emerge—in part as a result of the leadership of significant public figures, such as former vice president Al Gore, who won a Nobel Peace Prize in 2007 for his efforts to draw attention to the problem.

THE GLOBAL ENVIRONMENTAL MOVEMENT

An international movement for well over a century, environmentalism has grown rapidly throughout the world in the late twentieth and early twenty-first centuries. What began as a series of localized efforts to preserve wilderness sites and to clean up air and water has evolved into a broad effort to deal with concerns that affect, and threaten, the entire globe.

During the 1960s, 1970s, and 1980s, while long-standing American environmental associations such as the Wilderness Society, the Sierra Club, and the National Audubon Society were being rejuvenated, organizations elsewhere in the world sought to create an international environmental movement. The World Wildlife Fund (WWF), created in Switzerland in 1961, eventually attracted more than 5 million supporters in over 150 countries and now claims to be the world's largest independent conservation organization. Greenpeace was founded in Canada in 1971 to oppose U.S. nuclear testing off the coast of Alaska. It, too, has grown into an international organization, with 2.8 million financial supporters worldwide and a presence in forty nations.

Nongovernmental organizations (NGOs) such as Greenpeace and WWF were not the only institutions to recognize environmental concerns. In June 1972, the United Nations (UN) held its first Conference on the Human Environment in Stockholm, Sweden. Representatives of 113 countries attended the conference to discuss issues of global environmental importance—including the role of chlorofluorocarbons (CFCs), a chemical compound used in refrigerants and aerosol sprays, in depleting the ozone layer.

After the conference, the UN created the United Nations Environment Programme (UNEP) to help coordinate international efforts for environmentalism and encourage sustainable development in poorer nations around the world.

The world's first "Green" parties—political parties explicitly devoted to environmental concerns (and often to other issues of social justice)—appeared in 1972, beginning in New Zealand (the Values Party) and Tasmania (the United Tasmania Group). Since then, Green parties have proliferated throughout the world, including in the United States. The most powerful Green party to date has been *Die Grünen* in Germany, founded in 1980. *Die Grünen* allied with the Social Democratic Party in a governing coalition from 1998, and in 2000, this coalition successfully passed the Nuclear Exit Law, which set a timetable of twenty years for Germany's eventual abandonment of nuclear power and a switch to renewable energy.

Large-scale ecological catastrophes have often helped galvanize the global environmental movement. Among the more significant of these events was the Bhopal disaster of 1984, in which a gas leak at a Union Carbide pesticide plant in Bhopal, India, resulted in the deaths of between 3,000 and 15,000 people. Two years later, a nuclear reactor accident in the Soviet city of Chernobyl, in Ukraine, caused fifty-six direct deaths, with predictions of many thousands more deaths to follow as a result of exposure. The area around Chernobyl itself is expected to be partially contaminated for 24,000 years, the radioactive half-life of plutonium-239. A less catastrophic nuclear accident at Three Mile Island, Pennsylvania, in 1979 heightened antinuclear sentiment in the United States. In 1989, the oil tanker *Exxon Valdez* ran aground on Bligh Reef in Prince William Sound, Alaska, and spilled approximately 10.9 million gallons of crude oil. Eventually covering thousands of square miles of ocean water (and 1,300 miles of Alaska shoreline) in oil, the spill killed hundreds of thousands of animals instantly and devastated the fragile ecosystem of the sound. The 2010 explosion of the Deepwater Horizon well about 50 miles southeast of the Mississippi Delta caused the largest marine oil spill in history.

In developed, industrialized nations, environmental advocacy has largely focused on energy policy, conservation, clean technologies, and changing individual and social attitudes about consumption (as in the recycling movement). The growth of environmentalism is often linked to issues of human and democratic rights and freedom from First World exploitation. For example, the Green Belt Movement in Kenya, begun in 1977 by Wangari Maathai, encouraged Kenyan women to plant over 30 million trees across the nation to address the challenges of deforestation, soil erosion, and lack of water. The Green Belt Movement became an important human rights and women's rights organization, focused on reducing poverty and promoting peaceful democratic change through environmental conservation and protection. Maathai won the 2004 Nobel Peace Prize for her achievements.

Over the past two decades, the environmental movement has grown even more global in scope, with multilateral environmental treaties and worldwide summits becoming the principal strategies of advocates. In 1997, an international effort to reduce global warming by mandating the lowering of greenhouse gas emissions culminated in the Kyoto Protocol (which the United States did not join). While the George W. Bush administration rejected most efforts to limit carbon emissions, other leading Americans helped bring the issue of global warming to wide attention both in the United States and around the world. Perhaps most notable has been former vice president Al Gore, whose 2006 film *An Inconvenient Truth* may have done more to raise awareness of the threat of global warming than any other recent event—both in the United States and in many other nations. As a result of his efforts, Gore won the 2007 Nobel Peace Prize—an honor he shared with others, appropriately, given the global character of the movement he has championed. His cowinner was the Inter-governmental Panel on Climate Change, launched in Switzerland in 1988 and affiliated with the United Nations.

In the years since Gore's Nobel Peace Prize, climate change has become a major international issue. Overwhelming evidence that increased levels of atmospheric carbon dioxide produced by the use of fossil fuels has began to alter the world's climate has prompted world leaders to take notice. In particular, oceans have begun to rise slowly, large snow and ice bodies melt, and plants grow earlier in their life cycles. In 2015, 195 countries, including the United States, pledged to combat climate change by signing the Paris Accord. In 2017, however, President Trump removed America from the agreement. •

UNDERSTAND, ANALYZE, & EVALUATE

1. Why are environmental movements in developing nations often linked to issues of human rights and protection from exploitation by developed nations? How do developed nations threaten the environment of developing nations?
2. Why do you think the global environmental movement is growing in strength today?

In 1997, representatives of the major industrial nations met in Kyoto, Japan, and agreed to a broad treaty establishing steps toward reducing carbon emissions and thus slowing or reversing global warming. The Clinton administration formally signed the Kyoto Protocol, but nothing came of it. Indeed, Clinton never even submitted it for ratification because the Senate had earlier passed the Byrd-Hagel Resolution by a vote of 95 to 0 that formally rejected the treaty's key tenets. President George W. Bush, while proclaiming grave concern over climate concern, refused to support the Kyoto Protocol because it excluded developing countries like China and India.

Unlike Bush, President Obama met with some success on climate change issues. He championed and signed legislation raising fuel efficiency in passenger cars and trucks in 2012 and directed the Environmental Protection Agency to regulate coal ash, a major CO_2 emitter primarily used in creating electricity. In 2015, Obama notched one of his biggest and most personally meaningful victories despite continued Republican protest. With 195 other countries, he entered into the Paris Accord to combat global climate change. Under the Accord, the United States promised to cut its own greenhouse gas emissions somewhere between 26 and 28 percent of its 2005 levels by 2025. Obama then pledged up to $3 billion to help for poor countries develop ways to battle climate change.

But U.S. participation was short-lived. Five months after taking office, President Trump sharply reversed the American position. He informed other signees of the Paris Accord that the United States would withdraw from the international climate agreement, arguing that it imposed unjust standards on American businesses and consumers. Even though America's departure promises to limit global effort aimed at slowing or reversing global warming, the other signees to the Paris Accord have vowed to keep their work and press on.

AMERICA IN THE WORLD

The celebration of the beginning of a new millennium on January 1, 2000, was an important moment not just because of the change in the calendar. It was notable above all as a global event—a shared and for the most part joyous experience that united the world in its exuberance. But if the millennium celebrations suggested the bright promise of an interconnected world, other events at the dawn of the new century suggested its dark perils. Indeed, the United States' increasing role as an economic and military superpower triggered fears among many Americans about a foreign policy that was too aggressive and trade initiatives that took advantage of low-wage workers in other countries and unfairly benefited large international businesses. The rise of mass protests over America's global economic policies and terrorism painfully brought home the dangers of living in the twenty-first century.

OPPOSING THE "NEW WORLD ORDER"

In the United States and other industrial nations, opposition to globalization—or to what President George H. W. Bush once called the "new world order"—took several forms. To many Americans on both the political left and right, the nation's increasingly interventionist foreign policy was deeply troubling. Critics on the left charged that the United States was using military action to advance its economic interests, arguing that the 1991 Gulf War and the Iraq War that began in 2003 were primarily intended to preserve access to foreign oil.

Critics on the right complained that humanitarian interventions in Somalia in 1993 and the Balkans in the late 1990s were too costly and risky. Others worried that the United States was ceding its sovereignty to international organizations, such as United Nations–led peacekeeping missions.

Labor unions insisted that the rapid expansion of free-trade agreements unfairly led to the export of jobs from advanced nations to less developed ones. They pointed to the trend of American manufacturers relocating plants in foreign countries where labor was cheaper and government regulation less. Civil rights groups argued that the global economy was creating new classes of "slave laborers" working in conditions that few Western nations would tolerate. Environmentalists argued that globalization, in exporting industry to low-wage countries, also exported industrial pollution and toxic waste into nations that had no effective laws to control them, and contributed significantly to global warming. And still others opposed global economic arrangements on the grounds that they enriched and empowered large multinational corporations and threatened the freedom and autonomy of individuals and communities.

Varied opponents of globalization found a common enemy in the multinational institutions that policed and advanced the global economy. Among them were the World Trade Organization, which monitored the enforcement of the General Agreement on Tariffs and Trade (GATT) treaties of the 1990s; the International Monetary Fund (IMF), which controlled international credit and exchange rates; and the World Bank, which made money available for development projects in many countries. In November 1999, when leaders of leading industrial nations gathered for their annual meeting in Seattle, Washington, tens of thousands protested—most of them peacefully. But some of them clashed with police, smashed store windows, and all but paralyzed the city. A few months later, a smaller but still substantial demonstration disrupted meetings of the IMF and the World Bank in Washington, D.C. And in July 2001, at a meeting of the same leaders in Genoa, Italy, an estimated 50,000 demonstrators battled with police in a melee that left one protester dead and several hundred injured. The participants in the meeting responded to the demonstrations by pledging $1.2 billion to fight the AIDS epidemic in developing countries—and by deciding to hold future meetings in remote locations far from major cities.

The Rise of Terrorism

Outside the industrialized West, the impact of globalization sparked other controversies. Many citizens of nonindustrialized nations resented the way the world economy had left them in poverty. In their view, the developed world exploited and oppressed them. In some parts of the nonindustrialized world—particularly in some of the Islamic nations of the Middle East—the increasing reach of globalization created additional grievances, rooted not just in economics but also in religion and culture.

The Iranian Revolution of 1979, in which orthodox Muslims ousted a despotic government, was one of the first large and visible manifestations of a phenomenon that eventually reached across much of the Islamic world. It threatened the stability of the globe. Militants used isolated incidents of violence and mayhem, designed to disrupt societies and governments and to create fear among their peoples. Such tactics are known to the world as terrorism.

Terrorism refers to the use of violence as a form of intimidation against peoples and governments. It is neither a new term nor one confined to contemporary America. Acts of what came to be called terrorism have occurred in many parts of the world. Irish revolutionaries engaged in terrorism regularly against the English through much of the twentieth century. Jews used it in Palestine against the British before the creation of Israel, and Palestinians have used it frequently against Jews in Israel—particularly in the past several decades. Revolutionary groups in Italy, Germany, Japan, and France have engaged in terrorist acts intermittently over the past several decades.

The United States, too, has experienced terrorism for many years, much of it against American targets abroad—including the bombing of the Marine barracks in Beirut in 1983; the explosion that brought down an American airliner over Lockerbie, Scotland, in 1988; the bombing of American embassies in 1998; and the assault on the U.S. naval vessel *Cole* in 2000. Terrorist incidents were relatively rare, but not unknown, within the United States itself prior to September 11, 2001. Militants on the American left performed various acts of terror in the 1960s and early 1970s as part of antiwar and anarchist movements. Timothy McVeigh, part of a militant right-wing movement, executed the largest single terrorist act on American soil before 9/11 when he blew up a federal building in Oklahoma City in 1995, killing 168 people. A year later, serial bomber Eric Robert Rudolph wreaked havoc at the Summer Olympics in Atlanta. And in 1993, foreign Islamic militants launched a successful terrorist attack on American soil, detonating a bomb in the parking garage of the World Trade Center that killed six people, injured a thousand, and caused serious but not irreparable structural damage to the towers.

Most Americans, however, considered terrorism a problem mainly confined to other nations. That changed swiftly on September 11, 2001, when **Al Qaeda** terrorists, in a series of coordinated attacks, hijacked four planes. They drove two into the World Trade towers in New York, collapsing both structures; and another into the Pentagon outside Washington, damaging it heavily. The final plane, on route to Washington, crashed in rural Pennsylvania after passengers fought with the hijackers. Nearly 3,000 Americans

(©Robert J Fisch/Flickr Open/Getty Images)

SEPTEMBER 11, 2001 At 9:03 AM, hijackers crashed United Airlines Flight 175 into floors 75-85 of the New York City's World Trade Center South Tower, killing all on board and hundreds inside the building. Only 16 minutes earlier another group of hijackers had piloted American Airlines Flight 11 into floors 93-99 of the North Tower, seen here burning.

were killed. The **9/11 attacks** jolted Americans out of any sense of complacency and made them confront the dangers of international terrorism. They also initiated a new and aggressive campaign by the federal government and military to combat foreign threats to American security.

THE WAR ON TERROR

In the aftermath of September 11, 2001, the U.S. government launched what President Bush called a "war on terror." The attacks on the World Trade Center and the Pentagon, government intelligence indicated, had been planned and orchestrated by Middle Eastern agents of a powerful terrorist network known as Al Qaeda. Its leader, **Osama bin Laden**—until 2001 little known outside the Arab world—quickly became one of the most notorious figures in the world. The militant Taliban government of Afghanistan had sheltered and supported Al Qaeda previously, and most reports placed bin Laden in its continued care. In 2001, NATO, led by the United States, began a sustained campaign of bombing against the regime and sent in ground troops. Afghanistan's Taliban regime quickly collapsed, and its leaders—along with the Al Qaeda fighters allied with them—fled the capital, Kabul. American and anti-Taliban Afghan troops pursued them into the mountains but failed to capture bin Laden and the other leaders of his organization.

American forces in Afghanistan rounded up several hundred people with suspected connections to the Taliban and Al Qaeda and moved these prisoners (and eventually others) to a facility at the American military base in **Guantánamo**, Cuba. They were among the first suspected terrorists to be handled by the Bush administration in dealing with terrorism after September 11, 2001. They were held for months, and in some cases years, without access to lawyers, without facing formal charges, and were subjected to intensive interrogation and at times even torture. Critics denounced the dangers to basic civil liberties. At the same time, the federal government dramatically increased the approval of secret surveillance warrants against alleged foreign spies living in the United States. Overseeing these warrants is the Foreign Intelligence Surveillance (FISA) Court, established in 1978, whose proceedings are strictly shielded from public view. The covert nature of the court and its controversial rulings caused a long-running debate over the government's tactics to fight terror. Most notably, and as exposed in a cache of leaked documents by one-time CIA contractor Edward Snowden, the court compelled Verizon to turn over a log of customer cell phone records to the National Security Administration in 2013. Still, pointing to Guantánamo Bay and the newly expanded reach of the FISA Court, others argued that these new tactics were sadly necessary to protect Americans. In the matter of how to combat terrorism effectively and constitutionally, there were no easy answers. President Obama, in his first month in the White House, pledged to close the prison at Guantánamo in part because of the unfair treatment of its prisoners. But he soon found that the promise was impossible to keep during the war on terror.

THE IRAQ WAR

In his State of the Union address to Congress in January 2002, President Bush spoke of an "axis of evil," which included the nations of Iraq, Iran, and North Korea—all countries with anti-American regimes that either possessed or assumed to be trying to acquire nuclear weapons. Although Bush did not say so at the time, many people around the world interpreted these words to mean that the United States would soon try to topple the government of Saddam Hussein in Iraq.

For over a year, the Bush administration slowly built a public case for invading Iraq. Much it rested on two claims, neither of which directly implicated Hussein in the 1993 or 2001 deadly attacks on the World Trade Center in New York City. One was that Iraq was supporting terrorist groups that were hostile to the United States. The other, and eventually the more important, was that Iraq either had or was developing what came to be known as "weapons of mass destruction," which included nuclear weapons and agents of chemical and biological warfare. Less central to these arguments, at least in the United States, was the charge that the Hussein government was responsible for major violations of human rights. Except for the last, none of these claims turned out to be accurate.

In March 2003, American troops, with support from Great Britain and several other countries and partial authorization from the United Nations, invaded Iraq and quickly toppled the Hussein regime, beginning the **Iraq War**. Hussein himself went into hiding but was eventually captured in December 2003. He was executed in Iraq on December 30, 2006. In May 2003, shortly after the American capture of Baghdad, President Bush made a dramatic appearance on an aircraft carrier off the coast of California, where he declared victory in the Battle of Iraq, praised the military and allies in the war effort, and warned of the "difficult work to do in Iraq" while standing in front of a large sign reading "Mission Accomplished."

In the following months, however, events in Iraq suggested that the mission had only just begun. Of the more than 4,800 American soldiers killed in Iraq as of 2014, over 4,000 of them died after the "mission accomplished" speech. And despite significant efforts by the United States and its allies to hand over authority to an Iraqi government and to restore order to the country, insurgents continued to disrupt the recovery with persistent attacks and terrorist actions throughout the fragile nation.

Support for the war in the United States steadily declined in the years after the first claim of victory. The failure to find widespread and conclusive evidence of the weapons of mass destruction was a hammer blow to the war's credibility. Another blow came from reports of the torture and humiliation of Iraqi prisoners by American soldiers at the Abu Ghraib prison in Baghdad and other sites in Iraq and around the world.

The invasion of Iraq was the most visible evidence of a basic change in the long-term structure of modern American foreign policy. Ever since the late 1940s, the containment policy had become the cornerstone of America's role in the world. The United States had worked to maintain global stability by containing, but not often directly threatening or attacking, its adversaries. Even after the Cold War ended, the United States strove to practice containment and exercise military constraint despite its unchallenged military preeminence. In the administrations of George H. W. Bush and Bill Clinton, for example, American leaders still worked closely with the United Nations and NATO to achieve U.S. international goals and resisted taking unilateral military action.

There had always been those who criticized these constraints. They believed that America should do more than maintain stability and move actively to topple undemocratic regimes and destroy potential enemies of the United States. In the administration of George W. Bush, these critics took control of American foreign policy and began to reshape it. The legacy of containment was largely repudiated. Instead, the public stance of the American government was that the United States had the right and the responsibility to fight tyranny and spread freedom throughout the world—not just by exhortation and example but also, when necessary, by military force. In Latvia in May 2005, President Bush spoke of the decision at the end of World War II not to challenge Soviet domination of Eastern Europe. That decision had rested on the belief that such a challenge would lead the United States into another war. The controversial agreement negotiated at Yalta in 1945 by Roosevelt,

Churchill, and Stalin, which failed to end the Soviet occupation of Poland and other Eastern European nations, was, the president said, part of an "unjust tradition" by which powerful governments sacrificed the interests of small nations. "This attempt to sacrifice freedom for the sake of stability," the president continued, "left a continent divided and unstable." The lesson, Bush suggested, was that the United States and other great powers should value stability less and freedom more, and should be willing to take greater risks in the world to end tyranny and oppression.

NEW CHALLENGES IN THE MIDDLE EAST

The end of the American combat role in Iraq was already under way in the last year of the Bush administration. Obama brought it to a close in 2010 and withdrew the last combat troops in 2011. At the same time, he committed significant additional soldiers to the war in Afghanistan, where Americans had been fighting since 2001. Obama escalated the **Afghan war** in 2011. For almost ten years, a major goal of American foreign policy was to find Osama bin Laden, the head of Al Qaeda, the organization behind the destruction of 9/11. In May 2011, Navy Seals found and killed bin Laden. Shortly afterward, leaders from countries of the North Atlantic Treaty Organization drafted a plan for the withdrawal of international forces from Afghanistan and facilitated peace talks between the Afghan government and the Taliban. Obama ordered nearly all American troops to leave the country and cease combat operations by the close of 2014, in effect ending American involvement in the conflict.

Despite the end of the Iraq War and the killing of bin Laden, conflict in the Middle East continued to dominate American foreign policy under Obama. The president had appointed Hillary Clinton as his secretary of state and together they tried to create peace between Israel and Palestine—an effort that made little or no progress. Elsewhere they sought to improve relationships damaged by the Iraq War and to build new international trade opportunities. But resurgent turmoil in the Middle East created new challenges. The United States intervened in a civil war in Libya and helped end the regime of the long-standing leader Muammar al-Qaddafi. And in 2012, Obama and Clinton began to pressure Iran from creating nuclear weapons. Three years later, Iran signed an international pact effectively halting its development of any nuclear arms in exchange for lifting economic sanctions originally put in place to check its nuclear ambitions. Yet that deal is currently in danger of crumbling. President Trump openly doubts Iran will ever keep its word while Iran now says it could restart its nuclear program immediately if Trump follows through on his threat to cancel the deal.

On a different front, Syria, a country locked in violent civil war since 2011, experienced a new and terrifying level of bloodshed. Opponents of the Ba'ath government sought the ouster of President Bashar al-Assad and his repressive regime. Assad unleashed the army in response, killing an estimated 120,000 of his own people by September 2013. The displacement of hundreds of thousands of Syrians into neighboring countries threatened to further destabilize the region. Assad's use of chemical weapons triggered a strong condemnation by the United States and its European allies, such as Britain, France, and Germany. Working with Russia, a traditional ally of the Assad regime, the United States and Europe brokered a delicate deal to remove the stockpile of chemical weapons from the country. Obama, aware of his nation's unwillingness to become involved in another ground war, resisted calls for sending troops to dislodge Assad. But four months after Obama left office, in April 2017, Syria thumbed its nose at its earlier anti-chemical weapons pledge and gassed over eighty to death. President Trump swiftly ordered the firing of fifty-nine cruise missiles on the Syrian government air base from which the chemical attacks were launched.

A volatile element in the Syrian conflict—as well as politics in Iraq and throughout the Middle East and Europe—has been the rise of ISIS (the Islamic State of Iraq and Syria). Composed of former Al Qaeda fighters and their supporters, this powerful rebel group seeks not only to topple the Assad regime but more broadly to install itself as a conservative Islamic state that would stamp out any Western cultural and political influence throughout the world. As a result, it violently opposes Western nations like America and its allies, including Islamic countries such as Jordan and Saudi Arabia that support America's position. ISIS has steadily conducted campaigns of terror against Western nations, kidnapping and murdering American and British citizens and posting gruesome videos of beheadings to social media websites around the world. It has used online propaganda to radicalize individuals who have carried out more than 140 terrorist attacks in twenty-nine countries beyond Iraq and Syria, killing at least 2,000 people and injuring many more. In 2018, ISIS serves as a symbol of the persistent instability of the region and a reminder of the continuing threat of terrorism.

DIPLOMACY AND THREATS IN EAST ASIA

Even though Obama focused much of his foreign policy on the Middle East, China's growing military and economic power also grabbed his attention. Recognizing the need to open new doors of cooperation, Obama became the first president to visit China during his first year in office. Secretary of State Clinton followed by announcing a "pivot" of American diplomatic and military focus to Asia as a way to expand and protect American interests there.

(©Kirsty Wigglesworth/AP Photo)

DRONES   Unmanned combat air vehicles (UCAVs), also known as drones, have become weapons of choice during many U.S. military engagements throughout the world. Pilots operate these vehicles from remote sites, a practice that was unimaginable when the international laws of war were last drafted in 1949. In calling for an examination of the use of drones, critics have cited the unintended killing of citizens in Pakistan and the targeting of three American citizens by U.S. drones in Yemen.

In particular she intended to facilitate greater access to booming Chinese markets for struggling U.S. manufacturers and to defuse the threat of aggression and nuclear proliferation by China's close ally, North Korea. But Obama and Secretary Clinton were also wary of China's economic ambitions. When China established the Asian Infrastructure Investment Bank in 2016 as a way to bolster its leadership in regional trade, the Obama administration accelerated efforts to forge the Trans-Pacific Partnership with Asian and Pacific allies—a partnership that never came into being before Obama left office and, given President Trump's unfavorable opinion of it, probably never will.

China has become a major focus for the Trump administration during its early days as well, although for a very different reason—to help establish better relations with North Korea. North Korea has publicly bragged of getting close to developing a fully fledged nuclear program and begun to test long-range missiles capable of delivering a nuclear payload to American allies like South Korea and Japan and the American territory of Guam. North Korea's dictator, Kim Jong-un, has also boasted that his scientists are nearing completion of a new intercontinental ballistic missile capable of reaching Hawaii. In response, Trump officials have sought to enlist China in an effort to restrain North Korea's bellicosity and halt the progress of its nuclear program. At the same time, the United States had led a successful effort at the United Nations to impose economic sanctions on North Korea as a way of encouraging it to curb its nuclear ambitions and tamp down its aggressive posture. President Trump himself has sworn to respond militarily to any effort by North Korea to threaten or attach an American ally.

A New Cold War?

Turmoil in the Middle East and the threat of terrorism are not the only focal points of current American foreign policy. In a bold move that reignited memories of the Cold War, Russia, under the leadership of President **Vladimir Putin**, annexed the Ukrainian territory of Crimea in March 2014. Putin inserted military troops to support Russian separatists and quickly established a firm grip over the local government and untrammeled access to the city and Bay of Sevastopal, home to Russia's Black Sea fleet. Ignoring a flurry of international peace initiatives and sanctions imposed by the United States, its allies, and the United Nations, Putin tightened his hold over Crimea and even implemented sanctions of his own: he eliminated most agricultural imports from countries opposing him.

Closer to home, American intelligence services concluded that Russia meddled in the run-up to the 2016 presidential elections. Despite denials from Putin, they claim that Russian hackers penetrated Democratic Party electronic files and e-mails and leaked their contents as part of a concerted effort to benefit the Trump campaign. In summer 2017, the Justice Department appointed Robert S. Mueller, the former director of the Federal Bureau of Investigation, as special counsel to oversee a formal investigation into any links between the Russian government and the Trump presidential campaign. His work is ongoing. And in July 2018, President Trump visited Putin to improve relations between their countries but achieved no clear resolution.

The relationship between Russia and America remains tense, with no resolution satisfactory to both countries over the issue of Crimea or the 2016 presidential election in sight. It reminds us that major conflicts between the United States and countries in central and eastern Europe did not end with the fall of the Berlin Wall or collapse of the Soviet Union, but persist in the form of nations like Russia intent on aggressively expanding its sphere of international influence.

CONCLUSION

The United States in the first years of the twenty-first century battled new challenges and anxieties. U.S. foreign policy after the attacks of September 11, 2001, not only divided the American people but had also deeply alienated much of the world. Crises in the Middle East made it impossible to ignore the persistent threat of terrorism and extremism while conflict with Russia brought back Cold War fears of instability in eastern and central Europe. The American economy was struggling as early as 2007 and, in the fall of 2008, experienced the worst economic crisis since the Great Depression. By 2014 the economy had improved but polls indicated a continuing sense of uncertainty about the future among many Americans. Gridlock continued at the federal level, making it difficult to achieve sweeping reform in several key areas. Political divisions—not only among politicians but also among voters—are as great as they have been in many years.

The United States still remains the wealthiest and most powerful nation in the world, and it continues to cherish great ideals and great hopes. Moving forward into an uncertain future, Americans are burdened with serious problems and great challenges, but they are also armed with extraordinary resilience and energy that has allowed the nation—through its long and turbulent history—to endure, to flourish, and to imagine and strive for a better future.

KEY TERMS/PEOPLE/PLACES/EVENTS

Affordable Care Act 793
Afghan war 817
AIDS 805
Al Qaeda 814
Barack Obama 791
Defense of Marriage Act
  (DOMA) 806

Donald Trump 797
George W. Bush 789
Great Recession
  of 2008 792
Guantánamo 815
Hillary Rodham Clinton 786
Iraq War 816

9/11 attacks 815
Occupy Wall Street
  (OWS) 796
Osama bin Laden 815
Tea Party movement 793
terrorism 813
Vladimir Putin 819

RECALL AND REFLECT

1. How has partisanship affected how presidents governed in the last twenty-five years?
2. How has America's relationship to the rest of the world changed as a result of the war on terror and in particular the Iraq War?
3. How did the digital revolution affect the American economy?
4. What were the key causes of the Great Recession?

APPENDIX

The Declaration of Independence
The Constitution of the United States

THE DECLARATION OF INDEPENDENCE

In Congress, July 4, 1776,

THE UNANIMOUS DECLARATION OF THE THIRTEEN
UNITED STATES OF AMERICA

When, in the course of human events, it becomes necessary for one people to dissolve the political bands which have connected them with another, and to assume, among the powers of the earth, the separate and equal station to which the laws of nature and of nature's God entitle them, a decent respect to the opinions of mankind requires that they should declare the causes which impel them to the separation.

We hold these truths to be self-evident, that all men are created equal; that they are endowed by their Creator with certain unalienable rights; that among these, are life, liberty, and the pursuit of happiness. That, to secure these rights, governments are instituted among men, deriving their just powers from the consent of the governed; that, whenever any form of government becomes destructive of these ends, it is the right of the people to alter or to abolish it, and to institute a new government, laying its foundation on such principles, and organizing its powers in such form, as to them shall seem most likely to effect their safety and happiness. Prudence, indeed, will dictate that governments long established, should not be changed for light and transient causes; and, accordingly, all experience hath shown, that mankind are more disposed to suffer, while evils are sufferable, than to right themselves by abolishing the forms to which they are accustomed. But, when a long train of abuses and usurpations, pursuing invariably the same object, evinces a design to reduce them under absolute despotism, it is their right, it is their duty, to throw off such government and to provide new guards for their future security. Such has been the patient sufferance of these colonies, and such is now the necessity which constrains them to alter their former systems of government. The history of the present King of Great Britain is a history of repeated injuries and usurpations, all having, in direct object, the establishment of an absolute tyranny over these States. To prove this, let facts be submitted to a candid world:

He has refused his assent to laws the most wholesome and necessary for the public good.

He has forbidden his governors to pass laws of immediate and pressing importance, unless suspended in their operation till his assent should be obtained; and, when so suspended, he has utterly neglected to attend to them.

He has refused to pass other laws for the accommodation of large districts of people, unless those people would relinquish the right of representation in the legislature; a right inestimable to them, and formidable to tyrants only.

He has called together legislative bodies at places unusual, uncomfortable, and distant from the depository of their public records, for the sole purpose of fatiguing them into compliance with his measures.

He has dissolved representative houses repeatedly for opposing, with manly firmness, his invasions on the rights of the people.

He has refused, for a long time after such dissolutions, to cause others to be elected; whereby the legislative powers, incapable of annihilation, have returned to the people at large for their exercise; the state remaining, in the meantime, exposed to all the danger of invasion from without, and compulsions within.

He has endeavored to prevent the population of these States; for that purpose, obstructing the laws for naturalization of foreigners, refusing to pass others to encourage their migration hither, and raising the conditions of new appropriations of lands.

He has obstructed the administration of justice, by refusing his assent to laws for establishing judiciary powers.

He has made judges dependent on his will alone, for the tenure of their offices, and the amount and payment of their salaries.

He has erected a multitude of new offices, and sent hither swarms of officers to harass our people, and eat out their substance.

He has kept among us, in time of peace, standing armies, without the consent of our legislatures.

He has affected to render the military independent of, and superior to, the civil power.

He has combined, with others, to subject us to a jurisdiction foreign to our Constitution, and unacknowledged by our laws; giving his assent to their acts of pretended legislation:

For quartering large bodies of armed troops among us:

For protecting them by a mock trial, from punishment, for any murders which they should commit on the inhabitants of these States:

For cutting off our trade with all parts of the world:

For imposing taxes on us without our consent:

For depriving us, in many cases, of the benefit of trial by jury:

For transporting us beyond seas to be tried for pretended offences:

For abolishing the free system of English laws in a neighboring province, establishing therein an arbitrary government, and enlarging its boundaries, so as to render it at once an example and fit instrument for introducing the same absolute rule into these colonies:

For taking away our charters, abolishing our most valuable laws, and altering, fundamentally, the powers of our governments:

For suspending our own legislatures, and declaring themselves invested with power to legislate for us in all cases whatsoever.

He has abdicated government here, by declaring us out of his protection, and waging war against us.

He has plundered our seas, ravaged our coasts, burnt our towns, and destroyed the lives of our people.

He is, at this time, transporting large armies of foreign mercenaries to complete the works of death, desolation, and tyranny, already begun, with circumstances of cruelty and perfidy scarcely paralleled in the most barbarous ages, and totally unworthy the head of a civilized nation.

He has constrained our fellow citizens, taken captive on the high seas, to bear arms against their country, to become the executioners of their friends, and brethren, or to fall themselves by their hands.

He has excited domestic insurrections amongst us, and has endeavored to bring on the inhabitants of our frontiers, the merciless Indian savages, whose known rule of warfare is an undistinguished destruction of all ages, sexes, and conditions.

In every stage of these oppressions, we have petitioned for redress, in the most humble terms; our repeated petitions have been answered only by repeated injury. A prince, whose character is thus marked by every act which may define a tyrant, is unfit to be the ruler of a free people.

Nor have we been wanting in attention to our British brethren. We have warned them, from time to time, of attempts made by their legislature to extend an unwarrantable jurisdiction over us. We have reminded them of the circumstances of our emigration and settlement here. We have appealed to their native justice and magnanimity, and we have conjured them, by the ties of our common kindred, to disavow these usurpations, which would inevitably interrupt our connections and correspondence. They, too, have been deaf to the voice of justice and consanguinity. We must, therefore, acquiesce in the necessity which denounces our separation, and hold them as we hold the rest of mankind, enemies in war, in peace, friends.

We, therefore, the representatives of the United States of America, in general Congress assembled, appealing to the Supreme Judge of the world for the rectitude of our intentions, do, in the name, and by the authority of the good people of these colonies, solemnly publish and declare, that these united colonies are, and of right ought to be, free and independent states: that they are absolved from all allegiance to the British Crown, and that all political connection between them and the state of Great Britain is, and ought to be, totally dissolved; and that, as free and independent states, they have full power to levy war, conclude peace, contract alliances, establish commerce, and to do all other acts and things which independent states may of right do. And, for the support of this declaration, with a firm reliance on the protection of Divine Providence, we mutually pledge to each other our lives, our fortunes, and our sacred honor.

The foregoing Declaration was, by order of Congress, engrossed, and signed by the following members:

John Hancock

NEW HAMPSHIRE
Josiah Bartlett
William Whipple
Matthew Thornton

CONNECTICUT
Roger Sherman
Samuel Huntington
William Williams
Oliver Wolcott

NEW YORK
William Floyd
Philip Livingston
Francis Lewis
Lewis Morris

NEW JERSEY
Richard Stockton
John Witherspoon
Francis Hopkinson
John Hart
Abraham Clark

MASSACHUSETTS BAY
Samuel Adams
John Adams
Robert Treat Paine
Elbridge Gerry

PENNSYLVANIA
Robert Morris
Benjamin Rush
Benjamin Franklin
John Morton
George Clymer
James Smith
George Taylor
James Wilson
George Ross

DELAWARE
Caesar Rodney
George Read
Thomas M'Kean

MARYLAND
Samuel Chase
William Paca
Thomas Stone
Charles Carroll, of Carrollton

RHODE ISLAND
Stephen Hopkins
William Ellery

VIRGINIA
George Wythe
Richard Henry Lee
Thomas Jefferson
Benjamin Harrison
Thomas Nelson Jr.
Francis Lightfoot Lee
Carter Braxton

NORTH CAROLINA
William Hooper
Joseph Hewes
John Penn

SOUTH CAROLINA
Edward Rutledge
Thomas Heyward Jr.
Thomas Lynch Jr.
Arthur Middleton

GEORGIA
Button Gwinnett
Lyman Hall
George Walton

Resolved, That copies of the Declaration be sent to the several assemblies, conventions, and committees, or councils of safety, and to the several commanding officers of the continental troops; that it be proclaimed in each of the United States, at the head of the army.

THE CONSTITUTION
OF THE UNITED STATES[1]

We the People of the United States, in Order to form a more perfect Union, establish Justice, insure domestic Tranquility, provide for the common defence, promote the general Welfare, and secure the Blessings of Liberty to ourselves and our Posterity, do ordain and establish this CONSTITUTION for the United States of America.

Article I

Section 1.

All legislative Powers herein granted shall be vested in a Congress of the United States, which shall consist of a Senate and House of Representatives.

Section 2.

The House of Representatives shall be composed of Members chosen every second Year by the People of the several States, and the Electors in each State shall have the Qualifications requisite for Electors of the most numerous Branch of the State Legislature.

No Person shall be a Representative who shall not have attained to the Age of twenty-five Years, and been seven Years a Citizen of the United States, and who shall not, when elected, be an Inhabitant of that State in which he shall be chosen.

[Representatives and direct Taxes[2] shall be apportioned among the several States which may be included within this Union, according to their respective Numbers, which shall be determined by adding to the whole Number of free Persons, including those bound to Service for a Term of Years, and excluding Indians not taxed, three fifths of all other Persons.][3] The actual Enumeration shall be made within three Years after the first Meeting of the Congress of the United States, and within every subsequent Term of ten Years, in such Manner as they shall by Law direct. The Number of Representatives shall not exceed one for every thirty Thousand, but each State shall have at Least one Representative; and until such enumeration shall be made, the State of New Hampshire shall be entitled to chuse three, Massachusetts eight, Rhode-Island and Providence Plantations one, Connecticut five, New York six, New Jersey four, Pennsylvania eight, Delaware one, Maryland six, Virginia ten, North Carolina five, South Carolina five, and Georgia three.

When vacancies happen in the Representation from any State, the Executive Authority thereof shall issue Writs of Election to fill such Vacancies.

The House of Representatives shall chuse their Speaker and other Officers; and shall have the sole Power of Impeachment.

Section 3.

The Senate of the United States shall be composed of two Senators from each State, chosen by the Legislature thereof, for six Years; and each Senator shall have one Vote.

Immediately after they shall be assembled in Consequence of the first Election, they shall be divided as equally as may be into three Classes. The Seats of the Senators of the

---

1 This version, which follows the original Constitution in capitalization and spelling, was published by the United States Department of the Interior, Office of Education, in 1935.

2 Altered by the Sixteenth Amendment.

3 Negated by the Fourteenth Amendment.

first Class shall be vacated at the Expiration of the second Year, of the second Class at the Expiration of the fourth Year, and of the third Class at the Expiration of the sixth Year, so that one-third may be chosen every second Year; and if Vacancies happen by Resignation, or otherwise, during the Recess of the Legislature of any State, the Executive thereof may make temporary Appointments until the next Meeting of the Legislature, which shall then fill such Vacancies.

No Person shall be a Senator who shall not have attained to the Age of thirty Years, and been nine Years a Citizen of the United States, and who shall not, when elected, be an Inhabitant of that State for which he shall be chosen.

The Vice President of the United States shall be President of the Senate, but shall have no vote, unless they be equally divided.

The Senate shall chuse their other Officers, and also a President pro tempore, in the absence of the Vice President, or when he shall exercise the Office of President of the United States.

The Senate shall have the sole Power to try all Impeachments. When sitting for that purpose they shall be on Oath or Affirmation. When the President of the United States is tried, the Chief Justice shall preside: And no person shall be convicted without the Concurrence of two thirds of the Members present.

Judgment in Cases of Impeachment shall not extend further than to removal from Office, and disqualification to hold and enjoy any Office of honor, Trust, or Profit under the United States: but the Party convicted shall nevertheless be liable and subject to Indictment, Trial, Judgment, and Punishment, according to Law.

Section 4.
The Times, Places and Manner of holding Elections for Senators and Representatives, shall be prescribed in each State by the Legislature thereof; but the Congress may at any time by Law make or alter such Regulations, except as to the Places of Chusing Senators.

The Congress shall assemble at least once in every Year, and such Meeting shall be on the first Monday in December, unless they shall by Law appoint a different Day.

Section 5.
Each House shall be the Judge of the Elections, Returns and Qualifications of its own Members, and a Majority of each shall constitute a Quorum to do Business; but a smaller number may adjourn from day to day, and may be authorized to compel the Attendance of absent Members, in such Manner, and under such Penalties, as each House may provide.

Each House may determine the Rules of its Proceedings, punish its Members for disorderly Behaviour, and, with the Concurrence of two thirds, expel a Member.

Each House shall keep a Journal of its Proceedings, and from time to time publish the same, excepting such Parts as may in their Judgment require Secrecy; and the Yeas and Nays of the Members of either House on any question shall, at the Desire of one fifth of those Present, be entered on the Journal.

Neither House, during the Session of Congress, shall, without the Consent of the other, adjourn for more than three days, nor to any other Place than that in which the two Houses shall be sitting.

Section 6.
The Senators and Representatives shall receive a Compensation for their Services, to be ascertained by Law, and paid out of the Treasury of the United States. They shall in all

Cases, except Treason, Felony, and Breach of the Peace, be privileged from Arrest during their Attendance at the Session of their respective Houses, and in going to and returning from the same; and for any Speech or Debate in either House, they shall not be questioned in any other Place.

No Senator or Representative shall, during the Time for which he was elected, be appointed to any civil Office under the Authority of the United States, which shall have been created, or the Emoluments whereof shall have been increased, during such time; and no Person holding any Office under the United States shall be a Member of either House during his continuance in Office.

Section 7.

All Bills for raising Revenue shall originate in the House of Representatives; but the Senate may propose or concur with Amendments as on other bills.

Every Bill which shall have passed the House of Representatives and the Senate, shall, before it become a Law, be presented to the President of the United States; If he approve he shall sign it, but if not he shall return it, with his Objections, to that House in which it shall have originated, who shall enter the Objections at large on their Journal, and proceed to reconsider it. If after such Reconsideration two thirds of that House shall agree to pass the bill, it shall be sent, together with the objections, to the other House, by which it shall likewise be reconsidered, and if approved by two thirds of that House, it shall become a Law. But in all such Cases the Votes of both Houses shall be determined by Yeas and Nays, and the Names of the Persons voting for and against the Bill shall be entered on the Journal of each House respectively. If any Bill shall not be returned by the President within ten Days (Sundays excepted) after it shall have been presented to him, the Same shall be a Law, in like Manner as if he had signed it, unless the Congress by their Adjournment prevent its Return, in which Case it shall not be a Law.

Every Order, Resolution, or Vote to which the Concurrence of the Senate and House of Representatives may be necessary (except on a question of Adjournment) shall be presented to the President of the United States; and before the Same shall take Effect, shall be approved by him, or being disapproved by him, shall be repassed by two thirds of the Senate and House of Representatives, according to the Rules and Limitations prescribed in the Case of a Bill.

Section 8.

The Congress shall have Power To lay and collect Taxes, Duties, Imposts and Excises, to pay the Debts and provide for the common Defence and general Welfare of the United States; but all Duties, Imposts and Excises shall be uniform throughout the United States;

To borrow money on the credit of the United States;

To regulate Commerce with foreign Nations, and among the several States, and with the Indian Tribes;

To establish an uniform rule of Naturalization, and uniform Laws on the subject of Bankruptcies throughout the United States;

To coin Money, regulate the Value thereof, and of foreign Coin, and fix the Standard of Weights and Measures;

To provide for the Punishment of counterfeiting the Securities and current Coin of the United States;

To establish Post Offices and post Roads;

To promote the Progress of Science and useful Arts, by securing for limited Times to Authors and Inventors the exclusive Right to their respective Writings and Discoveries;

To constitute Tribunals inferior to the Supreme Court;

To define and punish Piracies and Felonies committed on the high Seas, and Offenses against the Law of Nations;

To declare War, grant Letters of Marque and Reprisal, and make Rules concerning Captures on Land and Water;

To raise and support Armies, but no Appropriation of Money to that Use shall be for a longer Term than two Years;

To provide and maintain a Navy;

To make Rules for the Government and Regulation of the land and naval forces;

To provide for calling forth the Militia to execute the Laws of the Union, suppress Insurrections and repel Invasions;

To provide for organizing, arming, and disciplining the Militia, and for governing such Part of them as may be employed in the Service of the United States, reserving to the States respectively, the Appointment of the Officers, and the Authority of training the Militia according to the discipline prescribed by Congress;

To exercise exclusive Legislation in all Cases whatsoever, over such District (not exceeding ten Miles square) as may, by Cession of particular States, and the acceptance of Congress, become the Seat of the Government of the United States, and to exercise like Authority over all Places purchased by the Consent of the Legislature of the State in which the Same shall be, for the Erection of Forts, Magazines, Arsenals, Dock-yards, and other needful Buildings;–And

To make all Laws which shall be necessary and proper for carrying into Execution the foregoing Powers, and all other Powers vested by this Constitution in the Government of the United States, or in any Department or Officer thereof.

Section 9.

The Migration or Importation of such Persons as any of the States now existing shall think proper to admit, shall not be prohibited by the Congress prior to the Year one thousand eight hundred and eight, but a tax or duty may be imposed on such Importation, not exceeding ten dollars for each Person.

The privilege of the Writ of Habeas Corpus shall not be suspended, unless when in Cases of Rebellion or Invasion the public Safety may require it.

No bill of Attainder or ex post facto Law shall be passed.

No capitation, or other direct, Tax shall be laid unless in Proportion to the Census or Enumeration herein before directed to be taken.

No Tax or Duty shall be laid on Articles exported from any State.

No Preference shall be given by any Regulation of Commerce or Revenue to the Ports of one State over those of another: nor shall Vessels bound to, or from, one State, be obliged to enter, clear, or pay Duties in another.

No Money shall be drawn from the Treasury, but in Consequence of Appropriations made by Law; and a regular Statement and Account of the Receipts and Expenditures of all public Money shall be published from time to time.

No Title of Nobility shall be granted by the United States: And no Person holding any Office of Profit or Trust under them, shall, without the Consent of the Congress, accept of any present, Emolument, Office, or Title, of any kind whatever, from any King, Prince, or foreign State.

Section 10.

No State shall enter into any Treaty, Alliance, or Confederation; grant Letters of Marque and Reprisal; coin Money; emit Bills of Credit; make any Thing but gold and silver Coin a Tender in Payment of Debts; pass any Bill of Attainder, ex post facto Law, or Law impairing the Obligation of Contracts, or grant any Title of Nobility.

No State shall, without the Consent of the Congress, lay any Imposts or Duties on Imports or Exports, except what may be absolutely necessary for executing its inspection Laws; and the net Produce of all Duties and Imposts, laid by any State on Imports or Exports, shall be for the use of the Treasury of the United States; and all such Laws shall be subject to the Revision and Control of the Congress.

No state shall, without the Consent of Congress, lay any duty of Tonnage, keep Troops, or Ships of War in time of Peace, enter into any Agreement or Compact with another State, or with a foreign Power, or engage in War, unless actually invaded, or in such imminent Danger as will not admit of delay.

Article II

Section 1.

The executive Power shall be vested in a President of the United States of America. He shall hold his Office during the Term of four years, and, together with the Vice President, chosen for the same Term, be elected, as follows:

Each State shall appoint, in such Manner as the Legislature thereof may direct, a Number of Electors, equal to the whole Number of Senators and Representatives to which the State may be entitled in the Congress: but no Senator or Representative, or Person holding an Office of Trust or Profit under the United States, shall be appointed an Elector.

[The Electors shall meet in their respective States, and vote by Ballot for two persons, of whom one at least shall not be an Inhabitant of the same State with themselves. And they shall make a List of all the Persons voted for, and of the Number of Votes for each; which List they shall sign and certify, and transmit sealed to the Seat of the Government of the United States, directed to the President of the Senate. The President of the Senate shall, in the Presence of the Senate and House of Representatives, open all the Certificates, and the Votes shall then be counted. The Person having the greatest Number of Votes shall be the President, if such Number be a Majority of the whole Number of Electors appointed; and if there be more than one who have such Majority, and have an equal Number of Votes, then the House of Representatives shall immediately chuse by Ballot one of them for President; and if no Person have a Majority, then from the five highest on the List the said House shall in like Manner chuse the President. But in chusing the President, the Votes shall be taken by States, the Representation from each State having one Vote; a quorum for this Purpose shall consist of a Member or Members from two-thirds of the States, and a Majority of all the States shall be necessary to a Choice. In every Case, after the Choice of the President, the Person having the greatest Number of Votes of the Electors shall be the Vice President. But if there should remain two or more who have equal votes, the Senate shall chuse from them by Ballot the Vice President.][4]

The Congress may determine the Time of chusing the Electors, and the Day on which they shall give their Votes; which Day shall be the same throughout the United States.

No person except a natural-born Citizen, or a Citizen of the United States, at the time of the Adoption of this Constitution, shall be eligible to the Office of President; neither

4 Revised by the Twelfth Amendment.

shall any Person be eligible to that Office who shall not have attained to the Age of thirty-five years, and been fourteen Years a Resident within the United States.

In Case of the Removal of the President from Office, or of his Death, Resignation, or Inability to discharge the Powers and Duties of the said Office, the same shall devolve on the Vice President, and the Congress may by Law provide for the Case of Removal, Death, Resignation, or Inability, both of the President and Vice President, declaring what Officer shall then act as President, and such Officer shall act accordingly, until the disability be removed, or a President shall be elected.

The President shall, at stated Times, receive for his Services a Compensation, which shall neither be increased nor diminished during the Period for which he shall have been elected, and he shall not receive within that Period any other Emolument from the United States, or any of them.

Before he enter on the execution of his Office, he shall take the following Oath or Affirmation:—"I do solemnly swear (or affirm) that I will faithfully execute the Office of President of the United States, and will, to the best of my Ability, preserve, protect, and defend the Constitution of the United States."

Section 2.

The President shall be Commander in Chief of the Army and Navy of the United States, and of the Militia of the several States, when called into the actual Service of the United States; he may require the Opinion, in writing, of the principal Officer in each of the executive Departments, upon any subject relating to the Duties of their respective Offices, and he shall have Power to Grant Reprieves and Pardons for Offenses against the United States, except in Cases of Impeachment.

He shall have Power, by and with the Advice and Consent of the Senate, to make Treaties, provided two-thirds of the Senators present concur; and he shall nominate, and by and with the Advice and Consent of the Senate, shall appoint Ambassadors, other public Ministers and Consuls, Judges of the supreme Court, and all other Officers of the United States, whose Appointments are not herein otherwise provided for, and which shall be established by Law: but the Congress may by Law vest the Appointment of such inferior Officers, as they think proper, in the President alone, in the Courts of Law, or in the Heads of Departments.

The President shall have Power to fill up all Vacancies that may happen during the Recess of the Senate, by granting Commissions which shall expire at the End of their next Session.

Section 3.

He shall from time to time give to the Congress Information of the State of the Union, and recommend to their Consideration such Measures as he shall judge necessary and expedient; he may, on extraordinary occasions, convene both Houses, or either of them, and in Case of Disagreement between them, with respect to the Time of Adjournment, he may adjourn them to such Time as he shall think proper; he shall receive Ambassadors and other public Ministers; he shall take care that the Laws be faithfully executed, and shall Commission all the Officers of the United States.

Section 4.

The President, Vice President and all civil Officers of the United States, shall be removed from Office on Impeachment for, and Conviction of, Treason, Bribery, or other high Crimes and Misdemeanors.

Article III

Section 1.

The judicial Power of the United States, shall be vested in one supreme Court, and in such inferior Courts as the Congress may from time to time ordain and establish. The Judges, both of the supreme and inferior Courts, shall hold their Offices during good Behaviour, and shall, at stated Times, receive for their Services, a Compensation, which shall not be diminished during their Continuance in Office.

Section 2.

The judicial Power shall extend to all Cases, in Law and Equity, arising under this Constitution, the Laws of the United States, and Treaties made, or which shall be made, under their Authority;—to all Cases affecting ambassadors, other public ministers and consuls;—to all cases of admiralty and maritime Jurisdiction;—to Controversies to which the United States shall be a Party;—to Controversies between two or more States;—between a State and Citizens of another State;[5]—between Citizens of different States—between Citizens of the same State claiming Lands under Grants of different States, and between a State, or the Citizens thereof, and foreign States, Citizens, or Subjects.

In all Cases affecting Ambassadors, other public Ministers and Consuls, and those in which a State shall be Party, the supreme Court shall have original Jurisdiction. In all the other Cases before mentioned, the supreme Court shall have appellate Jurisdiction, both as to Law and Fact, with such Exceptions, and under such Regulations as the Congress shall make.

The trial of all Crimes, except in Cases of Impeachment, shall be by Jury; and such Trial shall be held in the State where the said Crimes shall have been committed; but when not committed within any State, the Trial shall be at such Place or Places as the Congress may by Law have directed.

Section 3.

Treason against the United States, shall consist only in levying War against them, or in adhering to their Enemies, giving them Aid and Comfort. No Person shall be convicted of Treason unless on the Testimony of two Witnesses to the same overt Act, or on Confession in open Court.

The Congress shall have power to declare the Punishment of Treason, but no Attainder of Treason shall work Corruption of Blood, or Forfeiture except during the Life of the Person attained.

Article IV

Section 1.

Full Faith and Credit shall be given in each State to the public Acts, Records, and judicial Proceedings of every other State. And the Congress may by general Laws prescribe the Manner in which such Acts, Records and Proceedings shall be proved, and the Effect thereof.

Section 2.

The Citizens of each State shall be entitled to all Privileges and Immunities of Citizens in the several States.

5 Qualified by the Eleventh Amendment.

A Person charged in any State with Treason, Felony, or other Crime, who shall flee from Justice, and be found in another State, shall on demand of the executive Authority of the State from which he fled, be delivered up, to be removed to the State having Jurisdiction of the crime.

No Person held to Service or Labour in one State, under the Laws thereof, escaping into another, shall, in Consequence of any Law or Regulation therein, be discharged from such Service or Labour, but shall be delivered up on Claim of the Party to whom such Service or Labour may be due.

Section 3.
New States may be admitted by the Congress into this Union; but no new State shall be formed or erected within the Jurisdiction of any other State; nor any State be formed by the Junction of two or more States, or parts of States, without the Consent of the Legislatures of the States concerned as well as of the Congress.

The Congress shall have Power to dispose of and make all needful Rules and Regulations respecting the Territory or other Property belonging to the United States; and nothing in this Constitution shall be so construed as to Prejudice any Claims of the United States, or of any particular State.

Section 4.
The United States shall guarantee to every State in this Union a Republican Form of Government, and shall protect each of them against Invasion; and on Application of the Legislature, or of the Executive (when the Legislature cannot be convened) against domestic Violence.

Article V

The Congress, whenever two-thirds of both Houses shall deem it necessary, shall propose Amendments to this Constitution, or, on the Application of the Legislatures of two-thirds of the several States, shall call a Convention for proposing Amendments, which, in either Case, shall be valid to all Intents and Purposes, as part of this Constitution, when ratified by the Legislatures of three-fourths of the several States, or by Conventions in three-fourths thereof, as the one or the other Mode of Ratification may be proposed by the Congress; Provided that no Amendment which may be made prior to the Year One thousand eight hundred and eight shall in any Manner affect the first and fourth Clauses in the Ninth Section of the first Article; and that no State, without its Consent, shall be deprived of its equal Suffrage in the Senate.

Article VI

All Debts contracted and Engagements entered into, before the Adoption of this Constitution, shall be as valid against the United States under this Constitution, as under the Confederation.

This Constitution, and the Laws of the United States which shall be made in Pursuance thereof; and all Treaties made, or which shall be made, under the Authority of the United States, shall be the supreme Law of the Land; and the Judges in every State shall be bound thereby, any Thing in the Constitution or Laws of any State to the Contrary notwithstanding.

The Senators and Representatives before mentioned, and the Members of the several State Legislatures, and all executive and judicial Officers, both of the United States and of the several States, shall be bound by Oath or Affirmation to support this Constitution; but no religious Tests shall ever be required as a qualification to any Office or public Trust under the United States.

Article VII

The Ratification of the Conventions of nine States shall be sufficient for the Establishment of this Constitution between the States so ratifying the same.

Done in Convention by the Unanimous Consent of the States present the Seventeenth Day of September in the Year of our Lord one thousand seven hundred and Eighty seven, and of the Independence of the United States of America the Twelfth. In Witness whereof We have hereunto subscribed our Names.[6]

George Washington
President and deputy from Virginia

NEW HAMPSHIRE
John Langdon
Nicholas Gilman

MASSACHUSETTS
Nathaniel Gorham
Rufus King

CONNECTICUT
William Samuel Johnson
Roger Sherman

NEW YORK
Alexander Hamilton

NEW JERSEY
William Livingston
David Brearley
William Paterson
Jonathan Dayton

PENNSYLVANIA
Benjamin Franklin
Thomas Mifflin
Robert Morris
George Clymer
Thomas FitzSimons
Jared Ingersoll
James Wilson
Gouverneur Morris

DELAWARE
George Read
Gunning Bedford Jr.
John Dickinson
Richard Bassett
Jacob Broom

MARYLAND
James McHenry
Daniel of St. Thomas Jenifer
Daniel Carroll

VIRGINIA
John Blair
James Madison Jr.

NORTH CAROLINA
William Blount
Richard Dobbs Spaight
Hugh Williamson

SOUTH CAROLINA
John Rutledge
Charles Cotesworth
  Pinckney
Charles Pinckney
Pierce Butler

GEORGIA
William Few
Abraham Baldwin

Articles in Addition to, and Amendment of, the Constitution of the United States of America, Proposed by Congress, and Ratified by the Legislatures of the Several States, Pursuant to the Fifth Article of the Original Constitution.[7]

[Article I]

Congress shall make no law respecting an establishment of religion, or prohibiting the free exercise thereof; or abridging the freedom of speech, or of the press; or the right of the people peaceably to assemble, and to petition the Government for a redress of grievances.

[Article II]

A well regulated Militia, being necessary to the security of a free State, the right of the people to keep and bear Arms shall not be infringed.

---

6 These are the full names of the signers, which in some cases are not the signatures on the document.
7 This heading appears only in the joint resolution submitting the first ten amendments.

[Article III]

No Soldier shall, in time of peace, be quartered in any house, without the consent of the Owner, nor in time of war, but in a manner to be prescribed by law.

[Article IV]

The right of the people to be secure in their persons, houses, papers, and effects, against unreasonable searches and seizures, shall not be violated, and no Warrants shall issue, but upon probable cause, supported by Oath or affirmation, and particularly describing the place to be searched, and the persons or things to be seized.

[Article V]

No person shall be held to answer for a capital or otherwise infamous crime, unless on a presentment or indictment of a Grand Jury, except in cases arising in the land or naval forces, or in the Militia, when in actual service in time of War or public danger; nor shall any person be subject for the same offence to be twice put in jeopardy of life or limb; nor shall be compelled in any criminal case to be a witness against himself, nor be deprived of life, liberty, or property, without due process of law; nor shall private property be taken for public use, without just compensation.

[Article VI]

In all criminal prosecutions, the accused shall enjoy the right to a speedy and public trial, by an impartial jury of the State and district wherein the crime shall have been committed, which district shall have been previously ascertained by law, and to be informed of the nature and cause of the accusation; to be confronted with the witnesses against him; to have compulsory process for obtaining witnesses in his favour, and to have the Assistance of Counsel for his defense.

[Article VII]

In suits at common law, where the value in controversy shall exceed twenty dollars, the right of trial by jury shall be preserved, and no fact tried by a jury, shall be otherwise reexamined in any Court of the United States, than according to the rules of the common law.

[Article VIII]

Excessive bail shall not be required, nor excessive fines imposed, nor cruel and unusual punishments inflicted.

[Article IX]

The enumeration of the Constitution, of certain rights, shall not be construed to deny or disparage others retained by the people.

[Article X]

The powers not delegated to the United States by the Constitution, nor prohibited by it to the States, are reserved to the States respectively, or to the people.

[Amendments I–X, in force 1791.]

[Article XI][8]

The Judicial power of the United States shall not be construed to extend to any suit in law or equity, commenced or prosecuted against one of the United States by Citizens of another State, or by Citizens or Subjects of any Foreign State.

[Article XII][9]

The Electors shall meet in their respective States and vote by ballot for President and Vice-President, one of whom, at least, shall not be an inhabitant of the same State with themselves; they shall name in their ballots the person voted for as President, and in distinct ballots the person voted for as Vice-President, and they shall make distinct lists of all persons voted for as President, and of all persons voted for as Vice-President, and of the number of votes for each, which lists they shall sign and certify, and transmit sealed to the seat of the government of the United States, directed to the President of the Senate;—The President of the Senate shall, in the presence of the Senate and House of Representatives, open all the certificates and the votes shall then be counted;—The person having the greatest number of votes for President, shall be the President, if such number be a majority of the whole number of Electors appointed; and if no person have such majority, then from the persons having the highest numbers not exceeding three on the list of those voted for as President, the House of Representatives shall choose imme-diately, by ballot, the President. But in choosing the President, the votes shall be taken by states, the representation from each state having one vote; a quorum for this purpose shall consist of a member or members from two-thirds of the states, and a majority of all the states shall be necessary to a choice. And if the House of Representatives shall not choose a President whenever the right of choice shall devolve upon them, before the fourth day of March next following, then the Vice-President shall act as President, as in the case of the death or other constitutional disability of the President.—The person having the greatest number of votes as Vice-President, shall be the Vice-President, if such number be a majority of the whole number of Electors appointed, and if no person have a majority, then from the two highest numbers on the list, the Senate shall choose the Vice-President; a quorum for the purpose shall consist of two-thirds of the whole number of Senators, and a majority of the whole number shall be necessary to a choice. But no person constitutionally ineligible to the office of President shall be eligible to that of Vice-President of the United States.

[Article XIII][10]

Section 1.
Neither slavery nor involuntary servitude, except as a punishment for crime whereof the party shall have been duly convicted, shall exist within the United States, or any place subject to their jurisdiction.

Section 2.
Congress shall have power to enforce this article by appropriate legislation.

8 Adopted in 1798.
9 Adopted in 1804.
10 Adopted in 1865.

[Article XIV][11]

Section 1.
All persons born or naturalized in the United States, and subject to the jurisdiction thereof, are citizens of the United States and of the State wherein they reside. No State shall make or enforce any law which shall abridge the privileges or immunities of citizens of the United States; nor shall any State deprive any person of life, liberty, or property, without due process of law; nor deny to any person within its jurisdiction the equal protection of the laws.

Section 2.
Representatives shall be apportioned among the several States according to their respective numbers, counting the whole number of persons in each State, excluding Indians not taxed. But when the right to vote at any election for the choice of electors for President and Vice-President of the United States, Representatives in Congress, the Executive and Judicial officers of a State, or the members of the Legislature thereof, is denied to any of the male inhabitants of such State, being twenty-one years of age, and citizens of the United States, or in any way abridged, except for participation in rebellion, or other crime, the basis of representation therein shall be reduced in the proportion which the number of such male citizens shall bear to the whole number of male citizens twenty-one years of age in such State.

Section 3.
No person shall be a Senator or Representative in Congress, or elector of President and Vice-President, or hold any office, civil or military, under the United States, or under any State, who, having previously taken an oath, as a member of Congress, or as an officer of the United States, or as a member of any State legislature, or as an executive or judicial officer of any State, to support the Constitution of the United States, shall have engaged in insurrection or rebellion against the same, or given aid or comfort to the enemies thereof. But Congress may by a vote of two-thirds of each House, remove such disability.

Section 4.
The validity of the public debt of the United States, authorized by law, including debts incurred for payment of pensions and bounties for services in suppressing insurrection or rebellion, shall not be questioned. But neither the United States nor any State shall assume or pay any debts or obligation incurred in aid of insurrection or rebellion against the United States, or any claim for the loss or emancipation of any slave; but all such debts, obligations, and claims shall be held illegal and void.

Section 5.
The Congress shall have the power to enforce, by appropriate legislation, the provisions of this article.

[Article XV][12]

Section 1.
The right of citizens of the United States to vote shall not be denied or abridged by the United States or by any State on account of race, color, or previous condition of servitude—

Section 2.
The Congress shall have power to enforce this article by appropriate legislation.

11 Adopted in 1868.
12 Adopted in 1870.

[Article XVI][13]

The Congress shall have power to lay and collect taxes on incomes, from whatever source derived, without apportionment among the several States, and without regard to any census or enumeration.

[Article XVII][14]

The Senate of the United States shall be composed of two Senators from each State, elected by the people thereof, for six years; and each Senator shall have one vote. The electors in each State shall have the qualifications requisite for electors of the most numerous branch of the State legislatures.

When vacancies happen in the representation of any State in the Senate, the executive authority of such State shall issue writs of election to fill such vacancies: *Provided*, That the legislature of any State may empower the executive thereof to make temporary appointments until the people fill the vacancies by election as the legislature may direct.

This amendment shall not be so construed as to affect the election or term of any Senator chosen before it becomes valid as part of the Constitution.

[Article XVIII][15]

Section 1.
After one year from the ratification of this article the manufacture, sale, or transportation of intoxicating liquors within, the importation thereof into, or the exportation thereof from the United States and all territory subject to the jurisdiction thereof for beverage purposes is hereby prohibited.

Section 2.
The Congress and the several States shall have concurrent power to enforce this article by appropriate legislation.

Section 3.
This article shall be inoperative unless it shall have been ratified as an amendment to the Constitution by the legislatures of the several States, as provided in the Constitution, within seven years from the date of the submission hereof to the States by the Congress.

[Article XIX][16]

The right of citizens of the United States to vote shall not be denied or abridged by the United States or by any State on account of sex.

Congress shall have power to enforce this article by appropriate legislation.

[Article XX][17]

Section 1.
The terms of the President and Vice-President shall end at noon on the 20th day of January, and the terms of Senators and Representatives at noon on the 3d day of January,

13 Adopted in 1913.
14 Adopted in 1913.
15 Adopted in 1918.
16 Adopted in 1920.
17 Adopted in 1933.

of the years in which such terms would have ended if this article had not been ratified; and the terms of their successors shall then begin.

Section 2.
The Congress shall assemble at least once in every year, and such meeting shall begin at noon on the 3d day of January, unless they shall by law appoint a different day.

Section 3.
If, at the time fixed for the beginning of the term of the President, the President elect shall have died, the Vice-President elect shall become President. If a President shall not have been chosen before the time fixed for the beginning of his term or if the President elect shall have failed to qualify, then the Vice-President elect shall act as President until a President shall have qualified; and the Congress may by law provide for the case wherein neither a President elect nor a Vice-President elect shall have qualified, declaring who shall then act as President, or the manner in which one who is to act shall be selected, and such person shall act accordingly until a President or Vice-President shall have qualified.

Section 4.
The Congress may by law provide for the case of the death of any of the persons from whom the House of Representatives may choose a President whenever the right of choice shall have devolved upon them, and for the case of the death of any of the persons from whom the Senate may choose a Vice-President whenever the right of choice shall have devolved upon them.

Section 5.
Sections 1 and 2 shall take effect on the 15th day of October following the ratification of this article.

Section 6.
This article shall be inoperative unless it shall have been ratified as an amendment to the Constitution by the legislatures of three-fourths of the several States within seven years from the date of its submission.

[Article XXI][18]

Section 1.
The eighteenth article of amendment to the Constitution of the United States is hereby repealed.

Section 2.
The transportation or importation into any State, Territory, or possession of the United States for delivery or use therein of intoxicating liquors, in violation of the laws thereof, is hereby prohibited.

Section 3.
This article shall be inoperative unless it shall have been ratified as an amendment to the Constitution by conventions in the several States, as provided in the Constitution, within seven years from the date of the submission hereof to the States by the Congress.

18 Adopted in 1933.

[Article XXII][19]

No person shall be elected to the office of the President more than twice, and no person who has held the office of President, or acted as President, for more than two years of a term to which some other person was elected President shall be elected to the office of the President more than once.

But this Article shall not apply to any person holding the office of President when this Article was proposed by the Congress, and shall not prevent any person who may be holding the office of President, or acting as President, during the term within which this Article becomes operative from holding the office of President or acting as President during the remainder of such term.

This article shall be inoperative unless it shall have been ratified as an amendment to the Constitution by the legislatures of three-fourths of the several states within seven years from the date of its submission to the states by the Congress.

[Article XXIII][20]

Section 1.
The District constituting the seat of Government of the United States shall appoint in such manner as the Congress may direct:

A number of electors of President and Vice-President equal to the whole number of Senators and Representatives in Congress to which the District would be entitled if it were a State, but in no event more than the least populous State; they shall be in addition to those appointed by the States, but they shall be considered, for the purposes of the election of President and Vice-President, to be electors appointed by a State; and they shall meet in the District and perform such duties as provided by the twelfth article of amendment.

Section 2.
The Congress shall have power to enforce this article by appropriate legislation.

[Article XXIV][21]

Section 1.
The right of citizens of the United States to vote in any primary or other election for President or Vice President, for electors for President or Vice President, or for Senator or Representative in Congress, shall not be denied or abridged by the United States or any state by reason of failure to pay any poll tax or other tax.

Section 2.
The Congress shall have the power to enforce this article by appropriate legislation.

[Article XXV][22]

Section 1.
In case of the removal of the President from office or of his death or resignation, the Vice President shall become President.

19 Adopted in 1951.
20 Adopted in 1961.
21 Adopted in 1964.
22 Adopted in 1967.

Section 2.
Whenever there is a vacancy in the office of the Vice President, the President shall nominate a Vice President who shall take office upon confirmation by a majority vote of both Houses of Congress.

Section 3.
Whenever the President transmits to the President Pro Tempore of the Senate and the Speaker of the House of Representatives his written declaration that he is unable to discharge the powers and duties of his office, and until he transmits to them a written declaration to the contrary, such powers and duties shall be discharged by the Vice President as Acting President.

Section 4.
Whenever the Vice President and a majority of either the principal officers of the executive departments or of such other body as Congress may by law provide, transmit to the President Pro Tempore of the Senate and the Speaker of the House of Representatives their written declaration that the President is unable to discharge the powers and duties of his office, the Vice President shall immediately assume the powers and duties of the office as Acting President.

Thereafter, when the President transmits to the President Pro Tempore of the Senate and the Speaker of the House of Representatives his written declaration that no inability exists, he shall resume the powers and duties of his office unless the Vice President and a majority of either the principal officers of the executive departments or of such other body as Congress may by law provide, transmit within four days to the President Pro Tempore of the Senate and the Speaker of the House of Representatives their written declaration that the President is unable to discharge the powers and duties of his office. Thereupon Congress shall decide the issue, assembling within forty-eight hours for that purpose if not in session. If the Congress, within twenty-one days after receipt of the latter written declaration, or, if Congress is not in session, within twenty-one days after Congress is required to assemble, determines by two-thirds vote of both Houses that the President is unable to discharge the powers and duties of his office, the Vice President shall continue to discharge the same as Acting President; otherwise, the President shall resume the powers and duties of his office.

[Article XXVI][23]

Section 1.
The right of citizens of the United States, who are eighteen years of age or older, to vote shall not be denied or abridged by the United States or by any State on account of age.

Section 2.
The Congress shall have power to enforce this article by appropriate legislation.

[Article XXVII][24]

No law varying the compensation for the services of the Senators and Representatives shall take effect until an election of Representatives shall have intervened.

---

23 Adopted in 1971.
24 Adopted in 1992.

GLOSSARY

9/11 attacks A series of coordinated attacks on September 11, 2001, in which Al Qaeda operatives hijacked four planes, destroyed the World Trade towers in New York, damaged the Pentagon outside Washington, and caused the death of all aboard United Flight 93, altogether killing 3,000 people.

A. Philip Randolph Leader of the Brotherhood of Sleeping Car Porters and activist in the American labor and civil rights movements.

Aaron Burr Vice president of the United States during Thomas Jefferson's first term, he killed Alexander Hamilton in a duel in 1804 and was rumored to be involved in several plots that could destabilize the United States.

Abigail Adams Supporter of expanding women's rights and protections in the new United States; wife of John Adams.

abolitionist An advocate for the end of a state-approved practice or institution; the term is used most often in connection with the eradication of slavery.

Abraham Lincoln Lawyer and diplomat originally from Kentucky who served as the 16th president of the United States during the Civil War.

Abraham Lincoln Brigade A group of roughly 3,000 young Americans who traveled to Spain to join a fight against the fascists there.

Adams-Onís Treaty Agreement between the United States and Spain in 1819 that gave Florida to the United States in exchange for dropping its claims to Texas.

Adolf Hitler Leader of the German Nazi Party who took power in 1933; fascist whose assumption of dictatorial powers and belief in Aryan racial superiority resulted in the deaths of millions of innocent people including six million Jews in the Holocaust.

affirmative action A policy that grants special consideration in the hiring and promoting of members of groups that historically have faced discrimination.

Affordable Care Act Also known as Obamacare, health-care legislation meant to expand Americans' access to insurance.

Afghan war Post-9/11 military campaign against the Taliban in Afghanistan who were believed to aid Al Qaeda and harbor Osama bin Laden.

AFL-CIO New name of the 1955 merger of the labor groups American Federation of Labor and the Congress of Industrial Organizations.

Agricultural Adjustment Act Act that created a federal agency empowered to achieve parity by controlling the production of seven basic commodities.

Agricultural Marketing Act Proposed by President Hoover in April 1929, it established the first major government program to help farmers maintain prices.

AIDS Acquired immune deficiency syndrome, the set of symptoms and illnesses caused by the HIV virus that killed many Americans in the late twentieth century.

Al Qaeda Network of Islamic extremists responsible for the 9/11 attacks as well as other terrorist acts.

Alamo A Catholic mission in San Antonio that was the site of a major battle in the Texas Revolution in which Mexican forces put down insurgents seeking Texas independence.

Albany Plan Benjamin Franklin's 1754 proposal for a "general government" to manage relations between the colonies and Indians; rejected by the colonies at the beginning of the French and Indian War.

Alexander H. Stephens Vice president of the Confederacy.

Alexander Hamilton One of the country's founders, Hamilton championed a strong central government as a Federalist and was influential in Washington's cabinet.

Alexis de Tocqueville French aristocrat who toured the United States in the early 1830s and wrote *Democracy in America*.

Alger Hiss A high-ranking member of the State Department accused in 1948 of passing classified documents to a communist agent; eventually convicted of perjury.

Alice Paul Head of the National Woman's Party.

Alien and Sedition Acts A group of laws passed under President John Adams that limited new immigrants' access to citizenship and gave the federal government broad powers to limit criticism of the government.

Allies One of the two sides in the First World War, comprised of Britain, France, Russia, and in 1917, the United States.

American Federation of Labor (AFL) Union of skilled workers, formed in 1881 and led by Samuel Gompers, that used strikes to gain concessions from management.

American Indian Movement (AIM) Organization of Native American activists formed in 1968 to promote Indian self-determination.

American Patriots Term for supporters of American independence during the Revolutionary War.

American Plan A euphemism for the open shop; the crusade for this became a pretext for a harsh campaign of union-busting.

American Socialist Party Political party for economic reform created in 1901 that was closely aligned with organized labor.

American System Henry Clay's economic plan to bolster and unify the American economy by raising protective tariffs, developing the transportation system, and establishing a strong national bank.

Amistad Ship at the center of an 1841 Supreme Court case over the foreign slave trade; the Court decided that the Africans who had commandeered the ship had been illegally captured and sold and were granted freedom.

Andrew Carnegie Scottish immigrant who became a steel magnate and then philanthropist during the Gilded Age.

Andrew Jackson Seventh president of the United States; had distinguished himself at the Battle of New Orleans in the War of 1812 and as an Indian fighter.

Andrew Johnson Democrat from Tennessee who served as Lincoln's vice president and, upon Lincoln's assassination, became the seventeenth president; opposed Radical Republican policies on Reconstruction.

Anne Hutchinson Critic of the clerical doctrine of grace who sparked the Antinomian heresy that challenged the spiritual authority of established clergy.

antebellum The period before a war; in U.S. history, the term is commonly used to describe the pre-Civil War period.

Antietam Site of a Union victory on September 17, 1862, that stands as the single bloodiest day in American military history, blunted Confederate progress northward, and prompted Lincoln to issue the preliminary Emancipation Proclamation.

Antifederalists Term used by Federalists to describe those who were against ratification of the Constitution.

Antinomianism A belief that salvation comes from God's grace alone and not from good works.

Antonio Lopez de Santa Anna Politician and general who served multiple stints as president of Mexico and led Mexico in the war with the United States, 1846–1848.

Apollo program A NASA program to land an astronaut on the moon in the 1960s.

appeasement A foreign policy that accepts (rather than opposes) the aggressive moves of another state or actor.

Appomattox Court House Site of Lee's surrender to Grant.

Armory Show An event in New York City that displayed works of the French postimpressionists and of some American modern artists; supported by the Ashcan artists.

Army–McCarthy hearings One of the earliest televised hearings of Congress, the spectacle of Joseph McCarthy demeaning and bullying witnesses whom he accused of communist sympathies led to his loss of public support and official censure for unbecoming conduct.

Articles of Confederation The first adopted plan for union by the states that established a federal Congress with the power to tax and issue money; each state had one vote.

artisan An independent, skilled craftsperson.

Ashcan school Art movement whose members produced work startling in its naturalism and stark in its portrayal of the social realities of the era.

Atlanta Compromise This term describes Booker T. Washington's philosophy, stated in an 1895 speech, that blacks should forgo agitation for political rights and concentrate on self-improvement and preparation for equality.

Atlantic Charter Statement of shared aims issued by America and Britain in August 1941; the two nations called for a new world order based on self-determination, economic cooperation, and antimilitarism.

Atlantic World The peoples and empires around the Atlantic Ocean rim that became interconnected in the sixteenth century.

Ayatollah Ruhollah Khomeini Anti-American religious leader of Iran who took control in 1979 after the previous leader was deposed.

Baby Boom A period of increased birthrate; the term is used most often to describe such a demographic trend from 1946 to 1964.

Bacon's Rebellion A major conflict in Virginia pitting the ruling gentry class against black and white laborers and black slaves seeking greater freedoms and opportunities that resulted in a sharper definition between Indian and white spheres of influence.

Baltimore and Ohio Railroad The oldest railroad in the United States, originally built to help Maryland compete with canals in other states.

Bank War Term used for President Andrew Jackson's fight against Nicholas Biddle and supporters of the Bank of the United States; Jackson ultimately succeeded in eliminating the Bank.

Barack Obama Former U.S. senator from Illinois and first African American elected president who set a progressive agenda during his eight years in office.

Bartolomé de Las Casas Dominican friar who fought for fairer treatment of indigenous people in Spanish colonies.

Battle of Fallen Timbers The 1794 defeat of Indian group the Miami in the Ohio Valley, which forced the defeated Miami to agree to a treaty that ceded Indian lands to the United States.

Battle of the Bulge The last major battle on the Western Front during World War II, as the Germans were finally stopped at Bastogne.

Bay of Pigs Failed invasion of Cuban exiles supported by the United States to overthrow the Castro regime in 1961.

Beats Term used to describe artists and authors, like Jack Kerouac, who were critics of middle-class society and conformity.

Benedict Arnold Military hero early in the Revolution; he lost hope as the war progressed and ultimately conspired with the British.

Benito Mussolini Leader of Italy's Fascist Party before and during World War II.

Benjamin Franklin Inventor, author, diplomat, and one of the most famous people of the 1700s; served as a colonial agent in England during the early part of the conflict between the colonies and England.

Benjamin Harrison Republican senator who was elected president in 1888 in one of the most corrupt elections in American history.

Betty Friedan Author of the 1963 *The Feminine Mystique* who described the frustration of many women who found themselves limited socially, economically, and intellectually in postwar America.

Bill Clinton Former governor of Arkansas and forty-second president during a period of economic prosperity in the 1990s; impeached but acquitted on charges of obstructing justice and lying about an extramarital affair.

Bill of Rights First ten amendments to the U.S. Constitution; limited the new government's ability to infringe upon certain fundamental rights.

Black Codes State laws that developed after the Civil War in the former Confederate states to limit the political power and mobility of black Americans.

Black Hawk War Attack by Sauk (or Sac) and Fox Indians against white settlers from 1831 to 1832 that ended after a brutal response by American forces.

black power A philosophy of racial empowerment and distinctiveness as opposed to assimilation into white culture.

Bonus Army The group of more than 20,000 World War I veterans who marched in 1932 into Washington demanding payment of owed monies from the federal government.

Booker T. Washington The chief spokesman for a commitment to black education and the founder and president of Tuskegee University.

Boston Massacre Inflammatory description of a deadly clash between a mob and British soldiers on March 5, 1770, that became a symbol of British oppression for many colonists.

Boston Tea Party Dramatic attempt by Boston leaders to show colonial contempt for the Tea Act; they dumped British tea into Boston harbor and triggered similar acts of resistance in colonial cities.

Boxer Rebellion A revolt begun by Chinese nationalists against foreigners in China.

braceros Contract laborers from Mexico allowed into the United States during World War II in response to wartime labor shortages.

brinksmanship The attempt to gain a negotiating advantage by pushing a situation to the edge of war or other disaster.

Brotherhood of Sleeping Car Porters An important union dominated and led by African Americans, including A. Philip Randolph.

Browder v. Gayle The 1956 district court decision affirmed by the Supreme Court that ruled that Montgomery's bus segregation laws were unconstitutional.

Brown v. Board of Education of Topeka The 1954 Supreme Court Decision that overturned "separate but equal" opinion of *Plessy v. Ferguson* and provided federal support for the civil rights movement.

Bull Moose Party Also known as the Progressive Party, launched by Theodore Roosevelt ahead of the 1912 presidential election.

Cahokia Major trading center in the Mississippi River valley near modern-day St. Louis, Missouri, from the seventh to the thirteenth centuries.

Californios Hispanic residents of California.

Calvin Coolidge Former governor of Massachusetts and vice president under Warren Harding; became president when Harding died in office; elected to the office of president in 1924 but did not run again in 1928.

Camp David accords Peace treaty between Israel and Egypt brokered by President Carter in 1978.

Cane Ridge Kentucky site of the 1801 religious revival that lasted a number of days with thousands of attendees.

capitalist Owner of material or financial assets useful for the accumulation of additional wealth.

carpetbaggers Slang term used by white Southern Democrats to describe white men from the North, many of them veterans, who settled in the South as hopeful planters, businessmen, and professionals and supported Republican policies.

Cecilius Calvert The second Lord Baltimore who, with his father George Calvert, was instrumental in the founding of Baltimore.

Central Intelligence Agency (CIA) Replaced the World War II-era Office of Strategic Services in 1947; tasked with the collection of information rel-ated to national security from around the world through open and covert methods.

Central Powers One of the sides in the First World War, comprised of Germany, Austria-Hungary, and the Ottoman Empire.

César Chávez Leader of the mostly Hispanic United Farm Workers (UFW) in the 1970s.

Charles E. Coughlin A Catholic priest famous for his national radio broadcasts; he proposed a series of monetary reforms that he insisted would restore prosperity and ensure economic justice.

Charles Sumner United States Senator from Massachusetts who was a leading voice against slavery and for black liberties.

charter A formal order from a governmental leader or body, like the king of a court, often granting the recipient power over a body of land, a business, or a people.

checks and balances A system that grants the various branches of government the power to oversee or constrain other branches, so that no part grows too powerful.

Chester A. Arthur Became president when Garfield was assassinated.

Chief Joseph Leader of the Nez Percé tribe in the Pacific Northwest during the late 1870s who fought efforts to force the tribe onto a reservation in the Idaho territory.

Chinese Exclusion Act The federal law of 1882 that blocked Chinese immigration and prevented those Chinese already living in America from becoming citizens for ten years.

Christian Coalition A religious political coalition formed in the 1970s to elect candidates supportive of its evangelical values.

Christopher Columbus Sea captain working for the Spanish crown whose trans-Atlantic voyages helped introduce the "New World" to Europeans.

citizenship The legal recognition of a person's inclusion in a body politic by the extension of various rights and privileges and the expectation of various duties and obligations.

city beautiful movement Led by architect Daniel Burnham, the movement sought to impose order and symmetry on the disordered life of American cities.

Civilian Conservation Corps (CCC) Agency that created camps in national parks and forests for young unemployed men from the cities to work in a semi-military environment; projects included planting trees, building reservoirs, and improving agricultural irrigation.

Claudette Colvin An early leader in the civil rights movement who was arrested at the age of fifteen for not giving up her seat on a Montgomery bus nine months before Rosa Parks.

Clovis people Term used for the oldest inhabitants of the Americas most probably from modern-day Siberia who would have traveled the Bering Strait some 11,000 years ago.

Coercive Acts Parliament's retaliation against the Boston Tea Party that was meant to coerce Boston colonists by reducing the colony's self-government.

Cold War A simmering conflict between the United States and Soviet Union that emerged at the end of World War II, expressed in ideological terms of difference between capitalism and communism but often executed as a competition for power and security; tensions took many forms, including espionage, an arms race, and proxy wars around the world.

colonization A process by which a country or territory falls, usually by force, under the control of a hostile country or territory.

colony A geographic area in one nation under control by another nation and typically occupied at least partly by settlers from that other nation.

committees of correspondence First called for by Samuel Adams, the committees formed in Boston and other parts of the colonies to share information about British abuses of power.

Common Sense Thomas Paine's popular pamphlet that encouraged independence from England by arguing that colonists could never be truly free under the English constitution.

Commonwealth v. Hunt Massachusetts Supreme Court decision (1842) that established the legality of unions in Massachusetts.

Community Action programs Part of Johnson's "war on poverty," programs that employed members of poor communities in designing and administering local services.

Compromise of 1850 Seeking to diffuse tensions over slavery, this series of bills admitted California as a free state, abolished slavery in Washington, D.C., and established the Fugitive Slave Act.

Compromise of 1877 Rutherford B. Hayes's promise to withdraw federal troops from the South, effectively ending Reconstruction, in exchange for the support of Southern delegates in the disputed election of 1876 presidential election.

concentration policy U.S. government policy introduced in 1851 that forced Indian tribes to live in specific regions, thereby opening up new areas for settlement by non-Indians.

Coney Island The famous and popular amusement park located on a Brooklyn beach.

Confederate States of America Also known as the Confederacy, those slave states that seceded from the Union and declared an independent nation.

Confiscation Acts Two laws passed by the federal government during the Civil War, in 1861 and 1862, designed to free slaves held by Confederates.

Congress of Industrial Organizations (CIO) Led by John L. Lewis, this committee expanded the constituency of the American labor movement.

Congress of Racial Equality (CORE) Established in 1942, black organization that mobilized popular resistance to discrimination in new ways such as sit-ins and "Freedom Rides."

conquistador A European (especially Spanish and Portuguese) conqueror of the Americas (particularly Mexico and Peru) during the fifteenth and sixteenth centuries.

conscription The practice of requiring citizens to serve in the military or other national service; the draft.

conservationist A proponent of the protection of land for carefully managed development, as opposed to a preservationist, who seeks to protect nature from development altogether.

Constitution The legal framework of the United States created to resolve limitations of the Articles of Confederation.

consumerism An increased focus on purchasing goods for personal use; the protection or promotion of consumer interests.

containment The Cold War strategy that called for preventing the spread of communism, by force or by other means.

coolies Derogatory term for Chinese indentured servants whose conditions were close to slavery.

cotton kingdom Term used for the lower South to describe the economy and culture built on cotton production.

Cotton Mather Puritan theologian who, drawing from the knowledge of his slave, Onesimus, helped introduce smallpox immunizations to America.

counterculture A way of life opposed to the prevailing culture; the term typically refers to the revolution in lifestyles, values, and behavior among some young people of the 1960s.

Court-packing plan Derogatory nickname for one aspect of President Roosevelt's proposal to overhaul the federal court system.

covenant A Puritan belief that an individual's relationship with God and with others rested on mutual respect, duty, and consent.

Coxey's Army A group of unemployed who marched on Washington, led by an Ohio Populist, to demand relief from the depression.

Creole A person of European or African ancestry born in the Americas; also, a person of mixed European and African ancestry.

crop-lien system A credit system widely used in the South after the Civil War in which farmers promised a portion of their future crops in exchange for supplies from local merchants.

Cuban missile crisis A thirteen-day standoff between the USSR and the United States over Soviet nuclear missiles in Cuba that ended with the Kennedy–Khrushchev Pact.

cult of domesticity The early-nineteenth-century belief that women were the guardians of family and religious virtue within the home.

cult of honor A set of beliefs, associated with white southern males of the nineteenth century, that emphasized respect, reputation, and the protection of women.

D-Day The Allied attack of June 6, 1944, across the English Channel against Hitler's forces in France.

Dale Carnegie Author of the best-selling self-help manual *How to Win Friends and Influence People*, published in 1936.

Daniel Webster Prominent diplomat and politician of the early republic, serving as senator, representative, and secretary of state; regularly championed issues in defense of the Union.

Darwinism The argument that the human species had evolved from earlier forms of life through a process of "natural selection."

Daughters of Liberty Organization of women in the colonies that led the boycott against the Tea Act.

David Walker Black abolitionist who encouraged blacks to unite and take any necessary measures to fight slavery and other forms of discrimination.

Dawes Plan A 1924 agreement in which American banks would provide loans to Germany that would then be used to pay war reparations to Britain and France.

Dawes Severalty Act Legislation that provided for the gradual elimination of most tribal ownership of land and the allotment of tracts to individual owners.

Declaration of Independence A founding document of the United States, the declaration explained why the colonies were breaking away from England. Drafted by Thomas Jefferson who borrowed concepts from other works and edited by the Second Continental Congress, the declaration also appealed to foreign countries and spurred colonies to reform themselves as states.

Defense of Marriage Act (DOMA) A 1996 federal law that allowed states to decide whether or not to recognize same-sex marriages.

deism The belief that God created but does not actively control the universe.

Denmark Vesey A freed black living in Charleston, South Carolina, who in 1822 planned a thwarted slave rebellion that may have numbered over 9,000.

deregulation The process of removing government controls over industries such as airlines, trucking, electricity supply, and banking, with the intention of stimulating competition and innovation.

détente The easing of hostilities between countries, used especially in connection with the Cold War in the 1970s.

Dollar Diplomacy Foreign policies, especially those of the Taft administration in Latin America, that privileged American economic interests.

Dominion of New England Colonial entity formed when James II combined the government of Massachusetts with the government of the rest of the New England colonies and, later, also included New York and New Jersey.

Donald Trump New York Republican businessman and billionaire elected forty-fifth president in a surprising victory over Democrat Hillary Clinton.

Dorothea Dix Advocate for individuals with mental illness in America and Europe.

Dorr Rebellion Named after the leader, Thomas L. Dorr, the Dorr Rebellion was a failed attempt by a group in Rhode Island to set up a new state government with expanded voting rights.

Douglas MacArthur American general who headed the occupation of a conquered Japan at the end of World War II; also led UN forces against the North Koreans in the Korean War until relieved by President Truman for making insubordinate statements.

Dred Scott **decision** The 1857 Supreme Court ruling that effectively stated that a slave was not a citizen but was, instead, property and therefore could not bring a suit in the federal courts.

Dust Bowl A region that stretched north from Texas into the Dakotas and experienced a decade-long drought that began in 1930.

Dwight D. Eisenhower U.S. general in charge of the invasion of France across the English Channel, later the supreme Allied commander and then president of the United States elected in 1952.

Earth Day First started in 1970, a day of events meant to heighten public awareness of environmental issues.

Echo Park A national park on the border between Utah and Colorado that was threatened by development in the 1950s; environmental organizations rallied to block the dam project.

Edward Bellamy Author of the utopian novel *Looking Backward* (1888) in which government monopolies created an equitable society.

Eleanor Roosevelt Outspoken supporter of racial justice and source of continuous pressure on the federal government to ease discrimination against blacks; wife of Franklin Roosevelt.

Eli Whitney American inventor best known for developing the cotton gin.

Elizabeth Cady Stanton Abolitionist and women's rights advocate who co-organized the Seneca Falls Convention.

Elizabeth I Protestant Queen of England for the latter half of the 1500s who presided over the beginnings of English colonial enterprises in America.

Elizabeth Keckley Personal seamstress of Mary Todd Lincoln who bought freedom for herself and her son through sewing.

Emancipation Proclamation Lincoln's executive order of 1863 declaring that the slaves held in the Confederate states were forever free.

embargo A ban on trade with another country, especially the refusal to allow foreign ships to unload goods at port.

encomienda The right to extract tribute and labor from the natives on large tracts of land in Spanish America; also the name given to the land and village in such tracts.

Enforcement Acts Also known as the Ku Klux Klan Acts, these congressional acts in 1870 and 1871 prohibited states from discriminating against voters on the basis of race and gave the national government authority to prosecute crimes by individuals under federal law.

Enlightenment An intellectual movement that stressed the importance of science and reason in the pursuit of truth.

Erie Canal A constructed waterway that connected the Great Lakes to the Hudson River and transformed New York into an economic powerhouse of the young United States.

Eugene V. Debs Leader of the American Railway Union in the Pullman strike of 1894; presidential candidate for the Socialist Party.

eugenics The pseudo-scientific movement that attributed genetic weakness to various races and ethnicities; also describes efforts to control or isolate supposed hereditary traits through selective breeding, sterilization, immigration restriction, and other forms of social engineering.

evangelist A devout person who aims to convert others to the faith through preaching and missionary work.

Factory Girls Association The 1834 union originally formed by Lowell workers to protest pay cuts.

factory system A method of manufacturing involving powered machinery, usually run by water, that allowed the use of unskilled labor and greater output than in the artisan tradition.

Fair Deal Harry Truman's twenty-one-point domestic program supporting expansion of Social Security, an increase of the minimum wage, public housing, and environmental/public works planning.

Farm Security Administration Created in 1937, this agency provided loans to help famers cultivating submarginal soil to relocate to better lands; in the end, it moved no more than a few thousand.

Farmers' Alliances Began among southern farmers in 1875 but spread nationwide; formed cooperatives and other marketing mechanisms.

fascism A term originating with Mussolini's Fascist Party and applying to any antidemocratic regime with a supreme leader, intolerance of dissent, faith in militarism over diplomacy, and a belief in national or ethnic superiority.

Federal Deposit Insurance Corporation (FDIC) Established by the Glass-Steagall Act of June 1933, this guaranteed all bank deposits up to $2,500.

Federal Highway Act of 1956 Massive ten-year federal project to build over 40,000 miles of interstate highways initiated under President Eisenhower.

federalism A political system dividing powers between state and federal governments that together constitute a federation.

Federalists Term for supporters of the Constitution and later a political party that favored a strong central government.

Fidel Castro One of the leaders against Fulgencio Batista's dictatorship of Cuba, Fidel Castro took control of Cuba in 1959 and turned Cuba into a communist state with support from the Soviet Union.

Fifteenth Amendment An 1870 constitutional amendment that forbade the states and the federal government from denying suffrage to any male citizen on account of race, color, or previous condition of servitude.

fireside chats President Franklin Roosevelt's regular radio addresses during which he explained in simple terms his programs and plans to the people, helping build public confidence in the administration.

First Battle of Bull Run The first major battle of the Civil War; also known as First Battle of Manassas.

First Continental Congress Early gathering of colonial delegates in 1774 that called for the repeal of all oppressive laws of Parliament since 1763.

Five Civilized Tribes Term used for the five tribes of the American South that had adopted some Euro-American social structures and institutions by the 1830s.

flappers Young women who challenged traditional expectations in the mid-1920s.

Fort Necessity Site of the opening skirmish in the French and Indian War, this stockade in the Ohio Valley was unsuccessfully protected by Militia Colonel George Washington.

Fort Sumter Fort in Charleston, South Carolina, that was shelled by Confederate forces on April 12, 1861, forcing its surrender and marking the start of armed conflict in the Civil War.

Forty-niners A slang term for people who flocked to California in 1849 in search of gold.

Fourteen Points President Woodrow Wilson's list of principles for which he believed the nation should be fighting during the First World War.

Fourteenth Amendment An 1868 constitutional amendment that granted citizenship to all persons born in the United States and prohibited states from denying "life, liberty, or property, without due process of law" or equal protection under the law.

Frances Perkins First female member of the cabinet; appointed by Roosevelt as secretary of labor.

Francis Cabot Lowell Pioneer of American textile manufacturing who created one of the first complete mills in Waltham, Massachusetts.

Frank Capra Italian-born director whose films presented social messages; films included *Mr. Deeds Goes to Town*.

Franklin Delano Roosevelt Assistant secretary of the navy, governor of New York, and president from 1933 until his death in office in 1945; his campaign and subsequent administrations offered Americans "a new deal."

Frederick Douglass African American abolitionist and reformer who was a major voice against slavery in both his writings and in public speeches throughout America and Europe.

free silver Economic philosophy that advocated for the coining of silver; farmers and others believed that expanding the money supply in this way would increase prices for their products and ease their debt payments.

Free-Soil Party The antislavery party that emerged during the 1848 presidential and congressional elections.

Freedmen's Bureau U.S. bureau established in 1858 that aimed to help former enslaved people forge independent lives.

freedom rides Civil rights initiative in which groups of interracial students traveled by bus through segregated states.

Freedom Summer Attempt by civil rights activists in the summer of 1964 to encourage black voter registration mostly in segregated states like Alabama and Mississippi.

French and Indian War Colonists' name given to the Seven Years' War in the colonies that strained the relationship of England to its colonies and marked the decline of relationships between Native Americans and Europeans.

Gabriel Prosser Leader of a thwarted large-scale slave revolt outside Richmond, Virginia, in 1800.

Gadsden Purchase The 1853 American acquisition from Mexico of nearly 30,000 acres of land that now form modern southern Arizona and southwestern New Mexico.

George B. McClennan Union general who ran unsuccessfully as a Northern Democrat in the 1864 presidential election against Lincoln.

George Calvert The first Lord Baltimore who, with his son Cecilius, the second Lord Baltimore, was instrumental in the founding of Maryland.

George Grenville Prime Minister to King George III who increased troops and taxes in the colonies after the French and Indian War and made many colonists believe colonial self-rule was under attack.

George H. W. Bush Vice president under Reagan who served as the forty-first president during the first Gulf War and several years of economic downturn.

George III King of England in 1760 who wanted to reassert the crown's authority; he was mentally unstable for most of his reign.

George W. Bush Son of the forty-first president and former governor of Texas, he pushed through broad tax cuts and led the country after the 9/11 attacks, initiating an aggressive war against terror.

George Washington Military leader and one of the founders of the United States; served as first president.

Gerald R. Ford Vice president appointed by Richard Nixon in 1973 who took over the presidency in 1974 after Nixon's resignation.

Geronimo Apache chief and medicine man who led the fight against resettlement efforts by Mexico and then the United States.

Gettysburg Pennsylvania town that was the site of a major Civil War battle on July 1–3, 1863, in which the Union Army turned back the Confederate march northward.

GI Bill Officially known as the Servicemen's Readjustment Act of 1944; provided housing, education, and job-training subsidies to veterans.

Gibbons v. Ogden Supreme Court case of 1824 that strengthened federal authority over interstate commerce.

globalization The process of interaction and exchange between peoples and ideas from different parts of the globe.

Good Neighbor Policy Franklin Roosevelt's position regarding the countries of Latin America, marking a departure from traditional American intervention.

gospel of wealth Term popularized by Andrew Carnegie to argue that those with immense wealth carry a greater burden to use that wealth for social progress.

Grangers Founded in 1867, the first major farm organization in the country to mobilize against railroads and other special interests; predecessor to the farmers' alliances of the late nineteenth century.

Great Awakening The first major American religious revival, begun in earnest in the 1730s.

Great Depression The major economic downturn of the 1930s that ended with American entrance into World War II.

Great Migration The movement of nearly half a million black people from the rural South to industrial cities in the North in the era of the First World War.

Great Recession of 2008 Economic crisis fueled by the collapse of the housing market and poor regulation of financial industries.

Great Society LBJ's legislative initiatives that focused on addressing the social problems of poverty, decaying cities, and poor schools.

greenbacks Paper currency not backed by gold or silver.

Grover Cleveland Reform governor of New York who was elected president in 1884 and again in 1892.

Guadalcanal One of the southern Solomon Islands, American forces assaulted a Japanese garrison here for six months in 1942–1943 before successfully driving them out.

Guantánamo U.S. naval base in Cuba where suspected terrorists from the war on terror have been interrogated and detained since 2002.

Gulf of Tonkin Resolution Act of Congress in 1964 that gave President Johnson the authority to escalate the conflict in Vietnam based on questionable accounts of attacks made on American ships by the North Vietnamese.

Half-Breeds Political group within the Republican Party led by James G. Blaine of Maine, who favored reform.

Handsome Lake Seneca native and revivalist of the Second Great Awakening who called for a return to native traditions among the Iroquois tribes.

Harlem Renaissance Term used to describe the flourishing artistic life created by a new generation of black intellectuals in New York who focused on the richness of their own racial heritage.

Harpers Ferry Site of the federal arsenal raided by John Brown in 1859.

Harriet Beecher Stowe Abolitionist, best known for her novel *Uncle Tom's Cabin.*

Harry Hopkins Former director of New York State relief agency; appointed by Roosevelt to administer New Deal agencies FERA and the WPA.

Harry S. Truman Democratic senator from Missouri, then Franklin Roosevelt's vice presidential candidate in the 1944 election, and president of the United States from 1945 to 1953.

Hartford Convention Meeting of New Englanders, many of them Federalists, that denounced the War of 1812; they had just adjourned when news of Jackson's victory in New Orleans and the peace treaty became known.

Hawley-Smoot Tariff This 1930 act established the highest import duties in history and stifled global commerce; it contributed to the dramatic contraction of international trade leading up to the Great Depression.

Haymarket bombing In a clash between striking laborers and police in Chicago on May 1, 1886, an unknown person threw a bomb into a crowd killing seven police and injuring nearly seventy others.

headright system A grant system that allowed new settlers to acquire fifty acres of land in a variety of ways.

Henry Cabot Lodge The Republican senator and chair of the Foreign Relations Committee who obstructed and opposed the ratification of the Treaty of Versailles after the First World War.

Henry Clay Prominent politician from Kentucky, serving as Speaker of the House, senator, and secretary of state and running unsuccessfully for president three times; one of the founders of the Whig Party; helped bring about the Missouri Compromise of 1820 while Speaker.

Henry David Thoreau Transcendentalist who urged Americans to resist both social conformity and unjust laws.

Henry Ford Early leader of the automobile industry who stressed the standardization of parts and assembly lines.

Henry George Author of *Progress and Poverty* (1879), which argued for tax reform on land as a way to break the power of monopolies.

Herbert Hoover Elected president in 1928, he personified the modern, prosperous, middle-class society of the New Era, but also came to be associated with the failure to adequately respond to the Great Depression.

Herman Melville Author of the 1851 classic *Moby Dick* that captured harsh aspects of nineteenth-century American culture.

Hessians German mercenaries hired by England during the American Revolutionary War.

Hetch Hetchy Valley that was the object of a 1906 controversy that brought the contending views of the early conservation movement to a head.

Hideki Tojo General and leader of the war party in Japan; replaced more moderate prime minister in 1941.

Hillary Rodham Clinton Former first lady, senator of New York, secretary of state, and in 2016 the first woman to earn the presidential nomination of a major political party.

Hindenburg German dirigible that crashed in flames in Lakehurst, New Jersey, in 1937, broadcast live over the radio.

Hiroshima Japanese site of the first detonation of an atomic bomb against an enemy nation, dropped by the United States in 1945.

Ho Chi Minh Longtime supporter of Vietnamese independence who later became the leader of the communists of Vietnam.

Holocaust Systematic Nazi campaign of the 1930s and 1940s to exterminate Jews and other "undesirable" groups of Europe.

Homestead Act Federal legislation permitting any citizen or prospective citizen, including freed slaves, to purchase 160 acres of public land in the western United States for a small fee after living on it for five years.

Homestead Strike A strike of the steel mill union in 1892 that led to armed conflict and the involvement of state militia.

Hoovervilles The term used to describe the shantytowns that unemployed people established on the outskirts of cities during the Depression.

Horace Mann Educational reformer who promoted education as essential to a strong democracy.

Horatio Alger Author of Gilded Age books whose hardworking heroes go from "rags to riches."

horizontal integration A corporate combination where a group of businesses that do the same thing are consolidated.

House Un-American Activities Committee (HUAC) Congressional committee that held widely publicized investigations into communist subversion within the American government.

Hudson River school New York landscape painters known for their depictions of spectacular vistas.

Huey P. Long Senator from Louisiana known as "the Kingfish" who initially supported Roosevelt but broke with him; champion of the Share-Our-Wealth Plan, which would have guaranteed every American a home and income.

Hull House The most famous of the settlement houses, opened in Chicago in 1889.

Ida B. Wells African American journalist whose reporting in the late nineteenth century on racial violence launched what became an international antilynching movement.

Immigration Act of 1965 Legislation that revised laws from the 1920s, allowing for greater immigration from most areas and removing preferences for northern European immigrants.

impeachment The process of charging a public official with misconduct, with the potential for punishment including loss of office.

imperialism The process whereby an empire or nation pursues military, political, or economic advantage by extending its rule over external territories and peoples.

impressment The act of forcing people to serve in a navy or other military operation; the term is most commonly used in connection with the actions of British fleets against American sailors in the early 1800s.

indentured servitude The condition of being bound to an employer for a specific period of time, usually in exchange for the cost of passage to a new land. The labor practice was most commonly used in Britain's American colonies.

Indian Civil Rights Act Law passed by Congress in 1968 that extended Bill of Rights protection to reservation Indians and accepted Indian legal authority inside reservations.

Indian Removal Act An 1830 act that allowed the federal government to negotiate with American Indians to relocate them west of the Mississippi River.

Indian Territory Present-day Oklahoma, the land designated for American Indians forced to relocate west of the Mississippi River by the Indian Removal Act.

Industrial Revolution The transformation of the economy from manual to mechanized forms of production; started in Britain in the eighteenth century and later spread to other places, including in the United States in the nineteenth century.

Industrial Workers of the World (IWW) Known to its opponents as the "Wobblies," the radical labor organization led by "Big Bill" Haywood; advocated a single union for all workers.

Industrialization The process of a society changing from predominately agricultural production to a society based on factory production.

intercontinental ballistic missile (ICBM) Missile capable of traveling over oceans and into space to deliver nuclear strikes.

Interstate Commerce Act The first effective federal railroad regulation, passed in 1887; administered by a five-person agency.

Iran–Contra scandal Covert and illegal operation by members of the Reagan administration who funneled money gained from selling arms to the anti-American government of Iran to the anticommunist rebels or "Contras" in Nicaragua.

Iraq War An armed conflict (2003–2011) of Western countries led by the United States to depose Iraq leader Saddam Hussein, set up a more democratic government, and defend it against local insurgents.

Iroquois Confederacy Organization of five Indian nations that traded regularly with the French and English in the early colonial period, but their relationships with the colonists deteriorated during the mid to late 1700s.

isolationism A foreign policy that avoids forging alliances or lending support to other nations, especially in wartime.

Issei Japanese immigrants.

J. P. Morgan Banker and creator of U.S. Steel.

Jacob Leisler Colonist who raised a militia in 1689 and proclaimed himself the head of government in New York.

Jacob Riis New York newspaper photographer who wrote *How the Other Half Lives*, which used photos and words to expose the harshness of tenement life.

James A. Garfield Veteran Republican congressman from Ohio and a Half-Breed; won the presidency in the 1880 election; assassinated in 1881.

James Henry Hammond South Carolina senator who coined the expression "cotton is king."

James K. Polk North Carolinian and 11th president of the United States who served from 1845 to 1849.

James Madison Fourth president of the United States; instrumental in the creation of the U.S. Constitution.

James Oglethorpe Veteran British general who spearheaded the founding of Georgia.

Jamestown First colonial settlement of the London Company in North America.

Jane Addams Influential social worker and advocate of the settlement house movement.

Jarena Lee An African American woman who preached in public in contrast to rules and customs that prohibited her from doing so during the first half of the nineteenth century.

Jay's Treaty Crafted in response to continued British seizure of American ships in 1794 by the chief justice of the Supreme Court, John Jay; resolved the dispute by acknowledging American supremacy over the Northwest territory and producing a commercial relationship with Britain.

Jefferson Davis President of the Confederacy.

jeremiad A sermon of despair at society's lost moral virtue, usually warning about dire consequences in the world and the afterlife.

Jim Crow laws A dense network of state and local statutes that institutionalized an elaborate system of racial hierarchy.

Jimmy Carter Former governor of Georgia who served as the thirty-ninth president of the United States during a period of rising oil prices, economic recession, and the Iran hostage crisis.

jingoes A term coined in the late nineteenth century to refer to advocates for expanded U.S. economic, political, and military power in the world.

John Adams One of the country's founders; first vice president of the United States and the second president of the United States.

John Birch Society Ultra-conservative organization led by Robert Welch, who was convinced communism had infiltrated all levels of the American government.

John Brown Radical abolitionist who aimed to foment a slave insurrection in the South.

John Burgoyne General for British northern forces, defeated at Saratoga.

John C. Calhoun Prominent South Carolinian politician serving as senator, secretary of state, vice president, and secretary of war; supporter of slavery and of nullification, or the states' rights to nullify federal laws if they found them unconstitutional.

John Collier Commissioner of Indian affairs whose goal was to reverse the pressures of assimilation and instead champion Indian rights.

John D. Rockefeller Founder of Standard Oil, famous for horizontal and vertical integration, and the wealthiest man of the Gilded Age.

John Dos Passos Author of the *U.S.A.* trilogy in the 1930s, which attacked materialistic American culture.

John Foster Dulles Secretary of state under Eisenhower who advocated for aggressive action against communism, as well as brinksmanship as a strategy to gain concessions from foreign powers.

John J. Pershing The American general who led the expedition chasing Pancho Villa in 1916 and later commanded the American forces in the First World War.

John Kennedy First Catholic to be elected president after defeating Richard Nixon in 1960; assassinated in 1963.

John L. Lewis Leader of the United Mine Workers, champion of industrial unionism, and first president of the CIO.

John Marshall Chief Justice of the United States Supreme Court for over thirty years and a Federalist, Marshall most famously rendered the opinion in *Marbury v. Madison.*

John Muir The leading preservationist in the United States and founder of the Sierra Club.

John Peter Zenger New York publisher tried for libel whose case expanded free speech.

John Quincy Adams Son of John Adams, he served as secretary of state under James Monroe, president from 1825 to 1829, and later as a member of the House of Representatives.

John Smith World traveler and writer whose leadership helped the Jamestown colony survive.

John Steinbeck Author of *The Grapes of Wrath,* perhaps the best-known depiction of Depression-era American life.

John Tyler Virginian who became the tenth president after the death of William Henry Harrison

only a month into his administration; regularly clashed with his fellow Whigs and was not nominated for reelection by his party.

John Winthrop Governor of the Massachusetts Bay Company who dominated colonial politics.

Jonathan Edwards New England Congregationalist preacher who was famous for vivid descriptions of hell and damnation.

Josef Stalin Communist dictator of the Soviet Union from the 1920s until his death in 1953; responsible for the death or exile of millions of Soviet citizens.

Joseph and Mary Brant Mohawk brother and sister who allied with the British, thus harming the unity of the Iroquois Confederacy's neutrality during the Revolutionary War.

Joseph Smith Founder of the Mormon faith.

Judith Sargent Murray Essayist of the early republic who argued for a larger role for women in the new country.

Julius and Ethel Rosenberg New York couple accused, convicted, and executed for passing secret information regarding America's atomic bomb to the Soviets; Julius was likely guilty, Ethel likely innocent.

Kansas-Nebraska Act Passed by Congress in May 1854, it allowed residents of the territories of Kansas and Nebraska to decide whether slavery would be permitted there.

Kate Chopin A southern writer who explored the oppressive features of traditional marriage; known for her shocking novel *The Awakening.*

King Philip's War The most prolonged and deadly encounter between whites and Indians in the seventeenth century.

Knights of Labor Short-lived early national labor union that championed eight-hour workdays and the end of child labor, open to almost all workers.

Know-Nothings Name used for the anti-immigrant, anti-Catholic group that formed in 1850 and organized as the American Party.

Korematsu v. U.S. U.S. Supreme Court case that upheld the internment of more than 100,000 Japanese Americans to detention camps.

Ku Klux Klan One of many secret societies that used terrorism and physical violence to intimidate former slaves and undercut their constitutional rights, especially the right to vote.

Langston Hughes A leading writer of the Harlem Renaissance.

League of Nations The organization President Woodrow Wilson hoped would implement the principles of the Fourteen Points after the First World War; it ultimately came into being without the United States as a member.

lend-lease A system that allowed the Franklin Roosevelt administration to lend or lease arms to the British without explicitly violating the Neutrality Acts.

Levittowns Named after developer William Levitt, Levittowns were inexpensive suburban developments of similarly built homes.

Lewis and Clark On the direction of President Jefferson, Meriwether Lewis and William Clark led an expedition from Missouri to the Pacific in order to gather information on the lands acquired in the Louisiana Purchase.

Liberia African nation established in 1830 by freed blacks whose manumission and voyage was sponsored by the American Colonization Society (ACS).

Liberty League An organization founded by conservative business leaders, led by the Du Pont family, and focused on attacking the New Deal.

Life **magazine** New and enormously popular photographic journal, first published in 1936, it had the largest readership of any publication in the United States other than *Reader's Digest*.

Little Bighorn Site of the 1876 battle in which Colonel George Custer and his men were surprised and killed by a large army of Sioux warriors.

long drive A journey over grasslands that allowed western cattle ranchers to deliver their animals to railroad centers.

Lord Cornwallis British officer with early successes as leader of the Southern British forces but who was forced to surrender at Yorktown in 1781.

Lord Dunmore's Proclamation British promise of 1775 to grant freedom to people enslaved by Patriots in exchange for joining their military forces against the rebelling colonists.

Lost Generation Author Gertrude Stein used this term to describe the young Americans emerging from World War I.

Louis D. Brandeis Lawyer and Supreme Court justice; author of *Other People's Money*, which was about the "curse of bigness."

Louisa May Alcott Author of the *Little Women* series about an ambitious girl who fought conventional society to become a writer.

Lowell or Waltham system A factory system used to mass-produce textiles, primarily in New England, that relied on young women workers who lived in factory communities.

Loyalists (Tories) Supporters of England and the king, they may have represented a third of the white colonial population; many left America after the Revolution.

Lucretia Mott Abolitionist and women's rights advocate who co-organized the Seneca Falls Convention.

Lusitania The British passenger liner sunk by Germany in May 1915, killing almost 1,200 people, including 128 Americans.

Lyndon Johnson Often called LBJ, the president from 1963 to 1969 who promoted major social reform in his Great Society legislation and expanded America's military role in Vietnam.

Malcolm X Leader of the civil rights movement who promoted black power; assassinated in 1965.

Manhattan Project The American military's secret operation to develop an atomic bomb.

Manifest Destiny An ideology holding that God or fate intended the United States to expand its dominion across the North American continent.

manumission The act of freeing slaves.

Mao Zedong Leader of the communist armies of China in ongoing conflict with the nationalist government of Chiang Kai-shek in the 1930s and 1940s; won that battle and declared a communist China in 1949.

Marbury v. Madison Important decision of the United States Supreme Court that established the court's authority over the constitutionality of laws.

Marcus Garvey The African American leader who encouraged black people to reject assimilation into white society and develop pride in their own race and culture; he founded the Universal Negro Improvement Association (UNIA).

Margaret Sanger The pioneer of the American birth-control movement.

Mark Twain Pen name of Samuel Langhorne, nineteenth-century American author and humorist who wrote *The Adventures of Tom Sawyer* (1876) and *The Adventures of Huckleberry Finn* (1885).

Marshall Plan American program after World War II meant to spark economic recovery in Europe and thus cultivate economic ties and broader alliances between the Continent and the United States; eventually channeled $13 billion into the economies of sixteen participating countries.

Martin Luther King Jr. Baptist minister who came to prominence during the Montgomery bus boycott and went on to be the voice of the civil rights movement until his assassination in 1968.

Martin Van Buren Eighth president of the United States after serving as Andrew Jackson's vice president; nicknamed the little magician, but struggled as president during a difficult depression.

Massachusetts Bay Company Group of Puritan merchants in England who organized a new colonial venture in America.

Mayflower Compact Document that the Pilgrims signed to establish a government for themselves.

McCarthyism Name given to the anticommunist crusade of Senator Joseph McCarthy in the early 1950s, during which he recklessly persecuted alleged communists, often without evidence.

McCulloch v. Maryland Supreme Court case that confirmed the implied powers of Congress by upholding the constitutionality of the Bank of the United States.

Medicaid Social welfare program created during the Johnson administration that extended medical care to all ages in need.

Medicare Social welfare program created under the Johnson administration to provide health care to elderly Americans.

mercantilism An economic theory popular in Europe from the sixteenth through eighteenth centuries holding that nations were in competition with one another for wealth, and that the state should maximize its wealth by limiting imports and establishing new colonies that would provide access to precious minerals, spices, and slaves.

Mesoamerica Land area of the Archaic period including the lower portion of modern-day Mexico and the rest of Central America where many native societies flourished.

mestizo A person of mixed European and American descent, traditionally in Spanish-speaking territories and nations.

Metacom Leader of an attempt by Indians in seventeenth-century New England to drive out English settlers and resist encroachment on their lands.

middle grounds Places where European and Indian cultures interacted and where neither side had a military advantage.

middle passage The name given to the route used by slave ships between Africa and the Americas.

Mikhail Gorbachev Soviet leader who initiated broad economic reforms, government restructuring, and changes in military policy including a reduced Soviet presence in Eastern Europe and who resigned when the Soviet Union ceased to exist.

minstrel show Form of popular theater and entertainment from the early 1800s to the early 1900s that openly mocked and degraded African American culture.

Missouri Compromise Agreement of 1820 that defused sectional conflict by agreeing to admit Maine as a free state and Missouri as a slave state, and to henceforth prohibit slavery in the Louisiana Purchase territory in the regions north of the southern border of Missouri.

Molly Maguires A secret society of Irish-born coal miners willing to use violence to deal with management.

monopoly A business entity that controls an industry or market sector without competition.

Monroe Doctrine Articulated in 1823, the policy of the United States that warned against European interference in the American continents and promised the United States would stay out of European affairs.

Morse code System, designed by Samuel Morse, of long and short electrical bursts that made the telegraph system a viable, long-distance communication system.

muckraker A journalist who exposes scandal, corruption, and injustice; the term was especially popular during the progressive era.

My Lai massacre The deliberate killing of hundreds of Vietnamese villagers in the hamlet of My Lai in early 1968.

Nat Turner Leader of a slave revolt in 1831 in Southampton County, Virginia, that killed 60 white men, women, and children before being crushed.

Nathaniel Hawthorne Novelist, best known for *The Scarlet Letter* and *The House of the Seven Gables*, who wrote about the misery caused by egotism.

National Association for the Advancement of Colored People (NAACP) Founded in 1909 when the Niagara Movement joined with sympathetic white progressives; goal was equal rights.

National Consumers League (NCL) Formed in the 1890s under the leadership of Florence Kelley; goal was to force retailers and manufacturers to improve wages and working conditions.

National Labor Relations Board (NLRB) Part of the Wagner Act, this board was an enforcement mechanism that compelled employers to recognize and bargain with legitimate unions.

National Organization for Women A leading advocacy organization for women's rights, formed in 1966.

National Origins Act of 1924 Law that banned immigration from East Asia entirely and reduced the quota for European immigrants; the result was an immigration system that greatly favored northwestern Europeans.

National Recovery Administration (NRA) A federal agency that called on businesses to accept the regulation of wages, hours, prices, and other labor practices with the goal of stabilizing the economy, maintaining the workforce, and reducing competition; invalidated by the Supreme Court in 1935.

National Socialist (Nazi) Party Germany's National Socialist organization, headed by Adolf Hitler, that came to power in 1933.

nativism A belief in the superiority of native-born inhabitants over immigrants; in particular, an anti-immigrant movement that began in the early 1800s in the United States and crested with the passage of immigration restriction in 1924.

Navigation Acts Three acts that Parliament passed to regulate colonial commerce.

Nelson Mandela Leader of the African National Congress and force against apartheid who became the first black president of South Africa in 1994.

neoconservatives A small but influential group of conservative intellectuals who rejected liberalism after the turmoil of the 1960s.

Neutrality Acts Series of laws between 1935 and 1937 that created a mandatory arms embargo against both sides in any military conflict and legislated other inhibitors of American involvement in another foreign war.

New Deal The broad array of reform initiatives launched during the administration of Franklin Roosevelt in the 1930s that dramatically increased the impact of the federal government on economic life and the personal welfare of citizens.

New Freedom Presidential candidate Woodrow Wilson's 1912 program that supported a progressive agenda.

New Frontier JFK's campaign plan for progressive domestic reforms.

New Jersey Plan Plan presented by William Paterson of New Jersey during the Constitutional Convention to have a single legislative body with equal representation for all states regardless of population.

New Nationalism Presidential candidate Theodore Roosevelt's 1912 program supporting economic concentration and using government to regulate and control it.

New Right Conservative movement that began in the 1970s and culminated in the election of Ronald Reagan.

New South A term referring to the economic modernization and industrialization of the South after Reconstruction.

Nicholas Biddle Ran the Second Bank of the United States; fought ultimately unsuccessfully against President Andrew Jackson for the survival of the institution.

Nicola Sacco and Bartolomeo Vanzetti The two anarchists accused of murder who were eventually executed in the 1927 amid widespread nativist prejudices and fears.

Nineteenth Amendment The amendment to the constitution ratified in 1920 that guaranteed women the right to vote.

Nisei The American-born children of Japanese immigrants.

Nixon Doctrine Foreign policy plan under President Nixon to continue to support allies' military defense needs while cutting back on American forces.

Noah Webster Author, teacher, and promoter of the new American nation, best known for his dictionaries and spellers that helped standardize the American language.

North Atlantic Treaty Organization (NATO) The postwar alliance of the United States and many of the countries of Western Europe, unified against invasion by the Soviet Union.

Northwest Ordinance A 1787 decree that created a single political territory out of the land north of the Ohio River.

NSC-68 A 1950 report commissioned by the Truman administration and issued by the National Security Council; called for a major expansion of American military power to combat the threat of communism and the Soviet Union.

nullification The theory that individual states, as the original creators of the federal government, possess the right to invalidate federal laws if they find them unconstitutional.

Occupy Wall Street (OWS) Protest movement of 2011 against economic inequality that began as an encampment in a Wall Street area park.

Office of Price Administration (OPA) Unpopular federal organization during World War II tasked with fighting economic inflation.

Office of War Information (OWI) Agency charged with disseminating the official U.S. viewpoint and encouraging domestic war efforts during World War II.

Okies Collective term for families from the Dust Bowl (though not all came from Oklahoma) traveling to California in search of jobs.

Okinawa Fierce battle in the Pacific on an island 370 miles south of Japan; saw the use of kamikaze planes and the loss of over 100,000 Japanese troops.

Oneida "Perfectionists" Members of a Utopian experiment in upstate New York who rejected traditional notions of family and marriage in favor of communal bonds.

Open Door The metaphor Secretary of State John Hay used in 1898 to characterize the access to Chinese markets he desired for the United States; it was later expanded to refer to a policy of granting equal trade access to all countries.

Oregon Trail A 2,100-mile wagon route that linked the Missouri River to western Oregon and was a main passageway for white western settlers between the 1830s and early 1870s.

Osama bin Laden Leader of Al Qaeda from 1987 until 2011, when he was killed in Pakistan by U.S. military special forces.

Palmer Raids Led by U.S. Attorney General A. Mitchell Palmer, these 1919 and 1920 police actions targeted alleged radical centers throughout the country, often using extralegal means.

Panama Canal The canal finished in 1914 that linked the Atlantic and the Pacific by creating a channel through Central America.

Pancho Villa The Mexican revolutionary whom Gen. John Pershing unsuccessfully pursued into Mexico after Villa killed Americans along the border.

Panic of 1819 Six-year depression that began with a price collapse of American trade goods.

Panic of 1837 Triggered by an executive order that the government would accept payment for land only in gold or silver or a currency backed by one of the metals, this economic crisis included business failures, a spike in unemployment, falling prices, and even bread riots.

Panic of 1893 The beginning of the most severe depression the United States had experienced at the time; triggered by the Philadelphia and Reading Railroad bankruptcy.

parity A complicated formula for setting an adequate price for farm goods and ensuring that farmers would earn back at least their production costs no matter the fluctuations of national or world agricultural markets.

Patrick Henry Virginia politician who lead the fight against the Stamp Act and declared supporters of Parliament taxes were enemies of the colonies.

Paxton Boys A group of Pennsylvania frontiersmen who demanded tax relief and massacred Conestoga Indians.

Pearl Harbor American naval base in Hawaii and headquarters of the Pacific Fleet; attacked by Japanese on December 7, 1941.

peculiar institution Southern term for slavery as a special institution of the South.

Pendleton Act First national civil service measure, passed in 1883, that tested applicants' qualifications for federal jobs by a test rather than patronage connections; largely symbolic at first but grew in reach over time.

Pequot War War in Connecticut during 1637 between English settlers and Indians of the region.

Pinckney's Treaty Agreement between the United States and Spain that guaranteed access to the Mississippi River for American trade and protection from Native Americans in Spain's territories.

planter class Wealthy slaveholding planters of the South who dominated southern society despite their limited number.

Plessy v. Ferguson An 1896 Supreme Court decision that ruled that separate accommodations for blacks and whites were legal so long as they were equal.

Plymouth Plantation First Pilgrim settlement in Massachusetts.

Pontiac Ottawa chief who led a coalition of tribes to war against the British from 1763 to 1766; achieved some gains including pressuring the British to restrain their settlers from the trans-Appalachian west, but eventually undermined by internal divisions, disease, and the brutal violence of settlers and the British military.

Popé Indian religious leader who led a successful uprising against the Spanish in 1680.

Popular Front This was a broad coalition of antifascist groups on the left; communism was its driving force.

popular sovereignty A term coined by Stephen A. Douglas to adjudicate the expansion of slavery in the western territories by allowing settlers to decide the status of slavery for their territory.

Populism A reform movement of the 1890s that promoted federal government policies to redistribute wealth and power from national elites to common people; more generally, refers to a political doctrine that supports the rights of the people over the elite.

Powhatan Chief of the Powhatan Confederacy and father of Pocahontas.

preservationist Activist who believes in the protection of natural environments rather than their managed development.

Proclamation of 1763 Attempt by England to reduce violence between Native Indians and English colonists by legally barring settlement beyond the Appalachian Mountains.

progressivism The ideology that claimed that the nation's most pressing need was to impose order and justice on a society that seemed to be approaching chaos.

prohibition Complete ban on the sale and manufacture of alcoholic beverages; 1920 amendment put it into effect on a national level.

Protestant Reformation The schism in the Catholic Church that began in 1517 with Martin Luther and led to new forms of Christian denominations still recognizable today.

Public Health Service Organization created in 1912; goal was to prevent occupational diseases and create common health standards.

Puerto Rico Part of the Spanish Empire from 1508 until 1898, when it fell under the control of the United States; became an American territory in 1917.

Pullman strike A 1894 railroad strike that escalated to twenty-seven states and territories, ultimately broken by federal troops and resulting in management's victory.

Puritans A sect of Protestants of England that wished to "purify" the Church of England of its Catholic ceremonies and practices.

Quakers A Protestant sect that called themselves the Society of Friends and believed that all could attain salvation by cultivating their inherent divinity.

quasi war The name given to the undeclared war between the United States and France of 1798–1799.

Queen Liliuokalani Nationalist leader of Hawaii elevated to the throne in 1891.

Rachel Carson Author of the 1962 book *Silent Spring* who argued that overuse of pesticides was destroying the environment.

Radical Republicans A wing of the Republican Party in the mid-nineteenth century that aggressively opposed slavery and, after the Civil War, fought to expand and protect African American civil rights.

Ralph Waldo Emerson Transcendentalist philosopher who urged individuals to find fulfillment and self-improvement in nature.

range wars Conflicts between sheepmen and cattlemen, ranchers, and farmers.

Reagan Doctrine President Reagan's policy to combat communism by supporting anticommunist regimes and revolutionaries with money and military aid.

Reaganomics Supply-side economic policy embraced by Reagan and based on the idea that reducing taxes on corporations and the wealthy would encourage new investment and social well-being.

Rebecca Cox Jackson Radical African American religious figure who broke with the free black church movement in Philadelphia and ultimately joined the Shaker movement during the mid-nineteenth century.

Reconstruction The process by which the federal government, between 1865 and 1877, controlled the former Confederate states and set the conditions for their readmission to the Union.

Reconstruction Finance Corporation (RFC) The bill established a government agency to provide federal loans to troubled banks, railroads, and other businesses.

Red Scare A period of intense popular fear and government repression of real or imagined leftist radicalism; usually associated with the years immediately following World War I.

Redeemers Coalition of white southern landowners, business interests, and professionals who sought to "redeem" the South after the Civil War by limiting the influence of the Republican Party and violently overthrowing federal reconstruction policies and African American citizenship rights.

relocation centers Euphemistic name for areas of detention for more than 100,000 Japanese Americans during World War II, rounded up and evacuated against their will.

republicanism A system of governance in which power derives from the people, rather than from a ruling family, aristocratic class, or some other supreme authority.

Republicans Name for those who wished to limit the new government's power, in opposition to the Federalists.

Revolution of 1800 Thomas Jefferson's term for his election in 1800 which saw the peaceful transfer of power between ideologically opposed parties.

Richard Nixon Vice president under Dwight D. Eisenhower and president from 1969 until his resignation in 1974 as a result of the Watergate scandal.

Richard Wright Author of *Native Son*, a story of a young African American man broken by the system of racial oppression.

Roanoke The first English colony attempted in the North America.

Robert E. Lee Superintendent of West Point and later general of the Northern Army of Virginia, he won a string of early victories during the Civil War and later presided over the official surrender of the Confederacy.

Robert Fulton American inventor of the first commercially successful steamboat, the *Clermont*.

Robert M. La Follette Wisconsin senator and nationally known progressive.

Rocky Mountain school Group of late-nineteenth-century painters known for large-scale depictions of western landscapes.

Roe v. Wade Supreme Court ruling that allowed for legal abortions as part of a woman's right to privacy (Fourteenth Amendment) while also establishing conditions under which states can regulate abortion after the first trimester.

Roger B. Taney Appointed secretary of the treasury under President Jackson to remove federal deposits from the Bank of the United States; he was later appointed by Jackson as chief justice of the Supreme Court and wrote the *Dred Scott v. Sanford* decision in 1857.

Roger Williams Controversial minister who established the Rhode Island colony where people of different faiths could worship without interference.

Ronald Reagan Former governor of California elected as fortieth president in 1982 who led a conservative reform of American politics during his two terms.

Roosevelt Corollary President Theodore Roosevelt's amendment to the Monroe Doctrine, stating that the United States had the right not only to oppose European intervention in the Western Hemisphere but also to intervene in the domestic affairs of its neighbors should they be unable to maintain order and sovereignty.

Rosa Parks Civil rights activist who was arrested for not giving up her seat to a white passenger on a bus in Montgomery, Alabama, in 1955; her arrest spurred the Montgomery bus boycott.

Rosie the Riveter Popular image of a woman performing industrial work during World War II in America; became a symbol of female contributions to the war effort.

Rutherford B. Hayes Elected president in 1876 but largely ineffectual in office; the deals that led to his election are often described as marking the end of Reconstruction.

Saddam Hussein Iraqi leader whose invasion of Kuwait led to the first Gulf War; deposed by the United States in the second Gulf War.

Sagebrush Rebellion A late 1970s movement by western conservatives who opposed federal environmental regulations and restrictions on development.

Salem witchcraft trials An instance of the widespread hysteria in the 1680s regarding supposed satanic influences in New England that often targeted women.

Sam Houston A soldier, lawyer, congressman, and governor of Tennessee, he eventually moved to Texas where he commanded the Texas armies in their successful battle for independence from Mexico in 1836.

Samuel Gompers Union organizer under whose leadership the American Federation of Labor (AFL) grew by combining similar skilled unions together.

Sarah Bagley Creator of the Female Labor Reform Association that promoted better working conditions and shorter workdays in the mid-1840s.

Saratoga Site in New York where, with the help of Benedict Arnold, General Horatio Gates surrounded British General John Burgoyne and forced his surrender.

scalawags Slang term referring to Southern whites who supported the Republican Party and federal Reconstruction policies after the Civil War.

Scopes trial Tennessee case that attracted intense national attention to the debate over whether to teach evolution or creationism in the schools.

Scotch-Irish Scottish Presbyterians who had settled in northern Ireland in the early seventeenth century.

Scottsboro case A 1931 case that was among the most notorious examples of racism in the United States; an all-white jury convicted nine black teenagers of raping two white women despite overwhelming evidence of their innocence.

secession The act of asserting independence by withdrawing membership from a political state; it refers in particular to the South's departure from the United States in 1861.

Second Continental Congress Body of colonial representatives formed after the battles of Lexington and Concord to help resolve the conflict with Great Britain.

Second Great Awakening A wave of Protestant revival in the early 1800s signified by large congregations and dynamic sermons.

second middle passage Term coined by historian Ira Berlin to describe the forced movement of slaves with the United States, primarily from the upper South to the cotton states.

Second New Deal Launched in the spring of 1935 in response both to growing political pressures and continuing economic crisis, these new proposals represented a shift toward more openly anticorporate initiatives; this wave also included more long-term reforms including Social Security.

Securities and Exchange Commission (SEC) A federal government agency established in 1934 to police the stock market.

Selective Service Act The 1917 law that created a national draft to provide men to fight the First World War.

Seminole Wars Term used to describe a series of conflicts between United States forces and the Seminole, a mixture of Native Americans and black settlers in Florida; the first one, in 1816–1819, saw Andrew Jackson lead an invasion of Spanish Florida, during which Jackson's troops chased Seminole raiders and seized Spanish forts.

Seneca Falls Convention The 1848 meeting that produced the Declaration of Sentiments and Resolutions arguing for women's inalienable rights.

separation of powers The partitioning of authority to distinct branches of a government.

Seven Years' War Called the French and Indian War in the American colonies, the Seven Years' War was a global conflict between England and France ultimately won by England in 1763.

Shakers Utopian religious society committed to complete celibacy, equality of the sexes, and a simple ordered life.

sharecropping A farming system in which large landowners rent their fields to farmers, usually families, in return for a share of the crop's production.

Shays's Rebellion A 1786 uprising of poor Massachusetts farmers demanding relief from their debts.

Sherman Antitrust Act Aimed at prohibiting corporate combinations that restrained competition, and passed in 1890, it was largely ineffective.

Shiloh Name of battle site in southwestern Tennessee where, on April 6–7, 1862, Union forces won control of the upper Mississippi River.

silent majority Phrase coined by Richard Nixon to refer to conservative voters, as opposed to the more vocal counterculture.

sit-down strike A planned labor stoppage in which workers assume their positions in a factory or other workplace but refuse to perform their duties, thus preventing the use of strikebreakers.

slave codes Laws passed in the British colonies or in American states granting white masters absolute authority over the enslaved; these included laws depriving slaves of property, free movement, and legal defenses.

Social Darwinism The belief that societies are subject to the laws of natural selection and that some societies or peoples are innately superior to others.

Social Gospel The effort to make faith a tool of social reform; the movement was chiefly concerned with redeeming the nation's cities.

social justice A movement that seeks justice for whole groups or societies rather than individuals.

Social Security Act Passed in 1935; established several distinct programs including a pension program for workers (though many were excluded); also established a system of unemployment insurance and aid to people with disabilities as well to dependent children.

socialism A political theory that advocates government (rather than private) ownership and management of the means of production and distribution.

Sojourner Truth Former slave who lectured extensively on behalf of equal rights for blacks and women.

Sons of Liberty Groups of male colonists who organized against England's enforcement of the Stamp Act and who terrorized British officials.

sovereignty The authority to govern; popular sovereignty refers to the idea that the source of this authority is the people, who confer authority through elections.

Spanish Civil War The 1936–1939 war between Spain's liberal republican government and the conservative forces of General Francisco Franco.

Spanish-American War War of 1898 between the United States and Spain; took place in Cuba and the Philippines and resulted in American possession of or great influence over those areas and others.

specie circular Executive order issued by President Jackson that required gold or silver to buy public lands.

spoils system The process whereby elected officials give out government jobs as reward for political favors.

Sputnik The first earth-orbiting satellite launched by the Soviet Union in 1957.

stagflation An economic condition in which inflation is high, unemployment is high, and growth is low.

Stalwarts Political group within the Republican Party led by Roscoe Conkling of New York that favored traditional, professional machine politics.

Stamp Act Hated act passed by Prime Minister Grenville of England that required an official stamp on all paper documents in the colonies and united the colonies against England.

Stephen A. Douglas Democratic senator from Illinois who brokered the Compromise of 1850 and ran unsuccessfully against Lincoln and others in the presidential election of 1860.

Stephen F. Austin Immigrant from Missouri who established the first legal American settlement in the Mexican territory of Texas in 1822.

Stephen H. Long Dispatched by the United States government, he explored the Platte and South Platte Rivers in present-day Nebraska and Colorado.

Stonewall Riot Landmark 1969 event in the gay liberation movement that began as patrons of the Stonewall Inn, a gay nightclub, reacted violently against a police raid.

Stono Rebellion A slave revolt in South Carolina during the colonial period.

Strategic Defense Initiative (SDI) President Reagan's missile defense plan, which included ground and space-based antimissile defense weapons.

Students for a Democratic Society (SDS) Leading organization of student radicalism in the 1960s.

Sugar Act British act of 1764 designed to stop sugar smuggling in the colonies by lowering taxes on molasses but enforcing their payment and forcing compliance with trade laws.

Sunbelt The southeastern and southwestern regions of the United States.

Susan B. Anthony Abolitionist and one of the most iconic and active leaders of the early women's right movement.

Syngman Rhee Pro-Western though not reliably democratic leader of South Korea in 1950.

Taft-Hartley Act Officially known as the Labor-Management Relations Act of 1947; made it illegal to operate a business in which no worker could be hired without first being a member of a union.

Tallmadge Amendment Proposed amendment to Missouri's admission to statehood that would have gradually turned it from a slave state to a free state.

Tammany Hall Urban machine led by famously corrupt city boss William M. Tweed.

Taylorism Named for Frederick Winslow Taylor, an attempt to use scientific management to improve factory production.

Tea Act A 1773 act passed by England that gave the British East India Company the right to export tea to the colonies without paying the same taxes that were imposed on colonial merchants; the act enraged American merchants and colonists boycotted tea.

Tea Party movement Conservative political movement begun in 2009 to reduce taxes, government regulations, and federal efforts to implement universal health care.

Teapot Dome The location of rich naval oil reserves in Wyoming and part of a national scandal during the Harding administration.

Tecumseh A chief of the Shawnees who worked to unite native peoples against the threat of white expansion; died fighting for Britain in the War of 1812.

Tejanos The Mexican residents of Texas.

Teller Amendment The 1898 amendment to the war declaration against Spain that promised no American intention to occupy or control Cuba in the wake of an American victory.

temperance Self-restraint, especially concerning drink; the temperance movement pushed for bans on the sale and consumption of alcohol.

tenements By the late nineteenth century, this was a descriptor used for slum dwellings.

Tennessee Valley Authority (TVA) A regional planning program focused on water resources as a source of cheap electric power.

terrorism The use of violence as a form of intimidation against peoples and governments.

Tet offensive Large coordinated attack on January 31, 1968, of American strongholds in South Vietnam by communists forces that led to lost support for the Vietnam War in America.

Thaddeus Stevens U.S Representative from Pennsylvania who was an abolitionist and a leader of the Radical Republicans.

The Federalist Papers A collection of essays written by Alexander Hamilton, James Madison, and John Jay that supported ratification of the Constitution.

The Jazz Singer The first feature-length film with spoken dialogue, or "talkie."

The Other America Title of Michael Harrington's 1962 about the chronic problem of poverty in America.

the Prophet Also known as Tenskwatawa, the Shawnee prophet was a charismatic speaker, leader, and younger brother of Tecumseh; the Battle of Tippecanoe disillusioned many of his followers.

theocracy A form of government in which political power is believed to derive from a deity, and in which religious and government structures are intertwined.

Theodore Dreiser Author of *Sister Carrie*, which focused on the plight of single women.

Theodore Roosevelt Rough Rider during the Spanish-American War, governor of New York, Republican Party and progressive leader, vice president, and president of the United States from 1901 to 1909.

Thirteenth Amendment Passed on January 31, 1865, this constitutional amendment formally abolished slavery.

Thomas J. ("Stonewall") Jackson Confederate general who commanded troops in major Civil War engagements in the first half of war before being mortally wounded in the Battle of Chancellorsville in May 1863.

Thomas Jefferson One of the founders of the United States, he wrote most of the Declaration of Independence and served in all levels of government, both locally and nationally, in his long career.

Tiananmen Square Location in China of the 1989 student uprising that was brutally put down by Chinese authorities.

Townsend Plan Created by a California physician, this proposal focused on federal pensions for older adults.

Townshend Duties External taxes passed by England's Charles Townshend that taxed goods imported to the colonies; hated by the colonists, the taxes were later repealed after a colonial boycott of English goods.

Trail of Tears Term for the forced journey made by Native Americans to the Indian Territory that began in the winter of 1838, killing perhaps a quarter or more of the migrants.

transcendentalism A philosophical and literary movement of the early nineteenth century that sought beauty and truth in nature and the individual, rather than in formalized education, politics, or religion.

Treaty of Guadalupe Hidalgo Agreement to end the Mexican War in which the United States gained California and New Mexico and the Texas boundary was drawn at the Rio Grande.

trench warfare A common form of fighting in the First World War, whereby armies sought cover below ground from artillery bombardment, machine guns, and other military technologies.

Triangle Shirtwaist Company fire This disastrous event in New York was influential in finally passing a series of pioneering labor laws.

triangular trade A simplified description of the complex trade networks of the Atlantic World; the triangle metaphor refers to the trade in rum, slaves, and sugar among New England, Africa, and the West Indies.

Truman Doctrine Expressed policy of the United States, articulated in 1947, to support groups or governments fighting against communists around the world.

Turner thesis The theory articulated by Frederick Jackson Turner in 1893 that westward expansion into the frontier had defined and continually renewed American ideas about democracy and individualism.

U-2 Crisis A 1960 diplomatic incident between the United States and the Soviet Union when a U.S. U-2 spy plane was shot down by the Soviets after crossing Soviet air space.

U.S.S. *Maine* American vessel sunk in Havana harbor in February 1898; explosion was blamed on a Spanish mine and used by popular press to urge war; likely a mechanical error.

Ulysses S. Grant Chief of the Union armies (at the beginning of 1864) and eighteenth president who supervised much of Reconstruction.

United Nations An international organization, established in the peace talks after World War II, that contained a General Assembly and a Security Council of the five major powers.

United Service Organization (USO) Organization that recruited thousands of young women during World War II to serve as hostesses and sustain the morale of servicemen.

United States Sanitary Commission An organization of Northern civilian volunteers who raised money and support for the care of the sick and wounded during the Civil War; organized large numbers of female nurses to serve in field hospitals.

vaudeville A form of theater adapted from French models; the most popular urban entertainment into the first decades of the twentieth century.

vertical integration The arrangement by which a company takes ownership of businesses in various stages of production and distribution within the same industry.

Viet Cong Military arm of the National Liberation Front (NLF); communists in South Vietnam who fought against South Vietnamese rule and the American military with the support of the North Vietnamese.

Vietnamization Term used by President Nixon to describe transferring the responsibility for fighting the Vietnam War to the South Vietnamese.

Virginia and Kentucky Resolutions Written by Jefferson and Madison, respectively, in response to the Alien and Sedition Acts, the resolutions argued that states had the right to nullify federal laws.

Virginia House of Burgesses The first elected legislature in what would become the United States.

Virginia Plan James Madison's proposal during the Constitutional Convention for a two-house legislature where states would be represented in both bodies in proportion to their population.

Virginia Resolves Term used for a group of resolutions passed by the Virginia legislature declaring only the colonies' governments had the right to tax colonists.

virtual representation British political theory holding that members of Parliament represented all British subjects, not just those from the specific region that had elected them.

Vladimir Putin Political leader of Russia since 1999.

Voting Rights Act of 1965 Legislation that expanded the right to vote by providing federal protections to African Americans who had previously been barred by local and state regulations.

W. E. B. Du Bois Sociologist, historian, one of the first African Americans to receive a degree from Harvard, author of *The Souls of Black Folk*, chief spokesman for fighting for black civil rights, founding member of the Niagara Movement and the NAACP.

Wade-Davis Bill The 1864 bill stipulating that all Confederate states seeking readmission to the Union have a majority of its voters take a loyalty oath to the federal government; it never passed because Lincoln refused to sign it.

Walt Whitman Writer who helped define American literature with his book of poems, *Leaves of Grass*, and his focus on individual freedom.

War Hawks Term given to a group of congressmen who argued for war with Britain in 1812.

War Industries Board The 1917 agency created to coordinate government purchases of military supplies.

Warren G. Harding Senator from Ohio who was elected president in 1920; generally remembered as ill-suited for the office.

Warsaw Pact A Soviet-led alliance of its Eastern European satellite nations created in 1955.

Washington Irving Successful author in the early 1800s of historical works and short stories including "The Legend of Sleepy Hollow."

Washington, D.C. The capital of the United States designed by French engineer Pierre L'Enfant; took many years to develop into a major city.

Watergate Named after the site where Nixon's operatives were first arrested, the scandal involving Nixon's use of illegal campaign tactics and attempts to cover up those tactics.

Webster-Ashburton Treaty This 1842 treaty helped defined the northern border between British colonies (now Canada) and the United States and soothed American anger at British actions in the Caroline and Creole affairs.

Webster-Hayne debate Senate exchange between Daniel Webster and Robert Hayne that focused on the issue of states' rights versus national power, pitting the nullification advocate Hayne against the nationalist Webster.

welfare capitalism A corporate strategy for discouraging labor unrest by improving working conditions, hours, wages, and other elements of workers' lives.

Western Union Telegraph Company The dominant telegraph company by 1860, formed by a combination of smaller telegraph companies.

Whigs Political party formed during the presidency of Andrew Jackson to oppose Jackson and to support a more active federal government; favored industrial, commercial, and infrastructural development to promote economic growth.

Whiskey Rebellion A 1794 uprising of western Pennsylvania farmers opposed to a new federal whiskey tax; put down by troops led by President Washington.

Wilbur and Orville Wright Builders of the first self-powered airplane, successfully flown in 1903.

William Berkeley The royal governor of Virginia during Bacon's Rebellion.

William H. Seward Secretary of state in both President Lincoln's and President Johnson's administrations who negotiated purchase of Alaska from Russia in 1867.

William Henry Harrison Ninth president of the United States who died shortly after taking office; experienced Indian fighter at an early age and later governor of Indian Territory; defeated Tecumseh at the Battle of Tippecanoe.

William Howard Taft Theodore Roosevelt's most trusted lieutenant and his handpicked successor, who was elected president in 1908.

William Howe British commander who led troops in capturing New York in 1776 and Philadelphia in 1777, but who was largely seen as ineffective until replaced in 1778.

William James Harvard psychologist and most prominent publicist of pragmatism.

William Jennings Bryan Congressman from Nebraska, tireless 1896 presidential candidate, and author of the "Cross of Gold" speech; also later secretary of state under President Woodrow Wilson and a Christian fundamentalist witness in the Scopes trial.

William Lloyd Garrison Founder of *The Liberator*, a newspaper that focused on the harsh truths of slavery and argued for the immediate release of the enslaved and extension of citizenship to all.

William M. Tweed The famously corrupt boss of New York's political machine Tammany Hall.

William McKinley Governor of Ohio and former congressman who was elected president in 1896 and 1900; assassinated in 1901.

William Penn Outspoken Quaker who led the colony of Pennsylvania after receiving a royal land grant.

William Pitt Leading English secretary of state and prime minister who ran England's war effort during the Sevens Years' War.

William Randolph Hearst The most powerful U.S. newspaper chain owner; by 1914, he controlled nine newspapers and two magazines.

William T. Sherman Union general who captured Atlanta and in late 1864 marched his troops across Georgia and the Carolinas, burning crops and buildings as he went and crippling the Confederacy.

Wilmot Proviso Failed congressional plan to prohibit slavery in any territory acquired from Mexico.

Winston Churchill Outspoken British prime minister in power during most of World War II.

Women's Christian Temperance Union (WCTU) Led by Frances Willard after 1879 and advocate for abstinence from the consumption of alcohol; single largest women's organization in American history by 1911.

Woodrow Wilson Native Virginian, president of Princeton University, governor of New Jersey, Democratic Party and progressive leader, and president of the United States from 1913 to 1921.

Woodstock Music festival held in upstate New York in August of 1969 that became a symbol of the counterculture.

Worcester v. Georgia Supreme Court case of 1832 that affirmed federal authority over individual states' authority concerning the affairs of Indian tribes.

Works Progress Administration (WPA) Established in 1935, this was a system of work relief for the unemployed, but on a larger scale than earlier, similar endeavors; it included such programs as the Federal Art Project, the Federal Music Project, and the Federal Writers' Project.

Wounded Knee Located on the Pine Ridge Indian Reservation in South Dakota, it was the site of a massacre of between 150 and 300 Sioux, including women and children, by the U.S. Army on December 29, 1890.

XYZ Affair Name given to an international incident between U.S. and French diplomats that sparked the quasi war between France and the United States.

Yalta Conference A 1945 meeting between Roosevelt, Churchill, and Stalin that laid the groundwork for the United Nations, but otherwise established only murky or soon-violated agreements on the partition of Germany and the question of who would rule Poland.

yellow journalism Sensationalist reporting, particularly in newspapers of the late nineteenth and early twentieth centuries, so named for the color of a character in one of the papers' comic strips.

yeoman farmer Small farmer who worked his own soil and possessed no slave labor.

Yorktown Virginia site of the last major battle of the American Revolution, where Lord Cornwallis surrendered to George Washington and French forces in 1781.

Young America A political movement supporting free trade and territorial expansion in America during the late 1840s and 1850s.

Zachary Taylor American hero of the Mexican War who was elected president in 1848.

Zimmermann Telegram The communication intercepted in early 1917 from the German foreign secretary to the German ambassador in Mexico outlining a deal to draw the Mexicans into the war against the United States.

zoot suits Style of dress among Mexican American youths during World War II that featured padded shoulders and baggy pants; led to attacks by whites for flaunting wartime protocols to conserve clothing materials.

INDEX

AAA. *See* Agricultural Adjustment
    Administration
Abolitionism, 136–137
    Amistad case, 267–268, 293
    anti-, 292
    arguments for, 268–269
    black leaders for, 290–292
    division in, 292–293, 309
    early, 262, 290
    Fugitive slave laws, 309, 310, 311
    Garrison and, 290–293, 309
    global, 289
    influence of, 295
    in North, 121–122, 297
    political parties and, 309, 321
    violence and, 292
    Washington, D. C. and, 329
    women and, 285, 287
Abortion, 740, 741, 769, 804–805
Abraham Lincoln Brigade, 577
ACLU. *See* American Civil Liberties Union
ACS. *See* American Colonization Society
ADA. *See* Americans for Democratic Action
Adams, Abigail, 123, 124–125
Adams, Charles Francis, Jr., 337, 489
Adams, John, 97–98, 99, 128, 166
    correspondence with Abigail, 123, 124–125
    death of, 185
    Declaration of Independence, 111
    France negotiations by, 150
    independence support by, 107
    peace negotiations of, 120
    presidency of, 150, 151, 152–153
    on taverns, 101
    as vice president, 142–143
Adams, John Quincy
    Amistad case, 268
    Florida and, 191–192
    peace negotiations of, 183
    presidency of, 198–199
    as secretary of state, 191, 199
Adams, Samuel, 97–98, 101, 103, 107, 141
Adams-Onis Treaty, 192
Addams, Jane, 490
Adjustable rate mortgages (ARM), 792
Advanced Research Projects Agency (ARPA), 800
Advertising
    in 1920s, 548, 552–553
    in 1950s, 678
    railroad, 399
    television, 678
AEF. *See* American Expeditionary Forces
Affirmative action, 711, 740, 804
Affordable Care Act, 793, 797
Afghan War, 817
Afghanistan, Soviets in, 749
AFL. *See* American Federation of Labor
AFL-CIO. *See* American Federation of Labor and
    Congress of Industrial Organizations

Africa
    former colonies in, 749
    Liberia, 290
    slave trade, 17, 18, 55, 62, 63
    social and economic structures in, 16–18
    trade and, 18
    WWII in, 618, 619
African American women
    abolitionists, 285, 287
    in cities, 427
    clubs, 493
    employment of, 266, 366, 571
    preachers, 285–287
    during Reconstruction, 366
    slaves, 260, 263, 265, 266
    teachers, 493
African Americans. *See also* Civil rights; Civil War; Slaves;
    Voting rights
    abolitionists, 290–292
    baseball teams, 334
    Black Cabinet, 606
    black nationalism, 536–537
    black power, 714–715
    in cities, 427, 536–537, 545, 624, 685–686
    citizenship rights of, 137, 140–141, 352, 361, 368
    in Congress, 364, 379, 703
    education, 265, 283, 365, 375, 449, 803
    employment, 359, 568, 686, 711
    families, 270, 366–367, 677–678
    free, 140, 243, 267, 270, 363
    in Great Depression, 567–568
    Harlem Renaissance, 537, 553
    horse trainers and jockeys, 165
    incomes, 365–366
    land ownership, 365
    in legal system, 61, 624, 707
    life expectancies, 265
    lynchings, 328, 378–379, 536, 555, 656
    middle class of, 689, 803
    migration to cities, 427, 536–537, 545, 624
    military service, 325, 329, 330–331, 474, 517, 525, 621, 688
    music, 269, 684
    New Deal and, 606
    in New South, 360–361, 374–375
    performers, 376–377, 445
    police shootings, 711, 804
    population increase, 228
    populism and, 462–463
    post-civil rights era, 803–804
    poverty of, 267, 366
    reformers, 500–501
    religion of, 157, 158–159, 285–287, 363, 380
    resettlement to Caribbean and Africa, 290
    in Spanish-American War, 474–475, 476
    union members, 424, 463
    workers, 545–546
    writers, 553–554
    WWI and, 525, 536–537
    WWII and, 621, 624–625